Kishore Vaigyanik Protsahan Yojana

KVPY

STREAM SA

KVPY

STREAM SA

Authors
Lakshman Prasad *(Mathematics)*
Deepak Paliwal, Mansi Garg *(Physics)*
Neha Minglani Sachdeva *(Chemistry)*
Sanubia Saleem *(Biology)*

arihant
ARIHANT PRAKASHAN (Series), MEERUT

ARIHANT PRAKASHAN (Series), MEERUT

All Rights Reserved

ॐ **Administrative & Production Offices**

Regd. Office
'Ramchhaya' 4577/15, Agarwal Road, Darya Ganj, New Delhi -110002
Tele: 011- 47630600, 43518550; Fax: 011- 23280316

ॐ **Head Office**
Kalindi, TP Nagar, Meerut (UP) - 250002
Tel: 0121-7156203, 7156204

ॐ **Sales & Support Offices**
Agra, Ahmedabad, Bengaluru, Bareilly, Chennai, Delhi, Guwahati, Hyderabad, Jaipur, Jhansi, Kolkata, Lucknow, Nagpur & Pune.

ॐ **ISBN** : 978-93-26198-46-2

ॐ **Price :** ₹ 245.00

PO No : TXT-XX-XXXXXXX-X-XX

Published by Arihant Publications (India) Ltd.

For further information about the books published by Arihant
log on to www.arihantbooks.com or email to info@arihantbooks.com

Follow us on   

ABOUT THE EXAM

KVPY i.e. Kishore Vaigyanik Protsahan Yojana is a National Level Fellowship (scholarship) Program in Basic Science (Physics, Chemistry, Mathematics & Biology) upto Pre-Phd Level, run by Department of Science & Technology, Government of India and Conducted by IISC (Indian Institute of Science) Bangalore, Karnataka Annually.

It Was Started in 1999 to Encourage Basic Sciences Students to take up Research Career in Sciences. The Objective of the Exam is to Encourage Talented Students for Research Career in Sciences.

ELIGIBILITY CRITERIA

KVPY scholarships are given only to Indian Nationals to study in India. There are three streams in KVPY; SA, SB & SX. Eligibility criteria for different streams is discussed below;

- **For SA** Class 11 Students who passed class 10 with minimum 75% (65% for SC/ST/PWD) marks in Mathematics & Science.

  The fellowship of students selected in SA will be activated only if they pursue undergraduate courses in Basic Sciences (B.Sc./B.S./B.Stat./B.Math/Integrated M.Sc. or M.S.) and have secured a minimum of 60% (50% for SC/ST/PWD) marks in science subjects in class 12th.

- **For SX** Class 12 Students aspiring to pursue undergraduate program (B.Sc. etc) with basic sciences (Physics, Chemistry, Mathematics & Biology) who passed class 10 with minimum 75% (65% for SC/ST/PWD) marks in Mathematics & Science.

  The fellowship of students selected in SX will be activated only if they pursue undergraduate courses in Basic Sciences (B.Sc./B.S./B.Stat./B.Math/Integrated M.Sc. or M.S.) and have secured a minimum of 60% (50% for SC/ST/PWD) marks in science subjects in class 12th.

- **For SB** B.Sc. Ist year Students who passed class 12 with 60% marks in Maths & Sciences (PCMB) & class 10 with minimum 75% marks in Mathematics & Science.

  In order to activate fellowship, in the first year of undergraduate course they should secure minimum 60% (50% for SC/ST/PWD) marks.

Those students who are intending or pursuing undergraduate program under distance education scheme or correspondence course of any university are not eligible.

SYLLABUS OF KVPY

There is no prescribed syllabus for KVPY aptitude test, it aims to assess the understanding &
analytical ability of the students than his/her factual knowledge. However questions are
framed from syllabus upto class 10/12/Ist Year of Undergraduate Courses in basic sciences, as
applicable. There are two Questions Papers in KVPY; one for stream SA & Other for SB/SX
(Question Paper is same for SB & SX).

QUESTION PAPERS PATTERN

There are two Questions Papers in KVPY; one for stream SA & Other for SX/SB
(Question Paper is same for SB & SX).

- **Question Paper for SA Stream** caries 80 Questions for 100 marks. There are Two Parts in
  the Question Paper; Part I has 15 Questions of 1 mark each for Mathematics, Physics,
  Chemistry & Biology while Part II has 5 Questions of 2 marks each for Mathematics,
  Physics, Chemistry & Biology.

- **Question Paper for SB/SX Stream** caries 120 Questions for 160 marks. There are Two
  Parts in the Question Paper; Part I has 20 Questions of 1 mark each for Mathematics,
  Physics, Chemistry & Biology while Part II has 10 Questions of 2 marks each for
  Mathematics, Physics, Chemistry & Biology.

MODE OF EXAM

KVPY is conducted in Online Mode in English & Hindi Medium.

TIME OF EXAM

- Normally the notification or advertisement for KVPY appear in National Newspapers on
  May 11 (Technology Day) and Second Sunday of July every year.
- Generally the exam is conducted in the month of November.

SELECTION PROCESS

After scrutiny of application forms on the basis of eligibility criteria for various streams all
eligible students are called for Aptitude Test conducted in English & Hindi Medium at
different centers across the country. On the basis of performance in aptitude test shortlisted
students are called for an interview, which is the final stage of selection procedure.

FELLOWSHIPS

The selected students are eligible to receive KVPY fellowship after class 12th/Ist Year of Undergraduate course only if they pursue Undergraduate Courses in Basic Science, upto Pre-PhD or 5 Years whichever is earlier.

Details of fellowships are listed below;

Basic Science	Monthly Fellowship	Annual Contingency Grant
SA/SX/SB during Ist to IIIrd year of B.Sc./B.S./BB.Stat./B.Math/ Integrated M.Sc or M.S.	Rs. 5000	Rs. 20000
SA/SX/SB during M.Sc. / IVth to Vth years of Integrated M.Sc /M.S./ M.Math/ M.Stat.	Rs. 7000	Rs. 28000

CONTINUATION / RENEWAL OF FELLOWSHIP

- The fellow should continue to study basic science and should also maintain a minimum level of academic performance as Ist division or 60% (50% for SC/ST/PWD) marks in aggregate. Also the fellow has to pass all the subjects prescribed for that particular year.
- In each year marks are to be certified by the Dean or Head of the Institution.
- The fellowship will be discontinued if above marks are not obtained. However if fellow passed all the subjects & obtain marks more than 60% (50% for SC/ST/PWD) in subsequent year, the fellowship can be renewed only for that year onwards.
- If KVPY fellow opts out of the basic science at any stage then monthly fellowship and contingency grant will be forfeited from him.

KVPY Timeline 2022

IMPORTANT DATES

Opening of Application Portal	:	Ist Week of September 2022
Last Date of Submission of Online Application	:	Last Week of October 2022
KYPY Aptitude Test	:	Last Week of January 2023

APPLICATION FEE

For General Category	:	Rs. 1000/-
For SC/ST/PWD (Bank Charges Extra)	:	Rs. 500/-

For more details visit:www.kvpy.iisc.ernet.in

CONTENTS

QUESTION PAPER 2021
Stream : SA
[Exam Held on 22 May 2022, Shift I]

Time : 180 Min

MM : 100

Instructions

1. There are 80 questions in this paper.
2. This question paper contains two parts; Part I and Part II. There are four sections; Mathematics, Physics, Chemistry and Biology in each part.
3. Out of the four options given with each question, only one is correct.

➲ PART-I (1 Mark Questions)

MATHEMATICS

1. Let ABC be a scalene triangle with incentre I and circumcentre O. Suppose B, C, I, O are concyclic points. Then, $\angle B + \angle C$ is
   - (a) 60°
   - (b) 105°
   - (c) 120°
   - (d) 135°

2. Suppose $ABCD$ $(AB \parallel CD)$ is a trapezium such that the diagonals AC, BD bisect the angles $\angle DAB, \angle CBA$, respectively. Then,
   - (a) no two sides of the trapezium are equal
   - (b) exactly two sides of the trapezium are equal
   - (c) exactly three sides of the trapezium are equal
   - (d) None of the options above can be concluded

3. Suppose ABC is a triangle and D, E are points on the sides AB and AC respectively. If $AD : AB = 3 : 5$ and $AE : AC = 2 : 3$, then the ratio of the areas of the triangles ABC and ADE lies in the interval
   - (a) $(1, 2]$
   - (b) $\left(2, \dfrac{5}{2} \right]$
   - (c) $\left(\dfrac{5}{2}, 3 \right]$
   - (d) $\left(3, \dfrac{7}{2} \right]$

4. Let $ABCD$ be a convex quadrilateral in which $AC = BD$, $AB = CD, \angle BAC = 70°$ and $\angle BCD = 60°$. The acute angle between AC and BD is
   - (a) 70°
   - (b) 75°
   - (c) 80°
   - (d) 85°

5. Integers 1, 2, 3, ..., n, $(n \geq 3)$ are written on a blackboard and an integer k $(1 < k < n)$ is erased. The average of the remaining numbers is 16. Then, $n + k$ is
   - (a) 31
   - (b) 40
   - (c) 47
   - (d) 50

6. Let $p = 99$ and $q = 101$. Define $p_1 = \log\left(\dfrac{p + q}{2} \right)$ and $q_1 = \dfrac{1}{2} (\log p + \log q)$ and $p_2 = \log\left(\dfrac{p_1 + q_1}{2} \right)$, $q_2 = \dfrac{1}{2} (\log p_1 + \log q_1)$ where all logarithms have base 10. Then,
   - (a) $\log p_1 > p_2 > q_2 > \log q_1$
   - (b) $\log p_1 > q_2 > p_2 > \log q_1$
   - (c) $\log q_1 > p_2 > q_2 > \log p_1$
   - (d) $\log q_1 > q_2 > p_2 > \log p_1$

7. Let a be the largest real root and b be the smallest real root of the polynomial equation
$$x^6 - 6x^5 + 15x^4 - 20x^3 + 15x^2 - 6x + 1 = 0$$
Then, $\dfrac{a^2 + b^2}{a + b + 1}$ is

(a) $\dfrac{1}{2}$ (b) $\dfrac{2}{3}$ (c) $\dfrac{5}{4}$ (d) $\dfrac{13}{7}$

8. The number of ordered pairs (a, b) of integers such that $1 \le a, b \le 2021$ and the equations $x^2 - ax + b = 0$ and $x^3 - ax^2 + bx + a - b = 0$ have a common real root is

(a) 2017   (b) 2018   (c) 2019   (d) 2021

9. The number of positive integers x satisfying the equation $\dfrac{1}{x} + \dfrac{1}{x+1} + \dfrac{1}{x+2} = \dfrac{13}{12}$ is

(a) 0   (b) 1
(c) 2   (d) more than 2

10. A contractor has two teams of workers, team A and team B. Team A can complete a project P in 12 days and team B can complete P in 36 days. Team A starts working on P and team B joins team A after four days. Team A is withdrawn after another two days and team B is asked to double its efficiency. The number of additional days required for team B to complete P is

(a) 6   (b) 8   (c) 15   (d) 16

11. The number of positive integers n such that $n + 3$ divides $n^3 - 3$ is

(a) 3   (b) 4   (c) 5   (d) 8

12. Suppose we have an arithmetic progression $a_1, a_2, \ldots, a_n, \ldots$ with $a_1 = 1$, $a_2 - a_1 = 5$. The median of the finite sequence $a_1, a_2, \ldots, a_k$, where $a_k \le 2021$ and $a_{k+1} > 2021$ is

(a) 1011   (b) 1011.5   (c) 1013.5   (d) 1016

13. The value of the fifth root of $10^{10^{10}}$ is

(a) $10^{2 \times 10^9}$ (b) $10^{20 \times 10^9}$
(c) 10^{10^2} (d) $10^{2^{10}}$

14. Let A denote the set of all 2-digit numbers in base 10 that are equal to four times the sum of the factorial of their digits. The sum of the numbers in A is

(a) 12   (b) 34   (c) 44   (d) 54

15. In a class of 100 students, 15 students choose only Physics (but not Mathematics and Chemistry), 3 choose only Chemistry (but not Mathematics and Physics), and 45 choose only Mathematics (but not Physics and Chemistry). Of the remaining students, it is found that 23 have taken Physics and Chemistry, 20 have taken Physics and Mathematics, and 12 have taken Mathematics and Chemistry. The number of students who choose all the three subjects is

(a) 6   (b) 9   (c) 12   (d) 15

PHYSICS

16. You are holding a shallow circular container of radius R filled with water to a height $h (h \ll R)$. When you walk with speed v, it is seen that water starts spilling over. This happens due to the resonance of the periodic impulse given to the container (due to walking) with the oscillation of the water in the container. If the time-period of water oscillating in the container is inversely proportional to $\sqrt{h}$, then v is proportional to)

(a) R (b) $\sqrt{R}$
(c) $\dfrac{1}{\sqrt{R}}$ (d) $\dfrac{1}{R}$

17. A lens placed 10 cm away from a wall casts a sharp inverted image of a candle on it. It again casts a sharp image when the lens is moved 20 cm further away from the wall. Now, the candle and the lens are moved such that a sharp inverted image with unit magnification is formed on the wall. To achieve this configuration, the candle was moved

(a) 20 cm towards the wall
(b) 20 cm away from the wall
(c) 10 cm away from the wall
(d) 10 cm towards the wall

18. An electrical circuit consists of ten 100Ω resistors. Out of these 10 resistors, a group of n_1 resistors are connected in parallel and another group of n_2 resistors are separately connected in parallel. These two groups are then connected in series and this combination is connected to a voltage source of 100 V. If the net current through the circuit is 2.5 A, then the values of n_1 and n_2 are

(a) 6, 4   (b) 5, 5
(c) 2, 8   (d) 3, 7

19. A rectangular box has water in it. It is being pulled to the right with an acceleration a. Which of the following options shows the correct shape of water surface on it?

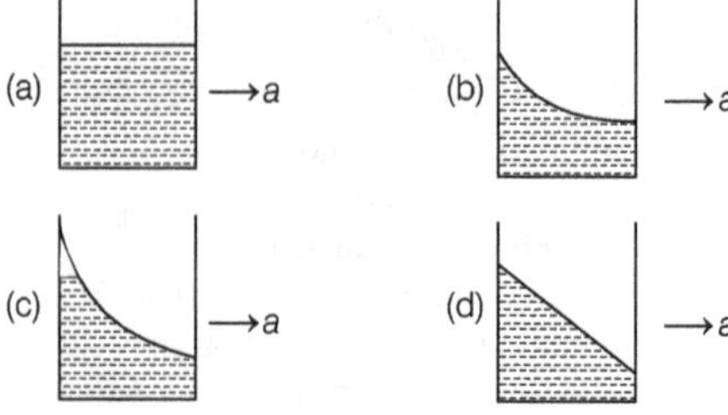

20. On fission a U^{235} nucleus releases 3×10^{-11} J of energy. In a 1 GW nuclear reactor 4.2% of the energy is converted to useful energy. The U^{235} consumed (in grams) in half an hour is closest to (Avogadro number, $N_A = 6.023 \times 10^{23}$)

(a) 5   (b) 50
(c) 500   (d) 1000

21. The International Avogadro Coordination project created the world's most perfect sphere using silicon in its crystalline form. The diameter of the sphere is 9.4 cm with an uncertainty of 0.2 nm. The atoms in the crystals are packed in cubes of side a. The side is measured with a relative error of 2×10^{-9} and each cube has 8 atoms in it. Then, the relative error in the mass of the sphere is closest to (Assume molar mass of silicon and Avogadro's number to be known precisely)

(a) 6.4×10^{-9} (b) 4.0×10^{-10}
(c) 1.2×10^{-8} (d) 5.0×10^{-8}

22. A laser beam is incident on a flat/ plane mirror at some angle and results in a reflected beam. The mirror is now rotated by an angle δ, while the direction of incident laser beam is kept the same. The angle between the new reflected beam and the reflected beam before the mirror was rotated is

(a) $2\,\delta$ (b) 0   (c) δ (d) $\dfrac{\delta}{2}$

23. Consider two charges, $+q$ and $-q$, $(q > 0)$ placed at a distance $2a$ from each other. At the point M (see figure below), the electric field makes an angle ϕ from the X-axis. The correct value of ϕ is

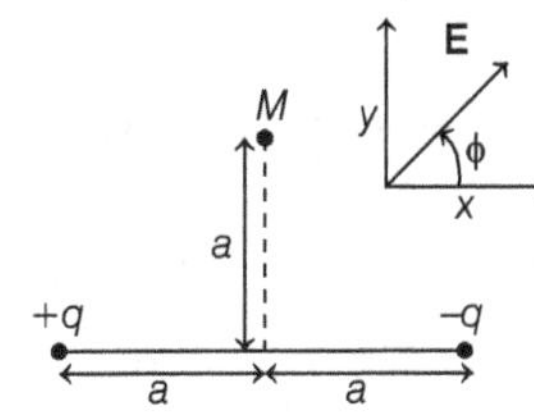

(a) $0°$ (b) $90°$ (c) $180°$ (d) $270°$

24. A particle starts from rest $x = 0$ m with an acceleration of $1\,\text{m/s}^2$. At $t = 5$ s it receives an additional acceleration in the same direction as its motion. At $t = 10$ s its speed and position are v and x, respectively. Had the additional acceleration not been provided, its speed and position would have been v_0 and x_0, respectively. It is found that $x - x_0$ is 12.5 m. Then, one can conclude that $v - v_0$ is

(a) 5 m/s   (b) 10 m/s
(c) 15 m/s   (d) 20 m/s

25. The heat required to change 1 kg of ice at –8°C into water at 20°C, at 1 atm of pressure, is closest to (Assume that ice has a specific heat capacity 2.1 kJ/kg/K, water has a specific heat capacity 4.2 kJ/kg/K and latent heat of fusion of ice is 333 kJ/kg)

(a) 414 kJ   (b) 424 kJ
(c) 434 kJ   (d) 444 kJ

26. A button battery is rated 3V and 225 mAh. A cricket ball (mass $= 0.163$ kg) having energy equal to that stored in the battery will have speed closest to

(a) 20 m/s   (b) 70 m/s
(c) 90 m/s   (d) 170 m/s

27. An airplane air speed indicator reads 100 m/s and its compass shows that it is heading 37° east of north. The meterological information provided to the navigator is that the wind velocity is 20 m/s towards east. The speed of the airplane relative to the ground is closest to

(a) 111 m/s   (b) 113 m/s
(c) 115 m/s   (d) 120 m/s

28. A white light is falling on a bi-convex lens. Which of the following options represents the correct qualitative behaviour of the focussing of this light?

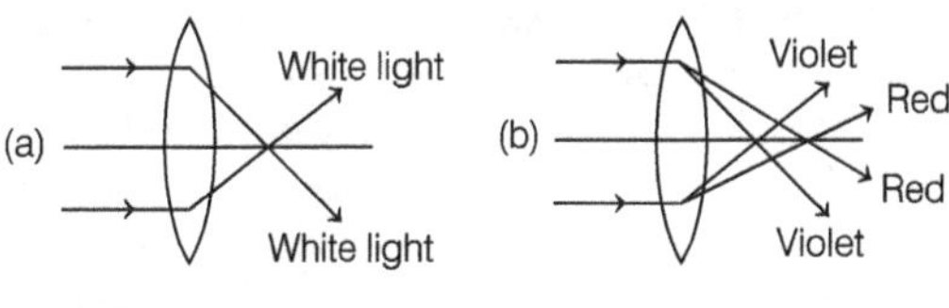

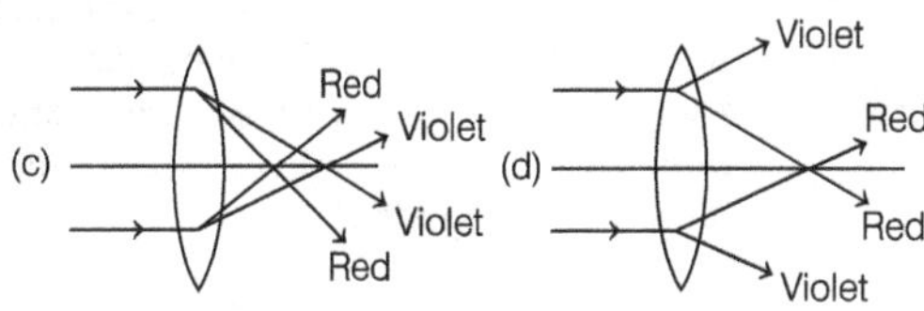

29. Shown in the figure is transparent tank of length 30 cm. A black strip of width 3.8 cm is stuck on its left wall. When a source of light is kept to the left of it, a shadow of width 7.6 cm is formed on the right wall.

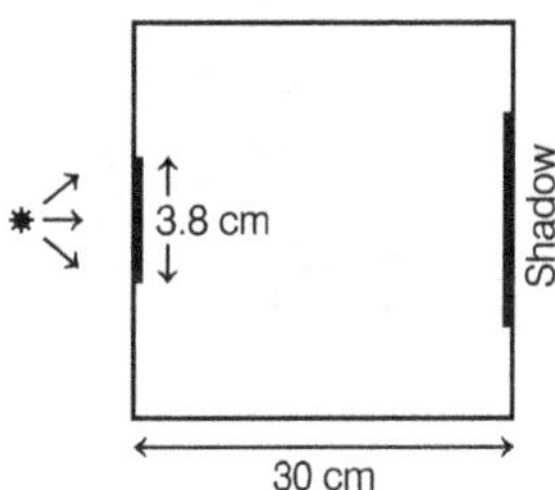

Now, the tank is filled with a liquid of refractive index n and the width of the shadow reduces to 6.4 cm. The value of n is closest to

(a) 1.20   (b) 1.35
(c) 1.45   (d) 1.55

30. Consider a mercury filled tube as shown in the figure below

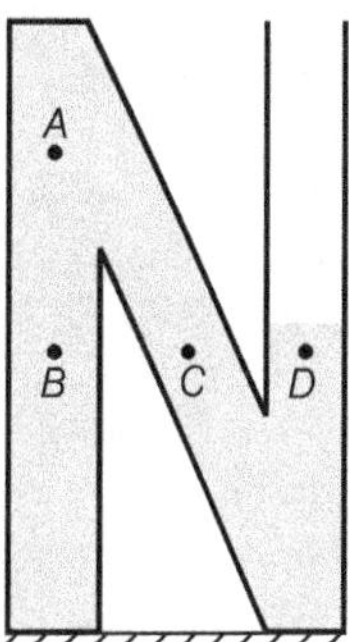

Which of the following options about the pressures at the lettered locations (A, B, C, D) is true?

(a) $p_B > p_A > p_C > p_D$ (b) $p_B = p_C = p_D > p_A$
(c) $p_B = p_C = p_D < p_A$ (d) $p_A = p_B = p_C = p_D$

CHEMISTRY

31. Consider the reaction, $P\,(aq) \rightleftharpoons Q(aq)$ with an equilibrium constant $K = 1.5$. The reaction is started in a vessel with a concentration of $[P]$ of 2 M and concentration of $[Q] = 0$. When the equilibrium is established, half the amount of P is removed, and the reaction is allowed to re-equilibrate. The concentration of Q in the vessel (in M) is closest to

(a) 0.64   (b) 0.96
(c) 0.24   (d) 1.20

32. A gas is reversible expanded from the same initial state to the same final volume using isobaric, isothermal and adiabatic processes. The correct order of the work done by the system on the surroundings in the three different methods is

(a) isobaric > isothermal > adiabatic
(b) isobaric > adiabatic > isothermal
(c) adiabatic > isothermal > isobaric
(d) isothermal > isobaric > adiabatic

33. When 22.4 L of $H_2\,(g)$ is mixed with 5.6 L of $Cl_2\,(g)$, each at S.T.P., the moles of HCl (g) formed after completion of the reaction is closest to

(a) 1.0   (b) 0.75   (c) 0.5   (d) 0.25

34. A bulb emits monochromatic yellow light of the wavelength 0.57 micron. If the rate of emission of quanta per second of the bulb is 14.33×10^{19}, the power of the bulb (in Watt) is

(a) 25   (b) 50   (c) 75   (d) 100

35. An isolated chamber is divided into two halves by a partition with an ideal gas in one half. By making a hole in the partition, the gas is allowed to expand to the full chamber. Among the following the parameter which changes in the process is

(a) internal energy   (b) heat
(c) temperature   (d) pressure

36. Iodination of a hydrocarbon (C—H $\rightarrow$ C—I) with molecular iodine is a slow and reversible reaction, However, it can be carried out in the presence of an oxidising agent such as

(a) H_3BO_3 (b) HIO_3
(c) H_3PO_4 (d) CH_3CO_2H

37. A mixture of 1 mole of benzene and 1 mole of nitrobenzene is reacted with 1 mole of acetyl chloride in the presence of $AlCl_3$. The major product (s) is/are

(a) acetophenone
(b) 3-nitroacetophenone
(c) 1 : 1 mixture of acetophenone and 3- nitroacetophenone
(d) 1-3-diacetyl benzene

38. The stability of the carbocations

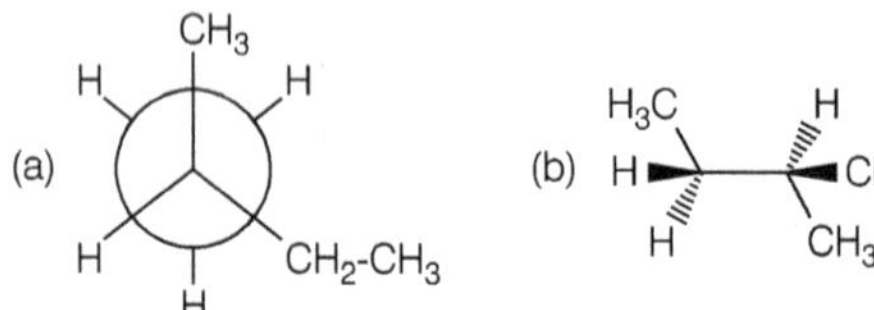

follows the order
(a) I > II > III > IV   (b) III > II > IV > I
(c) IV > II > I > III   (d) IV > I > III > II

39. Among the following the structure which does not represent 2- methyl butane is

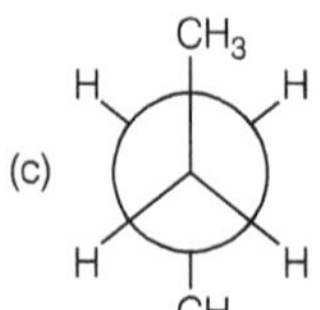

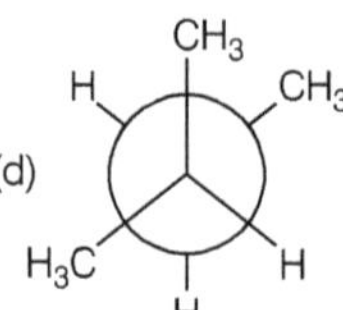

40. The reaction of 1- ethylcyclopentene with BH_3/ THF followed by treatment with H_2O_2/NaOH produces

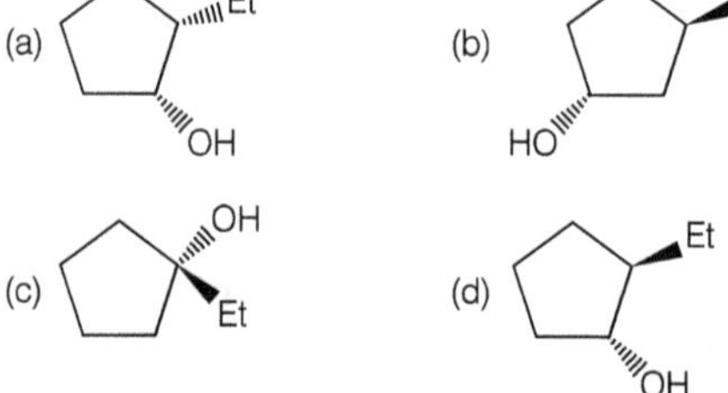

41. The similar chemical properties of lithium and magnesium arise due to their similar
(a) electron affinities   (b) ionic sizes
(c) ionisation potential   (d) hydration enthalpy

42. The incorrect statement about the dissolution of an alkali metal in liquid ammonia is
(a) it produces a blue colouration of the solution.
(b) the blue colouration occurs due to ammoniated electrons that absorbs in visible region of light.
(c) on standing, the blue solution liberates hydrogen gas.
(d) the blue solution is diamagnetic.

43. Among the following, the correct statement for thionyl tetrafluoride is
(a) the geometry of thionyl tetrafluoride is trigonal bipyramidal having the sulphur oxygen bond on the trigonal plane.
(b) the geometry of thionyl tetrafluoride is trigonal bipyramidal having the sulphur oxygen bond perpendicular to the trigonal plane.

(c) the geometry of thionyl tetrafluoride is square pyramidal having the sulphur oxygen bond on the square plane.

(d) the geometry of thionyl tetrafluoride is square pyramidal having the sulphur oxygen bond perpendicular to the square plane.

44. The thermal stability of the hydrides of group -16 elements follows the order

(a) $H_2Te < H_2S < H_2Se < H_2O$

(b) $H_2O < H_2Se < H_2S < H_2Te$

(c) $H_2Te < H_2Se < H_2O < H_2S$

(d) $H_2Te < H_2Se < H_2S < H_2O$

45. The number of acidic protons present in H_3PO_2, H_3PO_3 and H_3PO_4 respectively, are

(a) 1, 2 and 3   (b) 2, 3 and 3

(c) 1, 2 and 2   (d) 3, 3 and 3

BIOLOGY

46. Which one of the following biomolecules is an end product of amylolysis ?

(a) Amino acids   (b) Fatty acids

(c) Monosaccharides   (d) Nucleotides

47. Which one of the following is not used in constructing phylogenetic trees ?

(a) Nuclear DNA   (b) Mitochondrial DNA

(c) Anatomical features   (d) Habitat similarity

48. Caecum is located between

(a) ileum and ascending colon

(b) oesophagus and pharynx

(c) rectum and descending colon

(d) stomach and duodenum

49. Which one of the following plants is an invasive species that has spread to many parts of the Indian subcontinent?

(a) *Prosopis juliflora*   (b) *Ficus religiosa*

(c) *Cocos nucifera*   (d) *Lotus corniculatus*

50. Which one of the following processes maximally facilitates the ascent of sap?

(a) Guttation   (b) Photosynthesis

(c) Photorespiration   (d) Transpiration

51. Which one of the following biomolecules is not present in healthy colostrum ?

(a) Antibodies   (b) Lysozyme

(c) Carbohydrates   (d) Haemoglobin

52. You have made a mixed vegetarian curry with potato, cauliflower, radish and tomato, and spiced it with mustard, cinnamon and clove. The final product of this culinary adventure consists of

(a) root, flower, fruit, bark, leaf

(b) stem, flower, root, fruit, bark

(c) stem, meristem, root, fruit, seed, bark, bud

(d) stem, meristem, root, fruit, seed, bud, leaf

53. Which one of the following processes would be an immediate effect on a plant, if there is a sudden and large increase in soil salinity?

(a) Plasmolysis of root cells

(b) Closure of stomata

(c) Increase in transpiration

(d) Increase in root turgidity

54. High blood glucose in diabetic patients is known to induce cataract. This is because high glucose

(a) crystalises in the lens and blocks light

(b) causes osmotic changes in aqueous humor promoting lens impairment

(c) is polymerised into starch and is deposited in the lens

(d) reflects light from the lens thereby impairing vision

55. Which one of the following is most likely to occur because of climate change-driven temperature increase?

(a) Fish shift their ranges to shallower waters

(b) Mammals shift their ranges towards lower latitudes

(c) Frogs shift their ranges towards the equator

(d) Birds shift their ranges to higher elevations

56. Which one of the following cell types contains Nissl's granules?

(a) Eosinophils   (b) Hepatocytes

(c) Cardiomyocyte   (d) Neurons

57. Within the kingdom-Animalia, which one of the following features is primarily used for classification of the organism?

(a) Body symmetry   (b) Habitat

(c) Mode of nutrition   (d) Locomotory organs

58. In ureotelic animals, urea is produced through

(a) Cori cycle

(b) Kerbs' cycle

(c) Ornithine cycle

(d) Pentose phosphate pathway

59. Which of the following is incorrect about pollen grains?

(a) Angiosperm species can be identified from their pollen morphology

(b) Pollen movement is facilitated by flagella in angiosperms

(c) Pollen out numbers ovules in angiosperm flowers

(d) Pollen is found only in angiosperms

60. Food chains seldom exceed four or five trophic levels because

(a) only 10% of energy in all levels is available for decomposers to convert into nutrients for the entire ecosystem

(b) only 10% of energy at all heterotroph levels is available for conversion of biomass by autotrophs

(c) almost 90% of energy at the autotrophs level are converted to biomass by heterotrophs in all trophic levels

(d) almost 90% of energy in each heterotroph level is not converted into biomass at the next level

➔ **PART-II** (2 Marks Questions)

MATHEMATICS

61. The sum of the sides of a right-angled triangle is 42 and the difference between the median and altitude drawn from the vertex at the right angle is 2. The area of the triangle is
(a) 42   (b) 51   (c) 63   (d) $9\sqrt{51}$

62. The number of ordered pairs (a, b) of integers such that $a - b$ is a root of $x^2 + ax + b = 0$ is
(a) 3   (b) 4   (c) 5   (d) 6

63. Let a, b, c, d be positive integers. Consider the following statements.

I. If 9 divides $a^3 + b^3 + c^3$, then 3 divides abc.

II. If 9 divides $a^3 + b^3 + c^3 + d^3$, then 3 divides $abcd$.

Then,
(a) both I and II are true   (b) I is true but II is false
(c) I is false but II is true   (d) both I and II are false

64. Let λ be the positive root of the equation $x^2 - x - 1 = 0$ and set $a_n = \dfrac{1}{\sqrt{5}} (\lambda^n - (1 - \lambda)^n)$ for $n \in N$, where N is the set of all natural numbers. Consider the sets $A = \{ n \in N : a_n$ is a rational number, but not an integer$\}$ and $B = \{ n \in N : a_n$ is an irrational number$\}$ Then,
(a) both the sets A and B are empty
(b) the set A is empty but the set B is non-empty
(c) the set A is non-empty and the set B is empty
(d) both the sets A and B are non-empty

65. The number of integers q, $1 \le q \le 2021$, such that $\sqrt{q}$ is rational, and $\dfrac{1}{q}$ has a terminating decimal expansion, is
(a) 1   (b) 11   (c) 22   (d) 44

PHYSICS

66. A student of mass M is 1.5 m tall and has her centre of mass 1 m above ground when standing straight. She wants to jump up vetically. To do so, she bends her knees so that her centre of mass is lowerd by 0.2 m and then pushes the ground by a constant force F. As a result, she jumps up such that the maximum height of her feet is 0.3 m above ground. The ratio F / Mg is
(a) 1.5   (b) 2.5   (c) 3.5   (d) 4.5

67. The $45° - 45° - 90°$ prism of height 10 cm (see image below) has a refractive index 2, with a silvered-hypotenus surface.

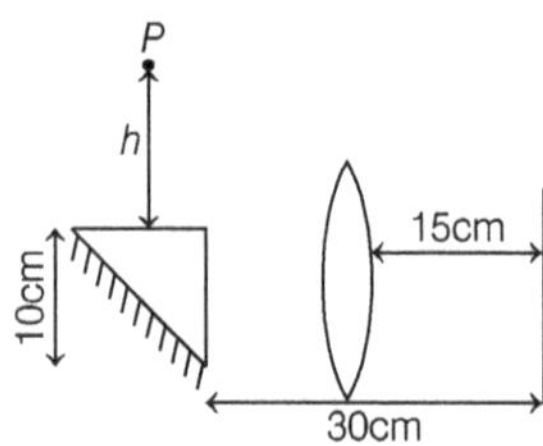

A convex lens of focal length 10 cm placed 15 cm in front of the wall produces a sharp image of P on it. The value of h (in cm) is closest to
(a) 20   (b) 15
(c) 10   (d) 5

68. When the resistance R (indicated in the figure below) is changed from 1 kΩ to 10 kΩ, the current flowing through the resistance R' does not change. What is the value of the resistor R'.

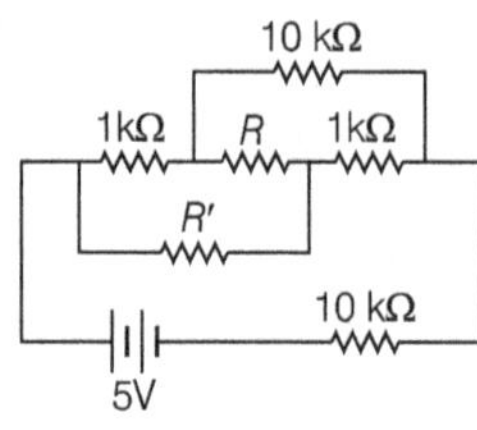

(a) 5 kΩ (b) 100 Ω
(c) 10 Ω (d) 1 Ω

69. A 20 cm long tube is closed at one end. It is held vertically and its open end is dipped in water until only half of it is outside the water surface. Consequently, water rises in it by height h as shown in the figure. The value of h is closest to (assume that the temperature remains constant, $p_{\text{atmosphere}} = 10^5 \, \text{N} / \text{m}^2$, density of water $= 10^3 \, \text{kg} / \text{m}^3$, and acceleration due to gravity, $g = 10 \text{m} / \text{s}^2$)

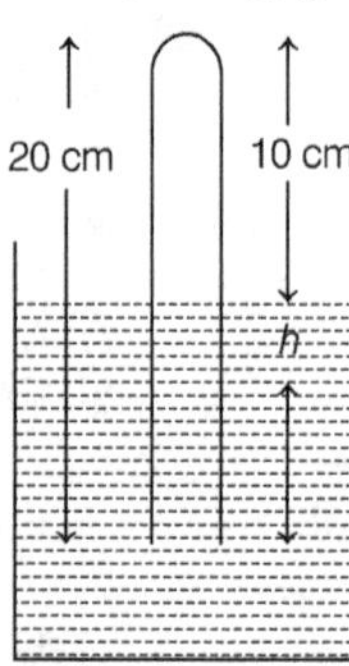

(a) 2 cm   (b) 1 cm
(c) 0.4 cm   (d) 0.2 cm

70. Two particles, one at the centre of a circle of radius R, and another at a point Q on the circle, start moving towards a point P on the circle at the same time (see figure below). Both are at rest initially and move with uniform velocities $\mathbf{v}_1$ and $\mathbf{v}_2$ respectively. They also reach the point P at the same time. If the angle between the velocities is θ and the angle subtended by P and Q at the centre is ϕ (as shown in the figure), then

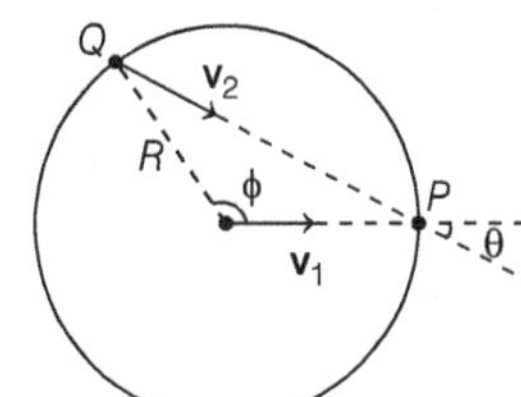

(a) $\tan\dfrac{\phi}{2} = \cot\theta$ (b) $\tan\phi = \cot\theta$

(c) $\cot\dfrac{\phi}{2} = \cot\theta$ (d) $\tan\dfrac{\phi}{2} = \cot\dfrac{\theta}{2}$

CHEMISTRY

71. A hydrocarbon having molecular formula C_5H_{10} produced a tertiary alcohol upon treatment with a few drops of conc. sulphuric acid and water. The same hydrocarbon when reacted with acidic potassium permanganate produced a ketone and a carboxylic acid. The hydrocarbon is
(a) cyclopentane   (b) 1- pentene
(c) 2- methyl-2-butene   (d) 2- pentene

72. Nitrogen present in an unknown organic compound was estimated by Dumas method to be 17.7% by weight. The compound is very likely to be
(a) nitrobenzene   (b) pyridine
(c) nitromethane   (d) aniline

73. A pink coloured aqueous solution of $Co(NO_3)_2$ turns blue on addition of HCl gradually. This colour change happens due to the formation of
(a) $[CoCl_4]^{2-}$ (b) $[CoCl_6]^{4-}$
(c) $[Co(H_2O)_4Cl_2]$ (d) $[Co(H_2O)_2Cl_4]^{2-}$

74. 50 mL of 0.1 M of a weak acid HA is titrated with 0.1 M of NaOH. The ionisation constant of HA (K_a) is 1.8×10^{-5}. Using the given information and from the options shown below, the best indicator for the titration of HA with NaOH is
(a) methyl orange (changes colour from red to yellow as the pH changes from 3.2 to 4.4)
(b) methyl red (changes colour from red to yellow as the pH changes from 4 to 6.3)
(c) phenolphthalein (changes from colourless to pink to as the pH changes from 8.3 to 11)
(d) sodium salt of Alizarin yellow (changes colour from yellow to red as the pH changes from 10 to 12)

75. Consider the p-V (pressure-volume) diagram given below where an ideal gas is reversibly converted from state A and B.

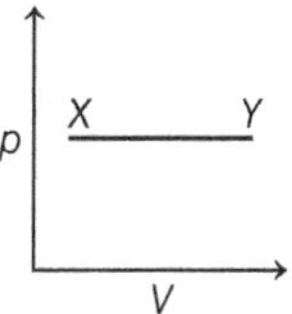

Among the following the correct T-S (temperature-entropy) diagram, which corresponds to this process is

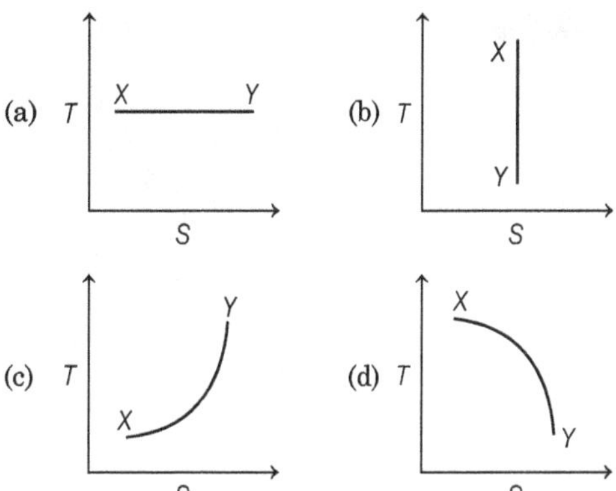

BIOLOGY

76. Which one of the following plots would best describe the relationship between human infant mortality and birth weight (1-10 kgs)?

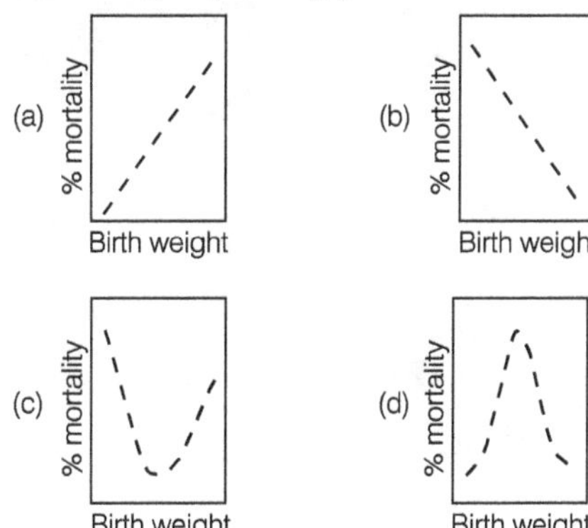

77. A genetic form of a locus would be called an allele only when
(a) its frequency in a population is > 0.01 and it is heritable
(b) its frequency in a population is > 0.01 irrespective of its heritability
(c) it is heritable irrespective of its frequency
(d) it is a tandem repeat irrespective of its frequency

78. A student conducted an experiment to determine the role of sunlight in photosynthesis. Two plants were used, while plant 1 was kept in the dark for 48 hours before the experiment, plant 2 was kept in the sunlight. The student covered one leaf from each plant with a black paper, as shown in the figure. Then, both the plants were kept in the sunlight for a few hours and the levels of starch was immediately examined in the leaves (leaf 1 from plant 1 and leaf 2 from plant 2). Which one of the following figures correctly represent the results of this experiment?

(a) Leaf 1 Leaf 2   (b) Leaf 1 Leaf 2

(c) Leaf 1 Leaf 2   (d) Leaf 1 Leaf 2

79. In the exponential population growth model, population growth rate is given by $dN/dt = rN$, where r is a measure of the population's intrinsic rate of increase and N is population size. The parameter 'r' is determined by
(a) birth rate and density   (b) death rate only
(c) birth rate only   (d) birth rate and death rate

80. Match the fibres in Column I with the primary constituents in Column II given below.

Column I	Column II
P. Cobweb	(i) Fibroin
Q. Silk	(ii) Sericin
R. Cotton	(iii) Keratin
S. Hair	(iv) Cellulose

Choose the correct combination.

Codes
(a) P-(i); Q-(i), (ii) ; R-(iv); S-(iii)
(b) P-(iii); Q-(ii); R-(iv); S-(i)
(c) P-(i), (i); Q-(ii); R-(iv); S-(iii)
(d) P-(i), (i); Q-(i), (ii); R-(iii); S-(i)

Answers

PART-I

1	(c)	2	(c)	3	(b)	4	(c)	5	(c)	6	(a)	7	(b)	8	(b)	9	(b)	10	(b)
11	(c)	12	(a)	13	(a)	14	(c)	15	(b)	16	(d)	17	(d)	18	(b)	19	(d)	20	(c)
21	(c)	22	(a)	23	(a)	24	(a)	25	(c)	26	(d)	27	(b)	28	(b)	29	(c)	30	(b)
31	(b)	32	(a)	33	(c)	34	(b)	35	(d)	36	(b)	37	(a)	38	(c)	39	(c)	40	(d)
41	(b)	42	(d)	43	(a)	44	(d)	45	(a)	46	(c)	47	(d)	48	(a)	49	(a)	50	(d)
51	(d)	52	(c)	53	(a)	54	(b)	55	(d)	56	(d)	57	(a)	58	(c)	59	(b)	60	(d)

PART-II

61	(c)	62	(b)	63	(b)	64	(a)	65	(b)	66	(b)	67	(c)	68	(b)	69	(d)	70	(a)
71	(c)	72	(b)	73	(a)	74	(c)	75	(c)	76	(c)	77	(a)	78	(b)	79	(d)	80	(a)

Solutions

1. *(c)* $\angle BOC = \angle BIC$ [$BCIO$ is cyclic quadrilateral]

$$\Rightarrow \quad 2A = 90° + \frac{A}{2}$$

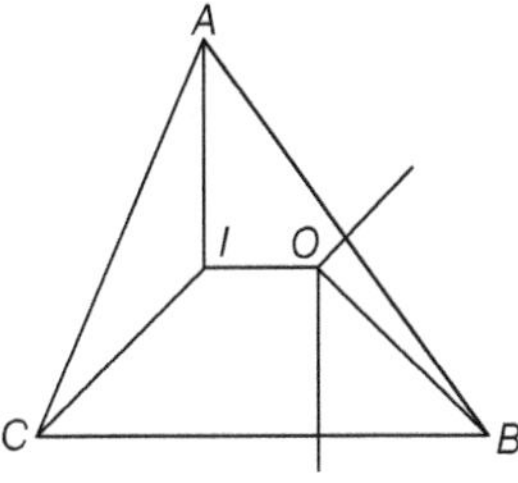

$$\angle BIC = 90° + \frac{A}{2}$$
$$\angle BOC = 2A$$
$$\Rightarrow \quad 90° + \frac{A}{2} = 2A$$
$$\Rightarrow \quad \frac{3A}{2} = 90°$$
$$\Rightarrow \quad A = 60°$$

Hence, $\angle B + \angle C = 120°$

2. *(c)*

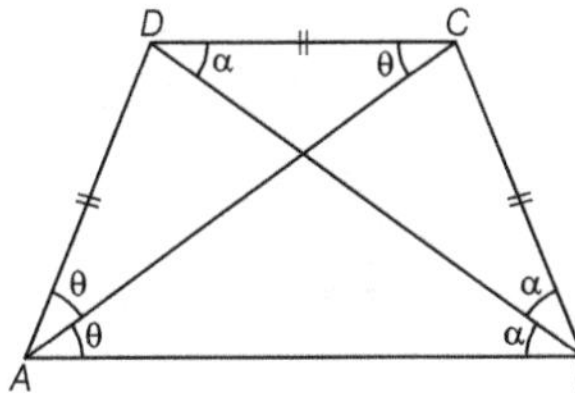

$\because AC$ is bisector of $\angle DAB$.

$\therefore \qquad \angle DAC = \angle CAB$ ...(i)

and $\qquad DC \parallel AB$

$\therefore \qquad \angle CAB = \angle ACD$ ...(ii)

$\therefore \qquad \angle DAC = \angle ACD$

Hence, $AD = DC$

Similarly, $BC = DC$

Hence, exactly three sides are equal.

3. *(b)* $\dfrac{AD}{AB} = \dfrac{3}{5}, \dfrac{AE}{AC} = \dfrac{2}{3}$

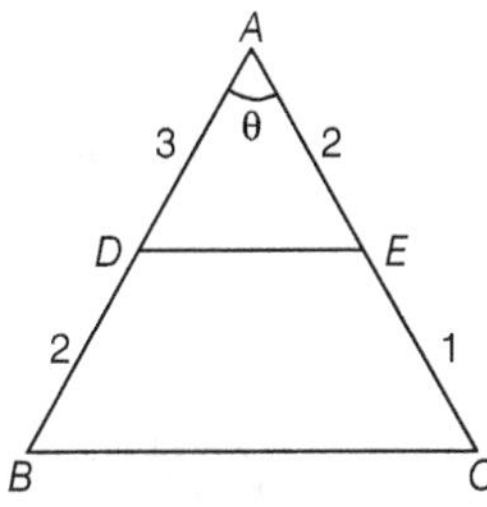

$$\frac{ar\,(\Delta ABC)}{ar\,(\Delta ADE)} = \frac{\frac{1}{2} \times AB \times AC \sin\theta}{\frac{1}{2} \times AD \times AE \sin\theta}$$
$$= \frac{5 \times 3}{3 \times 2} = \frac{5}{2}$$

Hence, area lies between $\left(2, \dfrac{5}{2}\right]$.

4. *(c)* $\Delta ABC \cong \Delta DCB$

$$\angle AOB = ?$$

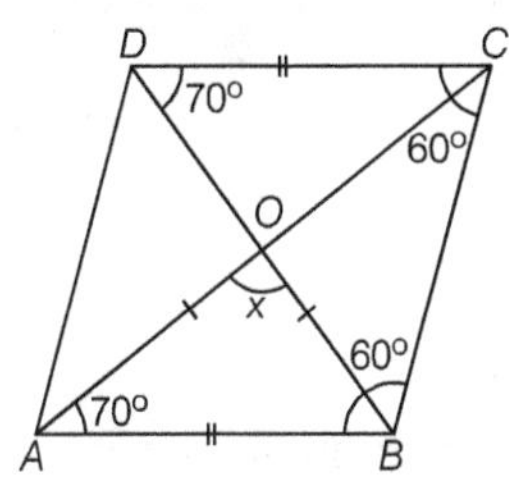

$\because \qquad \Delta ABC \cong \Delta DCB$

$\therefore \qquad \angle CAB = \angle BDC$

and $\qquad \angle ABC = \angle DCB$

Hence, $\angle AOB = 80°$

5. *(c)* $\dfrac{\dfrac{n(n+1)}{2} - k}{(n-1)} = 16$

$$\Rightarrow \quad \frac{n^2 - 31n + 32}{2} = k$$
$$\therefore \quad 1 < \frac{n^2 - 31n + 32}{2} < n$$

Here, $1 < \dfrac{n^2 - 31n + 32}{2}$

$$\Rightarrow \quad n^2 - 31n + 30 > 0$$
$$\Rightarrow \quad (n - 30)(n - 1) > 0 \qquad \text{... (i)}$$

Similarly, $\dfrac{n^2 - 31n + 32}{2} < n$

$$\Rightarrow \quad n^2 - 33n + 32 < 0 \qquad \text{... (ii)}$$

From Eqs. (i) and (ii), we get

$$n = 31$$
$$k = \frac{(31)^2 - 31(31) + 32}{2} = 16$$

So, $n + k = 31 + 16 = 47$

6. *(a)* Given, $p = 99, q = 101$

$$p_1 = \log\left(\frac{p+q}{2}\right) = \log\left(\frac{99 + 101}{2}\right)$$
$$= \log 100 = 2$$
$$q_1 = \frac{1}{2}(\log p + \log q)$$
$$= \log(pq)^{1/2} = \log(99 \times 101)^{1/2}$$
$$= \log(9999)^{1/2}$$

$$p_2 = \log\left(\frac{p_1 + q_1}{2}\right)$$
$$\Rightarrow \quad \log^{-1} p_2 = \frac{p_1 + q_1}{2} = \frac{p_1}{2} + \frac{q_1}{2}$$
$$= 1 + \frac{\log(9999)^{1/2}}{2} = 1 + \log(9999)^{1/4}$$
$$q_2 = \log(p_1 q_1)^{1/2}$$
$$\Rightarrow \quad \log^{-1} q_2 = (p_1 q_1)^{1/2}$$
$$= [2 \times \log(9999^{1/2})]^{1/2}$$

$$\begin{array}{cc} \log q_1 & q_2 \\ q_1 & \log^{-1} q_2 \\ \downarrow & \downarrow \end{array}$$
$$\log(9999)^{1/2} \quad [2 \times \log(9999^{1/2})]^{1/2}$$

$$\begin{array}{cc} & p_2 & \log p_1 \\ & \log^{-1} p_2 & p_1 \\ & \downarrow & \downarrow \end{array}$$
$$1 + \log(9999)^{1/4} \qquad 2$$

$$p_1 > \log^{-1} p_2 > \log^{-1} q_2 > q_1$$
$$\Rightarrow \quad \log p_1 > p_2 > q_2 > \log q_1$$

7. *(b)* $(x - 1)^6 = 0$

So, here all the roots are $x = 1, 1, 1, \ldots\ldots$

So, $\dfrac{a^2 + b^2}{a + b + 1} = \dfrac{1 + 1}{1 + 1 + 1} = \dfrac{2}{3}$

8. *(b)* If common root $= \alpha$

$$x^2 - ax + b = 0$$
$$x^3 - ax^2 + bx + a - b = 0$$
$$\Rightarrow \quad \alpha^3 - a\alpha^2 + b\alpha + (a - b) = 0 \qquad \text{... (i)}$$
$$\alpha^2 - a\alpha + b = 0 \qquad \text{... (ii)}$$
$$\Rightarrow \quad \alpha^3 - a\alpha^2 + b\alpha = 0 \qquad \text{... (iii)}$$

Multiply by α in Eq. (ii) and subtracting Eq. (iii) from Eq. (ii),

$$a - b = 0 \Rightarrow a = b$$

For real roots

$$b^2 - 4ac \geq 0$$
$$a^2 \geq 4a$$
$$(a - 4)\,a \geq 0$$

Total ordered pairs $= 2018$

9. *(b)* According to the graph, we can say only one positive integer satisfy the equation.

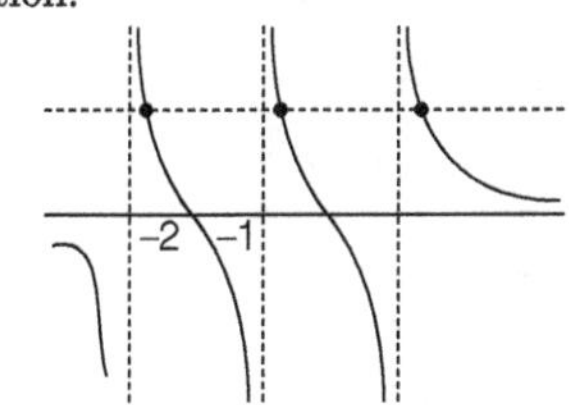

$$\frac{(x+1)(x+2) + x(x+2) + x(x+1)}{x(x+1)(x+2)} = \frac{13}{12}$$

$$36x^2 + 72x + 24 = 13(x^3 + 3x^2 + 2x)$$
$$(x - 2)(13x^2 + 29x + 12) = 0$$

Hence, only one positive integral value of

$$x = 2$$

10. *(b)* $\dfrac{4}{12} + 2\left(\dfrac{1}{12} + \dfrac{1}{36}\right) + \dfrac{2}{36}\, n = 1$

$\Rightarrow \qquad\qquad n = 8$

Hence, required days = 8

11. *(c)* $\dfrac{n^3 - 3}{n + 3}$

$\Rightarrow \qquad \dfrac{(n + 3)(n^2 - 3n + 9) - 30}{(n + 3)}$

$\Rightarrow \qquad \dfrac{(n + 3)(n^2 - 3n + 9)}{(n + 3)} - \dfrac{30}{(n + 3)}$

$\Rightarrow \qquad (n^2 - 3n + 9) - \dfrac{30}{n + 3}$

Here, $\dfrac{30}{n + 3}$ should be integer.

$\Rightarrow \qquad 30 = 2 \times 3 \times 5$

So, $n + 3 \rightarrow 16$ values possible

or we can say 16 values possible for n

So, 5 positive values are possible.

12. *(a)* $a_1 = 1, d = 5$ (given)

So, AP = 1, 6, 11, 16, 21, …

$$a_k = a + (k - 1)d$$
$$a_k = 1 + (k - 1)5$$
$$1 + (k - 1)5 \le 2021$$

$\Rightarrow \qquad (k - 1)5 \le 2020$

$\Rightarrow \qquad k - 1 \le 404$

$\Rightarrow \qquad k \le 405$

Or

$$a_{k+1} > 2021$$
$$1 + 5k > 2021$$

$\Rightarrow \qquad 5k > 2020 \Rightarrow k > 404$

Hence, $k = 405$

$$a_1, a_2, a_3, …, a_{405}$$

Now, median $= a_{203} = a + (203 - 1)\, d$

$$= 1 + (202)5 = 1 + 1010$$
$$= 1011$$

13. *(a)* $x = 10^{10^{10}} = 10^{10 \times 10^9}$

Fifth root $= x^{\frac{1}{5}} = (10^{10 \times 10^9})^{\frac{1}{5}}$

$$= 10^{10 \times 10^9 \times \frac{1}{5}} = 10^{2 \times 10^9}$$

14. *(c)* $ab = (a! + b!)$

$\because ab \le 99 \Rightarrow a! + b! \le \dfrac{99}{4}$

$a, b \le 4$

Check for $a = 1, 2, 3, 4$

$\qquad\qquad b = 0, 1, 2, 3, 4$

We get, 12, 32

Sum $= 12 + 32 = 44$

15. *(b)* Total = 100

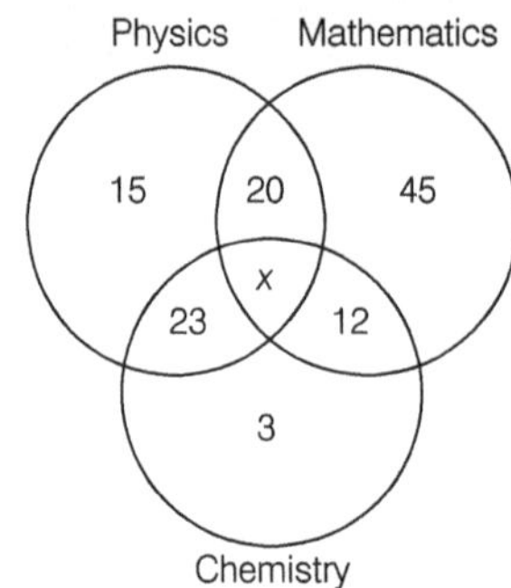

Remaining $= 100 - 15 - 3 - 45 = 37$

$$37 = (P \cap M) + (P \cap C) + (M \cap C)$$
$$\underset{20}{\uparrow} \qquad\quad \underset{23}{\uparrow} \qquad\quad \underset{12}{\uparrow}$$
$$- 2\underset{\underset{^6C_2}{\downarrow}}{(P \cap C \cap M)}$$

$\Rightarrow \qquad 37 = 55 - 2x$

$\Rightarrow \qquad 2x = 55 - 37$

$\Rightarrow \qquad 2x = 18 \Rightarrow x = 9$

16. *(d)* Impulse given is directly proportional to circumference and mass of water is directly proportional to area of container.

We have,

$$p = mv$$

$\Rightarrow \qquad v = \dfrac{p}{m} = \dfrac{k_1 \cdot 2\pi R}{k_2 \cdot \pi R^2}$

or $\qquad v \propto \dfrac{1}{R}$

17. *(d)*

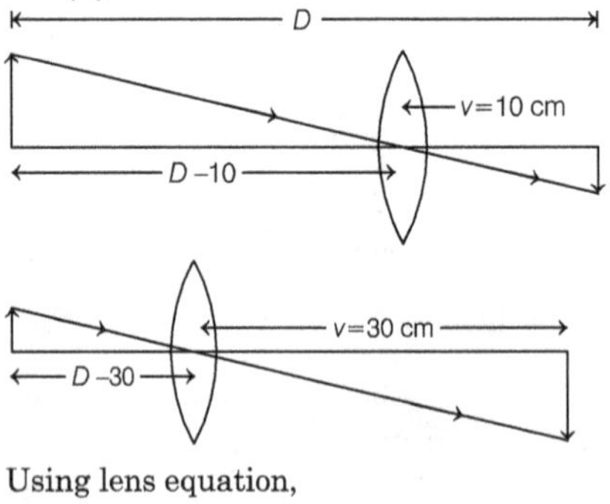

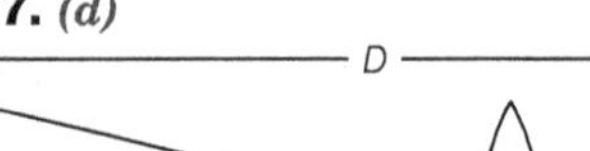

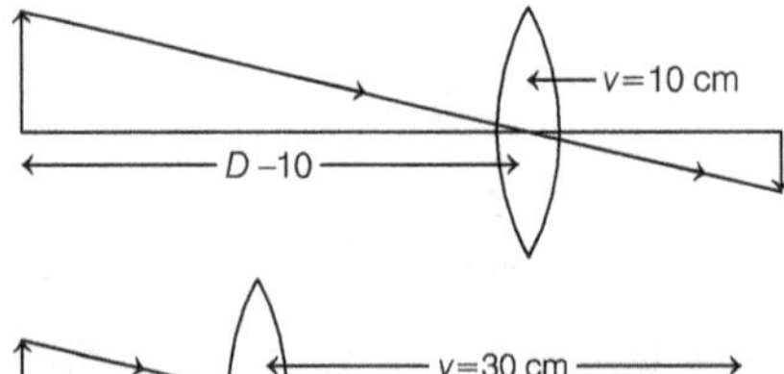

Using lens equation,

$$\dfrac{1}{10} - \dfrac{1}{-(D - 10)} = \dfrac{1}{f} \qquad …\,(i)$$

and $\qquad \dfrac{1}{30} - \dfrac{1}{-(D - 30)} = \dfrac{1}{f} \qquad …\,(ii)$

From Eqs. (i) and (ii), we get

$$\dfrac{1}{10} + \dfrac{1}{D - 10} = \dfrac{1}{30} + \dfrac{1}{D - 30}$$

or $\qquad\qquad D = 40\,\text{cm}$

Substituting D in Eq. (i), we get

$$f = 7.5\,\text{cm}$$

Hence, to obtain an image of same size, object distance must be kept $2f$ and distance of wall and candle must be $4f = 4 \times 7.5 = 30\,\text{cm}$.

Hence, candle must be moved 10 cm towards wall.

18. *(b)* The diagram is shown below

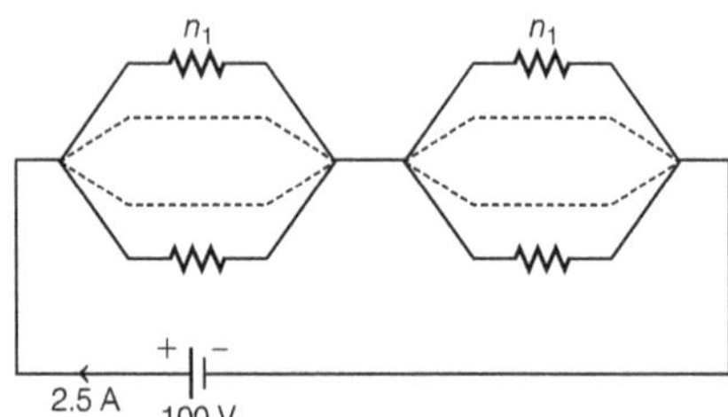

We have,

$$n_1 + n_2 = 10 \qquad\qquad …\,(i)$$

and $\qquad 100 = 2.5\left(\dfrac{R}{n_1} + \dfrac{R}{n_2}\right)$

Here, $\qquad R = 100\,\Omega$

$\Rightarrow \qquad 100 = 2.5 \times 100\left(\dfrac{1}{n_1} + \dfrac{1}{n_2}\right)$

$\Rightarrow \qquad \dfrac{1}{n_1} + \dfrac{1}{n_2} = \dfrac{2}{5}$

$\Rightarrow \qquad \dfrac{10}{n_1 n_2} = \dfrac{2}{5}$ or $n_1 n_2 = 25 \qquad …\,(ii)$

Now, $(n_1 - n_2)^2 = (n_1 + n_2)^2 - 4(n_1 n_2)$

$$= 10^2 - 4 \times 25 = 0$$

or $\qquad n_1 = n_2$

Hence, $n_1 = n_2 = 5$

19. *(d)* Forces on a water particle are shown below,

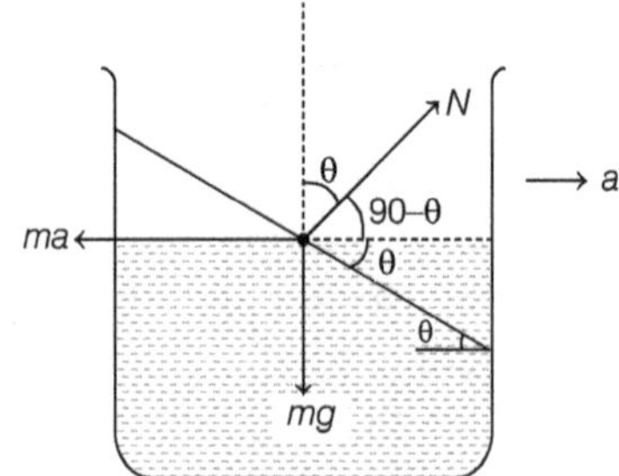

$$N \cos\theta = mg$$

and $\qquad N \sin\theta = ma$

$\Rightarrow \qquad a = g \cdot \tan\theta$

Also, profile of surface is a straight line.

20. *(c)* Useful power output of reactor in $\dfrac{1}{2}$ h is

$$P = 10^9 \times 1800\,\text{J}$$
$$= 1.8 \times 10^{12}\,\text{J}$$

This energy is only 4.2% of energy produced in fission of U^{235}.

Hence, total energy of fission,
$$E_1 = \frac{100}{4.2} \times 1.8 \times 10^{12}$$
$$= \frac{18}{42} \times 10^{14} \text{ J}$$

Now, 1 mole or 235 g of uranium produces energy,
$$E_2 = 3 \times 10^{-11} \times 6.023 \times 10^{23} \text{ J}$$

$\therefore$ 1 g of U^{235} produces energy of
$$= \frac{3 \times 10^{-11} \times 6.023 \times 10^{23}}{235} \text{ J}$$

Hence, mass of U^{235} in grams needed is
$$\frac{E_1}{E_2} = \frac{\left(\frac{18}{42} \times 10^{14}\right)}{\left(\frac{3 \times 10^{-11} \times 6.02 \times 10^{23}}{235}\right)}$$

$$\approx \left(\frac{\frac{18}{4^2}}{\frac{18}{235}}\right) \times 10^2$$

$$= \frac{235}{42} \times 10^2 = 559 \text{ g}$$

Nearest value is 500 g.

21. *(c)* Volume of sphere
$$= \frac{4}{3}\pi (D/2)^3 = \frac{\pi}{6}D^3$$

Volume of 1 cube $= a^2$

Number of atoms in sphere,
$$N = \frac{\text{Volume of sphere}}{\text{Volume of 1 cube}} \times 8$$

$$N = \frac{\frac{4}{3}\pi D^3}{a^2}$$

Now, mass of sphere,
$$M = N \times m_1 = \frac{\frac{4}{3}\pi D^3}{a^2} \times m_1,$$

(m_1 = mass of 1 silicon atom)

So, relative error in mass of sphere
$$= \frac{\Delta M}{M} = \frac{3\Delta D}{D} + \frac{2\Delta a}{a}$$
$$= \frac{3 \times 0.2 \times 10^{-9}}{9.4 \times 10^{-2}} + 2 \times 10^{-9} \approx 1.2 \times 10^{-8}$$

22. *(a)*

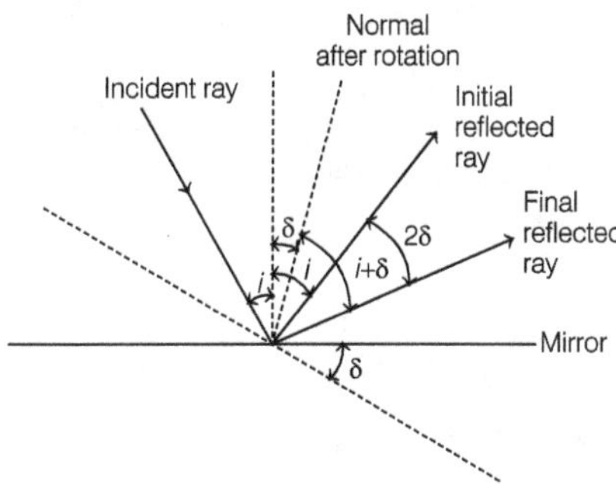

From diagram angle between previous normal and new reflected ray
$$= (i + \delta) + \delta = i + 2\delta$$

Angle between initial and final reflected rays $= (i + 2\delta) - i = 2\delta$

23. *(a)*

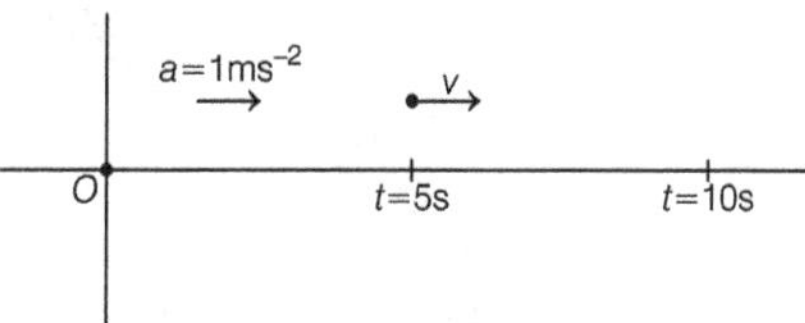

Charges are of equal magnitudes and fields of charges E_1 and E_2 are also of equal magnitudes.

Hence, resultant field **E** is along angle bisector of E_1 and E_2.

So, angle of **E** and X-axis is 0°.

24. *(a)* **Case I** Particle moving with acceleration of 1 ms^{-2}, $x = 0$, $x = 0$, $t = 0$,

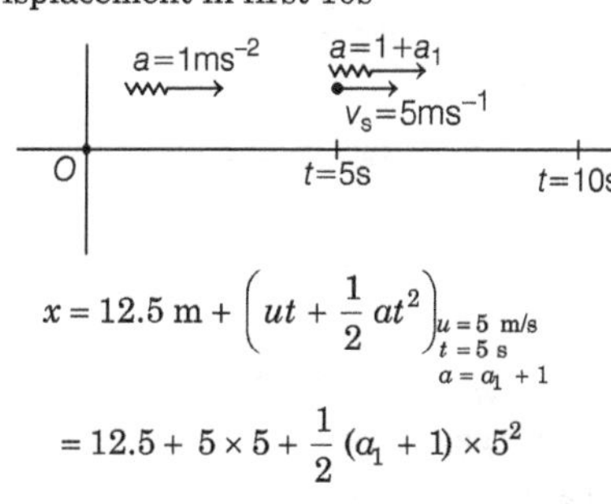

Velocity at $t = 5$s,
$$v_5 = u + at = 0 + 1 \times 5$$
$$= 5 \text{ ms}^{-1}$$

Velocity at $t = 10$s,
$$v_0 = 0 + 1 \times 10$$
$$\Rightarrow \quad = 10 \text{ ms}^{-1}$$

Also displacement at $t = 5$ s,
$$x_5 = ut + \frac{1}{2}at^2 = \frac{1}{2} \times 1 \times 5^2$$
$$= 12.5 \text{ m}$$

Also displacement at $t = 10$ s,
$$x_0 = \frac{1}{2} \times 1 \times 10^2 = 50 \text{ m}$$

Case II Particle moving with additional acceleration (a_1),

Displacement in first 10s

$$x = 12.5 \text{ m} + \left(ut + \frac{1}{2}at^2\right)_{\substack{u = 5 \text{ m/s} \\ t = 5 \text{ s} \\ a = a_1 + 1}}$$
$$= 12.5 + 5 \times 5 + \frac{1}{2}(a_1 + 1) \times 5^2$$

Velocity after 10s,
$$v = (x + (1 + a_1)t)_{\substack{u = 5 \text{ m/s} \\ t = 5 \text{ s}}}$$
$$= 5 + (1 + a_1) \times 5 = 10 + 5a_1 \quad \ldots \text{(i)}$$

Now, given $x - x_0 = 12.5$

So, $\left[12.5 + 25 + \frac{25}{2}(1 + a_1)\right] - [50] = 12.5$

$$\Rightarrow \quad \frac{25}{2}(a_1) = 12.5 \text{ or } a_1 = 1 \text{ m/s}^2$$

Substituting a_1 in Eq. (i), we get
$$v = 10 + 5 \times 1 = 15 \text{ m/s}$$

So, $v - v_0 = 15 - 10 = 15 \text{ m/s}$

25. *(c)*

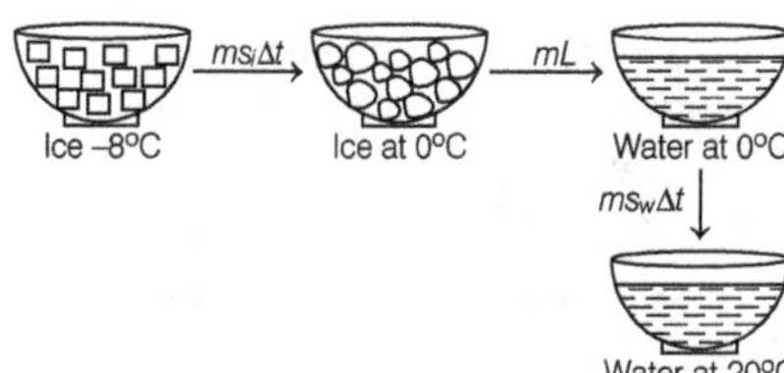

Heat required to convert ice at -8°C to ice at 0°C
$$= ms_{\text{ice}}\Delta t = 1 \times 2.1 \times 10^3 \times (0 - (-8))$$
$$= 16.8 \times 10^3 \text{ J}$$

Heat required to melt ice
$$= mL = 1 \times 333 \times 10^3 = 333 \times 10^3 \text{ J}$$

Heat required to heat water from 0°C to 20°C
$$= ms_w\Delta t = 1 \times 4.2 \times 10^3 \times 20$$
$$= 84 \times 10^3 \text{ J}$$

Total heat $= (16.8 + 333 + 84) \times 10^3$
$$= 433.8 \text{ kJ} \approx 434 \text{ kJ}$$

26. *(d)* Energy stored in battery,
$$E = \text{voltage} \times \text{ampere-hours}$$
$$= 3 \times 225 \times 10^{-3} \text{ (Watt-hours)}$$
$$= 3 \times 225 \times 10^{-3} \times 3600 \text{ J}$$

If this energy is stored in ball, then
$$\frac{1}{2}mv^2 = E$$
$$\text{or} \quad v^2 = \frac{2E}{m}$$

$$\Rightarrow \quad v^2 = \frac{2 \times 3 \times 225 \times 3600 \times 10^{-3}}{0.163}$$
$$= \frac{2 \times 3 \times 225 \times 3600}{16.3}$$

$$\Rightarrow \quad v^2 \approx \frac{15^2 \times 6^2 \times 10^2}{3^2 \times 3}$$

$$\Rightarrow \quad v = \frac{15 \times 6 \times 10}{3 \times \sqrt{3}}$$
$$= 5 \times 10 \times 2\sqrt{3}$$
$$= 170 \text{ m/s}$$

27. *(b)*

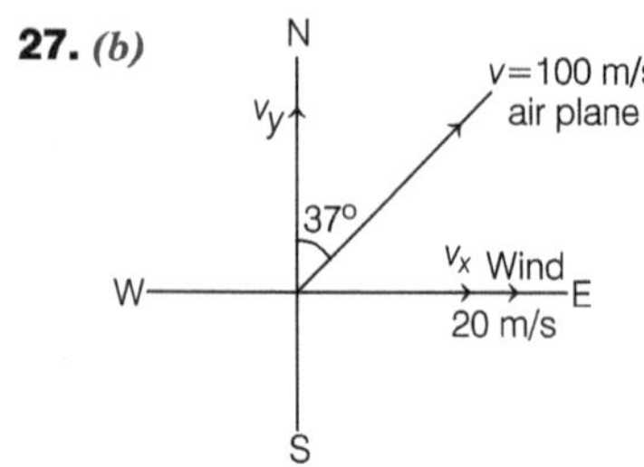

Velocity of plane in north and east directions are

$$v_y = v\cos 37° = 100 \times \frac{4}{5} = 80 \text{ m/s}$$

$$v_x = v\sin 37° = 100 \times \frac{3}{5} = 60 \text{ m/s}$$

Now, velocity of wind add up in v_x, so velocity components of plane are;

$$v_y = 80 \text{ m/s and}$$

and $\quad v_x' = 60 + 20 = 80 \text{ m/s}$

So, velocity of plane with respect to ground,

$$v = \sqrt{(v_x')^2 + (v_y)^2}$$
$$= \sqrt{80^2 + 80^2} = 80\sqrt{2}$$
$$= 113.13 \text{ m/s}$$

28. *(b)* Focal length of a lens depends on refractive index are

$$f \propto \frac{1}{n}$$

and $\quad n_{\text{violet}} > n_{\text{red}}$

$\Rightarrow \quad f_{\text{violet}} < f_{\text{red}}$

So, violet colour converges nearer to lens.

∴ Correct diagram is

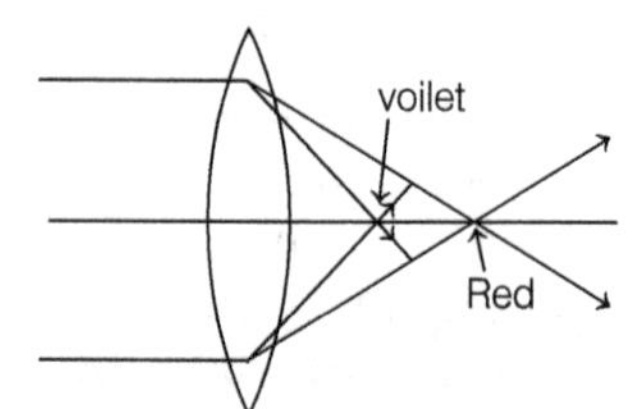

29. *(c)* Shadows length shortened due to refraction.

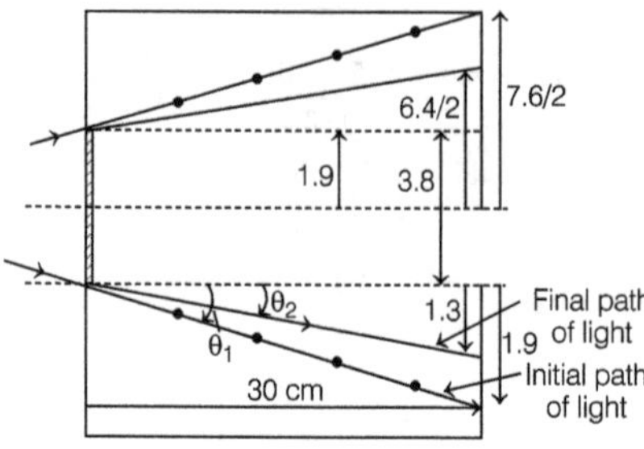

From diagram,

$$\sin\theta_1 = \frac{1.9}{H_1} \text{ and } \sin\theta_2 = \frac{1.3}{H_2}$$

where, H_1 and H_2 are hypotenuous lengths (path of light rays in two cases).

As $H_1 \approx H_2$, we have,

Refractive index, $n = \dfrac{\sin\theta_1}{\sin\theta_2} = \dfrac{1.9}{1.3} \Rightarrow n = 1.46$

30. *(b)* As, pressure of a liquid column ∝ height of liquid, this means pressure at points at same level is equal.

∴ $\qquad p_B = p_C = p_D$

Also p_A is less than p_B.

∴ $\qquad p_B = p_C = p_D > p_A$

Note *To visualise this imagine that a hole is made at point A, B, C or D and then calculate amount of fluid that comes out of hole.*

If fluid volume from two holes is found equal, then pressures at these are equal.

31. *(b)* $\quad P(aq) \rightleftharpoons Q(aq)$

When $t = 0 \quad 2M \qquad —$

$t_{\text{eq.}} \quad (2-x)\text{ M} \qquad x\text{ M}$

$$K = \frac{x}{2-x}$$

$$K = 1.5 \text{ (given in question)}$$

$$1.5 = \frac{x}{2-x} \Rightarrow x = 1.2$$

When the equilibrium is established.

$P(aq) \rightleftharpoons Q(aq)$

0.8 M $\qquad$ 1.2 M (before equilibrium)

0.4 M $\qquad$ 1.2 M (when half of the P is removed)

$0.4 + y \qquad 1.2 - y$ (Reaction is backward shifted)

$$K = \frac{1.2 - y}{0.4 + y} \Rightarrow 1.5 = \frac{1.2 - y}{0.4 + y}$$

$$y = 0.24$$

at equilibrium

$$|Q| = 1.2 - y = 1.2 - 0.24 = 0.96 \text{ M}$$

32. *(a)* Work done ∝ area under p-V curve.

If we draw a p-V curve for isobaric process then $\Delta p = 0$ and a straight line parallel to volume axis is obtained.

In p-V curve of isothermal process $\Delta T = 0$ and a hyperbolic curve from V_1 to V_2.

In p-V curve of adiabatic process we have pV^γ = constant, its graph is also hyperbolic, but slope of p-V curve in this case is V times slope of p-V curve in isothermal process.

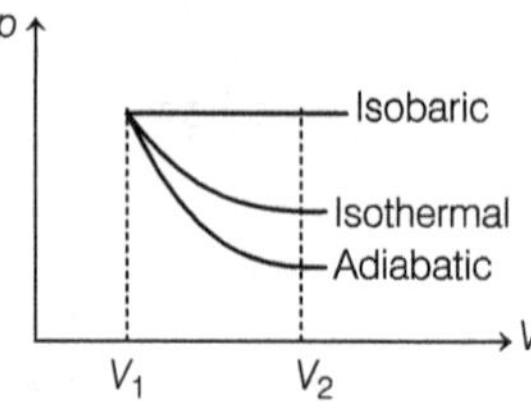

Thus, we have area under the p-V curve as:

isobaric > isothermal > adiabatic

33. *(c)* $\quad \underset{22.4 \text{ L}}{H_2} + \underset{5.6\,1\,\text{L}}{Cl_2} \longrightarrow 2HCl$

1 mole of chlorine form 2 moles of HCl

∴ 0.5 mole of chlorine form 1 mole of HCl

∴ When 22.4 L of $Cl_2(g)$ form 1 mole of HCl

∴ 5.6 L of Cl_2 form $\left(\dfrac{1}{22.4} \times 5.6\right)$ mole

of HCl = 0.25 moles of HCl

34. *(b)*

$$E = \frac{hc}{\lambda} = \frac{6.626 \times 10^{-34} \text{Js} \times 3 \times 10^8 \text{ m/s}}{0.57 \times 10^{-6}}$$

$$= 3.487 \times 10^{-19} \text{ J}$$

Rate of emission of quanta $= \dfrac{\text{Power}}{\text{Energy}}$

∴ $\qquad$ Power = Rate × Energy

$$= 14.33 \times 10^{19} \times 3.487 \times 10^{-19}$$
$$= 49.97 \text{ W} \approx 50 \text{ W}$$

35. *(d)* Since, it is an isolated chamber there is no exchange of heat.

∴ $\Delta Q = 0$, also work done by the ideal gas, while expansion is zero.

Thus, change in internal energy is zero.

Also, during free expansion of an ideal gas temperature remains constant, i.e. $\Delta T = 0$. Thus, only parameter out of the given once which is changes in the process is pressure.

36. *(b)* Iodination of hydrocarbons is carried out in presence of oxidising agents because one of the products is hydrogen iodide, which is a strong reducing agent and it converts alkyl iodide back to an alkane. Thus, oxidising agents like HNO_3 / HIO_3 are used to oxidising agent.

37. *(a)*

It is Friedel-Craft's reaction, in which acyl group substitutes one of the hydrogen atom on benzene to form acetophenone. Nitrobenzene does not give Friedel-Craft's acylation since —NO_2 group is a strong electron acceptor group causing decrease in electron density of benzene ring which thus do not show electrophilic addition.

Thus,

38. *(c)*

I	II	III	IV
Non-aro matic	Non-aro matic	Anti-aro matic	Aromatic
No π e^- hyper conjugati on stabilises	No conjugati on	Conjugat ion 2 resonatin g structure	Conjugat ion 4 resonatin g structure

Thus, the order is IV > II > I > III.

39. *(c)*

$$H_3C-\underset{\underset{H}{|}}{\overset{\overset{CH_3}{|}}{C}}-CH_2-CH_3 \text{ (2-methyl butane)}$$

(c) is not correct representation of 2-methyl butane.

40. *(d)* It is hydroboration reaction which follow anti-Markownikoff rule and the hydrogen atom goes to more substituted carbon atom.

Mechanism

1-ethylcyclopentene

syn-addition

41. *(b)* Li and Mg show diagonal relationship due to which there ionic sizes are almost similar. Due to small size lithium differ from other alkali metals but resembles magnesium, as its size is closer to lithium.

42. *(d)* Alkali metals are having one electron in its outermost shell which they can lose. Alkali metal atom in solution readily loses its valence electron. Both cation and the electron combine with ammonia to form ammoniated cation $[M(NH_3)_n]^+$ and ammoniated electron $[e(NH_3)_n]^-$. The ammoniated electron is responsible for blue colour of solution. The dilute solutions are paramagnetic in nature because they contain free ammoniated electron. But as the concentration increases, the ammoniated metal get bound by free electrons and solution colour changes to bronze.

$$2e^- \, [NH_3]_n \longrightarrow [e(NH_3)_n]_2$$

(Blue colour)   (Bronze colour)
Paramagnetic   Diamagnetic

43. *(a)* Thionyl tetrafluoride is an inorganic compound with formula SOF_4. Its shape is distorted trigonal bipyramidal, with the oxygen found on the equator.

Correct option is (a) the geometry of thionyl tetrafluoride is trigonal bipyramidal having the sulphur-oxygen bond on the trigonal plane.

44. *(d)* As the size of the element increases down the group, the bond dissociation energy of element-hydrogen bond decreases and hence the bond break more easily. Thus, thermal stability of hydrides of group-16 elements decreases down the group.

$$H_2O > H_2S > H_2Se > H_2Te$$

45. *(a)*

H_3PO_2 H_3PO_3 H_3PO_4

As is clearly visible from the structure of three compounds H_3PO_2 is monobasic due to presence of only one —OH groups, H_3PO_3 is dibasic with two —OH groups and H_3PO_4 is tribasic with three —OH groups.

46. *(c)* Monosaccharides are the end product of amylolysis. Amylolysis or amylase enzyme digestion turns polysaccharide starch into smaller molecules, ultimately yielding maltose, which in turn is cleaved into two glucose molecules (monosaccharide) by maltase enzyme. Amylase is found in our saliva.

47. *(d)* Habitat similarities between organisms are not used in constructing phylogenetic tree. A phylogenetic tree is a diagram that represents evolutionary relationships among organisms. The pattern of branching in a phylogenetic tree reflects how species or other groups evolved from a series of common ancestors. Nuclear and mitochondrial DNA as well as anatomical features of organisms are used in constructing phylogenetic tree.

48. *(a)* Caecum is located between the ileum (distal small bowel) and the ascending colon. The caecum is the most proximal part of the large intestine and

having served as a site for cellulose digestion in herbivorous animals.

49. *(a) Prosopis juliflora* is an invasive species that has spread many parts of Indian subcontinent. It is a shrub or small tree in the family–Fabaceae, a kind of mesquite. It is native to Mexico, South America and the Caribbean. It has shown itself to be a very aggressive invader, especially in frost-free arid and semi-arid natural grasslands, both in its native range and in particular, where introduced. It was introduced in India to meet the fuel wood requirement of the rural poor and to restore degraded lands.

50. *(d)* Transpiration maximally facilitates the ascent of sap in vascular plants. It helps in the ascent of sap by producing suction force acting from the bottom of the plant. Transpirational pull extends upto root hair through water column in xylem vessel. Due to transpirational pull water molecules enter into the roots hair from soil. Thus, transpiration helps in the absorption and upward movement of water and minerals dissolved in it from roots to the leaves.

51. *(d)* Haemoglobin is not present in healthy colostrum. It is present in red blood cells of blood. Colostrum is the first form of breastmilk that is released by the mammary glands after giving birth. It's nutrient-dense and high in antibodies and antioxidants to build a newborn baby's immune system. It also contains antibacterial lysozyme enzyme and lactose sugar as carbohydrate. It changes to breastmilk within two to four days after your baby is born.

52. *(c)* Potato, cauliflower, radish, tomato, mustard, cinnamon and clove are stem, meristem, root, fruit, seed, bark and bud, respectively.

- Edible part of potato is a modified underground stem (tuber).
- Edible part of cauliflower is its head, which is composed of a white inflorescence meristem.
- Edible part of radish is a modified fusiform root.
- Edible part of tomato is fruit.
- Edible part of mustard is seed.
- Edible part of cinnamon is bark.
- Edible part of clove is dried flower bud.

53. *(a)* Plasmolysis of root cells would be an immediate effect on a plant if there is a sudden and large increase in soil salinity. Plasmolysis is a typical response of plant cells exposed to hyperosmotic stress. The loss of turgidity of root cells leads to the shrinking of a cell membrane away from the cell wall. Water moves out of the cell and the protoplast shrinks away from the cell wall. It occurs due to higher concentration of soil solution due to increased salinity which leads to exosmosis of water from root cells to soil and causes plasmolysis and death of roots hairs.

54. *(b)* High blood glucose in diabetic patients is known to induce cataract, because high glucose level causes osmotic changes in aqueous humor promoting lens impairment. A cataract causes a part of the lens to become opaque, or cloudy. Thus, light does not pass through easily and vision becomes blurry. The aqueous humor is the space between the eyeballs and the lens of the cornea. It supplies nutrients and oxygen to the lens. When blood sugar rises, the lens swells, resulting in blurry vision. Uncontrolled blood sugar also causes enzymes in the lens to convert glucose to a substance called sorbitol. Too much sorbitol in the lens leads to cloudy vision, too.

55. *(d)* Birds may shift their range to higher elevations because of climate change driven temperature increase. Climate change affects birds both directly and indirectly. The distributions of birds are closely associated with both winter and summer temperatures, and increased temperatures due to climate change may directly affect birds by forcing them to use more energy for thermoregulation as well as forcing them to fly at higher elevations due to lower temperature at higher altitude.

56. *(d)* Nissl's granules are present in the cytoplasm of the cell body of the neurons along with other cell organelles like Golgi apparatus, endoplasmic reticulum, mitochondria, nucleus, etc. These granules give a slight coloured appearance to the cytoplasm of the cell body. They help in protein synthesis in the neurons.

57. *(a)* Body symmetry is primarily used for animal classification. Animals can be classified by three types of body plan symmetry: asymmetry, bilateral symmetry and radial symmetry.

- Only members of the phylum-Porifera (sponges) have no body plan symmetry.
- Bilateral symmetry involves the division of the animal through a sagittal plane, resulting in two mirror-image, right and left halves,

such as those in helminthes, annelids, arthropods, molluscs and chordates.

- Radial symmetry is the arrangement of body parts around a central axis, such as those in ctenophores, adult echinodermates and cnidarians.

58. *(c)* In ureotelic animals such as humans, urea is produced by Ornithine cycle. It helps in conversion of excess of amino acids into urea in the liver. Urea is produced in a series of reactions which take place in the mitochondrial matrix and cytosol of liver cells. Ornithine cycle is the series of biochemical reactions that converts ammonia, which is highly toxic, and carbon dioxide to the much less toxic urea during the excretion of metabolic nitrogen derived from the deamination of excess amino acids. The urea is ultimately excreted in solution in urine.

59. *(b)* Pollen movement is not facilitated by flagella in angiosperms. A flagellum is a hair-like appendage that protrudes from certain plant, protist, bacterial and animal cells to provide motility.

Rest statements are correct.

60. *(d)* Food chain seldom exceeds four or five trophic levels because almost 90 % energy in energy heterotrophy level is not converted into biomass at next level. According to Lindeman's 10% law of energy transfer, only 10% energy is transferred from one trophic level to the next higher level to get stored as secondary biomass. Rest of the energy is wastes in respiration and other biological activities. The loss of energy at each trophic level is so great that very little usable energy remains after four or five trophic levels. Hence, only 4 to 5 trophic levels are present in each food chain.

61. *(c)* $a + b + c = 42$

$$AD - AE = 2$$

Area of triangle = ?

Area of $\triangle ABC = \dfrac{1}{2} \times \text{Base} \times \text{height}$

$$\Delta = \frac{1}{2} \times 2R \times h = rS$$

[here $r = (s - a)\tan A/2$]

$$\Rightarrow \quad R(R - 2) = (21 - 2R) \times 1 \times 21$$
$$\Rightarrow \quad R = 9$$
$$h = 7$$
$$\text{Area} = \frac{1}{2} \times 2R \times h$$
$$= \frac{1}{2} \times 2 \times 9 \times 7 = 63$$

62. *(b)* $x^2 + ax + b = 0$

$$\text{Roots} = \frac{-a \pm \sqrt{a^2 - 4b}}{2}$$

$$\Rightarrow \quad \frac{-a + \sqrt{a^2 - 4b}}{2} = a - b$$
$$\Rightarrow \quad -a + \sqrt{a^2 - 4b} = 2a - 2b$$
$$\Rightarrow \quad \sqrt{a^2 - 4b} = 3a - 2b$$
$$\Rightarrow \quad a^2 - 4b = 9a^2 + 4b^2 - 12ab$$
$$\Rightarrow \quad 8a^2 + 4b^2 - 8ab = 0$$
$$\Rightarrow \quad \sqrt{a^2 - 6b} = 2b - 3a$$
$$\Rightarrow \quad a^2 - 6b = (2b - 3a)^2$$
$$\Rightarrow \quad a^2 - 6b = 4b^2 + 9a^2 - 12ab$$
$$\Rightarrow \quad 8a^2 + 4b^2 - 6b - 12ab$$

Both are quadratic equation.

Hence, total number of roots = 2 + 2 = 4.

63. *(b)* $a^3 + b^3 + c^3 = 9k_1 \Rightarrow abc = 3k_2$

Possibility of a, b, c can be $3k_1$, $3k_1 + 1$, $3k_2 + 2$

Case I $(3k_1)^3 + (3k_1 + 1)^3 + (3k_2 + 2)^3$
$$= 9k' + 9$$

divisible by 9 and abc is divisible by 3.

Case II $(3k_1)^3 + (3k_2)^3 + (3k_3)^3 = 9k'$

divisible by 9 and abc is divisible by 3.

Case III $(3k_1 + 1)^3 + (3k_2 + 1)^3 + (3k_3 + 1)^3$
$$= 9k' + 3$$

not divisible by 9.

Case IV $(3k_1 + 2)^3 + (3k_2 + 2)^3 + (3k_3 + 2)^3$

not divisible by 9.

Case V $(3k_1 + 2)^3 + (3k_2 + 2)^3 + (3k_3)^3$

not divisible by 9.

Case VI $(3k_1 + 1)^3 + (3k_2 + 1)^3 + (3k_3)^3$

not divisible by 9.

Hence, option (b) is true.

64. *(a)* $x^2 - x - 1 = 0$

$$x = \frac{1 \pm \sqrt{5}}{2}$$

$$\lambda = \frac{1 + \sqrt{5}}{2}, \quad 1 - \lambda = \frac{1 - \sqrt{5}}{2}$$

$$a_n = \frac{1}{\sqrt{5}}(\lambda^n - (1 - \lambda)^n) \; \forall \; n \in N$$

$$a_n = \frac{1}{\sqrt{5}}\left(\left(\frac{1 + \sqrt{5}}{2}\right)^n - \left(\frac{1 - \sqrt{5}}{2}\right)^n\right)$$

$$a_n = \frac{1}{\sqrt{5} \cdot 2^n}[(1+\sqrt{5})^n - (1-\sqrt{5})^n]$$

$$(1+\sqrt{5})^n = 1 + {}^nC_1\sqrt{5} + {}^nC_2(\sqrt{5})^2 + ...$$

$$(1-\sqrt{5})^n = 1 - {}^nC_1\sqrt{5} + {}^nC_2(\sqrt{5})^2 - ....$$

So, $\quad a_n = \dfrac{[{}^nC_1 + {}^nC_3 5 + {}^nC_5 5^2 + ...]}{2^{n-1}}$

$$a_n = \frac{2\Sigma\, {}^nC_r 5^r}{2^n} \text{ where } r \text{ is odd}$$

$$a_n = 3^n - (-2)^n \in I \;\forall\; n \in N$$

$\Rightarrow A \in \phi;\, B \in \phi$

Hence, the sets are empty.

65. *(b)* $q = 1^2, 2^2, 3^2, ..., 44^2$

Pick only those which have factors in the form of $2^a \times 5^b$.

So, $n = 11$

66. *(b)*

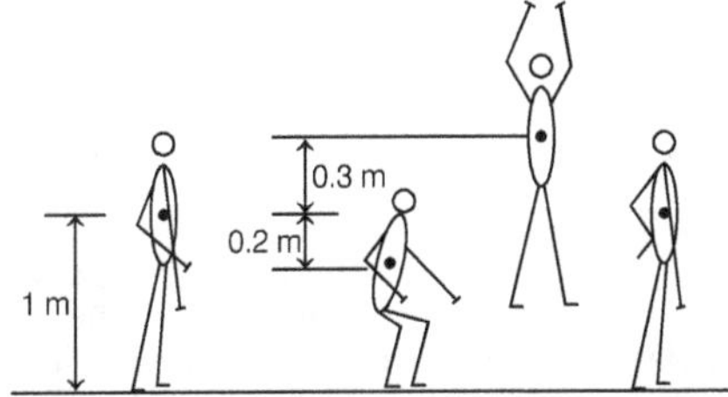

Centre of mass is pushed by 0.2 m only by the force.

So, work done by force $= M \times a \times 0.2$

and change in potential energy by force.

$= Mg \times 0.5$ (as total displacement is 0.5) m

Equating both, we get

$$Ma \times 0.2 = Mg \times 0.5$$

$$\Rightarrow \quad \frac{Ma}{Mg} = \frac{F}{Mg} = \frac{0.5}{0.2} = 2.5$$

67. *(c)*

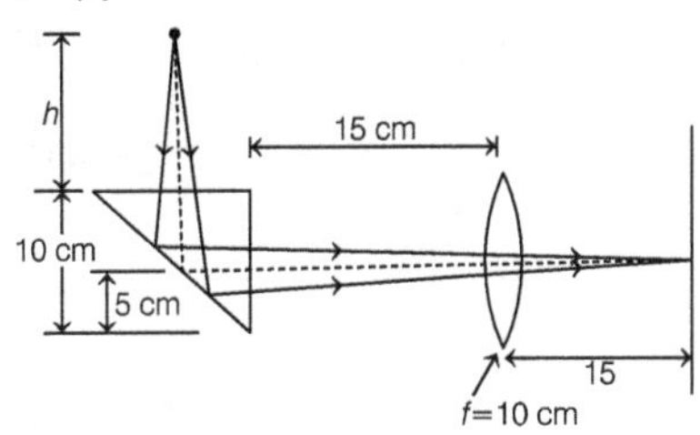

From figure,

Object distance $= 15 + 5 + h$

Also using lens formula,

$$\frac{1}{v} - \frac{1}{u} = \frac{1}{f}$$

Here, $v = 15\,cm$, $f = 10\,cm$

$$\Rightarrow \quad \frac{1}{15} - \frac{1}{10} = \frac{1}{u}$$

$$\Rightarrow \quad u = \frac{10 \times 15}{10 - 15} = -30\,cm$$

Hence, $15 + 5 + h = 30$

$$\Rightarrow \quad h = 10\,cm$$

68. *(b)* According to the given figure,

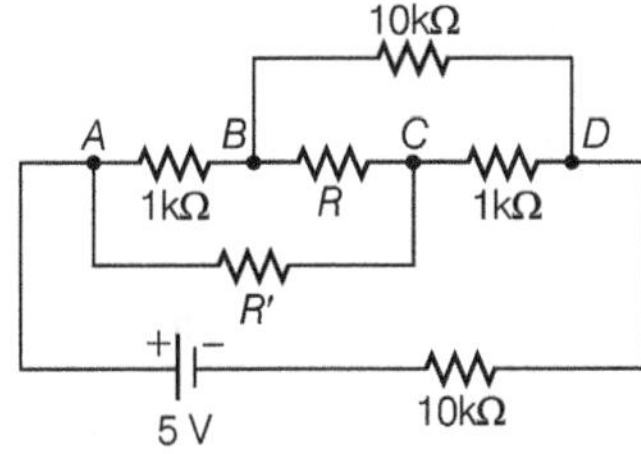

Given circuit is equivalent to following Wheatstones bridge.

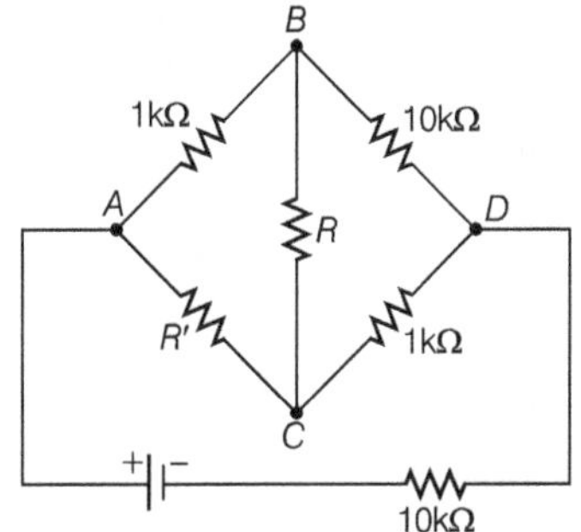

As changing value of R does not effect current values.

So, Wheatstones bridge must be balanced.

$$\Rightarrow \quad \frac{1\,k\Omega}{R'} = \frac{10\,k\Omega}{1\,k\Omega}$$

$$\Rightarrow \quad R' = \frac{1}{10}\,k\Omega = 100\,\Omega$$

69. *(d)*

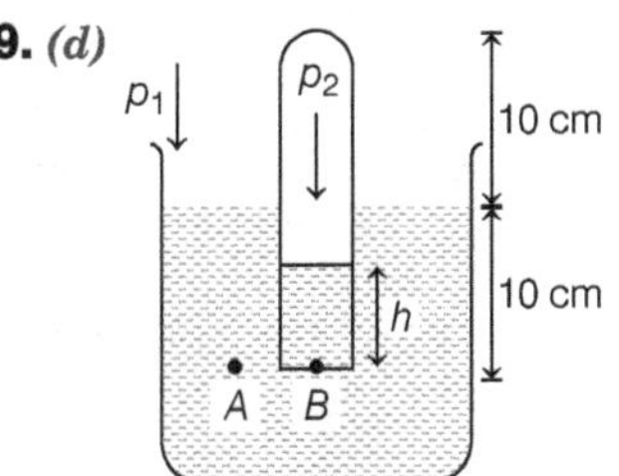

Equating pressures at A and B, we have

$$p_2 + 10^4\, h = 10^5 + 10^4 \times \frac{1}{10} \quad ...(i)$$

Also, for isothermal compression of air column,

$$p_1 \times 0.2 = p_2(0.2 - h) \quad ...(ii)$$

From Eqs. (i) and (ii), we have

$$\frac{10^5 \times 0.2}{0.2 - h} + 10^4 h = 10^5 + 10^3$$

Solving Eqs. (i) and (ii), we get

$$h = 0.002\,m = 0.2\,cm$$

70. *(a)*

From figure, In $\triangle AEF$,

$$\cos(\pi - \phi) = \frac{x}{R}$$

$$\Rightarrow \quad x = -R\cos\phi$$

$$\sin(\pi - \phi) = \frac{y}{R}$$

$$\Rightarrow \quad y = R\sin\phi$$

Also, $\quad x' = v_1 \times t = R$

$$x + x' = v_2\cos\theta \times t \quad ...(i)$$

$$y = v_2\sin\theta \times t \quad ...(ii)$$

Substituting t from Eqs. (ii) in Eq. (i), we have

$$v_1 t - R\cos\phi = v_2\cos\theta \times \frac{R\sin\phi}{v_2\sin\theta}$$

Also, $\quad v_1 t = R$

$$R(1 - \cos\phi) = \cot\theta \cdot \sin\phi \times R$$

$$\Rightarrow \quad \cot\theta = \frac{1 - \cos\phi}{\sin\phi}$$

$$= \frac{2\sin^2\phi/2}{2\sin\phi/2\cos\phi/2}$$

$$\cot\theta = \tan\frac{\phi}{2}$$

71. *(c)*

2-methyl-2-butene (C_5H_{10}) + H_2SO_4 (conc.)

$\longrightarrow$ (addition product with OSO_3H)

$\xrightarrow[H_2O]{\Delta}$ Tertiary alcohol

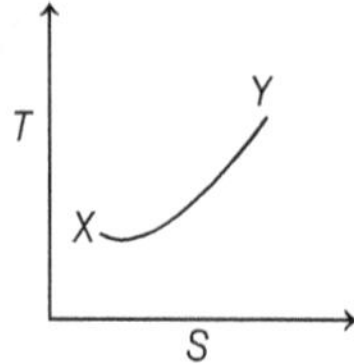

72. *(b)* During Dumas method an organic compound is heated with CuO in an atmosphere of CO_2, which gives free nitrogen alongwith CO_2 and H_2O.

$$C_xH_yN_z + \left(2x + \frac{y}{z}\right)CuO \longrightarrow xCO_2$$

$$+ \frac{y}{2}(H_2O) + \frac{z}{2}(N_2) + \left(2x + \frac{y}{z}\right)(Cu)$$

Since % of nitrogen in m g of compound is calculated as :

$$\% \text{ of nitrogen} = \frac{28 \times V_{N_2} \times 100}{22400 \times m}$$

Thus, pyridine is the correct option.

73. *(a)* $Co(NO_3)_2$ is pink in colour due to electronic transition of electron from t_{2g} to e_g energy level. When excess of HCl is added to this solution it changes into $[CoCl_4]^{2-}$ which is blue in colour. $[CoCl_4]^{2-}$ is tetrahedral with sp^3 hybridisation and Cl^- is a weak field ligand.

74. *(c)* $pK_a = -\log K_a$

$$= -\log(1.8 \times 10^{-5})$$
$$= 5 - \log 1.8$$
$$= 5 - 0.26$$
$$pK_a = 4.74$$

Since, at the end point.

Molarity of salt $= \dfrac{0.1 \text{ M}}{2} = 0.05 \text{ M} = c$

$$pH = \frac{pK_w + pK_a + \log c}{2}$$

$$= \frac{14 + 4.74 + \log 0.05}{2}$$

$$pH = \frac{14 + 4.74 - 1.3010}{2}$$

$$pH = \frac{14 + 4.74 - 1.3010}{2}$$

$$= \frac{17.439}{2}$$

$$pH = 8.7195$$

At this pH phenolphthalein (pH 8.3 – 11) works well.

75. *(c)* In $p\text{-}V$ diagram from X to Y the pressure is constant, so it is an isobaric process.

In isobaric process as heat is added temperature increases and entropy also increases. Thus, correct curve for representation of isobaric process is (c).

76. *(c)* Birth weight is an important indicator and prognostic factor for the health of newborns, as it reflects the nutritional and metabolic conditions of the mother, as well as fetal development during pregnancy. Under-weight and over-weight are both causes of infant mortality, thus, graph "c" is the correct representation of relationship between infant mortality and birth weight as average infant birth weight in India is 2.8 to 3.2 kg. At first phase as infant weight increases upto 4.5–5 kg mortality decrease and in second phase as infant weight further increases mortality also increase.

77. *(a)* A genetic form of a locus would be called an allele only when its frequency in a population is > 0.01 and it is heritable. An allele is a variant form of a gene. Some genes have a variety of different forms, which are located at the same position, or genetic locus, on a chromosome. Humans are called diploid organisms because they have two alleles at each genetic locus, with one allele inherited from each parent.

78. *(b)* In the given experiment of photosynthesis, when in first step a portion of leaf was covered with a black paper which blocks sunlight to prevent the photosynthesis and production of starch, that portion of leaf -1 remains light coloured in iodine test due to the absence of starch. But, second time when leaf is not covered by black paper photosynthesis and production of starch occur which give positive dark coloured result in iodine test.

79. *(d)* In exponential population growth model, population growth rate is given by $dN/dt = rN$, where r is a measure of the population's intrinsic and N is population size. The parameter r is determined by birth rate and death rate. "r" is known as the intrinsic rate of natural increase or the Malthusian parameter. This rate can be calculated as the number of births minus the number of deaths per generation time.

80. *(a)* P-i, Q-i,ii, R-iv and S-iii

- Cobweb (spider web) is made up of fibroin protein.
- Silk is made up of fibroin (75%) and sericin (22.5%) proteins.
- Cotton fibre is made up of polysaccharide cellulose.
- Hair is made up of keratin protein.

QUESTION PAPER 2020
Stream : SA

MM : 100

Instructions

1. There are 80 questions in this paper.
2. This question paper contains two parts; Part I and Part II. There are four sections; Mathematics, Physics, Chemistry and Biology in each part.
3. Out of the four options given with each question, only one is correct.

➲ PART–I (1 Mark Questions)

MATHEMATICS

1. Let $[x]$ be the greatest integer less than or equal to x, for a real number x. Then the equation $[x^2] = x + 1$ has
(a) two solutions
(b) one solution
(c) No solution
(d) More than two solutions

2. Let $p_1(x) = x^3 - 2020x^2 + b_1x + c_1$ and
$p_2(x) = x^3 - 2021x^2 + b_2x + c_2$ be polynomials having two common roots α and β. Suppose there exist polynomials $q_1(x)$ and $q_2(x)$ such that $p_1(x)q_1(x) + p_2(x)q_2(x) = x^2 - 3x + 2$. Then the correct identity is
(a) $p_1(3) + p_2(1) + 4028 = 0$
(b) $p_1(3) + p_2(1) + 4026 = 0$
(c) $p_1(2) + p_2(1) + 4028 = 0$
(d) $p_1(1) + p_2(2) + 4028 = 0$

3. Suppose p, q, r are positive rational numbers such that $\sqrt{p} + \sqrt{q} + \sqrt{r}$ is also rational. Then
(a) $\sqrt{p}, \sqrt{q}, \sqrt{r}$ are irrational

(b) $\sqrt{pq}, \sqrt{pr}, \sqrt{qr}$ are rational, but $\sqrt{p}, \sqrt{q}, \sqrt{r}$ are irrational
(c) $\sqrt{p}, \sqrt{q}, \sqrt{r}$ are rational
(d) $\sqrt{pq}, \sqrt{pr}, \sqrt{qr}$ are irrational

4. Let A, B, C be three points on a circle of radius 1 such that $\angle ACB = \dfrac{\pi}{4}$. Then, the length of the side AB is
(a) $\sqrt{3}$
(b) $\dfrac{4}{3}$
(c) $\dfrac{3}{\sqrt{2}}$
(d) $\sqrt{2}$

5. Let x and y be two positive real numbers such that $x + y = 1$. Then, the minimum value of $\dfrac{1}{x} + \dfrac{1}{y}$ is
(a) 2
(b) $\dfrac{5}{2}$
(c) 3
(d) 4

6. Let $ABCD$ be a quadrilateral such that there exists a point E inside the quadrilateral satisfying $AE = BE = CE = DE$. Suppose $\angle DAB, \angle ABC, \angle BCD$ is an arithmetic progression. Then the median of the set $\{\angle DAB, \angle ABC, \angle BCD\}$ is
(a) $\dfrac{\pi}{6}$
(b) $\dfrac{\pi}{4}$
(c) $\dfrac{\pi}{3}$
(d) $\dfrac{\pi}{2}$

7. The number of ordered pairs (x, y) of positive integers satisfying $2^x + 3^y = 5^{xy}$ is

(a) 1   (b) 2   (c) 5   (d) Infinite

8. If the integers from 1 to 2021 are written as a single integer like 123 ... 91011 ... 20202021, then the 2021st digit (counted from the left) in the resulting number is

(a) 0   (b) 1   (c) 6   (d) 9

9. In a ΔABC, a point D is chosen on BC such that $BD : DC = 2 : 5$. Let P be a point on the circumcircle ABC such that $\angle PDB = \angle BAC$. Then $PD : PC$ is

(a) $\sqrt{2} : \sqrt{5}$ (b) $2 : 5$ (c) $2 : 7$ (d) $\sqrt{2} : \sqrt{7}$

10. Let $[x]$ be the greatest integer less than or equal to x, for a real number x. Then the following sum

$$\left[\frac{2^{2020}+1}{2^{2018}+1}\right] + \left[\frac{3^{2020}+1}{3^{2018}+1}\right] + \left[\frac{4^{2020}+1}{4^{2018}+1}\right]$$
$$+ \left[\frac{5^{2020}+1}{5^{2018}+1}\right] + \left[\frac{6^{2020}+1}{6^{2018}+1}\right] \text{ is}$$

(a) 80   (b) 85   (c) 90   (d) 95

11. Let r be the remainder when 2021^{2020} is divided by 2020^2. Then r lies between

(a) 0 and 5   (b) 10 and 15

(c) 20 and 100   (d) 107 and 120

12. In a ΔABC, the altitude AD and the median AE divide $\angle A$ into three equal parts. If $BC = 28$, then the nearest integer to $AB + AC$ is

(a) 38   (b) 37   (c) 36   (d) 33

13. The number of permutations of the letters a_1, a_2, a_3, a_4, a_5 in which the first letter a_1 does not occupy the first position (from the left) and the second letter a_2 does not occupy the second position (from the left) is

(a) 96   (b) 78   (c) 60   (d) 42

14. There are m books in black cover and n books in blue cover, and all books are different. The number of ways these $(m + n)$ books can be arranged on a shelf so that all the books in black cover are put side by side is

(a) $m!n!$ (b) $m!(n + 1)!$

(c) $(n + 1)!$ (d) $(m + n)!$

15. A 5-digit number $\overline{abcde}$, when multiplied by 9, gives the 5-digit number $\overline{edcba}$. The sum of the digits in the number is

(a) 18   (b) 27   (c) 36   (d) 45

PHYSICS

16. A mouse jumps off from the 15th floor of a high-rise building and lands 12 m from the building. Assume that, each floor is of 3 m height. The horizontal speed with which the mouse jumps is closest to

(a) zero   (b) 5 km/h

(c) 10 km/h   (d) 15 km/h

17. Consider two wires of same material having their ratio of radii to be 2 : 1. If these two wires are stretched by equal force, then the ratio of stress produced in them is

(a) $\dfrac{1}{4}$ (b) $\dfrac{1}{2}$ (c) $\dfrac{3}{4}$ (d) 1

18. A submarine has a window of area 30×30 cm^2 on its ceiling and is at a depth of 100 m below sea level in a sea. If the pressure inside the submarine is maintained at the sea-level atmosphere pressure, then the force acting on the window is (consider density of sea water = 1.03×10^3 kg/m^3, acceleration due to gravity = 10 m/s^2)

(a) 0.93×10^5 N   (b) 0.93×10^3 N

(c) 1.86×10^5 N   (d) 1.86×10^3 N

19. A spacecraft which is moving with a speed u relative to the earth in the x-direction, enters the gravitational field of a much more massive planet which is moving with a speed $3u$ in the negative x-direction. The spacecraft exits following the trajectory as shown below.

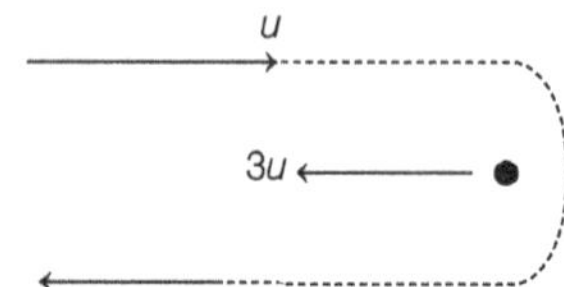

The speed of the spacecraft with respect to the earth a long a time after it has escaped the planet's gravity is given by

(a) u (b) $4u$ (c) $2u$ (d) $7u$

20. The earth's magnetic field was flipped by 180° a million years ago. This flip was relatively rapid and took 10^5 yrs. Then, the average change in orientation per year during the flip was closest to

(a) 1 s   (b) 5 s

(c) 10 s   (d) 30 s

21. The platelets are drifting with the blood flowing in a streamline flow through a horizontal artery as shown below

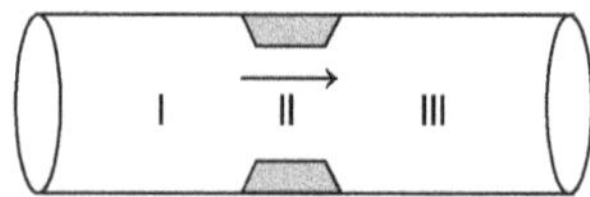

Artery is contracted in region II. Choose the correct statement.

(a) As the platelets enter a constriction, the platelets get squeesed closer together in the narrow region and hence the fluid pressure must rise there

(b) As the platelets enter a constriction, pressure is lower there

(c) The artery's cross-section area is smaller in the constriction and thus the pressure must be larger there because pressure equals the force divided by area

(d) Pressure is same in all the parts of the artery

22. Which of the following colourful patterns is due to diffraction of light?
(a) Rainbow
(b) White light dispersed using a prism
(c) Colours observed on compact disc
(d) Blue colour of sky

23. Two balls are projected with the same velocity but with different angles with the horizontal. Their ranges are equal. If the angle of projection of one is 30° and its maximum height is h, then the maximum height of other will be
(a) h (b) $3h$
(c) $6h$ (d) $10h$

24. Figure below shows a shampoo bottle in a perfect cylindrical shape.

In a simple experiment, the stability of the bottle filled with different amount of shampoo volume is observed. The bottle is tilted from one side and then released. Let the angle θ depicts the critical angular displacement resulting, in the bottle losing its stability and tipping over. Choose the graph correctly depicting the fraction f of shampoo filled ($f = 1$ corresponds to completely filled) *versus* the tipping angle θ.

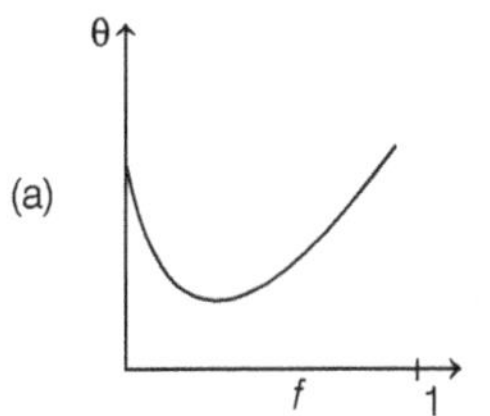

(a)

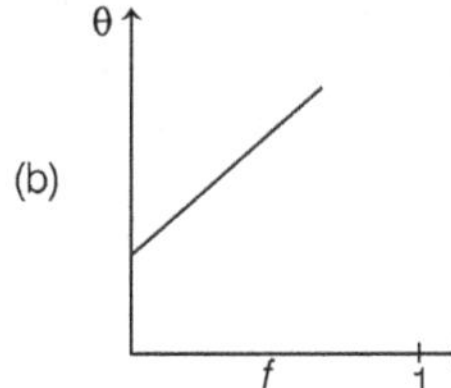

(b)

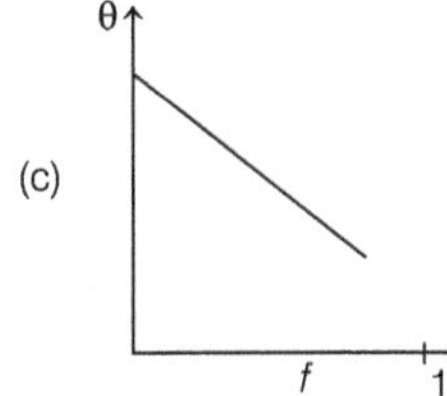

(c)

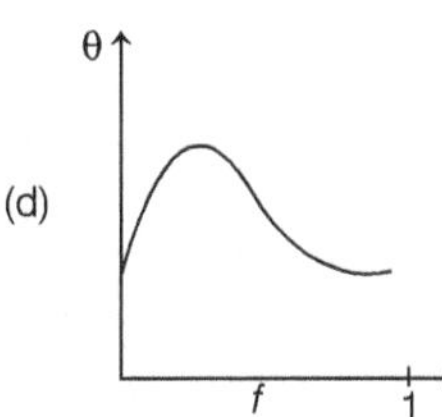

(d)

25. At a height of 10 km above the surface of earth, the value of acceleration due to gravity is the same as that of a particular depth below the surface of earth. Assuming uniform mass density for the earth, the depth is
(a) 1 km   (b) 5 km
(c) 10 km   (d) 20 km

26. The following graph depicts the inverse of magnification *versus* the distance between the object and lens data for a setup. The focal length of the lens used in the setup is

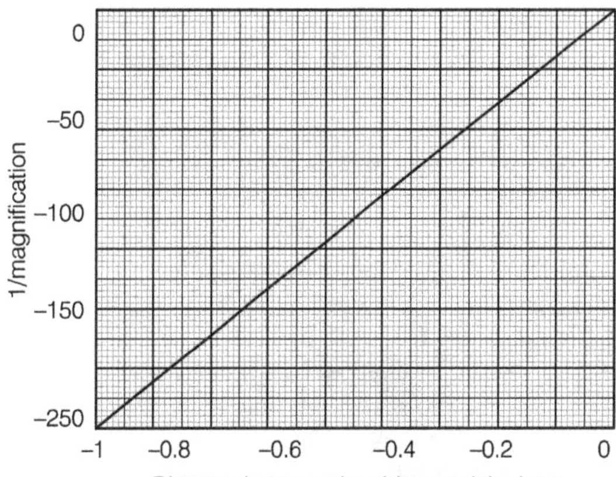

(a) 250 m   (b) 0.004 m
(c) 125 m   (d) 0.002 m

27. In a circus, a performer throws an apple towards a hoop held at 45 m height by another performer standing on a high platform (see figure). The thrower aims for the hoop and throws the apple with a speed of 24 m/s. At the exact moment that the thrower releases the apple, the other performer drops the hoop. The hoop falls straight down. At what height above the ground does the apple go through the hoop?

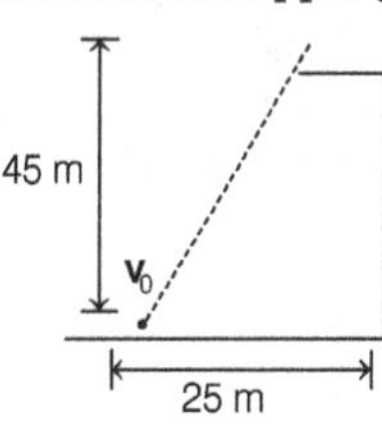

(a) 21 m   (b) 22 m
(c) 23 m   (d) 24 m

28. A student was trying to construct the circuit shown in the figure below marked (a), but ended up constructing the circuit marked (b). Realising her mistake, she corrected the circuit, but to her surprise, the output voltage (across R) did not change.

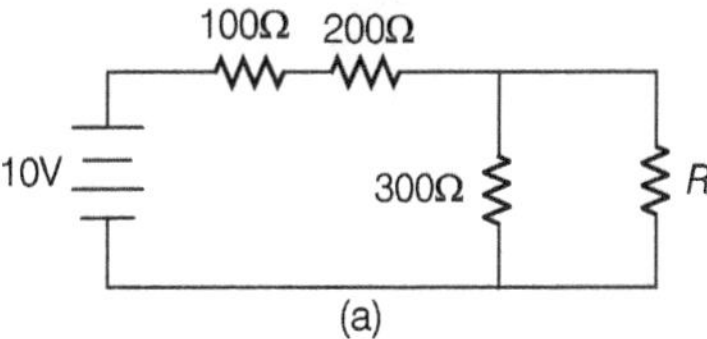

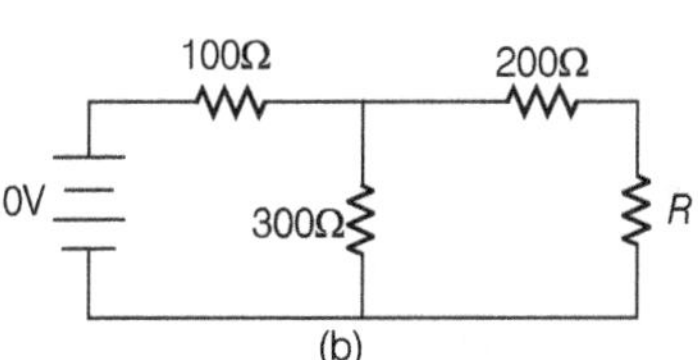

The value of resistance R is
(a) 100 Ω   (b) 150 Ω   (c) 200 Ω   (d) 300 Ω

29. The ratio of gravitational force and electrostatic repulsive force between two electrons is approximately (gravitational constant $= 6.7 \times 10^{-11}$ Nm^2/kg^2, mass of an electron $= 9.1 \times 10^{-31}$ kg, charge on an electron $= 1.6 \times 10^{-19}$ C)
(a) 24×10^{-24}
(b) 24×10^{-36}
(c) 24×10^{-44}
(d) 24×10^{-54}

30. A monochromatic beam of light enters a square enclosure with mirrored interior surfaces at an angle of incidence θ_i ($\neq 0$) (see figure). For some value(s) of θ_i, the beam is reflected by every mirrored wall (other than the one with the opening) exactly once and exits the enclosure through the same hole. Which of the following statements about this beam is correct?

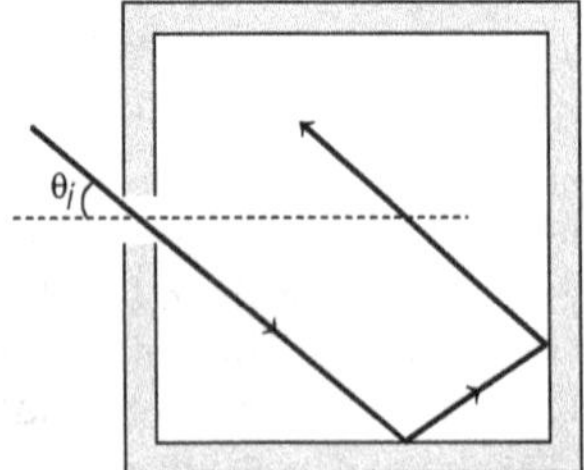

(a) The beam will not come out of the enclosure for any value of θ_i.
(b) The beam will come out for more than two values of θ_i.
(c) The beam will come out only at $\theta_i = 45$.
(d) The beam will come out for exactly two values of θ_i.

CHEMISTRY

31. The acidity of

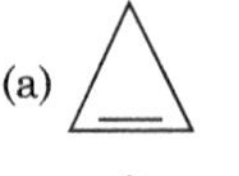

I   II   III   IV

follows the order
(a) I > II > III > IV
(b) IV > III > II > I
(c) III > IV > I > II
(d) III > II > IV > I

32. Among the following,

I   II   III
IV   V

The compounds which can exhibit optical activity are
(a) only II, IV and V
(b) only IV and V
(c) only I, II and V
(d) only I, II and IV

33. A molecule which has 1°, 2° and 3° carbon atoms is
(a) 2,3,4-trimethylpentane
(b) chlorocyclohexane
(c) 2,2-dimethylcyclohexane
(d) methylcyclohexane

34. The organic compound which can be purified by steam distillation is
(a) acetone   (b) aniline   (c) glucose   (d) ethanol

35. Among the following, the most acidic compound is
(a)
(b)
(b)
(d)

36. A closed 10 L vessel contains 1 L water gas (1 : 1 $CO : H_2$) and 9 L air (20% O_2 by volume) at STP. The contents of the vessel are ignited. The number of moles of CO_2 in the vessel is closest to
(a) 0.22 mol   (b) 0.022 mol   (c) 0.90 mol   (d) 3.60 mol

37. A certain metal has a work function of $\Phi = 2$ eV. It is irradiated first with 1 W of 400 nm light and later with 1 W of 800 nm light. Among the following, the correct statement is

[Given: Planck constant (h) $= 6.626 \times 10^{-34}$ m^2 kg s^{-1}; Speed of light (c) $= 3 \times 10^8$ ms^{-1}]

(a) both colours of light give rise to same number of photoelectrons.
(b) 400 nm light gives rise to less energetic photoelectrons than 800 nm light.
(c) only 400 nm light leads to ejection of photoelectrons.
(d) 800 nm light leads to more photoelectrons.

38. Among the following, the correct statement about the chemical equilibrium is
(a) equilibrium constant is independent of temperature.
(b) equilibrium constant tells us how fast the reaction reaches equilibrium.
(c) at equilibrium, the forward and the backward reactions stop so that the concentrations of reactants and products are constant.
(d) equilibrium constant is independent of whether you start the reaction with reactants or products.

39. Among the following, the plot that shows the correct marking of most probable velocity (V_{mp}), average velocity ($\overline{V}$), and root mean square velocity (V_{rms}) is

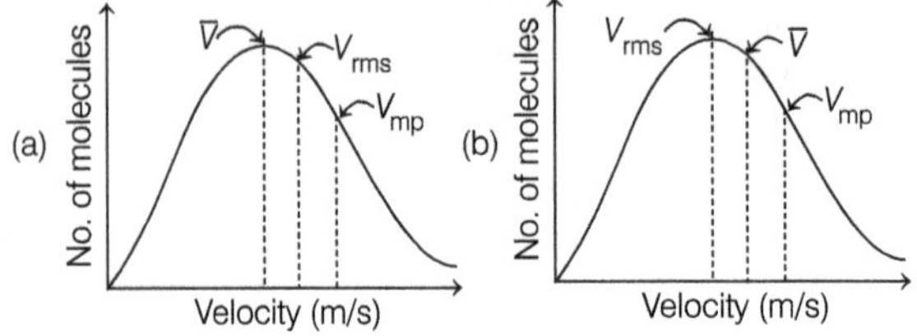

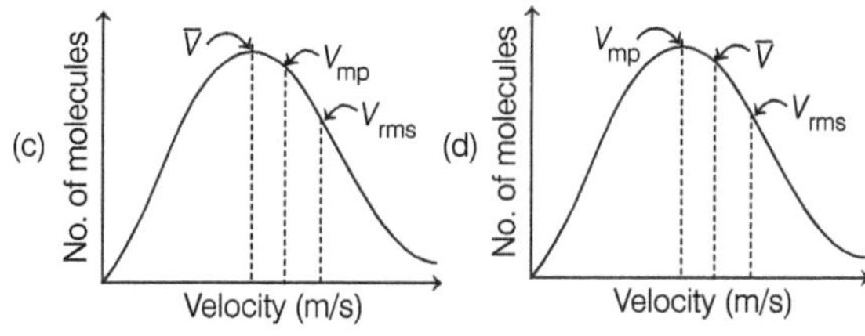

40. The correct set of quantum numbers for the unpaired electron of Cu atom is

(a) $n = 3, l = 2, m = -2, s = +\dfrac{1}{2}$

(b) $n = 3, l = 2, m = +2, s = -\dfrac{1}{2}$

(c) $n = 4, l = 0, m = 0, s = +\dfrac{1}{2}$

(d) $n = 4, l = 1, m = +1, s = +\dfrac{1}{2}$

41. Among the following, the most polar molecule is

(a) $AlCl_3$ (b) CCl_4 (c) $SeCl_6$ (d) $AsCl_3$

42. The covalent characters of $CaCl_2$, $BaCl_2$, $SrCl_2$ and $MgCl_2$ follow the order

(a) $CaCl_2 < BaCl_2 < SrCl_2 < MgCl_2$
(b) $BaCl_2 < SrCl_2 < CaCl_2 < MgCl_2$
(c) $CaCl_2 < BaCl_2 < MgCl_2 < SrCl_2$
(d) $SrCl_2 < MgCl_2 < CaCl_2 < BaCl_2$

43. Among the following, the correct statement is

(a) 100. has four significant figures.
(b) 1.00×10^2 has four significant figures.
(c) 2.005 has four significant figures.
(d) 0.0025 has four significant figures.

44. A thermodynamic cycle in the pressure (p) – volume (V) plane is given below

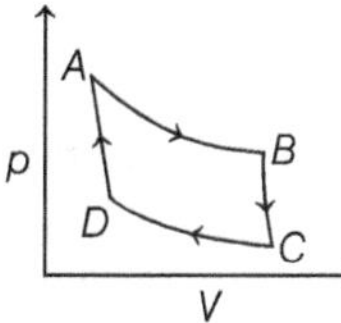

AB and CD are isothermal processes while BC and DA are adiabatic processes. The same cycle in the temperature (T) - entropy (S) plane is

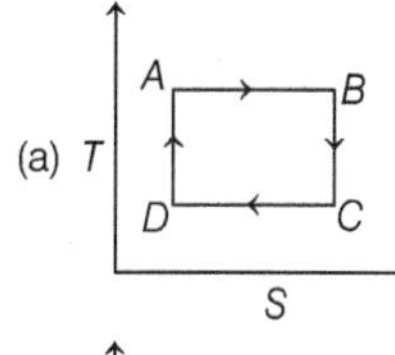
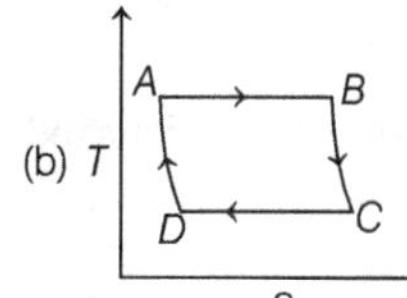
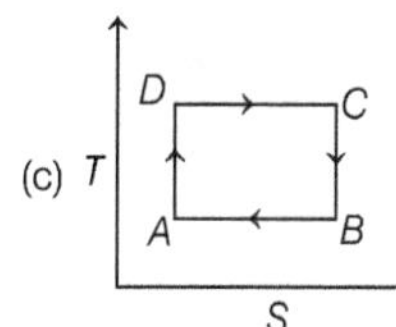
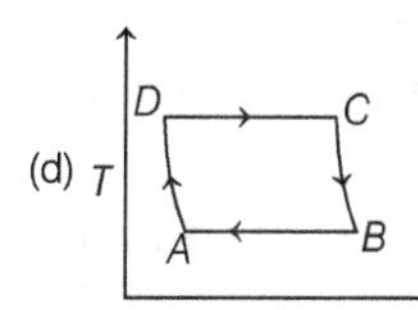

45. The first ionisation potential (IP) of the elements Na, Mg, Si, P, Cl and Ar are 5.14, 7.65, 8.15, 10.49, 12.97 and 15.76 eV, respectively. The IP (in eV) of K is closest to

(a) 13.3   (b) 18.2   (c) 4.3   (d) 6.4

BIOLOGY

46. Which one of the following chemicals serves as a substrate for carbonic anhydrase?

(a) O_2 (b) CO_2 (c) NO_2 (d) CO

47. Which one of the following is not a function of the small intestine?

(a) Absorption of end products of digestion
(b) Digestion of proteins
(c) Digestion of lipids
(d) Acidification of ingested food

48. Insulin stimulates the conversion of glucose to

(a) fructose   (b) glycogen
(c) sucrose   (d) starch

49. Which one of the following statements about ecosystem energetics is incorrect?

(a) The metabolic requirements of poikilotherms are higher than that of homeotherms.
(b) Autotrophs form the base of the food chain in natural ecosystems.
(c) In terrestrial ecosystems, most of the primary production is consumed by detritivores and not herbivores.
(d) Approximately 10% energy of one trophic level is transferred to the next level.

50. Proton motive force is created by pumping protons across the

(a) *trans*-Golgi network
(b) endoplasmic reticulum
(c) mitochondrial inner membrane
(d) early endosomal membrane

51. Which one of the following Mendelian diseases is an example of X-linked recessive disorder?

(a) Haemophilia   (b) Phenylketonuria
(c) Sickle-cell anaemia   (d) Beta thalassemia

52. Which one of the following pair gives rise to fruit and seed, respectively, in a typical angiosperm plant?

(a) Ovule and ovary   (b) Ovary and pollen
(c) Pollen and anther   (d) Ovary and ovule

53. The concept of vaccination arose from Edward Jenner's observation that

(a) injecting inactivated anthrax spores in sheep protected them from anthrax
(b) injecting humans with tuberculosis-infected lung extracts protected them from tuberculosis
(c) milk-maids previously infected with cowpox did not contract smallpox
(d) injecting inactivated rabies virus in humans protected them from rabies

54. A plant with genotype AABBCC is crossed with another plant with aabbcc genotype. How many different genotypes of pollens is possible in an F$_1$ plant if these three loci follow independent assortment?

(a) 8
(b) 4
(c) 2
(d) 1

55. Which one of the following sequences of events correctly represents mitosis?

(a) Metaphase, telophase, prophase, anaphase
(b) Anaphase, prophase, metaphase, telophase
(c) Prophase. anaphase, metaphase, telophase
(d) Prophase, metaphase, anaphase, telophase

56. The amount of air that is left behind in lungs after expiratory reserve volume has been exhaled is

(a) inspiratory reserve volume
(b) tidal volume
(c) residual volume
(d) vital capacity

57. Match the species in Column I with their respective feature of body organisation in Column II.

	Column I		Column II
P.	Mollusca	(i)	Pseudocoelom
Q.	Annelida	(ii)	Radula
R.	Nematoda	(iii)	Radial symmetry
S.	Echinodermata	(iv)	Segmentation

Choose the correct combination.

(a) P–(ii), Q–(i), R–iv, S–(iii)
(b) P–(ii), Q–(iv), R–i, S–(iii)
(c) P–(iii), Q–(iv), R–i, S–(ii)
(d) P–(iv), Q–(iii), R–ii, S–(i)

58. Who among the following scientists proposed the theory of natural selection independently of Charles Darwin?

(a) Alfred Russel Wallace   (b) Carl Linnaeus
(c) Georges Cuvier   (d) Jean-Baptiste Lamarck

59. The maximum concentration of harmful chemicals is expected to be found in organisms

(a) at the bottom of a food chain.
(b) at the middle of a food chain.
(c) at the top of a food chain.
(d) at any level in a food chain.

60. The genome of SARS-CoV-2 is composed of

(a) double-stranded DNA   (b) double-stranded RNA
(c) single-stranded DNA   (d) single-stranded RNA

➲ PART-II (2 Mark Questions)

MATHEMATICS

61. Let A denote the set of all 4-digit natural numbers with no digit being 0. Let $B \subset A$ consist of all numbers x such that no permutation of the digits of x gives a number that is divisible by 4. Then the probability of drawing a number from B with all even digits is

(a) $\dfrac{625}{1641}$ (b) $\dfrac{16}{641}$ (c) $\dfrac{16}{1641}$ (d) $\dfrac{1000}{1641}$

62. Let ABC be a triangle such that $AB = 4$, $BC = 5$ and $CA = 6$. Choose points D, E, F on AB, BC, CA respectively, such that $AD = 2$, $BE = 33$, $CF = 4$. Then

$$\frac{\text{area } \Delta DEF}{\text{area } \Delta ABC}$$

(a) $\dfrac{1}{4}$ (b) $\dfrac{3}{15}$ (c) $\dfrac{4}{15}$ (d) $\dfrac{7}{30}$

63. The number of ordered pairs (x, y) of integers satisfying $x^3 + y^3 = 65$ is

(a) 0   (b) 2   (c) 4   (d) 6

64. A bottle in the shape of a right-circular cone with height h contains some water. When its base is placed on a flat surface, the height of the vertex from the water level is a units. When it is kept upside down, the height of the base from the water level is $\dfrac{a}{4}$ units. Then the ratio $\dfrac{h}{a}$ is

(a) $\dfrac{1+\sqrt{85}}{4}$ (b) $\dfrac{1+\sqrt{85}}{8}$ (c) $\dfrac{1+\sqrt{65}}{4}$ (d) $\dfrac{1+\sqrt{65}}{8}$

65. Consider the following two statements :

I. If n is a composite number, then n divides $(n - 1)\,!$.

II. There are infinitely many natural numbers n such that $n^3 + 2n^2 + n$ divides $n!$

(a) I and II are true   (b) I and II are false
(c) I is true and II is false   (d) I is false and II is true

PHYSICS

66. A charge $+q$ is situated at a distance d away from both the sides of a grounded conducting L shaped sheet as shown in the figure.

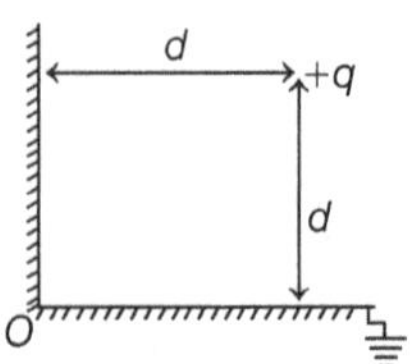

The force acting on the charge $+q$ is

(a) towards O, magnitude $\dfrac{q^2}{32\pi\varepsilon_0 d^2}(2\sqrt{2} + 1)$

(b) away from O, magnitude $\dfrac{q^2}{32\pi\varepsilon_0 d^2}(2\sqrt{2} + 1)$

(c) towards O, magnitude $\dfrac{q^2}{32\pi\varepsilon_0 d^2}(2\sqrt{2}-1)$

(d) away from O, magnitude $\dfrac{q^2}{32\pi\varepsilon_0 d^2}(2\sqrt{2}-1)$

67. Three balls, A, B and C are released and all reach the point X (shown in the figure). Balls A and B are released from two identical structures, one kept on the ground and the other at height h, from the ground as shown in the figure. They take time t_A and t_B respectively to reach X (time starts after they leave the end of the horizontal portion of the structure). The ball C is released from a point at height h, vertically above X and reaches X in time t_C. Choose the correct option.

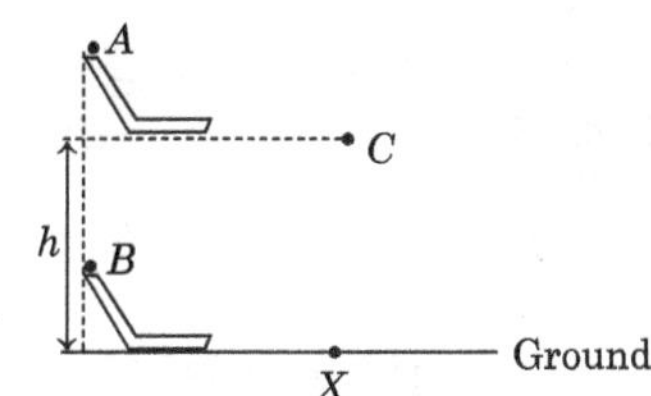

(a) $t_C < t_A < t_C$

(b) $t_C = t_A = t_C$

(c) $t_C = t_A < t_C$

(d) $t_B < t_A = t_C$

68. Four bulbs, red, green, white and blue (denoted by R, G, W and B respectively) are kept in front of a converging lens (as shown in the figure below). The observer sees that the green and blue bulbs are kept to the left of the principal axis, while the red and white bulbs are kept to the right of the principal axis. He also sees that the red and green bulbs are above principal axis, while the white and blue bulbs are below the principal axis. The screens S_1 and S_2 are set appropriate positions for the focusing to view the images.

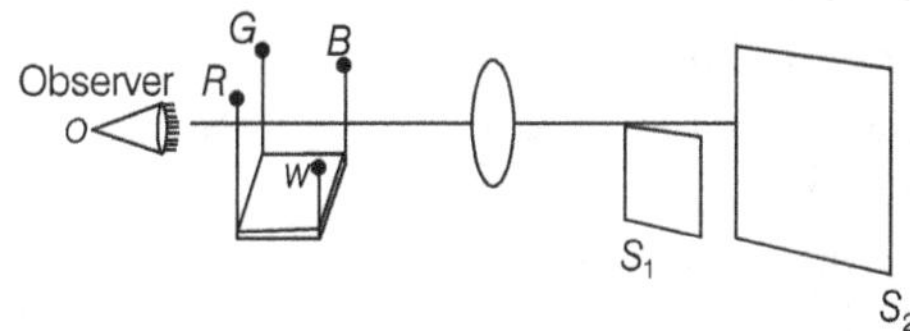

Choose the figure that correctly represents the images as seen by the observer.

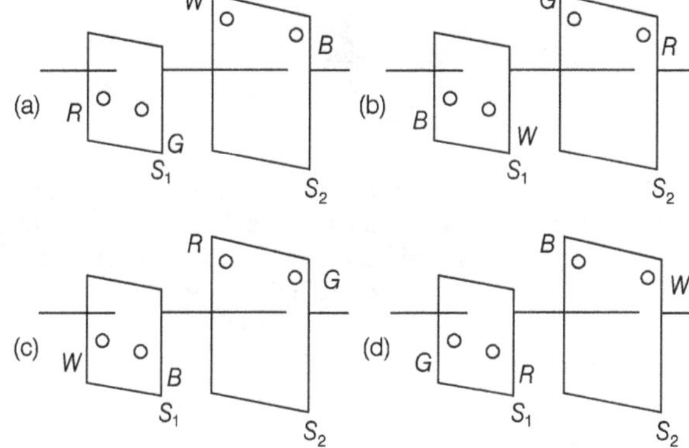

69. A wide bottom cylindrical massless plastic container of height 9 cm has 40 identical coins inside it and is floating on water with 3 cm inside the water. If we start putting more of such coins on its lid, it is observed that after N coins are put, its equilibrium changes from stable to unstable. Equilibrium in floating is stable if the geometric centre of the submerged portion is above the centre of the mass of the object). The value of N is closed to

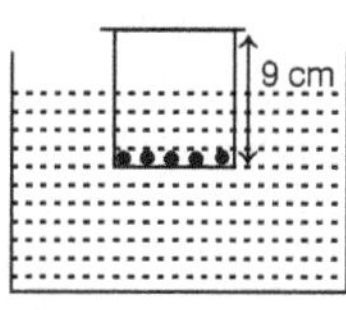

(a) 6   (b) 10

(c) 16   (d) 24

70. A small coin is fixed at the centre of the base of an empty cylindrical steel container having radius $R = 1$ m and height $d = 4$ m. At time $t = 0$, the container starts getting filled with water at a flowrate of $Q = 0.1$ m^3/s without disturbing the coin. Find the approximate time when the coin will first be seen by the observer O from the height of $H = 5.75$ m above and $L = 1.5$ m radially away from the coin as shown in the figure. (Take, refractive index of water, $n = 1.33$)

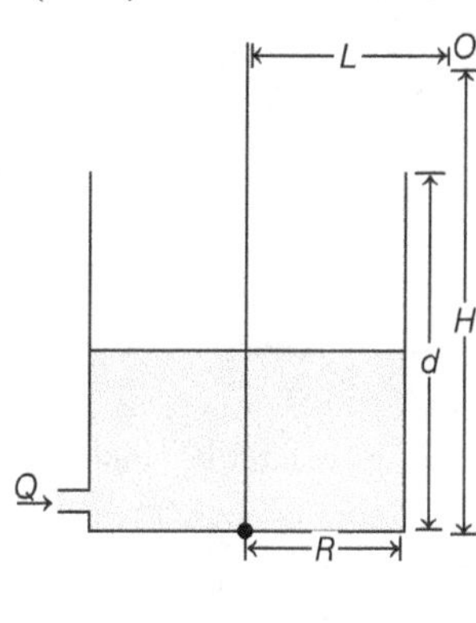

(a) Zero   (b) 32 s

(c) 63 s   (d) 150 s

CHEMISTRY

71. A hydrocarbon X with molecular formula C_4H_6 decolourises bromine water and forms a white precipitate in ethanolic $AgNO_3$ solution. Treatment of X with $HgCl_2$ in aqueous H_2SO_4 produces a compound, which gives a yellow precipitate when treated with I_2 and NaOH. The structure of X is

(a) 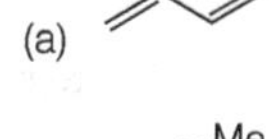

(b) 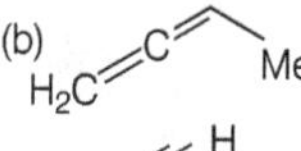

(c) 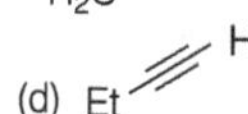

(d)

72. 0.102 g of an organic compound X was oxidised with fuming nitric acid. The resulting solution, after reaction with excess of aqueous $BaCl_2$, produce 0.233 g of $BaSO_4$ as a precipitate. Compound X is likely to be [Given: Atomic wt. of Ba = 137]

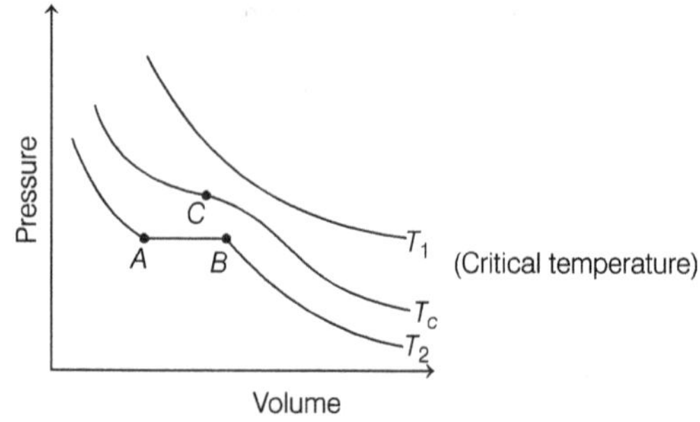

73. The specific heat of a certain substance is 0.86 J g^{-1} K^{-1}. Assuming ideal solution behaviour, the energy required (in J) to heat 10 g of 1 molal of its aqueous solution from 300 K to 310 K is closest to

[Given: Molar mass of the substance = 58 g mol^{-1}; specific heat of water = 4.2 J g^{-1} K^{-1}]

(a) 401.7 J　(b) 424.7 J　(c) 420.0 J　(d) 86.0 J

74. Strength of a H_2O_2 solution is labelled as 1.79 N. Its strength can also be expressed as closest to

(a) 20 volume (b) 5 volume (c) 10 volume (d) 15 volume

75. The isotherms of a gas are shown below:

Among the following

(i) At T_1, the gas cannot be liquefied.

(ii) At point B, liquid starts to appear at T_2.

(iii) T_c is the highest temperature at which the gas can be liquefied.

(iv) At point A, a small increase in pressure condenses the whole system to a liquid.

The correct statements are

(a) only (i) and (ii)　　(b) only (i), (iii) and (iv)
(c) only (ii), (iii) and (iv)　(d) (i), (ii), (iii) and (iv)

BIOLOGY

76. Anthropocene refers to the geological age during which

(a) the earliest hominids radiated from their ancestral forms

(b) human activity significantly influenced climate and environment

(c) arthropod radiation was highest

(d) arthropod radiation significantly influenced climate and environment

77. Match the vitamins listed in Column I with the diseases caused due to their deficiency in Column II.

	Column I		Column II
P.	Vitamin-A	(i)	Pellegra
Q.	Vitamin-B$_2$	(ii)	Rickets
R.	Vitamin-D	(iii)	Ariboflavinosis
S.	Vitamin-B$_{12}$	(iv)	Night blindness
		(v)	Pernicious anaemia

Codes
(a) P–(iv), Q–(ii), R–(iii), S–(v)
(b) P–(i), Q–(ii), R–(iv), S–(iii)
(c) P–(iv), Q–(iii), R–(ii), S–(v)
(d) P–(iii), Q–(iv), R–(v), S–(i)

78. An adult mammal with 50 kg body weight has the following functional parameters of its lungs.
Inspiratory reserve volume = 40 mL/kg body weight
Expiratory reserve volume = 15 mL/kg body weight
Vital capacity = 60 mL/kg body weight
Breathing rate = 20/min
The volume (in litre) of air that its lungs displaces in 24 hours is
(a) 72,000　　　　(b) 7,200
(c) 3,600　　　　(d) 1,200

79. In a breed of dog, long-haired phenotype is recessive to short-hair. In a litter one pup is short haired and its sibling is long-haired. Consider the following possible phenotypes of the parents.

I. Both parents are short-haired.

II. Both parents are long-haired.

III. One parent is short-haired and one is long-haired.

Choose the correct combination of the possible parental phenotypes.
(a) Only I　　　　(b) Only II
(c) Only III　　　(d) I and III

80. In medical diagnostics for a disease, sensitivity (denoted by a) of a test refers to the probability that a test result is positive for a person with the disease, whereas specificity (denoted by b) refers to the probability that a person without the disease tests negative. A diagnostic test for COVID-19 has the values of $a = 0.99$ and $b = 0.99$. If the prevalence of COVID-19 in a population is estimated to be 10%, what is the probability that a randomly chosen person tests positive for COVID-19?
(a) 0.099　　　　(b) 0.10
(c) 0.108　　　　(d) 0.11

Answers

Solutions

1. (c) We have, $[x^2] = x + 1$ ...(i)

Clearly, Eq. (i) $\Rightarrow x$ is an integer ...(ii)

$$x^2 - \{x^2\} = x + 1$$
$$\Rightarrow \quad x^2 - x - 1 = \{x^2\} \quad \text{(iii)}$$

Eq.(iii) $\Rightarrow x^2 - x - 1 < 1$
$$\Rightarrow \quad -1 < x < 2 \quad \text{...(iv)}$$

From Eqs. (ii) and (iv) $\Rightarrow$ possible values of x are 0 and 1.

But 0 and 1 do not satisfy Eq. (i).

$\therefore$ Equation $[x^2] = x + 1$ has no soltuion.

2. (a) Let $p_1(x) = x^3 - 2020x^2 + b_1 x + c_1$
$$= (x - \alpha)(x - \beta)(x - \gamma)$$
and $\quad p_2(x) = x^3 - 2021x^2 + b_2 x + c_2$
$$= (x - \alpha)(x - \beta)(x - \delta)$$

Since, $p_1(x) \cdot q_1(x) + p_2(x) \cdot q_2(x)$
$$= x^2 - 3x + 2$$

On comparing the coefficient of x^3, we get

$q_1(x) = -q_2(x) = q(x)$ (say)

So, $(x - \alpha)(x - \beta)[q(x)(\delta - \gamma)]$
$$= (x - 1)(x - 2)$$

$\therefore \quad \alpha = 1, \beta = 2, \gamma = 2017$ and $\delta = 2018$

$p_1(x) = (x - 1)(x - 2)(x - 2017)$
$$\Rightarrow \quad p_1(3) = -4028$$
$$p_2(x) = (x - 1)(x - 2)(x - 2018)$$
$$\Rightarrow \quad p_2(1) = 0$$

So, $\quad p_1(3) + p_2(1) + 4028 = 0$

3. (c) $\because p, q, r \in Q$ and $\sqrt{p} + \sqrt{q} + \sqrt{r} \in Q$
$$\Rightarrow \quad (\sqrt{p} + \sqrt{q} + \sqrt{r})^2 \in Q$$
$$\Rightarrow \quad \sqrt{pq} + \sqrt{qr} + \sqrt{rp} \in Q \quad \text{(i)}$$

Case I Let exactly one of $\sqrt{p}, \sqrt{q}, \sqrt{r}$ is irrational.

$\sqrt{p}, \notin Q$ but $\sqrt{r}, \sqrt{q} \in Q$

From Eq. (i), $\sqrt{p} \underbrace{(\sqrt{q} + \sqrt{r})}_{\text{rational}} \in Q$

which is contradiction.

Case II Let exactly two out of $\sqrt{p}, \sqrt{q}, \sqrt{r}$ are irrational.

$\sqrt{p}, \sqrt{q} \notin Q$ but $\sqrt{r} \in Q$

From Eq. (i),
$$\sqrt{p}\sqrt{q} + \sqrt{r}\sqrt{p} + \sqrt{r}\sqrt{q} + (\sqrt{r})^2 \in Q$$
$$\Rightarrow (\sqrt{p} + \sqrt{r})(\sqrt{q} + \sqrt{r}) \in Q$$

$\because$ Both $\sqrt{p} + \sqrt{r}$ and $\sqrt{q} + \sqrt{r}$ are irrational. Hence, they must be conjugate of each other. Which is contradiction.

Case III Let all $\sqrt{p}, \sqrt{q}, \sqrt{r}$ are irrational.

Let $\sqrt{p} + \sqrt{q} + \sqrt{r} = x$, when $x \in Q^+$

From Eq. (i), $\sqrt{p}(x - \sqrt{p}) + \sqrt{q}\sqrt{r} \in Q$
$$\Rightarrow x\sqrt{p} + \sqrt{q}\sqrt{r} \in Q$$

Which is contradiction.

Hence, all $\sqrt{p}, \sqrt{q}$ and $\sqrt{r}$ must be rational.

4. (d)

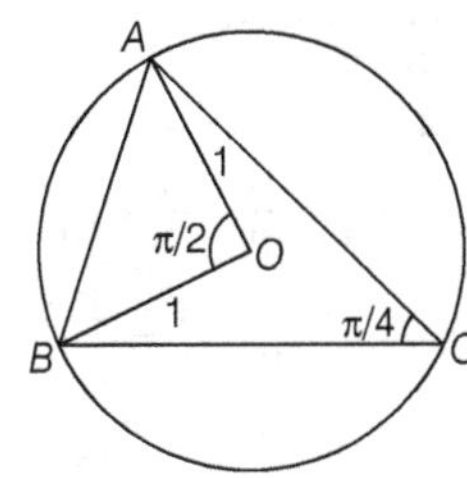

$$\angle AOB = 2\angle ACB$$

($\because$ The angle subtended by an arc at the centre is double the angle subtended by the arc in the remaining part of the circle).

In $\triangle AOB$,
$$AB^2 = 1^2 + 1^2 = 2$$
$$\therefore \qquad AB = \sqrt{2}$$

5. (d) We know that, $AM \geq HM$
$$\frac{x + y}{2} \geq \frac{2}{\dfrac{1}{x} + \dfrac{1}{y}} \Rightarrow (x + y)\left(\frac{1}{x} + \frac{1}{y}\right) \geq 4$$
$$\Rightarrow \quad \frac{1}{x} + \frac{1}{y} \geq 4 \qquad [\because (x + y = 1)]$$

6. (d) Since, $\angle DAB, \angle ABC$ and $\angle BCD$ are in AP $\therefore$ Let $\angle DAB = \theta - \alpha, \angle ABC = \theta$ and $\angle BCD = \theta + \alpha$

$\therefore$ Median of $\angle DAB, \angle ABC$ and $\angle BCD = \theta$

From point E all the vertices are at equal distance.

$\therefore ABCD$ is cyclic.

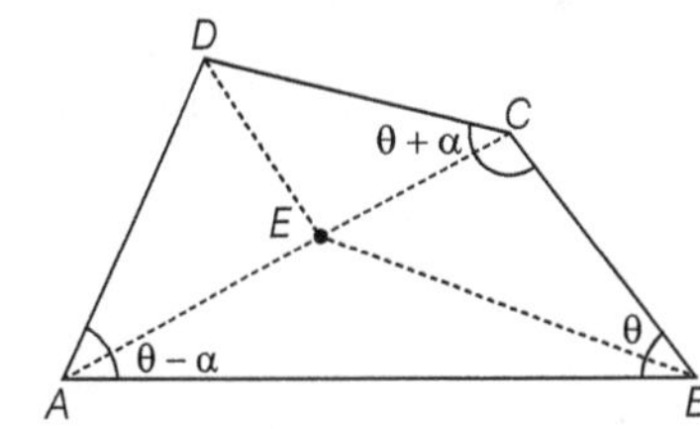

and $\angle ADC = 2\pi - (\theta - \alpha + \theta + \theta + \alpha)$
$$= 2\pi - 3\theta$$
and $\angle ADC + \angle ABC = \pi$
$$\Rightarrow 2\pi - 3\theta + \theta = \pi$$
$$\therefore \qquad \theta = \frac{\pi}{2}$$

7. (a) $\because 2^x + 3^y = 5^{xy}$

When $x = y = 1$, then $2 + 3 = 5$

and $\left(\dfrac{2}{5}\right)^x \cdot \dfrac{1}{5^y} + \left(\dfrac{3}{5}\right)^y \cdot \dfrac{1}{5^x} = 1$ here for any

$x, y \in Z^+$ LHS is not equal to 1 as both are less than $\dfrac{1}{2}$.

$\therefore$ Only one ordered pair (1, 1) is possible.

8. *(b)* Total number of digits used till
$99 = 9 + 90 \times 2 = 189$
The digits use in next 610 three digit
numbers = 1830
$\therefore$ Total digit used till the number
$710 = 189 + 1830 = 2019$
Next three digits are 711
$\therefore$ 2021st digit is 1.

9. *(d)* Given,

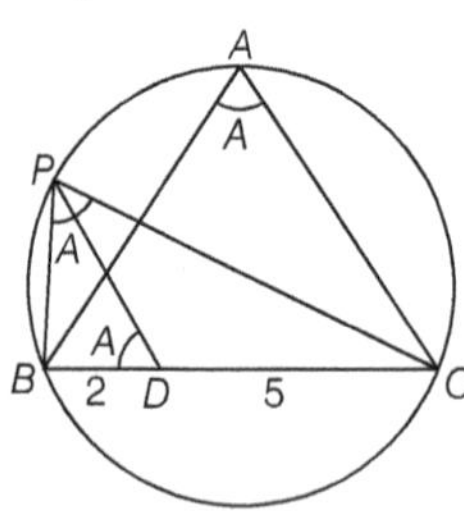

$$\angle PDB = \angle BAC = A \text{ (let)}$$
$$\therefore \quad \angle BPC = A$$
$$\text{Let} \quad \angle BPD = \phi$$
$$\Rightarrow \quad \angle DPC = A - \phi$$
$$\therefore \quad \angle PBD = 180° - \phi - A$$
$$\angle PDC = 180° - A$$
$$\therefore \quad \angle PCD = \phi$$
$$\Delta PDB \sim \Delta CPB \quad \text{(by AA similarity)}$$
$$\therefore \quad \frac{PB}{BC} = \frac{BD}{PB} = \frac{PD}{PC}$$
$$\Rightarrow \quad PB^2 = BD \cdot BC = \frac{2}{7} x \cdot x$$
$$\Rightarrow \quad PB = \sqrt{\frac{2}{7}} \, x$$
$$\therefore \quad \frac{PD}{PC} = \frac{\sqrt{2/7}\,x}{x} = \sqrt{\frac{2}{7}}$$

10. *(b)* $\dfrac{1 + x^{2020}}{1 + x^{2018}} = \dfrac{x^2(1 + x^{2018}) + 1 - x^2}{1 + x^{2018}}$

$$= x^2 + \frac{1 - x^2}{1 + x^{2018}}$$

Put $x = 2 \quad \therefore \left[4 + \dfrac{(-3)}{1 + 2^{2018}}\right] = 3$

Put $x = 3 \quad \therefore \left[9 - \dfrac{8}{1 + 3^{2018}}\right] = 8$

Similarly for $x = 4$, $\left[16 - \dfrac{15}{1 + 4^{2018}}\right] = 15$

For $x = 5$, $\left[25 - \dfrac{24}{1 + 5^{2018}}\right] = 24$

For $x = 6$, $\left[36 - \dfrac{35}{1 + 6^{2018}}\right] = 35$

$\therefore$ Required sum
$$= 3 + 8 + 15 + 24 + 35 = 85$$

11. *(a)* We have,
$$(2021)^{2020} = (1 + 2020)^{2020}$$
$$= {}^{2020}C_0 + {}^{2021}C_1 \cdot 2020 + {}^{2020}C_2 \cdot (2020)^2 + \dots$$
$$= 1 + (2020)^2 + (2020)^2 \times \lambda, \text{ where } \lambda \in Z^+$$
when divided by (2020) remainder will
be 1.

12. *(a)* Let $AD = h$ and $BD = x$

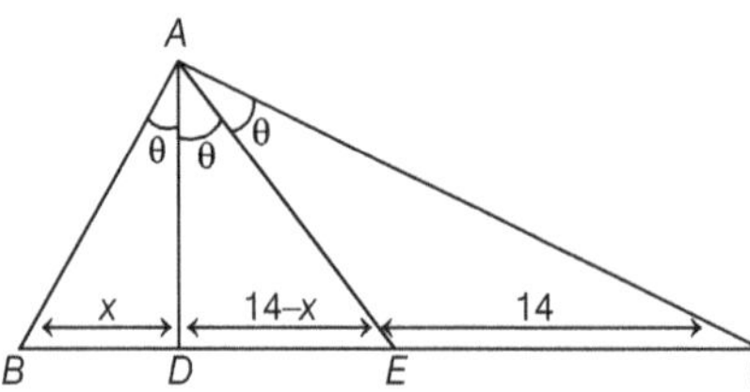

In ΔABD, $\tan\theta = \dfrac{x}{h}$ …(i)

and in ΔADE, $\tan\theta = \dfrac{14 - x}{h}$ …(ii)

From Eqs. (i) and (ii), $\dfrac{x}{h} = \dfrac{14 - x}{h} \Rightarrow x = 7$

Now in ΔADC, $\tan 2\theta = \dfrac{28 - x}{h}$ and in

ΔABD, $\tan\theta = \dfrac{x}{h}$

$$\therefore \quad \frac{\tan 2\theta}{\tan\theta} = \frac{28 - x}{x}$$
$$\Rightarrow \quad \frac{\dfrac{2\tan\theta}{1 - \tan^2\theta}}{\tan\theta} = \frac{28 - 7}{7} \quad (\because x = 7)$$
$$\Rightarrow \quad \frac{2}{1 - \tan^2\theta} = 3$$
$$\Rightarrow \quad 3 - 3\tan^2\theta = 2$$
$$\Rightarrow \quad \tan^2\theta = \frac{1}{3}$$
$$\Rightarrow \quad \tan\theta = \frac{1}{\sqrt{3}} \Rightarrow \theta = 30°$$
$\therefore \sin 30° = 7/AB \Rightarrow AB = 14$
and $\sin 60° = 14/AC \Rightarrow AC = 14\sqrt{3}$
$\therefore AB + AC = 14(1 + \sqrt{3}) = 38.248$

13. *(b)* Number of ways
$$= 5!\left(1 - \frac{1}{1!} + \frac{1}{2!} - \frac{1}{3!} + \frac{1}{4!} - \frac{1}{5!}\right)$$
$$+ 4! \, {}^3C_1 \left(1 - \frac{1}{1!} + \frac{1}{2!} - \frac{1}{3!} + \frac{1}{4!}\right)$$
$$+ 3! \, {}^3C_2 \left(1 - \frac{1}{1!} + \frac{1}{2!} - \frac{1}{3!}\right) + {}^3C_3 \cdot 1$$
$$= 44 + 27 + 6 + 1 = 78$$

14. *(b)* Here, m books will be considered
one thing. So, total $(n + 1)$ things to
arrange.
$\therefore$ Required number of ways $= (n + 1)! \, m!$

15. *(b)* $abcde \times 9 = abcde(10 - 1) = abcde0$

$$\begin{array}{r} -0abcde \\ \hline 0edcba \end{array}$$

$$(a - 1) - 0 = 0 \Rightarrow \boxed{a = 1}$$
$$10 - e = a \Rightarrow \boxed{e = 9}$$
$$b - a = e \Rightarrow \boxed{b = 0}$$
$$(e - 1) - d = b \Rightarrow \boxed{d = 8}$$
$$d - c = c \Rightarrow \boxed{c = 4}$$
$$\overline{abcde} = 10989$$
$\therefore$ Sum of digits = 27

16. *(d)* Given, distance of land from the
building, $s = 12$ m
Height of each floor, $h = 3$ m
Total height of building,
$$H = 15 \times 3 = 45 \text{ m}$$
The situation can be shown as,

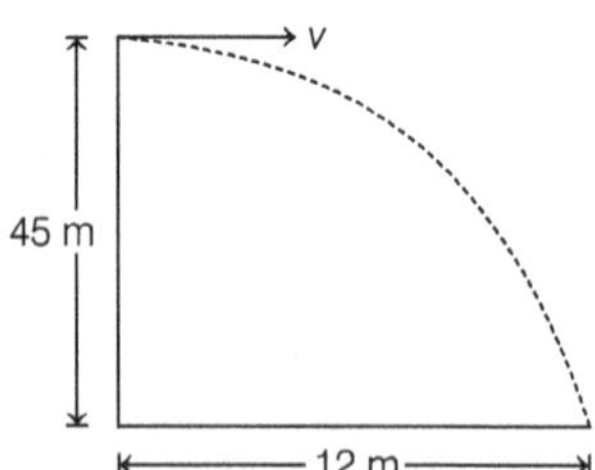

Using second equation of motion for
motion under gravity,
$$H = ut + \frac{1}{2} gt^2 = 0 + \frac{1}{2} gt^2$$
$$\Rightarrow \quad t = \sqrt{\frac{2H}{g}}$$
$$= \sqrt{\frac{2 \times 45}{10}} = 3 \text{ s}$$
If v be the horizontal speed, then
$$s = v \times t$$
$$\text{or} \quad v = \frac{s}{t}$$
$$= \frac{12}{3} = 4 \text{ ms}^{-1}$$
$$= 4 \times \frac{18}{5} \simeq 15 \text{ kmh}^{-1}$$

17. *(a)* Let r_1 and r_2 be the radii of two
wires, then
$$\frac{r_1}{r_2} = \frac{2}{1} \quad \text{(given)}$$

We know that, stress $= \dfrac{F}{A}$

As force applied is same, so
$$\frac{(\text{Stress})_1}{(\text{Stress})_2} = \frac{A_2}{A_1} = \frac{\pi r_2^2}{\pi r_1^2}$$
$$= \left(\frac{r_2}{r_1}\right)^2 = \left(\frac{1}{2}\right)^2 = \frac{1}{4}$$

18. *(a)* Given, area, $A = 30 \times 30$ cm^2
$$= 900 \times 10^{-4} \text{ m}^2$$
Depth, $h = 100$ m
Density of water, $\rho = 1.03 \times 10^3$ kg/m^3

Acceleration due to gravity, $g = 10 \text{ m/s}^2$

As we know that,

pressure, $p = \dfrac{\text{Force } (F)}{\text{Area } (A)}$

or $\quad F = p \times A = \rho g h A$

$\quad\quad = 1.03 \times 10^3 \times 10 \times 100 \times 900 \times 10^{-4}$

$\quad\quad = 9.27 \times 10^4 \simeq 9.3 \times 10^4$

$\quad\quad = 0.93 \times 10^5 \text{ N}$

19. *(d)* Initially, relative speed of spacecraft w.r.t. earth,

$\quad (\mathbf{u}_{SE})_i = u$

Relative speed of planet w.r.t. earth,

$\quad (\mathbf{u}_{PE})_i = -3u$

$\therefore$ Initially, relative speed of spacecraft w.r.t. planet,

$\quad (\mathbf{v}_{SP})_i = u - (-3u) = 4u$

Final relative speed of spacecraft w.r.t. planet,

$\quad (\mathbf{v}_{SP})_f = -(\mathbf{v}_{SP})_i = -4u$

$\therefore$ Finally, relative speed of spacecraft becomes,

$\quad (\mathbf{v}_{SE})_f = (\mathbf{v}_{SP})_f + (\mathbf{u}_{PE})_i$

$\quad\quad = -4u - 3u = -7u$

or $\quad |\mathbf{v}_{SE}| = 7u$

20. *(b)* As, $1° = (60 \times 60)\,\text{s}$

It is given that in 10^5 year, flip is $180°$.

$\therefore$ Average change in orientation per year $= \dfrac{180}{10^5}$ degree

$\quad\quad = \dfrac{180}{10^5} \times 60 \times 60\,\text{s} = 6.48\,\text{s}$

It is closest to 5 s.

21. *(b)* Let A_1 be the area of region I and v_1 be the velocity of blood in this region. Similarly, A_2 and v_2 be the area and velocity in region II.

Using equation of continuity,

$\quad A_1 v_1 = A_2 v_2$

As, $A_1 > A_2$, so $v_2 > v_1$

Now, using Bernoulli's theorem,

$\quad p + \dfrac{1}{2}\rho v^2 = \text{constant}$

As, $\quad v_2 > v_1$

$\therefore \quad p_2 < p_1$

Hence, the pressure is lower in region II, when platelets enters a constriction.

22. *(c)* Among given patterns, the colour observed on compact disc is due to diffraction of light.

The cause of rest of patterns are as :

(a) Rainbow occurs because of refraction, total internal reflection and dispersion of light.

(b) When white light passes through a prism, the colourful pattern formed is due to dispersion of light.

(d) Blue colour of the sky is due to scattering of light.

23. *(b)* As ranges are equal, so the angles of projection of two balls must be complementary.

i.e., $\quad\quad\quad \theta_1 + \theta_2 = 90°$

Given, $\quad\quad\quad \theta_1 = 30°$

$\therefore \quad\quad\quad\quad \theta_2 = 90° - 30° = 60°$

Maximum height of projectile (ball),

$H_{\max} = \dfrac{u^2 \sin^2 \theta}{2g}$

$\therefore \quad \dfrac{H_1}{H_2} = \dfrac{u_1^2 \sin^2 \theta_1}{2g} \times \dfrac{2g}{u_1^2 \sin^2 \theta_2}$

$\quad\quad = \dfrac{\sin^2 (30°)}{\sin^2 (60°)} \quad\quad (\because u_1 = u_2)$

$\quad \dfrac{h}{H_2} = \dfrac{\left(\dfrac{1}{2}\right)^2}{\left(\dfrac{\sqrt{3}}{2}\right)^2} = \dfrac{1}{3} \quad\quad (\because H_1 = h)$

or $\quad H_2 = 3h$

24. *(d)* The situation can be depicted as

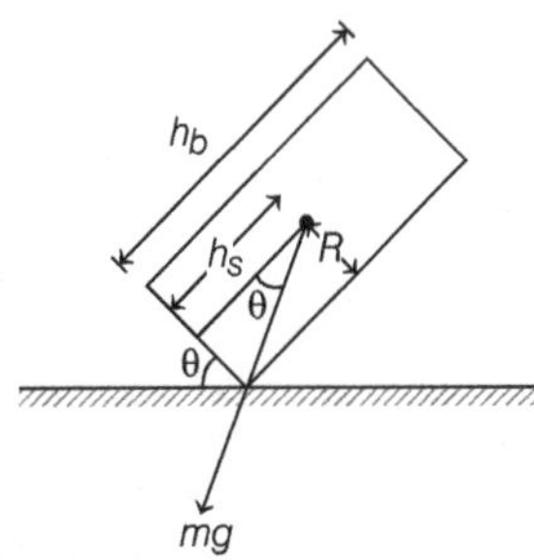

where, h_b = height of bottle,

$\quad\quad h_s$ = height of shampoo

and $\quad R$ = radius of bottle.

For critical angular displacement, mg would pass through tilted side as shown above.

From the above figure,

$\quad\quad \tan \theta = \dfrac{R}{h_s}$

Also, fraction of shampoo, $f = \dfrac{h_s}{h_b}$

$\Rightarrow \quad\quad h_s = f h_b$

$\quad\quad \tan \theta = \dfrac{R}{f h_b}$

or $\quad\quad \theta = \tan^{-1}\left(\dfrac{R}{f h_b}\right)$

$\therefore$ If f increases, then θ will increase upto $0.5\,f$ and afterward it decreases. It is correctly shown in graph (d).

25. *(d)* The value of acceleration due to gravity at a height h is

$\quad g_h = g\left(1 - \dfrac{2h}{R}\right)$

and at depth d is

$\quad g_d = g\left(1 - \dfrac{d}{R}\right)$

It is given that, $g_h = g_d$

$\Rightarrow \quad g\left(1 - \dfrac{2h}{R}\right) = g\left(1 - \dfrac{d}{R}\right)$

$\Rightarrow \quad \dfrac{2h}{R} = \dfrac{d}{R}$

$\Rightarrow \quad d = 2h = 2 \times 10 \quad (\because h = 10\,\text{km})$

$\quad\quad = 20\,\text{km}$

26. *(b)* Using lens formula,

$\quad \dfrac{1}{v} - \dfrac{1}{u} = \dfrac{1}{f}$

$\Rightarrow \quad \dfrac{u}{v} - 1 = \dfrac{u}{f}$

$\Rightarrow \quad m - 1 = \dfrac{u}{f} \quad\quad \left(\because m = \dfrac{v}{u}\right)$

or $\quad \dfrac{1}{m} = \dfrac{u}{f} + 1$

Comparing this with equation of straight line $y = nx + c$, where n is the slope of line, we get

Slope of given graph $\left(\dfrac{1}{m}\ versus\ u\right) = \dfrac{1}{f}$

$\Rightarrow \quad \dfrac{1}{f} = \dfrac{250 - 200}{1 - 0.8}$

$\quad\quad = \dfrac{50}{0.2} = 250$

or $\quad f = \dfrac{1}{250} = 0.004\,\text{m}$

27. *(b)* Given, velocity of projection of apple, $v = 24$ m/s

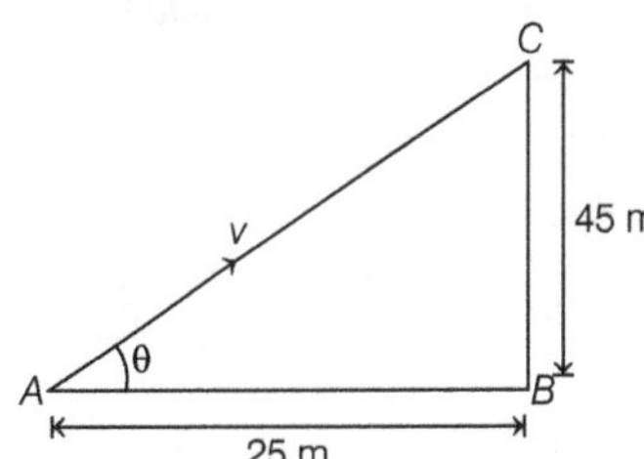

Distance between point of projection and hoop is given by

$AC = \sqrt{(25)^2 + (45)^2} = \sqrt{2650}\,\text{m}$

So, time taken by the ball to the hoop,

$\quad t = \dfrac{\sqrt{2650}}{24}\,\text{s}$

The distance covered by hoop is

$s = \dfrac{1}{2}gt^2 = \dfrac{1}{2} \times 10 \times \left(\dfrac{\sqrt{2650}}{24}\right)^2$

$$= 5 \times \frac{2650}{576} = \frac{13250}{576}$$

$\therefore$ Height above the ground where apple go through the hoop is

$$H = 45 - \frac{13250}{576}$$

$$= \frac{12670}{576} \simeq 22 \text{ m}$$

28. *(a)* For circuit (a), the equivalent resistance is

$$R_{eq} = \frac{300 \times R}{300 + R} + (100 + 200)$$

$$= \frac{300R + 300R + 90000}{(300 + R)}$$

The current through the circuit,

$$I = \frac{V}{R_{eq}}$$

$$= \frac{(300 + R) \times 10}{(600R + 90000)}$$

Using voltage division rule, voltage across R for circuit (a),

$$V_a = \frac{(300 + R) \times 10}{(600R + 90000)} \times \frac{300R}{(300 + R)}$$

$$= \frac{10R}{(2R + 300)}$$

For circuit (b), the equivalent resistance is

$$R_{eq} = \frac{(200 + R) \times 300}{(500 + R)} + 100$$

$$= \frac{110000 + 400R}{500 + R}$$

The current in circuit (b) is

$$I = \frac{V}{R_{eq}} = \frac{(500 + R) \times 10}{(110000 + 400R)}$$

Again, voltage across R for circuit (b),

$$V_b = \frac{(500 + R) \times 10}{(110000 + 400R)} \times \frac{300R}{(500 + R)}$$

$$= \frac{30R}{(1100 + 4R)}$$

According to question,

$$V_a = V_b$$

$$\frac{10R}{(2R + 300)} = \frac{30R}{(1100 + 4R)}$$

$$1100 + 4R = 6R + 900$$

$$\Rightarrow \qquad R = 100\,\Omega$$

29. *(c)* Given, gravitational constant $= 6.7 \times 10^{-11}$ $\text{Nm}^{-2}/\text{kg}^2$

Mass of an electron $= 9.1 \times 10^{-31}$ kg

Charge of an electron $= 1.6 \times 10^{-19}$ C

Gravitational force, $F_G = \dfrac{Gm_1 m_2}{r^2}$

$$= \frac{6.7 \times 10^{-11} \times (9.1 \times 10^{-31})^2}{r^2}$$

Electrostatic repulsive force,

$$F_E = \frac{Kq_1 q_2}{r^2}$$

$$= \frac{9 \times 10^9 \times (1.6 \times 10^{-19})^2}{r^2}$$

$$\therefore \quad \frac{F_G}{F_E} = \frac{6.7 \times 10^{-11} \times (9.1 \times 10^{-31})^2}{9 \times 10^9 \times (1.6 \times 10^{-19})^2}$$

$$= 24 \times 10^{-44}$$

30. *(c)* The situation for given question can be shown as,

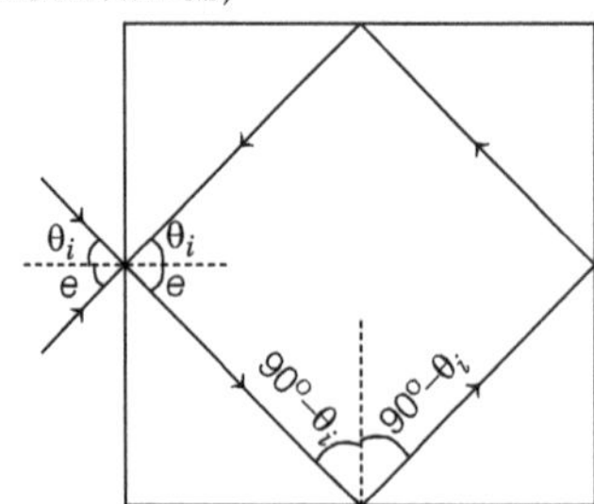

From symmetry,

$$e = \theta_i \quad \Rightarrow \quad 2\theta_i = 90°$$

or $\qquad \theta_i = 45°$

Hence, the beam will come out only at $\theta_i = 45°$.

31. *(c)* The correct acidity order is III > IV > I > II. In substituted phenols, the presence of electron withdrawing groups such as nitro ($-\text{NO}_2$) group enhances the acidic strength due to the effective delocalisation of negative charge in phenoxide ion. IV is stronger than III as ($-\text{NO}_2$) group at *para* position has more electron withdrawing effect due to ($-R$) effect.

On the other hand, electron releasing groups, such as $-$ OMe group, do not favour the formation of phenoxide ion resulting in decrease in acidic strength.

32. *(a)* Optical activity is shown by compounds that have an asymmetric carbon atom or the chiral carbon atom. It must have non-superimposable mirror image. It should not contain any element of symmetry. So, compounds II, IV and V exhibit optical activity whereas compounds I and III does not.

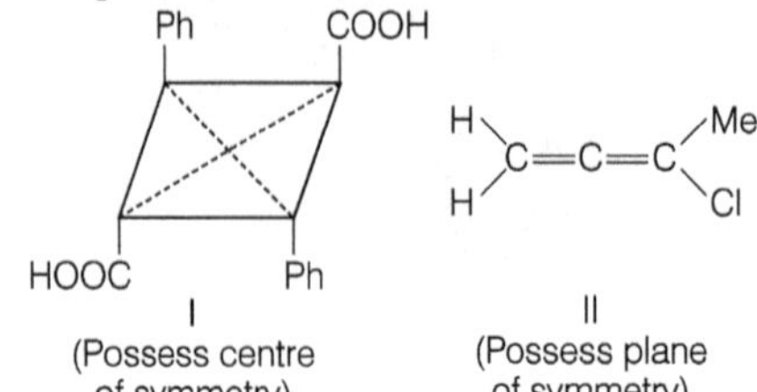

I
(Possess centre of symmetry)

II
(Possess plane of symmetry)

33. *(d)* A molecule which has 1°, 2° and 3° carbon atoms is methylcyclohexane.

So, number of 1° carbon atom = 1

number of 2° carbon atoms = 5

number of 3° carbon atom = 1

34. *(b)* Aniline compound can be purified by steam distillation. This method is used to separate the compounds which are steam volatile and are insoluble in water. In this method, steam from a steam generator is passed through a heating flask containing the liquid to be distilled. The mixture of steam and the volatile organic compound is condensed and collected in a receiver.

35. *(b)* The most acidic compound is cyclopent-1, 3-diene (option-b). More the stability of conjugate base formed by the hydrocarbon more will be acidic nature of hydrocarbon.

$6\,\pi e^{\ominus}$
(Aromatic species (highly stable))

36. *(b)* 1 L of water gas has 1 : 1 CO and H_2 gases. So, volume of hydrogen gas is equal to the carbon monoxide gas.

i.e. $V_{H_2} = V_{CO} = 0.5\,\text{L}$

So, volume of oxygen (V_{O_2}) in the vessel

$$= \frac{9 \times 20}{100} = 1.8\,\text{L}$$

Following reaction takes place on ignition

$$\underset{0.5\,\text{L}}{2CO(g)} + \underset{1.8\,\text{L}}{O_2(g)} \longrightarrow \underset{0.5\,\text{L}}{2CO_2(g)} \text{ at STP}$$

$\therefore$ Number of moles of CO_2 formed $= \dfrac{0.5}{22.4}$

$$= 0.022\,\text{mol}$$

37. *(c)* Given, Work function $(\phi) = 2$ eV

Wavelength $(\lambda_1) = 400$ nm

Wavelength $(\lambda_2) = 800$ nm

Planck constant (h)

$$= 6.626 \times 10^{-34}\ \text{m}^2\text{kg s}^{-1}$$

Speed of light $(c) = 3 \times 10^8\ \text{ms}^{-1}$

Energy associated with 1 W of 400 nm light is $E = \dfrac{hc}{\lambda_1} = \dfrac{6.626 \times 10^{-34} \times 3 \times 10^8}{400 \times 10^{-9}}\ \text{J}$

$$= 3.1\,\text{eV}$$

Similarly, energy associated with 1 W of 800 nm light is

$$E = \frac{hc}{\lambda_2}$$

$$= \frac{6.626 \times 10^{-34} \times 3 \times 10^8}{800 \times 10^{-9}}$$

$$= 1.5 \text{ eV}$$

Since, work function (ϕ) of the metal = 2 eV Therefore, only 400 nm light gives rise to ejection of photoelectrons.

38. *(d)* Statement (d) is correct whereas all other statements are incorrect.

Corrected statements are:

(a) Equilibrium constant is temperature dependent having one unique value for a particular reaction.

(b) It does not tells us how fast the reaction reaches equilibrium.

(c) At equilibrium, the rates of forward and reverse reactions are equal, dynamic and there is no net change in composition.

39. *(d)* Expression for most probable velocity (V_{mp}), average velocity ($\overline{V}$) and root mean square velocity (V_{rms}) is as follows :

$$V_{\text{rms}} = \sqrt{\frac{3RT}{M}}$$

$$\overline{V} = \sqrt{\frac{8RT}{\pi M}}$$

$$V_{\text{mp}} = \sqrt{\frac{2RT}{M}}$$

So, the decreasing order of various molecular speeds is $V_{\text{rms}} > \overline{V} > V_{\text{mp}}$ Hence, the correct plot is (d).

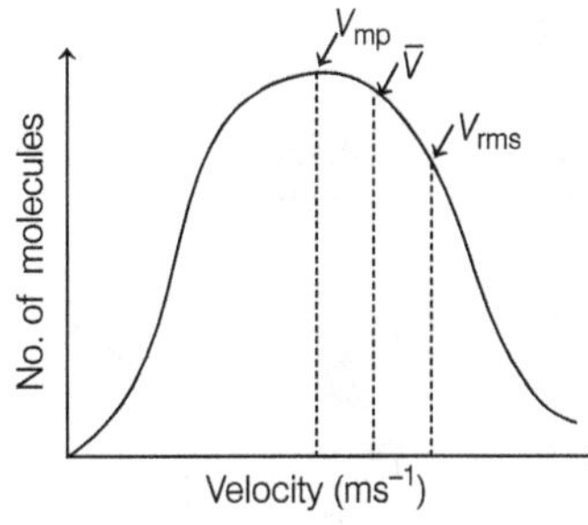

40. *(c)* Electronic configuration of Cu (29) is $1s^2, 2s^2, 2p^6, 3s^2, 3p^6, 3d^{10}, 4s^1$. Only one unpaired electron is present in $4s^1$.

So, the correct set of quantum number is

$$n = 4, \ l = 0, \ m = 0, \ s = +\frac{1}{2}.$$

41. *(d)* The most polar molecule is $AsCl_3$ whereas $AlCl_3$, CCl_4 and $SeCl_6$ are non-polar molecules since they possess zero dipole moment. Structures as follows:

($\mu = 0$) ($\mu = 0$) ($\mu = 0$)

The dipole moment of $AsCl_3$ is non-zero. So, it is a polar molecule.

42. *(b)* The correct order of covalent character is $BaCl_2 < SrCl_2 < CaCl_2 < MgCl_2$. It can be explained by the Fajan's rule. On moving down the group size of ion increases. With increase in size of cation, their polarising power decreases hence covalent character of chlorides also decreases.

43. *(c)* Statement (c) is correct whereas statement (a), (b) and (d) are incorrect. 2.005 has four significant figures. Zeros between two non-zero digits are significant.

Corrected statements

- 100. has three significant figures.
- 1.00×10^2 has three significant figures.
- 0.0025 has two significant figures.

44. *(a)* Thermodynamic cycle in pV plane when plotted under T-S plane is shown as follows:

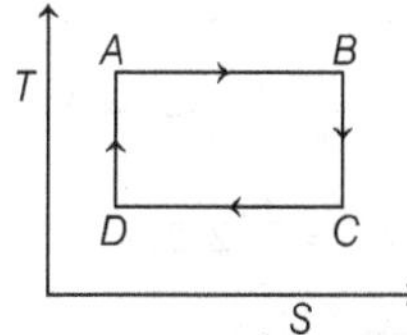

Step 1 ($A \rightarrow B$) : Process involved is isothermal expansion, i.e. $T_A = T_B$. Here, volume increases and p decreases. So, entropy will increase.

Step 2 ($B \rightarrow C$) : Process involved is adiabatic expansion, so cooling occur. Therefore, $T_B > T_C$.

Step 3 ($C \rightarrow D$) : Process involved is isothermal compression, i.e. $T_C = T_D$. Here, volume decreases and p increases. So, entropy will decrease.

Step 4 ($D \rightarrow A$) : Process involved is adiabatic compression, so heating occur and $T_A > T_D$. For adiabatic process, $\Delta S = 0$ means entropy remains same.

45. *(c)* On moving down in a group, ionisation potential generally (IP) decreases. So, ionisation potential of K should be less than that of Na. Hence, option (c) is correct.

46. *(b)* The carbonic anhydrases form a family of enzymes that catalyse the interconversion between carbon dioxide and the dissociated ions of carbonic acid. The active site of most carbonic anhydrases contain a zinc ion.

$$CO_2 + H_2O \rightleftharpoons H_2CO_3 \rightleftharpoons HCO_3^- + H^+$$
Substrate

47. *(d)* The small intestine is the part of the inestine where 90% of the digestion of carbohydrates, proteins and lipids, etc. and the adsorption of food occurs. The other 10% take place in the stomach and large intestine. The main function of the small intestine is absorption of nutrients and minerals from food. Acidification of digested food occurs in stomach due to the secretion of HCl from parietal cells.

48. *(b)* Insulin is a pancreatic hormone that regulates blood glucose level by the stimulating the conversion of glucose to glycogen (this process is called glycogenesis).

49. *(a)* Poikilotherms are also called 'ectotherms' cold blooded animals. Such creatures are the thermoregulatory opposite of 'endotherms' or 'homeothermic'. Since thermoregulation is energetically expensive, so homeotherms have relatively higher metabolic requirements than poikilotherms.

50. *(c)* The chemiosmotic hypothesis was proposed by Peter Mitchell. This hypothesis stated that a proton motive force was responsible for driving the synthesis of ATP. In this hypothesis protons would be pumped across the inner mitochondrial membrane as electrons went through the electron transfer chain.

51. *(a)* Haemophilia is an X-linked recessive disorder that is passed through generation and can be traced by using a pedigree.

Phenylketonuria, sickle-cell anaemia and β-thalassemia are autosomal recessive disorder.

52. *(d)* The seeds and fruits are the results of fertilisation or sexual reproduction in plants. The ovary in angiosperms develops into the fruit where as ovules become the seed.

53. *(c)* Edward Jenner observed that milk maids who had getten cowpox did not show any symptoms of smallpox after variolation. This is a case of active immunity in which infection of cowpox virus (similar to smallpox virus) in milkmaid stimulate the immunity system of milk maids against smallpox virus.

54. *(a)* Independent assortment states that the alleles of two (or more) different genes get sorted into gametes independently of one another.

Parents AABBCC aabbcc

F_1 AaBbCc

(Here n heterozygous locus = 3)

Gametes = $2^n = (2)^3 = 8$

Therefore, 8 different genotypes of pollen is possible in F_1 plant, when these three loci follow independent assortment.

55. *(d)* Mitosis is a process of cell duplication, in which one cell divides into two genetically identical daughter cells. The correct sequence of events of mitosis is

Prophase $\longrightarrow$ Metaphase $\longrightarrow$ Anaphase $\longrightarrow$ Telophase

56. *(c)* The residual volume (RV) is the amount of air that is left in the lungs even after maximum forceful expiration. And this forceful expiration is the expiratory reserve volume. It is about 1000-1100 mL.

57. *(b)* The radula is the anatomical structure used for feeding in most species of Mollusca.

Metameric segmentation is true segmentation in which external segmentation corresponds to the internal segmentation and the body is divided into a number of segments Animals belong to phylum–Annelida and Arthropoda exhibit metameric segmentation.

The pseudocoelom is a fluid filled body cavity lying inside the external body wall of the nematode that baths the internal organs, including the alimentary system and reproductive system.

Radial symmetry is the arrangement of body parts around a central axis, animals have top and bottom surface but no left and right sides or front or back. It is present in adult echinoderms.

58. *(a)* Alfred Russel Wallace who worked first in Amazon River basin and then in Malay Archipelago had also come to similar conclusions as that of Charles Darwin for natural selection in the year 1858 independently. This pushed him to publish his book on the origin of species.

59. *(c)* Biomagnification also known as bioamplification or biological magnification is any concentration of a toxin in the tissue of tolerant organisms along the food chain. The maximum

concentration is found in top consumers that occupy top of a food chain.

60. *(d)* Seveure acute respiratory syndrome corona virus-2 (SARS-CoV-2) has a positive sense single-stranded genomic RNA as a genetic material.

61. *(c)* For number not divisible by 4 and not having zero can be formed as

Number of ways to form

All digits odd numbers = 5^4

3 digits odd numbers + 1 even numbers (4 or 8) = $5^3 . 2 . 4$

2 digits odd numbers + 2 even numbers (4 or 8) = 0

1 digits odd numbers + 3 even numbers = 0

All even numbers = 2^4 (only 2 or 6 can be used)

$\therefore$ Required probability = $\dfrac{2^4}{5^4 + 5^3 \cdot 8 + 2^4}$

$= \dfrac{16}{1641}$

62. *(c)*

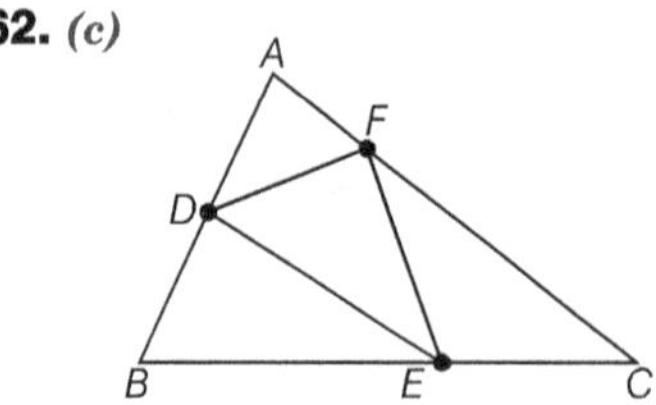

Here, $a = BC = 5$, $b = CA = 6$ and $c = AB = 4$

Area of $\Delta ADF = \dfrac{1}{2} \cdot 2 \cdot 2 \sin A = 2\sin A$

Area of $\Delta BDF = \dfrac{1}{2} \cdot 2 \cdot 3 \sin B = 3\sin B$

And area of $\Delta CEF = \dfrac{1}{2} \cdot 2 \cdot 4 \sin C = 4\sin C$

And area of $\Delta ABC = \Delta$

$\therefore$　$\dfrac{\text{Area of } \Delta DEF}{\text{Area of } \Delta ABC}$

$= \dfrac{\Delta - (2\sin A + 3\sin B + 4\sin C)}{\Delta}$

$= 1 - \dfrac{1}{\Delta}\left(2 \cdot \dfrac{2\Delta}{bc} + 3 \cdot \dfrac{2\Delta}{ac} + 4 \cdot \dfrac{2\Delta}{ab}\right)$

$= 1 - \dfrac{2(2a + 3b + 4c)}{abc}$

$= 1 - \dfrac{2(10 + 18 + 16)}{5 \cdot 6 \cdot 4} = \dfrac{16}{60} = \dfrac{4}{15}$

63. *(b)* $x^3 + y^3 = 65$

Let $x, y > 0$

Clearly, (1, 4) and (4, 1) holds for x or $y \geq 6$ difference of two cubes is always greater than or equal to 91. Hence, only 2 ordered pair possible.

64. *(b)*

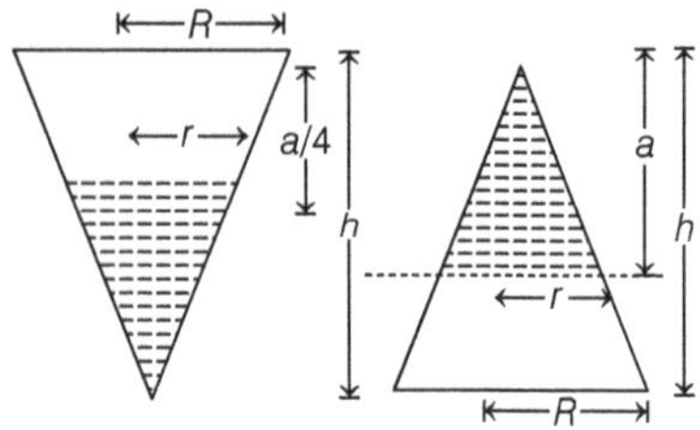

Volume of water in both the cases will be equal i.e.,

$\dfrac{1}{3}\pi r_1^2\left(h - \dfrac{a}{4}\right) = \dfrac{1}{3}\pi R^2 h - \dfrac{1}{3}\pi r^2 a$　...(i)

$\dfrac{r}{a} = \dfrac{R}{h}$　...(ii)

and $r_1 h = R\left(h - \dfrac{a}{4}\right)$　...(iii)

From Eqs. (i), (ii) and (iii), we get

$16\left(\dfrac{h}{a}\right)^2 - 4\left(\dfrac{h}{a}\right) - 21 = 0 \Rightarrow \dfrac{h}{a} = \dfrac{1 + \sqrt{85}}{8}$

65. *(d)* Since, Statement I does not hold for $n = 4$

$\Rightarrow$ Statement I is false.

For Statement II,

$n(n + 1)^2 \mid n!$

$\Rightarrow$　$(n + 1)^2 \mid (n - 1)!$

Let　$n = 3k - 1, k > 3, k \in N$

$n + 1 = 3k, n - 1 = 3k - 2$

$(n - 1)! = (3k - 2)!$

$= (3k - 2) \times (3(k - 1)) \times ... \times (2k + 1) (2k)$

$(2k - 1) ... \times (k + 1) k(k - 1) ... 3 \times 2 \times 1$

Since, RHS contains $3^2, k^2$

Hence, it is divisible by $(3k)^2$.

$\Rightarrow (n - 1)!$ is divisible by $(n + 1)^2$

$\Rightarrow$ Statement II is true.

66. *(c)* The given diagram can be shown by symmetry of four charges as,

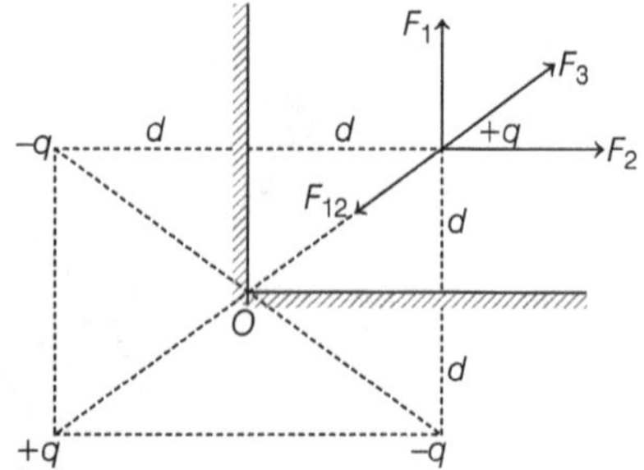

Let O be the centre and $2d$ be the distance between charges.

Forces between $-q$ and $+q$ is

$F_1 = \dfrac{Kq^2}{4d^2} = F_2$ (attractive)

and force between $+q$ and $+q$ is

$$F_3 = \frac{Kq^2}{(2\sqrt{2}d)^2} = \frac{Kq^2}{8d^2} \text{ (repulsive)}$$

So, net force acting on the charge is

$$F_{net} = F_{12} - F_3 = \sqrt{2}\,F_1 - F_3$$
$$\left(\because F_{12} = \sqrt{F_1^2 + F_1^2} = \sqrt{2}F_1\right)$$
$$= \frac{\sqrt{2}Kq^2}{4d^2} - \frac{Kq^2}{8d^2}$$
$$= \frac{q^2(2\sqrt{2} - 1)}{32\pi\varepsilon_0 d^2}, \text{ towards } O$$

67. (*) For ball A, the vertical velocity is zero, when it leaves the structure. So,

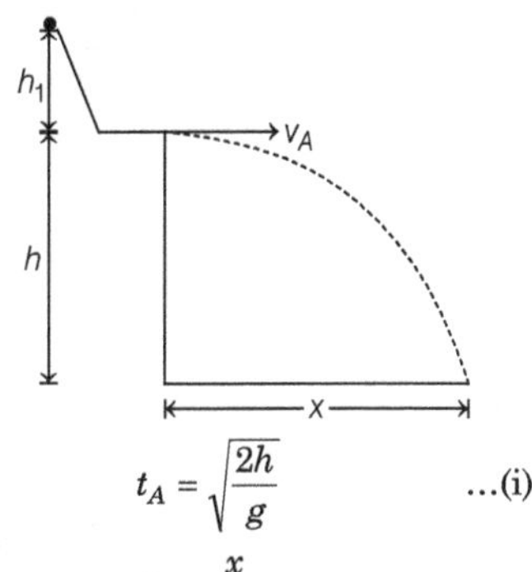

$$t_A = \sqrt{\frac{2h}{g}} \qquad \text{...(i)}$$

Also, $$t_A = \frac{x}{v_A}$$

where, v_A = horizontal velocity of ball A.
From energy conservation,
PE of A at height h_1 = KE of A

$$\Rightarrow \qquad mgh_1 = \frac{1}{2}mv_A^2$$
$$\Rightarrow \qquad v_A = \sqrt{2gh_1}$$
$$\therefore \qquad t_A = \frac{x}{\sqrt{2gh_1}} \qquad \text{...(ii)}$$

For ball B, using energy conservation,

$$mgh_1 = \frac{1}{2}mv_B^2$$
$$\Rightarrow \qquad v_B = \sqrt{2gh_1}$$
$$\therefore \qquad t_B = \frac{x}{v_B} = \frac{x}{\sqrt{2gh_1}} \qquad \text{...(iii)}$$

So, $t_A = t_B$ [using Eqs. (ii) and (iii)]
For ball C, the time can be given for motion under gravity,

$$t_C = \sqrt{\frac{2h}{g}} \qquad \text{...(iv)}$$

From Eqs. (i) and (iv), we get

$$t_C = t_A = t_B$$

Note Correct option can be (b) for $t_A = t_B = t_C$.

68. (a) As the images are formed on the screen, so they are real and inverted (due to converging lens).

Since the blue and white bulbs are below the principle axis, so their image should be above and similarly as the green and red are above, so their image should be below the principle axis. Also, the blue and white bulbs are neares to lens, so image will be far from lens compared to that of red and green bulbs. Hence, option (a) is correct.

69. (b) Let m be the mass of each coin. The centre of mass on N coins kept on lid is

$$\text{CM} = \frac{40m \times 0 + Nm \times 9}{(40 + N)\,m} = \frac{9N}{N + 40} \text{ cm}$$

The geometric centre of submerged part after keeping N coins will be

$$\text{GC} = \frac{3(40 + N)}{40} \text{ cm}$$

For equilibrium, CM = GC

$$\Rightarrow \qquad \frac{9N}{N + 40} = \frac{(40 + N)\,3}{40}$$
$$\Rightarrow 3N^2 - 480N + 4800 = 0$$

This gives, $N = 10.72$, which is closed to 10.

70. (c) The situation can be shown as,

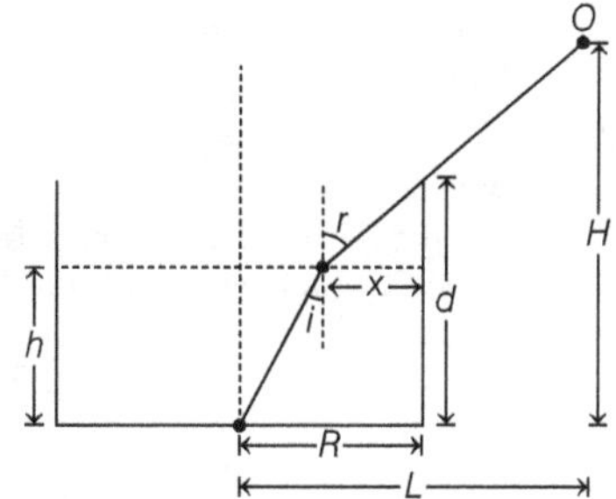

Here, $R = 1$ m, $L = 1.5$ m, $d = 4$ m and $H = 5.75$

$$\therefore \quad \tan r = \frac{L - R}{H - d} = \frac{1.5 - 1}{5.75 - 4}$$
$$= \frac{0.5}{1.75} = \frac{2}{7} = \frac{x}{d - h} \qquad \text{...(i)}$$

and $$\tan i = \frac{R - x}{h} \qquad \text{...(ii)}$$

From Snell's law,

$$\mu \sin i = \sin r$$
$$\Rightarrow \qquad \tan i = \frac{3}{\sqrt{203}}$$

Using Eqs. (i) and (ii)

$$x = (d - h)\tan r = R - h \tan i$$
$$\Rightarrow \qquad h = \frac{d \tan r - R}{\tan r - \tan i}$$

$$= \frac{4 \times \dfrac{2}{7} - 1}{\dfrac{2}{7} - \dfrac{3}{\sqrt{203}}} = 1.92 \text{ m}$$

Volume of water filled $= \pi R^2 h$

$$= \pi \times 1^2 \times 1.92$$

or $Q\,t = 6.0288$ (where, Q = flow rate)

$$\Rightarrow \quad t = \frac{6.0288}{0.1} = 60.288 \text{ s, which is close}$$

to 63 s.

71. (d) The hydrocarbon (X) is butyne (Et —≡— H). It decolourises bromine water and forms a white precipitate in ethanolic $AgNO_3$ solution.

$$\text{Et} \underset{\substack{\text{Butyne}\\(X)}}{\equiv} \text{H} \xrightarrow[\text{brown colour}]{\text{Br}_2 \text{ water}} \text{Et}-\overset{\overset{\text{Br}}{|}}{\underset{\underset{\text{Br}}{|}}{\text{C}}}-\overset{\overset{\text{Br}}{|}}{\underset{\underset{\text{Br}}{|}}{\text{C}}}-\text{H}$$

$$\text{Et} \underset{(X)}{\equiv} \text{H} \xrightarrow[\text{AgNO}_3]{\text{Ethanolic}} \text{C}_2\text{H}_5 - \text{C} \equiv \overset{\ominus \;\oplus}{\underset{\text{White ppt.}}{\text{C Ag}}}$$

Butyne (X) on treatment with $HgCl_2$ in aqueous H_2SO_4 produces butanone which gives yellow ppt. of CHI_3 on treatment with I_2 and NaOH as follows

$$\text{Et} \underset{(X)}{\equiv} \text{H} \xrightarrow{\text{HgCl}_2/\text{H}_2\text{SO}_4} \text{C}_2\text{H}_5 - \underset{\underset{\text{O}}{\|}}{\text{C}} - \text{CH}_3$$

$$\xrightarrow[\text{NaOH}]{\text{I}_2} \underset{\text{Yellow}}{\text{CHI}_3}{\downarrow} + \text{C}_2\text{H}_5\text{COO}^-$$

72. (d) Compound X is likely to be [cyclohexane-S ring]. % of S in compound

$$= \frac{32 \times \text{mass of } BaSO_4 \text{ formed} \times 100}{233 \times \text{mass of organic compound}}$$
$$= \frac{32 \times 0.233}{233 \times 0.102} \times 100 = 31.37\%$$

73. (a) Given, specific heat of a substance $= 0.86 \text{ Jg}^{-1}\text{K}^{-1}$

As, 1000 g solution has 1 mole (or 58 g) substance.

So, 10 g solution will have 0.58 g substance

and 10 g solution will have $(10-0.58)$ g water $= 9.42$ g water.

So, the energy required = heat required to raise the temperature of sample + heat required to raise the temperature of water.

$$= (0.58 \times 0.86 \times 10) + (9.42 \times 4.2 \times 10)$$
$$= 400.628 \text{ J} = 401.7 \text{ J}$$

74. (c) Given,

Strength of a $H_2O_2 = 1.79$ N

Volume strength $(H_2O_2) = 11.2 \times$ molarity

For H_2O_2, molarity $= \dfrac{\text{normality}}{2}$

So, volume strength (H_2O_2)

$$= 5.6 \times \text{normality} = 5.6 \times 1.79$$
$$= 10.024 = 10 \text{ volume}$$

75. *(d)* All given statements are correct.

In the graph, at T_1, the gas cannot be liquefied. In curve, T_2, at point B liquid of a particular volume appears. Further compression does not change the pressure. Liquid and gaseous state coexist and further application of pressure results in the condensation of more gas until the point A is reached. T_c is the highest temperature at which the gas can be liquefied. Above critical temperature (T_c) gas cannot liquefy even applying high pressure. It can be shown as follows.

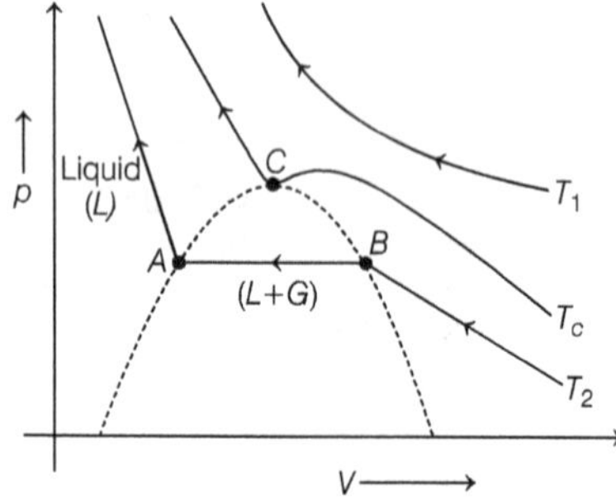

76. *(b)* Anthropocene epoch is an informal geologic time internal used to describe the most recent period in earth's history when human activity started to have a significant impact on the earth's climate and ecosystem.

77. *(c)* Impaired dark adaptation of the eyes, can lead to night blindness. It is a symptom of vitamin-A deficiency. Ariboflavinosis is caused by deficiency of vitamin-B_2 (riboflavin) and is characterised by soreness of the mouth.) Rickets is the softening and weakening of bones in children, usually because of an extreme and prolonged vitamin-D deficiency. Deficiency of vitamin-B_{12} causes pernicious anaemia. Pellagra is a disease caused by a lack of the vitamin–B_3 (niacin).

78. *(b)* Vital capacity is the maximum amount of air a person can expel from the lungs after a maximum inhalation

Vital capacity $(VC) - IRV + ERV + TV$

$TV = VC - (IRV + ERV)$

$$= 60 \text{ mL/kg} - (40 \text{ mL/kg} + 15 \text{ mL/kg})$$
$$= 5 \text{ mL/kg}$$

TV of an adult mammal of 50 kg body weight $= 5 \text{ mL/kg} \times 50 \text{ kg}$

$$= 250 \text{ mL}$$

$TV/min = 250 \text{ mL} \times 20 = 500 \text{ mL}$

Volume of air that lungs displace in 24 hours (TV/day)

$$= TV/min \times 60 \times 24$$
$$= 5000 \text{ mL} \times 60 \times 24$$
$$= 7,200,000 \text{ mL}$$
$$= 7200 \text{ L}$$

79. *(d)* Since long-haired phenotype is recessive to short hair

Genotype, Long haired dog $= ll$

Short haired dog $= LL$

One pup is short haired that can be $= LL$ or Ll and its sibling is long haired $= ll$

(i) Parents   Short hair   ×   Short hair
                  Ll   Ll

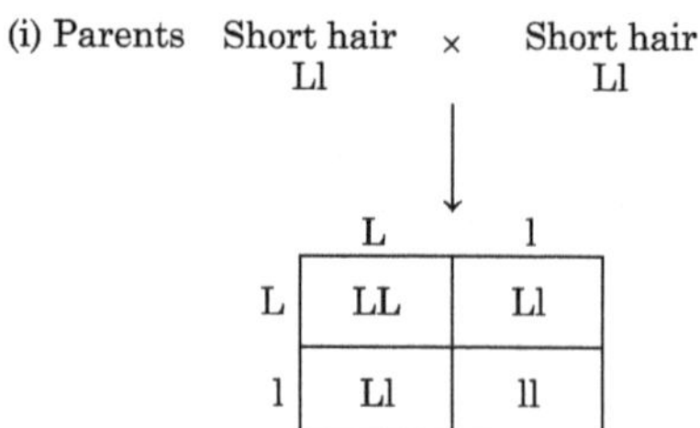

(ii) Parents   Short hair ×   Long hair
                   Ll   ll

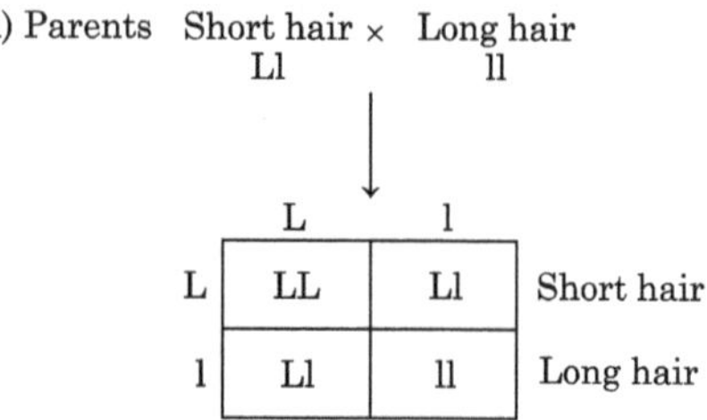

So both (i) and (iii) are possible.

80. *(c)* Probablity of getting positive report $= P(P_R)$

Probability of actual Covid-19 positive $= P(P_A)$

Probability of not actually Covid-19 positive $= P(\overline{P_A})$

$$P(P_R) = P\left(\frac{P_R}{P_A}\right) \cdot P(P_A) + P\left(\frac{P_R}{\overline{P_A}}\right) \cdot P(\overline{P_A})$$

$$= \left(\frac{99}{100} \times \frac{10}{100}\right) + \left(\frac{1}{100} \times \frac{90}{100}\right)$$

$$= \frac{990 + 90}{10,000}$$

$$= \frac{108}{1000} + 0.108$$

$$P(P_R) = 0.108$$

QUESTION PAPER 2019
Stream : SA

MM : 100

Instructions

1. There are 80 questions in this paper.
2. This question paper contains two parts; Part I and Part II. There are four sections; Mathematics, Physics, Chemistry and Biology in each part.
3. Out of the four options given with each question, only one is correct.

➲ PART-I (1 Mark Questions)

MATHEMATICS

1. Let ABC be an equilateral triangle with side length a. Let R and r denote the radii of the circumcircle and the incircle of triangle ABC respectively. Then, as a function of a, the ratio $\dfrac{R}{r}$

(a) strictly increases   (b) strictly decreases
(c) remains constant
(d) strictly increases for $a < 1$ and strictly decrease for $a > 1$

2. Let b be an non-zero real number. Suppose the quadratic equation $2x^2 + bx + \dfrac{1}{b} = 0$ has two distinct real roots. Then

(a) $b + \dfrac{1}{b} > \dfrac{5}{2}$ (b) $b + \dfrac{1}{b} < \dfrac{5}{2}$

(c) $b^2 - 3b > -2$ (d) $b^2 + \dfrac{1}{b^2} < 4$

3. Let $p(x) = x^2 + ax + b$ have two distinct real roots, where a, b are real number. Define $g(x) = p(x^3)$ for all real number x.

Then, which of the following statements are true?

    I. g has exactly two distinct real roots.

    II. g can have more than two distinct real roots.

    III. There exists a real number α such that $g(x) \geq \alpha$ for all real x.

(a) Only I   (b) Both I and III
(c) Only II   (d) Both II and III

4. Let a_n, $n \geq 1$, be an arithmetic progression with first term 2 and common difference 4. Let M_n be the average of the first n terms. Then the sum $\displaystyle\sum_{n=1}^{10} M_n$ is

(a) 110   (b) 335
(c) 770   (d) 1100

5. In a triangle ABC, $\angle BAC = 90°$; AD is the altitude from A on to BC. Draw DE perpendicular to AC and DF perpendicular to AB. Suppose $AB = 15$ and $BC = 25$. Then the length of EF is

(a) 12   (b) 10
(c) $5\sqrt{3}$ (d) $5\sqrt{5}$

6. The sides a, b, c of a triangle satisfy the relations $c^2 = 2ab$ and $a^2 + c^2 = 3b^2$. Then the measure of $\angle BAC$, in degrees, is
(a) 30   (b) 45
(c) 60   (d) 90

7. Let N be the least positive integer such that whenever a non-zero digit c is written after the last digit of N, the resulting number is divisible by c. The sum of the digits of N is
(a) 9   (b) 18
(c) 27   (d) 36

8. Let $x_1, x_2, \ldots, x_{11}$ be 11 distinct positive integers. If we replace the largest of these integers by the median of the other 10 integers, then
(a) the median remains the same
(b) the mean increases
(c) the median decreases
(d) the mean remains the same

9. The number of cubic polynomials $P(x)$ satisfying $P(1) = 2$, $P(2) = 4$, $P(3) = 6$, $P(4) = 8$ is
(a) 0
(b) 1
(c) more than one but finitely many
(d) infinitely many

10. A two-digit number $\overline{ab}$ is called almost prime if one obtains a two-digit prime number by changing at most one of its digits a and b. (For example, 18 is an almost prime number because 13 is a prime number). Then the number of almost prime two-digit numbers is
(a) 56   (b) 75   (c) 87   (d) 90

11. Let P be an interior point of a convex quadrilateral $ABCD$ and K, L, M, N be the mid-points of AB, BC, CD, DA respectively. If Area $(PKAN) = 25$, Area $(PLBK) = 36$, and Area $(PMDN) = 41$ then Area $(PLCM)$ is
(a) 20   (b) 29   (c) 52   (d) 54

12. The number of non-negative integer solutions of the equations $6x + 4y + z = 200$ and $x + y + z = 100$ is
(a) 3   (b) 5   (c) 7   (d) Infinite

13. Let $N_1 = 2^{55} + 1$ and $N_2 = 165$.

Then
(a) N_1 and N_2 are coprime
(b) the HCF (Highest Common Factor) of N_1 and N_2 is 55
(c) the HCF of N_1 and N_2 is 11
(d) the HCF of N_1 and N_2 is 33

14. Let $l > 0$ be a real number, C denote a circle with circumference l and T denote a triangle with perimeter l. Then
(a) given any positive real number α, we can choose C and T as above such that ratio $\dfrac{\text{Area }(C)}{\text{Area }(T)}$ is greater than α

(b) given any positive real number α, we can choose C and T as above such that ratio $\dfrac{\text{Area }(C)}{\text{Area }(T)}$ is less than α

(c) give any C and T as above, the ratio $\dfrac{\text{Area }(C)}{\text{Area }(T)}$ is independent of C and T

(d) there exist real numbers a and b such that for any circle C and triangle T as above, we must have $a < \dfrac{\text{Area }(C)}{\text{Area }(T)} < b$

15. The number of three digit numbers $\overline{abc}$ such that the arithmetic mean of b and c and the square of their geometric mean are equal is
(a) 9   (b) 18
(c) 36   (d) 54

PHYSICS

16. Various optical processes are involved in the formation of a rainbow. Which of the following provides the correct order in time in which these processes occur?
(a) Refraction, total internal reflection, refraction.
(b) Total internal reflection, refraction, total internal reflection.
(c) Total internal reflection, refraction, refraction.
(d) Refraction, total internal reflection, total internal reflection.

17. A specially designed Vernier calliper has the main scale least count of 1 mm. On the Vernier scale, there are 10 equal divisions and they match with 11 main scale divisions. Then, the least count of the Vernier calliper is
(a) 0.1 mm   (b) 0.909 mm
(c) 1.1 mm   (d) 0.09 mm

18. A steel ball is dropped in a viscous liquid. The distance of the steel ball from the top of the liquid is shown below. The terminal velocity of the ball is closest to

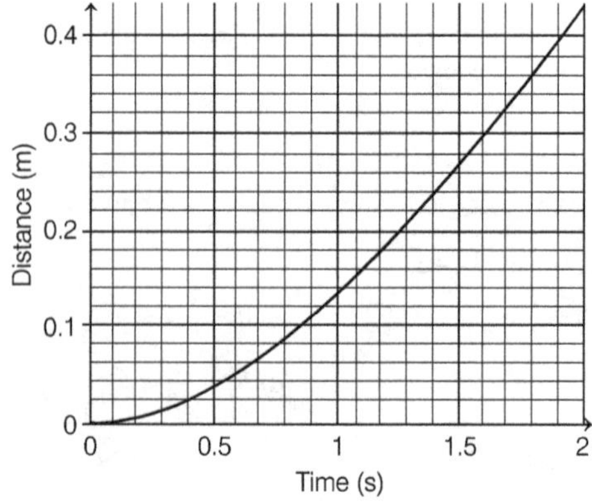

(a) 0.26 m/s   (b) 0.33 m/s
(c) 0.45 m/s   (d) 0.21 m/s

19. A student in a town in India, where the price per unit (1 unit = 1 kWh) of electricity is ₹ 5.00, purchases a 1 kVA UPS (uninterrupted power supply) battery. A day before the exam, 10 friends arrive to the student's home with their laptops and all connect their laptops to the UPS. Assume that each laptop has a constant power requirement of 90 W. Consider the following statements.

   I. All the 10 laptops can be powered by the UPS, if connected directly.

   II. All the 10 laptops can be powered, if connected using an extension box with a 3 A fuse.

   III. If all the 10 friends use the laptop for 5 h, then the cost of the consumed electricity is about ₹ 22.50.

Select the correct option with the true statements.

(a) I only   (b) I and II only
(c) I and III only   (d) II and III only

20. Frosted glass is widely used for translucent windows. The region, where a transparent adhesive tape is stuck over the frosted glass becomes transparent. The most reasonable explanation for this is

(a) diffusion of adhesive glue into glass
(b) chemical reaction at adhesive tape-glass interface
(c) refractive index of adhesive glue is close to that of glass
(d) adhesive tape is more transparent than glass

21. Consider two equivalent, triangular hollow prisms A and B made of thin glass plates and arranged with negligible spacing as shown in the figure. A beam of white light is incident on prism A from the left. Given that, the refractive index of water is inversely related to temperature, the beam to the right of prism B would not appear white, if

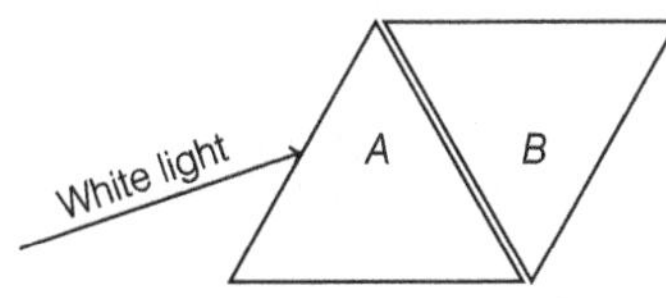

(a) both prisms are filled with hot water (70°C)
(b) both prisms are filled with cold water (7°C)
(c) both prisms are empty
(d) prism A is filled with hot water (70°C) and prism B with cold water (7°C)

22. A ball is moving uniformly in a circular path of radius 1 m with a time period of 1.5 s. If the ball is suddenly stopped at $t = 8.3$ s, the magnitude of the displacement of the ball with respect to its position at $t = 0$ s is closest to

(a) 1 m   (b) 33 m
(c) 3 m   (d) 2 m

23. A particle slides from the top of a smooth hemispherical surface of radius R which is fixed on a horizontal surface. If it separates from the hemisphere at a height h from the horizontal surface, then the speed of the particle is

(a) $\sqrt{(2g(R - h))}$
(b) $\sqrt{(2g(R + h))}$
(c) $\sqrt{2gR}$
(d) $\sqrt{2gh}$

24. The nuclear radius is given by $R = r_0 A^{1/3}$, where r_0 is constant and A is the atomic mass number. Then, the nuclear mass density of U^{238} is

(a) twice that of Sn^{119}
(b) thrice that of Sn^{119}
(c) same as that of Sn^{119}
(d) half that of Sn^{119}

25. The electrostatic energy of a nucleus of charge Ze is equal to $\dfrac{kZ^2e^2}{R}$, where k is a constant and R is the nuclear radius. The nucleus divides into two daughter nuclei of charges $\dfrac{Ze}{2}$ and equal radii. The change in electrostatic energy in the process when they are far apart is

(a) $\dfrac{0.375kZ^2e^2}{R}$ (b) $\dfrac{0.125kZ^2e^2}{R}$

(c) $\dfrac{kZ^2e^2}{R}$ (d) $\dfrac{0.5kZ^2e^2}{R}$

26. Two masses M_1 and M_2 carry positive charges Q_1 and Q_2, respectively. They are dropped to the floor in a laboratory set up from the same height, where there is a constant electric field vertically upwards. M_1 hits the floor before M_2. Then,

(a) $Q_1 > Q_2$ (b) $Q_1 < Q_2$
(c) $M_1 Q_1 > M_2 Q_2$ (d) $M_1 Q_2 > M_2 Q_1$

27. Which one of the following schematic graphs best represents the variation of pV (in Joules) *versus* T (in Kelvin) of one mole of an ideal gas? (The dotted line represents $pV = T$)

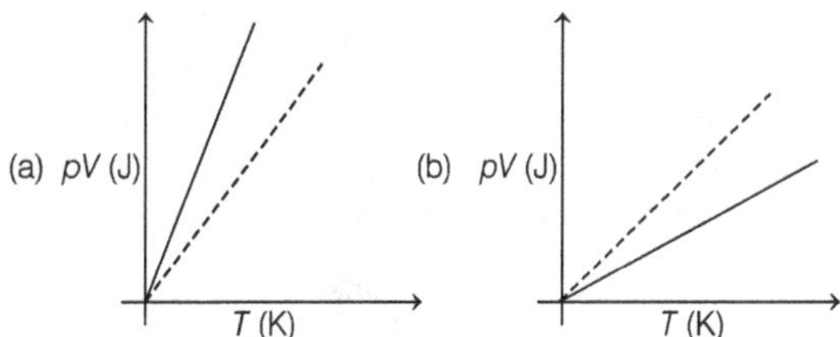

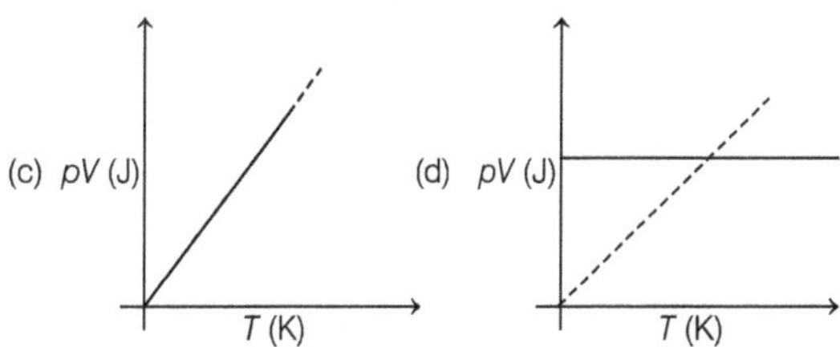

28. Mumbai needs 1.4×10^{12} L of water annually. Its effective surface area is 600 km^2 and it receives an average rainfall of 2.4 m annually. If 10% of this rain water is conserved, it will meet approximately
(a) 1% of Mumbai's water needs
(b) 10% of Mumbai's water needs
(c) 50% of Mumbai's water needs
(d) 100% of Mumbai's water needs

29. A mass M moving with a certain speed V collides elastically with another stationary mass m. After the collision, the masses M and m move with speeds V' and v, respectively. All motion is in one dimension. Then,
(a) $V = V' + v$
(b) $V' = V + v$
(c) $V' = \dfrac{(V + v)}{2}$
(d) $v = V + V'$

30. Four ray 1, 2, 3 and 4 are incident normally on the face PQ of an isosceles prism PQR with apex angle $\angle Q = 120°$. The refractive indices of the material of the prism for the above rays 1, 2, 3 and 4 are 1.85, 1.95, 2.05 and 2.15 respectively and the surrounding medium is air. Then, the rays emerging from the face QR are
(a) 4 only
(b) 1 and 2 only
(c) 3 and 4 only
(d) 1, 2, 3 and 4

CHEMISTRY

31. The hybridisations of N, C and O shown in the following compound

$$R\!-\!N\!=\!C\!=\!O$$

respectively, are
(a) sp^2, sp, sp^2
(b) sp^2, sp^2, sp^2
(c) sp^2, sp, sp
(d) sp, sp, sp^2

32. The following compounds

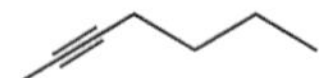 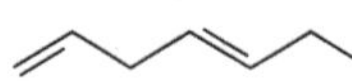

are
(a) geometrical isomers
(b) positional isomers
(c) optical isomers
(d) functional group isomers

33. The major product of the following reaction

is

(a) Ph$\equiv$H
(b)
(c)
(d)

34. IUPAC name of the following compound

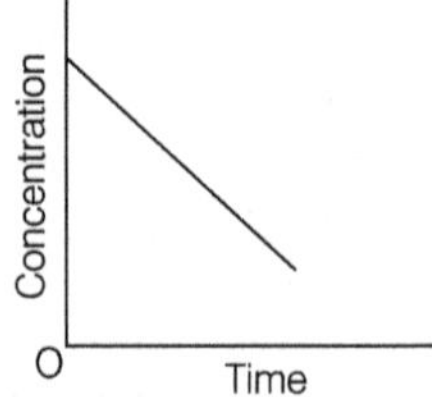

is
(a) 1-hydroxycyclohex-4-en-3-one
(b) 1-hydroxycyclohex-3-en-5-one
(c) 3-hydroxycyclohex-5-en-1-one
(d) 5-hydroxycyclohex-2-en-1-one

35. In water-gas shift reaction, hydrogen gas is produced from the reaction of steam with
(a) methane
(b) coke
(c) carbon monoxide
(d) carbon dioxide

36. Treatment with lime can remove hardness of water caused by
(a) $CaCl_2$
(b) $CaSO_4$
(c) $Ca(HCO_3)_2$
(d) $CaCO_3$

37. The most polarisable ion among the following is
(a) F$^-$
(b) I$^-$
(c) Na$^+$
(d) Cl$^-$

38. For a multi-electron atom, the highest energy level among the following is
(a) $n = 5, l = 0, m = 0, s = +\dfrac{1}{2}$
(b) $n = 4, l = 2, m = 0, s = +\dfrac{1}{2}$
(c) $n = 4, l = 1, m = 0, s = +\dfrac{1}{2}$
(d) $n = 5, l = 1, m = 0, s = +\dfrac{1}{2}$

39. The oxide, which is neither acidic nor basic is
(a) As_2O_3
(b) Sb_4O_{10}
(c) N_2O
(d) Na_2O

40. The element whose salts cannot be detected by flame test is
(a) Mg
(b) Na
(c) Cu
(d) Sr

41. The plot of concentration of a reactant vs time for a chemical reaction is shown below.

The order of this reaction with respect to the reactant is
(a) 0
(b) 1
(c) 2
(d) not possible to determine from this plot

42. During the free expansion of an ideal gas in an isolated chamber,
(a) internal energy remains constant
(b) internal energy decreases
(c) work done on the system is negative
(d) temperature increases

43. The number of moles of water present in a spherical water droplet of radius 1.0 cm is,

[Given : Density of water in the droplet = 1.0 g cm^{-3}]

(a) $\dfrac{\pi}{18}$ (b) $\dfrac{2\pi}{27}$

(c) 24π (d) $\dfrac{2\pi}{9}$

44. Among the following, the correct statement about cathode ray discharge tube is
(a) the electrical discharge can only be observed at high pressure and at low voltage.
(b) in the absence of external electrical or magnetic field, cathode rays travel in straight lines.
(c) the characteristics of cathode rays depend upon the material of electrodes.
(d) the characteristics of cathode rays depend upon the gas present in the cathode ray tube.

45. For a spontaneous process,
(a) enthalpy change of the system must be negative
(b) entropy change of the system must be positive
(c) entropy change of the surrounding must be positive
(d) entropy change of the system plus surrounding must be positive

BIOLOGY

46. Which one of the following is a CORRECT statement about primates' evolution?
(a) Chimpanzees and gorillas evolved from macaques
(b) Humans and chimpanzees evolved from gorillas
(c) Human, chimpanzees and gorillas evolve from a common ancestor
(d) Humans and gorillas evolved from chimpanzees

47. The crypts of Lieberkuhn are found in which one of the following parts of the human digestive tract?
(a) Oesophagus
(b) Small intestine
(c) Stomach
(d) Rectum

48. Removal of the pancreas impairs the breakdown of
(a) lipids and carbohydrates only
(b) lipids and proteins only
(c) lipids, proteins and carbohydrates
(d) proteins and carbohydrates only

49. Microscopic examination of a blood smear reveals an abnormal increase in the number of granular cells with multiple nuclear lobes. Which one of the following cell types has increased in number?
(a) Lymphocytes   (b) Monocytes
(c) Neutrophils   (d) Thrombocytes

50. Which one of the following genetic phenomena is represented by the blood group AB?
(a) Codominance   (b) Dominance
(c) Overdominance   (d) Semidominance

51. The mode of speciation mediated by geographical isolation is referred as
(a) adaptive radiation
(b) allopatric speciation
(c) parapatric speciation
(d) sympatric speciation

52. Which one of the following metabolic conversion requires oxygen?
(a) Glucose to pyruvate
(b) Glucose to CO_2 and ethanol
(c) Glucose to lactate
(d) Glucose to CO_2 and H_2O

53. Where are the proximal and distal convoluted tubules located within the human body?
(a) Adrenal cortex
(b) Adrenal medulla
(c) Renal cortex
(d) Renal medulla

54. In a diploid organism, when the locus X is inactivated, transcription of the locus Y is triggered. Based on this observation, which one of the following statements is CORRECT?
(a) X is dominant over Y
(b) X is epistatic to Y
(c) Y is dominant over X
(d) Y is epistatic to X

55. Which one of the following sequences represents the CORRECT taxonomical hierarchy?
(a) Species, genus, family, order
(b) Order, genus, family, species
(c) Species, order, genus, family
(d) Species, genus, order, family

56. Which one of the following organs is NOT a site for the production of white blood cells?
(a) Bone marrow   (b) Kidney
(c) Liver   (d) Spleen

57. Which one of the following anatomical structures is involved in guttation?
(a) Cuticle   (b) Hydathodes
(c) Lenticels   (d) Stomata

58. Which one of the following parts of the eye is affected in cataract?
(a) Cornea   (b) Conjunctiva
(c) Retina   (d) Lens

59. Which one of the following organisms is a bryophyte?
(a) Liverwort   (b) *Volvox*
(c) *Chlamydomonas*   (d) Fern

60. During oogenesis in mammals, the second meiotic division occurs
(a) before fertilisation
(b) after implantation
(c) before ovulation
(d) after fertilisation

↻ PART-II (2 Marks Questions)

MATHEMATICS

61. Let a, b, c, d be distinct real numbers such that a, b are roots of $x^2 - 5cx - 6d = 0$, and c, d are roots of $x^2 - 5ax - 6b = 0$. Then $b + d$ is

(a) 180   (b) 162   (c) 144   (d) 126

62. Let $S = \{1, 2, 3, \ldots, 100\}$. Suppose b and c are chosen at random from the set S. The probability that $4x^2 + bx + c$ has equal roots is

(a) 0.001   (b) 0.004   (c) 0.007   (d) 0.01

63. Let N be the set of positive integers. For all $n \in N$, let

$$f_n = (n + 1)^{1/3} - n^{1/3} \text{ and}$$

$$A = \left\{ n \in N : f_{n+1} < \frac{1}{3(n+1)^{2/3}} < f_n \right\}$$

Then,

(a) $A = N$

(b) A is a finite set

(c) the complement of A in N is nonempty, but finite

(d) A and its complement in N are both infinite

64. A prime number p is called special if there exist primes p_1, p_2, p_3, p_4 such that $p = p_1 + p_2 = p_3 - p_4$. The number of special primes is

(a) 0

(b) 1

(c) more than one but finite

(d) infinite

65. Let ABC be a triangle in which $AB = BC$. Let X be a point on AB such that $AX : XB = AB : AX$. If $AC = AX$, then the measure of $\angle ABC$ equals

(a) 18°   (b) 36°   (c) 54°   (d) 72°

PHYSICS

66. A water-proof laser pointer of length 10 cm placed in a water tank rotates about a horizontal axis passing through its centre of mass in a vertical plane as shown in the figure. The time period of rotation is 60 s. Assuming the water to be still and no reflections from the surface of the tank, the duration for which the light beam escapes the tank in one time period is close to (Take, refractive index of water = 1.33)

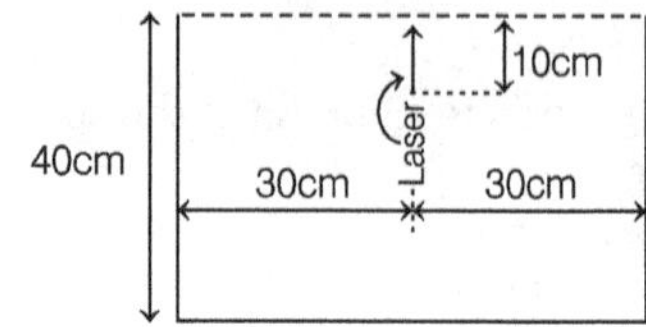

(a) 8.13 s   (b) 14.05 s

(c) 16.67 s   (d) 23.86 s

67. In an hour-glass approximately 100 grains of sand fall per second (starting from rest); and it takes 2 s for each sand particle to reach the bottom of the hour-glass. If the average mass of each sand particle is 0.2 g, then the average force exerted by the falling sand on the bottom of the hour-glass is close to

(a) 0.4 N   (b) 0.8 N

(c) 1.2 N   (d) 1.6 N

68. A student uses the resistance of a known resistor $(1\,\Omega)$ to calibrate a voltmeter and an ammeter using the circuits shown below. The student measures the ratio of the voltage to current to be $1 \times 10^3\,\Omega$ in circuit (a) and $0.999\,\Omega$ in circuit (b). From these measurements, the resistance (in Ω) of the voltmeter and ammeter are found to be close to

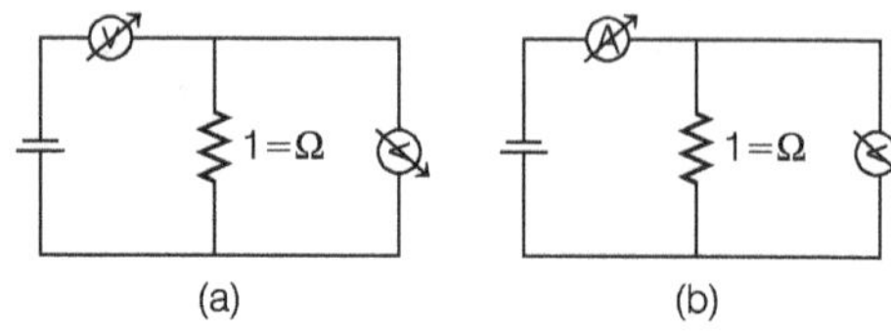

(a) 10^2 and 10^{-2} (b) 10^3 and 10^{-3}

(c) 10^{-2} and 10^2 (d) 10^{-2} and 10^3

69. A hot air balloon with a payload rises in the air. Assume that the balloon is spherical in shape with diameter of 11.7 m and the mass of the balloon and the payload (without the hot air inside) is 210 kg. Temperature and pressure of outside air are 27 °C and 1 atm $= 10^5$ N/m^2, respectively. Molar mass of dry air is 30 g. The temperature of the hot air inside is close to [The gas constant, $R = 8.31 \text{JK}^{-1}\text{mol}^{-1}$]

(a) 27 °C   (b) 52 °C

(c) 105 °C   (d) 171 °C

70. A healthy adult of height 1.7 m has an average blood pressure (BP) of 100 mm of Hg. The heart is typically at a height of 1.3 m from the foot. Take, the density of blood to be 10^3 kg/m^3 and note that 100 mm of Hg is equivalent to 13.3 kPa (kilo pascals). The ratio of BP in the foot region to that in the head region is close to

(a) one   (b) two

(c) three   (d) four

CHEMISTRY

71. PbO_2 is obtained from

(a) the reaction of PbO with HCl

(b) thermal decomposition of $Pb(NO_3)_2$ at 200°C

(c) the reaction of Pb_3O_4 with HNO_3

(d) the reaction of Pb with air at room temperature

72. For one mole of a van der Waals' gas, the compressibility factor $Z = \left(\dfrac{pV}{RT}\right)$ at a fixed volume will certainly decrease, if

[Given : "a" and "b" are standard parameters for van der Waals' gas]

(a) "b" increases and "a" decreases at constant temperature
(b) "b" decreases and "a" increases at constant temperature
(c) temperature increases at constant "a" and "b" values
(d) "b" increases at constant "a" and temperature

73. The correct statements among the following.

i. $E_{2s}(\text{H}) > E_{2s}(\text{Li}) < E_{2s}(\text{Na}) > E_{2s}(\text{K})$.
ii. The maximum number of electrons in the shell with principal quantum number n is equal to $2n^2$.
iii. Extra stability of half-filled subshell is due to smaller exchange energy.
iv. Only two electrons, irrespective of their spin, may exist in the same orbital are.

(a) i and ii   (b) ii and iii
(c) iii and iv   (d) i and iv

74. An organic compound contains 46.78% of a halogen X. When 2.00 g of this compound is heated with fuming HNO_3 in the presence of $AgNO_3$, 2.21 g AgX was formed. The halogen X is
[Given : atomic weight of Ag = 108, F = 19, Cl = 35.5, Br = 80, I = 127]
(a) F   (b) Cl   (c) Br   (d) I

75. An organic compound X with molecular formula C_6H_{10}, when treated with HBr, forms a *gem*-dibromide. The compound X upon warming with $HgSO_4$ and dil. H_2SO_4, produces a ketone, which gives a positive iodoform test. The compound X is

(a)    (b) 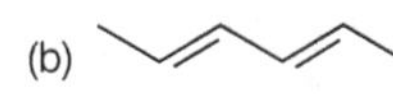

(c) 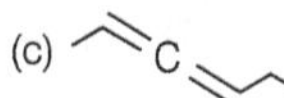   (d) 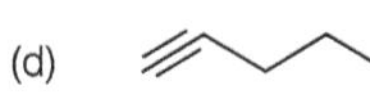

BIOLOGY

76. A cell weighing 1 mg grows to double its initial mass before dividing into two daughter cells of equal mass. Assuming no death, at the end of 100 divisions what will be the ratio of the mass of the entire population of these cells to that of the mass of the earth? Assume that mass of the earth is 10^{24} kg and 2^{10} is approximately equal to 1000.
(a) 10^{-28} (b) 10^{-3}
(c) 1   (d) 10^3

77. Papaya is a dioecious species with XY sexual genotype for male and XX for female. What will be the genotype of the embryos and endosperm nuclei after double fertilisation?
(a) 50% ovules would have XXX endosperm and YY embryo, while the other 50% would have XXY endosperm and XX embryo
(b) 100% ovules would have XXX endosperm and XY embryo
(c) 100% ovules would have XXY endosperm and XX embryo
(d) 50% ovules would have XXX endosperm and XX embryo, while the other 50% would have XXY endosperm and XY embryo

78. Solid and dotted lines represent the activities of pepsin and salivary amylase enzymes of the digestive tract, respectively. Which one of the following graphs best represents their activity *vs* pH?

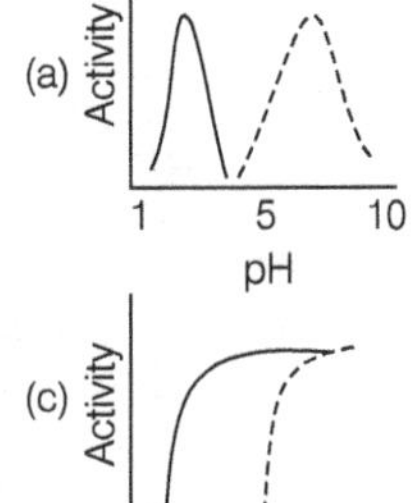
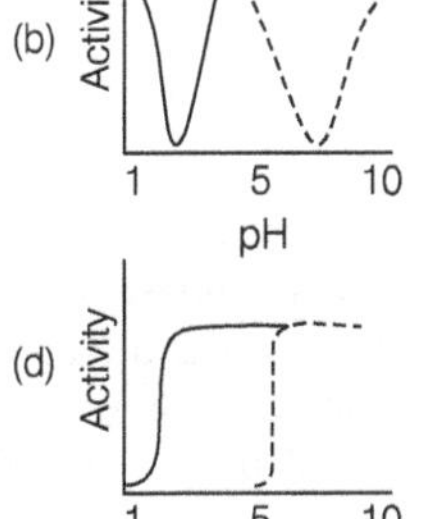

79. If the gene pool of the locus X in the human genome is 4, then what would be the highest possible number of genotypes in a large population?
(a) 6   (b) 8
(c) 10   (d) 16

80. Match the plant hormones in Column I with their primary function in Column II.

	Column I		Column II
P.	Abscisic acid	i.	Promotes disease resistance
Q.	Ethylene	ii.	Maintains seed dormancy
R.	Cytokinin	iii.	Promotes seed germination
S.	Gibberellin	iv.	Promotes fruit ripening
		v.	Inhibits leaf senescence

Choose the correct combination
(a) P–iii, Q–iv, R–i, S–ii
(b) P–ii, Q–iv, R–v, S–iii
(c) P–v, Q–iii, R–ii, S–i
(d) P–iv, Q–ii, R–iii, S–v

Answers

Solutions

1. *(c)* For an equilateral triangle ABC having side length a. If R and r are radii of the circumcircle and the incircle of triangle ABC respectively, then

$$R = \frac{a}{2}\sec 30° = \frac{a}{2}\left(\frac{2}{\sqrt{3}}\right) = \frac{a}{\sqrt{3}}$$

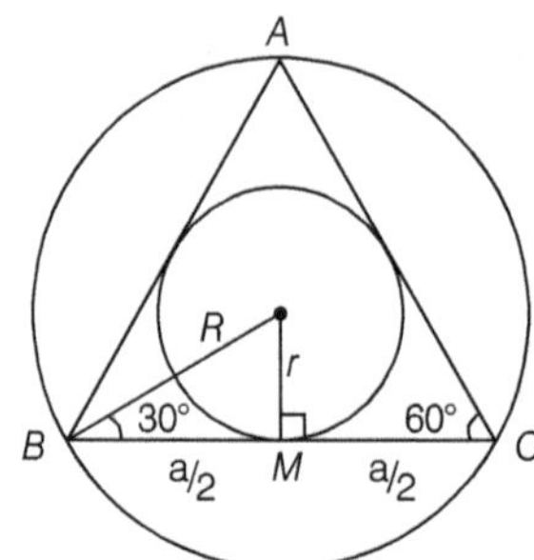

and $r = \dfrac{a}{2}\tan 30° = \dfrac{a}{2} \times \dfrac{1}{\sqrt{3}} = \dfrac{a}{2\sqrt{3}}$

$$\therefore \frac{R}{r} = \frac{\dfrac{a}{\sqrt{3}}}{\dfrac{a}{2\sqrt{3}}} = 2, \text{ which is independent of } a$$

and it is constant.

2. *(c)* Given quadratic equation $2x^2 + bx + \dfrac{1}{b} = 0$, has two distinct real roots, so

$$D > 0$$

$$\Rightarrow \qquad b^2 - 4(2)\left(\frac{1}{b}\right) > 0$$

$$\Rightarrow \qquad b^2 - \frac{8}{b} > 0 \Rightarrow \frac{b^3 - 8}{b} > 0$$

$$\Rightarrow \qquad \frac{(b-2)(b^2 + 2b + 4)}{b} > 0$$

$$\Rightarrow \qquad b \in (-\infty, 0) \cup (2, \infty) \qquad ...(i)$$

For option (c),

$$b^2 - 3b > -2$$

$$\Rightarrow \qquad b^2 - 3b + 2 > 0$$

$$\Rightarrow \qquad (b-2)(b-1) > 0$$

$$b \in (-\infty, 1) \cup (2, \infty)$$

mean if $b \in (-\infty, 0) \cup (2, \infty)$

then $b^2 - 3b > -2$

3. *(b)* Let the given quadratic polynomial $p(x) = x^2 + ax + b$ has two distinct real roots α and β, then

$p(x) = x^2 + ax + b = (x - \alpha)(x - \beta)$

and since $g(x) = p(x^3) = (x^3 - \alpha)(x^3 - \beta)$

let $\alpha = \alpha_1^3$ and $\beta = \beta_1^3$

then $g(x) = (x^3 - \alpha_1^3)(x^3 - \beta_1^3)$

$= (x - \alpha_1)(x - \beta_1)(x^2 + \alpha_1 x + \alpha_1^2)$

$$(x^2 + \beta_1 x + \beta_1^2)$$

$\because$ the discriminants of quadratic equations

$x^2 + \alpha_1 x + \alpha_1^2$ and $x^2 + \beta_1 x + \beta_1^2$ are negative.

$\therefore g(x)$ has exactly two distinct real roots and since $g(x) = x^6 + ax^3 + b$ is an even degree polynomial, so there exists a real number 'α' such that $g(x) \geq \alpha$ for all real x.

4. *(a)* The sum of first n, $n \geq 1$ terms of arithmetic progression with first term 2 and common difference 4, is

$$S_n = \frac{n}{2}[4 + (n-1)4] = 2n^2$$

So, the average of the first n terms

$$M_n = \frac{S_n}{n} = 2n$$

Now, $\displaystyle\sum_{n=1}^{10} M_n = 2\sum_{n=1}^{10} n$

$$= 2 \times \left(\frac{10 \times 11}{2}\right) = 110$$

5. *(a)* It is given that in triangle ABC, $\angle BAC = 90°$, AD is the altitude from A on to BC.

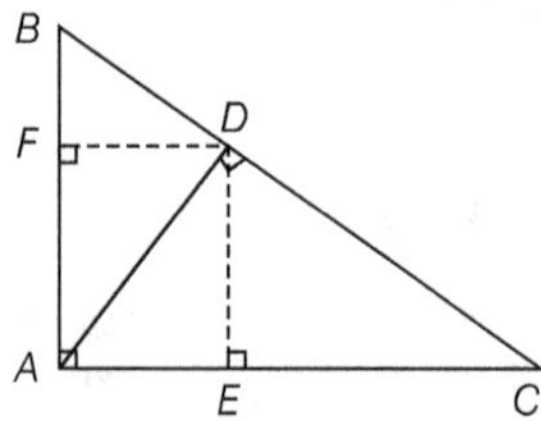

Since, $AB = 15$ and $BC = 25$

$$\therefore \qquad AC = \sqrt{BC^2 - AB^2} = \sqrt{625 - 225}$$

$$= \sqrt{400} = 20$$

Now, since area of $\Delta ABC = \frac{1}{2}(BC)(AD)$

$$= \frac{1}{2}(AB)(AC)$$

$$\Rightarrow \frac{1}{2}(BC)(AD) = \frac{1}{2} \times 15 \times 20$$

$$\Rightarrow \quad 25 \times AD = 300$$

$$\Rightarrow \quad\quad AD = 12$$

$\because AEDF$ is a rectangle, then
$EF = AD = 12$

6. *(b)* It is given that the sides of triangle, a, b and c satisfy the following relations

$$c^2 = 2ab \qquad\qquad ...(i)$$

and $\qquad a^2 + c^2 = 3b^2 \qquad\qquad ...(ii)$

From Eqs. (i) and (ii), we get

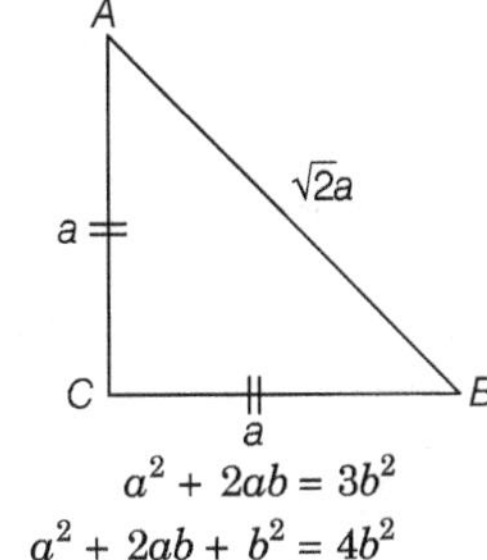

$$a^2 + 2ab = 3b^2$$

$$\Rightarrow \quad a^2 + 2ab + b^2 = 4b^2$$

$$\Rightarrow \quad (a + b)^2 = (2b)^2 = (b + b)^2$$

$$\Rightarrow \quad a = b, \text{ so } c = \sqrt{2}a$$

$$\therefore \quad\quad \angle A = \angle B = 45°$$

7. *(a)* As N be the least positive integer and when a non-zero digit C is written after the last digit of N, the resulting number is divisible by C.

So, $10N + C$ is divisible by C

$\therefore 10N$ must be divisible by C.

Now, the least integer (N) which is divisible by digit 'C' i.e. (1 to 9) must be L.C.M of $\{1, 3, 4, 6, 7, 9\}$.

$$= \text{L.C.M of } \{4, 7, 9\}$$

$$= 252 = N$$

and sum of digits of number 'N' is

$$2 + 5 + 2 = 9$$

8. *(c)* Let the given 11 distinct positive integers are in increasing order
$x_1, x_2, x_3, x_4, x_5, x_6, x_7, x_8, x_9, x_{10}, x_{11}$, so x_{11} is largest of these integers and the median is x_6.

Now, median of first 10 numbers is

$$\frac{x_5 + x_6}{2} = m \text{ (Let)}.$$

Now, we have to replace largest number x_{11} by m and then increasing order will be

$$x_1, x_2, x_3, x_4, x_5, m, x_6, x_7, x_8, x_9, x_{10}$$

$$\because \quad m < x_6 \text{ as } x_5 < \frac{x_5 + x_6}{2} < x_6$$

So, median decreases.

9. *(a)* Let the equation of a cubic polynomial

$$P(x) = ax^3 + bx^2 + cx + d$$

Now,

$$P(1) = a + b + c + d = 2 \qquad ...(i)$$

$$P(2) = 8a + 4b + 2c + d = 4 \qquad ...(ii)$$

$$P(3) = 27a + 9b + 3c + d = 6 \quad ...(iii)$$

$$P(4) = 64a + 16b + 4c + d = 8 \quad ...(iv)$$

From Eqs. (i) and (ii), we get

$$7a + 3b + c = 2 \qquad\qquad ...(v)$$

From Eqs. (ii) and (iii), we get

$$19a + 5b + c = 2 \qquad\qquad ...(vi)$$

From Eqs. (iii) and (iv), we get

$$37a + 7b + c = 2 \qquad\qquad ...(vii)$$

Now, from Eqs. (v) and (vi), we get

$$12a + 2b = 0 \qquad\qquad ...(viii)$$

and from Eqs. (vi) and (vii), we get

$$18a + 2b = 0 \qquad\qquad ...(ix)$$

From Eqs. (viii) and (ix), we get

$$a = 0 \text{ and } b = 0,$$

$$c = 2 \text{ and } d = 0.$$

So, $P(x) = 2x$

$\therefore$ no cubic polynomial is possible.

10. *(d)* Since in the group of first 10 two digit number 10-19, has atleast 1 prime number similarly in other groups of 10 two digits numbers 20-29, 30-39, 40-49, 50-59, 60-69, 70-79, 80-89 and 90-99 have almost 1 prime numbers.

So, the number of almost prime two-digit number is 90.

11. *(c)* Let a convex quadrilateral $ABCD$ and K, L, M, N be the mid-point of AB, BC, CD, DA respectively.

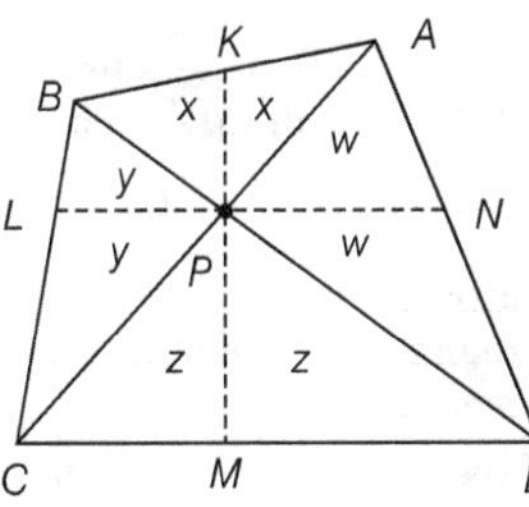

Now, as area $\triangle AKP = $ area $\triangle BKP = x$ (let)
Similarly

$$\triangle BLP = \triangle CLP = y$$

$$\triangle CPM = \triangle DPM = z$$

and $\triangle DNP = \triangle ANP = w$

It is given that Area $(PKAN) = x + w = 25$

area $(PLBK) = x + y = 36$

and area $(PMDN) = z + w = 41$

So area $(PLCM) = y + z$

$$= (x + y) + (z + w) - (x + w)$$

$$= \text{area } (PLBK) + \text{area } (PMDN) -$$
$$\text{area } (PKAN)$$

$$= 36 + 41 - 25 = 77 - 25 = 52$$

12. *(c)* Given equations

$$6x + 4y + z = 200, \qquad\qquad ...(i)$$

and $x + y + z = 100 \qquad\qquad ...(ii)$

By Eqs. (i) and (ii), we get

$$5x + 3y = 100$$

For non-negative integer solutions, when

$$x = 2, \text{ then } y = 30$$

$$x = 5, \text{ then } y = 25$$

$$x = 8, \text{ then } y = 20$$

$$x = 11, \text{ then } y = 15$$

$$x = 14, \text{ then } y = 10$$

$$x = 17, \text{ then } y = 5$$

and $x = 20$, then $y = 0$

In every case $z = 100 - (x + y) > 0$

So, total number of non-negative integral solutions are 7.

13. *(d)* It is given that, $N_2 = 165$

$$= 3 \times 5 \times 11 \text{ and } N_1 = 2^{55} + 1$$

As we know that, if n is odd integer then $x^n + y^n$ is divisible by $x + y$.

So, $N_1 = 2^{55} + 1^{55}$ is divisible by $2 + 1 = 3$

and $N_1 = 2^{55} + 1^{55}$

$$= (2^5)^{11} + (1^5)^{11} = (32)^{11} + (1)^{11}$$

is divisible by $32 + 1 = 33$

$\therefore$ the HCF of N_1 and N_2 is 33.

14. *(a)* It is given that circumference of circle C is l and the perimeter of triangle T is l.

Now, let the radius of circle C is r, so

$$2\pi r = l \Rightarrow r = \frac{l}{2\pi}$$

$\therefore$ area of circle C is $A_1 = \pi r^2 = \frac{l^2}{4\pi}$

Now, as we know that area of triangle will be maximum for given perimeter if it is an equilateral triangle, let the length of side of equilateral triangle is 'a', then

$$3a = l \Rightarrow a = \frac{l}{3}$$

and area of equilateral triangle is

$$A_2 = \frac{\sqrt{3}}{4}a^2$$

So, $A_2 = \frac{\sqrt{3}}{4}\left(\frac{l^2}{9}\right) = \frac{l^2}{12\sqrt{3}}$

$$\therefore \quad \frac{A_1}{A_2} = \frac{\dfrac{l^2}{4\pi}}{\dfrac{l^2}{12\sqrt{3}}} = \frac{3\sqrt{3}}{\pi} > 1$$

Since, as we took an equilateral triangle, which has maximum area. But we can take a triangle T such that the ratio $\dfrac{\text{area }(C)}{\text{area }(T)}$ is greater than any positive real number α.

15. *(b)* It is given that, the number of three digit number $\overline{abc}$, such that

$$\frac{b+c}{2} = bc \qquad \text{...(i)}$$

the above relation is true if $b = c = 0$

And if neither b nor c is zero, then

$\dfrac{1}{b} + \dfrac{1}{c} = 2$, and $b, c \in \{1, 2, 3, 4, 5, 6, 7, 8, 9\}$

Then $b = c = 1$

and $a \in \{1, 2, 3, 4, 5, 6, 7, 8, 9\}$

So, total number of such three digit number are $2 \times 9 = 18$

16. *(a)* Formation of rainbow is shown below.

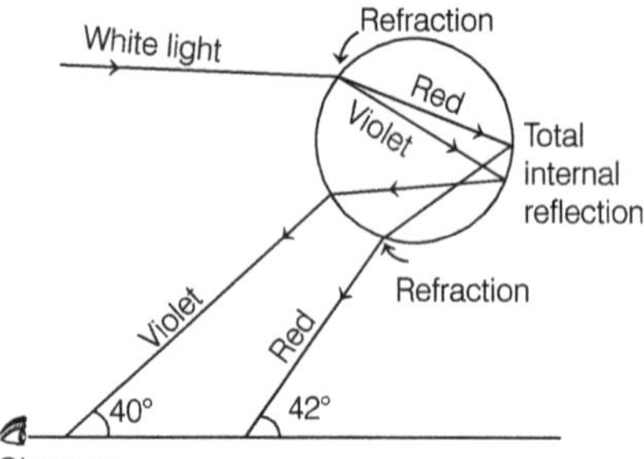

So, processes involved in formation of rainbow in correct order are: refraction, total internal reflection, refraction.

Hence, the correct order is given in option (a).

17. *(a)* Here, 10 divisions of vernier scall = 11 main scale divisions

So, 1 vernier scale division = $\dfrac{11}{10}$ main scale divisions

Now, we use formula for least count,

Least count = 1 main scale division – 1 vernier scale division.

$$\Rightarrow \quad LC = 1MSD - 1VSD$$

$$= \left(1 - \frac{11}{10}\right) MSD$$

$$= -\frac{1}{10} MSD$$

$$= -\frac{1}{10} \times 1\,mm$$

$$= -0.1\,mm$$

So, magnitude of least count is 0.1 mm.

18. *(b)* Velocity = Slope of distance – Time graph

Last portion of given graph is a straight line which indicates that velocity is constant, i.e. terminal velocity is reached.

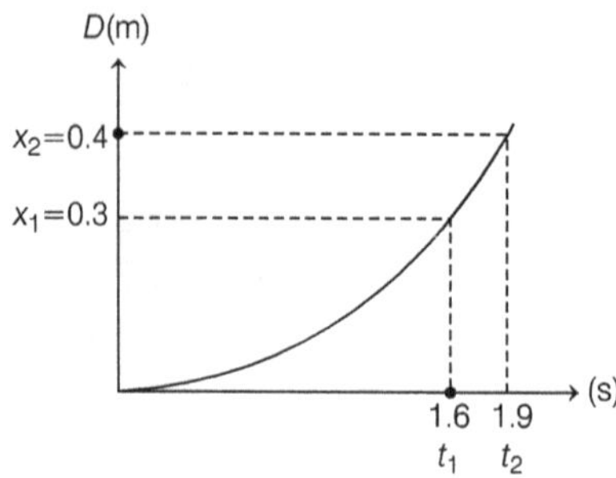

From data of graph,
Terminal velocity,

$$v = \frac{x_2 - x_1}{t_2 - t_1} = \frac{0.4 - 0.3}{1.9 - 1.6}$$

$$= \frac{0.1}{0.3} = 0.33 \text{ m/s}$$

19. *(c)* Power requirement for 1 laptop, $P_1 = 90\,W$

So, power requirement for 10 laptops,

$$P = 10 \times P_1 = 10 \times 90$$

$$= 900\,W = 0.9\,kW$$

In 5h, electrical energy used by all laptops,

$$E = P \times t = 0.9 \times 5$$

$$= 4.5\,kWh$$

Cost of electrical energy used is

$$\text{Cost} = E \times \text{Unit cost}$$

$$= 4.5 \times 5$$

$$= ₹\,22.50$$

So, statement III is correct.

For laptop charger, input voltage is 220 V.

So, current when all 10 laptops are connected through an extension,

$$I = \frac{P}{V} = \frac{900}{220} \approx 4.1A$$

As, line current exceeds current rating of fuse, therefore 3A fuse cannot be used. So, statement II is incorrect.

20. *(c)* Frosted glass has a rough layer which causes irregular refraction and makes glass translucent.

When a transparent tape which has refractive index close to that of glass is pasted over the rough surface of glass, the tape glue fills the roughness of glass.

This makes glass surface more smooth and so refraction is more regular. This makes region of tape transparent.

21. *(d)* Prism B is inverted relative to prism A. So, dispersion of light caused by prism A and B is in opposite direction.

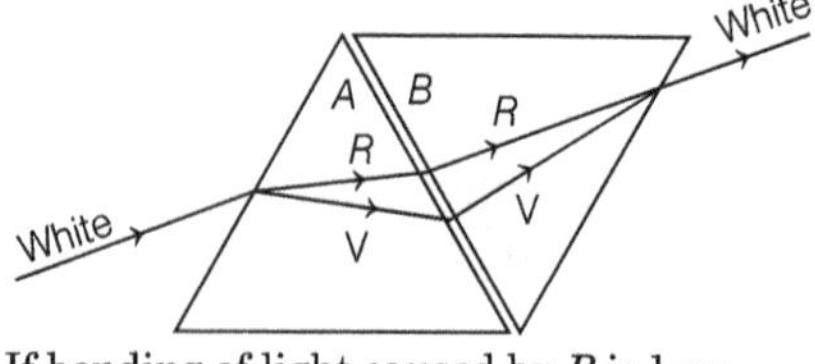

If bending of light caused by B is less than or more than that of A, then out going beam of light is not white.

So, when both prisms are filled with water at different temperatures, their refractive indices are different and the dispersion produced by A and B are not equal and opposite. Hence, with condition in (d) beam to right of prism B will be coloured.

22. *(d)* Time period of rotation of ball = 1.5 s

So, in time interval of 7.5 s (= 1.5×5) s ball completes 5 revolutions.

Also, ball covers one-fourth of circular path in time $\dfrac{1.5}{4} = 0.375$ s.

So, in remaining 0.8 s (= 8.3– 7.5s) ball is very near to other end of diameter as shown in the figure.

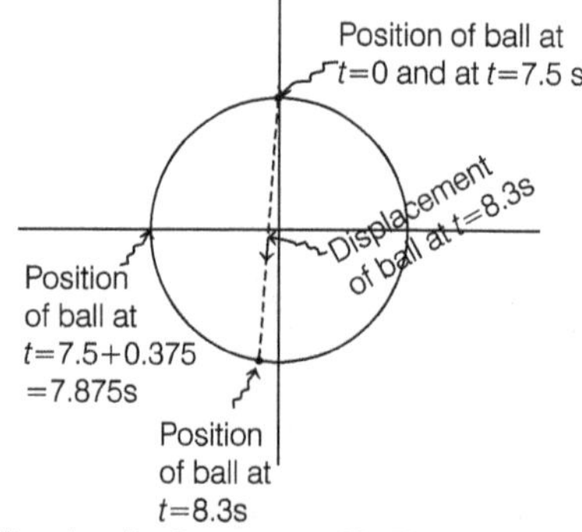

Clearly, displacement of ball is nearly equals to diameter (= 2 m) of circular path.

23. *(a)* Condition given in question is shown below.

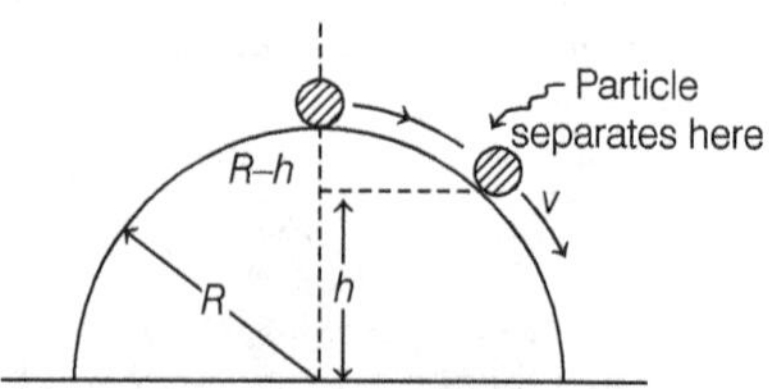

Let v = speed of particle when it separates from hemisphere.

As there is no friction, loss of potential energy appears in form of kinetic energy of particle.

$$\therefore \quad mg(R-h) = \frac{1}{2}mv^2$$
$$\Rightarrow \quad v = \sqrt{2g(R-h)}$$

24. *(c)* Given, nuclear radius is
$$R = r_0 A^{\frac{1}{3}}$$
Here, atomic mass number of nucleus = A

$\therefore$ Nuclear density d is given by
$$d = \frac{\text{Mass number}}{\text{Volume}}$$
$$\Rightarrow \quad d = \frac{A}{\frac{4}{3}\pi R^3} = \frac{A}{\frac{4}{3}\pi (r_0 A^{\frac{1}{3}})^3}$$
$$\Rightarrow \quad d = \frac{A}{\frac{4}{3}\pi r_0^3 \cdot A} = \frac{3}{4\pi r_0^3}$$

As $r_0 = $ a constant, so nuclear density is a constant quantity.

$\therefore$ Nuclear mass density of U^{238} is same as that of Sn^{119}.

25. *(a)* Electrostatic energy of a nucleus of charge Ze is
$$U_1 = \frac{kZ^2 e^2}{R} \qquad \text{...(i)}$$

When this nucleus is divided into two equal nuclei of radius r, then as density of nuclear matter is a constant, we have
initial density = final density
$$\frac{M}{\frac{4}{3}\pi R^3} = \frac{\frac{M}{2}}{\frac{4}{3}\pi r^3}$$
$$\Rightarrow \quad r^3 = \frac{R^3}{2} \text{ or } r = \frac{R}{2^{\frac{1}{3}}} \qquad \text{...(ii)}$$

Now, final electrostatic energy is given by
$$U_2 = 2 \times \frac{kZ'^2 e^2}{r} \Rightarrow U_2 = \frac{2k\left(\frac{Z}{2}\right)^2 e^2}{\left(\frac{R}{2^{\frac{1}{3}}}\right)}$$

[from Eq. (ii)] $= \frac{1}{2^{\frac{2}{3}}} \cdot \frac{kZ^2 e^2}{R}$

$$\Rightarrow \quad U_2 = \frac{1}{2^{\frac{2}{3}}} \cdot U_1$$

[from Eq. (i)] $= 0.63 U_1$

So, change in electrostatic energy in this process is
$$\Delta U = U_1 - U_2 \qquad (\because U_1 > U_2)$$
$$= U_1 - 0.63 U_1 = (1 - 0.63) U_1 = 0.375 U_1$$
$$= 0.375 \frac{kZ^2 e^2}{R} \qquad \text{[From Eq. (i)]}$$

26. *(d)* Time of fall $= \sqrt{\dfrac{2h}{a_{\text{net}}}}$

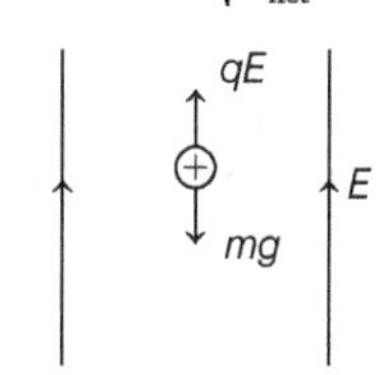

Net acceleration of charged masses is
$$a_{\text{net}} = g - \frac{qE}{m}$$

As, M_1 hits the floor before M_2.
$$\Rightarrow \quad \sqrt{\frac{2h}{a_1}} > \sqrt{\frac{2h}{a_2}}$$
$$\Rightarrow \quad \frac{1}{a_1} > \frac{1}{a_2}$$
$$\Rightarrow \quad a_2 > a_1$$

When reciprocal is taken in equality sign is reversed, then.
$$g - \frac{Q_1 E}{M_1} > g - \frac{Q_2 E}{M_2}$$
$$\Rightarrow \quad -\frac{Q_1 E}{M_1} > -\frac{Q_2 E}{M_2}$$
$$\Rightarrow \quad \frac{Q_1 E}{M_1} < \frac{Q_2 E}{M_2}$$

Here, multiplication with -1 reverse sign of inequality.

So, $\dfrac{Q_1}{M_1} < \dfrac{Q_2}{M_2}$

or $\quad M_2 Q_1 < M_1 Q_2$

$\Rightarrow \quad M_1 Q_2 > M_2 Q_1$

27. *(a)* From gas equation,
$$pV = nRT$$
Here, $n = 1$ mole
So, $pV = RT$ $\qquad$ ...(i)
Substituting the value of R in Eq. (i), we get
$$pV = 8.3\, T$$

Clearly, slope of pV *versus* T line is 8.3, which is greater than one. Hence, following graph is correct.

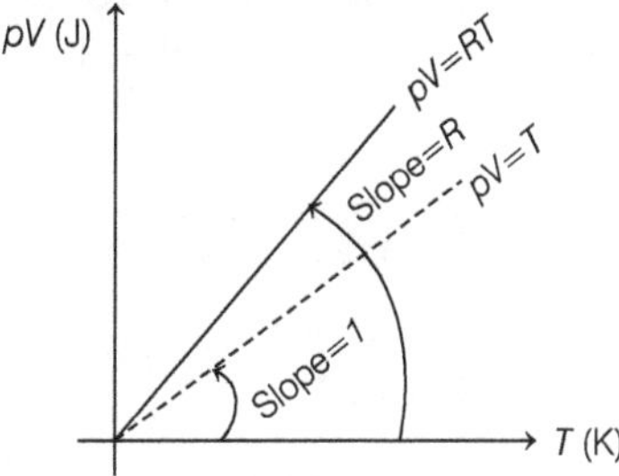

28. *(b)* Surface area over which rain is received, $A = 600\,\text{km}^2$
$$= 600 \times (10^3)^2 \,\text{m}^2$$
$$= 6 \times 10^8 \,\text{m}^2$$
Average rainfall, $h = 2.4\,\text{m}$
Volume of water received by rain, V
$$= A \times h = 6 \times 10^8 \times 2.4 \,\text{m}^3$$
Water conserved = 10% of volume received by rain
$$= 6 \times 10^8 \times \frac{10}{100} \times 2.4\,\text{m}^3 = 1.44 \times 10^8 \,\text{m}^3$$
$$= 1.4 \times 10^8 \times 10^3 \,\text{L} = 1.4 \times 10^{11}\,\text{L}$$

Percentage of total water consumption received by rain is
$$= \frac{1.4 \times 10^{11} \times 100}{1.4 \times 10^{12}} = 10\%$$

29. *(d)* Collision is elastic, so both linear momentum and kinetic energy are conserved.

We have following situation,

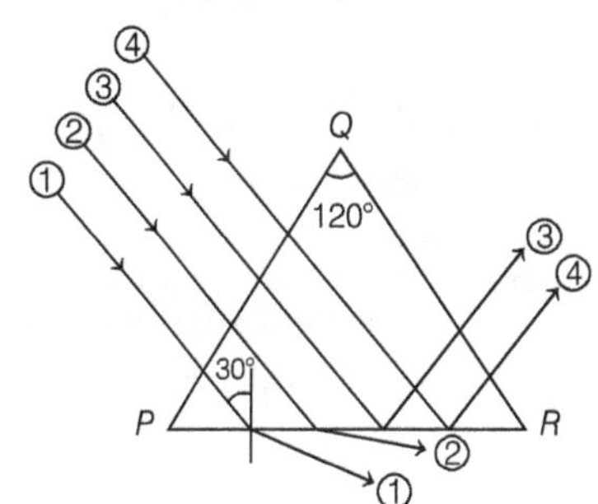

According to figure,
$MV = MV' + mv$ ...(i) (linear momentum conservation)
$$\frac{1}{2}MV^2 = \frac{1}{2}MV'^2 + \frac{1}{2}mv^2 \qquad \text{...(ii)}$$
$\qquad$ (kinetic energy conservation)
From Eqs. (i) and (ii), we get
$$M(V - V') = mv \qquad \text{...(iii)}$$
and $M(V^2 - V'^2) = mv^2$ $\qquad$ ...(iv)
Dividing Eq. (iv) by Eq. (iii), we have
$$\frac{M(V^2 - V'^2)}{M(V - V')} = \frac{mv^2}{mv}$$
or $V + V' = v$

30. *(c)* Total internal, reflection occurs when $n \geq \dfrac{1}{\sin i_c}$.

In given situation, angle of incidence of each of ray is 30° over face PR.

So, $i = 30°$

$\Rightarrow \quad \dfrac{1}{\sin i} = \dfrac{1}{\sin 30°} = 2$

Hence, for total internal reflection at surface PR, $n \geq 2$. As refractive index for 3 and 4 is more than 2, only rays 1 and 2, pass from face PR while rays 3 and 4 pass through face QR (as shown in diagram).

31. *(a)* Hybridisation is determined from the steric number (number of atoms bonded to the central atom + the number of lone pairs). Number of hybrid orbitals must be equal to the steric number.

From the Lewis structure.

$$R\diagdown \underset{\cdot\cdot}{N} = C = \underset{\cdot\cdot}{\ddot{O}}:$$

(i) Steric number of N-atom = 3 (2 bonded atoms + 1 lone pair), $\therefore$ Hybridisation $= sp^2$ (3 hybrid orbitals).

(ii) Steric number of C-atom = 2 (2 bonded atoms), $\therefore$ Hybridisation $= sp$ (2 hybrid orbitals).

(iii) Steric number of O-atom = 3 (1 bonded atom + 2 lone pair) $\therefore$ Hybridisation $= sp^2$ (3 hybrid orbitals).

32. *(d)* One isomer is an alkyne and the other one is an alkadiene. Since, they have two different functional groups, they are functional group isomers.

33. *(a)*

$$Ph{-}CHBr{-}CH_2Br \xrightarrow[-HBr]{1.\text{Excess alcoholic KOH}} Ph{-}CH{=}CHBr$$

$$Ph{-}CH{=}CHBr \xrightarrow[-2NH_3]{2.NaNH_2 \, / \, -HBr} Ph{-}C{\equiv}\overset{\ominus}{C} \, Na^+ \xrightarrow{3.H_3O^+} Ph{-}C{\equiv}CH$$

or $Ph{\equiv}H$

34. *(d)*

Principal functional group is ketone.

$\therefore C_1$ is carbonyl carbon atom.

Locants for hydroxyl groups and double bonds are 5 and 2, which are preferred over 3 and 5, since the lower number at first difference (2 compared to 3) is preferred.

Hence, the IUPAC name of given compound is 5-hydroxycyclohex-2-en-1-one.

35. *(d)* Water-gas shift reaction is

$$CO + H_2O \xrightarrow{\;FeO \cdot Cr_2O_3 \text{ (Catalyst)}\;} CO_2 + H_2$$

In this reaction, hydrogen gas is produced from the reaction of steam with carbon dioxide.

36. *(c)* Temporary hardness (caused by bicarbonates of calcium or magnesium) can be removed by using lime, $Ca(OH)_2$.

$$Ca(HCO_3)_2 + Ca(OH)_2 \longrightarrow 2CaCO_3 + 2H_2O$$

37. *(b)* Among anions with same charge, the one having greatest size has maximum polarisability. Thus, I^- ion having most polarisability.

38. *(b, d)* Among the orbitals of a multi-electron atom, the one with greatest value of $n + l$ has the greatest energy.

Between two orbitals with same value of $n + l$ e.g. options (b) and (d), the one with greater value of n has greater energy.

39. *(c)* N_2O is a neutral oxide, which is neither acidic nor basic.

40. *(a)* Of all the s-block elements, Mg and Be salts do not impart colour to flame.

41. *(a)*

For a reaction

$$X \longrightarrow Y,$$

$$\text{rate} = \dfrac{-d[X]}{dt}; [X] = \text{concentration of } X.$$

If reaction is nth order,

$$\text{rate} \propto [X]^n$$

From the graph, the slope $\dfrac{d[X]}{dt}$ is constant.

$\therefore$ Rate is constant at any concentration.

$\therefore \qquad\qquad n = 0$

42. *(a)* In a free expansion, external pressure $(p_{ex}) = 0$

$\therefore \qquad W = - p_{ex} \cdot \Delta V = 0$

and the system is isolated.

Heat does not enter or leave, $q = 0$.

$\Delta U = q + W = 0$, where $U =$ internal energy.

43. *(b)* Number of moles,

$$n = \dfrac{\text{mass } (m)}{\text{molar mass } (M)}$$

Given, radius = 1.0 cm,

$\therefore$ volume $= \dfrac{4\pi}{3}$ cm^3

Given, density = 1.0 g cm^{-3},

$\therefore$ Mass = volume × density $= \dfrac{4\pi}{3}$ g.

(Atomic weight of water = 18)

$\therefore \qquad n = \dfrac{4\pi}{3 \times 18} = \dfrac{2\pi}{27}$

44. *(b)* Cathode ray is observed only at low pressure and high voltage, which travel in straight line in the absence of electrical and magnetic fields. Characteristics of cathode rays are independent of the material of electrode or the gas present in the tube.

45. *(d)* For a spontaneous process in an isolated system, the change in entropy is positive, i.e, $\Delta S > O$.

However, if a system is not isolated, the entropy change of both the system and surroundings are to be taken into account because system and surroundings together constitute the isolated system thus, the total entropy change (ΔS_{total}) is sum of the change in entropy of the system (ΔS_{system}) and the change in entropy of the surroundings $(\Delta S_{surroundings})$,

i.e., $\Delta S_{total} = \Delta S_{system} + \Delta S_{Surroundings}$ for a spontenceus process, ΔS_{total} must be positive, i.e., ΔS_{total} is also termed as $\Delta S_{universe}$.

46. *(c)* The correct statement for primates' evolution is that human, chimpanzees and gorillas share a common ancestor. From fossil records, primatologists came to know that human, chimpanzee and gorilla are evolved from a common ancient ancestor about 10 million years ago. Recent studies on gorilla genome confirmed that gorilla diverged from the common ancestor about 6 million years ago.

47. *(b)* The crypts of Lieberkuhn are found in small intestine. Crypts are invagination of the epithelium around the villi and lined largely with younger epithelial cell which are involved in secretion of mucus.

48. *(c)* Removal of pancreas impairs the breakdown of lipids, proteins and carbohydrates because pancreas produces insulin and other important enzyme like trypsin, chymotrypsin, amylase and lipase which helps in breakdown of macromolecules.

49. *(c)* Microscopic examination of blood smear reveals an abnormal increase in neutrophils. Neutrophils have a multilobed nucleus and granulated cytoplasm.

Their number increases in blood in response of bacterial infection, acute inflammation and Eclampsia. Neutrophils are produced by hematopoiesis in the bone marrow and are active phagocytic cells.

Lymphocytes are white blood cells which occurs in blood, lymph and lymphoid organs.

Monocytes are mononuclear phagocytic cells.

Platelets are known as **thrombocytes** and helps in blood clotting.

50. *(a)* Blood group AB represents codominance. In codominance a heterozygous individual expresses both alleles simultaneously with blending. No single allele is dominant over the other. Expression of both A and B alleles at same time results in AB type blood.

51. *(b)* Allopatric speciation is a genetic divergence permitted by geographical isolation. It is a speciation that occurs when population of the same species becomes isolated due to geographic barriers such as mountain ranges and water bodies. The population is reproductively isolated and each of the population accumulates different mutation and become diverge.

52. *(d)* Conversion of glucose to CO_2 and H_2O requires oxygen. In aerobic respiration glucose reacts with oxygen forming ATP, carbon dioxide and water are released as byproducts.

$$C_6H_{12}O_6 + 6O_2 \longrightarrow 6CO_2 + 6H_2O + ATP$$

53. *(c)* Proxima and distal convoluted tubules are located in renal cortex. Convoluted means the tubules one tightly coiled. Proximal convoluted tubules are associated with the reabsorption of filtered water, Na^+, K^+. glucose, amino acid, Cl^-, HCO_3^-, Ca^{2+}, Mg^{2+} and secretion of H^+, NH_4^+, urea whereas distal convoluted tubules are associated with reabsorption of water, Na^+, Cl^- and Ca^{2+}.

54. *(d)* When one gene masks or modifies the expression of another gene at distinct locus is known as epistasis. Gene that masks other or expresses itself is epistatic gene and gene that is masked is hypostatic gene. Here, X is inactivated by Y and triggers its own expression that means Y is epistatic to loci X because it masks the expression of X.

55. *(a)* The correct taxonomic hierarchy is species, genus, family, order. Taxonomy is the branch of biology that deals with identification, nomenclature and classification. Carlous Linnaeus invented binomial nomenclature and developed a classification system known as taxonomic hierarchy. The various units of classification is kingdom, phylum, class, order, family, genus and species.

56. *(b)* Kidneys are not associated with the production of white blood cells. Kidneys regulate blood volume and composition, release erythropoietin and excrete waste in the urine.

Bone marrow is involved in hematopoiesis. It is the site of B-lymphocytes synthesis and maturation.

Liver produces monocytes (a type of white blood cells).

In spleen, B and T-lymphocytes are present. 50% of spleen cells are B-lymphocytes and 30-40% are T-lymphocytes.

57. *(b)* Hydathodes are involved in guttation. Hydathodes are specialised pore located along the leaf margins and tip which secrets water droplets. The exudation of water droplets from the tip or margin of the leaves is called guttation. Hydathodes mediated guttation occurs under high humidity and in the absence of transpiration.

Cuticle is an extracellular layer which covers the epidermis of plants which provides protection against dessication and external environmental stress.

Lenticels and **stomata** both regulates gaseous exchange between internal plant tissues and atmosphere and also regulates water movement through transpiration.

58. *(d)* Cataract affect the lens in eye. It occurs due to the clouding of lens and prevent light and image from reaching to retina. Cataract makes a person vision blurry and less colourful.

59. *(a)* **Liverwort** These are non-vascular plants and one of the three ancient lines of bryophytes (liverworts, hornworts and mosses).

Volvox It is a spherical multicellular green algae and used as a genetic model of morphogenesis.

Chlamydomonas It is a genus of unicellular green algae found in soil, freshwater and oceans.

Fern These are vascular plants that possess true roots, leaves and stem and are reproduced by spores. Ferns and lycophytes are pteridophytes.

60. *(d)* The second meiotic division occurs after fertilisation. Oogenesis is the formation of female gametes (egg). Oogenesis begins in female before birth. During early fetal development, germ cell differentiate into oogonia. After several mitotic divisions, oogonia begins meiosis and known as primary oocytes. It remains arrested after diplotene of prophase-I of meiosis-I until the female becomes sexually mature. After puberty, primary oocyte completes meiosis-I and produces secondary oocytes and it arrests at metaphase-II and it completes meiosis-II only after fertilisation.

61. *(c)* It is given that the quadratic equation $x^2 - 5cx - 6d = 0$ has roots a and b, then

$$a + b = 5c \qquad \text{...(i)}$$

and $ab = -6d \qquad \text{...(ii)}$

and, the quadratic equation $x^2 - 5ax - 6b = 0$ has roots c and d, then

$$c + d = 5a \qquad \text{...(iii)}$$

and $\qquad cd = -6b \qquad \text{...(iv)}$

Now, from Eqs. (i) and (iii), we have

$$(a + b) - (c + d) = 5c - 5a$$
$$\Rightarrow (a - c) + (b - d) = -5(a - c)$$
$$\Rightarrow \qquad (b - d) = 6(c - a) \qquad \text{...(v)}$$

$\therefore a$ and c are the roots of equations.

$x^2 - 5cx - 6d = 0$ and $x^2 - 5ax - 6b = 0$, respectively.

$$\therefore \qquad a^2 - 5ac - 6d = 0$$
and $\quad c^2 - 5ac - 6b = 0$
$$\Rightarrow (a^2 - c^2) - 6(d - b) = 0$$
$$\Rightarrow \quad a + c = \frac{6(d - b)}{a - c} = 36 \qquad \text{...(vi)}$$

From Eqs. (i) and (iii), we have

$$(a + b) + (c + d) = 5(a + c)$$
$$\Rightarrow \quad b + d = 4(a + c) = 4(36) \text{ [from Eq. (vi)]}$$
$$\Rightarrow \quad b + d = 144$$

62. *(a)* The quadratic equation
$$4x^2 + bx + c = 0$$

has equal roots if $b^2 - 16c = 0$
$$\Rightarrow \qquad b^2 = 2^4 c$$

Now, c should be chosen from the set $S = \{1, 2, 3, ..., 100\}$, such that it is a perfect square number, so

$c = 1, 4, 9, 16, 25, 36, 49, 64, 81, 100$

$\therefore$ number of ordered pair (b, c) will be 10.

So, required probability $= \dfrac{10}{100 \times 100}$

$$= \dfrac{1}{1000} = 0.001$$

63. *(a)* It is given that for $n \in N$

$$f_n = (n+1)^{1/3} - n^{1/3}$$

$$= \frac{(n+1) - n}{(n+1)^{2/3} + (n+1)^{2/3} \, n^{2/3} + n^{2/3}}$$

$$= \frac{1}{(n+1)^{2/3} + (n+1)^{2/3} \, n^{2/3} + n^{2/3}}$$

$\because \forall \, n \in N$

$$3n^{2/3} < (n+1)^{2/3} + (n+1)^{2/3} \, n^{2/3} + n^{2/3}$$
$$< 3(n+1)^{2/3}$$

$$\Rightarrow \frac{1}{3(n+1)^{2/3}}$$
$$< \frac{1}{(n+1)^{2/3} + (n+1)^{2/3} \, n^{2/3} + n^{2/3}} < \frac{1}{3n^{2/3}}$$

$$\Rightarrow \frac{1}{3(n+1)^{2/3}} < f_n < \frac{1}{3n^{2/3}}$$

Similarly,

$$\frac{1}{3(n+2)^{2/3}} < f_{n+1} < \frac{1}{3(n+1)^{2/3}}$$

$$\therefore \quad f_{n+1} < \frac{1}{3(n+1)^{2/3}} < f_{n+1}, \, \forall \, n \in N$$

So, set $A = N$.

64. *(b)* It is given that for prime numbers p_1, p_2, p_3, p_4 the special prime number

$$p = p_1 + p_2 = p_3 - p_4$$

Case I

If all p_1, p_2, p_3, p_4 are odd, then $(p_1 + p_2)$ and $(p_3 - p_4)$ are even, which is not possible.

Case II

If one of p_1 and p_2 is even, say p_2 is 2 and p_4 must be 2.

So, $p = p_1 + 2 = p_3 - 2$

the above equation is satisfied only if

$$p = 5, p_1 = 3 \text{ and } p_3 = 7$$

So, the number of special prime p is 1.

65. *(b)* It is given that in ΔABC,

$AB = BC$

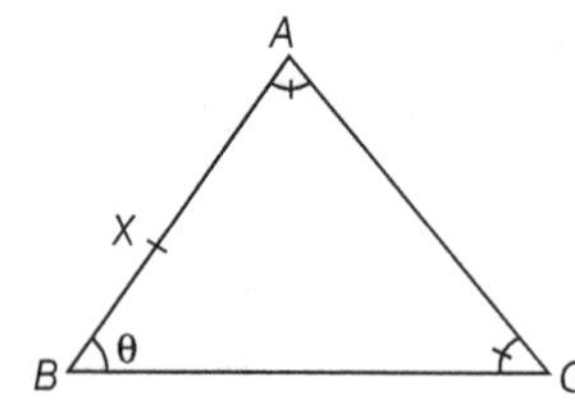

$$\text{and } \frac{AX}{XB} = \frac{AB}{AX} = \frac{1}{x} \text{ (say)}$$

$$\Rightarrow \quad AX = x \cdot AB$$

and $XB = xAX$

$$\therefore XB = x^2 \cdot AB$$

$\because \quad AB = AX + XB = x \cdot AB + x^2 \cdot AB$

$$\Rightarrow \quad x^2 + x - 1 = 0$$

$$\Rightarrow \quad x = \frac{-1 \pm \sqrt{1+4}}{2} = \frac{\pm\sqrt{5} - 1}{2}$$

$$\because \quad x > 0, \text{ so } x = \frac{\sqrt{5} - 1}{2}$$

Now, $\cos\theta = \dfrac{AB^2 + BC^2 - AC^2}{2(AB)(BC)}$

$$\Rightarrow \quad \cos\theta = \frac{2(AB^2) - (AX^2)}{2(AB^2)} \quad [\because AB = BC]$$

$$= \frac{2(AB^2) - (x^2 \cdot AB^2)}{2(AB^2)}$$

$$= \frac{2 - x^2}{2}$$

$$= \frac{2 - \left(\dfrac{\sqrt{5} - 1}{2}\right)^2}{2}$$

$$= \frac{8 - (5 + 1 - 2\sqrt{5})}{8}$$

$$= \frac{2\sqrt{5} + 2}{8}$$

$$= \frac{\sqrt{5} + 1}{4} = \cos 36°$$

So, $\theta = \angle ABC = 36°$

66. *(c)* When angle of incidence of laser on surface of water is less than critical incidence, it goes out otherwise reflected back into the tank.

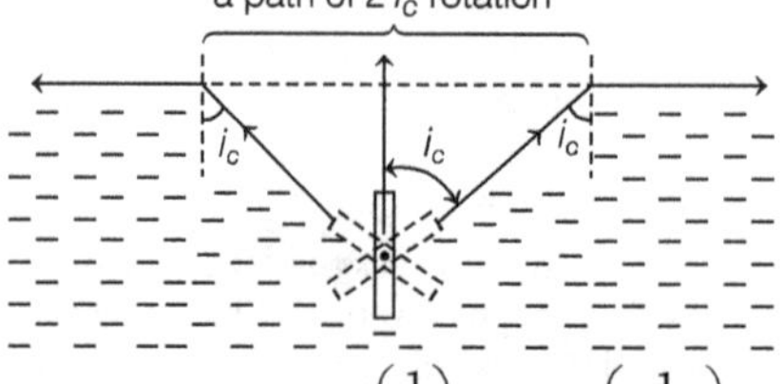

For water, $i_c = \sin^{-1}\left(\dfrac{1}{n}\right) = \sin^{-1}\left(\dfrac{1}{1.33}\right)$

$$\Rightarrow i_c = \sin^{-1}(0.75)$$

$$\Rightarrow i_c \approx 50°$$

If ω = angular speed and t = time to travel an arc of $2\,i_c$, then using $\omega t = 2i_c$.

We have, $t = \dfrac{2i_c}{\omega}$

$$= \frac{2 \times \dfrac{50}{180} \times \pi}{\left(\dfrac{2\pi}{60}\right)} = 16.67 \, \text{s}$$

67. *(a)* Force = Rate of change of momentum

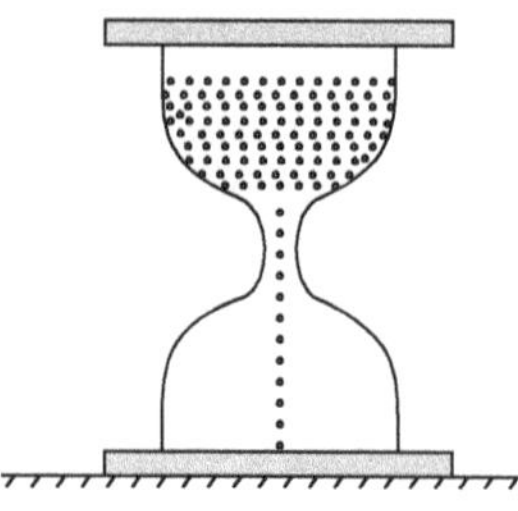

Velocity with which a sand particle strikes the bottom of hour-glass,

$$v = u + gt$$

$$\Rightarrow \quad v = 0 + 10 \times 2 = 20 \, \text{ms}^{-1}$$

Change in momentum of particle

$$= p_f - p_i = 0 - mv$$

$$= -0.2 \times 10^{-3} \times 20$$

$$= -4 \times 10^{-3} \, \text{kg-ms}^{-1}$$

Momentum imparted to base by the particle $= 4 \times 10^{-3}$ kg-ms^{-1}

Total change of momentum imparted per second by all 100 particles

$$= 4 \times 10^{-3} \text{kg-ms}^{-1} \times 100 \, \text{s}^{-1}$$

$$= 0.4 \, \text{kg-ms}^{-1}$$

So, force on bottom = 0.4 N

68. *(b)* When a voltmeter put in series, it still reads potential drop and when an ammeter is connected in parallel, it still shows current through it.

Case a

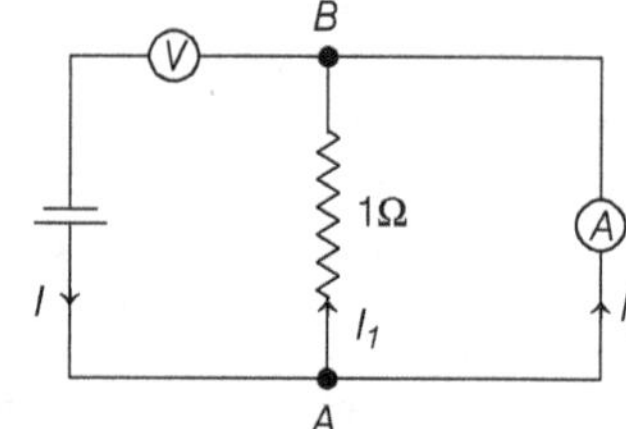

Let I = current through cell, then potential drop read by voltmeter is

$V = I \cdot R_V$ (this is reading of voltmeter)

Where, R_V is the resistance of voltmeter

In loop AB,

$$V_{AB} = I_1 \times 1 = I_2 \times R_A \text{ and } I = I_1 + I_2$$

Where, R_A is the resistance of ammeter

We substitute for I_1 from above equation to get

$$\Rightarrow \quad I = I_2 R_A + I_2 = I_2(R_A + 1)$$

$$\Rightarrow \quad I_2 = \frac{I}{(R_A + 1)}$$

(this is reading of ammeter)

Now given,

$$\frac{\text{voltmeter reading}}{\text{ammeter reading}} = 1 \times 10^3 = \frac{IR_V}{\left(\dfrac{I}{R_A + 1}\right)}$$

So, $R_V (R_A + 1) = 1000$ ...(i)

Case b

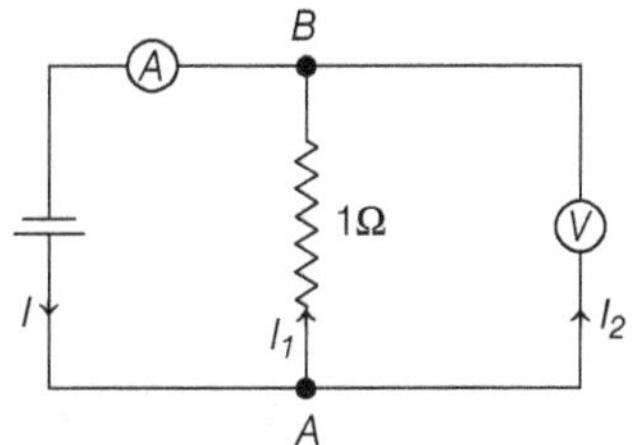

Let I = current through cell, then ammeter reading in this case is I.

Also, in loop AB,

$V_{AB} = I_1 \times 1 = I_2 \times R_V$

As, $I = I_1 + I_2 = I_2 R_V + I_2$

$\quad = I_2 (R_V + 1)$

So, $I_2 = \dfrac{I}{(R_V + 1)}$

Hence, voltmeter reading is $V = I_2 R_V$

$= \dfrac{IR_V}{(R_V + 1)}$ (this is reading of voltmeter)

Now given, voltmeter reading ÷ ammeter reading = 0.999 Ω.

So, $0.999 = \dfrac{\left[\dfrac{IR_V}{(R_V + 1)}\right]}{I}$

$\Rightarrow \quad 0.999 = \dfrac{R_V}{R_V + 1}$

So, $R_V = 999\,\Omega$ ...(ii)

$\approx 10^3\,\Omega$

Substituting R_V in Eq (i), we get

$R_A = \dfrac{1}{999}$

or $R_A = 10^{-3}\,\Omega$

69. *(c)* Hot air balloon will rise in the atmosphere when upthrust of buoyant force is greater than weight of balloon and its payload.

Upthrust = Weight of atmospheric air displaced by balloon

So, upthrust ≥ weight of balloon and its payload

$\Rightarrow$ (Volume of air displaced × density of atmospheric air × Acceleration due to gravity) ≥ (Volume of air of inside balloon × density of air inside balloon × acceleration due to gravity) + (Weight of payload of balloon)

$\Rightarrow V \cdot \rho_o \cdot g \geq V \cdot \rho_i \cdot g + 210 \times g$

where ρ_o = density of outside air and ρ_i = density of inside air.

$\Rightarrow \quad V(\rho_o - \rho_i) = 210$

$\Rightarrow \quad \rho_o - \rho_i = \dfrac{210 \times 3}{4\pi r^3} \quad \left(\because V = \dfrac{4}{3}\pi r^3\right)$

$\Rightarrow \dfrac{PM}{RT_o} - \dfrac{PM}{RT_i} = \dfrac{210 \times 3}{4 \times \pi \times \left(\dfrac{11.7}{2}\right)^3} \Rightarrow \dfrac{1}{T_o} - \dfrac{1}{T_i}$

$= \dfrac{680 \times 8 \times 8.31}{4 \times \pi \times (11.7)^3 \times 10^5 \times 30 \times 10^{-3}}$

$\Rightarrow \dfrac{T_i - T_o}{T_o T_i} = \dfrac{1}{1387}$

$\Rightarrow \quad T_o T_i = 1387\,(T_i - T_o)$

$\Rightarrow 300\,T_i = 1387\,T_i - 300 \times 1387$

$\quad\quad\quad$ (as, $T_o = 27°C = 300\,K$)

So, $T_i = \dfrac{300 \times 1387}{1087} \approx 383\,K$

$\therefore \quad T_i = 383 - 273 = 110°\,C$

So, temperature of hot air is near to 105° C.

70. *(c)*

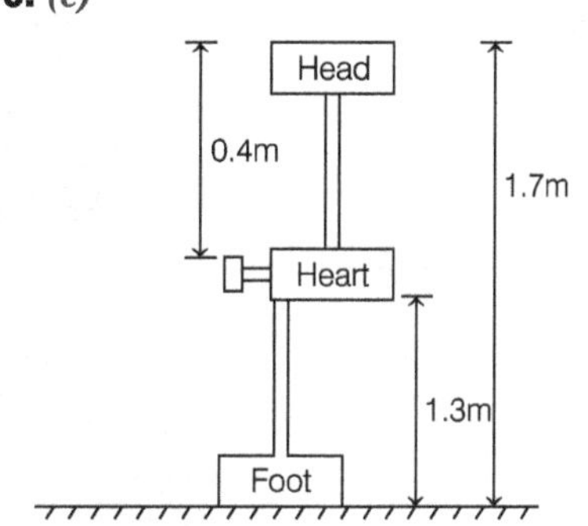

Pressure at head level = $p_{\text{heart}} - \rho g h$

$= 13.3 - 10^3 \times 10 \times 0.4$

$= 9.3\,\text{kPa}$

Pressure at foot level = $p_{\text{heart}} + \rho g h$

$= 13.3 + 10^3 \times 10 \times 1.3$

$= 26.3\,\text{kPa}$

So, ratio $= \dfrac{26.3}{9.3} \approx 2.9$ or 3

71. *(c)* (a) $PbO + HCl \longrightarrow PbCl_2 + H_2O$

$\quad\quad\quad\quad\quad$ (not correct option)

(b) $2Pb(NO_3)_2 \longrightarrow 2PbO + 4NO_2 + O_2$

$\quad\quad\quad\quad\quad$ (not correct option)

(c) $Pb_3O_4 + 4HNO_3 \longrightarrow 2Pb(NO_3)_2$

$\quad\quad\quad + PbO_2 + 2H_2O$ (correct option)

(d) $Pb + air$ (contains O_2, H_2O and CO_2)

$\xrightarrow[\text{temperature}]{\text{room}}$

Protective layer of varying composition, mainly $PbCO_3$ is formed only on the surface. (not correct option)

72. *(b)* If p_0 and V_0 are used as notation of ideal pressure and ideal volume of a

van der Waals' gas, the actual pressure and volume are:

$$p = p_0 - \dfrac{an^2}{V^2},\ V = V_0 + nb$$

$\therefore$ As "a" increases, p decreases, so $\dfrac{pV}{RT}$ decreases, when temperature is constant.

and, as "b" decreases, V decreases, so $\dfrac{pV}{RT}$ decreases, when temperature is constant.

Note option (c) : When temperature increases, pV also increases and therefore Z would not necessarily decrease.

73. *(a)* (i) Energy of the 2s orbital of different elements decreases as nuclear charge (equal to atomic number) of atom increases.

(ii) There are n^2 orbitals in a shell with principal quantum number n.

$\therefore$ total number of electrons = $2n^2$.

(iii) Extra stability of half-filled orbitals is due to greater exchange energy.

(iv) For two electrons will be in the same orbital, their spin quantum numbers must be different.

It is not irrespective of their spin.

74. *(c)* Mass of $AgX = 2.21\,g$

Mass of X = 46.78% of 2.00 g

$= \dfrac{46.78 \times 2.00}{100}$

$\cong 0.94\,g$

$\therefore$ Mass of Ag in AgX must be

$2.21 - 0.94\,g$

$= 1.27\,g$

$\therefore$ Number of moles of $Ag = \dfrac{1.27}{108}$,

which is also equal to number of moles of X.

$\therefore$ Atomic mass of $X = \dfrac{\text{mass}}{'n'}$

$= \dfrac{0.94 \times 108}{1.27} \cong 80$

$\therefore$ The halogen must be bromine (Br).

75. *(d)*

$$\text{(alkyne)} + 2HBr \longrightarrow \text{(gem-dibromide with Br, Br)}$$

(Hydrobromination, Markownikoff's product, which is a *gem*-dibromide).

$$X + H_2O \xrightarrow[+\ Hg^{2+}]{+\ H^+} \text{(ketone)}$$

$\quad\quad\quad$ (dil. H_2SO_4 + $HgSO_4$)

Acid catalysed hydration of alkyne gives ketone. In the case of terminal alkyne, the product is a methyl ketone, which gives haloform test.

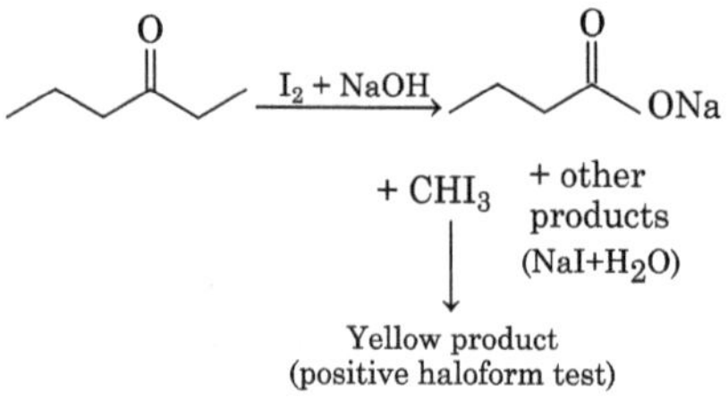

76. *(c)* Mass of one cell = 1 mg = 10^{-6} kg

Division in the cell is calculated as 2^n

So, after 100 divisions,

Number of cells = $2^n = 2^{100}$

Total mass of cells = Total no. of cells × Mass of one cell

$$= 2^{100} \times D10^{-6} \text{ kg}$$
$$= 2^{10} = 10^3$$
$$= (10^3)^{10} \times 10^{-6} \text{ kg}$$
$$= 10^{30} \times 10^{-6} \text{ kg}$$
$$= 10^{+24} \text{ kg}$$

Mass of earth is 10^{24} kg

$$\text{Ratio} = \frac{\text{Total mass of cells}}{\text{Mass of earth}}$$
$$= \frac{10^{24}}{10^{24}} = 1$$

So, option (c) is correct

77. *(d)* In papaya, sexual genotype for male is XY and for female is XX. In double fertilisation, the X nuclei fuses with egg and polar nuclei then resulting genotype of embryo and endosperm is XX and XXX. When Y nuclei fuses with the egg cell and polar nuclei then resulting genotype for embryo and endosperm is XY and XXY.

So, 50% XXX and XXY is genotype of endosperm and 50% XX and XY is genotype of embryo.

78. *(a)* Graph (a) represents the activity of pepsin at low pH and salivary amylase activity at high pH. Enzymes have a particular pH where they have the proper conformation to have maximum catalytic activity. Pepsin have maximum catalytic activity at a very low pH (2.0) and no longer functional once moved to alkaline condition and optimum pH for salivary amylase ranges from 6 to 7 and it is most active at pH 6.8.

Graph (b) represents minimum activity of pepsin and salivary amylase.

Graph (c) and (d) represents constant activity of both enzyme. At low pH activity of pepsin increases and become stable as pH is increasing and activity of amylase increases at above pH 5 and become stable at high pH.

79. *(c)* Gene pool of locus X = 4

$$\text{Possible genotype} = \frac{n}{2}(n+1)$$

n = Total number of gene for 'X' loucs

$$n = 4$$
$$= \frac{n}{2}(n+1)$$
$$= \frac{4}{2}(4+1) = 2(5) = 10$$

So, highest possible genotype in a population is 10.

80. *(b)* The correct combination of plant hormones with their function is as follows

(P) Abscisic acid—Maintains seed dormancy

(Q) Ethylene—Promotes fruit ripening

(R) Cytokinin—Inhibits leaf senescence

(S) Gibberellin—Promotes seed germination

QUESTION PAPER 2018
Stream : SA

MM : 100

Instructions

1. There are 80 questions in this paper.

2. This question paper contains two parts; Part I and Part II. There are four sections; Mathematics, Physics, Chemistry and Biology in each part.

3. Out of the four options given with each question, only one is correct.

➲ PART-I (1 Mark Questions)

MATHEMATICS

1. The number of pairs (a, b) of positive real numbers satisfying $a^4 + b^4 < 1$ and $a^2 + b^2 > 1$ is

(a) 0
(b) 1
(c) 2
(d) More than 2

2. The number of real roots of the polynomial equation $x^4 - x^2 + 2x - 1 = 0$ is

(a) 0
(b) 2
(c) 3
(d) 4

3. Suppose the sum of the first m terms of an arithmetic progression is n and the sum of its first n terms is m, where $m \neq n$. Then, the sum of the first $(m + n)$ terms of the arithmetic progression is

(a) $1 - mn$
(b) $mn - 5$
(c) $-(m + n)$
(d) $m + n$

4. Consider the following two statements

  I. Any pair of consistent liner equations in two variables must have a unique solution.

  II. There do not exist two consecutive integers, the sum of whose squares is 365.

Then

(a) both I and II are true
(b) both I and II are false
(c) I is true and II is false
(d) I is false and II is true

5. The number of polynomials $p(x)$ with integer coefficients such that curve $y = p(x)$ passes through $(2, 2)$ and $(4, 5)$ is

(a) 0
(b) 1
(c) more than 1 but finite
(d) infinite

6. The median of all 4-digit numbers that are divisible by 7 is

(a) 5797
(b) 5498.5
(c) 5499.5
(d) 5490

7. A solid hemisphere is attached to the top of a cylinder, having the same radius as that of the cylinder. If the height of the cylinder were doubled (keeping both radii fixed), the volume of the entire system would have increased by 50%. By what percentage would the volume have increased if the radii of the hemisphere and the cylinder were doubled (keeping the height fixed)?

(a) 300%
(b) 400%
(c) 500%
(d) 600%

8. Consider a $\triangle PQR$ in which the relation $QR^2 + PR^2 = 5\,PQ^2$ holds. Let G be the point of intersection of medians PM and QN. Then, $\angle QGM$ is always

(a) less than 45°
(b) obtuse
(c) a right angle
(d) acute and larger than 45°

9. Let a, b, c be the side-lengths of a triangle and l, m, n be the lengths of its medians. Put $K = \dfrac{l + m + n}{a + b + c}$.

Then, as a, b, c vary, K can assume every value in the interval

(a) $\left(\dfrac{1}{4}, \dfrac{2}{3}\right)$
(b) $\left(\dfrac{1}{2}, \dfrac{4}{5}\right)$
(c) $\left(\dfrac{3}{4}, 1\right)$
(d) $\left(\dfrac{4}{5}, \dfrac{5}{4}\right)$

10. Let x_0, y_0 be fixed real numbers such that $x_0^2 + y_0^2 > 1$. If x, y are arbitrary real numbers such that $x^2 + y^2 \le 1$, then the minimum value of $(x - x_0)^2 + (y - y_0)^2$ is

(a) $\left(\sqrt{x_0^2 + y_0^2} - 1\right)^2$
(b) $x_0^2 + y_0^2 - 1$
(c) $(|x_0| + |y_0| - 1)^2$
(d) $(|x_0| + |y_0|)^2 - 1$

11. Let PQR be a triangle is which $PQ = 3$. From the vertex R, draw the altitude RS to meet PQ at S. Assume that $RS = \sqrt{3}$ and $PS = QR$. Then, PR equals

(a) $\sqrt{5}$
(b) $\sqrt{6}$
(c) $\sqrt{7}$
(d) $\sqrt{8}$

12. A 100 mark examination was administered to a class of 50 students. Despite only integer marks being given, the average score of the class was 47.5. Then, the maximum number of students who could get marks more than the class average is

(a) 25
(b) 35
(c) 45
(d) 49

13. Let S be the sum of the digits of the number $15^2 \times 5^{18}$ in base 10. Then,

(a) $S < 6$
(b) $6 \le S < 140$
(c) $140 \le S < 148$
(d) $S \ge 148$

14. Let PQR be an acute-angled triangle in which $PQ < QR$. From the vertex Q draw the altitude QQ_1, the angle bisector QQ_2 and the median QQ_3, with Q_1, Q_2, Q_3 lying on PR. Then,

(a) $PQ_1 < PQ_2 < PQ_3$
(b) $PQ_2 < PQ_1 < PQ_3$
(c) $PQ_1 < PQ_3 < PQ_2$
(d) $PQ_3 < PQ_1 < PQ_2$

15. All the vertices of a rectangle are of the form (a, b) with a, b integers satisfying the equation $(a - 8)^2 - (b - 7)^2 = 5$. Then, the perimeter of the rectangle is

(a) 20
(b) 22
(c) 24
(d) 26

PHYSICS

16. A block of wood is floating on water at 0°C with volume V_0 above water. When the temperature of water increases from 0 to 10°C, the change in the volume of the block that is above water is best described schematically by the graph.

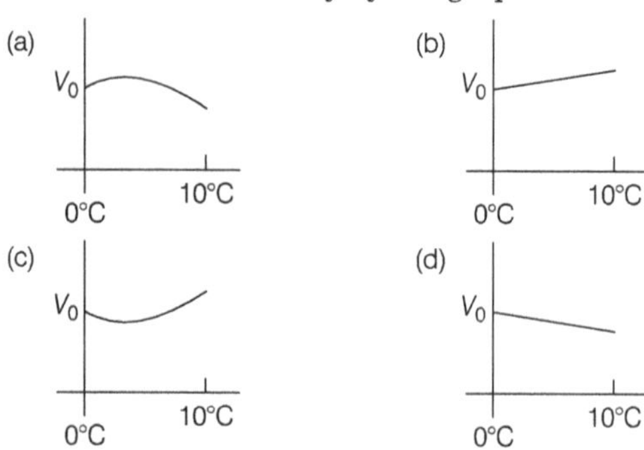

17. A very large block of ice of the size of a volleyball court and of uniform thickness of 8 m is floating on water. A person standing near its edge wishes to fetch a bucketful of water using a rope. The smallest length of rope required for this is about

(a) 3.6 m
(b) 1.8 m
(c) 0.9 m
(d) 0.4 m

18. A box filled with water has a small hole on its side near the bottom. It is dropped from the top of a tower. As it falls, a camera attached on the side of the box records the shape of the water stream coming out of the hole. The resulting video will show

(a) the water coming down forming a parabolic stream
(b) the water going up forming a parabolic stream
(c) the water coming out in a straight line
(d) no water coming out

19. An earthen pitcher used in summer cools water in it essentially by evaporation of water from its porous surface. If a pitcher carries 4 kg of water and the rate of evaporation is 20 g per hour, temperature of water in it decreases by ΔT in two hours. The value of ΔT is close to (ratio of latent of evaporation to specific heat of water is 540°C)

(a) 2.7°C
(b) 4.2°C
(c) 5.4°C
(d) 10.8°C

20. Two plane mirrors are kept on a horizontal table making an angle θ with each other as shown schematically in the figure. The angle θ is such that any ray of light reflected after striking both the mirrors returns parallel to its incident path. For this to happen, the value of θ should be

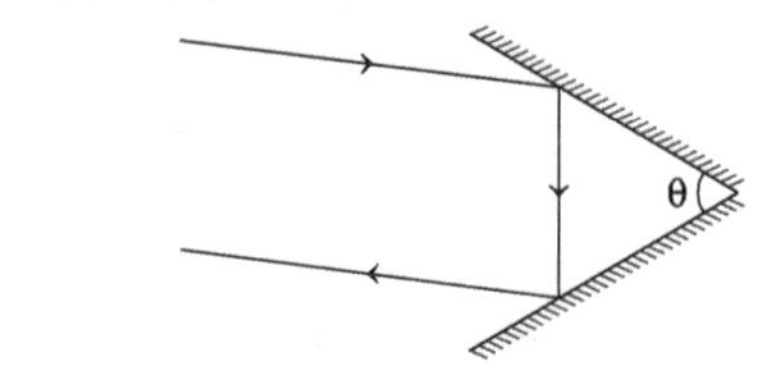

(a) 30°
(b) 45°
(c) 60°
(d) 90°

21. A certain liquid has a melting point of $-50°C$ and a boiling point of $150°C$. A thermometer is designed with this liquid and its melting and boiling points are designated at $0°L$ and $100°L$. The melting and boiling points of water on this scale are
(a) $25°L$ and $75°L$, respectively
(b) $0°L$ and $100°L$, respectively
(c) $20°L$ and $70°L$, respectively
(d) $30°L$ and $80°L$, respectively

22. One can define an alpha-volt (α-V) to be the energy acquired by an α-particle when it is accelerated by a potential of 1 V. For this problem, you may take a proton to be 2000 times heavier than an electron. Then,
(a) $1\,\alpha$-$V = 1eV/4000$ (b) $1\,\alpha$-$V = 2\,eV$
(c) $1\,\alpha$-$V = 8000\,eV$ (d) $1\,\alpha$-$V = 1eV$

23. In a particle accelerator, a current of $500\,\mu A$ is carried by a proton beam in which each proton has a speed of 3×10^7 m/s. The cross-sectional area of the beam is 1.50 mm^2. The charge density in this beam (in C/m^3) is close to
(a) 10^{-8} (b) 10^{-7} (c) 10^{-6} (d) 10^{-5}

24. Which of the following is not true about the total lunar eclipse?
(a) A lunar eclipse can occur on a new moon and full moon day
(b) The lunar eclipse would occur roughly every month, if the orbits of earth and moon were perfectly coplanar
(c) The moon appears red during the eclipse because the blue light is absorbed in earth's atmosphere and red is transmitted
(d) A lunar eclipse can occur only on a full moon day

25. Many exoplanets have been discovered by the transit method, where in one monitors, a dip in the intensity of the parent star as the exoplanet moves in front of it. The exoplanet has a radius R and the parent star has radius $100\,R$. If I_0 is the intensity observed on earth due to the parent star, then as the exoplanet transits
(a) the minimum observed intensity of the parent star is $0.9\,I_0$
(b) the minimum observed intensity of the parent star is $0.99\,I_0$
(c) the minimum observed intensity of the parent star is $0.999\,I_0$
(d) the minimum observed intensity of the parent star is $0.9999\,I_0$

26. A steady current I is set up in a wire whose cross-sectional area decreases in the direction of the flow of the current. Then, as we examine the narrowing region,
(a) the current density decreases in value
(b) the magnitude of the electric field increases
(c) the current density remains constant
(d) the average speed of the moving charges remains constant

27. Select the correct statement about rainbow.
(a) We can see a rainbow in the western sky in the late afternoon
(b) The double rainbow has red on the inside and violet on the outside
(c) A rainbow has an arc shape, since the earth is round
(d) A rainbow on the moon is violet on the inside and red on the outside

28. Remote sensing satellites move in an orbit that is at an average height of about 500 km from the surface of the earth. The camera onboard one such satellite has a screen of area A on which the images captured by it are formed. If the focal length of the camera lens is 50 cm, then the terrestrial area that can be observed from the satellite is close to
(a) $2 \times 10^3\,A$ (b) $10^6\,A$ (c) $10^{12}\,A$ (d) $4 \times 10^{12}\,A$

29. Letters A, B, C and D are written on a cardboard as shown in the figure below.

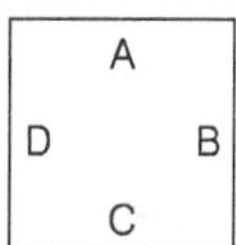

The cardboard is kept at a suitable distance behind a transparent empty glass of cylindrical shape. If the glass is now filled with water, one sees an inverted image of the pattern on the cardboard when looking through the glass. Ignoring magnification effects, the image would appear as

(a) 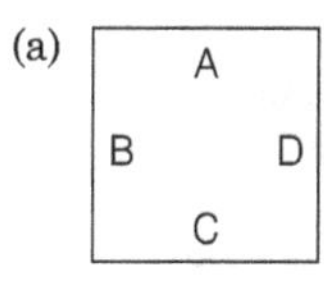
(b) 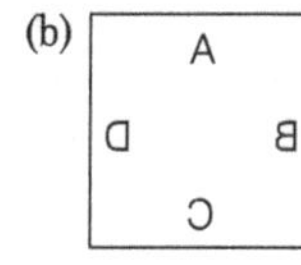
(c) 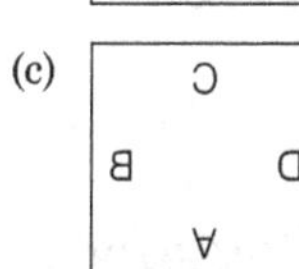
(d) 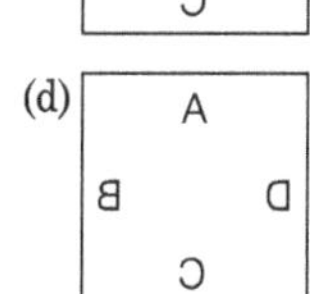

30. If a ball is thrown at a velocity of 45 m/s in vertical upward direction, then what would be the velocity profile as function of height? (Assume, $g = 10$ m/s^2)

(a) 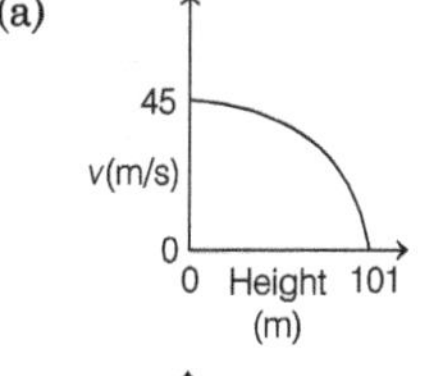
(b) 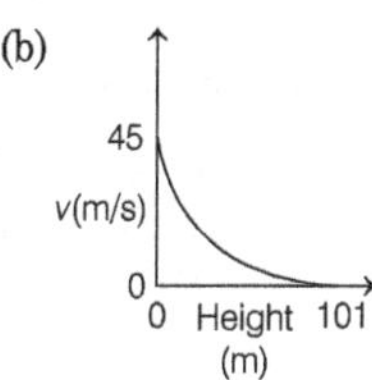
(c) 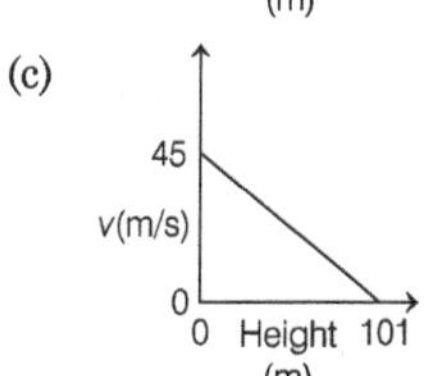
(d) 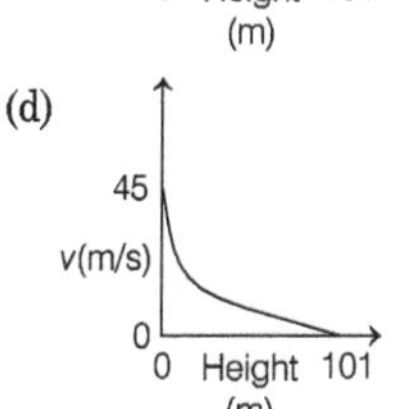

CHEMISTRY

31. The number of water molecules in 250 mL of water is closest to

[Given, density of water is 1.0 g mL^{-1}; Avogadro's number $= 6.023 \times 10^{23}$]

(a) 83.6×10^{23} (b) 13.9×10^{23}
(c) 1.5×10^{23} (d) 33.6×10^{23}

32. Among the following, the correct statement is

(a) pH decreases when solid ammonium chloride is added to a dilute aqueous solution of NH_3
(b) pH decreases when solid sodium acetate is added to a dilute aqueous solution of acetic acid
(c) pH decreases when solid NaCl is added to a dilute aqueous solution of NaOH
(d) pH decreases when solid sodium oxalate is added to a dilute aqueous solution of oxalic acid

33. The solubility of $BaSO_4$ in pure water (in g L^{-1}) is closest to

[Given; K_{sp} for $BaSO_4$ is 1.0×10^{-10} at 25°C. Molecular weight of $BaSO_4$ is 233 g mol^{-1}]

(a) 1.0×10^{-5}
(b) 1.0×10^{-3}
(c) 2.3×10^{-5}
(d) 2.3×10^{-3}

34. Among the following, the incorrect statement is

(a) no two electrons in an atom can have the same set of four quantum numbers
(b) the maximum number of electrons in the shell with principal quantum number, n is equal to $n^2 + 2$
(c) electrons in an orbital must have opposite spin
(d) in the ground state, atomic orbitals are filled in the order of their increasing energies

35. A container of volume 2.24 L can with stand a maximum pressure of 2 atm at 298 K before exploding. The maximum amount of nitrogen (in g) that can be safely put in this container at this temperature is closest to

(a) 2.8   (b) 5.6
(c) 1.4   (d) 4.2

36. The compound shown below

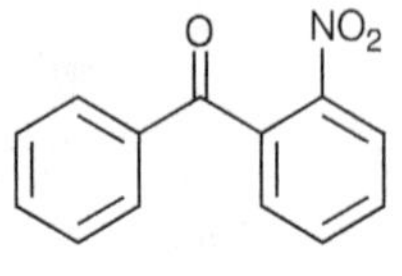

can be readily prepared by Friedel-Craft's reaction between

(a) benzene and 2-nitrobenzoyl chloride
(b) benzyl chloride and nitrobenzene
(c) nitrobenzene and benzoyl chloride
(d) benzene and 2-nitrobenzyl chloride

37. The correct statement about the following compounds

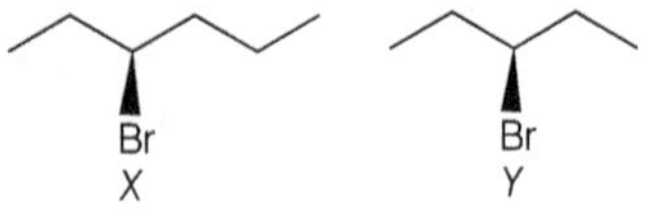

is
(a) Both are chiral
(b) Both are achiral
(c) X is chiral and Y is achiral
(d) X is achiral and Y is chiral

38. The most acidic proton and the strongest nucleophilic nitrogen in the following compound

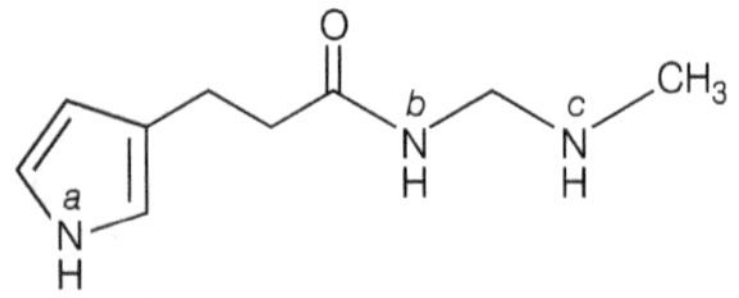

respectively, are
(a) $N^a – H; N^b$ (b) $N^b – H; N^c$
(c) $N^a – H; N^c$ (d) $N^c – H; N^a$

39. The chlorine atom of the following compound

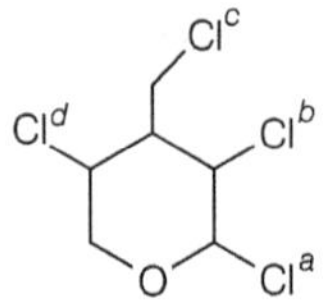

that reacts most readily with $AgNO_3$ to give a precipitate is

(a) Cl^a (b) Cl^b (c) Cl^c (d) Cl^d

40. Among the following sets, the most stable ionic species are

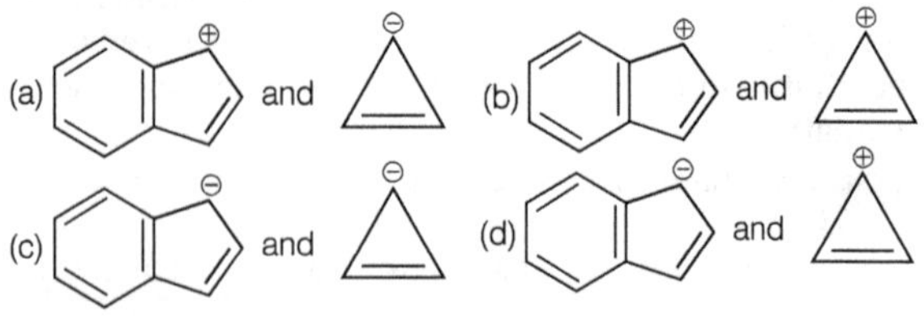

41. The correct order of energy of 2s-orbitals in H, Li, Na and K, is

(a) K < Na < Li < H   (b) Na < Li < K < H
(c) Na < K < H < Li   (d) H < Na < Li < K

42. The hybridisation of xenon atom in XeF_4 is

(a) sp^3 (b) dsp^2
(c) $sp^3 d^2$ (d) $d^2 sp^3$

43. The formal oxidation numbers of Cr and Cl in the ions $Cr_2O_7^{2-}$ and ClO_3^-, respectively are

(a) + 6 and +7   (b) +7 and +5
(c) +6 and +5   (d) +8 and +7

44. A filter paper soaked in salt X turns brown when exposed to HNO_3 vapor. The salt X is
(a) KCl   (b) KBr   (c) KI   (d) K_2SO_4

45. The role of haemoglobin is to
(a) store oxygen in muscles
(b) transport oxygen to different parts of the body
(c) convert CO to CO_2
(d) convert CO_2 into carbonic acid

BIOLOGY

46. Which one of the following molecules is a secondary metabolite?
(a) Ethanol   (b) Lactate
(c) Penicillin   (d) Citric acid

47. Lecithin is a
(a) carbohydrate   (b) phospholipid
(c) nucleoside   (d) protein

48. The water potential (ψ_p) of pure water at standard temperature and atmospheric pressure is
(a) 0   (b) 0.5   (c) 1.0   (d) 2.0

49. Action potential in neurons is generated by a rapid influx of
(a) chloride ions   (b) potassium ions
(c) calcium ions   (d) sodium ions

50. Erythropoietin is produced by
(a) heart   (b) kidney
(c) bone marrow   (d) adrenal gland

51. Tendrils are modifications of
(a) stem or leaf   (b) stem only
(c) leaf only   (d) aerial roots only

52. Which one of the following combinations of biomolecules is present in the ribosomes?
(a) RNA, DNA and protein
(b) RNA, lipids and DNA
(c) RNA and protein
(d) RNA and DNA

53. Which one of the following proteins does not play a role in skeletal muscle contraction?
(a) Actin   (b) Myosin
(c) Troponin   (d) Microtubule

54. Which one of the following reactions is catalysed by high-energy ultraviolet radiation in the stratosphere?
(a) $O_2 + O \longrightarrow O_3$ (b) $O_2 \longrightarrow O + O$
(c) $O_3 + O_3 \longrightarrow 3O_2$ (d) $O + O \longrightarrow O_2$

55. Which one of the following statements is true about trypsinogen?
(a) It is activated by enterokinase
(b) It is activated by renin
(c) It is activated by pepsin
(d) It does not need activation

56. Which one of the following organisms respires through the skin?
(a) Blue whale   (b) Salamander
(c) Platypus   (d) Peacock

57. Which one of the following human cells lacks a nucleus?
(a) Neutrophil   (b) Neuron
(c) Mature erythrocyte   (d) Keratinocyte

58. The first enzyme that the food encounters in human digestive system is
(a) pepsin   (b) trypsin
(c) chymotrypsin   (d) amylase

59. Glycoproteins are formed in which one of the following organelles?
(a) Peroxisome   (b) Lysosome
(c) Golgi apparatus   (d) Mitochondria

60. An example of nastic movement (external stimulus-dependent movement) in plants is
(a) folding up of the leaves of *Mimosa pudica*
(b) climbing of tendrils
(c) growth of roots from seeds
(d) growth of pollen tube towards the ovule

ꙩ PART-II (2 Marks Questions)

MATHEMATICS

61. What is the sum of all natural numbers n such that the product of the digits of n (in base 10) is equal to $n^2 - 10n - 36$?
(a) 12   (b) 13   (c) 124   (d) 2612

62. Let m (respectively, n) be the number of 5-digit integers obtained by using the digits 1, 2, 3, 4, 5 with repetitions (respectively, without repetitions) such that the sum of any two adjacent digits is odd. Then $\dfrac{m}{n}$ is equal to

(a) 9   (b) 12   (c) 15   (d) 18

63. The number of solid cones with integer radius and integer height each having its volume numerically equal to its total surface area is
(a) 0   (b) 1   (c) 2   (d) infinite

64. Let $ABCD$ be a square. An arc of a circle with A as centre and AB as radius is drawn inside the square joining the points B and D. Points P on AB, S on AD, Q and R on arc BD are taken such that $PQRS$ is a square.

Further suppose that PQ and RS are parallel to AC.
Then, $\dfrac{\text{area } PQRS}{\text{area } ABCD}$ is

(a) $\dfrac{1}{8}$ (b) $\dfrac{1}{5}$ (c) $\dfrac{1}{4}$ (d) $\dfrac{2}{5}$

65. Suppose $ABCD$ is a trapezium whose sides and height are integers and AB is parallel to CD. If the area of $ABCD$ is 12 and the sides are distinct, then $|AB - CD|$

(a) is 2

(b) is 4

(c) is 8

(d) cannot be determined from the data

PHYSICS

66. A coffee maker makes coffee by passing steam through a mixture of coffee powder, milk and water. If the steam is mixed at the rate of 50 g per minute in a mug containing 500 g of mixture, then it takes about t_0 seconds to make coffee at $70°$ C when the initial temperature of the mixture is 25°C. The value of t_0 is close to (ratio of latent heat of evaporation to specific heat of water is 540°C and specific heat of the mixture can be taken to be the same as that of water)

(a) 30   (b) 45   (c) 60   (d) 90

67. A person in front of a mountain is beating a drum at the rate of 40 per minute and hears no distinct echo. If the person moves 90 m closer to the mountain, he has to beat the drum at 60 per minute to not hear any distinct echo. The speed of sound is

(a) 320 ms^{-1} (b) 340 ms^{-1} (c) 360 ms^{-1} (d) 380 ms^{-1}

68. A glass beaker is filled with water up to 5 cm. It is kept on top of a 2 cm thick glass slab. When a coin at the bottom of the glass slab is viewed at the normal incidence from above the beaker, its apparent depth from the water surface is d cm. Value of d is close to (the refractive indices of water and glass are 1.33 and 1.5, respectively)

(a) 2.5 cm   (b) 5.1 cm   (c) 3.7 cm   (d) 6.0 cm

69. A proton of mass m and charge e is projected from a very large distance towards an α-particle with velocity v. Initially α-particle is at rest, but it is free to move. If gravity is neglected, then the minimum separation along the straight line of their motion will be

(a) $e^2/4\pi\varepsilon_0 mv^2$ (b) $5e^2/4\pi\varepsilon_0 mv^2$

(c) $2e^2/4\pi\varepsilon_0 mv^2$ (d) $4e^2/4\pi\varepsilon_0 mv^2$

70. A potential is given by $V(x) = k(x+a)^2/2$ for $x < 0$ and $V(x) = k(x-a)^2/2$ for $x > 0$. The schematic variation of oscillation period T for a particle performing periodic motion in this potential as a function of its energy E is

(a) 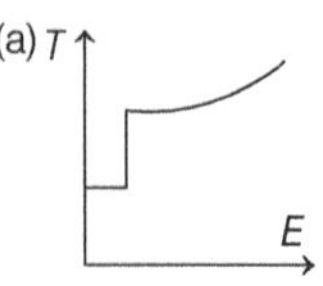

(b) 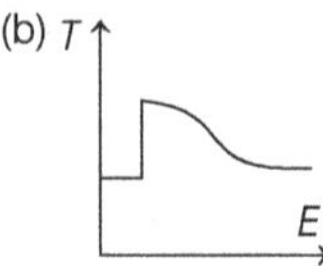

(c) 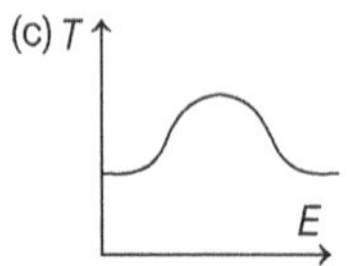

(d) 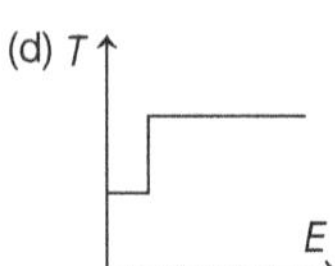

CHEMISTRY

71. Among the following, the species with identical bond order are

(a) CO and O_2^{2-} (b) O_2^- and CO

(c) O_2^{2-} and B_2 (d) CO and N_2^+

72. The quantity of heat (in J) required to raise the temperature of 1.0 kg of ethanol from 293.45 K to the boiling point and then change the liquid to vapor at that temperature is closest to

[Given, boiling point of ethanol 351.45 K. Specific heat capacity of liquid ethanol $2.44 \text{ J g}^{-1}\text{K}^{-1}$. Latent heat of vaporisation of ethanol 855 J g^{-1}]

(a) 1.42×10^2 (b) 9.97×10^2

(c) 1.42×10^5 (d) 9.97×10^5

73. A solution of 20.2 g of 1,2-dibromopropane in MeOH upon heating with excess Zn produces 3.58 g of an unsaturated compound X. The yield (%) of X is closest to   [Atomic weight of Br is 80.]

(a) 18   (b) 85   (c) 89   (d) 30

74. The lower stability of ethyl anion compared to methyl anion and the higher stability of ethyl radical compared to methyl radical, respectively, are due to

(a) $+I$-effect of the methyl group in ethyl anion $\sigma \rightarrow p$-orbital conjugation in ethyl radical

(b) $-I$-effect of the methyl group in ethyl anion and $\sigma \rightarrow \sigma^*$ conjugation in ethyl radical

(c) $+I$ effect of the methyl group in both cases

(d) $+I$- effect of the methyl group in ethyl anion and $\sigma \rightarrow \sigma^*$ conjugation in ethyl radical

75. The F-Br-F bond angles in BrF_5 and the Cl-P-Cl bond angles in PCl_5, respectively, are

(a) identical in BrF_5 but non-identical in PCl_5

(b) identical in BrF_5 and identical in PCl_5

(c) non-identical in BrF_5 but identical in PCl_5

(d) non-identical in BrF_5 and non-identical in PCl_5

BIOLOGY

76. If the genotypes determining the blood groups of a couple are $I^A I^O$ and $I^A I^B$, then the probability of their first child having type O blood is

(a) 0   (b) 0.25   (c) 0.50   (d) 0.75

77. A cross was carried out between two individuals heterozygous for two pairs of genes was carried out. Assuming segregation and independent assortment, the number of different genotypes and phenotypes obtained respectively would be
(a) 4 and 9
(b) 6 and 3
(c) 9 and 4
(d) 11 and 4

78. If the H⁺ concentration of an aqueous solution is 0.001 M, then the pOH of the solution would be
(a) 0.001
(b) 0.999
(c) 3
(d) 11

79. Consider the following vision defects listed in Columns I and II and the corrective measures in Column III. Choose the correct combination.

	Column I		Column II		Column III
P.	Hypermetropia	(i)	Near-sightedness	a.	Convex lens
Q.	Myopia	(ii)	Far-sightedness	b.	Concave lens

(a) P–ii–b
(b) Q–i–b
(c) P–i–a
(d) Q–i–a

80. Which one of the following properties causes the plant tendrils to coil around a bamboo stick?
(a) Tendril has spines
(b) The base of the tendril grows faster than the tip
(c) Part of the tendril in contact with the bamboo stick grows at a slower rate than the part away from it.
(d) The tip of the tendril grows faster than the base

Answers

PART-I

1	(d)	2	(b)	3	(c)	4	(b)	5	(a)	6	(b)	7	(c)	8	(c)	9	(c)	10	(a)
11	(c)	12	(d)	13	(b)	14	(a)	15	(a)	16	(a)	17	(c)	18	(d)	19	(c)	20	(d)
21	(a)	22	(b)	23	(d)	24	(a)	25	(d)	26	(b)	27	(*)	28	(c)	29	(d)	30	(a)
31	(a)	32	(a)	33	(d)	34	(b)	35	(d)	36	(a)	37	(c)	38	(b)	39	(a)	40	(d)
41	(a)	42	(c)	43	(c)	44	(c)	45	(b)	46	(c)	47	(b)	48	(a)	49	(d)	50	(b)
51	(a)	52	(c)	53	(d)	54	(b)	55	(a)	56	(b)	57	(c)	58	(d)	59	(c)	60	(a)

PART-II

61	(b)	62	(c)	63	(b)	64	(d)	65	(b)	66	(b)	67	(c)	68	(b)	69	(b)	70	(b)
71	(c)	72	(d)	73	(b)	74	(a)	75	(d)	76	(a)	77	(c)	78	(d)	79	(b)	80	(c)

** No options are correct.*

Solutions

1. *(d)* We have,
$$a^4 + b^4 < 1 \text{ and } a^2 + b^2 > 1$$
The graph of $x^2 + y^2 = 1$ and $x^4 + y^4 = 1$ are

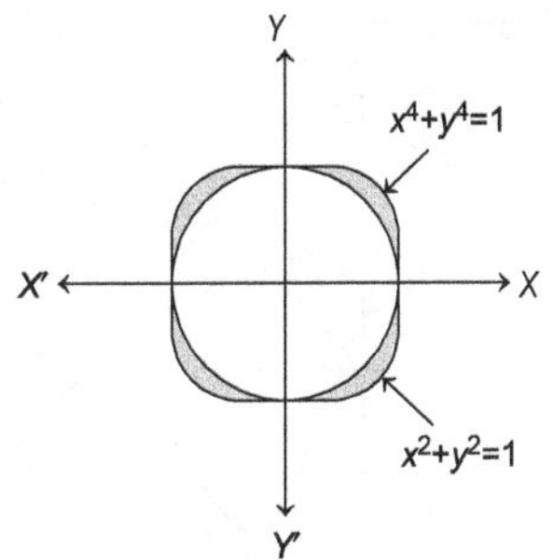

Clearly from graph.
There are many positive real number (a, b) satisfying $a^4 + b^4 < 1$ and $a^2 + b^2 > 1$.

2. *(b)* Given,
$$x^4 - x^2 + 2x - 1 = 0$$
$$\Rightarrow \quad x^4 - (x-1)^2 = 0$$
$$\Rightarrow (x^2 - x + 1)(x^2 + x - 1) = 0$$
$$\Rightarrow \quad x^2 - x + 1 = 0$$
or $$x^2 + x - 1 = 0$$
$$\Rightarrow x^2 - x + 1 = 0 \text{ has no real roots.}$$
$$\Rightarrow x^2 + x - 1 = 0 \text{ has two real roots}$$

3. *(c)* Given, $S_m = n$ and $S_n = m$
$$S_m = \frac{m}{2}[2a + (m-1)d] = n \quad ...(i)$$
$$S_n = \frac{n}{2}(2a + (n-1)d) = m \quad ...(ii)$$
On subtracting Eq. (ii) from Eq. (i), we get
$$(m-n)\,a + (m-n)(m+n-1)\frac{d}{2}$$

$$= -(m-n)$$
$$\Rightarrow \quad 2a + (m+n-1)d = -2 \quad [m \neq n]$$
$$\therefore \quad S_{m+n} = \frac{m+n}{2}(2a + (m+n-1)d)$$
$$= \frac{m+n}{2}(-2) = -(m+n)$$

4. *(b)* (I) Any pair of consistent linear equation in two variables must have a unique solution. This statement is false.
Consistent equation may have unique or infinite solution.

(II) There do not exists two consecutive integers the sum of whose square is 365. This statement is also false
$$13^2 + 14^2 = 365.$$

5. *(a)* Let
$$P(x) = a_n x^n + a_{n-1} x^{n-1} + a_{n-2} x^{n-2} + \ldots$$
$$+ a_1 x + a_0$$
$$a_0, a_1, a_2 \ldots \in I$$
Given, $P(2) = 2$ and $P(4) = 5$
$$2 = a_n 2^n + a_{n-1} 2^{n-1} + a_{n-2} 2^{n-2} + \ldots$$
$$+ a_1 2 + a_0 \ldots \text{(i)}$$
$$5 = a_n 4^n + a_{n-1} 4^{n-1} + a_{n-2} 4^{n-2} + \ldots$$
$$+ 4a_1 + a_0 \ldots \text{(ii)}$$
On subtracting Eq. (i) from Eq. (ii), we get
$$3 = a_n(4^n - 2^n) + a_{n-1}(4^{n-1} - 2^{n-1})$$
$$+ \ldots + 2a_1$$
Clearly, LHS is odd number and RHS is even number.

$\therefore$ No polynomials exists.

6. *(b)* Four digits number which is divisible by 7 are 1001, 1008, 1015, ..., 9996.

Hence, total number of such numbers
$$= 1286$$
$$\text{Median} = \frac{\left(\dfrac{N}{2}\right)^{\text{th}} \text{observation} + \left(\dfrac{N}{2}+1\right)^{\text{th}} \text{observation}}{2}$$
$$[\because N \text{ is even}]$$
$$\text{Median} = \frac{\left(\dfrac{1286}{2}\right)^{\text{th}} \text{observation} + \left(\dfrac{1286}{2}+1\right)^{\text{th}} \text{observation}}{2}$$
$$= \frac{643^{\text{th}} + 644^{\text{th}}}{2}$$
$$= \frac{(1001 + (642)7) + (1001) + (643)7}{2}$$
$$= \frac{2(1001) + 7(642 + 643)}{2}$$
$$= \frac{2(1001) + 7(1285)}{2}$$
$$= 1001 + 4497.5 = 5498.5$$

7. *(c)* Let the height and radius of cylinder are h are r, respectively.

$\therefore$ Volume of cylinder $= \pi r^2 h$

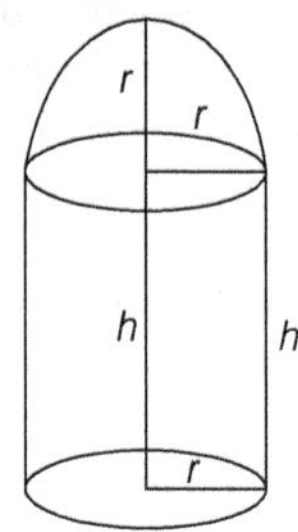

and volume of hemisphere $= \dfrac{2}{3}\pi r^3$

$\therefore$ Volume of solid $= \pi r^2 h + \dfrac{2}{3}\pi r^3$

When height of cylinder is doubled, then volume of solid $= 2\pi r^2 h + \dfrac{2}{3}\pi r^3$

$\therefore$
$$\frac{V_2}{V_1} = \frac{3}{2} = \frac{2\pi r^2 h + \dfrac{2}{3}\pi r^3}{\pi r^2 h + \dfrac{2}{3}\pi r^3}$$

$\Rightarrow$
$$\frac{2h + \dfrac{2}{3}r}{h + \dfrac{2}{3}r} = \frac{3}{2} \Rightarrow \frac{h}{2} = \frac{r}{3}$$

When the radius is doubled, then volume of solid $= 4\pi r^2 h + \dfrac{16\,\pi r^3}{3}$

$$\therefore \frac{V_2'}{V_1} = \frac{4h + \dfrac{16}{3}r}{h + \dfrac{2}{3}r} = \frac{4h + 8h}{h + h} = 6 \left[\because \frac{r}{3} = \frac{h}{2}\right]$$

Hence, volume is increased by 500%.

8. *(c)* In ΔPQR

Given, $QR^2 + PR^2 = 5PQ^2$

Median PM and QN intersect of G.

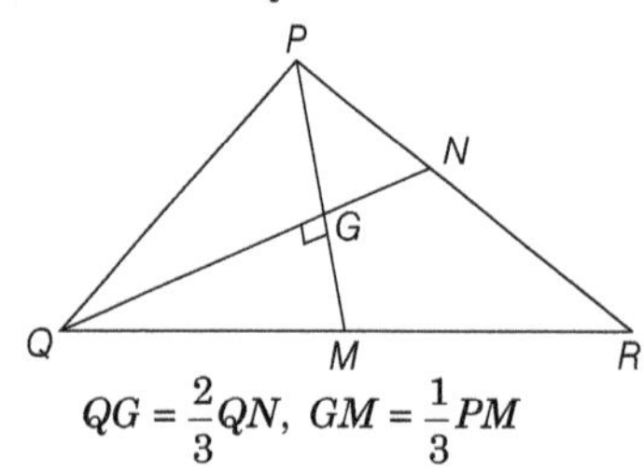

$$QG = \frac{2}{3}QN, \quad GM = \frac{1}{3}PM$$
$$\Rightarrow \quad QG^2 + GM^2 = \left(\frac{2}{3}QN\right)^2 + \left(\frac{1}{3}PM\right)^2$$
$$= \frac{4}{9}QN^2 + \frac{1}{9}PM^2$$
$$= \frac{4}{9}\left(\frac{2PQ^2 + 2QR^2 - PR^2}{4}\right)$$
$$+ \frac{1}{9}\left(\frac{2PQ^2 + 2PR^2 - QR^2}{4}\right)$$
$$= \frac{1}{9}\left[\frac{8PQ^2 + 8QR^2 - 4PR^2 + 2PQ^2 + 2PR^2 - QR^2}{4}\right]$$
$$= \frac{1}{9}\left[\frac{10PQ^2 + 7QR^2 - 2PR^2}{4}\right]$$
$$= \frac{1}{9}\left[\frac{2(5PQ^2 - PR^2) + 7QR^2}{4}\right]$$
$$= \frac{1}{9}\left[\frac{2QR^2 + 7QR^2}{4}\right] = \frac{1}{4}QR^2 = QM^2$$

$\therefore \quad OG^2 + GM^2 = QM^2$

$\therefore \quad \angle QGM = 90°$

9. *(c)* Let ΔABC
$$BC = a$$
$$AC = b$$
$$AB = c$$

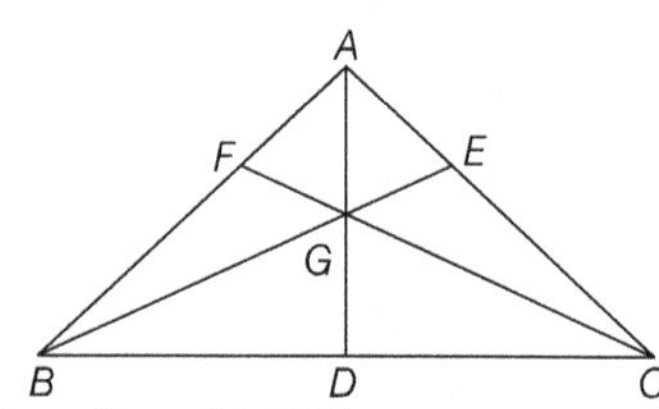

and median of ΔABC
$$AD = l$$
$$BE = m$$
$$CF = n$$

AD is median,

$\therefore \quad AD < \dfrac{AB + BC}{2}$

$\therefore \quad l < \dfrac{b + c}{2}$

Similarly, $m < \dfrac{a + b}{2}$ and $n < \dfrac{a + c}{2}$

$\therefore \quad l + m + n < a + b + c$

$\Rightarrow \quad \dfrac{l + m + n}{a + b + c} < 1 \qquad \ldots\text{(i)}$

Also in ΔBGC, $BG + GC > BC$

$\therefore \quad \dfrac{2}{3}(m + n) > a$

Similarly, $\dfrac{2}{3}(n + l) > b$ and $\dfrac{2}{3}(m + l) > c$

$\because \quad \dfrac{4}{3}(l + m + n) > a + b + c$

$\Rightarrow \quad \dfrac{l + m + n}{a + b + c} > \dfrac{3}{4} \qquad \ldots\text{(ii)}$

From Eqs. (i) and (ii), we get
$$\frac{l + m + n}{a + b + c} \in \left(\frac{3}{4}, 1\right)$$

10. *(a)* Let $P(x_0, y_0)$

Given $x^2 + y^2 \leq 1$

Let any arbitrary point $8(x, y)$.

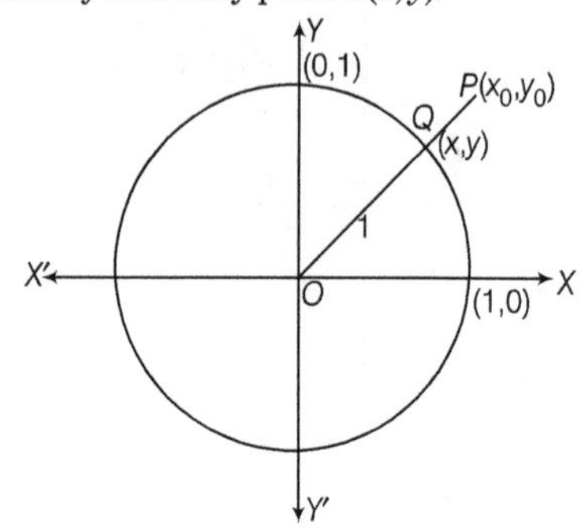

$$PQ^2 = (x - x_0)^2 + (y - y_0)^2$$
$$PQ^2 = (OP - OQ)^2$$
$$PQ^2 = (OP - OQ)^2$$
$$PQ^2 = (\sqrt{x_0^2 + x_0^2} - 1)^2 \qquad [\because OQ = 1]$$

$\therefore$ Minimimum value of PQ^2 is
$$(\sqrt{x_0^2 + y_0^2} - 1)^2$$

11. *(c)* Given, in ΔPQR
$$PQ = 3$$
Altitude $\quad RS = \sqrt{3}$
$\Rightarrow \qquad PS = QR$

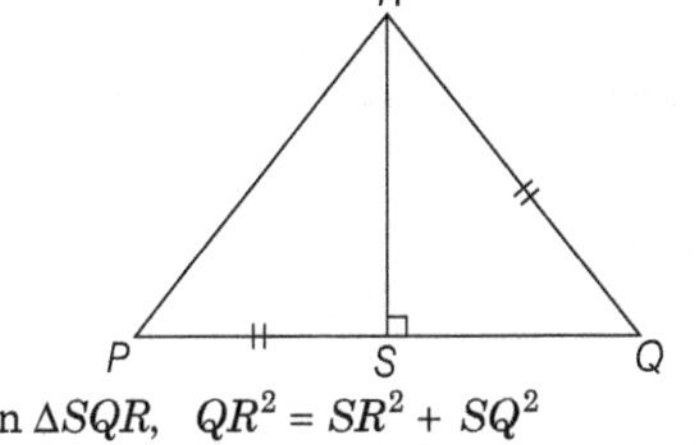

In $\Delta SQR, \quad QR^2 = SR^2 + SQ^2$
$$PS^2 = (\sqrt{3})^2 + (QP - PS)^2$$
$$[\because SQ = PQ - PS]$$
$$PS^2 = 3 + (3 - PS)^2$$
$$PS^2 = 3 + 9 - 6PS + PS^2 \Rightarrow PS = 2$$

In ΔPRS,
$$PR^2 = PS^2 + RS^2 = (2)^2 + (\sqrt{3})^2 = 4 + 3$$
$$PR = \sqrt{7}$$

12. *(d)* Total number of students = 50

Average marks of student = 47.5

$\therefore$ Total marks of students
$$= 50 \times 47.5 = 2375$$

Now, the student get integer marks Hence, the maximum number of students we will divide total mark by 48.
$$\therefore \qquad \frac{2375}{48} = 49$$

13. *(b)* Given number,
$$n = 15^2 \times 5^{18}$$
$$n = 3^2 \times 5^2 \times 5^{18}$$
$$n = 9 \times 5^{20}$$

Taking log base 10 both side
$$\log_{10} n = \log_{10} 9 + \log_{10} 5^{20}$$
$$= 2\log_{10} 3 + 20\log_{10} 5$$
$$= 2 \times 0.4771 + 20 \times (1 - 0.3010)$$
$$= 14 \text{ characters value}$$

Hence, the number have 15 digits

S = Sum of digits of the number

Now, n has last digit is 5.

$\therefore$ Minimum value of $S = 1 + 5 = 6$

Maximum value of $S = 9 \times 14 + 5$
$$= 126 + 5 = 131$$
$$\therefore \quad 6 \leq S < 140$$

14. *(a)* Given, PQR is an acute angle triangle.
$$PQ < QR$$

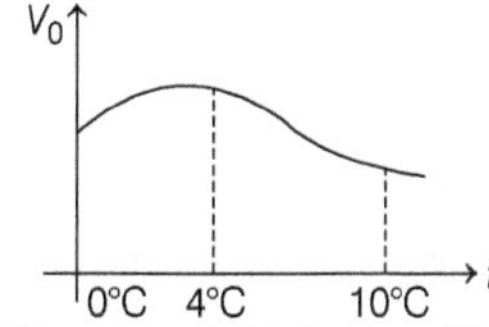

$$\angle QRP < \angle QPR$$
$$PQ_3 = \frac{1}{2} PR$$
$$PQ_2 : Q_2 R = r : p$$
$$PQ_2 = \left(\frac{r}{r + p}\right) PR$$

But $\qquad r < p$
$$PQ_2 < \frac{1}{2} PR$$

Comparison between altitude and angle bisector
$$\angle QPQ_2 + \angle PQ_2Q + \angle PQQ_2 = \angle RQQ_2$$
$$+ \angle QQ_2R + \angle QRQ_2$$
$$\therefore \angle PQQ_2 = \angle RQQ_2$$
[since, QQ_2 is angle bisector of $\angle Q$]
$$\angle QPQ_2 + \angle PQ_2Q = \angle QQ_2R + \angle QRQ_2$$
$$\therefore PQ < QR \text{ the } \angle QPQ_2 < \angle QRQ_2$$
Hence, $\angle QQ_2P < \angle QQ_2R$

But $\angle QQ_2P + \angle QQ_2R = 180°$

Hence, $\angle QQ_2P < 90°$ and $\angle QQ_2R > 90°$

$\because$ Foot from Q to side PR lie inside ΔPQQ_2
$$\Rightarrow \qquad PQ_1 < PQ_2 < PQ_3$$

15. *(a)* Given, $(a - 8)^2 - (b - 7)^2 = 5$
$$\Rightarrow \quad (a - 8 + b - 7)\,(a - 8 - b + 7) = 5$$
$$\Rightarrow \qquad (a + b - 15)\,(a - b - 1) = 5$$

There are four case
$$a + b - 15 = 5;\ a - b - 1 = 1 \qquad \dots \text{(i)}$$
$$a + b - 15 = 1;\ a - b - 1 = 5 \qquad \dots \text{(ii)}$$
$$a + b - 15 = -5;\ a - b - 1 = -1 \qquad \dots \text{(iii)}$$
$$a + b - 15 = -1;\ a - b - 1 = -5 \qquad \dots \text{(iv)}$$

On solving, we get

(i) $a = 11, b = 9$ \qquad (ii) $a = 11, b = 5$

(iii) $a = 5, b = 5$ \qquad (iv) $a = 5, b = 9$

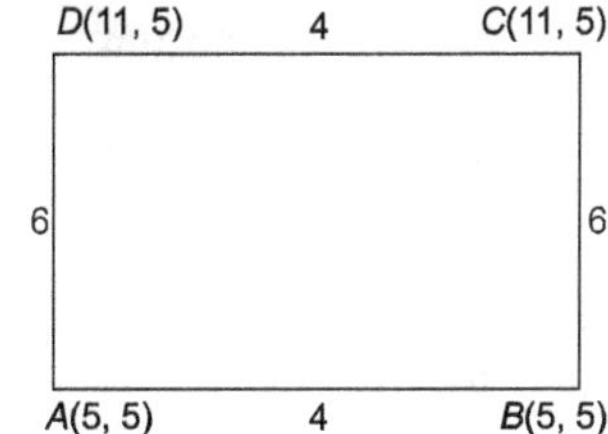

$\therefore$ Perimeter $= 2(4 + 6) = 20$

16. *(a)* As temperature of water is increased from 0°C to 10°C, density of water initially increases upto a maximum at 4°C and then it reduces.

So, buoyant force on block of wood also increases till temperature reaches 4°C and then decreases from 4°C to 10°C.

Hence, volume of block above water also increases upto 4°C and then decreases from 4°C to 10°C.

$\therefore$ Variation of V_0 *versus* t as shown below.

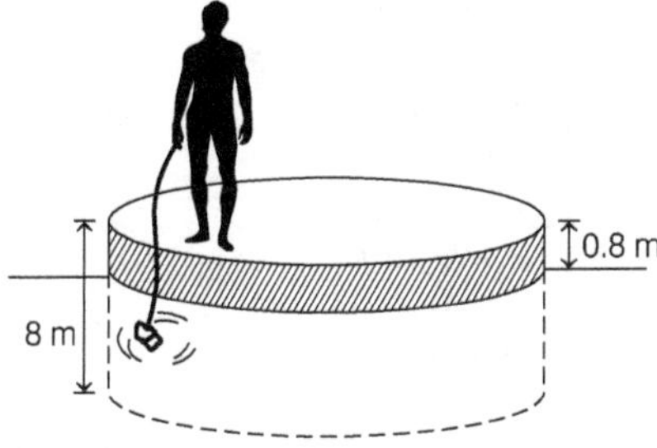

17. *(c)* Fraction of thickness of ice block out of water is
$$x = 1 - \left(\frac{\rho_{\text{ice}}}{\rho_{\text{water}}}\right) = 1 - \frac{0.9}{1} \text{ or } x = 0.1$$

So, minimum length of rope required $\approx$ thickness of ice $\times$ 0.1 = 8 $\times$ 0.1 = 0.8 m.

Hence, nearest option is 0.9 m.

18. *(d)* When box with hole is in free fall, both water and box cover equal distance downwards in equal time.

Hence, no water comes out of hole in free fall of box.

19. *(c)* Water evaporated in two hours
$$= m = 2\,\text{h} \times 20\,\text{g/h}$$
$$= 40\,\text{g} = 40 \times 10^{-3}\,\text{kg}$$

Heat absorbed by water during evaporation is

Q = Mass evaporated $\times$ Latent heat
$$Q = mL \qquad \dots\text{(i)}$$

Assuming this heat is taken entirely from water in earthen pot, if ΔT is decrease of temperature of pot then,
$$Q = Ms\Delta T \qquad \dots\text{(ii)}$$

where, M = mass of water in pot and s = specific heat of water.

Equating Eqs. (i) and (ii), we get
$$mL = Ms\Delta T$$
$$\text{or } \Delta T = \frac{m}{M} \times \frac{L}{s} = \frac{40 \times 10^{-3}}{4} \times 540 = 5.4°C$$

20. *(d)* As emergent ray is parallel to incident ray, deviation angle δ is 180°.

But $\qquad \delta = 360° - 2\theta$

where, θ = angle between inclined mirrors.

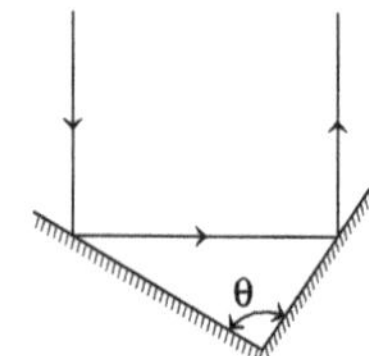

So, $\qquad 360° - 2\theta = 180°$

or $\qquad 2\theta = 180° \Rightarrow \theta = 90°$

21. *(a)* From principle of thermometry,

$\dfrac{T - T_{\text{LFP}}}{T_{\text{UFP}} - T_{\text{LFP}}}$ = a constant for every

thermometric scale.

Now, for any temperature L on a thermometer designed with given liquid and equivalent temperature C on centigrade scale, we have

$\left(\dfrac{L - T_{\text{LFP}}}{T_{\text{UFP}} - T_{\text{LFP}}} \right)_{\substack{\text{Liquid} \\ \text{based} \\ \text{scale}}} = \left(\dfrac{C - T_{\text{LFP}}}{T_{\text{UFP}} - T_{\text{LFP}}} \right)_{\substack{\text{Centigrade} \\ \text{scale}}}$

$\Rightarrow \qquad \dfrac{L - (-50)}{150 - (-50)} = \dfrac{C - 0}{100 - 0}$

$\dfrac{L + 50}{150 + 50} = \dfrac{C}{100}$

$\Rightarrow \qquad L + 50 = 2C$

Now at 0°L, centigrade scale reading will be

$0 + 50 = 2C$ or $C = \dfrac{50}{2} = 25°$ L

and at 100° L, centigrade scale reading will be

$100 + 50 = 2C$ or $C = \dfrac{150}{2} = 75°$ L

22. *(b)* An alpha-volt (α-V) is the energy acquired by an α-particle (charge 2e units) when accelerated by a potential difference of 1 V.

$\therefore \qquad 1\,\alpha\text{-}V = q\,(\Delta V)$

$\qquad\qquad = 2e \times 1V = 2\,eV$

23. *(d)* If Q is charge contained in L length of beam of area A, then

$\qquad L \times A \times \rho = Q$

where, ρ = charge density of beam.

So, $\qquad \rho = \dfrac{Q}{L \times A} = \dfrac{Q/t}{L/t \times A} = \dfrac{I}{v \times A}$

$\qquad = \dfrac{500 \times 10^{-6}}{3 \times 10^{7} \times 1.50 \times 10^{-6}}$

$\qquad = \dfrac{5}{3 \times 1.5} \times 10^{-5} = 1.1 \times 10^{-5} \ \text{Cm}^{-3}$

24. *(a)* A lunar eclipse occurs only on a full moon day.

So, option (a) is incorrect.

25. *(d)* Intensity of radiation (mainly visible light) emitted from surface of a star is proportional to its area.

So, $\qquad I \propto A$ or $I = kA$

where, k = constant.

Now, if I_0 = intensity of parent star.

Then, $I_0 = k\pi\,(100\,R)^2 = k\,\pi\,R^2 \times 10000$

When exoplanet is in front of star, observed intensity will be minimum. Let intensity minimum is $I_{\min}$, then

$\qquad I_{\min} = k\,[\pi\,(100\,R)^2 - \pi\,R^2]$

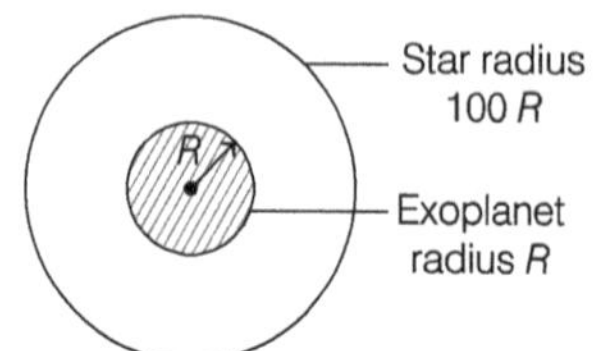

$\Rightarrow \qquad I_{\min} = k\pi R^2\,(10000 - 1)$

$\qquad\qquad = k\pi R^2 \times 9999$

So, $\qquad \dfrac{I_{\min}}{I_0} = \dfrac{k\pi R^2 \times 9999}{k\pi R^2 \times 10000}$

$\Rightarrow \qquad I_{\min} = I_0 \times 0.9999$

26. *(b)* When current flows through a conductor of tapered cross-section, current flow through every section remains constant.

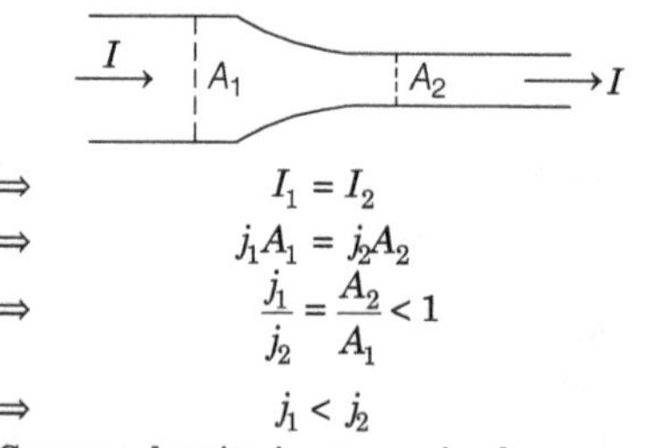

$\Rightarrow \qquad I_1 = I_2$

$\Rightarrow \qquad j_1 A_1 = j_2 A_2$

$\Rightarrow \qquad \dfrac{j_1}{j_2} = \dfrac{A_2}{A_1} < 1$

$\Rightarrow \qquad j_1 < j_2$

Current density increases in the narrow region.

Also, $\qquad j = nev_d$

$\Rightarrow \qquad nev_{d_1} < nev_{d_2}$

$\Rightarrow \qquad v_{d_1} < v_{d_2}$

Drift velocity increases in the narrow region.

and $\qquad j = \dfrac{E}{\rho}$

where, ρ = resistivity of material.

$\Rightarrow \qquad \dfrac{E_1}{\rho} < \dfrac{E_2}{\rho} \Rightarrow E_1 < E_2$

Electric field magnitude increases in the narrow region.

27. (No option is matching)

In late afternoon rainbow is visible in east side when light of sun in west side is reflected and refracted by a layer of water droplets.

Rainbow is circular because locous of reflected rays reaching eye of observer is a circle. Its roundness is not due to roundness of earth.

There is no rainbow on moon due to lack of atmosphere.

In case of a primary rainbow, violet colour is on inside and red colour is on outside of arc.

In case of a secondary rainbow, red colour is on inside and violet colour is on outside of arc.

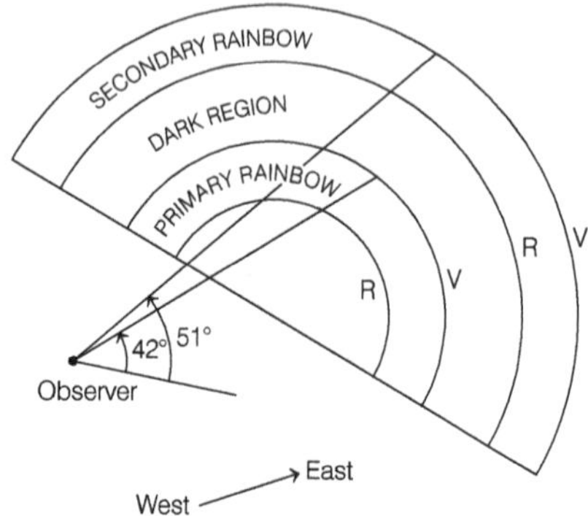

So, none of the option is correct. Option (b) is correct, if only secondary rainbow is considered.

28. *(c)* Consider the given diagram,

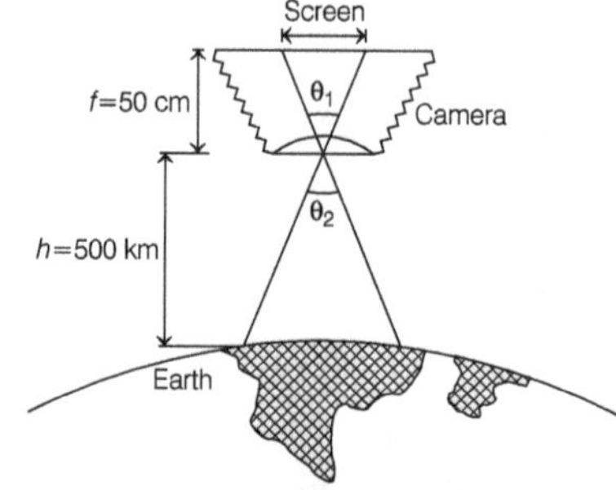

Assuming area observed and screen both circular, we have

$\qquad \theta_1 = \theta_2 \Rightarrow \dfrac{d_1}{f} = \dfrac{d_2}{h} \Rightarrow \dfrac{d_2}{d_1} = \dfrac{h}{f}$

where, d_1 = diameter of camera screen

and d_2 = diameter of area on earth.

Now, $\dfrac{\text{area observed on earth}}{\text{area of screen}} = \dfrac{A_0}{A}$

$\qquad = \dfrac{\left(\dfrac{\pi \cdot d_2^2}{4} \right)}{\left(\dfrac{\pi \cdot d_1^2}{4} \right)} = \dfrac{d_2^2}{d_1^2}$

$$\Rightarrow \quad \frac{A_0}{A} = \left(\frac{h}{f_1}\right)^2 = \left(\frac{500 \times 10^{+3}}{50 \times 10^{-2}}\right)^2$$

$$= (10 \times 10^3 \times 10^2)^2 = (10^6)^2 = 10^{12}$$

29. *(d)* A cylindrical lens produces erect and laterally inverted image.
So, image appears as shown below.

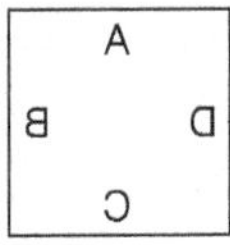

30. *(a)* For the ball, we have
$$u = 45 \text{ ms}^{-1}, \ g = -10 \text{ ms}^{-2}$$
Now using, $v^2 - u^2 = 2gh$, we have
$$v^2 = (45)^2 - 20h$$
$$\Rightarrow \quad v = \sqrt{2025 - 20h}$$
At $v = 0, \ h = \dfrac{2025}{20} \approx 101 \text{ m}$

at $h = 0, v = 45 \text{ ms}^{-1}$

As velocity decreases with height, slope of v-h graph must be negative at all points.
Hence, correct graph is (a).

31. *(a)* Given, density of water = 1.0 g mL^{-1}

         volume of water = 250 mL.
$\therefore$ Mass of water = density $\times$ volume
$$= 1.0 \times 250 = 250 \text{ g}$$
18 g of water contains
$$= 6.023 \times 10^{23} \text{ molecules}$$
$\therefore$ 250 g of water contains
$$= \frac{6.023 \times 10^{23}}{18} \times 250$$
$$= 83.65 \times 10^{23} \text{ molecules}$$

32. *(a)* Dil.aqueous solution of NH_3 is NH_4OH.
$$NH_4OH \rightleftharpoons NH_4^+ + OH^-$$
On adding solid ammonium chloride
$$NH_4Cl \longrightarrow NH_4^+ + Cl^-$$
The reaction moves backward due to common ion effect. The concentration of OH^- decreases and hence the pH decreases.

33. *(d)* Given, $K_{sp} = 1 \times 10^{-10}$
$$BaSO_4 \rightleftharpoons \underset{S}{Ba^{2+}} + \underset{S}{SO_4^{2-}}$$
Let the solubity of Ba^{2+} and SO_4^{2-} be S
$\therefore \qquad K_{sp} = S^2$
$$1 \times 10^{-10} = S^2$$
$$S = 10^{-5} \text{ mol/L}$$
Thus, solubility of $BaSO_4$ in pure water (in g/L)

Solubility (in mol/L) $\times$ Molecular weight
$$= 233 \times 10^{-5} = 2.3 \times 10^{-3}$$

34. *(b)* Consider the following statements.
(I) According to Pauli's exclusion principle, no two electrons in an atom can have the same set of four quantum numbers.
Thus, statement (a) is correct.
(II) The maximum number of electrons in the shell with principle quantum number, $n = 2n^2$.
Thus, statement (b) is incorrect.
(III) Electrons in an orbital must have opposite spin, i.e. $m_s = +\dfrac{1}{2}$ and $\dfrac{-1}{2}$. Thus, statement (c) is correct.
(IV) According to Aufbau principle, in the ground state of the atoms, the orbitals are filled in order of their increasing energies.
Thus, statement (d) is correct.

35. *(d)* From ideal gas equation
$$pV = nRT$$
maximum number of moles in container,
$$n = \frac{pV}{RT} = \frac{2 \times 2.24}{0.0821 \times 298}$$
$$= 0.18 \text{ moles}$$
Maximum weight of N_2 in container
$$= 0.183 \times 28 = 5.127 \text{ g}$$
At 5.127 g exploding can occur. Thus, it must be less than 5.127. Thus, the maximum amount of nitrogen that can be safely put in this container at 298 temperature and exert pressure less than 2 atm will be closest to 4.2 g.

36. *(a)*

This reaction is Friedal-Craft acylation. In this reaction, benzene reacts with acyl halide or acid anhydride in the presence of Lewis acid like $AlCl_3$ to yield acylbenzene.

37. *(c)*

Here, the marked carbon (*) is chiral as it has 4 different groups attached to it.

Here, the marked carbon (*) is achiral as it has 2 similar ethyl group attached to it.

38. *(b)*

In the given compound most acidic proton will be N^b — H. This is because its conjugate base will get resonance stabilised and the most nucleophilic nitrogen will be N^c. This is because the lone pair of electrons present on this N is localised over sp^3-hybrid orbital.

39. *(a)* The reaction between haloalkane and $AgNO_3$ gives carbocation intermediate. So, more easily it will be formed, more readily it will react to give precipitate.

In the given compound

Cl^a is easily lost from this compound and carbocation formation takes place readily. This is because this Cl^a is closest to electronegative atom O, which will attract the electron density towards itself and readily leaves C—Cl^a bond.
Hence, it will most readily react with $AgNO_3$ to give precipitate.

40. *(d)* The specie which follows Huckel's rule $(4n + 2)\pi$ will be most stable species.

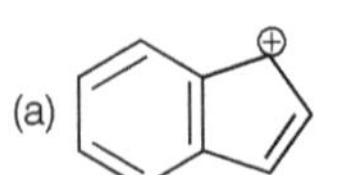 and 

(a)

It has $8\pi e^-$s, doesn't follow Huckel's rule

It has $4\pi e^-$s, doesn't follow Huckel's rule

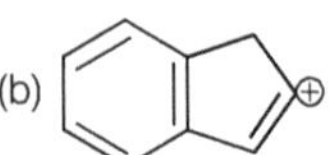

(b)

It has $8\pi e^-$s, doesn't follow Huckel's rule

It has $2\pi e^-$s, follows Huckel's rule

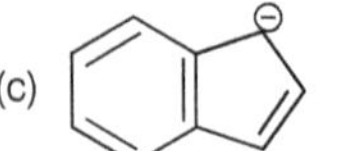

(c)

It has $10\pi e^-$s, follows Huckel's rule

It has $4\pi e^-$s, doesn't follow Huckel's rule

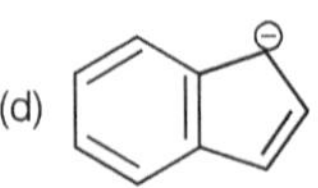

(d)

It has $10\pi e^-$s, follows Huckel's rule

It has $2\pi e^-$s, follows Huckel's rule

As both the species in option (d) follow Huckel's rule. Thus, it is correct option.

41. *(a)* As the atomic number increases, the energy of orbital decreases. This is because the atomic radii decreases (nuclear charge increases) with increase in atomic number. The atomic number of H, Li, Na and K respectively, are 1, 3, 11 and 19. Thus, the correct order of energy of $2s$-orbitals is

$$K < Na < Li < H.$$

42. *(c)* The hybridisation of any compound can be calculated as,

$$X = \frac{1}{2} \quad \text{[Valence electrons}$$

+ Number of monoatomic ∓ Anion/cations]

∴ For XeF_4 $(X) = \frac{1}{2}(8 + 4 - 0) = 6$

∴ The hybridisation is sp^3d^2.

43. *(c)* In $Cr_2O_7^{2-}$,

Let the oxidation state of Cr be x

∴ $2(x) + 7(-2) = -2$

$2x - 14 = -2$

$2x = 12$

$x = +6$

In ClO_3^-,

Let the oxidation state of Cl be x

∴ $1(x) + 3(-2) = -1$

$x - 6 = -1$

$x = +5$

44. *(c)* As, a filter paper soaked in salt X turns brown when exposed to HNO_3 vapour, then salt X must be a strong reducing agent which will reduce HNO_3 to NO_2 (brown gas).

Among the given salt, KI is the strongest reducing agent. Thus, salt X is KI.

$$2KI + 4HNO_3 \longrightarrow I_2 + 2NO_2 + 2KNO_3 + 2H_2O$$

45. *(b)* The role of haemoglobin is to transport oxygen from lungs or gills to different parts of the body. There it releases the oxygen to permit aerobic respirisation to provide energy to power the functions of the organism in the process called metabolism.

46. *(c)* Penicillin is a secondary metabolite. Secondary metabolites are organic compounds produced by bacteria, fungi or plants which are not directly involved in the normal growth, development or reproduction of the organism, e.g., antibiotics like penicillin, streptomycin, etc. Rest molecules like ethanol, lactate and citric acid are primary metabolites.

47. *(b)* Lecithin is a phospholipid that is important in cell structure and metabolism. Lecithins are composed of phosphoric acid, cholines, esters of glycerol and two fatty acids; the chain length, position and degree of unsaturation of these fatty acids vary and this variation results in different lecithins with different biological functions.

48. *(a)* Pure water at standard temperature and atmospheric pressure has a water potential of zero. As solute is added, its value becomes more negative. This causes water potential to decrease. Water potential is the measure of the potential energy in water. It is denoted by the Greek letter ψ *(Psi)* and is expressed in units of pressure (pressure is a form of energy) called Mega Pascals (MPa).

49. *(d)* An action potential is generated by the rapid influx of Na^+ ions followed by a slightly slower efflux of K^+ ions. The action potential is the mechanism by which nerve cells communicate and conduct information and muscle cells are induced to contract.

50. *(b)* Erythropoietin (EPO) is a hormone produced by the kidney that promotes the formation of red blood cells by the bone marrow. Chemically, erythropoietin is a protein with an attached sugar (a glycoprotein). It is produced by kidney cells when the body

experiences low oxygen level. The resulting rise in red-blood cells increases the oxygen carrying capacity of the blood.

51. *(a)* Tendrils are the modifications of stem or leaf. The tendril is a thread-like, twisting, clinging growth on the vines of the plant that enables it to attach itself to another object or another plant for support. Plants such as grapes, peas and cucumbers have tendrils.

52. *(c)* Ribosomes consist of two biomolecules (i.e. RNA and proteins). The small ribosomal subunits which read the RNA, and large subunits which join amino acids to form a polypeptide chain. Each subunit comprises one or more ribosomal RNA (rRNA) molecules and a variety of ribosomal proteins (r-protein).

53. *(d)* Microtubule does not play a role in skeletal muscle. Microtubules are hollow fibrous shafts whose main function is to help support and give shape to the cell. They also serve a transportation function as they are the routes upon which organelles move through the cell.

54. *(b)* In the stratosphere, ozone is created primarily by ultraviolet radiation. When high energy ultraviolet rays strike ordinary oxygen molecules (O_2), they split the molecule into two single oxygen atoms, known as atomic oxygen.

$$O_2 \rightarrow O + O$$

A freed oxygen then combines with another oxygen molecule to form a molecule of ozone (O_3).

55. *(a)* Trypsinogen is an inactive substance secreted by the pancreas, from which the digestive enzyme trypsin is formed in the duodenum. Trypsinogen is converted into its active form trypsin by an enzyme enterokinase. This results in the subsequent activation of pancreatic digestive enzymes.

56. *(b)* Salamanders are a group of amphibians typically characterised by a lizard-like appearance with slender bodies, blunt snouts, short limbs and a tail. Salamanders breath through their skin and the thin membranes in the mouth and throat.

57. *(c)* Mature human erythrocytes (Red blood cells) lack a nucleus. The absence of a nucleus is an adaptation of the red blood cell for its role. It allows the RBC to contain more haemoglobin and therefore carry more oxygen molecules. It also allows the cell to have its distinctive biconcave shape which aids diffusion.

58. *(d)* The first enzyme that the food encounters in the digestive system is amylase. Digestion begins in the mouth with the secretion of saliva and its digestive enzymes. Saliva contains the digestive enzyme amylase, which works on carbohydrate, starch like breads, potatoes or pasta to help break them down into simple sugars.

59. *(c)* Glycoproteins are formed in the Golgi apparatus of the cell. Glycoproteins are proteins that contain covalently attached sugar residues. Glycoproteins are present at the surface of cells where they function as membrane proteins and play a role in cell to cell interactions.

60. *(a)* An example of nastic movement in plants is folding up of the leaves of *Mimosa pudica*. Nastic movements in plants are reversible and repeatable movements in response to a stimulus whose direction is determined by the anatomy of the plant. The leaves of the *Mimosa pudica* fold up when touched and returns to full leaf in a few minutes. The leaves of the *Mimosa* achieve this rapid folding by a change in turgor pressure.

61. *(b)* Given, $n^2 - 10n - 36$

n is a natural number.

$\therefore$ Product of its digits is ≥ 0

$\therefore n^2 - 10n - 36 \geq 0$

$$n = \frac{10 \pm \sqrt{100 + 144}}{2}$$

$$n = 5 \pm \sqrt{61}$$

$\therefore \qquad n \in (-\infty, 5 - \sqrt{61}) \cup (5 + \sqrt{61}, \infty)$

But n is positive integer.

$\therefore \qquad n \geq 13$

When n is two digits numbers, then maximum product $= 9 \times 9 = 81$

$\therefore \qquad n^2 - 10n - 36 \leq 81$

$\qquad n^2 - 10n - 117 \leq 0$

$\therefore \qquad n \in [5 - \sqrt{142}, 5 + \sqrt{142}]$

n is taken two digit number.

$\therefore \qquad n \in [13,17) = 13, 14, 15, 16$

$\therefore$ Product of digits $= 3, 4, 5, 6$

When put $n = 13$

$\qquad 13^2 - 10 \times 13 - 36 = 169 - 166 = 3$

$n = 13$ satisfies

62. *(c)* We have, m is 5-digits number using digits 1, 2, 3, 4, 5 with repetition such that sum of two adjacent digit is odd and n is 5-digits number using digits 1, 2,

3, 4, 5 without repetitions such that sum of any two adjacent digits is odd.

Sum of two digits are odd if one is even and other is odd.

Even = 2, 4

Odd = 1, 3, 5

Case **I** Digit is repeated.

Two possibilities

(a) odd even odd even odd

$\qquad = 3 \times 2 \times 3 \times 2 \times 3 = 108$

(b) even odd even odd even

$\qquad = 2 \times 3 \times 2 \times 3 \times 2 = 72$

$\therefore \qquad m = 108 + 72 = 180$

Case **II** Digit is not repeated.

The possibility of arrangement is

odd even odd even odd

$\qquad = 3 \times 2 \times 2 \times 1 \times 1 = 12$

$\qquad n = 12$

$\therefore \qquad \dfrac{m}{n} = \dfrac{180}{12} = 15$

63. *(b)* Let height and radius of cone is h and r respectively, $h, r \in I$

Given volume of cone = Surface area of cone

$$\frac{1}{3} \pi r^2 h = \pi r l + \pi r^2$$

$\Rightarrow \qquad \dfrac{1}{3} \pi r^2 h = \pi r \sqrt{h^2 + r^2} + \pi r^2$

$\Rightarrow \qquad \dfrac{1}{3} r h = \sqrt{h^2 + r^2} + r \qquad [r \neq 0]$

$\Rightarrow \qquad r h - 3r = 3\sqrt{h^2 + r^2}$

$\Rightarrow r^2 h^2 + 9r^2 - 6hr^2 = 9h^2 + 9r^2$

$\Rightarrow h^2(r^2 - 9) = 6hr^2$

$\Rightarrow \qquad h = \dfrac{6r^2}{r^2 - 9}$

$\Rightarrow \qquad h = 6\left(\dfrac{r^2}{r^2 - 9}\right)$

$\Rightarrow \qquad h = 6 + \dfrac{54}{r^2 - 9}$

h and r are integer.

$\because r^2 - 9$ is a factor of 54.

$\therefore r^2 - 9 = 1, 2, 3, 6, 9, 18, 27, 54$

$\qquad r^2 = 10, 11, 12, 15, 18, 27, 36, 63$

$\therefore \qquad r = 6$ only possible value.

$\therefore \qquad h = 6 + \dfrac{54}{36 - 9}$

$\qquad = 6 + 2 = 8$

$\therefore \qquad r = 6, h = 8$

64. *(d)* Given, $ABCD$ is a square.

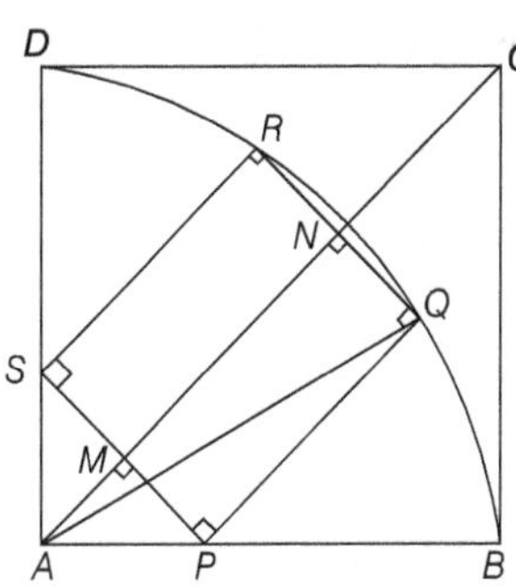

$\qquad \angle CAP = \angle MAP = 45°$

$\therefore \qquad AM = MP = QN$

$PQRS$ is a square,

$\because \qquad MN = PQ = PS$

$\qquad PS = 2PM = 2AM$

$\qquad AN = AM + MN = 3AM$

In $\triangle ABQ$,

$\qquad AQ^2 = AN^2 + QN^2$

$\qquad 1 = (3AM)^2 + AM^2 \ [\because AQ = 1]$

$\qquad 10 AM^2 = 1$

$\qquad AM^2 = 1$

$\qquad AM^2 = \dfrac{1}{10}$

Area of square $PQRS = PS^2$

$\qquad = 4AM^2 = \dfrac{4}{10} = \dfrac{2}{5}$

$\therefore \qquad \dfrac{\text{Area square } PQRS}{\text{Area of square } ABCD} = \dfrac{2}{5}$

65. *(b)* We have,

$ABCD$ is a trapezium.

AB is parallel to CD.

Area of trapezium = 12

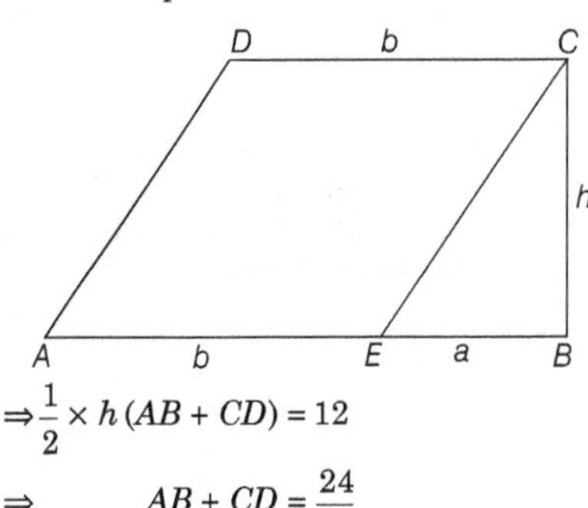

$\Rightarrow \dfrac{1}{2} \times h\,(AB + CD) = 12$

$\Rightarrow \qquad AB + CD = \dfrac{24}{h}$

Sides and height of trapezium are integer.

$\therefore h$ is a factor of 24

$h = 1, 2, 3, 4, 6, 8, 12, 24$

$\qquad AB + CD = 24, 12, 8, 6, 4, 3, 2, 1$

But $AB + CD > h$

$\qquad AB + CD = 24, 12, 8, 6$

In ΔBEC,

BEC is a right angled triangle.

$\therefore h$ must be 3 and 4

When $h = 3$, $BE = 4$, $CE = 5$

$$AB + CD = 8$$
$$AE + BE + AE = 8$$
$$2AE = 8 - BE = 8 - 4$$
$$AE = 2$$

$\therefore AB = 4 + 2 = 6$, $CD = 2$

$\therefore |AB - CD| = |6 - 2| = 4$

66. *(b)* Let m gram of steam is condensed in the process of heating mixture from 25°C to 70°C.

Then,

Heat lost by steam = Heat gained by mixture

$\Rightarrow$ Heat of condensation of steam + Heat given by water formed = Heat gained by mixture

$\Rightarrow \quad m \cdot L + ms_w \Delta T = M \cdot s_m \Delta T$

$\Rightarrow \quad mL + ms_w (100 - 70)$
$$= 500 \times s_w \times (70 - 25)$$

$\Rightarrow m = \dfrac{500 \times s_w \times 45}{L + 30 s_w}$

$\Rightarrow m = \dfrac{500 \times 45}{\left(\dfrac{L}{s_w} + 30\right)}$

$\Rightarrow m = \dfrac{500 \times 45}{(540 + 30)} \approx 40 \,\text{g}$

Now, in 1 min, 50 g of steam is condensed.

$\therefore$ 40 g of steam will be condensed in time t_0,

$t_0 = \dfrac{40 \times 60}{50} \,\text{s} = 48 \,\text{s}$

Nearest answer is 45 s.

67. *(c)* As drummer does not hear any echo this means time between two successive wavefronts is equal to time in which a wavefront reaches back to drummer.

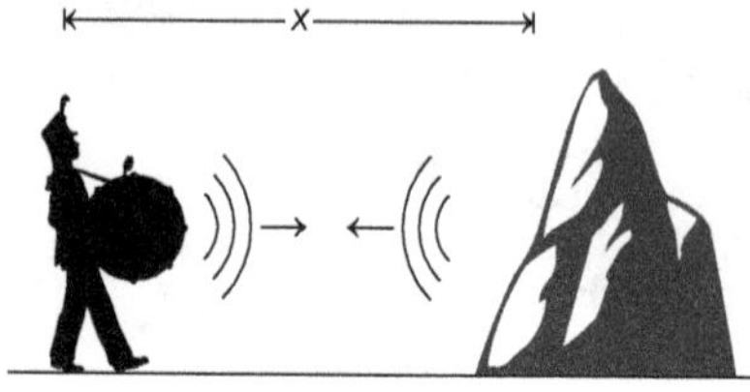

Distance covered by sound = $2x$

If v = speed of sound, then

$\dfrac{2x}{v}$ = time interval between two successive wavefronts.

So, we have

In case I, $\quad \dfrac{2x}{v} = \dfrac{60}{40}$ ...(i)

In case II, $\dfrac{2(x - 90)}{v} = \dfrac{60}{60}$ ...(ii)

Substituting for x from Eq. (i) in Eq. (ii), we get

$$2x - 180 = v$$
$\Rightarrow \quad \dfrac{3}{2}v - 180 = v$

$\Rightarrow \quad v = 360 \,\text{ms}^{-1}$

68. *(b)* Apparent depth d in case of more than one medium is

$$d = \dfrac{d_1}{\mu_1} + \dfrac{d_2}{\mu_2} + \ldots \quad \ldots(i)$$

where, d_1 and d_2 are the thickness of slabs of medium with refractive index μ_1 and μ_2, respectively.

Here, $d_1 = 5 \,\text{cm}$, $\mu_1 = 1.33$

$$d_2 = 2 \,\text{cm}, \mu_2 = 1.5$$

Substituting these values in Eq. (i), we get

Apparent depth, $d = \dfrac{5}{1.33} + \dfrac{2}{1.5}$

$$= 5.088 \,\text{cm} = 5.1 \,\text{cm}$$

69. *(b)* As α-particle is free to move, initial kinetic energy of system will be

$$k_i = \dfrac{1}{2}\mu v^2$$

where, μ = reduced mass of system

$$= \dfrac{m \cdot 4m}{m + 4m}.$$

Now, by energy conservation, we have

Initial kinetic energy = Potential energy at minimum separation r

$$\dfrac{1}{2}\left(\dfrac{m \cdot 4m}{m + 4m}\right)v^2 = \dfrac{1}{4\pi\varepsilon_0} \cdot \dfrac{2e^2}{r}$$

$\Rightarrow \quad r = \dfrac{5e^2}{4\pi\varepsilon_0 mv^2}$

70. *(b)* Given, potential function for the oscillating particle is

$$V(x) = \begin{cases} \dfrac{k(x + a)^2}{2}, & x < 0 \\[2mm] \dfrac{k(x - a)^2}{2}, & x > 0 \end{cases}$$

So, potential energy of the particle (mass m) is

$$U(x) = \begin{cases} \dfrac{km(x + a)^2}{2}, & x < 0 \\[2mm] \dfrac{km(x - a)^2}{2}, & x < 0 \end{cases}$$

$$\dfrac{dU}{dx} = \begin{cases} km(x + a), & x < 0 \\[1mm] km(x - a), & x > 0 \end{cases}$$

If $\dfrac{dU}{dx} = 0$, when $x = \pm a$.

Now, $\dfrac{d^2U}{dx^2} = km > 0$

So, particle is in unstable equilibrium at $x = \pm a$.

Hence, particle is unbounded for $-a > x$ and $x > a$.

In region, $-a \le x \le a$, time period of particle reduces from a maximum.

So, correct graph is (b).

71. *(c)* The bond order can be calculated as

$$\text{B.O} = \dfrac{1}{2}(N_b - N_a)$$

where, N_b = electrons in bonding orbitals

N_a = electrons in antibonding orbitals.

(a) CO and O_2^{2-}

The electronic configuration of CO (14) is

$\sigma 1s^2\ \sigma^* 1s^2\ \sigma 2s^2\ \sigma^* 2s^2\ \sigma^* 2p_z^2\ \pi\, 2p_x^2\ \pi 2p^2 y$

$\therefore \quad \text{B.O} = \dfrac{1}{2}(10 - 4) = \dfrac{6}{2} = 3$

The electronic configuration of O_2^{2-} (18) is

$\sigma 1s^2\ \sigma^* 1s^2\ \sigma 2s^2\ \sigma^* 2s^2 \sigma 2p_z^2\ \pi 2p_x^2$
$\pi 2py^2\ \pi^* 2p_x^2\ \pi^* 2py^2$

$$\text{B.O} = \dfrac{1}{2}(10 - 8) = 1$$

(b) O_2^- and CO

The electronic configuration of O_2^- (17) is

$\sigma 1s^2\ \sigma^* 1s^2\ \sigma 2s^2\ \sigma^* 2s^2 \sigma 2p_z^2\ \pi 2p_x^2$
$\pi 2p_y^2\ \pi^* 2p_x^2\ \pi^* 2p_y^1$

$$\text{B.O} = \dfrac{1}{2}(10 - 7) = \dfrac{3}{2} = 1.5$$

B.O of CO is 3

   [as calculated in option (a)]

(c) B.O of O_2^{2-} is 1

   [as calculated in option (a)]

The electronic configuration of B_2 (10) is

$\sigma 1s^2\ \sigma^* 1s^2\ \sigma 2s^2\ \sigma^* 2s^2\ \pi 2p_x^1 \pi 2p_y^1$

$$\text{B.O} = \dfrac{1}{2}[6 - 4] = \dfrac{2}{2} = 1$$

(d) B.O of CO is 3

   [as calculated in option (a)]

Electronic configuration of N_2^+ (13) is

$\sigma 1s^2\ \sigma^* 1s^2\ \sigma 2s^2\ \sigma^* 2s^2\ \pi 2p_x^2\ \pi 2p_y^2\ \sigma 2p_z^1$

$$\text{B.O} = \dfrac{1}{2}[9 - 4] = \dfrac{5}{2} = 2.5$$

Thus, option (c) is correct.

72. *(d)* Given, mass of ethanol = 1 kg
$$= 1000 \,\text{g}$$

Latent heat of vaporisation of ethanol
$$= 855 \,\text{Jg}^{-1}$$

Specific heat capacity of ethanol
$$= 2.44 \, J / gk^{-1}$$
Heat, $q = mc\Delta T$ + heat of vaporisation
$$= 1000 \times 2.44 \, (351.45 - 293.45)$$
$$+ \, 855 \times 1000 \, J$$
$$= 9.97 \times 10^{5} \, J$$

73. *(b)*

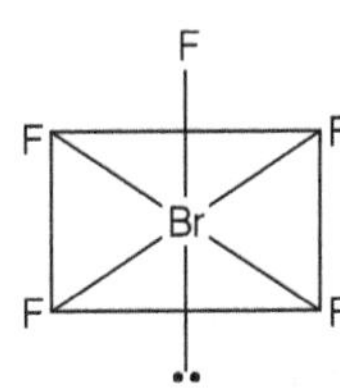

Moles of 1, 2-dibromo propane
$$= \frac{20.2}{202} = 0.1 \, mole$$

Moles of prop-1-ene $= \dfrac{3.58}{42}$
$$= 0.085 \, mole$$

% yield $= \dfrac{0.085}{0.1} \times 100 = 85\%$

74. *(a)* The lower stability of ethyl anion ($CH_3 \, \overset{-}{C}H_2$) compared to methyl anion ($\overset{-}{C}H_3$) is because of $+ I$-effect of methyl group of ethyl anion. The higher stability of ethyl radical compared to methyl radical is due to $\sigma - p$-orbital conjugation which is known as hyper conjugation in ethyl radical.

Hyper conjugation
in ethyl radical

75. *(d)* The geometry of BrF_5 is square pyramidal.

Here, the lone pair occupies the axial position and hence axial bonds will suffer more repulsion than axial bonds.
Thus, the axial Br—F bond length will be different than equitorial Br—F.

The geometry of PCl_5 is triangular pyramidal.

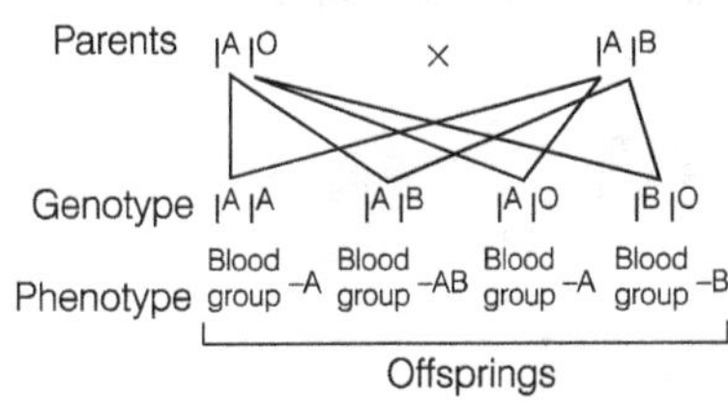

The axial bonds suffer more repulsions than equitorial bonds, so they are larger in bond length.

76. *(a)* The genotype of child having blood group-O with parents having $I^A I^O$ and $I^A I^B$ blood groups can be represented as

From the above cross, it is shown that none of the offsprings will be of blood group-O.
∴ The probability of their first child having type-O blood is zero.

77. *(c)* In the given question, both parents are heterozygous for two pairs of genes. This means the cross is a dihybrid cross.

Lets assume a dihybrid cross

Pure breeding traits — Yellow round seeds (YYRR), Wrinkled green seeds (yyrr)

Heterozygous trait — Yellow round seeds (YyRr)

Gametes → YR, Yr, yR, yr

♂ / ♀	YR	Yr	yR	yr
YR	YYRR yellow round	YYRr yellow round	YyRR yellow round	YyRr yellow round
Yr	YYRr yellow round	YYrr yellow wrinkled	YyRr yellow round	Yyrr yellow wrinkled
yR	YyRR yellow round	YyRr yellow round	yyRR green round	yyRr green round
yr	YyRr yellow round	Yyrr yellow wrinkled	yyRr green round	yyrr wrinkled green

The genotypic ratio is $1 : 2 : 1 : 2 : 4 : 2 : 1 : 2 : 1$
The phenotypic ratio is $9 : 3 : 3 : 1$
∴ The number of different genotypes and phenotypes obtained would be 9 and 4, respectively.

78. *(d)* The H^+ ion concentration of an aqueous solution is 0.001 M or 1×10^{-3} M
Since we know that pH $= - \log[H^+]$
Using this equation, by plugging in the values
pH $= - \log 10^{-3} = - (-3) \log 10 = 3$
pH $= 3$
We know that
$$pOH = 14 - pH = 14 - 3 = 11$$
∴　　$pOH = 11$

79. *(b)* Hypermetropia is far sightedness. A vision condition in which nearby objects are blurry. It is corrected by using convex lens.

Myopia is near sightedness. A condition in which close objects appear clearly but far ones do not. It is corrected using concave lens.

80. *(c)* The tendrils are sensitive to touch. When they come in contact with any support, the part of the tendril in contact with the object does not grow rapidly as the part of the tendril away from the object. This causes the tendril to circle around the object and thus cling to it. This process is known as positive thigmotropism. Thigmotropism is the directional response of a plant organ to touch or physical contact with a solid object. This differential response is generally caused by the induction of some pattern differential growth.

QUESTION PAPER 2017
Stream : SA (Nov 19)

MM : 100

Instructions

1. There are 80 questions in this paper.
2. This question paper contains two parts; Part I and Part II. There are four sections; Mathematics, Physics, Chemistry and Biology in each part.
3. Out of the four options given with each question, only one is correct.

➲ PART-I (1 Mark Questions)

MATHEMATICS

1. Suppose BC is a given line segment in the plane and T is a scalene triangle. The number of points A in the plane such that the triangle with vertices A, B, C (in same order) is similar to triangle T is
(a) 4   (b) 6   (c) 12   (d) 24

2. The number of positive integers n in the set $\{2, 3, \ldots, 200\}$ such that $\dfrac{1}{n}$ has a terminating decimal expansion is
(a) 16   (b) 18   (c) 40   (d) 100

3. If a, b, c are real numbers such that $a + b + c = 0$ and $a^2 + b^2 + c^2 = 1$, then $(3a + 5b - 8c)^2 + (-8a + 3b + 5c)^2 + (5a - 8b + 3c)^2$ is equal to
(a) 49   (b) 98
(c) 147   (d) 294

4. Let ABC be a triangle and M be a point on side AC closer to vertex C than A. Let N be a point on side AB such that MN is parallel to BC and let P be a point on side BC such that MP is parallel to AB. If the area of the quadrilateral $BNMP$ is equal to $\dfrac{5}{18}$ of the area of $\triangle ABC$, then the ratio AM / MC equals
(a) 5   (b) 6
(c) $\dfrac{18}{5}$ (d) $\dfrac{15}{2}$

5. Let $n \geq 4$ be a positive integer and let $l_1, l_2, \ldots, l_n$ be the lengths of the sides of arbitrary n sided non-degenerate polygon P. Suppose
$$\frac{l_1}{l_2} + \frac{l_2}{l_3} + \ldots + \frac{l_{n-1}}{l_n} + \frac{l_n}{l_1} = n$$
Consider the following statements:
  I. The lengths of the sides of P are equal.
  II. The angles of P are equal.
III. P is a regular polygon if it is cyclic.
Then,
(a) I is true and I implies II (b) II is true
(c) III is false   (d) I and III are true

6. Consider the following statements: For any integer n,
   I. $n^2 + 3$ is never divisible by 17.
   II. $n^2 + 4$ is never divisible by 17.
   Then,
   (a) both I and II are true   (b) both I and II are false
   (c) I is false and II is true   (d) I is true and II is false

7. Let S be the set of all ordered pairs (x, y) of positive integers, with HCF $(x, y) = 16$ and LCM $(x, y) = 48000$. The number of elements in S is
   (a) 4   (b) 8   (c) 16   (d) 32

8. Consider the set A of natural numbers n whose units digit is non-zero, such that if this units digit is erased, then the resulting number divides n. If K is the number of elements in the set A, then
   (a) K is infinite   (b) K is infinite but $K > 100$
   (c) $25 \le K \le 10$ (d) $K < 25$

9. There are exactly twelve Sundays in the period from January 1 to March 31 in a certain year. Then, the day corresponding to February 15 in that year is
   (a) Tuesday   (b) Wednesday
   (c) Thursday
   (d) not possible to determine from the given data

10. Consider a three-digit number with the following properties:
   I. If its digits in units place and tens place are interchanged, the number increases by 36;
   II. If its digits in units place and hundreds place are interchanged, the number decreases by 198.
   Now, suppose that the digits in tens place and hundreds place are interchanged. Then, the number
   (a) increases by 180   (b) decreases by 270
   (c) increases by 360   (d) decreases by 540

11. Consider four triangles having sides (5, 12, 9), (5, 12, 11), (5, 12, 13) and (5, 12, 15). Among these, the triangle having maximum area has sides.
   (a) (5,12, 9)   (b) (5, 12, 11)
   (c) (5, 12, 13)   (d) (5, 12, 15)

12. In a classroom, one-fifth of the boys leave the class and the ratio of the remaining boys to girls is 2 : 3. If further 44 girls leave the class, then class the ratio of boys to girls is 5 : 2. How many more boys should leave the class so that the number of boys equals that of girls?
   (a) 16   (b) 24   (c) 30   (d) 36

13. Let X, Y, Z be respectively the areas of a regular pentagon, regular hexagon and regular heptagon which are inscribed in a circle of radius 1. Then,
   (a) $\dfrac{X}{5} < \dfrac{Y}{6} < \dfrac{Z}{7}$ and $X < Y < Z$
   (b) $\dfrac{X}{5} < \dfrac{Y}{6} < \dfrac{Z}{7}$ and $X > Y > Z$
   (c) $\dfrac{X}{5} > \dfrac{Y}{6} > \dfrac{Z}{7}$ and $X > Y > Z$
   (d) $\dfrac{X}{5} > \dfrac{Y}{6} > \dfrac{Z}{7}$ and $X < Y < Z$

14. The least value of a natural number n such that $\binom{n-1}{5} + \binom{n-1}{6} < \binom{n}{7}$, where $\binom{n}{r} = \dfrac{n!}{(n-r)!\, r!}$, is
   (a) 12   (b) 13
   (c) 14   (d) 15

15. In a Mathematics test, the average marks of boys is $x\%$ and the average marks of girls is $y\%$ with $x \ne y$. If the average marks of all students is $z\%$, the ratio of the number of girls to the total number of students is
   (a) $\dfrac{z - x}{y - x}$ (b) $\dfrac{z - y}{y - x}$
   (c) $\dfrac{z + y}{y - x}$ (d) $\dfrac{z + x}{y - x}$

PHYSICS

16. Particles used in the Rutherford's scattering experiment to deduce the structure of atoms
   (a) had atomic number 2 and were fully ionised
   (b) had atomic number 2 and were neutral
   (c) had atomic number 4 and were fully ionised
   (d) had atomic number 4 and were neutral

17. The number of completely filled shells for the element $_{16}\text{S}^{32}$ is
   (a) 1   (b) 2
   (c) 3   (d) 4

18. In an experiment on simple pendulum to determine the acceleration due to gravity, a student measures the length of the thread as 63.2 cm and diameter of the pendulum bob as 2.256 cm. The student should take the length of the pendulum to be
   (a) 64.328 cm   (b) 64.3 cm
   (c) 65.456 cm   (d) 65.5 cm

19. A uniform metallic wire of length L is mounted in two configurations. In configuration 1 (triangle), it is an equilateral triangle and a voltage V is applied to corners A and B. In configuration 2 (circle), it is bent in the form of a circle and the potential V is applied at diametrically opposite points P and Q. The ratio of the power dissipated in configuration 1 to configuration 2 is

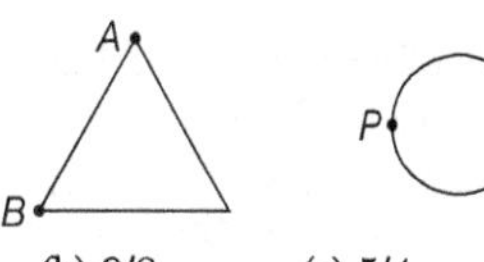

   (a) 2/3   (b) 9/8   (c) 5/4   (d) 7/8

20. Six objects are placed at the vertices of a regular hexagon. The geometric centre of the hexagon is at the origin with objects 1 and 4 on the X-axis (see figure). The mass of the kth object is $m_k = k^i M \, |\cos\theta_k|$, where i is an integer, M is a constant with dimension of mass and θ_k is the angular position of the kth vertex measured from the positive X-axis in the counter-clockwise sense.

If the net gravitational force on a body at the centroid vanishes, the value of i is

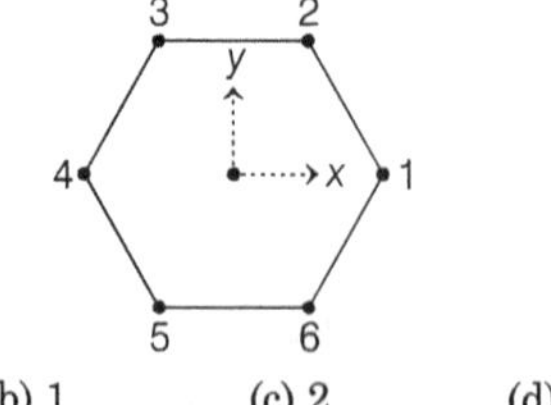

(a) 0   (b) 1   (c) 2   (d) 3

21. A mirror is placed at an angle of 30° with respect to Y-axis (see figure). A light ray travelling in the negative y-direction strikes the mirror. The direction of the reflected ray is given by the vector

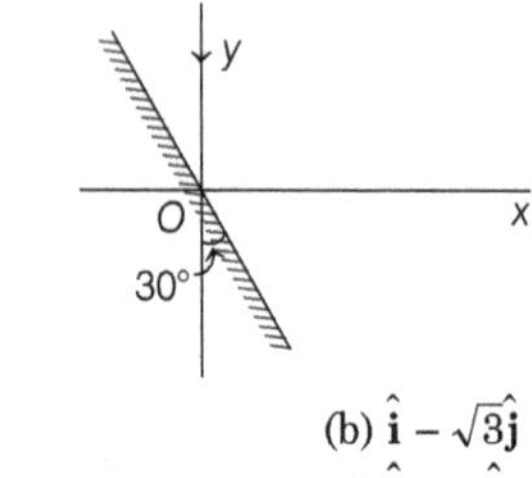

(a) $\hat{\mathbf{i}}$

(b) $\hat{\mathbf{i}} - \sqrt{3}\hat{\mathbf{j}}$

(c) $\sqrt{3}\hat{\mathbf{i}} - \hat{\mathbf{j}}$

(d) $\hat{\mathbf{i}} - 2\hat{\mathbf{j}}$

22. A total charge q is divided as q_1 and q_2 which are kept at two of the vertices of an equilateral triangle of side a. The magnitude of the electric field E at the third vertex of the triangle is to be depicted schematically as a function of $x = q_1/q$. Choose the correct figure.

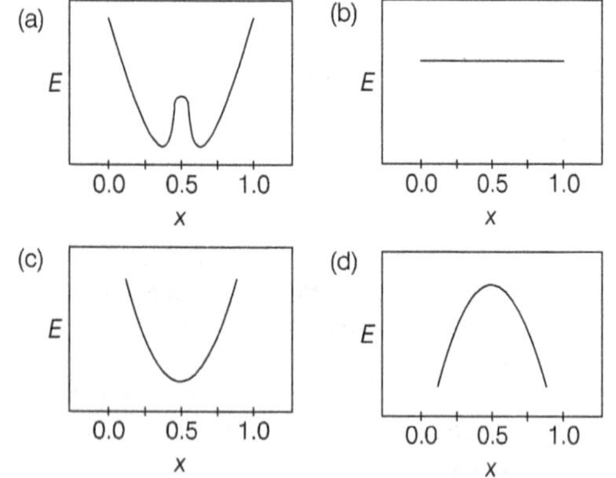

23. The refractive index of water in a biology laboratory tank varies as $1.33 + 0.002/\lambda^2$, where λ is the wavelength of light. Small pieces of organic matter of different colours are seen at the bottom of the tank using a travelling microscope. Then, the image of the organic matter appears

(a) deeper for the violet pieces than the green ones

(b) shallower for the blue pieces than the orange ones

(c) at the same depth for both the blue and orange pieces

(d) deeper for the green pieces than the red ones

24. Two students P and Q perform an experiment to verify Ohm's law for a conductor with resistance R. They use a current source and a voltmeter with least counts of 0.1 mA and 0.1 mV, respectively. The plots of the variation of voltage drop V across R with current I for both are shown below.

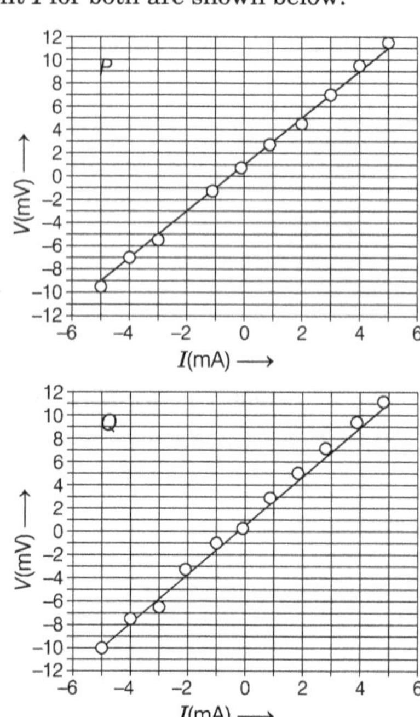

The statement which is most likely to be correct?

(a) P has only random error(s)

(b) Q has only systematic error(s)

(c) Q has both random and systematic errors

(d) P has both random and systematic errors

25. A cylindrical vessel of base radius R and height H has a narrow neck of height h and radius r at one end (see figure). The vessel is filled with water (density ρ_w) and its neck is filled with immiscible oil (density ρ_0). Then, the pressure at

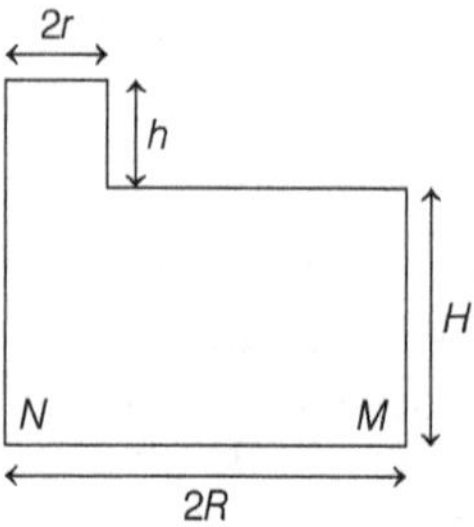

(a) M is $g(h\rho_0 + H\rho_w)$

(b) N is $g(h\rho_0 + H\rho_w)\dfrac{r^2}{R^2}$

(c) M is $gH\rho_w$

(d) N is $g\dfrac{\rho_w HR^2 + \rho_0 hr^2}{R^2 + r^2}$

26. Two cars S_1 and S_2 are moving in coplanar concentric circular tracks in the opposite sense with the periods of revolution 3 min and 24 min, respectively. At time $t = 0$, the cars are farthest apart. Then, the two cars will be
(a) closest to each other at $t = 12$ min and farthest at $t = 18$ min
(b) closest to each other at $t = 3$ min and farthest at $t = 24$ min
(c) closest to each other at $t = 6$ min and farthest at $t = 12$ min
(d) closest to each other at $t = 12$ min and farthest at $t = 24$ min

27. In the circuit shown below, a student performing Ohm's law experiment accidently puts the voltmeter and the ammeter as shown in the circuit below. The reading in the voltmeter will be close to

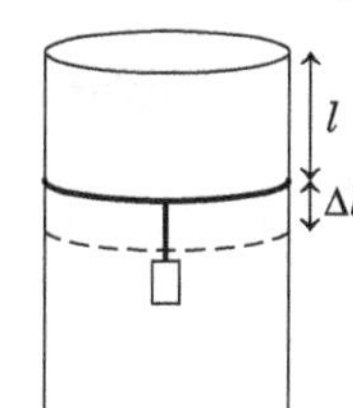

(a) 0 V (b) 4.8 V (c) 6.0 V (d) 1.2 V

28. The Bhagirathi and the Alaknanda merge at Deoprayag to form the Ganga with their speeds in the ratio $1 : 1 : 5$. The cross-sectional areas of the Bhagirathi, the Alaknanda and the Ganga are in the ratio $1 : 2 : 3$. Assuming streamline flow, the ratio of the speed of Ganga to that of the Alaknanda is
(a) $7 : 9$ (b) $4 : 3$ (c) $8 : 9$ (d) $5 : 3$

29. A long cylindrical pipe of radius 20 cm is closed at its upper end and has an airtight piston of negligible mass as shown. When a 50 kg mass is attached to the other end of piston, it moves down by a distance Δl before coming to equilibrium. Assuming air to be an ideal gas, $\Delta l / l$ (see figure) is close to ($g = 10$ m/s^2, atmospheric pressure is 10^5 Pa),

(a) 0.01 (b) 0.02 (c) 0.04 (d) 0.09

30. The word KVPY is written on a board and viewed through different lenses such that board is at a distance beyond the focal length of the lens.

First image   Second image

Ignoring magnification effects, consider the following statements.
(I) First image has been viewed from the planar side of a plano-concave lens and second image from the planar side of a plano-convex lens.
(II) First image has been viewed from the concave side of a plano-concave lens and second image from the convex side of a plano-convex lens.
(III) First image has been viewed from the concave side of a plano-concave lens and second image from the planar side of a plano-convex lens.
(IV) First image has been viewed from the planar side of a plano-concave lens and second image from the convex side of a plano-convex lens.

Which of the above statements are correct?
(a) Only statement III is correct
(b) Only statement II is correct
(c) Only statements III and IV are correct
(d) All statements are correct

CHEMISTRY

31. The IUPAC name for the following compound is

(a) 4,6-dimethylheptane (b) 1,3,5-trimethylhexane
(c) 2,4-dimethylheptane (d) 2,4,6-trimethylhexane

32. The stability of carbocations

$(CH_3)_3\overset{\oplus}{C}$ $(CH_3)_2\overset{\oplus}{C}(OCH_3)$ $CH_3CH_2CH_2\overset{\oplus}{C}H_2$ $CH_3\overset{\oplus}{C}HCH_2CH_3$
  I   II   III   IV

follows the order
(a) III < IV < II < I   (b) III < IV < I < II
(c) IV < III < II < I   (d) IV < III < I < II

33. The acidity of compounds I-IV in water
  I. ethanol   II. acetic acid
III. phenol   IV. acetonitrile
follows the order
(a) IV < I < III < II   (b) I < II < III < IV
(c) IV < I < II < III   (d) IV < III < I < II

34. In the following reaction,

the major product is

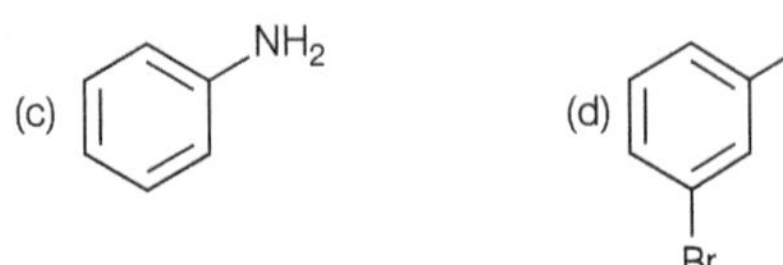

35. The reddish brown precipitate formed in the Fehling's test for aldehydes (RCHO) is due to the formation of

(a) Cu

(b) Cu$_2$O

(c) CuO

(d) (RCOO)$_2$Cu

36. The reducing ability of the metals K, Au, Zn and Pb follows the order

(a) K > Pb > Au > Zn

(b) Pb > K > Zn > Au

(c) Zn > Au > K > Pb

(d) K > Zn > Pb > Au

37. White phosphorus catches fire in air to produce dense white fumes. This is due to the formation of

(a) P$_4$O$_{10}$

(b) PH$_3$

(c) H$_3$PO$_3$

(d) H$_3$PO$_2$

38. The maximum number of electrons that can be filled in the shell with the principal quantum number $n = 4$ is

(a) 64 (b) 26 (c) 18 (d) 32

39. At a constant pressure p, the plot of volume (V) as a function of temperature (T) for 2 moles of an ideal gas gives a straight line with a slope 0.328 LK^{-1}. The value of p (in atm) is closest to

[Gas constant, $R = 0.0821$ L atm mol^{-1} K^{-1}]

(a) 0.25

(b) 0.5

(c) 1.0

(d) 2.0

40. Which of the following transformations can be carried out by using HI as a reducing agent, under acidic conditions?

[Given : I$_2$(s) $\rightarrow$ 2I$^-$; $E^\circ = 0.54$ V]

(i) Cu$^+$ $\rightarrow$ Cu(s); $E^\circ = 0.52$ V

(ii) Cr^{3+} $\rightarrow$ Cr^{2+}; $E^\circ = -0.41$ V

(iii) Fe^{3+} $\rightarrow$ Fe^{2+}; $E^\circ = 0.77$ V

(iv) Fe^{2+} $\rightarrow$ Fe(s); $E^\circ = -0.44$ V

(a) (i) and (iii)

(b) (ii) and (iv)

(c) Only (iii)

(d) Only (ii)

41. C$_{60}$ emerging from a source at a speed (v) has a de Broglie wavelength of 11.0 Å. The value of v (in ms^{-1}) is closest to

[Planck's constant $h = 6.626 \times 10^{-34}$ Js]

(a) 0.5 (b) 2.5 (c) 5.0 (d) 30

42. The lattice energies of NaCl, NaF, KCl and RbCl follow the order

(a) KCl < RbCl < NaCl < NaF

(b) NaF < NaCl < KCl < RbCl

(c) RbCl < KCl < NaCl < NaF

(d) NaCl < RbCl < NaF < KCl

43. The oxidation states of P atom in POCl$_3$, H$_2$PO$_3$ and H$_4$P$_2$O$_6$, respectively are

(a) +5, +4, +4

(b) +5, +5, +4

(c) +4, +4, +5

(d) +3, +4, +5

44. A solution (5 mL) of an acid X is completely neutralised by y mL of 1M NaOH. The same volume (y mL) of 1M NaOH is required to neutralise 10 mL of 0.6 M of H$_2$SO$_4$ completely. The normality (N) of the acid X is

(a) 1.2 (b) 2.4 (c) 4.8 (d) 0.6

45. 1.25 g of a metal (M) reacts with oxygen completely to produce 1.68 g of metal oxide. The empirical formula of the metal oxide is

[molar mass of M and O are 69.7 g mol^{-1} and 16.0 g mol^{-1}, respectively]

(a) M_2O (b) M_2O$_3$ (c) MO$_2$ (d) M_3O$_4$

BIOLOGY

46. According to Watson-Crick model, hydrogen bonding in a double-stranded DNA occurs between

(a) adenine and guanine

(b) adenine and thymine

(c) cytosine and adenine

(d) guanine and thymine

47. Which one of the following statements about mitosis is correct?

(a) One nucleus gives rise to 4 nuclei

(b) Homologous chromosomes synapse during anaphase

(c) The centromeres separate at the onset of anaphase

(d) Non-sister chromatids recombine

48. Gaseous exchange of oxygen and carbon dioxide between alveolar air and capillaries takes place by

(a) active transport

(b) diffusion

(c) carrier-mediated transport

(d) imbibition

49. Of the periods listed below, which one is the earliest period when ostracoderms, the jawless and finless fishes, appeared?

(a) Devonian period

(b) Cambrian period

(c) Carboniferous period

(d) Silurian period

50. Scurvy is caused by the deficiency of

(a) nicotinic acid

(b) ascorbic acid

(c) pantothenic acid

(d) retinoic acid

51. Optical activity of DNA is due to its

(a) bases

(b) sugars

(c) phosphates

(d) hydrogen bonds

52. The monarch butterfly avoids predators such as birds by

(a) changing colour frequently

(b) flying away from the predator swiftly

(c) producing a chemical obnoxious to the predator

(d) producing ultrasonic waves

53. Filariasis is caused by
(a) *Entamoeba histolytica* (b) *Plasmodium falciparum*
(c) *Trypanosoma brucei* (d) *Wuchereria bancrofti*

54. Which one of the following conversions does not happen under anaerobic conditions?
(a) Glucose to ethanol by *Saccharomyces*
(b) Lactose to lactic acid by *Lactobacillus*
(c) Glucose to CO_2 and H_2O by *Saccharomyces*
(d) Cellulose to glucose by *Cellulomonas*

55. An amount of 18 g glucose corresponds to
(a) 1.8 mole (b) 1 mole (c) 0.18 mole (d) 0.1 mole

56. The number of electrons required to reduce one molecule of oxygen to water during mitochondrial oxidation is
(a) 4 (b) 3 (c) 2 (d) 1

57. Which one of the following molecules is derived from pantothenic acid?
(a) Thiamine pyrophosphate
(b) Nicotinamide adenine dinucleotide phosphate
(c) Flavin adenine dinucleotide phosphate
(d) AcetylCo-A

58. Match the diseases given in Column I with the principal causal organisms in Column II and choose the correct combination.

	Column I		Column II
(P)	AIDS	(i)	HBV
(Q)	Syphilis	(ii)	*Neisseria* sp.
(R)	Viral hepatitis	(iii)	*Treponema* sp.
(S)	Gonorrhoea	(iv)	HIV

(a) P-iv, Q-iii, R-i, S-ii (b) P-iv, Q-ii, R-i, S-iii
(c) P-i, Q-ii, R-iv, S-iii (d) P-i, Q-iv, R-ii, S-iii

59. Chromosomes are classified based on the position of centromere. A chromosome having a terminal centromere is called
(a) metacentric (b) telocentric
(c) sub-metacentric (d) acrocentric

60. Which one of the following options lists the primary energy source(s) for all forms of life on the earth?
(a) Light, inorganic substances
(b) Inorganic substances, organic substances
(c) Light, organic substances
(d) N_2, CO_2

➲ PART-II (2 Marks Questions)

MATHEMATICS

61. Let $ABCD$ be a trapezium with parallel sides AB and CD such that the circle S with AB as its diameter touches CD. Further, the circle S passes through the mid-points of the diagonals AC and BD of the trapezium. The smallest angle of the trapezium is
(a) $\dfrac{\pi}{3}$ (b) $\dfrac{\pi}{4}$
(c) $\dfrac{\pi}{5}$ (d) $\dfrac{\pi}{6}$

62. Let S be the set of all points $\left(\dfrac{a}{b}, \dfrac{c}{d}\right)$ on the circle with radius 1 centred at $(0, 0)$ where a and b are relatively prime integers, c and d are relatively prime integers (that is HCF (a, b) = HCF (c, d) = 1), and the integers b and d are even. Then, the set S
(a) is empty
(b) has four elements
(c) has eight elements
(d) is infinite

63. Suppose we have two circles of radius 2 each in the plane such that the distance between their centers is $2\sqrt{3}$. The area of the region common to both circles lies between
(a) 0.5 and 0.6 (b) 0.65 and 0.7
(c) 0.7 and 0.75 (d) 0.8 and 0.9

64. Let C_1, C_2 be two circles touching each other externally at the point A and let AB be the diameter of circle C_1. Draw a secant BA_3 to circle C_2, intersecting circle C_1 at a point A_1 ($\neq A$), and circle C_2 at points A_2 and A_3. If $BA_1 = 2$, $BA_2 = 3$ and $BA_3 = 4$, then the radii of circles C_1 and C_2 are respectively
(a) $\dfrac{\sqrt{30}}{5}, \dfrac{3\sqrt{30}}{10}$ (b) $\dfrac{\sqrt{5}}{2}, \dfrac{7\sqrt{5}}{10}$
(c) $\dfrac{\sqrt{6}}{2}, \dfrac{\sqrt{6}}{2}$ (d) $\dfrac{\sqrt{10}}{3}, \dfrac{17\sqrt{10}}{30}$

65. Let a, b, c, d be real numbers between -5 and 5 such that
$$|a| = \sqrt{4 - \sqrt{5 - a}}, |b| = \sqrt{4 + \sqrt{5 - b}}, |c| = \sqrt{4 - \sqrt{5 + c}},$$
$$|d| = \sqrt{4 + \sqrt{5 + d}}$$
Then, the product $abcd$ is
(a) 11 (b) -11
(c) 121 (d) -121

PHYSICS

66. Persons A and B are standing on the opposite sides of a 3.5 m wide water stream which they wish to cross. Each one of them has a rigid wooden plank whose mass can be neglected. However, each plank is only slightly longer than 3 m. So, they decide to arrange them together as shown in the figure schematically.

With B (mass 17 kg) standing, the maximum mass of A, who can walk over the plank is close to

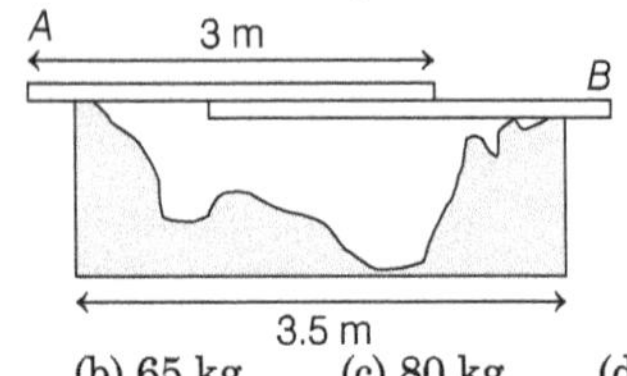

(a) 17 kg　　(b) 65 kg　　(c) 80 kg　　(d) 105 kg

67. Two different liquids of same mass are kept in two identical vessels, which are placed in a freezer that extracts heat from them at the same rate causing each liquid to transform into a solid. The schematic figure below shows that temperature T *versus* time t plot for the two materials. We denote the specific heat of materials in the liquid (solid) states to be C_{L1} (C_{S1}) and $C_{L2}(C_{S2})$, respectively.

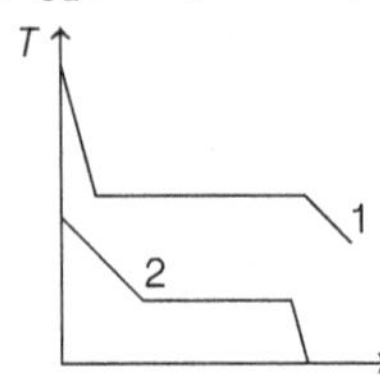

Choose the correct option given below.

(a) $C_{L1} < C_{L2}$ and $C_{S1} < C_{S2}$　　(b) $C_{L1} > C_{L2}$ and $C_{S1} < C_{S2}$
(c) $C_{L1} > C_{L2}$ and $C_{S1} > C_{S2}$　　(d) $C_{L1} < C_{L2}$ and $C_{S1} > C_{S2}$

68. A ray of light originates from inside a glass slab and is incident on its inner surface at an angle θ as shown below.

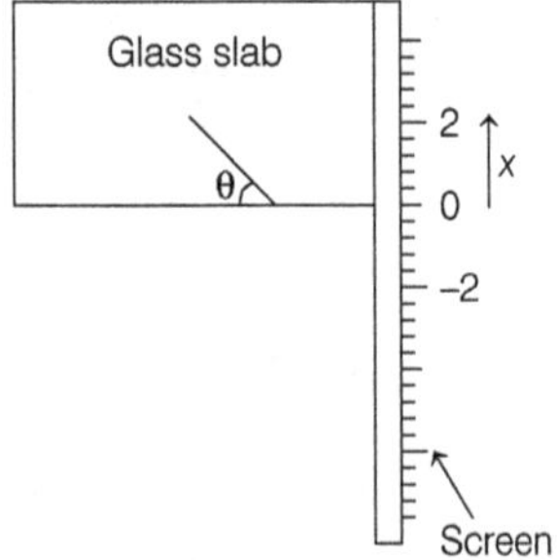

In this experiment, the location x of the spot where the ray hits the screen is recorded. Which of the following correctly shows the plot of variation of x with the angle θ ?

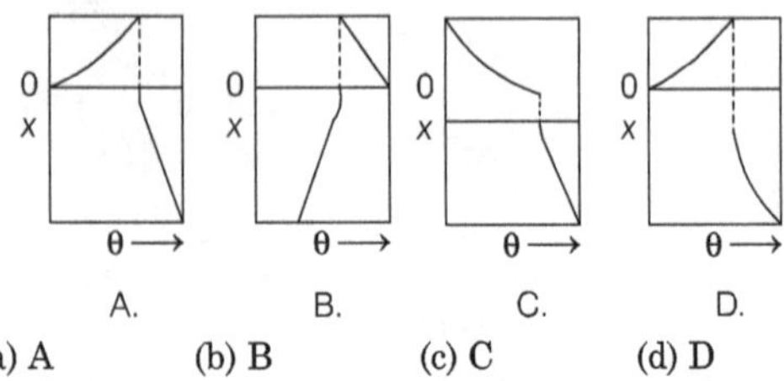

(a) A　　(b) B　　(c) C　　(d) D

69. Four identical pendulums are made by attaching a small ball of mass 100 g on a 20 cm long thread and suspended from the same point. Now, each ball is

given charge Q, so that balls move away from each other with each thread making an angle of 45° from the vertical. The value of Q is close to

$$\left(\frac{1}{4\pi\varepsilon_0} = 9 \times 10^9 \text{ in SI units}\right)$$

(a) $1\,\mu C$　　(b) $1.5\,\mu C$　　(c) $2\,\mu C$　　(d) $2.5\,\mu C$

70. Two parallel discs are connected by a rigid rod of length $L = 0.5$ m centrally. Each disc has a slit oppositely placed as shown in the figure. A beam of neutral atoms are incident on one of the discs axially at different velocities v, while the system is rotated at angular speed of 600 rev/second, so that atoms only with a specific velocity emerge at the other end. Calculate the two largest speeds (in metre/second) of the atoms that will emerge at the other end.

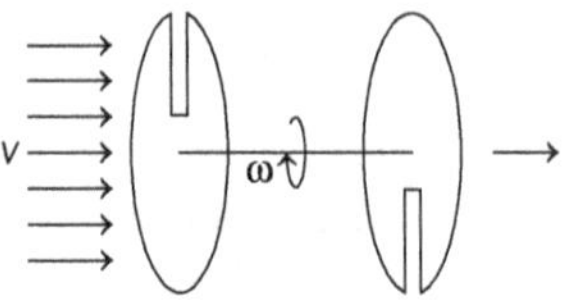

(a) 75, 25　　(b) 100, 50　　(c) 300, 100　　(d) 600, 200

CHEMISTRY

71. Among the following compounds, E/Z isomerism is possible for
(a) 2-methylbut-2-ene　　(b) 2-methylbut-1-ene
(c) 3-methylpent-1-ene　　(d) 3-methylpent-2-ene

72. In the reaction,

$$H_3C - C \equiv C - H \xrightarrow[\substack{2.\ x \\ 3.\ y}]{1.\ NaNH_2,\ \Delta} H_3C\text{---}\text{---}CH_3$$

x and y, respectively are
(a) $x = CH_3OH$; $y = Pd/BaSO_4$, quinoline, H_2
(b) $x = CH_3I$; $y = Pd/BaSO_4$, quinoline, H_2
(c) $x = CH_3I$; $y = Na$ in liq. NH_3
(d) $x = CH_3OH$; $y = Na$ in liq. NH_3

73. Among the following molecules, the one with the largest bond angle at the central atom is
(a) ClF_3　　(b) $POCl_3$　　(c) BCl_3　　(d) SO_3

74. A compound has the following composition by weight : Na = 18.60%, S = 25.80%, H = 4.02% and O = 51.58%. Assuming that all the hydrogen atoms in the compound are part of water of crystallisation, the correct molecular formula of the compound is
(a) $Na_2S_2O_3 \cdot 3H_2O$　　　　(b) $Na_2SO_4 \cdot 5H_2O$
(c) $Na_2SO_4 \cdot 10H_2O$　　　　(d) $Na_2S_2O_3 \cdot 5H_2O$

75. X g of ice at 0°C is added to 340 g of water at 20°C. The final temperature of the resultant mixture is 5°C. The value of X (in g) is closest to

[Heat of fusion of ice = 333 J/g; specific heat of water = 4.184 J/g.K]

(a) 80.4　　(b) 52.8　　(c) 120.6　　(d) 60.3

BIOLOGY

76. Considering ABO blood grouping system in humans, during blood transfusion some combinations of blood groups are compatible (✓), whereas the others are incompatible (✗). Which one of the following options is correct?

(a)

		Recipient			
		O	A	B	AB
Donor	O	✗	✗	✗	✓
	A	✓	✗	✓	✗
	B	✓	✓	✗	✗
	AB	✓	✓	✓	✓

(b)

		Recipient			
		O	A	B	AB
Donor	O	✗	✗	✗	✗
	A	✓	✗	✓	✗
	B	✓	✓	✗	✗
	AB	✓	✓	✓	✗

(c)

		Recipient			
		O	A	B	AB
Donor	O	✓	✗	✗	✗
	A	✓	✓	✗	✗
	B	✓	✗	✓	✗
	AB	✓	✓	✓	✓

(d)

		Recipient			
		O	A	B	AB
Donor	O	✓	✓	✓	✓
	A	✗	✓	✗	✓
	B	✗	✗	✓	✓
	AB	✗	✗	✗	✓

77. A 25,000 Da protein contains a single binding site for a molecule (ligand), whose molecular weight is 2,500 Da. Assuming high affinity and physiologically irreversible binding, the amount of the ligand required to occupy all the binding sites in 10 mg protein will be
(a) 0.1 mg
(b) 1 mg
(c) 10 mg
(d) 100 mg

78. In an *in vitro* translation experiment, poly (UC) RNA template produced poly (Ser-Leu), while poly (AG) RNA template produced poly (Arg-Glu) polypeptide. Which one of the following options represents correct interpretations of the codons assignments for Ser, Leu, Arg and Glu?
(a) Ser-UCU, Leu-CUC, Arg-AGA, Glu-GAG
(b) Ser-CUC, Leu-GAG, Arg-UCU, Glu-AGA
(c) Ser-AGA, Leu-UCU, Arg-GAG, Glu-CUC
(d) Ser-GAG, Leu-AGA, Arg-CUC, Glu-UCU

79. A single bacterium is actively growing in a medium that supports its growth to a number of 100 million. Assuming the division time of the bacterium as 3 hours and the lifespan of non-dividing bacteria as 5 hours, which one of the following represents the maximum number of bacteria that would be present at the end of 15 hours?
(a) 10
(b) 64
(c) 24
(d) 32

80. A couple has two sons and two daughters. Only one son is colourblind and the rest of the siblings are normal. Assuming colourblindness is sex-linked, which one of the following would be the phenotype of the parents?
(a) Mother would be colourblind, father would be normal
(b) Father would be colourblind, mother would be normal
(c) Both the parents would be normal
(d) Both the parents would be colourblind

Answers

PART-I

1	(c)	2	(b)	3	(c)	4	(a)	5	(d)	6	(d)	7	(b)	8	(d)	9	(c)	10	(d)
11	(c)	12	(b)	13	(d)	14	(c)	15	(a)	16	(a)	17	(b)	18	(b)	19	(b)	20	(a)
21	(c)	22	(c)	23	(b)	24	(d)	25	(a)	26	(d)	27	(c)	28	(c)	29	(c)	30	(d)
31	(c)	32	(b)	33	(a)	34	(c)	35	(b)	36	(d)	37	(a)	38	(d)	39	(b)	40	(c)
41	(*)	42	(c)	43	(a)	44	(b)	45	(b)	46	(b)	47	(c)	48	(b)	49	(b)	50	(b)
51	(b)	52	(c)	53	(d)	54	(c)	55	(d)	56	(a)	57	(d)	58	(a)	59	(b)	60	(a)

PART-II

61	(d)	62	(a)	63	(c)	64	(a)	65	(a)	66	(c)	67	(b)	68	(a)	69	(b)	70	(d)
71	(d)	72	(c)	73	(a)	74	(d)	75	(d)	76	(d)	77	(b)	78	(a)	79	(d)	80	(c)

** No option is correct.*

Solutions

1. *(c)* Let triangle T is PQR and other triangle is ABC.

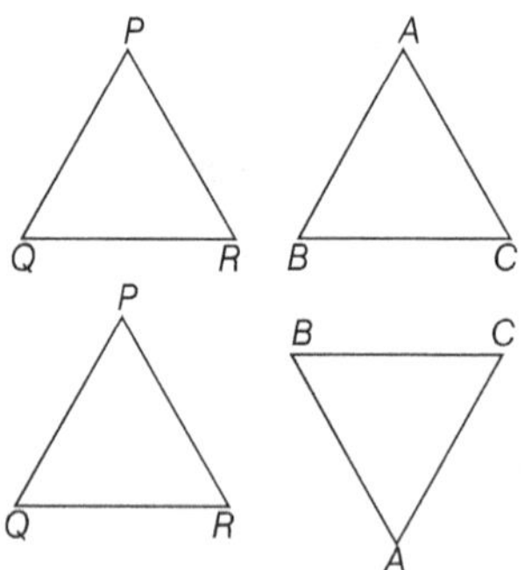

A can taken position if $\Delta ABC \sim \Delta PQR$.

We can arrange A, B, C in 3! ways

$$= 6 \text{ ways}$$

Total position of A can take $= 3! \times 2 = 12$ ways

2. *(b)* We have, $n \in \{2, 3, 4, 5, 6, ..., 200\}$

$\dfrac{1}{n}$ has terminating decimal of $n = 2^a \times 5^b$

$\therefore n = 2, 4, 5, 8, 10, 16, 20, 25, 32, 40, 50, 64, 80, 100, 125, 128, 160, 200$

$\therefore$ Total number of $n = 18$

3. *(c)* We have,

$$a + b + c = 0 \text{ and } a^2 + b^2 + c^2 = 1$$

Now $(3a + 5b - 8c)^2 + (- 8a + 3b + 5c)^2$
$$+ (5a - 8b + 3c)^2$$

$= 9a^2 + 25b^2 + 64c^2 - 48ac + 30ab$
$\qquad - 80bc + 64a^2 + 9b^2 + 25c^2 - 80ac$
$\qquad - 48ab + 30bc + 25a^2 + 64b^2 + 9c^2$
$\qquad + 30ac - 8ab - 48bc$

$= 98(a^2 + b^2 + c^2) - 98(ab + bc + ca)$

$= 98(a^2 + b^2 + c^2)$
$$\qquad - 98\left(\frac{(a + b + c)^2 - (a^2 + b^2 + c^2)}{2}\right)$$

$= 98(1) - 98\left(\dfrac{0 - 1}{2}\right) = 98 + 49 = 147$

4. *(a)* $\Delta ABC \sim \Delta ANM$

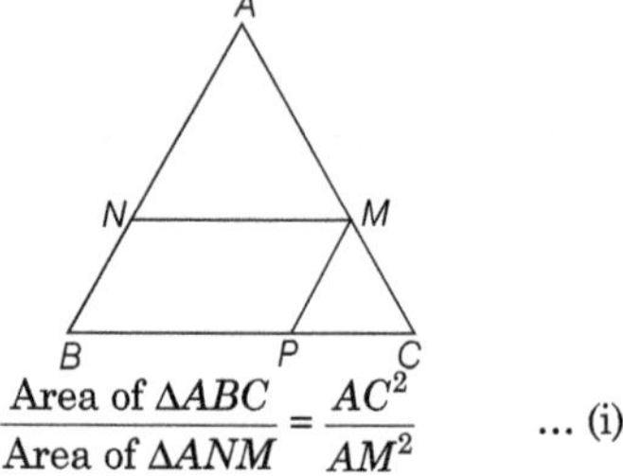

$\therefore \quad \dfrac{\text{Area of } \Delta ABC}{\text{Area of } \Delta ANM} = \dfrac{AC^2}{AM^2}$ ... (i)

$\Delta ABC \sim MPC$

$\dfrac{\text{Area of } \Delta ABC}{\text{Area of } \Delta MPC} = \dfrac{AC^2}{MC^2}$ ...(ii)

From Eqs. (i) and (ii), we get

$$\dfrac{\text{Area of } \Delta ANM}{\text{Area of } \Delta MPC} = \dfrac{AM^2}{MC^2}$$

$$\dfrac{\text{Area of } \Delta ANM + \text{Area of } \Delta MPC}{\text{Area of } \Delta MPC}$$

$$= \dfrac{AM^2 + MC^2}{MC^2}$$

Now, Area of ΔANM + Area of ΔMPC
$$= \text{Area of } \Delta ABC - \text{Area of } BNMP$$

$\therefore \quad \dfrac{13\ (\text{Area of } \Delta ABC)}{18\ (\text{Area of } \Delta MPC)} = \dfrac{AM^2 + MC^2}{MC^2}$

From Eq. (iii), $\dfrac{13}{18}\left(\dfrac{(AC^2)}{MC^2}\right) = \dfrac{AM^2 + MC^2}{MC^2}$

$\Rightarrow \quad 13\,(AM + MC)^2 = 18\,(AM^2 + MC^2)$

$\Rightarrow \quad \dfrac{AM}{MC} = 5$

5. *(d)* We have, $l_1, l_2, l_3 ..., l_n$ be the lengths of the side of arbitrary n sided non-degenerate polygon P and

$$\frac{l_1}{l_2} + \frac{l_2}{l_3} + \frac{l_3}{l_4} + ... + \frac{l_{n-1}}{l_n} + \frac{l_n}{l_1} = n,\ n \geq 4$$

Using AM $\geq$ GM, we get

$$\frac{\dfrac{l_1}{l_2} + \dfrac{l_2}{l_3} + \dfrac{l_3}{l_4} + ... + \dfrac{l_n}{l_1}}{n} \geq \left(\frac{l_1}{l_2} \times \frac{l_2}{l_3} \times ... \times \frac{l_n}{l_1}\right)^{1/n}$$

$\therefore \quad \dfrac{l_1}{l_2} + \dfrac{l_2}{l_3} + ... + \dfrac{l_n}{l_1} \geq n$

$\therefore \quad n \geq n \Rightarrow n = n$

So, $\qquad$ AM = GM

$\therefore \quad l_1 = l_2 = l_3 ... = l_n$

$\therefore$ The length of sides of P are equal and P is regular polygon of it is cyclic.

6. *(d)* Let $n^2 + 3$ is divisible by 17

$\therefore \qquad n^2 + 3 = 17K \qquad [K \in N]$

$\Rightarrow \qquad n^2 = 17K - 3$

$\Rightarrow \qquad n^2 = 3\,(17m - 1) \quad [\because K = 3m]$

$3\,(17m - 1)$ is a perfect square is not possible.

$\therefore n^2 + 3$ is never divisible by 17.

$n^2 + 4$ put $n = 9$

$(9)^2 + 4 = 81 + 4 = 85$ is divisible by 17.

$\therefore$ I is true and II is false.

7. *(b)* We have,

$$\text{HCF } (x, y) = 16$$
$$\text{LCM } (x, y) = 48000$$

We know,

Product of two number = HCF $\times$ LCM

$\therefore \qquad xy = 16 \times 48000$

$\qquad\qquad xy = 16 \times 16 \times (3^1 \times 2^3 \times 5^3)$

As HCF of $(x, y) = 16$

2^3 can be selected in 1 ways and 3^1 and 5^3 can be selected in $(1 + 1)(3 + 1) = 8$ ways

$\therefore$ Number of ordered pairs = 8

8. *(d)* Let two digits number
$$ab = 10a + b, b \neq 0$$

if b is erased.

Then, the resulting number is a.

$\therefore ab$ is divisible by a if ab is multiple of c.

$\therefore$ Such number are 11, 12, 13, 14, 15, 16, 17, 18, 19, 22, 24, 26, 28, 33, 36, 39, 44, 48, 55, 66, 77, 88, 99.

$\therefore$ Total number are 23.

Hence, $\qquad K < 25$

9. *(c)* There are 90 days from 1 January to 31 March (Non-leap year)

If year 13 leap year, then total number of days = 91 (13 weeks)

But we have 12 Sunday

$\therefore$ 12 weeks

$\therefore$ Ist Jan will be Monday as there will be 90 days January 1 to 31 March.

$\therefore$ 15th February will be Thursday.

10. *(d)* Let three digits number be
$$100x + 10y + z.$$

According to problem,

$$100x + 10y + z = 100x + 10z + y - 36$$

$\Rightarrow \quad 9y - 9z + 36 = 0$

$\Rightarrow \qquad y - z + 4 = 0 \qquad ...(i)$

$\Rightarrow \quad 100x + 10y + z = 100z + 10y + x + 198$

$\Rightarrow \qquad x - z - 2 = 0 \qquad ...(ii)$

Now, $(100x + 10y + z) - (100y + 10x + z)$
$$= 90(x - y)$$
$$= 90(6) \quad [\because \text{from Eqs. (i) and (ii)}]$$
$$= 540$$

$\therefore$ So, on interchanging for digit at tens place and hundred place, the value of number is decreased by 540.

11. *(c)* We have,

Four triangle having sides are

(5, 12, 9), (5, 12, 11), (5, 12, 13), (5, 12, 15)

A right triangle has maximum area.

$\therefore$ Among these the triangle whose sides (5, 12, 13) form a right angled triangle.

$\therefore$ It has maximum area.

12. *(b)* Let the number of boys and girls in classroom is x and y, respectively.

Given, $\dfrac{x - x/5}{y} = \dfrac{2}{3} \Rightarrow \dfrac{4x}{5y} = \dfrac{2}{3}$

$\Rightarrow \qquad \dfrac{x}{y} = \dfrac{5}{6}$ ...(i)

Also, $\dfrac{x - x/5}{y - 44} = \dfrac{5}{2} \Rightarrow \dfrac{4x}{5(y - 44)} = \dfrac{5}{2}$

$\Rightarrow \qquad 8x = 25y - 1100$ ... (ii)

From Eqs. (i) and (ii), we get

$$x = 50, \; y = 60$$

Let z number of boy leaves so number of boys and number of girls are equal.

$\therefore \qquad 50 - 10 - z = 60 - 44$

$$z = 40 - 16 = 24$$

13. *(d)* We have,

X, Y, Z be respectively the area of a regular pentagon, regular hexagon and regular heptagon which are inscribed in radius of unit circle.

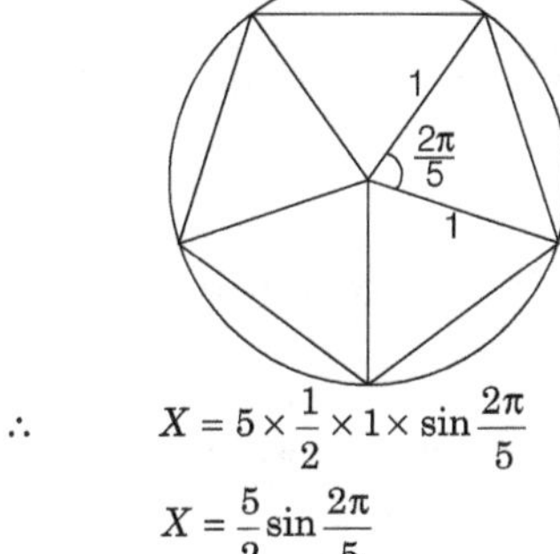

$\therefore \qquad X = 5 \times \dfrac{1}{2} \times 1 \times \sin \dfrac{2\pi}{5}$

$$X = \dfrac{5}{2} \sin \dfrac{2\pi}{5}$$

Similarly,

$$Y = \dfrac{6}{2} \sin \dfrac{2\pi}{6} \text{ and } Z = \dfrac{7}{2} \sin \dfrac{2\pi}{7}$$

$\dfrac{X}{5} = \dfrac{1}{2} \sin \dfrac{2\pi}{5}, \dfrac{Y}{6} = \dfrac{1}{2} \sin \dfrac{2\pi}{3}, \dfrac{Z}{7} = \dfrac{1}{2} \sin \dfrac{2\pi}{7}$

$\sin \dfrac{2\pi}{5} > \sin \dfrac{2\pi}{6} > \sin \dfrac{2\pi}{7}$

$\therefore \dfrac{X}{5} > \dfrac{Y}{6} > \dfrac{Z}{7}$ and $X < Y < Z$

14. *(c)* Given,

$$^{n-1}C_5 + {}^{n-1}C_6 < {}^{n}C_7$$
$$^{n}C_6 < {}^{n}C_7$$
$$[\because {}^{n}C_{r-1} + {}^{n}C_r = {}^{n+1}C_r]$$

$\Rightarrow \qquad \dfrac{n!}{(n-6)!6!} < \dfrac{n!}{(n-7)!7!}$

$\Rightarrow \qquad n - 6 > 7$

$\Rightarrow \qquad n > 13$

$\therefore$ Least value of $x = 14$

15. *(a)* Let the number of boy $= B$

and number of girls $= G$

Sum of marks obtained by boys $= Bx$

$\therefore$ Sum of marks obtained by girls $= Gy$

Now, given

$$\dfrac{Bx + Gy}{B + G} = z$$

$\Rightarrow B(x - z) = G(z - y) = \dfrac{B}{G} = \dfrac{z - y}{x - z}$

Now, $\dfrac{G}{B + G} = \dfrac{1}{\dfrac{B}{G} + 1} = \dfrac{1}{\dfrac{z-y}{x-z} + 1} = \dfrac{x - z}{x - y}$

$\Rightarrow \qquad \dfrac{G}{B + G} = \dfrac{z - x}{y - x}$

16. *(a)* Particles used in Rutherford's scattering experiment (Geiger-Marsden experiment) are α-particles derived from a tube of radium emanation (or radon). α-particles are helium nuclei $^4_2$He, they are fully ionised and have atomic number 2.

17. *(b)* Atomic number of $_{16}S^{32}$ is 16. Its electronic configuration using $2n^2$ rule is

$$_{16}S = \underbrace{1s^2, 2s^2p^6}_{[\text{Ne}]}, \underbrace{3s^2p^4}_{\text{Unfilled}}$$

So, number of fully filled orbits or shells is 2.

18. *(b)* Length of pendulum = Length of thread + Radius of bob

$$= 63.2 + \dfrac{2.256}{2} = 63.2 + 1.128$$

$$= 64.328 \, \text{cm}$$

But now the student must apply rule for taking significant digits in a measurement.

In addition or subtraction,

Number of digits after decimal in result

= Least number of digits after decimal in quantities added

So, length of pendulum = 64.3 cm.

19. *(b)* Let a = side length of equilateral triangle, r = radius of circle and x = resistance per unit length of wire used.

Then, $L = 3a = 2\pi r$ or $a = \dfrac{L}{3}$ and $r = \dfrac{L}{2\pi}$

Now, in case I,

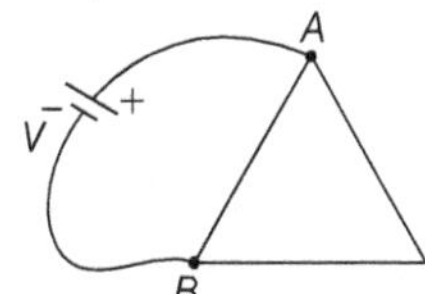

Equivalent resistance across AB is

$$R_{AB} = (ax \parallel 2ax) = \dfrac{ax \times 2ax}{ax + 2ax}$$

$$= \dfrac{2a^2x^2}{3ax} = \dfrac{2}{3} ax$$

$\Rightarrow \qquad R_{AB} = \dfrac{2}{3} \times \dfrac{L}{3} \times x$

Power dissipated is

$$P_1 = \dfrac{V^2}{R_{AB}} = \dfrac{9V^2}{2Lx} \qquad \text{...(i)}$$

In case II,

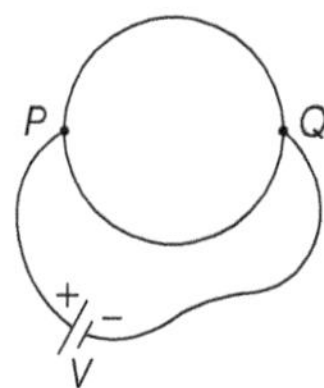

$$R_{PQ} = (\pi rx \parallel \pi rx) = \dfrac{\pi rx \times \pi rx}{\pi rx + \pi rx} = \dfrac{\pi^2 r^2 x^2}{2\pi rx}$$

$$= \dfrac{1}{2} \pi rx = \dfrac{1}{2} \pi \times \dfrac{L}{2\pi} x = \dfrac{Lx}{4}$$

So, power dissipated is

$$P_2 = \dfrac{V^2}{R_{PQ}} = \dfrac{4V^2}{Lx}$$

Ratio of power dissipated in two cases is

$$\dfrac{P_1}{P_2} = \dfrac{9V^2/2Lx}{4V^2/Lx} = \dfrac{9}{8}$$

20. *(a)* For a mass m at centroid of hexagon (at origin), net force is zero when $\quad \Sigma F_x = 0$ and $\Sigma F_y = 0$.

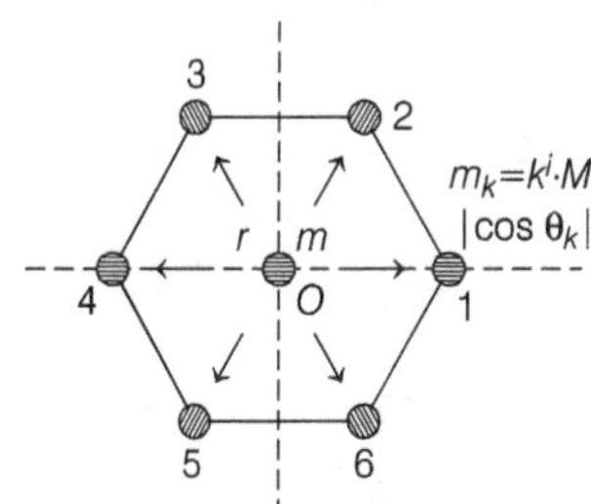

Now, ΣF_x = sum of all x-components of forces on m due to masses at vertices of hexagon.

$$= \dfrac{Gm}{r^2} (\Sigma (k^i M \mid \cos \theta_k \mid \cdot \cos \theta_k))$$

$$= \dfrac{GmM}{r^2} (1^i \mid \cos 0° \mid \cdot \cos 0° + 2^i \mid \cos 60° \mid$$
$$\cdot \cos 60° + 3^i \mid \cos 120° \mid \cdot \cos 120°$$
$$+ 4^i \mid \cos 180° \mid \cdot \cos 180°$$
$$+ 5^i \mid \cos 240° \mid \cdot \cos 240°$$
$$+ 6^i \mid \cos 300° \mid \cdot \cos 300°)$$

$$= \dfrac{GMm}{r^2} \cdot \left(1^i + \dfrac{2^i}{4} - \dfrac{3^i}{4} - 4^i - \dfrac{5^i}{4} + \dfrac{6^i}{4} \right)$$

As $\Sigma F_x = 0$, for net force on m to be zero. we have

$$1^i + \dfrac{2^i}{4} - \dfrac{3^i}{4} - 4^i - \dfrac{5^i}{4} + \dfrac{6^i}{4} = 0$$

Above equation is satisfied with $i = 0$.

21. *(c)* Following laws of reflection, reflected ray makes an angle of 30° with mirror as shown below.

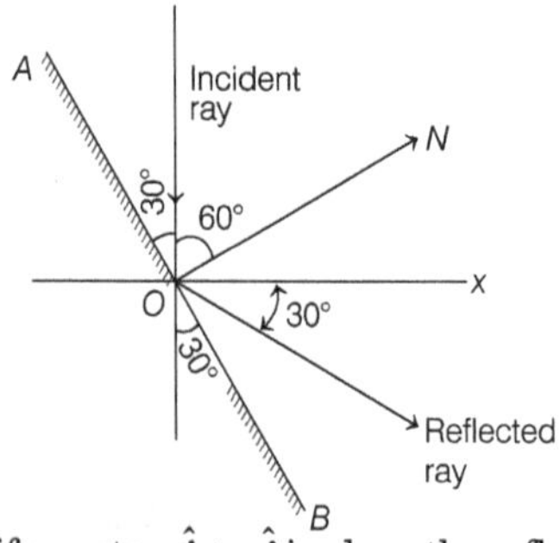

So, if a vector $x\hat{\mathbf{i}} + y\hat{\mathbf{j}}$ is along the reflected ray, then

$$\tan(-30°) = \frac{y}{x} \text{ or } \frac{y}{x} = -\frac{1}{\sqrt{3}}$$

This is correct with option (c).

22. *(c)* When q_1 and q_2 are the magnitudes of charges at two vertices of an equilateral triangle of side a, magnitude of electric field at third vertex is

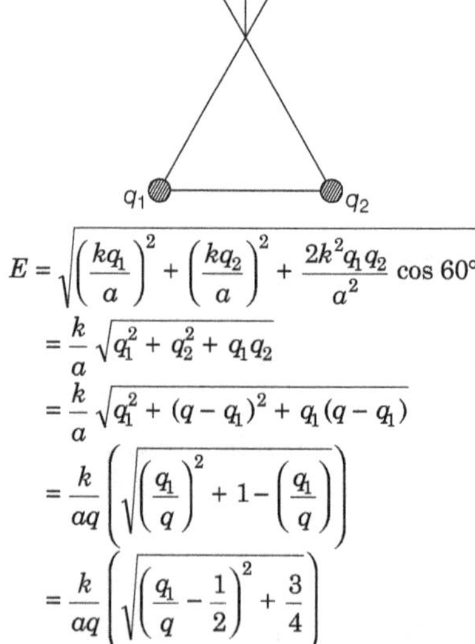

$$E = \sqrt{\left(\frac{kq_1}{a}\right)^2 + \left(\frac{kq_2}{a}\right)^2 + \frac{2k^2 q_1 q_2}{a^2}\cos 60°}$$

$$= \frac{k}{a}\sqrt{q_1^2 + q_2^2 + q_1 q_2}$$

$$= \frac{k}{a}\sqrt{q_1^2 + (q - q_1)^2 + q_1(q - q_1)}$$

$$= \frac{k}{aq}\left(\sqrt{\left(\frac{q_1}{q}\right)^2 + 1 - \left(\frac{q_1}{q}\right)}\right)$$

$$= \frac{k}{aq}\left(\sqrt{\left(\frac{q_1}{q} - \frac{1}{2}\right)^2 + \frac{3}{4}}\right)$$

So, field is minimum when $\dfrac{q_1}{q} = \dfrac{1}{2}$.

This condition is satisfied in graph (c).

23. *(b)* As, refractive index,

$$\mu = 1.33 + \frac{0.002}{\lambda^2}$$

So, μ is more for small wavelengths.

i.e. $\mu_{\text{orange}} < \mu_{\text{green}} < \mu_{\text{blue}}$

As, $\mu = \dfrac{\text{real depth}}{\text{apparent depth}}$

$\Rightarrow$ Apparent depth $\propto \dfrac{1}{\mu}$

Now, $\mu_{\text{orange}} < \mu_{\text{blue}}$

$\Rightarrow$ (Apparent depth)$_{\text{blue}}$

       < (Apparent depth)$_{\text{orange}}$

24. *(d)* For P errors are both positive and negative.

For Q errors are only positive.

So, P has both random and systematic errors.

25. *(a)* Pressure is same at all the points of base.

i.e. Pressure at M = Pressure at N

Also, pressure applied anywhere to the fluid is equally transmitted in all directions.

So, pressure at base = pressure due to oil column of height h + pressure due to water column of height H.

$$\Rightarrow \ \rho_o gh + \rho_w gH \Rightarrow g(\rho_0 \cdot h + \rho_w H)$$

26. *(d)*

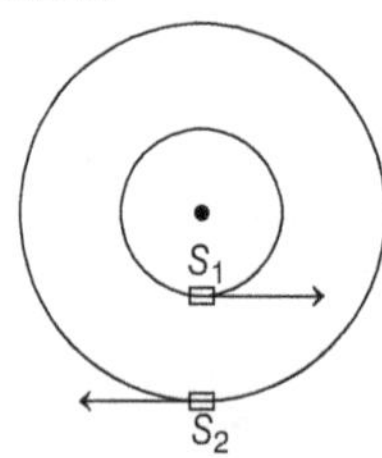

Positions of cars at t = 0s

At $t = 12$ min, car S_1 has completed three rounds and it is at its position.

At $t = 12$ min, car S_2 completed half round and it is at diametrically opposite point as shown below.

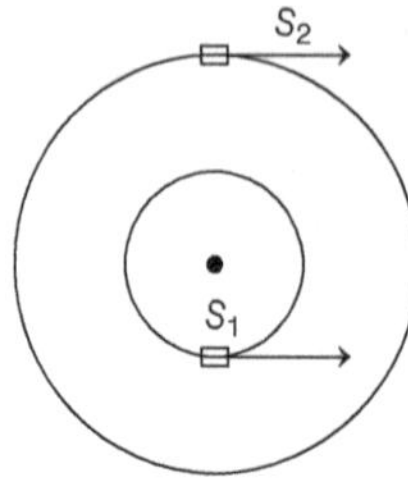

Positions of cars at t = 12 min

So, cars are closest at $t = 12$ min.

At $t = 24$ min, cars S_1 and S_2 are both at their initial positions and so are farthest, as shown below.

Hence, cars are farthest from each other at $t = 24$ min.

27. *(c)* The resistance of voltmeter is very high and resistance of ammeter is very low. When ammeter is put in parallel to 8 kΩ resistor, nearly whole of current goes through the ammeter. Hence, circuit is equivalent to following.

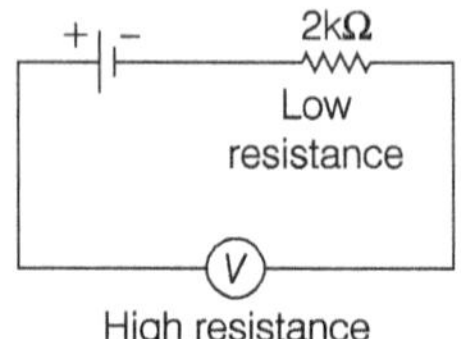

So, maximum potential drop occurs in the voltmeter (high resistance). Hence, reading of voltmeter is nearly 6 V.

28. *(c)* As water is not stored anywhere. So, volume flow rate of Ganga = volume flow rate of Bhagirathi + volume flow rate of Alaknanda

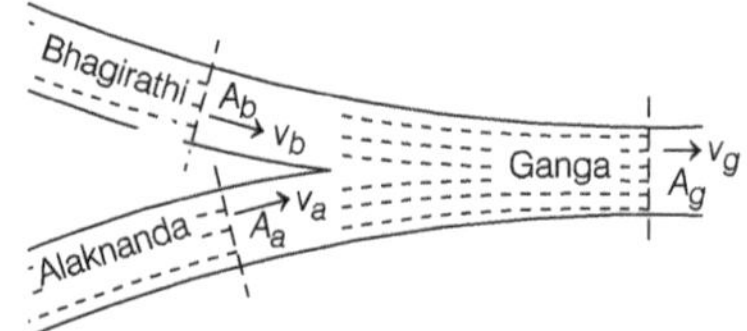

$\therefore$ By equation of continuity, we have

$$\Rightarrow \qquad A_g v_g = A_b v_b + A_a v_a \qquad \text{...(i)}$$

It is given that area of flow of Ganga, Alaknanda and Bhagirathi are in ratio,

$$A_g : A_a : A_b = 3 : 2 : 1$$

or $\qquad A_g = 3x, A_a = 2x, A_b = x$

Also, ratio of speeds of Bhagirathi and Alaknanda is

$$v_b : v_a = 1 : \frac{3}{2}$$

or $\qquad v_b = y, v_a = \frac{3}{2}y$

Substituting these values in Eq. (i), we get

$$3x \cdot v_g = x \cdot y + 2x \cdot \frac{3}{2}y = 4xy$$

So, $\qquad v_g = \frac{4}{3}y$

$\therefore$ Ratio of speed of Ganga to that of Alaknanda is

$$\frac{v_g}{v_a} = \frac{\frac{4}{3}y}{\frac{3}{2}y} = \frac{8}{9}$$

29. *(c)* Initially pressure inside the cylinder is atmospheric pressure p_0.

When mass m is attached to piston and it comes down by a distance Δl, let pressure is p.

Then, in equilibrium,
$$p_0 V_0 = pV \Rightarrow p_0(A)(l) = pA(l + \Delta l)$$

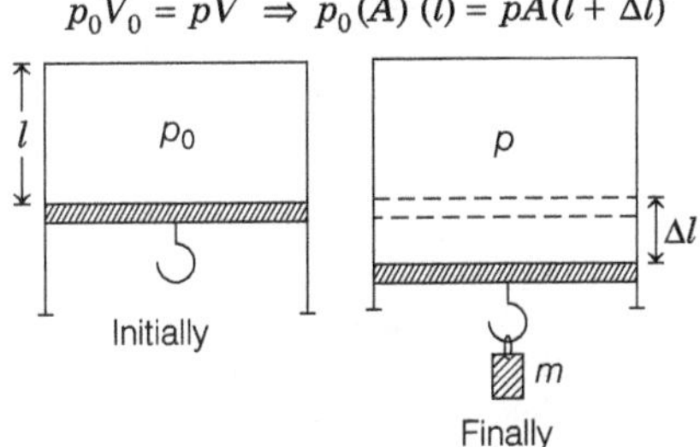

So, final pressure will be
$$p = \frac{p_0 Al}{A(l + \Delta l)} = \frac{p_0 l}{(l + \Delta l)}$$

In equilibrium, weight of mass m is balanced by force of suction due to reduced pressure p.

$\because$
$$(p_0 - p)A = mg$$
$$\Rightarrow \left(p_0 - \frac{p_0 l}{l + \Delta l}\right)A = mg \Rightarrow \frac{p_0 A}{mg} = \frac{l}{\Delta l} + 1$$
$$\Rightarrow \frac{10^5 \times \pi \times (20 \times 10^{-2})^2}{50 \times 10} = \frac{l}{\Delta l} + 1$$
$$\Rightarrow \frac{22 \times 8}{7} - 1 = \frac{l}{\Delta l}$$
$$\Rightarrow \frac{l}{\Delta l} = \frac{169}{7} \text{ or } \frac{\Delta l}{l} \approx 0.04$$

30. *(d)* For a plano-concave lens, when view is from concave side. Radius of curvature of surface 1 is $R_1 = \infty$ and radius of curvature of surface 2 is $R_2 = R$.

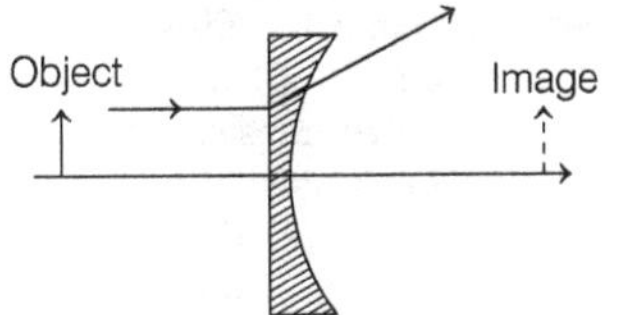

So, focal length of lens using
$$\frac{1}{f} = (\mu - 1)\left(\frac{1}{R_1} - \frac{1}{R_2}\right) \left[\mu = \frac{3}{2} \text{ for glass}\right]$$

we have, when viewed from curved side,
$$f = \frac{-R}{(\mu - 1)}$$
and $\qquad R_1 = -R, R_2 = \infty.$

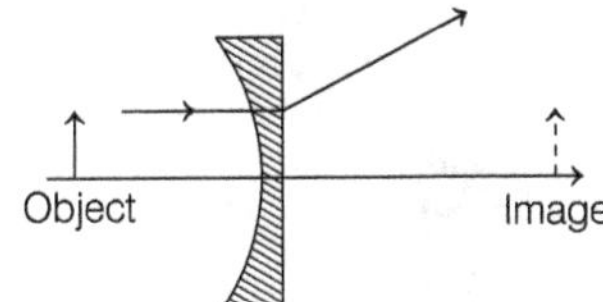

When viewed from plane side,
$$\frac{1}{f} = (\mu - 1)\left(-\frac{1}{R}\right)$$
$$\Rightarrow \qquad f = \frac{-R}{(\mu - 1)}$$

So, a plano-concave lens acts like a diverging lens weather object is viewed from plane side or curved side.

Hence, image appears erect in both cases.

$\therefore$ First image appears same when viewed from plane or curved side of a plano-concave lens.

Similarly, a plano-convex lens is a converging lens from both side view.

So, second image appears always inverted in both cases.

31. *(c)* The IUPAC name for the following compound is

2, 4-dimethylheptane

32. *(b)* As the size of alkyl group goes on increasing, the $+I$ effect exerted by it becomes strong and, thus the carbocation will be more stable. So, among 1°, 2° and 3° carbocation, 3° will be most stable.

Although $(CH_3)_2 \overset{+}{C}(OCH_3)$ will be highly stable among the given carbocations due to resonance stabilisation.

$$(CH_3)_2 - \overset{+}{C} - \overset{..}{\underset{..}{O}} - CH_3 \longleftrightarrow$$
$$(CH_3)_2 - C = \overset{+}{\underset{..}{O}} - CH_3$$

Thus, the correct order of stability of carbocations will be

$$CH_3CH_2CH_2\overset{+}{C}H_2 < CH_3\overset{+}{C}HCH_2CH_3 <$$
$$\underset{III}{(1°)} \qquad\qquad \underset{IV}{(2°)}$$
$$(CH_3)_3C^+ < (CH_3)_2\overset{+}{C}(OCH_3)$$
$$\underset{I}{(3°)} \qquad\qquad\qquad II$$

33. *(a)* The acidity of compounds in water depends upon the ease with which it can lose H^+ ions. Acetic acid is the strongest acid as the negative charge on carboxylate ion (conjugate base) is delocalised over two oxygen atoms. Hence, H^+ ion can be easily lost. The next strongest acidic compound phenol. This is because the phenoxide ion is resonance stabilised. This easily allows the H to leave as H^+ ion. Among acetonitrile and ethanol, ethanol is more acidic, this is because in ethanol the H-atom is directly attached to more electronegative atom, O.

Thus, the correct order of acidity of compound I-IV in water will be
IV < I < III < II.

34. *(c)*

This reaction is known as Hofmann bromamide reaction. It is used for preparing amine containing one carbon less than the starting amide. In this reaction, migration of an alkyl or aryl group takes place from carbonyl carbon of the amide to N-atom.

35. *(b)* Fehling's reagent is a mixture of aqueous copper sulphate and alkaline sodium potassium tartarate. When an aldehyde is heated with Fehling's reagent a reddish brown precipitate is obtained and the aldehydes are oxidised to corresponding carboxylate anion. This reddish brown precipitate is due to the formation of copper oxide.

$$RCHO + 2Cu^{2+} + 5OH^- \xrightarrow{\Delta} RCOO^-$$
(Fehling's solutions)
$$+ Cu_2O\downarrow + 3H_2O$$
Red brown (ppt).

36. *(d)* The reducing ability of metals can be determined by electrochemical series. In this series, various elements are arranged according to their decreasing values of standard reduction potentials. The reducing ability of the metal increases as you go up the series. The increasing order of $E°$ values of given metals are,

$$K < Zn < Pb < Au.$$

Thus, the correct order of reducing ability of metals K, Au, Zn and Pb follows the order

$$K > Zn > Pb > Au.$$

37. *(a)* White phosphorus is highly reactive and catches fire when exposed to air and produces white dense fumes of phosphorus oxide, P_4O_{10}.

$$P_4 + 5O_2 \rightarrow P_4O_{10}$$

38. *(d)* The maximum number of electrons that can be filled in the shell with principle quantum number, $n = 2n^2$

For $\qquad n = 4$

Maximum number of electrons $= 2(4)^2 = 32$

39. *(b)* According to ideal gas equation
$$pV = nRT \Rightarrow \frac{V}{T} = \frac{nR}{p} = \text{slope}$$

Given, slope $= 0.328$, $n = 2$

$\therefore \quad p = \dfrac{nR}{\text{slope}} = \dfrac{2 \times 0.0821}{0.328} = 0.500 \text{ atm}$

40. *(c)* The more positive $E°$ value of metal, feasible transformation can be carried out by using HI as reducing agent under acidic conditions.

As $E° = 0.77\,V\ (Fe^{3+} \to Fe^{2+})$ is more positive than, $E° = 0.54\ (I_2(s) \to 2I^-)$ thus can be used for carrying out transformation as it is the strongest oxidising agent among the other given options.

41. *(*)* According to de-Broglie wavelength

$$\lambda = \frac{h}{mv}$$

Mass of $C_{60} = 12 \times 60 = 720\,g$

Given, $\lambda = 11.0\overset{\circ}{A} = 11 \times 10^{-10}\,m$

$$h = 6.626 \times 10^{-34}\,Js$$
$$= 6.626 \times 10^{-34}\,kg\ m^2s^{-1}$$

$$\therefore\ v = \frac{h}{m\lambda} = \frac{6.626 \times 10^{-34}\ kgm^2s^{-1}}{720 \times 10^{-3}\ kg \times 11 \times 10^{-10}\,m}$$

$$= 0.8 \times 10^{-18}\,m/s$$

No option is correct in the given format as the value of wavelength is given in Å which gives the large difference in answer.

42. *(c)* Lattice energy is the energy required to completely separate one mole of a solid ionic compound into gaseous constituent. Lattice energy increases with decrease in the size of ions.

This is because as the size of ion is less, intermolecular distance will be less and so forces of attraction is greater.

Thus, the correct increasing order of lattice energies is,

RbCl < KCl < NaCl < NaF.

43. *(a)* Let the oxidation state of P-atom in $POCl_3$, H_2PO_3 and $H_4P_2O_6$ be x.

(i) $POCl_3$
$$x + 1\,(-2) + 3(-1) = 0$$
$$x - 2 - 3 = 0$$
$$x = + 5$$

(ii) H_2PO_3
$$2(1) + x + 3(-2) = 0$$
$$2 + x - 6 = 0$$
$$x = + 4$$

(iii) $H_4P_2O_6$
$$4(1) + 2x + 6(-2) = 0$$
$$4 + 2x - 12 = 0$$
$$2x = 8$$
$$x = + 4$$

44. *(b)* Number of equivalents
$$= M \times V \times \text{acidity/basicity}$$
Number of equivalents of NaOH
$$= 1 \times y \times 1 = y$$

Number of equivalents of H_2SO_4
$$= 0.6 \times 10 \times 2 = 12$$
(Number of equivalents)$_{NaOH}$
$$= (\text{Number of equivalents})_{H_2SO_4}$$
$$= y = 12\,mL$$
Also, number of equivalents of acid
$$= \text{Number of equivalents of NaOH}$$
$$N \times 5 = 1 \times 12 \times 1\quad [N = M \times \text{basicity}]$$
$$N = \frac{12}{5} = 2.4$$

45. *(b)* $M + O_2 \to MO_2$

Percentage of $M = \frac{1.25}{1.68} \times 100 = 74.4\%$

Percentage of oxygen in oxide
$$= 100 - 74.4\% = 25.6\%$$

To calculate empirical formula

Eleme-nt	% of element	At mass of element	Moles of element	Simplest molar ratio	Simplest whole no.
M	74.4	69.7	$\frac{74.4}{69.7} = 1.06$	$\frac{1.06}{1.06} = 1$	$1 \times 2 = 2$
O	25.6	16	$\frac{25.6}{16} = 1.6$	$\frac{1.6}{1.06} = 1.50$	$1.50 \times 2 = 3$

$\therefore$ Empirical formula of metal oxide is M_2O_3.

46. *(b)* In 1953, JD Watson and FHC Crick proposed a 3-D model of physiological DNA. They proposed that DNA is a double-stranded helical molecule. It consists of two sugar-phosphate backbones on the outside, held together by hydrogen bonds between pairs of nitrogenous bases on the inside. The bases adenine (A) always pairs with thymine (T) by two hydrogen bonds and guanine always pairs with cytosine (C) by three hydrogen bonds. This complimentarity is known as the base pairing rule.

47. *(c)* In anaphase, sister chromatids separate from centromeres so, number of chromosome becomes double. Other statements about mitosis can be corrected as Mitosis is a single nuclear division that results in two nuclei.

Synapsis takes place during prophase-I of meiosis not during mitosis. Non-sister chromatids recombine during prophase-I of meiosis. During mitosis, each sister chromatid separates and moves to opposite pole of the cell at anaphase.

48. *(b)* Gaseous exchange occurs at the alveoli in the lungs and takes place by diffusion. The alveoli are surrounded by capillaries so, oxygen and carbon dioxide diffuse between the air in the alveoli and the blood in the capillaries. Diffusion is the movement of gas from an area of high concentration to an area of low concentration.

49. *(b)* The class Ostracodermi is represented by the fossil vertebrates of late Cambrian period. The earliest known vertebrates to appear in fossil record were jawless primitive fish-like animals collectively called ostracoderms. These animals resembled the present day cyclostomes (lampreys and hagfishes) in many respects.

50. *(b)* Scurvy is caused by the deficiency of vitamin-C (Ascorbic acid) in the body. It can lead to anaemia, debility, exhaustion, spontaneous bleeding, pain in the limbs and especially the legs, swelling in some parts of the body and sometimes ulceration of the gums and loss of teeth.

51. *(b)* DNA polymer is made up of nitrogenous base, a sugar and one or more phosphate. Optical activity results due to the molecular asymmetry. The nucleic acid bases have a plane of symmetry. Hence, they do not induce optical activity. Sugars are asymmetric and cause optical activity of DNA.

52. *(c)* The monarch butterfly avoids predators such as birds by producing a chemical obnoxious to the predator. Monarchs lay their eggs on milkweed (swan plants), a member of the genus *Asclepias*. As the caterpillars eat the milkweed leaves, they ingest chemicals called cardiac glycosides. Birds or other animals that eat the caterpillars (or milkweed itself) become sick and vomit.

The caterpillars sequester (hold onto) this toxin as they pupate and the toxins are transferred to the adult butterflies. Birds or other creatures that eat the monarchs become sick, so they learn to leave both the butterflies and larvae alone.

53. *(d)* Filariasis is caused by *Wuchereria bancrofti*. It lives in lymphatic vessels and causes swelling of lower limbs and scrotum. *Entamoeba histolytica* causes amoebiasis. *Plasmodium falciparum* causes malaria. *Trypanosoma brucei* causes African sleeping sickness.

54. *(c)* Conversion of glucose to CO_2 and H_2O by *Saccharomyces* is a reaction which takes place in aerobic conditions, i.e. in the presence of oxygen.

$$C_6H_{12}O_6 + 6O_2 \to 6CO_2 + 6H_2O$$

55. *(d)* A mole is the quantity of a substance whose weight in grams is equal to the molecular weight of the substance. 1 mole is equal to 1 moles Glucose, or 180.15588 grams.

$\therefore$ 18 g of glucose = x mole $\times$ 180 g

x mole = $\dfrac{18}{180}$ = 0.1 mole

$\therefore$ An amount of 18 g glucose corresponds to 0.1 mole.

56. *(a)* Four electrons are required to reduce one molecule of oxygen to water during mitochondrial oxidation.

$O_2 + 4e^- + 4H^+ \to 2H_2O$

This process mentioned above takes place during oxidative phosphorylation. It is the metabolic pathway in which cells use enzymes to oxidise nutrients, thereby releasing energy which is used to produce ATP.

57. *(d)* Vitamin-B_5 is pantothenic acid or pantothenate, that is required in the synthesis of acetyl Co-A. In all living organisms, Co-A is synthesised in a five step process that requires four molecules of ATP, pantothenate and cysteine.

58. *(a)* HIV is the causative organism for AIDS.

Syphilis is a bacterial infection caused by *Treponema* sp. It spreads by sexual contact that starts as a painless sore. Viral hepatitis caused by HBV is an infection that causes liver inflammation and damage organs.

Gonorrhoea is caused by *Neisseria* sp. It is sexually transmitted bacterial infection that if let untreated may cause infertility.

59. *(b)* Telocentric chromosome is a chromosome like a straight rod with the centromere in terminal position.

Metacentric chromosome is a X-shaped chromosome, with the centromere in the middle so that the two arms of the chromosomes are almost equal. Acrocentric chromosome is a chromosome in which the centromere is located quite near one end of the chromosome. Sub-metacentric chromosome is a chromosome whose centromere is located near the middle.

60. *(a)* Living organisms require energy to grow, reproduce and respond to the environment. Energy sources include primarily light and inorganic compounds. The most common source of energy on the earth is photosynthesis, which transforms sunlight into food. Life forms usually

contain specific combinations of inorganic elements including carbon, hydrogen, nitrogen and oxygen that combine to form proteins and nucleic acids.

61. *(d)* Given,

$ABCD$ is a trapezium where AB is parallel to CD. A circle S with AB as diametre touch CD and also circle passes through the mid-points of diagonal AC and BD.

$$AR = RC$$
$$\angle ARB = 90°$$

$\therefore \Delta ABC$ is isosceles

$$AB = BC \qquad \ldots \text{(i)}$$

Similarly, in ΔABD

$$BQ = QD$$
$$\angle AQB = 90°$$

$\therefore \Delta ABD$ is isosceles.

$$\therefore \qquad AB = AD \qquad \ldots \text{(ii)}$$

From Eqs. (i) and (ii),

$$AB = BC = AD$$

$\therefore$ Trapezium is isosceles.

In ΔADM,

$$\sin \angle ADM = \frac{AM}{AD} = \frac{OP}{AD} = \frac{OP}{2OP}$$
$$\left[\because OP = \frac{1}{2} AB \right]$$

$\Rightarrow \qquad \sin (\angle ADM) = \dfrac{1}{2}$

$\Rightarrow \qquad \angle ADM = 30° = \dfrac{\pi}{6}$

62. *(a)* Let the equation of circle is $x^2 + y^2 = 1, \left(\dfrac{a}{b}, \dfrac{c}{d} \right)$ lie on circle.

$\therefore \qquad \dfrac{a^2}{b^2} + \dfrac{c^2}{d^2} = 1$

$\Rightarrow \qquad \dfrac{c}{d} = \pm \dfrac{1}{b}\sqrt{b^2 - a^2}$

c and d are relatively prime.

$\therefore \dfrac{c}{d}$ is rational.

So, $\quad b^2 - a^2 = \lambda^2$ [$\because b$ is even; $\therefore a$ is odd]

b is even, a is odd.

$\therefore \lambda^2$ is odd $\Rightarrow b^2 = \lambda^2 + a^2$

$\Rightarrow \qquad b^2 = (2k + 1)^2 + (2m + 1)^2$

$\Rightarrow \qquad b^2 = 4k^2 + 4k + 1 + 4m^2 + 4m + 1$

$\Rightarrow \qquad b^2 = 4 (k^2 + m^2 + k + m) + 2$

$\therefore b$ is even; $\therefore b^2$ is multiple of 4.

But $4 (k^2 + m^2 + k + m) + 2$ is not multiple of 4.

$\therefore$ Not possible.

$\therefore S$ is empty set.

63. *(c)* Given,

Two circle each of radius is 2 and difference between their centre is $2\sqrt{3}$

$$AB = 2\sqrt{3} \Rightarrow AC = \frac{1}{2} AB$$
$$AC = \sqrt{3}$$

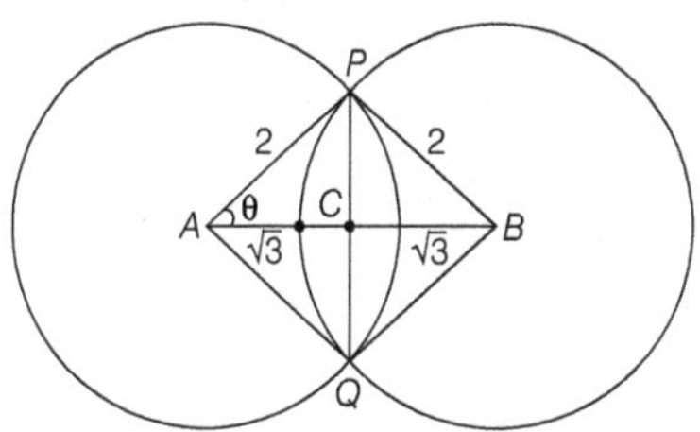

In ΔAPC, $\qquad \cos\theta = \dfrac{AC}{AP} = \dfrac{\sqrt{3}}{2}$

$$\theta = 30°$$

Area of common region

$= 2$ (Area of sector $-$ Area of ΔAPQ)

$= 2 \left(\dfrac{60}{360} \times \pi(2)^2 - \dfrac{1}{2} \times (2)^2 \times \sin 60° \right)$

$= 2 \left(\dfrac{4\pi}{6} - \dfrac{4\sqrt{3}}{4} \right)$

$= 2 \left(\dfrac{2}{3}(3.14) - (1.73) \right)$

$= 2 (2.09 - 1.73) = 2 (0.36) = 0.72$

$\therefore$ Area of region lie between 0.7 and 0.75.

64. *(a)* Given,

AB is diameter of circle C_1.

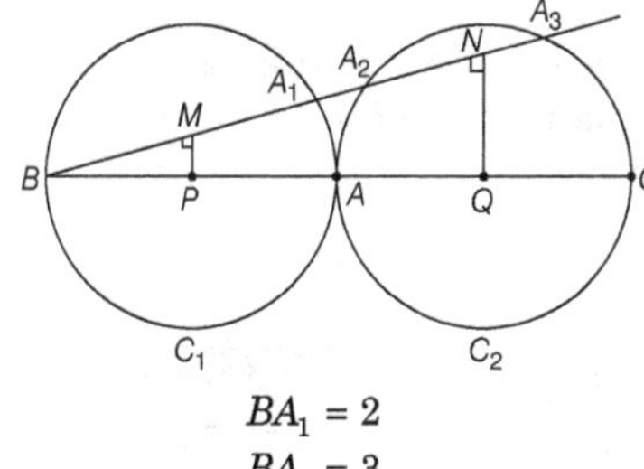

$$BA_1 = 2$$
$$BA_2 = 3$$
$$BA_3 = 4$$

Let radius of circle $C_1 = r_1$ and radius of circle $C_2 = r_2$

$\therefore \qquad BA = 2r_1$ and $AC = 2r_2$

$\Rightarrow \qquad BM = \dfrac{1}{2} BA_1 = 1$

$\Rightarrow \qquad BN = BA_2 + \dfrac{1}{2} A_2 A_3$

$= 3 + \dfrac{1}{2} = \dfrac{7}{2}$

In $\triangle BMP$ and $\triangle BNQ$,

$$\triangle BMP \sim \triangle BNQ$$

$\therefore$
$$\frac{BM}{BN} = \frac{BP}{BQ}$$

$\Rightarrow$
$$\frac{1}{7/2} = \frac{r_1}{2r_1 + r_2}$$

$\Rightarrow \qquad 2r_2 = 3r_1 \qquad \ldots \text{(i)}$

Now, $\quad BA_2 \times BA_3 = BA \times BC$

$\Rightarrow \qquad 3 \times 4 = 2r_1(2r_1 + 2r_2)$

$\Rightarrow \qquad 12 = 4(r_1^2 + r_1 r_2)$

$\Rightarrow \qquad r_1^2 + r_1 r_2 = 3 \qquad \ldots \text{(ii)}$

From Eqs. (i) and (ii), we get

$$r_1 = \sqrt{\frac{6}{5}} = \frac{\sqrt{30}}{5} \text{ and } r_2 = \frac{3\sqrt{30}}{10}$$

65. (a) Given,

$$|a| = \sqrt{4 - \sqrt{5 - a}}$$
$$|b| = \sqrt{4 + \sqrt{5 - b}}$$
$$|c| = \sqrt{4 - \sqrt{5 + c}}$$
$$|d| = \sqrt{4 + \sqrt{5 + d}}$$

On squaring, we get

$$a^2 = 4 - \sqrt{5 - a}$$
$$= a^2 - 4 = -\sqrt{5 - a}$$

Again squaring, we get

$$a^4 - 8a^2 + 16 = 5 - a$$

$\Rightarrow \quad a^4 - 8a^2 + a + 11 = 0$

Similarly, squaring other given equation and solving we can say that

$a, b, -c, -d$ are roots of equation

$$x^4 - 8x^2 + x + 11 = 0$$

$\therefore$ The product of roots

i.e. $\qquad abcd = 11$

66. (c) When planks are arranged as given in question, we have following situation.

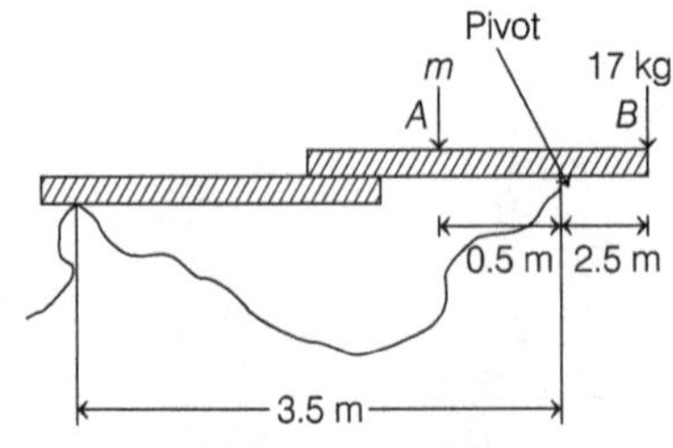

Let m = maximum mass of A.

Then, for safe crossing,

$$mg \times 0.5 = 17 \times g \times 2.5$$

$\Rightarrow \qquad m = \dfrac{17 \times 2.5}{0.5} = 85 \text{ kg}$

So, a man of mass upto 80 kg can pass over planks.

67. (b) Let Q = rate of heat removal.

Then, $\qquad Q \cdot t = mcT$

$\Rightarrow \qquad T = \dfrac{Q}{mc} \cdot t$

Comparing this with $y = mx$,

Slope of T-t line $\propto \dfrac{1}{\text{Specific heat}}$

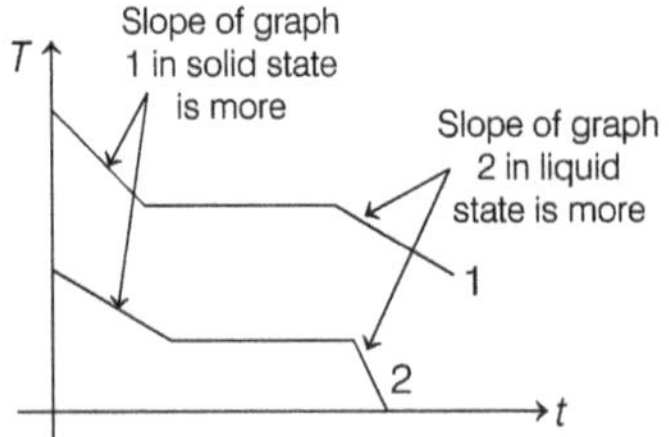

From graph,

$\therefore \qquad C_{S1} < C_{S2}$

and $\qquad C_{L1} > C_{L2}$

68. (a) As θ increases, angle of incidence $(i = 90 - \theta)$ decreases. Initially upto $i = i_c$ angle of critical incidence, reflection takes place and x is positive. Also, x increases till θ is such that $i = i_c$, after that refraction takes place and x becomes negative.

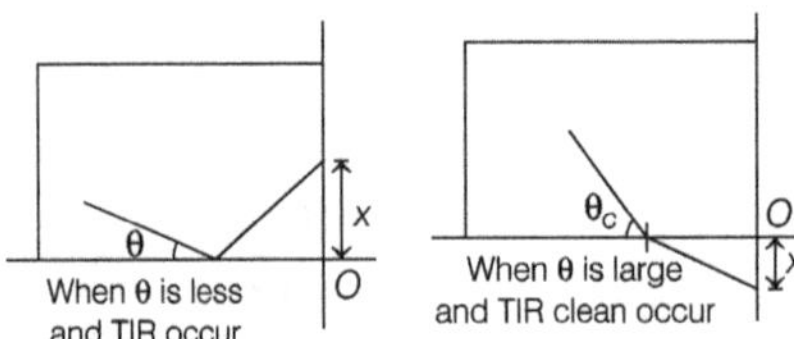

69. (b) Electrostatic force on any of the ball is (let x = separation between two adjacent balls).

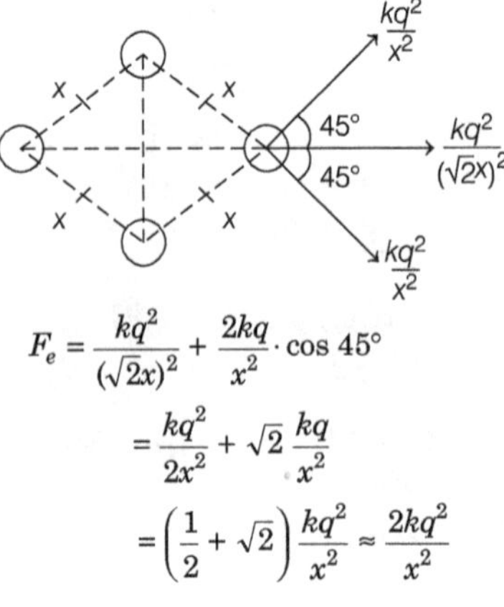

$$F_e = \frac{kq^2}{(\sqrt{2}x)^2} + \frac{2kq}{x^2} \cdot \cos 45°$$

$$= \frac{kq^2}{2x^2} + \sqrt{2}\,\frac{kq}{x^2}$$

$$= \left(\frac{1}{2} + \sqrt{2}\right)\frac{kq^2}{x^2} \approx \frac{2kq^2}{x^2}$$

As each ball is at an angle of 45° from each other, so in equilibrium, we have

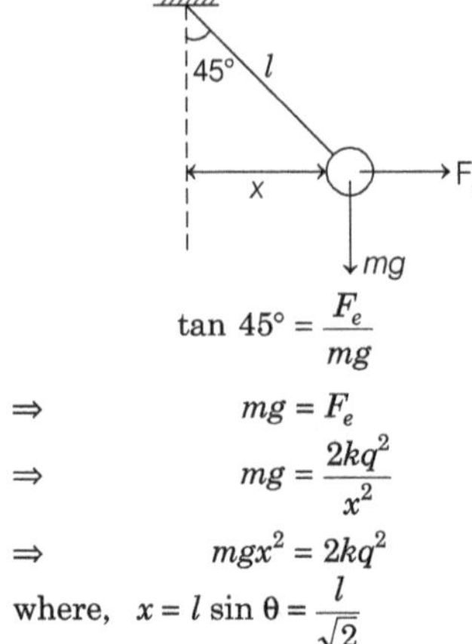

$$\tan 45° = \frac{F_e}{mg}$$

$\Rightarrow \qquad mg = F_e$

$\Rightarrow \qquad mg = \dfrac{2kq^2}{x^2}$

$\Rightarrow \qquad mgx^2 = 2kq^2$

where, $\quad x = l\sin\theta = \dfrac{l}{\sqrt{2}}$

So, substituting values, we get

$$\Rightarrow 100 \times 10^{-3} \times 10 \times \left(\frac{20 \times 10^{-2}}{\sqrt{2}}\right)^2$$

$$= 2 \times 9 \times 10^9 \times q^2$$

$\Rightarrow \qquad q^2 = \dfrac{10^{-2}}{9 \times 10^9}$

$\Rightarrow \qquad q^2 > 10^{-12}$

(slightly higher than 10^{-12})

$\Rightarrow \qquad q > 10^{-6} \text{ C}$

So, nearest answer is $1.5\,\mu\text{C}$.

70. (d) Time at which discs gaps are alined,

$$t = \frac{\pi}{\omega}, \frac{3\pi}{\omega}, \frac{5\pi}{\omega}, \ldots$$

So, speeds of atoms that emerges on other side are

$$v_1 = \frac{0.5}{\dfrac{\pi}{600} \times 2\pi} = 600 \text{ ms}^{-1}$$

and $\quad v_2 = \dfrac{0.5}{\dfrac{3\pi}{600} \times 2\pi} = 200 \text{ ms}^{-1}$

71. (d) If alkenes have two different substituents (x, y) at each end of the $C = C$, then only they can show E/Z isomerism.

(a) 2-methylbut-2-ene

As $x = y$, this alkene will not show E/Z isomerism.

(b) 2-methylbut-1-ene

Here also $x = y$

$\therefore$ It will not show E/Z isomerism.

(c) 3-methylpent-1-ene

$$x\,\textcircled{H}\quad\textcircled{H}\,x$$
$$\diagdown C = C \diagup$$
$$y\,\textcircled{H}\quad \boxed{CH_2(CH_3)CH_2CH_3}\,y$$

This compound will not show E/Z isomerism.

(d) 3-methylpent-2-ene

$$x\,\textcircled{H}\quad \boxed{CH_2CH_3}\,x$$
$$\diagdown C = C \diagup$$
$$y\,\textcircled{H$_3$C}\quad \textcircled{CH$_3$}\,y$$

As $x \neq y$, thus this alkene will show E/Z is isomerism.

72. *(c)*

$$CH_3 - C \equiv C - H \xrightarrow{\text{(i) Na}^{\oplus}\ \text{NH}_2^{\ominus}} CH_3\,C \equiv C^{\ominus}\,Na^{\oplus}$$

$$\downarrow \text{(ii) } CH_3{}_{\delta^+} - I{}_{\delta^-}\ (x)$$

$$HC = CH \xleftarrow[(y)]{\text{(iii) Na/liq. NH}_3} CH_3 C \equiv C CH_3 + NaI$$

with CH_3 substituents *(Trans form)*

Thus, in the given reaction,

$x = CH_3 I$ and $y = Na/liq.\ NH_3$.

73. *(a)* The bond angle depends upon the electronegativity of the central atom. More is the electronegativity of the central, larger is the bond angle. Thus, among the given central atom Cl has the highest electronegativity. Therefore, ClF_3 has the largest bond angle at the central atom.

74. *(d)*

Elements	% of element	At mass of element	Moles of element	Simplest molar ratio	Simplest whole no.
Na	18.6	23	$\dfrac{18.6}{23} = 0.8$	$\dfrac{0.8}{0.8} = 1$	$1 \times 2 = 2$
S	25.8	32	$\dfrac{25.8}{32} = 0.8$	$\dfrac{0.8}{0.8} = 1$	$1 \times 2 = 2$
O	51.58	16	$\dfrac{51.58}{16} = 3.22$	$\dfrac{3.22}{0.8} = 4$	$4 \times 2 = 8$
H	4.02	1	$\dfrac{4.02}{1} = 4.02$	$\dfrac{4.02}{0.8} = 5$	$5 \times 2 = 10$

Thus, the empirical formula of compound is $Na_2S_2H_{10}O_8$.

As it is given the all the hydrogen atoms in the compound are part of water of crystallisation, therefore molecular formula will be $Na_2S_2O_3 \cdot 5H_2O$.

75. *(d)* Given, latent heat of fusion of ice = 333 J/g

Specific heat of water = 4184 J/g K

First X g of ice at 0°C melts and then its temperature increases by gaining heat from 340 g of water at 20°C.

$\therefore$ Energy gained by X g of ice = energy lost by 340 g of water

$$[E = mc\,\Delta T]$$

$$X\,(333) + X \times 4184\,(278 - 273) = 340 \times 4184\,(293 - 278)$$

$$333X + 20.92X = 21338.4 \Rightarrow 353.92X = 21338.4$$

$$X = 60.29 \approx 60.3\ g$$

76. *(d)* Blood group-O individuals are called universal donor as they can give blood to person with blood group-A, B, AB and O.

Blood group-AB individuals can only give blood to persons with blood group-AB but can receive blood from all other blood groups.

Therefore, the correct table for the blood transfusion compatibility for ABO blood group system in human is

(d)

		Recipient			
		O	A	B	AB
Donor	O	✓	✓	✓	✓
	A	✗	✓	✗	✓
	B	✗	✗	✓	✓
	AB	✗	✗	✗	✓

77. *(b)* Assuming x as the amount of ligand to occupy all the binding sites in 10 mg protein.

$$\frac{x\ \text{mg}}{\text{Protein in grams}} = \frac{\text{Ligand molecular weight}}{\text{Protein molecular weight}}$$

$$x = \frac{2500}{25000} \times 10 = 1\,\text{mg}$$

78. *(a)* Serine is coded by UCU, UCC, UCA, UCG, AGU, AGC

Leucine is coded by CUU, CUC, CUA, CUG, UUA, UUG

Arginine is coded by AGA, AGG, CGU, CGC, CGA, CGG

Glutamic acid is coded by GAA, GAG

Therefore, option (a) is the correct interpretation of the assigned amino acids.

Ser-UCU, Leu-CUC, Arg-AGA, Glu-GAG

79. *(d)* The number of bacteria after 15 hours will be 32. This happens as each bacterium doubles up after every 3 hours, i.e. it will double $\dfrac{15}{3} = 5$ times in 15 hours.

Therefore, the sequence in which the growth of bacteria taking place will be

$$1 \xrightarrow{\text{3 hours}} 2 \xrightarrow{\text{3 hours}} 4 \xrightarrow{\text{3 hours}} 8 \xrightarrow{\text{3 hours}} 16 \xrightarrow{\text{3 hours}} 32$$

80. *(c)* Colourblindness is a X-linked recessive disease, i.e. an heterozygous mother does not show the disease and is a carrier. But a father cannot be a carrier of the disease as it has single X-chromosome.

In the given question, the son is colourblind which means it had inherited X^c from the mother. But another son is normal. This shows that the mother is heterozygous for the disease.

The expected cross for the question will be

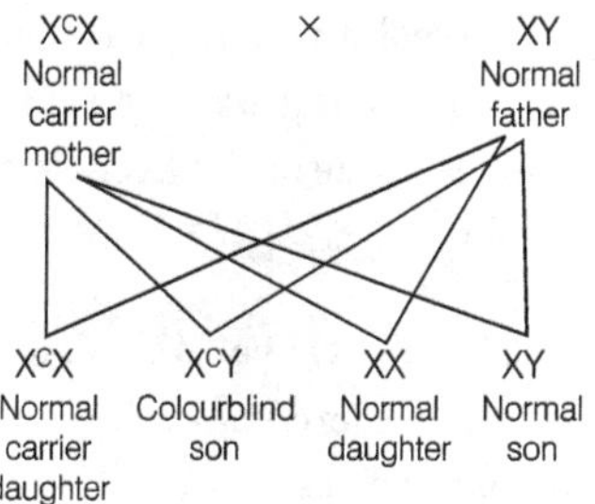

This shows that **both the parents would be normal** if they have one colourblind son and one normal son.

QUESTION PAPER 2017

Stream : SA (Nov 05)

MM : 100

Instructions

1. There are 80 questions in this paper.
2. This question paper contains two parts; Part I and Part II. There are four sections; Mathematics, Physics, Chemistry and Biology in each part.
3. Out of the four options given with each question, only one is correct.

➔ PART-I (1 Mark Questions)

MATHEMATICS

1. A quadrilateral has distinct integer side lengths. If the second-largest side has length 10, then the maximum possible length of the largest side is

(a) 25   (b) 26   (c) 27   (d) 28

2. The largest power of 2 that divides $\dfrac{200!}{100!}$ is

(a) 98   (b) 99   (c) 100   (d) 101

3. Let a_1, a_2, a_3, a_4 be real numbers such that $a_1 + a_2 + a_3 + a_4 = 0$ and $a_1^2 + a_2^2 + a_3^2 + a_4^2 = 1$. Then, the smallest possible value of the expression $(a_1 - a_2)^2 + (a_2 - a_3)^2 + (a_3 - a_4) + (a_4 - a_1)^2$ lies in the interval

(a) (0, 1.5)   (b) (1.5, 2.5)   (c) (2.5, 3)   (d) (3, 3.5)

4. Let S be the set of all ordered pairs (x, y) of positive integers satisfying the condition $x^2 - y^2 = 12345678$. Then,

(a) S is an infinite set

(b) S is the empty set

(c) S has exactly one element

(d) S is a finite set and has at least two elements.

5. Let $A_1\,A_2\,A_3\dots A_9$ be a nine-sided regular polygon with side length 2 units. The difference between the lengths of the diagonals A_1A_5 and A_2A_4 equals

(a) $2 + \sqrt{12}$ (b) $\sqrt{12} - 2$ (c) 6   (d) 2

6. Let $a_1, a_2, \dots, a_n$ be n non-zero real numbers, of which p are positive and remaining are negative. The number of ordered pairs $(j, k), j < k$, for which $a_j a_k$ is positive, is 55. Similarly, the number of ordered pairs $(j, k), j < k$, for which $a_j a_k$ is negative, is 50. Then, the value of $p^2 + (n - p)^2$ is

(a) 629   (b) 325   (c) 125   (d) 221

7. If a, b, c, d are four distinct numbers chosen from the set $\{1, 2, 3, \dots, 9\}$, then the minimum value of $\dfrac{a}{b} + \dfrac{c}{d}$ is

(a) $\dfrac{3}{8}$ (b) $\dfrac{1}{3}$ (c) $\dfrac{13}{36}$ (d) $\dfrac{25}{72}$

8. If $72^x \cdot 48^y = 6^{xy}$, where x and y are non-zero rational numbers, then $x + y$ equals

(a) 3 (b) $\dfrac{10}{3}$ (c) -3 (d) $-\dfrac{10}{3}$

9. Let AB be a line segment of length 2. Construct a semicircle S with AB as diameter. Let C be the mid-point of the arc AB. Construct another semicircle T external to the $\triangle ABC$ with chord AC as diameter. The area of the region inside the semi-circle T but outside S is

(a) $\dfrac{\pi}{2}$ (b) $\dfrac{1}{2}$ (c) $\dfrac{\pi}{\sqrt{2}}$ (d) $\dfrac{1}{\sqrt{2}}$

10. Let $r(x)$ be the remainder when the polynomial $x^{135} + x^{125} - x^{115} + x^5 + 1$ is divided by $x^3 - x$. Then,

(a) $r(x)$ is the zero polynomial
(b) $r(x)$ is a non-zero constant
(c) degree of $r(x)$ is one (d) degree of $r(x)$ is two

11. It is given that the number 43361 can be written as a product of two distinct prime number p_1, p_2. Further, assume that there are 42900 numbers which are less than 43361 and are coprime to it. Then, $p_1 + p_2$ is

(a) 462 (b) 464 (c) 400 (d) 402

12. Let ABC be a triangle with $\angle C = 90°$. Draw CD perpendicular to AB. Choose points M and N on sides AC and BC respectively such that DM is parallel to BC and DN is parallel to AC. If $DM = 5$, $DN = 4$, then AC and BC are respectively equal to

(a) $\dfrac{41}{4}, \dfrac{41}{5}$ (b) $\dfrac{39}{4}, \dfrac{39}{5}$ (c) $\dfrac{38}{4}, \dfrac{38}{5}$ (d) $\dfrac{37}{4}, \dfrac{37}{5}$

13. Let A, G and H be the arithmetic mean, geometric mean and harmonic mean, respectively of two distinct positive real numbers. If α is the smallest of the two roots of the equation $A(G - H)x^2 + G(H - A)x + H(A - G) = 0$ then,

(a) $-2 < \alpha < -1$ (b) $0 < \alpha < 1$
(c) $-1 < \alpha < 0$ (d) $1 < \alpha < 2$

14. In the figure, $ABCD$ is a unit square. A circle is drawn with centre O on the extended line CD and passing through A. If the diagonal AC is tangent to the circle, then the area of the shaded region is

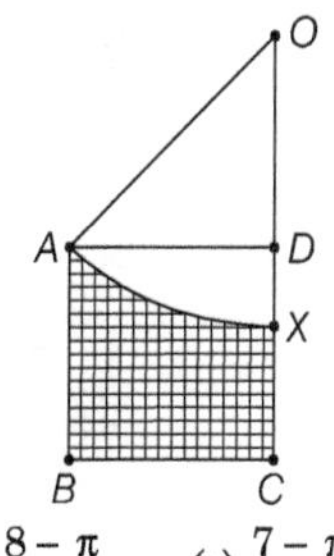

(a) $\dfrac{9 - \pi}{6}$ (b) $\dfrac{8 - \pi}{6}$ (c) $\dfrac{7 - \pi}{4}$ (d) $\dfrac{6 - \pi}{4}$

15. The sum of all non-integer roots of the equation $x^5 - 6x^4 + 11x^3 - 5x^2 - 3x + 2 = 0$ is

(a) 6 (b) –11 (c) -5 (d) 3

PHYSICS

16. Consider the following statements (X and Y stand for two different elements):

(I) $^{65}_{32}X$ and $^{65}_{33}Y$ are isotopes.

(II) $^{86}_{42}X$ and $^{85}_{42}Y$ are isotopes.

(III) $^{174}_{85}X$ and $^{177}_{88}Y$ have the same number of neutrons.

(IV) $^{235}_{92}X$ and $^{235}_{94}Y$ are isobars.

Which of the above statements are correct?
(a) Only statements II and IV are correct
(b) Only statements I, II and IV are correct
(c) Only statements II, III and IV are correct
(d) All statements are correct

17. A student performs an experiment to determine the acceleration due to gravity g. The student throws a steel ball up with initial velocity u and measures the height h travelled by it at different times t. The graph the student should plot on a graph paper to readily obtain the value of g is
(a) h versus t (b) h versus t^2
(c) h versus $\sqrt{t}$ (d) h / t versus t

18. A person goes from point P to point Q covering 1 /3 of the distance with speed 10 km/h, the next 1/3 of the distance at 20 km/h and the last 1/3 of the distance at 60 km/h. The average speed of the person is
(a) 30 km/h (b) 24 km/h (c) 18 km/h (d) 12 km/h

19. A person looks at the image of two parallel finite length lines PQ and RS in a convex mirror (see figure).

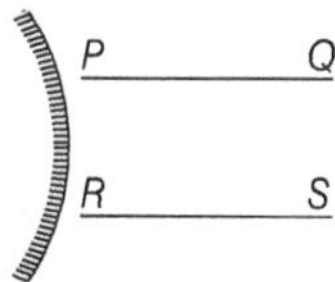

Which of the following represents schematically the image correctly?

Note Letters P, Q, R and S are used only to denote the endpoints of the lines.

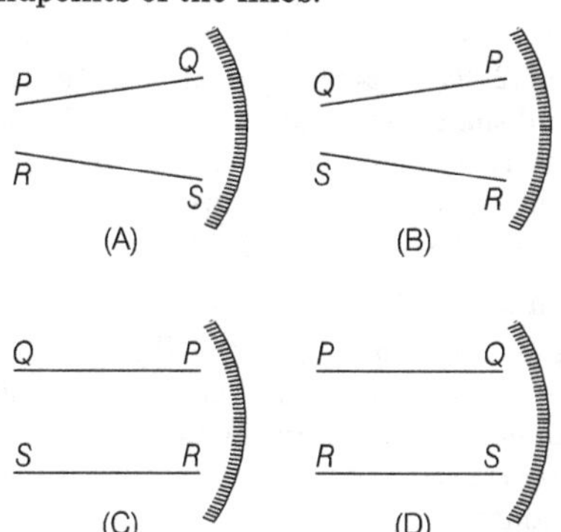

(a) A (b) B (c) C (d) D

20. In Guericke's experiment to show the effect of atmospheric pressure, two copper hemispheres were tightly fitted to each other to form a hollow sphere and the air from the sphere was pumped out to create vacuum inside. If the radius of each hemisphere is R and the atmospheric pressure is p, then the minimum force required (when the two hemispheres are pulled apart by the same force) to separate the hemispheres is

(a) $2p\pi R^2$ (b) $4p\pi R^2$ (c) $p\pi R^2$ (d) $\dfrac{p}{2}\pi R^2$

21. Positive point charges are placed at the vertices of a star shape as shown in the figure. Direction of the electrostatic force on a negative point charge at the centre O of the star is

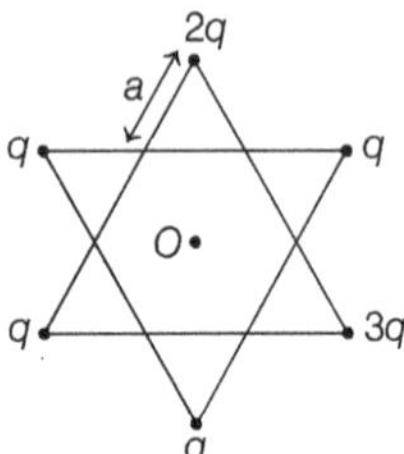

(a) towards right   (b) vertically up
(c) towards left   (d) vertically down

22. A total solar eclipse is observed from the earth. At the same time an observer on the moon view's the earth. She is most likely to see (E denotes the earth)

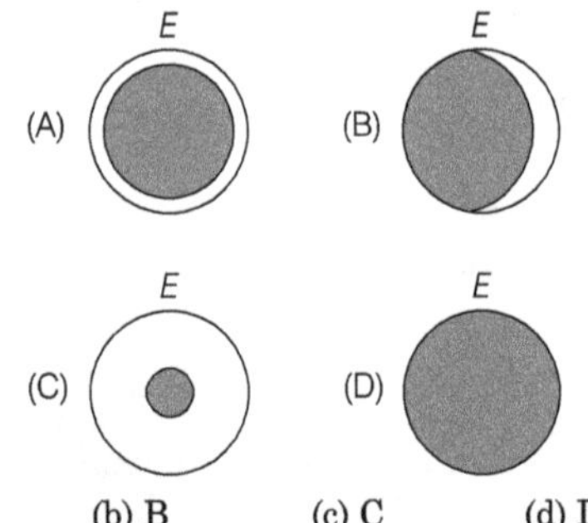

(a) A   (b) B   (c) C   (d) D

23. Ice in a freezer is at $-7°C$. 100 g of this ice is mixed with 200 g of water at $15°C$. Take the freezing temperature of water to be $0°C$, the specific heat of ice equal to 2.2 J/g $°C$, specific heat of water equal to 4.2 J/g$°C$ and the latent heat of ice equal to 335 J/g. Assuming no loss of heat to the environment, the mass of ice in the final mixture is closest to

(a) 88 g   (b) 67 g   (c) 54 g   (d) 45 g

24. A point source of light is placed at $2f$ from a converging lens of focal length f. A flat mirror is placed on the other side of the lens at a distance d such that rays reflected from the mirror are parallel after passing through the lens again. If $f = 30$ cm, then d is equal to

(a) 15 cm   (b) 30 cm   (c) 45 cm   (d) 75 cm

25. The word KVPY is written on a board and viewed through different lenses such that board is at a distance beyond the focal length of the lens.

First image   Second image

Ignoring magnification effects, consider the following statements:

(I) First image has been viewed from the planar side of a plano-convex lens and second image from the convex side of a plano-convex lens.

(II) First image has been viewed from the concave side of a plano-concave lens and second image from the convex side of a plano-convex lens.

(III) First image has been viewed from the concave side of a plano-concave lens and second image from the planar side of a plano-convex lens.

(IV) First image has been viewed from the planar side of a plano-concave lens and second image from the convex side of a plano-convex lens.

Which of the above statements are correct?

(a) All statements are correct
(b) Only statement III is correct
(c) Only statement IV is correct
(d) Only statements II, III and IV are correct

26. A ball is dropped vertically from height h and is bouncing elastically on the floor (see figure). Which of the following plots best depicts the acceleration of the ball as a function of time.

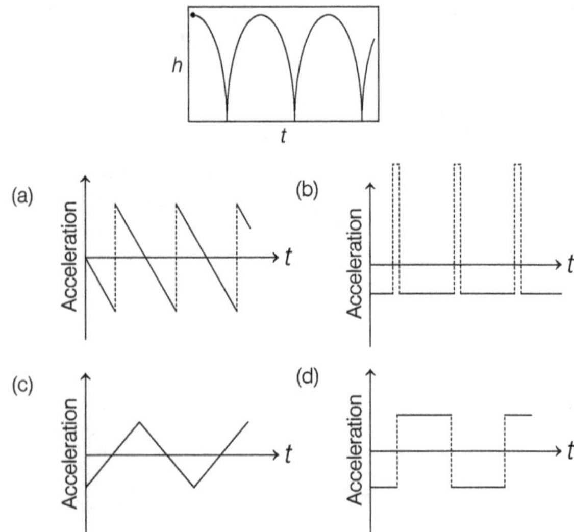

27. A student studying the similarities and differences between a camera and the human eye makes the following observations:

I. Both the eye and the camera have convex lenses.

II. In order to focus, the eye lens expands or contracts while the camera lens moves forward or backward.

III. The camera lens produces upside down real images while the eye lens produces only upright real images.

IV. A screen in camera is equivalent to the retina in the eyes.

V. A camera adjusts the amount of light entering in it by adjusting the aperture of the lens. In the eye, the cornea controls the amount of light.

Which of the above statements are correct?

(a) Statements I, II and IV are correct

(b) Statements I, III and V are correct

(c) Statements I, II, IV and V are correct

(d) All statements are correct

28. A particle starts moving along a line from zero initial velocity and comes to rest after moving distance d. During its motion, it had a constant acceleration f over 2/3 of the distance and covered the rest of the distance with constant retardation. The time taken to cover the distance is

(a) $\sqrt{2d/3f}$ (b) $2\sqrt{d/3f}$ (c) $\sqrt{3d/f}$ (d) $\sqrt{3d/2f}$

29. If the image formed by a thin convex lens of power P has magnification m, then image distance v is

(a) $v = \dfrac{1-m}{P}$ (b) $v = \dfrac{1+m}{P}$ (c) $v = \dfrac{m}{P}$ (d) $v = \dfrac{1+2m}{P}$

30. A long cylindrical pipe of radius 20 cm is closed at its upper end and has an airtight piston of negligible mass as shown. When a 50 kg mass is attached to the other end of the piston, it moves down. If the air in the enclosure is cooled from temperature T to $T - \Delta T$, the piston moves back to its original position. Then $\Delta T / T$ is close to (Assuming air to be an ideal gas, $g = 10$ m/s^2, atmospheric pressure is 10^5 Pa)

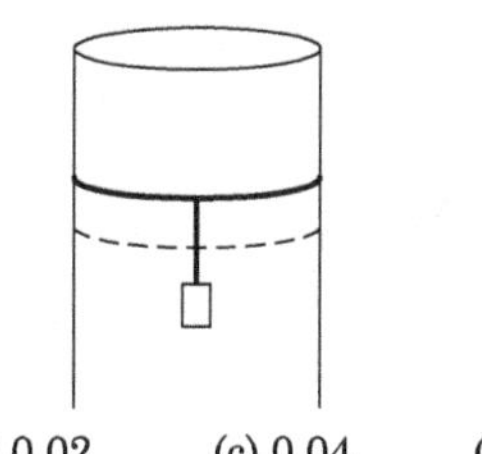

(a) 0.01   (b) 0.02   (c) 0.04   (d) 0.09

CHEMISTRY

31. The structure of 3-methylpent-2-ene is

(a)   (b)

(c)   (d)

32. The stability of carbanions

$$CH_3CH_2CH_2\overset{\ominus}{C}H_2 \qquad CH_3\overset{\ominus}{C}HCH_2CH_3$$
$$\text{I} \qquad\qquad\qquad \text{II}$$
$$(CH_3)_3\overset{\ominus}{C} \qquad CH_3\overset{\ominus}{C}(Ph)CH_2CH_3$$
$$\text{III} \qquad\qquad\qquad \text{IV}$$

follows the order

(a) III < IV < I < II   (b) I < II < IV < III

(c) III < II < I < IV   (d) IV < III < II < I

33. In the following reaction

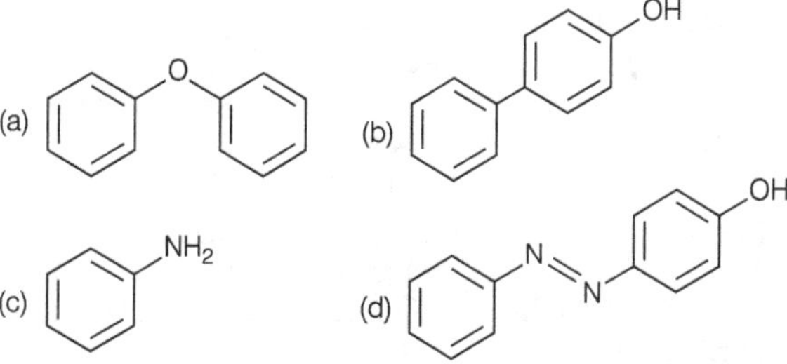

the major product is

(a)   (b)

(c)   (d)

34. In the reaction of 1-bromo-3-chlorocyclobutane with two equivalents of sodium in ether, the major product is

(a)   (b)

(c)   (d)

35. The order of basicity of

in water is

(a) IV < III < I < II   (b) II < I < IV < III

(c) IV < I < III < II   (d) II < III < I < IV

36. The first ionisation energy of Na, B, N and O atoms follows the order

(a) B < Na < O < N   (b) Na < B < O < N

(c) Na < O < B < N   (d) O < Na < N < B

37. Among P_2O_5, As_2O_3, Sb_2O_3 and Bi_2O_3, the most acidic oxide is

(a) P_2O_5 (b) As_2O_3 (c) Sb_2O_3 (d) Bi_2O_3

38. Among K, Mg, Au and Cu, the one which is extracted by heating its ore in air is

(a) K   (b) Mg   (c) Au   (d) Cu

39. The metal ion with total number of electrons same as S^{2-} is

(a) Na^+ (b) Ca^{2+} (c) Mg^{2+} (d) Sr^{2+}

40. X g of Ca [atomic mass = 40] dissolves completely in concentrated HCl solution to produce 5.04 L of H_2 gas at STP. The value of X is closest to

(a) 4.5   (b) 8.1   (c) 9.0   (d) 16.2

41. A 20 g object is moving with velocity 100 ms^{-1}. The de Broglie wavelength (in m) of the object is [Planck's constant $h = 6.626 \times 10^{-34}$ Js]

(a) 3.313×10^{-34} (b) 6.626×10^{-34}

(c) 3.313×10^{-31} (d) 6.626×10^{-31}

42. In a closed vessel at STP, 50 L of CH_4 is ignited with 750 L of air (containing 20% O_2). The number of moles of O_2 remaining in the vessel on cooling to room temperature is closest to

(a) 5.8   (b) 2.2   (c) 4.5   (d) 6.7

43. CO_2 is passed through lime water. Initially the solution turns milky and then becomes clear upon continued bubbling of CO_2. The clear solution is due to the formation of

(a) $CaCO_3$ (b) CaO

(c) $Ca(OH)_2$ (d) $Ca(HCO_3)_2$

44. The maximum number of electrons that can be filled in the shell with the principal quantum number $n = 3$ is

(a) 18   (b) 9   (c) 8   (d) 2

45. The atomic radii of Li, F, Na and Si follow the order

(a) Si > Li > Na > F   (b) Li > F > Si > Na

(c) Na > Si > F > Li   (d) Na > Li > Si > F

BIOLOGY

46. The major excretory product of birds is

(a) urea   (b) uric acid

(c) nitrates   (d) ammonia

47. Codon degeneracy means that

(a) several amino acids are coded by more than one codon

(b) one codon can code for many amino acids

(c) one amino acid can be coded by only one codon

(d) the codons are triplet nucleotide sequences

48. In cell cycle, during interphase

(a) two daughter cells are produced

(b) the nucleus is divided into two daughter nuclei

(c) the chromosome condenses

(d) the DNA is replicated

49. Transfer of genetic material between population is best defined as

(a) gene flow   (b) genetic drift

(c) genetic shift   (d) speciation

50. Which one of the following statements is correct about the tobacco mosaic virus?

(a) It affects all monocotyledonous plants

(b) It affects photosynthetic tissue of the infected plant

(c) It does not infect other species belonging to the Solanaceae

(d) It infects gymnosperms

51. Which one of the following statements is correct about placenta?

(a) Placenta is permeable to all bacteria

(b) Oxygen and carbon dioxide cannot diffuse through the placenta

(c) Waste products diffuse out of placenta into maternal blood

(d) Placenta does not secrete chorionic gonadotropins

52. The respiratory quotient of the reaction given below is

$2(C_{51}H_{98}O_6) + 145O_2 \rightarrow 102CO_2 + 90H_2O + Energy$

(a) 0.703   (b) 0.725   (c) 0.960   (d) 1.422

53. Which one of the following statements is incorrect about nucleosomes?

(a) They contain DNA

(b) They contain histones

(c) They are membrane-bound organelle

(d) They are a part of chromosomes

54. The immediate precursor of thyroxine is

(a) tyrosine   (b) tryptophan

(c) pyridoxine   (d) thymidine

55. The maximum number of oxygen molecules that can bind to one molecule of haemoglobin is

(a) 8   (b) 6   (c) 4   (d) 2

56. Which one of the following biomolecules is synthesised in smooth endoplasmic reticulum?

(a) Proteins   (b) Lipids

(c) Carbohydrates   (d) Nucleotides

57. The products of light reaction during photosynthesis include

(a) ATP and NADPH   (b) O_2 and $NADP^+$

(c) O_2 and H_2O (d) $NADP^+$ and H_2O

58. Hypothalamus directly controls the production of which of the following hormones?

(a) Glucocorticoid and insulin

(b) Insulin and glucagon

(c) Atrial natriuretic factor and gastrin

(d) Glucocorticoids and androgens

59. Which one of the following drug is not obtained from fungal or plant sources?

(a) Penicillin   (b) Reserpine

(c) Acetaminophen   (d) Quinine

60. Jean Baptiste Lamarck explained evolution based on

(a) natural selection

(b) survival of the fittest

(c) mutations

(d) inheritance of acquired characteristics

➲ PART-II (2 Marks Questions)

MATHEMATICS

61. Let S be the circle in XY-plane which touches the X-axis at point A, the Y-axis at point B and the unit circle $x^2 + y^2 = 1$ at point C externally. If O denotes the origin, then the angle OCA equals

(a) $\dfrac{5\pi}{8}$ (b) $\dfrac{\pi}{2}$ (c) $\dfrac{3\pi}{4}$ (d) $\dfrac{3\pi}{4}$

62. In an isosceles trapezium, the length of one of the parallel sides, and the lengths of the non-parallel sides are all equal to 30. In order to maximise the area of the trapezium, the smallest angle should be

(a) $\dfrac{\pi}{6}$ (b) $\dfrac{\pi}{4}$ (c) $\dfrac{\pi}{3}$ (d) $\dfrac{\pi}{2}$

63. Let A_1, A_2, A_3 be regions in the XY-plane defined by

$$A_1 = \{(x, y) : x^2 + 2y^2 \le 1\}$$
$$A_2 = \{(x, y) : |x^3| + 2\sqrt{2}\,|y|^3 \le 1\}$$
$$A_3 = \{(x, y) : \max(|x|, \sqrt{2}\,|y|) \le 1\}$$

Then,

(a) $A_1 \supset A_2 \supset A_3$ (b) $A_3 \supset A_1 \supset A_2$
(c) $A_2 \supset A_3 \supset A_1$ (d) $A_3 \supset A_2 \supset A_1$

64. Let $ABCD$ be a square and E be a point outside $ABCD$ such that E, A, C are collinear in that order. Suppose $EB = ED = \sqrt{130}$ and the areas to ΔEAB and square $ABCD$ are equal. Then, the area of square $ABCD$ is

(a) 8   (b) 10   (c) $\sqrt{120}$ (d) $\sqrt{125}$

65. Consider the set $A = \{1, 2, 3, \ldots, 30\}$. The number of ways in which one can choose three distinct number from A so that the product of the chosen numbers is divisible by 9 is

(a) 1590   (b) 1505   (c) 1110   (d) 1025

PHYSICS

66. Two different liquids of same mass are kept in two identical vessels, which are placed in a freezer that extracts heat from them at the same rate causing each liquid to transform into a solid. The schematic figure below shows the temperature T *versus* time t plot for the two materials. We denote the specific heat in the liquid states to be C_{L1} and C_{L2} for materials 1 and 2, respectively and latent heats of fusion U_1 and U_2, respectively.

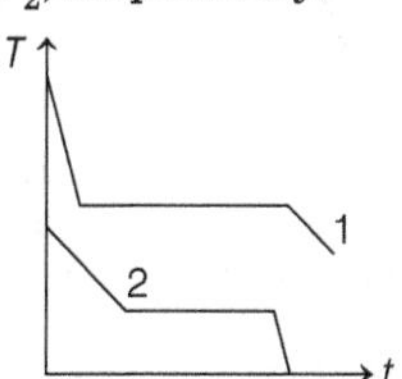

Choose the correct option.

(a) $C_{L1} > C_{L2}$ and $U_1 < U_2$ (b) $C_{L1} > C_{L2}$ and $U_1 > U_2$
(c) $C_{L1} < C_{L2}$ and $U_1 > U_2$ (d) $C_{L1} < C_{L2}$ and $U_1 < U_2$

67. A long horizontal mirror is next to a vertical screen (seen figure).

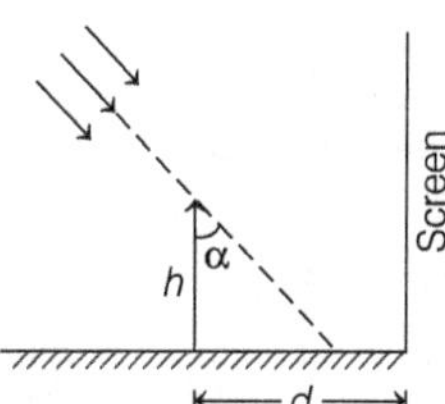

Parallel light rays are falling on the mirror at an angle α from the vertical. If a vertical object of height h is kept on the mirror at a distance $(d > h) \tan\alpha$. The length of the shadow of the object on the screen would be

(a) $\dfrac{h}{2}$ (b) $h \tan\alpha$

(c) $2h$ (d) $4h$

68. A spherical marble of radius 1 cm is stuck in a circular hole of radius slightly smaller than its own radius (for calculation purpose, both can be taken same) at the bottom of a bucket of height 40 cm and filled with water up to 10 cm.

If the mass of the marble is 20 g, then the net force on the marble due to water is close to

(a) 0.02 N upwards   (b) 0.02 N downwards
(c) 0.04 N upwards   (d) 0.04 N downwards

69. In the circuit shown below (on the left) the resistance and the emf source are both variable.

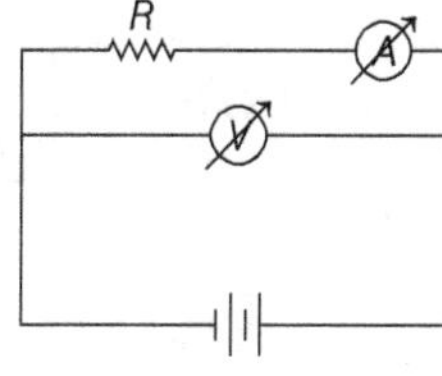

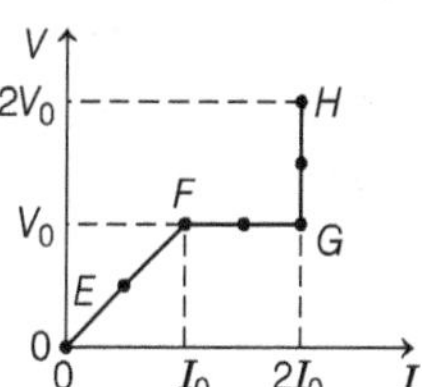

The graph of seven readings of the voltmeter and the ammeter (V and I, respectively) for different settings of resistance and the emf, taken at equal intervals of time Δt, are shown below (on the right) by the dots connected by the curve $EFGH$. Consider the internal resistance of the battery to be negligible and the voltmeter an ammeter to be ideal devices. (Take, $R_0 \equiv \dfrac{V_0}{I_0}$).

Then, the plot of the resistance as a function of time corresponding to the curve $EFGH$ is given by

(a)
(b)
(c)
(d)

70. Stokes' law states that the viscous drag force F experienced by a sphere of radius a, moving with a speed v through a fluid with coefficient of viscosity η, is given by $F = 6\pi\eta av$. If this fluid is flowing through a cylindrical pipe of radius r, length l and pressure difference of p across its two ends, then the volume of water V which flows through the pipe in time t can be written as $\dfrac{V}{t} = k\left(\dfrac{p}{l}\right)^a \eta^b r^c$, where k is a dimensionless constant. Correct values of a, b and c are

(a) $a = 1, b = -1, c = 4$ (b) $a = -1, b = 1, c = 4$
(c) $a = 2, b = -1, c = 3$ (d) $a = 1, b = -2, c = -4$

CHEMISTRY

71. The reaction of an alkene X with bromine produces a compound Y, which has 22.22% C, 3.71% H and 74.07% Br. The ozonolysis of alkene X gives only one product. The alkene X is,

[Given, atomic mass of C = 12; H = 1; Br = 80]

(a) ethylene   (b) 1-butene
(c) 2-butene   (d) 3-hexene

72. In the following reaction,

$$H_3C - C \equiv C - H \xrightarrow[H_3O^+]{Hg^{2+}} X \xrightarrow[PhCHO]{dil.\ NaOH} Y$$

X and Y, respectively, are

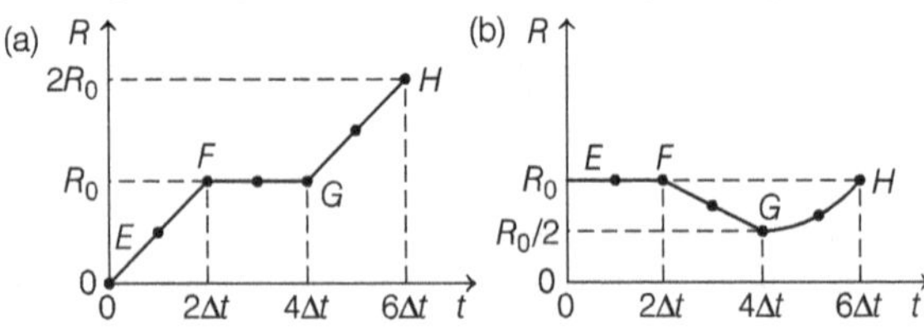

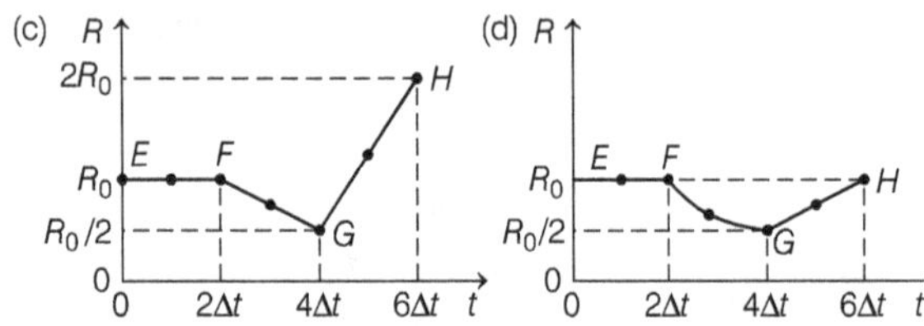

73. $KMnO_4$ reacts with H_2O_2 in an acidic medium. The number of moles of oxygen produced per mole of $KMnO_4$ is

(a) 2.5   (b) 5   (c) 1.25   (d) 2

74. The photoelectric behaviour of K, Li, Mg and Ag metals is shown in the plot below. If light of wavelength 400 nm is incident on each of these metals, which of them will emit photoelectrons?

[Planck's constant $h = 6.626 \times 10^{-34}$ Js; velocity of light $c = 3 \times 10^8$ m s^{-1}; 1 eV $= 1.6 \times 10^{-19}$ J]

(a) K   (b) K and Li
(c) K, Li and Mg   (d) K, Li, Mg and Ag

75. A piece of metal weighing 100 g is heated to 80°C and dropped into 1 kg of cold water in an insulated container at 15°C. If the final temperature of the water in the container is 15.69°C, the specific heat of the metal in J/g.°C is

(a) 0.38   (b) 0.24
(c) 0.45   (d) 0.13

BIOLOGY

76. The nucleus of a diploid organism contains 3 ng of DNA in G_1-phase. Which one of the following statements describes the state of the cell at the end of S-phase?

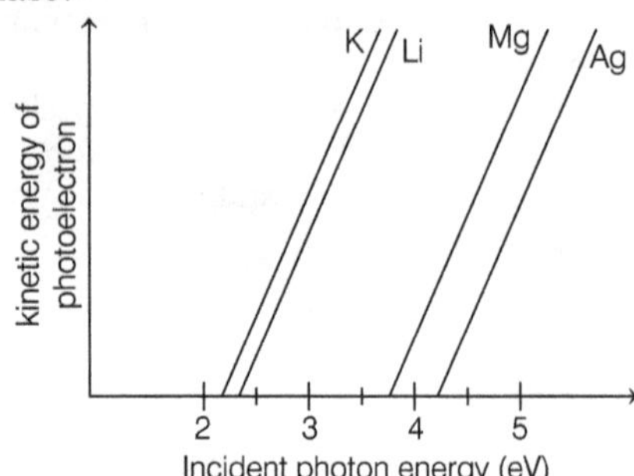

(a) The nucleus divides into two and each nucleus contains 3 ng of DNA

(b) The nucleus does not divide and it contains 3 ng of DNA

(c) The nucleus divides into two and each nucleus contains 1.5 ng of DNA

(d) The nucleus does not divide and it contains 6 ng of DNA

77. Three cellular processes are listed below. Choose the correct combination of processes that involve proton gradient across the membrane.

   I. Photosynthesis   II. Aerobic respiration
III. Anaerobic respiration

(a) II and III   (b) I and II
(c) I, II and III   (d) I and III

78. The concentration of OH^- ions in a solution with the H^+ ions concentration of 1.3×10^{-4} M is

(a) 7.7×10^{-4} M   (b) 1.3×10^{-4} M
(c) 2.6×10^{-8} M   (d) 7.7×10^{-11} M

79. Given that tidal volume is 600 mL, inspiratory reserve volume is 2500 mL and expiratory reserve volume is 800 mL, what is the value of vital capacity of lung?

(a) 3900 mL   (b) 3300 mL
(c) 3100 mL   (d) 1400 mL

80. Which of the following organisms produces sperm without involving meiosis?

(a) Sandfly and fruitfly   (b) Housefly and grasshopper
(c) Honeybee and ant   (d) Zebra fish and frog

Answers

PART-I

1	(b)	2	(c)	3	(b)	4	(b)	5	(d)	6	(c)	7	(d)	8	(d)	9	(b)	10	(c)
11	(a)	12	(a)	13	(b)	14	(d)	15	(d)	16	(c)	17	(d)	18	(c)	19	(b)	20	(c)
21	(a)	22	(c)	23	(b)	24	(c)	25	(d)	26	(b)	27	(c)	28	(c)	29	(a)	30	(c)
31	(a)	32	(c)	33	(d)	34	(d)	35	(c)	36	(b)	37	(a)	38	(d)	39	(b)	40	(c)
41	(a)	42	(b)	43	(d)	44	(a)	45	(d)	46	(b)	47	(a)	48	(d)	49	(a)	50	(b)
51	(c)	52	(a)	53	(c)	54	(a)	55	(c)	56	(b)	57	(a)	58	(d)	59	(c)	60	(d)

PART-II

61	(a)	62	(c)	63	(d)	64	(b)	65	(a)	66	(c)	67	(c)	68	(*)	69	(d)	70	(a)
71	(c)	72	(b)	73	(a)	74	(b)	75	(c)	76	(d)	77	(b)	78	(d)	79	(a)	80	(c)

Solutions

1. *(b)* We have, side of quadrilateral has distinct integer second largest size has length 10.

Let $a = 8$, $b = 9$, $c = 10$, (All are distinct)

We know, in quadrilateral Sum of three sides is greater than fourth side

$\therefore a + b + c > d \Rightarrow 8 + 9 + 10 > d \Rightarrow d < 27$

$\therefore$ Maximum length of 4th side is 26.

2. *(c)* Exponent of 2 in 200!.

$$= \left[\frac{200}{2}\right] + \left[\frac{200}{2^2}\right] + \left[\frac{200}{2^3}\right] + \left[\frac{200}{2^4}\right] + \left[\frac{200}{2^5}\right]$$
$$+ \left[\frac{200}{2^6}\right] + \left[\frac{200}{2^7}\right] + \left[\frac{200}{2^8}\right]$$

$= 100 + 50 + 25 + 12 + 6 + 3 + 1 = 197$

Exponent of 2 in 100!

$$= \left[\frac{100}{2}\right] + \left[\frac{100}{2^2}\right] + \left[\frac{100}{2^3}\right] + \left[\frac{100}{2^4}\right] + \left[\frac{100}{2^5}\right]$$
$$+ \left[\frac{100}{2^6}\right] + \left[\frac{100}{2^7}\right]$$

$= 50 + 25 + 12 + 6 + 3 + 1 = 97$

$\therefore$ Exponent of 2.

In $\dfrac{200!}{100!} = \dfrac{2^{197}}{2^{97}} = 2^{100}$

$\therefore$ The largest power of 2 is 100.

3. *(b)* Given, $a_1 + a_2 + a_3 + a_4 = 0$

and $\qquad a_1^2 + a_2^2 + a_3^2 + a_4^2 = 1$

It is possible only

when, $a_1 = a_2 = \dfrac{1}{2}$ and $a_3 = a_4 = -\dfrac{1}{2}$

$\therefore (a_1 - a_2)^2 + (a_2 - a_3)^2 + (a_3 - a_4)^2$
$$+ (a_4 - a_1)^2$$

$\left(\dfrac{1}{2} - \dfrac{1}{2}\right)^2 + \left(\dfrac{1}{2} + \dfrac{1}{2}\right)^2 + \left(-\dfrac{1}{2} + \dfrac{1}{2}\right)^2 + \left(-\dfrac{1}{2} - \dfrac{1}{2}\right)^2$

$\qquad 0 + 1 + 0 + 1 = 2$

The value lies between (1.5, 2.5).

4. *(b)* x and y are positive integer

$\qquad x^2 - y^2 = 12345678$

RHS 12345678 is and even number and last digit is 8.

$\therefore$ The last digit of x be 3, 7

and the last digit of y be 1, 9.

$\therefore x$ and y must be odd and square of difference is multiple of 8 but RHS is not multiple of 8.

$\therefore S$ is the empty set.

5. *(d)* Given, A_1, A_2, A_3, ..., A_9 are nine-side regular polygon of each side 2 units.

$\therefore \qquad A_1 A_2 = A_2 A_3 = A_3 A_4 = ... = A_8 A_9 = 2$

$\angle A_1 O A_2 = \dfrac{2\pi}{9}$

$\therefore \angle A_1 O A_5 = \dfrac{2\pi}{9} \times 4 = \dfrac{8\pi}{9} \Rightarrow \angle A_2 O A_4 = \dfrac{4\pi}{9}$

$OA_1 = OA_2 = r$

In $\Delta A_1 O A_2$,

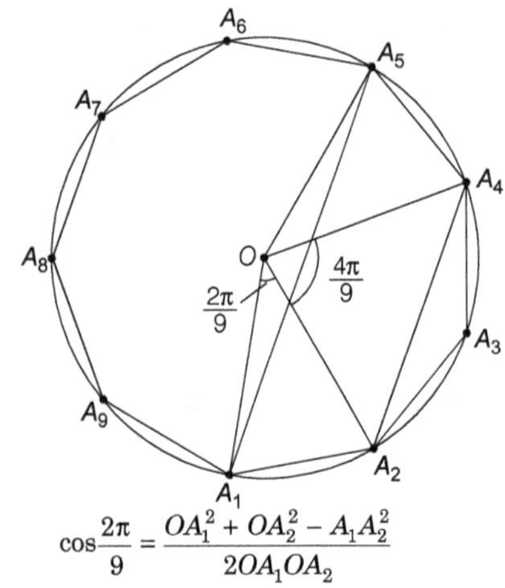

$\cos\dfrac{2\pi}{9} = \dfrac{OA_1^2 + OA_2^2 - A_1 A_2^2}{2 OA_1 OA_2}$

$\cos\dfrac{2\pi}{9} = \dfrac{2r^2 - 4}{2r^2}$

$r^2 \cos\dfrac{2\pi}{9} = r^2 - 2$

$r^2 = \dfrac{2}{1 - \cos\dfrac{2\pi}{9}} = \dfrac{2}{2\sin^2\dfrac{\pi}{9}}$

$r = \dfrac{1}{\sin\dfrac{\pi}{9}}$

In $\Delta A_1 O A_5$, $\cos\dfrac{8\pi}{9} = \dfrac{r^2 + r^2 - A_1 A_5^2}{2r^2}$

$\Rightarrow \qquad A_1 A_5 = 2r \sin\dfrac{4\pi}{9}$

Similarly, $\Delta A_2 O A_4$,

$\qquad A_2 A_4 = 2r \sin\dfrac{2\pi}{9}$

$\therefore A_1 A_5 - A_2 A_4 = 2r\left(\sin\dfrac{4\pi}{9} - \sin\dfrac{2\pi}{9}\right)$

$\qquad = 2r, \left(2\sin\dfrac{\pi}{9}\cos\dfrac{\pi}{3}\right)$

$\qquad = \dfrac{2}{\sin\dfrac{\pi}{9}} \times 2\sin\dfrac{\pi}{9} \times \dfrac{1}{2} \quad \left[\because r = \dfrac{1}{\sin\dfrac{\pi}{9}}\right]$

$\qquad = 2$

6. *(c)* Let p are positive number from $a_1, a_2, a_3, ..., a_n$

$\therefore n - p$ are negative number.

Given a_j, a_k is positive $j < k$ and $a_j a_k = 55$

$a_j a_k$ is positive.

$\therefore a_j$ and a_k are both positive or negative.

$\therefore \qquad {}^P C_2 + {}^{n-P} C_2 = 55$

and $a_j a_k$ is negative $j < k$

$\qquad a_j a_k = 50$

any one of a_j and a_k are positive:

$\therefore \qquad {}^P C_1 \times {}^{n-P} C_1 = 50 \Rightarrow P(n - P) = 50$

$\Rightarrow \qquad {}^P C_2 + {}^{n-P} C_2 = 55$

$\Rightarrow P(P - 1) + (n - P)(n - P - 1) = 110$

$\Rightarrow P^2 - P + (n - P)^2 - (n - P) = 110$

$\Rightarrow P^2 + (n - P)^2 - n = 110$

$\Rightarrow \{P + (n - P)\}^2 - 2P(n - P) - n = 110$

$\Rightarrow n^2 - 100 - n - 110 = 0 \ [\because P(n - P) = 50]$

$\therefore \qquad n^2 - n - 210 = 0$

$\Rightarrow (n - 15)(n + 14) = 0$

$\qquad\qquad n = 15, n \neq -14$

$\therefore \qquad P(15 - p) = 50$

$\Rightarrow p^2 - 15p + 50 = 0$

$\qquad (P - 10)(P - 5) = 0, \ p = 5 \text{ or } 10$

$\therefore \quad p^2 + (n - P)^2 = 5^2 + 10^2$

$\qquad\qquad\qquad = 25 + 100 = 125$

7. *(d)* We have,

a, b, c, d are four distinct number from the set $\{1, 2, 3, ..., 9\}$.

The minimum value of $\dfrac{a}{b} + \dfrac{c}{d}$ is possible

when $a = 2$, $b = 9$, $c = 1$, $d = 8$

$\therefore \qquad \dfrac{2}{9} + \dfrac{1}{8} = \dfrac{16 + 9}{72} = \dfrac{25}{72}$

8. *(d)* Given, $72^x \cdot 48^y = 6^{xy}$

$(2^3 \cdot 3^2)^x \cdot (2^4 \cdot 3)^y = 2^{xy} \cdot 3^{xy}$

$2^{3x + 4y} \cdot 3^{2x + y} = 2^{xy} \cdot 3^{xy}$

Equating the exponent of 2 and 3, we get

$3x + 4y = xy$ and $2x + y = xy$

On solving these equation, we get

$\qquad x = \dfrac{-15}{3}$ and $y = \dfrac{5}{3}$

$\therefore \qquad x + y = \dfrac{-15}{3} + \dfrac{5}{3} = \dfrac{-10}{3}$

9. *(b)* Given,

AB is diameter of circle S and C is the mid-point of arc length of AB.

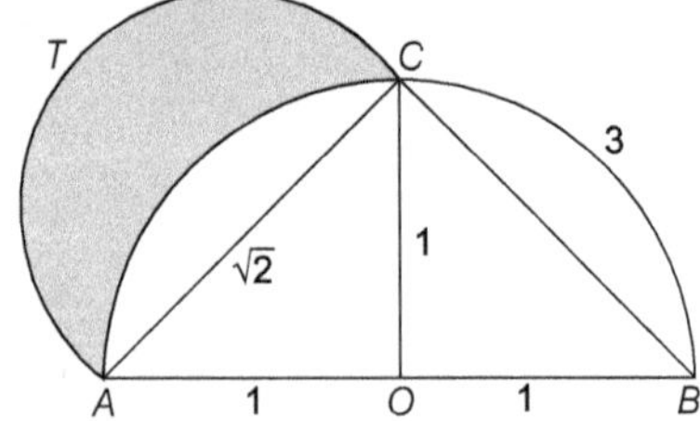

AC is diameter of circle T.

$$AB = 2$$

$$\therefore \quad OA = OB = OC = 1$$

Area of shaded region

= Area of semi-circle T + Area of $\triangle OAC$ – Area of quadrant of circle S

$$= \frac{\pi}{2}\left(\frac{\sqrt{2}}{2}\right)^2 + \frac{1}{2}\times 1 \times 1 - \frac{\pi}{4}\times (1)^2$$

$$= \frac{\pi}{4} + \frac{1}{2} - \frac{\pi}{4} = \frac{1}{2}$$

10. *(c)* Let $p(x) = x^{135} + x^{125} - x^{115} + x^5 + 1$, $q(x) = x^3 - x$ and $p(x) = q(x)k + r(x)$

$$x^{135} + x^{125} - x^{115} + x^5 + 1$$
$$= (x^3 - x)k + ax^2 + bx + c$$
$$[\because r(x) = ax^2 + bx + c]$$

Put $x = 0$,

$$\therefore \quad c = 1$$

Put $x = 1$, $3 = a + b + c \Rightarrow 3 = a + b + 1$

$$\Rightarrow \quad a + b = 2 \qquad \ldots \text{(i)}$$

Put $x = -1$, $-1 = a - b + c \Rightarrow -1 = a - b + 1$

$$\Rightarrow \quad a - b = -2 \qquad \ldots \text{(ii)}$$

From Eqs. (i) and (ii), we get

$$a = 0, b = 2$$

$$\therefore \quad r(x) = 2x + 1$$

$$\therefore \quad \text{Degree of } r(x) = 1$$

11. *(a)* The distinct prime factor of

$$43361 = 131 \times 331$$

where $p_1 = 131$ and $p_2 = 331$

$$\therefore \quad p_1 + p_2 = 131 + 331 = 462$$

12. *(a)* Given, ABC is right angled triangle

$$\angle C = 90°$$

CD is perpendicular on AB, DN and DM are parallel to AC and BC, respectively.

$DN = 4$ and $DM = 5$

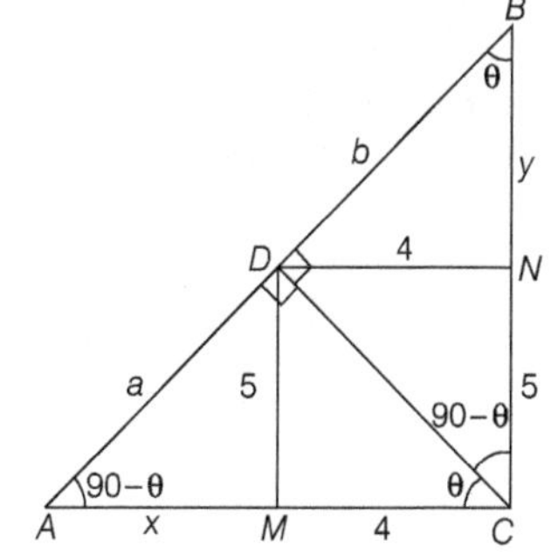

In $\triangle DMC$ and $\triangle DNB$,

$$\triangle DMC \sim \triangle DNB$$

$$\therefore \quad \frac{DM}{DN} = \frac{MC}{NB}$$

$$\Rightarrow \quad \frac{5}{4} = \frac{4}{NB} \Rightarrow NB = \frac{16}{5}$$

$$\therefore \quad BC = CN + NB = 5 + \frac{16}{5} = \frac{41}{5}$$

In $\triangle DNC$ and $\triangle DMA$,

$$\triangle DNC \sim \triangle DMA$$

$$\Rightarrow \quad \frac{DN}{DM} = \frac{NC}{MA}$$

$$\Rightarrow \quad \frac{4}{5} = \frac{5}{MA} \Rightarrow MA = \frac{25}{4}$$

$$\therefore \quad AC = MC + AM = 4 + \frac{25}{4} = \frac{41}{4}$$

13. *(b)* We have, A, G, H be arithmetic, geometric and harmonic mean respectively of two distinct positive real numbers.

$$A(G - H)x^2 + G\,(H - A)x + H\,(A - G) = 0$$

Let α and β be roots of the given equation

$$\alpha < \beta$$

$$\therefore \alpha + \beta = \frac{-G\,(H - A)}{A\,(G - H)} \Rightarrow \alpha\beta = \frac{H(A - G)}{A\,(G - H)}$$

$\beta = 1$ is satisfied the equation,

i.e. $AG - AH + GA - GA + HA - HG = 0$

$\therefore$ One of root is 1

$$\alpha = \frac{H(A - G)}{A(G - H)}$$

$$\Rightarrow \quad \alpha = \frac{AH - GH}{AG - AH}$$

$$\alpha = \frac{G^2 - GH}{AG - AH} \qquad [\because AH = G^2]$$

$$\alpha = \frac{G(G - H)}{A(G - H)} \Rightarrow \alpha = \frac{G}{A} \qquad [\because A > G]$$

$$\alpha < 1$$

Hence, $\quad 0 < \alpha < 1$

14. *(d)* Given, $ABCD$ is a square

$$AB = CD = AD = BC = 1$$

AC is tangent of circle

$$\angle OAC = 90°$$

$$\angle CAD = 45°$$

$$\therefore \quad \angle OAD = 45°$$

$$\therefore \quad OA = \sqrt{2}$$

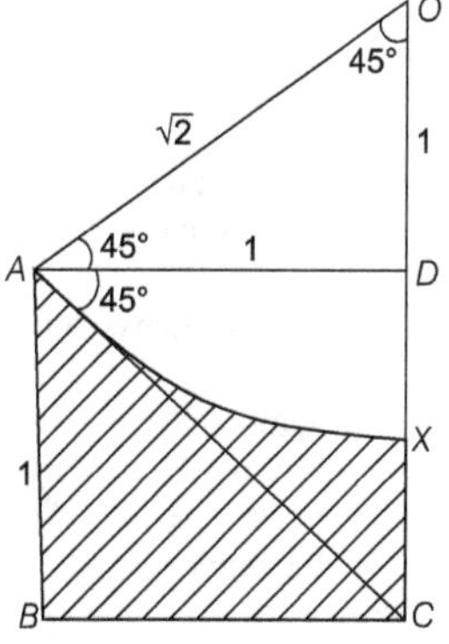

$\therefore$ Area of shaded region

= Area of square + Area of $\triangle AOD$ – Area of sector

$$= 1 + \frac{1}{2}\times 1 - \frac{45}{360}\times (\sqrt{2})^2 \cdot \pi$$

$$= 1 + \frac{1}{2} - \frac{\pi}{4} = \frac{3}{2} - \frac{\pi}{4} = \frac{6 - \pi}{4}$$

15. *(d)* Given,

$$x^5 - 6x^4 + 11x^3 - 5x^2 - 3x + 2 = 0$$

$$(x - 1)\,(x - 2)\,(x^3 - 3x^2 + 1) = 0$$

The sum of non-integer roots are sum of roots of equation

$$x^3 - 3x^2 + 1 = 0 \text{ i.e. } 3.$$

16. *(c)* For a nucleus, $_Z^A X$

Mass number, $A = N + Z$

where, N = number of neutrons

and Z = number of protons.

In $_{32}^{65}X$ and $_{33}^{65}Y$, number of protons are different. So, these are not isotopes.

In $_{42}^{86}X$ and $_{42}^{85}Y$, number of protons are equal. So, these are isotopes.

In $_{85}^{174}X$ and $_{88}^{177}Y$, number of neutrons are $174 - 85 = 89$ and $177 - 88 = 89$.

So, both have same number of neutrons.

In $_{92}^{235}X$ and $_{94}^{235}Y$, both have same mass number, so these are isobars.

17. *(d)* For thrown ball,

$$h = ut - \frac{1}{2}gt^2 \Rightarrow \frac{h}{t} = u - \frac{1}{2}gt$$

$$\Rightarrow \quad \frac{h}{t} = \frac{-g}{2}\cdot t + u$$

Comparing with $y = mx + c$, graph of $\frac{h}{t}$ *versus* t is a straight line with slope $\frac{-g}{2}$.

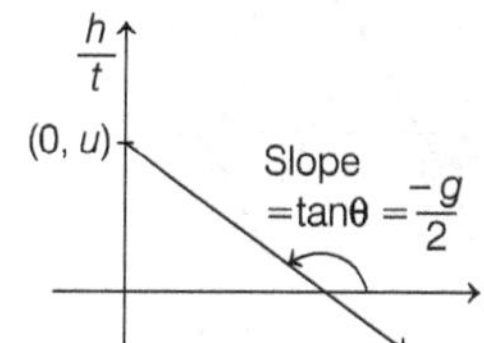

From above graph, value of acceleration due to gravity can be obtained by multiplying its slope with 2.

18. *(c)* Let total distance is $3x$ km.

For first part, time taken is $t_1 = \dfrac{x}{10}$ h

For second part, time taken is $t_2 = \dfrac{x}{20}$ h

For third part, time taken is $t_3 = \dfrac{x}{60}$ h

Average speed for PQ distance

$$= \frac{\text{Total distance}}{\text{Total time}} = \frac{3x}{\dfrac{x}{10} + \dfrac{x}{20} + \dfrac{x}{60}}$$

$$= \frac{3x}{\left(\dfrac{6x + 3x + x}{60}\right)} = 18\,\text{km/h}$$

19. *(b)* For points P and Q ray diagram will be as shown below.

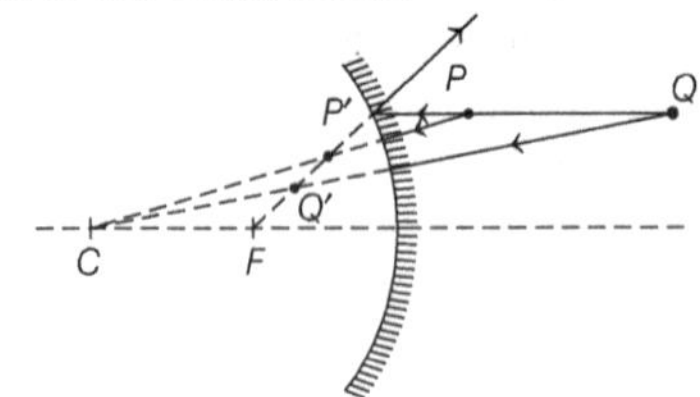

Clearly image will be

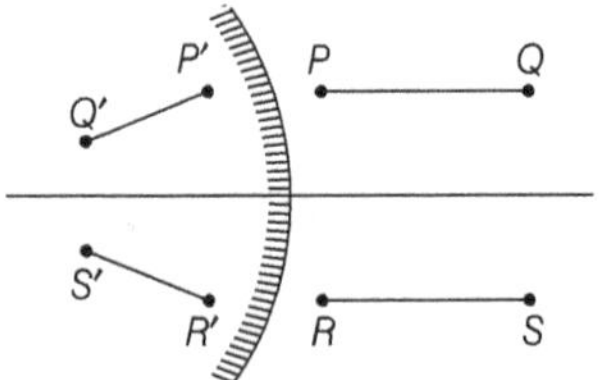

20. *(c)* In Guericke's experiment,

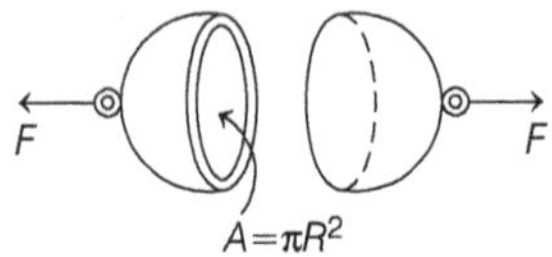

$$A = \pi R^2$$

If pressure difference between outside and inside is p, then

$$\frac{F}{A} = p \text{ or } F = pA = p\pi R^2$$

21. *(a)* Net resultant force is due to unbalanced forces of $3q$ and $2q$ charges.

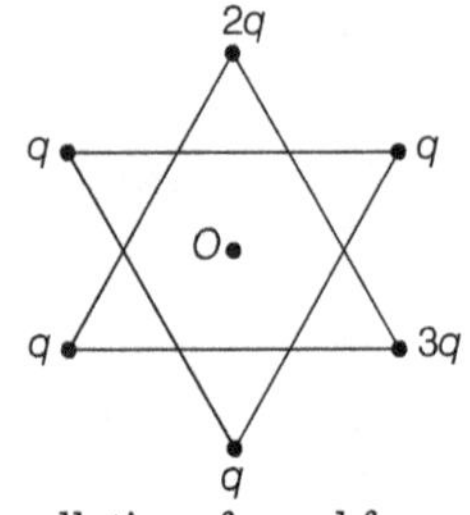

After cancellation of equal forces, we have following configuration:

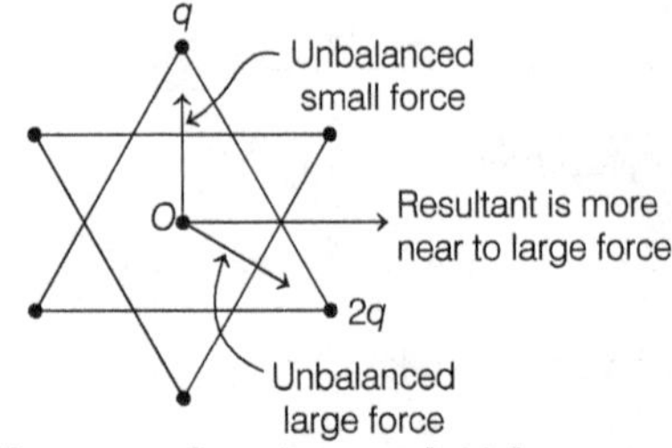

Hence, net force is towards right.

22. *(c)* Size of moon is very small compared to that of earth also, moon is much nearer to earth in comparison to sun.

Hence, shadow of moon covers only a small part of earth as shown in the figure given below.

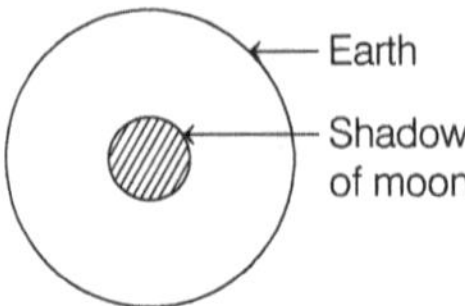

23. *(b)* Let m gram of ice melt and water reaches 0°C.

Then,

Heat lost by ice = Heat gained by water

$$\Rightarrow m_{ice}L_{ice} + m_{ice}\,c_{ice}\Delta T_{ice} = m_w c_w \Delta T_w$$
$$\Rightarrow m(335) + m(2.2)\,(0 - (-7))$$
$$= 200\,(4.2)\,(15 - 0)$$
$$\Rightarrow m(335 + 15.4) = 12600$$
$$\Rightarrow m = \frac{12600}{350.4} \approx 36\,g$$

So, ice left in mixture is $100 - 36 \approx 64\,g$.

Hence, nearest option is 67 g.

24. *(c)* Let S is the source placed at distance $2f (= 60\text{ cm})$.

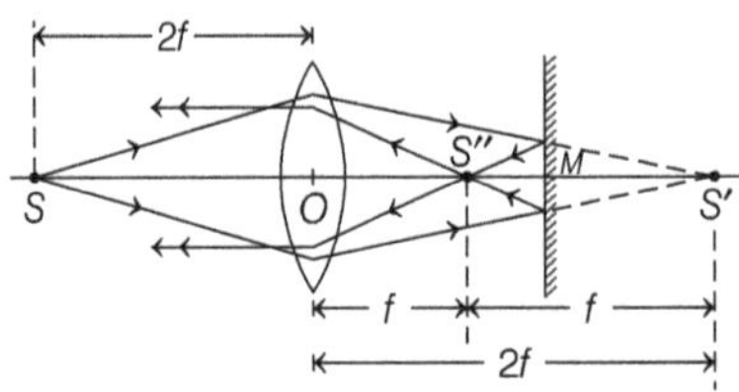

Image of S is formed at S' ($OS' = 60$ cm). As light rays after reflection from mirror are parallel after passing through lens, this is possible when they cross through focus as shown in figure.

For plane mirror, $MS'' = MS'$

So, $OM = d = OS'' + S''M$

$$= f + \frac{f}{2} = 30 + \frac{30}{2} = 45 \text{ cm}$$

25. *(d)* A plano-concave lens is a diverging lens and a plano-convex lens is a converging lens.

Image formed by a plano-concave lens is always erect and virtual.

Image formed by a plano-convex lens is real and inverted when object is placed at a distance larger than focal length of lens.

Plano-convex lens is a converging lens. Hence, image formed by a plano-convex lens is inverted.

So, all statements are correct.

26. *(b)* Acceleration of ball at all instances is $-9.8\,\text{ms}^{-2}$.

So, correct graph of acceleration and time will be as shown below.

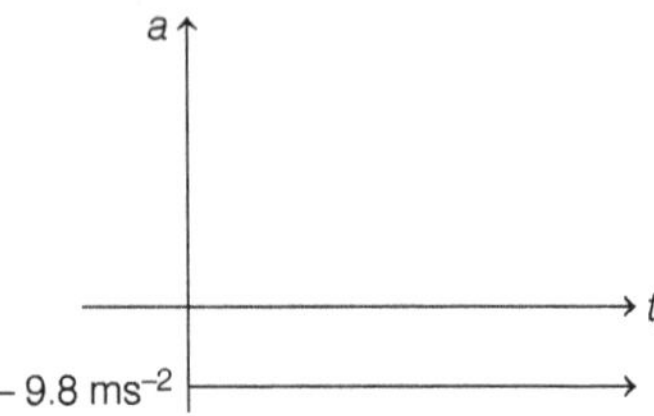

27. *(c)* Image produced on retina are real and inverted. We are able to perceive them as erect because of processing of our brain.

Only statement III is incorrect all other are correct.

28. *(c)*

Acceleration=f Retardation=a

$t=0$ v_1 d

A $v_2=0$

$u=0$ B C

$\frac{2}{3}d$

Velocity of particle at the end of $\frac{2}{3}$ distance is v_1.

Now, by equation of motion,

$$\Rightarrow v^2 - u^2 = 2as, \text{ we have}$$
$$\Rightarrow v_1^2 - 0^2 = 2f \times \frac{2}{3}d$$
$$\Rightarrow v_1^2 = \frac{4}{3}fd \Rightarrow v_1 = \frac{2}{\sqrt{3}} \cdot \sqrt{fd}$$

As, final velocity is zero, so for next part of journey is

$$v^2 - u^2 = 2as$$

Gives, $$0 - v_1^2 = 2a\left(\frac{1}{3}d\right)$$
$$\Rightarrow -\frac{4}{3}fd = \frac{2}{3}ad$$

or deacceleration, $a = -2f$

Now, using $v = u + at$, for first part of journey,

$$v = u + at$$
$$\Rightarrow v_1 = 0 + ft_1$$
$$\Rightarrow \frac{2}{\sqrt{3}}\sqrt{fd} = ft_1 \Rightarrow t_1 = \frac{2}{\sqrt{3}} \cdot \sqrt{\frac{d}{f}}$$

For second part of journey,

$$v = u + at$$
$$\Rightarrow 0 = v_1 - 2ft_2$$
$$\Rightarrow \frac{2}{\sqrt{3}}\sqrt{fd} = 2ft_2$$
$$\Rightarrow t_2 = \frac{1}{\sqrt{3}}\sqrt{\frac{d}{f}}$$

So, total time is

$$t = t_1 + t_2$$
$$= \frac{2}{\sqrt{3}}\sqrt{\frac{d}{f}} + \frac{1}{\sqrt{3}}\sqrt{\frac{d}{f}}$$
$$= \sqrt{3}\sqrt{\frac{d}{f}} = \sqrt{\frac{3d}{f}}$$

29. *(a)* Magnification is given by

$$m = \frac{v}{u} = \frac{f - v}{f}$$
$$\Rightarrow \qquad fm = f - v$$
$$\Rightarrow \qquad v = f(1 - m)$$
$$\Rightarrow \qquad v = \frac{1 - m}{P}$$

30. *(c)* Initial pressure in cylinder is atmospheric pressure p_0.

When mass m is attached to piston, then

pressure $= p_0 - \dfrac{mg}{A}$.

As, temperature remains constant during expansion

$$\Rightarrow \qquad p_i V_i = p_f V_f$$
$$\Rightarrow \qquad p_0 V_i = \left(p_0 - \frac{mg}{A}\right) \cdot V_f$$
$$\Rightarrow \qquad \frac{V_f}{V_i} = \frac{p_0}{\left(p_0 - \dfrac{mg}{A}\right)}$$
$$\frac{V_i}{V_f} = 1 - \frac{mg}{p_0 A} \Rightarrow \frac{mg}{p_0 A} = 1 - \frac{V_i}{V_f}$$
$$\Rightarrow \qquad \frac{mg}{p_0 A} = \frac{V_f - V_i}{V_f} = \frac{\Delta V}{V_f}$$

Now, when temperature is reduced by ΔT, the volume of gas again contracts to its original volume.

$$\Rightarrow \qquad \frac{V}{T} = \text{constant}$$
$$\text{or} \qquad \frac{\Delta V}{V} = \frac{\Delta T}{T}$$
$$\Rightarrow \qquad \frac{\Delta T}{T} = \frac{\Delta V}{V_f} = \frac{mg}{p_0 A}$$
$$\Rightarrow \qquad \frac{\Delta T}{T} = \frac{mg}{p_0 A}$$
$$= \frac{50 \times 10}{10^5 \times 3.14 \times (0.2)^2}$$
$$= \frac{5}{3.14 \times 4} \times \frac{10^2}{10^5 \times 10^{-2}}$$
$$= 0.4 \times 10^{-1} = 0.04$$

31. *(a)* The structure of 3-methylpent-2-ene is

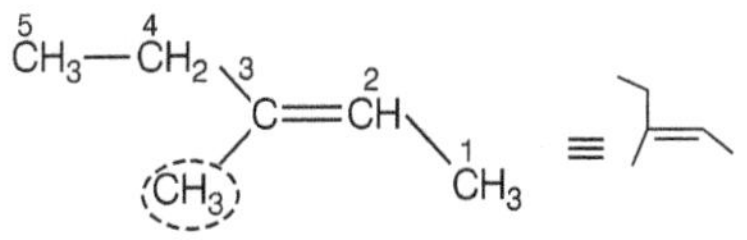

32. *(c)* Among the given carbanions compound IV has maximum stability as it is resonance stabilised, i.e.

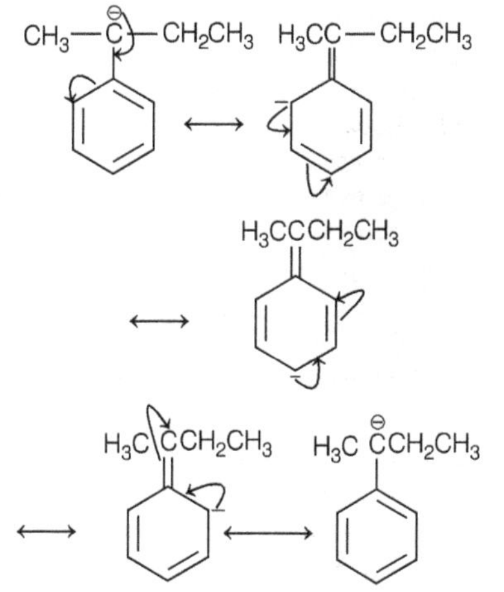

Among the other given carbanions, stability order of carbanion decreases as we move from 1° to 3° anion because of $+ I$ effect of methyl groups. There is an increased intensity of negative charge on central carbon of 3° carbanion which further makes it unstable. Thus, the correct increasing order is

$$(CH_3)_3\overset{\ominus}{C} < CH_3\overset{\ominus}{C}HCH_2CH_3$$
$$\underset{\text{III}}{3°} \qquad \underset{\text{II}}{2°}$$
$$< CH_3CH_2CH_2\overset{\ominus}{C}H_2 < CH_3\overset{\ominus}{C}(Ph)CH_2CH_3$$
$$\underset{\text{I}}{1°} \qquad\qquad \text{IV}$$

33. *(d)*

Diazonium salt   Phenol

p-hydroxy azobenzene (azodye)

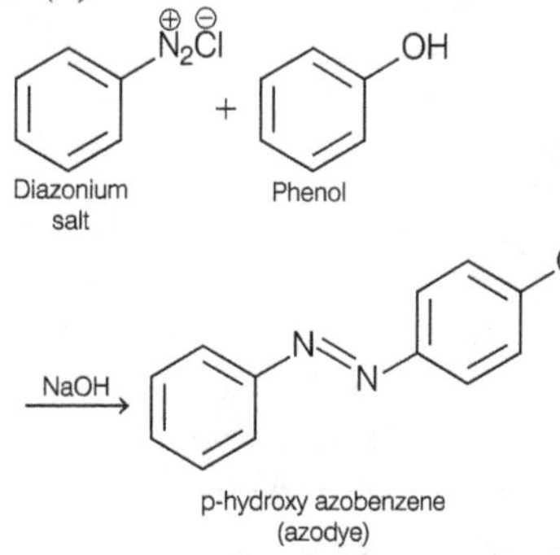

This reaction is known as coupling reaction. In this reaction electrophilic aromatic substitution takes place where aryl diazonium cation is the electrophile and the activated arene is a nucleophile.

34. *(d)* In the reaction of 1-bromo-3-chlorocyclobutane with two equivalents of sodium in ether gives bicyclo [1.1.0] as a major product.

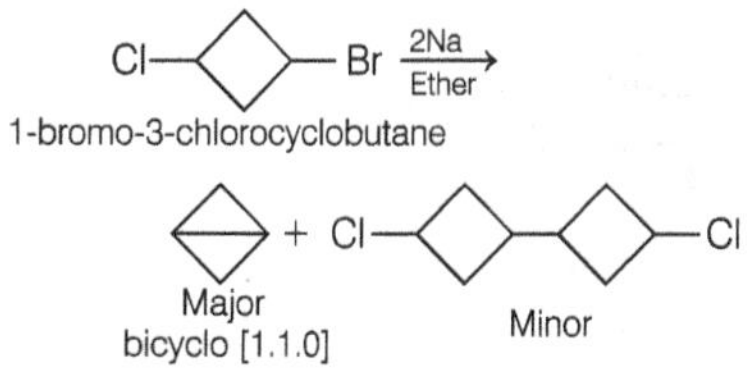

1-bromo-3-chlorocyclobutane

Major bicyclo [1.1.0]   Minor

This reaction is an example of Wurtz' reaction.

35. *(c)* Among the given compounds IV will have the least basicity as the lone pair on nitrogen takes part in resonance and will not be available for donation. Compound I will have more basicity than IV, because of the availability of lone pair of NH_2 group. But its basicity will be less than II and III because of the $-I$ effect of NO_2 which decreases the basicity of aniline.

Now between compounds II and III, II will be most basic. This is because it is an aliphatic amine and also in III, the nitrogen is present within the ring, so its electron will not be as much available as in II.

Thus, the order of basicity will be,
$$\text{IV} < \text{I} < \text{III} < \text{II}.$$

36. *(b)* As Na is an alkali metal it has least ionisation energy due to its large size. Rest of the three elements B, N and O are non-metal and lie in same period. So, as we move from left to right in a period the ionisation energy increases due to increased nuclear charge. But, N has half-filled configuration which is stable, thus it will have maximum ionisation energy. Thus, the correct order is, Na < B < O < N.

37. *(a)* P_2O_5, As_2O_3 are acidic oxides, Sb_2O_3 is an amphoteric while Bi_2O_3 is basic oxide but P_2O_5 is most acidic among them all. This is because down the group, metallic character increases and metal oxides are more basic, thus the basicity of metallic oxides also increases.

38. *(d)* Metal with low reactivity can be extracted by heating ore in air. This process of extraction is known as roasting. Among the given metals, Cu has least reactivity, so it can be directly extracted by heating its ore in air.

$$2Cu_2S + 3O_2 \rightarrow 2Cu_2O + 2SO_2 \uparrow$$

39. *(b)* Total number of electrons in
$$S^{2-} = 16 + 2 = 18$$

Total number of electrons present in the elements given in options are as follows :

(i) Na^+

Total number of electrons in
$Na^+ = 11 - 1 = 10$

(ii) Ca^{2+}

Total number of electrons in $Ca^{2+} = 20 - 2 = 18$

(iii) Mg^{2+}

Total number of electrons in $Mg^{2+} = 12 - 2 = 10$

(iv) Sr^{2+}

Total number of electrons in $Sr^{2+} = 38 - 2 = 36$

Thus, S^{2-} and Ca^{2+} have same number of electrons.

40. *(c)* $Ca + 2HCl \rightarrow CaCl_2 + H_2$

At STP 22.4 L of H_2 = 1 mole of H_2

$\therefore$ 5.04 of $H_2 = \dfrac{1}{22.4} \times 5.04 = 0.225$ mole

Number of moles of $Ca = \dfrac{X}{40}$

1 mole of Ca reacts to produce 1 mole of H_2.

$\therefore \dfrac{X}{40}$ moles of Ca reacts to produce 0.225 moles of H_2 gas.

$\therefore \qquad \dfrac{X}{40} = 0.225$

$\qquad\qquad X = 9.000$

41. *(a)* Given, mass of an object = 20 g

Velocity of an object = 100 ms^{-1}

According de Broglie

$$\lambda = \dfrac{h}{mv} = \dfrac{6.626 \times 10^{-31}}{20 \times 10^{-3} \times 100}$$

$$= 3.313 \times 10^{-34} \text{ m}$$

42. *(b)* $CH_4 + 2O_2 \rightarrow CO_2 + 2H_2O$

of O_2 in 750 L of air (containing 20% of O_2)

$$= \dfrac{20}{100} \times 750 = 150\,L$$

Some of CH_4 is ignited with 100 mL of O_2.

$\therefore$ Remaining volume of O_2 in vessel = 50 L

22.4 L contains 1 mole of O_2

$\therefore$ 50 L contains = $1/22.4 \times 50 = 2.2$ mole.

43. *(d)* CO_2 is passed through lime water which initially turns the solution milky because of formation of calcium carbonate. On continuous bubbling of CO_2 the solution becomes clear due to the formation of calcium bicarbonate.

$$\underset{\text{Lime water}}{Ca(OH)_2} + CO_2 \rightarrow \underset{\text{(Milky)}}{CaCO_3 \downarrow} + H_2O$$

$$\underset{\text{Excess}}{CaCO_3} + CO_2 + H_2O \rightarrow \underset{\substack{\text{Calcium bicarbonate}\\ \text{(Soluble in water)}}}{Ca(HCO_3)_2}\,(aq)$$

44. *(a)* Maximum number of electrons that can be accommodated in the shell. Principal quantum with number,

$$n = 2n^2$$

For $\qquad n = 3$

$\therefore$ Maximum number of electrons in shell with $(n = 3) = 2(3)^2 = 18$.

45. *(d)* Among the given elements Li and Na belong to group 1, i.e. they are alkali metals. So, they will have maximum atomic radii. Between Li and Na, Na will have the largest atomic radii. This is because as we move down the group atomic radii increases.

Si belongs to group 14 and F belongs to group 17. So, as we move from left to right in period the atomic radii decreases. Thus, Si will have large atomic radii than F but less than Li.

So, the correct order of atomic radii of given elements is, Na > Li > Si > F.

46. *(b)* The major excretory product of birds is uric acid. Nitrogenous wastes in the body of animals tend to form toxic ammonia, which must be excreted. Mammals such as humans excrete urea, while birds, reptiles and some terrestrial invertebrates produce uric acid as waste excretory product.

47. *(a)* There are 64 codons present in each living organism, out of which, 61 codons represent or code for amino acids and rest three are stop codons. Thus, there are more codon combinations than there are amino acids. The genetic code is described as degenerate because more than one codon sequence can code for the same amino acid.

48. *(d)* In cell cycle, during interphase, the DNA is replicated. Interphase begins with G_1-phase. During this phase, the cell makes a variety of proteins that are needed for DNA replication. G_1-phase is followed by synthetic or S-phase. This phase is responsible for the synthesis or replication of DNA. The aim of this process is to produce double the amount of DNA, providing the basis for the chromosome sets of the daughter cells.

49. *(a)* Gene flow is the transfer of genetic variation from one population to another. Genetic drift is a change in the frequency of an allele within a population over time. Speciation is the formation of new and distinct species in the course of evolution. Genetic shift is a major change within a population which changes the population altogether.

50. *(b)* Tobacco Mosaic Virus (TMV) affects photosynthetic tissue of the infected plant. Other statements can be corrected as TMV affects all dicotyledonous plants, of which most important are tobacco and tomato. But it does not affect any monocotyledonous plant. TMV is a *ss*RNA virus, it infects a wide range of plants, especially tobacco and other members of the family Solanaceae. TMV does not infect gymnosperms.

51. *(c)* Placenta allows the foetus to transfer waste products to the mother's blood. Other statements can be corrected as Placenta gives protection against most bacteria and does not allow infections to enter the foetus.

Placenta allows gaseous exchange *via* the mother's blood supply, i.e. it allows diffusion of O_2 and CO_2. Placenta produces hormones like human Chorionic Gonadotropin (hCG), progesterone, oestrogen and human Placental Lactogen (hPL).

52. *(a)* Respiratory Quotient (RQ) measures the ratio of the volume of carbon dioxide (V_C) produced by an organism to the volume of oxygen consumed (V_O). The RQ for the given equation is

$$RQ = \dfrac{CO_2 \text{ produced}}{O_2 \text{ consumed}} = \dfrac{102}{145} = 0.703$$

$$RQ = 0.703$$

53. *(c)* Nucleosome is a structural unit of a eukaryotic chromosome, consisting of a length of DNA coiled around a core histone. Thus, nucleosome is not a membrane bound organelle of a cell.

54. *(a)* Tyrosine is the immediate precursor of the thyroxine hormone. Thyroxine is produced in the thyroid gland from tyrosine and iodine. Thyrotropin Releasing Hormone (TRH) is produced by the hypothalamus which induces the release of thyroxine.

55. *(c)* The haemoglobin molecule has four binding sites for oxygen molecules. Thus, each Hb tetramer can bind four oxygen molecules. Haemoglobin is the oxygen transporting protein of red blood cells and is a globular protein with quaternary structure. Haemoglobin consists of four polypeptide subunits, 2α chains and 2β chains.

56. *(b)* The smooth endoplasmic reticulum functions in lipid synthesis and metabolism, the production of steroid hormones and detoxification. Smooth Endoplasmic Reticulum (SER) is a meshwork of five disc-like tubular membrane vesicles, part of a continuous membrane organelle within the cytoplasm of eukaryotic cells.

57. *(a)* The light dependent reaction of photosynthesis uses light energy to make two molecules needed for the next stage of photosynthesis. These include the energy storage molecule ATP and the reduced electron carrier NADPH. The light reaction takes place in the thylakoid membranes of chloroplasts.

58. *(d)* Hypothalamus directly controls the production of glucocorticoids and androgens. These hormones are secreted in response to ACTH (Adrenocorticotropic Hormone), which is secreted from the anterior pituitary gland. The ACTH is released in response to corticotropin releasing hormone from the hypothalamus. The pathway can be explained as

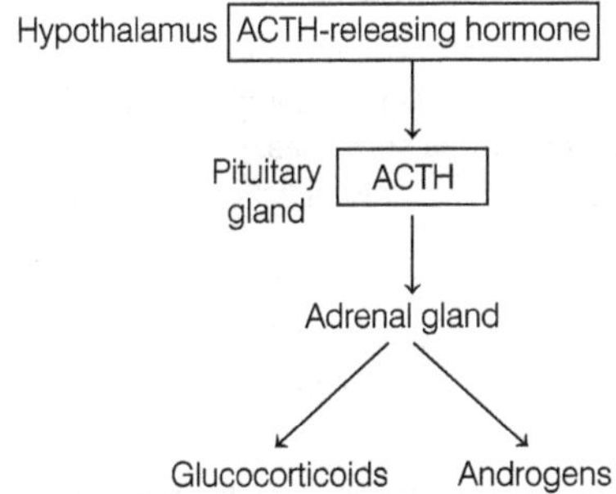

59. *(c)* Acetaminophen, also known as paracetamol is not produced by plant or fungi, it is artificially formed. The starting material for the manufacturing of paracetamol is phenol which is nitrated to give a mixture of the ortho and para-nitrotoluene.

Other drugs are obtained as, penicillin is an antibiotic obtained from ascomycetous fungi *Penicillium notatum*. Reserpine is an alkaloid derived from the roots of *Rauwolfia serpentina* plant. Quinine comes from the bark of the *Cinchona* tree.

60. *(d)* Lamarck is best known for his theory of Inheritance of Acquired Characteristics', first presented in 1801. It states that if an organism changes

during his life in order to adapt to its environment, those changes are passed on to its offsprings.

61. *(a)* $OC = 1$ radius of circle $x^2 + y^2 = 1$
$$OA = AP$$
$$\therefore \quad \angle AOP = \angle OPA = 45°$$

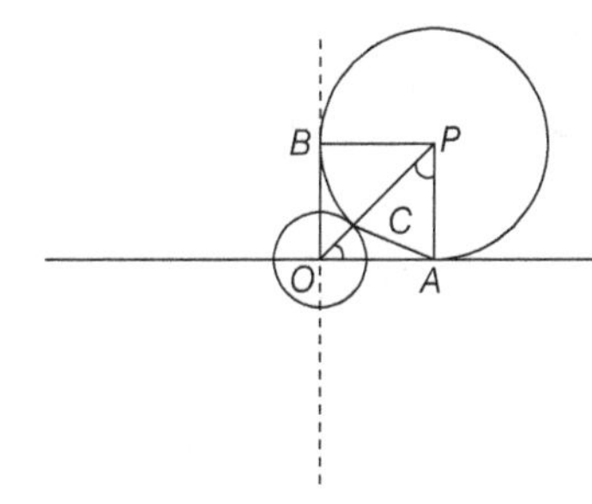

$AP = PC$ radius of circle
In $\triangle PCA$,
$$\therefore \angle PCA + \angle PAC + \angle CPA = 180°$$
$$\Rightarrow 2\angle PCA + 45° = 180°$$
$$\Rightarrow \quad \angle PCA = \frac{135°}{2}$$
$$\Rightarrow \quad \angle OCA = 180° - \angle PCA$$
$$\Rightarrow \quad \angle OCA = 180° - \frac{135°}{2} = \pi - \frac{3\pi}{8}$$
$$\Rightarrow \quad \angle OCA = \frac{5\pi}{8}$$

62. *(c)* Given $ABCD$ is trapezium
$$AD = BC = CD = 30$$
Let the smallest angle be θ.

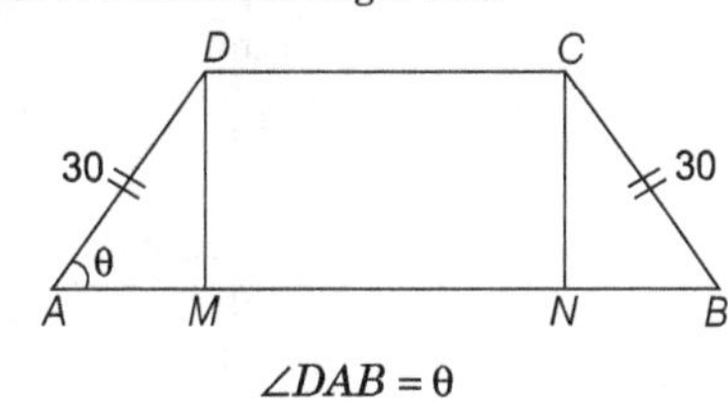

$$\angle DAB = \theta$$
In $\triangle AMD$,
$$\cos\theta = \frac{AM}{30} \Rightarrow AM = 30\cos\theta$$
$$\sin\theta = \frac{DM}{30} = DM = 30\sin\theta$$
Area of trapezium $= \frac{1}{2}(AB + CD)\,DM$
$$\Rightarrow \quad A = \frac{1}{2}(60 + 60\cos\theta)\,30\sin\theta$$
$$\Rightarrow \quad A = 900\,(\sin\theta + \sin\theta\cos\theta)$$
$$\Rightarrow \quad \frac{dA}{d\theta} = 900\,(\cos\theta - \sin^2\theta + \cos^2\theta)$$
For maximum or minimum, put $\frac{dA}{d\theta} = 0$
$$\therefore \quad \cos\theta - \sin^2\theta + \cos^2\theta = 0$$
$$\Rightarrow \quad \cos\theta + \cos 2\theta = 0$$
$$\Rightarrow \quad 2\cos\frac{3\theta}{2}\cos\frac{\theta}{2} = 0$$

$$\Rightarrow \quad \frac{3\theta}{2} = \frac{\pi}{2} \text{ or } \frac{\theta}{2} = \frac{\pi}{2}$$
$$\Rightarrow \quad \theta = \frac{\pi}{3} \text{ or } \theta = \pi$$
For maximum $\theta = \frac{\pi}{3}$

63. *(d)* Given, $A_1 = \{(x, y) : x^2 + 2y^2 \le 1\}$
$$A_2 = \{(x, y) : |x|^3 + 2\sqrt{2}\,|y|^3 \le 1\}$$
$$A_3 = \{(x, y) : \max(|x|, \sqrt{2}|y|) \le 1\}$$
Graph of A_1, A_2 and A_3 are

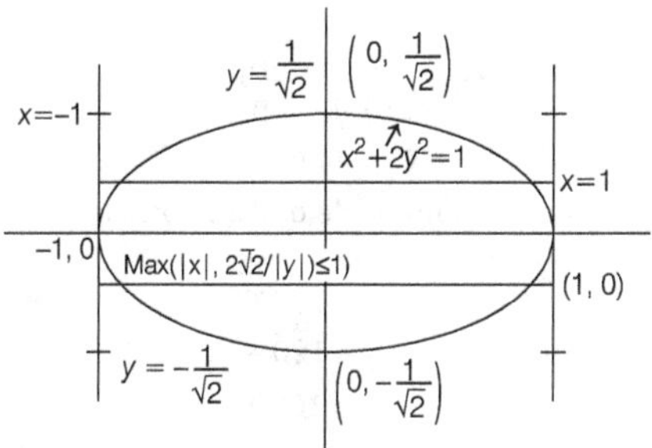

Clearly from graph $A_1 \subset A_2 \subset A_3$

64. *(b)* Given, area of $\triangle EAB =$ area of square $ABCD$
$$EB = ED = \sqrt{130}$$
Let side of square $= x$
$$BM = \frac{x}{\sqrt{2}} = AM$$

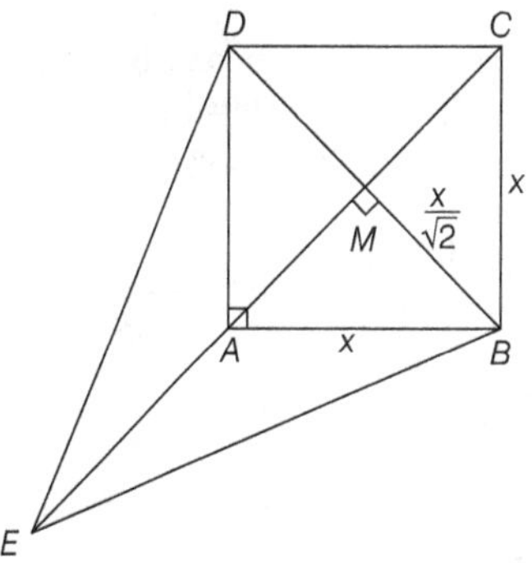

Area of $\triangle AEB =$ Area of $\triangle BEM -$ area of $(\triangle AMB)$
$$= \frac{1}{2}EM \times BM - \frac{1}{2}AM \times BM$$
$$= \frac{1}{2}BM\,(EM - AM)$$
$$= \frac{1}{2}\frac{x}{\sqrt{2}}\left(\sqrt{130 - \frac{x^2}{2}} - \frac{x}{\sqrt{2}}\right)$$
$$\therefore \quad \frac{1}{2}\cdot\frac{x}{\sqrt{2}}\left(\sqrt{130 - \frac{x^2}{2}} - \frac{x}{\sqrt{2}}\right) = x^2$$
$$\Rightarrow \quad \sqrt{130 - \frac{x^2}{2}} = 2\sqrt{2}\,x + \frac{x}{\sqrt{2}}$$

$$\Rightarrow \quad 130 - \frac{x^2}{2} = \left(\frac{5x}{\sqrt{2}}\right)^2$$

$$\Rightarrow \quad 130 - \frac{x^2}{2} = \frac{25x^2}{2}$$

$$\Rightarrow \quad 13x^2 = 130 \Rightarrow x^2 = 10$$

$\therefore$ Area of square $= 10$

65. *(a)* Given, $A = \{1, 2, 3, ..., 30\}$

Case **I** All three number are multiple of 3 then product of three number are divisible by 9.

$\therefore \qquad {}^{10}C_3 = 120$

Case **II** Two number are multiple of 3 and other are not multiple of 9.

i.e. $\qquad {}^{10}C_2 \times {}^{20}C_1 = 900$

Case **III** One are multiple of 9 and other two are not multiple of 3.

$${}^{3}C_1 \times {}^{20}C_2 = 570$$

$\therefore$ Total number of ways $= 120 + 900 + 570$
$$= 1590$$

66. *(c)* We have, heat extracted from a liquid during solidification,

$$U = Qt = mL \Rightarrow L \propto U$$

Also, heat extracted from liquid during cooling,

$$H = Qt = mc\Delta T$$

Temperature of liquid,

$$T = \frac{Q}{mc} \cdot t + T_i$$

Slope of T *versus* t line is inversely proportional to specific heat c.

Now, from given graph, we get

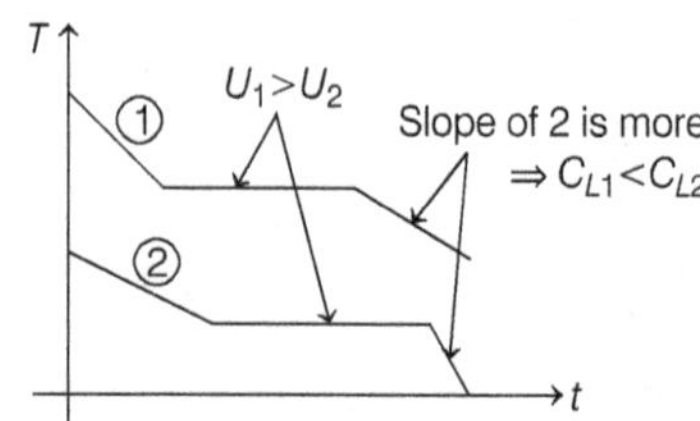

we get, $U_1 > U_2$ and $C_{L1} < C_{L2}$

67. *(c)* From geometry of figure, shadow length is CD $(= H)$.

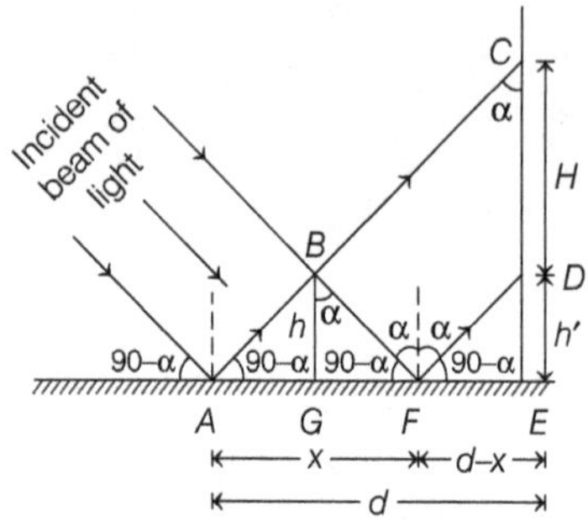

From similar triangles ΔBGF and ΔDEF, we have

$$\frac{DE}{BG} = \frac{FE}{GF}$$

$$\frac{h'}{h} = \left(\frac{d-x}{x}\right)$$

$$\Rightarrow \quad \frac{d}{x} = \frac{h'+h}{h} \qquad ...(i)$$

Now, from similar triangles ΔABG and ΔACE, we have

$$\frac{CE}{AE} = \frac{BG}{AG}$$

$\therefore \qquad \Delta ABG \cong \Delta FBG$

and $\qquad AG = GF = x$

$$\Rightarrow \quad \frac{H+h'}{d+x} = \frac{h}{x}$$

$$\Rightarrow \quad \frac{d}{x} = \frac{H+h'-h}{h} \qquad ...(ii)$$

Equating Eqs. (i) and (ii), we get

$$\frac{h'+h}{h} = \frac{H+h'-h}{h}$$

$$\Rightarrow \quad 2h = H$$

Hence, height of shadow on wall is $2h$.

68. (No option is matching)

Net force on marble due to water is

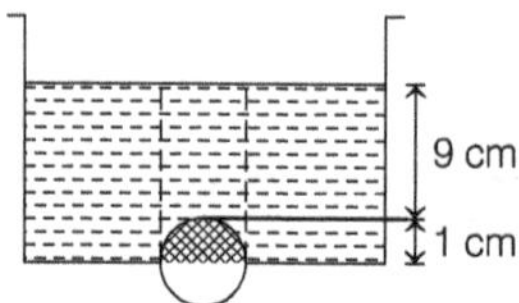

F_{net} = (Force of water column of height $\sim$ 9 cm) $-$ (Buoyant force on marble)

$\qquad = \pi r^2 \rho_w gh -$ Volume of marble
$\qquad\qquad\qquad$ under water $\times \rho_w \times g$

$\qquad = \pi r^2 \rho_w gh - \frac{2}{3}\pi r^3 \rho_w g$

$\qquad = \pi r^2 \rho_w g \left(h - \frac{2}{3}r\right)$

$\qquad \approx 3.14 \times (1 \times 10^{-2})^2 \times 1000 \times 10$
$$\left(9 - \frac{2}{3}\right) \times 10^{-2}$$

$\qquad = 26 \times 10^{-2} = 0.26\,\text{N (downwards)}$

69. *(d)* In given V-I graph,

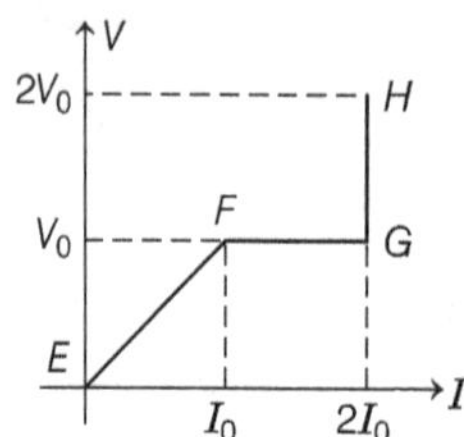

From E to F,

$$V_0 = I_0 R_0$$

$\Rightarrow \qquad$ s lope $= R_0$

$\therefore$ At F, resistance $= R_0 = \dfrac{V_0}{I_0}$

From F to G,

$$V = V_0 = \text{constant}$$

But current increases, so resistance must decreases.

At G, resistance $= \dfrac{R_0}{2} = \dfrac{V_0}{2I_0}$.

From G to H, current is constant but voltage increases, so resistance decreases.

At H, resistance $= \dfrac{2V_0}{2I_0} = \dfrac{V_0}{I_0} = R_0$

So, correct option is (d).

70. *(a)* From $\dfrac{V}{t} = k \left(\dfrac{p}{l}\right)^a \eta^b r^c$,

we have

$$[\text{L}^3\text{T}^{-1}] = \left[\frac{\text{ML}^{-1}\text{T}^{-2}}{\text{L}}\right]^a [\text{ML}^{-1}\text{T}^{-1}]^b [\text{L}]^c$$

Equating powers of M, L and T, we get
$$a + b = 0 \Rightarrow -2a - b + c = 3$$
$$-2a - b = -1$$

Solving, we get $a = 1$, $b = -1$ and $c = 4$

71. *(c)* Skeletal diagram for the given information can be shown as:

$$X + Br_2 \longrightarrow Y$$

$$O_3/Zn, H_2O \downarrow$$

One product

Emperical formula for Y can be calculated as,

Elements	% of element	At mass	Moles of element	Simplest molar ratio	Simplest whole no.
C	22.22%	12	22.22/12 = 1.85	1.85/0.92 = 2.01	2×2
H	3.71%	1	3.71/1 = 3.71	3.71/0.92 = 4.03	4×2
Br	74.07%	80	74.07/80 = 0.92	0.92/0.92 = 1	1×2

$\therefore$ The emperical formula of Y is $C_4H_8Br_2$.
According to retero synthesis.

$$CH_3-CH=CH-CH_3 + Br_2$$
$$(X)$$
$$\text{2-butene}$$
$$CH_3-CH-CH-CH_3$$
$$\left(\begin{array}{cc} Br & Br \end{array}\right)$$
$$(Y)$$
$$\text{2, 3-dibromobutane}$$

Also,

$$CH_3-CH=CH-CH_3 + O_3$$
$$(X)$$

$$CH_3-CH \quad CH-CH_3$$
$$O-O$$

$$\downarrow Zn/H_2O$$

$$2CH_3C-H$$
Acetaldehyde

72. *(b)*

$$CH_3-C\equiv C-H \xrightarrow[H_3O^+]{Hg^{2+}} H_3C-C-H_3C$$
$$(X)$$

$$\xrightarrow[\text{(aldol condensation)}]{PhCHO \mid \text{dil. NaOH}}$$

$$CH_3-C-CH=CH-Ph$$
$$(Y)$$
(α, β-unsaturated ketone)

In first step one molecule of water adds to alkyne on warming with mercuric sulphate and dilute sulphuric acid to form carbonyl compound, i.e. acetone. In second step 2 molecules of acetone condense in presence of dil. NaOH to form α, β-unsaturated ketone. This reaction is known as aldol condensation.

73. *(a)* For the reaction,

$$2\overset{+7}{Mn}O_4^- + 5\overset{-4}{H_2}O_2 + 6H^+ \longrightarrow$$
$$2Mn^{2+} + 8H_2\overset{-2}{O} + 5O_2$$

Let the number of moles of oxygen produced per mole $KMnO_4$ be x.

Number of equivalent = Number of moles
$$\times \text{ change in oxidation state}$$

Number of equivalent of $KMnO_4 = 1 \times 5$
Number of equivalent of $H_2O_2 = x \times 2$

$\therefore$ (Number of eq.)$_{KMnO_4}$
$$= \text{(Number of eq.)}_{H_2O_2}$$
$$1 \times 5 = x \times 2$$
$$x = \frac{5}{2} = 2.5$$

74. *(b)* Given, wavelength $\lambda = 400$ nm
$$= 400 \times 10^{-9} \text{ m}$$

Energy of photon $E = \dfrac{hc}{\lambda}$

$$E = \frac{6.626 \times 10^{-34} \text{ Js} \times 3 \times 10^8 \text{ m/s}}{400 \times 10^{-9} \text{ m}}$$

$$E = 4.97 \times 10^{-19} \text{ J}$$

$$= 4.97 \times 10^{-19} \times \frac{1 \text{ eV}}{1.6 \times 10^{-19} \text{ J}}$$

$$E = 3.1 \text{ eV}$$

If the energy of incident light $\geq$ work function of light. Then photoelectrons will be ejected.

Thus, K and Li will emit photoelectrons as their threshold energy (obtained from graph) is less than 3.1 eV.

75. *(c)* Given,

weight of metal = 100 g
$$T_2 = 15.69°C, \ T_1 = 80°C$$

Specific heat of water = 4.184 J/g°C
Heat gained by 100 g of metal = Heat lost by 1000 g of water.

We know, $Q = mc \, \Delta T$

$$\therefore 100 \times x \times (80 - 15.69)$$
$$= 1000 \times 4.184 \, (15.69 - 15)$$
$$= 100x \, (64.31) = 2886.96$$
$$x = \frac{2886.96}{6431} = 0.448 \approx 0.45 \text{ J/g.°C}$$

76. *(d)* In the G_1-phase of cell cycle, the cell grows in size, i.e. the cell synthesises various enzymes and nutrients that are needed later on for DNA replication. The next phase of cell cycle is S-phase during which the DNA amount doubles up, i.e. a cell with 3 ng of DNA in G_1-phase will now have 6 ng of DNA. G_2-phase comes after S-phase. It is second growth phase but here the DNA content will remain 6 ng.

77. *(b)* In photosynthesis, photophosphorylation and in aerobic respiration, oxidative phosphorylation occurs that requires proton gradient. The sunlight-driven production of ATP from ADP and inorganic phosphate is called photophosphorylation. It occurs in the chloroplast. Oxidative phosphorylation is the process in which ATP is formed by the transfer of electrons from NADH or $FADH_2$ to O_2 by a series of electron carriers. It occurs inside the mitochondria.

78. *(d)* $[H^+][OH^-] = 10^{-14}$

$$1.3 \times 10^{-4} \times [OH^-] = 10^{-14}$$

$$[OH^-] = \frac{1}{1.3} \times 10^{+4} \times 10^{-14}$$

$$= \frac{1}{1.3} \times 10^{-10} = 0.769 \times 10^{-10}$$

$$= 0.77 \times 10^{-10} = 7.7 \times 10^{-11} \text{ M}$$

79. *(a)* Vital capacity = Inspiratory reserve volume + Tidal volume + Expiratory reserve volume
$$= 2500 \text{ mL} + 800 \text{ mL} + 600 \text{ mL} = 3900 \text{ mL}$$
Vital capacity is the volume of air breathed out after the deepest inhalation.

80. *(c)* All haploid sexually reproducing organisms would produce sperms/male gametes without the process of meiosis, e.g. Honeybee (*Apis*) and Ant (*Formica*). Haploid parents produce gametes by mitotic division. This happens because meiosis is reductional division in which the daughter cells contain half the number of chromosomes as the parent cell. Therefore, haploid organisms do not show meiosis to further disturb their ploidy.

QUESTION PAPER 2016
Stream : SA

MM : 100

Instructions

1. There are 80 questions in this paper.
2. This question paper contains two parts; Part I and Part II. There are four sections; Mathematics, Physics, Chemistry and Biology in each part.
3. Out of the four options given with each question, only one is correct.

➲ PART-I (1 Mark Questions)

MATHEMATICS

1. Suppose the quadratic polynomial $P(x) = ax^2 + bx + c$ has positive coefficients a, b, c in arithmetic progression in that order. If $P(x) = 0$ has integer roots α and β. Then, $\alpha + \beta + \alpha\beta$ is equal to

(a) 3   (b) 5   (c) 7   (d) 14

2. The number of digits in the decimal expansion of $16^5 5^{16}$ is

(a) 16   (b) 17   (c) 18   (d) 19

3. Let t be real number such that $t^2 = at + b$ for some positive integers a and b. Then, for any choice of positive integers a and b, t^3 is never equal to

(a) $4t + 3$ (b) $8t + 5$ (c) $10t + 3$ (d) $6t + 5$

4. Consider the equation $(1 + a + b)^2 = 3(1 + a^2 + b^2)$, where a, b are real numbers. Then,

(a) there is no solution pair (a, b)
(b) there are infinitely many solution pairs (a, b)
(c) there are exactly two solution pairs (a, b)
(d) there is exactly one solution pair (a, b)

5. Let $a_1, a_2, \ldots, a_{100}$ be non-zero real numbers such that
$$a_1 + a_2 + \ldots + a_{100} = 0$$
Then,

(a) $\Sigma_{i=1}^{100} a_i 2^{a_i} > 0$ and $\Sigma_{i=1}^{100} a_i 2^{-a_i} < 0$
(b) $\Sigma_{i=1}^{100} a_i 2^{a_i} \geq 0$ and $\Sigma_{i=1}^{100} a_i 2^{-a_i} \geq 0$
(c) $\Sigma_{i=1}^{100} a_i 2^{a_i} \leq 0$ and $\Sigma_{i=1}^{100} a_i 2^{-ai} \leq 0$
(d) The sign of $\Sigma_{i=1}^{100} a_i 2^{a_i}$ or $\Sigma_{i=1}^{100} a_i 2^{-a_i}$ depends on the choice of a_i's

6. Let $ABCD$ be a trapezium, in which AB is parallel to CD, $AB = 11$, $BC = 4$, $CD = 6$ and $DA = 3$. The distance between AB and CD is

(a) 2   (b) 2.4   (c) 2.8
(d) Not determinable with the data

7. The points A, B, C, D, E are marked on the circumference of a circle in clockwise direction such that $\angle ABC = 130°$ and $\angle CDE = 110°$. The measure of $\angle ACE$ in degree is

(a) 50°   (b) 60°
(c) 70°   (d) 80°

8. Three circles of radii 1, 2 and 3 units respectively touch each other externally in the plane. The circumradius of the triangle formed by joining the centers of the circles is

(a) 1.5　　(b) 2　　(c) 2.5　　(d) 3

9. Let P be a point inside a ΔABC with $\angle ABC = 90°$. Let P_1 and P_2 be the images of P under reflection in AB and BC respectively. The distance between the circumcenters of ΔABC and P_1PP_2 is

(a) $\dfrac{AB}{2}$

(b) $\dfrac{AP + BP + CP}{3}$

(c) $\dfrac{AC}{2}$

(d) $\dfrac{AB + BC + AC}{2}$

10. Let a and b be two positive real numbers such that $a + 2b \le 1$. Let A_1 and A_2 be respectively the areas of circles with radii ab^3 and b^2. Then, the maximum possible value of $\dfrac{A_1}{A_2}$ is

(a) $\dfrac{1}{16}$

(b) $\dfrac{1}{64}$

(c) $\dfrac{1}{16\sqrt{2}}$

(d) $\dfrac{1}{32}$

11. There are two candles of same length and same size. Both of them burn at uniform rate. The first one burns in 5 hr and the second one burns in 3 h. Both the candles are lit together. After how many minutes the length of the first candle is 3 times that of the other?

(a) 90　　(b) 120　　(c) 135　　(d) 150

12. Consider a cuboid all of whose edges are integers and whose base is a square. Suppose the sum of all its edges is numerically equal to the sum of the areas of all its six faces. Then, the sum of all its edges is

(a) 12　　(b) 18　　(c) 24　　(d) 36

13. Let $A_1, A_2, \ldots, A_m$ be non-empty subsets of $\{1, 2, 3, \ldots, 100\}$ satisfying the following conditions:

1. The numbers $|A_1|, |A_2|, \ldots, |A_m|$ are distinct.

2. $A_1, A_2, \ldots, A_m$ are pairwise disjoint.

(Here $|A|$ donotes the number of elements in the set A)

Then, the maximum possible value of m is

(a) 13　　(b) 14　　(c) 15　　(d) 16

14. The number of all 2-digit numbers n, such that n is equal to the sum of the square of digit in its tens place and the cube of the digit in units place is

(a) 0　　(b) 1　　(c) 2　　(d) 4

15. Let f be a function defined on the set of all positive integers such that $f(xy) = f(x) + f(y)$ for all positive integers x, y. If $f(12) = 24$ and $f(8) = 15$. The value of $f(48)$ is

(a) 31　　(b) 32　　(c) 33　　(d) 34

PHYSICS

16. A person walks 25.0° north of east for 3.18 km. How far would she have to walk due north and then due east to arrive at the same location?

(a) Towards north 2.88 km and towards east 1.34 km

(b) Towards north 2.11 km and towards east 2.11 km

(c) Towards north 1.25 km and towards east 1.93 km

(d) Towards north 1.34 km and towards east 2.88 km

17. The length and width of a rectangular room are measured to be 3.95 ± 0.05 m and 3.05 ± 0.05 m, respectively. The area of the floor is

(a) 12.05 ± 0.01 m^2

(b) 12.05 ± 0.005 m^2

(c) 12.05 ± 0.34 m^2

(d) 12.05 ± 0.40 m^2

18. A car goes around uniform circular track of radius R at a uniform speed v once in every T seconds. The magnitude of the centripetal acceleration is a_c. If the car now goes uniformly around a larger circular track of radius $2R$ and experiences a centripetal acceleration of magnitude $8a_c$. Then, its time period is

(a) $2T$　　(b) $3T$　　(c) $T/2$　　(d) $3/2T$

19. The primary and the secondary coils of a transformer contain 10 and 100 turns, respectively. The primary coil is connected to a battery that supplies a constant voltage of 1.5 V. The voltage across the secondary coil is

(a) 1.5 V　　(b) 0.15 V　　(c) 0.0 V　　(d) 15 V

20. Water falls down a 500.0 m shaft to reach a turbine which generates electricity. How much water must fall per second in order to generate 1.00×10^9 W of power ? (Assume 50% efficiency of conversion and $g = 10$ ms^{-2})

(a) 250 m^3

(b) 400 m^3

(c) 500 m^3

(d) 200 m^3

21. The diagram below shows two circular loops of wire (A and B) centred on and perpendicular to the X-axis and oriented with their planes parallel to each other. The Y-axis passes vertically through loop A (dashed line). There is a current I_B in loop B as shown in the diagram. Possible actions which we might perform on loop A are

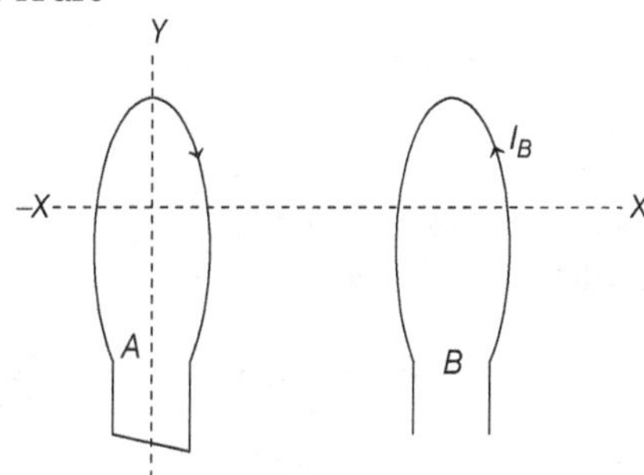

(I) move A to the right along X-axis closer to B

(II) move A to the left along X-axis away from B

(III) as viewed from above, rotate A clockwise about Y-axis

(IV) as viewed from above, rotate A anti-clockwise about Y-axis

Which of the actions will induce a current in A only in the direction shown?

(a) Only (I)   (b) Only (II)

(c) Only (I) and (IV)   (d) Only (II) and (III)

22. A rigid ball rolls without slipping on a surface shown below:

Which one of the following is the most likely representation of the distance travelled by the ball *versus* time graph?

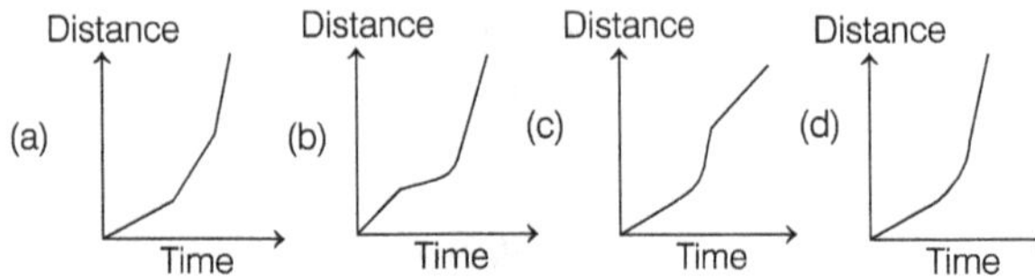

23. In an experiment, set up A consists of two parallel wires which carry currents in opposite directions as shown in the figure. A second set up B is identical to set up A, except that there is a metal plate between the wires.

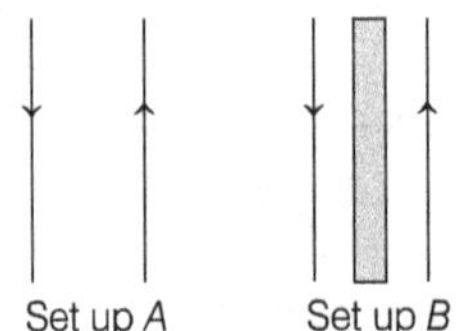

Set up A Set up B

Let F_A and F_B be the magnitude of the force between the two wires in setup A and setup B, respectively.

(a) $F_A > F_B \neq 0$ (b) $F_A < F_B$

(c) $F_A = F_B \neq 0$ (d) $F_A > F_B = 0$

24. In the circuit, wire 1 is of negligible resistance. Then,

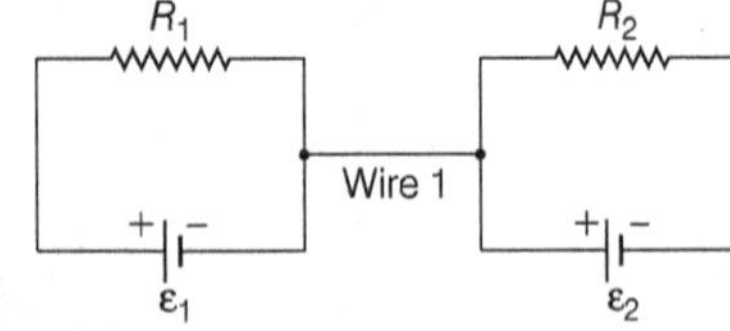

(a) current will flow through wire 1, if $\varepsilon_1 \neq \varepsilon_2$

(b) current will flow through wire 1, if $\dfrac{\varepsilon_1}{R_1} \neq \dfrac{\varepsilon_2}{R_2}$

(c) current will flow through wire 1, if $\dfrac{\varepsilon_1 + \varepsilon_2}{(R_1 + R_2)} \neq \dfrac{\varepsilon_1 - \varepsilon_2}{(R_1 - R_2)}$

(d) no current will flow through wire 1

25. The radius of a nucleus is given by $r_0 A^{1/3}$, where $r_0 = 1.3 \times 10^{-15}$ m and A is the mass number of the

nucleus. The lead nucleus has $A = 206$. The electrostatic force between two protons in this nucleus is approximately

(a) 10^2 N   (b) 10^7 N   (c) 10^{12} N   (d) 10^{17} N

26. A hollow lens is made of thin glass and in the shape of a double concave lens. It can be filled with air, water of refractive index 1.33 or CS_2 of refractive index 1.6. It will act as a diverging lens, if it is

(a) filled with air and immersed in water

(b) filled with water and immersed in CS_2

(c) filled with air and immersed in CS_2

(d) filled with CS_2 and immersed in water

27. A stone thrown down with a speed u takes a time t_1 to reach the ground, while another stone thrown upwards from the same point with the same speed takes time t_2. The maximum height the second stone reaches from the ground is

(a) $\dfrac{1}{2} g t_1 t_2$ (b) $g/8(t_1 + t_2)^2$

(c) $g/8(t_1 - t_2)^2$ (d) $\dfrac{1}{2} g t_2^2$

28. An electric field due to a positively charged long straight wire at a distance r from it is proportional to r^{-1} in magnitude. Two electrons are orbiting such a long straight wire in circular orbits of radii 1 A and 2A. The ratio of their respective time periods is

(a) $1:1$ (b) $1:2$ (c) $2:1$ (d) $4:1$

29. Two particles of identical mass are moving in circular orbits under a potential given by $V(r) = Kr^{-n}$, where K is a constant. If the radii of their orbits are $r_1 . r_2$ and their speeds are $v_1 . v_2$, respectively. Then,

(a) $v_1^2 r_1^n = v_2^2 r_2^n$ (b) $v_1^2 r_1^{-n} = v_2^2 r_2^{-n}$

(c) $v_1^2 r_1 = v_2^2 r_2$ (d) $v_1^2 r_1^{2-n} = v_2^2 r_2^{2-n}$

30. Mercury is often used in clinical thermometers. Which one of the following properties of mercury is not a reason for this ?

(a) The coefficient of the thermal expansion is large

(b) It is shiny

(c) It is a liquid at room temperature

(d) It has high density

CHEMISTRY

31. One mole of one of the sodium salts listed below, having carbon content close to 14.3% produces 1 mole of carbon dioxide upon heating (atomic mass of Na = 23, H = 1, C = 12, O = 16). The salt is

(a) C_2H_5COONa (b) $NaHCO_3$

(c) $HCOONa$ (d) CH_3COONa

32. Among formic acid, acetic acid, propanoic acid and phenol, the strongest acid in water is

(a) formic acid   (b) acetic acid

(c) propanoic acid   (d) phenol

33. According to Graham's law, the rate of diffusion of CO, O_2, N_2 and CO_2 follows the order
(a) $CO = N_2 > O_2 > CO_2$
(b) $CO = N_2 > CO_2 > O_2$
(c) $O_2 > CO = N_2 > CO_2$
(d) $CO_2 > O_2 > CO = N_2$

34. The major product formed when 2-butene is reacted with O_3 followed by treatment with Zn/H_2O is
(a) CH_3COOH (b) CH_3CHO
(c) CH_3CH_2OH (d) $CH_2 = CH_2$

35. The IUPAC name for the following compound is

$$CH_3-CH_2-CH_2-CH_2-\underset{\underset{CH_2}{\overset{||}{}}}{C}-CH_2-CH_2-CH_3$$

(a) 2-propylhex-1-ene   (b) 2-butylpent-1-ene
(c) 2-propyl-2-butylethene   (d) Propyl-1-butylethene

36. The major products obtained in the reaction of oxalic acid with conc. H_2SO_4 upon heating are
(a) CO, CO_2, H_2O (b) CO, SO_2, H_2O
(c) H_2S, CO, H_2O (d) $HCOOH$, H_2S, CO

37. $LiOH$ reacts with CO_2 to form Li_2CO_3 (atomic mass of $Li = 7$). The amount of CO_2 (in g) consumed by 1 g of $LiOH$ is closest to
(a) 0.916   (b) 1.832
(c) 0.544   (d) 1.088

38. The oxidation number of sulphur is -4 in
(a) H_2S (b) CS_2
(c) Na_2SO_4 (d) Na_2SO_3

39. Al_2O_3 reacts with
(a) only water   (b) only acids
(c) only alkalis   (d) both acids and alkalis

40. The major product formed in the oxidation of acetylene by alk. $KMnO_4$ is
(a) ethanol   (b) acetic acid
(c) formic acid   (d) oxalic acid

41. In a closed vessel, an ideal gas at 1 atm is heated from 27°C to 327°C. The final pressure of the gas will approximately be
(a) 3 atm   (b) 0.5 atm
(c) 2 atm   (d) 12 atm

42. Among the elements Li, N, C and Be, one with the largest atomic radius is
(a) Li   (b) N
(c) C   (d) Be

43. A redox reaction among the following is
(i) $CdCl_2 + 2KOH \longrightarrow Cd(OH)_2 + 2KCl$
(ii) $BaCl_2 + K_2SO_4 \longrightarrow BaSO_4 + 2KCl$
(iii) $CaCO_3 \longrightarrow CaO + CO_2$
(iv) $2Ca + O_2 \longrightarrow 2CaO$
(a) (i)   (b) (ii)   (c) (iii)   (d) (iv)

44. The electronic configuration, which obeys Hund's rule for the ground state of carbon atom is

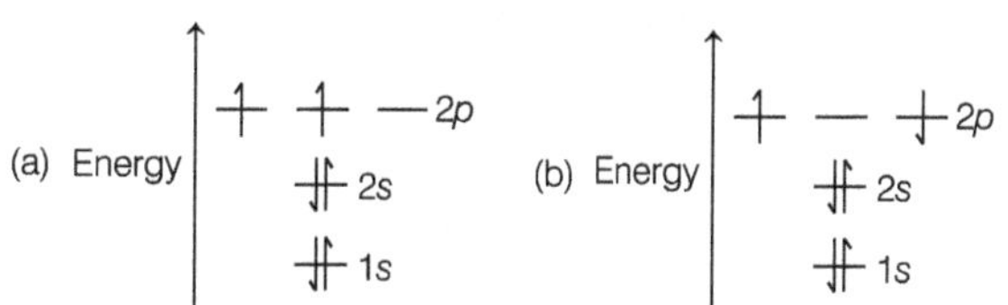

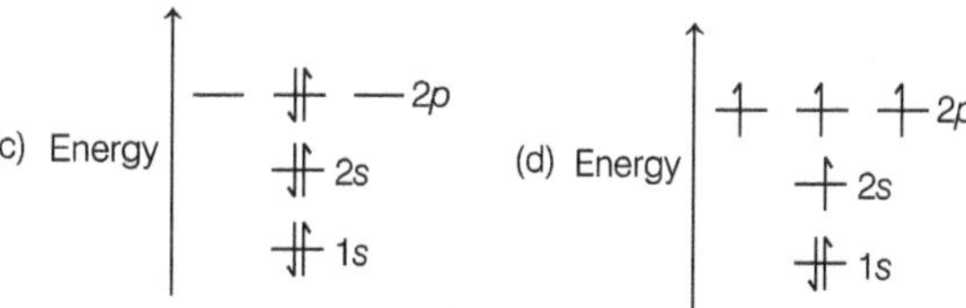

45. The graph that depicts Einstein's photoelectric effect for a monochromatic source of frequency above the threshold frequency is

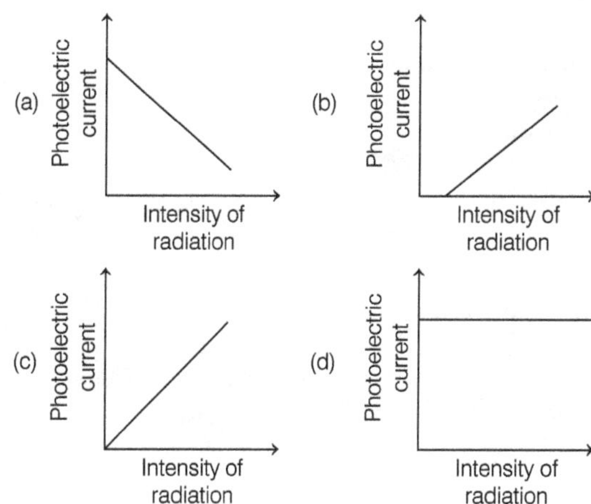

BIOLOGY

46. What is the length of human DNA containing 6.6×10^9 bp?
(a) 22 nm   (b) 0.22 mm
(c) 2.2 m   (d) 22 m

47. The Diphtheria, Pertussis, Tetanus (DPT) vaccine consists of
(a) live attenuated strains of diphtheria, pertussis, Tetanus
(b) toxoid of diphtheria, tetanus and heat-killed whole cells of Pertussis
(c) whole cell lysate of diphtheria, pertussis, tetanus
(d) heat-killed strains of diphtheria, pertussis, tetanus

48. Which of the following is not an enzyme?
(a) Lipase   (b) Amylase
(c) Trypsin   (d) Bilirubin

49. The pH of the avian blood is maintained by
(a) HCO_3^- (b) $H_2PO_4^-$ (c) CH_3COO^- (d) Cl^-

50. Podocyte layer that provides outer lining to the surface of glomerular capillaries are found in
(a) Bowman's capsule (b) loop of Henle
(c) renal artery (d) ureter

51. If a *ds*DNA has 20% adenine, what would be its cytosine content?
(a) 20% (b) 30%
(c) 40% (d) 80%

52. Which one of the following is incapable of curing pellagra?
(a) Niacine (b) Nicotine
(c) Nicotinamide (d) Tryptophan

53. In *Escherichia coli*, how many codons code for the standard amino acids?
(a) 64 (b) 60
(c) 61 (d) 20

54. *Bombyx mori* (silkworm) belongs to the order
(a) Lepidoptera (b) Diptera
(c) Hymenoptera (d) Coleoptera

55. The source of mammalian hormone 'relaxin' is
(a) ovary (b) stomach
(c) intestine (d) pancreas

56. Which one of the following animals is a connecting link between reptiles and mammals?
(a) Platypus (b) Bat
(c) Armadillo (d) Frog

57. What is the number of chromosomes in an individual with Turner's syndrome?
(a) 44 (b) 45
(c) 46 (d) 47

58. 'Chipko Movement' in the year 1974 in Garhwal Himalayas involved
(a) protecting tigers
(b) preventing soil erosion by planting trees
(c) preventing pollution by closing down industries
(d) hugging trees to prevent the contractors from felling them

59. Which of the following amino acids is not involved in gluconeogenesis?
(a) Alanine (b) Lysine
(c) Glutamate (d) Arginine

60. Which of the following entities causes syphilis?
(a) *Treponema pallidum* (b) *Neisseria gonorrhoeae*
(c) HIV (d) Hepatitis-B

➲ PART-II (2 Marks Questions)

MATHEMATICS

61. Suppose a is a positive real number such that $a^5 - a^3 + a = 2$. Then,
(a) $a^6 < 2$ (b) $2 < a^6 < 3$
(c) $3 < a^6 < 4$ (d) $4 \leq a^6$

62. Consider the quadratic equation $nx^2 + 7\sqrt{n}x + n = 0$, where n is a positive integer. Which of the following statements are necessarily correct?

I. For any n, the roots are distinct.

II. There are infinitely many values of n for which both roots are real.

III. The product of the roots is necessarily an integer.

(a) III only (b) I and III
(c) II and III (d) I, II and III

63. Consider a semicircle of radius 1 unit constructed on the diameter AB and let O be its centre. Let C be a point on AO such that $AC : CO = 2 : 1$. Draw CD perpendicular to AO with D on the semi-circle. Draw OE perpendicular to AD with E on AD. Let OE and CD intersect at H. Then, DH equals
(a) $\dfrac{1}{\sqrt{5}}$ (b) $\dfrac{1}{\sqrt{3}}$ (c) $\dfrac{1}{\sqrt{2}}$ (d) $\dfrac{\sqrt{5}-1}{2}$

64. Let S_1 be the sum of areas of the squares whose sides are parallel to coordinate axes. Let S_2 be the sum of areas of the slanted squares as shown in the figure. Then, $\dfrac{S_1}{S_2}$ is equal to

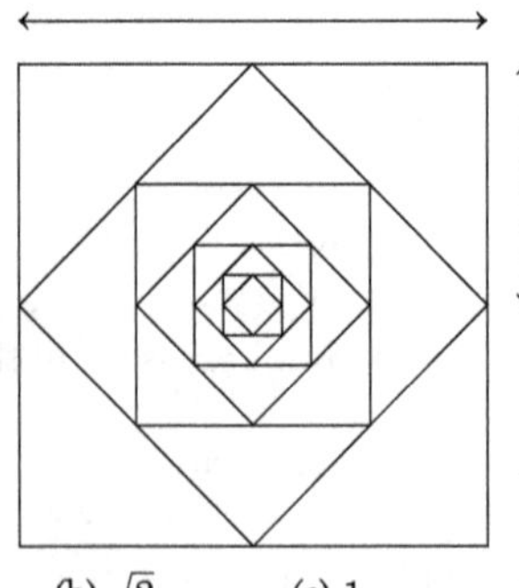

(a) 2 (b) $\sqrt{2}$ (c) 1 (d) $\dfrac{1}{\sqrt{2}}$

65. If a 3-digit number is randomly chosen. What is the probability that either the number itself or some permutation of the number (which is a 3-digit number) is divisible by 4 and 5?
(a) $\dfrac{1}{45}$ (b) $\dfrac{29}{180}$ (c) $\dfrac{11}{60}$ (d) $\dfrac{1}{4}$

PHYSICS

66. Which one of the following four graphs best depict the variation with x of the moment of inertia I of a uniform triangular lamina about an axis parallel to its base at a distance x from it?

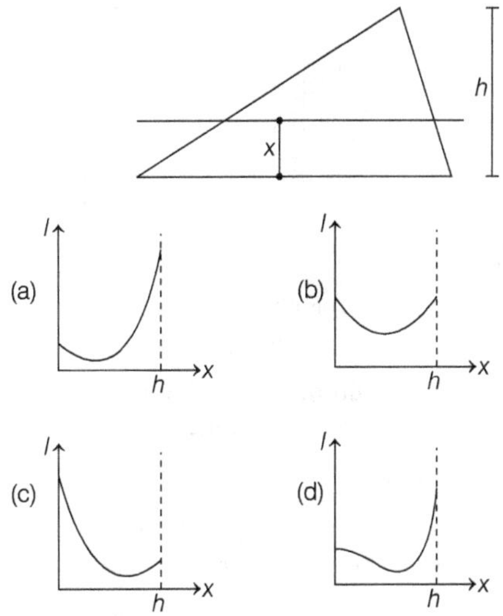

67. A rectangular block is composed of three different glass prisms (with refractive indices μ_1, μ_2 and μ_3) as shown in the figure below. A ray of light incident normal to the left face emerges normal to the right face. Then, the refractive indices are related by

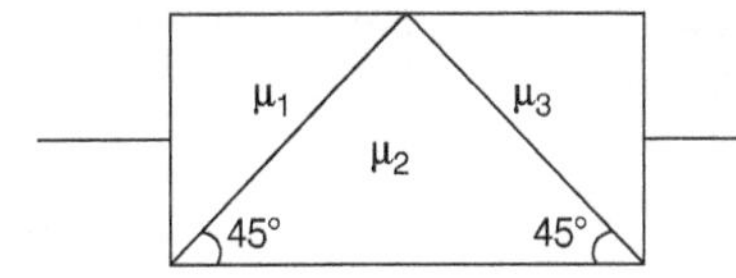

(a) $\mu_1^2 + \mu_2^2 = 2\mu_3^2$

(b) $\mu_1^2 + \mu_2^2 = \mu_3^2$

(c) $\mu_1^2 + \mu_3^2 = 2\mu_2^2$

(d) $\mu_2^2 + \mu_3^2 = 2\mu_1^2$

68. A uniform metal plate shaped like a triangle ABC has a mass of 540 g. The length of the sides AB, BC and CA are 3 cm, 5 cm and 4 cm, respectively. The plate is pivoted freely about the point A. What mass must be added to a vertex, so that the plate can hang with the long edge horizontal?

(a) 140 g at C

(b) 540 g at C

(c) 140 g at B

(d) 540 g at B

69. A 20 g bullet whose specific heat is 5000 J kg°C and moving at 2000 m/s plunges into a 1.0 kg block of wax whose specific heat is 3000 J kg°C. Both bullet and wax are at 25°C and assume that (i) the bullet comes to rest in the wax and (ii) all its kinetic energy goes into heating the wax. Thermal temperature of the wax (in °C) is close to

(a) 28.1   (b) 31.5   (c) 37.9   (d) 42.1

70. A V-shaped rigid body has two identical uniform arms. What must be the angle between the two arms, so that when the body is hung from one end the other arm is horizontal?

(a) $\cos^{-1}(1/3)$

(b) $\cos^{-1}(1/2)$

(c) $\cos^{-1}(1/4)$

(d) $\cos^{-1}(1/6)$

CHEMISTRY

71. In the following reaction, X, Y and Z are

(a) $X = CH_3Cl$; $Y = $ Anhydrous $AlCl_3$; $Z = HNO_3 + H_2SO_4$

(b) $X = CH_3COCl$; $Y = $ Anhydrous $AlCl_3$; $Z = HNO_3 + H_2SO_4$

(c) $X = CH_3Cl$; $Y = $ Conc. H_2SO_4; $Z = HNO_3 + H_2SO_4$

(d) $X = CH_3Cl$; $Y = $ Dil. H_2SO_4; $Z = HNO_3$

72. 2,3-dibromobutane can be converted to 2-butyne in a two steps reaction using

(a) (i) HCl and (ii) NaH

(b) (i) alc.KOH and (ii) $NaNH_2$

(c) (i) Na and (ii) NaOH

(d) (i) Br_2 and (ii) NaH

73. Given, $NO(g) + O_3(g) \longrightarrow NO_2(g) + O_2(g)$;

$$\Delta H = -198.9 \text{ kJ/mol}$$

$$O_3(g) \longrightarrow 3/2\, O_2(g);\ \Delta H = -142.3 \text{ kJ/mol}$$

$$O_2(g) \longrightarrow 2O(g);\ \ \ \ \Delta H = +495.0 \text{ kJ/mol}$$

The enthalpy change (ΔH) for the following reaction is

$$NO(g) + O(g) \longrightarrow NO_2(g)$$

(a) -304.1 kJ/mol

(b) $+304.1$ kJ/mol

(c) -403.1 kJ/mol

(d) $+403.1$ kJ/mol

74. A 1.85 g sample of an arsenic containing pesticide was chemically converted to AsO_4^{3-} (atomic mass of As = 74.9) and titrated with Pb^{2+} to form $Pb_3(AsO_4)_2$. If 20 mL of 0.1 M Pb^{2+} is required to reach the equivalence point, the mass percentage of arsenic in the pesticide sample is closest to

(a) 8.1   (b) 2.3

(c) 5.4   (d) 3.6

75. When treated with conc. HCl. MnO_2 yields a gas (X) which further reacts with $Ca(OH)_2$ to generate a white solid (Y). The solid Y reacts with dil. HCl to produce the same gas X. The solid Y is

(a) CaO

(b) $CaCl_2$

(c) $Ca(OCl)Cl$

(d) $CaCO_3$

BIOLOGY

76. The atmospheric pressure is 760 mm Hg at the sea level. Which of the following ranges is nearest to the partial pressure of CO_2 in mm Hg?
(a) 0.30-0.31   (b) 0.60-0.61
(c) 3.0-3.1   (d) 6.0-6.1

77. A breeder crossed a pure bred tall plant having white flowers to a pure bred short plant having blue flowers. He obtained 202 F_1 progeny and found that they are all tall having white flowers. Upon selfing these F_1 plants, he obtained a progeny of 2160 plants. Approximately, how many of these are likely to be short and having blue flowers?
(a) 1215   (b) 405
(c) 540   (d) 135

78. Match the different types of heart given in Column I with organisms given in Column II. Choose the correct combination.

Column I		Column II
P.	Neurogenic heart	i. Human
Q.	Bronchial heart	ii. King crab
R.	Pulmonary heart	iii. Shark

(a) P-ii, Q-iii, R-i
(b) P-iii, Q-ii, R-i
(c) P-i, Q-iii, R-ii
(d) P-ii, Q-i, R-iii

79. Given below are the four schematics that describe the dependence of the rate of an enzymatic reaction on temperature. Which of the following combinations is true for thermophilic and psychrophilic organisms?

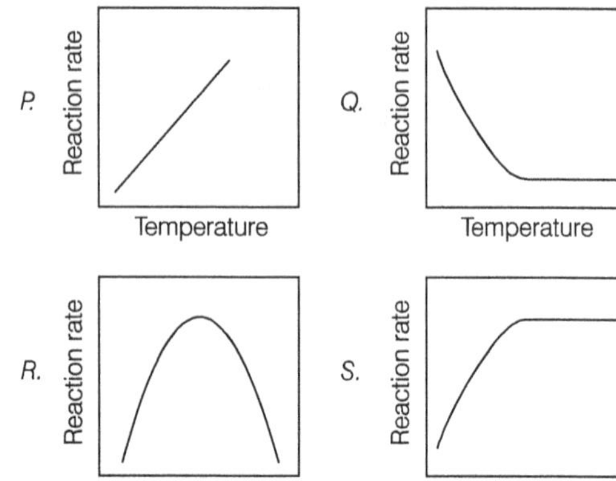

(a) P and P (b) P and S
(c) P and R (d) R and R

80. Match the enzymes in Column I with the reactions in Column II. Select the correct combination.

Column I		Column II
P.	Hydrolase	i. Inter-conversion of optical isomers
Q.	Lyase	ii. Oxidation and reduction of two substrates
R.	Isomerase	iii. Joining of two compounds
S.	Ligase	iv. Removal of a chemical group from a substance
		v. Transfer of a chemical group from one substrate to another

(a) P-iv, Q-ii, R-iii, S-i   (b) P-v, Q-iv, R-i, S-iii
(c) P-iv, Q-i, R-iii, S-v   (d) P-i, Q-iv, R-v, S-ii

Answers

PART-I

1	(c)	2	(c)	3	(b)	4	(d)	5	(a)	6	(b)	7	(b)	8	(c)	9	(c)	10	(b)
11	(d)	12	(c)	13	(a)	14	(c)	15	(d)	16	(d)	17	(c)	18	(c)	19	(c)	20	(b)
21	(a)	22	(d)	23	(c)	24	(d)	25	(a)	26	(d)	27	(b)	28	(b)	29	(a)	30	(d)
31	(b)	32	(a)	33	(a)	34	(b)	35	(a)	36	(a)	37	(a)	38	(*)	39	(d)	40	(d)
41	(c)	42	(a)	43	(d)	44	(a)	45	(c)	46	(c)	47	(b)	48	(d)	49	(a)	50	(a)
51	(b)	52	(b)	53	(c)	54	(a)	55	(a)	56	(a)	57	(b)	58	(d)	59	(b)	60	(a)

PART-II

61	(c)	62	(b)	63	(c)	64	(a)	65	(b)	66	(a)	67	(c)	68	(c)	69	(c)	70	(a)
71	(a)	72	(b)	73	(a)	74	(c)	75	(c)	76	(a)	77	(d)	78	(a)	79	(d)	80	(b)

** No option is correct.*

Solutions

1. *(c)* We have, $p(x) = ax^2 + bx + c$, where a, b, c are in AP and a, b, c are positive real.

α, β are root of $p(x) = 0$, where α and β are integers.

$$p(x) = ax^2 + bx + c = 0$$
$$\alpha + \beta = \frac{-b}{a}, \alpha\beta = \frac{c}{a}$$

α, β are integer.

$$\therefore \quad \alpha + \beta = \frac{-b}{a} = -\lambda, \lambda \in I$$
$$\Rightarrow \quad b = a\lambda$$

a, b, c are in AP.

$$\therefore \quad b = \frac{a+c}{2} \Rightarrow \frac{a+c}{2} = a\lambda$$
$$\Rightarrow \quad c = a(2\lambda - 1)$$
$$\therefore \quad ax^2 + a\lambda x + a(2\lambda - 1) = 0$$
$$\Rightarrow \quad x^2 + \lambda x + (2\lambda - 1) = 0 \quad [\because a \neq 0]$$

$D = \lambda^2 - 4(2\lambda - 1)$ is a perfect square for integral roots.

$$\because \quad \lambda^2 - 8\lambda + 4 = k^2$$
$$\Rightarrow \quad (\lambda - 4)^2 - 12 = k^2$$
$$\Rightarrow \quad (\lambda - 4 - k)(\lambda - 4 + k) = 2 \times 6$$
$$\Rightarrow \lambda - 4 - k = 2 \text{ and } \lambda - 4 + k = 6$$
$$\because \lambda = 8 \text{ and } k = 2$$
$$\therefore \quad \alpha + \beta + \alpha\beta = \frac{-b}{a} + \frac{c}{a}$$
$$= \frac{-a\lambda + a(2\lambda - 1)}{a}$$
$$= \frac{a(\lambda - 1)}{a}$$
$$= \lambda - 1 = 8 - 1 = 7$$

2. *(c)* We have,
$$16^5 \cdot 5^{16} = 16 \cdot 16^4 \cdot 5^{16}$$
$$= 16 \times 2^{16} \cdot 5^{16}$$
$$= 16 \times (10)^{16}$$
$\therefore$ Total number of digits in $16^5 \cdot 5^{16} = 18$

3. *(b)* Given,

$t^2 = at + b$, where a, b are positive integers. $t^3 = at^2 + bt$

$$\Rightarrow \quad t^3 = a(at + b) + bt$$
$$\Rightarrow \quad t^3 = a^2t + bt + ab$$
$$\Rightarrow \quad t^3 = (a^2 + b)t + ab$$

(i) $4t + 3$
$$a^2 + b = 4, ab = 3$$
$a = 1, b = 3$ it is possible

(ii) $8t + 5$
$$a^2 + b = 8, ab = 5$$
It is not possible

(iii) $10t + 3$
$$a^2 + b = 10, ab = 3$$
$a = 3, b = 1$ it is possible

(iv) $6t + 5$
$$a^2 + b = 6, ab = 5$$
$a = 1, b = 5$ it is also possible
Hence, option (b) is correct.

4. *(d)* Given,
$$(1 + a + b)^2 = 3(1 + a^2 + b^2)$$
$$1 + a^2 + b^2 + 2a + 2b + 2ab$$
$$= 3 + 3a^2 + 3b^2$$
$$\Rightarrow 2a^2 + 2b^2 - 2a - 2b - 2ab + 2 = 0$$
$$\Rightarrow \quad (a^2 - 2a + 1) + (b^2 - 2b + 1)$$
$$+ (a^2 + b^2 - 2ab) = 0$$
$$\Rightarrow \quad (a-1)^2 + (b-1)^2 + (a-b)^2 = 0$$
$$\therefore \quad a - 1 = 0, \quad b - 1 = 0, a - b = 0$$
$$\Rightarrow \quad a = 1, b = 1, a = b$$
$$\therefore \quad a = b = 1$$

Exactly one pair.

5. *(a)* We have, $a_1, a_2, a_3, ..., a_{100}$ be non-zero real number and
$$a_1 + a_2 + a_3 + ... + a_{100} = 0$$
$$a_i \cdot 2^{a_i} > a_i \text{ and } a_i \cdot 2^{-a_i} < a_i$$
$$\therefore \sum_{i=1}^{100} a_1 \cdot 2^{ai} > \sum_{i=1}^{100} a_i \text{ and } \sum_{i=1}^{100} a_1 \cdot 2^{-a_i} < \sum_{i=1}^{100} a_i$$
$$\Rightarrow \sum_{i=1}^{100} a_1 \cdot 2^{a_i} > 0 \text{ and } \sum_{i=1}^{100} a_1 \cdot 2^{-a_i} < 0$$

Hence, option (a) is correct.

6. *(b)* $ABCD$ is a trapezium.

AB is parallel to CD.

$AB = 11$, $BC = 4$, $CD = 6$ and $DA = 3$

Construct CE is parallel to DA.

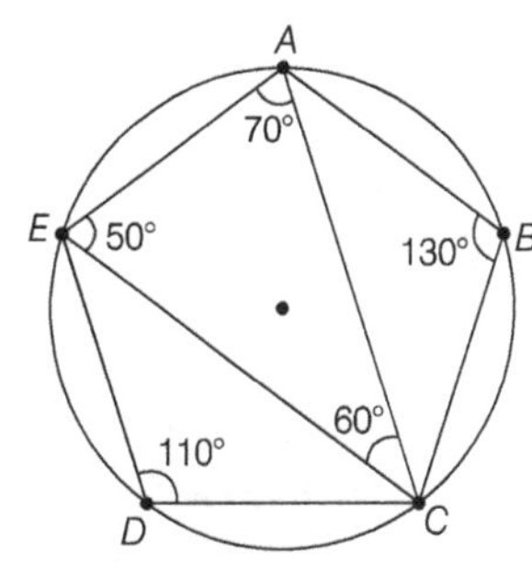

$$\therefore \quad CE = 3$$
$$BC = 4$$
$$BE = 5$$
$\therefore \angle BCE$ is a right angled triangle.

$\therefore$ Area of $\triangle BCE = \frac{1}{2} EC \times BC$

$$= \frac{1}{2} \times 3 \times 4 \quad \text{...(i)}$$

Also, area of
$$\triangle BCE = \frac{1}{2} \times BE \times h$$
$$= \frac{1}{2} \times 5 \times h \quad \text{...(ii)}$$

From Eqs. (i) and (ii),
$$\frac{1}{2} \times 3 \times 4 = \frac{1}{2} \times 5 \times h$$
$$\Rightarrow \quad h = 2.4$$

7. *(b)* Given,
$$\angle ABC = 130°$$
$$\angle CDE = 110°$$
$ABCE$ is a cyclic quadrilateral.

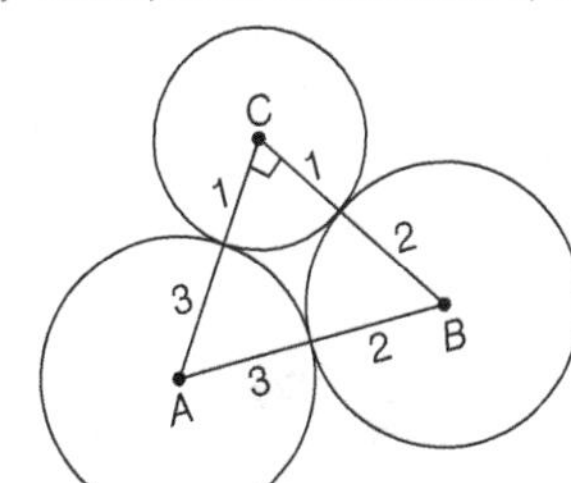

$$\therefore \quad \angle ABC + \angle AEC = 180°$$
$$\Rightarrow \quad \angle AEC = 50°$$
$ACDE$ is also cyclic quadrilateral.
$$\therefore \quad \angle CDE + \angle EAC = 180°$$
$$\Rightarrow \quad \angle EAC = 70°$$
In $\triangle AEC$,
$$\angle EAC + \angle AEC + \angle ACE = 180°$$
$$\Rightarrow \quad 70° + 50° + \angle ACE = 180°$$
$$\Rightarrow \quad \angle ACE = 60°$$

8. *(c)* Given, radii of circle are 1, 2 and 3.

$\therefore$ Side of $\triangle ABC$ are
$$AB = 5$$
$$BC = 3$$
$$AC = 4$$

$\therefore \Delta ABC$ is formed a right angled triangle where AB is hypotenuse of triangle.

We know circumradius of a right angled triangle is the half of the hypotenuse.

$\therefore$ Circumradius $= \dfrac{1}{2} \times AB$

$\qquad = \dfrac{1}{2} \times 5 = 2.5$

9. *(c)* ABC is a right angled triangle, $\angle ABC = 90°$

Circumcentre of ΔABC is mid-point of AC i.e. M.

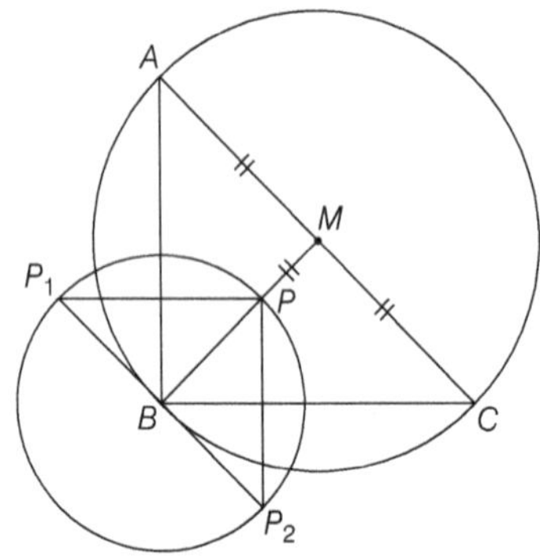

Circumcentre of ΔP_1PP_2 is mid-point of P_1P_2.

AB is perpendicular bisector of PP_1 and BC is perpendicular bisector of PP_2.

Perpendicular bisector of PP_1 and PP_2 intersect at B.

$\therefore B$ is circumcentre of ΔP_1PP_2.

$\therefore$ Distance between

$$BM = AM = MC = \frac{AC}{2}.$$

10. *(b)* Given, $a + 2b \le 1$ a, b are positive real number.

Radius of circle $C_1 = ab^3$

Radius of circle $C_2 = b^2$

$\therefore$ Area of circle $C_1 = A_1 = \pi a^2 b^6$

and area of circle $C_2 = A_2 = \pi b^4$

Now, $\quad \dfrac{A_1}{A_2} = \dfrac{\pi a^2 b^6}{\pi b^4} = a^2 b^2$

$\qquad\quad a + 2b \le 1$

$\Rightarrow \qquad \dfrac{a + 2b}{2} \ge \sqrt{2ab}$

$\qquad\qquad\qquad\qquad [\because \text{AM} \ge \text{GM}]$

$\Rightarrow \qquad 1 \ge (a + 2b)^2 \ge 8ab$

$\Rightarrow \qquad 8ab \le 1$

$\Rightarrow \qquad a^2 b^2 \le \dfrac{1}{64}$

$\therefore \qquad \dfrac{A_1}{A_2} \le \dfrac{1}{64}$

$\therefore$ Maximum value of $\dfrac{A_1}{A_2} = \dfrac{1}{64}$

11. *(d)* We have, length and size of two candles are same. Let L be the length of candles.

Given, first candle burns in 5 h and second candle burns in 3 h.

In one hours length of candles are $\dfrac{L}{5}$ and $\dfrac{L}{3}$, respectively.

Let after time t h the length of candles are L_1 and L_2.

$\therefore \qquad L_1 = L - \dfrac{L}{5}t$ and $L_2 = L - \dfrac{L}{3}t$

According to the problem,

$$L_1 = 3L_2$$

$\therefore \qquad L - \dfrac{L}{5}t = 3\left(L - \dfrac{L}{3}t\right)$

$\Rightarrow \quad 1 - \dfrac{1}{5}t = 3 - t \Rightarrow t\left(1 - \dfrac{1}{5}\right) = 3 - 1$

$\Rightarrow \qquad \dfrac{4t}{5} = 2 \Rightarrow t = \dfrac{5}{2}$ h

$\Rightarrow \qquad t = \dfrac{5}{2} \times 60 = 150 \min$

12. *(c)* Given, a cuboid has all edges are integers and base is square.

Let the length, breadth and height of cuboid is x, x, y.

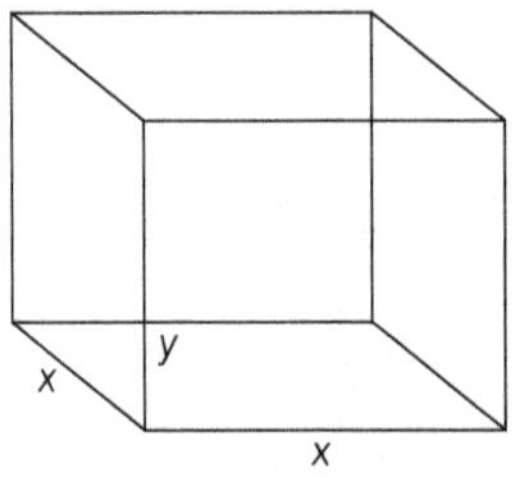

Sum of all edges of cuboid $= 4x + 4x + 4y$

Sum of area of all faces $= 2x^2 + 2xy + 2xy$

Given,

Sum of all edges of cuboid $=$ Sum of area of all faces

$\therefore \quad 4x + 4x + 4y = 2(x^2 + xy + xy)$

$\Rightarrow \qquad 4(2x + y) = 2(x^2 + 2xy)$

$\Rightarrow x^2 + 2xy - 4x - 2y = 0$

$\Rightarrow x^2 + 2x(y - 2) - 2y = 0$

$\Rightarrow \quad x = \dfrac{-2(y-2) \pm \sqrt{4(y-2)^2 + 4(2y)}}{2}$

$\Rightarrow \quad x = y - 2 \pm \sqrt{y^2 - 2y + 4}$

x is integer, when $y = 2$

$\therefore \qquad\qquad y = 2, x = 2$

Hence, sum of edges $= 8x + 4y = 16 + 8 = 24$

13. *(a)* We have, $A_1, A_2, A_3 \ldots, A_m$ are non-empty subsets of $\{1, 2, 3, \ldots, 100\}$

$|A_1|, |A_2|, \ldots, |A_m|$ are distincts.

$A_1 \cap A_2 \cap A_3 \ldots \cap A_m = \phi$

$\therefore A_1 \cap A_2 \cup A_3 \ldots \cup A_m = \{1, 2, 3, \ldots, 100\}$

Let $|A_1| = 1|A_2| = 2 \ldots |A_m| = M$

$A_1, A_2, A_3 \ldots, A_m$ are disjoint set.

$\therefore |A_1| + |A_2| \ldots + |A_m| = 100$

$1 + 2 + 3 \ldots + m = 100$

$$\dfrac{m(m+1)}{2} = 100$$

$$m^2 + m - 200 = 0$$

$= \dfrac{-b \pm \sqrt{b^2 - 4ac}}{2a} = \dfrac{-1 \pm \sqrt{1 + 4 \cdot 1 \cdot 200}}{2 \cdot 1}$

$= \dfrac{-1 \pm \sqrt{1 + 800}}{2} = \dfrac{-1 + \sqrt{801}}{2}$

$= \dfrac{-1 + 28.30}{2} = \dfrac{27.30}{2} = 16.65$

$m = \dfrac{1 + 28.30}{2} = \dfrac{29.30}{2} = 14.65$

$\therefore m < 14$

$\therefore$ Maximum possible of m is 13.

(14th set will have same size as that of previous size)

14. *(c)* Let two-digits number be $n = 10a + b$

Given, $\qquad n = a^2 + b^3$

$\therefore \qquad 10a + b = a^2 + b^3$

$\Rightarrow \qquad a^2 - 10a + b^3 - b = 0$

$\Rightarrow a(a - 10) + b(b + 1)(b - 1) = 0$

$\Rightarrow \qquad b(b+1)(b-1) = a(10 - a)$

$b \ne 1$ if $b = 1$ then $a = 10$ not possible

if $b = 2$, $a(10 - a) = 6$, no value of a

$b = 3$, $a(10 - a) = 24$, $a = 4, 6$

Numbers are 43 and 63.

If $b = 4$, $a(10 - a) = 60$ no value of a

If $b = 5$, $a(10 - a) = 120$ not possible

$\therefore$ Numbers are 43 and 63.

15. *(d)* Given, $f(xy) = f(x) + f(y)$

$\qquad f(12) = 24 \Rightarrow f(8) = 15$

$f(8) = f(2 \cdot 2 \cdot 2) = f(2) + f(2) + f(2)$

$\Rightarrow \qquad 15 = 3f(2) \Rightarrow f(2) = 5$

$\therefore f(48) = f(12 \cdot 2 \cdot 2) = f(12) + f(2) + f(2)$

$\qquad\qquad = 24 + 5 + 5 = 34$

16. *(d)* Displacement of person is

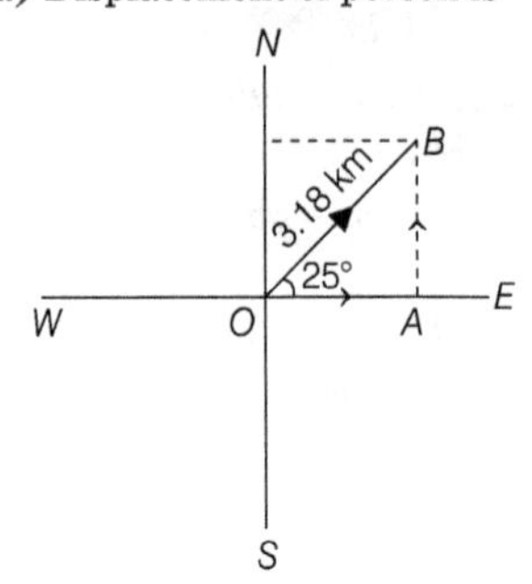

From above figure, distance travelled along north direction is

$AB = OB \sin 25° = 3.18 \times \sin 25° = 1.34$ km

Distance travelled along east direction is

$OA = 3.18 \times \cos 25° = 2.88$ km

17. *(c)* Area, $A = l \times b$

$$= 3.95 \times 3.05 = 12.05 \text{ m}^2$$

Now, $\qquad A = l \times b$

$\Rightarrow \qquad \dfrac{dA}{A} = \dfrac{dl}{l} + \dfrac{db}{b}$

$\Rightarrow \qquad \Delta A = \left(\dfrac{\Delta l}{l} + \dfrac{\Delta b}{b}\right) \times A$

$$= \left(\dfrac{0.05}{3.95} + \dfrac{0.05}{3.05}\right) \times 12.05$$

$$\approx 0.34$$

So, area of floor is $A = 12.05 \pm 0.34 \text{ m}^2$.

18. *(c)* When car goes around track of radius R, then

Time period, $\qquad T = \dfrac{2\pi R}{v}$

Centripetal acceleration, $a_c = \dfrac{v^2}{R}$

When car goes around circular track of radius $2R$, then

Centripetal acceleration,

$$a_c' = \dfrac{v'^2}{2R} = \dfrac{8v^2}{R} \Rightarrow v' = 4v$$

So, time period of car is

$$T' = \dfrac{2\pi R'}{v'} = \dfrac{2\pi (2R)}{4v}$$

$$= \dfrac{1}{2} \times \dfrac{2\pi R}{v} = \dfrac{T}{2}$$

19. *(c)* As primary voltage is constant, there is no change of magnetic flux of secondary coil.

So, there is no induction and hence voltage across secondary is zero.

20. *(b)* Power output, $P = 50\%$ of potential energy of water

Received by generator per second

$$= \dfrac{50}{100} \times \left(\dfrac{mgh}{t}\right)$$

$$= 0.5 \times \left(\dfrac{V}{t}\right) \rho \times g \times h \qquad \text{...(i)}$$

Here, $P = 1 \times 10^9$ W,

$g = 10 \text{ ms}^{-2}, \rho = 1000 \text{ kgm}^{-3}$

and $\quad h = 500$ m.

Substituting these values in Eq. (i), we get

Volume flow rate of water $= \dfrac{V}{t}$

$$= \dfrac{1 \times 10^9}{0.5 \times 1000 \times 10 \times 500} = 400 \text{ m}^3\text{s}^{-1}$$

21. *(a)* Current in loop is shown anti-clockwise.

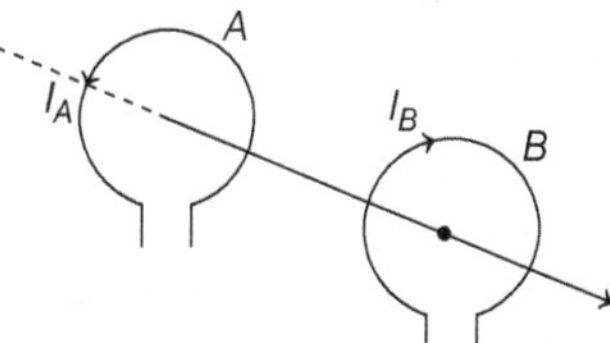

Hence to induce a anti-clockwise current in A, flux going into A must be increased and by bringing A closer to B, we get a anti-clockwise current in A. This is in accordance with Lenz's law.

22. *(d)* As ball moves from point A to point D,

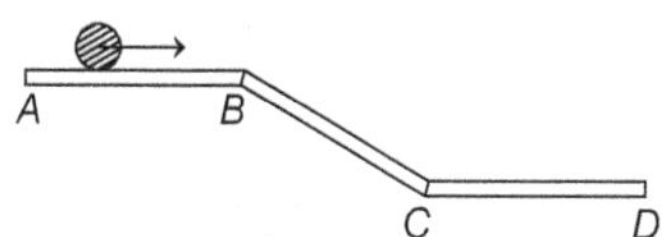

Velocity of ball increases rapidly in region BC. Then, from C to D, it moves with a constant velocity. So, graph is parabolic in region BC and slope of AB is less than slope of CD, as shown below.

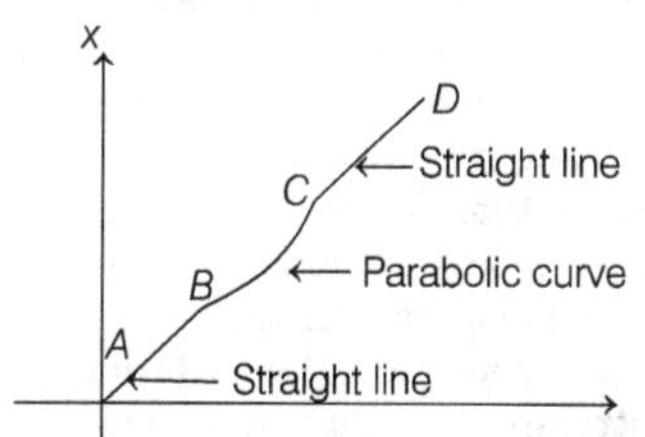

Note Velocity change is not very abrupt.

23. *(c)* Metal plate between wires may modify field pattern within the metal volume but number of field lines is not changed.

So, force between wires is same in both cases and is non-zero.

i.e. $\qquad F_A = F_B \neq 0.$

24. *(d)*

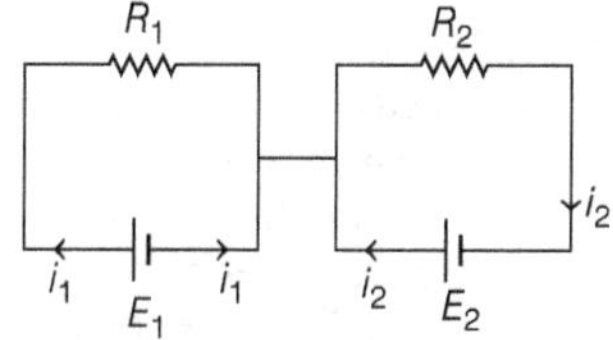

Current leaving the cell must be equal to current going into the cell.

So, current going from first loop to second loop must be zero for any value of E or R.

Hence, there is no current through the wire connecting loops.

25. *(a)* Taking protons at dimetrically opposite points of nucleus,

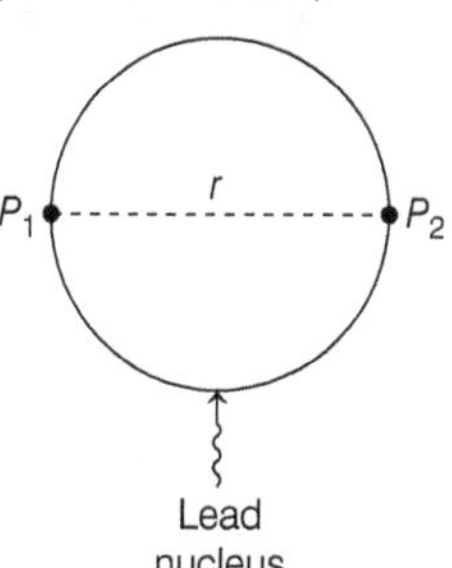

Force of electrostatic repulsion,

$$F = \dfrac{k(e)\,(e)}{r^2} = \dfrac{ke^2}{(r_0 A^{1/3})^2} = \dfrac{k \cdot e^2}{r_0^2 \cdot A^{2/3}}$$

Substituting values in above equation, we get

$$F = \dfrac{9 \times 10^9 \times (1.6 \times 10^{-19})^2}{(1.3 \times 10^{-15})^2 \,(206)^{2/3}}$$

$$= 0.039 \times 10^2 \text{ N}$$

26. *(d)* When medium outside a lens is denser than medium of lens, then a concave lens will acts like a convex lens and *vice-versa*.

Now, when hollow lens is filled with CS_2 ($\eta = 1.6$) and immersed in water ($\eta = 1.33$), its nature remains diverging as refractive index of medium of lens is more than refractive index of surrounding medium.

27. *(b)* For first stone,

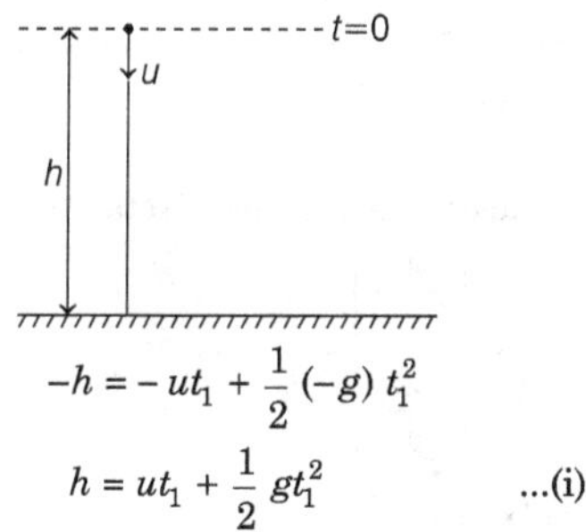

$$-h = -ut_1 + \dfrac{1}{2}(-g)\, t_1^2$$

or $\qquad h = ut_1 + \dfrac{1}{2} gt_1^2 \qquad \text{...(i)}$

For second stone,

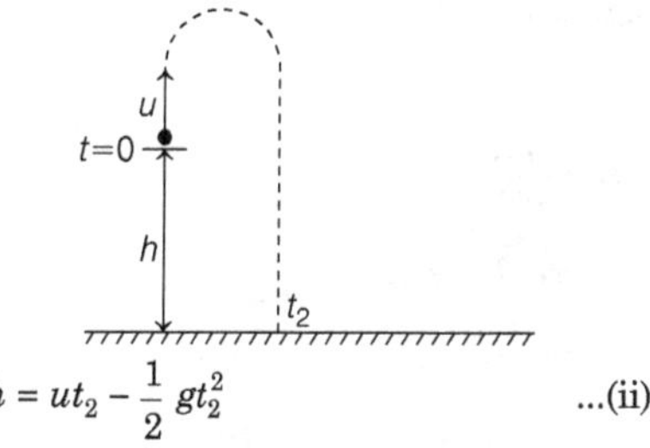

$$-h = ut_2 - \dfrac{1}{2} gt_2^2 \qquad \text{...(ii)}$$

Adding Eqs. (i) and (ii), we get

$$0 = u(t_1 + t_2) - \dfrac{1}{2} g(t_1^2 - t_2^2)$$

$$\Rightarrow \qquad u = \frac{g}{2}(t_1 - t_2)$$

Maximum height attained by second stone is

$$H = h + \frac{u^2}{2g}$$

$$\Rightarrow \qquad H = ut_1 + \frac{1}{2}gt_1^2 + \frac{u^2}{2g}$$

Substituting for u and rearranging, we get

$$H = \frac{g}{8}(t_1 + t_2)^2$$

28. *(b)* Electron revolve around wire due to its electrostatic force of attraction.

As field $\quad E \propto r^{-1} \Rightarrow E = kr^{-1}$

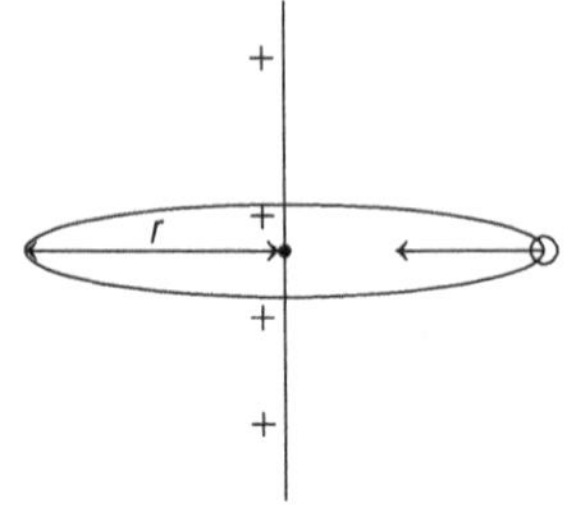

So, force on electron is

$$F = eE = ker^{-1}$$

This force is necessary centripetal force. So,

$$\frac{mv^2}{r} = \frac{ke}{r}$$

$$\Rightarrow \qquad v = \sqrt{\frac{ke}{m}}$$

As velocity of electron is independent of radius of paths,

$$\Rightarrow \qquad v_1 = v_2$$

Now, ratio of time periods of rotation are

$$\frac{T_1}{T_2} = \frac{\left(\dfrac{2\pi r_1}{v_1}\right)}{\left(\dfrac{2\pi r_2}{v_2}\right)} = \frac{r_1}{r_2} = \frac{1\text{Å}}{2\text{Å}} = \frac{1}{2}$$

29. *(a)* Given,

Potential, $V = Kr^{-n}$

So, magnitude of field,

$$E = -\frac{dV}{dr} = -\frac{d}{dr}(Kr^{-n})$$

$$\Rightarrow \qquad E = \frac{nK}{r^{n+1}}$$

Hence, force, $F = mE = \dfrac{mnK}{r^{n+1}}$

As particles are rotating in circular path,

$$F = \frac{mv^2}{r} = \frac{mnK}{r^{n+1}}$$

$$\Rightarrow \qquad v^2 r^n = nK = \text{constant}$$

So, $\qquad v_1^2 r_1^n = v_2^2 r_2^n$

30. *(d)* Fluid used in a thermometer must be easily visible, expands uniformly and significantly and it must be a liquid at room temperature.

So, density of mercury is not a feature for selecting mercury in clinical thermometers.

31. *(b)* $NaHCO_3$ which is a sodium salt only produces carbon dioxide on heating while the other salts produce ions on heating. Also, its carbon content which is close to 14.3%.

$$2NaHCO_3 \xrightarrow{\Delta} Na_2CO_3 + H_2O + CO_2$$

Molecular mass of $NaHCO_3$

$$= 23 + 1 + 12 + 16 \times 3 = 84$$

$$\% \text{ of C} = \frac{12}{84} \times 100 = 14.28\%$$

32. *(a)* **Key Idea**

- The substituents attached to benzoic acid having $+I$ effects tends to decrease its acidity.
- Carboxylic acids are more acidic than phenol as they are more resonance stabilised.

Among the three carboxylic acids given in the options, the $+I$ effect of CH_3 group intensifies the negative charge on the carboxylate ion thereby making acetate ion less stable than formate ion. As a result, the release of H^+ ion from acetic acid will become more difficult as compared to formic acid. Hence, formic acid is a stronger acid than acetic acid.

Further since $+I$ effect of alkyl groups increases in the order $CH_3 \!-\!\!< CH_3CH_2-$ the relative acid strength will decrease in the same order, i.e.,

$$\underset{\overset{\|}{O}}{H\,C}OH > CH_3COOH > CH_3CH_2COOH$$

Now between carboxylic acids and phenol, carboxylic acids are stronger acids than phenol because carboxylate ion is more resonance stabilised. This is because the negative charge on the carboxylate ion is delocalised over two electronegative oxygen atoms.

Thus, the order of acidic strength of given compounds is

$$\underset{\substack{\| \\ O \\ \text{Formic} \\ \text{acid}}}{HCOH} > \underset{\substack{\text{Acetic} \\ \text{acid}}}{CH_3COOH} > \underset{\substack{\text{Propanoic} \\ \text{acid}}}{CH_3CH_2COOH} > \underset{\text{Phenol}}{\bigcirc}$$

Hence, formic acid is a strongest acid.

33. *(a)* According to Graham's law, rate of diffusion is inversely proportional to the square root of molar mass, i.e.

$$r \propto \frac{1}{\sqrt{M}}$$

Thus, rate of diffusion decrease with increase in molecular weight. Therefore, the order of rate of diffusion will be

$$CO = N_2 > O_2 > CO_2$$
$$(28\text{ g}) \ (28\text{ g}) \ (32\text{ g}) \ (44\text{ g})$$

34. *(b)* The major product, formed when 2-butene is reacted with O_3 followed by treatment with Zn / H_2O is acetaldehyde. This reaction is known as reductive ozonolysis.

35. *(a)* The IUPAC name of the following is

$$\overset{6}{C}H_3\ \overset{5}{C}H_2\ \overset{4}{C}H_2\ \overset{3}{C}H_2\ \overset{2}{C}CH_2\ CH_2CH_3$$
$$\underset{\overset{1}{C}H_2}{\|}$$

2 propylhex-1-ene

36. *(a)* The major products obtained in the reaction of oxalic acid with conc. H_2SO_4 upon heating are carbon monoxide, carbon dioxide and water.

$$\underset{\text{Oxalic acid}}{\overset{\text{COOH}}{\underset{\text{COOH}}{|}}} \xrightarrow[H_2SO_4]{\Delta} CO + CO_2 + H_2O$$

37. *(a)* $2LiOH + CO_2 \longrightarrow Li_2CO_3 + H_2O$

Number of moles of LiOH $= \dfrac{1}{24}$ moles

2 moles of LiOH reacts with 1 mole of CO_2 to form 1 mole of Li_2CO_3 and H_2O.

$\therefore$ Number of moles of $CO_2 = \dfrac{1}{24 \times 2}$

$$= \dfrac{1}{48} \text{ moles}$$

1 mole of CO_2 = 44 g

$\dfrac{1}{48}$ moles of $CO_2 = \dfrac{1}{48} \times 44 = 0.916$ g

38. *(*)* The oxidation number of S in given compounds are as follows :

(i) H_2S

Let the oxidation state of S be x

$\therefore \quad 2 + x = 0$

$\qquad x = -2$

(ii) CS_2

$\qquad 4 + 2x = 0 \Rightarrow x = -2$

(iii) Na_2SO_4

$\qquad 2(+1) + x + 4(-2) = 0$

$\qquad\qquad 2 + x - 8 = 0$

$\qquad\qquad\qquad x = +6$

(iv) Na_2SO_3

$\qquad 2(+1) + x + 3(-2) = 0$

$\qquad\qquad 2 + x - 6 = 0$

$\qquad\qquad\qquad x = +4$

No, option is correct.

39. *(d)* Al_2O_3 is an amphoteric oxide (those oxides which show both the properties of acids and bases), so it can react both with acids and alkalis, e.g.

$$Al_2O_3 + HCl \longrightarrow AlCl_3 + H_2O$$
$$Al_2O_3 + NaOH + H_2O \longrightarrow Na[Al(OH)_4]$$

40. *(d)* The major product formed in the oxidation of acetylene by alk. $KMnO_4$ is oxalic acid.

$$\underset{\text{Acetylene}}{\overset{\text{CH}}{\underset{\text{CH}}{|||}}} + 2[O] \xrightarrow{\text{Alk. }KMnO_4} \underset{\text{Glyoxal}}{\left[\overset{\text{CH}=O}{\underset{\text{CH}=O}{|}}\right]} \xrightarrow[\text{Alk. }KMnO_4]{2[O]}$$

$$\underset{\substack{\text{Oxalic acid}\\\text{(Major product)}}}{\overset{\text{COOH}}{\underset{\text{COOH}}{|}}}$$

41. *(c)* According to ideal gas equation,

$$pV = nRT$$
$$p = \dfrac{nRT}{V}$$

At constant volume and number of moles

$$p \propto T$$

$\therefore \qquad \dfrac{p_1}{p_2} = \dfrac{T_1}{T_2}$

$\qquad T_1 = 27°C = 27 + 273 = 300K$

$\qquad T_2 = 327°C$

$\qquad\quad = 327 + 273 = 600K$

$\therefore \qquad \dfrac{1}{p_2} = \dfrac{300}{600}$

$\Rightarrow \qquad p_2 = 2\,\text{atm}$

42. *(a)* As the given elements Li, N, C and Be belong to same period i.e. 2nd period, so on moving from left to right in a period the atomic radius decreases because the effective nuclear charge increases. Thus, Li has the largest atomic radius among them all.

43. *(d)* A redox reaction is one in which the oxidation and reduction reactions occur simultaneously.

(i) $CdCl_2 + 2KOH \longrightarrow Cd(OH)_2 + 2KCl$

This is an example of double displacement reaction.

(ii) $BaCl_2 + K_2SO_4 \longrightarrow BaSO_4 + 2KCl$

This is a double displacement reaction.

(iii) $\overset{\overbrace{\qquad\text{Reduction}\qquad}}{CaCO_3 \longrightarrow CaO + CO_2}$

(iv) $\overset{\overbrace{\qquad\text{Reduction}\qquad}}{2\overset{0}{Ca} + \overset{0}{O_2} \longrightarrow 2\overset{+2}{Ca}\overset{-2}{O}}_{\underbrace{\qquad\text{Oxidation}\qquad}}$

As both oxidation and reduction reaction occurs simultaneously, so it is a redox reaction.

44. *(a)* According to Hund's rule, 'pairing of electrons in the orbitals belonging to same subshell does not take place until each orbital belonging to that subshell has got one electron each, i.e. it is singly occupied.

The electronic configuration, which obeys Hund's rule for ground state of carbon is $1s^2 2s^2 2p^2$.

$$\begin{array}{l}\uparrow\;\,\uparrow\;\;—2p\\[4pt]\uparrow\downarrow\;\;2s\\[4pt]\uparrow\downarrow\;\;1s\end{array}$$

45. *(c)* According to photoelectric effect, the number of electrons ejected is proportional to the intensity of radiation. Thus on increasing the intensity of radiation, the value of photoelectric current also increases, i.e. photoelectric current $\propto$ intensity of radiation. Hence, its graph would be linear.

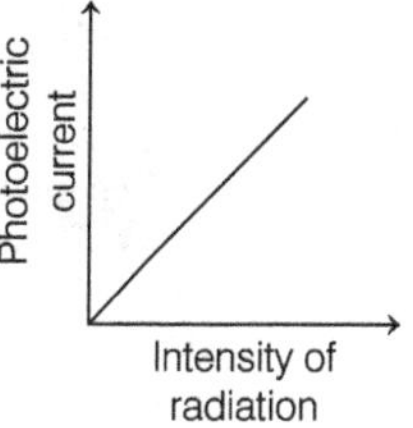

46. *(c)* The distance between 2 nucleotides/nitrogen bases is 0.34×10^{-9} m or 3.4 Å.
Therefore the length of human DNA containing 6.6×10^9 bp would be

$\qquad = 0.34 \times 10^{-9}$ m $\times\, 6.6 \times 10^9$ bp

$\qquad = 2.244$ m or 2.2 m

47. *(b)* DPT is a class of combination vaccines against three infectious diseases in humans, i.e. diphtheria, pertussis (whooping cough) and tetanus. The vaccine components include diphtheria and tetanus toxoids and killed whole cells of the bacterium that causes pertussis.

48. *(d)* Bilirubin is an orange yellow pigment formed in the liver by the breakdown of haemoglobin and excreted in bile. It is not an enzyme. Other options like lipase, amylase and trypsin are lipid digesting, starch digesting and endopeptidase enzymes.

49. *(a)* The pH of the avian blood is maintained by bicarbonate (HCO_3^-) ions. A variety of buffering systems exist in the body of birds that helps to maintain the pH between 7.35 and 7.45. Since the bicarbonate (HCO_3^-) ion is a base, it helps neutralise the acid in the blood and increases the pH above 7.

50. *(a)* Podocytes are cells of squamous epithelium of Bowman capsule of nephron. The Bowman's capsule filters the blood, retaining large molecules such as proteins while smaller molecules such as water, salts and sugars are filtered as the first step in the formation of urine.

51. *(b)* If *ds*DNA has 20% adenine, then according to the Chargaff's rule, it would have 20% thymine. The remaining 60% represents both G + C. Since guanine and cytosine are always present in equal numbers, the percentage of cytosine molecule is 30%.

52. *(b)* Pellagra cannot be cured by nicotine. Instead, pellagra can be cured by giving niacine, nicotinamide and tryptophan. Pellagra is a disease caused by a lack of the vitamin niacin (vitamin-B_3) which includes both nicotinic acid and nicotinamide and its precursors, i.e. the amino acid tryptophan. The main symptoms of pellagra are dermatitis, dementia and diarrhoea.

53. *(c)* In all living organisms, there are 64 codons and out of which 3 codons are stop or termination codons, i.e. UAA, UAG and UGA which do not code for any amino acids. Therefore, 61 codons code for the standard 20 amino acids.

54. *(a)* The order of silkworm (*Bombyx mori*) is Lepidoptera. It is the order of insects that includes butterflies and moths. About 1,80,000 species of the Lepidoptera are described till now.

55. *(a)* Relaxin hormone is produced by the ovary and the placenta with important effects in the female reproductive system and during pregnancy. In preparation for childbirth, it relaxes the ligaments in the pelvis and softens and widens the cervix.

56. *(a)* Platypus is a connecting link between reptiles and mammals. They have few mammalian characters such as hair, mammary glands, diaphragm whereas it lays eggs with yolk and egg shell similar to reptiles.

57. *(b)* The people with Turner's syndrome have 44 + XO chromosomes, so there are a total of 45 chromosomes only in each cell. Such persons are sterile females who have rudimentary ovaries, undeveloped breasts, small uterus, short stature and abnormal intelligence.

58. *(d)* 'Chipko Movement' was headed by social activist Sunder Lal Bahuguna in Uttarakhand to save trees from felling. The movement got its name due to people's action of hugging trees in order to prevent them from cutting down by state forest contractors.

59. *(b)* Lysine is not involved in gluconeogenesis. Gluconeogenesis is the biosynthesis of new glucose from certain non-carbohydrate carbon substrates like amino acids, etc. Out of the 20 amino acids, 18 are glucogenic (i.e. can be converted to glucose upon gluconeogenesis) while the remaining two amino acids, i.e. lysine and leucine are purely ketogenic (i.e. can be degraded into acetyl-Co-A).

60. *(a)* Causative agent of syphilis is *Treponema pallidum*. Syphilis is a bacterial infection usually spreads by sexual contact that starts as a painless sore.

Neisseria gonorrhoeae causes gonorrhoea. HIV causes AIDS. Hepatitis-B virus causes hepatitis, i.e. a liver infection.

61. *(c)* Given, $a^5 - a^3 + a = 2$

$$\Rightarrow \qquad a^5 - a^3 + a - 2 = 0$$

Let $f(a) = a^5 - a^3 + a - 2$

$$f'(a) = 5a^4 - 3a^2 + 1$$
$$f'(a) > 0, \forall\, a \in R$$

$\therefore\ a^5 - a^3 + a - 2 = 0$ has only one roots.

for $a^6 = 3 \Rightarrow a = (3)^{1/6} = 1.2$ [by calculation]

$f(4^{1/6}) > 0$ and at $a^6 = 4,\ a = (4)^{1/6}$

So one root lies in (3, 4).

$$\therefore\ 3 < a^6 < 4$$

62. *(b)* Given, $nx^2 + 7\sqrt{n}\,x + n = 0$

$$D = 49n - 4n^2 = n\,(49 - 4n)$$
$$D \neq 0;\quad \therefore \forall\, n \in I^+$$

$\therefore$ Roots are distinct.

For roots are real $D \geq 0$

$$\therefore\ n\,(49 - 4n) \geq 0 \Rightarrow n \leq \frac{49}{4}$$

So, $n \in \{1, 2, 3, 4, \ldots, 12\}$

So, x have finite value.

Product of roots is $\dfrac{n}{n} = 1$

$\therefore$ Products of root is necessarily integer. Hence, option (b) is correct.

63. *(c)* Given,

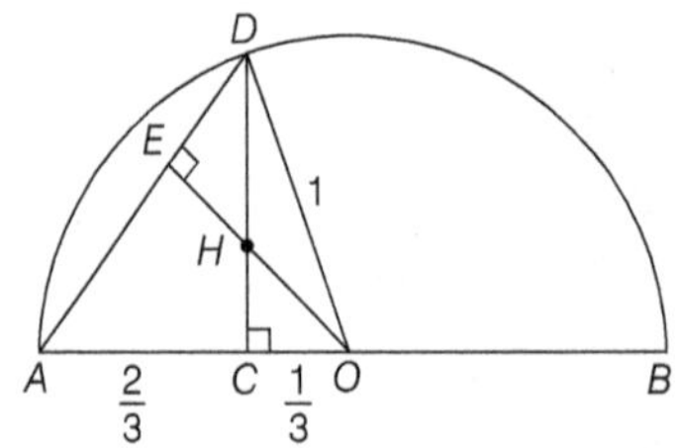

AB is diameter of circle.
O is centre of circle.

$$\therefore \qquad OA = OB = \frac{1}{2} AB = 1$$

C is a point on AO such that

$$\frac{AC}{OC} = \frac{2}{1} \Rightarrow AC = 2OC$$

CD is perpendicular to AO.

$\therefore\ OD = OA$ radius of circle

OE is perpendicular on AD.

$\therefore\ AOD$ is isosceles triangle.

$\therefore\ E$ is mid-point of AD.

$$\therefore \qquad OA = 1, OC = \frac{1}{3}, AC = \frac{2}{3}, OD = 1$$

In ΔOCD,

$$CD = \sqrt{OD^2 - OC^2} = \sqrt{1 - \frac{1}{9}} = \frac{2\sqrt{2}}{3}$$

In ΔACD,

$$AD = \sqrt{CD^2 + AC^2} = \sqrt{\frac{8}{9} + \frac{4}{9}}$$
$$= \frac{2\sqrt{3}}{3} = \frac{2}{\sqrt{3}}$$

In $\Delta DEH \sim \Delta OEA$

$$\frac{DE}{OE} = \frac{DH}{OA} \Rightarrow \frac{1/\sqrt{3}}{\sqrt{2}/\sqrt{3}} = \frac{DH}{1}$$

$$\Rightarrow\ DH = \frac{1}{\sqrt{2}} \qquad \left[\begin{array}{l} \because DE = \dfrac{1}{2} AD \\[2mm] OE = \sqrt{OA^2 - \left(\dfrac{1}{2} AD\right)^2} \end{array}\right]$$

64. *(a)* Here,

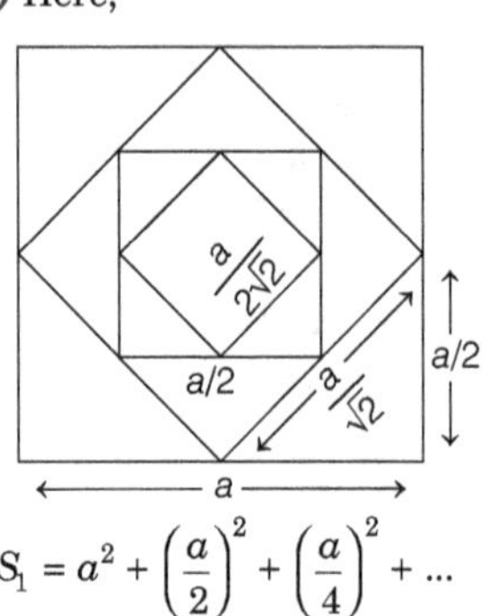

$$S_1 = a^2 + \left(\frac{a}{2}\right)^2 + \left(\frac{a}{4}\right)^2 + \ldots$$

$$S_2 = \left(\frac{a}{\sqrt{2}}\right)^2 + \left(\frac{a}{2\sqrt{2}}\right)^2 + \ldots$$

$$S_1 = a^2 + \frac{a^2}{4} + \frac{a^2}{16} + \ldots = \frac{a^2}{1 - \dfrac{1}{4}} = \frac{4a^2}{3}$$

$$S_2 = \frac{a^2}{2} + \frac{a^2}{8} + \frac{a^2}{32} + \ldots = \frac{a^2/2}{1 - \dfrac{1}{4}} = \frac{4a^2}{6}$$

$$\therefore \quad \frac{S_1}{S_2} = \frac{\dfrac{4a^2}{3}}{4a^2/6} = 2$$

65. *(b)* The 3-digit number which is divisible by 4 and 5 both.

i.e. last digits are 00, 20, 40, 60, 80

Now ending with 00 are (100, 200, 300 … 900) = 9

If digit repeat other than 0' then they are (220, 440, 660, 880) but 220 number can be permuted according to condition as (220, 202).

Similarly, for 440 as (440, 404), 660 and 880, so there are 8 favourable cases.

If the number have no digit repeated like 120, 120 can be permuted in 4 ways.

So, such number are $8 \times 4 \times 4 = 128$

Total favourable cases $= 9 + 8 + 128 = 145$

Required probability $= \dfrac{145}{900} = \dfrac{29}{180}$

66. *(a)* By parallel axes theorem, moment of inertia of triangular lamina about a parallel axes, which passes below its centre of mass is

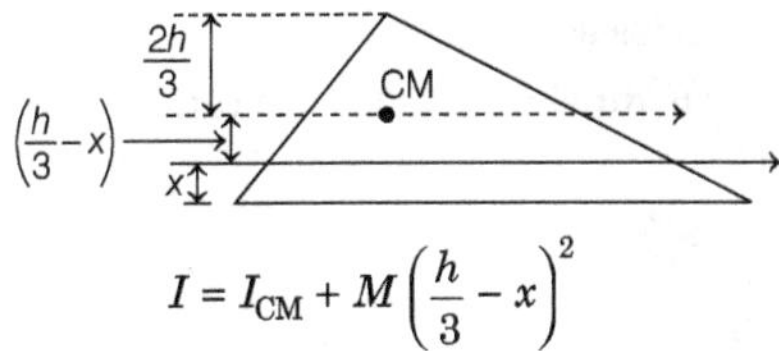

$$I = I_{CM} + M\left(\frac{h}{3} - x\right)^2$$

When axis of rotation of lamina, passes above its centre of mass and its moment of inertia is

$$I = I_{CM} + M\left(x - \frac{h}{3}\right)^2$$

Clearly, I *versus* x is a parabolic graph. Also, I first reduces axis of rotation comes closer to centre of mass and then it again increases.

So, correct variation of I with x is

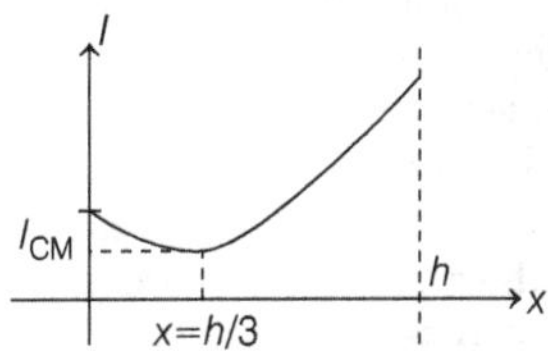

67. *(c)* Ray diagram of ray through the composition of prisms will be

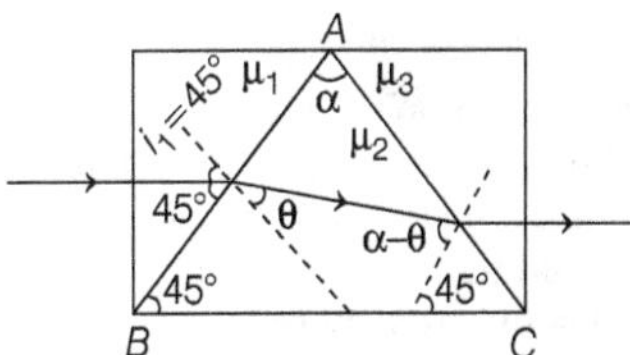

By Snell's law on surface AB and AC, we have $\mu_1 \sin 45° = \mu_2 \sin \theta$ ...(i)

and $\mu_3 \sin 45° = \mu_2 \cos \theta$ ...(ii)

As $\alpha - \theta = 45°$, from figure

Squaring and adding Eqs (i) and (ii),

we get $\dfrac{\mu_1^2}{2} + \dfrac{\mu_3^2}{2} = \mu_2^2$

68. *(c)* Given situation is

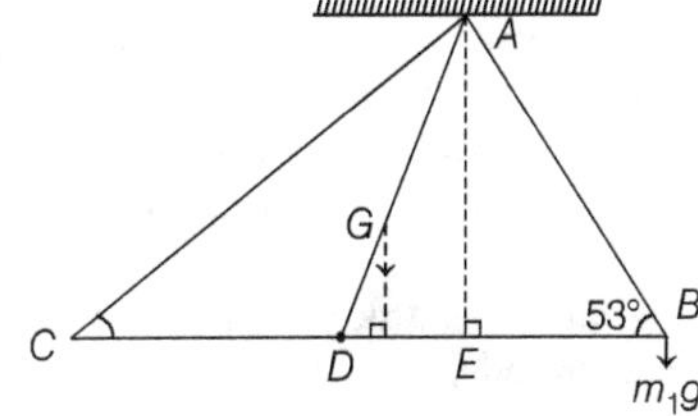

Weight of lamina acts through its centroid G to prevent tilting of lamina, let a mass m_1 is added at vertex B. From A, perpendicular AE is dropped on BC. AD is medium and G is centroid of ΔABC.

Now, consider ΔABC and ΔEBA.

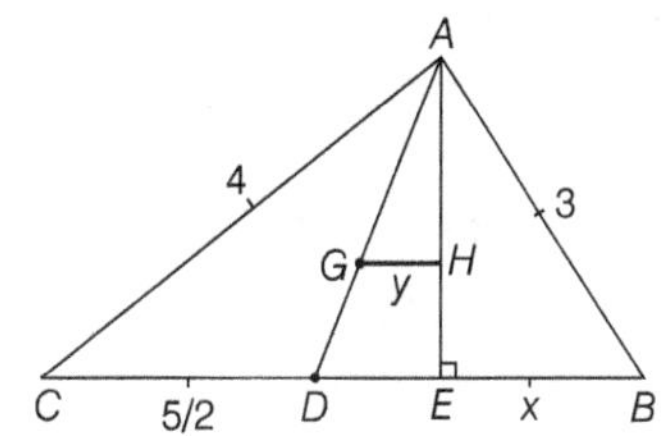

$\Delta ABC \sim \Delta EBA$

$\dfrac{AB}{EB} = \dfrac{BC}{AB} \Rightarrow EB = x = \dfrac{AB^2}{BC} \Rightarrow EB = x = \dfrac{9}{5}$

So, $DE = BD - EB$

$= \dfrac{5}{2} - \dfrac{9}{5} = \dfrac{25 - 18}{10} = \dfrac{7}{10}$ cm

Now, consider ΔADE, G is centroid of ΔABC.

So, $\dfrac{AG}{GD} = \dfrac{2}{1}$ or $AG = \dfrac{2}{3} AD$

Also, GH is parallel to DE.

So, $\dfrac{AG}{AD} = \dfrac{GH}{DE}$

$\Rightarrow GH = \dfrac{AG \times DE}{AD} = \dfrac{\frac{2}{3} AD \times DE}{AD}$

$= \dfrac{2}{3} \times \dfrac{7}{10} = \dfrac{14}{30} = \dfrac{7}{15}$ cm

For BC to remain horizontal, torque of $m_1 g$ about A must be balanced by torque of mg about A.

$\Rightarrow$ $mg \times GH = m_1 g \times BE$

$\Rightarrow$ $540 \times \dfrac{7}{15} = m_1 \times \dfrac{9}{5}$

$\Rightarrow$ $m_1 = \dfrac{540 \times 7 \times 5}{15 \times 9} = 140\,g$

So, mass of 140 g must be added to vertex B, so that BC remains horizontal.

69. *(c)* As kinetic energy of bullet is used up in heating and melting the wax.

By energy conservation, we have

$$\frac{1}{2} m_b v_b^2 = m_w c_w\, (\Delta T_w) + m_b c_b\, (\Delta T_b)$$

As both bullet and wax initially are at same temperature ($T_i = 25°$C).

So, $\Delta T_w = \Delta T_b = \Delta T$ (say)

Then, $\dfrac{1}{2} m_b v_b^2 = (m_w c_w + m_b c_b)\, \Delta T$

or $\Delta T = \dfrac{m_b v_b^2}{2(m_w c_w + m_b c_b)}$

Substituting values in above equation, we get

$$\Delta T = \dfrac{20 \times 10^{-3} \times (2000)^2}{2(20 \times 10^{-3} \times 5000 + 1 \times 3000)}$$

$\Rightarrow$ $\Delta T = \dfrac{400}{31} = 12.9 \Rightarrow T_f - T_i = 12.9$

or $T_f = 25 + 12.9 = 37.9°$C

70. *(a)* Let length of each of rod is l and angle between them is θ.

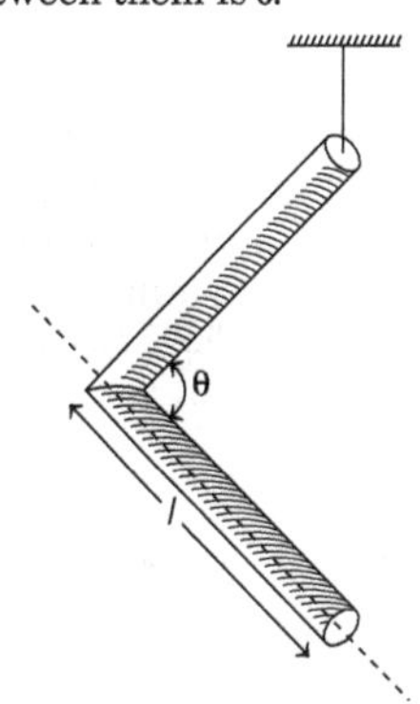

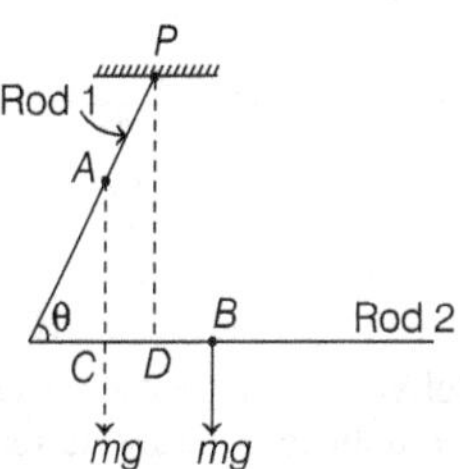

Let the lower rod is horizontal and upper rod makes θ angle with horizontal. Weights of rods acts vertically downwards from their centres A and B as shown in above figure.

Now, perpendicular distance of weight acting through point A from point D is

$$CD = l \cos \theta - \frac{l}{2} \cos \theta$$

$$CD = \frac{l}{2} \cos \theta$$

and perpendicular distance of weight acting through B from point D is

$$BD = \frac{l}{2} - l \cos \theta = \frac{l}{2}\,(1 - 2 \cos \theta)$$

At equilibrium torque of these two weights about D must balance each other,

i.e. $mg \times \dfrac{l}{2} \cos \theta = mg \times \dfrac{l}{2}\,(1 - 2 \cos \theta)$

$\Rightarrow$ $\dfrac{3}{2} \cos \theta = \dfrac{1}{2}$

$\Rightarrow$ $\cos \theta = \dfrac{1}{3}$

or $\theta = \cos^{-1}\left(\dfrac{1}{3}\right)$

71. *(a)* For the given reaction,

Benzene $+ CH_3Cl$ $\xrightarrow[\text{Friedel-Craft's reaction}]{\text{Anhyd. AlCl}_3 \ (Y)}$ (X) Toluene (CH_3)

$\xrightarrow[\text{Nitration}]{HNO_3/H_2SO_4; (Z)}$ 2-nitro toluene (CH_3, NO_2)

When benzene reacts with CH_3Cl in presence of anhyd.$AlCl_3$, then toluene is formed. This reaction is known as Friedel-Craft's reaction. The formed toluene then undergoes nitration to give 2-nitrotoluene.

72. *(b)* For the conversion of 2,3-dibromobutane to 2-butyne following steps can be used

Step 1

$$H_3C-\underset{\underset{Br}{|}}{C}H-\underset{\underset{Br}{|}}{C}H-CH_3 \xrightarrow[-HBr]{Alc.KOH}$$
2, 3-dibromobutane

$$CH_3-CH=\underset{\underset{Br}{|}}{C}-CH_3$$
2-bromo but-2-ene

In this step, dehydrohalogenation occurs where 2,3-dibromobutane gets converted into 2-bromobut-2-ene.

Step 2

$$CH_3-CH=\underset{\underset{Br}{|}}{C}-CH_3 + NaNH_2 \xrightarrow[-NH_3]{-NaBr}$$

$$CH_3-C\equiv C-CH_3$$

In this step, also dehydrohalogenation occurs where alkenyl halide on treatment with soda amide gives 2-butyne.

73. *(a)* Given,

$$NO(g) + O_3(g) \longrightarrow NO_2(g) + O_2(g);$$
$$\Delta H_1 = -198.9 \text{ kJ/mol}$$

$$O_3 \longrightarrow \frac{3}{2} O_2(g) \ \Delta H_2$$
$$= -142.3 \text{ kJ/mol}$$

$$O_2 \longrightarrow 2O_2(g) \ \Delta H_3 = +495.0 \text{ kJ/mol}$$

For the reaction,

$$NO(g) + O(g) \longrightarrow NO_2(g)$$
$$\Delta H = \Delta H_1 - \Delta H_2 - \frac{1}{2} \Delta H_3$$
$$= -198.9 - (-142.3) - \frac{1}{2} \times 495$$
$$= -304.1 \text{ kJ/mol}$$

74. *(c)* $3Pb^{2+} + 2AsO_4 \longrightarrow Pb_3(AsO_4)_2$

3 moles of Pb^{2+} reacts with 2 moles AsO_4

$\therefore$ 1 mole of Pb will react with

$$= \frac{2}{3} \text{ moles of } AsO_4$$

Normality = Molarity $\times$ Volume

$$N_{Pb^{2+}} = 0.1 \times \frac{20}{1000} = 2 \times 10^{-3}$$

$$\therefore \quad N_{AsO_4} = \frac{2}{3} \times 2 \times 10^{-3} = 0.00133$$

$$N_{As} = N_{AsO_4^{3-}} = 0.00133$$

$$W_{As} = N_{As} \times Mass_{As}$$
$$= 0.00133 \times 74.9$$
$$= 0.0996$$

$$\% \text{ of As} = \frac{0.0996}{1.85} \times 100$$
$$\approx 5.38$$
$$\approx 5.4\%$$

75. *(c)* When treated with conc.HCl, MnO_2 yields a chlorine gas (X), which further reacts with $Ca(OH)_2$ to generate calcium oxychloride $CaOCl_2$ (Y), which is a white solid that then reacts with dil. HCl to produce again chlorine gas (X). The equations can be written as

$$MnO_2 + HCl \text{ (conc.)} \longrightarrow \underset{X}{Cl_2(g)}$$

$$Ca(OH)_2 + Cl_2 \longrightarrow \underset{Y}{CaOCl_2}$$

$$CaOCl_2 + \text{dil. HCl} \longrightarrow \underset{(X)}{Cl_2} + CaCl_2 + H_2O$$

Thus, solid Y is Ca(OCl)Cl.

76. *(a)* $pCO_2 = 0.30 - 0.31$ mm Hg in air.

Air contains 0.04% of carbon dioxide. This means that in every 100 molecules of air, 0.04 will be CO_2 molecules. The number of moles of carbon dioxide in 100 molecules of air will be

$$nCO_2 = 0.04 \text{ molecules} \times N_A = 0.04 \times N_A$$

The total number of moles in the sample of air will be

$$n_{\text{total}} = 100 \text{ molecules} \times N_A = 100N_A$$

This means that mole fraction of carbon dioxide in the mixture will be

$$XCO_2 = \frac{0.04N_A}{100N_A} = 0.0004$$

Carbon dioxide's partial pressure in air will thus be

$$pCO_2 = 0.0004 \times 760 \text{ mm Hg}$$
$$= 0.304 \text{ mm Hg}$$

$\therefore$ We can say it ranges between 0.30-0.31 mm Hg.

77. *(d)*

$$\begin{pmatrix}\text{TTWW} \\ \text{Tall plant} \\ \text{with white} \\ \text{flowers}\end{pmatrix} \times \begin{pmatrix}\text{ttww} \\ \text{Short plant} \\ \text{with blue} \\ \text{flowers}\end{pmatrix}$$

$\downarrow$

TtWw
(Tall plant with white flower) (202 plants)
$\downarrow$ Selfing

Obtained 2160 plants total

According to dihybrid phenotypic ratio 9 : 3 : 3 : 1,

TW — 9

Tw — 3

tW — 3

tw — 1

The total number of short and blue flowered plants is

$$\frac{1}{16} \times 2130 = \frac{1080}{8} = 135$$

78. *(a)* P–ii, Q–iii, R–i

- A neurogenic heart requires nervous input to contract. It is seen in crustaceans like king crab.
- Bronchial hearts are myogenic accessory pumps found in coleoid cephalopods like shark that supplement the action of the main, systemic heart.
- Pulmonary heart is found in humans where the portion of the circulatory system carries deoxygenated blood away from the right ventricle of the heart to the lungs and returns oxygenated blood to the left atrium and ventricle of the heart.

79. *(d)* Both thermophiles and psychrophiles will show same enzymatic reaction graph. Mostly proteinaceous enzymes are labile to temperature. Thermophiles live at very high temperature while psychrophiles live in the range of −20°C to +10°C. In either case, rising temperature will first raise the rate of reaction but if temperature is still raised continuously, enzymes get denatured, hence reaction rate decreases.

80. *(b)* P–v, Q–iv, R–i, S–iii

- Hydrolases catalyse transfer of a chemical group from one substrate to another.
- Lyase catalyses removal of chemical groups from a substrate.
- Isomerase catalyses interconversion of optical, geometric or positional isomers.
- Ligase catalyses linking together of two compounds.

QUESTION PAPER 2015
Stream : SA

MM : 100

Instructions

1. There are 80 questions in this paper.
2. This question paper contains two parts; Part I and Part II. There are four sections; Mathematics, Physics, Chemistry and Biology in each part.
3. Out of the four options given with each question, only one is correct.

➔ PART–I (1 Mark Questions)

MATHEMATICS

1. Two distinct polynomials $f(x)$ and $g(x)$ are defined as follows:

$f(x) = x^2 + ax + 2$; $g(x) = x^2 + 2x + a$.

If the equations $f(x) = 0$ and $g(x) = 0$ have a common root, then the sum of the roots of the equation $f(x) + g(x) = 0$ is

(a) $-\dfrac{1}{2}$ (b) 0   (c) $\dfrac{1}{2}$ (d) 1

2. If n is the smallest natural number such that $n + 2n + 3n + \ldots + 99n$ is a perfect square, then the number of digits of n^2 is

(a) 1   (b) 2   (c) 3   (d) more than 3

3. Let x, y, z be positive reals. Which of the following implies $x = y = z$?

   I. $x^3 + y^3 + z^3 = 3xyz$ II. $x^3 + y^2z + yz^2 = 3xyz$

   III. $x^3 + y^2z + z^2x = 3xyz$ IV. $(x + y + z)^3 = 27xyz$

(a) I, IV only   (b) I, II and IV only

(c) I, II and III only   (d) All of them

4. In the figure given below, a rectangle of perimeter 76 units is divided into 7 congruent rectangles.

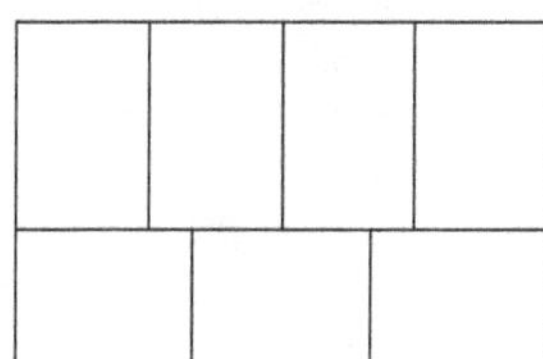

What is the perimeter of each of the smaller rectangles?

(a) 38   (b) 32   (c) 28   (d) 19

5. The largest non-negative integer k such that 24^k divides 13! is

(a) 2   (b) 3   (c) 4   (d) 5

6. In a $\triangle ABC$, points X and Y are on AB and AC, respectively, such that XY is parallel to BC. Which of the two following equalities always hold? (Here $[PQR]$ denotes the area of $\triangle PQR$).

   I. $[BCX] = [BCY]$

   II. $[ACX] \cdot [ABY] = [AXY] \cdot [ABC]$

(a) Neither I nor II　　　　(b) Only I
(c) Only II　　　　　　　　(d) Both I and II

7. Let P be an interior point of a $\triangle ABC$. Let Q and R be the reflections of P in AB and AC, respectively. If Q, A, R are collinear, then $\angle A$ equals

(a) 30°　　　(b) 60°　　　(c) 90°　　　(d) 120°

8. Let $ABCD$ be a square of side length 1, and Γ a circle passing through B and C, and touching AD. The radius of Γ is

(a) $\dfrac{3}{8}$　　　(b) $\dfrac{1}{2}$　　　(c) $\dfrac{1}{\sqrt{2}}$　　　(d) $\dfrac{5}{8}$

9. Let $ABCD$ be a square of side length 1. Let P, Q, R, S be points in the interiors of the sides AD, BC, AB, CD respectively, such that PQ and RS intersect at right angles. If $PQ = \dfrac{3\sqrt{3}}{4}$, then RS equals

(a) $\dfrac{2}{\sqrt{3}}$　　　　　　(b) $\dfrac{3\sqrt{3}}{4}$

(c) $\dfrac{\sqrt{2}+1}{2}$　　　　　(d) $4-2\sqrt{2}$

10. In the figure given below, if the areas of the two regions are equal then which of the following is true?

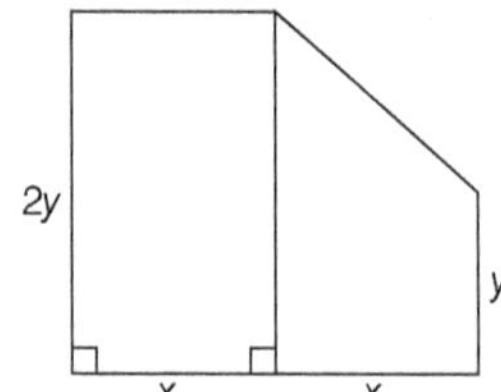
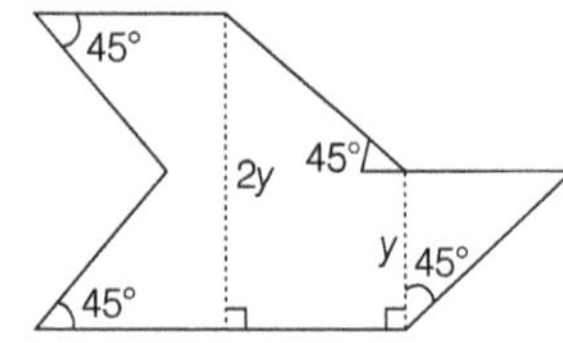

(a) $x = y$　　　　　　(b) $x = 2y$
(c) $2x = y$　　　　　(d) $x = 3y$

11. A man standing on a railway platform noticed that a train took 21 s to cross the platform (this means the time elapsed from the moment the engine enters the platform till the last compartment leaves the platform) which is 88 m long, and that it took 9 s to pass him. Assuming that the train was moving with uniform speed, what is the length of the train in meters?

(a) 55　　　　　　　(b) 60
(c) 66　　　　　　　(d) 72

12. The least positive integer n for which $\sqrt[3]{n+1} - \sqrt[3]{n} < \dfrac{1}{12}$ is

(a) 6　　　(b) 7　　　(c) 8　　　(d) 9

13. Let $n > 1$ be an integer. Which of the following sets of numbers necessarily contains a multiple of 3?

(a) $n^{19} - 1, n^{19} + 1$　　　(b) $n^{19}, n^{38} - 1$
(c) $n^{38}, n^{38} + 1$　　　　　(d) $n^{38}, n^{19} - 1$

14. The number of distinct primes dividing $12! + 13! + 14!$ is

(a) 5　　　(b) 6　　　(c) 7　　　(d) 8

15. How many ways are there to arrange the letters of the word **EDUCATION** so that all the following three conditions hold?

— the vowels occur in the same order (EUAIO),

— the consonants occur in the same order (DCTN),

— no two consonants are next to each other.

(a) 15　　　(b) 24　　　(c) 72　　　(d) 120

PHYSICS

16. In an experiment, mass of an object is measured by applying a known force on it, and then measuring its acceleration. If in the experiment, the measured values of applied force and the measured acceleration are $F = 10.0 \pm 0.2$ N and $a = 1.00 \pm 0.01$ m/s^2, respectively. Then, the mass of the object is

(a) 10.0 kg　　　　　　(b) 10.0 ± 0.1 kg
(c) 10.0 ± 0.3 kg　　　(d) 10.0 ± 0.4 kg

17. A hollow tilted cylindrical vessel of negligible mass rests on a horizontal plane as shown. The diameter of the base is a and the side of the cylinder makes an angle θ with the horizontal. Water is then slowly poured into the cylinder. The cylinder topples over when the water reaches a certain height h, given by

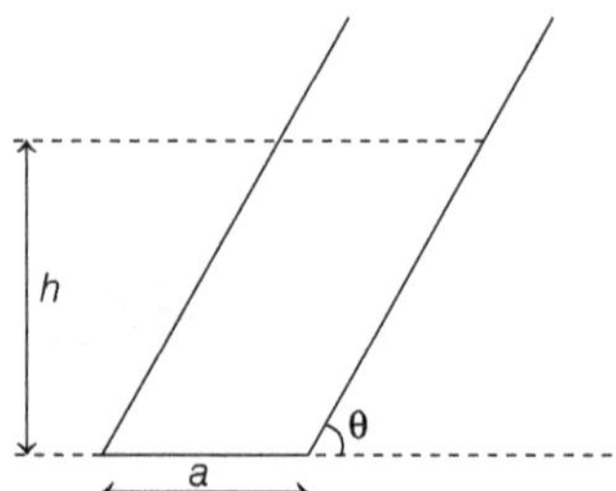

(a) $h = 2a\tan\theta$　　　　　(b) $h = a\tan^2\theta$
(c) $h = a\tan\theta$　　　　　　(d) $h = \dfrac{a}{2}\tan\theta$

18. An object at rest at the origin begins to move in the $+x$-direction with a uniform acceleration of 1 m/s^2 for 4 s and then it continues moving with a uniform velocity of 4 m/s in the same direction. The x-t graph for object's motion will be

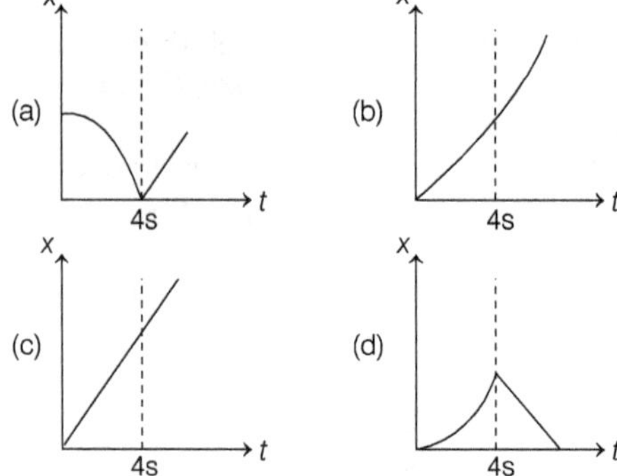

19. If the axis of rotation of the earth were extended into space, then it would pass close to
(a) the moon
(b) the sun
(c) the pole star
(d) the centre of mass of all the planets in the solar system

20. Methane is a greenhouse gas because
(a) it absorbs longer wavelengths of the electromagnetic spectrum while transmitting shorter wavelengths
(b) it absorbs shorter wavelengths of the electromagnetic spectrum while transmitting longer wavelengths
(c) it absorbs all wavelengths of the electromagnetic spectrum
(d) it transmits all wavelengths of the electromagnetic spectrum

21. A parachutist with total weight 75 kg drops vertically onto a sandy ground with a speed of 2 ms^{-1} and comes to halt over a distance of 0.25 m. The average force from the ground on her is close to
(a) 600 N   (b) 1200 N
(c) 1350 N   (d) 1950 N

22. The β-particles of a radioactive metal originate from
(a) the free electrons in the metal
(b) the orbiting electrons of the metal atoms
(c) the photons released from the nucleus
(d) the nucleus of the metal atoms

23. An optical device is constructed by fixing three identical convex lenses of focal lengths 10 cm each inside a hollow tube at equal spacing of 30 cm each. One end of the device is placed 10 cm away from a point source. How much does the image shift when the device is moved away from the source by another 10 cm?
(a) 0   (b) 5 cm   (c) 15 cm   (d) 45 cm

24. An isosceles glass prism with base angles 40° is clamped over a tray of water in a position such that the base is just dipped in water. A ray of light incident normally on the inclined face suffers total internal reflection at the base. If the refractive index of water is 1.33, then the condition imposed on the refractive index μ of the glass is
(a) μ < 2.07   (b) μ > 2.07
(c) μ < 1.74   (d) μ > 1.74

25. A point source of light is moving at a rate of 2 cms^{-1} towards a thin convex lens of focal length 10 cm along its optical axis. When the source is 15 cm away from the lens, the image is moving at
(a) 4 cms^{-1} towards the lens
(b) 8 cms^{-1} towards the lens
(c) 4 cms^{-1} away from the lens
(d) 8 cms^{-1} away from the lens

26. A light bulb of resistance $R = 16\,\Omega$ is attached in series with an infinite resistor network with identical resistances r as shown below. A 10 V battery drives current in the circuit. What should be the value of r such that the bulb dissipates about 1 W of power.

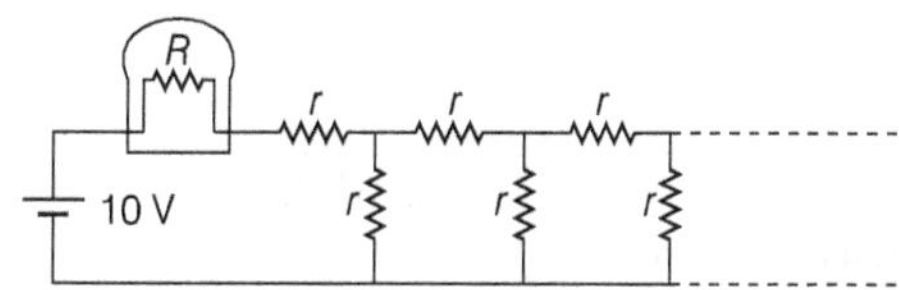

(a) 14.8 Ω   (b) 29.6 Ω   (c) 7.4 Ω   (d) 3.7 Ω

27. A ball is launched from the top of Mt. Everest which is at elevation of 9000 m. The ball moves in circular orbit around earth. Acceleration due to gravity near the earth's surface is g. The magnitude of the ball's acceleration while in orbit is
(a) close to $g/2$ (b) zero
(c) much greater than g (d) nearly equal to g

28. A planet is orbiting the sun in an elliptical orbit. Let U denote the potential energy and K denote the kinetic energy of the planet at an arbitrary point on the orbit. Choose the correct statement.
(a) $K < |U|$ always
(b) $K > |U|$ always
(c) $K = |U|$ always
(d) $K = |U|$ for two positions of the planet in the orbit

29. One mole of ideal gas undergoes a linear process as shown in the figure below. Its temperature expressed as a function of volume V is

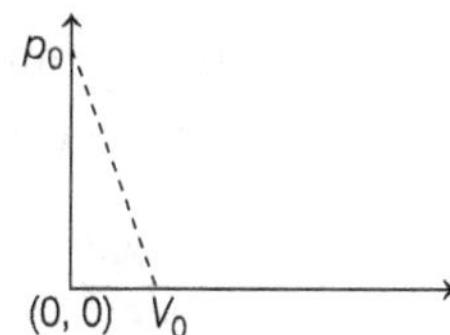

(a) $\dfrac{p_0 V_0}{R}$ (b) $\dfrac{p_0 V}{R}$

(c) $\dfrac{p_0 V}{R}\left(1 - \dfrac{V}{V_0}\right)$ (d) $\dfrac{p_0 V_0}{R}\left(1 - \left(\dfrac{V}{V_0}\right)^2\right)$

30. The international space station is maintained in a nearly circular orbit with a mean altitude of 330 km and a maximum of 410 km. An astronaut is floating in the space station's cabin. The acceleration of astronaut as measured from the earth is
(a) zero
(b) nearly zero and directed towards the earth
(c) nearly g and directed along the line of travel of the station
(d) nearly g and directed towards the earth

CHEMISTRY

31. The percentage of nitrogen by mass in ammonium sulphate is closest to (atomic masses of H = 1, N = 14, O = 16, S = 32)
(a) 21%
(b) 24%
(c) 36%
(d) 16%

32. Mendeleev's periodic law states that the properties of elements are a periodic function of their
(a) reactivity of elements
(b) atomic size
(c) atomic mass
(d) electronic configuration

33. Maximum number of electrons that can be accommodated in the subshell with azimuthal quantum number $l = 4$, is
(a) 10
(b) 8
(c) 16
(d) 18

34. The correct order of acidity of the following compounds is

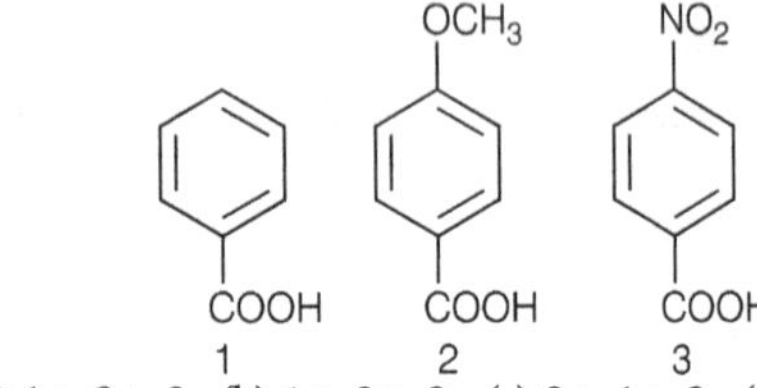

(a) $1 > 2 > 3$
(b) $1 > 3 > 2$
(c) $3 > 1 > 2$
(d) $3 > 2 > 1$

35. Reaction of 2-butene with acidic $KMnO_4$ gives
(a) CH_3CHO
(b) $HCOOH$
(c) CH_3CH_2OH
(d) CH_3COOH

36. The gas released when baking soda is mixed with vinegar is
(a) CO
(b) CO_2
(c) CH_4
(d) O_2

37. The element which readily forms an ionic bond has the electronic configuration
(a) $1s^2 2s^2 2p^3$
(b) $1s^2 2s^2 2p^1$
(c) $1s^2 2s^2 2p^2$
(d) $1s^2 2s^2 2p^6 3s^1$

38. The major products of the following reaction,
$$ZnS(s) + O_2(g) \xrightarrow{\text{Heat}} \ldots\ldots\ldots \text{ are}$$
(a) ZnO and SO_2
(b) $ZnSO_4$ and SO_3
(c) $ZnSO_4$ and SO_2
(d) Zn and SO_2

39. If Avogadro's number is A_0, the number of sulphur atoms present in 200 mL of 1N H_2SO_4 is
(a) $\dfrac{A_0}{5}$
(b) $\dfrac{A_0}{2}$
(c) $\dfrac{A_0}{10}$
(d) A_0

40. The functional group present in a molecule having the formula $C_{12}O_9$ is
(a) carboxylic acid
(b) anhydride
(c) aldehyde
(d) alcohol

41. A sweet smelling compound formed by reacting acetic acid with ethanol in the presence of hydrochloric acid is
(a) $CH_3COOC_2H_5$
(b) C_2H_5COOH
(c) $C_2H_5COOCH_3$
(d) CH_3OH

42. Among Mg, Cu, Fe, Zn the metal that does not produce hydrogen gas in reaction with hydrochloric acid is
(a) Cu
(b) Zn
(c) Mg
(d) Fe

43. The maximum number of isomeric ethers with the molecular formula $C_4H_{10}O$ is
(a) 2
(b) 3
(c) 4
(d) 5

44. The number of electrons required to reduce chromium completely in $Cr_2O_7^{2-}$ to Cr^{3+} in acidic medium, is
(a) 5
(b) 3
(c) 6
(d) 2

45. At constant pressure, the volume of a fixed mass of a gas varies as a function on temperature as shown in the graph

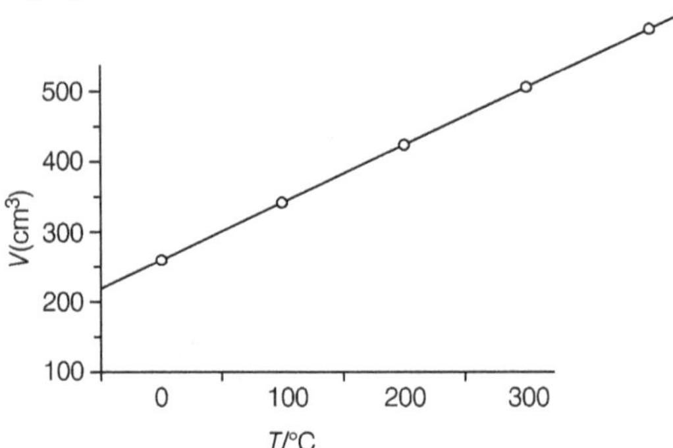

The volume of the gas at 300°C is larger than that at 0°C by a factor of
(a) 3
(b) 4
(c) 1
(d) 2

BIOLOGY

46. Excess salt inhibits bacterial growth in pickles by
(a) endosmosis
(b) exosmosis
(c) oxidation
(d) denaturation

47. Restriction endonucleases are enzymes that are used by biotechnologists to
(a) cut DNA at specific base sequences
(b) join fragments of DNA
(c) digest DNA from the 3′ end
(d) digest DNA from the 5′ end

48. Enzyme X extracted from the digestive system hydrolyses peptide bonds. Which of the following is probable candidate to be enzyme X?
(a) Amylase
(b) Lipase
(c) Trypsin
(d) Maltase

49. A person with blood group AB has
(a) antigen A and B on RBCs and both anti-A and anti-B antibodies in plasma
(b) antigen A and B on RBCs, but neither anti-A nor anti-B antibodies in plasma
(c) no antigen on RBCs but both anti-A and anti-B antibodies are present in plasma
(d) antigen A on RBCs and anti-B antibodies in plasma

50. Glycolysis is the breakdown of glucose to pyruvic acid. How many molecules of pyruvic acid are formed from one molecule of glucose?
(a) 1　　(b) 2　　(c) 3　　(d) 4

51. The process of the transfer of electrons from glucose to molecular oxygen in bacteria and mitochondria is known as
(a) TCA cycle　　(b) oxidative phosphorylation
(c) fermentation　　(d) glycolysis

52. Which one of the following cell types is a part of innate immunity?
(a) Skin epithelial cells　　(b) B-cells
(c) T-lymphocytes　　(d) Liver cells

53. Deficiency of which one of the following vitamins can cause impaired blood clotting?
(a) Vitamin-B　　(b) Vitamin-C
(c) Vitamin-D　　(d) Vitamin-K

54. Which one of the following is detrimental to soil fertility?
(a) Saprophytic bacteria　　(b) *Nitrosomonas*
(c) *Nitrobacter*　　(d) *Pseudomonas*

55. In which one of the following phyla is the body segmented?
(a) Porifera　　(b) Platyhelminthes
(c) Annelida　　(d) Echinodermata

56. Widal test is prescribed to diagnose
(a) typhoid　　(b) pneumonia
(c) malaria　　(d) filaria

57. Which among grass, goat, tiger and vulture in a food chain, will have the maximum concentration of harmful chemicals in its body due to contamination of pesticides in the soil?
(a) Grass since it grows in the contaminated soil
(b) Goat since it eats the grass
(c) Tiger since it feeds on the goat which feeds on the grass
(d) Vulture since it eats the tiger, which in turn eats the goat, which eats the grass

58. Considering the average molecular mass of a base to be 500 Da, what is the molecular mass of a double-stranded DNA of 10 base pairs?
(a) 500 Da　　(b) 5 kDa　　(c) 10 kDa　　(d) 1 kDa

59. Which of the following pairs are both polysaccharides?
(a) Cellulose and glycogen
(b) Starch and glucose
(c) Cellulose and fructose
(d) Ribose and sucrose

60. Which one of the following is a modified leaf?
(a) Sweet potato　　(b) Ginger
(c) Onion　　(d) Carrot

ꜱ PART–II (2 Marks Questions)

MATHEMATICS

61. A triangular corner is cut from a rectangular piece of paper and the resulting pentagon has sides 5, 6, 8, 9, 12 in some order. The ratio of the area of the pentagon to the area of the rectangle is
(a) $\dfrac{11}{18}$　　(b) $\dfrac{13}{18}$　　(c) $\dfrac{15}{18}$　　(d) $\dfrac{17}{18}$

62. For a real number x, let $[x]$ denote the largest integer less than or equal to x, and let $\{x\} = x - [x]$. The number of solutions x to the equation $[x]\{x\} = 5$ with $0 \le x \le 2015$ is
(a) 0　　(b) 3　　(c) 2008　　(d) 2009

63. Let $ABCD$ be a trapezium with AD parallel to BC. Assume there is a point M in the interior of the segment BC such that $AB = AM$ and $DC = DM$. Then, the ratio of the area of the trapezium to the area of $\triangle AMD$ is
(a) 2
(b) 3
(c) 4
(d) not determinable from the data

64. Given are three cylindrical buckets X, Y, Z whose circular bases are of radii 1, 2, 3 units, respectively. Initially water is filled in these buckets upto the same height. Some water is then transferred from Z to X so that they both have the same volume of water. Some water is then transferred between X and Y so that they both have the same volume of water. If h_Y, h_Z denote the heights of water at this stage in the buckets Y, Z, respectively, then the ratio $\dfrac{h_Y}{h_Z}$ equals
(a) $\dfrac{4}{9}$　　(b) 1　　(c) $\dfrac{9}{4}$　　(d) $\dfrac{81}{40}$

65. The average incomes of the people in two villages are P and Q, respectively. Assume that $P \ne Q$. A person moves from the first village to the second village. The new average incomes are P' and Q', respectively. Which of the following is not possible?
(a) $P' > P$ and $Q' > Q$　　(b) $P' > P$ and $Q' < Q$
(c) $P' = P$ and $Q' = Q$　　(d) $P' < P$ and $Q' < Q$

PHYSICS

66. A girl sees through a circular glass slab (refractive index 1.5) of thickness 20 mm and diameter 60 cm to the bottom of a swimming pool. Refractive index of water is 1.33. The bottom surface of the slab is in contact with the water surface.

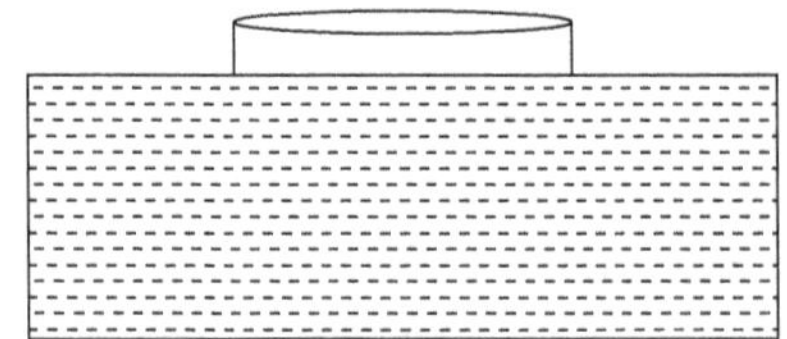

The depth of swimming pool is 6 m. The area of bottom of swimming pool that can be seen through the slab is approximately

(a) 100 m^2 (b) 160 m^2 (c) 190 m^2 (d) 220 m^2

67. 1 kg of ice at $-20°C$ is mixed with 2 kg of water at $90°C$. Assuming that there is no loss of energy to the environment, what will be the final temperature of the mixture? (Assume, latent heat of ice = 334.4 kJ/kg, specific heat of water and ice are 4.18 kJ kg^{-1}K^{-1} and 2.09 kJ kg^{-1}·K^{-1}, respectively.)

(a) 30°C   (b) 0°C   (c) 80°C   (d) 45°C

68. A rigid body in the shape of a V has two equal arms made of uniform rods. What must the angle between the two rods be so that when the body is suspended from one end, the other arm is horizontal?

(a) $\cos^{-1}\left(\dfrac{1}{3}\right)$ (b) $\cos^{-1}\left(\dfrac{1}{2}\right)$

(c) $\cos^{-1}\left(\dfrac{1}{4}\right)$ (d) $\cos^{-1}\left(\dfrac{1}{6}\right)$

69. A point object is placed 20 cm left of a convex lens of focal length $f = 5$ cm (see in the below figure). The lens is made to oscillate with small amplitude A along the horizontal axis. The image of the object will also oscillate along the axis with

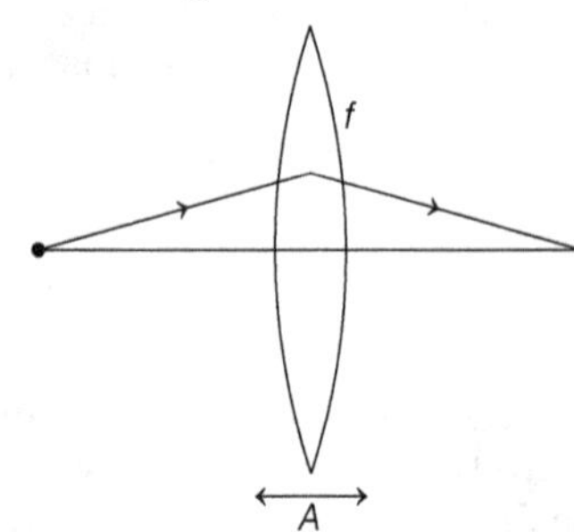

(a) amplitude $A / 9$, out of phase with the oscillations of the lens
(b) amplitude $A / 3$, out of phase with the oscillations of the lens
(c) amplitude $A / 3$, in phase with the oscillations of the lens
(d) amplitude $A / 9$, in phase with the oscillations of the lens

70. Stokes' law states that the viscous drag force F experienced by a sphere of radius a, moving with a speed v through a fluid with coefficient of viscosity η, is given by $F = 6\pi\eta av$.
If this fluid is flowing through a cylindrical pipe of radius r, length l and a pressure difference of p across its two ends, then the volume of water V which flows through the pipe in time t can be written as

$$\frac{v}{t} = k \left(\frac{p}{l}\right)^a \eta^b r^c$$

where, k is a dimensionless constant. Correct value of a, b and c are

(a) $a = 1, b = -1, c = 4$
(b) $a = -1, b = 1, c = 4$
(c) $a = 2, b = -1, c = 3$
(d) $a = 1, b = -2, c = -4$

CHEMISTRY

71. When 262 g of xenon (atomic mass = 131) reacted completely with 152 g of fluorine (atomic mass = 19), a mixture of XeF$_2$ and XeF$_6$ was produced. The molar ratio XeF$_2$: XeF$_6$ is

(a) 1 : 2   (b) 1 : 4
(c) 1 : 1   (d) 1 : 3

72. Reaction of ethanol with conc. sulphuric acid at 170°C produces a gas which is then treated with bromine in carbon tetrachloride. The major product obtained in this reaction is

(a) 1,2-dibromoethane
(b) ethylene glycol
(c) bromoethane
(d) ethyl sulphate

73. When 22.4 L of C$_4$H$_8$ at STP is burnt completely, 89.6 L of CO$_2$ gas at STP and 72 g of water are produced. The volume of the oxygen gas at STP consumed in the reaction is closest to

(a) 89.6 L   (b) 112 L
(c) 134.4 L   (d) 22.4 L

74. The amount of Ag (atomic mass = 108) deposited at the cathode when a current of 0.5 amp is passed through a solution of AgNO$_3$ for 1 h is closest to

(a) 2 g   (b) 5 g
(c) 108 g   (d) 11 g

75. The major product of the reaction is

(a) I   (b) II   (c) III   (d) IV

BIOLOGY

76. Genomic DNA is digested with Alu I, a restriction enzyme which is a four base-pair cutter. What is the frequency with which it will cut the DNA assuming a random distribution of bases in the genome?

(a) 1/4   (b) 1/24   (c) 1/256   (d) 1/1296

77. If rice is cooked in a pressure cooker on the Siachen glacier at sea beach and on Deccan plain, which of the following is correct about the time taken for cooking rice?

(a) Gets cooked faster on the Siachen glacier
(b) Gets cooked faster at sea beach
(c) Gets cooked faster on Deccan plain
(d) Gets cooked at the same time at all the three places

78. A few rabbits are introduced in an uninhabited island with plenty of food. If these rabbits breed in the absence of any disease, natural calamity and predation, which one of the following graphs best represents their population growth?

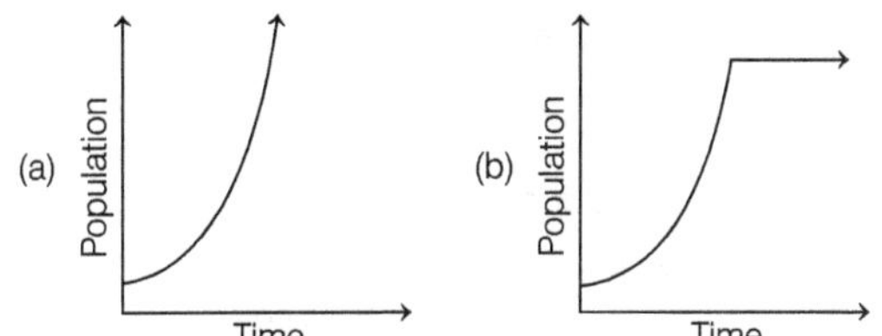

79. What is the advantage of storing glucose as glycogen in animals instead of a monomeric glucose?

(a) Energy obtained from glycogen is more than that from the corresponding glucose monomers
(b) Glucose present as monomers within the cell exerts more osmotic pressure than a single glycogen molecule, resulting in loss of water from the cells
(c) Glucose present as monomers within the cell exerts more osmotic pressure than a single glycogen molecule, resulting in excess water within the cells
(d) Glycogen gives more rigidity to the cells

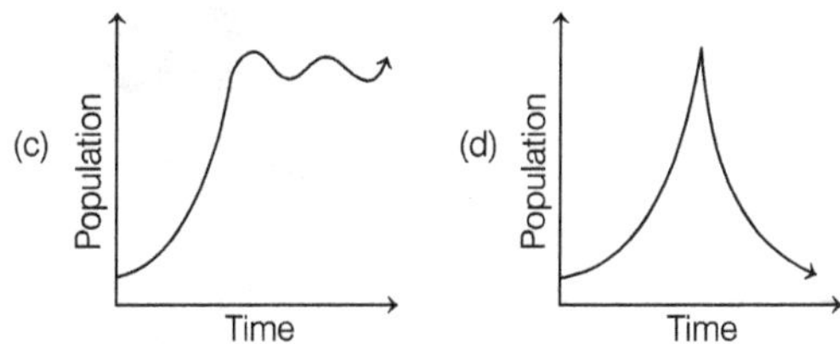

80. A line is drawn from the exterior of an animal cell to the centre of the nucleus, crossing through one mitochondrion. What is the minimum number of membrane bilayers that the line will cross?

(a) 4
(b) 3
(c) 8
(d) 6

Answers

PART-I

1	(c)	2	(c)	3	(b)	4	(c)	5	(b)	6	(d)	7	(c)	8	(d)	9	(b)	10	(b)
11	(c)	12	(c)	13	(b)	14	(a)	15	(a)	16	(c)	17	(c)	18	(b)	19	(c)	20	(a)
21	(c)	22	(d)	23	(a)	24	(b)	25	(d)	26	(a)	27	(d)	28	(a)	29	(c)	30	(d)
31	(a)	32	(c)	33	(d)	34	(c)	35	(d)	36	(b)	37	(d)	38	(a)	39	(c)	40	(b)
41	(a)	42	(a)	43	(b)	44	(c)	45	(d)	46	(b)	47	(a)	48	(c)	49	(b)	50	(b)
51	(b)	52	(a)	53	(d)	54	(d)	55	(c)	56	(a)	57	(d)	58	(c)	59	(a)	60	(c)

PART-II

61	(d)	62	(d)	63	(b)	64	(d)	65	(c)	66	(b)	67	(a)	68	(a)	69	(a)	70	(a)
71	(c)	72	(a)	73	(c)	74	(a)	75	(a)	76	(c)	77	(b)	78	(a)	79	(c)	80	(a)

Solutions

1. *(c)* We have,

$f(x) = x^2 + ax + 2$ and $g(x) = x^2 + 2x + a$

Let α be the common root of $f(x) = 0$ and $g(x) = 0$.

$\therefore \qquad \alpha^2 + a\alpha + 2 = 0$

and $\qquad \alpha^2 + 2\alpha + a = 0$

$\therefore \qquad \dfrac{\alpha^2}{a^2 - 4} = \dfrac{-\alpha}{a - 2} = \dfrac{1}{2 - a}$

$$\dfrac{\alpha^2}{a^2 - 4} = \dfrac{\alpha}{2 - a}$$

$\Rightarrow \alpha = \dfrac{a^2 - 4}{2 - a} = \dfrac{(a + 2)(a - 2)}{-(a - 2)} = -(a + 2)$

and $\qquad \dfrac{\alpha}{2 - a} = \dfrac{1}{2 - a} \Rightarrow \alpha = 1$

$\therefore \qquad -(a + 2) = 1$

$a + 2 = -1 \Rightarrow a = -3$

Now $\qquad f(x) + g(x) = 0$

$\therefore x^2 - 3x + 2 + x^2 + 2x - 3 = 0$

$\qquad 2x^2 - x - 1 = 0$

Sum of roots $= \dfrac{1}{2} \qquad \left[\because \alpha + \beta = \dfrac{-b}{a}\right]$

2. *(c)* We have,

$n + 2n + 3n + \dots + 99n$ is a perfect square

$n(1 + 2 + \dots + 99), \dfrac{n \times 99 \times 100}{2}$

$n \times 11 \times 9 \times 2 \times 25$

$= (3)^2 \times (5)^2 \times 2 \times 11 \times n$ is a perfect square

$\therefore n$ must be 22.

$\therefore \qquad n^2 = (22)^2 = 484$

Number of digit of n^2 is 3.

3. *(b)* We have,

$x = y = z$, x, y, z positive reals.

I. $x^3 + y^3 + z^3 = 3xyz$

We know,

$x^3 + y^3 + z^3 - 3xyz = (x + y + z)$

$\qquad (x^2 + y^2 + z^2 - xy - yz - zx)$

$\qquad = \dfrac{1}{2}(x + y + z)[(x - y)^2$

$\qquad\qquad + (y - z)^2 + (z - x)^2]$

When $x = y = z$

Then, $(x - y)^2 + (y - z)^2 + (z - x)^2 = 0$

$\therefore \qquad x^3 + y^3 + z^3 = 3xyz$

II. $x^3 + y^2z + yz^2 = 3xyz$

Put $x = y = z$

Then, LHS = RHS

III. Put $x = z = 1$ and $y = 2$

Then, it is also true.

So, we cannot say only for $x = y = z$ for true

IV. $(x + y + z)^3 = 27xyz$

$\qquad\qquad x = y = z$

Then, $(3x)^3 = 27x^3$

Hence option (iv) is also true.

4. *(c)* Given,

Perimeter of rectangle is 76 units.

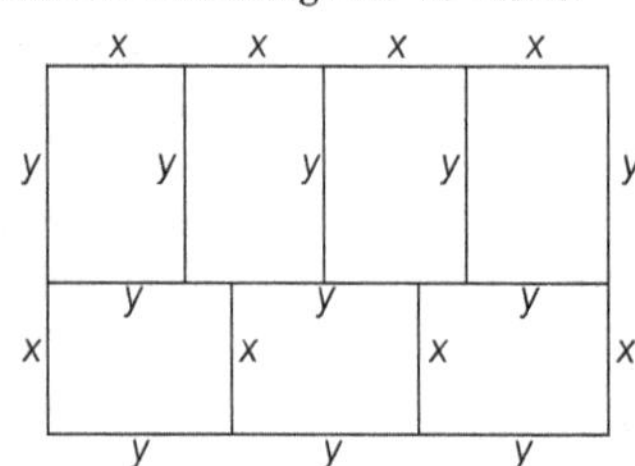

Let x and y are sides of each rectangles.

$\therefore$ Perimetre of rectangle $= 6x + 5y = 76$

$\qquad\qquad\qquad\qquad\qquad \dots\text{(i)}$

and $\qquad\qquad 4x = 3y \qquad \dots\text{(ii)}$

On solving Eqs. (i) and (ii), we get

$\qquad x = 6, y = 8$

$\therefore$ Perimeter of each rectangle

$\qquad = 2(x + y) = 2(6 + 8) = 28$ units

5. *(b)* $\quad 13! = 2 \times 3 \times 4 \times 5 \times 6 \times 7$

$\qquad\qquad \times 8 \times 9 \times 10 \times 11 \times 12 \times 13$

$\qquad = 2^{10} \times 3^5 \times 5^2 \times 7 \times 11 \times 13$

$24^k = (2^3 \times 3)^k$

When 13! is divide by 24^k

$\therefore \quad \dfrac{2^{10} \times 3^5 \times 5^2 \times 7 \times 11 \times 13}{2^{3k} \cdot 3^k}$

$\qquad = 2^{10 - 3k} \cdot 3^{5 - k} \cdot 5^2 \times 7 \times 11 \times 13$

$\therefore \quad 10 - 3k = $ integer

Then, maximum value of $k = 3$

6. *(d)* ABC is a triangle points X and Y on AB and AC respectively.

XY is parallel to BC.

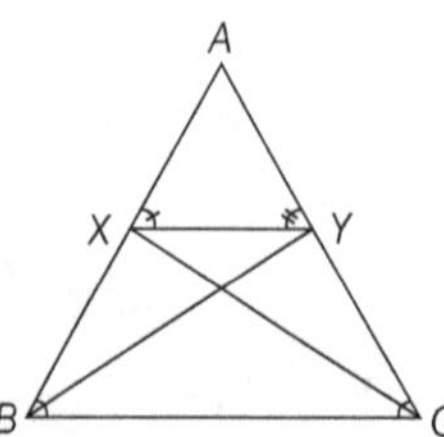

I. Area of BCX : Area of BCY

It is true because same base between same parallels.

II. Area of $\triangle ACX = \dfrac{1}{2}(AX)(AC)\sin A$

$\qquad$ Area of $\triangle ABY = \dfrac{1}{2}(AY)(AB)\sin A$

$\therefore$ (Area of $\triangle ACX$) (Area of $\triangle ABY$)

$\qquad = \dfrac{1}{2}(AX)(AC)\sin A \times \dfrac{1}{2}(AY)(AB)\sin A$

$\qquad = \dfrac{1}{2}(AX)(AY)\sin A \times \dfrac{1}{2}(AB)(AC)\sin A$

$\qquad = $ (Area of $\triangle AXY$) (Area of $\triangle ABC$)

Hence, I and II both are true.

7. *(c)* ABC is a triangle. P be interior point of a $\triangle ABC$, Q and R be the reflections of P in AB and AC respectively.

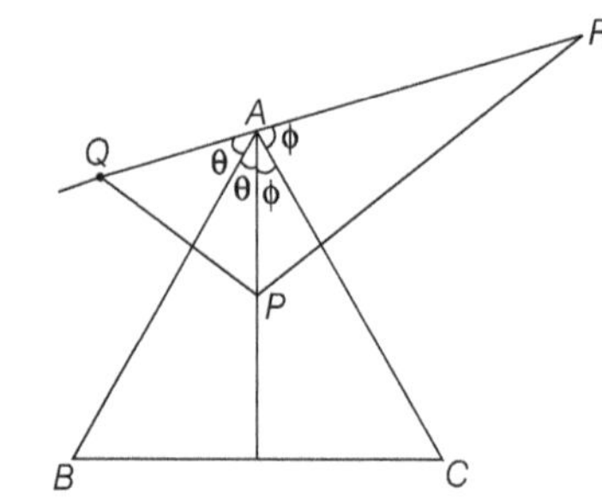

QAR are collinear

$\therefore \qquad \angle QAR = 180°$

Q is reflection of P on AB

$\therefore \qquad \angle QAB = \angle PAB$

R is reflection of P on AC

$\therefore \qquad \angle RAC = \angle PAC$

$\qquad \angle QAR = 180°$

$\therefore 2(\angle PAB + \angle PAC) = 180°$

$\qquad \angle PAB + \angle PAC = 90°$

$\Rightarrow \qquad \angle BAC = 90°$

8. *(d)* $ABCD$ is a square

$AB = BC = CD = AD = 1\,$unit

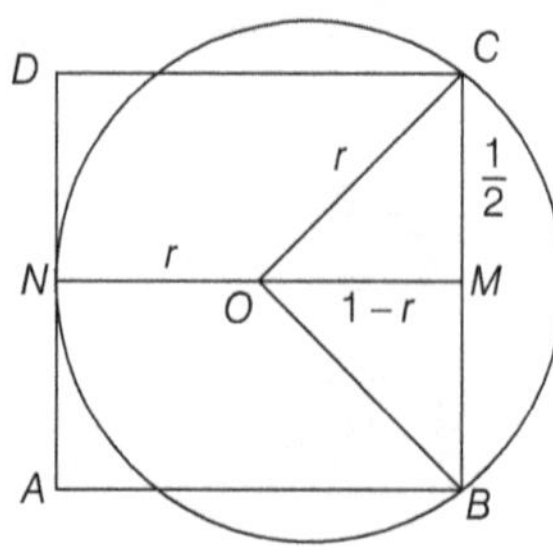

A circle Γ passing through B and C and touching AD.

BC is chord of circle.

$\therefore OM$ bisects the chord AB

$\therefore \qquad CM = MB = \dfrac{1}{2}BC = \dfrac{1}{2}$

$\Rightarrow \qquad OM = MN - ON = 1 - r$

In $\triangle OMC$, $OC^2 = OM^2 + CM^2$

$\Rightarrow \quad r^2 = (1-r)^2 + \left(\dfrac{1}{2}\right)^2$

$\Rightarrow \quad r^2 = 1 - 2r + r^2 + \dfrac{1}{4} \Rightarrow r = \dfrac{5}{8}$

9. *(b)* $ABCD$ is square

$\qquad AB = BC = CD = AD = 1$

PQ is perpendicular to RS

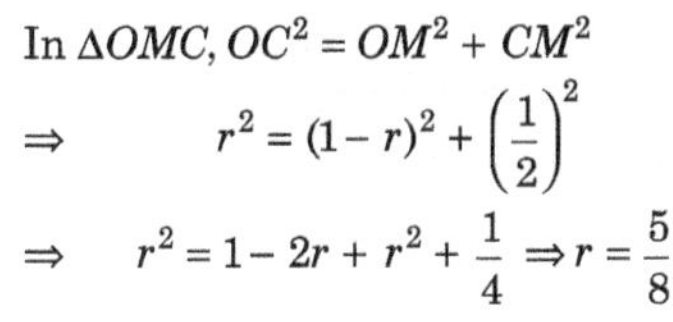

$\because$ Slope of $PQ \times$ Slope of $RS = -1$

$\therefore \quad \dfrac{q-p}{1-0} \times \dfrac{1-0}{s-r} = -1$

$\Rightarrow \qquad q - p = r - s \qquad \ldots(i)$

$\Rightarrow \qquad (PQ)^2 = (1-0)^2 + (q-p)^2$

$\Rightarrow \qquad \left(\dfrac{3\sqrt{3}}{4}\right)^2 = 1 + (q-p)^2$

$\Rightarrow \qquad (q-p)^2 = \dfrac{27}{16} - 1 = \dfrac{11}{16}$

$\Rightarrow \qquad (r-s)^2 = \dfrac{11}{16} \quad [\because q-p = r-s]$

$\Rightarrow \qquad RS = \sqrt{(1-0)^2 + (r-s)^2}$

$\Rightarrow \qquad RS = \sqrt{1 + \dfrac{11}{16}}$

$\therefore \qquad RS = \sqrt{\dfrac{27}{16}} = \dfrac{3\sqrt{3}}{4}$

10. *(b)* Given,

Area of both figures are equal

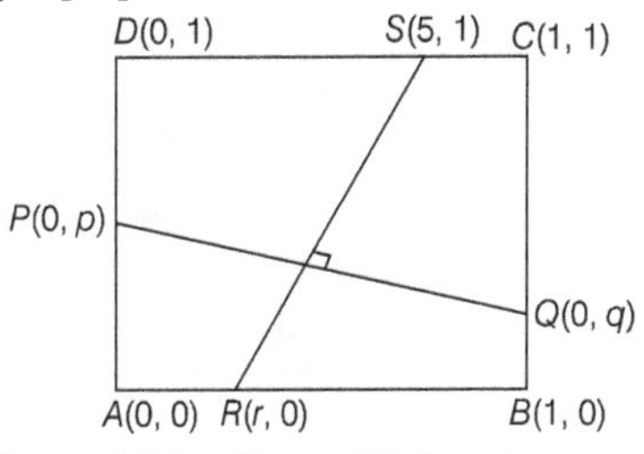

Area of fig. (i) $= 2xy + \dfrac{1}{2} \cdot x(3y)$

$\qquad = 2xy + \dfrac{3xy}{2} = \dfrac{7xy}{2}$

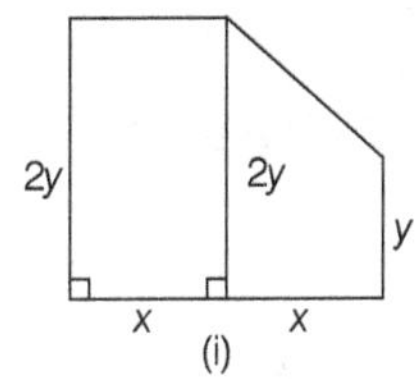

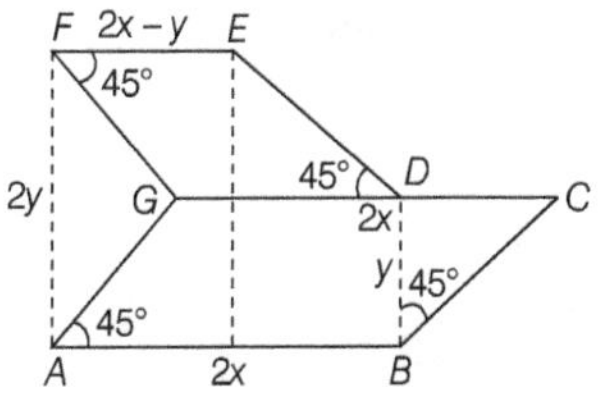

Area of fig. (ii)

Area of $ABCG$ + Area of $DEFG$

$\qquad = 2xy + (2x - y)\,y$

$\qquad = 2xy + 2xy - y^2 = 4xy - y^2$

$\therefore \quad \dfrac{7xy}{2} = 4xy - y^2 \Rightarrow y^2 = \dfrac{1}{2}xy \Rightarrow 2y = x$

11. *(c)* Let the length of trains be x meter.

Time taken by train h cross person = 9 s

$\therefore$ Speed of trains $= \dfrac{x}{9}$ m/s

Time taken by train to cross platform = 21 s

$\therefore \qquad \dfrac{x}{9} = \dfrac{x+88}{21}$

$\qquad [\because$ length of plateform = 88 m]

$\Rightarrow \qquad 21x = 9x + 9 \times 88$

$\Rightarrow \qquad 12x = 9 \times 88$

$\Rightarrow \qquad x = \dfrac{9 \times 88}{12} = 66\,\text{m}$

12. *(c)* We have,

$\qquad \sqrt[3]{n+1} - \sqrt[3]{n} < \dfrac{1}{12}$

$\qquad \sqrt[3]{n+1} < \sqrt[3]{n} + \dfrac{1}{12}$

Cubing both sides, we get

$n+1 < n + 3(n)^{2/3} \times \dfrac{1}{12} + 3\sqrt[3]{n} \times \dfrac{1}{144} + \dfrac{1}{1728}$

$\Rightarrow \quad 1 < \dfrac{3n^{1/3}}{12}\left(n^{1/3} + \dfrac{1}{12}\right) + \dfrac{1}{1728}$

$\Rightarrow \quad \dfrac{n^{1/3}}{4}\left(n^{1/3} + \dfrac{1}{12}\right) > 1 - \dfrac{1}{1728}$

$\Rightarrow \quad n^{1/3}\left(n^{1/3} + \dfrac{1}{12}\right) > \dfrac{1727}{432}$

Put $n = 8$ only possible least positive integers.

13. *(b)* Let $n = 3q + r$

$\qquad 0 \le r < 3$

$\therefore \qquad n = 3q, 3q + 1, 3q + 2$

If n is multiple of 3

i.e. $\qquad n = 3q$

Then, n^{19} is also multiple of 3.

When $n = 3q + 1$ and $3q + 2$

$\quad n^{38} = (3q + 1)^{38}$

$\qquad = (3q + 1)^{36}\,(3q + 1)^2$

$\qquad = (36k + 1)\,(9q^2 + 6q + 1)$

$\qquad\qquad [\because (x+1)^x = nk + 1]$

$\qquad = 36k\,(9q^2 + 6q + 1) + 9q^2 + 6q + 1$

$\qquad = 3k + 3\lambda + 1$

$\therefore n^{38} - 1 = 3k + 3\lambda + 1 - 1 = 3m$

$\therefore n^{38} - 1$ is multiple of 3

Similarly, when $n = 3q + 2$

$n^{38} - 1$ is also multiple of 3.

14. *(a)* We have, $12! + 13! + 14!$

$\qquad 12!(1 + 13 + 13 \times 14)$

$\qquad 12!\,(1 + 13\,(1 + 14))$

$\qquad 12! \times 196$

The number of distinct prime of $12! \times 196$ is 2, 3, 5, 7, 11.

15. *(a)* Given, EDUCATION

Vowel occurs in same order

$\qquad$ _E_U_A_I_O_

There are 6 place for letter DCTN

$\therefore$ Total number of arrangement is $^6C_4 = 15$.

16. *(c)* As, force $F = ma$

$\Rightarrow \dfrac{\Delta F}{F} = \dfrac{\Delta m}{m} + \dfrac{\Delta a}{a} \Rightarrow \dfrac{\Delta m}{m} = \dfrac{\Delta F}{F} - \dfrac{\Delta a}{a}$

$\Rightarrow \dfrac{\Delta m}{m} = \left(\dfrac{\pm 0.2}{10}\right) - \left(\dfrac{\pm 0.01}{1}\right)$

So, $\left(\dfrac{\Delta m}{m}\right)_{\max} = \dfrac{0.2}{10} + \dfrac{0.01}{1} = 0.03$

Maximum error in mass occurs when error in force and acceleration are of different signs.

So, $\Delta m = 0.03 \times m = 0.03 \times 10 \Rightarrow \Delta m = 0.3$ kg

Hence, mass of object is $m = 10 \pm 0.3$ kg.

17. *(c)* Cylinder will topple when centre of mass of filled cylinder lies outside the right edge of base. As centre of mass of filled cylinder lies at its mid-point.

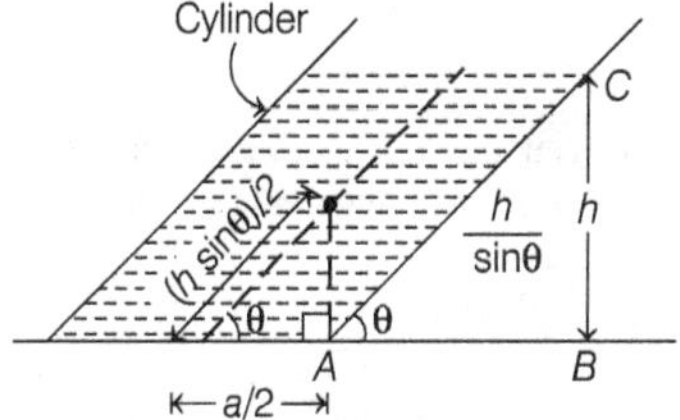

Now, from above diagram, we have

$\sin\theta = \dfrac{BC}{AC} \Rightarrow AC = \dfrac{h}{\sin\theta}$

So, $\cos\theta = \left(\dfrac{\dfrac{a}{2}}{\dfrac{h}{2}\sin\theta}\right)$ or $h = a\tan\theta$

18. *(b)* Initially, the velocity is increasing, so the $(x$-$t)$ graph must be with increasing slope or parabolic.

For first 4-s, $x = ut + \dfrac{1}{2}at^2$

$\Rightarrow \qquad x = t^2/2$ (parabola).

After 4 s, particle is moving with a constant velocity, so its graph is a straight line of constant slope after 4 s. After 4 s, velocity is constant.

$\therefore x = vt = (4 + at)t = 4t$ (straight line)

Hence, best suited option is (b).

19. *(c)* Axis of rotation of earth as shown below.

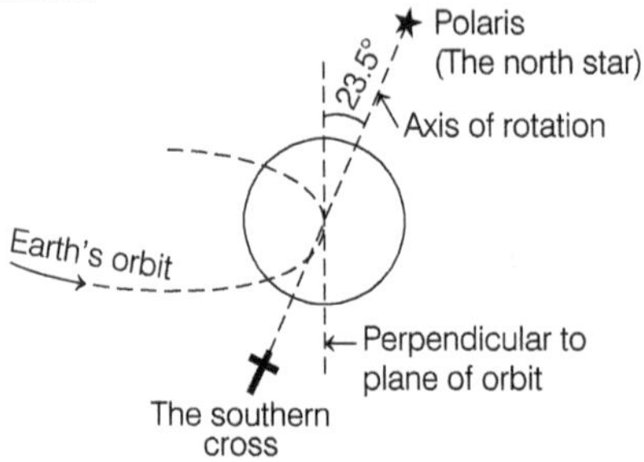

Axis of rotation of earth passes close to polaris, the polar star.

20. *(a)* Heat through sun reaches earth in form of infrared radiations of higher frequency range approx 10^{14} Hz. This heat is absorbed by solids on earth's surface and they re-radiate this heat in form of infrared radiations of lower frequency range approx 10^{10} Hz. These radiations are absorbed by greenhouse gases like methane and does not escapes into space causing warming of earth's atmosphere.

21. *(c)* As parachutist lands on earth's surface, there are two forces acting on her.

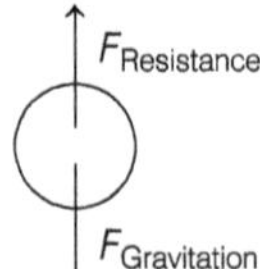

Now, before writing Newton's second law equation, we calculate acceleration of parachutist using
$$v^2 - u^2 = 2as$$
$$0 - (-2)^2 = 2(a)(-0.25)$$
So, retardation of parachutist is
$a = 8 \text{ ms}^{-2}$ (directed upwards)
Now, using $F_{net} = ma$, we have
$$F_R - F_g = ma \Rightarrow F_R - mg = ma$$
or $F_R = m(g + a) \Rightarrow F_R = 75(10 + 8) = 1350 \text{ N}$
So, resistive force of ground on parachutist is 1350 N.

22. *(d)* β^--particles are emitted from following nuclear reaction:
$$_0^1 n \longrightarrow {}_1^1 p + {}_{-1}^0 e + \bar{\nu}$$
A neutron in nucleus is converted into a proton with emission of a β^--particle and an antineutrino. This converts emitting nucleus into another nucleus of higher proton number.
$$_Z^A X \longrightarrow {}_{z+1}^A Y + {}_{-1}^0 e + \bar{\nu}$$
This decay is characteristics of nuclii for which, $\dfrac{N}{Z} < 1$

23. *(a)* Initially given situation is

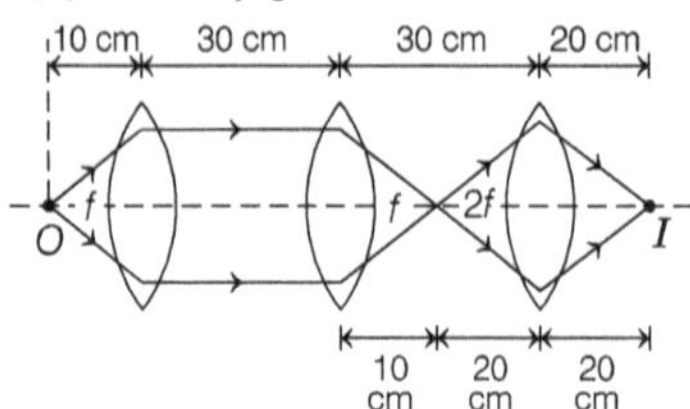

When device is moved away from source O, then situation is as shown below.

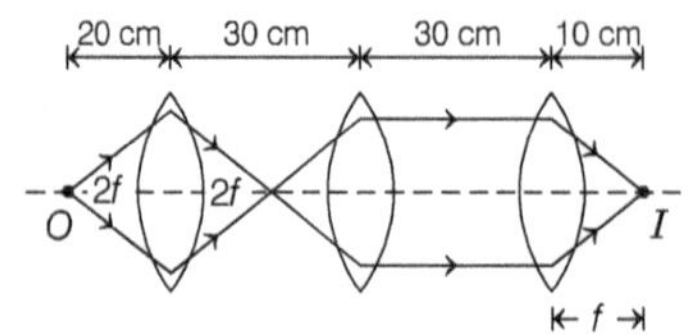

So, distance between object and image in both cases is 90 cm. Hence, there is no shift in image's position.

24. *(b)* Base angles of prism is given 40°. So, angle of prism $A = 180° - 80° = 100°$.

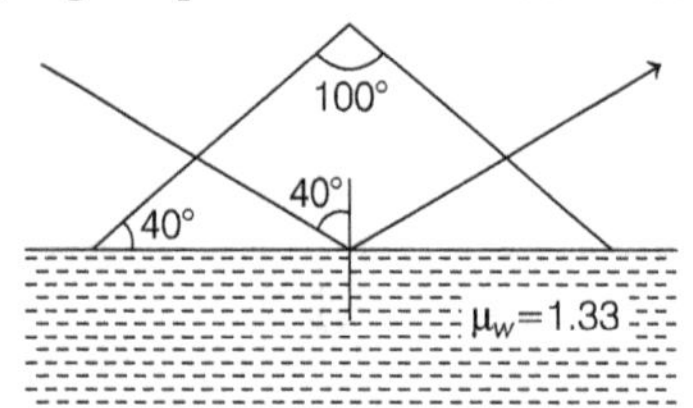

For TIR, $i > \theta_c \Rightarrow \sin 40° > \sin \theta_c$
$$\Rightarrow \sin 40° > \frac{\mu_w}{\mu_g} \Rightarrow \mu_g > \frac{1.33}{\sin 40°} \approx 2.07$$
or $\mu_g > 2.07$

25. *(d)* From mirror formula, we have
$$\frac{1}{v} - \frac{1}{u} = \frac{1}{f} \qquad ...(i)$$
Here, $f = +10 \text{ cm}, u = -15 \text{ cm}$
$$\Rightarrow v = \frac{10 \times -15}{-15 + 10} = 30 \text{ cm}$$
Now differentiating Eq. (i) with respect to time, we get
$$\frac{dv}{dt} = \frac{v^2}{u^2}\left(\frac{du}{dt}\right)$$
$$\therefore \quad \frac{dv}{dt} = \frac{(+30)^2}{(-15)^2} \times (+2 \text{ cm s}^{-1})$$
$$\Rightarrow \frac{dv}{dt} = +8 \text{ cm s}^{-1}$$
So, image is moving away from lens.

26. *(a)*

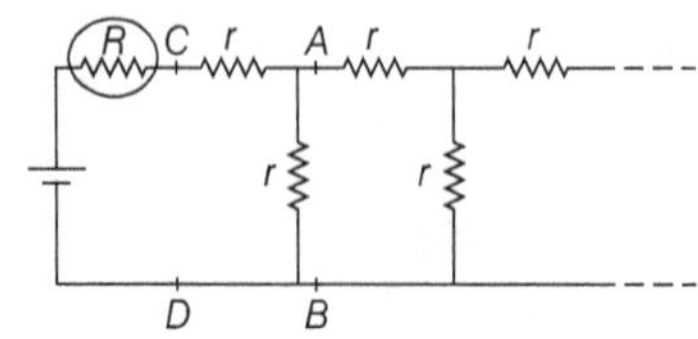

Adding or removing one of repeating member does not alters the resistance of an infinite network. Let $R_{AB} = x$, then $R_{AB} = R_{CD}$.
$$\Rightarrow x = r + \frac{rx}{r + x}$$
$$\Rightarrow x^2 - rx - x = 0$$
From sridharacharya formula, we have
$$x = \frac{-b \pm \sqrt{b^2 - 4ac}}{2a}$$
$$\Rightarrow x = -\frac{(-r) \pm \sqrt{r^2 + 4r^2}}{2}$$
$$\Rightarrow x = \frac{r(1 + \sqrt{5})}{2}$$
Now, power consumed by bulb of resistance R is 1 W,
$$i^2 R = 1 \Rightarrow i^2 = \frac{1}{16} \Rightarrow i = \frac{1}{4} \text{ A}$$
Now, current in circuit is
$$i = \frac{V}{R_{total}} \Rightarrow i = \frac{V}{R + R_{CD}}$$
$$\Rightarrow \frac{1}{4} = \frac{10}{16 + \frac{r}{2}(1 + \sqrt{5})}$$
$$\Rightarrow 16 + \frac{r}{2}(1 + \sqrt{5}) = 40 \Rightarrow r = 14.8 \ \Omega$$

27. *(d)* Let orbital radius of ball is r then orbital velocity of ball is
$$v = \sqrt{\frac{GM}{r}}$$
Here, $r = R + h$
$$\Rightarrow r = 6400 \text{ km} + 9 \text{ km}$$
or $r \approx 6400 \text{ km}$
$$\Rightarrow r = R \text{ (radius of earth)}$$
Now, acceleration of ball in orbit is
$$a = \frac{v^2}{r} = \frac{GM}{r^2} \approx \frac{GM}{R^2} \text{ or } a \approx g$$
So, acceleration of ball is nearly equal to g.

28. *(a)* For a satellite or planet, if total energy is E, then
kinetic energy, $K = -E$
and potential energy, $U = 2E$
where, E is negative.
So, $|U| > K$.

29. *(c)* Process given is

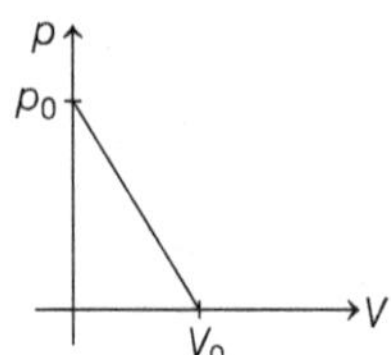

To find process equation, we use two point form of equation of straight line,

$$y - y_1 = \frac{y_2 - y_1}{x_2 - x_1}(x - x_1)$$

Here, $(x, y_1) = (0, p_0)$ and $(x_2, y_2) = (V_0, 0)$

Process equation is

$$p = p_0 - \frac{p_0}{V_0}.V$$

As, $\qquad p = \dfrac{RT}{V}$

$$\Rightarrow \qquad \frac{RT}{V} = p_0 - \frac{p_0}{V_0}.V$$

$$\Rightarrow \qquad T = \frac{p_0 V}{R}\left(1 - \frac{V}{V_0}\right)$$

30. (d) At height h, acceleration due to gravity is $g_h = \dfrac{GM}{(R + h)^2}$

For $\qquad h << R,$

$$g_h \approx \frac{GM}{R^2} = g$$

Direction is towards centre of earth.

31. (a) Total mass of ammonium sulphate $(NH_4)_2 SO_4$

$$= 2 \times 18 + 32 + 16 \times 4$$
$$= 36 + 96 = 132$$

Mass of nitrogen in $(NH_4)_2 SO_4 = 28$

% of N by mass in $(NH_4)_2 SO_4 = \dfrac{28}{132} \times 100$

$$= 21.2\%$$

32. (c) According to Mendeleev's periodic law, the physical and chemical properties of the elements are a periodic function of their atomic mass.

33. (d) Maximum number of electrons that can be accommodated in a subshell $= 2(2l + 1)$

When $l = 4$

Maximum number of electrons

$$= 2(2 \times 4 + 1) = 18$$

34. (c) Electron donating substituents tends to decrease the acidic strength while electron withdrawing substituents tends to increase the acidic strength of substituted benzoic acids relative to benzoic acid. OCH_3 exerts $+M$ effect which destabilises the conjugate base

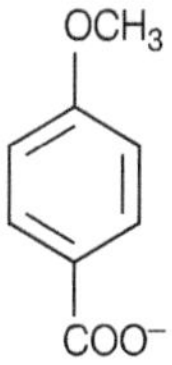

of the compound 2 and hence decreases the acidity, whereas NO_2 exerts $-M$ effect and stabilises the conjugate

base of the compound 3 and hence increases the acidity. Thus, the correct order of acidity of the given compounds are

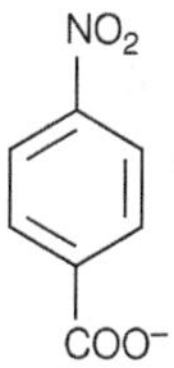

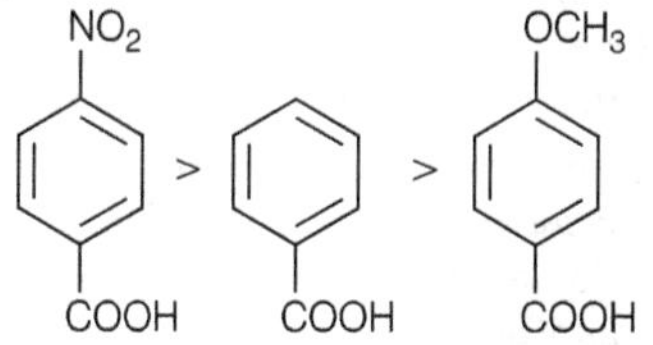

$$\underset{3}{NO_2} > \underset{1}{} > \underset{2}{OCH_3}$$

35. (d) Acidic potassium permanganate oxides alkenes to ketones or acids depending upon the nature of the alkene. Thus, reaction of 2-butene with acidic $KMnO_4$ gives acetic acid.

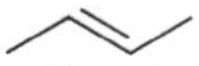

$$\underset{\text{2 butene}}{\diagup\diagdown} \xrightarrow[\substack{\text{Strong} \\ \text{oxidising} \\ \text{agent}}]{KMnO_4/H^+} \underset{\text{Acetic acid}}{2\ CH_3COOH}$$

36. (b) When baking soda is mixed with vinegar aqueous solution of sodium acetate is formed with the evolution of carbon dioxide gas

$$\underset{\text{Vinegar}}{CH_3COOH} + \underset{\text{Baking soda}}{NaHCO_3} \longrightarrow \underset{\substack{\text{Sodium} \\ \text{acetate}}}{CH_3CO\overset{-}{O}\overset{+}{N}a}\ (aq)$$

$$+ \underset{\text{Carbon dioxide gas}}{H_2O\ (l) + CO_2(g)}$$

37. (d) Alkali metals have the highest tendency to form ionic bond as they have low ionisation energy. The general electronic configuration of alkali metal is ns^1. Among the given electronic configuration, $1s^2 2s^2 2p^6 3s^1$ corresponds to the configuration of Na, which is an alkali metal and hence forms ionic bond readily.

38. (a)

$$2ZnS(s) + 3O_2(g) \xrightarrow{\Delta} 2ZnO + 2SO_2$$

This process is known as roasting where the sulphide ore is heated in a regular supply of air to give its oxide form at a temperature below the melting point of the metal.

39. (c) Given,

Normality of $H_2SO_4 = 1\ N$

Avogadro's number $= A$

Volume of $H_2SO_4 = 200\ mL$

Normality = Basicity $\times$ Molarity

For H_2SO_4, basicity $= 2$

$$\therefore \qquad 1 = 2 \times M$$

$$M = 0.5\ mol/L$$

$\therefore$ No. of moles of $H_2SO_4 =$ No. of moles of S

atom $= \dfrac{0.5 \times 200}{1000} = 0.1\ mol$

[No. of moles = Volume $\times$ Molarity]

1 mol of S $= A_0$ atoms

$\therefore$ 0.1 mole of S $= A_0 \times \dfrac{1}{10} = \dfrac{A_0}{10}$ atoms.

40. (b) The structure of $C_{12}O_9$ is as follows

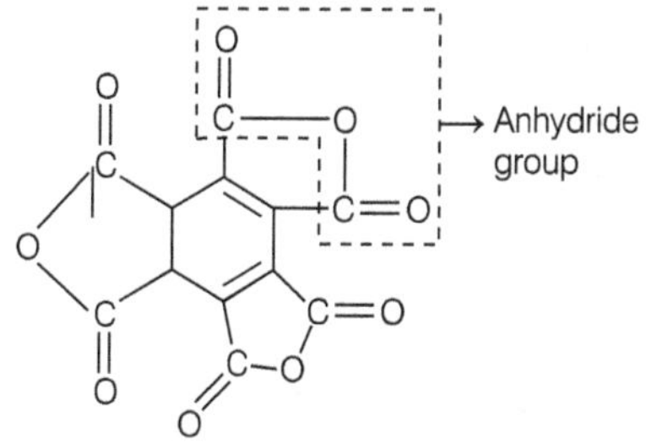

Mellitic anhydride

Thus, the functional group present in a molecule having $C_{12}O_9$ is an anhydride group.

41. (a) When acetic acid reacts with ethanol in the presence of hydrochloric acid then ethyl acetate (ester) is formed which is a sweet smelling compound.

$$\underset{\text{Acetic acid}}{CH_3COOH} + \underset{\text{Ethanol}}{C_2H_5OH} \longrightarrow \underset{\substack{\text{Ethyl acetate} \\ \text{(sweet smelling} \\ \text{compound)}}}{CH_3COOC_2H_5} + H_2O$$

42. (a) The metals that are present below hydrogen in reactivity series will not produce hydrogen gas in reaction with hydrochloric acid. Among the given metals, Cu is present below H in reactivity series, i.e. it is less reactive than H, will not produce H_2 gas in reaction with HCl acid.

43. (b) Isomers of compound with molecular formula $C_4H_{10}O$ are as follows

$$CH_3 CH_2 CH_2 CH_2 OH$$
$$CH_3 CH(OH)CH_2 CH_3$$
$$CH_3 - O - CH_2 CH_2 CH_3$$
$$CH_3 CH_2 OCH_2 CH_3$$
$$CH_3 - O - \underset{\underset{CH_3}{|}}{CH} - CH_3$$

Thus, there are 3 isomeric ethers with molecular formula $C_4H_{10}O$.

44. (c) $\overset{+6}{C}r_2O_7^{2-} + 14H^+ \rightarrow 2Cr^{3+} + 7H_2O$

As in the above reaction, there are net twelve positive charges on the left side and only six positive charges on right side.

Therefore, 6 electrons are required to reduce chromium completely in $Cr_2O_7^{2-}$ to Cr^{3+} in acidic medium

$$Cr_2O_7^{2-}\,(aq) + 14H^+\,(aq) + 6e^- \longrightarrow 2Cr^{3+}\,(aq) + 7H_2O$$

45. *(d)*

Volume of gas at 0°C

$$V_1 = 250 \text{ cm}^3$$

Volume of gas at 300°C

$$V_2 = 500 \text{ cm}^3$$

$$\therefore \quad \frac{V_2}{V_1} = \frac{500}{250} = 2$$

Thus, the volume of the gas at 300°C is larger than that at 0°C by a factor of 2.

46. *(b)* Excess salt inhibits growth in pickles by exosmosis. Salt kills and inhibits the growth of microorganisms by drawing water out of the cells of both the microbe and the food through osmosis (or more specifically exosmosis). Due to hypertonic solution outside the bacterial cell, bacteria will die by plasmolysis.

47. *(a)* Restriction endonuclease is an enzyme that cuts *ds*DNA into fragments at or near specific recognition sites (palindromic sequence) within the molecule known as restriction sites.

These enzymes are found in bacteria and archaea and provide a defence mechanism against invading viruses.

48. *(c)* In duodenum, trypsin enzyme catalyses the hydrolysis of peptide bonds, breaking down proteins into smaller peptides. Amylase hydrolyses starch into maltose inside the mouth. Lipase breaks down dietary fats into fatty acids and glycerol. Maltase hydrolyses maltose into simple sugar glucose.

49. *(b)* Person with blood group AB have both A and B antigen in the membrane of his red blood cell but lacks both antibodies (a, b) in his plasma. Due to this reason, blood group AB is called universal recipient.

50. *(b)* Glycolysis starts with one molecule of glucose and ends with two molecules of pyruvate (pyruvic acid) molecules, a total of four ATP molecules and two molecules of NADH.

51. *(b)* Oxidative phosphorylation is the process in which ATP is formed as a result of the transfer of electrons from NADH or $FADH_2$ (produced during glycolysis from glucose) to molecular oxygen (O_2) by a series of electron carriers. It takes place in the mitochondria in eukaryotes and in cytoplasm in prokaryotes.

52. *(a)* Innate immunity refers to non-specific defence mechanisms that come into play immediately or within hours of an antigen's appearance in the body. These mechanisms include physical barriers such as skin epithelial cells, chemicals in the blood and immune system cells that attack foreign cells in the body.

53. *(d)* Vitamin-K is a cofactor for the enzyme responsible for chemical reactions that maintains blood clotting factors : prothrombin; factor VII, IX, X; and proteins. Thus vitamin-K plays a key role in helping the blood clot thereby preventing excessive bleeding.

54. *(d) Pseudomonas* is denitrifying bacteria. Denitrifying bacteria are microorganisms whose action results in the conversion of nitrates in soil to free atmospheric nitrogen, thus depleting soil fertility and reducing agricultural productivity.

55. *(c)* Annelida shows metameric segmentation. It is the repetition of organs and tissues at intervals along the body of an animal, thus dividing the body into a linear series of similar parts or segments (metameres).

56. *(a)* The widal test is one method used to diagnose enteric fever also known as typhoid fever. Typhoid is caused by *Salmonella typhi* bacteria. Widal test was based on demonstrating the presence of agglutinin (antibody) in the serum of an infected patient, against the 'H' (flagellar) and 'O' (somatic) antigens of *Salmonella typhi*.

57. *(d)* The increase in concentration of harmful chemical substance like pesticides in the body of living organisms at each trophic level of a food chain is called biological magnification. The organism which occurs at the highest trophic level in the food chain will have the maximum concentration of harmful chemicals in its body. Since vulture occupies the top level as it eats the tiger, which eats the goat, which eats the grass in the food chain, it will have the maximum concentration of harmful chemicals in its body.

58. *(c)* Molecular mass of a base = 500 Da

Number of base in a *ds*DNA = 10 BP or 20 bases

Thus, molecular mass of a *ds*DNA with 20 bases = $20 \times 500 = 10\,kDa$

59. *(a)* A carbohydrate (e.g. starch, cellulose or glycogen) is a molecule consisting of a number of sugar molecules bonded together by glycosidic linkages and on hydrolysis give its constituent monosaccharides or oligosaccharides. Cellulose is a polymer of β, D-glucose and glycogen of α, D-glucose. Glucose, fructose and ribose are monosaccharides.

60. *(c)* Onion is a bulb, i.e. it is a modified leaf. A bulb is an underground pyriform-spherical structure that possesses a reduced convex or slightly conical disc-shaped stem and several fleshy scales enclosing a terminal bud. In Onion, the fleshy scales represent leaf bases in the outer part and scale leaves in the central region.

61. *(d)* We have,

A rectangular corner is cut form a rectangular piece of paper.

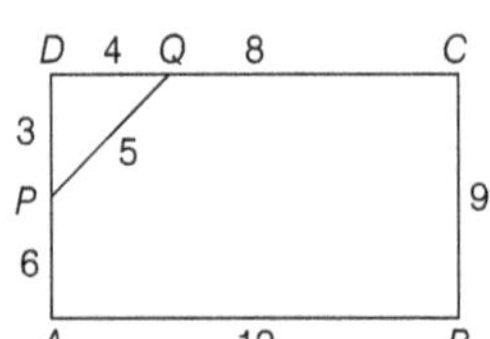

Area of rectangle

$$= 12 \times 9 = 108 \text{ sq units}$$

Area of pentagon

$$= \text{Area of rectangle} - \text{Area of triangle}$$

$$= 108 - 6 = 102$$

$$\therefore \text{ Ratio} = \frac{102}{108} = \frac{17}{18}$$

62. *(d)* We have,

$$[x]\,\{x\} = 5$$

$$x \in [0, 2015]$$

$$\Rightarrow \quad \{x\} = \frac{5}{[x]}$$

$$\{x\} \in [0,1)$$

$$\therefore \quad \frac{5}{[x]} < 1$$

$$[x] > 5$$

$\therefore$ Total number of solution is 2009.

63. *(b)* Given,

$ABCD$ is a trapezium.

AD is parallel to BC

M is point on BC

such that $AB = AM$ and $DC = DM$

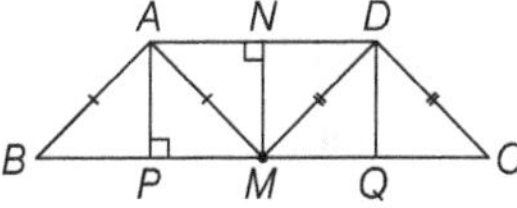

In $\triangle AMD$,

Area of $\triangle AMD$ = Area of $\triangle AMN$

$\qquad\qquad\qquad$ + Area of $\triangle DMN$

Area of $\triangle AMN$ = Area of $\triangle AMP$

$\qquad\qquad\qquad$ = Area of $\triangle ABP$

Area of $\triangle DMN$ = Area of $\triangle DQM$

$\qquad\qquad\qquad$ = Area of $\triangle DQC$

$\therefore$ Area of trapezium $ABCD$

$\qquad$ = Area of $\triangle ABM$ + Area of $\triangle AMD$

$\qquad\qquad\qquad$ + Area of $\triangle MDC$

$\qquad$ = 3 [Area of $\triangle APM$ + Area of $\triangle DMN$)

$\qquad$ = 3 Area of $\triangle AMD$

$\therefore \quad \dfrac{\text{Area of trapezium } ABCD}{\text{Area of } \triangle AMD}$

$\qquad = \dfrac{3\,[\text{Area of } \triangle ADM]}{\text{Area of } \triangle ADM} = \dfrac{3}{1} = 3:1$

64. *(d)* Let h_X, h_Y and h_Z are height of cylindrical bucket of X, Y and Z respectively and r_x, r_y and r_z are radii of bases of cylindrical bucket X, Y and Z respectively.

$\therefore \qquad V_X = \pi r_X^2 \times h_X$

$\qquad\qquad V_Y = \pi r_Y^2 \times h_Y$

$\qquad\qquad V_Z = \pi r_Z^2 \times h_Z$

$\qquad\qquad V_X = \pi h_X \qquad [\because r_x = 1]$

$\qquad\qquad V_Y = 4\pi h_Y \qquad [\because r_y = 2]$

$\qquad\qquad V_Z = 9\pi h_Z \qquad [\because r_z = 3]$

At initial stage $h_X = h_Y = h_Z = h$

$\therefore \quad V_X = \pi h, V_Y = 4\pi h, V_Z = 9\pi h$

At second stage some water transfer Z to X, then volume are equal

$\therefore \quad V_X = V_Z = 5\pi h \quad [\because V_X + V_Y = 10\pi h]$

At third stage some water is transferred between x and y.

$\qquad V_X = V_Y = \dfrac{9\pi h}{2} \quad [\because V_X + V_Y = 9\pi h]$

Volume of water at third stage

$\qquad V_Y = 4\pi h_Y = \dfrac{9}{2}\pi h$

and $V_Z = 9\pi h_Z = 5\pi h$

$\qquad \dfrac{V_Y}{V_Z} = \dfrac{4\pi h_Y}{9\pi h_Z} = \dfrac{\frac{9}{2}\pi h}{5\pi h} = \dfrac{81}{10}$

$\Rightarrow \qquad \dfrac{h_Y}{h_Z} = \dfrac{81}{40}$

65. *(c)* Let the number of people in two villages are x and y respectively.

Given, average income of x people $= P$ and average income of y people $= Q$

$\therefore$ Total income of people in two villages are P_x and Q_y respectively.

One person moves from first village to second village.

Then, number of people in first village $= x - 1$ and second village $= y + 1$

Average income $= P'$ and Q'

$\therefore$ Total income $= P'(x - 1)$ and $Q'(y + 1)$

Total income in both cases are same

$\therefore \quad Px + Qy = P'(x - 1) + Q'(y + 1)$

$\Rightarrow \quad Px - P'(x - 1) = Q'(y + 1) - Qy$

$\Rightarrow \quad x(P - P') + P' = y(Q' - Q) + Q'$

$\therefore \quad P' \neq P$ and $Q' \neq Q$

Hence, option (c) is correct.

66. *(b)* Girl can observe only those light rays which are refracted and leaves the glass slab at angle of 90° or less as shown below.

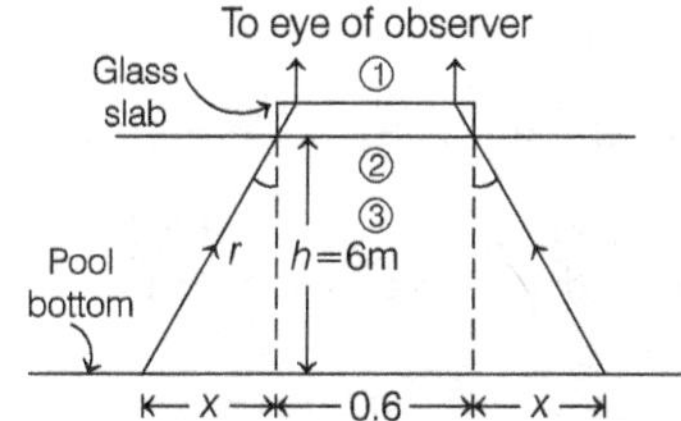

Now, from Snell's law in layer 1 and 3, we have

$\qquad\qquad n_1 \sin i = n_2 \sin r$

$\Rightarrow \qquad 1 \times \sin 90° = \dfrac{4}{3} \times \sin r$

$\qquad\qquad \sin r = \dfrac{3}{4}$

Now, from Pythagoras theorem, we have

$\Rightarrow \qquad \tan r = \dfrac{3}{\sqrt{7}}$

So, from figure, we have

$\qquad\qquad \tan r = \dfrac{x}{h}$

$\Rightarrow \qquad x = h \tan r = \dfrac{6 \times 3}{\sqrt{7}} = 6.8\,\text{m}$

Hence, area of pool visible through glass slab is $A = \dfrac{\pi d^2}{4} = \dfrac{\pi \times (2x + 0.6)^2}{4} \approx 160\,\text{m}^2$

67. *(a)* Let final temperature of mixture is $T\,°\text{C}$. Then,

Heat lost by 2 kg water at 90°C to cool down at $T°$C = Heat gained by 1 kg ice at −20°C to reach at 0°C + Heat gained by 1 kg ice at 0°C to change its state from ice to water + Water 1 kg formed at 0°C is now absorbs heat to reach temperature of $T°$C

$\Rightarrow \qquad m_w s_w \Delta T = m_i s_i (0 - (-20°\,\text{C}))$

$\qquad\qquad\qquad + m_i L + m_i s_w (T - 0)$

$\Rightarrow 2 \times 4.18 \times (90 - T) = 1 \times 2.09 \times 20$

$\qquad\qquad\qquad + 1 \times 334.4 + 1 \times 4.18 \times T$

$\Rightarrow \qquad 752.4 - 376.2 = 3 \times 4.18 \times T$

$\Rightarrow \qquad\qquad T = 30°\text{C}$

So, final temperature of mixture is 30°C.

68. *(a)* Let length of each of rod is l and angle between them is θ.

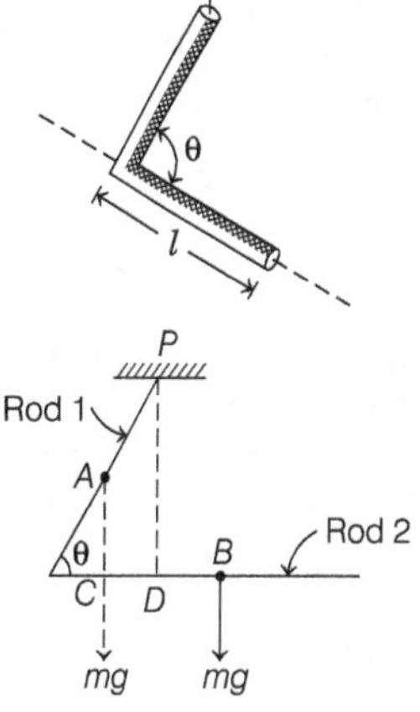

Let the lower rod is horizontal and upper rod makes θ angle with horizontal. Weights of rods acts vertically downwards from their centres A and B as shown in the above figure.

Now, perpendicular distance of weight acting through A from point D is

$$CD = l\cos\theta - \dfrac{l}{2}\cos\theta$$

$$CD = \dfrac{l}{2}\cos\theta$$

and perpendicular distance of weight acting through B from point D is

$$BD = \dfrac{l}{2} - l\cos\theta = \dfrac{l}{2}(1 - 2\cos\theta)$$

At equilibrium torque of these two weights about D must balance each other.

i.e. $\quad mg \times \dfrac{l}{2}\cos\theta = mg \times \dfrac{l}{2}(1 - 2\cos\theta)$

$\Rightarrow \qquad \dfrac{3}{2}\cos\theta = \dfrac{1}{2} \Rightarrow \cos\theta = \dfrac{1}{3}$

or $\qquad\qquad \theta = \cos^{-1}\left(\dfrac{1}{3}\right)$

69. *(a)* From lens equation, we have

$$\dfrac{1}{v} - \dfrac{1}{u} = \dfrac{1}{f}$$

Now, differentiating above equation with respect to time, we get

$$\dfrac{dv}{dt} = \dfrac{v^2}{u^2}\left(\dfrac{du}{dt}\right) \text{ or } \dfrac{dv}{dt} = m^2\left(\dfrac{du}{dt}\right)$$

As, $\dfrac{v}{u}$ = magnification (m)

$\Rightarrow \qquad \Delta v = m^2 \cdot \Delta u \qquad \ldots(i)$

i.e. if object oscillates with an amplitude Δu, then image also oscillates with amplitude Δv given by i.

Also, magnification,

$$m = \dfrac{v}{u} = \left(\dfrac{f}{f + u} \right) \qquad \ldots(ii)$$

Now, in given question,

$$u = -20\,cm, f = 5\,cm$$

So, $\quad m = \dfrac{f}{f + u} = \dfrac{5}{5 - 20} \Rightarrow m = -\dfrac{1}{3}$

From Eq. (i), we have

$$\Delta v = \left(-\dfrac{1}{3} \right)^2 \times \Delta u$$

or $\qquad \Delta v = \dfrac{1}{9} \times A \qquad$ [given, $\Delta u = A$]

As object is placed between ∞ and $2f$ distance, so on moving object near to lens, its image moves away from lens. So, oscillations of object and image are out of phase.

70. *(a)* By Stokes' law,

$$F = 6\pi\eta av$$

We have, $\quad \eta = \dfrac{F}{6\pi av}$

Dimensions of viscosity index η are

$$\Rightarrow \quad [\eta] = \left[\dfrac{MLT^{-2}}{L \cdot LT^{-1}} \right] = [ML^{-1}T^{-1}]$$

Now, given relation of volume flow rate is

$$\dfrac{V}{t} = k \left(\dfrac{p}{l} \right)^a \cdot \eta^b \cdot r^c$$

Substituting dimensions of physical quantities and equating dimensions on both sides of equation, we have

$$\dfrac{[L^3]}{[T]} = [ML^{-2}T^{-2}]^a \cdot [ML^{-1}T^{-1}]^b \cdot [L]^c$$

$$\Rightarrow [M^0 L^3 T^{-1}] = [M^{a+b} L^{-2a-b+c} T^{-2a-b}]$$

Equating dimensions, we have

$$a + b = 0 \qquad \ldots(i)$$
$$-2a - b + c = 3 \qquad \ldots(ii)$$
$$-2a - b = -1 \qquad \ldots(iii)$$

From Eqs. (ii) and (iii), we have

$$c = 4$$

From Eqs. (i) and (iii), we have

$$b = -1$$

Substituting b in Eq. (i), we have

$$a = 1$$

So, $a = 1, b = -1$ and $c = 4$.

71. *(c)* $2Xe + 4F_2 \longrightarrow XeF_2 + XeF_6$

No. of initial moles of Xe $= \dfrac{262}{131} = 2\,mol$

No. of initial moles of $F_2 = \dfrac{152}{38} = 4\,mol$

2 moles of Xe react completely with 4 moles of F_2 to give 1 mol of XeF_2 and 1 mol of XeF_6.

Thus, the molar ratio of $XeF_2 : XeF_6$ is $1 : 1$.

72. *(a)* When ethanol reacts with conc. sulphuric acid at 170°C produces ethene gas which is then treated with bromine in carbon tetrachloride to give 1,2-dibromoethane as a major product.

$$CH_3CH_2OH \xrightarrow[\substack{170°C \\ \text{(Dehydration} \\ \text{of alcohol)}}]{\text{Conc. } H_2SO_4} CH_2 = CH_2$$

Ethanol   Ethene

$$\xrightarrow[Br_2]{\substack{CCl_4 \\ \text{(Addition} \\ \text{reaction)}}}$$

$$\underset{\substack{| \qquad | \\ Br \quad\; Br}}{CH_2 - CH_2}$$

1, 2 dibromoethane (major)

73. *(c)* $C_4H_8(g) + 6O_2(g) \longrightarrow 4CO_2(g)$

At STP   22.4 L   89.6 L

$$+ \underset{72L}{4H_2O(g)}$$

No. of moles of water at STP $= \dfrac{72}{18} = 4\,mol$

1 mole of C_4H_8 burns completely with 6 moles of O_2 to give 4 moles of CO_2 and 4 moles of H_2O.

At STP 1 mole of O_2 contains $= 22.4\,L$

6 moles of O_2 contain $= 22.4 \times 6 = 134.4\,L$

74. *(a)* Given, current, $I = 0.5\,A$

Time, $t = 1hr = 3600\,s$

According to Faraday's IInd law of electrolysis,

$$W = \dfrac{\text{Atomic mass} \times I \times t}{96500}$$

$$= \dfrac{108}{96500} \times 0.5 \times 36000 = 2\,g$$

75. *(a)*

The addition of water to alkenes in the presence of an acid form alcohols which occurs through electrophilic addition mechanism and follows Markownikoff rule.

Hence, option (a) is correct.

76. *(c)* Alu I has the cut site 5'AGCT3' 3'TCGA5'

So, it is evident that wherever there will be the above sequence in the DNA fragment, Alu I will make blunt cuts over there.

Now according to question, if there is random distribution of bases in the genome, the probability of occurrence of the above cut sides will be

$$\dfrac{1}{4 \times 4 \times 4 \times 4} = \dfrac{1}{256} \text{ [since Alu I is a 4 base}$$

pair cutter]

So, the frequency will be $\dfrac{1}{256}$.

77. *(b)* The cooking of rice in open vessels is favoured at low temperatures and higher altitudes due to the atmospheric pressure. When the rice is cooked in the pressure cooker, then the rice will be cooked faster at the sea beach because the temperature is higher and pressure is lower at sea level than higher altitude. This will allow the water to boil faster inside the pressure cooker and the rice will be cooked faster.

78. *(a)* In the absence of disease, natural calamities and predation growth of rabbit is exponential. When resources are unlimited, populations exhibit exponential growth, resulting in a J-shaped curve (i.e. option a).

79. *(c)* Glucose is a monosaccharide and an osmotically active molecule which increases osmotic pressure in cell. So, water enters in cell while glycogen is osmotically inert molecule does not change the osmotic pressure. This is the reason why glucose is not stored in the cell instead glycogen is stored in the animal body.

80. *(a)* There will be four membrane bilayers that the line will cross

1 = Cell membrane

2 = Mitochondrion

1 = Nucleus

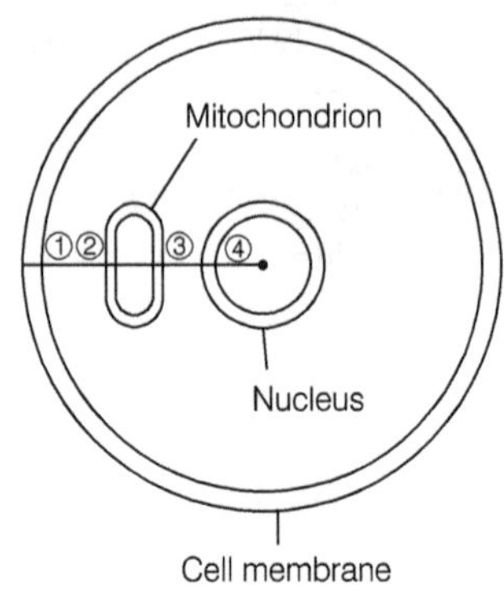

QUESTION PAPER 2014
Stream : SA

MM : 100

Instructions

1. There are 80 questions in this paper.

2. This question paper contains two parts; Part I and Part II. There are four sections; Mathematics, Physics, Chemistry and Biology in each part.

3. Out of the four options given with each question, only one is correct.

➲ PART-I (1 Mark Questions)

MATHEMATICS

1. Let r be a root of the equation $x^2 + 2x + 6 = 0$. The value of $(r + 2)(r + 3)(r + 4)(r + 5)$ is equal to
(a) 51   (b) – 51   (c) – 126   (d) 126

2. Let R be the set of all real numbers and let f be a function from R to R such that
$$f(x) + \left(x + \frac{1}{2}\right) f(1 - x) = 1, \text{ for all } x \in R. \text{ Then}$$
$2f(0) + 3f(1)$ is equal to
(a) 2   (b) 0   (c) – 2   (d) – 4

3. The sum of all positive integers n for which
$$\frac{1^3 + 2^3 + \ldots + (2n)^3}{1^2 + 2^2 + \ldots + n^2} \text{ is also an integers is}$$
(a) 8   (b) 9   (c) 15   (d) Infinite

4. Let x and y be two 2-digit numbers such that y is obtained by reversing the digits of x. Suppose they also satisfy $x^2 - y^2 = m^2$ for some positive integer m. The value of $x + y + m$ is
(a) 88   (b) 112   (c) 144   (d) 154

5. Let $p(x) = x^2 - 5x + a$ and $q(x) = x^2 - 3x + b$, where a and b are positive integers. Suppose HCF $(p(x), q(x)) = x - 1$ and $k(x) = 1 \text{ cm } (p(x), q(x))$ If the coefficient of the highest degree term of $k(x)$ is 1, then sum of the roots of $(x - 1) + k(x)$ is
(a) 4   (b) 5   (c) 6   (d) 7

6. In a quadrilateral $ABCD$, which is not a trapezium, it is known that $\angle DAB = \angle ABC = 60°$. Moreover, $\angle CAB = \angle CBD$. Then,
(a) $AB = BC + CD$ (b) $AB = AD + CD$
(c) $AB = BC + AD$ (d) $AB = AC + AD$

7. A semi-circle of diameter 1 unit sits at the top of a semi-circle of diameter 2 units.

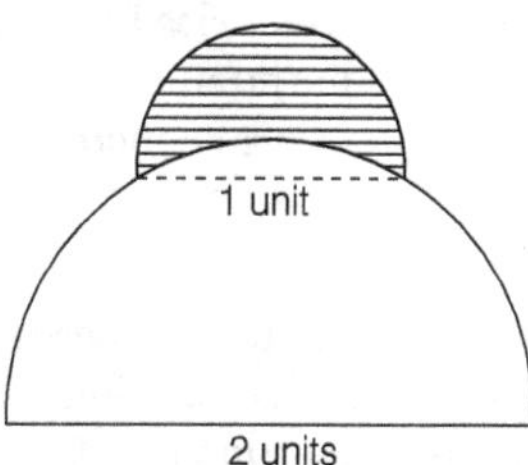

The shaded region inside the smaller semi-circle but outside the larger semi-circle is called a lune. The area of the lune is

(a) $\dfrac{\pi}{6} - \dfrac{\sqrt{3}}{4}$ (b) $\dfrac{\sqrt{3}}{4} - \dfrac{\pi}{24}$ (c) $\dfrac{\sqrt{3}}{4} - \dfrac{\pi}{12}$ (d) $\dfrac{\sqrt{3}}{4} - \dfrac{\pi}{8}$

8. The angle bisectors BD and CE of a $\triangle ABC$ are divided by the incentre I in the ratios $3 : 2$ and $2 : 1$ respectively. Then, the ratio in which I divides the angle bisector through A is

(a) $3 : 1$ (b) $11 : 4$
(c) $6 : 5$ (d) $7 : 4$

9. Suppose S_1 and S_2 are two unequal circles, AB and CD are the direct common tangents to these circles. A transverse common tangent PQ cuts AB in R and CD in S. If $AB = 10$, then RS is

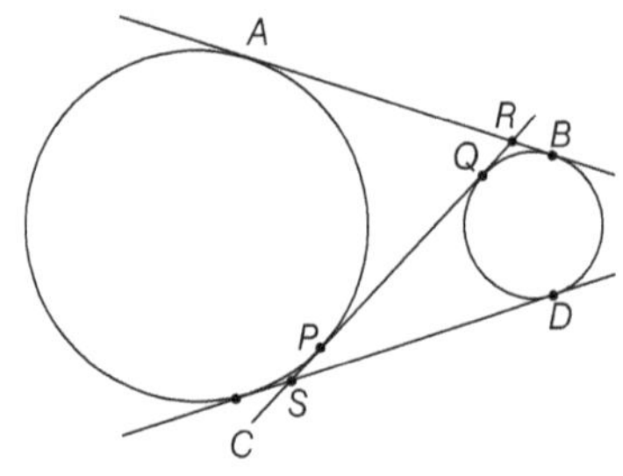

(a) 8   (b) 9   (c) 10   (d) 11

10. On the circle with center O, points A and B are such that $OA = AB$. A point C is located on the tangent at B to the circle such that A and C are on the opposite sides of the line OB and $AB = BC$. The line segment AC intersects the circle again at F. Then, the ratio $\angle BOF : \angle BOC$ is equal to

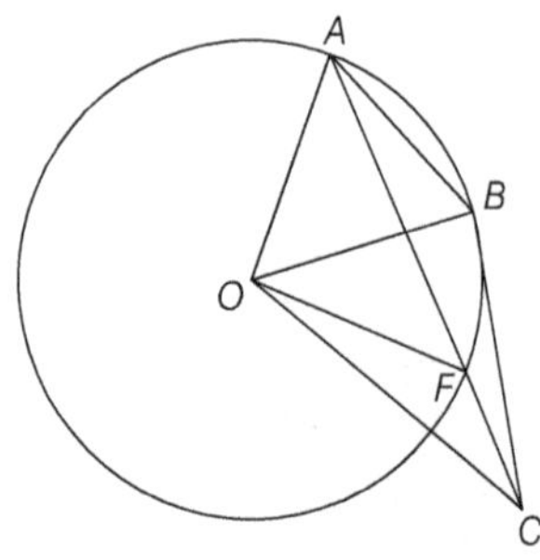

(a) $1 : 2$ (b) $2 : 3$ (c) $3 : 4$ (d) $4 : 5$

11. In a cinema hall, the charge per person is ₹ 200. On the first day, only 60% of the seats were filled. The owner decided to reduce the price by 20% and there was an increase of 50% in the number of spectators on the next day. The percentage increase in the revenue on the second day was

(a) 50   (b) 40   (c) 30   (d) 20

12. The population of cattle in a farm increases so that the difference between the population in year $n + 2$ and that in year n is proportional to the population in year $n + 1$. If the populations in years 2010, 2011 and 2013 were 39, 60 and 123, respectively,then the population in 2012 was

(a) 81   (b) 84   (c) 87   (d) 90

13. The number of 6-digit numbers of the form $ababab$ (in base 10) each of which is a product of exactly 6 distinct primes is

(a) 8   (b) 10   (c) 13   (d) 15

14. The houses on one side of a road are numbered using consecutive even numbers. The sum of the numbers of all the houses in that row is 170. If there are at least 6 houses in that row and a is the number of the sixth house, then

(a) $2 \le a \le 6$ (b) $8 \le a \le 12$
(c) $14 \le a \le 20$ (d) $22 \le a \le 30$

15. Suppose $a_2, a_3, a_4, a_5, a_6, a_7$ are integers such that

$$\frac{5}{7} = \frac{a_2}{2!} + \frac{a_3}{3!} + \frac{a_4}{4!} + \frac{a_5}{5!} + \frac{a_6}{6!} + \frac{a_7}{7!},$$

where $0 \le a_j < j$ for $j = 2, 3, 4, 5, 6, 7$. The sum of $a_2 + a_3 + a_4 + a_5 + a_6 + a_7$ is

(a) 8   (b) 9   (c) 10   (d) 11

PHYSICS

16. In the following displacement x *versus* time t graph, at which among the points P, Q and R is the object's speed increasing?

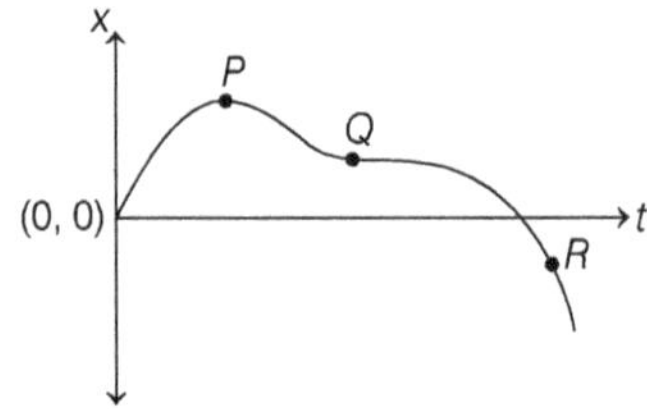

(a) R only   (b) P only
(c) Q and R only   (d) P, Q and R

17. A box when hung from a spring balance shows a reading of 50 kg. If the same box is hung from the same spring balance inside an evacuated chamber, the reading on the scale will be

(a) 50 kg because the mass of the box remains unchanged.
(b) 50 kg because the effect of the absence of the atmosphere will be identical on the box and the spring balance
(c) less than 50 kg because the weight of the column of air on the box will be absent
(d) more than 50 kg because the atmospheric buoyancy force will be absent

18. Two positively charged spheres of masses m_1 and m_2 are suspended from a common point at the ceiling by identical insulating massless strings of length l. Charges on the two spheres are q_1 and q_2, respectively. At equilibrium, both strings make the same angle θ with the vertical. Then

(a) $q_1 m_1 = q_2 m_2$ (b) $m_1 = m_2$
(c) $m_1 = m_2 \sin\theta$ (d) $q_2 m_1 = q_1 m_2$

19. A box when dropped from a certain height reaches the ground with a speed v. When it slides from rest from the same height down a rough inclined plane inclined at an angle 45° to the horizontal, it reaches the ground with a speed $v/3$. The coefficient of sliding friction between the box and the plane is (Take, acceleration due to gravity is 10 ms^{-2})

(a) $\dfrac{8}{9}$ (b) $\dfrac{1}{9}$ (c) $\dfrac{2}{3}$ (d) $\dfrac{1}{3}$

20. A thin paper cup filled with water does not catch fire when placed over a flame. This is because
(a) the water cuts off oxygen supply to the paper cup
(b) water is an excellent conductor of heat
(c) the paper cup does not become appreciably hotter than the water it contains
(d) paper is a poor conductor of heat

21. Ice is used in a cooler in order to cool its contents. Which of the following will speed up the cooling process?
(a) Wrap the ice in a metal foil
(b) Drain the water from the cooler periodically
(c) Put the ice as a single block
(d) Crush the ice

22. The angle of a prism is 60°. When light is incident at an angle of 60° on the prism, the angle of emergence is 40°. The angle of incidence i for which the light ray will deviate the least is such that
(a) $i < 40°$ (b) $40° < i < 50°$
(c) $50° < i < 60°$ (d) $i > 60°$

23. A concave lens made of material of refractive index 1.6 is immersed in a medium of refractive index 2.0. The two surfaces of the concave lens have the same radius of curvature 0.2 m. The lens will behave as a
(a) divergent lens of focal length 0.4 m
(b) divergent lens of focal length 0.5 m
(c) convergent lens of focal length 0.4 m
(d) convergent lens of focal length 0.5 m

24. A charged particle initially at rest at O, when released follows a trajectory as shown alongside. Such a trajectory is possible in the presence of 
(a) electric field of constant magnitude and varying direction
(b) magnetic field of constant magnitude and varying direction
(c) electric field of constant magnitude and constant direction
(d) electric and magnetic fields of constant magnitudes and constant directions which are parallel to each other

25. Two equal charges of magnitude Q each are placed at a distance d apart. Their electrostatic energy is E. A third charge $-Q/2$ is brought midway between these two charges. The electrostatic energy of the system is now
(a) $-2E$ (b) $-E$ (c) 0 (d) E

26. A bar magnet falls with its north pole pointing down through the axis of a copper ring. When viewed from above, the current in the ring will be
(a) clockwise, while the magnet is above the plane of the ring and counter clockwise, while below the plane of the ring
(b) counter clockwise throughout
(c) counter clockwise, while the magnet is above the plane of the ring and clockwise, while below the plane of the ring
(d) clockwise throughout

27. Two identical bar magnets are held perpendicular to each other with a certain separation, as shown below. The area around the magnets is divided into four zones.

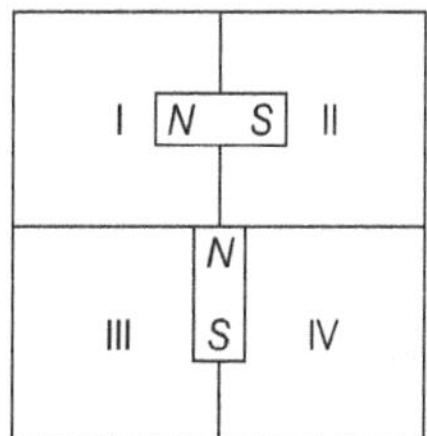

Given that there is a neutral point it is located in
(a) zone I (b) zone II (c) zone III (d) zone IV

28. A large number of random snap shots using a camera are taken of a particle in a simple harmonic motion between $x = -x_0$ and $x = +x_0$ with origin $x = 0$ as the mean position. A histogram of the total number of times the particle is recorded about a given position (Event no.) would most closely resemble.

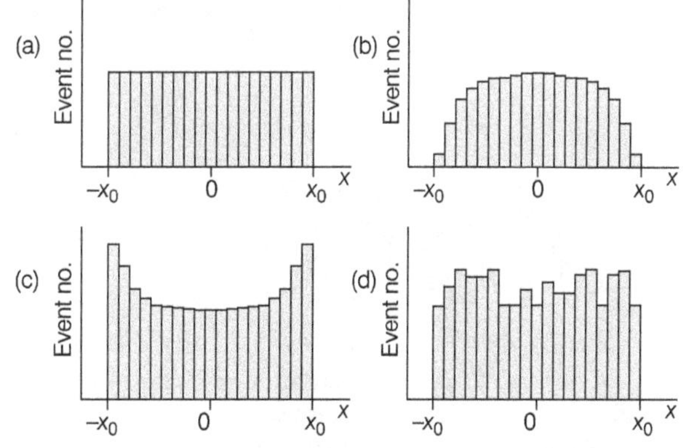

29. In 1911, the physicist Ernest Rutherford discovered that atoms have a tiny, dense nucleus by shooting positively charged particles at a very thin gold foil. A key physical property which led Rutherford to use gold was that it was
(a) electrically conducting (b) highly malleable
(c) shiny (d) non-reactive

30. Consider the following statements:
I. All isotopes of an element have the same number of neutrons.

II. Only one isotope of an element can be stable and non-radioactive.

III. All elements have isotopes.

IV. All isotopes of carbon can form chemical compounds with oxygen-16.

Choose the correct option regarding an isotope.

(a) Statements III and IV are correct

(b) Statements II, III and IV are correct

(c) Statements I, II and III are correct

(d) Statements I, III and IV are correct

CHEMISTRY

31. The isoelectronic pair is

(a) CO, N_2　　(b) O_2, NO　　(c) C_2, HF　　(d) F_2, HCl

32. The numbers of lone pairs and bond pairs in hydrazine are, respectively

(a) 2 and 4　　(b) 2 and 6　　(c) 2 and 5　　(d) 1 and 5

33. The volume of oxygen at STP required to burn 2.4 g of carbon completely is

(a) 1.12 L　　(b) 8.96 L　　(c) 2.24 L　　(d) 4.48 L

34. The species that exhibits the highest R_f value in a thin layer chromatogram using a non-polar solvent on a silica gel plate is

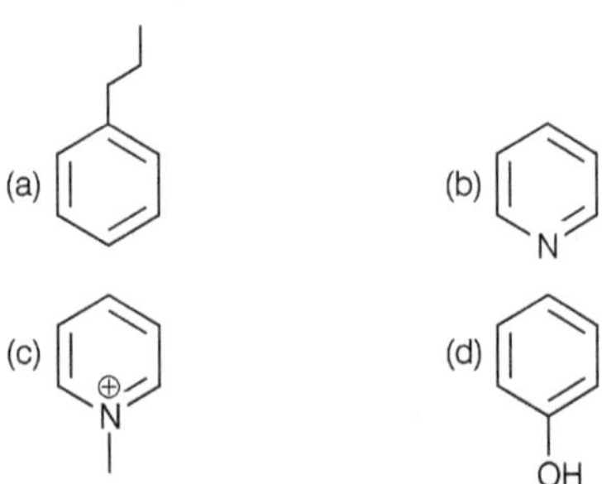

35. The number of C—C sigma bonds in the compound

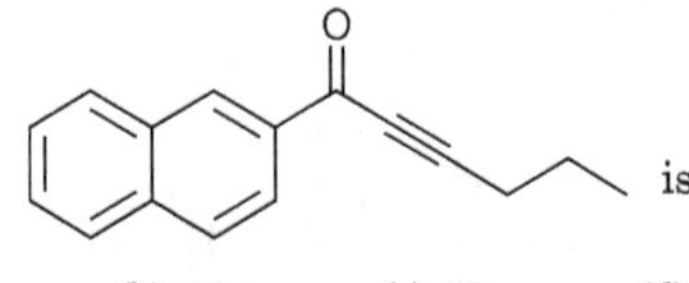

is

(a) 16　　(b) 17　　(c) 18　　(d) 11

36. If the radius of the hydrogen atom is 53 pm, the radius of the He^+ ion is closest to

(a) 108 pm　　(b) 81 pm

(c) 27 pm　　(d) 13 pm

37. The diamagnetic species is

(a) NO　　(b) NO_2　　(c) O_2　　(d) CO_2

38. The pH of 0.1 M aqueous solutions of NaCl, CH_3COONa and NH_4Cl will follow the order

(a) $NaCl < CH_3COONa < NH_4Cl$

(b) $NH_4Cl < NaCl < CH_3COONa$

(c) $NH_4Cl < CH_3COONa < NaCl$

(d) $NaCl < NH_4Cl < CH_3COONa$

39. At room temperature, the average speed of helium is higher than that of oxygen by a factor of

(a) $2\sqrt{2}$　　(b) $6/\sqrt{2}$　　(c) 8　　(d) 6

40. Ammonia is not produced in the reaction of

(a) NH_4Cl with KOH　　(b) AlN with H_2O

(c) NH_4Cl with $NaNO_2$　　(d) NH_4Cl with $Ca(OH)_2$

41. The number of isomers which are ethers and having the molecular formula $C_4H_{10}O$, is

(a) 2　　(b) 3　　(c) 4　　(d) 5

42. The major product of the reaction of 2-butene with alkaline $KMnO_4$ solution is

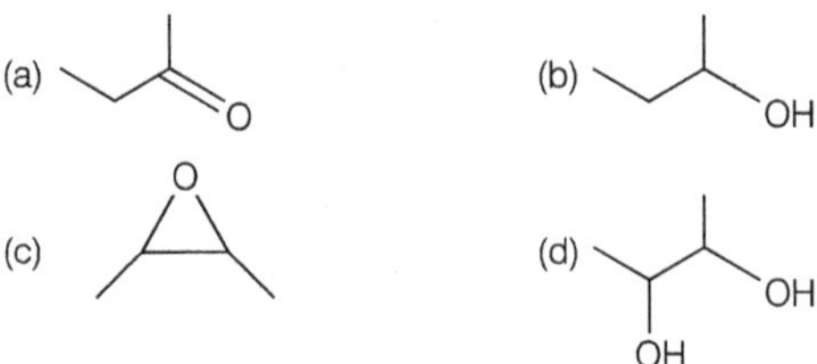

43. Among the compounds I-IV, the compound having the lowest boiling point is

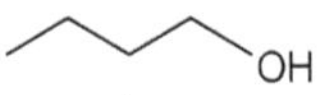

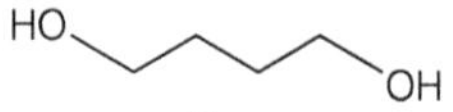

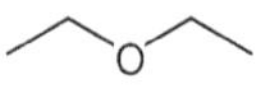

(a) I　　(b) II　　(c) III　　(d) IV

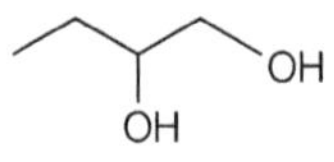

44. Of the following reactions

(i) $A \rightleftharpoons B$, $\Delta G° = 250$ kJ mol^{-1}

(ii) $D \rightleftharpoons E$, $\Delta G° = -100$ kJ mol^{-1}

(iii) $F \rightleftharpoons G$, $\Delta G° = -150$ kJ mol^{-1}

(iv) $M \rightleftharpoons N$, $\Delta G° = 150$ kJ mol^{-1}

The reaction with the largest equilibrium constant is

(a) (i)　　(b) (ii)　　(c) (iii)　　(d) (iv)

45. The first ionisation enthalpies for three elements are 1314, 1680 and 2080 kJ mol^{-1}, respectively. The correct sequence of the elements is

(a) O, F and Ne　　(b) F, O and Ne

(c) Ne, F and O　　(d) F, Ne and O

BIOLOGY

46. Individuals of one kind occupying a particular geographic area at a given time are called

(a) community　　(b) population

(c) species　　(d) biome

47. What fraction of the assimilated energy is used in respiration by the herbivores?

(a) ~ 10 per cent　　(b) ~ 60 per cent

(c) ~ 30 per cent　　(d) ~ 80 per cent

48. Athletes are often trained at high altitude because
(a) training at high altitude increases muscle mass
(b) training at high altitude increases the number of red blood cells
(c) there is less chance of an injury at high altitude
(d) athletes sweat less at high altitude

49. In human brain, two cerebral hemispheres are connected by a bundle of fibres which is known as
(a) medulla oblongata　　(b) cerebrum
(c) cerebellum　　(d) corpus callosum

50. Which one of the following hormones is produced by the pancreas?
(a) Prolactin　　(b) Glucagon
(c) Luteinising hormone　　(d) Epinephrine

51. The stalk of a plant leaf is derived from which one of the following types of plant tissue?
(a) Sclerenchyma　　(b) Parenchyma
(c) Chlorenchyma　　(d) Collenchyma

52. Which of the following muscle types cannot be used voluntarily?
(a) Both striated and smooth
(b) Both cardiac and striated
(c) Both smooth and cardiac
(d) Cardiac, striated and smooth

53. The pulmonary artery carries
(a) deoxygenated blood to the lungs
(b) oxygenated blood to the brain
(c) oxygenated blood to the lungs
(d) deoxygenated blood to the kidney

54. Both gout and kidney stone formation is caused by
(a) calcium oxalate　　(b) uric acid
(c) creatinine　　(d) potassium chloride

55. The auditory nerve gets its input from which of the following?
(a) The sense cells of the cochlea
(b) Vibration of the last ossicle
(c) Eustachian tube
(d) Vibration of the tympanic membrane

56. Which of the following organelles contain circular DNA?
(a) Peroxisomes and mitochondria
(b) Mitochondria and Golgi complex
(c) Chloroplasts and lysosomes
(d) Mitochondria and chloroplast

57. A reflex action does not involve
(a) neurons　　(b) brain
(c) spinal cord　　(d) muscle fibre

58. Which one of the following options is true in photosynthesis?
(a) CO_2 is oxidised and H_2O is reduced
(b) H_2O is oxidised and CO_2 is reduced
(c) Both CO_2 and H_2O are reduced
(d) Both CO_2 and H_2O are oxidised

59. Human mature Red Blood Cells (RBCs) do not contain
(a) iron　　(b) cytoplasm
(c) mitochondria　　(d) haemoglobin

60. A person was saved from poisonous snake bite by anti-venom injection.

Which of the following immunities explains this form of protection?
(a) Naturally acquired active immunity
(b) Artificially acquired active immunity
(c) Naturally acquired passive immunity
(d) Artificially acquired passive immunity

➔ PART-II (2 Marks Questions)

MATHEMATICS

61. Let a, b, c be non-zero real numbers such that $a + b + c = 0$, let $q = a^2 + b^2 + c^2$ and $r = a^4 + b^4 + c^4$. Then,
(a) $q^2 < 2r$ always
(b) $q^2 = 2r$ always
(c) $q^2 > 2r$ always
(d) $q^2 - 2r$ can take both positive and negative values

62. The value of $\sum\limits_{n=0}^{1947} \dfrac{1}{2^n + \sqrt{2^{1947}}}$ is equal to
(a) $\dfrac{487}{\sqrt{2^{1945}}}$　(b) $\dfrac{1946}{\sqrt{2^{1947}}}$　(c) $\dfrac{1947}{\sqrt{2^{1947}}}$　(d) $\dfrac{1948}{\sqrt{2^{1947}}}$

63. The number of integers a in the interval $[1, 2014]$ for which the system of equations $x + y = a$,
$$\dfrac{x^2}{x-1} + \dfrac{y^2}{y-1} = 4$$
has finitely many solutions is

(a) 0　　(b) 1007　　(c) 2013　　(d) 2014

64. In a $\triangle ABC$ with $\angle A = 90°$, P is a point on BC such that $PA : PB = 3 : 4$. If $AB = \sqrt{7}$ and $AC = \sqrt{5}$, then $BP : PC$ is
(a) $2 : 1$　(b) $4 : 3$　(c) $4 : 5$　(d) $8 : 7$

65. The number of all 3-digit numbers abc (in base 10) for which $(a \times b \times c) + (a \times b) +$
$(b \times c) + (c \times a) + a + b + c = 29$ is
(a) 6　　(b) 10　　(c) 14　　(d) 18

PHYSICS

66. A uniform square wooden sheet of side a has its centre of mass located at point O as shown in the figure below on the left. A square portion of side b of this sheet is cut out to produce an L-shaped sheet as shown in the figure on the right.

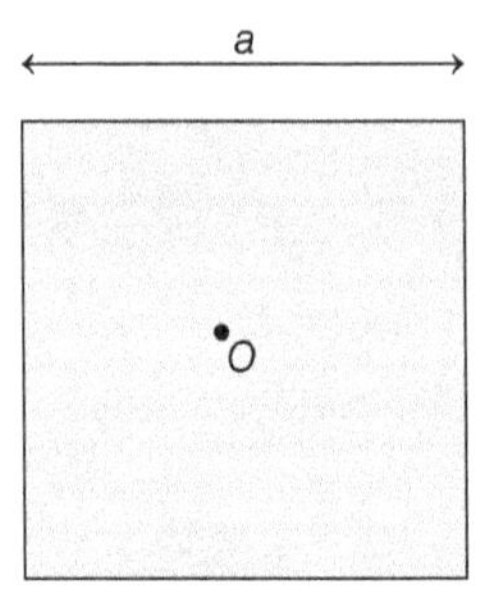 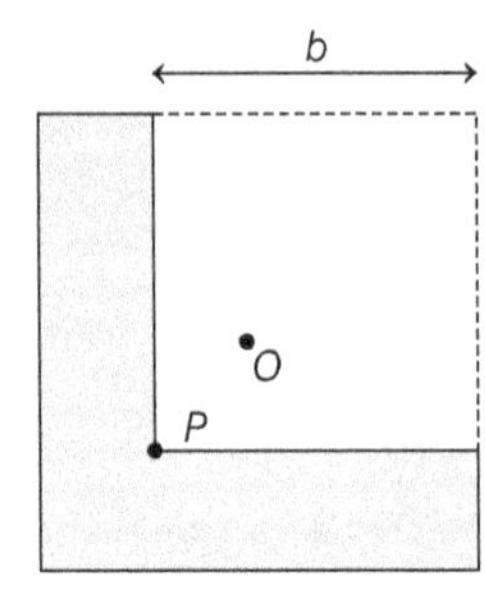

The centre of mass of the L-shaped sheet lies at the point P (in the above diagram), when

(a) $a/b = (\sqrt{5} - 1)/2$ (b) $a/b = (\sqrt{5} + 1)/2$
(c) $a/b = (\sqrt{3} - 1)/2$ (d) $a/b = (\sqrt{3} + 1)/2$

67. A machine is blowing spherical soap bubbles of different radii filled with helium gas. It is found that, if the bubbles have a radius smaller than 1 cm, then they sink to the floor in still air. Larger bubbles float in the air. Assume that the thickness of the soap film in all bubbles is uniform and equal. Assume that the density of soap solution is same as that of water ($= 1000$ kg m^{-3}). The density of helium inside the bubbles and air are 0.18 kg m^{-3} and 1.23 kg m^{-3}, respectively. Then, the thickness of the soap film of the bubbles is (**Note** $1\,\mu m = 10^{-6}$ m)

(a) $0.50\,\mu m$ (b) $1.50\,\mu m$
(c) $7.00\,\mu m$ (d) $3.50\,\mu m$

68. An aluminium piece of mass 50 g initially at 300°C is dipped quickly and taken out of 1 kg of water, initially at 30°C. If the temperature of the aluminium piece immediately after being taken out of the water is found to be 160°C, what is the temperature of the water? Then, specific heat capacities of aluminium and water are 900 Jkg^{-1}K^{-1} and 4200 Jkg^{-1}K^{-1}, respectively.

(a) 165°C (b) 45°C (c) 31.5°C (d) 28.5°C

69. A ray of light incident parallel to the base PQ of an isosceles right-angled triangular prism PQR suffers two successive total internal reflections at the faces PQ and QR before emerging reversed in direction as shown below.

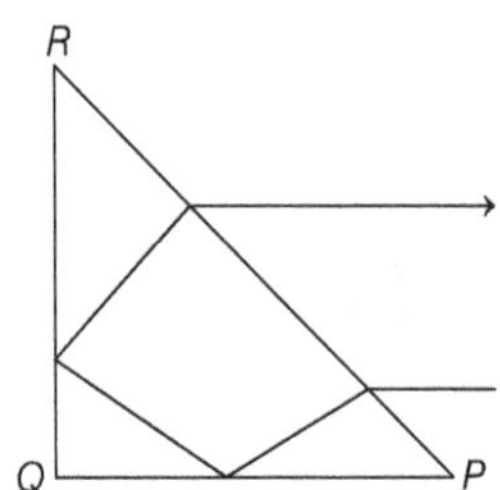

If the refractive index of the material of the prism is μ, then

(a) $\mu > \sqrt{5}$ (b) $\sqrt{3} < \mu < \sqrt{5}$
(c) $\sqrt{2} < \mu < \sqrt{3}$ (d) $\mu < \sqrt{2}$

70. Consider the circuit shown below where all resistors are 1 kΩ.

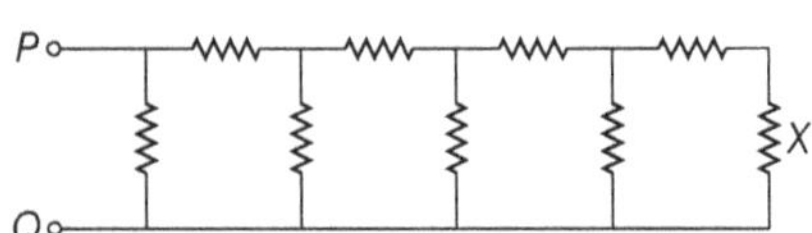

If a current of magnitude 1 mA flows through the resistor marked X, what is the potential difference measured between points P and Q?

(a) 21 V (b) 68 V
(c) 55 V (d) 34 V

CHEMISTRY

71. 10 moles of a mixture of hydrogen and oxygen gases at a pressure of 1 atm at constant volume and temperature, react to form 3.6 g of liquid water. The pressure of the resulting mixture will be closest to

(a) 1.07 atm (b) 0.97 atm
(c) 1.02 atm (d) 0.92 atm

72. The ammonia evolved from 2 g of a compound in Kjeldahl's estimation of nitrogen neutralises 10 mL of 2 M H_2SO_4 solution. The weight percentage of nitrogen in the compound is

(a) 28 (b) 14
(c) 56 (d) 7

73. Complete reaction of 2.0 g of calcium (at. wt. = 40) with excess HCl produces 1.125 L of H_2 gas. Complete reaction of the same quantity of another metal M with excess HCl produces 1.85 L of H_2 gas under identical conditions. The equivalent weight of M is closest to

(a) 23 (b) 9
(c) 7 (d) 12

74. A compound X formed after heating coke with lime reacts with water to give Y which on passing over red-hot iron at 873 K produces Z. The compound Z is

(a) 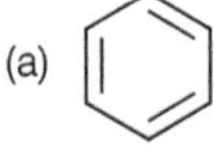 (b)

(c) (d)

75. In the following reaction sequence,

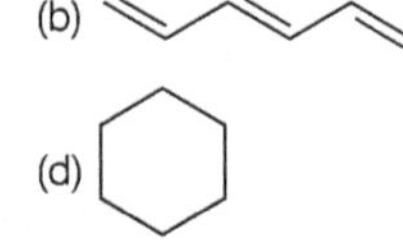

X and Y respectively are,

(a) $Ph-C\equiv C-H$ and [structure: acetophenone with NO_2 substituent]

(b) [structure: Ph-CH(OH)-CH$_2$-NH$_2$] and [structure: aryl ketone with NH_2 and NO_2]

(c) [structure: Ph-CH(NH$_2$)-CH$_2$-OH] and [structure: H_2N-CO-aryl with NO_2]

(d) [structure: Ph-CH(OH)-CH$_2$-NH$_2$] and [structure: aldehyde with NO_2]

BIOLOGY

76. In which of the following cellular compartments do respiratory reactions occur?
(a) Cytoplasm and endoplasmic reticulum
(b) Mitochondria and Golgi complex
(c) Mitochondria and cytoplasm
(d) Only mitochondria

77. A woman heterozygous for colourblindness marries a colourblind man. What would be the ratios of carrier daughters, colourblind daughters, normal sons and colourblind sons in the F_1-generation?
(a) $1:2:2:1$
(b) $2:1:1:2$
(c) $1:1:1:1$
(d) $1:1:2:2$

78. Two semipermeable bags containing 2% sucrose are placed in two beakers, 'P' containing water and 'Q' containing 10% sucrose. Which one of the following outcomes is true?
(a) Bag in 'P' becomes flaccid due to exosmosis
(b) Bag in 'P' becomes turgid due to endosmosis
(c) Bag in 'Q' becomes turgid due to endosmosis
(d) Concentration of sucrose remains unchanged in both

79. Children suffering from phenylketonuria are given food low in phenylalanine and supplemented with tyrosine. This is because they
(a) are unable to utilise phenylalanine
(b) do not require phenylalanine
(c) have increased tyrosine anabolism
(d) have increased tyrosine catabolism

80. Two bottles were half-filled with water from Ganga ('P') and Kaveri ('Q') and kept under identical airtight conditions for 5 days. The oxygen was determined to be 2% in bottle ('P') and 10% in bottle ('Q'). What could be the cause of this difference?
(a) Ganga is more polluted than Kaveri
(b) Both the rivers are equally polluted
(c) Kaveri is more polluted than Ganga
(d) Kaveri has more minerals than Ganga

Answers

PART-I

1	(c)	2	(c)	3	(a)	4	(d)	5	(d)	6	(c)	7	(b)	8	(b)	9	(c)	10	(b)
11	(d)	12	(b)	13	(c)	14	(c)	15	(b)	16	(a)	17	(d)	18	(b)	19	(a)	20	(c)
21	(d)	22	(b)	23	(d)	24	(a)	25	(b)	26	(c)	27	(a)	28	(c)	29	(b)	30	(a)
31	(a,d)	32	(c)	33	(d)	34	(a)	35	(b)	36	(c)	37	(d)	38	(b)	39	(a)	40	(c)
41	(b)	42	(d)	43	(c)	44	(c)	45	(a)	46	(b)	47	(c)	48	(b)	49	(d)	50	(b)
51	(d)	52	(c)	53	(a)	54	(b)	55	(a)	56	(d)	57	(b)	58	(b)	59	(c)	60	(d)

PART-II

61	(b)	62	(a)	63	(d)	64	(a)	65	(d)	66	(b)	67	(d)	68	(c)	69	(a)	70	(d)
71	(b)	72	(a)	73	(d)	74	(a)	75	(a)	76	(c)	77	(c)	78	(b)	79	(a)	80	(a)

Solutions

1. *(c)* We have, r be root of the equation
$$x^2 + 2x + 6 = 0$$
$$\because \quad r^2 + 2r + 6 = 0$$
$$r^2 = -(2r + 6)$$
Now, $(r + 2)(r + 3)(r + 4)(r + 5)$
$$= (r^2 + 5r + 6)(r^2 + 9r + 20)$$
$$= (-2r - 6 + 5r + 6)(-2r - 6 + 9r + 20)$$
$$= (3r)(7r + 14) = 21(r^2 + 2r)$$
$$= 21 \times (-6) \qquad [\because r^2 + 2r = -6]$$
$$= -126$$

2. *(c)* Given,
$$\Rightarrow f(x) + \left(x + \frac{1}{2}\right) f(1-x) = 1 \qquad \text{... (i)}$$
Put $x = 1 - x$, we get
$$f(1-x) + \left(1 - x + \frac{1}{2}\right) f(1 - (1-x)) = 1$$
$$\Rightarrow f(1-x) + \left(\frac{3}{2} - x\right) f(x) = 1 \qquad \text{...(ii)}$$
Eq. (ii) multiply by $\left(x + \frac{1}{2}\right)$, we get
$$\left(\frac{3}{2} - x\right)\left(x + \frac{1}{2}\right) f(x) + \left(x + \frac{1}{2}\right)$$
$$f(1-x) = x + \frac{1}{2} \qquad \text{...(iii)}$$
On subtracting Eq. (iii) from Eq. (i), we get
$$f(x)\left[1 - \left(\frac{3}{4} + x - x^2\right)\right] = 1 - x - \frac{1}{2}$$
$$\Rightarrow f(x) = \frac{\frac{1}{2} - x}{x^2 - x + \frac{1}{4}} \Rightarrow f(0) = 2 \text{ and } f(1) = -2$$
$$\because 2f(0) + 3f(1) - 2(2) + 3(-2) = 4 - 6 = -2$$

3. *(a)* Given, $\dfrac{1^3 + 2^3 + 3^3 + ... + (2n)^3}{1^2 + 2^2 + 3^2 + ... + n^2}$
$$= \frac{\dfrac{(2n)^2(2n+1)^2}{4}}{\dfrac{n(n+1)(2n+1)}{6}} \quad \left[\begin{array}{l} \because \Sigma n^3 = \dfrac{n^2(n+1)^2}{4} \\ \Sigma n^2 = \dfrac{n(n+1)(2n+1)}{6} \end{array}\right]$$
$$= \frac{\dfrac{4n^2(2n+1)^2}{4}}{\dfrac{n(n+1)(2n+1)}{6}} = \frac{6n(2n+1)}{n+1}$$
$$= \frac{12n^2 + 6n}{n+1} = (12n - 6) + \frac{6}{n+1}$$
$\because \dfrac{6}{n+1}$ is an integer if $n + 1$ is factor of 6.
$$\because n + 1 = 1, 2, 3, 6 \Rightarrow n = 1, 2, 5$$
Sum of $n = 1 + 2 + 5 = 8$

4. *(d)* We have,
x and y be two-digit numbers.
Let $x = 10a + b$, where b is units place and a is ten's place.
$$\because \qquad y = 10b + a$$
$$x^2 - y^2 = m^2$$
$$\because \quad (10a + b)^2 - (10b + a)^2 = m^2$$
$$\Rightarrow (10a + b + 10b + a)$$
$$(10a + b - 10b - a) = m^2$$
$$\Rightarrow \quad 11(a + b) \cdot 9(a - b) = m^2$$
$$\Rightarrow \qquad 99(a^2 - b^2) = m^2$$
$$\Rightarrow \qquad 3^2 \times 11(a^2 - b^2) = m^2$$
Now, $3^2 \times 11(a^2 - b^2)$ is a perfect square.
$\because a^2 - b^2 = 11 \Rightarrow (a + b)(a - b) = 11 \times 1$
$$a + b = 11 \text{ and } a - b = 11$$
On solving, we get $a = 6, b = 5$
$\because$ Number $x = 60 + 5 = 65$
$$y = 56$$
and $m^2 = (65)^2 - (56)^2 = (65 + 56)(65 - 56)$
$$\Rightarrow \quad m^2 = 121 \times 9 \Rightarrow m = 33$$
$$\because \quad x + y + m = 65 + 56 + 33 = 154$$

5. *(d)* We have,
$p(x) = x^2 - 5x + a$ and $q(x) = x^2 - 3x + b$
Given, $(x - 1)$ is HCF of $p(x)$ and $q(x)$.
$$\because p(1) = 0 \text{ and } q(1) = 0$$
$$\because p(1) = 0 = 1 - 5 + a \text{ and } q(1) = 0 = 1 - 3 + b$$
$$\Rightarrow \quad a = 4 \text{ and } b = 2$$
$\because p(x) = x^2 - 5x + 4$ and $q(x) = x^2 - 3x + 2$
$$\Rightarrow \quad p(x) = (x - 1)(x - 4)$$
and $q(x) = (x - 1)(x - 2)$
LCM of $p(x)$ and $q(x) = k(x)$
$$\because \quad k(x) = \frac{p(x) \cdot q(x)}{\text{HCF of } p(x) \text{ and } q(x)}$$
$$k(x) = \frac{(x-1)(x-4) \cdot (x-1)(x-2)}{x-1}$$
$$k(x) = (x-1)(x-2)(x-4)$$
Now, $x - 1 + k(x)$
$$= x - 1 + (x - 1)(x - 2)(x - 4)$$
$$= (x - 1)(1 + x^2 - 6x + 8)$$
$$= (x - 1)(x - 3)(x - 3)$$
$\because$ Roots of $x - 1 + k(x)$ are 1, 3, 3.
Sum of roots are $1 + 3 + 3 = 7$

6. *(c)* $ABCD$ is a quadrilateral
$$\angle DAB = \angle ABC = 60°$$
and $\qquad \angle CAB = \angle CBD$
Construction, AD and BC produced to meet at such that
$\triangle AEB$ is an equilateral.

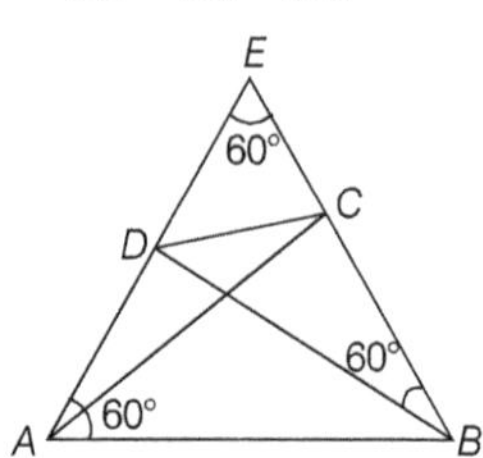

$$\because \qquad AB = BE = AE$$

In $\triangle BDE$ and $\triangle ABC$,
$$\angle BED = \angle ABC$$
$$\Rightarrow \qquad \angle DBE = \angle CAB \text{ given,}$$
$$[\because \angle DBE = \angle DBC]$$
$$\because \qquad \triangle BED \sim \triangle ABC$$
$$\because \quad \frac{BE}{AB} = \frac{BD}{AC} = \frac{ED}{BC} \Rightarrow \frac{BE}{AB} = \frac{ED}{BC}$$
$$\Rightarrow \qquad \frac{AB}{AB} = \frac{AE - AD}{BC}$$
$$\Rightarrow \quad AE - AD = BC \Rightarrow AB = AD + BC$$

7. *(b)* Area of lune = Area of semi-circle $ACBD$ – Area of segment $AEBA$

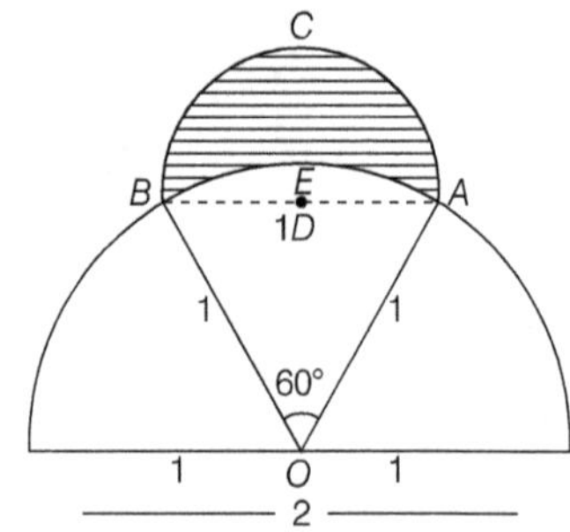

$$= \frac{1}{2}\pi\left(\frac{1}{2}\right)^2 - \left[\frac{60°}{360} \times \pi \times (1)^2 - \frac{\sqrt{3}}{4}(1)^2\right]$$
$$= \frac{\pi}{8} - \left[\frac{\pi}{6} - \frac{\sqrt{3}}{4}\right] = \frac{\pi}{8} - \frac{\pi}{6} + \frac{\sqrt{3}}{4} = \frac{\sqrt{3}}{4} - \frac{\pi}{24}$$

8. *(b)* Given,
In $\triangle ABC$

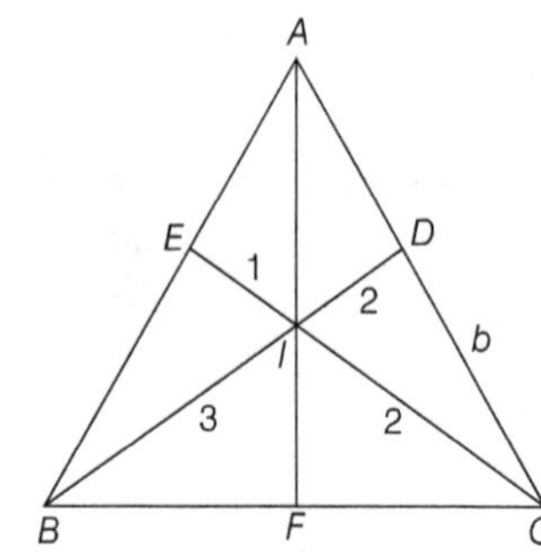

The angle bisector BD and CE are divided by incentre I in the ratio $3 : 2$ and $2 : 1$ respectively.

$\because$ $\qquad \dfrac{BI}{ID} = \dfrac{3}{2}$

and $\qquad \dfrac{CI}{IC} = \dfrac{2}{1}$

We know, $\dfrac{AI}{IF} = \dfrac{b + c}{a}, \dfrac{BI}{ID} = \dfrac{a + c}{b},$

$\qquad \dfrac{CI}{IE} = \dfrac{a + b}{c}$

$\because$ $\dfrac{BI}{ID} = \dfrac{a + c}{b} = \dfrac{3}{2} \Rightarrow 2(a + c) = 3b$ ...(i)

and $\dfrac{CI}{IE} = \dfrac{a + b}{c} = \dfrac{2}{1} \Rightarrow a + b = 2c$ ...(ii)

On solving Eqs. (i) and (ii), we get

$$b = \dfrac{3}{2}a \text{ and } c = \dfrac{5}{4}a$$

$\because$ $\dfrac{AI}{IF} = \dfrac{b + c}{a} = \dfrac{\dfrac{3}{2}a + \dfrac{5}{4}a}{a} = \dfrac{11}{4}$

Hence, ratio = 11 : 4.

9. *(c)* Given,

AB and CD are direct common tangents on circle PQ is transverse common tangent PQ cuts AB in R and CD in S.

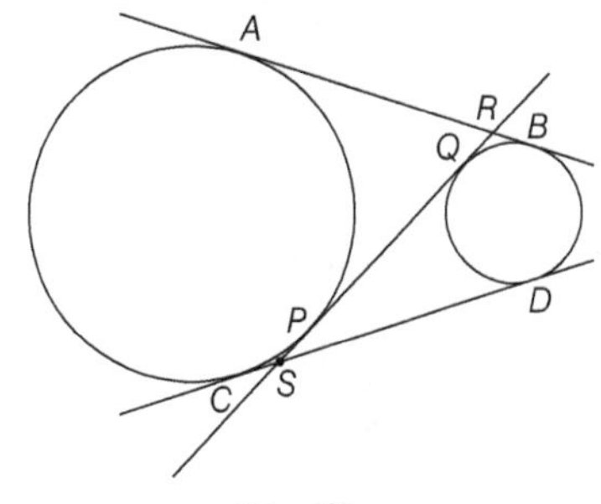

$$AB = 10$$
$$RP = RA$$

[$\because$ tangents from external point on a circle are equal]

Similarly

$$RQ = RB$$
$$SP = SC$$
$$RS = SP + PQ + RQ$$
$$RS = SP + RP$$
$$RS = SP + RA$$
$$RS = SP + AB - RB \quad \text{...(i)}$$

Also, $\qquad SQ = SD$

$$RS - QR = CD - CS$$
$$RS = QR + CD - CS$$
$$RS = RB + AB - SP \quad \text{...(ii)}$$

From Eqs. (i) and (ii), we get

$$SP = RB$$

$\because$ $\qquad RS = SP + AB - RB$

$$RS = AB = 10$$

10. *(b)* Given,

$OA = OB = OF$ radii of circle

BC is tangent on circle at B

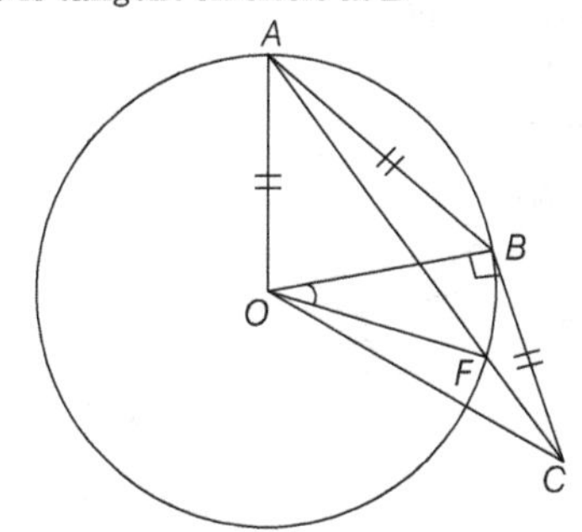

$$AB = BC$$
$$OA = AB$$

In $\triangle AOB$,

$$AO = OB = AB$$

$\because$ $\qquad \angle ABO = 60°$

[$\because ABC$ is an equilateral triangle]

In $\triangle ABC$,

$$AB = BC$$

$\because$ $\qquad \angle BAC = \angle BCA$

$\Rightarrow \angle BAC + \angle BCA + \angle ABC = 180°$

$\Rightarrow \qquad 2\angle BAC = 180° - 90° - 60°$

$\Rightarrow \qquad \angle BAC = 15°$

In $\triangle OBC$, $\qquad OB = OC$

$\because$ $\qquad \angle BOC = \angle BCO = 45°$

$\Rightarrow \qquad \angle BOF = 2\angle BAF$

[$\because$ angle subtend on centre of circle is twice the angle subtend an arc of circle]

$$\angle BOF = 30°$$

$\because$ $\qquad \dfrac{\angle BOF}{\angle BOC} = \dfrac{30°}{45°} = \dfrac{2}{3}$

11. *(d)* Let total seats = x

Ticket price of each seat = ₹ 200

On first day 60% of seats over filled

$\because$ Total revenue $= \dfrac{60}{100}x \times 200 = 120x$

On second day

Ticket price = 200 − 20% of 200 = 160

Total seat filled on 2nd day

$$= \dfrac{60}{100}x + \dfrac{50}{100} \times \dfrac{60x}{100} = \dfrac{90x}{100}$$

Total revenue on 2nd day

$$= \dfrac{90x}{100} \times 160 = 144x$$

Percentage increase in revenue on 2nd day

$$= \left(\dfrac{144x - 120x}{120x}\right) \times 100$$

$$= \dfrac{24}{120} \times 100 = 20\%$$

12. *(b)* Given,

Population in year 2010, 2011 and 2013 were 39, 60 and 123 respectively.

According to problems,

The population of cattle in farm increases such that difference between in year $n + 2$ and that in year n is proportional to the year $n + 1$.

$\because$ $\qquad (n + 2) - (n) = k \, (n + 1)$

$\because$ Let population in year 2012 = x

Year	Population
2010	39
2011	60
2012	x
2013	123

$\because$ $\qquad \dfrac{x - 39}{60} = k$ ... (i)

and $\qquad \dfrac{123 - 60}{x} = k$ ... (ii)

From Eqs. (i) and (ii), we get

$$\dfrac{x - 39}{60} = \dfrac{123 - 60}{x}$$

$\Rightarrow \qquad x^2 - 39x - 3780 = 0$

$\Rightarrow \qquad (x - 84)(x + 40) = 0$

$\therefore \qquad x = 84$

13. *(c)* We have,

6-digits number are $ababab$.

$\because ababab = 10^5 a + 10^4 b + 10^3 a + 10^2 b + 10a + b$

$$= (10^5 + 10^3 + 10)a + (10^4 + 10^2 + 1)b$$
$$= (10^4 + 10^2 + 1)(10a + b)$$
$$= (10000 + 100 + 1)(10a + b)$$
$$= (10101)(10a + b)$$
$$= 3 \times 7 \times 13 \times 37 (10a + b)$$

Since, 6-digit number are product of exactly 6 primes.

$\because 10a + b$ is product of 2 primes,

$10a + b$ is lie between 10 to 99.

$\because \qquad 10a + b = 10 = 2 \times 5$
$$22 = 2 \times 11$$
$$34 = 2 \times 17$$
$$38 = 2 \times 19$$
$$46 = 2 \times 23$$
$$55 = 5 \times 11$$
$$58 = 2 \times 29$$
$$62 = 2 \times 31$$
$$74 = 2 \times 37$$
$$82 = 2 \times 41$$
$$85 = 5 \times 17$$
$$94 = 2 \times 47$$
$$95 = 5 \times 19$$

$\because$ 13, 6-digits number.

14. *(c)* Let the number of houses be
$x, x + 2, x + 4, x + 6, x + 8, x + 10, ...$
6th number of house is a.

$\because$ $x + 10 = a \Rightarrow x = a - 10$

$\therefore$ $x > 10$

Now, $S_n = \dfrac{n}{2}(2x + (n-1)2)$

$S_n = n(x + n - 1)$

$\Rightarrow$ $170 = n(a - 10 + n - 1)$

$\Rightarrow n^2 + (a - 11)n - 170 = 0$

$\Rightarrow$ $n = -\dfrac{(a-11) \pm \sqrt{(a-11)^2 + 680}}{2}$

$\Rightarrow$ $n = \dfrac{(11-a) \pm \sqrt{(a-11)^2 + 680}}{2}$

$n \geq 6$

$\therefore$ $\dfrac{(11-a) \pm \sqrt{(a-11)^2 + 680}}{2} \geq 6$

$\Rightarrow$ $a \leq \dfrac{800}{24} \leq 33.33$

$\because$ $12 \leq a \leq 32$

$a = 12, 14, 16, 18, ...$

When, $a = 18, n = 10$, then $S_n = 170$

$\because$ $a = 18$

15. *(b)* We have,
$a_2, a_3, a_4, a_5, a_6, a_7$ are integers.

$\dfrac{5}{7} = \dfrac{a_2}{2!} + \dfrac{a_3}{3!} + \dfrac{a_4}{4!} + \dfrac{a_5}{5!} + \dfrac{a_6}{6!} + \dfrac{a_7}{7!}$

and $0 \leq a_j < j$

$\dfrac{5}{7} = \dfrac{2520a_2 + 840a_3 + 210a_4 + 42a_5 + 7a_6 + a_7}{7!}$

$\Rightarrow 3600 = 2520a_2 + 840a_3 + 210a_4$
$\qquad\qquad\qquad + 42a_5 + 7a_6 + a_7$

$\qquad 0 \leq a_j < j$

$\because$ $a_2 = 1$

$a_3 \in \{1, 2\}$

If $a_3 = 2$, then $2520 + (840) \times 2 > 3600$

$\because a_3$ must be 1

$a_4 \in \{1, 2, 3\}$

If $a_4 = 2$, then $2520 + 840 + 210(2) > 3600$

$\because a_4$ must be 1

$\because$ $3600 = 2520 + 840 + 210 + 42a_5$
$\qquad\qquad\qquad\qquad + 7a_6 + a_7$

$\Rightarrow$ $30 = 42a_5 + 7a_6 + a_7$

$a_5 \in \{1, 2, 3, 4\}$

If $a_5 = 1$

$30 < 42 + 7a_6 + a_7$

$\because$ $a_5 = 0$

Put $a_5 = 0$, then $30 = 7a_6 + a_7$

$\because a_6 = 4$ and $a_7 = 2$

$\because a_2 + a_3 + a_4 + a_5 + a_6 + a_7$
$\qquad\qquad = 1 + 1 + 1 + 0 + 4 + 2 = 9$

16. *(a)* In given displacement-time graph, velocity at a particular point is given by the slope of tangent to curve drawn at that point.

Speed is the magnitude of velocity, so magnitude of slope gives speed.

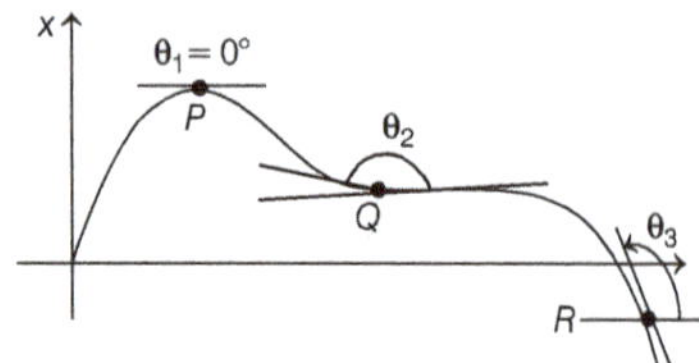

As angle of tangent at $R(\theta_3)$ is maximum, so slope's magnitude $|m| = |\tan\theta_3|$ is maximum at R. Hence, speed is increasing at point R.

17. *(d)* In an evacuated chamber, buoyant force of air is absent, so reading of spring balance is more than 50 kg.

18. *(b)* In given situation, forces on each of charged sphere are

(i) gravitational pull (mg)

(ii) electrostatic repulsion $\left(\dfrac{kq_1q_2}{r^2}\right)$

(iii) tension of string (T)

as shown below.

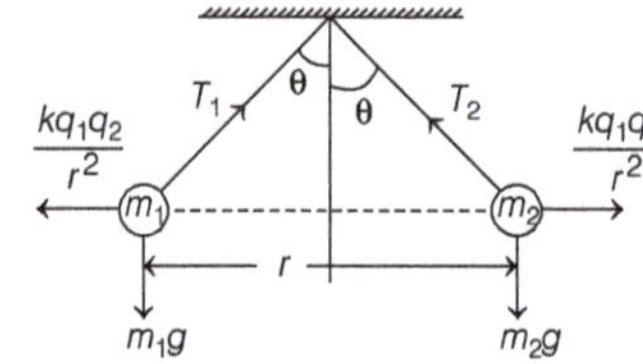

If we resolve tension in horizontal and vertical directions, we have following situation in equilibrium.

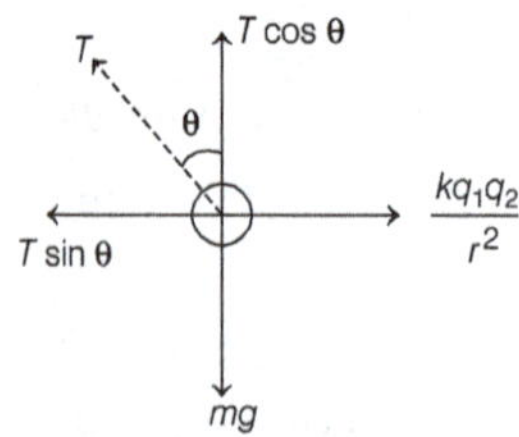

So, $T \sin\theta = \dfrac{kq_1q_2}{r^2}$ and $T \cos\theta = mg$

$\Rightarrow$ $\tan\theta = \dfrac{kq_1q_2}{r^2 \cdot mg}$

As angle θ is same for both spheres, we have

$\tan\theta_1 = \tan\theta_2$

or $\dfrac{kq_1q_2}{r^2 m_1 g} = \dfrac{kq_1q_2}{r^2 m_2 g}$

$\Rightarrow$ $m_1 = m_2$

19. *(a)* When box is dropped from height h, its speed when it reaches the ground is
$$v = \sqrt{2gh}$$

When block slides down the inclined plane $\theta = 45°$,

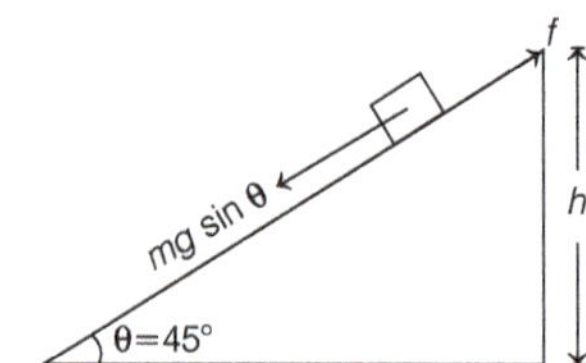

Net downward acceleration of block is
$$a = \dfrac{mg \sin\theta - f}{m}$$

where, f = friction force.

$\Rightarrow$ $a = \dfrac{mg \sin\theta - \mu mg \cos\theta}{m}$

$= g(\sin\theta - \mu \cos\theta)$

$= \dfrac{g}{\sqrt{2}}(1 - \mu)$

$\left[\because \sin\theta = \cos\theta = \dfrac{1}{\sqrt{2}}, \text{ when } \theta = 45°\right]$

Velocity of block when it reaches bottom of inclined plane is
$$v' = \sqrt{2as}$$

where, s = slope length of inclined plane.

$\Rightarrow$ $v' = \sqrt{2ah / \sin\theta}$

$= \sqrt{\left(2\dfrac{gh}{\sqrt{2}}(1-\mu) \times \sqrt{2}\right)}$

$= \sqrt{2gh(1-\mu)}$

$= \dfrac{v}{3}$ (given)

So, $\sqrt{2gh(1-\mu)} = \dfrac{1}{3}\sqrt{2gh}$

$\Rightarrow$ $1 - \mu = \dfrac{1}{9}$

$\Rightarrow$ $\mu = 1 - \dfrac{1}{9} = \dfrac{8}{9}$

20. *(c)* Thermal resistance of thin layer of paper is quite less, so heat reaches across the paper and water absorbs that heat. Temperature of paper does not rises beyond 100°C and upto its burning temperature.

$\therefore$ Paper cup does not catches fire.

21. *(d)* When ice is crushed, total surface area of ice that comes in contact with surrounding air increases. As a result crushing the ice speed up the cooling process.

22. *(b)* Graph of deviation δ *versus* angle of incidence i is as shown below (for an equilateral glass, $\mu = \dfrac{3}{2}$ prism).

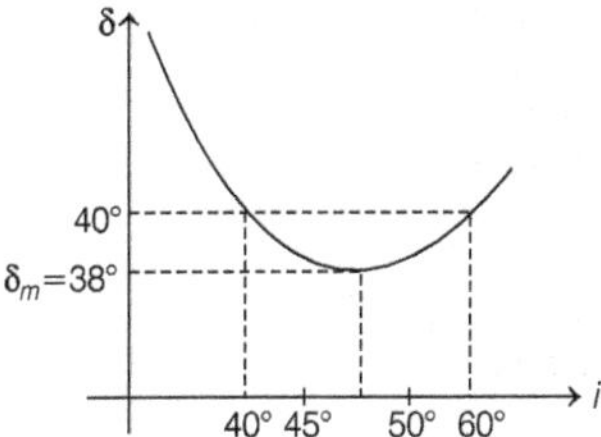

Clearly, angle of incidence for least deviation lies between $40° < i < 50°$.

23. *(d)* In air, focal length f of concave lens is given by

$$\frac{1}{f_{air}} = (\mu - 1)\left(\frac{1}{R_1} - \frac{1}{R_2}\right)$$

Here, $n_{ga} = 1.6, R_1 = -0.2\,m$
and $R_2 = +0.2\,m$

$$\therefore \quad \frac{1}{f_{air}} = (1.6 - 1)\left(\frac{-2}{0.2}\right) = \frac{-0.6 \times 2}{0.2}$$

$$\Rightarrow \quad f_{air} = -\frac{1}{6}\,m$$

When this lens is dipped in a medium of refractive index $n_{ea} = 2.0$, then

$$\frac{f_{liquid}}{f_{air}} = \frac{n_{ga} - 1}{n_{ge} - 1} = \frac{n_{ga} - 1}{\left(\dfrac{n_{ga}}{n_{ea}} - 1\right)}$$

$$\Rightarrow \quad \frac{f_e}{f_a} = \frac{1.6 - 1}{\left(\dfrac{1.6}{2} - 1\right)} \Rightarrow \frac{f_e}{f_a} = \frac{0.6}{0.8 - 1}$$

$$\Rightarrow \quad f_e = \frac{1}{6} \times \frac{0.6}{0.2} = \frac{1}{2}\,m = 0.5\,m$$

Hence, lens acts like a convergent lens of 0.5 m.

24. *(a)* As particle is initially at rest, so to move the charged particle an electric field is required.

As path of particle is a curve, so direction of electric field must be changing with distance.

25. *(b)* Electrostatic energy of two equal charges of magnitude Q placed d distance apart is

$$E = \frac{k q_1 q_2}{r_{12}} = \frac{kQ^2}{d} \qquad \ldots (i)$$

Now, when a third charge $\left(-\dfrac{Q}{2}\right)$ is placed at mid-point of these charges, then electrostatic energy of system is

$$E' = \frac{k q_1 q_2}{r_{12}} + \frac{k q_2 q_3}{r_{23}} + \frac{k q_1 q_3}{r_{13}}$$

$$= \frac{kQ^2}{d} - \frac{kQ^2/2}{d/2} - \frac{kQ^2/2}{d/2}$$

$$= -\frac{kQ^2}{d} = -E$$

[from Eq. (i)]

26. *(c)* Direction of current in ring is given by Lenz's law,

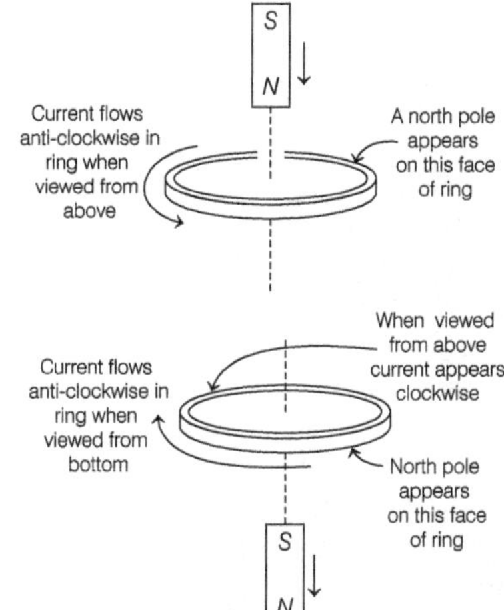

27. *(a)* Neutral point appears in region in which fields of magnets are in opposite directions.

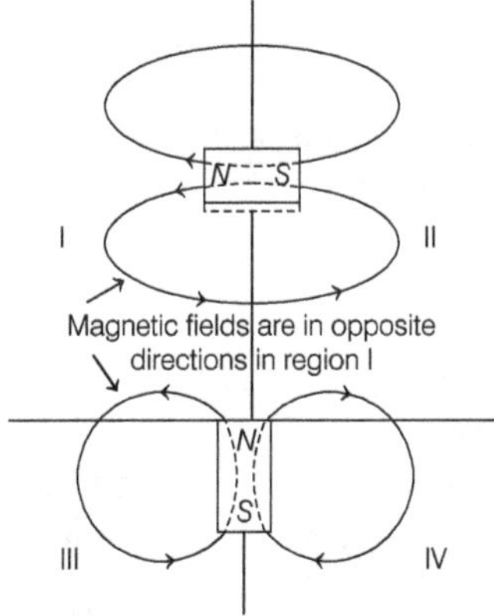

From above figure, we can conclude that magnetic fields cancel each other in region I only.

28. *(c)* In a simple harmonic motion, oscillating particle passes extreme positions two times, while it crosses mean position once in each half of oscillation.

So, graph (c) most closely resembles this situation.

29. *(b)* In Geiger-Marsden experiment, objective is to target α-particles towards an atom. This is possible only when target is a very thin metal foil.

As gold is very malleable, it is possible to produce a foil which is only few atoms thick.

30. *(a)* Isotopes have same number of protons. All isotopes of few elements are stable and non-radioactive. Also, all isotopes of few elements are unstable and radioactive. All elements have isotopes.

All isotopes of carbon can form compounds with oxygen.

So, only statements III and IV are correct.

31. *(a, d)* Isoelectronic species are those species, which have same number of electrons. The total number of electrons in each pair given in the options are as follows

(a) CO, N_2

    No. of electrons in CO $= 6 + 8 = 14$

    No. of electrons in $N_2 = 7 + 7 = 14$

(b) O_2, NO

    No. of electrons in $O_2 = 8 + 8 = 16$

    No. of electrons in NO $= 7 + 8 = 15$

(c) C_2, HF

    No. of electrons in $C_2 = 6 + 6 = 12$

    No. of electrons in HF $= 1 + 9 = 10$

(d) F_2, HCl

    No. of electrons in $F_2 = 9 + 9 = 18$

    No. of electrons in HCl $= 1 + 17 = 18$

Thus, CO and N_2, F_2 and HCl are isoelectronic pairs.

32. *(c)* The molecular formula of hydrazine is NH_2NH_2.

From the structure, it is clear that it has 2 lone pairs and 5 bond pairs (4 N — H and 1 N–N).

33. *(d)* $C(s) + O_2(g) \longrightarrow CO_2(g)$

1 mole of carbon reacts completely with 1 mole of oxygen to produce 1 mole of CO_2.

12 g of C reacts $= 1$ mole of O_2

2.4 g of C reacts with $= \dfrac{1}{12} \times 2.4$

$$= 0.2 \text{ mole of } O_2$$

At STP 1 mole of O_2 contains $= 22.4\,L$

$\therefore$ 0.2 mole of O_2 contains $= 22.4 \times 0.2$

$$= 4.48\,L$$

34. *(a)* The most often used stationary phase gel and alumina are polar material. Consequently, the least polar compound will have the highest R_f value, as they will be least bounded to the stationary phase and moves quickly up the TLC plate.

Among the given compound, compound (a) is least polar, so its R_f value will be maximum.

35. *(b)*

Thus, the number of C — C sigma bonds in the above given compound are 17.

36. *(c)* According to Bohr's radius of an atom

$$r_n = \frac{52.9 n^2}{Z} \text{ pm}$$

where, n = charge on atom

Z = atomic number

$$r_{\text{He}^+} = \frac{52.9 \times 1^2}{2} = 26.45 \approx 27 \text{ pm}$$

Thus, the radius of He^+ ion is closest to 27 pm.

37. *(d)* Diamagnetic species are those species which have paired electrons in their molecular orbitals.

The electronic configurations of molecules given in the options are as follows

(i) **NO**

Total number of electrons = 7 + 8 = 15

The electronic configuration of NO will be

$\sigma 1s^2, \sigma * 1s^2, \sigma 2s^2, \sigma * 2s^2, \sigma 2p_z^2, \pi 2p_x^2$

$= \pi z p_y^2, \pi * 2p_x^1$

(ii) **NO_2**

Total number of electrons = 7 + 8 + 8 = 23

The electronic configuration of NO_2 will be $[_{18}\text{Ar}] \, \sigma * 2p_z^2, \sigma 3s^2, \sigma * 3s^1$

(iii) **O_2**

Total number of electrons in O_2 = 16

Electronic configuration of O_2 will be

$\sigma 1s^2 \, \sigma * 1s^2 \, \sigma 2s^2 \, \sigma * 2s^2 \, \sigma 2p_z^2$
$\pi 2p_x^2 \, \pi 2p_y^2 \, \pi * 2p_x^1 \, \pi * 2p_y^1$

(iv) **CO_2**

Total number of electrons in CO_2 = 6 + 8 + 8 = 22

The electronic configuration of CO_2 will be $[_{18}\text{Ar}] \, \sigma * 2p_z^2 \, \sigma 3s^2$

Thus, CO_2 is a diamagnetic species.

38. *(b)* NaCl (NaOH + HCl) is a neutral salt, NH_4Cl (HCl + NH_4OH) is an acidic salt while CH_3COONa (CH_3COOH + NaOH) is a basic salt.

The value of pH of acidic salt is less than 7, while for neutral salt pH value is equal to 7 and for basic salt pH value is greater than 7. Thus, the increasing order of pH 0.1 M aqueous solutions of NaCl, CH_3COONa and NH_4Cl will be $\text{NH}_4\text{Cl} < \text{NaCl} < \text{CH}_3\text{COONa}$.

39. *(a)* At room temperature

$$V_{\text{avg}} = \sqrt{\frac{8RT}{\pi M}}$$

$\therefore$ Average speed $\propto \dfrac{1}{\sqrt{M}}$

$$\frac{V_{\text{He}}}{V_{\text{O}_2}} = \sqrt{\frac{M_{\text{O}_2}}{M_{\text{He}}}} = \sqrt{\frac{32}{4}} = \sqrt{8}$$

$$\Rightarrow \quad \frac{V_{\text{He}}}{V_{\text{O}_2}} = 2\sqrt{2}$$

Thus, the average speed of helium is higher than of oxygen by a factor of $2\sqrt{2}$.

40. *(c)* The products formed in each reaction given in the options are as follows

(i) $\text{NH}_4\text{Cl} + \text{KOH} \longrightarrow \text{KCl} + \text{NH}_3 + \text{H}_2\text{O}$

(ii) $\text{AlN} + 3\text{H}_2\text{O} \longrightarrow \text{Al(OH)}_3 + \text{NH}_3$

(iii) $\text{NH}_4\text{Cl} + \text{NaNO}_2 \longrightarrow \text{NaCl} + \text{N}_2 + 2\text{H}_2\text{O}$

(iv) $\text{NH}_4\text{Cl} + \text{Ca(OH)}_2 \longrightarrow \text{CaCl}_2 + \text{NH}_3 + \text{H}_2\text{O}$

Thus, ammonia is not produced in reaction given in option (c).

41. *(b)* Isomers of compound of molecular formula $\text{C}_4\text{H}_{10}\text{O}$ are as follows

$$\text{CH}_3\text{CH(OH)CH}_2\text{CH}_3$$
$$\text{CH}_3\text{CH}_2\text{CH}_2\text{CH}_2\text{OH}$$
$$\text{CH}_3 — \text{O} — \text{CH}_2 — \text{CH}_2\text{CH}_3$$
$$\text{CH}_3 — \text{CH}_2\text{OCH}_2\text{CH}_3$$

$$\text{CH}_3 — \text{O} — \overset{\overset{\displaystyle \text{CH}_3}{|}}{\text{CH}} — \text{CH}_3$$

Thus, there are 3 isomers which are ethers having the molecular formula $\text{C}_4\text{H}_{10}\text{O}$.

42. *(d)* The major product of the reaction of 2-butene (alkene) with alk. KMnO_4 solution is a vicinal glycol, i.e. butane-2,3 diol.

Butane-2, 3-diol

43. *(c)* The boiling point of a compound depends upon the extent of H-bond present in it. As compound I, II and IV are alcohols, so they can easily form H-bonds while compound III is an ether and cannot form H-bonds. Thus compound III, i.e. has lowest boiling point.

44. *(c)* The relation between Gibbs free energy and equilibrium constant can be given as

$$\Delta G° = - 2.303 RT \log K_{\text{eq}}$$
$$\log K_{\text{eq}} = - \Delta G° / 2.303 RT$$

The reaction having most negative value of $\Delta G°$ will have the largest equilibrium constant. Thus, the reaction with largest equilibrium constant will be

$$\text{F} \rightleftharpoons \text{G}, \, \Delta G° = - 150 \text{ kJ mol}^{-1}$$

45. *(a)* As O, F and Ne belong to same period, i.e. 2nd period, the ionisation energies increases on moving from left to right. This increase in ionisation energy is due to decrease in the atomic radii across a period. Thus, the first ionisation enthalpies for O, Fe and Ne are 1314, 1680 and 2080, respectively. So, the correct sequence of the element is O, F and Ne.

46. *(b)* Population is a group of individuals belonging to same species occupying a particular geographic area in a given time. A community is a group of people living in the same place or having a particular characteristic in common. Biome is a large naturally occurring community of flora and fauna occupying a major habitat. Species is a group of living organisms consisting of similar individuals capable of interbreeding.

47. *(c)* The energy assimilated by the herbivores is used in respiration and a fraction of unassimilated energy is transferred to decomposers (e.g. faecal matter). With increasing trophic levels, the respiration cost also increases sharply. On an average, producers consume about 20% of their gross productivity in respiration. The herbivores consume about 30% of assimilated energy in respiration. In carnivores, the proportion of assimilated energy consumed in respiration rises to about 60%.

48. *(b)* Athletes are often trained at high altitude because the air is 'thinner' at high altitudes, means there are fewer oxygen molecules per volume of air. Every breath taken at high altitude delivers less of what working muscles require. To compensate for the decrease in oxygen there occurs more production of red blood cells to aid in oxygen delivery to the muscles.

49. *(d)* Corpus callosum is nervous band which attaches both cerebral hemispheres of mammals. It is a thick band of nerve fibres that divides the cerebral cortex lobes into left and right hemispheres. It connects the left and right sides of the brain allowing for communication between both hemispheres.

50. *(b)* Glucagon is secreted from alpha cells of pancreas. Prolactin is secreted by the anterior pituitary. Luteinising hormone is secreted by the gonadotropic cells in the anterior pituitary. Epinephrine (or adrenaline) is secreted by the medulla of the adrenal gland.

51. *(d)* The stalk of plant leaf (petiole) is derived from collenchyma. Collenchyma cells are elongated cells with irregular thick cell walls that provide structural support, particularly in growing shoots and leaves. Their thick cell walls are composed of the compounds cellulose and pectin.

52. *(c)* Both smooth muscle (unstriated muscle) and cardiac muscle are functionally involuntary. Muscles that are under our conscious control are called voluntary muscles, while muscles that are not under our conscious control are called involuntary muscles. Striated muscles are voluntary muscles.

53. *(a)* Pulmonary artery arises from left ventricle and carries deoxygenated blood to the lungs.

The pulmonary artery begins in the heart at the base of the right ventricle.

54. *(b)* Gout is caused by the deposition of uric acid in joints. Composition of kidney stone is calcium oxalate, calcium phosphate, uric acid, xanthine and indigo calculi. Researches have shown that kidney stones are a complication of gout because extra uric acid can collect in the urinary tract and crystallise into stones.

55. *(a)* Cochlea is the main hearing organ. It is composed of sensory cells called hair cells, which convert vibrations into neural messages. These messages are then passed to the auditory nerve and carried up to the brain.

56. *(d)* Mitochondria and chloroplast contain circular DNA. Even though both organelles are found in eukaryotic cell, both mitochondria and chloroplast have characteristics often found in prokaryotic cells. These prokaryotic cell's characteristics include enclosed double membrane, circular DNA and bacteria like ribosomes.

57. *(b)* Reflex actions do not involve the brain in the decision making process. Reflex action is a rapid, spontaneous and involuntary activity that is produced in response to a stimulus. It is controlled by spinal cord.

Its pathway is as discussed below

Receptor $\longrightarrow$ Sensory neuron $\longrightarrow$
(Skin)

Integration centre
(Spinal cord)

$\downarrow$

Effector $\longleftarrow$ Motor neuron
(muscle)

58. *(b)* In photosynthesis,

Light reaction $\rightarrow$ Photolysis of water (H_2O is oxidised)

$2H_2O \rightarrow O_2 + 4\,[H]$ requires light reaction

Dark reaction $\rightarrow CO_2$ is reduced for sugar formation

$4\,[H] + CO_2 \rightarrow (CH_2O) + H_2O$ (Reduction)

59. *(c)* A mature RBC lacks nucleus, mitochondria and endoplasmic reticulum. In humans, mature RBCs are flexible and oval biconcave disks. They lack a cell nucleus and most organelles, in order to accommodate maximum space for haemoglobin.

60. *(d)* Antivenom injection provides artificial acquired passive immunity. Passive immunity is the transfer of active humoral immunity of readymade antibodies. It can occur naturally, when maternal antibodies are transferred to foetus through placenta and it can be induced artificially when high level of antibodies specific to a pathogen or toxin are transferred to non-immune persons through blood products that contain antibodies, such as antivenom injections are given.

61. *(b)* Given, $a + b + c = 0 \Rightarrow a, b, c \in R$

$\Rightarrow \quad a^2 + b^2 + c^2 = q$

$\Rightarrow \quad a^4 + b^4 + c^4 = r$

$\Rightarrow \quad (a^2 + b^2 + c^2)^2 = a^4 + b^4 + c^4$
$$+ 2\,(a^2b^2 + b^2c^2 + c^2a^2)$$

$\Rightarrow \quad (a^2 + b^2 + c^2)^2 = a^4 + b^4 + c^4 + 2$
$$[(ab + bc + ca)^2 - 2abc(a + b + c)]$$

$\Rightarrow \quad q^2 = r + 2[(ab + bc + ca)^2 - 2(abc)(0)]$

$\Rightarrow \quad q^2 = r + 2\,[ab + bc + ca]^2$

$\Rightarrow \quad q^2 = r + 2$
$$\left[\frac{(a + b + c)^2 - (a^2 + b^2 + c^2)}{2}\right]^2$$

$\Rightarrow \quad q^2 = r + 2\left(\dfrac{0 - q}{2}\right)^2$

$\Rightarrow \quad q^2 = r + \dfrac{2q^2}{4}$

$\Rightarrow \quad q^2 - \dfrac{1}{2}q^2 = r$

$\Rightarrow \quad q^2 = 2r$

62. *(a)* We have,

$$\sum_{n=0}^{1947} \frac{1}{2^n + \sqrt{2^{1947}}}$$

Let $\quad f(n) = \dfrac{1}{2^n + \sqrt{2^{1947}}}$

$$f(0) + f(1947) = \frac{1}{1 + 2^{\frac{1947}{2}}} + \frac{1}{2^{1947} + 2^{\frac{1947}{2}}}$$

$$= \frac{1}{1 + 2^{\frac{1947}{2}}} + \frac{1}{2^{\frac{1947}{2}}\left(2^{\frac{1947}{2}} + 1\right)}$$

$$= \frac{2^{\frac{1947}{2}} + 1}{2^{\frac{1947}{2}}\left(2^{\frac{1947}{2}} + 1\right)} = \frac{1}{2^{\frac{1947}{2}}}$$

Similarly, $f(1) + f(1946) = \dfrac{1}{2^{\frac{1947}{2}}}$

$\because \displaystyle\sum_{n=0}^{1947} f(x) = f(0) + f(1) + f(2) + f(3) +$
$$\ldots + f(1947)$$

$= (f(0) + f(1947)) + (f(1) + f(1946)) + \ldots$
$$\ldots + (f(973) + f(974))$$

$= 974 \times \dfrac{1}{2^{\frac{1947}{2}}}$

$\displaystyle\sum_{n=0}^{1947} f(n) = \dfrac{2 \times 487}{2 \times 2^{\frac{1945}{2}}} = \dfrac{487}{\sqrt{2^{1945}}}$

63. *(d)* Given,

$$x + y = a \Rightarrow a \in [1, 2014]$$

and $\quad \dfrac{x^2}{x - 1} + \dfrac{y^2}{y - 1} = 4$

$\therefore \quad \dfrac{x^2}{x - 1} + \dfrac{y^2}{y - 1} = 4$

$\Rightarrow x^2 y - x^2 + xy^2 - y^2 = 4(x - 1)(y - 1)$

$\Rightarrow \, x^2 y + xy^2 = 4(xy - (x + y) + 1) + x^2 + y^2$

$\Rightarrow \, xy\,(x + y) = 4(xy - a + 1)$
$$+ (x + y)^2 - 2xy$$

$\Rightarrow \quad xy(a) = 4xy - 4a + 4 + a^2 - 2xy$

$\Rightarrow xya - 2xy = a^2 - 4a + 4$

$\Rightarrow xy\,(a - 2) = (a - 2)^2$

$\Rightarrow \quad (a - 2)^2 - xy\,(a - 2) = 0$

$\Rightarrow \quad (a - 2)\,(a - 2 - xy) = 0$

$\Rightarrow \qquad a = 2 \text{ or } xy = a - 2$

or $\qquad x\,(a - x) = a - 2 \quad [\because y = a - x]$

$\Rightarrow \qquad x^2 - ax + a - 2 = 0$

Since, $x \in R$

$\because \qquad\qquad D \geq 0$

$\because \qquad\qquad a^2 - 4(a-2) \geq 0$

$\qquad a^2 - 4a + 8 \geq 0, \forall\, a \in R$

$\because \qquad\qquad a \in [1, 2014]$

64. *(a)* Given,

ABC is right angled triangle.

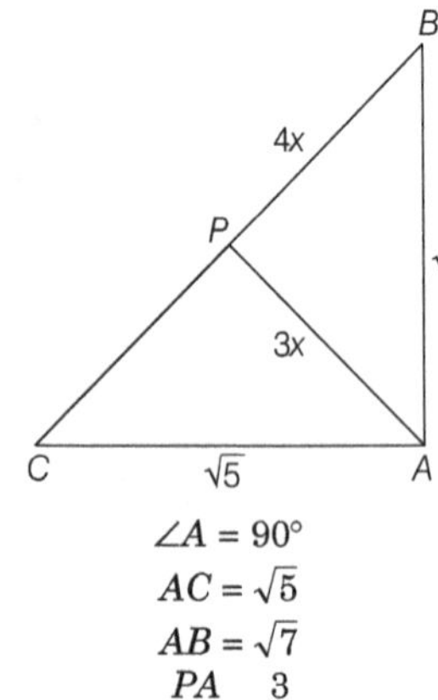

$\angle A = 90°$

$AC = \sqrt{5}$

$AB = \sqrt{7}$

$\dfrac{PA}{PB} = \dfrac{3}{4}$

In $\triangle ABC$

$\qquad BC^2 = AB^2 + AC^2 = 5 + 7 = 12$

$\qquad BC = \sqrt{12} = 2\sqrt{3}$

In $\triangle ABP$,

$\qquad \cos B = \dfrac{AB^2 + PB^2 - AP^2}{2AB \cdot PB}$

$\Rightarrow \quad \dfrac{\sqrt{7}}{2\sqrt{3}} = \dfrac{7 + 16x^2 - 9x^2}{2 \cdot \sqrt{7} \times 4x}$

$$\left[\because \cos B = \dfrac{AB}{BC} = \dfrac{\sqrt{7}}{2\sqrt{3}}\right]$$

$\Rightarrow \quad \dfrac{28x}{\sqrt{3}} = 7 + 7x^2 \Rightarrow 28x = 7\sqrt{3}\,(x^2 + 1)$

$\Rightarrow \quad \sqrt{3}\,x^2 - 4x + \sqrt{3} = 0$

$\Rightarrow \quad \sqrt{3}x^2 - 3x - x + \sqrt{3} = 0$

$\Rightarrow \quad (\sqrt{3}x - 1)(x - \sqrt{3}) = 0$

$\because \qquad x = \sqrt{3}, \dfrac{1}{\sqrt{3}}, x \neq \sqrt{3}$

$\because \qquad\qquad PB = 4/\sqrt{3}$

$PC = BC - BP = 2\sqrt{3} - \dfrac{4}{\sqrt{3}} = \dfrac{2}{\sqrt{3}}$

$\because \qquad \dfrac{BP}{PC} = \dfrac{4/\sqrt{3}}{2/\sqrt{3}} = 2:1$

65. *(d)* abc is three-digits number

$abc = 100a + 10b + c$

$100 \leq abc < 999,\, a \in \{1, 2, 3, ..., 9\}\, b, c \in \{0, 1, 2, 3, ..., 9\}$

Now, $(a \times b \times c) + (a \times b) + (b \times c)$

$\qquad\qquad + (c \times a) + a + b + c = 29$

$\Rightarrow (a \times b)(c + 1) + b(c + 1) + a(c + 1)$

$\qquad\qquad\qquad\qquad + (c + 1) = 30$

$\Rightarrow (c + 1)(a \times b + b + a + 1) = 30$

$\Rightarrow (c + 1)(b(a + 1) + 1(a + 1)) = 30$

$\Rightarrow \qquad (a + 1))(b + 1)(c + 1) = 30$

$\qquad\qquad\qquad 1 \leq a \leq 9,\, 0 \leq b, c \leq 9$

$\because$ Total number of solution $= 18$

66. *(b)* Centre of mass of square wooden plate with respect to chosen axis is at centre of plate.

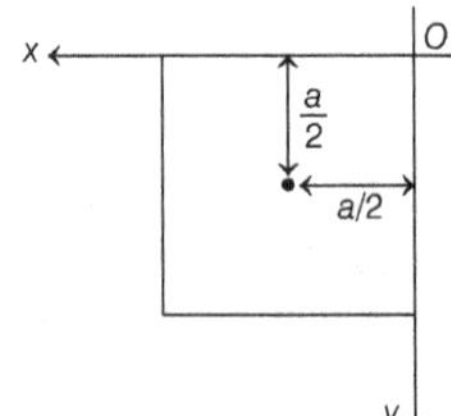

Coordinates of centre of mass are

$$x_1 = \dfrac{a}{2},\, y_1 = \dfrac{a}{2}$$

Mass of square plate, $m_1 = ka^2$ where, $k =$ mass per unit area.

Coordinates of centre of mass of removed portion and its mass with respect to axes chosen are

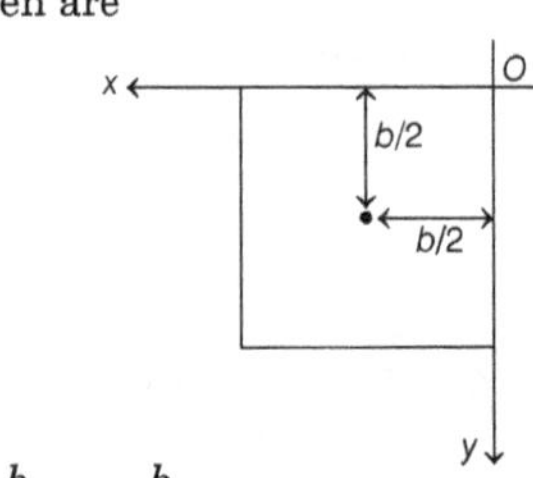

$$x_2 = \dfrac{b}{2},\, y_2 = \dfrac{b}{2}$$

and mass of removed portion,

$$m_2 = kb^2$$

Now, centre of mass of remaining L-shaped portion is given at point P whose coordinates are (b, b) with respect to chosen axes.

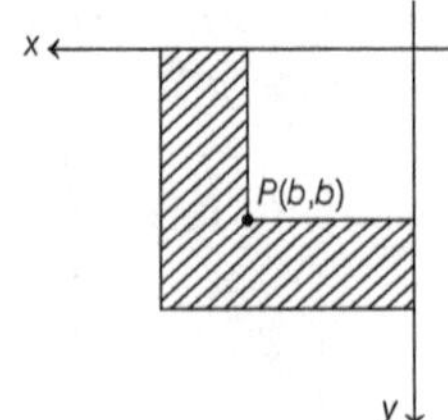

Now, using $X_{CM} = \dfrac{m_1 x_1 - m_2 x_2}{m_1 - m_2}$, we have

$$b = \dfrac{ka^2\left(\dfrac{a}{2}\right) - kb^2\left(\dfrac{b}{2}\right)}{ka^2 - kb^2} \Rightarrow b = \dfrac{a^3 - b^3}{2(a^2 - b^2)}$$

Rearranging, we get

$\Rightarrow \quad \left(\dfrac{a}{b}\right)^2 - \left(\dfrac{a}{b}\right) - 1 = 0$

$\Rightarrow \qquad\qquad \dfrac{a}{b} = \dfrac{1 \pm \sqrt{1 + 4}}{2}$

$\Rightarrow \qquad\qquad \dfrac{a}{b} = \dfrac{\sqrt{5} + 1}{2}$

Note *Choice of a different origin gives a different value of $\dfrac{a}{b}$.*

67. *(d)* For a soap bubble floating in air, Gravitational force = Buoyant force

$\Rightarrow g$ (mass of helium + mass of soap film) = Weight of air displaced by bubble ...(i)

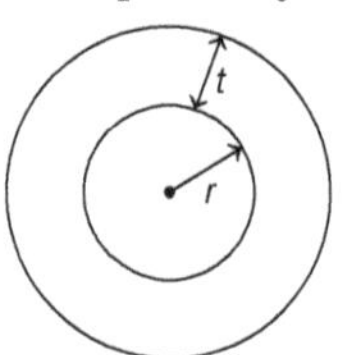

Let $r =$ inner radius of soap bubble and $t =$ thickness of film.

Then, from Eq. (i), we have

$\Rightarrow \quad \dfrac{4}{3}\pi r^3 \times \rho_{\text{He}} + 4\pi r^2 \times t \times \rho_{\text{soap}}$

$$= \dfrac{4}{3}\pi r^3 \times \rho_{\text{air}}$$

Substituting values in above equation, we get

$\Rightarrow \dfrac{4}{3} \times \pi \times (10^{-2})^3 \times 0.18 + 4\pi \times (10^{-2})^2$

$$\times t \times 1000$$

$$= \dfrac{4}{3} \times \pi \times (10^{-2})^3 \times 1.23$$

Rearranging, we get

$\Rightarrow 4\pi\,(10^{-2}) \cdot t \cdot 1000 = \dfrac{4}{3}\pi\,(10^{-6})\,(1.08)$

$\Rightarrow \qquad\qquad (10^5)\,t = 0.35$

or $\qquad\qquad t = 3.5 \times 10^{-6}$ m

$\qquad\qquad\qquad = 3.50\,\mu\text{m}$

68. *(c)* As heat lost by aluminium piece = heat gained by water

$\{ms(T_i - T_f)\}_{\text{aluminium}} = \{ms(T_f - T_i)\}_{\text{water}}$

Substituting given values, we get

$\Rightarrow \quad 50 \times 10^{-3} \times 900 \times (300 - 160)$

$$= 1 \times 4200 \times (T - 30)$$

$\Rightarrow \qquad 6300 = 4200\,(T - 30)$

$\Rightarrow \qquad\quad T = 30 + 1.5$

or $\qquad\quad T = 31.5°\text{C}$

So, temperature of water after taking out aluminium piece is 31.5°C.

69. *(a)* From the geometry of given figure,

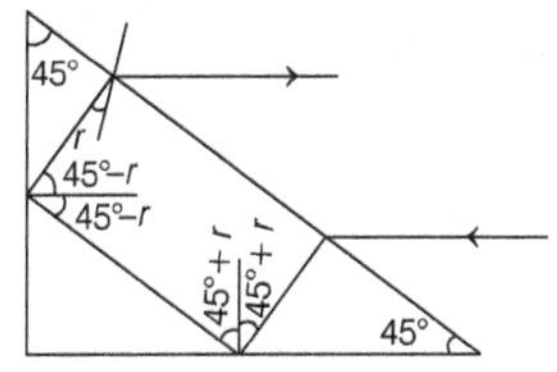

We have, for total internal reflections

$$45° + r > \theta_c \qquad ...(i)$$

and $\qquad 45° - r > \theta_c \qquad ...(ii)$

or $\qquad 90° > 2\theta_c \Rightarrow \sin 45° > \sin\theta_c$

$$\Rightarrow \qquad \frac{1}{\sqrt{2}} > \frac{1}{\mu} \text{ or } \mu > \sqrt{2} \qquad ...(iii)$$

From Eq. (ii), we have

$$45 - \theta_c > r$$

$$\sin(45 - \theta_c) > \sin r$$

$$\Rightarrow \frac{1}{\sqrt{2}}\cos\theta_c - \frac{1}{\sqrt{2}}\sin\theta_c > \frac{\sin 45°}{\mu}$$

$$\Rightarrow \frac{\sqrt{\mu^2 - 1}}{\mu} - \frac{1}{\mu} > \frac{1}{\mu} \Rightarrow \sqrt{\mu^2 - 1} > 2$$

$$\Rightarrow \qquad \mu > \sqrt{5} \qquad ...(iv)$$

Common solution of Eqs. (iii) and (iv) is $\mu > \sqrt{5}$.

70. *(d)* Let current through resistor X is be i.

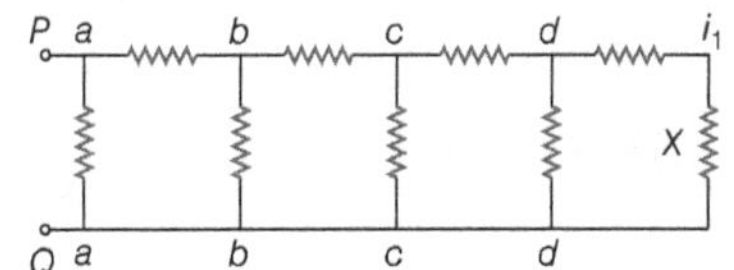

Now, we consider section dd,

Equating potential across dd, we get

$$i_2 R = i_1 (2R)$$

or $\qquad i_2 = 2i_1$

Hence, current i is

$$i_3 = i_1 + i_2 = i_1 + 2i_1 = 3i_1$$

Now, we consider section cc,

Equating potentials, we get

$$i_4 R = i_3 \left(R + \frac{2}{3}R \right)$$

$$i_4 = i_3 \left(\frac{5}{3} \right)$$

So, current, $i_5 = i_4 + i_3 = \dfrac{5}{3}i_3 + i_3 = \dfrac{8}{3}i_3$

$$= \frac{8}{3}(3i_1) = 8\,i_1$$

Similarly, across section bb,

$$\Rightarrow \qquad Ri_6 = \left(\frac{13}{8}R \right) i_5 \text{ or } i_6 = \frac{13}{8}i_5$$

So, current,

$$i_7 = \frac{13}{8}i_5 + i_5 = \frac{21}{8}i_5 = \frac{21}{8}(8i_1) = 21\,i_1$$

Now, for section aa, we have

$$Ri_8 = i_7 \left(\frac{13}{21} + 1 \right)R$$

$$Ri_8 = i_7 \left(\frac{34}{21}R \right)$$

$$\Rightarrow \qquad i_8 = i_7 \times \frac{34}{21}$$

Hence, current i is

$$i = i_7 + i_8$$

$$= i_7 + \frac{34}{21}i_7 = \frac{55}{21}i_7$$

$$= \frac{55}{21} \times 21 i_1$$

$$= 55 i_1 = 55 \times 10^{-3} \text{ A}$$

$$(\because i_1 = 1\,\text{mA, given})$$

Total resistance across PQ is

$$R_{\text{eq}} = \frac{34}{55}\,\text{k}\Omega$$

$$= \frac{34 \times 1000}{55}\,\Omega$$

So, potential drop across, PQ

$$= i R_{\text{eq}} = 55 \times 10^{-3} \times \frac{34}{55} \times 10^3 \text{ V}$$

$$= 34\,\text{V}$$

71. *(b)* 18 g of $H_2O = 1$ mole

$$3.6 \text{ of } H_2O = \frac{1}{18} \times 3.6 = 0.2 \text{ mole}$$

$$2H_2(g) \ + \ O_2(g) \ \longrightarrow \ 2H_2O(l)$$

Initially	x mol	$(10 - x)$ mol	0
After reaction	$x - 0.2$	$10 - x - \dfrac{0.2}{2}$	0.2 mol

$\therefore$ Resulting moles of gases in mixture

$$= x - 0.2 + 10 - x - 0.1 = 9.7$$

At constant temperature and volume,

$$\frac{p_1}{n_1} = \frac{p_2}{n_2}$$

$$\Rightarrow \qquad \frac{1}{10} = \frac{p_2}{9.7}$$

$$\Rightarrow \qquad p_2 = 0.97\,\text{atm}$$

72. *(a)* $2NH_3 + H_2SO_4 \longrightarrow (NH_4)_2SO_4$

Eq. of $H_2SO_4 = 2 \times 2 \times 10 \times 10^{-3}$

$$\text{[basicity of } H_2SO_4 = 2]$$

Eq. of $H_2SO_4 = $ Eq. of $NH_3 = $ No. of moles of ammonia $= 4 \times 10^{-2}$

1 mole of $NH_3 = 17$ g

$\therefore 4 \times 10^{-2}$ moles of $NH_3 = 17 \times 4 \times 10^{-2}$

$\therefore W_{NH_3} = 17 \times 4 \times 10^{-2}$ g

$$\Rightarrow W_N = \frac{14}{17} \times 17 \times 4 \times 10^{-2}$$

$$= 0.56\,\text{g}$$

$$\% \text{ of N} = \frac{0.56}{2} \times 100 = 28\%$$

73. *(d)* Let the equivalent weight of metal $M = x$

$$\frac{(\text{eq})_{\text{Ca}}}{(\text{eq})_M} = \frac{(\text{eq})_{H_2}, \text{ released}}{(\text{eq})_{H_2}, \text{ released}}$$

$$\Rightarrow \qquad \frac{\dfrac{2}{20}}{\dfrac{2}{x}} = \frac{\dfrac{1125}{(\text{eq vol})_{H_2}}}{\dfrac{185}{(\text{eq vol.})_{H_2}}}$$

$$\therefore \qquad \frac{x}{20} = \frac{1.125}{1.85}$$

$$\Rightarrow \qquad x = \frac{1.125}{1.85} \times 20$$

$$= 12.16 \approx 12$$

74. *(a)* When coke is heated with lime (CaO), then $CaC_2(X)$ is formed which then reacts with water to form acetylene (Y) as a major product. This acetylene on passing over red hot iron at 873 K produces benzene (Z).

75. *(a)*

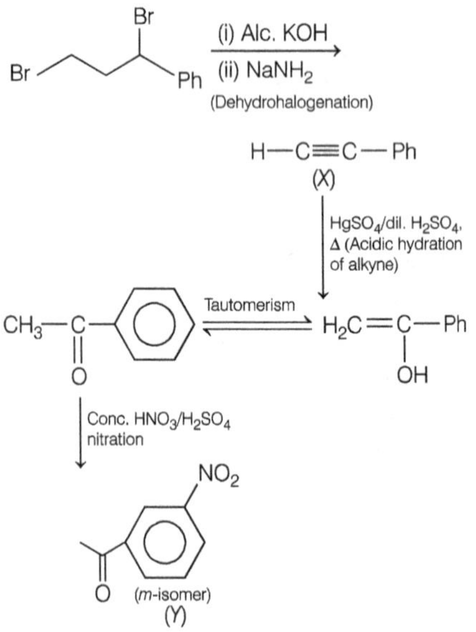

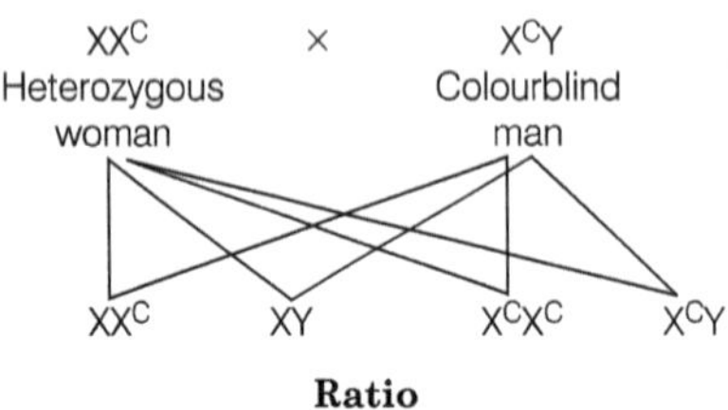

(i) Alc. KOH
(ii) NaNH₂
(Dehydrohalogenation)

$$H\!-\!C\!\equiv\!C\!-\!Ph$$
(X)

HgSO₄/dil. H₂SO₄, Δ (Acidic hydration of alkyne)

Tautomerism

$$CH_3\!-\!\underset{O}{\overset{}{C}}\!-\!\!\bigcirc \rightleftharpoons H_2C\!=\!\underset{OH}{\overset{}{C}}\!-\!Ph$$

Conc. HNO₃/H₂SO₄ nitration

(m-isomer)
(Y)

76. *(c)* Respiratory reactions occur in the mitochondria and cytoplasm. Respiratory reactions include glycolysis, Kreb's cycle and Electron Transport Chain (ETC). The glycolysis always occurs in the cytoplasm of all living cells. The Kreb's cycle occurs in the cytoplasm of all prokaryotes and in the mitochondrial matrix in eukaryotes.

The ETC occurs in the plasma membrane of prokaryotes and the inner mitochondrial membrane of eukaryotes.

77. *(c)* Colourblindness is X-linked recessive disorder.

$$XX^C \quad\times\quad X^C Y$$
Heterozygous woman　　　　Colourblind man

$$XX^C \qquad XY \qquad X^C X^C \qquad X^C Y$$

Ratio

	Genotype	F₁ ratio
Carrier daughter	XX^C	1
Colourblind daughter	$X^C X^C$	1
Normal son	XY	1
Colourblind son	$X^C Y$	1

78. *(b)* Osmosis is the net movement of solvent molecules into a region of higher solute concentration through a semipermeable membrane. In the given question, one of the 2 sucrose containing bags (semipermeable) is placed in a water containing beaker. Clearly, the concentration in the bag is more than the beaker and as a result, water will move through the semipermeable membrane (endosmosis) and make the bag turgid.

On the other hand, the second beaker contains 10% sucrose solution which is more concentrated than the semipermeable bag's sucrose concentration. Hence, water will move out of the bag to the beaker and make the bag flaccid (exosmosis). Thus, the answer (b) is correct.

79. *(a)* Phenylketonuria is an autosomal recessive disorder with mutation in gene for enzyme Phenylalanine Hydroxylase (PAH), making it non-functional.

$$\text{Phenylalanine} \xrightarrow[X]{PAH} \text{Tyrosine}$$

Such person cannot metabolise the above reaction leading to accumulation of phenylalanine. So, are given food low in phenylalanine and supplemented with tyrosine.

80. *(a)* Ganga is more polluted than Kaveri → lower DO [Dissolved Oxygen] indicates polluted water

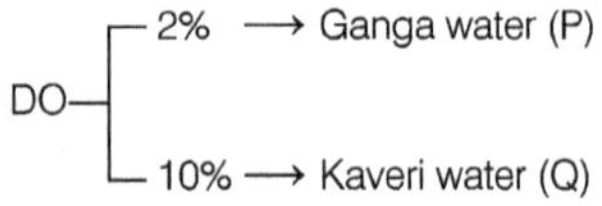

$$DO\begin{cases} 2\% \longrightarrow \text{Ganga water (P)} \\ 10\% \longrightarrow \text{Kaveri water (Q)} \end{cases}$$

Dissolved oxygen refers to the level of free oxygen present in water levels that are too high or too low can harm aquatic life and affect water quality.

QUESTION PAPER 2013
Stream : SA

MM : 100

Instructions

1. There are 80 questions in this paper.
2. This question paper contains two parts; Part I and Part II. There are four sections; Mathematics, Physics, Chemistry and Biology in each part.
3. Out of the four options given with each question, only one is correct.

➲ PART-I (1 Mark Questions)

MATHEMATICS

1. Let x, y, z be three non-negative integers such that $x + y + z = 10$. The maximum possible value of $xyz + xy + yz + zx$ is
(a) 52   (b) 64   (c) 69   (d) 73

2. If a, b are natural numbers such that $2013 + a^2 = b^2$, then the minimum possible value of ab is
(a) 671   (b) 668
(c) 658   (d) 645

3. The number of values of b for which there is an isosceles triangle with sides of lengths $b + 5, 3b - 2$ and $6 - b$ is
(a) 0   (b) 1   (c) 2   (d) 3

4. Let a, b be non-zero real numbers. Which of the following statements about the quadratic equation $ax^2 + (a + b)x + b = 0$ is necessarily true?

   I. It has at least one negative root.

   II. It has at least one positive root.

   III. Both its roots are real.

(a) I and II only   (b) I and III only
(c) II and III only   (d) All of them

5. Let x, y, z be non-zero real numbers such that $\dfrac{x}{y} + \dfrac{y}{z} + \dfrac{z}{x} = 7$ and $\dfrac{y}{x} + \dfrac{z}{y} + \dfrac{x}{z} = 9$, then $\dfrac{x^3}{y^3} + \dfrac{y^3}{z^3} + \dfrac{z^3}{x^3} - 3$ is equal to
(a) 152   (b) 153   (c) 154   (d) 155

6. In a $\triangle ABC$ with $\angle A < \angle B < \angle C$, points D, E, F are on the interior of segments BC, CA, AB respectively. Which of the following triangles cannot be similar to $\triangle ABC$?
(a) $\triangle ABD$ (b) $\triangle BCE$ (c) $\triangle CAF$ (d) $\triangle DEF$

7. Tangents to a circle at points P and Q on the circle intersect at a point R. If $PQ = 6$ and $PR = 5$, then the radius of the circle is
(a) $\dfrac{13}{3}$ (b) 4
(c) $\dfrac{15}{4}$ (d) $\dfrac{16}{5}$

8. In an acute angled $\triangle ABC$, the altitudes from A, B, C when extended intersect the circumcircle again at points A_1, B_1, C_1 respectively. If $\angle ABC = 45°$, then $\angle A_1 B_1 C_1$ equals
(a) 45°   (b) 60°   (c) 90°   (d) 135°

9. In a rectangle $ABCD$, points X and Y are the mid-points of AD and DC, respectively. Lines BX and CD when extended intersect at E, lines BY and AD when extended intersect at F. If the area of $ABCD$ is 60, then the area of BEF is

(a) 60   (b) 80   (c) 90   (d) 120

10. In the figure given below, $ABCDEF$ is a regular hexagon of side length 1, $AFPS$ and $ABQR$ are squares. Then, the ratio $\mathrm{ar}(APQ)/\mathrm{ar}(SRP)$ equals

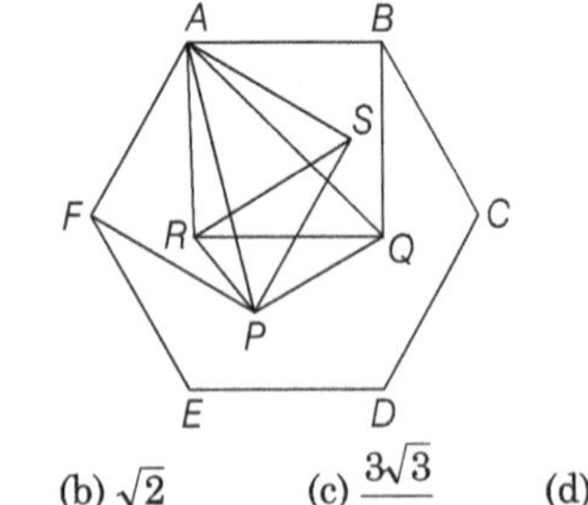

(a) $\dfrac{\sqrt{2}+1}{2}$ (b) $\sqrt{2}$ (c) $\dfrac{3\sqrt{3}}{4}$ (d) 2

11. A person X is running around a circular track completing one round every 40 s. Another person Y running in the opposite direction meets X every 15 s. The time, expressed in seconds, taken by Y to complete one round is

(a) 12.5   (b) 24   (c) 25   (d) 55

12. The least positive integer n for which
$\sqrt{n+1}-\sqrt{n-1}<0.2$ is

(a) 24   (b) 25
(c) 26   (d) 27

13. How many natural numbers n are there such that $n!+10$ is a perfect square?

(a) 1   (b) 2
(c) 4   (d) infinitely many

14. Ten points lie in a plane so that no three of them are collinear. The number of lines passing through exactly two of these points and dividing the plane into two regions each containing four of the remaining points is

(a) 1
(b) 5
(c) 10
(d) dependent on the configuration of points

15. In a city, the total income of all people with salary below ₹ 10000 per annum is less than the total income of all people with salary above ₹ 10000 per annum. If the salaries of people in the first group increases by 5% and the salaries of people in the second group decreases by 5%, then the average income of all people

(a) increases
(b) decreases
(c) remains the same
(d) cannot be determined from the data

PHYSICS

16. A man inside a freely falling box throws a heavy ball towards a side wall. The ball keeps on bouncing between the opposite walls of the box. We neglect air resistance and friction. Which of the following figures depicts the motion of the centre of mass of the entire system (man, the ball and the box)?

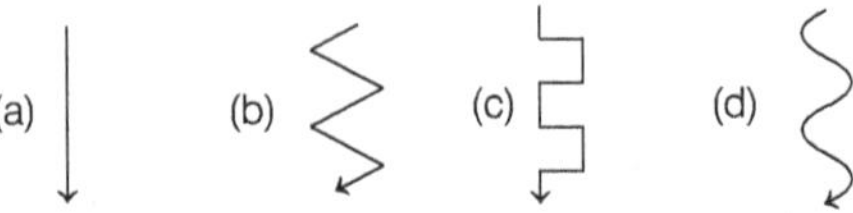

17. A ball is thrown horizontally from a height with a certain initial velocity at time $t=0$. The ball bounces repeatedly from the ground with the coefficient of restitution less than 1 as shown below.

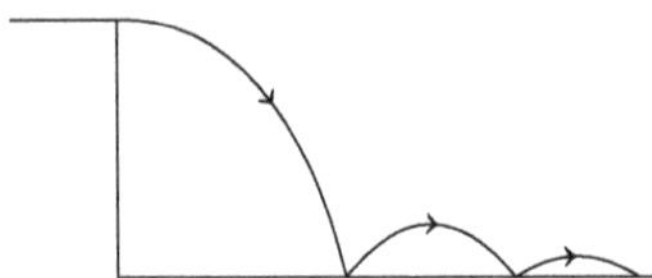

Neglecting air resistance and taking the upward direction as positive, which figure qualitatively depicts the vertical component of the ball's velocity v_y as a function of time t?

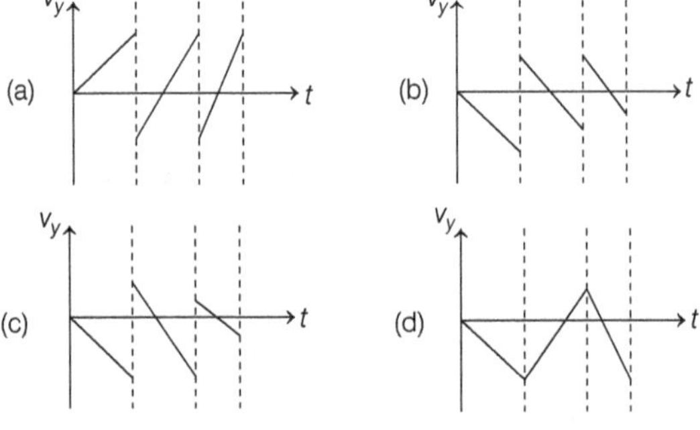

18. A tall tank filled with water has an irregular shape as shown. The wall CD makes an angle of 45° with the horizontal, the wall AB is normal to the base BC. The lengths AB and CD are much smaller than the height h of water (figure not to scale).

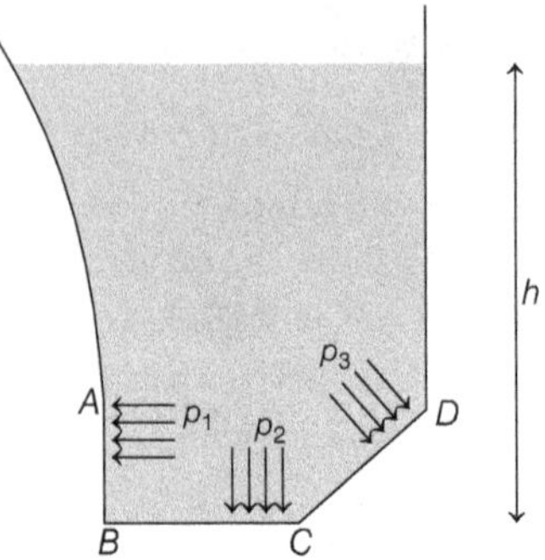

Let p_1, p_2 and p_3 be the pressures exerted by the water on the wall AB, base BC and the wall CD respectively. Density of water is ρ and g is acceleration due to gravity. Then, approximately

(a) $p_1 = p_2 = p_3$

(b) $p_1 = 0, p_3 = \dfrac{1}{\sqrt{2}} p_2$

(c) $p_1 = p_3 = \dfrac{1}{\sqrt{2}} p_2$

(d) $p_1 = p_3 = 0, p_2 = h\rho g$

19. The accompanying graph of position x *versus* time t represents the motion of a particle. If p and q are both positive constants, the expression that best describes the acceleration a of the particle is

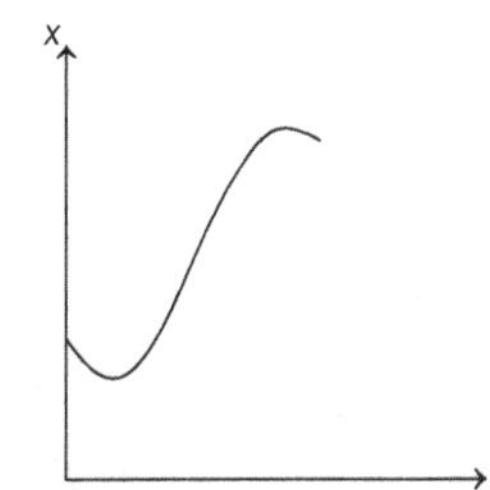

(a) $a = -p - qt$

(b) $a = -p + qt$

(c) $a = p + qt$

(d) $a = p - qt$

20. Two stones of masses m_1 and m_2 (such that $m_1 > m_2$) are dropped Δt time apart from the same height towards the ground. At a later time t, the difference in their speed is Δv and their mutual separation is Δs. While both stones are in flight

(a) Δv decreases with time and Δs increases with time

(b) Both Δv and Δs increase with time

(c) Δv remains constant with time and Δs decreases with time

(d) Δv remains constant with time and Δs increases with time

21. The refractive index of a prism is measured using three lines of a mercury vapour lamp. If μ_1, μ_2 and μ_3 are the measured refractive indices for these green, blue and yellow lines respectively, then

(a) $\mu_2 > \mu_3 > \mu_1$

(b) $\mu_2 > \mu_1 > \mu_3$

(c) $\mu_3 > \mu_2 > \mu_1$

(d) $\mu_1 > \mu_2 > \mu_3$

22. A horizontal parallel beam of light passes through a vertical convex lens of focal length 20 cm and is then reflected by a tilted plane mirror, so that it converges to a point I. The distance PI is 10 cm.

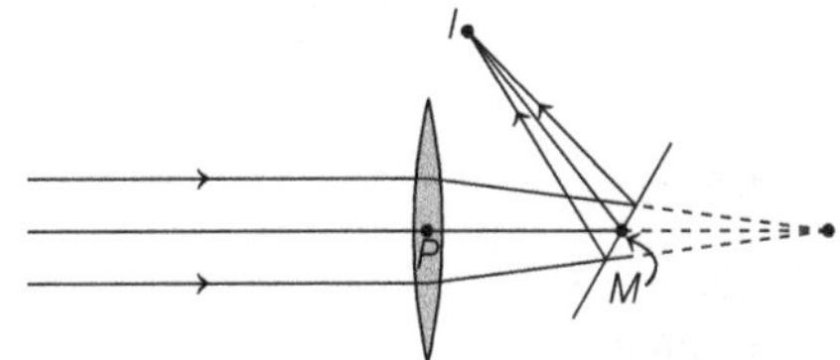

M is a point at which the axis of the lens intersects the mirror. The distance PM is 10 cm. The angle which the mirror makes with the horizontal is

(a) 15°
(b) 30°
(c) 45°
(d) 60°

23. In a car, a rear view mirror having a radius of curvature 1.50 m forms a virtual image of a bus located 10.0 m from the mirror. The factor by which the mirror magnifies the size of the bus is close to

(a) 0.06
(b) 0.07
(c) 0.08
(d) 0.09

24. Consider the following circuit shown below.

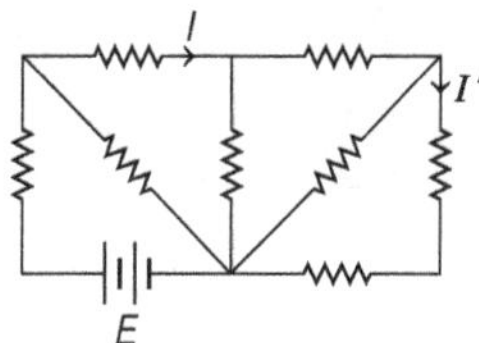

All the resistors are identical. The ratio of I / I' is

(a) 8
(b) 6
(c) 5
(d) 4

25. The figure shows a bar magnet and a metallic coil. Consider four situations:

  (I) Moving the magnet away from the coil.

  (II) Moving the coil towards the magnet.

  (III) Rotating the coil about the vertical diameter.

  (IV) Rotating the coil about its axis.

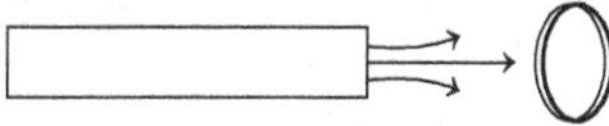

An emf in the coil will be generated for the following situations.

(a) I and II only

(b) I, II and IV only

(c) I, II, and III only

(d) I, II, III, and IV

26. A current of 0.1 A flows through a 25 Ω resistor represented by the circuit diagram. The current in 80 Ω resistor is

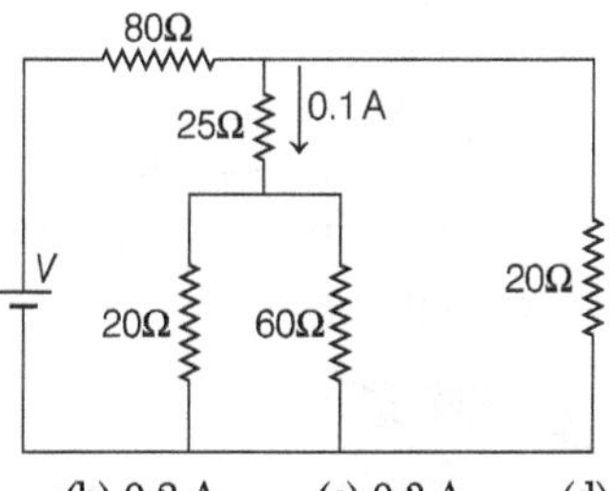

(a) 0.1 A
(b) 0.2 A
(c) 0.3 A
(d) 0.4 A

27. Solar energy is incident normally on the earth's surface at the rate of about 1.4 kW m^{-2}. The distance between the earth and the sun is 1.5×10^{11} m. Energy E and mass m are related by Einstein equation $E = mc^2$, where $c = 3 \times 10^8$ ms^{-1} is the speed of light in free space. The decrease in the mass of the sun is

(a) 10^9 kg s^{-1}

(b) 10^{30} kg s^{-1}

(c) 10^{26} kg s^{-1}

(d) 10^{11} kg s^{-1}

28. If the current through a resistor in a circuit increases by 3%, then the power dissipated by the resistor

(a) increases approximately by 3%

(b) increases approximately by 6%

(c) increases approximately by 9%

(d) decreases approximately by 3%

29. An ideal gas filled in a cylinder occupies volume V. The gas is compressed isothermally to the volume $V/3$. Now, the cylinder valve is opened and the gas is allowed to leak keeping temperature same. What percentage of the number of molecules should escape to bring the pressure in the cylinder back to its original value?

(a) 66%   (b) 33%   (c) 0.33%   (d) 0.66%

30. An electron enters a chamber in which a uniform magnetic field is present as shown below.

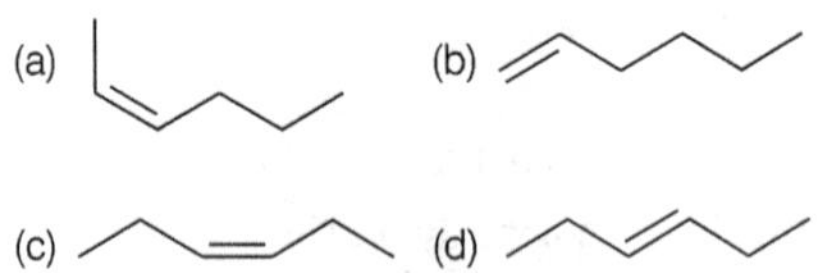

An electric field of appropriate magnitude is also applied, so that the electron travels undeviated without any change in its speed through the chamber. We are ignoring gravity. Then, the direction of the electric field is

(a) opposite to the direction of the magnetic field
(b) opposite to the direction of the electron's motion
(c) normal to the plane of the paper and coming out of the plane of the paper
(d) normal to the plane of the paper and into the plane of the paper

CHEMISTRY

31. The molecule having a formyl group is

(a) acetone   (b) acetaldehyde
(c) acetic acid   (d) acetic anhydride

32. The structure of *cis*-3-hexene is

(a)   (b)

(c)   (d)

33. The number of sp^2-hybridised carbon atoms in

$$HC \equiv C - CH_2 - \overset{O}{\overset{\|}{C}} - CH_2 - CH = CH_2, \text{ is}$$

(a) 3   (b) 5   (c) 4   (d) 6

34. The number of valence electrons in an atom with electronic configuration $1s^2 2s^2 2p^6 3s^2 3p^3$ is

(a) 2   (b) 3   (c) 5   (d) 11

35. The pair of atoms having the same number of neutrons is

(a) $^{12}_{6}C$, $^{24}_{12}Mg$ (b) $^{23}_{11}Na$, $^{19}_{9}F$ (c) $^{23}_{11}Na$, $^{24}_{12}Mg$ (d) $^{23}_{11}Na$, $^{39}_{19}K$

36. Which of the following molecules has no dipole moment?

(a) CH_3Cl (b) $CHCl_3$ (c) CH_2Cl_2 (d) CCl_4

37. The decay profiles of three radioactive species A, B and C are given below :

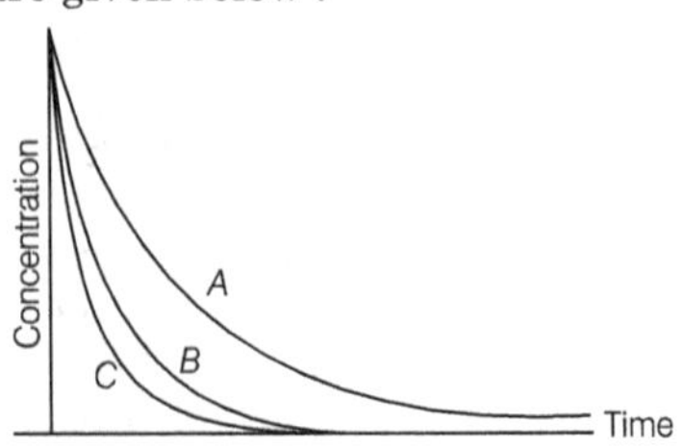

These profiles imply that the decay constants k_A, k_B and k_C follow the order

(a) $k_A > k_B > k_C$ (b) $k_A > k_C > k_B$
(c) $k_B > k_A > k_C$ (d) $k_C > k_B > k_A$

38. A specific volume of H_2 requires 24 s to diffuse out of a container. The time required by an equal volume of O_2 to diffuse out under identical conditions, is

(a) 24 s   (b) 96 s   (c) 384 s   (d) 192 s

39. Acetic acid reacts with sodium metal at room temperature to produce

(a) CO_2 (b) H_2 (c) H_2O (d) CO

40. The equilibrium constant, k_c for

$$3\,C_2H_2(g) \rightleftharpoons C_6H_6(g)$$

is $4\,L^2\,mol^{-2}$. If the equilibrium concentration of benzene is $0.5\,mol\,L^{-1}$, that of acetylene in $mol\,L^{-1}$ must be

(a) 0.025   (b) 0.25   (c) 0.05   (d) 0.5

41. The weight per cent of sucrose (formula weight $= 342$ g mol^{-1}) in an aqueous solution is 3.42. The density of the solution is $1\,g\,mL^{-1}$, the concentration of sucrose in the solution in mol L^{-1} is

(a) 0.01   (b) 0.1   (c) 1.0   (d) 10

42. The order of reactivity of K, Mg, Au and Zn with water is

(a) K > Zn > Mg > Au   (b) K > Mg > Zn > Au
(c) K > Au > Mg > Zn   (d) Au > Zn > K > Mg

43. Which of the following is an anhydride?

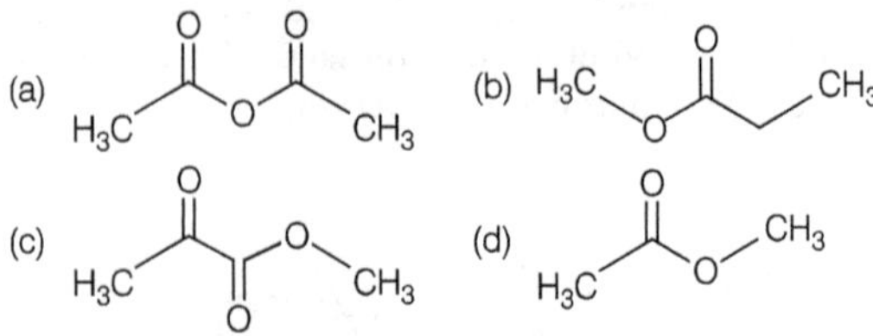

44. Which of the following metals will precipitate copper from copper sulphate solution?

(a) Hg   (b) Sn   (c) Au   (d) Pt

45. The radii of the first Bohr orbit of H (r_H), He$^+$ (r_{He^+}) and Li^{2+} ($r_{Li^{2+}}$) are in the order

(a) $r_{He^+} > r_H > r_{Li^{2+}}$ (b) $r_H < r_{He^+} < r_{Li^{2+}}$
(c) $r_H > r_{He^+} > r_{Li^{2+}}$ (d) $r_{He^+} < r_H > r_{Li^{2+}}$

BIOLOGY

46. The Bowman's capsule, a part of the kidney is the site of
(a) filtration of blood constituents
(b) reabsorption of water and glucose
(c) formation of ammonia
(d) formation of urea

47. In human brain, the sensation of touch, pain and temperature is controlled by the
(a) parietal lobe of cerebrum
(b) limbic lobe of cerebrum
(c) temporal lobe of cerebrum
(d) frontal lobe of cerebrum

48. A pathogen which cannot be cultured in an artificial medium is
(a) protozoan   (b) virus   (c) bacterium   (d) fungus

49. Meiosis-I and meiosis-II are characterised by the separation of
(a) homologous chromosomes; sister chromatids
(b) sister chromatids; homologous chromosomes
(c) centromere; telomere
(d) telomere; centromere

50. People suffering from albinism cannot synthesise
(a) suberin   (b) melanin   (c) keratin   (d) collagen

51. Short-sightedness in humans can be corrected by using
(a) concave lens   (b) convex lens
(c) cylindrical lens   (d) plain glass

52. A person with blood group 'A' can (i) donate blood to and (ii) receive blood from
(a) (i) person with blood group 'AB' and (ii) persons with any blood group
(b) (i) person with blood group 'A' or 'AB' and (ii) 'A' or 'O' blood groups
(c) (i) person with blood group 'B' or 'AB' and (ii) 'B' or 'O' blood groups
(d) (i) person with any blood group and (ii) 'O' blood group only

53. Animal cells after removal of nuclei still contained DNA. The source of this DNA is
(a) nucleosomes   (b) mitochondria
(c) peroxisomes   (d) lysosome

54. Which one of the following combinations is found in DNA?
(a) Guanine and guanidine (b) Guanidine and cytosine
(c) Guanine and cytosine   (d) Adenine and guanidine

55. Which one of the following is not a mode of asexual reproduction?
(a) Binary fission   (b) Multiple fission
(c) Budding   (d) Conjugation

56. Which one of the following classes of animals constitutes the largest biomass on the earth?
(a) Insects   (b) Fishes
(c) Mammals   (d) Reptilians

57. In the digestive system, the pH of the stomach and the intestine, respectively are
(a) alkaline, acidic   (b) acidic, alkaline
(c) acidic, neutral   (d) acidic, acidic

58. The major nitrogenous excretory product in mammals is
(a) amino acids   (b) ammonia
(c) urea   (d) uric acid

59. Which of the following plant traits (characters) is not an adaptation to dry (xeric) habitats?
(a) Sunken stomata on leaves
(b) Highly developed root system
(c) Thin epidermis without a cuticle on stem and leaves
(d) Small leaves and photosynthetic stem

60. Biological diversity increases with the productivity of an ecosystem. In which of the following habitats do we see the greatest diversity of species?
(a) Tropical dry grasslands
(b) Temperate deciduous forests
(c) Alpine grasslands
(d) Tropical evergreen forests

➲ PART-II (2 Marks Questions)

MATHEMATICS

61. Let a, b, c, d, e be natural numbers in an arithmetic progression such that $a + b + c + d + e$ is the cube of an integer and $b + c + d$ is square of an integer. The least possible value of the number of digits of c is
(a) 2   (b) 3
(c) 4   (d) 5

62. On each face of a cuboid, the sum of its perimeter and its area is written. Among the six numbers so written, there are three distinct numbers and they are 16, 24 and 31. The volume of the cuboid lies between
(a) 7 and 14   (b) 14 and 21
(c) 21 and 28   (d) 28 and 35

63. Let $ABCD$ be a square and let P be a point on segment CD such that $DP : PC = 1 : 2$. Let Q be a point on segment AP such that $\angle BQP = 90°$. Then, the ratio of the area of quadrilateral $PQBC$ to the area of the square $ABCD$ is
(a) $\dfrac{31}{60}$ (b) $\dfrac{37}{60}$ (c) $\dfrac{39}{60}$ (d) $\dfrac{41}{60}$

64. Suppose the height of a pyramid with a square base is decreased by $p\%$ and the lengths of the sides of its square base are increased by $p\%$ (where, $p > 0$). If the volume remains the same, then
(a) $50 < p < 55$ (b) $55 < p < 60$
(c) $60 < p < 65$ (d) $65 < p < 70$

65. There are three kinds of liquids X, Y, Z. Three jars J_1, J_2, J_3 contains 100 ml of liquids X, Y, Z respectively. By an operation we mean three steps in the following order
– stir the liquid in J_1 and transfer 10 ml from J_1 into J_2,
– stir the liquid in J_2 and transfer 10 ml from J_2 into J_3,
– stir the liquid in J_3 and transfer 10 ml from J_3 into J_1.
After performing the operation four times, let x, y, z be the amounts of X, Y, Z respectively, in J_1. Then,
(a) $x > y > z$ (b) $x > z > y$ (c) $y > x > z$ (d) $z > x > y$

PHYSICS

66. Two identical uniform rectangular blocks (with longest side L) and a solid sphere of radius R are to be balanced at the edge of a heavy table such that the centre of the sphere remains at the maximum possible horizontal distance from the vertical edge of the table without toppling as indicated in the figure.

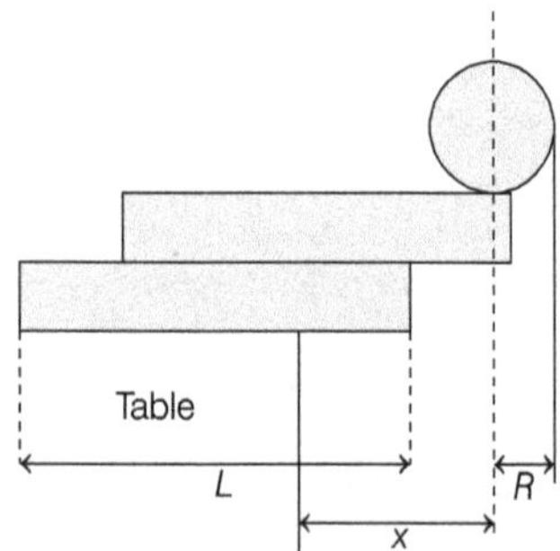

If the mass of each block is M and of the sphere is $M/2$, then the maximum distance x that can be achieved is
(a) $8L/15$ (b) $5L/6$
(c) $(3L/4 + R)$ (d) $(7L/15 + R)$

67. Two skaters P and Q are skating towards each other. Skater P throws a ball towards Q every 5 s such that it always leaves her hand with speed 2 ms^{-1} with respect to the ground. Consider two cases:
(I) P runs with speed 1 ms^{-1} towards Q, while Q remains stationary.
(II) Q runs with speed 1 ms^{-1} towards P, while P remains stationary.

Note That irrespective of speed of P, ball always leaves P's hand with speed 2 ms^{-1} with respect to the ground. Ignore gravity. Balls will be received by Q.
(a) One every 2.5 s in case (I) and one every 3.3 s in case (II)
(b) One every 2 s in case (I) and one every 4 s in case (II)
(c) One every 3.3 s in case (I) and one every 2.5 s in case (II)
(d) One every 2.5 s in case (I) and one every 2.5 s in case (II)

68. A 10.0 W electrical heater is used to heat a container filled with 0.5 kg of water. It is found that the temperature of the water and the container rose by 3 K in 15 min. The container is then emptied, dried and filled with 2 kg of an oil. It is now observed that the same heater raises the temperature of the container-oil system by 2 K in 20 min. Assuming no other heat losses in any of the processes, the specific heat capacity of the oil is
(a) 2.5×10^3 JK^{-1}kg^{-1}
(b) 5.1×10^3 JK^{-1}kg^{-1}
(c) 3.0×10^3 JK^{-1}kg^{-1}
(d) 1.5×10^3 JK^{-1}kg^{-1}

69. A ray of light incident on a transparent sphere at an angle $\pi/4$ and refracted at an angle r, emerges from the sphere after suffering one internal reflection. The total angle of deviation of the ray is
(a) $\dfrac{3\pi}{2} - 4r$ (b) $\dfrac{\pi}{2} - 4r$
(c) $\dfrac{\pi}{4} - r$ (d) $\dfrac{5\pi}{2} - 4r$

70. An electron with an initial speed of 4.0×10^6 ms^{-1} is brought to rest by an electric field. The mass and charge of an electron are 9×10^{-31} kg and 1.6×10^{-19} C, respectively. Identify the correct statement.
(a) The electron moves from a region of lower potential to higher potential through a potential difference of 11.4 μV
(b) The electron moves from a region of higher potential to lower potential through a potential difference of 11.4 μV
(c) The electron moves from a region of lower potential to higher potential through a potential difference of 45 V
(d) The electron moves from a region of higher potential to lower potential through a potential difference of 45 V

CHEMISTRY

71. The degree of dissociation of acetic acid (0.1 mol L^{-1}) in water (K_a of acetic acid is 10^{-5}) is
(a) 0.01   (b) 0.5
(c) 0.1   (d) 1.0

72. Compound X on heating with Zn dust gives compound Y which on treatment with O_3 followed by reaction with Zn dust gives propionaldehyde. The structure of X is

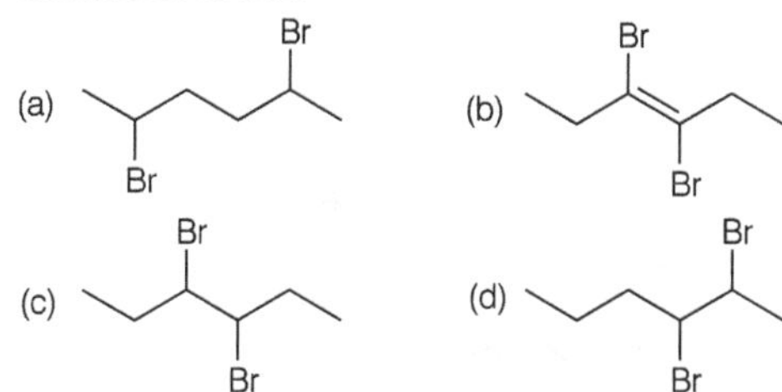

73. The amount of metallic Zn (atomic weight = 65.4) required to react with aqueous sodium hydroxide to produce 1 g of H_2, is
(a) 32.7 g   (b) 98.1 g   (c) 65.4 g   (d) 16.3 g

74. Natural abundances of ^{12}C and ^{13}C isotopes of carbon are 99% and 1%, respectively. Assuming they only contribute to the mol. wt. of C_2F_4, the percentage of C_2F_4 having a molecular mass of 101 is
(a) 1.98   (b) 98   (c) 0.198   (d) 99

75. 2,3-dimethylbut-2-ene when reacted with bromine forms a compound which upon heating with alcoholic KOH produces the following major product.

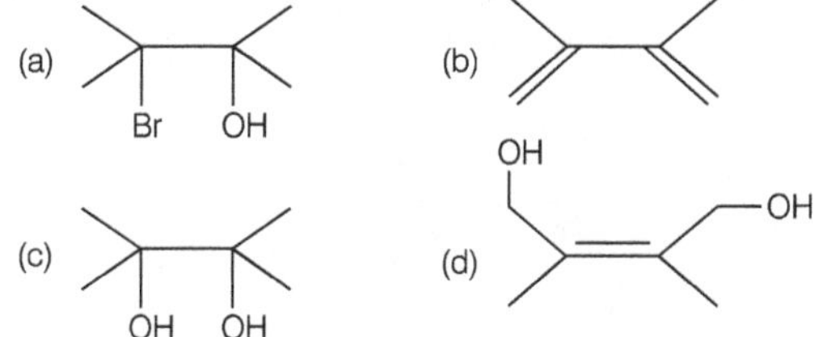

BIOLOGY

76. Sister chromatids of a chromosome have
(a) different genes at the same locus
(b) different alleles of the same gene at the same locus
(c) same alleles of the same gene at the same locus
(d) same alleles at different loci

77. A diabetic individual becomes unconscious after self-administering insulin. What should be done immediately to revive the individual?
(a) Provide him sugar
(b) Give him higher dose of insulin
(c) Provide him salt solution
(d) Provide him lots of water

78. A regular check on the unborn baby of a lady towards the end of her pregnancy showed a heart rate of 80 beats per minute. What would the doctor infer about the baby's heart condition from this?
(a) Normal heart rate
(b) Faster heart rate
(c) Slower heart rate
(d) Defective brain function

79. Three uniformly watered plants i, ii and iii were kept in 45% relative humidity, 45% relative humidity with blowing wind and 95% relative humidity, respectively. Arrange, these plants in the order (fastest to slowest) in which they will dry up.
(a) i → ii → iii   (b) ii → i → iii
(c) iii → ii → i   (d) iii → i → ii

80. Many populations colonising a new habitat show a logistic population growth pattern over time, as shown in the figure below

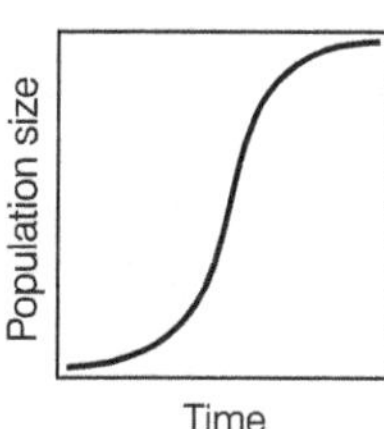

In such a population, the population growth rate
(a) stays constant over time
(b) increases and then reaches a asymptote
(c) decreases over time
(d) increases to a maximum and then decreases

Answers

PART-I

1	(c)	2	(c)	3	(c)	4	(b)	5	(c)	6	(a)	7	(c)	8	(c)	9	(c)	10	(d)
11	(b)	12	(c)	13	(a)	14	(b)	15	(b)	16	(a)	17	(b)	18	(a)	19	(d)	20	(c)
21	(b)	22	(d)	23	(b)	24	(a)	25	(c)	26	(c)	27	(a)	28	(b)	29	(a)	30	(c)
31	(b)	32	(c)	33	(a)	34	(b)	35	(c)	36	(d)	37	(d)	38	(b)	39	(b)	40	(d)
41	(b)	42	(b)	43	(a)	44	(b)	45	(c)	46	(a)	47	(a)	48	(b)	49	(a)	50	(b)
51	(a)	52	(b)	53	(b)	54	(c)	55	(d)	56	(a)	57	(b)	58	(c)	59	(c)	60	(d)

PART-II

61	(b)	62	(d)	63	(d)	64	(c)	65	(b)	66	(a)	67	(a)	68	(a)	69	(a)	70	(d)
71	(a)	72	(c)	73	(a)	74	(a)	75	(b)	76	(c)	77	(a)	78	(c)	79	(b)	80	(d)

Solutions

1. *(c)* We have, $x + y + z = 10$

Let three number $x + 1, y + 1, z + 1$

$AM \geq GM$

$$\frac{(x + 1) + (y + 1) + (z + 1)}{3} \geq$$
$$[(x + 1)(y + 1)(z + 1)]^{1/3}$$

$$\Rightarrow \frac{x + y + z + 3}{3} \geq$$
$$(xyz + xy + yz + xz + x + y + z + 1)^{1/3}$$

$$\Rightarrow \left(\frac{13}{3}\right)^3 \geq xyz + xy + yz + xz + 11$$

Now, x, y, z are integer.

$\therefore xyz + xy + yz + xz + 11$ is also integer.

$\therefore \left(\frac{13}{3}\right)^3$ is also integer.

$$\therefore \left[\left(\frac{13}{3}\right)^3\right] = 81 \left[\because \left(\frac{13}{3}\right)^3 = 81.37\right]$$

$\therefore xyz + xy + yz + xz + 11 \leq 81$

$$\Rightarrow xyz + xy + yz + xz \leq 70$$

$\therefore$ Maximum value of $xyz + xy + yz + xz$ is 69.

2. *(c)* Given, $2013 + a^2 = b^2$

$$\Rightarrow b^2 - a^2 = 2013$$
$$\Rightarrow (b - a)(b + a) = 3 \times 11 \times 61$$

ab is minimum.

When $b - a = 33$ and $b + a = 61$

On solving, we get $a = 14$ and $b = 47$

$\therefore$ Minimum value of $ab = 14 \times 47 = 658$

3. *(c)* We have sides of triangle are,

$$b + 5, 3b - 2, 6 - b$$

Triangle are isosceles.

$\therefore$ Two sides are equal.

Case I $b + 5 = 3b - 2$

$$\therefore b = \frac{7}{2}$$

So, sides are $\frac{17}{2}, \frac{17}{2}, \frac{5}{2}$.

Case II $3b - 2 = 6 - b \Rightarrow b = 2$

$\therefore$ Sides are 7, 4, 4

Case III $b + 5 = 6 - b \Rightarrow b = \frac{1}{2}$

Sides are $\frac{11}{2}, -\frac{1}{2}, \frac{11}{2}$ which is not possible.

$\therefore$ Only for two values of b, triangles are isosceles.

4. *(b)* We have,

$$\Rightarrow ax^2 + (a + b)x + b = 0$$
$$\Rightarrow ax^2 + ax + bx + b = 0$$
$$\Rightarrow (ax + b)(x + 1) = 0$$
$$\Rightarrow x = -\frac{b}{a}, -1$$

It has at least one negative root, i.e. -1.
So, it has both roots are real.

$\therefore$ Option (b) is correct.

5. *(c)* Given,

$$\Rightarrow \frac{x}{y} + \frac{y}{z} + \frac{z}{x} = 7 \Rightarrow \frac{y}{x} + \frac{z}{y} + \frac{x}{z} = 9$$

We know that,

$$a^3 + b^3 + c^3 - 3abc = (a + b + c)$$
$$(a^2 + b^2 + c^2 - ab - bc - ca)$$

$$\therefore a^3 + b^3 + c^3 - 3abc$$
$$= [(a + b + c)^2 - 3(ab + bc + ca)]$$

$$\Rightarrow \left(\frac{x}{y}\right)^3 + \left(\frac{y}{z}\right)^3 + \left(\frac{z}{x}\right)^3 - 3 = \left(\frac{x}{y} + \frac{y}{z} + \frac{z}{x}\right)$$
$$\left[\left(\frac{x}{y} + \frac{y}{z} + \frac{z}{x}\right)^2 - 3\left(\frac{x}{y} + \frac{y}{z} + \frac{z}{x}\right)\right]$$

$$\therefore \frac{x^3}{y^3} + \frac{y^3}{z^3} + \frac{z^3}{x^3} - 3 = (7)[7^2 - 3 \times 9]$$
$$= 7(49 - 27) = 7 \times 22 = 154$$

6. *(a)* In $\triangle ABC$, $\angle A < \angle B < \angle C$

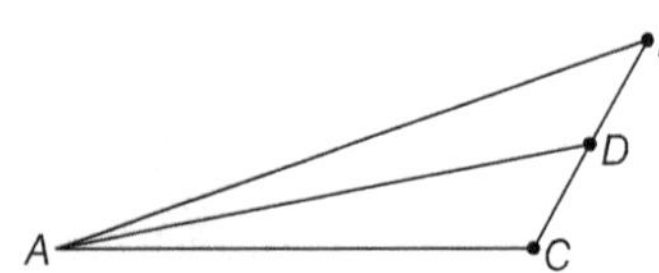

In $\triangle ABD$, $\angle D > \angle C$

So, $\triangle ABD$ not similar to $\triangle ABC$.

7. *(c)* Given,

PR and QR are tangents.

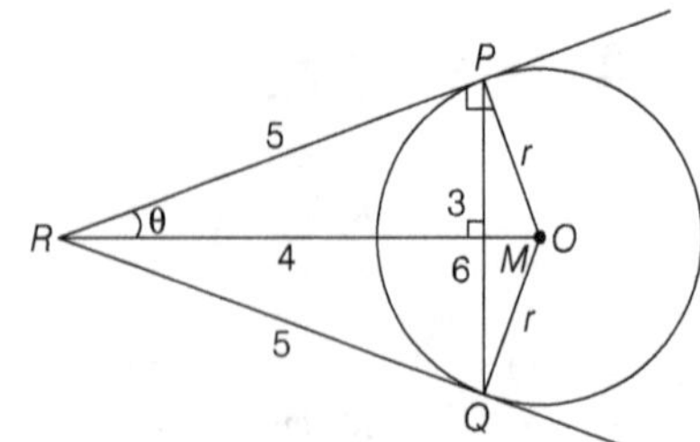

$$PQ = 6$$
$$PR = 5$$
$$PM = \frac{1}{2}PQ$$
$$\therefore PM = \frac{1}{2} \times 6 = 3$$

In $\triangle PRM$,

$$RM^2 = PR^2 - PM^2 = 25 - 9 = 16$$
$$RM = 4$$

In $\triangle PRM$, $\tan\theta = \dfrac{PM}{RM} = \dfrac{3}{4}$ ...(i)

In $\triangle POR$, $\tan\theta = \dfrac{OP}{PR} = \dfrac{r}{5}$ ...(ii)

From Eqs. (i) and (ii), we get

$$\frac{3}{4} = \frac{r}{5} \Rightarrow r = \frac{15}{4}$$

8. *(c)* Given, ABC is an acute angle triangle.

$$\angle B = 45°$$

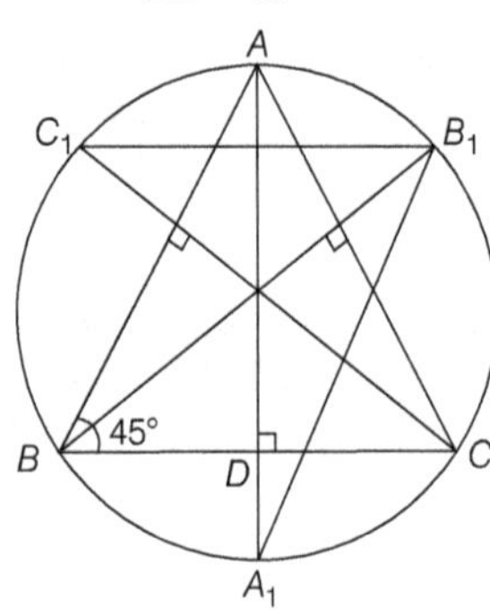

$$\angle ADC = 90°$$
$$[\because AD \text{ is altitude}]$$
$$\angle BAD = 45° = \angle BAA'$$

Similarly, $\angle BCC_1 = 45°$

$\therefore \angle BAA_1 = \angle BB_1A_1$

$[\because$ angle on same segment are equal]

$\angle BCC_1 = \angle BB_1C_1$

$[\because$ angle on same segment are equal]

$$\therefore \angle A_1B_1C_1 = \angle BB_1A_1 + \angle BB_1C_1$$
$$= 45° + 45° = 90°$$

9. *(c)* Given, $ABCD$ is rectangle.

$$\therefore AB = CD, BC = AD$$

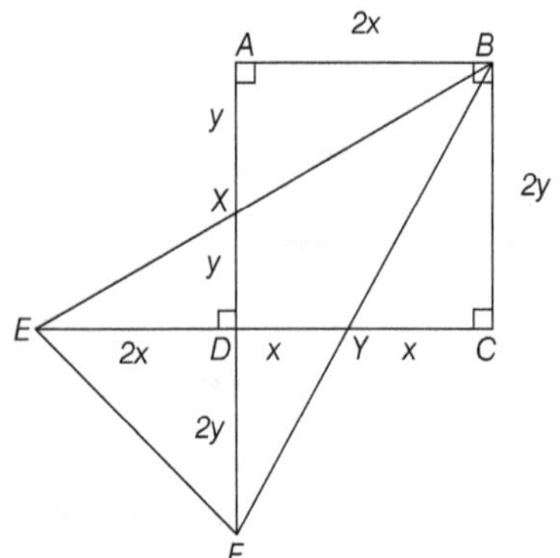

X and Y are mid-point of AD and CD respectively.

Let $AB=2x$, $BC=2y$

$\therefore AX = XD = y$

$DY = YC = x$

Area of rectangle $ABCD = 4xy = 60$

$\Rightarrow xy = 15$

In $\triangle ABX$ and $\triangle DEX$,

$$\triangle ABX \simeq \triangle DEX$$

$\therefore \qquad DE = AB = 2x$

Similarly, $\triangle CBY \simeq \triangle DFY$

$\therefore FD = BC = 2y$

$\therefore$ Area of $\triangle BEF$

$\quad = $ Area of $\triangle EFX +$ Area of $\triangle BFX$

$\quad = \dfrac{1}{2} FX \cdot DE + \dfrac{1}{2} FX \cdot AB$

$\quad = \dfrac{1}{2} \times 3y \times 2x + \dfrac{1}{2} \times 3y \times 2x$

$\quad = 6xy$

$\quad = 6 \times 15 = 90 \qquad [\because xy = 15]$

10. *(d)* Given,

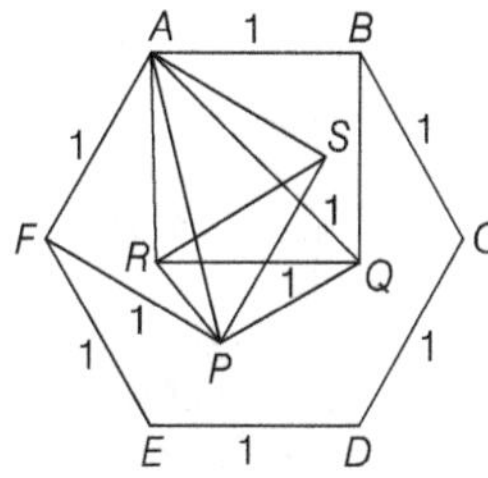

$ABCDEF$ is a regular hexagon of side length 1.

$ABQR$ and $AFPS$ is a square of each side length also 1.

$ADCDEF$ is a regular hexagon

$\therefore \qquad \angle FAB = 120°$

In square $ABQR$,

$$AB = BQ = 1$$

AQ is a diagonal of square

$\therefore \qquad AQ = \sqrt{AB^2 + BQ^2} = \sqrt{2}$

$\Rightarrow \angle BAS = \angle FAB - \angle FAS$

$\quad = 120° - 90° = 30°$

$\Rightarrow \angle SAR = \angle BAR - \angle BAS$

$\quad = 90° - 30° = 60°$

$\Rightarrow \angle ASR = 60°$

$\qquad [\because \triangle ARS$ is an equilateral triangle]

$\Rightarrow \angle RSP = \angle ASP - \angle ASR$

$\quad = 90° - 60° = 30°$

$\Rightarrow \angle FAB = \angle FAP + \angle PAQ + \angle QAB$

$\Rightarrow \ 120° = 45° + \angle PAQ + 45°$

$\qquad [\because \angle FAP = \angle QAB = 45°$

$\qquad FA = FP$ and $AB = BQ]$

$\therefore \ \angle PAQ = 30°$

$\therefore \dfrac{\text{Area of } \triangle PAQ}{\text{Area of } \triangle RSP} = \dfrac{\dfrac{1}{2} \times AQ \times AP \times \sin 30°}{\dfrac{1}{2} \times RS \times PS \times \sin 30°}$

$\qquad = \dfrac{\sqrt{2} \times \sqrt{2}}{1} = 2$

$\qquad [\because AQ = AP = \sqrt{2}, RS = PS = 1]$

11. *(b)* Given,

X complete one round in 40 s.

$\therefore \qquad 2\pi = 40 \text{ s}$

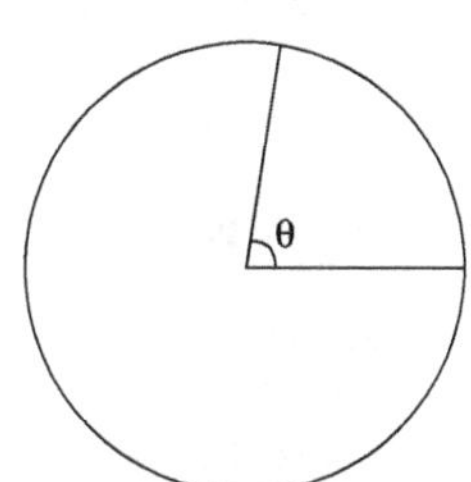

In one second, he complete, $\left(\dfrac{2\pi}{40}\right)$ round

In 15 s, he complete $\left(\dfrac{2\pi \times 15}{40}\right)$ round

Let Y complete one round in t s

$\therefore \qquad 2\pi = t$

In one second Y complete $\left(\dfrac{2\pi}{t}\right)$ round

In 15 s, Y complete $\left(\dfrac{2\pi}{t}\right) \times 15$ round

Since, both are move in opposite direction.

$\therefore \qquad \dfrac{2\pi}{40} \times 15 + \dfrac{2\pi}{t} \times 15 = 2\pi$

$\Rightarrow \qquad 15\left(\dfrac{1}{40} + \dfrac{1}{t}\right) = 1$

$\Rightarrow \qquad \dfrac{1}{t} = \dfrac{1}{15} - \dfrac{1}{40}$

$\Rightarrow \qquad \dfrac{1}{t} = \dfrac{8-3}{120}$

$\qquad = \dfrac{5}{120} = \dfrac{1}{24}$

$\therefore \qquad t = 24 \text{ s}$

12. *(c)* We have,

$$\sqrt{n+1} - \sqrt{n-1} < 0.2,\ n \in N$$

$\Rightarrow \qquad \sqrt{n+1} < 0.2 + \sqrt{n-1}$

On squaring both side, we get

$\quad n + 1 < 0.04 + n - 1 + 0.4 \sqrt{n-1}$

$\Rightarrow \ n + 1 - n + 1 - 0.04 < 0.4 \sqrt{n-1}$

$\Rightarrow \qquad \dfrac{2 - 0.04}{0.4} < \sqrt{n-1}$

$\Rightarrow \qquad 4.9 < \sqrt{n-1}$

$\Rightarrow \qquad n - 1 > (4.9)^2$

$\Rightarrow \qquad n > 1 + 24.01$

$\Rightarrow \qquad n > 25.01$

$\therefore$ Minimum value of $n = 26$

13. *(a)* Given, $n! + 10$

Put $\qquad n = 1, 2, 4, 5$

$n! + 10$ is not a perfect square.

Put $n = 3$, $3! + 10 = 6 + 10 = 16$ is a perfect square.

If $\qquad n > 5$

$n!$ is multiple of 10.

$\therefore \qquad n! = 10k$

$n! + 10 = 10k + 10 = 10(k + 1)$

$\qquad\qquad$ (when, k is even)

$\qquad = 10 (2m + 1)$

$\qquad = 2 \times 5 (2m + 1)$

$\therefore$ Product of odd and even is not a perfect square.

14. *(b)* We have 10 points lie a plane such that no three of them are collinear.

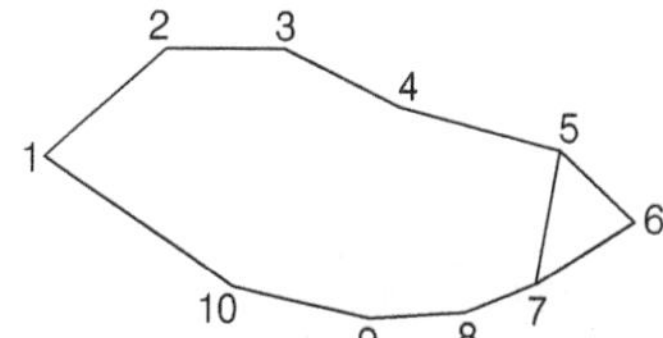

According to question only 5 ways are possible i.e. 1-6, 2-7, 3-8, 4-9 and 5-10.

15. *(b)* Let total number of people whose salary less than ₹ 10000 per annum $= x$

and annual salary of each person $= a$

$\therefore$ Total salary $= ax$

and total number of people whose salary more than ₹ 10000 per annum $= y$

and annual salary of each person $= b$

$\therefore$ Total salary $= bx$

When 5% increase of salary of people x

i.e. $\qquad x(a + 5\% \text{ of } a) = \dfrac{105ax}{100}$

and 5% decrease of salary of people y

i.e. $y(b - 5\% \text{ of } b) = \dfrac{95by}{100}$

$\dfrac{\text{Average salary after}}{\text{Average salary before}} = \dfrac{\dfrac{105ax}{100} + \dfrac{95by}{100}}{ax + by}$

$\qquad = 1 + \dfrac{5}{100}\left(\dfrac{ax - by}{ax + by}\right)$

$\qquad ax - by < 0$

$\therefore$ Average salary after be decreases.

16. *(a)* As centre of mass is subjected to a downward external force only, so its motion is along the direction of external force, i.e. downwards. Any internal force does not change position of centre of mass.

17. *(b)* When ball is released, vertical component of ball's velocity first increases in negative direction (downwards), then on collision with floor, its velocity is reversed (upwards).

As acceleration remains constant, so lines are parallel to each other as given in option (b).

18. *(a)* Pressure of a fluid column depends only on height of fluid column and as pressure is scalar, its magnitude does not depend on orientation of surface over which pressure acts.

19. *(d)* We have following observations from position x *versus* time t graph.

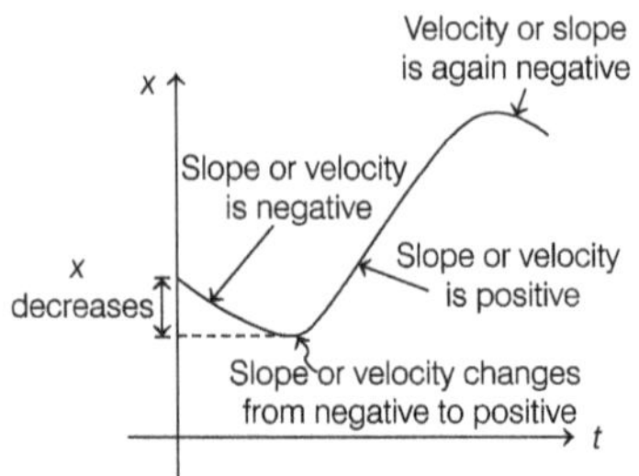

From above graph we can draw following velocity v *versus* time t graph.

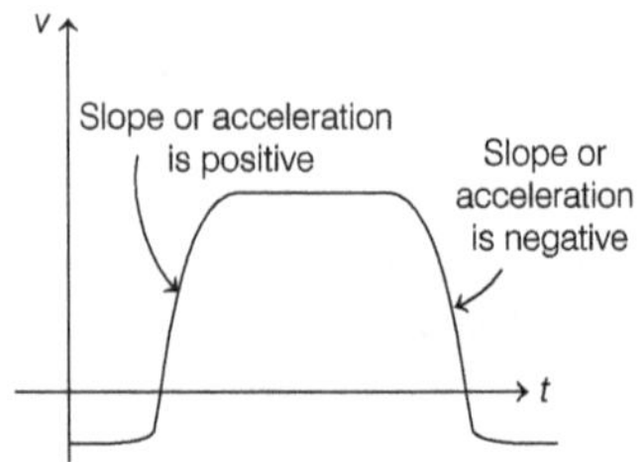

So, acceleration of given particle is initially positive but with time it becomes negative.

Hence, $a = p - qt$ is best suited option.

20. *(c)* Let first stone mass m_1 is dropped at instant $t = 0$.

Then at time t, its velocity and displacement respectively, are

$$v_1 = -gt \text{ and } s_1 = -\frac{1}{2}gt^2$$

As, second stone mass m_2 is dropped Δt time after, so its velocity and displacement at instant t respectively, are

$$v_2 = -g(t - \Delta t)$$

and

$$s_2 = -\frac{1}{2}(g)(t - \Delta t)^2$$

Difference in speeds of stones is

$$\Delta v = v_1 - v_2$$
$$= (-gt) - (-g(t - \Delta t))$$
$$= -gt + gt - g\Delta t = -g\Delta t$$

As both g and Δt are constants.

$\therefore \Delta v$ is constant and its value does not changes with time t.

The mutual separation Δs of the stones is

$$\Delta s = s_1 - s_2$$
$$= -\frac{1}{2}gt^2 - \left(-\frac{1}{2}g(t - \Delta t)^2\right)$$
$$= \frac{1}{2}g((t - \Delta t)^2 - t^2)$$
$$= \frac{1}{2}g(t^2 + \Delta t^2 - 2t\Delta t - t^2)$$
$$= \frac{1}{2}g(-2t\Delta t + \Delta t^2)$$
$$\Rightarrow \quad \Delta s = \frac{1}{2}g(\Delta t^2 - 2t\Delta t)$$

Clearly, Δs decreases with time and becomes zero when $2t = \Delta t$.

21. *(b)* Refractive index of a material is inversely proportional to wavelength of light.

$$\Rightarrow \quad \mu \propto \frac{1}{\lambda}$$

Now,
$$\lambda_{yellow} > \lambda_{green} > \lambda_{blue}$$
$$\Rightarrow \quad \mu_{yellow} < \mu_{green} < \mu_{blue}$$
or
$$\mu_3 < \mu_1 < \mu_2$$

22. *(d)* As focal length of lens is 20 cm, point of

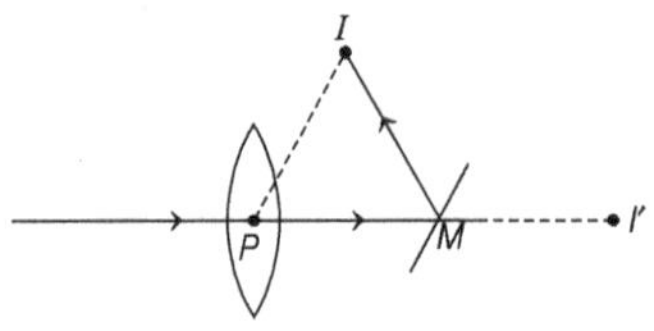

convergence of a parallel beam of light is also 20 cm.

Now, given $PM = 10\,\text{cm}$

So, $PI' = PM + MI = 20\,\text{cm}$

or $MI = 20 - 10 = 10\,\text{cm}$

As, $PI = 10\,\text{cm}$

$\therefore \Delta PMI$ is an equilateral triangle of side 10 cm.

Now, if MN is normal to mirror, as angle of incidence and reflection are equal, we have following situation

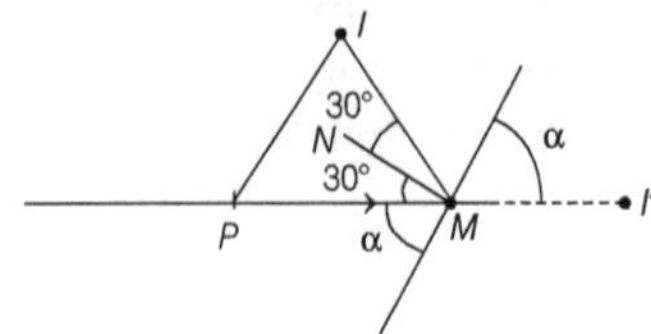

From above figure, we have

$$\alpha + 30° = 90° \Rightarrow \alpha = 60°$$

Hence, mirror makes an angle of 60° with the horizontal.

23. *(b)* Rear view mirror is a convex mirror.

Here, $u = -10\,\text{m}$

$$\therefore \quad f = \frac{R}{2} = +\left(\frac{1.5}{2}\right)\text{m}$$

Now, from mirror equation,

$$\frac{1}{v} + \frac{1}{u} = \frac{1}{f} \text{ or } \frac{1}{v} = \frac{1}{f} - \frac{1}{u} = \frac{2}{1.5} - \frac{1}{(-10)}$$
$$= \frac{4}{3} + \frac{1}{10} = \frac{43}{30} \text{ or } v = \frac{30}{43}\,\text{m}$$

Now, magnification,

$$m = \frac{-v}{u} = \frac{-\left(\dfrac{30}{43}\right)}{-10} = 0.069 \text{ or } m = 0.07$$

24. *(a)* first we distribute current in circuit given as

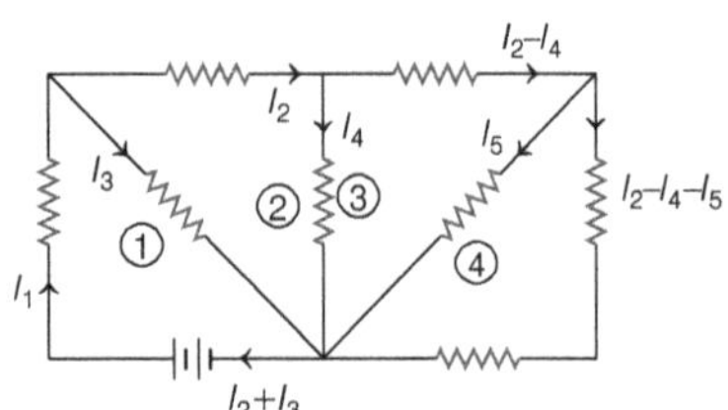

Current distribution must follows Kirchhoff's junction rule.

Now, from closed loops marked 1, 2, 3 and 4, we have following set of equations by application of Kirchhoff's loop rule,

$$I_1 = I_2 + I_3 \qquad \text{...(i)}$$
$$I_3 = I_2 + I_4 \qquad \text{...(ii)}$$
$$I_4 = I_2 - I_4 + I_5$$
$$\Rightarrow \quad 2I_4 = I_2 + I_5 \qquad \text{...(iii)}$$
$$I_5 = 2(I_2 - I_4 - I_5)$$
$$\Rightarrow \quad I_5 = 2I_2 - 2I_4 - 2I_5 \qquad \text{...(iv)}$$
$$3I_5 = 2I_2 - 2I_4 \qquad \text{...(v)}$$

From Eqs. (iii) and (v), we have

$$3I_5 = 2I_2 - (I_2 + I_5)$$
$$\Rightarrow \quad 4I_5 = I_2 \qquad \text{...(vi)}$$

From Eqs. (iii) and (vi), we have

$$2I_4 = 4I_5 + I_5 \Rightarrow I_4 = \frac{5}{2}I_5 \qquad \text{...(vii)}$$

From Eqs. (ii), (vi) and (vii), we have

$$I_3 = 4I_5 + \frac{5}{2}I_5 = \frac{13}{2}I_5 \qquad \text{...(viii)}$$

Now, marked currents I and I' in the given circuit are

$$I' = (I_2 - I_4 - I_5) = \left(4I_5 - \frac{5}{2}I_5 - I_5\right)$$
$$= \left(\frac{8 - 5 - 2}{2}\right)I_5 = \frac{I_5}{2} \qquad \text{...(ix)}$$

And $I = I_2 = 4I_5$

Hence, ratio of $I / I' = (4I_5) / (I_5 / 2) = 8.$

25. *(c)* An emf is induced in the coil when there is a flux change in the coil or when field lines are cut by the coil.

When coil rotates about its axis, there is no change in flux as no field line is cut by the coil.

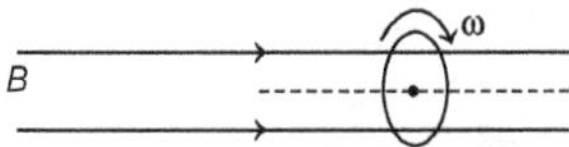

So, no emf is generated in coil when it is rotated about its axis. In all other cases an emf is induced in the coil.

26. *(c)* Given circuit is

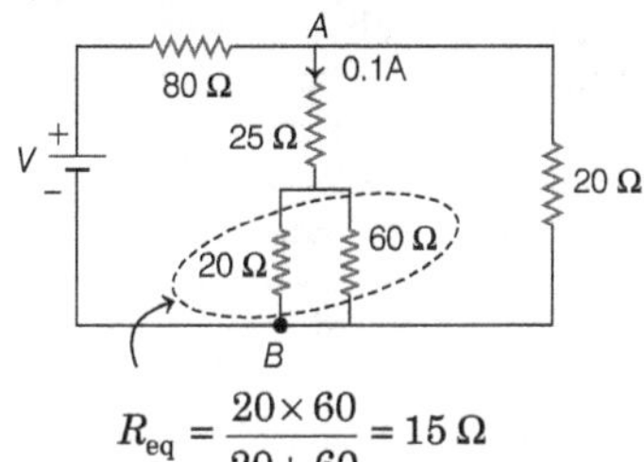

$$R_{eq} = \frac{20 \times 60}{20 + 60} = 15\,\Omega$$

We can redraw the circuit as

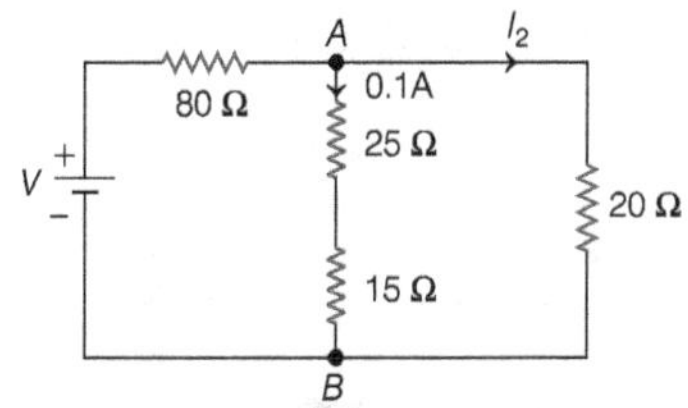

Let current through $20\,\Omega$ resistor is I_2, then

$$V_{AB} = 0.1\,(25 + 15) = I_2 \times 20$$

or $\quad I_2 = \dfrac{0.1 \times 40}{20} = 0.2\,\text{A}$

So, by Kirchhoff's junction rule, current through $8\,\Omega$ resistance is

$I = 0.1 + 0.2 = 0.3\,\text{A}$.

27. *(a)* Energy from sun is radiated in a sphere of radius $(r = 1.5 \times 10^{11}\text{m})$.

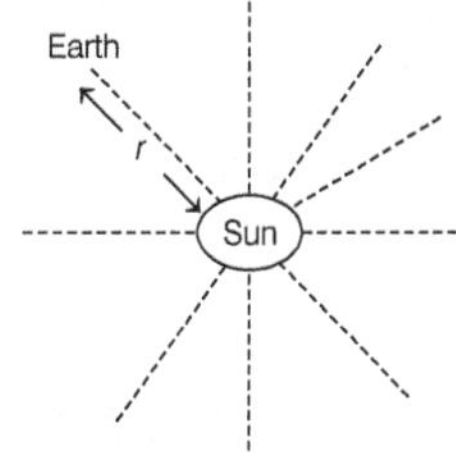

So, total energy radiated per second from sun is

$$\Delta E = 4\pi r^2 \times 1.4 \times 10^3$$
$$= 4 \times \frac{22}{7} \times 1.4 \times 10^3 \times (1.5 \times 10^{11})^2$$

From $E = mc^2$, we have

$$\Rightarrow \quad \Delta m = \frac{\Delta E}{c^2}$$

$$= \frac{4 \times 22 \times 1.4 \times 10^3 \times (1.5 \times 10^{11})^2}{7 \times (3 \times 10^8)^2}$$
$$\approx 10^9\,\text{kg s}^{-1}$$

So, mass reduction per second is around 10^9 kg.

28. *(b)* Power dissipated by resistor is

$$P = I^2 R \Rightarrow \frac{\Delta P}{P} = \frac{2\Delta I}{I}$$

or $\quad \dfrac{\Delta P}{P} \times 100 = \dfrac{2\Delta I}{I} \times 100$

Per cent change in power dissipation
$$= 2 \times \text{Per cent change in current}$$
$$= 2 \times 3\% = 6\%$$

29. *(a)* Initially let pressure is p, then

$$pV = n_1 RT$$

Finally pressure is p and volume is $\dfrac{V}{3}$.

Let number of moles of gas left is n_2, then

$$p\frac{V}{3} = n_2 RT$$

Dividing both equations, we get

$$\frac{n_2}{n_1} = \frac{1}{3} \text{ or } 1 - \frac{n_2}{n_1} = 1 - \frac{1}{3} \text{ or } \frac{n_1 - n_2}{n_1} = \frac{2}{3}$$

Hence, $\dfrac{n_1 - n_2}{n_1} \times 100 = \dfrac{2}{3} \times 100 = 66\%$

or percentage of number of molecules escaped = 66%.

30. *(c)* Using right hand rule, direction of magnetic force can be found. It acts outward from the plane of paper in given case.

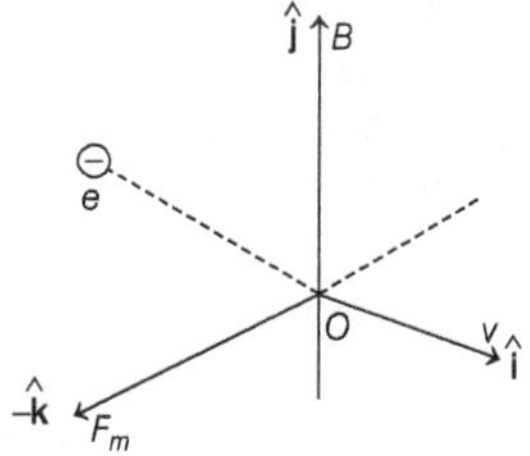

To avoid deflection of electron, electric field must be applied normal to the plane of paper (XOY-plane in diagrams) and pointing outward.

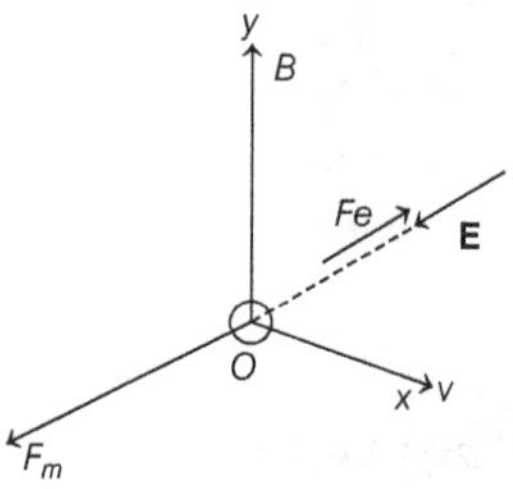

Magnitude of electric field applied is such that $F_m = F_e$.

31. *(b)* A formyl group is one which consists of a carbonyl group attached to a hydrogen, i.e.,

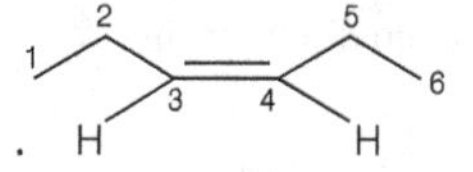

The structure of the given organic compounds are as follows

(i) Acetone — CH_3—C—CH_3, $\overset{\parallel}{O}$

(ii) Acetaldehyde — CH_3—C—H, $\overset{\parallel}{O}$

(iii) Acetic acid — CH_3OH

(iv) Acetic anhydride—CH_3—C—O—C—CH_3

As acetaldehyde has R—C—H group, $\overset{\parallel}{O}$

Thus, the correct option is (b).

32. *(c)* The structure of *cis*-3-hexene is

33. *(a)* Generally a sp^2-hybridised carbon atom is one which has a double bond.

$$HC\equiv C - CH_2 - \overset{O}{\overset{\parallel}{C}} - CH_2 - CH = CH_2$$

Thus, the given structure has $3sp^2$-hybridised carbon atoms.

34. *(b)* Valence electrons are those electrons which are present in the outermost shell of an element.

In the given electronic configuration, $1s^2 2s^2 2p^6 3s^2 3p^3$, $3p$ is the outermost shell, thus the number of valence electrons are 3.

35. *(c)* Number of neutrons in the pairs given in options are as follows

(a) $^{12}_{6}C$, $^{24}_{12}Mg$

No. of neutrons in C = 12 – 6 = 6
No. of neutrons in Mg = 24 – 12 = 12

(b) $^{23}_{11}Na$, $^{19}_{9}F$

No. of neutrons in Na = 23 – 11 = 12
No. of neutrons in F = 19 – 9 = 10

(c) $^{23}_{11}Na$, $^{24}_{12}Mg$

No. of neutrons in Na = 23 – 11 = 12
No. of neutrons in Mg = 24 – 12 = 12

(d) $_{11}^{23}Na$, $_{19}^{39}K$

No. of neutrons in Na = 23 − 11 = 12

No. of neutrons in K = 39 − 19 = 20

Thus, option (c) is correct.

36. *(d)* A molecule which has a symmetrical geometry will have no dipole moment, as the magnitude of all the bond moments cancel each other.

The structure of compounds given in options are as follows

CH_3Cl
($\mu = 0$)

$CHCl_3$
($\mu = 0$)

CCl_4
Symmetrical molecule, $\mu = 0$

Thus, CCl_4 has no dipole moment.

37. *(d)* As the species are radioactive, so they follow Ist order kinetics.

For Ist order $\quad C_t = C_0 e^{-kt}$

$\therefore \qquad\qquad k \propto \dfrac{1}{t}$

From the graph it can be concluded that species A takes maximum time to decay while species C takes least time. Thus, decay constant follows the order $k_C > k_B > k_A$.

38. *(b)* The ratio of rate of diffusion of two gases, O_2 and H_2 can be given as

$$\frac{r_{O_2}}{r_{H_2}} = \sqrt{\frac{M_{H_2}}{M_{O_2}}}$$

$$\frac{r_{O_2}}{r_{H_2}} = \sqrt{\frac{2}{32}} = \frac{1}{4}$$

$$r_{O_2} : r_{H_2} = 1 : 4$$

Also, rate of diffusion

$$= \frac{\text{Volume of diffused gas}}{\text{Time of diffused gas}}$$

$\therefore \quad \dfrac{r_{O_2}}{r_{H_2}} = \dfrac{t_{H_2}}{t_{O_2}} = \dfrac{1}{4} = \dfrac{24}{t_{O_2}} = 96\,s$

39. *(b)* Whenever an acid reacts with a metal, hydrogen gas is evolved. So, when acetic acid reacts with a sodium metal, hydrogen gas is produced.

$$CH_3COOH + Na \longrightarrow CH_3CO\bar{O}Na^+ + H_2 \uparrow$$

40. *(d)* For the reaction,

$$3C_2H_2(g) \rightleftharpoons C_6H_6(g)$$

$$K_c = \frac{[C_6H_6]}{[C_2H_2]^3} \Rightarrow 4 = \frac{0.5}{[C_2H_2]^3}$$

$$[C_2H_2]^3 = \frac{0.5}{4} = \frac{1}{8}$$

$$[C_2H_2] = \frac{1}{2} = 0.5\,mol/L$$

41. *(b)* Given,

$$\text{Weight of sucrose} = \frac{3.42}{100} = 0.0342\,g$$

$$\text{Molar mass of sucrose} = 342\,g$$

$$\text{Mass of solution} = 100\,g$$

$$\text{Density of solution} = 1\,g\,mL^{-1}$$

$\therefore \quad \text{No. of moles of sucrose} = \dfrac{0.0342}{342}$

Also, density $= \dfrac{\text{Mass}}{\text{Volume}}$

$\therefore \quad \text{Volume} = \dfrac{100}{1} = 100\,mL$

Concentration of solution is calculated in terms of molarity

$$\text{Molarity} = \frac{\text{No. of moles of sucrose}}{\text{Vol. of solution in litres}}$$

$$= \frac{\dfrac{0.0342}{100}}{1000} = \frac{0.0342}{100} \times 1000 = 0.1\,mol/L$$

42. *(b)* The reactivity of K, Mg, Au and Zn with water can be determined by the reactivity series of metals.

According to reactivity series, the decreasing order of reactivity will be

$$K > Mg > Zn > Au$$

43. *(a)* An anhydride is a compound that has two acyl groups bonded to same oxygen atom, i.e.

This type of structure is given in option (a).

2- acyl groups
attached to O-atoms

Thus, option (a) is correct.

44. *(b)* More reactive metal than Cu can precipitate copper from copper sulphate solution. The increasing order of reactivity of given element is

$$Au < Hg < Cu < Sn$$

As Sn is more reactive than Cu, so it would precipitate Cu from $CuSO_4$.

45. *(c)* According to Bohr's radius of an atom

$$r = 0.529 \times \frac{n^2}{Z} \Rightarrow r \propto \frac{1}{Z}$$

where, Z is the atomic number.

Thus, more is the atomic number lesser will the Bohr's radius. Therefore, the correct order is

$$r_H > r_{He^+} > r_{Li^{2+}}$$

46. *(a)* In Bowman's capsule ultrafiltration of blood occurs. Bowman's capsule is a cup-like sack at the beginning of the tubular component of a nephron in the mammalian kidney that performs the first step in the filtration of blood to form urine. Fluids from blood in the glomerular are collected in the Bowman's capsule (i.e. glomerular filtrate) and further processed along the nephron to form urine. This process is known as ultrafiltration.

47. *(a)* Parietal lobe is sensory lobe for touch, pain and temperature. The cerebral cortex is divided into four sections, called 'lobes'. Out of these, the parietal lobe is associated with movement, orientation, recognition and perception of stimuli. Thus, the parietal lobe functions in registration of sensory perception of touch, pain, heat and cold, knowledge about position in space, taking in information from environment, organising it and communicating to rest of brain.

48. *(b)* Virus cannot be cultured in an artificial medium. It multiples only in living cells. Viruses are obligate intracellular parasites.

They lack metabolic machinery to generate energy or to synthesise proteins, instead they rely on their host cells to carry out these functions.

49. *(a)* **Meiosis-I** Reduction division ($2n \to n$), separation of homologous chromosomes results in reduction of chromosome ploidy to half.

Meiosis-II Similar to mitosis where sister chromatids separate.

50. *(b)* Melanin pigment synthesised from tyrosine amino acid, imparts colour to skin. People suffering from albinism cannot synthesise melanin. Albinism is a disease, in which a person has partial or complete loss of pigmentation (colouring) of the skin, eyes and hair. There is a cell called the melanocyte that is responsible for giving eyes, skin and hair pigmentation.

In albinism, there occurs genetic mutation in melanocytes which interfere with their pigment.

51. *(a)* Short-sightedness (myopia) is corrected by using concave lens. These lens work by bending the light rays slightly outwards, so that they can focus further back on the retina.

Myopia is an eye defect in which the eyeball grows slightly too long. This means that light does not focus on the light sensitive tissue (retina) at the back of the eye properly. Instead, the light rays focus just in front of the retina, resulting in distant objects appearing blurred.

52. *(b)* A person with blood group 'O' is a universal donor, whereas person with blood group 'AB' is a universal recipient. Blood group 'O' do not have any antigen on their RBC whereas blood group 'AB' do not have any antibody in their blood plasma, but both the antigens A and B on their RBC.

Therefore, a person with blood group 'A' can donate blood to a person with blood group 'A' or 'AB' and can receive blood from a person with blood group 'A' or 'O'.

53. *(b)* Mitochondria are structures within cells that convert the energy from food into a form that cells can use. Although most DNA is packaged in chromosomes within the nucleus, mitochondria also have a small amount of their own DNA. This genetic material is known as mitochondrial DNA or *mt*DNA. Thus, after the removal of nuclei, the cell still have *mt*DNA.

54. *(c)* The correct combination present in DNA is guanine and cytosine. The DNA consists of four types of nitrogen bases, i.e. adenine (A), thymine (T), guanine (G) and cytosine (C). Whereas guanidine is a strong base that found in urine as a normal product of protein metabolism and not present in DNA.

55. *(d)* Conjugation is the transfer of genetic material between bacterial cells by direct cell to cell contact or by a bridge-like connection between two cells (e.g. bacteria). Thus, conjugation is a process of genetic recombination not asexual reproduction.

56. *(a)* Insects (class–Insecta or Hexapoda) are the animals constituting the largest biomass on the earth. In the world, about 900 thousand different kinds of living insects are known. This represents approximately 80% of the world's animal species.

57. *(b)* In the digestive system, the pH of stomach and intestine are acidic and alkaline, respectively. The pH of stomach is 1.5-2.5 (i.e. acidic) and the pH of intestine is 7.4-7.6 (i.e. alkaline).

58. *(c)* The major nitrogenous excretory product in mammals is urea. Nitrogenous wastes in the body of animals tend to form toxic NH_3, which must be excreted. NH_3 is converted to urea in hepatocytes of the body.

59. *(c)* Thin epidermis without a cuticle on stem and leaves is not an adaptation to dry habitat. This is because the cuticle is a waxy layer on the epidermis which prevents the entire leaf from losing water from the surface. Thus, thick cuticle prevents water loss.

60. *(d)* Diversity of species is highest in the tropical evergreen forests primarily because there are fewer ecological obstacles for biodiversity. Like the climate is wet and warm, plants and animals have the greatest access to consistent energy, water and carbon, etc. This reduces the selection for traits that emphasise the ability to withstand environmental stresses such as cold and drought, etc., and promotes higher rates of speciation.

61. *(b)* We have,

a, b, c, d, e are natural number and in AP.

Let D is common difference of AP.

∴ Let
$$c = C$$
$$a = C - 2D$$
$$b = C - D$$
$$d = C + D$$
$$e = C + 2D$$
$$a + b + c + d + e = 5C$$
and $\quad b + c + d = 3C$

Given, $a + b + c + d + e$ is a cube of number

∴ $\qquad 5C = \lambda^3$ ...(i)

and $b + c + d$ is a square of number

∴ $\qquad 3C = u^2$ ...(ii)

From Eqs. (i) and (ii), we get
$$\frac{\lambda^3}{5} = \frac{u^2}{3}$$

λ^3 and u^2 is a multiple of 15.

∴ Smallest possible value of $\lambda = 15$ and $u = 45$

∴ $\qquad c = \dfrac{u^2}{3} = \dfrac{(45)^2}{3} = 675$

∴ Number of digits = 3

62. *(d)* Let the length, breadth and height of cuboid be x, y and z respectively.

∴ Perimeter of face $PQRS = 2(x + y)$

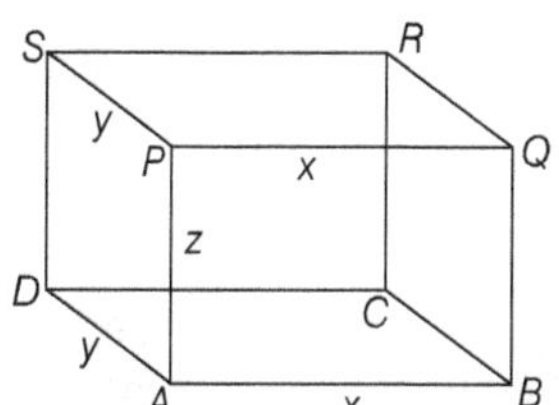

Area of $PQRS = xy$

∴ $\qquad 2(x + y) + xy = 16$ ...(i)

Similarly, for face $APSD$,
$$2(y + z) + yz = 24 \qquad \text{...(ii)}$$

and for face $APQB$,
$$2(x + z) + xz = 31 \qquad \text{...(iii)}$$

From Eqs. (ii) and (iii), we get
$$(x - y)(2 + z) = 7 \qquad \text{...(iv)}$$

From Eqs. (ii) and (iv), we get
$$4x = 2 + 5y \qquad \text{...(v)}$$

On solving Eqs. (i) and (v), we get
$$x = 3, y = 2, z = 5$$

∴ Volume of cuboid = $xyz = 3 \times 2 \times 5 = 30$

Hence, option (d) is correct.

63. *(d)* Given, $ABCD$ is a square.

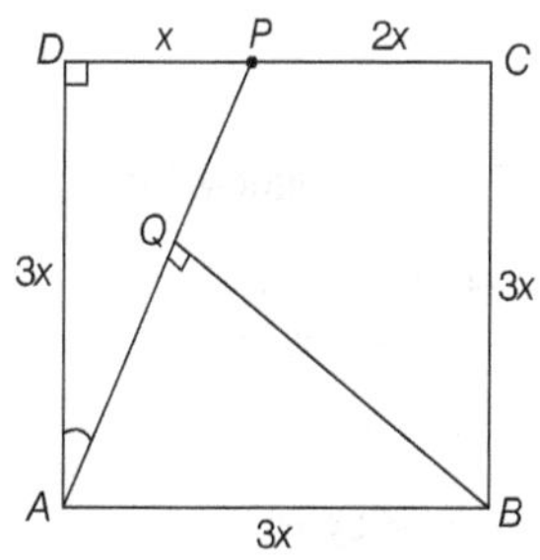

Let $\qquad AB = BC = CD = AD = 3x$
$$PD : PC = 1 : 2$$

∴ $\qquad PD = x$
$$PC = 2x$$

In ΔDAP and ΔQBA,
$$\angle DAP = \angle QBA$$
$$\angle D = \angle Q = 90°$$

∴ $\qquad \Delta DAP \sim \Delta QBA$

∴ $\qquad \dfrac{DA}{QB} = \dfrac{AP}{BA} = \dfrac{DP}{QB}$

⇒ $\qquad \dfrac{3x}{QB} = \dfrac{\sqrt{10}\,x}{3x} = \dfrac{x}{QA}$

$$[\because AP = \sqrt{9x^2 + x^2} = \sqrt{10}\,x]$$

∴ $\qquad QB = \dfrac{9}{\sqrt{10}}x \Rightarrow QA = \dfrac{3}{\sqrt{10}}x$

Area of quadrilateral $BQPC$ = area of square $ABCD$ − (area of $\triangle APD$ + area of $\triangle ABQ$)

$$= (3x)^2 - \left(\frac{1}{2} \times 3x \times x + \frac{1}{2} \times \frac{9}{\sqrt{10}} x \times \frac{3}{\sqrt{10}} x \right)$$

$$= 9x^2 - \left(\frac{3}{2} x^2 + \frac{27}{20} x^2 \right) = \frac{123x^2}{20}$$

$$\frac{\text{Area of quadrilateral } PQBC}{\text{Area of square } ABCD} = \frac{\dfrac{123x^2}{20}}{9x^2}$$

$$= \frac{41}{60}$$

64. *(c)* Let the side of square base of pyramid is x m and height of pyramid is y m.

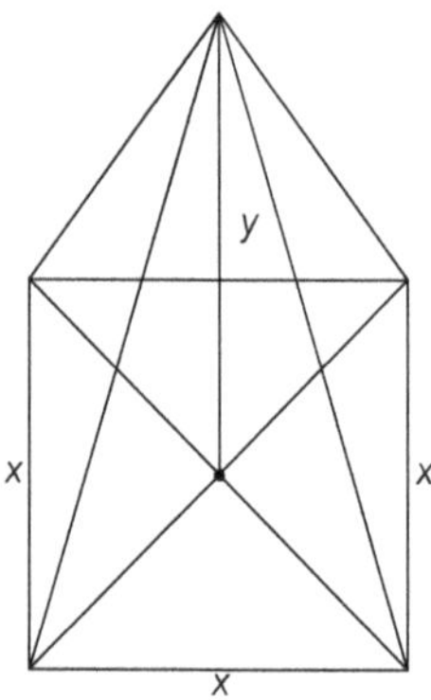

Volume of pyramid

$$= \frac{1}{3} \text{ area of base} \times \text{height} = \frac{1}{3} x^2 y$$

When x is increased by $p\%$, then new length $= x + p\%$ of

$$x = \left(\frac{100 + p}{100} \right) x$$

When y is decreased by $p\%$, then new height

$$= y - p\% \text{ of } y = \left(\frac{100 - p}{100} \right) y$$

Now, volume is same.

$$\therefore \frac{1}{3} x^2 y = \frac{1}{3} \left(\frac{100 + p}{100} x \right)^2 \left(\frac{100 - p}{100} \right) y$$

$$\Rightarrow 1 = \left(\frac{100 + p}{100} \right)^2 \left(\frac{100 - p}{100} \right)$$

$$\Rightarrow (100)^2 (100) = (10000 + 200p + p^2)$$
$$(100 - p)$$

$$\Rightarrow p^2 + 100p - 100^2 = 0$$
$$\Rightarrow p^2 + 100p + (50)^2 = (100)^2 + (50)^2$$
$$\Rightarrow (p + 50)^2 = 12500$$
$$\Rightarrow p + 50 = \sqrt{12500} = 111.80$$
$$\Rightarrow p = 111.80 - 50$$
$$\Rightarrow p = 61.80$$
$$\therefore 60 < p < 65$$

65. *(b)* We have, three kind of liquids x, y, z and three jars J_1, J_2, J_3 contains 100 ml of liquids X, Y, Z respectively.

When 10 ml of J_1 transfer to J_2

$\therefore J_1 = 90$ ml of X, $J_2 = 100$ ml of Y and 10 ml of X.

When 10 ml of J_2 transfer to J_3

$J_2 = \dfrac{1000}{11}$ of Y and $\dfrac{100}{11}$ of X, $J_3 = 100$ ml

of Z, $\dfrac{100}{11}$ of Y and $\dfrac{10}{11}$ of X

When 10 ml of J_3 transfer to J_1

$J_3 = \dfrac{1100}{11}$ of Z, $\dfrac{1100}{11}$ of Y, $\dfrac{110}{11}$ of X and

$J_1 = 90 + 10 \times \left(\dfrac{1}{11} \right)^2$ of X_1, $\dfrac{100}{121}$ of Y and

$\dfrac{100}{11}$ of Z

Similarly, we can find four operation of amount of X, Y, Z in J_1.

We get $x > z > y$.

66. *(a)* For system to be in equilibrium without toppling, following conditions must be fulfilled.

(i) Centre of mass C_1 of sphere and upper block must lie inside the edge of lower block.

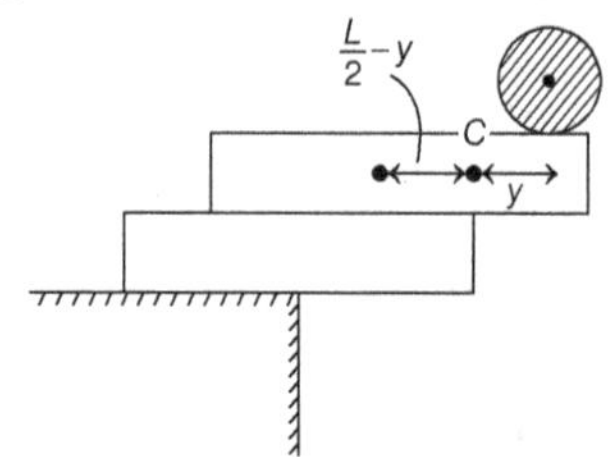

Taking origin of axes choosen at C, we have

$$\frac{M}{2} \times y = M \left(\frac{L}{2} - y \right)$$

$$\Rightarrow \frac{y}{2} + y = \frac{L}{2} \text{ or } y = \frac{L}{3}$$

(ii) Centre of mass of both of block and sphere must lie inside the edge of table.

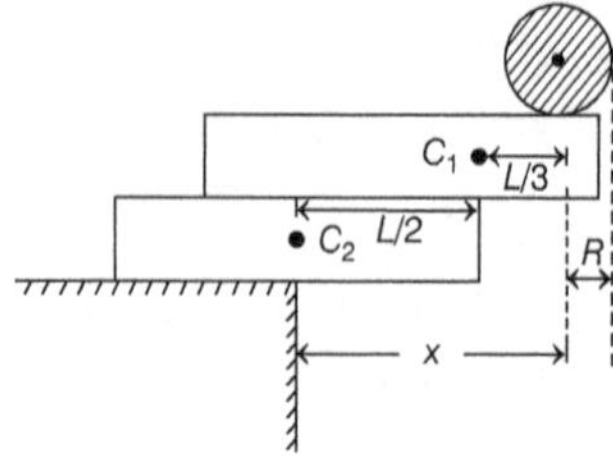

So, again taking centre of mass C_2 as origin,

$$\frac{3M}{2} \left(x - \frac{L}{3} \right) + M \left(x - \frac{L}{3} - \frac{L}{2} \right) = 0$$

$$\Rightarrow \frac{3x}{2} - \frac{L}{2} + x - \frac{L}{3} - \frac{L}{2} = 0$$

$$\Rightarrow \frac{5x}{2} = \frac{4L}{3}$$

$$\Rightarrow x = \frac{8L}{15}$$

67. *(a)* **Case I** P runs towards Q, while Q is stationary.

$$P \bullet \!\!\longrightarrow\!\bullet Q$$

First ball is received at time $t_1 = \dfrac{x}{2}$.

$\therefore$ Next ball is received at time t_2

$$= \frac{x - 5}{2} + 5 = \frac{x}{2} + \frac{5}{2}$$

So, $\quad \Delta t = t_2 - t_1 = \dfrac{5}{2}$ s $= 2.5$ s

Case II Q runs towards P, while P is stationary.

$$P \bullet\!\longleftarrow\!\!\bullet Q$$

First ball is received at time $t_1 = \dfrac{x}{3}$.

$\therefore$ Next ball is received at time t_2

$$= \frac{x - 5}{3} + 5$$

$$= \frac{x}{3} + \frac{10}{3}$$

So, $\quad \Delta t = t_2 - t_1 = \dfrac{10}{3}$ s $= 3.3$ s

68. *(a)* Energy supplied by heater = Heat absorbed by water + Heat absorbed by oil

So, with water in container,

$$P \Delta t = m_w s_w \Delta T + m_o s_o \Delta T$$

$$\Rightarrow 10 \times 15 \times 60 = 0.5 \times 4200 \times 3 + m_o s_o \times 3$$

$$\Rightarrow \quad m_o s_o = 900 \text{ J K}^{-1}$$

Now with oil in container,

$$P \Delta t = m_o s_o \Delta T + m_c s_c \Delta T$$

$$\Rightarrow 10 \times 20 \times 60 = 2 \times s_o \times 2 + 900 \times 2$$

$$\Rightarrow \quad s_o = \frac{10200}{4} = 2.5 \times 10^3 \text{ J K}^{-1}\text{kg}^{-1}$$

69. *(a)* According to condition given in question, ray diagram of sphere is

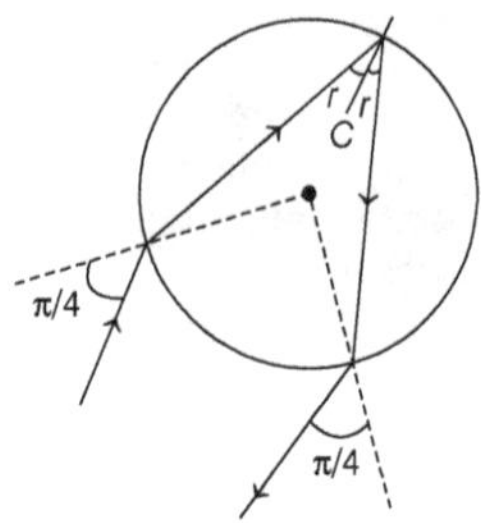

So, deviations are

$$\delta_1 = \frac{\pi}{4} - r$$

$$\delta_2 = \pi - 2r$$

$$\delta_3 = \frac{\pi}{4} - r$$

Total deviation of light ray is

$$\delta = \delta_1 + \delta_2 + \delta_3 = \frac{3\pi}{2} - 4r$$

70. *(d)* From, $qV = \frac{1}{2}mv^2$

where, V is stopping potential.

$$V = \frac{mv^2}{2q}$$

$$= \frac{9 \times 10^{-31} \times (4 \times 10^6)^2}{2 \times 16 \times 10^{-19}}$$

$$\approx 45\,V$$

So, electron must move across a potential difference of 45 V from higher to lower potential.

71. *(a)* Given,

Concentration of acetic acid, $C = 0.1\,M$

K_a of acetic acid $= 10^{-5}$

According to Ostwald dilution law,

$$K_a = \alpha^2 C$$

$$10^{-5} = \alpha^2 \times 0.1$$

$$\frac{10^{-5}}{0.1} = 10^{-5} \times 10 = \alpha^2$$

$$\alpha^2 = 10^{-4}$$

$$\alpha = 10^{-2}$$

72. *(c)* Skeletal diagram of given information can be drawn

$$X \xrightarrow{\text{Zn}} Y \xrightarrow{O_3/\text{Zn, H}_2O} 2CH_3CH_2CHO$$
$$\text{Propionaldehyde}$$

On retro synthesis.

73. *(a)*

$$Zn + 2NaOH(aq) \longrightarrow Na_2ZnO_4 + H_2 \uparrow$$

1 mole of H_2 is produced by 1 mole of Zn, i.e. 2 g of H_2 is produced by 65.4 g of Zn

$\therefore$ 1 g of H_2 is produced by $= \frac{65.4}{2}\,g = 32.7\,g$

74. *(a)* In molecular formula of C_2F_4, there are 4 F atoms. F has atomic mass of 19, so 4 F would have atomic mass of 76 g. So, possible molar mass of C_2F_4 are $100\,(76 + 12 + 12)$, $102\,(76 + 13 + 13)$ or $101\,(76 + 12 + 13)$.

Now according to % abundance

% of C_2F_4 of molar mass 100 (when both the C are ^{12}C)

$$= \frac{1}{100} \times \frac{1}{100} \times 100 = 0.01\%$$

% of C_2F_4 of molar mass 102 (when both the C are ^{13}C)

$$= \frac{99}{100} \times \frac{99}{100} \times 100 = 98.01\%$$

% of C_2F_4 of molar mass 101

$$= 100 - (98.01 + 0.01) = 1.98\%$$

75. *(b)* 2,3 dimethylbut-2-ene when reacts with bromine forms 2,3 dibromo 2,3 dimethyl butane which upon heating with alcoholic KOH produces 2,3 dimethylbut-1,3-diene as a major product. The reaction can be written as

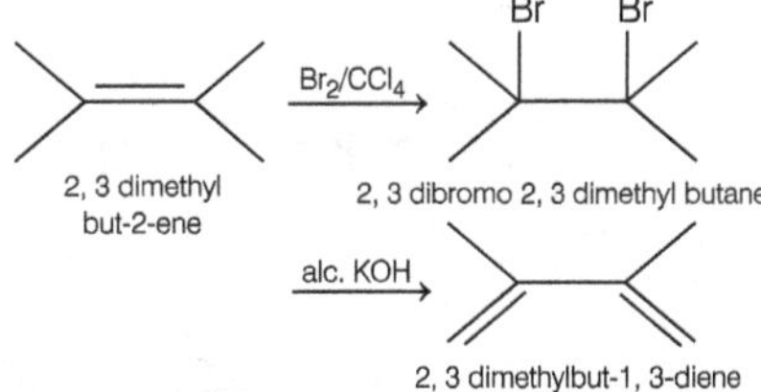

76. *(c)* Sister chromatids contain the same allele of the same gene at the same loci whereas non-sister chromatids contain different alleles of the same gene in the same loci.

Sister chromatids are the two chromatids of a replicated chromosome, which are connected by the centromere. They are identical to each other since they are produced by DNA replication.

77. *(a)* Insulin lowers blood sugar level and in this case, brain is getting inadequate sugar/glucose. Therefore, the person becomes unconscious. In order to revive the individual we need to provide him sugar, so that the blood sugar level becomes normal.

78. *(c)* A normal Foetal Heart Rate (FHR) usually ranges from 120-160 beats per minute. It is measurable sonographically. Therefore in this case, where the foetal heart rate is 80 beats per minute is a slower heart rate (foetal bradycardia).

79. *(b)* The plants in the order (fastest to slowest) in which they will dry up is ii → i → iii.

Relative humidity is the amount of water vapour present in air expressed as a percentage of the amount needed for saturation at the same temperature. As plants transpire, the humidity around saturates leaves with water vapour. When relative humidity levels are too high or there is a lack of air circulation, a plant cannot make water evaporate by transpiration or draw nutrients from the soil. Therefore 95% relative humidity will dry up the slowest, and the 45% relative humidity with blowing wind will dry up the fastest.

80. *(d)* The population growth pattern shown here is S-shaped (Sigmoidal curve). It is a population growth curve that shows an initial rapid growth (exponential growth) and then it slows down (decreases) as the carrying capacity is reached. Carrying capacity is the maximum number of individuals in a population that the environment can support.

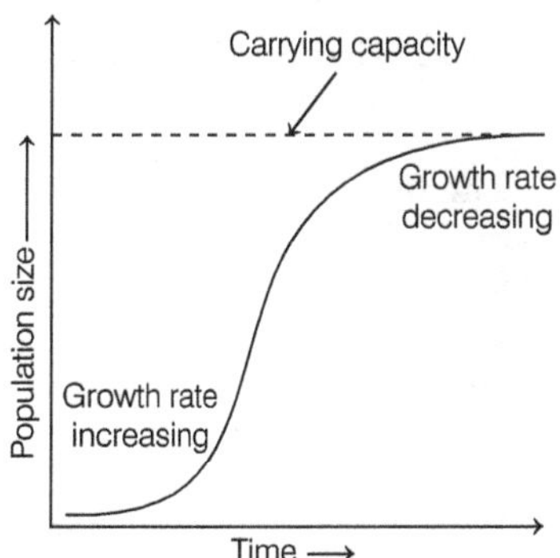

QUESTION PAPER 2012
Stream : SA

MM : 100

Instructions

1. There are 80 questions in this paper.

2. This question paper contains two parts; Part I and Part II. There are four sections; Mathematics, Physics, Chemistry and Biology in each part.

3. Out of the four options given with each question, only one is correct.

➲ PART-I (1 Mark Questions)

MATHEMATICS

1. Let $f(x)$ be a quadratic polynomial with $f(2) = 10$ and $f(-2) = -2$. Then, the coefficient of x in $f(x)$ is

(a) 1   (b) 2   (c) 3   (d) 4

2. The square root of $\dfrac{(0.75)^3}{1 - (0.75)} + [0.75 + (0.75)^2 + 1]$ is

(a) 1   (b) 2   (c) 3   (d) 4

3. The sides of a triangle are distinct positive integers in an arithmetic progression. If the smallest side is 10, the number of such triangles is

(a) 8   (b) 9

(c) 10   (d) infinitely many

4. If a, b, c, d are positive real numbers such that $\dfrac{a}{3} = \dfrac{a+b}{4} = \dfrac{a+b+c}{5} = \dfrac{a+b+c+d}{6}$, then $\dfrac{a}{b+2c+3d}$ is

(a) $\dfrac{1}{2}$ (b) 1

(c) 2   (d) not determinable

5. For $\dfrac{2^2 + 4^2 + 6^2 + \ldots + (2n)^2}{1^2 + 3^2 + 5^2 + \ldots + (2n-1)^2}$ to exceed 1.01, the maximum value of n is

(a) 99   (b) 100   (c) 101   (d) 150

6. In $\triangle ABC$, let AD, BE and CF be the internal angle bisectors with D, E and F on the sides BC, CA and AB respectively. Suppose AD, BE and CF concur at I and B, D, I, F are concyclic, then $\angle IFD$ has measure

(a) 15°

(b) 30°

(c) 45°

(d) any value $\leq 90°$

7. A regular octagon is formed by cutting congruent isosceles right angled triangles from the corners of a square. If the square has side length 1, the side length of the octagon is

(a) $\dfrac{\sqrt{2} - 1}{2}$ (b) $\sqrt{2} - 1$

(c) $\dfrac{\sqrt{5} - 1}{4}$ (d) $\dfrac{\sqrt{5} - 1}{3}$

8. A circle is drawn in a sector of a larger circle of radius r, as shown in the figure given below.

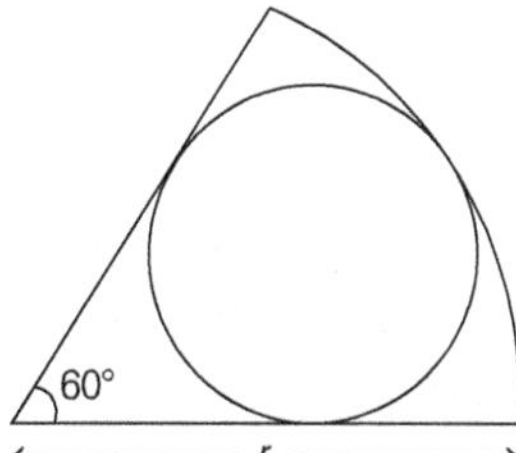

The smaller circle is tangent to the two bounding radii and the arc of the sector. The radius of the small circle is

(a) $\dfrac{r}{2}$ (b) $\dfrac{r}{3}$

(c) $\dfrac{2\sqrt{3}r}{5}$ (d) $\dfrac{r}{\sqrt{2}}$

9. In the figure, $AHKF$, $FKDE$ and $HBCK$ are unit squares, AD and BF intersect in X. Then, the ratio of the areas of triangles AXF and ABF is

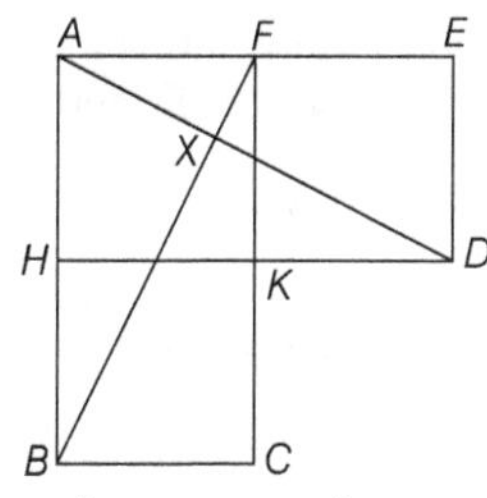

(a) $\dfrac{1}{4}$ (b) $\dfrac{1}{5}$ (c) $\dfrac{1}{6}$ (d) $\dfrac{1}{8}$

10. Suppose Q is a point on the circle with centre P and radius 1, as shown in the figure, R is a point outside the circle such that $QR = 1$ and $\angle QRP = 2°$. Let S be the point where the segment RP intersects the given circle. Then, measure of $\angle RQS$ equals

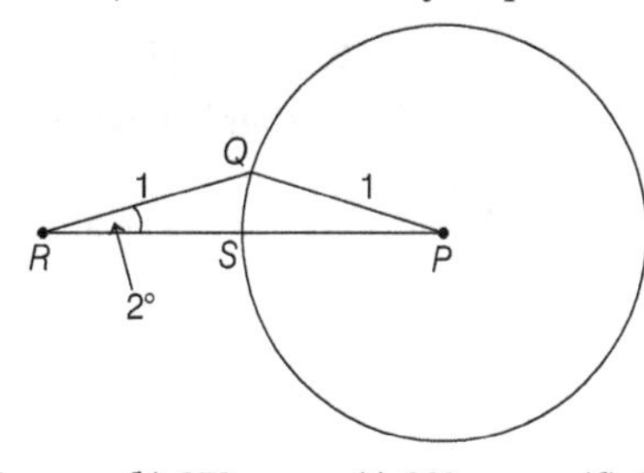

(a) 86°   (b) 87°   (c) 88°   (d) 89°

11. Observe that, at any instant, the minute and hour hands of a clock make two angles between them whose sum is 360°. At 6:15 the difference between these two angles is

(a) 165°   (b) 170°   (c) 175°   (d) 180°

12. Two workers A and B are engaged to do a piece of work. Working alone, A takes 8 h more to complete the work than, if both worked together. On the other hand, working alone, B would need $4\dfrac{1}{2}$ h more to complete the work than if both worked together. How much time would they take to complete the job working together?

(a) 4 h   (b) 5 h   (c) 6 h   (d) 7 h

13. When a bucket is half full, the weight of the bucket and the water is 10 kg. When the bucket is two-thirds full, the total weight is 11 kg. What is the total weight (in kg), when the bucket is completely full?

(a) 12   (b) $12\dfrac{1}{2}$ (c) $12\dfrac{2}{3}$ (d) 13

14. How many ordered pairs of (m, n) integers satisfy $\dfrac{m}{12} = \dfrac{12}{n}$?

(a) 30   (b) 15   (c) 12   (d) 10

15. Let $S = \{1, 2, 3, ..., 40\}$ and let A be a subset of S such that no two elements in A have their sum divisible by 5. What is the maximum number of elements possible in A?

(a) 10   (b) 13   (c) 17   (d) 20

PHYSICS

16. A clay ball of mass m and speed v strikes another metal ball of same mass m, which is at rest. They stick together after collision. The kinetic energy of the system after collision is

(a) $mv^2/2$ (b) $mv^2/4$ (c) $2\,mv^2$ (d) mv^2

17. A ball falls vertically downward and bounces off a horizontal floor. The speed of the ball just before reaching the floor (u_1) is equal to the speed just after leaving contact with the floor (u_2), $u_1 = u_2$. The corresponding magnitudes of accelerations are denoted respectively by a_1 and a_2. The air resistance during motion is proportional to speed and is not negligible. If g is acceleration due to gravity, then

(a) $a_1 < a_2$ (b) $a_1 > a_2$

(c) $a_1 = a_2 \neq g$ (d) $a_1 = a_2 = g$

18. Which of the following statements is true about the flow of electrons in an electric circuit?

(a) Electrons always flow from lower to higher potential

(b) Electrons always flow from higher to lower potential

(c) Electrons flow from lower to higher potential, except through power sources

(d) Electrons flow from higher to lower potential, except through power sources

19. A boat crossing a river moves with a velocity v relative to still water. The river is flowing with a velocity $v/2$ with respect to the bank. The angle with respect to the flow direction with which the boat should move to minimize the drift is

(a) 30°   (b) 60°   (c) 150°   (d) 120°

20. In the Arctic region, hemispherical houses called Igloos are made of ice. It is possible to maintain a temperature inside an Igloo as high as 20°C because
(a) ice has high thermal conductivity
(b) ice has low thermal conductivity
(c) ice has high specific heat
(d) ice has higher density than water

21. In the figure below, $PQRS$ denotes the path followed by a ray of light as it travels through three media in succession. The absolute refractive indices of the media are μ_1, μ_2 and μ_3, respectively. (The line segment RS in the figure is parallel to PQ).

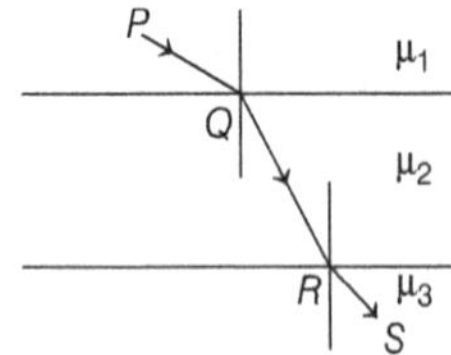

Then,
(a) $\mu_1 > \mu_2 > \mu_3$
(b) $\mu_1 = \mu_3 < \mu_2$
(c) $\mu_1 < \mu_2 < \mu_3$
(d) $\mu_1 < \mu_3 < \mu_2$

22. A ray of white light is incident on a spherical water drop whose centre is C as shown below.

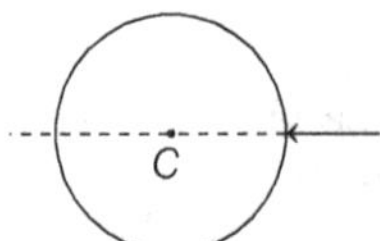

When observed from the opposite side, the emergent light
(a) will be white and will emerge without deviating
(b) will be internally reflected
(c) will split into different colours such that the angles of deviation will be different for different colours
(d) will split into different colours such that the angles of deviation will be the same for all colours

23. A convex lens of focal length 15 cm is placed in front of a plane mirror at a distance 25 cm from the mirror. Where on the optical axis and from the centre of the lens should a small object be placed such that the final image coincides with the object?
(a) 15 cm and on the opposite side of the mirror
(b) 15 cm between the mirror and the lens
(c) 7.5 cm and on the opposite side of the mirror
(d) 7.5 cm and between the mirror and the lens

24. Following figures show different combinations of identical bulb(s) connected to identical battery(ies). Which option is correct regarding the total power dissipated in the circuit?

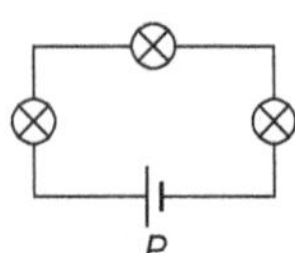 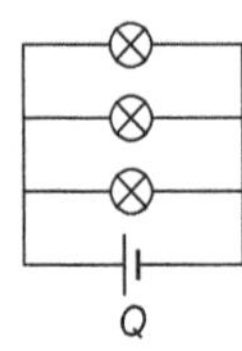

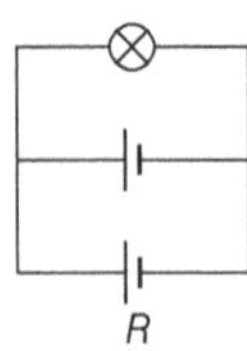 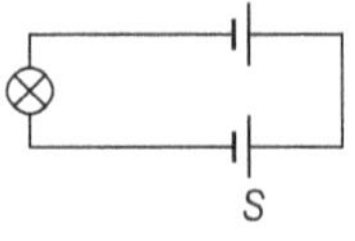

(a) $P < Q < R < S$
(b) $P < Q < R = S$
(c) $R < Q < P < S$
(d) $P > R > Q > S$

25. A circular metallic ring of radius R has a small gap of width d. The coefficient of thermal expansion of the metal is α in appropriate units. If we increase the temperature of the ring by an amount ΔT, then width of the gap
(a) will increase by an amount $d\alpha\Delta T$
(b) will not change
(c) will increase by an amount $(2\pi R - d)\,\alpha\Delta T$
(d) will decrease by an amount $d\alpha\Delta T$

26. A girl holds a book of mass m against a vertical wall with a horizontal force F using her finger, so that the book does not move. The frictional force on the book by the wall is
(a) F and along the finger but pointing towards the girl
(b) μF upwards, where μ is the coefficient of static friction
(c) mg and upwards
(d) equal and opposite to the resultant of F and mg

27. A solid cube and a solid sphere both made of same material are completely submerged in water but to different depths. The sphere and the cube have same surface area. The buoyant force is
(a) greater for the cube than the sphere
(b) greater for the sphere than the cube
(c) same for the sphere and the cube
(d) greater for the object that is submerged deeper

28. $^{238}_{92}$U atom disintegrates to $^{214}_{84}$Po with a half of 4.5×10^9 years by emitting six α-particles and n electrons. Here, n is
(a) 6　　　(b) 4　　　(c) 10　　　(d) 7

29. Which statement about the Rutherford model of the atom is not true?
(a) There is a positively charged centre in an atom called the nucleus
(b) Nearly all the mass of an atom resides in the nucleus
(c) Size of the nucleus is comparable to the atom
(d) Electrons occupy the space surrounding the nucleus

30. A girl brings a positively charged rod near a thin neutral stream of water from a tap. She observes that the water stream bends towards her. Instead, if she were to bring a negatively charged rod near to the stream, it will
(a) bend in the same direction
(b) bend in the opposite direction
(c) not bend at all
(d) bend in the opposite direction above and below the rod

CHEMISTRY

31. The weight of calcium oxide formed by burning 20 g of calcium in excess oxygen is
(a) 36 g   (b) 56 g   (c) 28 g   (d) 72 g

32. The major products in the reaction $Br_3CCHO \xrightarrow{NaOH}$ are

(a) $CHBr_3 +$ 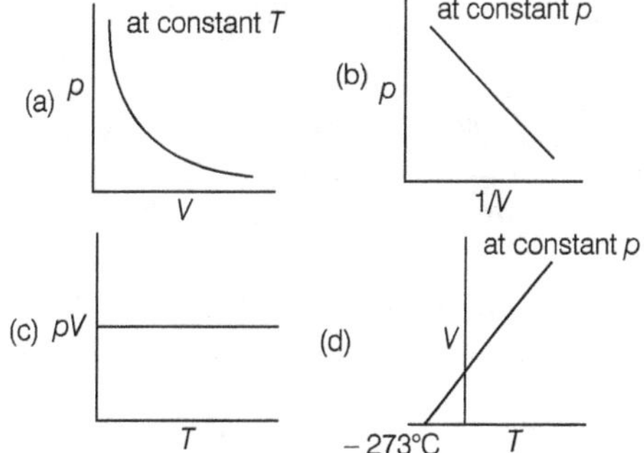

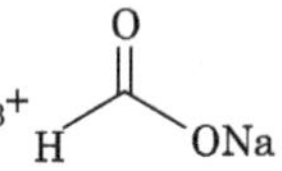

(b) $NaBr +$ 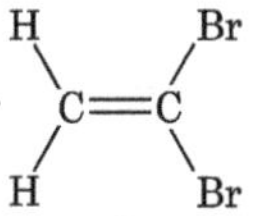 (C=C with H, Br groups)

(c) $NaOBr +$ (aldehyde D, H)

(d) (tribromo structures) OH + ... ONa

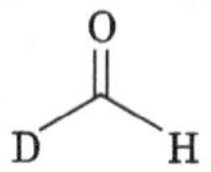

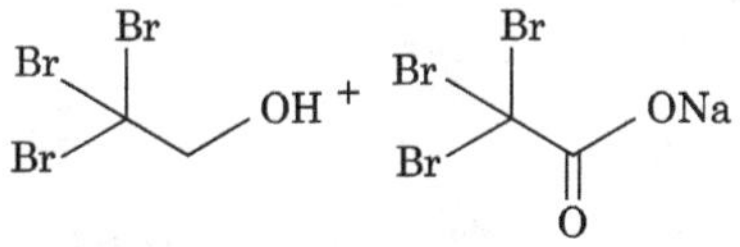

33. The number of electrons plus neutrons in $_{19}^{40}K^+$ is
(a) 38   (b) 59   (c) 39   (d) 40

34. Among the following, the most basic oxide is
(a) Al_2O_3 (b) P_2O_5 (c) SiO_2 (d) Na_2O

35. By dissolving 0.35 mole of sodium chloride in water, 1.30 L of salt solution is obtained. The molarity of the resulting solution should be reported as
(a) 0.3 M   (b) 0.269 M
(c) 0.27 M   (d) 0.2692 M

36. Among the quantities, density (ρ), temperature (T), enthalpy (H), heat capacity (C_p), volume (V) and pressure (p), a set of intensive variables are
(a) (ρ, T, H) (b) (H, T, V)
(c) (V, T, C_p) (d) (ρ, T, p)

37. The value of x in $KAl(SO_4)_x \cdot 12H_2O$ is
(a) 1   (b) 2   (c) 3   (d) 4

38. Among the following substituted pyridines, the most basic compound is

(a) 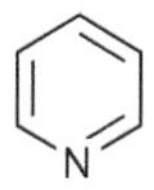 (pyridine)   (b) 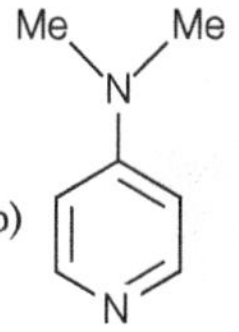 (4-dimethylamino pyridine)

(c) 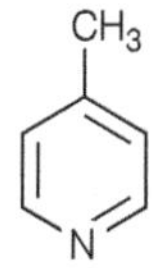 (4-methyl pyridine)   (d) 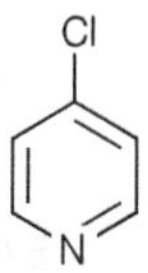 (4-chloro pyridine)

39. The major product in the following reaction is
$$H_3C-C\equiv C-H + HBr \text{ (excess)}$$
(a) 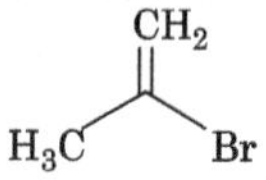 (H₃C, CH₂, Br structure)
(b) 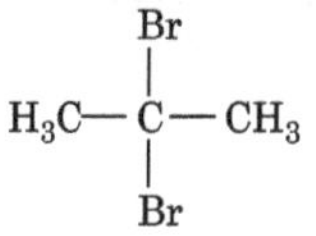 $H_3C-\underset{Br}{\overset{Br}{C}}-CH_3$
(c) $H_3C-\underset{Br}{\overset{H}{C}}-\underset{Br}{CH_2}$
(d) 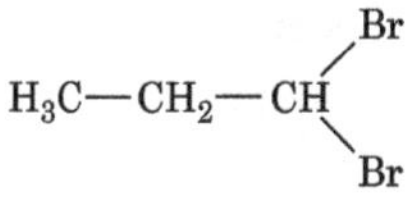 $H_3C-CH_2-CH(Br)_2$

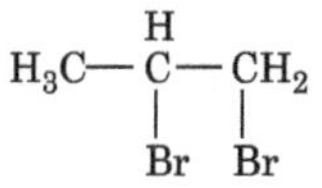

40. The major product in the following reaction at 25°C is $CH_3COOH \xrightarrow{CH_3CH_2NH_2}$
(a) $CH_3CONHCH_2CH_3$
(b) $CH_3CH=NCH_2CH_3$
(c) $NH_3^+CH_2CH_3 \cdot CH_3COO^-$
(d) $CH_3CON=CHCH_3$

41. A reaction with reaction quotient Q_C and equilibrium constant K_C, will proceed in the direction of the products when
(a) $Q_C = K_C$ (b) $Q_C < K_C$
(c) $Q_C > K_C$ (d) $Q_C = 0$

42. Acetyl salicylic acid is a pain killer and is commonly known as
(a) paracetamol   (b) aspirin
(c) ibuprofen   (d) penicillin

43. The molecule which does not exhibit strong hydrogen bonding is
(a) methyl amine   (b) acetic acid
(c) diethyl ether   (d) glucose

44. The following two compounds are

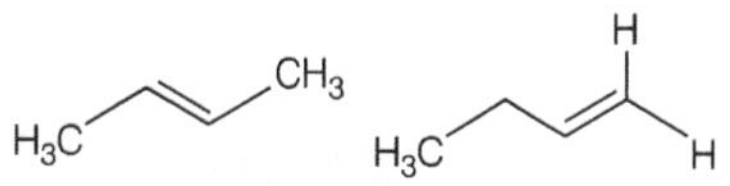

(two alkene structures)

(a) geometrical isomers
(b) positional isomers
(c) functional group isomers
(d) optical isomers

45. The graph that does not represent the behaviour of an ideal gas is

(a) p vs V at constant T
(b) p vs $1/V$ at constant p
(c) pV vs T
(d) V vs T at constant p

BIOLOGY

46. A smear of blood from a healthy individual is stained with a nuclear stain called hematoxylin and then observed under a light microscope. Which of the following cell types would be highest in number?
(a) Neutrophils
(b) Lymphocytes
(c) Eosinophils
(d) Monocytes

47. Which of the following biological phenomena involves a bacteriophage?
(a) Transformation
(b) Conjugation
(c) Translocation
(d) Transduction

48. In which compartment of a cell does the process of glycolysis take place?
(a) Golgi complex
(b) Cytoplasm
(c) Mitochondria
(d) Ribosomes

49. Huntington's disease is a disease of the
(a) nervous system
(b) circulatory system
(c) respiratory system
(d) excretory system

50. A cell will experience the highest level of endosmosis when it is kept in
(a) distilled water
(b) sugar solution
(c) salt solution
(d) protein solution

51. When the leaf of the 'touch-me-not' (chui-mui, *Mimosa pudica*) plant is touched, the leaf droops because
(a) a nerve signal passes through the plant
(b) the temperature of the plant increases
(c) water is lost from the cells at the base of the leaf
(d) the plant dies

52. If you are seeing mangroves around you, which part of India are you visiting?
(a) Western Ghats
(b) Thar desert
(c) Sunderbans
(d) Himalayas

53. Myeloid tissue is a type of
(a) haematopoietic tissue
(b) cartilage tissue
(c) muscular tissue
(d) areolar tissue

54. The heart of an amphibian is usually
(a) two-chambered
(b) three-chambered
(c) four-chambered
(d) three and half-chambered

55. Gigantism and acromegaly are due to defects in the function of which of the following glands?
(a) Adrenals
(b) Thyroid
(c) Pancreas
(d) Pituitary

56. The pH of 10^{-8} M HCl solution is
(a) 8
(b) close to 7
(c) 1
(d) 0

57. Which one of the following organelles can synthesise some of its own proteins?
(a) Lysosome
(b) Golgi apparatus
(c) Vacuole
(d) Mitochondrion

58. Maltose is a polymer of
(a) one glucose and one fructose molecule
(b) one glucose and one galactose molecule
(c) two glucose molecules
(d) two fructose molecules

59. The roots of some higher plants get associated with a fungal partner. The roots provide food to the fungus while the fungus supplies water to the roots. The structure so formed is known as
(a) lichen
(b) *Anabaena*
(c) mycorrhiza
(d) *Rhizobium*

60. Prehistoric forms of life are found in fossils. The probability of finding fossils of more complex organisms
(a) increases from lower to upper strata
(b) decreases from lower to upper strata
(c) remains constant in each stratum
(d) uncertain

➲ PART-II (2 Marks Questions)

MATHEMATICS

61. Let a, b, c be positive integers such that $\dfrac{a\sqrt{2}+b}{b\sqrt{2}+c}$ is a rational number, then which of the following is always an integer?
(a) $\dfrac{2a^2+b^2}{2b^2+c^2}$
(b) $\dfrac{a^2+b^2-c^2}{a+b-c}$
(c) $\dfrac{a^2+2b^2}{b^2+2c^2}$
(d) $\dfrac{a^2+b^2+c^2}{a+b-c}$

62. The number of solutions (x, y, z) to the system of equations $x+2y+4z=9$, $4yz+2xz+xy=13$, $xyz=3$, such that at least two of x, y, z are integers is
(a) 3
(b) 5
(c) 6
(d) 4

63. In a ΔABC, it is known that $AB=AC$. Suppose D is the mid-point of AC and $BD=BC=2$. Then, the area of the ΔABC is
(a) 2
(b) $2\sqrt{2}$
(c) $\sqrt{7}$
(d) $2\sqrt{7}$

64. A train leaves Pune at 7:30 am and reaches Mumbai at 11:30 am. Another train leaves Mumbai at 9:30 am and reaches Pune at 1:00 pm. Assuming that the two trains travel at constant speeds, at what time do the two trains cross each other?
(a) 10:20 am
(b) 11:30 am
(c) 10:26 am
(d) data not sufficient

65. In the given figures, which has the shortest path?

(a) 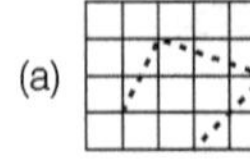
(b) 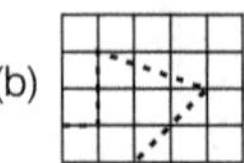
(c) 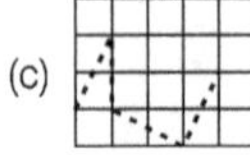
(d) 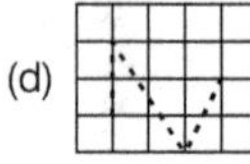

PHYSICS

66. In the circuit shown, n-identical resistors R are connected in parallel ($n > 1$) and the combination is connected in series to another resistor R_0. In the adjoining circuit n resistors of resistance R are all connected in series alongwith R_0.

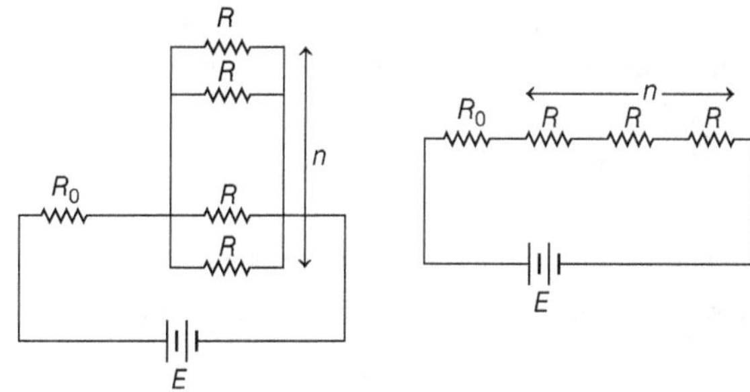

The batteries in both circuits are identical and net power dissipated in the n resistors in both circuits is same. The ratio R_0/R is

(a) 1   (b) n (c) n^2 (d) $1/n$

67. A firecracker is thrown with velocity of 30 ms^{-1} in a direction which makes an angle of 75° with the vertical axis. At some point on its trajectory, the firecracker splits into two identical pieces in such a way that one piece falls 27 m far from the shooting point. Assuming that all trajectories are contained in the same plane, how far will the other piece fall from the shooting point? (Take, $g = 10$ ms^{-2} and neglect air resistance)

(a) 63 m or 144 m   (b) 72 m or 99 m
(c) 28 m or 72 m   (d) 63 m or 117 m

68. A block of mass m is sliding down an inclined plane with constant speed. At a certain instant t_0, its height above the ground is h. The coefficient of kinetic friction between the block and the plane is μ. If the block reaches the ground at a later instant t_g, then the energy dissipated by friction in the time interval $(t_g - t_0)$ is

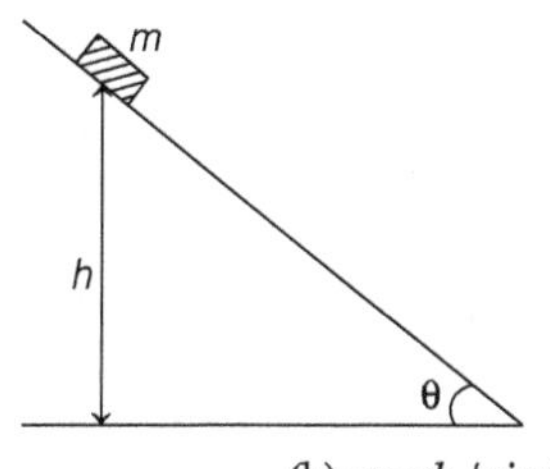

(a) μmgh (b) $\mu mgh / \sin\theta$
(c) mgh (d) $\mu mgh / \cos\theta$

69. A circular loop of wire is in the same plane as an infinitely long wire carrying a constant current i. Four possible motions of the loop are marked by N, E, W, and S as shown below.

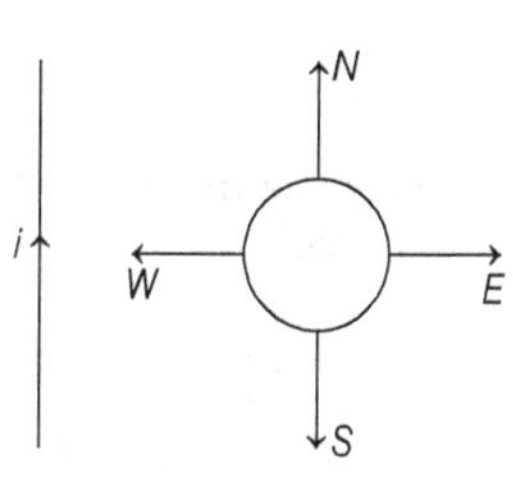

A clockwise current is induced in the loop when loop is pulled towards

(a) N (b) E (c) W (d) S

70. 150 g of ice is mixed with 100 g of water at temperature 80°C. The latent heat of ice is 80 cal/g and the specific heat of water is 1 cal/g°C. Assuming no heat loss to the environment, the amount of ice which does not melt is

(a) 100 g   (b) 0   (c) 150 g   (d) 50 g

CHEMISTRY

71. Upon fully dissolving 2.0 g of a metal in sulphuric acid, 6.8 g of the metal sulphate is formed. The equivalent weight of the metal is

(a) 13.6 g   (b) 20.0 g   (c) 4.0 g   (d) 10.0 g

72. Upon mixing equal volumes of aqueous solutions of 0.1 M HCl and 0.2 M H_2SO_4, the concentration of H^+ in the resulting solution is

(a) 0.30 mol/L (b) 0.25 mol/L (c) 0.15 mol/L (d) 0.10 mol/L

73. The products X and Y in the following reaction sequence are

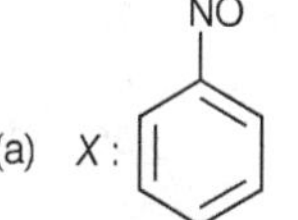

(a) X : 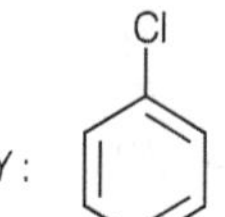 Y :

(b) X : 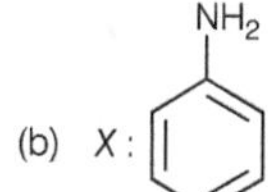 Y : 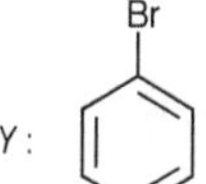

(c) X : 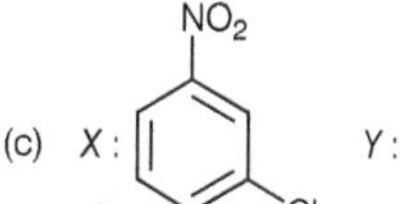 Y : 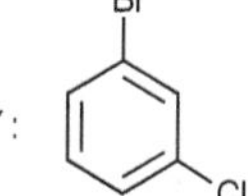

(d) X : 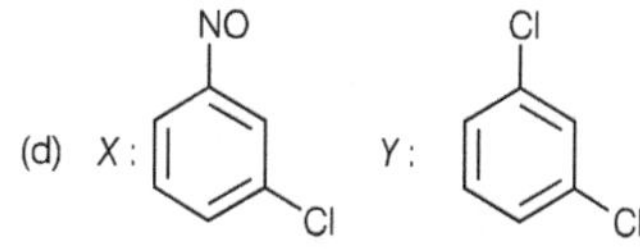 Y :

74. A plot of the kinetic energy $\left(\frac{1}{2}mv^2\right)$ of ejected electrons as a function of the frequency (v) of incident radiation for four alkali metals (M_1, M_2, M_3, M_4) is shown below.

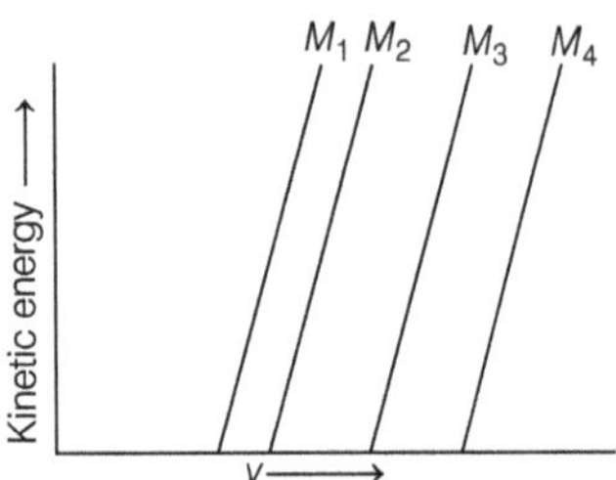

The alkali metals M_1, M_2, M_3 and M_4 are, respectively
(a) Li, Na, K and Rb
(b) Rb, K, Na and Li
(c) Na, K, Li and Rb
(d) Rb, Li, Na and K

75. The number of moles of Br_2 produced when two moles of potassium permanganate are treated with excess potassium bromide in aqueous acid medium is
(a) 1
(b) 3
(c) 2
(d) 4

BIOLOGY

76. A baby is born with the normal number and distribution of rods, but no cones in his eyes. We would expect that the baby would be
(a) colourblind   (b) nightblind
(c) blind with both eyes   (d) blind with one eye

77. In mammals, pleural membranes cover the lungs as well as insides of the ribcage. The pleural fluid in between the two membranes
(a) dissolves oxygen for transfer to the alveoli
(b) dissolves CO_2 for transfer to the blood
(c) provides partial pressure
(d) reduces the friction between the ribs and the lungs

78. At which phase of the cell cycle, DNA polymerase activity is at its highest?
(a) Gap 1 (G_1) (b) Mitotic (M)
(c) Synthetic (S)   (d) Gap 2 (G_2)

79. Usain Bolt, an olympic runner, at the end of a 100 metre sprint, will have more of which of the following in his muscles?
(a) ATP   (b) Pyruvic acid
(c) Lactic acid   (d) Carbon dioxide

80. Desert temperature often varies between 0-50°C. The DNA polymerase isolated from a camel living in the desert will be able to synthesise DNA most efficiently at
(a) 0°C   (b) 37°C   (c) 50°C   (d) 25°C

Answers

PART-I

1 (c)	2 (b)	3 (b)	4 (a)	5 (d)	6 (b)	7 (b)	8 (b)	9 (b)	10 (b)
11 (a)	12 (c)	13 (d)	14 (a)	15 (c)	16 (b)	17 (a)	18 (c)	19 (d)	20 (b)
21 (b)	22 (a)	23 (a)	24 (d)	25 (a)	26 (b)	27 (b)	28 (b)	29 (c)	30 (a)
31 (c)	32 (a)	33 (c)	34 (d)	35 (c)	36 (d)	37 (b)	38 (b)	39 (b)	40 (c)
41 (b)	42 (b)	43 (c)	44 (b)	45 (b, c)	46 (a)	47 (d)	48 (b)	49 (a)	50 (a)
51 (c)	52 (c)	53 (a)	54 (b)	55 (d)	56 (b)	57 (d)	58 (c)	59 (c)	60 (a)

PART-II

61 (d)	62 (b)	63 (c)	64 (c)	65 (d)	66 (a)	67 (d)	68 (c)	69 (b)	70 (d)
71 (b)	72 (b)	73 (b)	74 (b)	75 (*)	76 (a)	77 (d)	78 (c)	79 (c)	80 (b)

** No option is correct.*

Solutions

1. *(c)* Let $f(x) = ax^2 + bx + c$

$$[\because f(x) \text{ is quadratic polynomial}]$$

$$f(2) = 4a + 2b + c = 10 \qquad ...(i)$$

$$[\because f(2) = 10]$$

$$f(-2) = 4a - 2b + c = -2 \qquad ...(ii)$$

$$[\because f(-2) = -2]$$

On subtracting Eq. (ii) from Eq.(i), we get

$$4b = 12 \Rightarrow b = 3$$

$\therefore$ Coefficient of x in $f(x) = b = 3$

2. *(b)* Let $x = 0.75$

According to the question,

$$\frac{x^3}{1-x} + (x + x^2 + 1)$$

$$= \frac{x^3 + (1-x)(1+x+x^2)}{1-x}$$

$$= \frac{x^3 + 1 - x^3}{1-x} = \frac{1}{1-x}$$

Now, put the value of x

$$\frac{1}{1-0.75} = \frac{1}{0.25}$$

$$= \frac{100}{25} = 4$$

So, square root of the equation $= \sqrt{4} = 2$

3. *(b)* Given, sides of triangle are positive integer in an AP and the smallest side is 10.

$\therefore$ Sides of triangle are

$$10, 10 + d, 10 + 2d , d \in N$$

We know in triangle sum of two sides is greater than third sides.

$\therefore$

$$10 + 10 + d > 10 + 2d \qquad ...(i)$$

$$10 + 10 + 2d > 10 + d \qquad ...(ii)$$

$$10 + d + 10 + 2d > 10 \qquad ...(iii)$$

From Eqs. (i), (ii) and (iii), we get

$$d < 10$$

$\therefore \quad d = 1, 2, 3, 4, 5, 6, 7, 8, 9$

Hence, there are 9 triangles possible.

4. *(a)* We have,

$$\frac{a}{3} = \frac{a+b}{4} = \frac{a+b+c}{5} = \frac{a+b+c+d}{6} = k$$

On solving, we get

$$a = 3k, \ b = k, \ c = k, \ d = k$$

$\therefore$

$$\frac{a}{b + 2c + 3d} = \frac{3k}{k + 2k + 3k}$$

$$= \frac{3k}{6k} = \frac{1}{2}$$

5. *(d)* We have,

$$\frac{2^2 + 4^2 + 6^2 + ... + (2n)^2}{1^2 + 3^2 + 5^2 + ... + (2n-1)^2} > 101$$

$$\Rightarrow \quad \frac{\Sigma (2n)^2}{\Sigma (2n-1)^2} > \frac{101}{100}$$

$$\Rightarrow \quad \frac{4\Sigma n^2}{\Sigma(4n^2 - 4n + 1)} > \frac{101}{100}$$

$$\Rightarrow \quad \frac{4\Sigma n^2}{4\Sigma n^2 - 4\Sigma n + \Sigma 1} > \frac{101}{100}$$

$$\Rightarrow \quad \frac{\dfrac{4(n)(n+1)(2n+1)}{6}}{\dfrac{4n(n+1)(2n+1)}{6} - \dfrac{4n(n+1)}{2} + n} > \frac{101}{100}$$

$$\Rightarrow \quad \frac{4n(n+1)(2n+1)}{n[4(2n^2 + 3n + 1) - 12n - 12 + 6]} > \frac{101}{100}$$

$$\Rightarrow \quad \frac{4(n+1)(2n+1)}{8n^2 - 2} > \frac{101}{100}$$

$$\Rightarrow \quad \frac{4(2n+1)(n+1)}{2(2n+1)(2n-1)} > \frac{101}{100}$$

$$\Rightarrow \quad \frac{2n+2}{2n-1} > \frac{101}{100}$$

$$\Rightarrow \quad 200n + 200 > 202n - 101$$

$$\Rightarrow \quad 2n < 301$$

$$\Rightarrow \quad n < \frac{301}{2}$$

$\therefore$ Maximum value of $n = 150$

6. *(b)* Given,

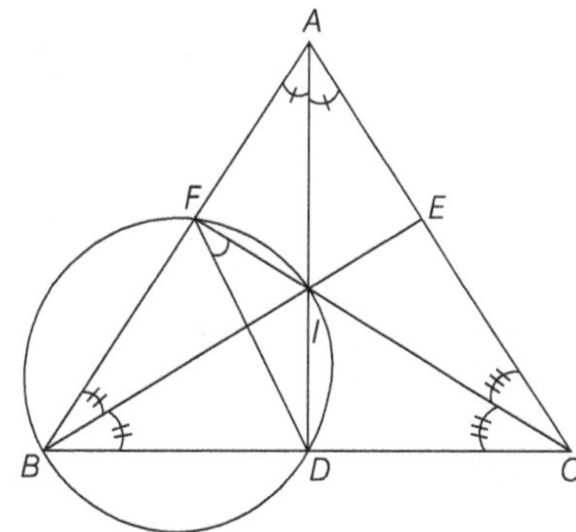

AD, BE, CF are angle bisectors of angle A, B and C respectively.

I is the concurrent point of angle bisector and $BD\ IF$ are concyclic.

Now, $BDIF$ is concyclic.

$\therefore$

$$\angle IFD = \angle IBD = \frac{\angle B}{2}$$

$$[\because \text{angle on same segments are equals}]$$

$$\Rightarrow \quad \angle FBD + \angle FID = 180°$$

$$[\because \text{sum of interior opposite angle of cyclic}$$
$$\text{quadrilateral is } 180°]$$

Now, $\angle FID = \angle ADC + \angle ICD$

$$[\because \text{sum angle properties}]$$

$$\Rightarrow \quad \angle FID = \angle BAD + \angle ABD + \angle ICD$$

$$= \frac{A}{2} + B + \frac{C}{2}$$

$$= \frac{A + C + 2B}{2}$$

$$= \frac{A + B + C + B}{2}$$

$$= \frac{180° + B}{2}$$

$\therefore \angle FBD + \angle FID = 180°$

$$= B + \frac{180° + B}{2} = 180°$$

$$\Rightarrow 3B = 180° \Rightarrow B = 60°$$

$$\therefore \angle IFD = \frac{\angle B}{2} = \frac{60}{2} = 30°$$

7. *(b)* Given,

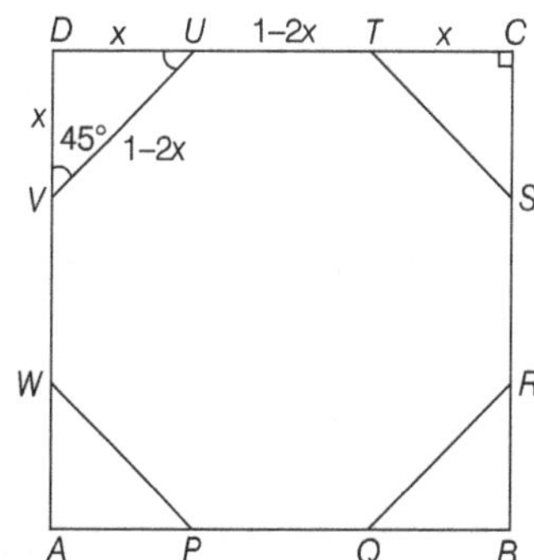

$ABCD$ is square of length 1 unit and a regular octagon is formed by cutting congruent isosceles triangle.

Let DUV is isosceles right angled triangle.

$\therefore \qquad \angle D = 90°$

$\therefore \qquad \angle DVU = 45°$

In ΔDVU,

$$\cos 45° = \frac{x}{1 - 2x}$$

$$\Rightarrow \quad \frac{1}{\sqrt{2}} = \frac{x}{1 - 2x}$$

$$\Rightarrow \quad \sqrt{2} = \frac{1 - 2x}{x}$$

$$\Rightarrow \quad \sqrt{2} = \frac{1}{x} - 2$$

$$\Rightarrow \quad \frac{1}{x} = 2 + \sqrt{2}$$

$$\Rightarrow \quad x = \frac{1}{\sqrt{2}(\sqrt{2}+1)} = \frac{\sqrt{2}-1}{\sqrt{2}}$$

$\therefore$ Side of regular octagon $= 1 - 2x$

$$= 1 - \frac{2(\sqrt{2}-1)}{\sqrt{2}}$$
$$= 1 - \sqrt{2}(\sqrt{2}-1)$$
$$= 1 - 2 + \sqrt{2}$$
$$= \sqrt{2} - 1$$

8. *(b)* Given, $OA = OB = r$

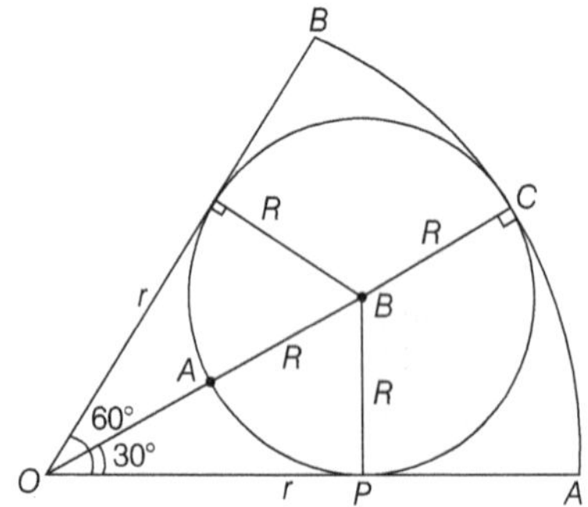

Also, OC is radius of sector

$\therefore \qquad OC = r$

Now, $OC = OB + BC$

$OC = OB + R \qquad [BC \text{ is radius of circle}]$

In $\triangle OPB$,

$$\sin 30° = \frac{BP}{OB} \quad [\because \angle BOP = 30°]$$

$$\Rightarrow \qquad \frac{1}{2} = \frac{R}{OB}$$

$$\Rightarrow \qquad OB = 2R$$

$$\therefore \qquad OC = 2R + R = 3R$$

$$\Rightarrow \qquad r = 3R$$

$$\Rightarrow \qquad R = \frac{r}{3}$$

9. *(b)* We have,

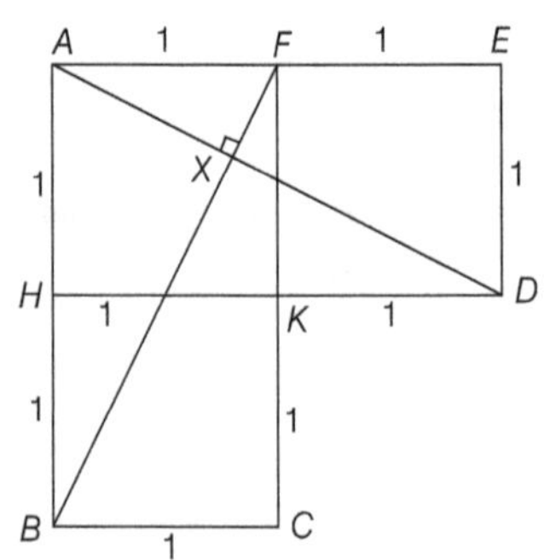

$AHKF, FKDE$ and $HBCK$ is a unit square.

AD and BF intersect at X.

In $\triangle ABF$, $\qquad AB = 2$

$$AF = 1$$

$\therefore \ FB^2 = AB^2 + AF^2 = 4 + 1 = 5$

In $\triangle AXF$ and $\triangle BAF$,

$$\angle F = \angle F \qquad \text{(common)}$$
$$\angle X = \angle A = (90°)$$
$$\therefore \qquad \triangle AXF \sim \triangle BAF$$
$$\therefore \qquad \frac{\text{ar}(\triangle AXF)}{\text{ar}(BAF)} = \frac{AF^2}{BF^2} = \frac{1}{5}$$

10. *(b)* Given,

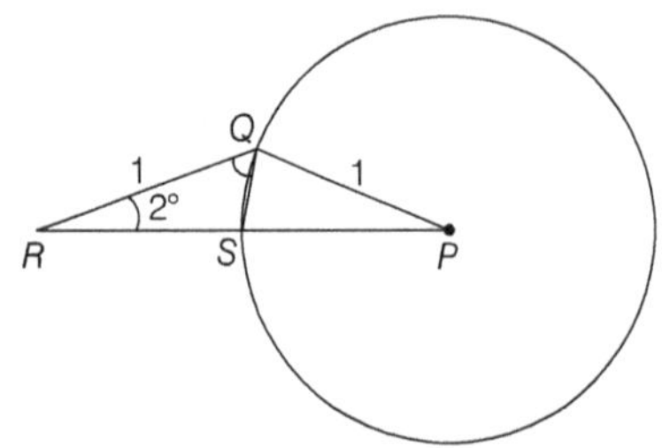

$$\angle QRP = 2°$$
$$PQ = QR = 1$$
$$\therefore \qquad \angle QPR = 2°$$
$$\angle RQP = 180° - 4° = 176°$$
$$SP = SQ \text{ radii of circle}$$
$$\therefore \qquad \angle SQP = \angle QSP$$
$$= \frac{180° - 2°}{2}$$
$$= \frac{178°}{2} = 89°$$
$$\angle RQS = \angle RQP - \angle SQP$$
$$= 176° - 89° = 87°$$

11. *(a)* At 6 : 15,

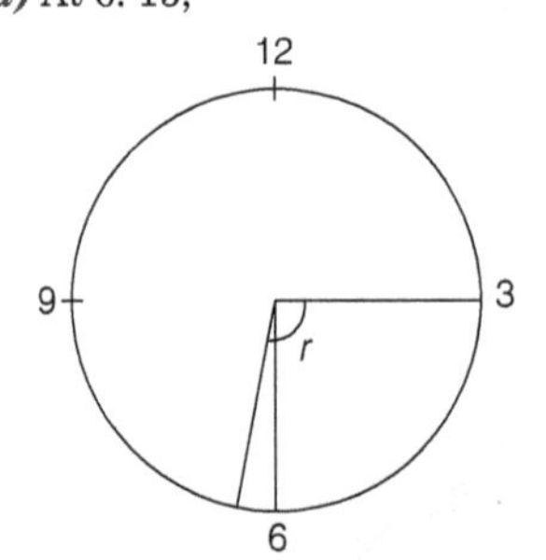

the minutes hand makes an angle is α.

$$\therefore \qquad \alpha = 90° + 15 \times \left(\frac{1}{2}\right)^°$$
$$\alpha = \left(\frac{195}{2}\right)^°$$

and hour hand is β.

Given, $\alpha + \beta = 360°$

$$\therefore \quad \beta = 360° - \alpha$$
$$= 360° - \left(\frac{195}{2}\right)^° = \left(\frac{525}{2}\right)^°$$

Difference between their angles

$$= \frac{525}{2} - \frac{195}{2} = \frac{330}{2} = 165°$$

12. *(c)* Let the time taken by A to complete the job $= x$ h and time taken by B to complete the job $= y$ h

A and B together works then they complete the work $= \left(\dfrac{1}{x} + \dfrac{1}{y}\right)$ in 1 h

Let the complete work in t h

$$t\left(\frac{1}{x} + \frac{1}{y}\right) = \frac{t+8}{x}$$

$$\Rightarrow \qquad \frac{t}{y} = \frac{8}{x} \qquad \text{...(i)}$$

$\qquad\qquad [B \text{ would } 4\frac{1}{2} \text{ h more to}$

$\qquad\qquad\qquad$ complete the work]

$$\because \qquad t\left(\frac{1}{x} + \frac{1}{y}\right) = \frac{t + \frac{9}{2}}{y}$$

$$\Rightarrow \qquad \frac{t}{x} = \frac{9}{2y} \qquad \text{...(ii)}$$

From Eqs. (i) and (ii),

$$t^2 = 36$$

$$\Rightarrow \qquad t = 6 \text{ h}$$

13. *(d)* Let the weight of bucket be x kg and the weight of water completely full be y kg.

According to the problem,

$$x + \frac{y}{2} = 10 \qquad \text{...(i)}$$

and $\qquad x + \dfrac{2y}{3} = 11 \qquad \text{...(ii)}$

On solving Eqs. (i) and (ii), we get

$$x = 7, \ y = 6$$

$\therefore$ Total weight, when bucket is completely full is $(x + y)$ kg i.e. $7 + 6 = 13$ kg

14. *(a)* We have,

$$\frac{m}{12} = \frac{12}{n}$$

$$\Rightarrow \qquad mn = 144$$

$$\Rightarrow \qquad mn = 2^4 \times 3^2$$

Total number of divisor of 144 is $(4+1)(2+1) = 15$

When m and n are positive integers.

If m and n are negative integers, then also number of divisor is 15.

$\therefore$ Total ordered pairs of (m, n) when m and n are integers $= 15 + 15 = 30$

15. *(c)* We have,

$$S = \{1, 2, 3, 4, ..., 40\}$$

A is subset of S whose sum of two element of A is not divisible by 5.

Possible set $A = \{$ 1, 2, 5, 6, 7, 11, 12, 16, 17, 21, 22, 26, 27, 31, 32, 36, 37$\}$

$\therefore$ Maximum number of elements in A is 17.

16. *(b)* Given situation is

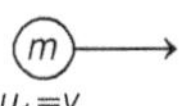

Initially one of the ball is at rest

Finally both balls moves with same speed together

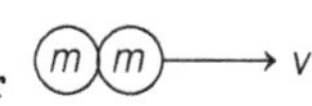

Conservation of momentum, gives

$$mv = 2mV \Rightarrow V = \frac{v}{2}$$

So, kinetic energy after collision is

$$K_f = \frac{1}{2}(2m)V^2 = \frac{1}{2} \times 2m \times \left(\frac{v}{2}\right)^2$$

$$= \frac{1}{4}mv^2$$

17. *(a)* Air resistance is same in both case. When ball is moving down, air resistance is directed away from g.

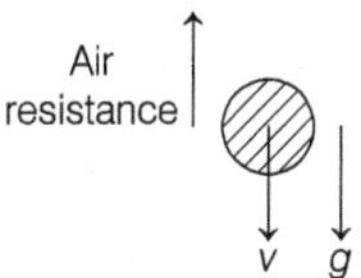

So, acceleration of ball moving downwards is

$$a_1 = \frac{mg - kv}{m}$$

or $\qquad a_1 = \left(g - \frac{k}{m}v\right)$

where, k is constant.

When ball is moving up, air resistance and g both are directed downwards.

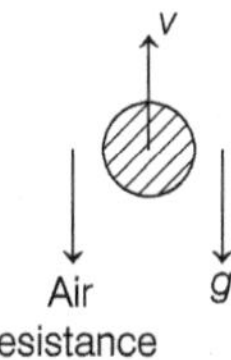

So, acceleration while moving upwards is

$$a_2 = g + \frac{k}{m}v$$

Clearly, $\qquad a_2 > a_1$.

18. *(c)* The free electrons experiences electrostatic force in the direction opposite to the direction of electric fired being is of negative charge. The electric field always directed from higher potential to lower potential. Therefore electrostatic force and negative charge or electrons always flows from lower to higher potential until the potantials become equal.

Hence, option (c) is correct.

19. *(d)* To minimize drift, let angle at which boat is directed by θ, as shown below.

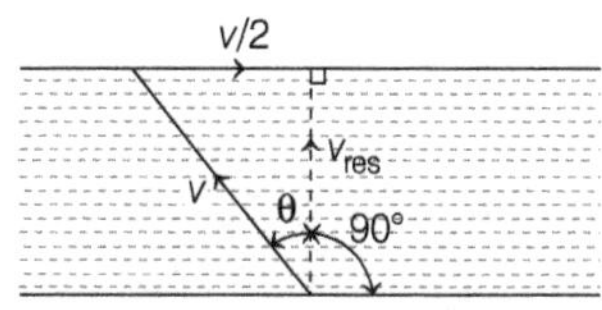

From above velocity triangle,

$$\sin\theta = \frac{v/2}{v} = \frac{1}{2} \text{ or } \theta = 30°$$

So, angle with respect to direction of flow is $90° + \theta° = 90° + 30° = 120°$.

20. *(b)* Ice is a bad conductor of heat, its thermal conductivity is very low. So, no exchange of heat from outside surrounding occurs in an Igloo. Thermal conductivity of ice is $1.6\,\text{Wm}^{-1}\,\text{K}^{-1}$.

21. *(b)* Light ray bends towards normal at point Q and it bends away from normal at point R.

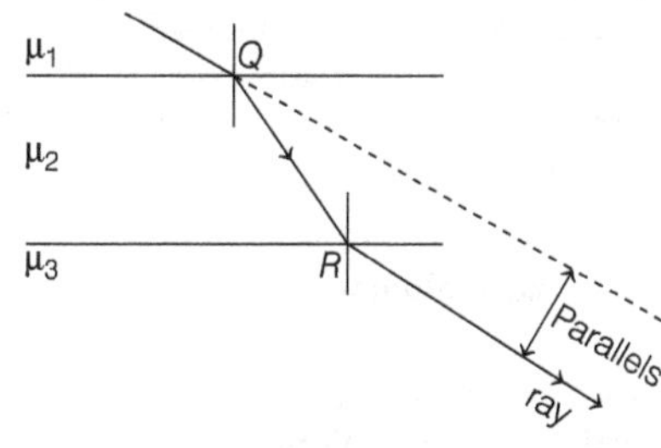

Also, the emergent ray is parallel to incident ray.

Hence, $\mu_1 = \mu_3 < \mu_2$ is correct option.

22. *(a)* As, incident light is normal to the surface, so no deviation or dispersion occurs.

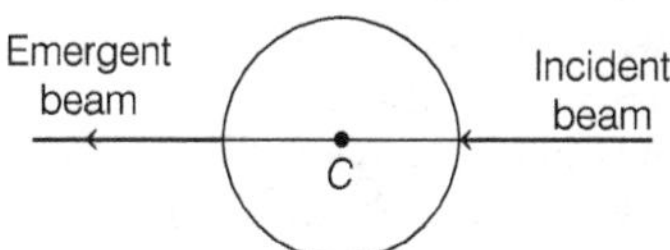

23. *(a)* If object is placed

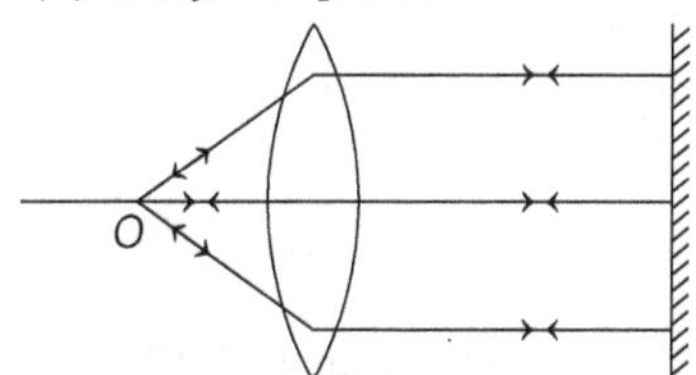

at the focus of lens on opposite side of mirror, then light rays after refraction from lens become parallel to the principal axis.

These parallel rays are reflected back over same path and again converges at focus.

24. *(d)* Power consumed in each case is

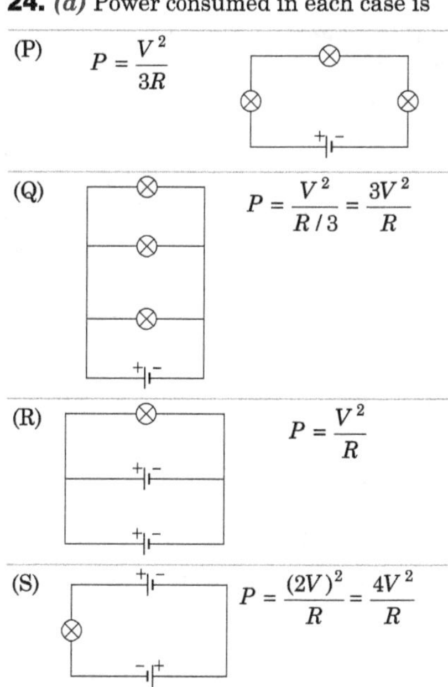

(P) $\qquad P = \dfrac{V^2}{3R}$

(Q) $\qquad P = \dfrac{V^2}{R/3} = \dfrac{3V^2}{R}$

(R) $\qquad P = \dfrac{V^2}{R}$

(S) $\qquad P = \dfrac{(2V)^2}{R} = \dfrac{4V^2}{R}$

So, order of increasing power consumption is $P > R > Q > S$.

25. *(a)* Gap or cavity also expands at same rate as that of metal.

Hence, width of gap also increases by same amount.

$\therefore$ Width of gap increases by $\Delta d = d\alpha\Delta T$.

26. *(b)*

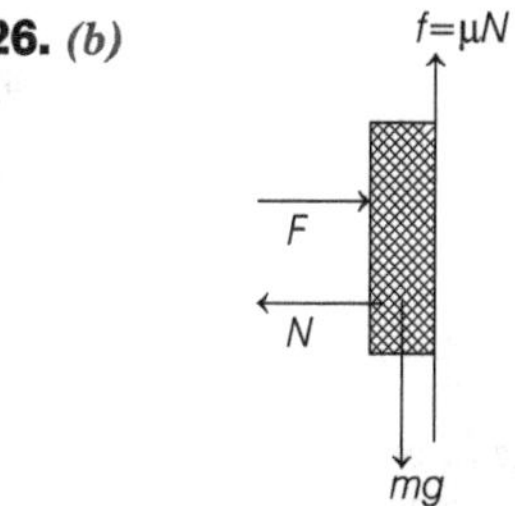

Minimum force F must be such that generated friction is able to balance weight mg of book.

So, $\qquad f = \mu N = \mu F$.

27. *(b)* Given,

Surface area of cube = Surface area of sphere

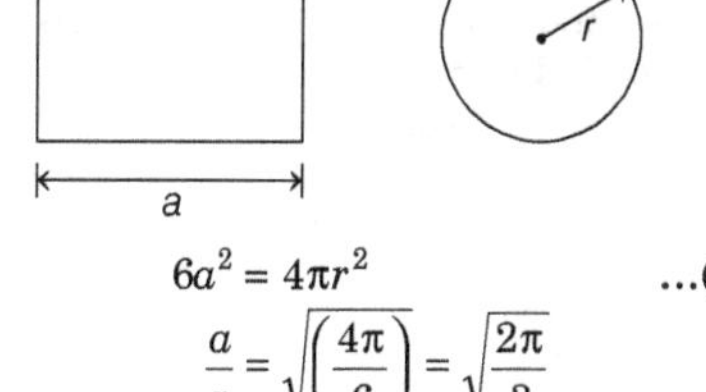

$\Rightarrow \qquad 6a^2 = 4\pi r^2 \qquad\qquad …(i)$

$\Rightarrow \qquad \dfrac{a}{r} = \sqrt{\left(\dfrac{4\pi}{6}\right)} = \sqrt{\dfrac{2\pi}{3}}$

Now, buoyant force is $F_B = V_{in} \cdot \rho_f \cdot g$

So, ratio of buoyant force on cube and sphere is

$$\frac{(F_B)_{cube}}{(F_B)_{sphere}} = \frac{V_{cube}}{V_{sphere}}$$

$$= \frac{a^3}{\frac{4}{3}\pi r^3} = \frac{3}{4\pi} \times \left(\frac{2\pi}{3}\right)^{\frac{3}{2}}$$

$$= \sqrt{\frac{9 \times 8 \times \pi^3}{16 \times \pi^2 \times 27}} = \sqrt{\frac{\pi}{6}}$$

$\therefore \qquad (F_B)_{cube} < (F_B)_{sphere}$

28. *(b)* Decay is

$$^{238}_{92}U \longrightarrow ^{214}_{84}Po + 6\,^4_2He + ne^-$$

Conservation of mass number and atomic number gives,

$$\Rightarrow \qquad 92 = 84 + 12 - n \Rightarrow n = 4$$

29. *(c)* In Rutherford model, positive charge acquires a very small place at centre of atom in nucleus.

So, option (c) is incorrect.

30. *(a)* Neutral objects are always attracted towards both positively and negatively charged objects. So, water stream still bends in same direction.

31. *(c)* $2Ca + O_2 \xrightarrow[\text{Excess}]{\Delta} 2CaO$

Number of moles of Ca $= \dfrac{20}{40} = \dfrac{1}{2}$ mole

1 mole of Ca produces 1 mole of CaO

$\therefore \dfrac{1}{2}$ mole of Ca will produces $\dfrac{1}{2}$ mole of CaO

1 mole of CaO = 56 g

$\dfrac{1}{2}$ mole of CaO $= 56 \times \dfrac{1}{2} = 28$ g

Thus, 28 g of CaO is formed by burning 20 g of Ca in excess oxygen.

32. *(a)*

$$Br_3CCHO \xrightarrow{NaOH} CHBr_3 + HCO^-Na^+$$

This reaction is known as bromoform reaction where the carbonyl carbon gets oxidised by sodium hydroxide to sodium salts of corresponding carboxylic acid having one carbon atom less than of carbonyl compound and the methyl group is converted to bromoform.

33. *(c)* For, $^{40}_{19}K^+$

Number of electrons in $K^+ = 18$

Number of neutrons in $K^+ = 40 - 19 = 21$

$\Rightarrow$ Sum of electron + neutron

$$= 18 + 21 = 39$$

34. *(d)* All the central atom of the given oxide belong to 2nd period, as we move from left to right in a period the basicity of oxide decreases.

$\therefore$ The order of increasing basicity of oxide would be

$$P_2O_5 < SiO_2 < Al_2O_3 < Na_2O$$

Thus, the most basic oxide would be Na_2O.

35. *(c)* Given,

Number of moles of solute NaCl

$$= 0.35 \text{ mole}$$

Volume of the solution $= 1.30$ L

$$\text{Molarity} = \frac{\text{Number of moles of solute}}{\text{Volume of solution in litres}}$$

$$= \frac{0.35}{1.30} = 0.269 \approx 0.27 \text{ M}$$

36. *(d)* Intensive variables are those variables which don't depend upon the quantity or size of matter. Among the given quantities density, temperature and pressure are intensive variables whereas heat capacity, enthalpy and volume are an extensive variables. Thus, the correct option is (d).

37. *(b)* $KAl(SO_4)_x \cdot 12H_2O$ is an empirical formula for potash alum which is double salt.

Potash alum is $K_2SO_4 \cdot Al_2(SO_4)_2 \cdot 24H_2O$

$\therefore$ Empirical formula is $KAl(SO_4)_2 \cdot 12H_2O$

Thus, $x = 2$.

38. *(b)* Pyridine is basic in nature due to the presence of free lone pair. Its basicity gets affected by the presence of different substituents attached to it. The electron withdrawing group decreases the basicity of pyridine, whereas electron releasing groups increases its basicity.

Substituents like $N(Me)_2$ and CH_3 are electron releasing but $N(Me)_2$ is more activating group than CH_3.

So,

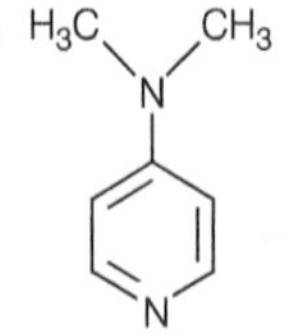

basicity would be maximum while Cl is an electron withdrawing group, so

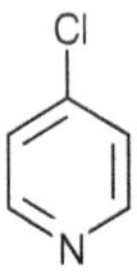

is basicity would be least.

The increasing order of basicity of compounds given in options will be

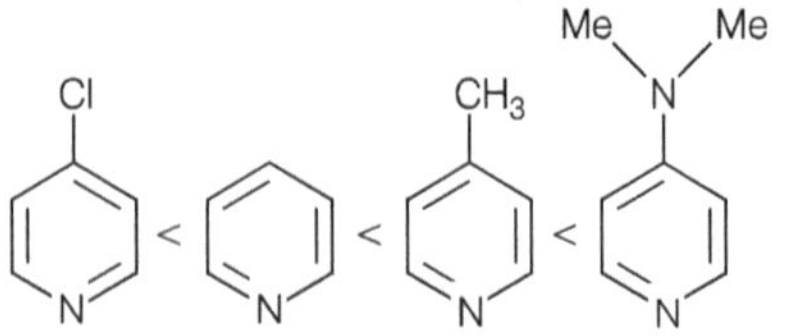

Thus, basicity of [pyridine] will be maximum.

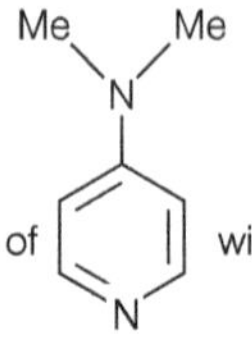

39. *(b)*

$$H_3C-C\equiv C-H + HBr \text{ (Excess)} \xrightarrow[\text{addition}]{\text{Markownikoff}}$$

$$\underset{\text{(Major)}}{H_3C-\overset{Br}{\underset{Br}{C}}-CH_3} \xleftarrow{HBr} H_3C-\underset{Br}{C}=CH_2$$

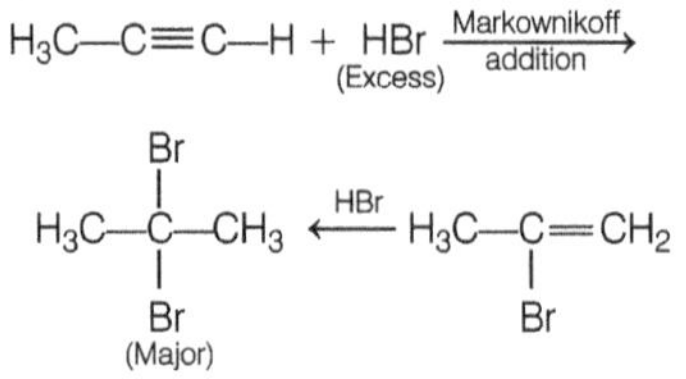

This is an electrophilic addition reaction which proceeds *via* carbonium ion formation and follows Markownikoff rule.

40. *(c)* As the reaction is occurring at room temperature, (25°C) so it will be an acid base reaction.

$$H_3C-COOH + CH_3CH_2NH_2 \xrightarrow[\substack{\text{Acid-base} \\ \text{reaction}}]{25°C}$$

$$NH_3^+CH_2CH_3 \cdot CH_3COO^-$$

41. *(b)* For an equilibrium reaction,

$$A + B \rightleftharpoons C + D;$$

$$Q_C = \frac{[C][D]}{[A][B]}$$

If $Q_C = K_C$, the reaction is in equilibrium.

If $Q_C > K_C$, the reaction proceeds in backward reaction.

If $Q_C < K_C$, the reaction proceeds in forward reaction.

Thus, the reaction will proceed in the direction of products i.e., forward reaction when $Q_C < K_C$.

42. *(b)* Acetyl salicylic which is a pain killer commonly known as aspirin.

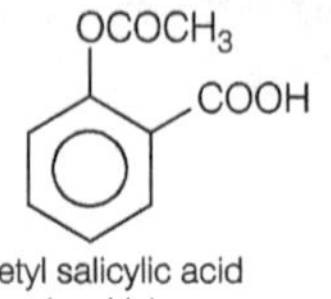

Acetyl salicylic acid (aspirin)

43. *(c)* Hydrogen bonding occurs in a molecule when a hydrogen atom is directly linked to an electronegative atom like F, O and N.

In case of diethyl ether ($H_5C_2OC_2H_5$), H is not directly linked to oxygen atom and hence will not exhibit strong hydrogen bonding.

44. *(b)*

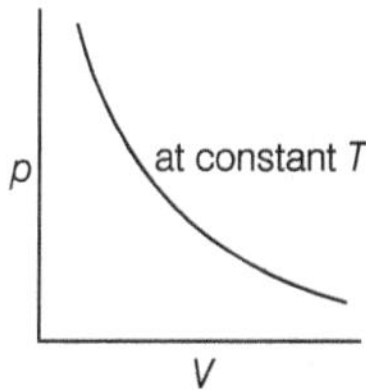

Both the compounds, but-2-ene and but-1-ene are positional isomers of each other because they differ in the position of double bond.

45. *(b, c)* $pV = nRT$

$$p = \frac{RT}{V} \text{ (for 1 mole)}$$

At constant T, p would be inversely proportional to V.

So, plot of p *versus* V would

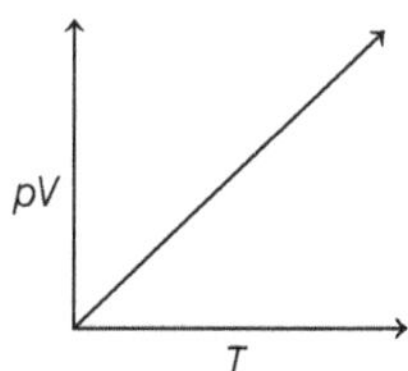

Thus, plot (a) is correct.

According to ideal gas equation.

$$pV = nRT \text{ or } \frac{pV}{T} = nR$$

As R is a gas constant, so plot between pV *versus* T would be linear and slope will be n. i.e.

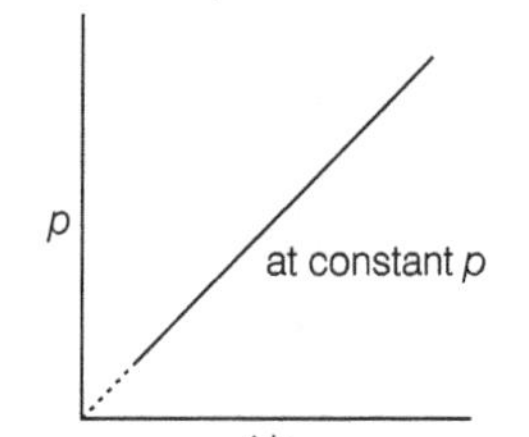

Also, from ideal gas equation p is directly proportional to $\dfrac{1}{V}$. Therefore, plot between p *versus* $\dfrac{1}{V}$ is a straight line, i.e.

Thus, plot (b) is incorrect.

46. *(a)* A smear of blood from a healthy individual if viewed under the microscope will show highest number of neutrophils. There are three types of blood cells in an individual, i.e. red blood cells (erythrocytes), white blood cells (leukocytes) and platelets (thrombocytes). RBCs and platelets are devoid of nucleus, thus are not stained by haematoxylin nuclear stain. Therefore, only WBCs are stained. In a healthy individual, there are five types of WBCs, i.e. neutrophils (accounts for 40-75% of leukocytes), eosinophils (1-6%), basophils (0-1%), lymphocytes (20-45%) and monocytes (2-10%).

47. *(d)* Transduction is a method of gene transfer in bacteria from donor to recipient using bacteriophage. In transduction, at first bacteriophage infects donor bacteria and then carries some part of donor genome with it. When this bacteriophage infects new bacterial cell, it transfers that DNA into recipient cell.

48. *(b)* Glycolysis is the first stage of cellular respiration that involves the breaking down of glucose into smaller molecules to produce ATP (cellular energy). Glycolysis occurs in the cytoplasm of all living organisms because that is where glucose and other related enzymes can be found in high concentrations.

49. *(a)* Huntington's disease is a disease of the nervous system. It is a fatal genetic disorder that causes the progressive breakdown of nerve cells in the brain. It deteriorates a person's physical and mental abilities during their prime working years and has no cure.

50. *(a)* A cell will experience the highest level of endosmosis when it is kept in distilled water. Endosmosis is the process by which water molecules move into the cell. Distilled water has far less solute concentration than cell fluid. Thus, it is a hypotonic solution which allows maximum endosmosis. Other solutions like sugar solution, salt solution and protein solution are hypertonic solutions compared to distilled water. Cell performs exosmosis in hypertonic solutions.

51. *(c)* The leaves of touch-me-not plant (*Mimosa pudica*) are very sensitive, they droop on touching because of autotrophic effect. As, water within the cells of this plant applies a turgour pressure, which makes to leaves its stay upright. So,

when any external pressure is applied like shaking or touching (seismonastic movement), activates the certain contractile proteins including potassium ions. These chemicals make water and electrolytes flow/diffuse out of the cell, resulting in a loss of cell pressure. This causes the cell to collapse, which squeezes the leaves close. Stimulus, in the form of touch is sometimes transmitted to neighbouring leaves as well and causing the closing of other neighbour leaves too.

52. *(c)* The Sundarbans delta is the largest mangrove forest in the world and is intersected by a complex network of tidal waterways, mudflats and small islands of salt-tolerant mangrove forests. It lies at the mouth of the Ganges. A mangrove is a shrub or small tree that grows in coastal saline or brackish water.

53. *(a)* The process by which new blood cells are formed is called haematopoiesis. The group of cells performing haematopoiesis are called hematopoietic tissue. These are of two kinds, i.e. myeloid tissue and lymphoid tissue. Myeloid tissue is red bone marrow, which produces erythrocytes, platelets and most of the leukocytes (including the B-lymphocytes). Lymphoid tissue consists of the lymphatic nodules, lymph nodes, spleen and thymus (which produces only T-lymphocytes).

54. *(b)* Vertebrate hearts can be categorised by the number of chambers they have, like two-chambered (one atrium and one ventricle) in fishes, **three-chambered** (two atria and one ventricle) in **amphibians** and reptiles; and four-chambered (two atria and two ventricles) in birds and mammals.

55. *(d)* Gigantism and acromegaly are syndromes of excessive secretion of growth hormone from pituitary gland. Acromegaly is a condition that affects adults, usually between the age of 30 and 50, while gigantism affects children with the same excess growth hormone but in a way that can delay puberty as well as causes excessive physical growth.

56. *(b)* The pH of 10^{-3} M HCl is close to 7, i.e., 6.98. It can be calculated as, pH $= -\log[H_3O^+]$, we get pH equal to 8. But this is not correct because an acidic solution cannot have pH greater than 7. It may be noted that in very dilute acidic solution, when H^+ concentrations from acid and water are comparable, the concentration of H^+ from water cannot be neglected.

Therefore, $[H^+]_{total} = [H^+]_{acid} + [H^+]_{water}$

Since HCl is a strong acid and is completely ionised $[H^+]_{HCl} = 1.0 \times 10^{-8}$

The concentration of H^+ from ionisation is equal to the $[OH^-]$ from water,

$$[H^+]_{H_2O} = [OH^-]_{H_2O} = x \text{ (say)}$$
$$[H^+]_{total} = 1.0 \times 10^{-8} + x$$

But $[H^+][OH^-] = 1.0 \times 10^{-14}$

$$(1.0 \times 10^{-8} + x)(x) = 1.0 \times 10^{-14}$$
$$x^2 + 10^{-8}x - 10^{-14} = 0$$

Solving of x, we get $x = 9.5 \times 10^{-8}$

Therefore $[H^+] = 1.0 \times 10^{-8} + 9.5 \times 10^{-8}$
$$= 10.5 \times 10^{-8} = 1.05 \times 10^{-7}$$

$\text{pH} = -\log[H^+] = -\log(1.05 \times 10^{-7}) = 6.98$

57. *(d)* Mitochondria have their own DNA and ribosomes. Ribosomes are the site of protein synthesis. Therefore, mitochondria are capable of making their own protein. Mitochondria are also capable of synthesising their own genetic material.

58. *(c)* Maltose is a polymer composed of two glucose molecules. It is a disaccharide formed when two units of glucose are joined with $\alpha(1 \to 4)$ bond. Maltose is also known as malt sugar and is found in foods in which starch is fermented by yeast or enzymes, such as in bread or brewed beverages.

59. *(c)* A mycorrhiza is a symbiotic association between roots of higher plant and a fungus. The plant makes organic molecules such as sugar by photosynthesis and supplies them to the fungus and the fungus supplies to the plant water and mineral nutrients, such as phosphorus, taken from the soil.

Lichen is a symbiotic partnership of a fungus and an alga. *Rhizobium* are nitrogen-fixing bacteria found in root nodules of legumes. *Anabaena* is a genus of filamentous cyanobacteria.

60. *(a)* During the course of evolution simple organisms evolved first while complex organisms evolved later. Fossilisation of complex organisms took later in upper strata of earth crust.

61. *(d)* We have, a, b, c are positive integers and $\dfrac{a\sqrt{2} + b}{b\sqrt{2} + c}$ is a rational number.

$$\therefore \left(\frac{a\sqrt{2}+b}{b\sqrt{2}+c}\right)\left(\frac{b\sqrt{2}-c}{b\sqrt{2}-c}\right)$$
$$= \frac{2ab - ac\sqrt{2} + b^2\sqrt{2} - bc}{2b^2 - c^2}$$

$$= \frac{2ab - bc + (b^2 - ac)\sqrt{2}}{2b^2 - c^2}$$

Since a, b, c are positive integers and $\dfrac{a\sqrt{2}+b}{b\sqrt{2}+c}$ is rational.

$$\therefore \qquad b^2 - ac = 0$$

$\therefore a, b, c$ are in GP.

Let $a = a$, $b = ar$, $c = ar^2$, where r is also positive integer.

(a) $\dfrac{2a^2 + b^2}{2b^2 + c^2}$

$$= \frac{2a^2 + a^2 r^2}{2a^2 r^2 + a^2 r^4} = \frac{1}{r^2} \text{ not integer}$$

(b) $\dfrac{a^2 + b^2 - c^2}{a + b - c} = \dfrac{a^2 + a^2 r^2 - a^2 r^4}{a + ar - ar^2}$

$$= a\left(\frac{1 + r^2 - r^4}{1 + r - r^2}\right) \text{ not integer}$$

(c) $\dfrac{a^2 + 2b^2}{b^2 + 2c^2}$

$$= \frac{a^2 + 2a^2 r^2}{a^2 r^2 + 2a^2 r^4} = \frac{1}{r^2} \text{ not integer}$$

(d) $\dfrac{a^2 + b^2 + c^2}{a + b - c} = \dfrac{a^2 + a^2 r^2 + a^2 r^4}{a + ar - ar^2}$

$$= \frac{a^2}{a}\left[\frac{1 + r^2 + r^4}{1 + r - r^2}\right]$$

$$= a(1 + r + r^2) \text{ integer}$$

62. *(b)* We have,

$$x + 2y + 4z = 9 \qquad \text{...(i)}$$
$$4yz + 2xz + xy = 13 \qquad \text{...(ii)}$$
$$xyz = 3$$
$$\Rightarrow \qquad x + 2y = 9 - 4z$$

From Eq. (ii),

$$2z(2y + x) + xy = 13$$
$$\Rightarrow \qquad 2z(9 - 4z) + \frac{3}{z} = 13 \qquad \left[\because xy = \frac{3}{z}\right]$$
$$\Rightarrow \qquad 8z^3 - 18z^2 + 13z - 3 = 0$$
$$\Rightarrow \qquad (z - 1)(2z - 1)(4z - 3) = 0$$
$$\Rightarrow \qquad z = 1, \frac{1}{2}, \frac{3}{4}$$

Put $z = 1$, then $x + 2y = 5$ and $xy = 3$

On solving, we get $x = 3$, $y = 1$ and $x = 2$, $y = \dfrac{3}{2}$

$\therefore$ Solutions are $(3, 1, 1)$ and $\left(2, \dfrac{3}{2}, 1\right)$.

Put $z = \dfrac{1}{2}$, then $x + 2y = 7$

$$xy = 6$$

On solving, we get $x = 3$, $y = 2$ and $x = 4$, $y = \dfrac{3}{2}$

$\therefore$ Solutions are $\left(3, 2, \dfrac{1}{2}\right)\left(4, \dfrac{3}{2}, \dfrac{1}{2}\right)$.

Put $z = \dfrac{3}{4}$, then $x + 2y = 6$

$$xy = 4$$

On solving, we get $x = 4$, $y = 1$ and $x = 2$, $y = 2$

$\therefore$ Solutions are $\left(4, 1, \dfrac{3}{4}\right)$ and $\left(2, 2, \dfrac{3}{4}\right)$.

At least two of x, y, z are integer is

$(3, 1, 1), \left(2, \dfrac{3}{2}, 1\right), \left(3, 2, \dfrac{1}{2}\right),$

$\left(4, 1, \dfrac{3}{4}\right), \left(2, 2, \dfrac{3}{4}\right)$

Hence, 5 solutions.

63. *(c)* Given, in $\triangle ABC$,

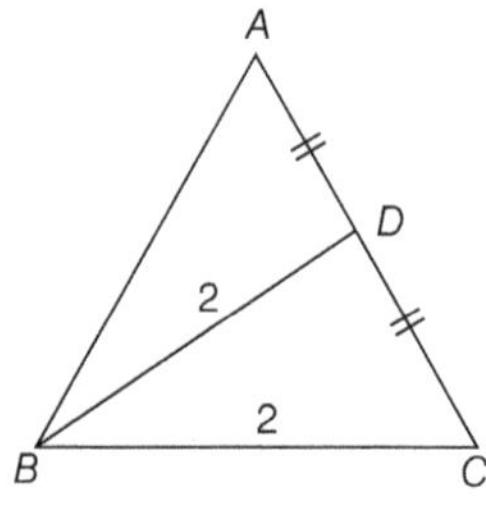

$$AB = AC$$

D is mid-point of AC.

$$\therefore \qquad AD = CD = \frac{AC}{2} = \frac{AB}{2}$$

In $\triangle ABD$,

$$\cos A = \frac{AB^2 + AD^2 - 2^2}{2 \cdot AB \cdot AD}$$

$$\cos A = \frac{4AD^2 + AD^2 - 4}{4AD^2}$$

$$[\because AB = 2AD]$$

$$\cos A = \frac{5AD^2 - 4}{4AD^2} \qquad \text{...(i)}$$

In $\triangle ABC$,

$$\cos A = \frac{AB^2 + AC^2 - 2^2}{2AB \cdot AC}$$

$$\cos A = \frac{4AD^2 + 4AD^2 - 4}{8AD^2}$$

$$\cos A = \frac{8AD^2 - 4}{8AD^2} \qquad \text{...(ii)}$$

From Eqs. (i) and (ii), we get

$$\frac{5AD^2 - 4}{4AD^2} = \frac{8AD^2 - 4}{8AD^2}$$

$$\Rightarrow \qquad 10AD^2 - 8 = 8AD^2 - 4$$
$$\Rightarrow \qquad AD = \sqrt{2}$$
$$\Rightarrow \qquad AB = 2\sqrt{2}$$

Area of $\triangle ABC = \dfrac{1}{2} AB \cdot AC \sin A$

$= \dfrac{1}{2} \times (2\sqrt{2})^2 \sqrt{1 - \cos^2 A}$

$= \dfrac{1}{2} \times 8 \times \sqrt{1 - \dfrac{9}{16}}$ $\qquad \left[\because \cos A = \dfrac{3}{5} \right]$

$= \sqrt{7}$

64. *(c)* Let the distance between Pune and Mumbai be x km.

Time taken by 1st train = 4 h

$\therefore$ Speed of 1st train $= \dfrac{x}{4}$ km/h

Time taken by 2nd train $= \dfrac{7}{2}$ h

$\therefore$ Speed of 2nd train $= \dfrac{x}{(7/2)} = \dfrac{2x}{7}$ km/h

1st train starts from 7 : 30 am and 2nd train starts from 9 : 30 am.

Distance travelled by 1st train in 2 h

$$= \dfrac{x}{2} \text{ km}$$

Let they meet at time t.

$\therefore \qquad \dfrac{x}{2} = \left(\dfrac{x}{4} \times t \right) + \left(\dfrac{2x}{7} \right) t$

$\Rightarrow \qquad t = \left(\dfrac{14}{15} \right) \text{h}$

$\Rightarrow \qquad t = \left(\dfrac{14}{15} \times 60 \right) \text{min} = 56 \text{ min}$

$\therefore$ They meet at $9 : 30 + 56 = 10 : 26$ am

65. *(d)*

(a) In figure

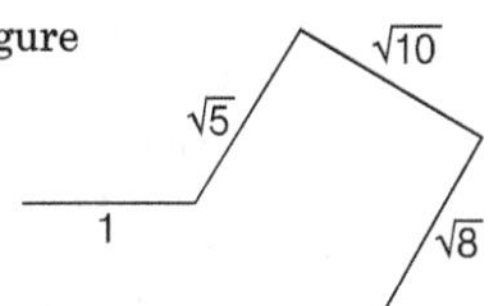

Path $= 1 + \sqrt{5} + \sqrt{10} + \sqrt{8}$

$\qquad = 1 + 2.23 + 3.16 + 2.82 = 9.21$

(b) In figure

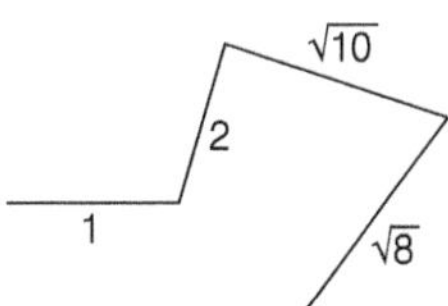

Path $= 1 + 2 + \sqrt{10} + \sqrt{8}$

$\qquad = 1 + 2 + 3.16 + 2.82 = 8.98$

(c) In figure

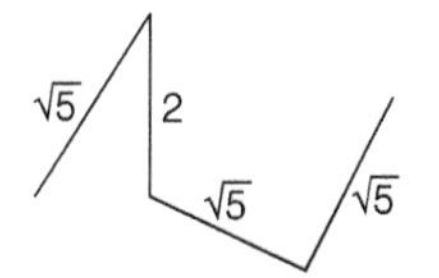

Path $= \sqrt{5} + 2 + \sqrt{5} + \sqrt{5} = 3\sqrt{5} + 2$

$\qquad = 3(2.23) + 2 = 8.69$

(d) In figure

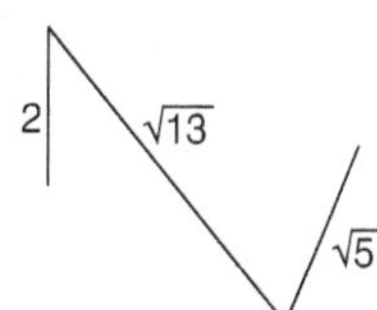

Path $= 2 + \sqrt{13} + \sqrt{5}$

$\qquad = 2 + 3.60 + 2.23 = 7.83$

$\therefore$ Shortest path have option fig (d).

Hence, option (d) is correct.

66. *(a)* In case I,

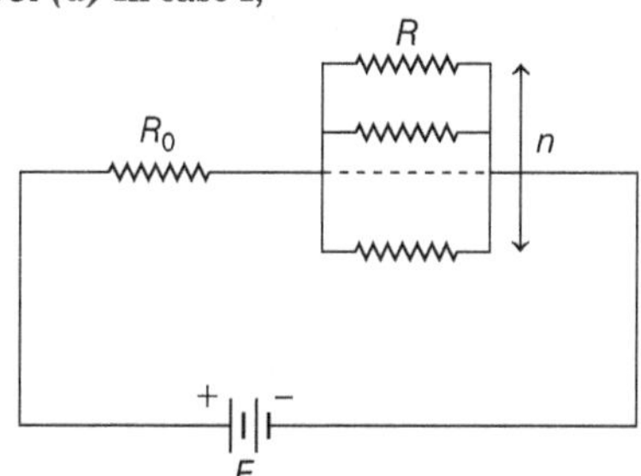

Total circuit resistance,

$$R_{eq} = R_0 + \dfrac{R}{n} = \dfrac{nR_0 + R}{n}$$

Circuit current $= i_1 = \dfrac{E}{R_{eq}} \Rightarrow i_1 = \dfrac{nE}{nR_0 + R}$

Power dissipated in n resistors,

$$P_1 = i_1^2 \cdot \left(\dfrac{R}{n} \right) = \dfrac{nE^2 R}{(nR_0 + R)^2}$$

In case II,

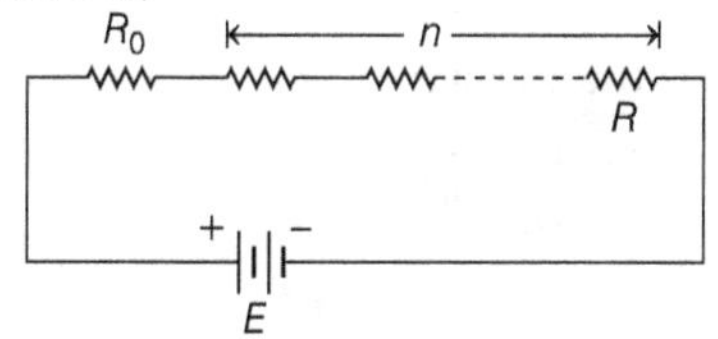

Total circuit resistance, $R_{eq} = R_0 + nR$

Current in circuit is

$$i_2 = \dfrac{E}{R_{eq}} = \dfrac{E}{R_0 + nR}$$

Power dissipated in n resistors,

$$P_2 = (i_2^2)(nR) = \dfrac{nE^2 R}{(R_0 + nR)^2}$$

As, $\qquad P_1 = P_2$

$\Rightarrow \qquad \dfrac{nE^2}{(nR_0 + R)^2} = \dfrac{nE^2 R}{(R_0 + nR)^2}$

$\Rightarrow \quad nR_0 + R = R_0 + nR$

$\Rightarrow \quad (n - 1)R_0 = (n - 1)R$

$\Rightarrow \qquad R_0 = R \text{ or } \dfrac{R_0}{R} = 1$

67. *(d)* Given situation is

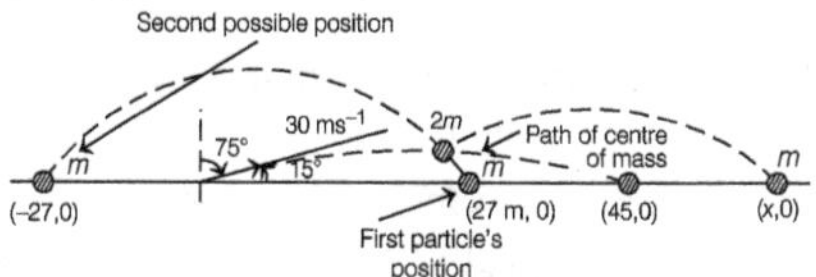

As explosion force which splits the firecracker is internal to system, path of centre of mass of system remains same.

Now, range of centre of mass of system is

$$R = \dfrac{u^2 \sin 2\theta}{g}$$

Here, $\quad u = 30 \text{ ms}^{-1}, \theta = 15°$

$\therefore \qquad R = \dfrac{30 \times 30 \times \sin(2 \times 15°)}{10} = 45 \text{ m}$

So, position (or x-coordinate) of centre of mass is at 45 m distance from origin.

Now using, $X_{CM} = \dfrac{m_1 x_1 + m_2 x_2}{m_1 + m_2}$, we get

$$45 = \dfrac{m(\pm 27) + mx}{m + m}$$

$\Rightarrow \qquad 45 = \dfrac{\pm 27 + x}{2}$

Solving, we get

$\qquad x = 90 \pm 27 \Rightarrow x = 63 \text{ m}$ or $x = 117 \text{ m}$

So, other piece may fell at 63 m or 117 m mark.

68. *(c)* As block is sliding with a constant speed, so change in kinetic energy of block when it reaches bottom is zero.

Now, by work-energy theorem,

Total work done = Change in kinetic energy

$\Rightarrow W_{friction} + W_{gravitation} = \Delta KE$

$\Rightarrow \qquad W_{friction} = - W_{gravitation}$

or $\qquad W_{friction} = - mgh$

So, energy dissipated due to friction $= mgh$.

69. *(b)* Magnetic field linked with loop is downwards.

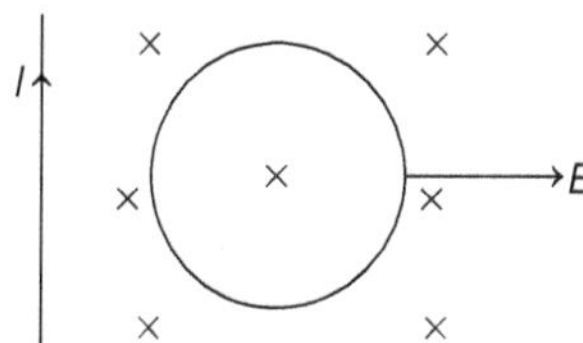

When loop is pulled away from wire, flux linked with loop decreases. This induces a current in loop which tries to oppose this change (in accordance with Lenz's law).

So, current induced in loop is clockwise.

70. *(d)* Let m gram of ice melts and this causes final temperature of mixture at 0°C. Further melting of ice is then stopped. As there is no heat loss

Heat lost by ice = Heat gained by water

$$\Rightarrow \qquad mL = m_w s_w (\Delta T)$$
$$\Rightarrow \qquad m\,80 = 100 \times 1 \times (80 - 0)$$
$$\Rightarrow \qquad m\,80 = 100 \times 80$$
$$\Rightarrow \qquad m = \frac{100 \times 80}{80}$$
$$\Rightarrow \qquad m = 100\,g$$

So, 50 g of ice does not melts.

71. *(b)* Let the equivalent weight of metal be x g.

Number of equivalents of metal
= Number of equivalents of metal sulphate

$$\frac{\text{Wt. of metal}}{\text{Eq. wt. of metal}} = \frac{\text{Wt. of metal sulphate}}{\text{Eq. wt. of metal sulphate}}$$

$$\frac{2}{x} = \frac{6.8}{x + 48} = 6.8x = 2x + 96$$

$$4.8x = 96$$
$$x = \frac{96}{4.8} = 20.0\,g$$

72. *(b)* Let the volume of HCl and H_2SO_4 be V [No. of moles = Molarity × Basicity × Volume]

Moles of H^+ ions in HCl
$$= 0.1 \times 1 \times V = 0.1\,V$$

Moles of H^+ ions in H_2SO_4
$$= 0.2 \times 2 \times V = 0.4\,V$$

Thus, resulting moles of H^+ ions in solution $= (0.1 + 0.4)\,V = 0.5\,V$

Resulting volume of a solution $= 2V$

$$[H^+] = \frac{\text{Moles}}{\text{Volume}} = \frac{0.5\,V}{2\,V}$$
$$= 0.25\,\text{mol L}$$

73. *(b)*

NO₂ — Nitrobenzene — Sn/HCl [Reduction] → NH₂ — Aniline (X) — (i) NaNO₂/HCl [Diazotisation] → Diazonium salt ($N \equiv NCl^-$) — (ii) CuBr, Δ (Sandmeyer reaction) → Br (Y) Bromobenzene

74. *(b)* According to the conservation of energy, the kinetic energy of the ejected electron is given as

$$h\nu = h\nu_0 + \frac{1}{2}mv^2 \Rightarrow \frac{1}{2}mv^2 = h\nu - h\nu_0$$

or $\dfrac{1}{2}mv^2 = h\nu - W_0$

where, $W_0 = h\nu_0 = $ Work function (minimum energy required to eject the electron).

Higher is the threshold frequency (ν_0) more will be the work function. Thus,

$$M_1 \to \text{Rb}, \; M_2 \to \text{K}, \; M_3 \to \text{Na}, \; M_4 \to \text{Li}$$

75. *(*)* $\text{KMnO}_4 + \text{KBr} + \text{H}_2\text{SO}_4$
$$\longrightarrow \text{MnSO}_4 + \text{K}_2\text{SO}_4 + \text{Br}_2 + \text{H}_2\text{O}$$

Balancing the above equation,
$$2\text{KMnO}_4 + 10\text{KBr} + 8\text{H}_2\text{SO}_4 \to 2\text{MnSO}_4 + 5\text{Br}_2 + 6\text{K}_2\text{SO}_4 + 8\text{H}_2\text{O}$$

No. of eq. of KMnO_4 = No. of eq. of Br_2
$$\text{Mole} \times n_{\text{KMnO}_4} = \text{Mole} \times n_{\text{Br}_2}$$

where, n is the balancing factor
$$n_{\text{KMnO}_4} = 5$$
$$n_{\text{Br}_2} = 2$$

$$2 \times 5 = 2 \times \text{moles}$$
$$= \text{moles}_{\text{Br}_2} = 5 \text{ mol}$$

76. *(a)* Absence of cone cells in eyes is known as total colour blindness or monochromacy. This person views everything as if it were in a black and white television. Monochromacy occurs when 2 or all 3 of cone pigments are missing and colour and light vision is reduced to one dimension.

77. *(d)* Pleural fluid is a serous fluid produced by the serous membrane covering normal pleurae. The pleural fluid acts as a lubricant and allows the pleurae to slide effortlessly against each other during respiratory movements, thus reducing the friction between the ribs and the lungs.

78. *(c)* DNA polymerase is an enzyme that synthesises DNA molecules from deoxyribonucleotides, the building blocks of DNA. These enzymes are essential for DNA replication. S-phase or synthetic phase is significant due to DNA synthesis. Thus, DNA polymerase activity is highest at S-phase of cell cycle.

79. *(c)* During vigorous muscular activity like running, muscles perform anaerobic respiration after a while due to scarcity of oxygen. During anaerobic respiration in muscles, lactic acid is produced as a byproduct. Thus a runner will have lactic acid in his muscles after a 100 metre sprint.

80. *(b)* Camel belongs to class–Mammalia. Both birds and mammals are homeothermic and have a fixed 37°C body temperature. So, the DNA polymerase isolated from a camel will work efficiently at temperature near its body temperature.

QUESTION PAPER 2011
Stream : SA

MM : 100

Instructions

1. There are 80 questions in this paper.

2. This question paper contains two parts; Part I and Part II. There are four sections; Mathematics, Physics, Chemistry and Biology in each part.

3. Out of the four options given with each question, only one is correct.

➲ PART-I (1 Mark Questions)

MATHEMATICS

1. Suppose a, b, c are three distinct real numbers, let
$$P(x) = \frac{(x-b)(x-c)}{(a-b)(a-c)} + \frac{(x-c)(x-a)}{(b-c)(b-a)} + \frac{(x-a)(x-b)}{(c-a)(c-b)}.$$

When simplified, $P(x)$ becomes
(a) 1
(b) x
(c) $\dfrac{x^2 + (a+b+c)(ab+bc+ca)}{(a-b)(b-c)(c-a)}$
(d) 0

2. Let a, b, x, y be real numbers such that $a^2 + b^2 = 81$, $x^2 + y^2 = 121$ and $ax + by = 99$. Then, the set of all possible values of $ay - bx$ is
(a) $\left(0, \dfrac{9}{11}\right]$ (b) $\left(0, \dfrac{9}{11}\right)$ (c) $\{0\}$ (d) $\left[\dfrac{9}{11}, \infty\right)$

3. If $x + \dfrac{1}{x} = a$, $x^2 + \dfrac{1}{x^3} = b$, then $x^3 + \dfrac{1}{x^2}$ is
(a) $a^3 + a^2 - 3a - 2 - b$ (b) $a^3 - a^2 - 3a + 4 - b$
(c) $a^3 - a^2 + 3a - 6 - b$ (d) $a^3 + a^2 + 3a - 16 - b$

4. Let a, b, c, d be real numbers such that $|a - b| = 2$, $|b - c| = 3, |c - d| = 4$. Then, the sum of all possible values of $|a - d|$ is
(a) 9   (b) 18
(c) 24   (d) 30

5. Below are four equations in x. Assume that $0 < r < 4$. Which of the following equations has the largest solution for x?
(a) $5\left(1 + \dfrac{r}{\pi}\right)^x = 9$ (b) $5\left(1 + \dfrac{r}{17}\right)^x = 9$
(c) $5(1 + 2r)^x = 9$ (d) $5\left(1 + \dfrac{1}{r}\right)^x = 9$

6. Let ABC be a triangle with $\angle B = 90°$. Let AD be the bisector of $\angle A$ with D on BC. Suppose $AC = 6$ cm and the area of the $\triangle ADC$ is 10 cm^2. Then, the length of BD in cm is equal to
(a) $\dfrac{3}{5}$ (b) $\dfrac{3}{10}$
(c) $\dfrac{5}{3}$ (d) $\dfrac{10}{3}$

7. A piece of paper in the shape of a sector of a circle (see Fig. 1) is rolled up to form a right-circular cone (see Fig. 2). The value of the angle θ is

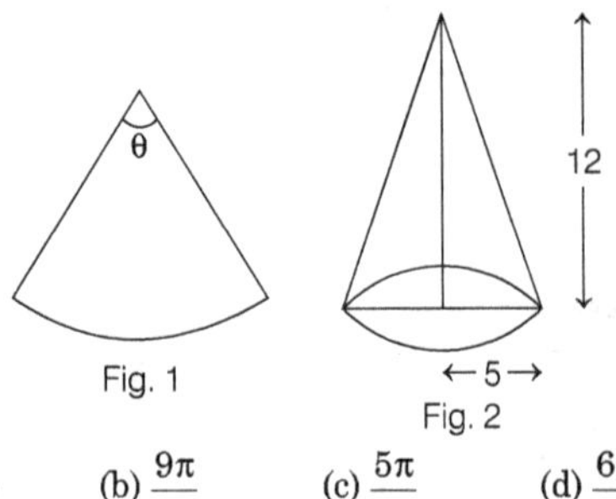

(a) $\dfrac{10\pi}{13}$ (b) $\dfrac{9\pi}{13}$ (c) $\dfrac{5\pi}{13}$ (d) $\dfrac{6\pi}{13}$

8. In given figure, $AB = 12$ cm, $CD = 8$ cm, $BD = 20$ cm, $\angle ABD = \angle AEC = \angle EDC = 90°$. If $BE = x$, then

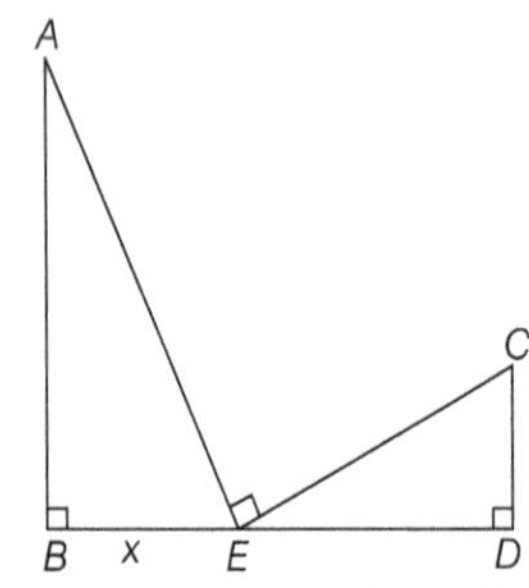

(a) x has two possible values whose difference is 4
(b) x has two possible values whose sum is 28
(c) x has only one value and $x \geq 12$
(d) x cannot be determined with the given information

9. Three circles each of radius 1 touch one another externally and they lie between two parallel lines. The minimum possible distance between the lines is
(a) $2 + \sqrt{3}$ (b) $3 + \sqrt{3}$
(c) 4   (d) $2 + \dfrac{1}{\sqrt{3}}$

10. The number of distinct prime divisors of the number $(512)^3 - (253)^3 - (259)^3$ is

(a) 4   (b) 5   (c) 6   (d) 7

11. Consider an incomplete pyramid of balls on a square base having 18 layers, and having 13 balls on each side of the top layer. Then, the total number N of balls in that pyramid satisfies
(a) $9000 < N < 10000$ (b) $8000 < N < 9000$
(c) $7000 < N < 8000$ (d) $10000 < N < 12000$

12. A man wants to reach a certain destination. One-sixth of the total distance is muddy while half the distance is tar road. For the remaining distance he takes a boat. His speed of travelling in mud, in water, on tar road is in the ratio 3 : 4 : 5. The ratio of the durations he requires to cross the patch of mud, stream and tar road is
(a) $\dfrac{1}{2} : \dfrac{4}{3} : \dfrac{5}{2}$ (b) 3 : 8 : 15   (c) 10 : 15 : 18   (d) 1 : 2 : 3

13. A frog is presently located at the origin (0, 0) in the XY-plane. It always jumps from a point with integer coordinates to a point with integer coordinates moving a distance of 5 units in each jump. What is the minimum number of jumps required for the frog to go from (0, 0) to (0, 1)?
(a) 2   (b) 3   (c) 4   (d) 9

14. A certain 12-hour digital clock displays the hour and the minute of a day. Due to a defect in the clock whenever the digit 1 is supposed to be displayed it displays 7. What fraction of the day will the clock show the correct time ?
(a) $\dfrac{1}{2}$ (b) $\dfrac{5}{8}$ (c) $\dfrac{3}{4}$ (d) $\dfrac{5}{6}$

15. There are 30 questions in a multiple-choice test. A student gets 1 mark for each unattempted question, 0 mark for each wrong answer and 4 marks for each correct answer. A student answered x questions correctly and scored 60. Then, the number of possible value of x is
(a) 15   (b) 10   (c) 6   (d) 5

PHYSICS

16. A simple pendulum oscillates freely between points A and B.

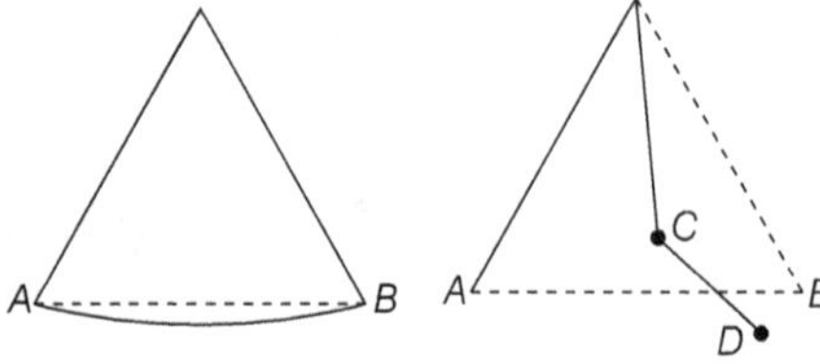

We now put a peg (nail) at the point C as shown in above figure. As the pendulum moves from A to the right, the string will bend at C and the pendulum will go to its extreme point D. Ignoring friction, the point D
(a) will lie on the line AB
(b) will lie above the line AB
(c) will lie below the line AB
(d) will coincide with B

17. A small child tries to move a large rubber toy placed on the ground. The toy does not move but gets deformed under her pushing force **F**, which is obliquely upward as shown in the figure.

Then,

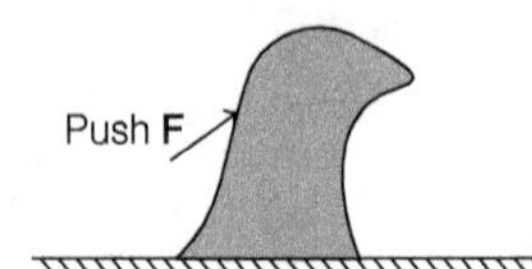

(a) the resultant of the pushing force **F**, weight of the toy, normal force by the ground on the toy and the frictional force is zero

(b) the normal force by the ground is equal and opposite to the weight of the toy

(c) the pushing force **F** of the child is balanced by the equal and opposite frictional force

(d) the pushing force **F** of the child is balanced by the total internal force in the toy generated due to deformation

18. A juggler tosses a ball up in the air with initial speed u. At the instant, it reaches its maximum height H, he tosses up a second ball with the same initial speed. The two balls will collide at a height

(a) $\dfrac{H}{4}$　　(b) $\dfrac{H}{2}$　　(c) $\dfrac{3H}{4}$　　(d) $\sqrt{\dfrac{3}{4}}H$

19. On a horizontal frictionless frozen lake, a girl 36 kg and a box 9 kg are connected to each other by means of a rope. Initially, they are 20 m apart. The girl exerts a horizontal force on the box, pulling it towards her. How far has the girl travelled when she meets the box?

(a) 10 m

(b) Since, there is no friction, the girl will not move

(c) 16 m

(d) 4 m

20. The following three objects (1) a metal tray, (2) a block of wood and (3) a woolen cap are left in a closed room overnight. Next day, the temperature of each is recorded as T_1, T_2 and T_3, respectively. The likely situation is

(a) $T_1 = T_2 = T_3$　　　　(b) $T_3 > T_2 > T_1$

(c) $T_3 = T_2 > T_1$　　　　(d) $T_3 > T_2 = T_1$

21. We sit in the room with windows open. Then,

(a) air pressure on the floor of the room equals the atmospheric pressure but the air pressure on the ceiling is negligible

(b) air pressure is nearly the same on the floor, the walls and the ceiling

(c) air pressure on the floor equals the weight of the air column inside the room (from floor to ceiling) per unit area

(d) air pressure on the walls is zero, since the weight of air acts downward

22. A girl standing at point P on a beach wishes to reach a point Q in the sea as quickly as possible. She can run at $6\,\mathrm{kmh^{-1}}$ on the beach and swim at $4\,\mathrm{kmh^{-1}}$ in the sea. She should take the path

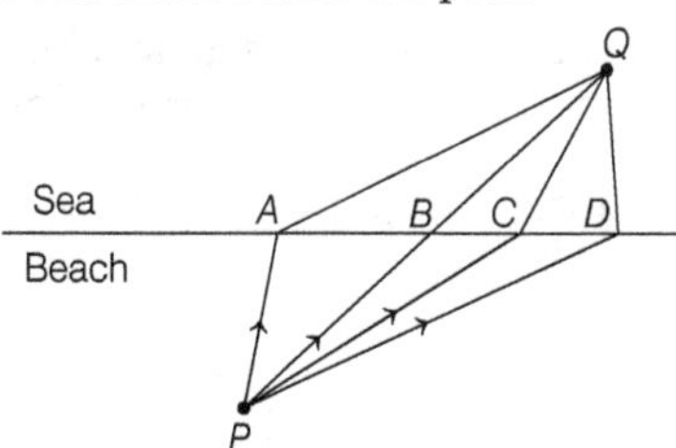

(a) PAQ　　(b) PBQ　　(c) PCQ　　(d) PDQ

23. Light enters an isosceles right triangular prism at normal incidence through face AB and undergoes total internal reflection at face BC as shown below.

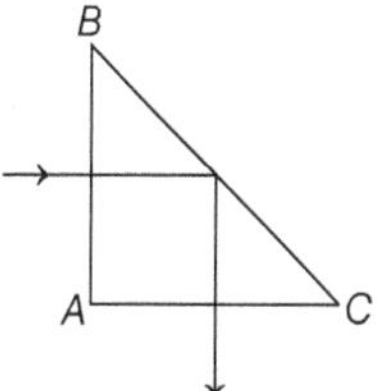

The minimum value of the refractive index of the prism is close to

(a) 1.10　　(b) 1.55　　(c) 1.42　　(d) 1.72

24. A convex lens is used to form an image of an object on a screen. If the upper half of the lens is blackened, so that it becomes opaque, then

(a) only half of the image will be visible

(b) the image position shifts towards the lens

(c) the image position shifts away from the lens

(d) the brightness of the image reduces

25. A cylindrical copper rod has length L and resistance R. If it is melted and formed into another rod of length $2L$, then the resistance will be

(a) R　　(b) $2R$　　(c) $4R$　　(d) $8R$

26. Two charges $+Q$ and $-2Q$ are located at points A and B on a horizontal line as shown below.

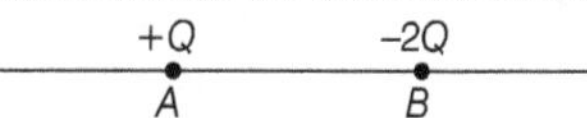

The electric field is zero at a point which is located at a finite distance

(a) on the perpendicular bisector of AB

(b) left of A on the line

(c) between A and B on the line

(d) right of B on the line

27. A 750 W motor drives a pump which lifts 300 L of water per minute to a height of 6 m. The efficiency of the motor is nearly

(Take, acceleration due to gravity to be $10\,\mathrm{m/s^2}$)

(a) 30%　　(b) 40%　　(c) 50%　　(d) 20%

28. Figure below shows a portion of an electric circuit with the currents in amperes and their directions. The magnitude and direction of the current in the portion PQ is

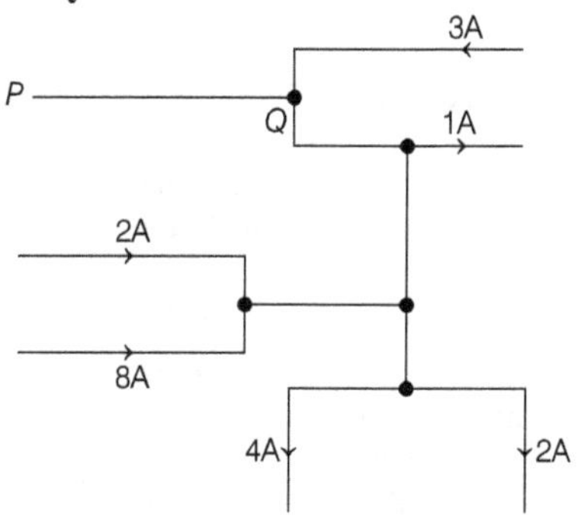

(a) zero

(b) 3 A from P to Q

(c) 4 A from Q to P

(d) 6 A from Q to P

29. A nucleus of lead Pb_{82}^{214} emits two electrons followed by an α-particle. The resulting nucleus will have
(a) 82 protons and 128 neutrons
(b) 80 protons and 130 neutrons
(c) 82 protons and 130 neutrons
(d) 78 protons and 134 neutrons

30. The number of air molecules in a (5m × 5m × 4m) room at standard temperature and pressure is of the order of
(a) 6×10^{23} (b) 3×10^{24} (c) 3×10^{27} (d) 6×10^{30}

CHEMISTRY

31. Two balloons A and B containing 0.2 mole and 0.1 mole of helium at room temperature and 2.0 atm, respectively, are connected. When equilibrium is established, the final pressure of He in the system is
(a) 1.0 atm
(b) 1.5 atm
(c) 0.5 atm
(d) 2.0 atm

32. In the following set of aromatic compounds

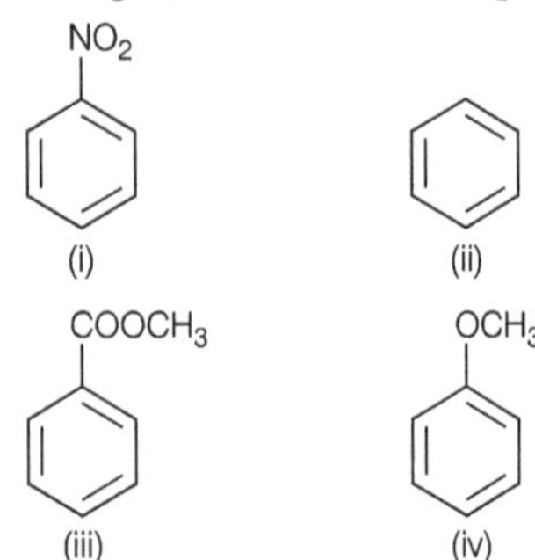

The correct order of reactivity toward Friedel-Crafts alkylation is
(a) i > ii > iii > iv
(b) ii > iv > iii > i
(c) iv > ii > iii > i
(d) iii > i > iv > ii

33. The set of principal (n), azimuthal (l) and magnetic (m_l) quantum numbers that is not allowed for the electron in H-atom is
(a) $n = 3, l = 1, m_l = -1$
(b) $n = 3, l = 0, m_l = 0$
(c) $n = 2, l = 1, m_l = 0$
(d) $n = 2, l = 2, m_l = -1$

34. At 298 K, assuming ideal behaviour, the average kinetic energy of a deuterium molecule is
(a) two times that of a hydrogen molecule
(b) four times that of a hydrogen molecule
(c) half of that of a hydrogen molecule
(d) same as that of a hydrogen molecule

35. An isolated box, equally partitioned contains two ideal gases A and B as shown

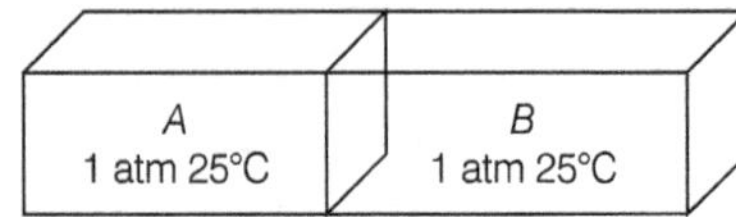

When the partition is removed, the gases mix. The changes in enthalpy (ΔH) and entropy (ΔS) in the process, respectively, are
(a) zero, positive
(b) zero, negative
(c) positive, zero
(d) negative, zero

36. The gas produced from thermal decomposition of $(NH_4)_2Cr_2O_7$ is
(a) oxygen
(b) nitric oxide
(c) ammonia
(d) nitrogen

37. The solubility curve of KNO_3 in water is shown below.

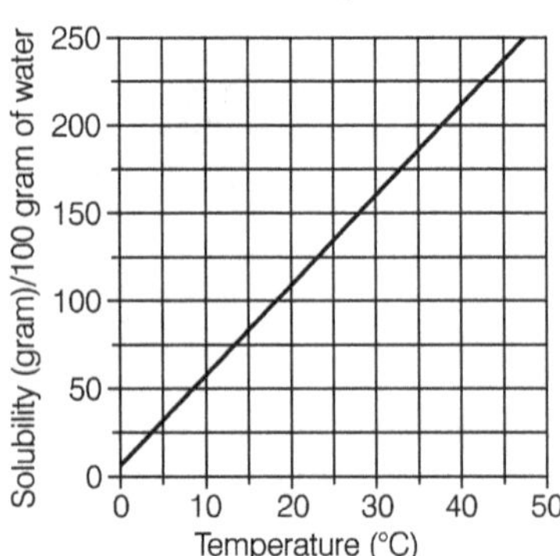

The amount of KNO_3 that dissolves in 50 g of water at 40°C is closest to
(a) 100 g (b) 150 g (c) 200 g (d) 50 g

38. A compound that shows positive iodoform test is
(a) 2-pentanone
(b) 3-pentanone
(c) 3-pentanol
(d) 1-pentanol

39. After 2 hours the amount of a certain radioactive substance reduces to 1/16th of the original amount (the decay process follows first-order kinetics). The half-life of the radioactive substance is
(a) 15 min (b) 30 min (c) 45 min (d) 60 min

40. In the conversion of a zinc ore to zinc metal, the process of roasting involves
(a) $ZnCO_3 \rightarrow ZnO$
(b) $ZnO \rightarrow ZnSO_4$
(c) $ZnS \rightarrow ZnO$
(d) $ZnS \rightarrow ZnSO_4$

41. The number of P–H bond(s) in H_3PO_2, H_3PO_3 and H_3PO_4, respectively, is
(a) 2, 0, 1 (b) 1, 1, 1 (c) 2, 0, 0 (d) 2, 1, 0

42. When chlorine gas is passed through an aqueous solution of KBr, the solution turns orange brown due to the formation of
(a) KCl (b) HCl (c) HBr (d) Br_2

43. Among

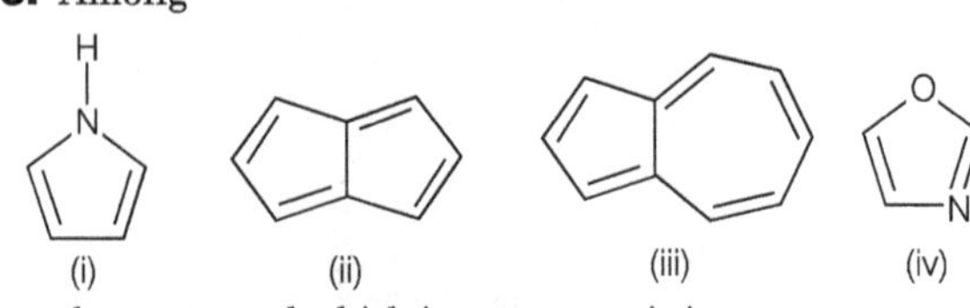

the compound which is not aromatic is
(a) i (b) ii (c) iii (d) iv

44. Among the following compounds

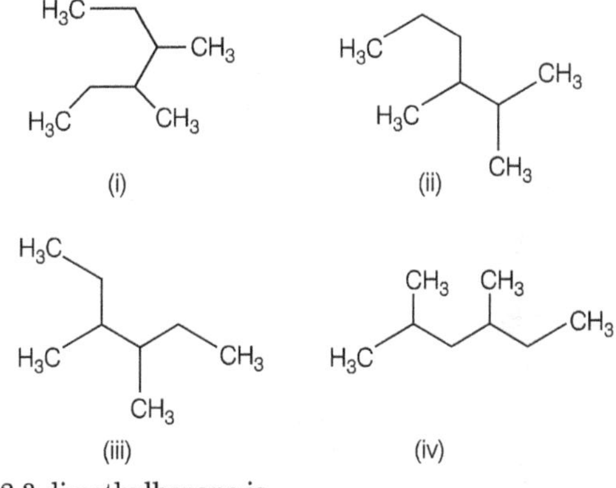

(i)   (ii)   (iii)   (iv)

2,3-dimethylhexane is

(a) i   (b) ii   (c) iii   (d) iv

45. The major product formed in the reaction,

is

(a) i   (b) ii   (c) iii   (d) iv

BIOLOGY

46. If parents have free earlobes and the offspring has attached earlobes, then the parents must be

(a) homozygous   (b) heterozygous
(c) codominant   (d) nullizygous

47. During meiosis, there is

(a) one round of DNA replication and one division
(b) two rounds of DNA replication and one division
(c) two rounds of DNA replication and two divisions
(d) one round of DNA replication and two divisions

48. Blood clotting involves the conversion of

(a) prothrombin to thromboplastin
(b) thromboplastin to prothrombin
(c) fibrinogen to fibrin
(d) fibrin to fibrinogen

49. The gall bladder is involved in

(a) synthesising bile
(b) storing and secreting bile
(c) degrading bile
(d) producing insulin

50. Which one of the following colours is the least useful for plant life?

(a) Red   (b) Blue
(c) Green   (d) Violet

51. At rest, the volume of air that moves in and out per breath is called

(a) resting volume   (b) vital capacity
(c) lung capacity   (d) tidal volume

52. How many sex chromosomes does a normal human inherit from father?

(a) 1   (b) 2
(c) 23   (d) 46

53. In the 16th century, sailors who travelled long distances had diseases related to malnutrition, because they were not able to eat fresh vegetables and fruits for months at a time. Scurvy is a result of the deficiency of

(a) carbohydrates   (b) proteins
(c) vitamin-C   (d) vitamin-D

54. Which of the following structures is not found in plant cells?

(a) Vacuole   (b) Nucleus
(c) Centriole   (d) Endoplasmic reticulum

55. The cell that transfers information about pain to the brain is called a

(a) neuron   (b) blastocyst
(c) histoblast   (d) haemocyte

56. The presence of nutrients in the food can be tested. Benedict's test is used to detect

(a) sucrose   (b) glucose
(c) fatty acid   (d) vitamins

57. Several minerals such as iron, iodine, calcium and phosphorus are important nutrients. Iodine is found in

(a) thyroxine   (b) adrenaline
(c) insulin   (d) testosterone

58. The principle upon which a lactometer works is

(a) viscosity   (b) density
(c) surface tension   (d) presence of protein

59. Mammalian liver cells will swell up when kept in

(a) hypertonic solution   (b) hypotonic solution
(c) isotonic solution   (d) isothermal solution

60. The form of cancer called 'carcinoma' is associated with

(a) lymph cells   (b) mesodermal cells
(c) blood cells   (d) epithelial cells

➷ PART-II (2 Marks Questions)

MATHEMATICS

61. Let $f(x) = ax^2 + bx + c$, where a, b, c are integers, Suppose $f(1) = 0$, $40 < f(6) < 50$, $60 < f(7) < 70$ and $1000t < f(50) < 1000(t+1)$ for some integer t. Then, the value of t is

(a) 2 　　(b) 3 　　(c) 4 　　(d) 5 or more

62. The expression
$$\frac{2^2 + 1}{2^2 - 1} + \frac{3^2 + 1}{3^2 - 1} + \frac{4^2 + 1}{4^2 - 1} + \ldots + \frac{(2011)^2 + 1}{(2011)^2 - 1}$$

lies in the interval

(a) $\left(2010, 2010\frac{1}{2}\right)$ 　　(b) $\left(2011 - \frac{1}{2011}, 2011 - \frac{1}{2012}\right)$

(c) $\left(2011, 2011\frac{1}{2}\right)$ 　　(d) $\left(2012, 2012\frac{1}{2}\right)$

63. The diameter of one of the bases of a truncated cone is 100 mm. If the diameter of this base is increased by 21% such that it still remains a truncated cone with the height and the other base unchanged, the volume also increases by 21%. The radius of the other base (in mm) is

(a) 65 　　(b) 55 　　(c) 45 　　(d) 35

64. Two friends A and B are 30 km apart and they start simultaneously on motorcycles to meet each other. The speed of A is 3 times that of B. The distance between them decreases at the rate of 2 km per minute. Ten minutes after they start, A's vehicle breaks down and A stops and waits for B to arrive. After how much time (in minutes) A started riding, does B meet A?

(a) 15 　　(b) 20 　　(c) 25 　　(d) 30

65. Three taps A, B, C fill up a tank independently in 10 h, 20 h, 30 h, respectively. Initially the tank is empty and exactly one pair of taps is open during each hour and every pair of taps is open at least for one hour. What is the minimum number of hours required to fill the tank?

(a) 8 　　(b) 9 　　(c) 10 　　(d) 11

PHYSICS

66. An object with uniform density ρ is attached to a spring that is known to stretch linearly with applied force as shown below.

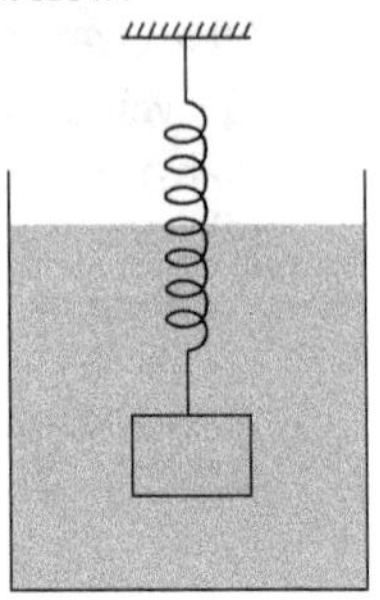

When the spring object system is immersed in a liquid of density ρ_1 as shown in the above figure, the spring stretches by an amount x_1 ($\rho > \rho_1$). When the experiment is repeated in a liquid of density ($\rho_2 < \rho_1$), the spring stretches by an amount x_2. Neglecting any buoyant force on the spring, the density of the object is

(a) $\rho = \dfrac{\rho_1 x_1 - \rho_2 x_2}{x_1 - x_2}$ 　　(b) $\rho = \dfrac{\rho_1 x_2 - \rho_2 x_1}{x_2 - x_1}$

(c) $\rho = \dfrac{\rho_1 x_2 + \rho_2 x_1}{x_1 + x_2}$ 　　(d) $\rho = \dfrac{\rho_1 x_1 + \rho_2 x_2}{x_1 + x_2}$

67. A body of 0.5 kg moves along the positive X-axis under the influence of a varying force F (in newton) as shown below.

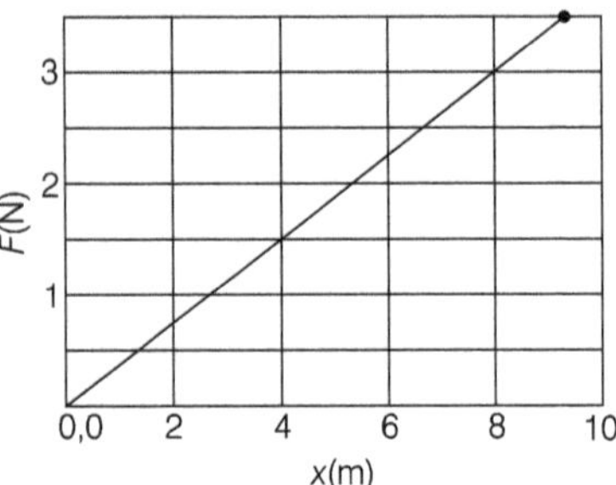

If the speed of the object at $x = 4$ m is 3.16 ms^{-1}, then its speed at $x = 8$ m is

(a) 3.16 ms^{-1} 　(b) 9.3 ms^{-1} 　(c) 8 ms^{-1} 　(d) 6.8 ms^{-1}

68. In a thermally isolated system, two boxes filled with an ideal gas are connected by a valve. When the valve is in closed position, states of the box 1 and 2 respectively, are (1 atm, V, T) and (0.5 atm, $4V$, T). When the valve is opened, then the final pressure of the system is approximately

(a) 0.5 atm 　(b) 0.6 atm 　(c) 0.75 atm 　(d) 1.0 atm

69. A student sees the top edge and the bottom centre C of a pool simultaneously from an angle θ above the horizontal as shown in the figure. The refractive index of water which fills up to the top edge of the pool is $\dfrac{4}{3}$. If $\dfrac{h}{x} = \dfrac{7}{4}$, then $\cos\theta$ is

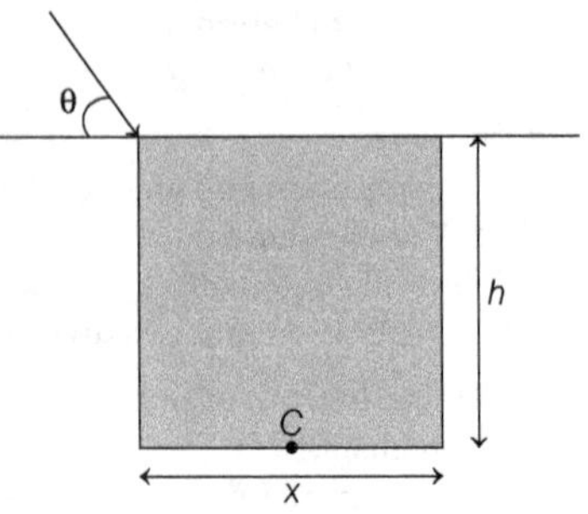

(a) $\dfrac{2}{7}$ 　　(b) $\dfrac{8}{3\sqrt{45}}$ 　　(c) $\dfrac{8}{3\sqrt{53}}$ 　　(d) $\dfrac{8}{21}$

70. In the following circuit, 1Ω resistor dissipates power P. If the resistor is replaced by $9\ \Omega$, the power dissipated in it is

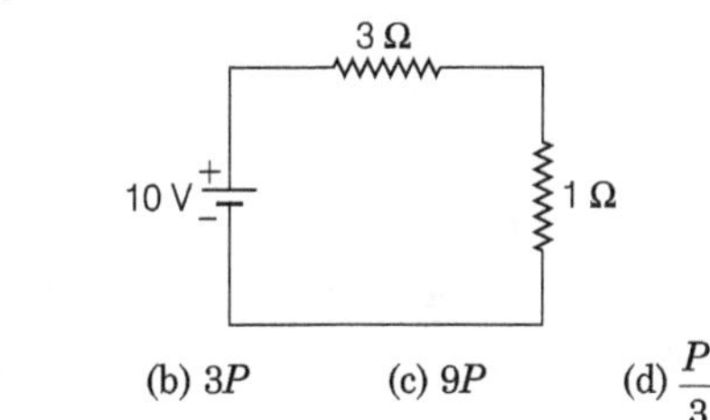

(a) P (b) $3P$ (c) $9P$ (d) $\dfrac{P}{3}$

CHEMISTRY

71. An aqueous buffer is prepared by adding 100 mL of $0.1\ \text{mol L}^{-1}$ acetic acid to 50 mL of $0.2\ \text{mol L}^{-1}$ of sodium acetate. If pK_a of acetic acid is 4.76, the pH of the buffer is

(a) 4.26   (b) 5.76   (c) 3.76   (d) 4.76

72. The maximum number of structural isomers possible for the hydrocarbon having the molecular formula C_4H_6, is

(a) 12   (b) 3   (c) 9   (d) 5

73. In the following reaction sequence, X and Y, respectively, are

(a) H_2O_2; $LiAlH_4$ (b) $C_6H_5\,COOH$; $LiAlH_4$
(c) $C_6H_5\,COOH$; $Zn/Hg \cdot HCl$ (d) alk. $KMnO_4$; $LiAlH_4$

74. Among (i) $[Co(NH_3)_6]Cl_3$, (ii) $[Ni(NH_3)_6]Cl_2$, (iii) $[Cr(H_2O)_6]Cl_3$, (iv) $[Fe(H_2O)_6]Cl_2$ the complex which is diamagnetic is

(a) i   (b) ii   (c) iii   (d) iv

75. At 783 K in the reaction, $H_2(g) + I_2(g) \rightleftharpoons 2HI(g)$, the molar concentrations (mol L^{-1}) of H_2, I_2 and HI at some instant of time are 0.1, 0.2 and 0.4, respectively. If the equilibrium constant is 46 at the same temperature, then as the reaction proceeds

(a) the amount of HI will increase
(b) the amount of HI will decrease
(c) the amount of H_2 and I_2 will increase
(d) the amount of H_2 and I_2 will not change

BIOLOGY

76. You remove four fresh tobacco leaves of similar size and age. Leave 'leaf 1' as it is, smear 'leaf 2' with vaseline on the upper surface, 'leaf 3' on the lower surface and 'leaf 4' on both the surfaces. Hang the leaves for a few hours and you observe that 'leaf 1' wilts the most, 'leaf 2' has wilted, 'leaf 3' wilted less than 'leaf 2' and 'leaf 4' remains fresh. Which of the following conclusions is most logical?

(a) Tobacco leaf has more stomata on the upper surface
(b) Tobacco leaf has more stomata on the lower surface
(c) Stomata are equally distributed in upper and lower surfaces
(d) No conclusion on stomatal distribution can be drawn from this experiment

77. Vestigial organs such as the appendix exist because

(a) they had an important function during development which is not needed in the adult
(b) they have a redundant role to play if an organ with similar function fails
(c) nature cannot get rid of structures that have already formed
(d) they were inherited from an evolutionary ancestor in which they were functional

78. Mendel showed that unit factors, now called alleles, exhibit a dominant/recessive relationship. In a monohybrid cross, the .... trait disappears in the first filial generation.

(a) dominant   (b) codominant
(c) recessive   (d) semi-dominant

79. If a man with an X-linked dominant disease has six sons with a woman having a normal complement of genes, then the sons will

(a) not show any symptoms of the disease
(b) show strong symtpoms of the disease
(c) three will show a disease symptom, while three will not
(d) five will show a disease symptom, while one will not

80. In evolutionary terms, an Indian school boy is more closely related to

(a) an Indian frog
(b) an American snake
(c) a Chinese horse
(d) an African shark

Answers

PART-I

1 (a)	2 (c)	3 (a)	4 (b)	5 (b)	6 (d)	7 (a)	8 (a)	9 (a)	10 (c)
11 (b)	12 (c)	13 (b)	14 (a)	15 (c)	16 (a)	17 (a)	18 (c)	19 (d)	20 (a)
21 (b)	22 (c)	23 (c)	24 (d)	25 (c)	26 (b)	27 (b)	28 (d)	29 (a)	30 (c)
31 (d)	32 (c)	33 (d)	34 (d)	35 (a)	36 (d)	37 (a)	38 (a)	39 (b)	40 (c)
41 (d)	42 (d)	43 (b)	44 (b)	45 (c)	46 (b)	47 (d)	48 (c)	49 (b)	50 (c)
51 (d)	52 (a)	53 (c)	54 (c)	55 (a)	56 (b)	57 (a)	58 (b)	59 (b)	60 (d)

PART-II

61 (c)	62 (c)	63 (b)	64 (d)	65 (a)	66 (b)	67 (d)	68 (b)	69 (c)	70 (a)
71 (d)	72 (c)	73 (b)	74 (a)	75 (a)	76 (b)	77 (d)	78 (c)	79 (a)	80 (c)

Solutions

1. *(a)* Given,
$$P(x) = \frac{(x-b)(x-c)}{(a-b)(a-c)} + \frac{(x-c)(x-a)}{(b-c)(b-a)}$$
$$+ \frac{(x-a)(x-b)}{(c-a)(c-b)}$$
$$P(a) = 1 + 0 + 0 = 1$$
$$P(b) = 0 + 1 + 0 = 1$$
$$P(c) = 0 + 0 + 1 = 1$$

$P(x)$ is a polynomial of degree atmost 2 and also attains same value i.e. 1 for distinct values of x (i.e. a, b, c).

$\therefore P(x)$ is an identity with only value equal to 1 for all R.

$$\therefore \frac{(x-b)(x-c)}{(a-b)(a-c)} + \frac{(x-c)(x-a)}{(b-c)(b-a)} +$$
$$\frac{(x-a)(x-b)}{(c-a)(c-b)} = 1$$

2. *(c)* Given, $a^2 + b^2 = 81$
$$\Rightarrow \quad x^2 + y^2 = 121$$
$$\Rightarrow \quad ax + by = 99$$
Now, $(a^2 + b^2)(x^2 + y^2) = 81 \times 121$
$$a^2x^2 + b^2y^2 + a^2y^2 + b^2x^2 = 81 \times 121 \quad \text{...(i)}$$
and $\quad (ax + by) = 99$
$$\Rightarrow \quad (ax + by)^2 = 99^2$$
$$\Rightarrow \quad a^2x^2 + b^2y^2 + 2axby = 99^2 \quad \text{...(ii)}$$
On subtracting Eq. (i) from Eq. (ii), we get
$$a^2y^2 + b^2x^2 - 2axby = 0$$
$$\Rightarrow \quad (ay - bx)^2 = 0$$
$$\Rightarrow \quad ay - bx = 0$$

3. *(a)* Given, $x + \dfrac{1}{x} = a$ and $x^2 + \dfrac{1}{x^3} = b$

Now, squaring both sides, we get
$$\left(x + \frac{1}{x}\right)^2 = a^2$$
$$\Rightarrow \quad x^2 + \frac{1}{x^2} + 2 = a^2 \quad \text{...(i)}$$
On cubing both sides, we get
$$\left(x + \frac{1}{x}\right)^3 = x^3 + \frac{1}{x^3} + 3\left(x + \frac{1}{x}\right) = a^3 \quad \text{...(ii)}$$
On adding Eqs. (i) and (ii), we get
$$\left(x^2 + \frac{1}{x^3}\right) + \left(x^3 + \frac{1}{x^2}\right) + 2 + 3\left(x + \frac{1}{x}\right)$$
$$= a^3 + a^2$$
$$\Rightarrow \quad b + \left(x^3 + \frac{1}{x^2}\right) + 2 + 3a = a^3 + a^2$$
$$\Rightarrow \quad x^3 + \frac{1}{x^2} = a^3 + a^2 - 3a - b - 2$$

4. *(b)* Given, $|a - b| = 2$, $|b - c| = 3$ and $|c - d| = 4$
$$\therefore \quad a - b = \pm 2, \ b - c = \pm 3 \text{ and } c - d = \pm 4$$
Possible value of $(a - d)$ are $\pm 9, \pm 5, \pm 3, \pm 1$.
$$\therefore \quad |a - d| = 9, 5, 3, 1$$
Sum of $|a - d| = 9 + 5 + 3 + 1 = 18$

5. *(b)* Given, $\quad 0 < r < 4$
$$A = 5\left(1 + \frac{r}{\pi}\right)^x = 9$$
$$\Rightarrow \quad \left(1 + \frac{r}{\pi}\right)^x = \frac{9}{5}$$
$$B = \left(1 + \frac{r}{17}\right)^x = \frac{9}{5}$$
$$C = (1 + 2r)^x = \frac{9}{5}$$
$$D = \left(1 + \frac{1}{r}\right)^x = \frac{9}{5}$$

All A, B, C, D are in the form of $(a)^x = b$
x is largest when a is smallest.
$\therefore$ In A, B, C, D
$$0 < r < 4$$
$1 + \dfrac{r}{17}$ is smallest
$\therefore$ Option (b) is correct.

6. *(d)* Given,
ABC is right angled triangle with B is 90°.

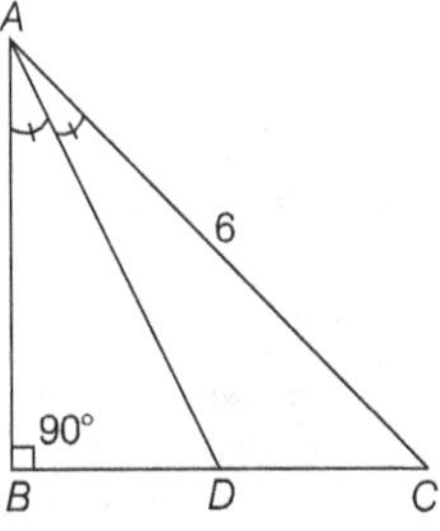

AD is angle bisector of $\angle A$.
$$\therefore \quad \frac{AB}{AC} = \frac{BD}{DC}$$
$$\Rightarrow \quad AB \cdot CD = BD \cdot AC$$
Area of $\triangle ADC = 10$
$$\Rightarrow \quad \frac{1}{2} \times AB \cdot CD = 10$$
$$\Rightarrow \quad \frac{1}{2} \times BD \cdot AC = 10$$
$$\Rightarrow \quad BD = \frac{20}{AC}$$
$$\Rightarrow \quad BD = \frac{20}{6} \quad [\because AC = 6]$$
$$\Rightarrow \quad BD = \frac{10}{3}$$

7. *(a)* We know, $\theta = \dfrac{AB}{OB}$

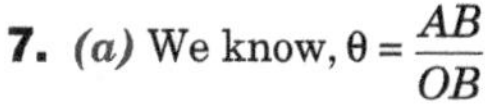
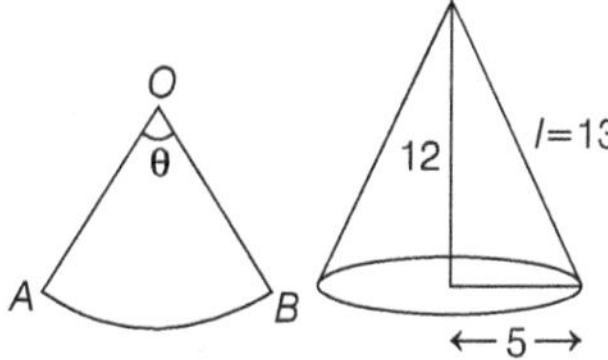

From first figure,

$$AB = 2\pi r$$
$$OB = 13$$

$\therefore \qquad 2\pi(5) = 13\theta \Rightarrow \theta = \dfrac{10\pi}{13}$

8. *(a)* $\Delta ABE \sim \Delta EDC$

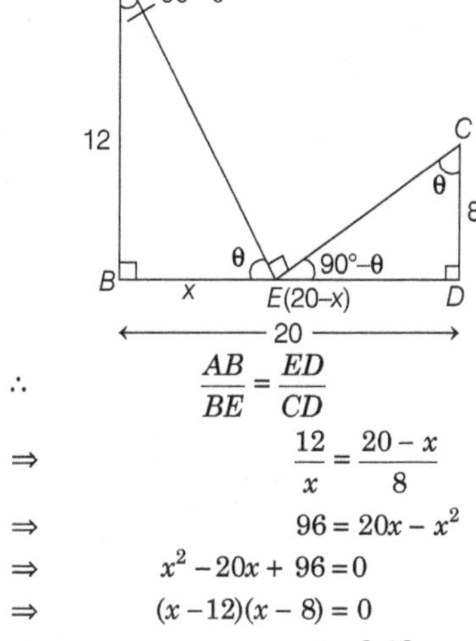

$\therefore \qquad \dfrac{AB}{BE} = \dfrac{ED}{CD}$

$\Rightarrow \qquad \dfrac{12}{x} = \dfrac{20 - x}{8}$

$\Rightarrow \qquad 96 = 20x - x^2$

$\Rightarrow \qquad x^2 - 20x + 96 = 0$

$\Rightarrow \qquad (x - 12)(x - 8) = 0$

$\Rightarrow \qquad x = 8, 12$

Hence, x has two values 8 and 12 and their difference is 4.

9. *(a)* Given, radius of each circle = 1

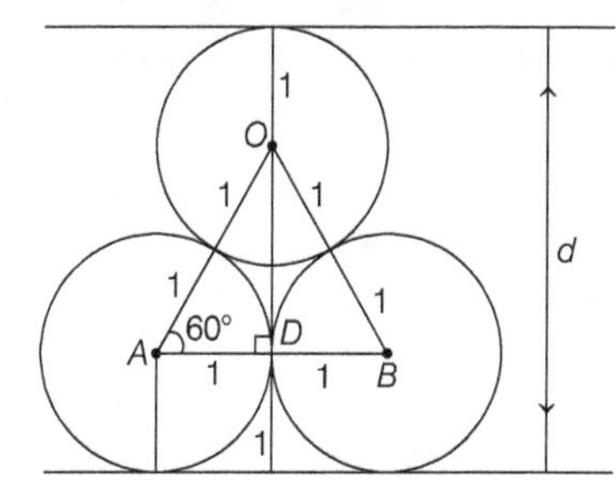

touch externally

$\therefore \qquad OA = OB = AB = 2$

In ΔOAD, $\quad \sin 60° = \dfrac{OD}{OA}$

$\Rightarrow OD = OA \sin 60° = 2 \times \dfrac{\sqrt{3}}{2} = \sqrt{3}$

$\therefore \ d = 1 + OD + 1 = 1 + \sqrt{3} + 1 = \sqrt{3} + 2$

10. *(c)* We have,

$$(512)^3 - (253)^3 - (259)^3$$
$$\Rightarrow \quad (512)^3 + (-253)^3 + (-259)^3$$

Now, $\quad 512 - 253 - 259 = 0$

We know that, $a + b + c = 0$ then

$$a^3 + b^3 + c^3 = 3abc$$

$\therefore \ (512)^3 - (253)^3 - (259)^3$

$$= 3(512)(-253)(-259)$$
$$= 3 \cdot 512 \cdot 253 \cdot 259$$
$$= 3 \cdot 2^9 \cdot 11 \times 23 \times 7 \times 37$$

$\therefore$ There are 6 distinct prime divisors.

11. *(b)* Given, square base pyramid is incomplete.

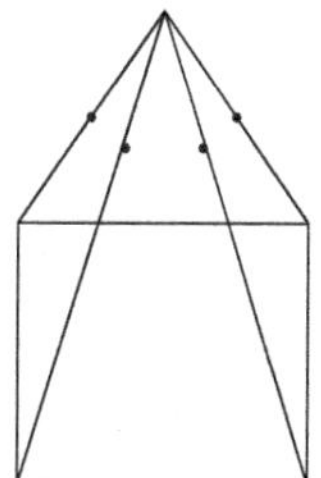

The top layer = 13 balls
There are 18 layer completed.
So, total number of balls

$N = 13^2 + 14^2 + 15^2 + 16^2 + \ldots + 30^2$

$N = (1^2 + 2^2 + 3^2 + 4^2 + \ldots + 30^2)$
$$\qquad\qquad - (1^2 + 2^2 + 3^2 \ldots 12^2)$$

$\Rightarrow N = \dfrac{30 \times 31 \times 61}{6} - \dfrac{12 \times 13 \times 25}{6}$

$\Rightarrow N = 5 \times 31 \times 61 - 2 \times 13 \times 25$

$$= 9455 - 650$$
$$= 8805$$

$\therefore \qquad 8000 < N < 9000$

12. *(c)* Let the total distance = x

Muddy distance = $\dfrac{x}{6}$

Water distance = $\dfrac{x}{2} - \dfrac{x}{6} = \dfrac{x}{3}$

Tar distance = $\dfrac{x}{2}$

Speed travelling in mud = $3y$

Speed travelling by stream = $4y$

Speed travelling in tar = $5y$

Ratio of time = $\dfrac{x/6}{3y} : \dfrac{x/3}{4y} : \dfrac{x/2}{5y}$

$$= \dfrac{1}{18} : \dfrac{1}{12} : \dfrac{1}{10}$$

$$= \dfrac{10}{180} : \dfrac{15}{180} : \dfrac{18}{180}$$

$$= 10 : 15 : 18$$

13. *(b)* We have, initial position of frog = (0,0)

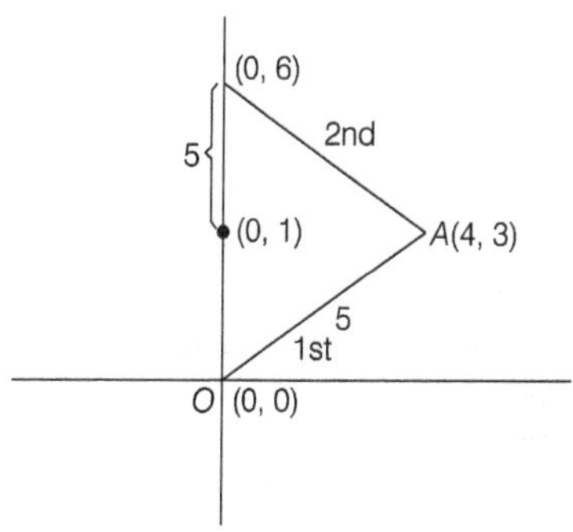

After 1st jump position of frog at (4, 3).
At 2nd jump position of frog at (0,6).
At 3rd jump position of frog at (0,1).
$\therefore$ Minimum number of jumps required for the frog to go from (0,0) to (0,1) and each distance is 5 units is 3.

14. *(a)* Digit 1 appears in 1, 10, 11, and 12 in hour.
$\therefore$ The clock will show the incorrect time between $1 - 2, 10 - 11, 11 - 12, 12 - 1$ day and night both incorrect time
$(8 \times 60) = 480 \min$

Digit 1 appear in minutes 1, 10, 11, 12, 13, 14, 15, 16, 17, 18, 19, 21, 31, 41, 51
$$= 15 \min$$

$\therefore$ It will shows the incorrect time

$$= 16 \times 15$$
$$= 240 \min$$

Total incorrect time = $240 + 480$
$$= 720 \min$$

Correct time = $24 \times 60 - 720$

Fraction of correction time

$$= \dfrac{24 \times 60 - 720}{24 \times 60}$$

$$= \dfrac{1}{2}$$

15. *(c)* Let the student answered correct
$$= x$$

Student answer wrong = y

Student unattempted = z

According to the question,

$$x + y + z = 30, \text{ and } 4x + z = 60$$

$$x = 15, \ y = 15, \ z = 0$$
$$x = 14, \ y = 12, \ z = 4$$
$$x = 13, \ y = 9, \ z = 8$$
$$x = 12, \ y = 6, \ z = 12$$
$$x = 11, \ y = 3, \ z = 16$$
$$x = 10, \ y = 0, \ z = 20$$

Total number of cases = 6

16. *(a)* Total length of a pendulum remains same, so extreme point D lies on the line AB, as shown below.

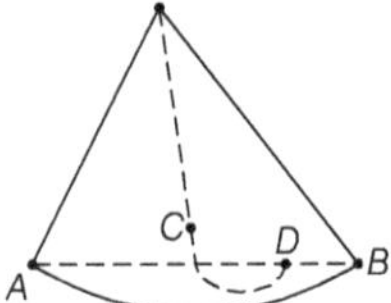

This can be proved by applying energy conservation between extreme positions A and D (its given friction is abscent),

$$K_A + U_A = K_B + U_B = K_D + U_D$$
$$\Rightarrow \quad 0 + U_A = 0 + U_B = 0 + U_D$$
$$\Rightarrow \quad U_A = U_B = U_D \Rightarrow h_A = h_B = h_D$$

17. *(a)* Taking boy, toy and ground as a composite system, we can say that there is no external force acting on the system, net acceleration of the system is zero.

$$A_{\text{system}} = 0 \Rightarrow (F_{\text{net}})_{\text{system}} = 0$$
$$\Rightarrow F + (mg)_{\text{boy}} + (N)_{\text{ground}} + (f)_{\text{friction}} = 0$$

18. *(c)* Let first ball reaches upto height H and it fells by a distance $H - h$, where it collided with second ball which rises upto height h.

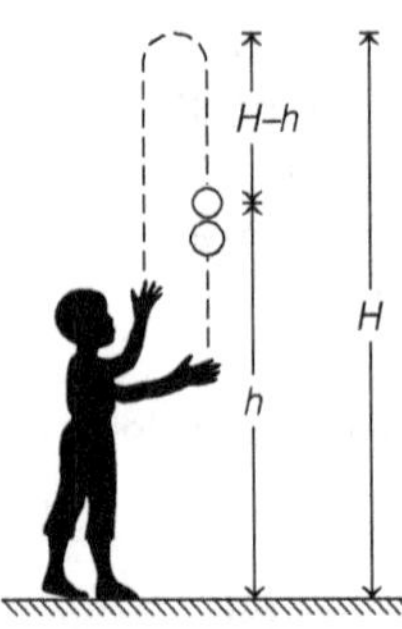

Equation of motion for first and second ball,

$$H - h = \frac{1}{2}gt^2 \qquad \text{...(i)}$$
$$h = ut - \frac{1}{2}gt^2 \qquad \text{...(ii)}$$

From Eqs. (i) and (ii), we have

$$H = ut \text{ or } t = \frac{H}{u} = \frac{u^2/2g}{u} = \frac{u}{2g}$$

Substituting the value of t in Eq. (ii), we have

$$h = u \times \frac{u}{2g} - \frac{1}{2}g \times \frac{u^2}{4g^2}$$
$$h = \frac{u^2}{2g} - \frac{u^2g}{8g^2}$$
$$h = \frac{u^2}{2g} - \frac{u^2}{8g} = \frac{4u^2 - u^2}{8g}$$

$$\text{or } h = 3u^2/8g = \frac{3}{4} \times \frac{u^2}{g} = \frac{3}{4} \cdot H \left[\because H = \frac{u}{2g} \right]$$

19. *(d)* As there is no external force, centre of mass of a system remains at same position.

Initially,

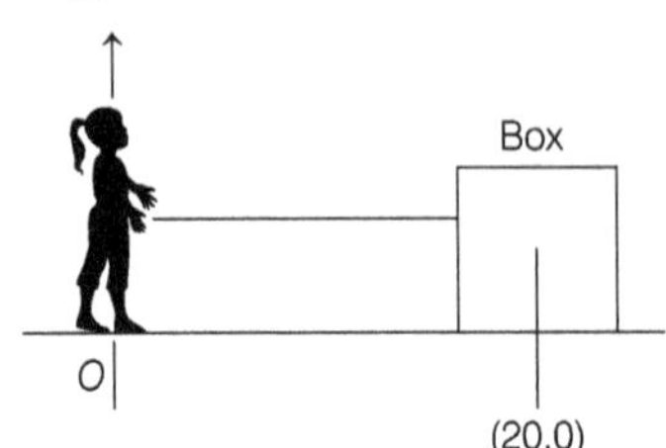

Position of centre of mass of a system taking girl at origin is

$$X_{\text{CM}} = \frac{36 \times 0 + 9 \times 20}{36 + 9} = \frac{9 \times 20}{45}$$

Finally,

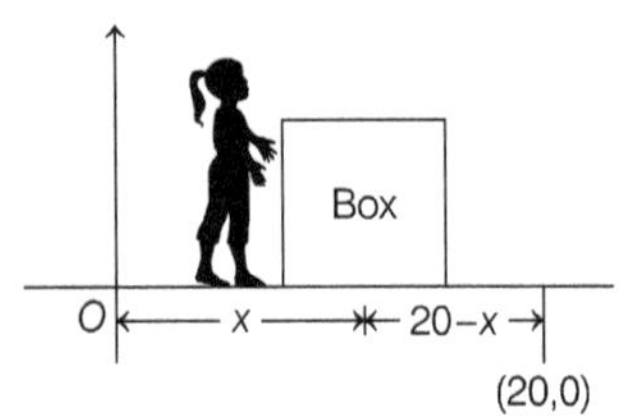

Position of centre of mass when girl and box are at same position is

$$X'_{\text{CM}} = \frac{(36 \times x) + (9 \times x)}{36 + 9} = \frac{36x + 9x}{45}$$

As, $X_{\text{CM}} = X'_{\text{CM}} \Rightarrow \dfrac{9 \times 20}{45} = \dfrac{36x + 9x}{45}$

$$\Rightarrow \quad 9 \times 20 = 45x \Rightarrow x = 4 \text{ m}$$

So, girl travelled by 4m, when she meet with box.

20. *(a)* Most likely each of the object is in thermal equilibrium with its surroundings. So, $T_1 = T_2 = T_3$.

21. *(b)* Gas molecules move randomly and effect of gravity on them is insignificantly low. So, pressure exerted by gas molecules is same everywhere.

22. *(c)* To reach point Q, using Fermat's principle, girl must bend her path towards normal as on beach velocity of girl is more than her velocity at sea.

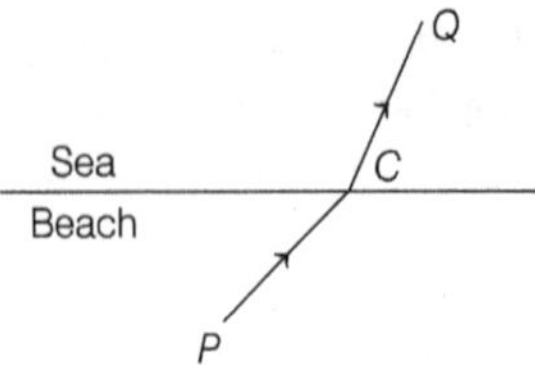

So, correct path is PCQ to reach in shortest time.

Note *Laws of refraction of light follows from Fermat's principle.*

23. *(c)* As total internal reflection occurs at angle of incidence, $i = 45°$.

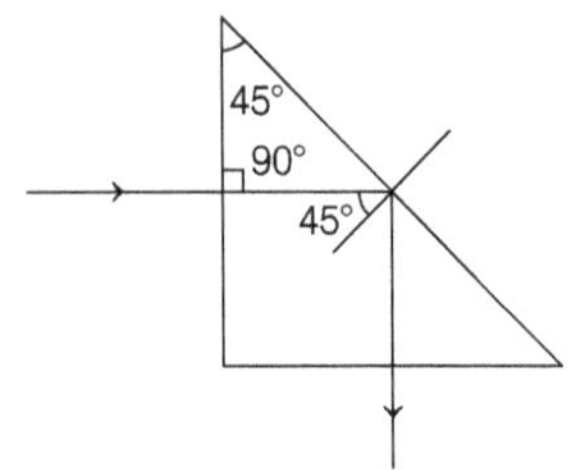

So, using $\mu = \dfrac{1}{\sin C}$, we have

$$\mu = \frac{1}{\sin 45°} = \sqrt{2} \text{ or } \mu \approx 1.42$$

24. *(d)* When a lens is cut into half or its half part is blackened, image is formed at same place but its intensity is reduced.

25. *(c)* As material of rod is not changed, resistivity of both rods is same.

Also, volume of material is same for both rods, so

$$A_1 l_1 = A_2 l_2$$
$$\text{or} \quad A_1 L = A_2 (2L)$$
$$\Rightarrow \quad A_2 = \frac{A_1}{2}$$

Now, using $R = \rho \dfrac{l}{A}$, we have

$$R_2 = \rho \frac{2L}{(A_1/2)} = 4\left(\frac{\rho L}{A_1}\right)$$
$$\text{or} \quad R_2 = 4R$$

26. *(b)* As direction of fields of charges at points A and B,

$$\overset{E_A}{\longleftarrow} \quad \overset{E_A}{\longrightarrow} \quad \overset{E_B}{\longleftarrow}$$
$$\underset{A}{\xrightarrow{E_B} + Q \xrightarrow{E_B} - 2Q \xrightarrow{E_A}}$$

are in opposite directions to left of A or right of B, so fields can be zero in these regions. But in right side of B, field cannot be zero as E_A is very smaller than E_B (charge at A is smaller magnitude and its distance from B is also large).

So, field can be zero in region left of A.

27. *(b)* Useful power

$$= \frac{\text{Work done by motor}}{\text{Time duration}}$$
$$\Rightarrow P_{\text{input}} \times \eta = \frac{W}{\Delta t}$$
$$\Rightarrow P_{\text{input}} \times \eta = \frac{mgh}{t}$$
$$\Rightarrow \quad \eta = \frac{300 \times 10 \times 6}{60 \times 750} = 0.4$$

So, per cent efficiency is, $\eta = 40\%$

28. *(d)* Using Kirchhoff's junction rule, directions and magnitudes of currents are as,

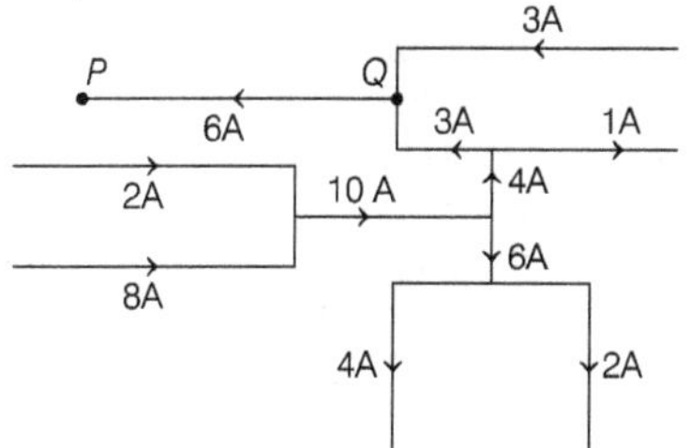

Clearly, current in the portion PQ is from Q to P is 6A.

29. *(a)* Decay scheme is as given below

$$^{214}_{82}Pb \longrightarrow ^{214}_{84}A + ^{0}_{-1}e$$
$$^{210}_{82}X + ^{4}_{2}He$$

Following conservation of mass number and atomic numbers, we have
Number of neutrons in X is
$$N = A - Z = 210 - 82 = 128$$
and number of protons is 82.

30. *(c)* From ideal gas equation,
$$pV = nRT \Rightarrow pV = Nk_BT \text{ or } N = \frac{pV}{k_BT}$$

Substituting given values, we get
$$\Rightarrow \quad N = \frac{10^5 \times 100}{138 \times 10^{-23} \times 273}$$
$$\Rightarrow \quad N = 3 \times 10^{27} \text{ molecules}$$

31. *(d)* Since the pressure of the helium gas in both the balloons A and B are same. Therefore, the final pressure of He will not change. Hence, the correct option is (d).

32. *(c)* The electron releasing groups attached to benzene increases the reactivity towards Friedel-Crafts alkylation whereas the electron withdrawing groups decreases the reactivity.

Among the given groups,—NO_2 and $COOCH_3$ are electron withdrawing group EWG, so they will decrease the reactivity where NO_2 shows stronger $-I$ effect than $COOCH_3$. So, the reactivity of nitrobenzene towards Friedel-Craft alkylation will be least. OCH_3 is an electron donating group, so it will increasing the reactivity.

Thus, the order of reactivity towards Friedel-Craft alkylation is
$$(iv) > (ii) > (iii) > (i)$$

33. *(d)* For any set of principal (n), azimuthal (l) and magnetic (m_l) quantum numbers, the conditions that are allowed for an electron is

(i) values of l should range from 0 to $n - 1$
(ii) values of m should range from $-l$ to l
Thus, the set that is not allowed for electron in H- atom is
$$n = 2, l = 2, m = -1$$
The allowed set of quantum numbers for H - atom having $n = 2$ will be
$$l = 0 \text{ to } 1$$
$$m_l = -1, 0, 1$$

34. *(d)* Average kinetic energy depends upon the temperature and not on the type of gases involved.

For any gas, $(K.E)_{avg} = \dfrac{3kT}{2}$ per molecule

The $(K.E)_{avg}$ of a deuterium molecule is same as that of hydrogen molecule.

35. *(a)* ΔH for this process = $C_V \Delta T = 0$
(at constant temperature)

ΔS for this process will be positive that is $\Delta S > 0$, the randomness increases the molecules of gases A and B gets intermixed with each other, when the partition is removed.

Thus, the correct option is (a).

36. *(d)* The thermal decomposition of $(NH_4)_2Cr_2O_7$ gives chromium oxide (Cr_2O_3), nitrogen gas and water.

$$(NH_4)_2Cr_2O_7 \xrightarrow{\Delta} Cr_2O_3 + N_2 + 4H_2O$$

37. *(a)* From the graph it can be seen that solubility of KNO_3 in water at 40°C is approximately 200 g per 100 of water.

∴ Amount of KNO_3 that dissolve (or solubility) in 50 g of water will
$$= \frac{200}{100} \times 50 = 100 \text{ g}$$

38. *(a)* Iodoform test with sodium hypoiodite is used for the detection of CH_3CO group or $CH_3CH(OH)$ group which produces CH_3CO group on oxidation.

Iodoform reaction with the given compounds are as follows :

(a) $CH_3—CH_2—CH_2—\underset{\underset{O}{\|}}{C}—CH_3 + \underset{NaOH}{I_2}$

2-pentanone

$$\xrightarrow{H^+/H_2O} \underset{\text{Butanoic acid}}{CH_3CH_2CH_2COOH} + \underset{\text{Iodoform}}{CHI_3}$$

If gives positive iodoform test due to the presence of CH_3CO group.

(b) $CH_3—CH_2—\underset{\underset{O}{\|}}{C}—CH_2—CH_3 + I_2/NaOH$

3-pentanone $\xrightarrow{H^+/H_2O}$ no reaction

It gives negative iodoform test.

(c) $\underset{\text{3-pentanol}}{CH_3CH_2\underset{\underset{H}{|}}{\overset{OH}{\underset{\,}{C}}}HCH_2CH_3} + I_2/NaOH \xrightarrow{H^+/H_2O}$

No reaction

It doesn't give positive iodoform test.

(d) $\underset{\text{1-pentanol}}{CH_3CH_2CH_2CH_2CH_2OH} + I_2 / NaOH$
$$\xrightarrow{H^+/H_2O} \text{no reaction}$$

It also give negative iodoform test.

39. *(b)* For first order reaction
$$k = \frac{2.303}{t} \log\left(\frac{a}{a - x}\right)$$
also $k = \dfrac{0.693}{t_{1/2}}$

∴
$$\frac{0.693}{t_{1/2}} = \frac{2.303}{t} \log\left(\frac{a}{a - x}\right)$$

According to question,
$$\frac{0.693}{t_{1/2}} = \frac{2.303}{2 \times 60} \log \frac{a}{a/16}$$
$$\Rightarrow \quad t_{1/2} = 30 \text{ min}$$

40. *(c)* In the process of roasting, sulphide ore is converted into an oxide ore with a regular supply of air in a furnace at a temperature below the melting point of the metal.

Thus, the conversion of sulphide ore into metal oxide is given the reaction
$$ZnS \longrightarrow ZnO, \text{ hence option (c) is correct.}$$

41. *(d)* The structures of given compounds can be drawn as follows :

$$\underset{H_3PO_2}{\overset{\overset{\displaystyle O}{\|}}{\underset{\underset{H}{|}}{\overset{|}{P}}}}_{H\quad OH} , \quad \underset{H_3PO_3}{\overset{\overset{\displaystyle O}{\|}}{\underset{\underset{OH}{|}}{\overset{|}{P}}}}_{HO\quad H} , \quad \underset{H_3PO_4}{\overset{\overset{\displaystyle O}{\|}}{\underset{\underset{OH}{|}}{\overset{|}{P}}}}_{HO\quad OH}$$

Thus, the number of P– H bond(s) in H_3PO_2, H_3PO_3 and H_3PO_4 respectively are 2, 1, 0.

42. *(d)* When chlorine gas is passed through an aqueous solution of KBr, the solution turns orange brown due to the evolution of bromine gas. The equation for the above reaction can be written as
$$Cl_2 + 2KBr \longrightarrow 2KCl + \underset{\text{Orange brown}}{Br_2} \uparrow$$

43. *(b)* The conditions for a compound to be aromatic are
(i) the molecule should be planar.
(ii) it should be cyclic with alternate single and double bonds.
(iii) it should follows Huckel's rule, *i.e.* should have $(4n + 2)$ π electrons.

π electrons present in given compounds are as follows :

(i) (4n+2)π electrons = 6π electrons

∴ Follows Huckel's rule

(ii) (4n+2)π electrons = 8π electrons

Doesn't follow Huckel's rule.

(iii) (4n+2)π electrons = 10π electrons

Follows Huckel's rule.

(iv) (4n+2)π electrons = 6π electrons

Follows Huckel's rule.
Thus, compound (ii) is not aromatic.

44. *(b)* The IUPAC nomenclature of the structures given in the options are as follows

(i) — 3, 4-dimethyl hexane

(ii) — 2, 3-dimethyl hexane

(iii) — 3, 4-dimethyl hexane

(iv) — 2, 4-dimethyl hexane

Hence, the correct option is (b).

45. *(c)*

This reaction involves $S_N 2$ mechanism where CN^- is substituted over Cl^- as it is a good leaving group as compared to Br and I, and occurs at a primary carbon (sp^3-hybridised).

46. *(b)* Attached earlobes is an autosomal recessive trait. Thus, a heterozygous parent with free earlobes will have offspring with attached earlobes.

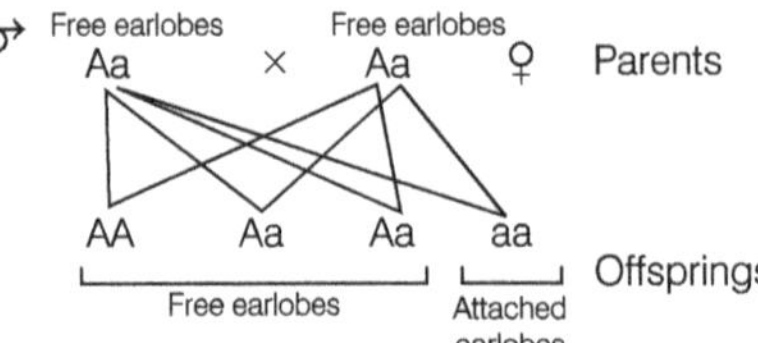

47. *(d)* For a complete meiotic cell division, there takes place one round of DNA replication during the S-phase and two divisions. This is because meiosis is a process where a single cell divides twice to produce four cells containing half the original amount of genetic information.

48. *(c)* Blood clotting involves the conversion of fibrinogen to fibrin. The blood clotting mechanism takes place as follows

Injury in blood vessels
↓
Platelets clump at the wound
↓
Platelets release thrombokinase
↓
Thrombin ← Thrombokinase ← Prothrombin ← Vitamin-K
Fibrin Fibrinogen
↓
Clot forms to prevent further blood loss

49. *(b)* The gall bladder is involved in storing and secreting bile. The gall bladder is a pear-shaped, hollow structure located under the liver and on the right side of the abdomen. Its primary function is to store and concentrate bile, a yellow brown digestive enzyme produced by the liver.

50. *(c)* Green light is not at all useful for photosynthesis. This is because, plant reflects green light and due to this same reason, plants appear green in colour.

51. *(d)* Tidal volume is the volume of inspired/expired air moving in and out of the lungs with each breath.

Vital capacity is the volume that can be inspired/expired after full expiration/inspiration.

Total lung capacity refers to the total amount of air in the lungs after taking the deepest breath possible.

52. *(a)* A normal human inherits only one sex chromosome (either X or Y chromosome) from father. Sex chromosomes, determine whether an individual is male or female. In human and other mammals these are designated by scientists as X and Y. In humans, the sex chromosomes comprise one pair of the total of 23 pairs of chromosomes. The other 22 pairs of chromosomes are called autosomes.

53. *(c)* Scurvy is a result of the deficiency of vitamin-C. Vitamin-C is mainly found in fruits such as oranges, grapefruit, lemons, strawberries and melons or it is found in vegetables such as broccoli and bell peppers. Therefore, malnutrition causes vitamin-C deficiency. Protein deficiency malnutrition is known as kwashiorkor and marasmus. Vitamin-D deficiency causes rickets. Carbohydrates deficiency causes weakness, nausea, dehydration, etc.

54. *(c)* Centriole is not found in plant cells, it is found only in animal cells. These paired organelles are typically located together near the nucleus in the centrosome, a granular mass that serves as an organising centre for microtubules. Centriole is involved in the development of spindle fibres in cell division.

55. *(a)* The brain and spinal cord are made up of many cells, including neurons and glial cells. Neurons are cells that send and receive electro-chemical signals for pain or pleasure to and from the brain and nervous system.

- Blastocyst is a structure formed in the early development of mammals. It possesses an Inner Cell Mass (ICM) which subsequently forms the embryo.
- Histoblast is a cell or cell group possessing broad histogenetic capacity, i.e. capable of forming tissue.
- Haemocyte is a cell of the haemolymph of various invertebrates, especially arthropods.

56. *(b)* Benedict's test is used to detect reducing sugars such as glucose. Sucrose is a non-reducing sugar, it gives negative result for Benedict's test. Benedict's reagent is a complex mixture of sodium carbonate, sodium citrate and copper (II) sulphate petahydrate.

57. *(a)* Iodine is found in thyroxine. Thyroxine, also called 3, 5, 3′, 5′-tetraiodothyronine or T_4, is one of the two major hormones secreted by the thyroid gland (the other is triiodothyronine). Thyroxine's principal function is to stimulate the consumption of oxygen and thus the metabolism of all cells and tissues in the body. Thyroxine is formed by the molecular addition of iodine to the amino acid tyrosine while the latter is bound to the protein thyroglobulin.

58. *(b)* Lactometer is a device used for testing the purity of milk. It measures relative density of milk with respect to water, which is also called specific gravity. If the specific gravity of a sample of milk is within the approved ranges, the milk is pure. If it is not, then there is some adulteration in milk.

59. *(b)* When mammalian liver cells are kept in a hypotonic solution, endosmosis occurs as the cell is hypertonic. Due to the endosmosis, the cellular protoplasm is filled with water, it swells and the cells become turgid. Swelling is seen because the water flows from lower concentration of solute to the higher concentration of solute.

60. *(d)* Carcinoma is a category of types of cancer that develops from epithelial cells. Lymphoma is the cancer that occurs in lymph cells. Leukemia is blood cancer that originates in the blood and bone marrow. Mesoderm is one of the germ layer from which skeletal muscle, bone, connective tissue, heart and the urogenital system originate.

61. *(c)* We have,
$$f(x) = ax^2 + bx + c, \quad a,b,c, \in Z$$
Also $f(1) = 0, \; 40 < f(6) < 50, \; 60 < f(7) < 70$
$$\therefore a + b + c = 0, \; 40 < 36a + 6b + c < 50,$$
$$60 < 49a + 7b + c < 70$$
$$c = -a - b \qquad \text{...(i)}$$
$$\therefore \quad 40 < 36a + 6b - a - b < 50$$
$$\text{and} \quad 60 < 49a + 7b - a - b < 70$$
$$\Rightarrow \qquad 40 < 35a + 5b < 50$$
$$\text{and} \qquad 60 < 48a + 6b < 70$$
$$\Rightarrow 8 < 7a + b < 10 \text{ and } 10 < 8a + b < \frac{70}{6}$$
Now, a and b are integer
$$\therefore \quad 7a + b = 9 \text{ and } 8a + b = 11$$
On solving these equation, we get
$$a = 2, \, b = -5$$
Put the value of a, b in Eq (i), we get
$$c = 3$$

$$\therefore \qquad f(x) = 2x^2 - 5x + 3$$
$$f(50) = 2(50)^2 - 5(50) + 3$$
$$= 5000 - 250 + 3 = 4753$$
Now, $1000t < f(50) < 1000(t+1)$
$$\therefore \qquad 1000t < 4753 < 1000(t+1)$$
$$\Rightarrow \qquad t < 4.753 < t + 1$$
$$\therefore t = 4, \, t \text{ is integer.}$$

62. *(c)* Let
$$S = \frac{2^2 + 1}{2^2 - 1} + \frac{3^2 + 1}{3^2 - 1} + \frac{4^2 + 1}{4^2 - 1} + ... + \frac{(2011)^2 + 1}{(2011)^2 - 1}$$
Here, $\qquad T_r = \dfrac{r^2 + 1}{r^2 - 1}$
$$\Rightarrow \qquad T_r = \frac{r^2 - 1 + 2}{r^2 - 1}$$
$$= 1 + \frac{2}{r^2 - 1} = 1 + \frac{2}{(r-1)(r+1)}$$
$$\Rightarrow \qquad T_r = 1 + \frac{1}{r-1} - \frac{1}{r+1}$$
$$\Rightarrow \qquad S = \sum_{r=2}^{2011} T_r$$
$$= \sum_{r=2}^{2011} \left[1 + \frac{1}{r-1} - \frac{1}{r+1} \right]$$
$$\Rightarrow \qquad S = T_2 + T_3 + T_4 + ... + T_{2011}$$
$$\Rightarrow S = \left(1 + \frac{1}{1} - \frac{1}{3} \right) + \left(1 + \frac{1}{2} - \frac{1}{4} \right)$$
$$+ \left(1 + \frac{1}{3} - \frac{1}{5} \right) + ... + \left(1 + \frac{1}{2010} - \frac{1}{2012} \right)$$
$$\Rightarrow S = 2010 + 1 + \frac{1}{2} - \frac{1}{2012} - \frac{1}{2011}$$
$$\Rightarrow S = 2011 + \frac{1}{2} - \left[\frac{1}{2011} + \frac{1}{2012} \right]$$
$$\Rightarrow S \text{ is lie between } \left(2011, 2011\frac{1}{2} \right).$$

63. *(b)* Given,
Diameter of base $= 100$ mm
$$\therefore \text{Radius of base} = \frac{100}{2} \text{ mm} = 50 \text{mm} = 5 \text{ cm}$$
Let other radius of base $= r$
And height of truncated cone $= h$
Volume of initially truncated cone $= V$
$$\therefore \qquad V = \frac{\pi h}{3} \{(5)^2 + 5r + r^2\}$$
When radius increase by 21%
$$\therefore \text{Radius of base} = 5 + \frac{21}{100} \times 5 = \frac{605}{100}$$
When volume increase by 21%
Then, $V^1 = V + \dfrac{21V}{100} = \dfrac{121V}{100}$
Now, $\quad V^1 = \dfrac{\pi h}{3} \left[\left(\dfrac{605}{100} \right)^2 + \dfrac{605}{100} r + r^2 \right]$
$$[\because r \text{ and } h \text{ are same}]$$

$$\Rightarrow \frac{121V}{100} = \frac{\pi h}{3} \left[\frac{(605)^2 + 60500r + (100r)^2}{(100)^2} \right]$$
$$\Rightarrow \frac{121}{100} \times \frac{\pi h}{3} (25 + 5r + r^2)$$
$$= \frac{\pi h}{3} \left[\frac{(605)^2 + 60500r + (100r)^2}{10000} \right]$$
$$\Rightarrow 100(3025 + 605r + 121r^2)$$
$$= 366025 + 60500r + (100r)^2$$
$$\Rightarrow 100 \times 121r^2 - 10000r^2$$
$$= 366025 - 302500$$
$$\Rightarrow \qquad 2100r^2 = 63525$$
$$\Rightarrow \qquad r^2 = \frac{63525}{2100} = 30.25$$
$$\Rightarrow \qquad r = \sqrt{30.25} = 5.5 \text{ cm} = 55 \text{ mm}$$

64. *(d)* Let the speed of $B = x$ km/h
and the speed of $A = 3x$ km/h
Distance between A and $B = 30$ km
Given, distance between them decrease at 2 km per minutes.
$$\therefore \text{ Distance decrease in one hour}$$
$$= 2 \times 60 = 120 \text{ km}$$
$\therefore$ Total distance travelled by A and B in one hour $= (x + 3x)$ km $= 4x$ km
$$\therefore \text{Speed} = \frac{120}{4} = 30 \text{ km/h}$$
Hence, speed of $B = 30$ km/h
Speed of $A = 90$ km/h
Distance travelled by A and B after 10 min $= 2 \times 10 = 20$ km
So, remaining distance $= (30 - 20) = 10$ km
Time taken by B to distance travelled
$$10 \text{ km} = \left(\frac{10}{30} \times 60 \right) = 20 \text{ min}$$
Total time taken by $A = 20 + 10 = 30$ min

65. *(a)* Taps A, B, C fill up a tank independently 10 h, 20 h, 30 h, respectively.

Given, exactly one pairs of taps is open during each hour and every pairs of taps is open at least one hour.

First A and B are open for one hour, then B and C and then C and A
$$\therefore \left(\frac{1}{10} + \frac{1}{20} \right) + \left(\frac{1}{20} + \frac{1}{30} \right) + \left(\frac{1}{30} + \frac{1}{10} \right)$$
$$= \frac{1}{5} + \frac{1}{10} + \frac{1}{15} = \frac{12 + 6 + 4}{60}$$
$$= \frac{22}{60} = \frac{11}{30}$$
In three hours the tank will be filled $\left(\dfrac{11}{30} \right)$th part. Now, for minimum time, the rest of tank must be filled with A and B taps.

$\therefore$ $$\left(\frac{1}{10} + \frac{1}{20}\right) = \frac{30}{20}$$

So, the rest of $\left(1 - \frac{11}{30}\right)$th $= \left(\frac{19}{30}\right)$th part of tank will taks 5 h more.

So, the tank will be filled in 8 h.

66. *(b)* For equilibrium of block hung from string,

Spring force + Buoyant force = Weight of block

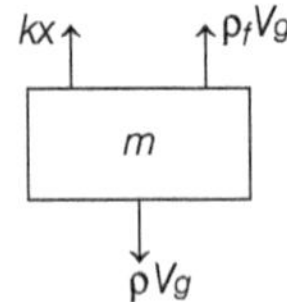

So, we have

$$kx_1 + \rho_1 Vg = \rho Vg \qquad \text{...(i)}$$

and $$kx_2 + \rho_2 Vg = \rho Vg \qquad \text{...(ii)}$$

Eliminating k, we get

$$\rho = \frac{\rho_1 x_2 - \rho_2 x_1}{x_2 - x_1}$$

67. *(d)* By work-kinetic energy theorem, work done is equal to change in kinetic energy.

So, $$\int_{x=4}^{x=8} F dx = \Delta K$$

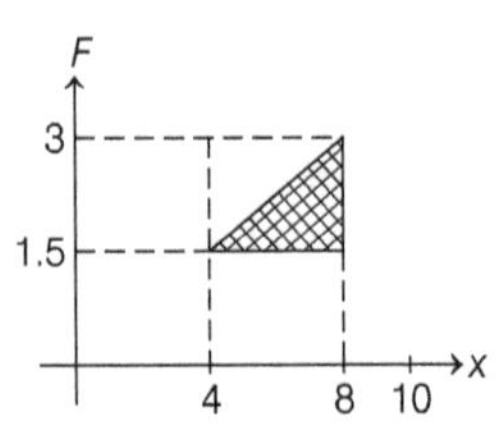

$\Rightarrow$ Area under force-displacement graph from $x = 4$ to $x = 8 = \frac{1}{2} m (v_f^2 - v_i^2)$

$$\Rightarrow \frac{1}{2} (3 - 1.5) \times (8 - 4) = \frac{1}{2} \times \frac{1}{2} \times (v_f^2 - (3.16)^2)$$

$$\Rightarrow v_f = 6.8 \text{ ms}^{-1}$$

68. *(b)* Given situation is

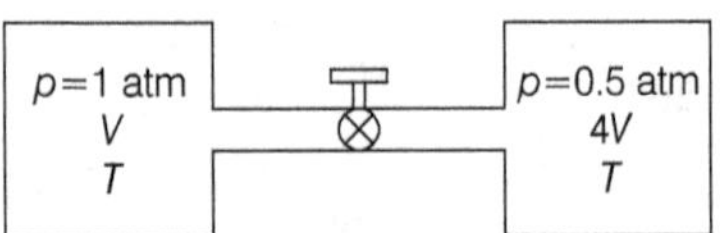

Let final temperature after opening the valve is T_f, then $\Delta W_{ext} = 0$ and $\Delta Q_{ext} = 0$

So, from first law of thermodynamics,

$$\Delta U = 0$$

$$\Rightarrow n_1 C_V T + n_2 C_V T = (n_1 + n_2) C_V T_f$$

$$\Rightarrow T_f = T$$

Now, by gas equation, we have

As, $$n_1 + n_2 = n$$

$$\Rightarrow \frac{V}{RT} + \frac{4V \times 0.5}{RT} = \frac{5V \times p_1}{RT}$$

$$\Rightarrow p = 0.6 \text{ atm}$$

69. *(c)* Ray diagram for pool is as shown below.

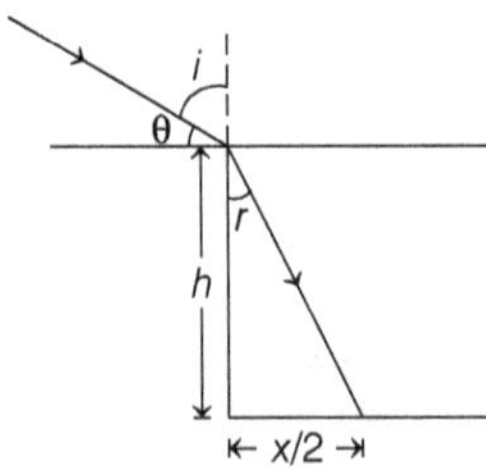

Using $n_1 \cdot \sin i = n_2 \cdot \sin r$, we have

$$1 \times \sin (90° - \theta) = \frac{4}{3} \sin r \qquad \text{...(i)}$$

Also, $$\tan r = \frac{x}{2h} = \frac{4}{7 \times 2} = \frac{2}{7}$$

$$\Rightarrow \sin r = \frac{2}{\sqrt{53}}$$

Substituting $\sin r$ in Eq. (i), we have

$$\cos \theta = \frac{4}{3} \times \frac{2}{\sqrt{53}} = \frac{8}{3\sqrt{53}}$$

70. *(a)* From given circuit, if $i = $ circuit current, then

$$V = iR_{eq} \Rightarrow i = \frac{10}{4} = 2.5 \text{ A}$$

So, power dissipated by circuit is

$$P = i^2 R = (2.5)^2 \times 1 = \frac{25}{4} \text{ W}$$

When 1Ω resistor is replaced by a 9Ω resistor, then power dissipated in $9\,\Omega$ resistor is

$$P' = \left(\frac{10}{12}\right)^2 \times (9)$$

$$= \frac{100 \times 9}{12 \times 12} = \frac{25}{4} \text{ W}$$

So, $P' = P$

71. *(d)* M_{eq} of $CH_3COOH = 100 \times 0.1 = 10$

M_{eq} of $CH_3COONa = 50 \times 0.2 = 10$

According to Henderson equation

$$pH = pK_a + \log \frac{[\text{salt}]}{[\text{acid}]}$$

$$pH = pK_a + \frac{\log [CH_3COO^-]}{\log [CH_3COOH]}$$

$$pH = 4.76 + \log \frac{10}{10}$$

$$pH = 4.76 + \log 1$$

$$\Rightarrow pH = 4.76$$

72. *(c)* Nine structure isomers are possible for the hydrocarbon having molecular formula C_4H_6.

These are as follows :

$CH_2 = C = CH - CH_3$, $CH_3CH_2C \equiv CH$,
$CH_3 - C \equiv C - CH_3$,
$CH_2 = CH - CH = CH_2$

73. *(b)* In the first sequence of reaction, an alkene is getting converted into epoxy group, so an oxidising agent is required both H_2O_2 and C_6H_5COOH are oxidising agent but C_6H_5COOH is used as they are not very sensitive to solvent polarity while, in 2nd sequence of reaction, the epoxy group is being reduced into an alcoholic group, thus a reducing agent is required. Thus, the suitable reagents are

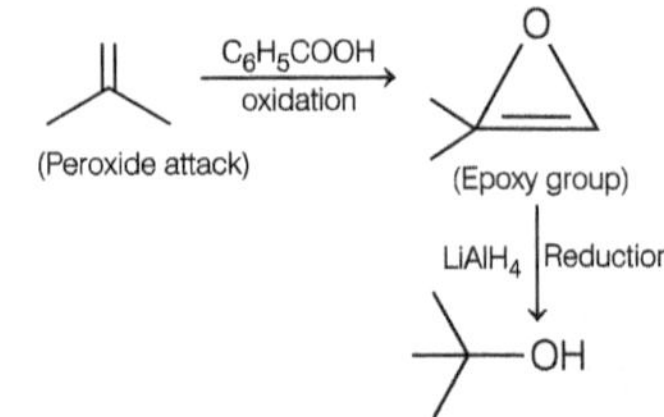

74. *(a)* The magnetic character of the given complexes are as follows :

(i) $Co(NH_3)_6]^{3+}$

Oxidation state of Co in $[Co(NH_3)_6]^{3+}$ is $+3$.

The electronic configuration of Co^{3+} is $3d^6 4s^0$.

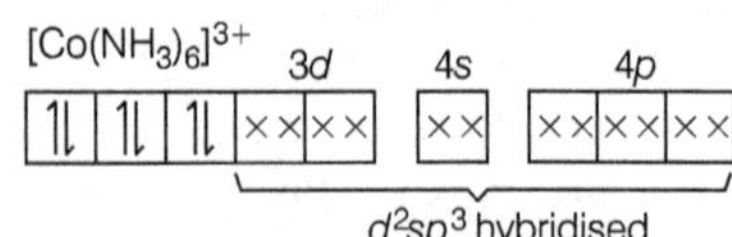

As NH_3 is a strong field ligand, paring of electrons occur

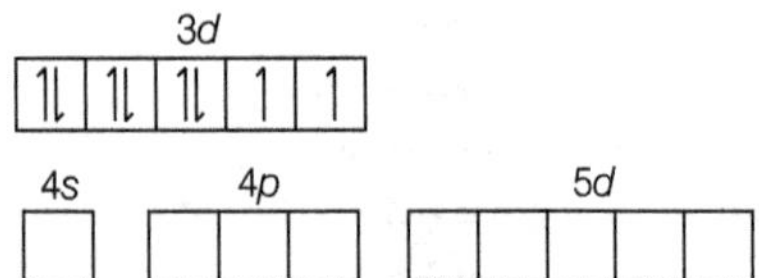

Thus, the complex is diamagnetic.

(ii) $[Ni(NH_3)_6]^{2+}$

Oxidation state of Ni in $[Ni(NH_3)_6]^{2+}$ is $+2$.

The electronic configuration for Ni^{2+} is $3d^8 4s^0$.

Though NH_3 is a strong ligand pairing will not occur because, if pairing would occur then also $2, d$-orbitals will not be available for hybridisation.

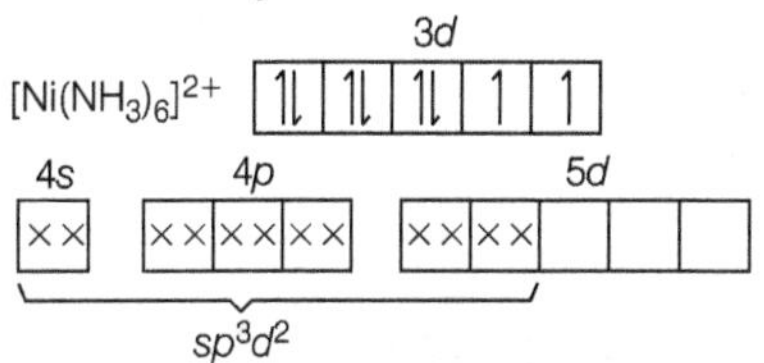

Thus, the complex is paramagnetic.

(iii) $[Cr(H_2O)_6]^{3+}$

Oxidation state of Cr in $[Cr(H_2O_6)]^{3+}$ is $+3$.

The electronic configuration of Cr^{3+} is $[Ar]\ 3d^3\ 4s^0$.

$[Cr(H_2O)_6]^{3+}$

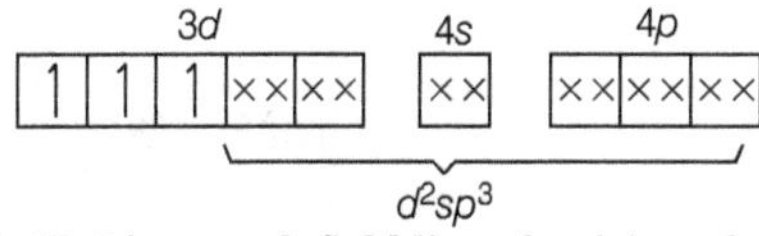

As H_2O is a weak field ligand pairing of electrons will not occur and the complex is paramagnetic.

(iv) $[Fe(H_2O)_6]^{2+}$

Oxidation state of Fe in $[Fe(H_2O_6)]^{2+}$ is $+2$.

The electronic configuration of Fe^{2+} is $[Ar]\ 3d^6\ 4s^0$.

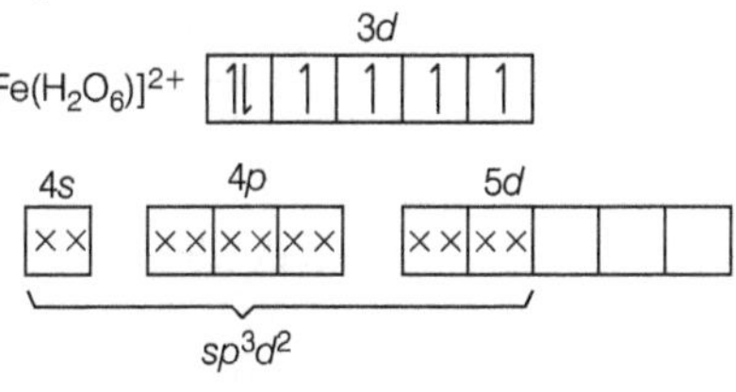

As H_2O is a weak field ligand, pairing of electrons will not occur and thus the complex will be paramagnetic.

75. *(a)* For the reaction,

$$H_2(g) + I_2(g) \rightleftharpoons 2HI(g) \qquad [K_C = 46]$$

$$Q_C = \frac{[HI]^2}{[H_2]\,[I_2]}$$

$$Q_C = \frac{0.4 \times 0.4}{0.1 \times 0.2} \implies Q_C = 8$$

As $Q_C < K_C$

So, the reaction will proceeds in forward direction. Hence, amount of HI increases.

76. *(b)* Tobacco is a dicot plant, thus its leaves have more number of stomata on its lower surface. If you cover the leaves of a healthy plant with vaseline, it will block its stomata and therefore it will not lose water through transpiration, so the upward movement of the water in the plant will stop. This will not allow the plant to wilt quickly.

The leaf '2' is smeared with vaseline on the upper surface, so the plant will lose water from the lower surface and in leaf '3', vaseline is smeared on the lower surface therefore the water is lost from the upper surface. But the number of stomata are more on the lower surface therefore leaf '2' will wilt more quickly than leaf '3'.

77. *(d)* Vestigial organs are those organs which are no longer in use. They were used to play an important role in our ancestors, but as and when we developed and evolved, some of these organs lost their functionality but managed to stay in our body. Appendix, coccyx, external ears, etc. are some examples of vestigial organs in human body.

78. *(c)* Gregor Mendel studied inheritance of traits in pea plants. In a monohybrid cross, the recessive trait disappears in the first filial generation. The traits that were visible in the F_1-generation are referred to as dominant traits. This happens because recessive allele does not express itself in the presence of dominant allele.

79. *(a)* An individual gets one sex chromosome from each parent during fertilisation.

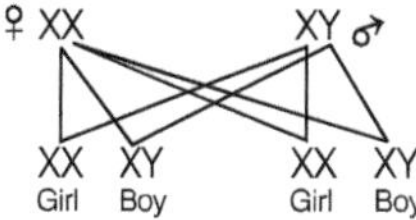

We see from the above cross that sons get their Y-chromosome from father and X-chromosome from mother.

Therefore, if a man with an X-linked dominant disease has six sons with a woman having a normal complement of genes, their sons will show no symptom of the disease.

80. *(c)* In evolutionary terms, an Indian school boy is more closely related to Chinese horse. Human and horse irrespective of their country are more generally similar in their chromosomal management, than to rest of the species mentioned here. This is because human and horse both belong to class Mammalia. Other options like frog, snake and shark belong to class– Amphibia, Reptilia and Chondrichthyes.

QUESTION PAPER 2010
Stream : SA

MM : 100

Instructions

1. There are 52 questions in this paper.
2. This question paper contains two parts; Part I and Part II.
3. Each question of part I carries 1 mark, for which only one option out of given four is correct.
4. Each question of part II carries 5 marks.

➲ PART-I (1 Mark Questions)

MATHEMATICS

1. A student notices that the roots of the equation $x^2 + bx + a = 0$ are each 1 less than the roots of the equation $x^2 + ax + b = 0$. Then, $a + b$ is
   (a) possibly any real number   (b) −2
   (c) −4   (d) −5

2. If x, y are real numbers such that
   $$3^{(x/y)+1} - 3^{(x/y)-1} = 24,$$
   then the value of $(x + y)/(x - y)$ is
   (a) 0   (b) 1   (c) 2   (d) 3

3. The number of positive integers n in the set {1, 2, 3, ..., 100} for which the number
   $$\frac{1^2 + 2^2 + 3^2 + ... + n^2}{1 + 2 + 3 + ... + n}$$ is an integer is
   (a) 33   (b) 34   (c) 50   (d) 100

4. The three different face diagonals of a cuboid (rectangular parallelopiped) have lengths 39, 40, 41. The length of the main diagonal of the cuboid which joins a pair of opposite corners is
   (a) 49   (b) $49\sqrt{2}$ (c) 60   (d) $60\sqrt{2}$

5. The sides of a $\triangle ABC$ are positive integers. The smallest side has length 1. Which of the following statements is true?
   (a) The area of $\triangle ABC$ is always a rational number
   (b) The area of $\triangle ABC$ is always an irrational number
   (c) The perimeter of $\triangle ABC$ is an even integer
   (d) The information provided is not sufficient to conclude any of the statements A, B or C above

6. Consider a square $ABCD$ of side 12 and let M, N be the midpoints of AB, CD respectively. Take a point P on MN and let $AP = r, PC = s$. Then, the area of the triangle whose sides are $r, s, 12$ is
   (a) 72   (b) 36   (c) $\dfrac{rs}{2}$ (d) $\dfrac{rs}{4}$

7. A cow is tied to a corner (vertex) of a regular hexagonal fenced area of side a m by a rope of length $\dfrac{5a}{2}$ m in a grass field. (The cow cannot graze inside the fenced area). What is the maximum possible area of the grass field to which the cow has access to graze?
   (a) $5\pi a^2$ (b) $\dfrac{5}{2}\pi a^2$ (c) $6\pi a^2$ (d) $3\pi a^2$

8. A closed conical vessel is filled with water fully and is placed with its vertex down. The water is let out at a constant speed. After 21 min, it was found that the height of the water column is half of the original height. How much more time in minutes does it require to empty the vessel?

(a) 21   (b) 14   (c) 7   (d) 3

9. I carried 1000 kg of watermelon in summer by train. In the beginning the water content was 99%. By the time I reached the destination, the water content had dropped to 98%. The reduction in the weight of the watermelon was

(a) 10 kg   (b) 50 kg   (c) 100 kg   (d) 500 kg

10. A rectangle is divided into 16 sub-rectangles as in the figure, the number in each sub-rectangle represents the area of that sub-rectangle. What is the area of the rectangle *KLMN* ?

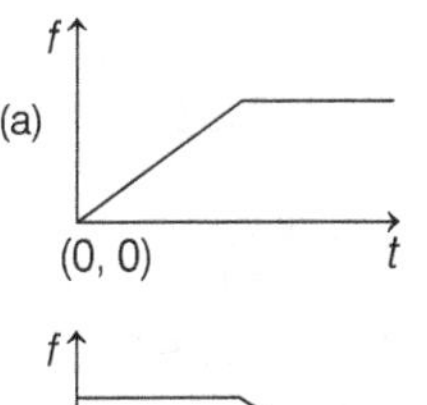

(a) 20   (b) 30   (c) 40   (d) 50

PHYSICS

11. A hollow pendulum bob filled with water has a small hole at the bottom through which water escapes at a constant rate. Which of the following statements describes the variation of the time period T of the pendulum as the water flows out?

(a) T decreases first and then increases
(b) T increases first and then decreases
(c) T increases throughout
(d) T does not change

12. A block of mass M rests on a rough horizontal table. A steadily increasing horizontal force is applied such that the block starts to slide on the table without toppling. The force is continued even after sliding has started. Assume the coefficients of static and kinetic friction between the table and the block to be equal. The correct representation of the variation of the frictional force f, exerted by the table on the block with time t is given by

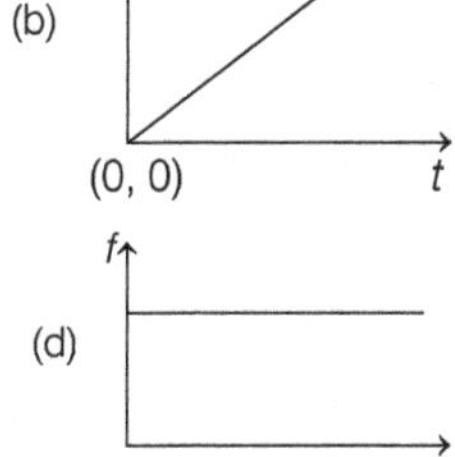

13. A soldier with a machine gun, falling from an airplane gets detached from his parachute. He is able to resist the downward acceleration, if he shoots 40 bullets a second at the speed of 500 m/s. If the weight of a bullet is 49 g, what is the weight of the man with the gun ? Ignore resistance due to air and assume the acceleration due to gravity, $g = 9.8 \text{ ms}^{-2}$.

(a) 50 kg   (b) 75 kg   (c) 100 kg   (d) 125 kg

14. A planet of mass is moving around a star of mass M and radius R in a circular orbit of radius r. The star abruptly shrinks to half its radius without any loss of mass. What change will be there in the orbit of the planet?

(a) The planet will escape from the star
(b) The radius of the orbit will increase
(c) The radius of the orbit will decrease
(d) The radius of the orbit will not change

15. Figure (i) below shows a Wheatstone's bridge in which P, Q, R and S are fixed resistances, G is a galvanometer and B is a battery. For this particular case, the galvanometer shows zero deflection. Now, only the positions of B and G are interchanged, as shown in figure (ii). The new deflection of the galvanometer

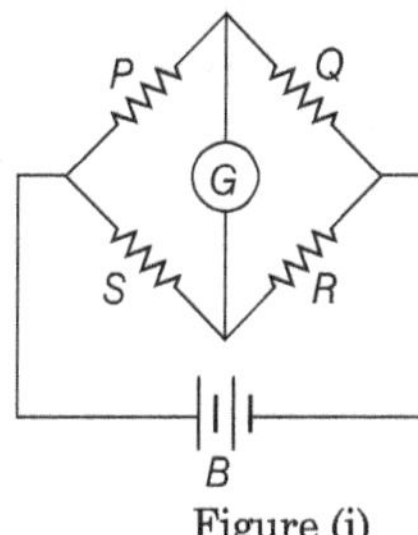

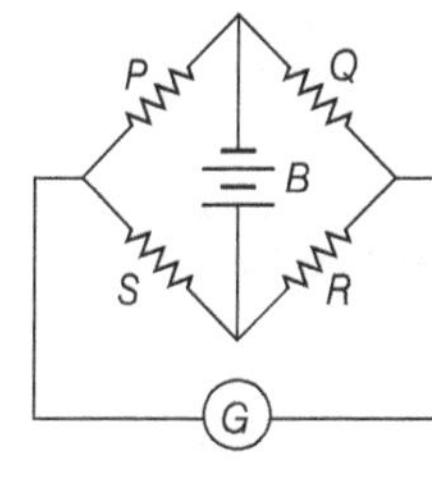

Figure (i)   Figure (ii)

(a) is to the left
(b) is to the right
(c) is zero
(d) depends on the values of P, Q, R and S

16. 12 positive charges of magnitude q are placed on a circle of radius R in a manner that they are equally spaced. A charge Q is placed at the centre, if one of the charges q is removed, then the force on Q is

(a) zero
(b) $\dfrac{qQ}{4\pi\varepsilon_0 R^2}$ away from the position of the removed charge
(c) $\dfrac{11qQ}{4\pi\varepsilon_0 R^2}$ away from the position of the removed charge
(d) $\dfrac{qQ}{4\pi\varepsilon_0 R^2}$ towards the position of the removed charge

17. An electric heater consists of a nichrome coil and runs under 220 V, consuming 1 kW power. Part of its coil burned out and it was reconnected after cutting off the burnt portion. The power it will cunsume now is

(a) more than 1 kW   (b) less than 1 kW, but not zero
(c) 1 kW   (d) 0 kW

18. White light is split into a spectrum by a prism and it is seen on a screen. If we put another identical inverted prism behind it in contact, what will be seen on the screen ?

(a) Violet will appear where red was

(b) The spectrum will remains same

(c) There will be no spectrum, but only the original light with no deviation

(d) There will be no spectrum, but the original light will be laterally displaced

19. Two identical blocks of metal are at 20°C and 80°C, respectively. The specific heat of the material of the two blocks increases with temperature. Which of the following is true about the final temperature T_f when the two blocks are brought into contact (assuming that no heat is lost to the surroundings)?

(a) T_f will be 50°C

(b) T_f will be more than 50°C

(c) T_f will be less than 50°C

(d) T_f can be either more than or less than 50° C depending on the precise variation of the specific heat with temperature

20. A new temperature scale uses X as a unit of temperature, where the numerical value of the temperature t_x in this scale is related to the absolute temperature T by $t_x = 3T + 100$. If the specific heat of a material using this unit is 1400 J kg^{-1}K^{-1}, its specific heat in the SI system of units is

(a) 4200 J kg^{-1} K^{-1}

(b) 1400 J kg^{-1} K^{-1}

(c) 466.7 J kg^{-1} K^{-1}

(d) impossible to determine from the information provided

CHEMISTRY

21. The boiling point of 0.01 M aqueous solutions of sucrose, NaCl and $CaCl_2$ would be

(a) the same   (b) highest for sucrose solution

(c) highest for NaCl solution   (d) highest for $CaCl_2$ solution

22. The correct electronic configuration for the ground state of silicon (atomic number = 14) is

(a) $1s^2 2s^2 2p^6 3s^2 3p^2$ (b) $1s^2 2s^2 2p^6 3p^4$

(c) $1s^2 2s^2 2p^4 3s^2 3p^4$ (d) $1s^2 2s^2 2p^6 3s^1 3p^5$

23. The molar mass of $CaCO_3$ is 100 g. The maximum amount of carbon dioxide that can be liberated on heating 25 g of $CaCO_3$ is

(a) 11 g   (b) 5.5 g

(c) 22 g   (d) 2.2 g

24. The atomic radii of the elements across the second period of the periodic table

(a) decrease due to increase in atomic number

(b) decrease due to increase in effective nuclear charge

(c) decrease due to increase in atomic weights

(d) increase due to increase in the effective nuclear charge

25. Among NH_3, BCl_3, Cl_2 and N_2, the compound that does not satisfy the octet rule is

(a) NH_3 (b) BCl_3 (c) Cl_2 (d) N_2

26. The gas produced on heating MnO_2 with conc. HCl is

(a) Cl_2 (b) H_2 (c) O_2 (d) O_3

27. The number of covalent bonds in C_4H_7Br, is

(a) 12   (b) 10   (c) 13   (d) 11

28. An aqueous solution of HCl has a pH of 2.0. When water is added to increase the pH to 5.0, the hydrogen ion concentration

(a) remains the same   (b) decreases three-fold

(c) increases three-fold   (d) decreases thousand-fold

29. Consider two sealed jars of equal volume. One contains 2 g of hydrogen at 200 K and the other contains 28 g of nitrogen at 400 K. The gases in the two jars will have

(a) the same pressure

(b) the same average kinetic energy

(c) the same number of molecules

(d) the same average molecular speed

30. Identify the stereoisomeric pair from the following choices.

(a) $CH_3CH_2CH_2OH$ and $CH_3CH_2OCH_3$

(b) $CH_3CH_2CH_2Cl$ and $CH_3CHClCH_3$

(c) $CH_3 - C = C - CH_3$ and $CH_3 - \overset{H}{\underset{H}{C}} - \overset{}{\underset{H}{C}} - CH_3$ (with H above each C)

(d)
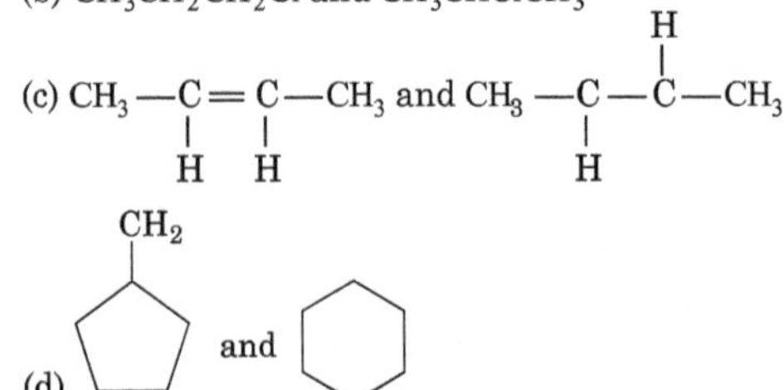

BIOLOGY

31. Which of the following is a water borne disease?

(a) Tuberculosis   (b) Malaria

(c) Chicken pox   (d) Cholera

32. In his seminal work on genetics, Gregor Mendel described the physical traits in the pea plant as being controlled by two 'factors'. What term is used to define these factors today?

(a) Chromosomes   (b) Genes

(c) Alleles   (d) Hybrids

33. A majority of the tree species of peninsular Indian origin fruit in the months of

(a) April-May   (b) August-September

(c) December-January   (d) All months of the year

34. In frogs, body proportions do not change with their growth. A frog that is twice as long as another will be heavier by approximately

(a) two-fold   (b) four-fold   (c) six-fold   (d) eight-fold

35. Which of the following has the widest angle of binocular vision?
(a) Rat   (b) Duck   (c) Eagle   (d) Owl

36. The two alleles of a locus which an offspring receives from the male and female gametes are situated on
(a) two different homologs of the same chromosome
(b) two different chromosomes
(c) sex chromosomes
(d) a single chromosome

37. Ants locate sucrose by
(a) using a strong sense of smell
(b) using a keen sense of vision
(c) physical contact with sucrose
(d) sensing the particular wavelength of light emitted/reflected by sucrose

38. The interior of a cow dung pile kept for a few days is quite warm. This is mostly because
(a) cellulose present in the dung is a good insulator
(b) bacterial metabolism inside the dung releases heat
(c) undigested material releases heat due to oxidation by air
(d) dung is dark and absorbs a lot of heat

39. Which one of these is the correct path for a reflex action?
(a) Receptor → Motor neuron→ Spinal cord → Sensory neuron→ Effector
(b) Effector→ Sensory neuron→ Spinal cord → Motor neuron→ Receptor
(c) Receptor→ Sensory neuron→ Spinal cord→ Motor neuron→ Effector
(d) Sensory neuron → Receptor→ Motor neuron→ Spinal cord→ Effector

40. Insectivorous plants digest insects to get an essential nutrient. Other plants generally get this nutrient from the soil. What is this nutrient?
(a) Oxygen   (b) Nitrogen
(c) Carbon dioxide   (d) Phosphates

➲ PART-II (5 Marks Questions)

MATHEMATICS

1. In a $\triangle ABC$, D and E are points on AB, AC respectively such that DE is parallel to BC. Suppose BE, CD intersect of O. If the areas of the triangles ADE and ODE are 3 and 1 respectively. Find the area of the $\triangle ABC$, with justification.

2. Leela and Madan pooled their music CD's and sold them. They got as many rupees for each CD as the total number of CD's they sold. They share the money as follows: Leela first takes 10 rupees, then Madan takes 10 rupees and they continue taking 10 rupees alternately till Madan is left out with less than 10 rupees to take. Find the amount that is left out for Madan at the end, with justification.

3. (a) Show that for every natural number n relatively prime to 10, there is another natural number m all of whose digits are 1's such that n divides m.

    (b) Hence or otherwise show that every positive rational number can be expressed in the form $\dfrac{a}{10^b(10^c - 1)}$ for some natural numbers a, b, c.

PHYSICS

4. Consider the two circuits P and Q shown below, which are used to measure the unknown resistance R.

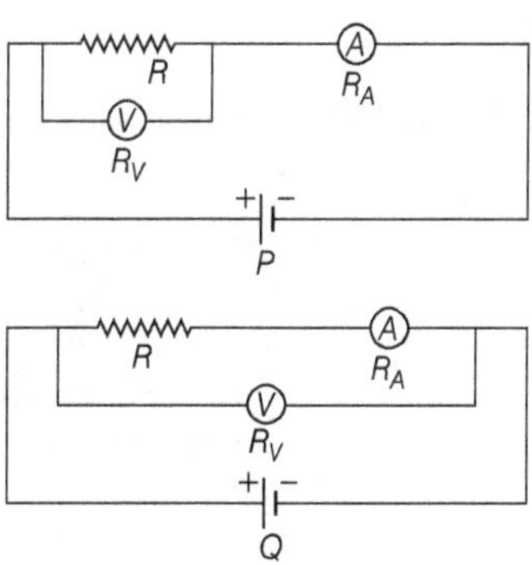

In each case, the resistance is estimated by using Ohm's law $R_{est} = \dfrac{V}{I}$, where V and I are the readings of the voltmeter and the ammeter, respectively. The meter resistances R_V and R_A are such that $R_A \ll R \ll R_V$. The internal resistance of the battery may be ignored. The absolute error in the estimate of the resistance is denoted by $\delta R = |R - R_{est}|$.
(a) Express δR_p in terms of the given resistance values.
(b) Express δR_Q in terms of the given resistance values.
(c) For what value of R will $\delta R_p \approx \delta R_Q$?

5. A point source is placed 20 cm to the left of a concave lens of focal length 10 cm.
(a) Where is the image formed?
(b) Where to the right of the lens would you place a concave mirror of focal length 5 cm, so that the final image is coincident with the source?
(c) Where would the final image be formed, if the concave mirror is replaced by a plane mirror at the same position?

6. A block of mass m is sliding on a fixed frictionless concave surface of radius R. It is released from rest at point P which is at a height of $H \ll R$ from the lowest point Q.

(a) What is the potential energy as a function of θ, taking the lowest point Q as the reference level for potential energy?

(b) What is the kinetic energy as a function of θ?

(c) What is the time takes for the particle to reach from point P to the lowest point Q?

(d) How much force is exerted by the block on the concave surface at the point Q?

CHEMISTRY

7. Copper in an alloy is estimated by dissolving in conc. nitric acid. In this process, copper is converted to cupric nitrate with the evolution of nitric oxide (NO). The mixture when treated with potassium iodide forms cupric iodide, which is unstable and decomposes to cuprous iodide and iodine.

The amount of copper in the alloy is estimated by titrating the liberated iodine with sodium thiosulphate. The reactions are

$$a\,Cu + b\,HNO_3 \rightarrow c\,Cu(NO_3)_2 + d\,NO + e\,H_2O$$
$$f\,CuI_2 \rightarrow g\,Cu_2I_2 + h\,I_2$$
$$i\,Na_2S_2O_3 + j\,I_2 \rightarrow k\,Na_2S_4O_6 + l\,NaI$$

(Fill up the blanks)

(a) The coefficients are : $a = $ ......, $b = $ ......, $c = $ ......, $d = $ ...... and $e = $ ....

(b) The coefficients are : $f = $ ......, $g = $ ...... and $h = $ ....

(c) The coefficients are : $i = $ ......, $j = $ ......, $k = $ ...... and $l = $ ....

(d) If 2.54 g of I_2 is evolved from a 2.0 g sample of the alloy, what is the percentage of copper in the alloy? (atomic weights of iodine and copper are 127 and 63.5, respectively).

8. You have been given four bottles marked A, B, C and D each containing one of the organic compounds given below

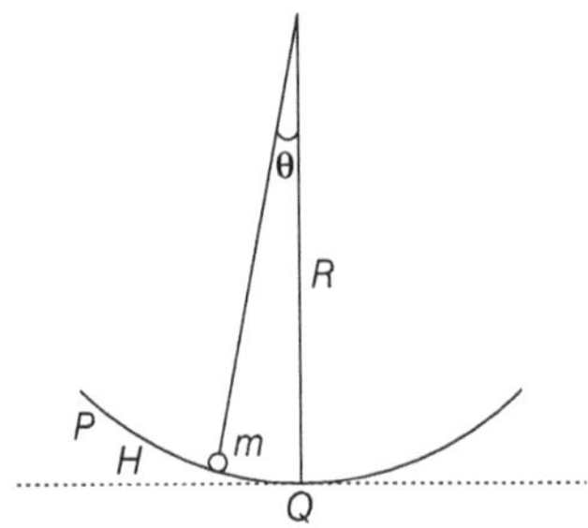

The following observations were made.

(i) The compound in the bottle A did not dissolve in either 1 N NaOH or 1 N HCl.

(ii) The compound in the bottle B dissolved in 1 N NaOH but not in 1 N HCl.

(iii) The compound in the bottle C dissolved in both 1 N NaOH and 1 N HCl.

(iv) The compound in the bottle D did not dissolve in 1 N NaOH but dissolved in 1 N HCl.

(Fill up the blanks)

(a) Indicate the compounds in : bottle $A = $ ......, bottle $B = $ ......, bottle $C = $ ...... and bottle $D = $ ....

(b) The compound with the highest solubility in distilled water is ....

(Indicate the answers by the compound numbers)

9. Assume that a human body requires 2500 kcal of energy each day for metabolic activity and sucrose is the only source of energy, as per the equation

$$C_{12}H_{22}O_{11}(s) + 12\,O_2(g) \longrightarrow 12\,CO_2(g) + 11H_2O(l);$$
$$\Delta H = -5.6 \times 10^6 \text{ J.}$$

(Fill up the blanks)

(a) The energy requirement of the human body per day is .... kJ.

(b) The mass of sucrose required to provide this energy is .... g and the volume of CO_2 (at STP) produced is .... litres.

BIOLOGY

10. Mohini, a resident of Chandigarh went to Shimla with her parents. There she found the same plant that they have in their backyard, at home. However, she observed that while the plants in their backyard bore white flowers, those in Shimla had pink flowers. She brought home some seeds of the plant from Shimla and planted them in Chandigarh. Upon performing self-breeding for several generations she found that the plant from Shimla produced only white flowers.

(a) According to you what might be the reason for this observation, genetic or environmental factors?

(b) Suggest a simple experiment to determine whether this variation is genetic in nature.

(c) Suggest another experiment to check whether this variation in flower colour is due to environmental factors.

11. The breakdown of glucose in a cell occurs in any one of the following pathways :

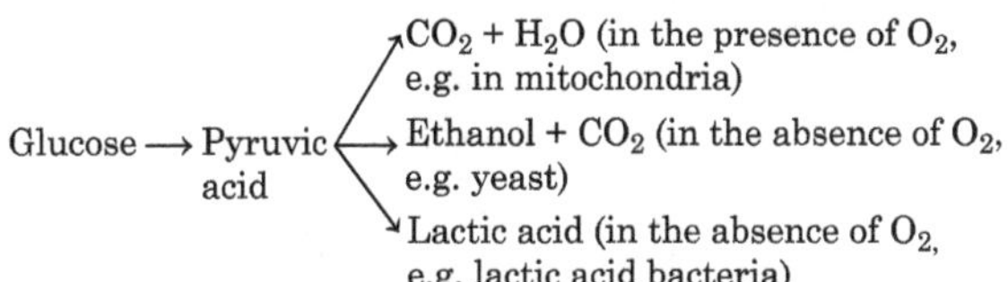

Three experiments (A, B, C) have been set up. In each experiment, a flask contains the organism in growth medium, glucose and a brown dye that changes its colour to yellow when the pH decreases.

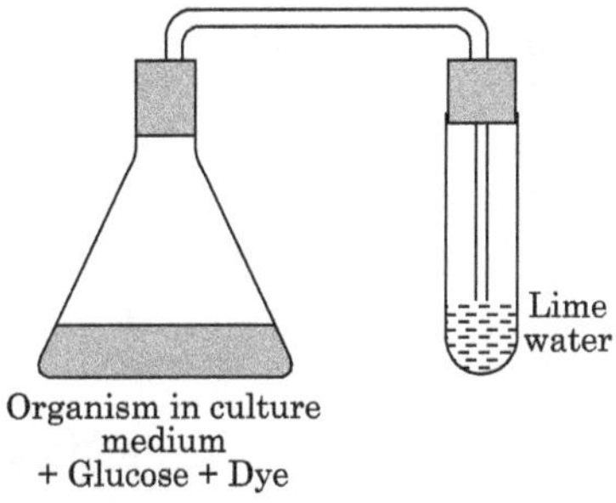

The mouth of the flask is attached to a test tube containing lime water (calcium hydroxide as shown in the figure). In C, but not in A and B, air is removed from the flask before beginning the experiment.

After a period of growth, the following observations were made

A. Lime water turns milky; the dye colour remains the same.

B. The dye colour changes; lime water does not turn milky.

C. Lime water turns milky; the dye colour remains the same.

(a) **Question** Identify which of the reactions in the pathways depicted above is taking place in each experiment. Give reasons for your answer.

(b) **Question** Identify which of the reactions in the pathways depicted above is expected to occur in Red Blood Cells (RBCs).

12. A scientist has a house just beside a busy highway. He collects leaves from some plants growing in his garden to do radio-carbon dating (to estimate the age of the plant by estimating the amount of a radioisotope of carbon in its tissues). Surprisingly the radio-carbon dating shows that the plant is a few thousand years old.

(a) Was the result of the radio-carbon dating wrong or can you propose a reason for such an observation?

(b) What simple experiment can be done to test the reason that you have proposed?

Answers

PART-I

1	(c)	2	(d)	3	(b)	4	(a)	5	(b)	6	(b)	7	(a)	8	(d)	9	(d)	10	(d)
11	(b)	12	(a)	13	(c)	14	(d)	15	(c)	16	(d)	17	(a)	18	(d)	19	(b)	20	(c)
21	(d)	22	(a)	23	(a)	24	(b)	25	(b)	26	(a)	27	(a)	28	(d)	29	(c)	30	(c)
31	(d)	32	(c)	33	(a)	34	(d)	35	(d)	36	(a)	37	(c)	38	(b)	39	(c)	40	(b)

Solutions

PART 1

1. *(c)* We have,
$$x^2 + bx + a = 0 \quad \text{...(i)}$$
$$x^2 + ax + b = 0 \quad \text{...(ii)}$$
Let α, β are the roots of equation
$$x^2 + bx + a = 0$$
$$\therefore \qquad \alpha + \beta = -b, \alpha\beta = a$$
Now, given roots of the equation
$x^2 + ax + b = 0$ is greater than 1 of the
roots of Eq. (i).
$$\therefore \alpha + 1 + \beta + 1 = -a \text{ and } (\alpha+1)(\beta+1) = b$$
$$\alpha + \beta + 2 = -a \text{ and } \alpha\beta + \alpha + \beta + 1 = b$$
$$\Rightarrow -b + 2 = -a \text{ and } a - b + 1 = b$$
$$\Rightarrow b - a = 2 \text{ and } 2b - a = 1$$
On solving these equations, we get
$a = -3, b = -1,$
$$\therefore \qquad a + b = -3 - 1 = -4$$

2. *(d)* We have,
$$3^{(x/y)+1} - 3^{(x/y)-1} = 24$$
$$\Rightarrow \quad 3 \cdot 3^{x/y} - \frac{3^{x/y}}{3} = 24 \Rightarrow \frac{8}{3} \cdot 3^{x/y} = 24$$
$$\Rightarrow \qquad 3^{x/y} = 9 \Rightarrow 3^{x/y} = 3^2$$
$$\Rightarrow \qquad \frac{x}{y} = 2$$
Using componendo and dividendo, we get
$$\frac{x+y}{x-y} = \frac{2+1}{2-1} \Rightarrow \frac{x+y}{x-y} = 3$$

3. *(b)* We have,
$$\frac{1^2 + 2^2 + 3^2 + 4^2 + \dots + n^2}{1 + 2 + 3 + 4 + \dots + n}$$
$$= \frac{\dfrac{n(n+1)(2n+1)}{6}}{\dfrac{n(n+1)}{2}}$$
$$= \frac{2n+1}{3} = k \text{ (let)}$$
$$\therefore \quad n = \frac{3k-1}{2}$$
Now, $1 \le \dfrac{3k-1}{2} \le 100$
$$\Rightarrow \quad 2 \le 3k - 1 \le 200$$
$$\Rightarrow \quad 2 + 1 \le 3k \le 200 + 1$$
$$\Rightarrow \quad 3 \le 3k \le 201$$
$$\Rightarrow \quad 1 \le k \le \frac{201}{3}$$
$$\Rightarrow \quad 1 \le k \le 67$$
Number of odd integer = 34

4. *(a)* Let the length, breadth and height
of cuboid is l, b and h respectively.

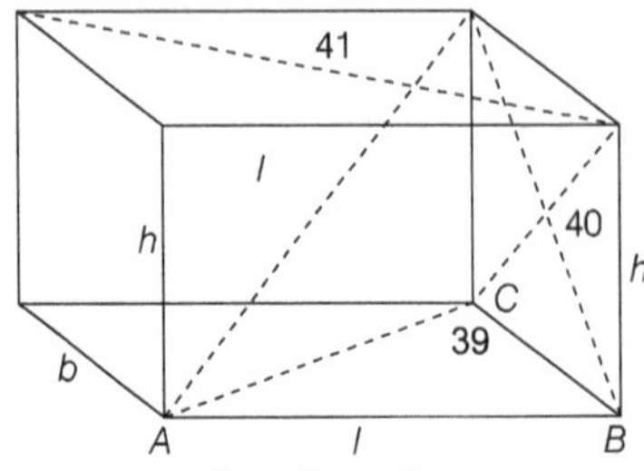

Given, $\qquad l^2 + h^2 = 39^2$
$$\Rightarrow \qquad b^2 + h^2 = 40^2$$
$$\Rightarrow \qquad l^2 + b^2 = 41^2$$
$$\Rightarrow \quad 2(l^2 + b^2 + h^2) = 39^2 + 40^2 + 41^2$$
$$\Rightarrow \qquad l^2 + b^2 + h^2 = 2401$$
$\therefore$ Length of longest diagonal
$$= \sqrt{l^2 + b^2 + h^2}$$
$$= \sqrt{2401} = 49$$

5. *(b)* We have,
sides of ΔABC are positive integer and
length of smallest side is 1.

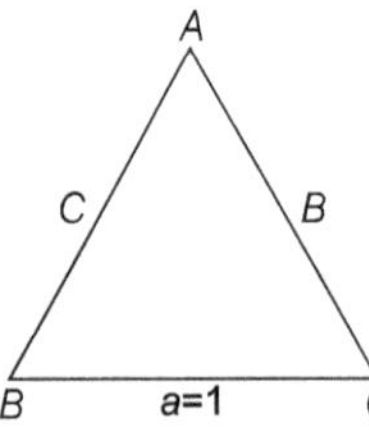

We know that the sum of two sides of
triangle is greater than third side.
$$\therefore \qquad b + 1 > c$$
$$\Rightarrow \qquad c - b < 1$$
$$1 + c > b$$
$$\Rightarrow \qquad b - c < 1$$
$$-1 < b - c < 1$$
b, c are integers.
$$\therefore \qquad b - c = 0 \Rightarrow b = c$$
Semi-perimeter $= \dfrac{a+b+c}{2}$
$$= \frac{2b+1}{2} = b + \frac{1}{2}$$
Area $A = \sqrt{s(s-a)(s-b)(s-c)}$
$$= \sqrt{\left(b + \frac{1}{2}\right)\left(b + \frac{1}{2} - 1\right)\left(b + \frac{1}{2} - b\right)\left(b + \frac{1}{2} - b\right)}$$
$$= \sqrt{\left(b + \frac{1}{2}\right)\left(b - \frac{1}{2}\right)\left(\frac{1}{2}\right)\left(\frac{1}{2}\right)} = \frac{1}{2}\sqrt{b^2 - \frac{1}{4}}$$
Since, b is integer.
$\therefore$ Area of ΔABC is always irrational
number.

6. *(b)* Given $ABCD$ is square

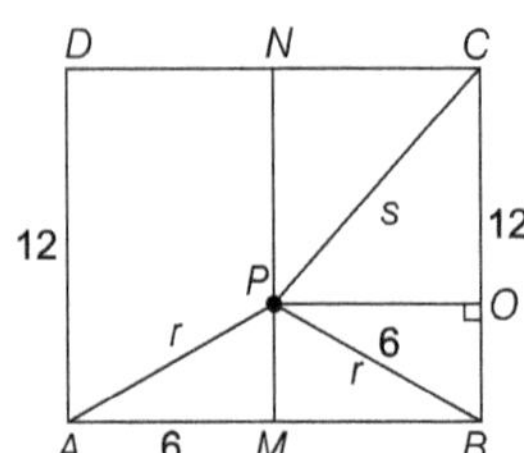

$AB = BC = 12$ units
M is mid-point of AB,
N is mid-point of CD,
P is point of MN and $CP = S$
$\because APB$ is an isosceles triangle,
$$\therefore \qquad AP = PB = r$$
$$OP = MB = 6 \text{ units}$$

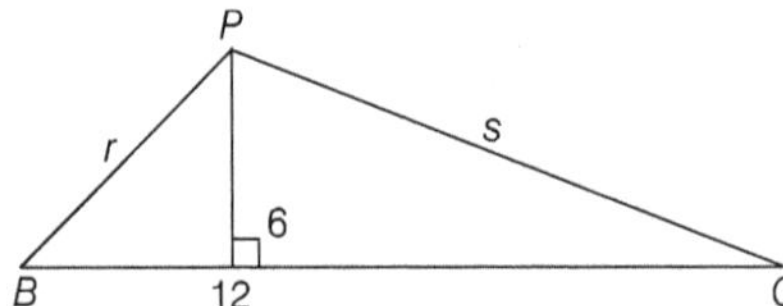

Area of triangle whose sides r, s and 12
are the area of ΔPBC
$$= \frac{1}{2} \times \text{Base} \times \text{Height} = \frac{1}{2} \times BC \times OP$$
$$= \frac{1}{2} \times 12 \times 6 = 36 \text{ sq units}$$

7. *(a)* Total area of the grass field graze
by the cow = 2 (area of sector APQ + area
of sector BQR + area of sector CRS)

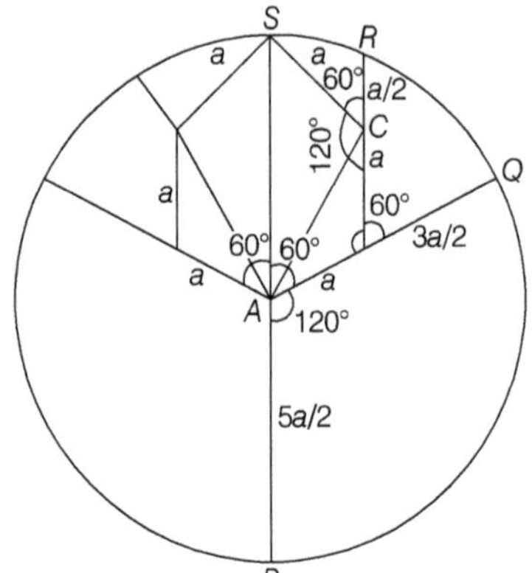

$$= 2\left(\frac{120}{360} \times \pi \times \left(\frac{5a}{2}\right)^2 + \frac{60}{360} \times \pi \times \left(\frac{3a}{2}\right)^2 \right.$$
$$\left. + \frac{60}{360} \times \pi \times \left(\frac{a}{2}\right)^2 \right)$$

$$= \frac{2\pi}{3}\left[\frac{25a^2}{4} + \frac{9a^2}{8} + \frac{a^2}{8}\right]$$

$$= \frac{2\pi}{3}\left[\frac{60a^2}{8}\right] = 5\pi a^2$$

8. *(d)* Let r and h be radius and height of cone, respectively.

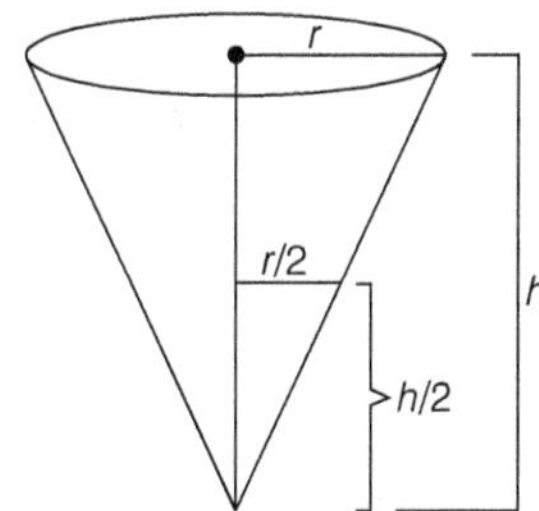

$\therefore$ Volume of cone $= \dfrac{1}{3}\pi r^2 h$

Given, rate of outflow of water in 21 min, then h changes to $\dfrac{h}{2}$

$\therefore$ Rate of outflow of water

$$= \frac{1}{3}\left(\pi r^2 h - \frac{\pi r^2}{4}\times\frac{h}{2}\right) = 21\,\text{min}$$

$$\Rightarrow \frac{7\pi r^2 h}{8\times 3} = 21\,\text{min} \Rightarrow \frac{1}{3}\frac{\pi r^2 h}{8} = 3\,\text{min}$$

$\therefore$ Time required to empty vessels in 3 min.

9. *(d)* We have,

1000 kg of watermelon in which 99% are water.

$\therefore$ 990 kg water and 10 kg rest.

Now, x kg watermelon has

$$= \frac{98}{100}x \text{ water} + \frac{2x}{100} \text{ rest}$$

Weight of solid part should remain same

$$\therefore \qquad \frac{2x}{100} = 10 \Rightarrow x = 500$$

$\therefore$ Weight reduction $= (1000 - 500)\text{kg}$

$$= 500\,\text{kg}$$

10. *(d)* Given,

10	c	4		
a		b		
N	d	M 12	d 15	
a		b		
	f		f 25	e
K	L			

Area of rectangles are

$$ac = 10$$
$$bc = 4$$
$$bd = 12$$
$$de = 15$$
$$ef = 25$$

$$\therefore \qquad \frac{ac}{bc}\times\frac{bd}{de}\times ef = \frac{10}{4}\times\frac{12}{15}\times 25$$

$$\Rightarrow \qquad af = 50$$

Area of rectangle $KLMN = af = 50$

11. *(b)* Time period of a pendulum depends on its length as

$$T \propto \sqrt{l}$$

where, l = length of pendulum.

As water flows out of the bob of pendulum, centre of mass of bob go down as the level of water falls. But when bob is completely emptied, centre of mass of bob again reaches to its centre. Hence, effective length of pendulum first increases then decreases.

So, time period of pendulum first increases then decreases.

12. *(a)* Force of friction is self adjusting. When applied force is increased friction, first increases till it reaches a maximum value called limiting friction.

If applied force is further increased, then friction does not increases further and body begins to move.

Force of friction then remains constant and its value is given by

$$f = \mu N$$

13. *(c)* In given case, rate of momentum change of bullets is equal to weight of soldier.

If M = mass of soldier and his gun and m = mass of bullet. Then,

$$Mg = \frac{N}{\Delta t}\times m(v - 0)$$

$$\Rightarrow \qquad M = \frac{(N/\Delta t)\times mv}{g}$$

where, $\dfrac{N}{\Delta t}$ is the number of bullets fired per second.

$$\Rightarrow \qquad M = \frac{40\times 49\times 10^{-3}\times 500}{9.8}$$

$$= 100\,\text{kg}$$

14. *(d)* When star shrinks without losing its mass, its gravitational acceleration on its surface increases but there is no change in force exerted by this star on a distant object like a planet. Force of gravitational attraction of star on planet is

$$F = \frac{GMm}{r^2}$$

where, M = mass of star, m = mass of planet and r = orbital radius of planet.

As, this force remains same there is no change in orbital radius of planet.

15. *(c)*

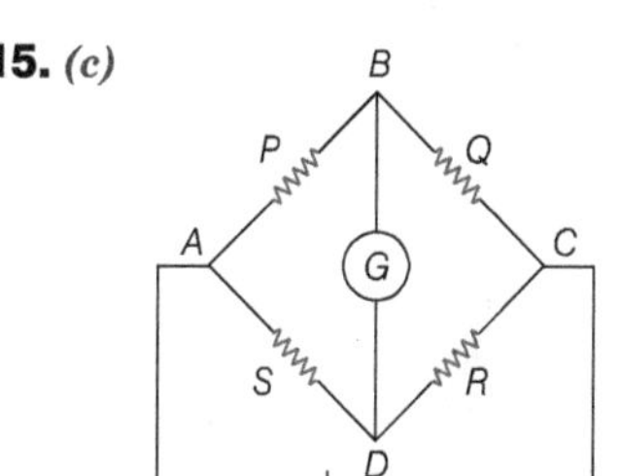

In case (i), galvanometer shows zero deflection.

$\therefore V_B = V_D$

$$\Rightarrow \qquad \frac{P}{S} = \frac{Q}{R} \qquad \text{...(i)}$$

When battery B and galvanometer G are interchanged, position of galvanometer is as shown below,

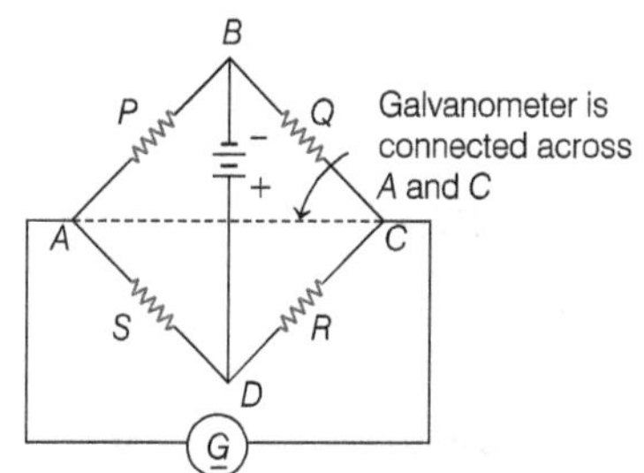

Now, ratio of resistances across galvanometer is

$$\frac{S}{P} \text{ and } \frac{R}{Q}$$

As from Eq. (i), $\dfrac{S}{P} = \dfrac{R}{Q}$

Hence, galvanometer still shows zero deflection because Wheatstone's bridge is balanced.

16. *(d)* Force on charge Q is initially zero as forces of 12 charges balances each other.

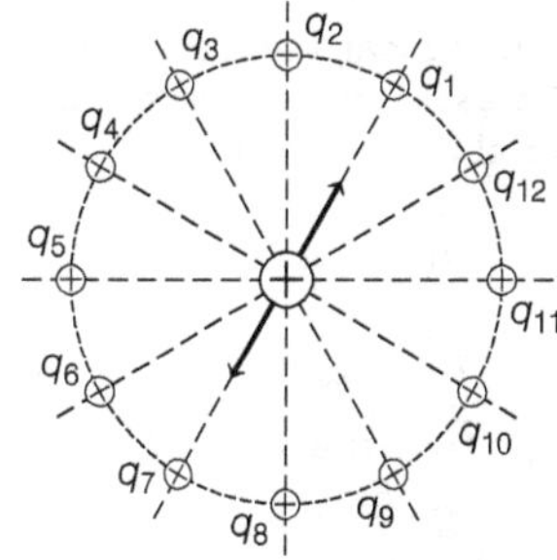

As shown in above figure, forces of diametrically opposite charges balances each other, hence net force on Q is zero. When one of the charge q (let q_1) is removed, net force on Q is now the unbalanced force of diametrically opposite charge.

i.e. Force, $F = \dfrac{kqQ}{R^2} = \dfrac{qQ}{4\pi\varepsilon_0 R^2}$

and this force vector points towards the position of the removed charge.

17. *(a)* Power $P = \dfrac{V^2}{R}$ as V remains constant in given condition, while current changes as resistance is reduced.

Power consumed by heater coil $P \propto \dfrac{1}{R}$.

On cutting part of coil, its resistance decreases. So, power consumed by coil increases and it will be more than 1 kW.

18. *(d)* First prism separates white light into its constituent colours which are then recombined by the second inverted prism into white light.

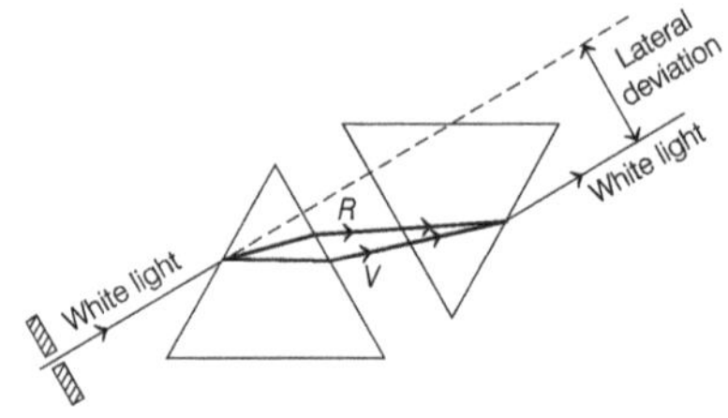

As two prisms combinedly form a glass slab, light beam is deviated on a parallel path.

19. *(b)* When blocks are brought into contact, hotter one lost heat and colder one gains that heat.

Let T = final temperature of the blocks.

Then,

Heat lost by hotter block = Heat gained by colder block

$\Rightarrow ms_1 (T_i - T_f)_{\text{Hot block}} = ms_2 (T_f - T_i)_{\text{Cold block}}$

or $\dfrac{s_1}{s_2} = \dfrac{(T_f - T_i)_{\text{Cold block}}}{(T_i - T_f)_{\text{Hot block}}}$

Here, we are using two different specific heats s_1 and s_2 as it is given that specific heat of material increases with temperature. So, $s_1 > s_2$.

$\Rightarrow \dfrac{s_1}{s_2} > 1$

$\Rightarrow \dfrac{(T_f - T_i)_{\text{Cold block}}}{(T_i - T_f)_{\text{Hot block}}} > 1$

$\Rightarrow \dfrac{T - 20}{80 - T} > 1$

$\Rightarrow T - 20 > 80 - T$

$\Rightarrow T + T > 80 + 20$

$\Rightarrow 2T > 100$

$\Rightarrow T > 50°C$

20. *(c)* Given, $t_x = 3T + 300$

So, change in temperatures in two systems are related as

$t_{x_2} - t_{x_1} = (3T_2 + 300) - (3T_1 + 300)$
$= 3 (T_2 - T_1)$

or $\Delta t_x = 3\Delta T$

Now to convert units, we use

$N_1 u_1 = N_2 u_2$

$\dfrac{1400\,\text{J}}{\Delta t_x \text{ kg}} = \dfrac{N_2 \text{J}}{\Delta T \text{ kg}}$

$\Rightarrow \dfrac{1400}{3\Delta T} = \dfrac{N_2}{\Delta T}$

$\Rightarrow N_2 = \dfrac{1400 \Delta T}{3\Delta T}$

$\Rightarrow N_2 = \dfrac{1400}{3} = 466.7$

Hence, in SI system, value of specific heat is $c = 466.7\,\text{J kg}^{-1}\,\text{K}^{-1}$.

21. *(d)* As boiling point is a colligative property, it depends only on the number of particles present in a solution. Aqueous solution having more number of particles will have highest elevation in boiling point.

$C_{12}H_{22}O_{11}(aq) \rightleftharpoons$ No ions

$NaCl \rightleftharpoons Na^+ + Cl^-$ (Total ions = 2)

$CaCl_2 \rightleftharpoons Ca^{2+} + 2Cl^-$ (Total ions = 3)

Thus, $CaCl_2$ will have highest boiling point.

22. *(a)* As silicon belongs to group 14 whose general configuration is ns^2np^2. Thus, the correct electronic configuration of Si is $1s^2 2s^2 2p^6 3s^2 3p^2$.

23. *(a)* $CaCO_3 \xrightarrow{\Delta} CaO + CO_2$

No. of moles of $CaCO_3 = \dfrac{25}{100} = \dfrac{1}{4}$ mole

1 mole of $CaCO_3$ gives 1 mole of CO_2.

$\therefore \dfrac{1}{4}$ mole of $CaCO_3$ gives $\dfrac{1}{4}$ mole of CO_2.

1 mole of $CO_2 = 44\,\text{g}$

So, $\dfrac{1}{4}$ mole of $CO_2 = \dfrac{44}{4} = 11\,\text{g}$

Thus, 11 g of CO_2 is released on heating 25 g of $CaCO_3$.

24. *(b)* On moving across the second period of the periodic table, the atomic radii of the elements decrease, due to increase in effective nuclear charge, the electrons of all the shells are pulled little closer to nucleus thereby making each individual shell smaller and smaller.

25. *(b)* According to octet, the atoms of different elements combine with each other in order to complete their respective octets (*i.e.*, 8 electrons in their outermost shell or 2 electrons in case of H, Li and Be to attain stable nearest noble gas configuration).

The Lewis structures of given molecules are as follows

(a) NH_3— H×·N̈·×H
$\qquad\qquad$ H

As the octet is complete, hence it follows octet rule.

(b) BCl_3 ××C̈l× ·Ḃ· ×C̈l××

Octet rule is not followed in this case as there are total 6 electrons in the outermost shell of B even after bonding.

(c) Cl_2 , :C̈l· ×C̈l××

Octet rule is followed in case of Cl_2.

(d) N_2, :N⦂ ⦂N:

As both the N have complete octet. Thus, it follows octet rule.

Hence, the correct option is (b).

26. *(a)* On heating MnO_2 with conc. HCl, $MnCl_2$ and H_2O are released with the evolution of Cl_2 gas. The chemical equation for it can be written as

$MnO_2 + 4HCl \longrightarrow MnCl_2 + 2H_2O + Cl_2$

27. *(a)* The structure of C_4H_7Br can be written as

$$\text{H—C}=\text{C—C—C—Br}$$

Thus, total number of covalent bonds in C_4H_7Br is 12.

28. *(d)* As we know

$$pH = -\log [H^+]$$

As the initial pH of aqueous solution = 2

$\therefore$ Concentration of H^+, $[H^+] = 10^{-2}$

As the final pH of aqueous solution = 5

$\therefore \qquad [H^+] = 10^{-5}$

$\therefore \qquad \dfrac{[H^+]_f}{[H^+]_i} = \dfrac{10^{-5}}{10^{-2}}$

$= 10^{-3}$

Thus, H^+ concentration decreases by thousand fold.

29. *(c)* For Ist jar

No. of moles of $H_2 = \dfrac{2}{2} = 1$

∴ No. of molecules of H_2 in 1 mole
$$= 6.022 \times 10^{23}$$

For 2nd jar

No. of moles of $N_2 = \dfrac{28}{28} = 1$

∴ No. of molecules of N_2 in 1 mole
$$= 6.022 \times 10^{23}$$

Thus, the gases in two jars will have same number of molecules.

30. *(c)* The type of isomers in the given options are as follows

(a) $CH_3 CH_2CH_2OH$ and $CH_3 CH_2OCH_3$
They are functional isomers.

(b) $CH_3 CH_2CH_2Cl$ and $CHCHClCH_3$
They are positional isomers.

(c) $H_3C—C\!\!=\!\!C—CH_3$ with H, H below
Cis

and $CH_3C\!\!=\!\!C—CH_3$ with H above and H below
Trans

As they are *cis* and *trans* form, so they are geometrical isomers which are a type of stereoisomers.

(d)

These are structural isomers.

Thus, the correct option is (c).

31. *(d)* Water borne diseases such as cholera is caused by drinking contaminated or dirty water. Cholera is caused by the bacterium *Vibrio cholerae.*

32. *(c)* The term allele was formerly used by Mendel for the factors representing the two alternate forms of a character, e.g. tallness and dwarfness in case of height in pea (T and t).

33. *(a)* This happens because the temperature starts to increase all over the country in March and by April. The interior parts of the peninsular record mean daily temperature of 30-35°C. Maximum temperature rises sharply exceeding 45°C by the end of May. The warm temperature can affect the ripening process of fruits and vegetables by speeding up the production of ethylene gas which rushes the ripening or fruiting process.

34. *(d)* A frog that is twice as long as another will be heavier by approximately eight folds. It is because their weight is determined by their folds, so by applying unitary method it is eight folds. Frog shape is triangular.

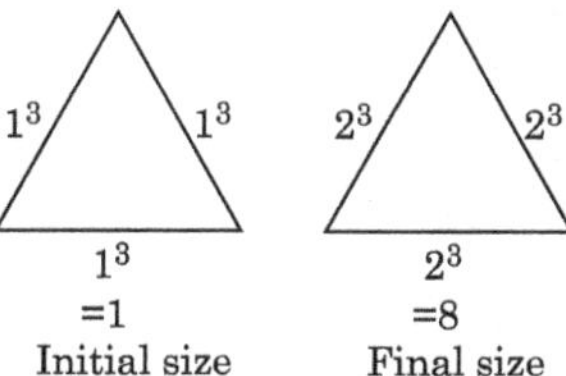

35. *(d)* Owl's eye have the widest angle of binocular vision among rat, duck and eagle. Binocular vision is the vision using two eyes with overlapping fields of view, allowing good perception of depth. Unlike many birds with eyes that sit at an angle, owl's eye face directly forward giving them incredible binocular vision. Although their large eyes cannot move or roll-like human eyes can, owls can move their heads nearly all the way around, allowing them to have a 270 degree range of vision without moving their bodies.

36. *(a)* An allele is a varient form of gene. Some genes have a variety of different forms, which are located at the same position on a chromosome. Humans are called diploid organisms because they have two alleles at each genetic locus, with one allele inherited from each parent. Each pair of alleles represents the genotype of a specific gene.

37. *(c)* Ants locate sucrose by physical contact with sucrose. Ants can smell food using their antennae, which can detect minute odours. But sugars actually do not have a smell. Therefore, when the scout worker ants locate sugar while foraging, they take a piece back home to the colony, while doing this, the ant will leave a chemical trial which the other ants can follow.

38. *(b)* The interior of a cow dung pile kept for a few days is quite warm. This is because bacterial metabolism inside the dung releases heat in the form of biogas $(CH_4 + CO_2)$. This happens by anaerobic digestion of cow dung by methanogenic bacteria.

39. *(c)* The correct path for a reflex action is

Receptor → Sensory neuron → Spinal cord → Motor neuron → Effector

The sensory nerve fibres bring sensory impulses from the receptor organ to the central nervous system (brain and spinal cord). The motor nerve fibres relay the motor impulses from the central nervous system to the effector organs. Reflex action is a form of animal behaviour in which the stimulation of a sensory organ (receptor) results in the activity of some organ without the intervention of will.

40. *(b)* Insectivorous plants mostly thrive in marshes and rocky outcrops or other nitrogen poor areas where sunlight and water are abundant. These plants have evolved the ability to trap and digest insects, which are an excellent source of nitrogen as they contain around 10% nitrogen by mass. Insectivorous plants are able to obtain between 10-80% of their total nitrogen from insects.

PART 2

1. Given in $\triangle ABC$, D and E are points on AB, AC respectively such that DE is parallel to BC.

BE and CD intersect at O.

Area of $\triangle ADE = 3$ sq units

Area of $\triangle DOE = 1$ sq units

Area of $\triangle BEC =$ Area of $\triangle BDC$

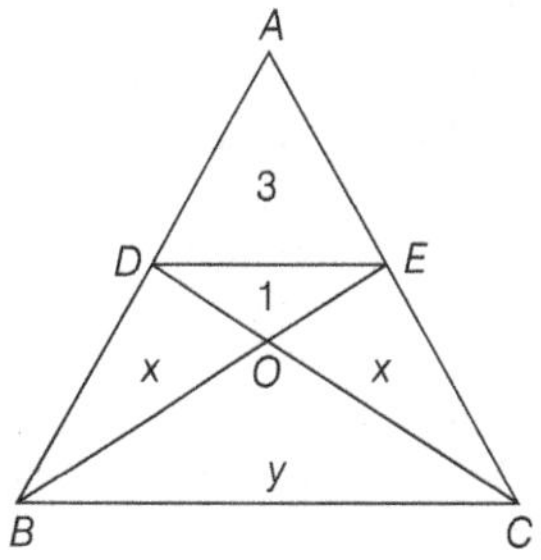

[same base between same parallels]

$\Rightarrow$
$(BOD) + ar(DOE) = ar(COE) + ar(DOE)$
$\Rightarrow ar(BOD) = ar(COE) = x$
$\Rightarrow \qquad ar(BOC) = y$

We know that area of two triangle having equal altitude is the same as the ratio of their respective bases.

∴ $\qquad \dfrac{x}{1} = \dfrac{BO}{OE} = \dfrac{y}{x}$

$\Rightarrow \qquad y = x^2$

Now, $\triangle ADE$ and $\triangle ABC$ are similar.

∴ $\quad \dfrac{ar(ADE)}{ar(ABC)} = \dfrac{DE^2}{BC^2} = \dfrac{ar(ODE)}{ar(OBC)}$

$\Rightarrow \quad \dfrac{3}{4 + 2x + y} = \dfrac{1}{y}$

$$\Rightarrow \qquad 3y = 4 + 2x + y$$
$$\Rightarrow \qquad 2y = 2(2 + x)$$
$$\Rightarrow \qquad y = x + 2$$
$$\Rightarrow \quad x^2 - x - 2 = 0 \qquad [\because y = x^2]$$
$$\Rightarrow \qquad (x - 2)(x + 1) = 0$$
$$\Rightarrow \qquad x = 2,\ x \neq -1$$
$\therefore$ Area of $\Delta ABC = 4 + 2x + y$
$$= 4 + 4 + 4 = 12 \text{ sq units}$$

2. Let the total number of CD's sold by the Leela and Madan together $= x$
Total money obtained by them
$$= (x \times x) = x^2$$
They divided x^2 in such that,
$x^2 = 10$ (an odd number) + a number less than 10
$$\Rightarrow \qquad x = 10q + r \qquad [\because 0 \le r < 10]$$
$$\Rightarrow \qquad x^2 = (10q + r)^2$$
$$\Rightarrow \qquad x^2 = 100q^2 + 20qr + r^2$$
$r^2 = 10$ (an odd number) + a number less than 10
$$0 \le r < 10$$
$\therefore$ Taking $r = 0, 1, 2, 3, ..., 9$, we get $r = 4$ or 6
$$r = 16 \text{ or } 36$$
$$r^2 = 10 + 6 \text{ or } 3(10) + 6$$
Hence, the amount left for Madan at the end is 6 rupees.

3. (a) We have,
A natural number 'm' whose all digits are 1
$\therefore m = 1, 111, 1111, 11111, ..., (1111 ... 1)$
A natural number 'n' which is relatively prime to 10 when $n + 1$ number
$1, 111, 1111, 11111, ..., (1111...1)$ divides by n, then $n + 1$ remainder obtained.
$\therefore$ Possibilities of remainder are 0, 1, 2, 3, ..., $n - 1$ which are n in numbers, where two remainder are same.
Let two numbers $x = 11\,1... 1$ and $y = 111... 1$ having say i digits and j digits respectively which leave the same remainder after division by n.
We take, $\qquad i < j$
$y - x$ is divisible by n;
But $y - x = 11... 1000 ... 0$ where $j - i$ number of 1's and remaining zero. Since, n is coprime to 10. We see that n divides $m = 111...1$ a number having 1's as its digits.

(b) Let the positive rational number is
$$\frac{p}{q}, \text{ where } q \neq 0$$
and $q = 2^r \cdot 5^s \cdot t$ where t is coprime to 10 Choose any number m having only is as its digit and is divisible by t.

Consider $9m$, which has only 9 as its digits and b divisible by t.
Let $\qquad k = \dfrac{9m}{t}$
$\therefore \quad 9k = 9m \cdot 2^r \cdot 5^s = (10^c - 1) 2^r \cdot 5^s$
where, c is the number of digits in m.
We can find d such that
$qd = 10^b (10^c - 1)$
　　　[such that 10^b is a suitable power of 2 if $s > r$ and a suitable power of s if $r > s$]
$\therefore \qquad \dfrac{p}{q} = \dfrac{pd}{qd} = \dfrac{a}{10^b (10^c - 1)}$
where, $pd = a$.

4. (a) In case P,

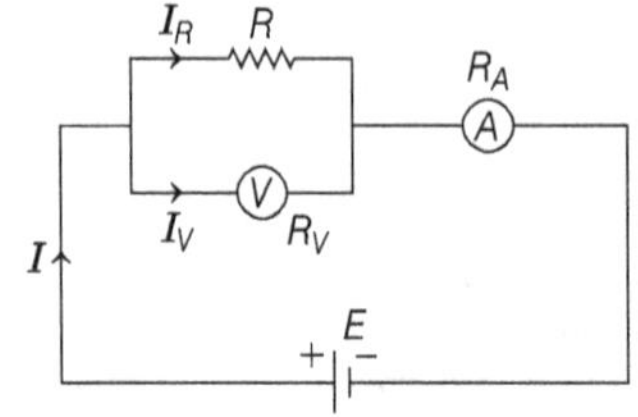

Current through cell is
$$I = I_R + I_V = V / R + V / R_V$$
where, $V =$ potential drop across resistance R.
$$\Rightarrow \qquad I = V\left(\frac{1}{R} + \frac{1}{R_V}\right) = V\left(\frac{R + R_V}{RR_V}\right)$$
$$\Rightarrow \qquad RR_V = \frac{V}{I}(R + R_V)$$
$$\Rightarrow \left(R_V - \frac{V}{I}\right) R = \frac{VR_V}{I}$$
$$\Rightarrow \qquad R = \frac{VR_V}{I(R_V - V/I)}$$
$$\Rightarrow \qquad R = \frac{V}{I} \cdot \left(\frac{R_V}{R_V - \dfrac{V}{I}}\right)$$
But $\dfrac{V}{I} = R_{\text{est}} =$ estimated resistance
$$\therefore \qquad R = R_{\text{est}} \left(\frac{R_V}{R_V - R_{\text{est}}}\right)$$
$$= R_{\text{est}} \cdot \left(\left(1 - \frac{R_{\text{est}}}{R_V}\right)^{-1}\right)$$
$$= R_{\text{est}} \left(1 + \frac{R_{\text{est}}}{R_V}\right)$$
Using binomial approximation and neglecting higher order terms.
Now, error in case P is
$$\delta R_P = |R_{\text{est}} - R|$$
$$= \frac{R_{\text{est}}^2}{R_V}$$

(b) In case Q,

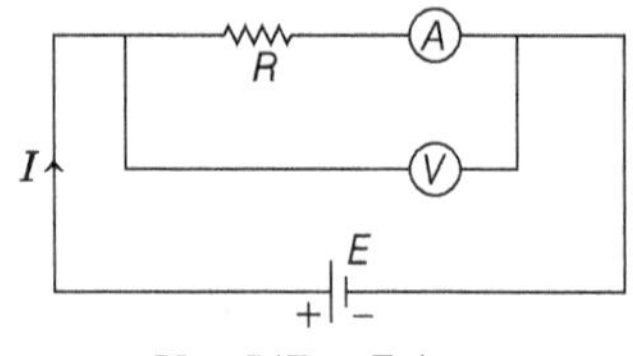

$$V = I(R + R_A)$$
$$\Rightarrow \qquad R = \left(\frac{V}{I}\right) - R_A = R_{\text{est}} - R_A$$
So, error in case Q is
$$\Rightarrow \qquad \delta R_Q = |R_{\text{est}} - R| = R_A$$
(c) If $R = \sqrt{R_A R_V}$ then,
$$\frac{\delta R_P}{\delta R_Q} = \frac{R_{\text{est}}^2}{R_A R_V} = \frac{R_{\text{est}}^2}{R^2} \approx 1$$

5. Given situation is

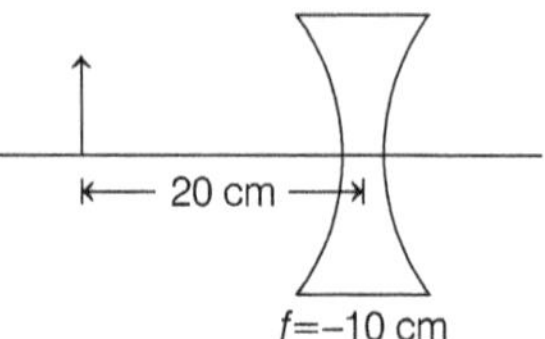

(a) We use lens formula to get position of image $u = -20$ cm, $f = -10$ cm.
As, $\quad \dfrac{1}{v} - \dfrac{1}{u} = \dfrac{1}{f}$
$$\Rightarrow \qquad \frac{1}{v} = \frac{1}{f} + \frac{1}{u} = \frac{-1}{10} - \frac{1}{20}$$
$$\Rightarrow \qquad \frac{1}{v} = \frac{-2 - 1}{20} = \frac{-3}{20}$$
$$\Rightarrow \qquad v = \frac{-20}{3} \text{ cm}$$
Image is virtual and it is in front of lens at $\dfrac{20}{3}$ cm.

(b) Concave mirror again converge rays and its image formed is coincident with object.

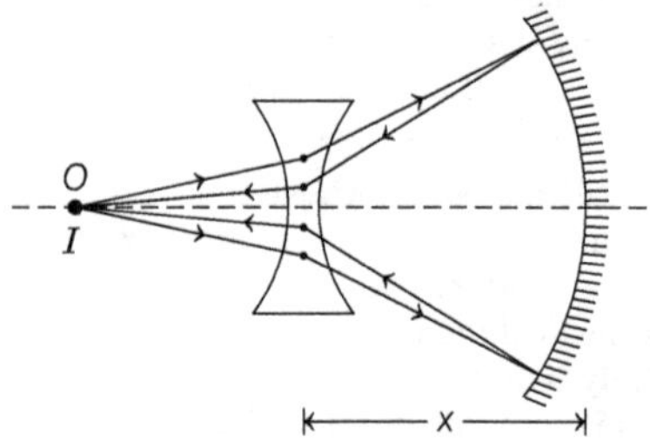

Let mirror is placed at distance x behind the lens. Now, first image I_1 of lens acts like object for mirror.
Hence, for mirror,
$$u = -\left(\frac{20}{3} + x\right) \text{cm}.$$

Given, $f = -5\,cm$

By lens equation, we get position of image I_2 from concave mirror as

$$\frac{1}{v} + \frac{1}{u} = \frac{1}{f}$$

or

$$\frac{1}{v} = -\frac{1}{u} + \frac{1}{f}$$

$$\Rightarrow \quad \frac{1}{v} = \frac{-1}{-\left(\dfrac{20}{3} + x\right)} + \frac{1}{(-5)}$$

$$\Rightarrow \quad \frac{1}{v} = \frac{1}{\left(\dfrac{20}{3} + x\right)} - \frac{1}{5} = \frac{5 - \left(\dfrac{20}{3} + x\right)}{5\left(\dfrac{20}{3} + x\right)}$$

$$\frac{1}{v} = \frac{-(3x + 5)}{15\left(\dfrac{20}{3} + x\right)} = \frac{-(3x + 5)}{5(20 + 3x)}$$

As this image is acting like an object for lens, so we have from lens equation,

$$u = -\frac{5(20 + 3x)}{(3x + 5)}\,cm, f = -10\,cm$$

and

$$v = +20\,cm$$

$$\Rightarrow \quad \frac{1}{v} + \frac{1}{u} = \frac{1}{f}$$

$$\Rightarrow \quad \frac{1}{20} - \frac{(3x + 5)}{5(20 + 3x)} = \frac{-1}{10}$$

$$\Rightarrow \frac{5(20 + 3x) - 20(3x + 5)}{20 \times 5(20 + 3x)} = -\frac{1}{10}$$

$$\Rightarrow \quad \frac{100 + 15x - 60x - 100}{2000 + 300x} = -\frac{1}{10}$$

$$2000 = 150x$$

$$\frac{2000}{150} = x$$

$$\Rightarrow \quad x = \frac{40}{5}\,cm = 13.33\,cm$$

So, mirror is placed at 13.33 cm behind the concave lens.

(c) When a plane mirror is placed at same position, then

For plane mirror is $f = \infty$,

$$u = -\left(\frac{20}{3} + x\right)$$

$$= -\left(\frac{20}{3} + \frac{40}{5}\right)$$

$$= -\frac{60}{5} = -12\,cm$$

Now, by mirror equation,

$$\frac{1}{v} + \frac{1}{u} = \frac{1}{f}$$

or

$$\frac{1}{v} = -\frac{1}{u}$$

$$\Rightarrow \quad \frac{1}{v} = -\left(\frac{-1}{12}\right)$$

So, $\quad v = 12\,cm$

As there is lens in between, so final image formed is calculated as

$$\frac{1}{v} - \frac{1}{u} = \frac{1}{f}$$

$$\frac{1}{v} = \frac{1}{-10} + \frac{1}{12} = -\frac{2}{120}$$

$$\therefore \qquad v = -60\,cm$$

So, final image is formed at a distance of 60 cm left of lens.

6. (a) Mass m is at height H from point Q, where potential energy is taken zero.

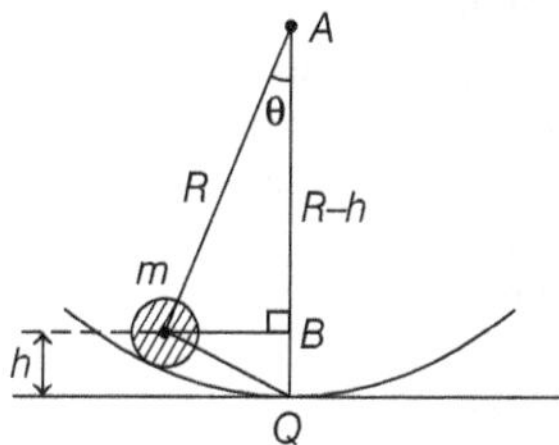

From geometry of above figure, if at some angle θ, height of mass m above lowest point Q is h, then from $\triangle ABC$,

$$\cos\theta = \frac{R - h}{R} \Rightarrow h = R\,(1 - \cos\theta)$$

Hence, potential energy of m as a function of θ is

$$PE = U(\theta) = mgh$$

$$\Rightarrow \qquad U(\theta) = mgR\,(1 - \cos\theta)$$

(b) Kinetic energy at position θ = Loss of potential energy that occurred in reaching this position

$$\Rightarrow \text{Kinetic energy is } K(\theta) = mgH - U(\theta)$$

$$\Rightarrow \qquad K(\theta) = mgH - mgR(1 - \cos\theta)$$

$$= mg\,(H - R\,(1 - \cos\theta))$$

(c) For $H << R$, mass m will oscillate about mean position in SHM. Time period of oscillation of m is

$$T = \frac{1}{2\pi}\sqrt{\frac{R}{g}}$$

Time taken to travel from P to Q is one-fourth of this time period.

i.e.

$$t = \frac{1}{8\pi}\sqrt{\frac{R}{g}}$$

(d) From energy conservation at lowest point, if m has velocity v, then

$$\frac{1}{2}mv^2 = mgH$$

$$\Rightarrow \quad mv^2 = 2mgH \text{ or } \frac{mv^2}{R} = \frac{2mgH}{R}$$

But this centripetal force is resultant of force of normal reaction N and weight of body.

$$\Rightarrow \qquad N - mg = \frac{mv^2}{R}$$

$$\Rightarrow \qquad N = mg + \frac{2mgH}{R}$$

$$\Rightarrow \qquad N = mg\left(1 + \frac{2H}{R}\right)$$

This is the force by block on the concave surface.

7. The balanced chemical equations for the given equations can be written as

(i) $3Cu + 8HNO_3 \longrightarrow 3Cu(NO_3)_2 + 2NO + 4H_2O$

(ii) $2CuI_2 \longrightarrow Cu_2I_2 + I_2$

(iii) $2Na_2S_2O_3 + I_2 \longrightarrow Na_2S_4O_6 + 2NaI$

Thus,

(a) The coefficients are : $a = 3, b = 8, c = 3, d = 2$ and $e = 4$

(b) The coefficients are : $f = 2, g = 1, h = 1$

(c) The coefficients are : $i = 2, j = 1, k = 1$ and $l = 2$

(d) No. of moles of $I_2 = \dfrac{2.54}{254} = 0.01\,mol$

Moles of $CuI_2 = 2$ moles of I_2

$= 1$ mole of Cu

$= 2 \times 0.01 = 0.02$

Weight = mole × atomic weight

Weight of Cu $= 0.02 \times 63.5 = 1.27\,g$

% of copper present in the alloy

$$= \frac{1.27}{2} \times 100 = 63.5\%$$

8. Conclusions that can be made from the given observations are as follows

(a) (i) As the compound in the bottle A did not dissolve in either 1 N NaOH or 1 N HCl. This indicates that the molecule is neutral. Thus, the compound A is (III).

CH_3

(ii) As the compound in the bottle B dissolved in 1 N NaOH but not in 1 N HCl shows that the compound is acidic in nature, thus the compound in bottle B is (II).

CO_2H

(iii) The compound in bottle C dissolved in both 1 N NaOH and 1 N HCl indicates that the compound is amphoteric in nature. Thus, the compound in bottle C is (IV).

CO_2H
NH_2

(amphoteric because of its Zwitter ion)

(iv) The compound in bottle D dissolved in both 1 N NaOH, but dissolve in 1 N HCl shows that the compound is a base, thus the compound is (I).

$\text{C}_6\text{H}_5\text{—CH}_2\text{—NH}_2$

(b) The compound with highest solubility in distilled water is (iv),

$\text{C}_6\text{H}_5\text{—CH}_2\text{—CH(NH}_2\text{)—COOH}$

This is due to Zwitter ion formation which can be shown as

$\text{C}_6\text{H}_5\text{—CH}_2\text{—CH(}^+\text{NH}_3\text{)—COO}^-$

9. $C_{12}H_{22}O_{11}(s) + 12 O_2(g)$
$$\longrightarrow 12CO_2(g) + 11H_2O(l)$$
$$\Delta H = -5.6 \times 10^5 \text{ J}$$

(a) 1 kcal = 4.18 kJ
$\therefore 2500$ kcal $= 2500 \times 4.18$ kJ $= 10450$ kJ
So, the energy requirement of the human body per day is 10450 kJ.

(b) No. of moles of sucrose
$$= \frac{10450 \times 10^3 \text{ J}}{5.6 \times 10^6 \text{ J}} = 1.866 \text{ mol}$$

Weight of sucrose
$$= \text{molar mass} \times \text{number of moles}$$

$= 342 \times 1.866$

$= 638.172$ g

1 mole of $C_{12}H_{22}O_{11}$ gives 12 moles of CO_2
$\therefore 1.866$ moles of $C_{12}H_{22}O_{11}$ gives
$= 1.866 \times 12$ moles of CO_2
$= 22.392$ moles of CO_2

At STP 1 mole of $CO_2 = 22.4$ L
22.392 moles of $CO_2 = 22.4 \times 22.392$ L
$= 501.5808$ L

10. (a) Difference in flower colour is most likely due to environmental factors.

(b) Perform cross-breeding between the plants from Chandigarh and those from Shimla to find out whether we get any pink flowers or flowers with any shade of colour between pink and white in the F_1-generation.

(c) Grow the plants from Chandigarh in Shimla and check whether they still produce white flowers or bear pink flowers.

11. (a) In experiment A, ethanol fermentation occurs producing CO_2, turning lime water milky. Since acid is not produced, the dye colour does not change.

In experiment B, lactic acid fermentation takes place, which produces acid but does not produce CO_2. Hence, dye colour changes to yellow but the lime water does not turn milky.

In experiment C, since the lime water turns milky, ethanol fermentation is occurring. In addition, since removal of air did not affect the reaction, the fermentation is anaerobic and yeast must be the organism in the flask.

(b) In RBCs, lactic acid fermentation occurs.

12. (a) The result of radio-carbon dating was correct.

Reason Vehicles running on the highway beside the house emitted carbon dioxide from the combustion of petrol or diesel, which are fossil fuels. The carbon in this carbon dioxide, coming from living material that has been converted into petroleum millions of years ago, would get assimilated into the tissues of the plant as it uses carbon dioxide from the surrounding atmosphere for photosynthesis. Therefore, tissues of the plant, when used for radio-carbon dating, would show the age of the plant to be many thousands of years old.

(b) A simple experiment to test the validity of this explanation would be to collect seeds from the plants and grow them in a plot of land away from the highway or other sources of CO_2 coming from the burning of fossil fuels. Radio-carbon dating of plants growing from these seeds should show them as young plants.

QUESTION PAPER 2009
Stream : SA

MM : 100

Instructions

1. There are 80 questions in this paper.

2. This question paper contains two parts; Part I and Part II. There are four sections; Mathematics, Physics, Chemistry and Biology in each part.

3. Out of the four options given with each question, only one is correct.

➲ PART–I (1 Mark Questions)

MATHEMATICS

1. The real numbers x satisfying $\dfrac{\sqrt{x+5}}{1-x} > 1$ are precisely those which satisfy

(a) $x < 1$ (b) $0 < x < 1$ (c) $-5 < x < 1$ (d) $-1 < x < 1$

2. Let t_n denote the number of integral-sided triangles with distinct sides chosen from $\{1, 2, 3, ..., n\}$. Then, $t_{20} - t_{19}$ equals

(a) 81   (b) 153   (c) 163   (d) 173

3. The number of pairs of reals (x, y) such that $x = x^2 + y^2$ and $y = 2xy$ is

(a) 4   (b) 3   (c) 2   (d) 1

4. How many positive real numbers x satisfy the equation $x^3 - 3|x| + 2 = 0$?

(a) 1   (b) 3   (c) 4   (d) 6

5. Let $(1 + 2x)^{20} = a_0 + a_1x + a_2x^2 + ... + a_{20}x^{20}$. Then, $3a_0 + 2a_1 + 3a_2 + 2a_3 + 3a_4 + 2a_5 + ... + 2a_{19} + 3a_{20}$ equals

(a) $\dfrac{5 \cdot 3^{20} - 3}{2}$ (b) $\dfrac{5 \cdot 3^{20} + 3}{2}$ (c) $\dfrac{5 \cdot 3^{20} + 1}{2}$ (d) $\dfrac{5 \cdot 3^{20} - 1}{2}$

6. Let P_1, P_2, P_3, P_4, P_5 be five equally spaced points on the circumference of a circle of radius 1, centred at O. Let R be the set of points in the plane of the circle that are closer to O than any of P_1, P_2, P_3, P_4, P_5. Then, R is a

(a) circular region

(b) pentagonal region

(c) rectangular region

(d) oval region that is not circular

7. A company situated at $(2, 0)$ in the XY-plane charges ₹ 2 per km for delivery. A second company at $(0, 3)$ charges ₹ 3 per km for delivery.

The region of the plane where it is cheaper to use the first company is

(a) the inside of the circle $(x + 5.4)^2 + y^2 = 18.72$

(b) the outside of the circle $(x + 1.6)^2 + (y - 5.4)^2 = 18.72$

(c) the inside of the circle $(x - 1.6)^2 + (y + 5.4)^2 = 18.72$

(d) the outside of the circle $(x - 5.4)^2 + (y + 1.6)^2 = 18.72$

8. In a right $\triangle ABC$, the incircle touches the hypotenuse AC at D. If $AD = 10$ and $DC = 3$, the inradius of ABC is

(a) 5   (b) 4   (c) 3   (d) 2

9. The sides of a quadrilateral are all positive integers and three of them are 5, 10, 20. How many possible value are there for the fourth side?

(a) 29   (b) 31   (c) 32   (d) 34

10. If the volume of a sphere increases by 72.8%, then its surface area increases by

(a) 20%   (b) 44%   (c) 24.3%   (d) 48.6%

11. If the decimal $0.d25d25d25...$ is expressible in the form $n/27$, then $d + n$ must be

(a) 9   (b) 28   (c) 30   (d) 34

12. At what time between 10 O'clock and 11 O'clock are the two hands of a clock symmetric with respect to the vertical line (give the answer to the nearest second)?

(a) 10h 9m 13s   (b) 10h 9m 14s

(c) 10h 9m 22s   (d) 10h 9m 50s

13. A woman has 10 keys out of which only one opens a lock. She tries the keys one after the another (keeping aside the failed ones) till she succeeds in opening the lock. What is the chance that it is the seventh key that works?

(a) $\dfrac{7}{10}$ (b) $\dfrac{1}{2}$ (c) $\dfrac{3}{10}$ (d) $\dfrac{1}{10}$

14. In a certain school, 74% students like cricket, 76% students like football and 82% like tennis. Then, all the three sports are liked by at least

(a) 68%   (b) 32%   (c) 77%   (d) 36%

15. Let S_n be the sum of all integers k such that $2^n < k < 2^{n+1}$, for $n \geq 1$. Then, 9 divides S_n if and only if

(a) n is odd   (b) n is of the form $3k + 1$

(c) n is even   (d) n is of the form $3k + 2$

PHYSICS

16. A boy standing on the footpath tosses a ball straight up and catches it. The driver of a car passing by moving with uniform velocity sees this.

The trajectory of the ball as seen by the driver will be

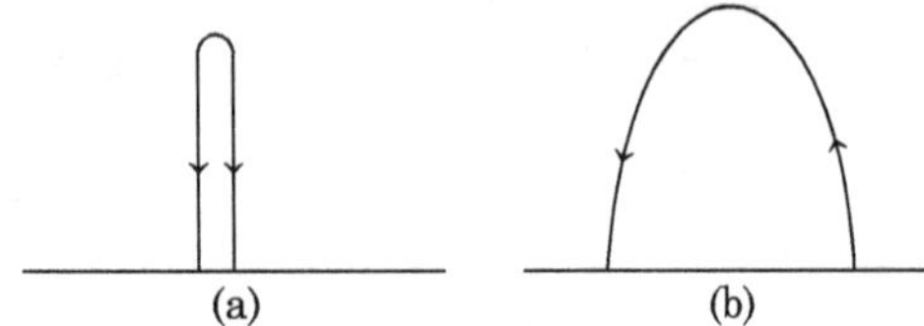

17. Consider two spherical planets of same average density. Second planet is 8 times as massive as first planet. The ratio of the acceleration due to gravity of the second planet to that of the first planet is

(a) 1   (b) 2   (c) 4   (d) 8

18. Two immiscible liquids A and B are kept in an U-tube. If the density of liquid A is smaller than the density of liquid B, then the equilibrium situation is

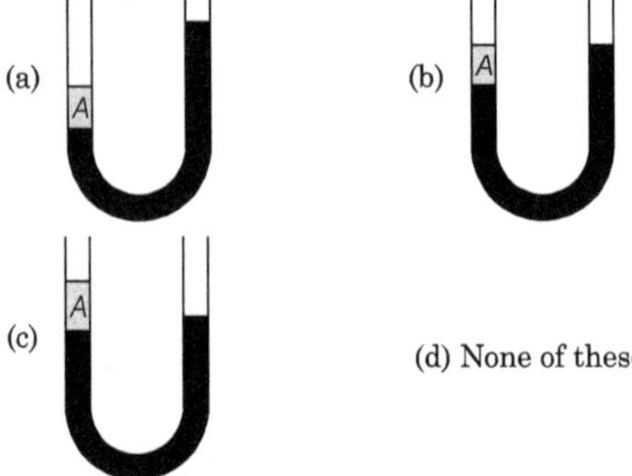

(d) None of these

19. In the figure given below, a ray of light travelling in a medium of refractive index μ passes through two different connected rectangular blocks of refractive indices μ_1 and μ_2 ($\mu_2 > \mu_1$).

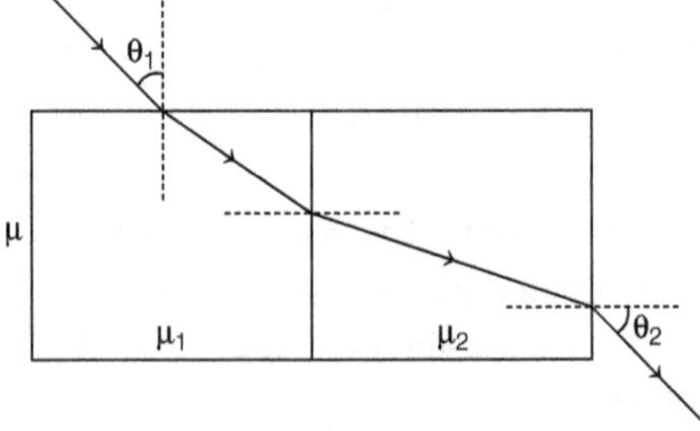

The angle of incidence θ_1 is increased slightly. Then, the angle θ_2 is

(a) increases (b) decreases (c) remains same

(d) increases or decreases depending on the value of (μ_1/μ_2)

20. Two charges of same magnitude move in two circles of radii $R_1 = R$ and $R_2 = 2R$ in a region of constant uniform magnetic field $\mathbf{B}_0$.

The work W_1 and W_2 done by the magnetic field in the two cases respectively, are such that

(a) $W_1 = W_2 = 0$ (b) $W_1 = W_2 \neq 0$

(c) $W_1 = W_2$ (d) $W_1 < W_2$

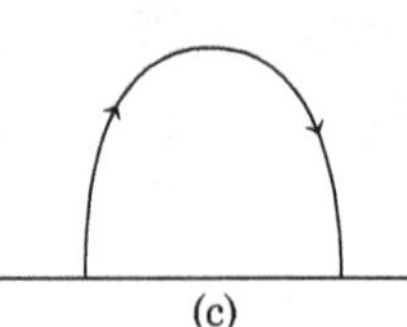
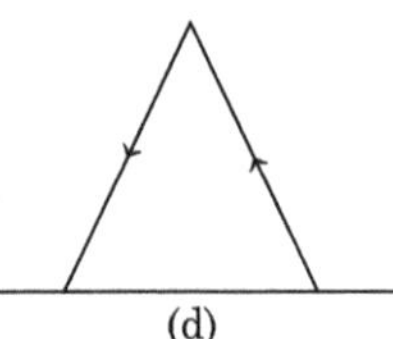

21. Two charges $+q$ and $-q$ are placed at a distance b apart as shown in the figure given below.

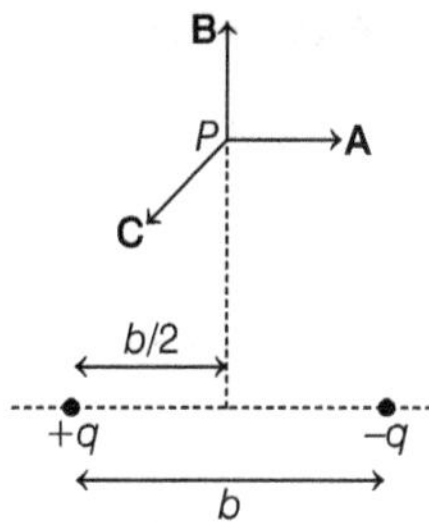

The electric field at a point P on the perpendicular bisector as shown is
(a) along vector **A** (b) along vector **C**
(c) along vector **B** (d) zero

22. A block of mass M is at rest on a plane surface inclined at an angle θ to the horizontal. The magnitude of force exerted by the plane on the block is
(a) $Mg \cos\theta$ (b) $Mg \tan\theta$ (c) $Mg \sin\theta$ (d) Mg

23. We are able to squeeze snow and make balls out of it because of
(a) anomalous behaviour of water
(b) large latent heat of ice
(c) large specific heat of water
(d) low melting point of ice

24. Which of the following phenomena can be demonstrated by light, but not with sound waves in an air column?
(a) Reflection (b) Diffraction
(c) Refraction (d) Polarisation

25. The temperature of a metal coin is increased by $100°C$ and its diameter increases by 0.15%. Its area increases by nearly
(a) 0.15% (b) 0.30% (c) 0.60% (d) 0.0225%

26. The note "Saa" on the Sarod and the Sitar have the same pitch. The property of sound that is most important in distinguishing between the two instruments is
(a) fundamental frequency (b) displacement amplitude
(c) intensity (d) waveform

27. $^{235}_{92}U$ atom disintegrates to $^{207}_{82}Pb$ with a half-life of 10^9 yr. In the process, it emits 7α particles and $n\beta^-$ particles. Here, n is
(a) 7 (b) 3 (c) 4 (d) 14

28. Consider the following circuit given below.

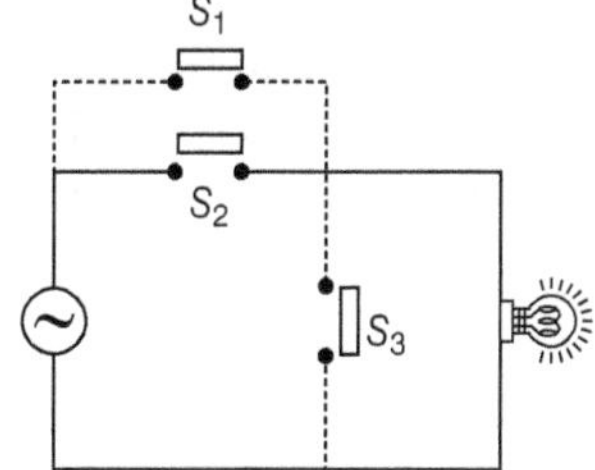

The bulb will light up, if
(a) S_1, S_2 and S_3 are all closed
(b) S_1 is closed but S_2 and S_3 are open
(c) S_2 and S_3 are closed but S_1 is open
(d) S_1 and S_3 are closed but S_2 is open

29. Two bulbs, one of 200 W and the other of 100 W are connected in series with a 100 V battery which has no internal resistance.

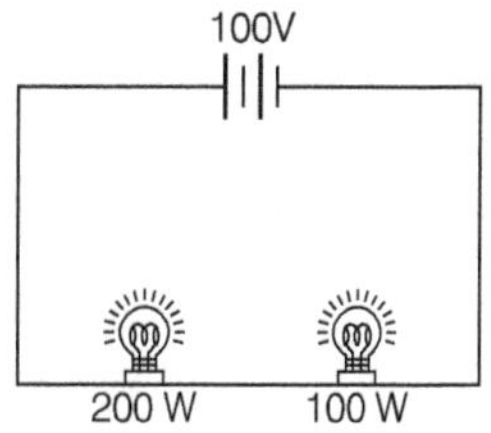

Then,
(a) the current passing through the 200 W bulb is more than that through the 100 W bulb
(b) the power dissipation in the 200 W bulb is more than that in the 100 W bulb
(c) the voltage drop across the 200 W bulb is more than that across the 100 W bulb
(d) the power dissipation in the 100 W bulb is more than that in the 200 W bulb

30. A solid cube and a solid sphere of identical material and equal masses are heated to the same temperature and left to cool in the same surroundings. Then,
(a) the cube will cool faster because of its sharp edges
(b) the cube will cool faster because it has a larger surface area
(c) the sphere will cool faster because it is smooth
(d) the sphere will cool faster because it has a larger surface area

CHEMISTRY

31. The element X which forms a stable product of the type XCl_4 is
(a) Al (b) Na (c) Ca (d) Si

32. A mixture of NH_4Cl and $NaCl$ can be separated by
(a) filtration (b) distillation
(c) sublimation (d) decantation

33. The pair in which the first compound is ionic and the second compound is covalent, is
(a) $Fe(OH)_2$, CH_3OH (b) $Fe(OH)_2$, $Cu(OH)_2$
(c) CH_3OH, CH_3CH_2OH (d) $Ca(OH)_2$, $Cu(OH)_2$

34. In the reaction, $SO_2 + 2H_2S \longrightarrow 3S + 2H_2O$, the substance that is oxidised is
(a) SO_2 (b) H_2O (c) S (d) H_2S

35. Sodium oxide dissolves in water to give sodium hydroxide which indicates its
(a) acidic character (b) basic character
(c) amphoteric character (d) ionic character

36. For an ideal gas, Boyle's law is best described by

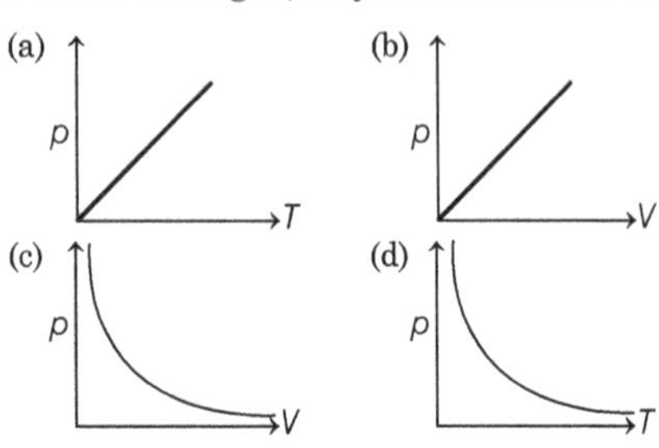

37. The pH values of (i) 0.1 M HCl (*aq*), (ii) 0.1 M KOH, (iii) tomato juice and (iv) pure water follow the order.
(a) (i) < (iii) < (iv) < (ii)   (b) (iii) < (i) < (iv) < (ii)
(c) (i) < (ii) < (iii) < (iv)   (d) (iv) < (iii) < (ii) < (i)

38. When calcium carbide is added to water, the gas that is evolved is
(a) carbon dioxide   (b) hydrogen
(c) acetylene   (d) methane

39. The atomic radii of the alkali metals follow the order
(a) Li > Na > K > Cs   (b) K > Cs > Li > Na
(c) Na > K > Cs > Li   (d) Cs > K > Na > Li

40. The number of possible structural isomers of C_3H_4 is
(a) 1   (b) 2   (c) 3   (d) 4

41. Among the four compounds, (i) acetone, (ii) propanol, (iii) methyl acetate and (iv) propionic acid, the two that are isomeric are
(a) methyl acetate and acetone
(b) methyl acetate and propanol
(c) propionic acid and methyl acetate
(d) propionic acid and acetone

42. One mole of nitrogen gas on reaction with 3.01×10^{23} molecules of hydrogen gas produces
(a) one mole of ammonia
(b) 2.0×10^{23} molecules of ammonia
(c) 2 moles of ammonia
(d) 3.01×10^{23} molecules of ammonia

43. Saponification is
(a) hydrolysis of an ester (b) hydrolysis of an amide
(c) hydrolysis of an ether (d) hydrolysis of an acid chloride

44. A concentrated solution of lead nitrate in water can be stored in
(a) an iron vessel   (b) a copper vessel
(c) a zinc vessel   (d) a magnesium vessel

45.

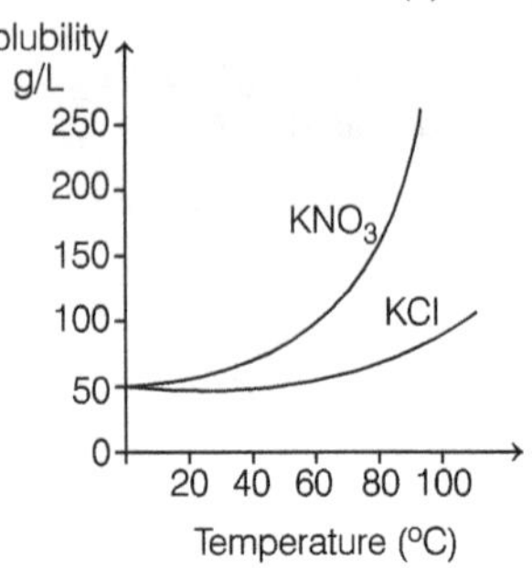

Given the solubility curves of KNO_3 and KCl, which of the following statements is not true ?
(a) At room temperature, the solubility of KNO_3 and KCl are not equal
(b) The solubilities of both KNO_3 and KCl increase with temperature
(c) The solubility of KCl decreases with temperature
(d) The solubility of KNO_3 increases much more compared to that of KCl with increase in temperature

BIOLOGY

46. Which one of the following is the smallest in size?
(a) Bacteria   (b) Mitochondrion
(c) Mammalian cell   (d) Virus

47. If birds are moved from 30°C - 10°C, their body temperature
(a) changes from 30°C - 10°C
(b) increases by 10°C
(c) does not change at all
(d) decreases by 10°C

48. Ascorbic acid is a/an
(a) strong inorganic acid   (b) hormone
(c) vitamin   (d) enzyme

49. Bile salts
(a) breakdown polypeptide chains
(b) emulsify fats and solubilise them
(c) digest fats
(d) help breakdown of polysaccharides

50. Dietary fibres are composed of
(a) cellulose   (b) proteins
(c) amylase   (d) unsaturated fats

51. '*On the Origin of Species, by Means of Natural Selection*' was written by
(a) Hugo de Vries   (b) Charles Dickens
(c) Charles Darwin   (d) Alfred Russell Wallace

52. Unlike humans, dogs cannot perspire to get rid of excess metabolic heat. They lose metabolic heat by
(a) panting
(b) taking a bath
(c) running in windy conditions
(d) rolling in the mud

53. Haemodialysis is a treatment option for patients with malfunctions of
(a) kidney   (b) liver
(c) heart   (d) lungs

54. An individual has 'O' blood group if his/her blood sample
(a) clumps only when antiserum A is added
(b) clumps only when antiserum B is added
(c) clumps when both antiserum A and antiserum B are added
(d) does not clump when either antiserum A or antiserum B is added

55. In warmer weather, curd from milk forms faster because
(a) bacteria diffuse better in warmer milk
(b) the rate of bacterial multiplication increases
(c) lactogen is better dissolved
(d) it is easier to separate protein from water

56. Seedlings grown in dark are
(a) similar to those grown in light
(b) taller than those grown in light
(c) shorter than those grown in light
(d) they do not grow at all

57. In humans, Rhesus condition can arise when
(a) father is Rh^+ and mother is Rh^-
(b) father is Rh^- and mother is Rh^+
(c) either father or mother is Rh^+
(d) either father or mother is Rh^-

58. The part of the human brain that governs memory and intelligence is
(a) cerebrum
(b) medulla
(c) hypothalamus
(d) cerebellum

59. Saturated dietary fats increase the risk of heart disease by
(a) widening arteries by thinning their walls
(b) narrowing veins by carbohydrate deposition
(c) narrowing arteries by fat deposition
(d) narrowing arteries by carbohydrate deposition

60. Rotation of crops is carried out to
(a) increase variation in the mineral content of the soil
(b) increase diversity of plant habitats
(c) increase in nitrogen content of the soil
(d) increase convenience for the farmer

➲ PART-II (2 Marks Questions)

MATHEMATICS

61. Let $\log_a b = 4$, $\log_c d = 2$, where a, b, c, d are natural numbers. Given that $b - d = 7$, the value of $c - a$ is
(a) 1   (b) -1
(c) 2   (d) -2

62. Let $P(x) = 1 + x + x^2 + x^3 + x^4 + x^5$. What is the remainder when $P(x^{12})$ is divided by $P(x)$?
(a) 0   (b) 6
(c) $1 + x$ (d) $1 + x + x^2 + x^3 + x^4$

63. In a $\triangle ABC$, the altitudes from B and C on to the opposite sides are not shorter than their respective opposite sides. Then, one of the angles of ABC is
(a) 30°   (b) 45°
(c) 60°   (d) 72°

64. In a $\triangle ABC$, $AB = AC = 37$. Let D be a point on BC such that $BD = 7$, $AD = 33$. The length of CD is
(a) 7   (b) 11
(c) 40   (d) not determinable

65. A line segment l of length a cm is rotated about a vertical line L keeping the line l in one of the following three positions (I) l is parallel to L and is at a distance of r cm from L, (II) l is perpendicular to L and its mid-point is at a distance r cm from L, (III) l and L are in the same plane and l is inclined to L at an angle 30° with its mid-point at a distance r cm from L. Let A_1, A_2, A_3 be the areas so generated. If $r > (a/2)$, then
(a) $A_1 < A_3 < A_2$ (b) $A_2 < A_1 < A_3$
(c) $A_1 = A_3 < A_2$ (d) $A_1 = A_2 = A_3$

PHYSICS

66. A spring balance A reads 2 kg with a block of mass m suspended from it. Another balance B reads 3 kg when a beaker with a liquid is put on its pan. The two balances are now so arranged that the hanging mass m is fully immersed inside the liquid in the beaker as shown in the figure given below.

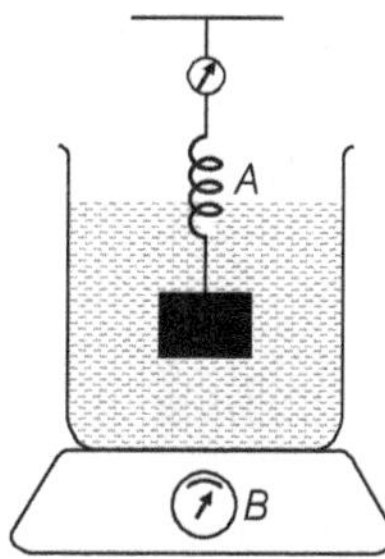

In this situation,
(a) the balance A will read 2 kg and B will read 5 kg
(b) the balance A will read 2 kg and B will read 3 kg
(c) the balance A will read less than 2 kg and B will read between 3 kg and 5 kg
(d) the balance A will read less than 2 kg and B will read 3 kg

67. According to the quantum theory, a photon of electromagnetic radiation of frequency ν has energy $E = h\nu$, where h is known as Planck's constant. According to the theory of relativity, a particle of mass m has equivalent energy $E = mc^2$, where c is speed of light. Thus, a photon can be treated as a particle having effective mass $m = \dfrac{h\nu}{c^2}$.

If a flash of light is sent horizontally in earth's gravitational field, then photons while travelling a horizontal distance d would fall through a distance given by

(a) $\dfrac{gd^2}{2c^2}$ (b) $\dfrac{h}{mc}$ (c) $\dfrac{mcd^2}{h}$ (d) zero

68. A solid square plate is spun around different axes with the same angular speed. In which of the following choice of axis of rotation will the kinetic energy of the plate be the largest?
(a) Through the centre, normal to the plate
(b) Along one of the diagonals of the plate
(c) Along one of the edges of the plate
(d) Through one corner normal to the plate

69. An object is placed 0.40 m from one of the two lenses L_1 and L_2 of focal lengths 0.20 m and 0.10 m respectively, as depicted in the figure. The separation between the lenses is 0.30 m.

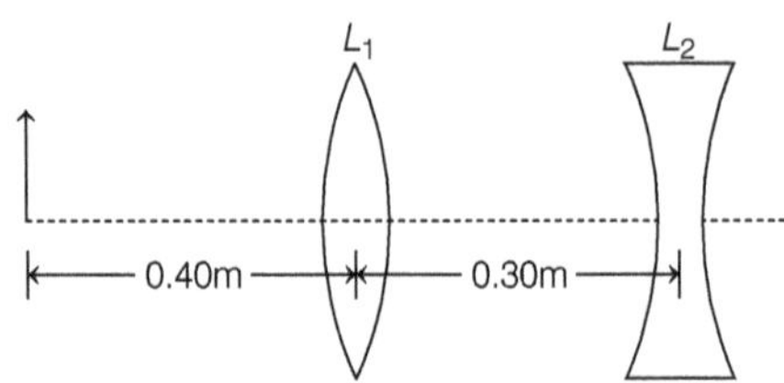

The final image formed by these two lenses system is at
(a) 0.13 m to the right of the second lens
(b) 0.05 m to the right of the second lens
(c) 0.13 m to the left of the second lens
(d) infinity

70. 5 charges each of magnitude 10^{-5} C and mass 1 kg are placed (fixed) symmetrically about a movable central charge of magnitude 5×10^{-5} C and mass 0.5 kg as shown in the figure given below. The charge at P_1 is removed. The acceleration of the central charge is

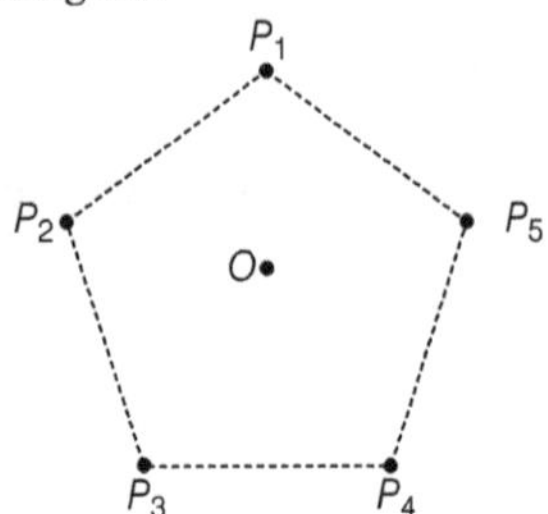

[Given,
$$OP_1 = OP_2 = OP_3 = OP_4 = OP_5 = 1 \text{ m}, \frac{1}{4\pi\varepsilon_0} = 9 \times 10^9]$$

(a) 9 ms^{-2} upwards
(b) 9 ms^{-2} downwards
(c) 4.5 ms^{-2} upwards
(d) 4.5 ms^{-2} downwards

CHEMISTRY

71. Reaction of NaCl with conc. H_2SO_4 liberates a gas, X that turns moist blue litmus paper red. When gas X is passed into a test tube containing egg shell powder suspended in water another gas, Y is generated which when passed through lime water makes it milky. The gases X and Y, respectively, are
(a) HCl and CO_2 (b) Cl_2 and CO_2
(c) SO_2 and CO_2 (d) SO_2 and HCl

72. 10 mL of an aqueous solution containing 222 mg of calcium chloride (mol. wt. = 111) is diluted to 100 mL. The concentration of chloride ion in the resulting solution is
(a) 0.02 mol/L   (b) 0.01 mol/L
(c) 0.04 mol/L   (d) 2.0 mol/L

73. Aluminium reduces manganese dioxide to manganese at high temperature. The amount of aluminium required to reduce one g mole of manganese dioxide is
(a) 1/2 g mol   (b) 3/4 g mol
(c) 1 g mol   (d) 4/3 g mol

74. Ethanol on reaction with alk. $KMnO_4$ gives X which when reacted with methanol in the presence of an acid gives a sweet smelling compound Y, X and Y respectively, are
(a) acetaldehyde and acetone
(b) acetic acid and methyl acetate
(c) formic acid and methyl formate
(d) ethylene and ethyl methyl ether

75. The pH of a 10 mL aqueous solution of HCl is 4. The amount of water to be added to this solution in order to change its pH from 4 to 5 is
(a) 30 mL   (b) 60 mL   (c) 90 mL   (d) 120 mL

BIOLOGY

76. Proteins are synthesised on
(a) cytoskeleton   (b) mitochondria
(c) ribosomes   (d) Golgi apparatus

77. Which of the following allows light to focus in visual perception?
(a) Retina   (b) Iris
(c) Retinal pigment   (d) Cornea

78. During cell division, if there is one round of chromosome duplication followed by one round of cell division, the number of chromosomes the daughter cells will have as compared to the mother is
(a) equal   (b) double   (c) half   (d) one fourth

79. Similar type of vegetation can be observed, in the same
(a) latitude   (b) longitude   (c) country   (d) continent

80. Which of the following ecological food chains does not represent an erect pyramid of numbers ?
(a) Grass–Rodent–Snake   (b) Tree–Bird–Avian parasite
(c) Grass–Deer–Tiger   (d) Insect–Chicken–Human

Answers

PART-I

1 (d)	2 (a)	3 (a)	4 (a)	5 (c)	6 (b)	7 (b)	8 (d)	9 (a)	10 (b)
11 (d)	12 (b)	13 (d)	14 (b)	15 (c)	16 (b)	17 (b)	18 (c)	19 (b)	20 (a)
21 (a)	22 (a)	23 (*)	24 (d)	25 (b)	26 (d)	27 (c)	28 (c)	29 (d)	30 (b)
31 (d)	32 (c)	33 (a)	34 (d)	35 (b)	36 (c)	37 (a)	38 (c)	39 (d)	40 (b)
41 (c)	42 (b)	43 (a)	44 (b)	45 (c)	46 (d)	47 (c)	48 (c)	49 (b)	50 (a)
51 (c)	52 (a)	53 (a)	54 (d)	55 (b)	56 (b)	57 (c)	58 (a)	59 (c)	60 (a)

PART-II

61 (a)	62 (b)	63 (b)	64 (c)	65 (d)	66 (c)	67 (a)	68 (d)	69 (d)	70 (c)
71 (a)	72 (c)	73 (d)	74 (b)	75 (c)	76 (c)	77 (d)	78 (a)	79 (a)	80 (b)

* *No option is correct.*

Solutions

1. (d) We have,

$$\frac{\sqrt{x+5}}{1-x} > 1$$

$$\sqrt{x+5} > 0,\ 1-x > 0$$

$$\therefore \qquad x > -5 \qquad \text{...(i)}$$

$$x < 1 \qquad \text{...(ii)}$$

Again, $\dfrac{\sqrt{x+5}}{1-x} > 1$

$$\Rightarrow \qquad \sqrt{x+5} > 1-x$$

$$\Rightarrow \qquad x+5 > (1-x)^2$$

[squaring both sides]

$$\Rightarrow \qquad x+5 > 1+x^2-2x$$

$$\Rightarrow \qquad x^2-3x-4 < 0$$

$$\Rightarrow \qquad (x-4)(x+1) < 0$$

$$\Rightarrow \qquad x \in (-1, 4) \qquad \text{...(iii)}$$

From Eqs. (i), (ii) and (iii), we get

$$x \in (-1, 1)$$

$$\therefore \qquad -1 < x < 1$$

2. (a) t_n denotes the number of integral sided triangle with distincts sides from $\{1, 2, 3, ..., n\}$. t_{19} is the number of triangle formed by the sides from $\{1, 2, 3, ..., 19\}$ and t_{20} is the number of triangle formed by the distinct sides from $\{1, 2, 3, ..., 20\}$.

Any triangle counted in t_{19} is also counted in t_{20}, but $t_{20} - t_{19}$ is the number of triangle counted in t_{20} but not in t_{19}. A triangle is counted in t_{20} but no t_{19} if and only if its largest side is 20.

The middle side of is a and the smallest side can be $21-a$ to $a-1$.

So, the number of triangle with largest side 20 and middle side.

$a = 11$, then other sides are $21-11, 11-1$ i.e. 10, 10 (11, 10, 10) 1 triangle. Similarly $a = 12$, (smallest sides are (9, 10, 11) = 3 triangle $a = 13$, smallest sides are (8, 9, 10, 11, 12) = 5 triangle

$\therefore$ Total number of triangles on

$$1+3+5+7+....+17 = 81$$

3. (a) We have,

$$x = x^2 + y^2 \qquad \text{...(i)}$$

and $\qquad y = 2xy \qquad \text{...(ii)}$

$$\because \qquad y - 2xy = 0$$

$$\Rightarrow \qquad y(1-2x) = 0$$

$$\Rightarrow \qquad y = 0,\ x = \frac{1}{2}$$

Put $y = 0$ in Eq. (i), we get

$$x = x^2 + 0$$

$$\Rightarrow \qquad x - x^2 = 0$$

$$\Rightarrow \qquad x(1-x) = 0$$

$$\Rightarrow \qquad x = 0,\ x = 1$$

Put $x = \dfrac{1}{2}$ in Eq. (i), we get

$$\frac{1}{2} = \left(\frac{1}{2}\right)^2 + y^2$$

$$\Rightarrow \qquad y^2 = \frac{1}{2} - \frac{1}{4}$$

$$\Rightarrow \qquad y^2 = \frac{1}{4} \Rightarrow y = \pm\frac{1}{2}$$

$\therefore$ Value of (x, y) are (0, 0) (0, 1)

$$\left(\frac{1}{2}, \frac{1}{2}\right)\left(\frac{1}{2}, \frac{-1}{2}\right).$$

4. (a) We have,

$$x^3 - 3|x| + 2 = 0$$

Case I $x > 0$

$$\therefore \qquad x^3 - 3x + 2 = 0$$

$$\Rightarrow \qquad (x-1)(x-1)(x+2) = 0$$

$$\Rightarrow \qquad x = 1, -2$$

Since, $\qquad x > 0$

$$\therefore \qquad x \neq -2$$

$$x = 1$$

Case II $x < 0$

$$\therefore \qquad x^3 + 3x + 2 = 0$$

Graph of $x^3 + 3x + 2$

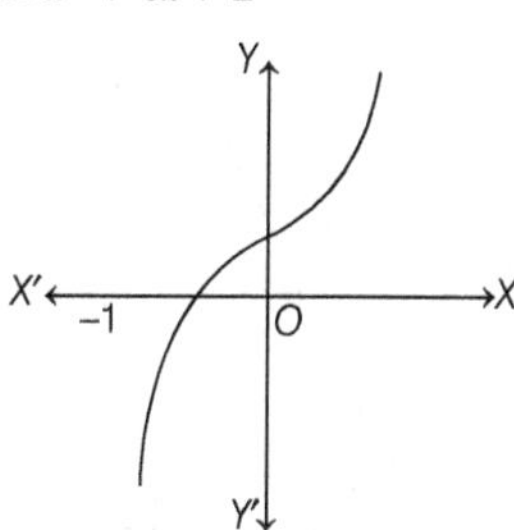

Clearly, from graph.

It has one solution lie between $(-1, 0)$.

$\therefore$ Positive value of $x = 1$

Hence, only one solutions.

5. (c) We have,

$$(1+2x)^{20} = a_0 + a_1 x + a_2 x^2 + ... + a_{20} x^{20}$$

Put $x = 1$,

$$3^{20} = a_0 + a_1 + a_2 + ... + a_{20} \qquad \text{...(i)}$$

Put $x = -1$,

$$1 = a_0 - a_1 + a_2 - a_3 + ... + a_{20} \qquad \text{...(ii)}$$

On adding Eqs. (i) and (ii), we get

$$\frac{3^{20}+1}{2} = a_0 + a_2 + a_4 + \ldots + a_{20}$$

On subtracting Eq. (ii) from Eq. (i), we get

$$\frac{3^{20}-1}{2} = a_1 + a_3 + a_5 + \ldots + a_{19}$$

Now, we have

$$3a_0 + 2a_1 + 3a_2 + 2a_3 + \ldots + 2a_{19} + 3a_{20}$$
$$= 3\,(a_0 + a_2 + a_4 + \ldots + a_{20})$$
$$\qquad\qquad + 2(a_1 + a_3 + \ldots + a_{19})$$
$$= 3\left(\frac{3^{20}+1}{2}\right) + 2\left(\frac{3^{20}-1}{2}\right)$$
$$= \frac{5 \cdot 3^{20}+1}{2}$$

6. *(b)* P_1, P_2, P_3, P_4, P_5 be five equally spaced points on the circumference of circle of radius 1.

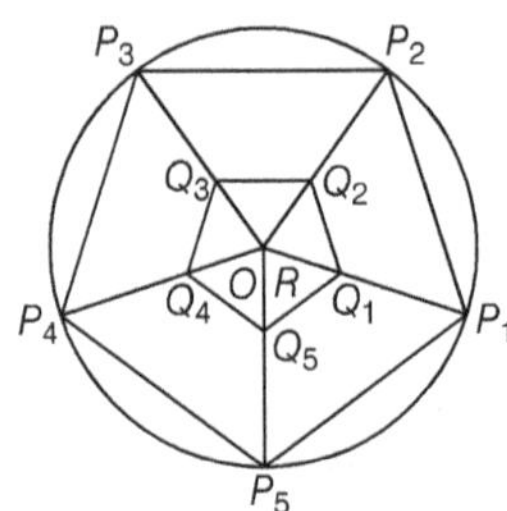

Let R which is near to point O.

$\therefore$ OR is lie between the pentagonal region Q_1, Q_2, Q_3, Q_4, Q_5.

7. *(b)* Let $P(x, y)$ be any point lie in XY-plane.

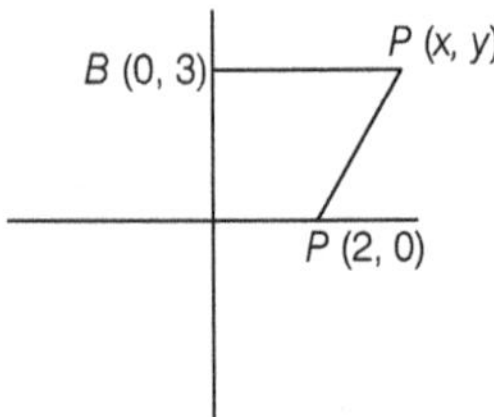

According to problem, $2PA < 3PB$

$$4PA^2 < 9PB^2$$
$$\Rightarrow \quad 4\,[(x-2)^2 + (y-0)^2] < 9$$
$$[(x-0)^2 + (y-3)^2]$$
$$\Rightarrow \quad 4\,(x^2 - 4x + 4 + y^2) < 9$$
$$(x^2 + y^2 - 6x + 9)$$
$$\Rightarrow \quad 5x^2 + 5y^2 - 54y + 16x + 65 > 0$$
$$\Rightarrow \quad x^2 + y^2 - 10.8y + 3.2x + 13 > 0$$
$$\Rightarrow \quad (x+1.6)^2 + (y-5.4)^2 > 18.72$$

Hence, the region is outside the
$$(x+1.6)^2 + (y-5\cdot4)^2 = 18.72$$

8. *(d)* We have,

ABC is a right angled triangle. AC is hypotenuse of ΔABC. The incircle touch the hypotenuse at D.

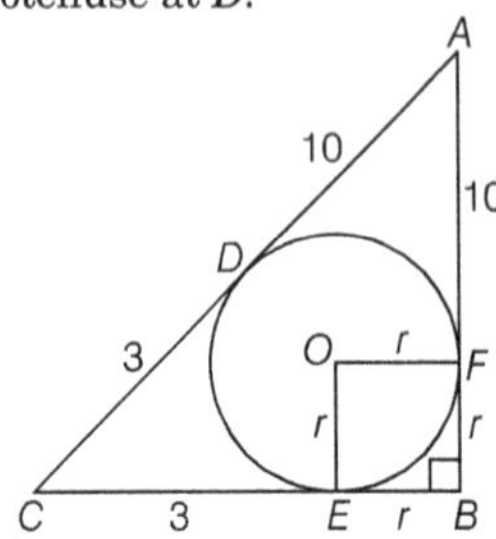

Given, $\qquad AD = 10$

$$CD = 3$$
$$OE = OF = r\,(\text{radius of circle})$$
$$OE = BE = BF = r$$
$$AD = AF = 10$$

[AD and AF are tangents on a circle from external points are equal]

Similarly, $\quad CD = CE = 3$

In ΔABC, $\quad AC^2 = AB^2 + BC^2$

$$(13)^2 = (10+r)^2 + (3+r)^2$$
$$\Rightarrow \quad 169 = 100 + 20r + r^2 + 9 + 6r + r^2$$
$$\Rightarrow \quad 2r^2 + 26r - 60 = 0$$
$$\Rightarrow \quad r^2 + 13r - 30 = 0$$
$$\Rightarrow \quad (r+15)\,(r-2) = 0$$
$$\Rightarrow \quad r = 2,\ r \neq -15$$

9. *(a)* We have three sides of quadrilateral are 5, 10, 20.

Let the fourth sides of quadrilateral = x

We know that in quadrilateral. Sum of three side is greater than fourth sides

$$\therefore \qquad 5 + 10 + 20 > x \qquad \ldots(i)$$
$$5 + 10 + x > 20 \qquad \ldots(ii)$$
$$5 + 20 + x > 10 \qquad \ldots(iii)$$
$$10 + 20 + x > 5 \qquad \ldots(iv)$$

From Eq. (i) $x < 35$

From Eq. (ii) $x > 5$

From Eq. (iii) $x > -15$

From Eq. (iv) $x > -25$

Now, x is a positive integer.

$\therefore$ From Eqs. (i), (ii), (iii) and (iv),

$$5 < x < 35$$

$\therefore$ Value of x is 6, 7, 8, 9, 10, 11, 12, 13, 14, 15, 16, 17, 18, 19, 20, 21, 22, 23, 24, 25, 26, 27, 28, 29, 30, 31, 32, 33, 34

$\therefore$ There are 29 possible values of x.

10. *(b)* Let initial volume of sphere is V and radius is r.

$$\therefore \qquad V = \frac{4}{3}\pi r^3$$

Volume of sphere after increase is V' and radius is r'.

$$\therefore \qquad V' = \frac{4}{3}\pi r'^3$$
$$\Rightarrow \qquad V' = (V + 72.8\% \text{ of } V)$$
$$= V\left(1 + \frac{728}{1000}\right) = \frac{1728v}{1000}$$
$$\Rightarrow \qquad V' = \frac{1728}{1000}\left(\frac{4}{3}\pi r^3\right)$$
$$\therefore \quad \frac{1728}{1000} \cdot \frac{4}{3}\pi r^3 = \frac{4}{3}\pi r'^3$$
$$\Rightarrow \qquad \frac{r'^3}{r^3} = 1.728 \Rightarrow \frac{r'}{r} = 1.2$$

$\therefore$ Increase in surface area of sphere

$$= \left(\frac{r'}{r}\right)^2 = 1.44 = 144\%$$

$\therefore$ Surface area increase $= (144 - 100)\%$
$$= 44\%$$

11. *(d)* Let $\quad x = 0.\overline{d25d25}d25 \qquad \ldots(i)$
$$1000x = d25.\overline{d25d25} \qquad \ldots(ii)$$

On subtracting Eq. (i) from Eq. (ii), we get

$$999x = d25 \Rightarrow x = \frac{d25}{999}$$

But given, $\qquad x = \frac{n}{27}$

$$\therefore \qquad \frac{n}{27} = \frac{d25}{999} \Rightarrow n = \frac{d25}{37}$$

$$d \in \{1, 2, 3, 4, 5, 6, 7, 8, 9\}$$

n is integer.

$\therefore d25$ is a multiple of 37.

When, put $d = 9$

Then, n is multiple of 37.

$$\therefore \qquad n = \frac{925}{37} = 25$$

$$\therefore \qquad n + d = 25 + 9 = 34$$

12. *(b)* Exactly at 10 O'clock the hour hand has travelled 300° from 12 O'clock.

One hour = 60 minute.

One minute hand moves 1° and hour clock hand move $\left(\dfrac{30}{360}\right)^\circ = \left(\dfrac{1}{12}\right)^\circ$

Assuming we have made it to 10 O'clock and now the hour and the minute hand start moving spontaneously.

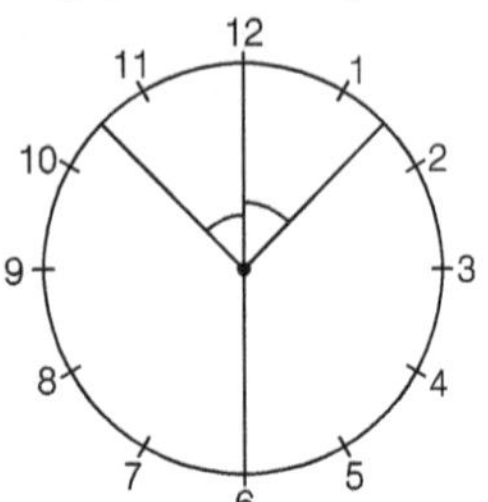

If the hands of the watch are symmetric with vertical line.

Supposing this happens when x minutes have passed x minutes = $(6x)°$ have been covered our hour hand would cover.

$$\left[(6x)\left(\frac{1}{12}\right)\right]° = \left(\frac{1}{2}x\right)°$$

$\therefore$ Our hand has covered $\left(300 + \frac{x}{2}\right)°$

On subtracting this from 360° to find the angle from 12 O'clock anti-clockwise, we get

$$360° - \left(300 + \frac{x}{2}\right)° = \left(60 - \frac{x}{2}\right)°$$

So, they are symmetric.

$$\therefore \qquad 60 - \frac{x}{2} = 6x$$

$$\Rightarrow \qquad x = \left(\frac{120}{13}\right)° = 9\,\text{min}\,13.8\,\text{s}$$

$\therefore$ Time = 10 h 9 m 14 s

13. (d) Woman has 10 keys out of which only one opens a lock.

The first keys works with probability $\frac{1}{10}$

The conditional probability that the second keys works given that first failed = $\frac{1}{9}$.

$\therefore$ Required probability (seventh key works)

$= P$ (I fails) $\cdot P$ (2nd/I fails) $\cdot P$ (III /2 fails) $\qquad P$ (7th/6th fails)

$$= \frac{9}{10} \times \frac{8}{9} \times \frac{7}{8} \times \frac{6}{7} \times \frac{5}{6} \times \frac{4}{5} \times \frac{1}{4} = \frac{1}{10}$$

14. (b) Given, 74% students like cricket

76% students like football

82% students like tennis

$\therefore$ 26% student not like cricket

24% student not like football

18% student not like tennis

Student all the three sports like at least

$= 100\% -$ (sport not likes)

$= 100\% - (26 + 24 + 18)\%$

$= 100\% - 68\% = 32\%$

15. (c) We have, $2^n < k < 2^{n+1}, k \in N$

Number of integer between 2^n and 2^{n+1} is i.e $k = 2^{n+1} - 2^n - 1$

First term = $2^n + 1$

Last term = $2^{n+1} - 1$

$$\therefore S_n = \frac{2^{n+1} - 2^n - 1}{2}[2^n + 1 + 2^{n+1} - 1]$$

$$S_n = \frac{2^{n+1} - 2^n - 1}{2}(2^n)(1 + 2)$$

$$S_n = \frac{(2^n - 1)(2^n) \cdot 3}{2}$$

But $S_n = 9m$, $m \in I$

$$\therefore \qquad \frac{(2^n - 1)2^n \cdot 3}{2} = 9m$$

$$\Rightarrow \qquad (2^n - 1)2^{n-1} = 3m$$

$$\Rightarrow \qquad 2^n(2^n - 1) = 6m$$

It is possible when, n is even.

16. (b) Velocity of a ball is measured relative to a fixed object or frame. If frame of reference is moving, then object will have a velocity opposite to that of frame of reference. In given case, car is frame of reference. Due to motion of car, the ball has two velocities

(i) vertical velocity

(ii) horizontal velocity opposite to motion of car.

Because of there two velocities, path of ball will be parabolic in car frame.

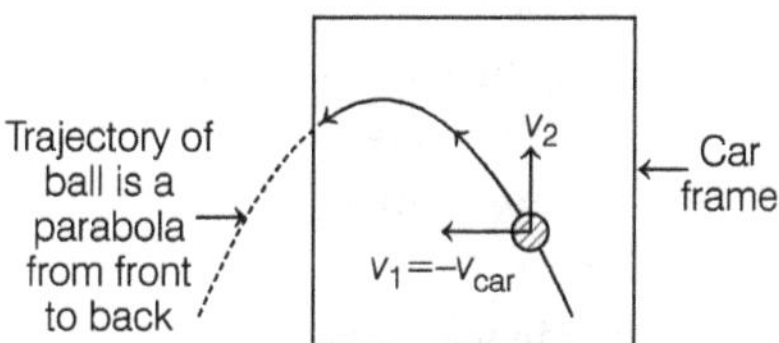

So, trajectory of ball will be as that of option (c).

17. (b) Given, mass of second planet

$$= 8 \times \text{mass of first planet}$$

$$\Rightarrow \qquad M_2 = 8 M_1 \qquad \dots \text{(i)}$$

$$\Rightarrow \qquad \frac{4}{3}\pi R_2^3 \times \rho = 8 \times \frac{4}{3}\pi R_1^3 \times \rho$$

$\therefore$ Density of both planets is same.

$$\Rightarrow \qquad R_2^3 = 8R_1^3$$

$$\text{or} \qquad R_2 = 2R_1 \qquad \dots \text{(ii)}$$

So, ratio of acceleration due to gravity of the second planet to that of the first planet is

$$\frac{g_2}{g_1} = \frac{\left(\dfrac{GM_2}{R_2^2}\right)}{\left(\dfrac{GM_1}{R_1^2}\right)} = \left(\frac{M_2}{M_1}\right) \times \left(\frac{R_1}{R_2}\right)^2$$

$$= \frac{8M_1}{M_1} \times \left(\frac{R_1}{2R_1}\right)^2 = \frac{2}{1}$$

So, $\qquad g_2 = 2g_1$.

18. (c) As density of B is more than that of A, a small volume of B weighs equals to a large volume of A.

Hence, if we draw a horizontal line from bottom of column of A, then a lesser

length column of B must appear above this line in other limb of U-tube. It is as shown below.

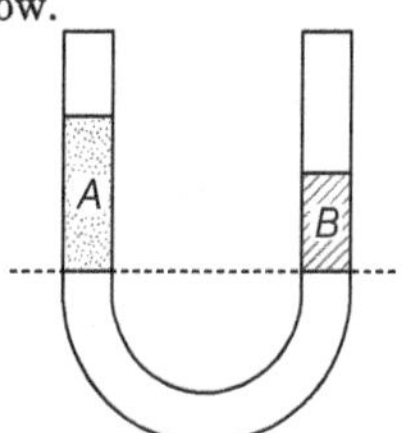

This is shown in option (c).

19. (b) Given situation is

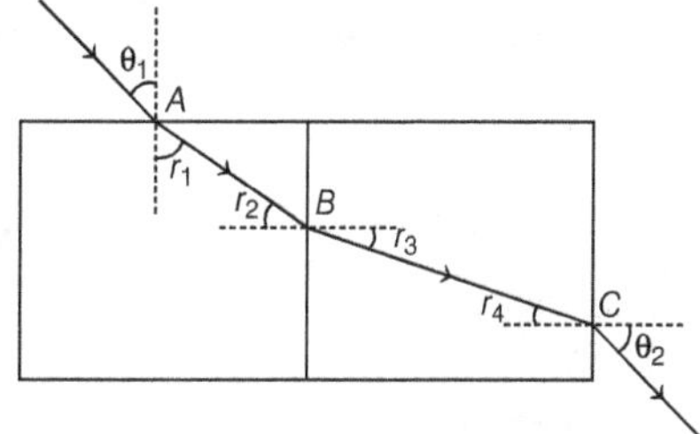

When θ_1 is increased at point A following Snell's law ($i \propto r$), then r_1 increases.

When r_1 increases, r_2 decreases at point B.

Decrease of r_2 causes a decrease of r_3 as ($i \propto r$).

Also $r_3 = r_4$, so when r_3 decreases, r_4 also decreases. This causes a decrease in value of θ_2.

So, a increase of θ_1 causes a decrease in θ_2.

20. (a) Force on a charged particle moving in region of magnetic field is

$$\mathbf{F} = q(\mathbf{v} \times \mathbf{B})$$

Clearly, $\mathbf{F}$ is perpendicular to both $\mathbf{v}$ and $\mathbf{B}$.

As, magnetic force is perpendicular to velocity of moving charged particle. So, work done in time Δt is

$$W = (\mathbf{F} \cdot \mathbf{v})\, \Delta t = 0$$

Hence, $\qquad W_1 = W_2 = 0$

21. (a) Given situation is

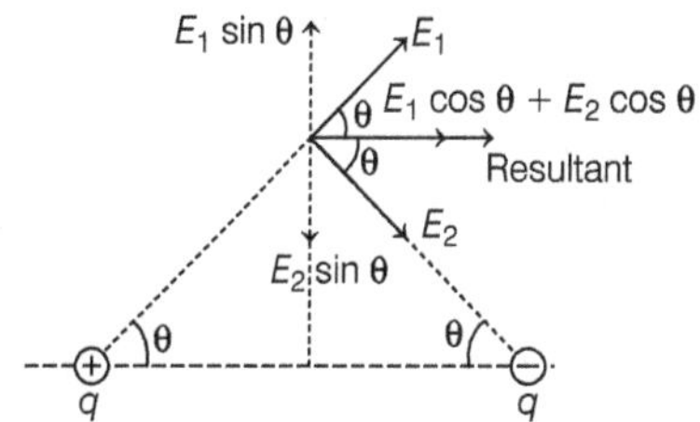

As charges are of equal magnitude, direction of resultant field is along the angle bisector of the angle formed by field vectors.

22. *(a)* Weight of mass M can be resolved into components parallel and perpendicular to inclined plane as shown below.

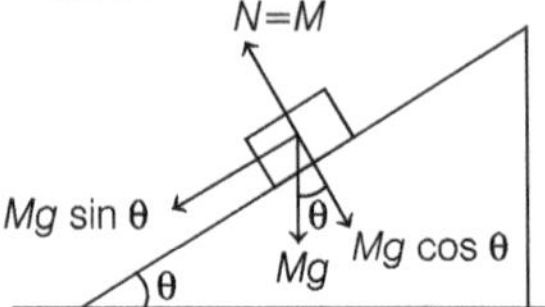

Force of block on incline is $Mg\cos\theta$, so force exerted by block on mass M is $Mg\cos\theta$ directed perpendicularly up the plane.

23. (No option is matching)

When we squeeze the snow due to increased pressure, melting point of ice (snow) is lowered and it melts. As pressure is removed, water formed is again frozen because melting point is again raised. This process is called regelation of ice.

None of the option given is correct.

24. *(d)* Polarisation is a process of alignment of electric vectors (or plane of oscillation of particles) in a particular direction when an electromagnetic wave (or a mechanical transverse wave) passes through a narrow slit. Sound waves in air are longitudinal waves, so they cannot be polarised. Polarisation is shown only by transverse waves.

25. *(b)* Percentage increase in area

$$= \frac{\text{Final area} - \text{Initial area}}{\text{Initial area}} \times 100$$

$$= \frac{\pi\,(r_2^2 - r_1^2)}{\pi r_1^2} \times 100$$

$$= \frac{(r_1 + \Delta r)^2 - r_1^2}{r_1^2} \times 100$$

where, Δr = increase in radius.

$$= \left(\frac{r_1^2 + 2r_1\Delta r + \Delta r^2 - r_1^2}{r_1^2}\right) \times 100$$

$$= \frac{2r_1\Delta r + \Delta r^2}{r_1^2} \times 100$$

As Δr is small, we can neglect Δr^2.

$$\approx \frac{2r_1\Delta r}{r_1^2} \times 100$$

$$= 2\left(\frac{\Delta r}{r_1} \times 100\right)$$

$$= 2 \times 0.15\% = 0.30\%$$

26. *(d)* Property of sound that makes difference between two sounds having same frequency and amplitude is called timber or quality of sound. This is how amplitude rises or falls in a given time duration.

This is shown by waveform of sound wave. Two waves can have same amplitude and frequency but can have different waveforms. As shown here.

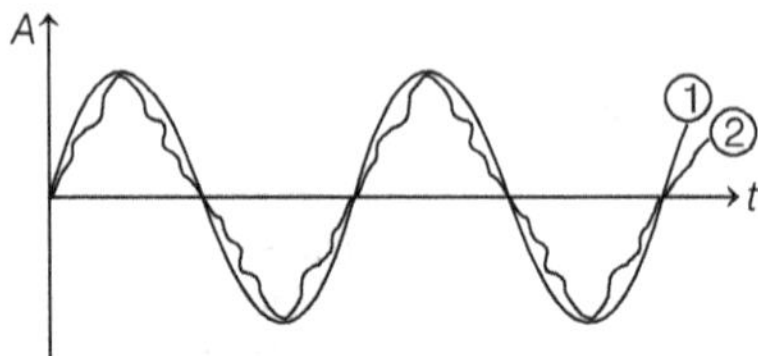

27. *(c)* Given, 7 α particles are emitted from $^{235}_{92}$U.

$$\Rightarrow \quad {}^{235}_{92}\text{U} \longrightarrow {}^{207}_{78}A + 7({}^{4}_{2}\text{He})$$

Now, $n\beta^{-}$ particles are emitted to produce $^{207}_{82}$Pb.

$$\Rightarrow \quad {}^{207}_{78}A \longrightarrow {}^{207}_{82}\text{Pb} + n({}^{0}_{-1}\beta)$$

Conservation of atomic number, gives

$$78 = 82 - n \Rightarrow n = 82 - 78 = 4$$

So, $4\,\beta^{-}$ particles are emitted in given nuclear reaction.

28. *(c)* In given circuit, when S_1 and S_3 both are closed, then source is short circuited. Closing either S_1 or S_3 does not completes any of path. Hence, they produce no change in circuit.

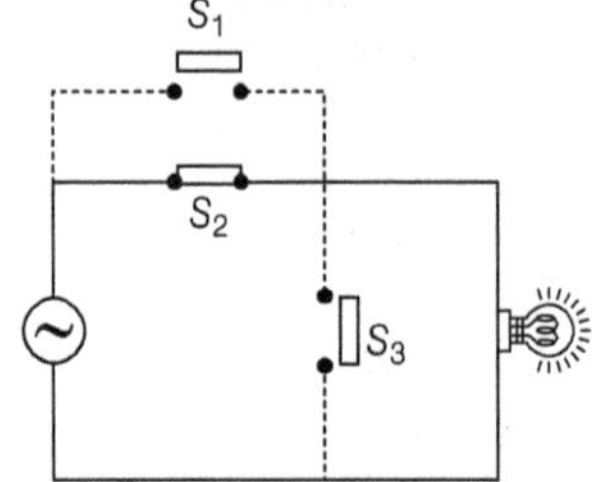

On closing S_2 alone the circuit containing bulb is complete. Hence, bulb will light up when S_2 is closed alongwith S_3 but S_1 is open. Option (c) is correct.

29. *(d)* Resistance of bulb is inversely proportional to its rated power.

$$\Rightarrow \quad R = \frac{V_{\text{rated}}^2}{P_{\text{rated}}} \Rightarrow R \propto \frac{1}{P_{\text{rated}}}$$

As bulbs are in series, so same current flows through them at all instances. Power dissipation in a series combination is

$$P = I^2 R \Rightarrow P \propto R$$

or $\quad P \propto \dfrac{1}{P_{\text{rated}}}$

So, power dissipation is more in the 100 W bulb. This makes option (d) correct.

30. *(b)* Area of cube is more than that of a sphere for same mass and density. Cube also have sharp edges that radiates more effectively than a flat surface.

So, rate of cooling for cube is much rapid than sphere. Effect of sharp edges is prominent only at very high temperatures. So, option (b) is correct.

31. *(d)* As element X is forming a stable product of the type XCl_4, so X must be tetravalent. Among the given elements Al is trivalent, Na is monovalent, Ca is divalent and Si is tetravalent. Thus, option (d) is correct.

32. *(c)* A mixture of NH_4Cl and NaCl can be separated by the process of sublimation. In this process, solid directly changes to gaseous state without passing into liquid state. NH_4Cl sublimes to gaseous NH_3 and HCl upon heating whereas NaCl does not sublime, the reaction can be written as

$$NH_4Cl(s) \longrightarrow NH_3(g) + HCl(g)$$

33. *(a)* An ionic compound is formed when metal and a non-metal reacts whereas covalent compound is formed when 2 non-metals react with each other. In the given options, $Fe(OH)_2$, $Ca(OH)_2$ and $Cu(OH)_2$ are ionic while CH_3OH, CH_3CH_2OH are covalent.

Thus, the correct pair in which first compound is ionic and the second compound is covalent is given in option (a).

34. *(d)* In the given reaction,

$$\overset{\text{Reduction}}{\overbrace{\underset{\underset{\text{Oxidation}}{\underbrace{}}}{SO_2 + 2H_2S \longrightarrow 3S + 2H_2O}}}$$

Here, H_2S is getting oxidised to H_2O.

35. *(b)* $\underset{\text{Sodium Oxide}}{Na_2O} + H_2O \longrightarrow \underset{\substack{\text{Sodium}\\\text{hydroxide}}}{2NaOH}$

As Na_2O is a metal oxide which on dissolving with water gives NaOH which is metal hydroxide, indicates the basic character of Na_2O.

36. *(c)* According to Boyle's law, the pressure of a given mass of an ideal gas is inversely proportional to its volume at a constant temperature.

$$\therefore \quad p \propto \frac{1}{V}$$

Both option c and b is showing relationship between p and V but the correct option is (c), as it is showing inverse relationship and option (b) is showing a linear relationship.

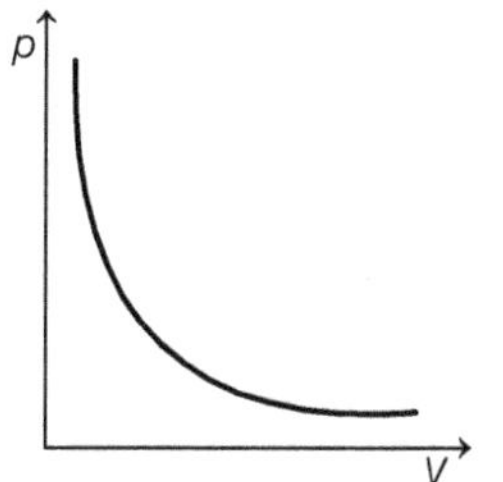

37. *(a)* pH stands for potenz (power) of hydrogen. The pH values for acidic solution ranges from 0 to 7, for pure water its value is 7 and for basic solution, it ranges from 7-14.

As HCl is a strong acid, the pH value will be least. On the other hand, KOH is a strong base, its pH value will be maximum, tomato juice contains citric acid which is a weak acid, so its pH value will be more than HCl, but will be less than H_2O and KOH.

Thus, the correct order of pH values will be

$$(i) < (iii) < (iv) < (ii)$$

38. *(c)* When calcium carbide is added to water, acetylene gas is evolved. The reaction can be written as

$$CaC_2 + 2H_2O \longrightarrow Ca(OH)_2 + CH\equiv CH$$
(Calcium carbide)   (Acetylene)

39. *(d)* On moving down the group, as the atomic number of alkali metal increases, their atomic radii also increases because here shielding effect predominates over nuclear charge. Thus, the correct order of atomic radii of alkali metal is

$$Cs > K > Na > Li$$

40. *(b)* Two structural isomers of C_3H_4 are possible, which are propyne and cyclopropane.

$$CH_3C\equiv CH$$
(Propyne)   (Cyclopropene)

41. *(c)* The molecular formulas for the given compounds are as follows

acetone – C_3H_6O propanol – C_3H_8O
methyl acetate – $C_3H_6O_2$
propionic acid – $C_3H_6O_2$.

As molecular formula for both propionic acid ($CH_3CH_2\overset{\|}{\underset{O}{C}}OH$) and methyl acetate

functional ($CH_3-\overset{\|}{\underset{O}{C}}OCH_3$) are same but

have different functional groups, so they are functional isomers.

42. *(b)* $N_2 + 3H_2 \rightleftharpoons 2NH_3$

6.022×10^{23} molecules of $H_2 = 1$ mole

$\therefore 3.011 \times 10^{23}$ molecules of $H_2 = 0.5$ mole.

3 moles of H_2 reacts with 2 moles of NH_3.

So, 1 mole of H_2 reacts $= \dfrac{2}{3}$ moles of NH_3.

$\therefore 0.5$ mole of H_2 react with $\dfrac{2}{3} \times 0.5$

$$= \dfrac{1}{3} \text{ mole}$$

1 mole of NH_3 contains 6.022×10^{23} molecules.

So, $\dfrac{1}{3}$ mole of NH_3 will have

$$= 6.022 \times 10^{23} \times \dfrac{1}{3}$$
$$= 2.0 \times 10^{23} \text{ molecules.}$$

43. *(a)* Saponification is the process of hydrolysis of glyceryl ester of stearic acid with sodium hydroxide, which produces glycerol and soap. The reaction can be written as

$$
\begin{array}{l}
CH_2-O-\overset{\overset{\displaystyle O}{\|}}{C}-C_{17}H_{35} \\
CH-O-\overset{\overset{\displaystyle O}{\|}}{C}-C_{17}H_{35} \ +3NaOH \ \overset{\Delta}{\longrightarrow} \\
CH_2-O-\underset{\underset{\displaystyle O}{\|}}{C}-C_{17}H_{35}
\end{array}
$$

$$3C_{17}H_{35}COO^-Na^+$$
(soap)
$$+$$
$$CH_2OH$$
$$|$$
$$CHOH$$
$$|$$
$$CH_2OH$$
Glycerol

44. *(b)* A concentrated solution of lead nitrate in water can be stored in copper vessel as copper can not react with lead nitrate solution because it is less reactive than lead. Whereas, all other given metals are more reactive than lead and can easily react (displace) it from its solution.

45. *(c)* The solubility of KCl increases with increase in temperature. Thus, the statement (c) is incorrect.
(a) From the graph, it is clear that at room temperature the solubility of KNO_3 and KCl are not equal. Thus, the statement (a) is correct.
(b) The solubility of both KNO_3 and KCl increases with temperature. Thus, statement (b) is correct.
(d) From the graph, it can be seen that the solubility of KNO_3 increases

much more compared to that of KCl with increase in temperature. Thus, the statement (a) is correct.

46. *(d)* Virus is the smallest in size among bacteria, mammalian cell and mitochondrion. Virus ranges in size from about 20-400 nm in diameter. Bacterial cells range in size from 0.2-10 μm. Mammalian cells are between 10-100 μm in diameter. Mitochondria are commonly between 0.75-3 μm in diameter.

47. *(c)* Birds and mammals are endothermic animals, i.e. their core body temperature is kept nearly constant through thermal homeostasis. Therefore, if birds are moved from 30°-10°C their body temperature does not change at all.

48. *(c)* Ascorbic acid is also known as vitamin-C, a vitamin found in citrus fruits and is an essential nutrient involved in the repair of connective tissue and the enzymatic production of certain neurotransmitters. In the body, it acts as an antioxidant, helping to protect cells from the damage caused by free radicals.

49. *(b)* Bile salts consist of sodium bicarbonate, sodium glycocholate and sodium taurocholate. These are the primary components of bile produced in the liver. Their main function is emulsification of fat (i.e. breakdown of large fat molecules into small droplets) and their solubilisation.

50. *(a)* Dietary fibres are composed of non-starch polysaccharides such as cellulose, dextrins, inulin, lignin, chitins, pectins, beta-glucans, waxes and oligosaccharides. Dietary fibres, also known as roughage is the portion of plant derived food that cannot be completely broken down by digestive enzymes.

Rest others, i.e. amylase, proteins and unsaturated fats are although basic components of diet but are not considered as dietary fibres.

51. *(c)* 'On the Origin of Species, by Means of Natural Selection' or 'The Preservation of Favoured Races in the Struggle for Life', published on 24 November 1859 is a work of scientific literature by Charles Darwin which is considered to be the foundation of evolutionary biology.

52. *(a)* Panting refers to breathing quickly and loudly through mouth. It helps dogs to get rid of excess metabolic heat when they are hot or engaged in vigorous exercise.

This happens because panting helps dogs to circulate the necessary air through their bodies to cool down.

53. *(a)* Haemodialysis is a process of purifying the blood of a person whose kidneys are not working normally. It helps to filter waste, removes extra fluid and balances electrolytes (sodium, potassium, bicarbonate, chloride, calcium, magnesium and phosphate). During haemodialysis, blood is removed from the body and filtered through a man-made membrane called a dialyser, or artificial kidney and then the filtered blood is returned to the body.

54. *(d)* An individual has 'O' blood group if his/her blood sample does not clump when either antiserum 'A' or antiserum 'B' is added. Antiserum is a blood serum containing antibodies against specific antigens. Clumping or Agglutination is the process that occurs if an antigen is mixed with its corresponding antibody. A person with 'O' blood group neither have 'A' nor 'B' antigens on his/her red blood cells, but both 'a' and 'b' antibodies in his/her plasma. Thus, they are also called as universal donor.

55. *(b)* The rate of bacterial multiplication increases in warmer weather thereby forming curd from milk faster. This happens because *Lactobacillus* (i.e. bacteria that turns milk into curd) is more active in summers and develops more, which inturn accelerates the fermentation process.

56. *(b)* Seedlings grown in dark are taller than those grown in light as they develop long hypocotyls (embryonic shoot) and their cotyledons remain closed around the epicotyl in an apical hook. This process is referred to as etiolation.

57. *(c)* In humans, Rhesus condition can arise when either father or mother is Rh positive. Rhesus (Rh) factor is an inherited protein found on the surface of red blood cells. If an individual's blood has the protein, he/she is Rh positive and if his/her blood lacks the protein, he/she is Rh negative. A baby may have the blood type and Rh-factor of either parent or a combination of both parents. Rh factor follows a common pattern of law of dominance because Rh-positive gene is a dominant gene.

58. *(a)* The part of the human brain that governs memory and intelligence is cerebrum. It is the largest part of the human brain associated with most critical and intelligent brain function such as thoughts and actions.

59. *(c)* Saturated dietary fats increase the risk of heart disease by narrowing arteries by fat deposition. Saturated fat raises the level of cholesterol in your blood. High levels of Low Density Lipid (LDL) cholesterol in blood are responsible for their deposition in blood vessel, thus narrowing the lumens and increasing the risk of heart diseases and stroke.

60. *(a)* Rotation of crops is carried out to increase variation in the mineral content of the soil. Prolonged planting of the same crop type leads to the depletion of specific nutrients in the soil.

61. *(a)* We have, $\log_a b = 4$,

$\log_c d = 2$, $a, b, c, d \in N$

$\Rightarrow \qquad b = a^4, d = c^2$

$\Rightarrow \qquad b - d = 7 = a^4 - c^2$

$\Rightarrow \qquad 7 = (a^2 + c)(a^2 - c)$

$\Rightarrow \qquad 7 \times 1 = (a^2 + c)(a^2 - c)$

$\therefore \qquad a^2 + c = 7 \text{ and } a^2 - c = 1$

On solving, we get $a = 2$ and $c = 3$

$\therefore \qquad c - a = 3 - 2 = 1$

62. *(b)* We have,

$P(x) = 1 + x + x^2 + x^3 + x^4 + x^5$

$P(x) = \dfrac{1 - x^6}{1 - x}$

$\left[\because a + ar + ar^2 + \ldots + ar^n = \dfrac{a(-r^n)}{1 - r} \right]$

It has 5 roots let $\alpha_1, \alpha_2, \alpha_3, \alpha_4, \alpha_5$ they are 6th roots of unity

Now,

$P(x^{12}) = 1 + x^{12} + x^{24} + x^{36} + x^{48} + x^{60}$

$\therefore P(x^{12}) = P(x) \cdot Q(x) + R(x)$

Here, $R(x)$ is a polynomial of maximum degree 4.

Put $x = \alpha_1, \alpha_2, \alpha_3, \alpha_4, \alpha_5$; we get

$R(\alpha_1) = 6 = R(\alpha_2) = R(\alpha_3)$
$\qquad\qquad = R(\alpha_4) = R(\alpha_5)$

$\therefore R(x) - 6 = 0$ has 6 roots, which contradicts that $R(x)$ is maximum of degree 4.

$\therefore$ So it is an identity.

$\because \qquad\qquad R(x) = 6$

63. *(b)* ABC is a triangle in which BE and CF are altitude.

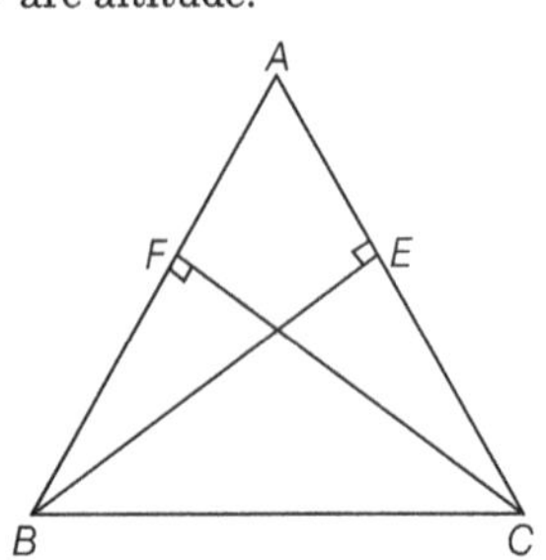

Given, $\qquad BE \geq AC$

$\qquad\qquad CF \geq AB$

In $\triangle ABE$, $\quad \sin A = \dfrac{BE}{AB}$

$\qquad\qquad AB \sin A = BE$

$\qquad\qquad AB \sin A \geq AC \quad [\because BE \geq AC] \ldots\text{(i)}$

Similarly in $\triangle ACF$,

$\qquad\qquad \sin A = \dfrac{CF}{AC}$

$\Rightarrow \qquad AC \sin A = CF$

$\Rightarrow \qquad AC \sin A \geq AB \quad [\because CF \geq AB] \ldots\text{(ii)}$

From Eqs. (i) and (ii), we get

$(AB + AC)\sin A \geq (AB + AC) \Rightarrow \sin A \geq 1$

$\Rightarrow \qquad\qquad \sin A = 1 \qquad [0 \leq \sin A \leq 1]$

$\Rightarrow \qquad\qquad A = 90° \qquad [\because \sin 90° = 1]$

Now, from Eqs. (i) and (ii), we get

$\qquad\qquad AB \geq AC$

and $\qquad\qquad AC \geq AB$

$\therefore \qquad\qquad AB = AC$

Hence, angles are 45°, 45°, 90°.

64. *(c)* Given, $\quad AB = AC = 37$

$\qquad\qquad AD = 33$

$\qquad\qquad BD = 7$

In $\triangle ABE$,

$\qquad\qquad AB^2 = AE^2 + BE^2 \qquad\qquad \ldots\text{(i)}$

In $\triangle ADE$,

$\qquad\qquad AD^2 = AE^2 + DE^2 \qquad\qquad \ldots\text{(ii)}$

$\Rightarrow \quad AB^2 - AD^2 = BE^2 - DE^2$

$\Rightarrow \quad AB^2 - AD^2 = (BE + DE)(BE - DE)$

$$\Rightarrow \quad AB^2 - AD^2 = (CE + DE)(BD)$$
$$[\because BE = CE]$$
$$\Rightarrow \quad AB^2 - AD^2 = CD \cdot BD$$
$$\Rightarrow \quad CD = \frac{AB^2 - AD^2}{BD}$$
$$\Rightarrow \quad CD = \frac{37^2 - 33^2}{7} \quad \text{[given]}$$
$$\Rightarrow \quad CD = \frac{(37 + 33)\,(37 - 33)}{7}$$
$$\Rightarrow \quad CD = \frac{70 \times 4}{7} = 40$$

65. *(d)* **Case I** Area is generated by line segment l is curved surface area of cylinder = $2\pi ra$

$$\therefore \quad A_1 = 2\pi ra$$

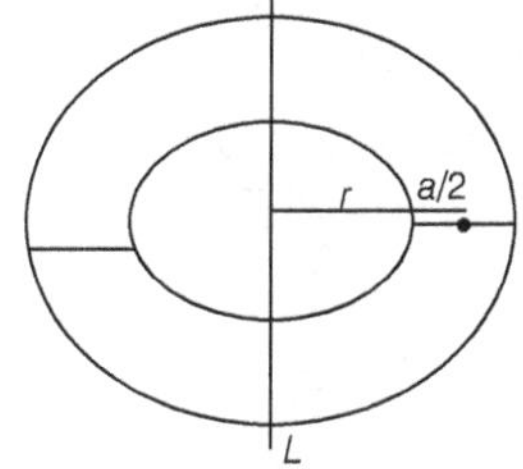

Case II Area is formed in circle.

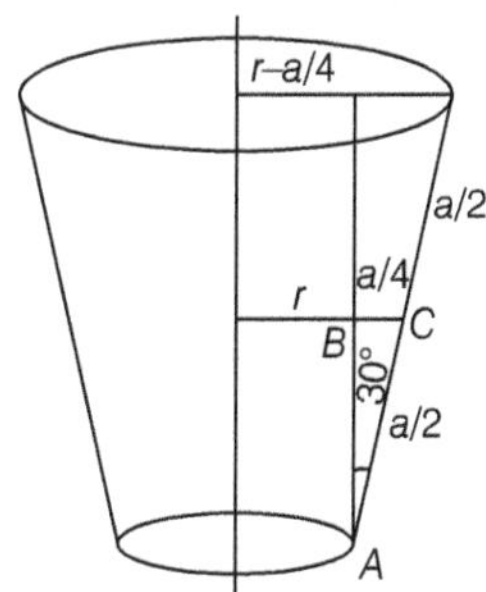

Area of circular region

$$A_2 = \pi \left[\left(r + \frac{a}{2} \right)^2 - \left(r - \frac{a}{2} \right)^2 \right]$$
$$= 2\pi ra$$

Case III Area generated to form a frustrum.

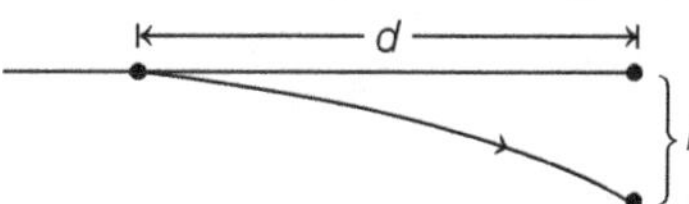

In $\triangle ABC$,
$$\sin 30° = \frac{BC}{AC}$$

$$\frac{1}{2} = \frac{B/C}{a/2}$$
$$\Rightarrow \quad BC = \frac{9}{4}$$
$$\therefore \quad A_3 = \pi a \left(r - \frac{a}{4} + r + \frac{a}{4} \right)$$
$$\Rightarrow \quad A_3 = 2\pi ra$$
$$\therefore \quad A_1 = A_2 = A_3$$

66. *(c)* When block is dipped in water, it displaces some water which exerts buoyant force on block. As a result, reading on scale A will be lower than 2 kg. Due to reaction of block (which is equal to buoyant force), beaker of water is pushed. So, reading of scale B will be more than 3 kg.

67. *(a)* In time t, a particle of mass m falls by a distance
$$h = \frac{1}{2} g t^2$$
Now, distance covered horizontally = d and speed in horizontal direction = c.

Time to travel distance, $d = t = \dfrac{d}{c}$

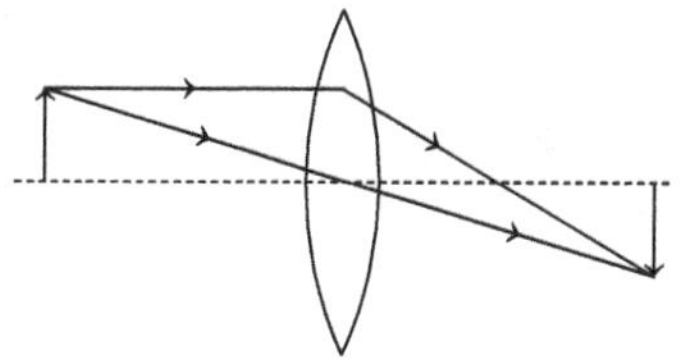

So, photons falls through a distance,
$$h = \frac{1}{2} g t^2 = \frac{1}{2} \times g \times \left(\frac{d}{c} \right)^2 = \frac{gd^2}{2c^2}$$

68. *(d)* Kinetic energy of a rotating body is
$$K = \frac{1}{2} I \omega^2$$

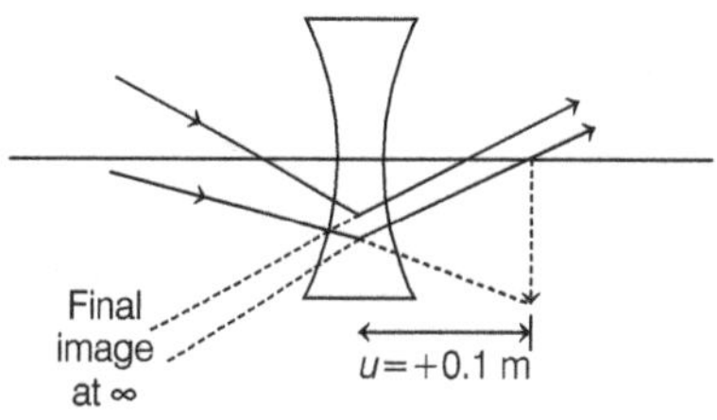

where, I = moment of inertia of a body. For square plate, moment of inertia is largest along an axis perpendicular to plane of plate and through its one of corner. As mass distribution is now farthest from axis of rotation.

So, kinetic energy of plate is largest in option (d).

69. *(d)* Image of first lens acts like object for second lens.

Now, for first lens,
$$u = -0.40 \text{ m}, f = +0.20 \text{ m}$$

By lens equation,
$$\frac{1}{v} - \frac{1}{u} = \frac{1}{f}$$
$$\text{or} \quad \frac{1}{v} = \frac{1}{f} + \frac{1}{u} = \frac{1}{0.2} + \frac{1}{(-0.4)}$$
$$\Rightarrow \quad \frac{1}{v} = \frac{1}{0.4}$$
$$\Rightarrow \quad v = 0.4 \text{ m}$$

Now, this image acts like a virtual object for second lens.

For second lens, $u = +0.1 \text{ m}, f = -0.1 \text{ m}$

By lens equation,
$$\frac{1}{v} = \frac{1}{f} + \frac{1}{u} = \frac{1}{-0.1} + \frac{1}{0.1}$$
$$\Rightarrow \quad \frac{1}{v} = 0 \Rightarrow v = \infty$$

Hence, final image is formed at infinity.

Alternate Method For lens L_1, $u = -(2f)$ so image is formed at $2f$ distance. Now, image distance for L_2 is 0.1 m and focal length of L_2 is also 0.1 m. Hence, object for L_2 is at focus, so its image is formed at infinity.

70. *(c)* Forces on charge at point O, initially balances each other as it is given that acceleration occurs when charge at point P_1 is removed. This means resultant of force due to charges at points P_2, P_3, P_4 and P_5 is equal and opposite to force due to at point P_1.

Hence, acceleration of charge at point O is directed along OP_1.

$$\text{Acceleration} = \frac{F}{m}$$

$$= \frac{\left(\dfrac{Kq_1 q_2}{r^2} \right)}{m} = \frac{9 \times 10^9 \times 10^{-5} \times 5 \times 10^{-5}}{(1)^2 \times 1}$$

$$= 4.5 \text{ ms}^{-2}$$

71. *(a)* When concentrated sulphuric acid reacts with NaCl, then sodium bisulphate and HCl gas (*X*) is formed. The HCl gas released is acidic in nature and turns blue litmus red.

$$2NaCl + H_2SO_4 \longrightarrow Na_2SO_4 + 2HCl$$
$$(X)$$

When HCl gas (*X*) is passed into a testtube containing egg shell powder which contains calcium carbonate suspended in water another gas CO_2 (*Y*) is released, which turns lime water milky.

$$\underset{\substack{(X)}}{HCl} + \underset{\substack{Egg\ shell \\ powder}}{CaCO_3} \longrightarrow CaCO_2 + \underset{\substack{(Y)}}{CO_2} + H_2O$$

$$CO_2 + Ca(OH)_2 \longrightarrow \underset{\substack{Milky}}{CaCO_3} + H_2O$$

Thus, the gases *X* and *Y* respectively are HCl and CO_2.

72. *(c)* Initial concentration of $CaCl_2$ in

$$\text{solution} = \frac{222 \times 10^{-3}}{111 \times 10 \times 10^{-3}} = 0.2\,M$$

On dilution,

$$M_1V_1 = M_2V_2$$
$$0.2 \times 10 = M_2 \times 100$$
$$M_2 = 0.02\,M$$

∴ On dilution, the final concentration of $CaCl_2$ will become 0.02 *M*.

$$\underset{\substack{0.02M}}{CaCl_2} \longrightarrow \underset{\substack{0.02M}}{Ca^{2+}} + \underset{\substack{2 \times 0.02}}{2Cl^-}$$

∴ The concentration of Cl^- ion in the resulting solution = 0.04 mol/L.

73. *(d)* $4Al + 3MnO_2 \longrightarrow 3Mn + 2Al_2O_3$

3 moles of MnO_2 reacts with 4 moles of Al.

∴ 1 mole of MnO_2 reacts = $\dfrac{4}{3}$ moles of Al

⇒ Amount of Al required to reduce 1 g mole of MnO_2 = $\dfrac{4}{3}$ g mol.

74. *(b)* Ethanol on reaction with alkaline $KMnO_4$ gives acetic acid (*X*), which when reacts with methanol in the presence of an acid gives methyl acetate (*Y*), which is a sweet smelling compound.

$$\underset{\substack{Ethanol}}{CH_3CH_2OH} \xrightarrow[KMnO_4]{Alkaline} \underset{\substack{Acetic\ Acid}}{CH_3COOH}(X)$$

$$CH_3COOH + \underset{\substack{Methanol}}{CH_3OH} \xrightarrow{H^+}$$

$$\underset{\substack{Methyl\ acetate \\ (Sweet\ smell)}}{CH_3COOCH_3}\,(Y) + H_2O$$

Thus, *X* and *Y* respectively are acetic acid and methyl acetate.

75. *(c)* Given,

pH of 10 mL of HCl solution = 4

∴ Concentration of H^+ ions = 10^{-4} M

After dilution,

pH of HCl becomes = 5

∴ Concentration of H^+ ions = 10^{-5} M

As we know,

$$M_1V_1 = M_2V_2$$
$$= 10^{-4} \times 10 = 10^{-5} \times V_2$$
$$V_2 = 100\,mL$$

So, 90 mL of water should be added for the pH change from 4 to 5.

76. *(c)* Ribosomes are the site where RNA is translated into protein. This process is called protein synthesis. Protein is needed for many cell functions such as repairing damage or directing chemical processes. Ribosomes can be found floating within the cytoplasm or attached to the endoplasmic reticulum.

77. *(d)* The cornea acts as the eye's outer most lens. It functions like as window that controls and focusses the entry of light into the eye (visual perception). The cornea contributes between 65-75 per cent of the eye's total focussing power. When light strikes the cornea, it bends or refracts the incoming light on to the lens. The cornea covers the pupil (the opening at the centre of the eye), iris (the coloured part of the eye), and anterior chamber (the fluid filled inside of the eye).

78. *(a)* One round of chromosome duplication followed by one round of cell division leads to equal number of chromosomes in the daughter cells as compared to the mother cell.

79. *(a)* Latitude and temperature are related to each other in a way that, as we approaches the equator, the temperature gets warmer and as we approaches the poles, it gets cooler. Since, same vegetation grows in the same climatic zone, therefore similar type of vegetation can be observed in the same latitude.

80. *(b)* Tree–Bird–Avian parasite does not represent an erect pyramid of number. Instead, it is an inverted pyramid of number. All ecological pyramids of number are erect except in parasitic food chain, where one primary producer supports numerous parasites which further support more hyperparasites.

PRACTICE
SETS (1-5)

PRACTICE SET 1
Stream : SA

MM : 100

Instructions

1. There are 80 questions in this paper.

2. This question paper contains two parts; Part I and Part II. There are four sections; Mathematics, Physics, Chemistry and Biology in each part.

3. Out of the four options given with each question, only one is correct.

➲ PART-I (1 Mark Questions)

MATHEMATICS

1. If $x = \sqrt{3} + 1$, then value of $x^4 + \dfrac{16}{x^4}$ is

(a) 54   (b) 55
(c) 58   (d) 56

2. Three friends Ajay, Vijay and Sanjay move along a circular path of length 1.2 km with speeds of 6 km/h, 8 km/h and 9 km/h respectively. Ajay and Vijay move in the same direction but Sanjay move in opposite direction, if they all start at the same time and from same place. How many time will Ajay and Sanjay meets anywhere on the path by the time Ajay and Vijay for the first time anywhere on the path?

(a) 6 times   (b) 7 times
(c) 8 times   (d) 9 times

3. A cone is within the cylinder and cylinder is within a cube touch by all vertical faces with same bases and height, then the ratio of their volume will be

(a) $14 : 11 : 13$ (b) $42 : 33 : 11$
(c) $56 : 36 : 22$ (d) None of these

4. When 10 is subtracted from each of the given observation, the mean is reduced to 60%. If 5 is added to all the given observation, the mean will be

(a) 25   (b) 30   (c) 60   (d) 65

5. In the given figure, AB is the diameter of the circle centered at O. If $\angle COA = 60°$, $AB = 2r$, $AC = d$ and $CD = l$, then l is equal to

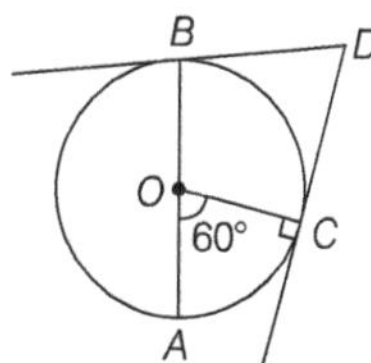

(a) $d\sqrt{3}$ (b) $\dfrac{d}{\sqrt{3}}$ (c) $3d$ (d) $\dfrac{\sqrt{3}d}{2}$

6. The sum of all integers x for which $x^4 + x^3 + x^2 + x + 1$ is a perfect square

(a) 2   (b) 4   (c) 3   (d) 6

7. The sum of all 3-digit numbers which are equal to 11 times the sum of squares of their digits is
(a) 1212 (b) 1353 (c) 1452 (d) 1364

8. If $2f(xy) = \{f(x)\}^y + \{f(y)\}^x$ for all $x, y \in R$, and $f(1) = 2$, then the value $f(5) - f(3)$ is equal to
(a) 12 (b) 24 (c) 36 (d) 48

9. A job has to completed by 12 boys in 15 days. If three boys are absent from the first day, then by what percentage should the remaining boys increase their rate of working to complete the job
(a) $33\dfrac{1}{3}\%$ (b) $22\dfrac{1}{2}\%$
(c) $40\dfrac{2}{3}\%$ (d) $30\dfrac{1}{3}\%$

10. The number of positive integer x which satisfies the condition $\left[\dfrac{x}{99}\right] = \left[\dfrac{x}{101}\right]$, where x is greatest integer functions
(a) 2499 (b) 2500
(c) 2501 (d) None of these

11. In a regular heptagon $ABCDEFG$ the side of heptagon is 1, then diagonals $\dfrac{1}{AC} + \dfrac{1}{AD}$ is equal to
(a) $\dfrac{1}{2}$ (b) $\dfrac{2}{3}$ (c) 1 (d) $\dfrac{1}{4}$

12. In the given figure, the length of AB is

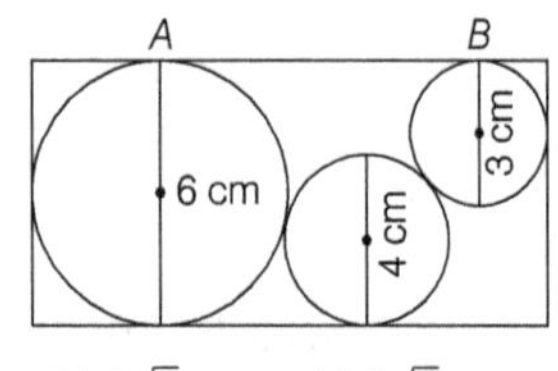

(a) 3 (b) $2\sqrt{6}$ (c) $3\sqrt{6}$ (d) 4

13. There are 20 units cubes all of whose faces are white, and 44 units cubes all of whose faces are red. They are put together to form a bigger cube ($4 \times 4 \times 4$). What is the minimum number of white visible on this larger cube?
(a) 20 (b) 14 (c) 12 (d) 8

14. A larger tanker can be filled by two pipes A and B in 60 min and 40 min respectively. How many minutes will take to fill the empty tanker if only B is used in the first half of the time and A and B are both used in the second half of the time?
(a) 15 (b) 20 (c) 27.5 (d) 30

15. If α and β are acute angles such that
$$\cos^2\alpha + \cos^2\beta = \frac{3}{2} \text{ and } \sin\alpha - \sin\beta = \frac{1}{4}, \text{ then } \alpha + \beta$$
equals
(a) $\dfrac{\pi}{6}$ (b) $\dfrac{\pi}{4}$ (c) $\dfrac{\pi}{3}$ (d) $\dfrac{\pi}{2}$

PHYSICS

16. A solid cylinder of mass m and length l is placed vertically on the ground.
If Y = Young's modulus of cylinder's material, then strain energy stored is

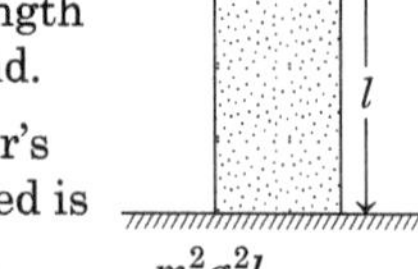

(a) $\dfrac{m^2g^2l}{3AY}$ (b) $\dfrac{m^2g^2l}{6AY}$ (c) $\dfrac{m^2g^2l}{2AY}$ (d) $\dfrac{m^2g^2l}{AY}$

17. A metallic wire is loaded at ends with two masses is placed over a slab of ice.

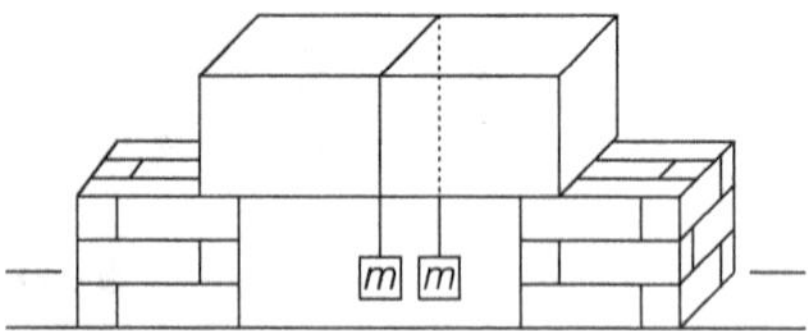

This wire passes through slab without splitting it into two pieces. This is due to
(a) depression of melting point
(b) elevation of melting point
(c) high conductivity of metal wire
(d) high specific heat of ice

18. Two identical boxes one of them is filled with nitrogen and other is filled with helium are put on a fast moving train.
If train is suddenly stopped, then what will be the ratio of rise of temperature of two boxes nearly?
(a) 2 : 1 (b) 1 : 4 (c) 4 : 7 (d) 1 : 1

19. A gas expands from state a to state b as shown below.

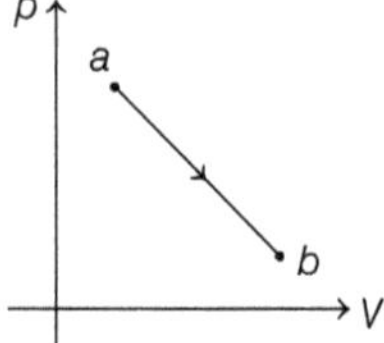

Temperature of gas during the above expansion process
(a) decreases continuously (b) increases continuously
(c) decreases then increases (d) increases then decreases

20. An elastic ball of mass m is suspended with an ideal thread. Another ball of same mass hits ball with velocity v_0 as shown below.

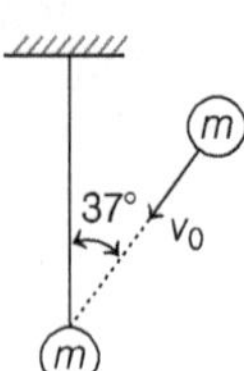

Impulsive tension in the string due to collision is
(a) mv_0 (b) $\dfrac{5}{7}mv_0$ (c) $\dfrac{18}{17}mv_0$ (d) $\dfrac{4}{9}mv_0$

21. A stationary radioactive nucleus decays as:

$$X \longrightarrow {}^{4}_{2}\text{He} + Y$$

If speed of α-particle is v, then speed of daughter nucleus Y will be

(a) $\dfrac{4v}{A-4}$ (b) $\dfrac{2v}{A-4}$

(c) $\dfrac{4v}{A+4}$ (d) $\dfrac{2v}{A+4}$

22. 30 g ice at 0°C is mixed with 25 g of steam at 100°C. The resulting mixture is

(Latent heat of fusion = 80 cal/g, latent heat of vapourisation = 540 cal/g and specific heat of water = 1 cal)

(a) water and ice at 0°C
(b) water at 100°C
(c) water and steam at 100°C
(d) water, ice and steam at 50°C

23. An object falling freely from rest covers a distance s in 5th second. Then, distance travelled by object in 7th second is

(a) $\dfrac{13}{9}s$ (b) $\dfrac{9}{13}s$ (c) $\dfrac{9}{11}s$ (d) $\dfrac{11}{9}s$

24. A pendulum bob is given a push when it is suspended freely.

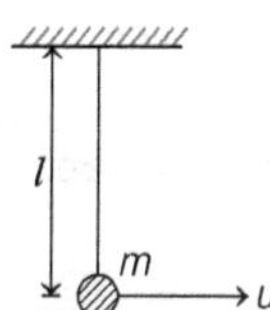

If bob successfully completes the vertical circle, then least ratio of kinetic energies at bottom and top of the circle is

(a) 2 : 1   (b) 5 : 1   (c) 7 : 1   (d) 1 : 2

25. A wood block is floating in benzene at 0°C.

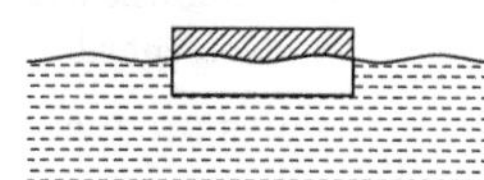

It is given,

Density of wood = 880 kg m^{-3}

Density of benzene = 900 kg m^{-3}

Cubical expansion coefficient of wood = 1.5×10^{-4} K^{-1}

Cubical expansion coefficient of benzene
$$= 1.2 \times 10^{-3} \text{ K}^{-1}$$

Minimum temperature at which wooden block just sink in is

(a) 22°C   (b) 10°C   (c) 12°C   (d) 15°C

26. Mass of the largest stone that can be moved by flowing water stream depends on density of water, acceleration due to gravity and velocity of flow. Then, mass m is proportional to

(a) v^2 (b) v^4 (c) v^6 (d) v^{-1}

27. A body falls through a viscous fluid starting from rest towards ground. Then, after a long time, which of the most likely to be correct?

(a) No energy is dissipated by body
(b) Rate of potential energy dissipation is constant
(c) Rate of kinetic energy dissipation is constant
(d) Whole of the energy of body can be dissipated before reaching ground

28. Identical blocks of wood are piled over each other as shown below.

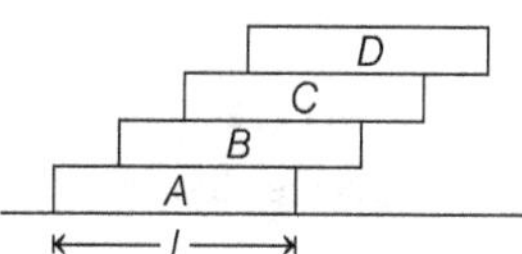

If length of each block is l, then maximum possible projection for topmost block is

(a) $\dfrac{l}{2}$ (b) $\dfrac{l}{3}$ (c) $\dfrac{l}{4}$ (d) $\dfrac{l}{6}$

29. For a two particle systems, kinetic energy K and potential energy U varies with separation r of particles as

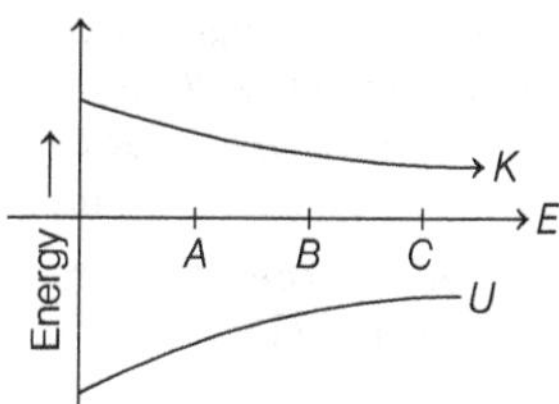

The system is a bound system for

(a) $r = r_A$ (b) $r = r_B$
(c) $r = r_C$ (d) all points A, B and C

30. A point source of light S, placed at a distance L in front of the centre of a plane mirror of width 1 m, hangs vertically on a wall.

A man walks in front of mirror along a line parallel.

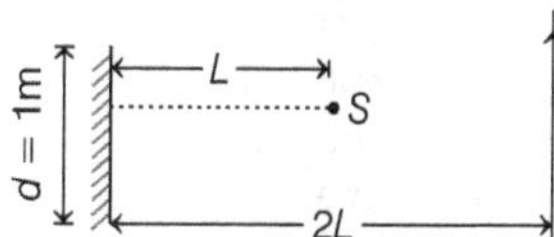

To the mirror at a distance $2L$ from mirror as shown in the above figure. Distance upto which source is visible to man is

(a) 1 m   (b) 2 m   (c) 3 m   (d) 4 m

CHEMISTRY

31. The correct order of the lattice energies of the following ionic compounds is

(a) $NaCl > MgBr_2 > CaO > Al_2O_3$
(b) $NaCl > CaO > MgBr_2 > Al_2O_3$
(c) $Al_2O_3 > MgBr_2 > CaO > NaCl$
(d) $Al_2O_3 > CaO > MgBr_2 > NaCl$

32. Average volume available to a molecule in a sample of ideal gas at STP is
(a) 3.72×10^{-20} cm^3 (b) 2.69×10^{19} cm^3
(c) 22400 cm^3 (d) $22400 \times 6.02 \times 10^{23}$ cm^3

33. Among the quantities, boiling point (I), entropy (II), pH (III) and emf of a cell (IV), intensive properties are
(a) Both I and II   (b) I, II and III
(c) I, III and IV   (d) All of these

34. The number of radial nodes of $3s$ and $2p$ -orbitals are respectively
(a) 2, 0   (b) 0, 2   (c) 1, 2   (d) 2, 1

35. A sulphur containing species that cannot be a reducing agent is
(a) SO_2 (b) SO_3^{2-} (c) H_2SO_4 (d) S^{2-}

36. The energy (in J) corresponding to light of wavelength 45 nm, is closest to
($h = 6.63 \times 10^{-34}$ Js, speed of light $= 3 \times 10^8$ ms^{-1})
(a) 6.63×10^8 (b) 6.67×10^{11}
(c) 4.42×10^{-15} (d) 4.42×10^{-18}

37. The reaction $N_2 + 3H_2 \longrightarrow 2NH_3$ is used to produce ammonia. When 450 g of hydrogen was reacted with nitrogen, 1575 g of ammonia were produced. The percentage yield of reaction is closest to
(a) 61.8   (b) 72.4   (c) 51.8   (d) 89.1

38. The number of isomers for the compound with the molecular formula $C_2BrClFI$ is
(a) 3   (b) 4   (c) 5   (d) 6

39. Time required to deposit one millimole of aluminium metal by the passage of 9.65 A through molten electrolyte containing aluminium ion is
(a) 30 s   (b) 10 s   (c) 30,000 s   (d) 10,000 s

40. The IUPAC name of the following compound is

(a) 4, 4, 3-trimethyl hex-1-yne
(b) 4, 4, 3-trimethyl hex-1-ene
(c) 3, 4, 4-trimethyl hex-1-yne
(d) 3, 4, 4-trimethyl hex-1-ene

41. Which of the following compounds will not undergo aldol condensation?
(a) Methanal   (b) 2-methyl pentanal
(c) Cyclohexanone   (d) 1-phenyl propanone

42. Which is the most basic compound among the given options?

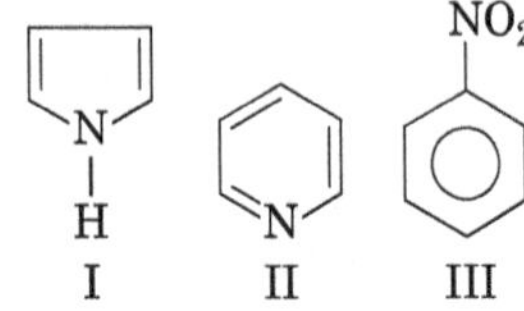

(a) I   (b) II   (c) III   (d) Both I and III

43. Clemmensen reduction of ketone is carried out in the presence of which of the following reagents?
(a) Zn-Hg with HCl   (b) LiAlH$_4$
(c) H$_2$ and Pt as a catalyst (d) Glycol with KOH

44. Standard electrode potential of three metals X, Y and Z are -1.2 V, $+0.5$ V and -3.0 V, respectively. The reducing power of these metals will be
(a) $Y > X > Z$ (b) $Z > X > Y$
(c) $X > Y > Z$ (d) $Y > Z > X$

45. When white phosphorus is heated with caustic soda, the compounds formed are
(a) $PH_3 + NaH_2PO_3$ (b) $PH_3 + NaH_2PO_2$
(c) $PH_3 + Na_2HPO_3$ (d) $PH_3 + NaH_2PO_4$

BIOLOGY

46. During urine formation, the filtration of blood at the glomerulus is
(a) an active process
(b) an osmotic process
(c) a pressure dependent physical process
(d) a non-energy-mediated transport process

47. Grave's disease is associated with
(a) insufficiency of thyroid hormones
(b) excess of thyroid hormones
(c) insufficiency of corticosteroids
(d) excess of growth hormones

48. 'Imperfect fungi' is a group represented by fungal species which have
(a) simple mycelia
(b) no known mechanism of sexual reproduction
(c) unknown phylogenetic relationship
(d) lost its survival mechanism against harsh environment

49. Which of the following is not a characteristic of phylum Chordata?
(a) Pharyngeal slits   (b) Amniotic egg
(c) Post-anal tail   (d) Notochord

50. The energy rich fuel molecules produced in the TCA cycle are
(a) 2 GTP, 2 NADH and 1 FADH$_2$
(b) 1 GTP, 2 NADH and 2 FADH$_2$
(c) 1 GTP, 3 NADH and 1 FADH$_2$
(d) 2 GTP and 3 NADH

51. In *Drosophila melanogaster* males, homologous chromosomes pair and segregate during meiosis but crossing over does not occur. At which stage of meiosis does segregation of 2 alleles of a gene take place in their individuals?
(a) Zygotene   (b) Diakinesis
(c) Anaphase-I   (d) Anaphase-II

52. Excess oxygen consumed after a vigorous exercise is
(a) to pump out lactic acid from muscle
(b) to increase the concentration of lactic acid in muscle
(c) to reduce dissolved carbon dioxide in blood
(d) to make ATP for gluconeogenesis

53. Mark the correct relationship
(a) $\psi_w = \psi_p - (\psi_\pi + \psi_m)$
(b) $\psi_w = \psi_p + \psi_s + \psi_m$
(c) $\psi_w = \psi_p + \psi_\pi - \psi_m$
(d) None of these

54. Hydrogen bonds occur between which of the following constituents of DNA?
(a) Sugar and base
(b) Phosphate and base
(c) Complementary bases
(d) Phosphate and sugar

55. Which one of the following neurotransmitters is secreted by the pre-ganglionic neurons of sympathetic nervous system?
(a) Epinephrine
(b) Acetylcholine
(c) Dopamine
(d) Nor-epinephrine

56. Which of the following statements about evolution is incorrect?
(a) Evolution is the product of natural selection
(b) Evolution is goal-oriented
(c) Prokaryotes evolve faster than eukaryotes
(d) Evolution need not always lead to a better phenotype

57. Which one of the following compounds is generally translocated in the phloem?
(a) Sucrose
(b) D-glucose
(c) D-mannose
(d) D-fructose

58. Which organelles would be more prominent in a secretory cell than in a non-secretory cell?
(a) Golgi bodies
(b) Lysosomes
(c) Mitochondria
(d) Pinocytic vesicles

59. In the conversion of RuBP to GP (PGA)
(a) a molecule of carbon dioxide is accepted
(b) a stable six-carbon molecule is produced
(c) ATP is generated
(d) hydrogen is combined with oxygen to form water

60. Adventitious roots develop in
(a) creepers
(b) trailers
(c) twinners
(d) All of these

➔ PART-II (2 Marks Questions)

MATHEMATICS

61. Let $P(a, b)$ be a variable point satisfying $4 \le a^2 + b^2 \le 9$ and $b^2 - 4ab + a^2 \le 0$. Let R be the complete equation represented in XY-plane in which P can lie, the area of region R is
(a) $\dfrac{2\pi}{3}$
(b) π
(c) $\dfrac{4\pi}{3}$
(d) $\dfrac{5\pi}{3}$

62. Let $S_1(n)$ be the sum of first n terms of arithmetic progression 8, 12, 16, ... and let $S_2(n)$ be the sum of the first n terms of arithmetic progression 17, 19, 21, ... if for some value of n, $S_1(n) = S_2(n)$, then this common sum is
(a) 216
(b) 260
(c) 200
(d) None of these

63. On a card, the following three statements are found
  1. on this card exactly one statement is false
  2. on this card exactly two statement are false
  3. on this card exactly three statement are false

The number of false statement on the card is exactly
(a) 0
(b) 1
(c) 2
(d) 3

64. $\triangle ABC$ is right angled at A. The circle with centre A and radius AB cuts BC and AC internally at D and E respectively. If $BD = 20$ and $DC = 16$, then the length AC equals
(a) $6\sqrt{21}$
(b) $6\sqrt{26}$
(c) 30
(d) 32

65. The coefficient of x^{30} in the expansion of $(1 + 2x + 3x^2 + \dots + 20x^{19} + 21x^{20})^2$ is
(a) 2706
(b) 2450
(c) 1481
(d) 256

PHYSICS

66. A thin rod of length $f/3$ is placed along the principal axis of a concave mirror of focal length f such that its image which is real and elongated just touches the rod. Linear magnification obtained is
(a) 1
(b) $\dfrac{3}{2}$
(c) $\dfrac{1}{2}$
(d) $\dfrac{5}{2}$

67. Cube of side a is located in three dimensional cartesian space as shown in the figure given below.

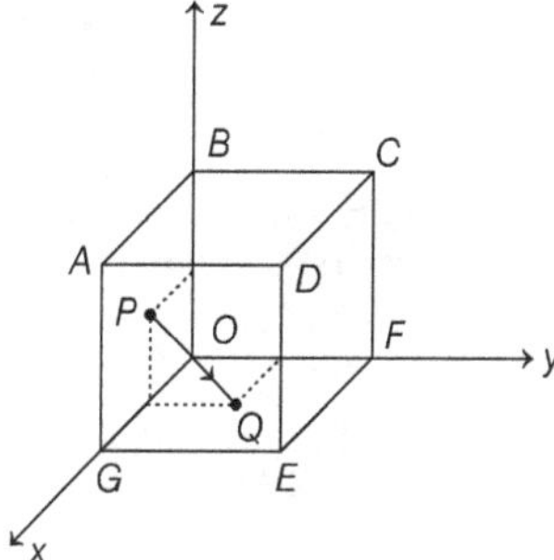

Unit vector in the direction PQ (from centre of face $ABOG$ to centre of face $OGEF$) is
(a) $-\sqrt{2}\hat{j} - \sqrt{2}\hat{k}$
(b) $-\sqrt{2}\hat{j} + \sqrt{2}\hat{k}$
(c) $\dfrac{1}{\sqrt{2}}\hat{j} - \dfrac{1}{\sqrt{2}}\hat{k}$
(d) $-\dfrac{1}{2}\hat{j} + \dfrac{1}{\sqrt{2}}\hat{k}$

68. In given circuit, cells have zero internal resistances. Power dissipated in resistors $R_1 = 20\,\Omega$ and $R_2 = 20\,\Omega$ is

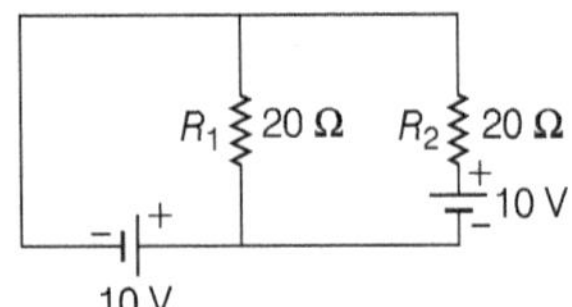

(a) $P_1 = 5\,\text{W}, P_2 = 0\,\text{W}$ (b) $P_1 = 10\,\text{W}, P_2 = 5\,\text{W}$
(c) $P_1 = 5\,\text{W}, P_2 = 5\,\text{W}$ (d) $P_1 = 5\,\text{W}, P_2 = 10\,\text{W}$

69. A piece of wood of mass 0.03 kg is dropped from the top of a 100 m high building. At same instant, a bullet of mass 0.02 kg is fired from the ground, with a velocity of 100 ms^{-1} along same vertical line. Bullet gets embedded in block of wood. Height to which combined system rises above the top of the building is (Take, $g = 10\,\text{ms}^{-2}$)

(a) 10 m   (b) 40 m   (c) 30 m   (d) 20 m

70. If force F, length L and time T are chosen as fundamental quantities, then mass is

(a) $[FL^{-1}\,T^{-2}]$ (b) $[FL^{-1}T^{2}]$
(c) $[FL\,T^{-2}]$ (d) $[FL^{0}\,T^{-2}]$

CHEMISTRY

71. 10 dm^3 of an ideal monoatomic gas at 27°C and 1.01×10^5 N·m^{-2} pressure heated at constant pressure to 127°C. Thus, entropy change in JK^{-1} is

(a) 2.422   (b) 5.98
(c) -2.422 (d) -5.981

72. What is the mass of precipitate formed when 50 mL of 16.9% solution of $AgNO_3$ is mixed with 50 mL of 5.8% NaCl solution ?
(Molar mass of Ag = 107.8, N = 14, O = 16, Na = 23 and Cl = 35.5)

(a) 28 g   (b) 3.5 g   (c) 7 g   (d) 14 g

73. Which of the following diatomic molecules would be stabilised by removal of an electron?

(a) C_2 (b) CN
(c) N_2 (d) O_2

74. When calcium carbide is hydrolysed, compound X is formed as a major product, which then reacts with dilute sulphuric acid in the presence of mercuric sulphate, a compound Y is formed. Compounds X and Y are

(a) C_2H_2 and CH_3CHO
(b) CH_4 and HCOOH
(c) C_2H_4 and CH_3COOH
(d) C_2H_2 and CH_3COOH

75. $C_5H_{12} + Cl_2 \xrightarrow{\text{Light}} \underset{B}{C_5H_{11}Cl} \xrightarrow{\text{Na/ether}} C$
   $\underset{A}{}$

Only one structure is possible for B. Identify A, B and C in the reaction

(a) $CH_3C(CH_3)_2CH_3$, $CH_3C(CH_3)_2CH_2Cl$, $CH_3C(CH_3)_2CH_2CH_2C(CH_3)_2CH_3$
(b) $CH_3CHCH_2CH_3$, $CH_3C(Cl)(CH_3)CH_2CH_3CH_3$, $CH_2C(CH_3)_2C(CH_3)_2CH_2CH_3$
(c) Both (a) and (b)
(d) None of the above

BIOLOGY

76. Which one of the following statements regarding plant growth hormones is correct?

(a) Gibberellins do not play any role in flowering
(b) Auxin and cytokinin inhibit cell division
(c) ABA inhibits root growth and promotes shoot growth at low water potential
(d) ABA promotes leaf senescence independent of ethylene

77. A woman with one gene for haemophilia and a gene for colourblindness on one of the X-chromosomes marries a normal man. How will the progeny be?

(a) All sons and daughters haemophilic and colourblind
(b) 50% haemophilic colourblind sons and 50% colourblind carrier daughters
(c) 50% haemophilic daughters and 50% colourblind daughters
(d) Haemophilic and colourblind daughters

78. Which one of the following relationships is true in water at 25°C?

(a) $[OH^-] = [H_2O^-]$ (b) $[H^+] = [H_2O]$
(c) $K_w > 1 \times 10^{-14}$ (d) $[H^+] = [OH^-]$

79. Identify the correct match between the animal (flatworm, earthworm, roundworm) and its body cavity type (acoelomate, coelomate, pseudocoelomate).

(a) Roundworm–Pseudocoelomate; Earthworm–Acoelomate; Flatworm–Coelomate
(b) Roundworm–Acoelomate; Earthworm–Coelomate; Flatworm–Acoelomate
(c) Roundworm–Pseudocoelomate; Earthworm–Coelomate; Flatworm–Acoelomate
(d) Roundworm–Coelomate; Earthworm–Pseudocoelomate; Flatworm–Acoelomate

80. A sequence of amino acids may end in either an amino group (—NH$_2$) or a carboxyl group (—COOH). What is the theoretical number of chemically different dipeptides that may be assembled from 20 different amino acids?

(a) 40   (b) 80   (c) 160   (d) 400

Answers

1	*(d)*	2	*(b)*	3	*(b)*	4	*(b)*	5	*(a)*	6	*(a)*	7	*(b)*	8	*(b)*	9	*(a)*	10	*(a)*
11	*(c)*	12	*(c)*	13	*(c)*	14	*(d)*	15	*(c)*	16	*(b)*	17	*(a)*	18	*(a)*	19	*(d)*	20	*(c)*
21	*(a)*	22	*(c)*	23	*(a)*	24	*(b)*	25	*(a)*	26	*(c)*	27	*(b)*	28	*(d)*	29	*(d)*	30	*(c)*
31	*(d)*	32	*(a)*	33	*(c)*	34	*(a)*	35	*(c)*	36	*(c)*	37	*(a)*	38	*(d)*	39	*(a)*	40	*(c)*
41	*(a)*	42	*(b)*	43	*(a)*	44	*(b)*	45	*(b)*	46	*(c)*	47	*(b)*	48	*(b)*	49	*(b)*	50	*(c)*
51	*(c)*	52	*(d)*	53	*(b)*	54	*(c)*	55	*(b)*	56	*(b)*	57	*(a)*	58	*(a)*	59	*(a)*	60	*(a)*

61	*(d)*	62	*(b)*	63	*(c)*	64	*(b)*	65	*(a)*	66	*(b)*	67	*(b)*	68	*(a)*	69	*(b)*	70	*(b)*
71	*(a)*	72	*(c)*	73	*(d)*	74	*(a)*	75	*(a)*	76	*(d)*	77	*(b)*	78	*(d)*	79	*(c)*	80	*(d)*

Solutions

1. *(d)* We have, $x = \sqrt{3} + 1$

Both sides squarring, we get

$\Rightarrow \quad x^2 = 3 + 2\sqrt{3} + 1 = 4 + 2\sqrt{3}$

$\Rightarrow \quad \dfrac{4}{x^2} = \dfrac{4}{4 + 2\sqrt{3}} = \dfrac{4}{2(2 + \sqrt{3})}$

$\qquad = 2(2 - \sqrt{3}) = 4 - 2\sqrt{3}$

$\Rightarrow x^4 + \dfrac{16}{x^4} = \left(x^2 + \dfrac{4}{x^2}\right)^2 - 8$

$\qquad = (4 + 2\sqrt{3} + 4 - 2\sqrt{3})^2 - 8$

$\qquad = (8)^2 - 8 = 64 - 8 = 56$

2. *(b)* Time taken by Ajay and Vijay to meet first time anywhere on the path

$= \dfrac{\text{Distance}}{\text{Relative speed}} = \dfrac{1.2}{8.6} = 0.6\,\text{h}$

Time taken by Ajay and Sanjay to meet anywhere

$= \dfrac{\text{Distance}}{\text{Relative speed}} = \dfrac{1.2}{9 + 6} = 0.8\,\text{h}$

The number of times Ajay and Sanjay meets anywhere on the path by the time Ajay and Vijay meets each other for the

first time $= \dfrac{36}{4.8} = 7\dfrac{1}{2}$, i.e. 7 times.

3. *(b)* Let the side of cube $= x$

$\therefore$ Radius of cylinder = Radius of cone $= \dfrac{x}{2}$

Height of cylinder = Height of cone $= x$

Volume of cube $(V_1) = x^3$

Volume of cylinder

$(V_2) = \pi \left(\dfrac{x}{2}\right)^2 \cdot x = \dfrac{\pi x^3}{4}$

Volume of cone

$(V_3) = \dfrac{1}{3} \pi \left(\dfrac{x}{2}\right)^2 \cdot x = \dfrac{\pi x^3}{12}$

$\therefore V_1 : V_2 : V_3 = x^3 : \dfrac{\pi x^3}{4} : \dfrac{\pi x^3}{12}$

$\qquad = 1 : \dfrac{\pi}{4} : \dfrac{\pi}{12}$

$\qquad = 1 : \dfrac{22}{28} : \dfrac{22}{84}$

$\qquad = 42 : 33 : 11$

4. *(b)* Let the observation are

$x_1, x_2, x_3, \ldots, x_n$

$\therefore \quad \bar{x} = \dfrac{\displaystyle\sum_{i=1}^{n} x_i}{n}$

When 10 is subtracted from each observation, then mean $= \bar{x} - 10$

$\therefore \quad \bar{x} - 10 = 60\%$ of $\bar{x}$

$\Rightarrow \bar{x} - 10 = \dfrac{60}{100} \bar{x}$

$\Rightarrow \bar{x} - \dfrac{3}{5} \bar{x} = 10 \Rightarrow \bar{x} = 25$

When 5 is added to each observation, then new mean is $25 + 5 = 30$

5. *(a)* Given, $\angle COA = 60°$

$AO = OB = OC = r$

In $\triangle AOC$, $AO = CO = r$ and $\angle COA = 60°$

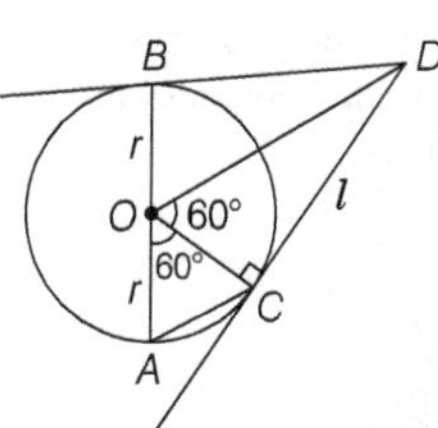

$\therefore \triangle AOC$ is an equilateral triangle.

$\therefore \qquad AC = d = r$

$DB = DC = l$

[$\because$ two tangents are equal from external points]

$\Rightarrow \quad \angle BOD = \angle COD = \dfrac{1}{2} \angle BOC$

$\Rightarrow \quad \angle BOC = 180° - \angle COA$

$\qquad = 180° - 60° = 120°$

$\Rightarrow \quad COD = \dfrac{1}{2} \angle BOC = \dfrac{1}{2} \times 120° = 60°$

In $\triangle OCD$, $\tan \angle COA = \dfrac{CD}{OC}$

$\Rightarrow \quad \tan 60° = \dfrac{l}{d}$

$\Rightarrow \qquad l = d\sqrt{3}$

6. *(a)* Let $y^2 = x^4 + x^3 + x^2 + x + 1$

Consider $\left(x^2 + \dfrac{x}{2}\right)^2 = x^4 + x^3 + \dfrac{x^2}{4}$

$\qquad = x^4 + x^3 + x^2 + x + 1 - \left(\dfrac{3}{4} x^2 + x + 1\right)$

$\qquad = y^2 - \dfrac{1}{4} (3x^2 + 4x + 4)$

As discriminant of $3x^2 + 4x + 4$ is negative.

$\therefore \qquad 3x^2 + 4x + 4 > 0$

Thus, $\left(x^2 + \dfrac{x}{2}\right)^2 < y^2$

$\Rightarrow \qquad |y| > \left|x^2 + \dfrac{x}{2}\right|$

But $x^2 + \dfrac{x}{2} = \left(x + \dfrac{1}{2}\right) x$ is non-negative,

$\forall x \in I$

$\left|x^2 + \dfrac{x}{2}\right| = x^2 + \dfrac{x}{2} < |y|$

If x is even, then $|y| \ge x^2 + \dfrac{x}{2} + 1$

$\Rightarrow \qquad y^2 \ge x^4 + x^3 + x^2 + x + 1 + \dfrac{5}{4}x^2$

$\Rightarrow \qquad y^2 \ge y^2 + \dfrac{5}{4}x^2$

which is not possible.

If $x \ne 0$, then $x = 0$ is the only solution when x is even.

If x is odd, then $x^2 + \dfrac{x}{2} + \dfrac{1}{x}$ is an integer.

So, $|y| \ge \left(x^2 + \dfrac{x}{2}\right) + \dfrac{1}{2}$

In this case,

$y^2 \ge x^4 + x^3 + x^2 + x + 1 + \left(\dfrac{x^2}{4} - \dfrac{x}{2} - \dfrac{3}{4}\right)$

i.e. $\quad y^2 \ge y^2 + \left(\dfrac{x^2}{4} - \dfrac{x}{2} - \dfrac{3}{4}\right)$

$\qquad = y^2 + \dfrac{1}{4}(x^2 - 2x - 3)$

and hence $\dfrac{1}{4}(x^2 - 2x - 3) \le 0$

$\qquad x^2 - 2x - 3 \le 0 \qquad x \in [-1, 3]$

$\therefore$ There are exactly 3 integer $0, -1$ and 3 for which the expression is perfect square and sum $= 0 - 1 + 3 = 2$

7. *(b)* Let three-digits number are

$\qquad 100a + 10b + c$

Given, $100a + 10b + c = 11(a^2 + b^2 + c^2)$ ...(i)

$(99a + 11b) + (a - b + c) = 11(a^2 + b^2 + c^2)$

$99a + 11b$ is divisible by 11.

$\therefore a + b + c$ is must divisible by 11.

Hence, so, $a - b + c$

$\qquad -8 \le a - b + c \le 18$

We conclude $a - b + c$ is either 0 or 11.

Now, putting $b = a + c$ in Eq. (i), we get

$100a + 10(a + c) + c = 11[a^2 + (a + c)^2 + c^2]$

$\Rightarrow \quad 2a^2 + (2c - 10)a + 2c^2 - c = 0$

$\therefore$ The first two terms of this expression are even third term should be even as well

$\Rightarrow c$ is even

$D = (2c - 10)^2 - 4 \times 2(2c^2 - c)$

$\quad = 4(-3c^2 - 8c + 25)$ is a square of $c = 0$

When $c = 0$

$\therefore \quad 2a^2 - 10a = 0 \Rightarrow a = 5, a \ne 0$

$b = a + c \Rightarrow b = 5 + 0 = 5$

$\therefore$ Number are 550

Now, when $b = a + c - 11$

$\therefore 2a^2 + (2c - 32a) + 2c^2 - 23c + 131 = 0$

$D = 4(-3c^2 + 14c - 16)$ is square $c = 3$

$\because 2a^2 - 26a + 80 = 0, a = 5, a \ne 8$

$\therefore b = a + c = 5 + 3 = 8$

$\therefore$ Number are 803

$\therefore$ Sum $= 550 + 803 = 1353$

8. *(b)* We have,

$\qquad 2f(xy) = \{f(x)\}^y + \{f(y)\}^x$

Putting $y = 1$

$\therefore \qquad 2f(x) = f(x) + \{f(1)\}^x$

$\qquad f(x) = 2^x$

$\therefore \qquad f(5) = 2^5 = 32$ and $f(3) = 2^3 = 8$

$\qquad f(5) - f(3) = 32 - 8 = 24$

9. *(a)* $M_1 = 12$ boys, $D_1 = 15$ days,

$R_1 = $ Rate of working

$M_2 = 9$ boys, $D_2 = 15$ days, $R_2 = $ Rate of working

$\therefore \qquad M_1 D_1 R_1 = M_2 D_2 R_2$

$\Rightarrow \quad 12 \times 15 \times R_1 = 9 \times 15 \times R_2$

$\Rightarrow \qquad \dfrac{R_1}{R_2} = \dfrac{9}{12} = \dfrac{3}{4}$

$\Rightarrow \qquad \dfrac{R_2}{R_1} = \dfrac{4}{3}$

Percentage increase $= \dfrac{(R_2 - R_1)}{R_1} \times 100$

$\qquad = \left(\dfrac{R_2}{R_1} - 1\right) \times 100$

$\qquad = \left(\dfrac{4}{3} - 1\right) \times 100$

$\qquad = \dfrac{1}{3} \times 100$

$\qquad = 33\dfrac{1}{3}\%$

10. *(a)* We know,

$\left[\dfrac{x}{K - 1}\right] = \left[\dfrac{x}{K + 1}\right]$ when $K \ge 2$

Then, $x = \dfrac{K^2 - 4}{4}$ when K is even and

$\dfrac{K^2 - 5}{4}$ is when K is odd.

$\therefore \quad \left[\dfrac{x}{100 - 1}\right] = \left[\dfrac{x}{100 + 1}\right]$

$K = 100$ which is even.

$\therefore$ Positive integers of $x = \dfrac{100^2 - 4}{4}$

$\qquad = (25)^2 - 1 = 2500 - 1$

$\qquad = 2499$

11. *(c)* Reflect the heptagon with AG as an axis to obtain another heptagon $AB'C'D'E'F'G'$

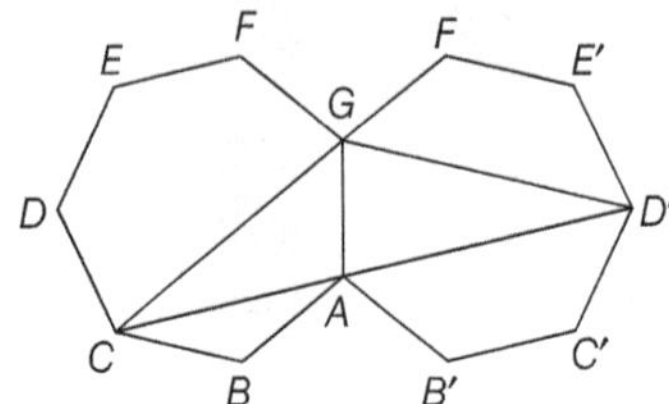

$\angle ABC = \dfrac{5\pi}{7}$

$\qquad BC = AC$

$\therefore \qquad \angle BAC = \angle BCA$

$\qquad = \dfrac{1}{2}\left(\pi - \dfrac{5\pi}{7}\right) = \dfrac{\pi}{7}$

$\therefore \angle GAC + \angle GAD' = \dfrac{4\pi}{7} + \dfrac{3\pi}{7} = \pi$

Hence, CAD' are collinear.

$\qquad \angle GCA = \angle GD'A = \dfrac{\pi}{7}$

$\Rightarrow \qquad \angle CAB = \angle ACB$

$\therefore \qquad \Delta GCD' \sim \Delta BAC$

$\qquad \dfrac{GC}{BA} = \dfrac{CD'}{AC} = \dfrac{GD'}{BC}$

$\Rightarrow \qquad \dfrac{AC}{BA} = \dfrac{CD'}{GC} = \dfrac{CA + AD'}{AD}$

$\qquad\qquad [\because GC = GD = AD]$

$\Rightarrow \qquad \dfrac{AC}{AB} = \dfrac{AC + AD}{AD}$

$\Rightarrow \dfrac{1}{AB} = \dfrac{AC + AD}{AC \cdot AD} = \dfrac{1}{AC} + \dfrac{1}{AD}$

$\Rightarrow \dfrac{1}{AC} + \dfrac{1}{AD} = \dfrac{1}{AB} = 1 \qquad [\because AB = 1]$

12. *(c)* We have, radius of circle are 3, 2 and 1.5, respectively.

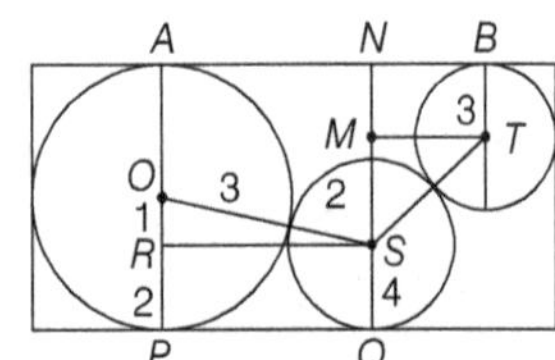

In ΔORS,

$\qquad OR = OP - RP$

$\Rightarrow \qquad OR = 3 - 2 = 1 [\because RP = SQ = 2]$

$\Rightarrow \qquad OS = 3 + 2 = 5$

$\therefore \qquad RS^2 = PQ^2 = OS^2 - OR^2$

$\qquad = (5)^2 - (1)^2 = 25 - 1 = 24$

$\Rightarrow \qquad PQ = \sqrt{24} = 2\sqrt{6}$

In ΔSMT,

$\qquad SM = QM - SQ$

$\qquad = 4.5 - 2 = 2.5$

$\qquad\qquad [\because QM = AP - BT]$

$\qquad ST = 2 + 1.5 = 3.5$

$\qquad MT^2 = ST^2 - SM^2$

$\qquad = (3.5)^2 - (2.5)^2$

$\qquad = 12.25 - 6.25 = 6$

$\qquad MT = \sqrt{6}$

$\therefore \qquad AB = AN + NB$

$\qquad = PQ + MT$

$\qquad = 2\sqrt{6} + \sqrt{6} = 3\sqrt{6}$

13. *(c)* Given, $4 \times 4 \times 4$ cubes is made 64 faces $1 \times 1 \times 1$ cubes.

Total cubes = 64, White = 20, Red = 44

To find minimum number of visible white box counting total visible faces of unit cube.

Total number of faces of small cube on bigger cube except boundary cubes

$$= 4 \times 6 = 24$$

Counting boundary cubes

$$= 16 + 8 + 8 = 32$$

$\therefore$ Total visible faces = 56

But we have 44 red cube.

$\therefore$ Minimum number of white faces cubes which are visible = $56 - 44 = 12$

14. *(d)* Let x minute will be taken. In one minute A can fill the $\dfrac{1}{60}$ part of tanker and in one minute B can fill the $\dfrac{1}{40}$ part of tanker.

Both can fill in t minute

$$\frac{t}{60} + \frac{t}{40} = 1$$

$$\Rightarrow \qquad t = 24 \text{ min}$$

Both can fill in one minute $\dfrac{1}{24}$ part of tanker

$$1 = \left(\frac{x}{2}\right)\left(\frac{1}{40}\right) + \frac{x}{2} \cdot \left(\frac{1}{24}\right)$$

$$\Rightarrow \frac{x}{2}\left(\frac{1}{40} + \frac{1}{24}\right) = 1$$

$$\Rightarrow \quad \frac{x}{2}\left(\frac{3+5}{120}\right) = 1 \Rightarrow x = \frac{120 \times 2}{8}$$

$$\Rightarrow \qquad x = 30 \text{ min}$$

15. *(c)* We have,

$$\Rightarrow \qquad \cos^2 \alpha + \cos^2 \beta = \frac{3}{2}$$

$$\Rightarrow \quad \frac{1 + \cos 2\alpha}{2} + \frac{1 + \cos 2\beta}{2} = \frac{3}{2}$$

$$\Rightarrow \qquad \cos 2\alpha + \cos 2\beta = 1$$

$$\Rightarrow \quad 2 \cos (\alpha + \beta) \cos (\alpha - \beta) = 1$$

$$\Rightarrow \quad \cos (\alpha + \beta) \cos (\alpha - \beta) = \frac{1}{2} \qquad \text{...(i)}$$

and $$\qquad \sin \alpha \sin \beta = \frac{1}{4}$$

$$\Rightarrow \qquad 2 \sin \alpha \sin \beta = \frac{1}{2}$$

$$\Rightarrow \quad \cos (\alpha - \beta) - \cos (\alpha + \beta) = \frac{1}{2} \qquad \text{...(ii)}$$

From Eqs. (i) and (ii), we get

$$\cos (\alpha + \beta) \cos (\alpha - \beta) - \cos (\alpha - \beta)$$
$$+ \cos (\alpha + \beta) = 0$$

$$\Rightarrow \quad \cos (\alpha + \beta) = \frac{1}{2} \text{ and } \cos (\alpha - \beta) = 1$$

$$\therefore \qquad \alpha + \beta = \frac{\pi}{3}$$

16. *(b)* $dU = \dfrac{1}{2}\left(\dfrac{mgx}{9A}\right)^2 \cdot A \cdot dx$

$$U = \frac{1}{2} \frac{m^2 g^2 A}{l^2 A^2 Y} \int_0^l x^2 \, dx$$

$$= \frac{m^2 g^2 l}{6 A Y}.$$

17. *(a)* Ice melts at lower temperature due to increase in pressure. As wire passes, the water formed is again freezes and hence wire passes without cutting ice.

18. *(a)* Conservation of energy gives,

$$\frac{1}{2} m u^2 = \Delta U$$

$$\Rightarrow \qquad \frac{1}{2} m u^2 = n C_V \Delta T$$

$$\Rightarrow \qquad \Delta T = \frac{m u^2}{2 n C_V} = \frac{n M u^2}{2 n C_V} = \frac{M u^2}{2 C_V}$$

$$\therefore \frac{\Delta T_{N_2}}{\Delta T_{He}} = \frac{(M_{N_2} \cdot C_{V_{He}})}{(M_{He} \cdot C_{V_{N_2}})} = \frac{14}{4} \times \frac{\frac{3}{2} R}{\frac{5}{2} R}$$

$$= \frac{21}{10} \approx \frac{2}{1}$$

19. *(d)* We plot process along with isotherms.

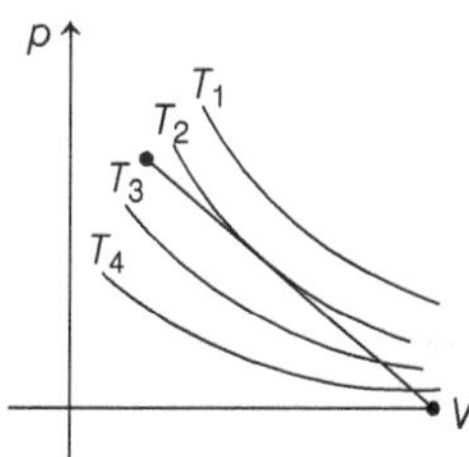

Clearly, temperature initially increases then decreases.

20. *(c)* Linear momentum is conserved in the horizontal direction.

$$\Rightarrow m v_0 \sin 37° + 0 = m V - m v \sin 37°$$

Along common normal,

$$e(v_0 - 0) = V \sin 37° + v$$

$$\Rightarrow \qquad V = \frac{27}{34} v_0 \text{ and } v = \frac{11}{34} v_0$$

So, impulsive tension

$$= m v_0 \cos 37° + m v \cos 37°$$

$$= m v_0 \left(\frac{4}{5}\right) + m v_0 \left(\frac{11}{34} \times \frac{4}{5}\right)$$

$$= m v_0 \left(\frac{18}{17}\right)$$

21. *(a)* By momentum conservation,

$$4v = (A - 4)v'$$

$$\Rightarrow \qquad v' = \frac{4v}{A - 4}$$

22. *(c)* Heat required to melt ice

$$= Q_1 = mL = 30 \times 80 = 240 \text{ cal}$$

Heat taken by water formed to reach at 100°C, $Q_2 = ms\Delta T = 3000$ cal

Heat given by steam on condensation

$$= Q_3 = mL = 25 \times 540 = 13500 \text{ cal}$$

As heat taken by ice is less than heat given by steam on condensation. So, resulting mixture is at 100°C.

Steam condensed

$$= \frac{\text{Maximum heat absorbed by ice}}{\text{Latent heat of vapourization}}$$

$$= \frac{5400}{50} = 10 \text{ g}$$

So, resulting mixture contains $(30 + 10 = 40 \text{ g})$ of water and $(25 - 10 = 15 \text{ g})$ of steam at 100°C.

23. *(a)* For a freely falling body, distances travelled in each successive second increases in the ratio of successive odd integers.

i.e. $s_1 : s_2 : s_3 : s_4 : s_5 : s_6 : s_7 :: 1 : 3 : 5 : 7 : 9 : 11 : 13$

$$\Rightarrow \qquad \frac{s_5}{s_7} = \frac{9}{13} \Rightarrow s_7 = \frac{13}{9} s_5$$

24. *(b)* For successful rotation,

$$v_{\text{bottom}} = \sqrt{5gl}$$

$$v_{\text{top}} = \sqrt{gl}$$

These values are minimum possible values.

So, ratio of kinetic energies,

$$\frac{K_{\text{bottom}}}{K_{\text{top}}} = \frac{\frac{1}{2} m v_{\text{bottom}}^2}{\frac{1}{2} m v_{\text{top}}^2} = 5 : 1$$

25. *(a)* Wooden block sinks, when Density of wood = Density of benzene

$$\Rightarrow \qquad \frac{\rho_w}{1 + r_w \Delta T} = \frac{\rho_b}{1 + r_b \Delta T}$$

$$\Rightarrow \qquad \Delta T = \frac{\rho_b - \rho_w}{\rho_w r_w - \rho_b r_b} = 21.7°\text{C}$$

So, at 22°C wood block sinks in benzene.

26. *(c)* $m = k \rho^a g^b v^c$

$$\Rightarrow \quad [M] = [M^a L^{-3a + b + c} T^{-2b - c}]$$

$$\Rightarrow \qquad a = 1, b = -3, c = 6$$

$$\therefore \qquad m \propto v^6$$

27. *(b)* After a long time, terminal velocity is attained to kinetic energy is constant and only potential energy is dissipated at a constant rate.

28. *(d)* $2wx = w\left(\dfrac{l}{2} - x\right) \Rightarrow x = \dfrac{l}{6}$

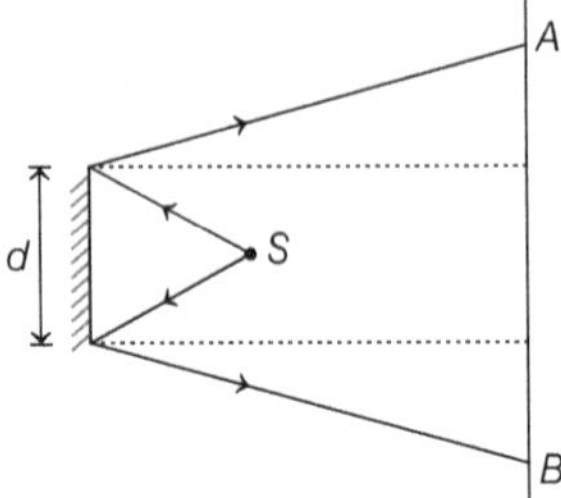

29. *(d)* As total energy of system $(U + K)$ is negative for all values of r, system is a bound system.

30. *(c)* From ray diagram,

Distance, $AB = d + d + d = 3d$

∴ Distance required $= 3$ m.

31. *(d)* Lattice energy is defined as the amount of energy required to completely seperate one mole of a solid ionic compound into gaseous constituent ions. It is directly proportional to the charge of the ions. Thus, greater the ionic charge, larger is the lattice energy.

Hence, correct order is

$$Al_2O_3 > CaO > MgBr_2 > NaCl$$

32. *(a)* One mole of ideal gas at STP (22.4 L) contains 6.022×10^{23} atoms i.e., 6.022×10^{23} atoms are present in 22400 mL.

∴ Average volume per molecule

$$= \dfrac{22400}{6.022 \times 10^{23}} \text{ cm}^3$$

$$= 3.72 \times 10^{-20} \text{ cm}^3$$

33. *(c)* Intensive properties are those properties which do not depend upon the quantity or size of matter. Among the given quantities, boiling point (I), pH (III) and emf (IV) are intensive properties whereas entropy (II) is an extensive property.

34. *(a)* Number of radial nodes

$$= n - l - 1$$

For 3 s-orbital

$$n = 3, l = 0$$

∴ Number of radial nodes $= 3 - 0 - 1 = 2$

For 2p-orbital, $n = 2, l = 1$

Number of radial nodes $= 2 - 1 - 1 = 0$

35. *(c)* If the specie is a reducing agent, it means it can be oxidised easily thus it should have an oxidation number less than the maximum values of oxidation number. Oxidation number of S in the given species are

(i) SO_2

$$x + 2(-2) = 0$$
$$x = +4$$

(ii) SO_3^{2-}

$$x + 3(-2) = -2$$
$$x - 6 = -2$$
$$x = +4$$

(iii) H_2SO_4

$$2(1) + x + 4(-2) = 0$$
$$2 + x - 8 = 0$$
$$x = +6$$

(iv) S^{2-}

$$x = -2$$

As the maximum value of oxidation number of S is -2. Thus, H_2SO_4 can not act as a reducing agent.

36. *(d)* The wavelength of light is related to its energy by the equation $E = \dfrac{hc}{\lambda}$

Given, $\lambda = 45$ nm

$$= 45 \times 10^{-9} \text{ m} \quad [\because 1 \text{ nm} = 10^{-9} \text{ m}]$$

Hence, $E = \dfrac{6.63 \times 10^{-34} \text{ Js} \times 3 \times 10^8 \text{ ms}^{-1}}{45 \times 10^{-9} \text{ m}}$

$$= 4.42 \times 10^{-18} \text{ J}$$

37. *(a)* $N_2 + 3H_2 \longrightarrow 2NH_3$

6 g of hydrogen produces 34 g of NH_3

∴ 450 g of hydrogen produces

$$= \dfrac{34}{6} \times 450 = 2550 \text{ g of } NH_3$$

Actual ammonia produced in the solution

$$= 1575 \text{ g}$$

∴　　% yield $= \dfrac{1575}{2550} \times 100$

$$= 61.76 \% \approx 61.8\%$$

38. *(d)* The possible isomer of $C_2BrClFI$ are as follows

Therefore, the above compound has 6 isomers.

39. *(a)* 1 mole of Al requires

$$= 3 \times 96500 \text{ C}$$

10^{-3} moles of Al requires

$$= 3 \times 96500 \times 10^{-3} \text{ C}$$
$$= 3 \times 96.5 \text{ C} \qquad [1C = As]$$
$$= 3 \times 9.65 \text{ As}$$

Time (s) $= \dfrac{3 \times 96.5}{9.65 \text{ A}}$ As $= 30$ s

40. *(c)* The IUPAC name of the following compound is

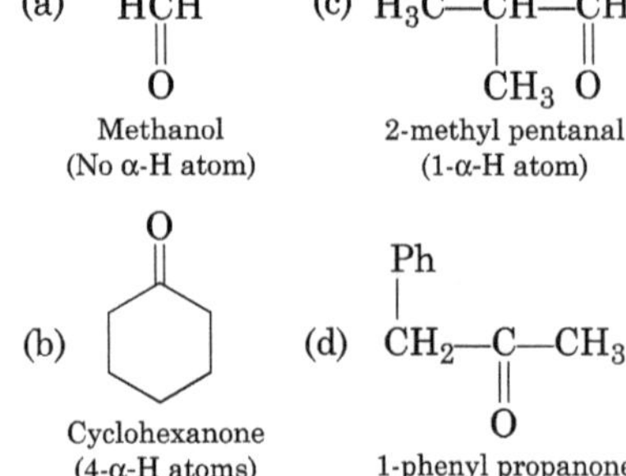

3, 4, 4-trimethylhex-1-yne .

41. *(a)* Aldehydes or ketones having atleast one α –H atom undergo aldol condensation. The structures of given compounds are as follows:

(a) HCH, O — Methanol (No α-H atom)

(b) Cyclohexanone (4-α-H atoms)

(c) H_3C—CH—CH, CH_3, O — 2-methyl pentanal (1-α-H atom)

(d) CH_2—C—CH_3, Ph, O — 1-phenyl propanone (5-α-H atoms)

Thus, among the given compounds, methanal has no α-H atom.
Hence, it will not give aldol condensation.

42. *(b)* Compound II is most basic among the given compounds. This is because the lone pair present on nitrogen in pyridine does not take part in delocalisation and hence they are available for donation. Whereas, in compound I and III the lone pair on N atom takes part in resonance and will not be available for donation, so their basicity will be less.

43. *(a)* In Clemmensen reduction, ketones are reduced to alkanes with the help of Zn-Hg in the presence of HCl.

For example,

$$\underset{H_3C}{\overset{H_3C}{{>}}}C{=}O \xrightarrow[\text{HCl}]{\text{Zn-Hg}} \underset{H_3C}{\overset{H_3C}{{>}}}CH_2$$

44. *(b)* Higher the reduction potential of a metal, lesser will its reducing power.

As the reduction potentials of a metal is decreasing in the order $Y > X > Z$, thus the reducing power will decrease in the order $Z > X > Y$.

45. *(b)* When white phosphorus is heated with caustic soda , then sodium hypophosphite with phosphine is formed.

$$\underset{\substack{\text{White}\\\text{phosphorus}}}{4P} + \underset{\substack{\text{Caustic}\\\text{soda}}}{3NaOH} + 3H_2O \longrightarrow$$

$$\underset{\substack{\text{Sodium}\\\text{hypophosphite}}}{NaH_2PO_2} + \underset{\text{Phosphine}}{PH_3}$$

46. *(c)* The filtration of blood at the glomerulus is a pressure dependent physical process known as renal ultrafiltration. The force of hydrostatic pressure in the glomerulus (the force of pressure exerted from the pressure of the blood vessel itself) is the driving force that pushes filtrate out of the capillaries and into the slits in the nephron.

47. *(b)* Grave's disease is an immune system disorder that results in the overproduction of thyroid hormones (hyperthyroidism). Its symptoms include anxiety, irritability, tremor, heat sensitivity, enlargement of thyroid gland, change in menstrual cycle, etc.

48. *(b)* The 'imperfect fungi' belongs to class Deuteromycetes. They are called as imperfect because sexual reproduction is absent in these forms. They reproduce only by asexual spores called conidia.

49. *(b)* Presence of amniotic egg is not a characteristic of phylum Chordata. The four features shared by all chordates are presence of a single notochord, a dorsal hollow nerve cord, pharyngeal slits and a post-anal tail. Amniotic eggs are present in reptiles, birds and mammals only.

50. *(c)* TCA cycle or Citric acid cycle is a series of reactions that produces one GTP or ATP as well as three NADH molecules and one $FADH_2$ molecule in each turn, which will be used in further steps of cellular respiration to produce ATP for the cell.

51. *(c)* During anaphase-I, no crossing over leads to segregation of alleles. Anaphase-I begins when the two chromosomes of each bivalent (tetrad) separate and start moving toward opposite poles of the cell as a result of the action of the spindle, but their centromeres are still attached.

52. *(d)* After vigorous exercise, excess oxygen is required by the body to make ATP for gluconeogenesis, to metabolise lactic acid, to replenish phosphocreatine and glycogen and to pay back any oxygen that has been borrowed from haemoglobin.

53. *(b)* Water potential (ψ_w) is actually determined by taking into account factors like osmotic (or solute) potential (ψ_s), pressure potential (ψ_p) and matrix or capillary potential (ψ_m). The formula for calculating water potential is

$$\psi_w = \psi_s + \psi_p + \psi_m$$

54. *(c)* Hydrogen bonding in DNA occurs between complementary bases in order to keep the two strands of DNA helix together. These bonds occur as 2 hydrogen bonds between adenine and thymine and 3 hydrogen bonds between cytosine and guanine.

55. *(b)* Both sympathetic and parasympathetic preganglionic neurons are cholinergic meaning they release Acetylcholine (Ach) at the synapse in the ganglion. Ach basic functions involve the control of skeletal muscles *via* activation of the motor neurons as well as stimulating the muscles of the body.

56. *(b)* Evolution is not goal oriented. Evolution simply depends on the environment, which the organisms live and try to survive. The environment is fit for strongest individual who can survive and reproduce. Evolution uses the theory of natural selection where there is variation. We have variations of traits, heredity and different reproductive strategies as a result of natural selection.

57. *(a)* The sucrose is actively transported against its concentration gradient into the phloem cells using the electrochemical potential of the proton gradient. This is coupled to the uptake of sucrose with a carrier protein called the sucrose-H^+ symporter.

58. *(a)* A secretory cell would need secretory enzymes and glycoproteins required in secretions, which are produced in Golgi bodies.

59. *(a)* Riboluse 1,5-Biphosphate (RuBP) is the first acceptor of CO_2 in the formation of two molecules of 3-Phosphoglyceraldehyde (PGA) during the Calvin cycle of photosynthesis.

60. *(a)* Horizontal stem of creepers often develop adventitious roots from the nodes. Adventitious roots are the roots which arise from an organ other than a root. They generally develop from stem nodes, internodes, leaves, etc.

61. *(d)* Given, $4 \le a^2 + b^2 \le 9$
and $\qquad b^2 - 4ab + a^2 \le 0$

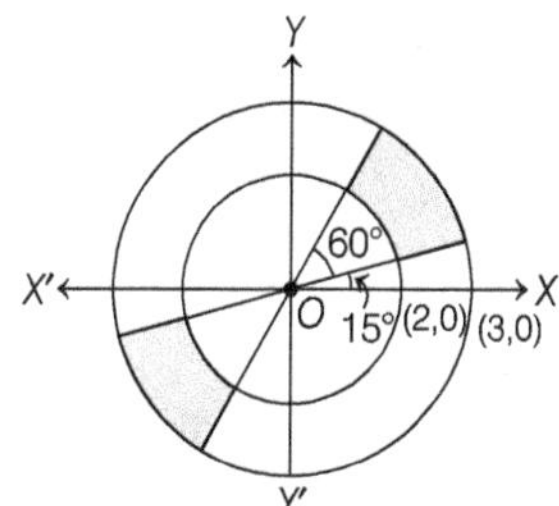

Let $\dfrac{b}{a} = \tan\theta$

$$\left(\frac{b}{a}\right)^2 - \frac{4b}{a} + 1 \le 0$$

$$\Rightarrow \quad \tan^2\theta - 4\tan\theta + 1 \le 0$$

$$\Rightarrow \quad \tan\theta \in [2 - \sqrt{3}, 2 + \sqrt{3}]$$

$$\Rightarrow \quad \theta \in [15°, 75°]$$

Area of region $= \dfrac{\pi}{3} (3^2 - 2^2)$

$$= \frac{\pi}{3} (9 - 4) = \frac{5\pi}{3}$$

62. *(b)* Given,

$$S_1(n) = 8 + 12 + 16 + \ldots + n \text{ terms}$$

$$S_1(n) = \frac{n}{2} [16 + (n - 1) 4] = \frac{n}{2} (12 + 4n)$$

and $S_2(n) = 17 + 19 + 21 + \ldots + n$ terms

$$S_2(n) = \frac{n}{2} [34 + (n - 1) 2] = \frac{n}{2} (32 + 2n)$$

$$S_1(n) = S_2(n)$$

$$\because \frac{n}{2} (12 + 4n) = \frac{n}{2} (32 + 2n) \Rightarrow n = 10$$

$$\because \quad S_1(10) = 5(16 + 36) = 260 = S_2(10)$$

$\because$ Common sum $= 260$

63. *(c)* If any statement is true, then remaining 2 are false.

64. *(b)* Given, $\triangle ABC$ is right angled at A. A is centre of circle and AB is radius of circle.

$$BD = 20$$
$$CD = 16$$

In $\triangle ABC$, $AC^2 + r^2 = BC^2$

$$AC^2 + r^2 = (36)^2 \qquad \ldots\text{(i)}$$

CB and CF are secant of circle.

$$\because \qquad CE - CF = CD \times CB$$

$$\Rightarrow (AC - r)(AC + r) = 16 \times 36$$

$$AC^2 - r^2 = 16 \times 36 \qquad \ldots\text{(ii)}$$

From Eqs. (i) and (ii), we get
$$2AC^2 = 36(36 + 16) = 36 \times 52$$
$$\Rightarrow \quad AC = 6\sqrt{26}$$

65. *(a)* We have,
$$(1 + 2x + 3x^2 + \ldots + 21x^{20})^2$$
$$= (1 + 2x + 3x^2 + \ldots + 21x^{20})$$
$$(21x^{20} + 20x^{19} + \ldots + 3x^2 + 2x + 1)$$
Coefficient of x^{30} is
$$11 \times 21 + 12 \times 20 + \ldots + 21 \times 11$$
$$= 2(11 \times 21 + 12 \times 20 + 13 \times 19 + 14 \times 18$$
$$+ 15 \times 17) + 16 \times 16$$
$$= 2(231 + 240 + 247 + 252 + 255) + 256$$
$$= 2(1225) + 256 = 2450 + 256 = 2706$$

66. *(b)* Given situation is

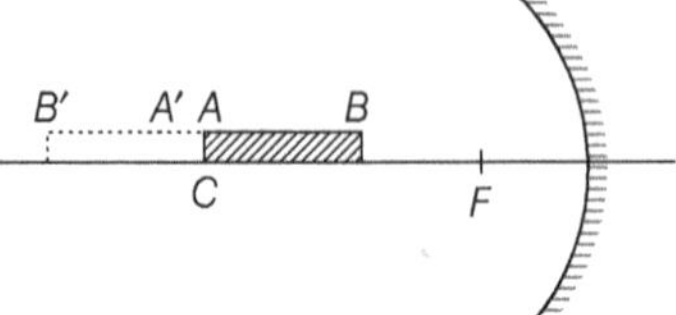

By mirror formula,
$$\frac{1}{v_B} - \frac{1}{\dfrac{5}{3}f} = -\frac{1}{f} \Rightarrow v_B = -\frac{5f}{2}$$

Hence, image length is $l' = f\left(\dfrac{5}{2} - 2\right) = \dfrac{f}{2}$

So, magnification is $m = \dfrac{l'}{l} = \dfrac{f/2}{f/3} = \dfrac{3}{2}$

67. *(b)* Coordinates of points P and Q are
$$P : \left(\frac{a}{2}, 0, \frac{a}{2}\right) \text{and } Q : \left(\frac{a}{2}, \frac{a}{2}, 0\right)$$

So, unit vector along PQ is
$$\hat{PQ} = \frac{\mathbf{PQ}}{|\mathbf{PQ}|} = \frac{-\dfrac{a}{2}\hat{\mathbf{j}} + \dfrac{a}{2}\hat{\mathbf{k}}}{\sqrt{\dfrac{a^2}{4} + \dfrac{a^2}{4}}}$$
$$= \sqrt{2}\,(-\hat{\mathbf{j}} + \hat{\mathbf{k}})$$

68. *(a)* By KVL, $I_1 = \dfrac{10}{20}$
$$\Rightarrow \quad P_1 = I_1^2 R_1 = \frac{100}{400} \times 20 = 5\,\text{W}$$
and $\quad I_2 = 0 \Rightarrow P_2 = 0$

69. *(b)*

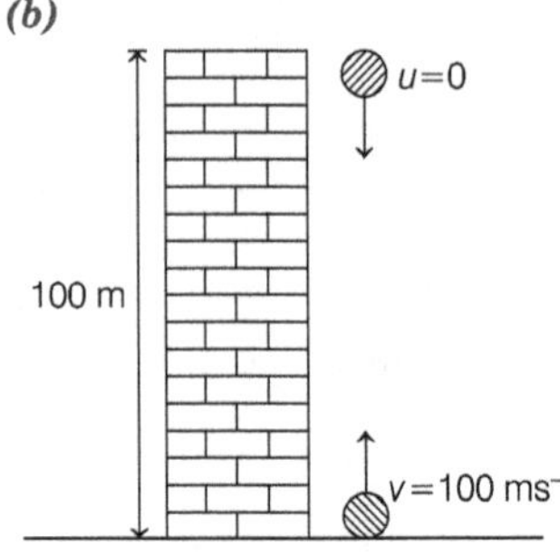

Time at which bullet and block collide is
$$t = \frac{d}{v} = \frac{100}{100 - 0} = 1\,\text{s}$$

Speed of wood just before collision
$$= gt = 100\,\text{ms}^{-1}$$

Speed of bullet at $t = 1\,\text{s}$ is
$$= v - gt = 100 - 10 \times 1 = 90\,\text{ms}^{-1}.$$

Let v' = velocity of bullet + block system after collision. Then, by momentum conservation, we have
$$- (0.03) \times 10 + (0.02) \times 90 = (0.05)\,v'$$
$$\Rightarrow \qquad\qquad v' = 30\,\text{ms}^{-1}$$

Now, maximum height reached
$$= \frac{v^2}{2g} - \text{distance through}$$
$$\text{which block fells in 1 s}$$
$$= \left(\frac{30 \times 30}{2 \times 10}\right) - \left(\frac{1}{2} \times 10 \times 1^2\right) = 45 - 5$$
$$= 40\,\text{m}$$

70. *(b)* $M = kF^a L^b T^c$
where, k is a constant.
$$[M] = [MLT^{-2}]^a L^b T^c$$
Equating dimensions, we have
$$a = 1 \qquad\qquad \ldots(i)$$
$$b + a = 2 \qquad\qquad \ldots(ii)$$
$$-2a + c = 0 \qquad\qquad \ldots(iii)$$
Putting value of a from Eq. (i) in Eq. (ii), we get
$$b + a = 0$$
$$b + 1 = 0$$
$$b = -1 \qquad\qquad \ldots(iv)$$
Again putting value of a from Eq. (i) in Eq. (iii), we get
$$-2a + c = 0$$
$$-2 \times 1 + c = 0$$
$$-2 + c = 0$$
$$c = 2$$
$$\Rightarrow \quad a = 1, b = -1 \text{and } c = 2$$
So, $\quad [M] = [FL^{-1}T^2]$

71. *(a)* From ideal gas equation,
$$pV = nRT$$
$$n = \frac{pV}{RT} = \frac{1.01 \times 10^5\,\text{N}\cdot\text{m}^{-2} \times 10 \times 10^{-3}\,\text{m}^3}{8.314\,\text{J mol}^{-1}\text{K}^{-1} \times 300\,\text{K}}$$
$$= 0.405\,\text{mol} \qquad [1\text{N}\cdot\text{m} = 1\,\text{J}]$$

For monoatomic gases, $C_p = \dfrac{5}{2}R = 2.5R$

$T_1 = 300\,\text{K}$ and $T_2 = 400\,\text{K}$
$R = 8.314\,\text{J mol}^{-1}\,\text{K}^{-1}$
$$\Delta S = 2.303\,nC_p \log \frac{T_2}{T_1}$$
$$= 2.303 \times 0.405 \times 2.5 \times 8.314 \log \frac{400}{300}$$
$$\Delta S = 2.422\,\text{JK}^{-1}$$

72. *(c)* 16.9% solution of $AgNO_3$ means 16.9 g $AgNO_3$ is present in 100 mL solution.

$\therefore$ 8.45 g $AgNO_3$ will be present in 50 mL solution.

Similarly, 5.8 g NaCl is present in 100 mL solution.

$\therefore$ 2.9 g NaCl is present in 50 mL solution.

	$AgNO_3$ +	NaCl $\rightarrow$	AgCl +	$NaNO_3$
Initial moles	$\dfrac{8.45}{169.8}$ $= 0.049$	$\dfrac{2.9}{58.5}$ $= 0.049$	0	0
After reaction	0	0	0.049	0.049

Mass of compound = moles $\times$ molar mass
$\therefore$ Mass of AgCl precipitated
$$= 0.049 \times 143.5 = 7.03\,\text{g}$$

73. *(d)* The species formed after removal of an electron from the given diatomic molecules are as follows
(a) $C_2 \longrightarrow C_2^+ + e^-$
(b) $CN \longrightarrow CN^+ + e^-$
(c) $N_2 \longrightarrow N_2^+ + e^-$
(d) $O_2 \longrightarrow O_2^+ + e^-$

The stability of diatomic molecule can be determined by calculating its bond order. More is the bond order, more is the stability of a molecule.
$$\text{B.O} = \frac{1}{2}\,(N_b - N_a)$$

$\therefore$ The bond orders of diatomic molecules with their ionic species are given below.

		B.O
(i)	C_2	2.0
(ii)	C_2^+	1.5
(iii)	CN	2.5
(iv)	CN^+	2.0
(v)	N_2	3
(vi)	N_2^+	2.5
(vii)	O_2	2
(viii)	O_2^+	2.5

As the bond order increases from 2 to 2.5 when an e^- is removed from O_2 molecule (O_2^+), so it become stabilised.

74. *(a)* Calcium carbide on hydrolysis gives acetylene as a major product which then reacts with dil H_2SO_4 in the presence of $HgSO_4$ to give acetaldehyde.

$$\underset{\substack{\text{Calcium} \\ \text{carbide}}}{CaC_2} + 2H_2O \longrightarrow \underset{(X)}{\underset{\text{Acetylene}}{C_2H_2}} + Ca(OH)_2$$

$$\underset{\text{CH}}{\overset{\text{CH}}{\underset{\|}{}}} \xrightarrow{\text{dil } H_2SO_4/HgSO_4} \underset{\substack{\text{O} \\ (Y) \\ \text{Acetaldehyde}}}{CH_3 - C - H}$$

75. *(a)* As only one structure of *B* with molecular formula $C_5H_{11}Cl$ is possible, thus the structure of *B* would be

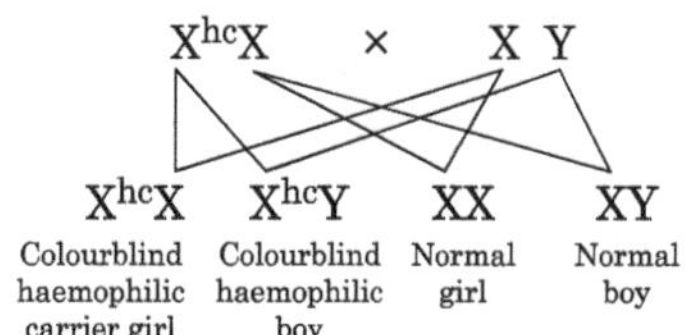

76. *(d)* ABA or Abscisic Acid promotes leaf senescence independent of ethylene. Other statements can be corrected as

Gibberellins play the most important role in flowering. It is seen that treatment of gibberellin on biennials or long day plants, stem elongation occurs before flower primordia are formed. Auxin and cytokinin promote cell division.

It is seen that ABA and ethylene can control and induce root and shoot growth under water stress or low water potential.

77. *(b)* The cross for the given question would be

$X^{hc}X$ × X Y

$X^{hc}X$ $X^{hc}Y$ XX XY

| Colourblind haemophilic carrier girl | Colourblind haemophilic boy | Normal girl | Normal boy |

∴ The progeny be 50% haemophilic colourblind sons and 50% colourblind carrier daughters.

78. *(d)* In pure water, the concentration of hydrogen ions and concentration of hydroxyl ions are equal. Consequently water is neither acidic nor basic, but neutral. Therefore, water at 25°C will have $H^+ = OH^-$.

79. *(c)* **Acoelomate** Animals like sponges, coelenterates and flatworms are without a coelom or any other internal cavity except the digestive tract.

Pseudocoelomate Roundworms have a body cavity derived directly from the blastocoel of the embryo. It is called pseudocoel because like true coelom, it is not lined by peritoneum but is bounded with ectoderm on the outer side and endoderm on the inner side.

Coelomate Animals with a tube within a tube body plan have a fluid-filled body cavity between the body wall and the digestive tract as like in earthworms. It is derived from embryonic mesoderm and is lined by peritoneum.

80. *(d)* A dipeptide is made up of 2 amino acids which may be same or different. The total possible number of different dipeptides that may be assembled from 20 different amino acids will thus be

$$20^n = 20^2 = 20 \times 20 = 400$$

PRACTICE SET 2

Stream : SA

MM : 100

Instructions

1. There are 80 questions in this paper.
2. This question paper contains two parts; Part I and Part II. There are four sections; Mathematics, Physics, Chemistry and Biology in each part.
3. Out of the four options given with each question, only one is correct.

➲ PART-I (1 Mark Questions)

MATHEMATICS

1. The remainder when 5^{99} is divided by 13
(a) 6
(b) 8
(c) 9
(d) 10

2. A polynomial $p(x)$ when divided by $x^2 - 3x + 2$ leaves remainder $2x - 3$, then
(a) $p(x)$ must have a root between 0 and 3
(b) $p(x)$ cannot have a root between 0 and 3
(c) $p(x)$ must have a real root but may or may not be between 0 and 3
(d) $p(x)$ need not have a real root

3. A shopkeeper increases the price of a commodity by $x\%$ some time later, he reduces the new price by $y\%$ and notices that the price is now the same as it was originally. The value of $\dfrac{1}{y} - \dfrac{1}{x}$ is
(a) $-\dfrac{1}{100}$
(b) 0
(c) $\dfrac{1}{100}$
(d) None of these

4. Difference between the corresponding roots $x^2 + ax + b = 0$ and $x^2 + bx + a = 0$ is same and $a \neq b$, then
(a) $a + b + 4 = 0$
(b) $a + b - 4 = 0$
(c) $a - b - 4 = 0$
(d) $a - b + 4 = 0$

5. Let P be a point in the interior of the rectangle $ABCD$, which of the following sets of numbers can form the areas of the four triangles PAB, PBC, PCD, PDA in same order
(a) 10, 9, 12, 5
(b) 21, 15, 6, 12
(c) 10, 9, 8, 6
(d) 12, 8, 7, 5

6. Let $x_1, x_2, \ldots, x_n$ be n observation such that $\displaystyle\sum_{i=1}^{n} x_i^2 = 400$ and $\displaystyle\sum_{i=1}^{n} x_i = 80$. Then, a possible value of n among the following is
(a) 15
(b) 18
(c) 9
(d) 12

7. The set $S = \{1, 2, 3, \ldots, 12\}$ is to be partitioned into three sets A, B, C of equal size. Thus, $A \cup B \cup C = S$, $A \cap B = B \cap C = A \cap C = \phi$. The number of ways of partition S is
(a) $\dfrac{12!}{3! \, (4!)^3}$
(b) $\dfrac{12!}{3! \, (3!)^4}$
(c) $\dfrac{12!}{(4!)^3}$
(d) $\dfrac{12!}{(3!)^4}$

8. You have a measuring cup with capacity 25 ml and another with capacity 110 ml, the cups have no markings showing intermediate volumes. Using large container and as much tap water as you wish. What is the smallest amount of water you can measure accurately?

(a) 1 ml   (b) 5 ml
(c) 10 ml   (d) 25 ml

9. Let A, B, C, D be collinear points in that order. Suppose $AB : CD = 3 : 2$ and $BC : AD = 1 : 5$. Then, $AC : BD$ is

(a) 1 : 1   (b) 11 : 10
(c) 16 : 1   (d) 17 : 13

10. Let ABC be triangle with $AB = AC = 6$. If the circumradius of the triangle is 5, then BC equals

(a) $\dfrac{25}{3}$ (b) 9
(c) $\dfrac{48}{5}$ (d) 10

11. Two cars start together in the same direction from the same place. The first goes with a speed of 10 km/h. The second goes at a speed of 8 km/h in the first hour and increase the speed by $\dfrac{1}{2}$ km each succeeding hour.

After how many hours will the second car overtake the first, if both go non-stop.

(a) 9 h   (b) 5 h
(c) 7 h   (d) 8 h

12. If x, y are natural numbers such that $x^2 + 2013 = y^2$, then the minimum value of xy is

(a) 645   (b) 658
(c) 668   (d) 671

13. A cube has each edge 2 cm and a cuboid is 1 cm long, 2 cm wide and 3 cm high. The paint in a certain container is sufficient to paint an area equal to 54 cm^2. Which one of the following is true?

(a) Both cube and cuboid are painted
(b) Only cube can be painted
(c) Only cuboid can be painted
(d) Neither cube nor cuboid can be painted

14. How many positive real number x are there such that $(x)^{x\sqrt{x}} = (x\sqrt{x})^{x}$?

(a) 1   (b) 2
(c) 4   (d) Infinite

15. Let $0 < a < b < c$ be three distinct digits. The sum of all 3-digit number formed by using all the 3-digit number once each is 1554. The value of b is

(a) 1   (b) 2   (c) 3   (d) 4

PHYSICS

16. A box is falling freely inside the box, a particle is projected with some velocity v with respect to the box at angle θ.

For an observer sitting in the box, path of particle is

(a) 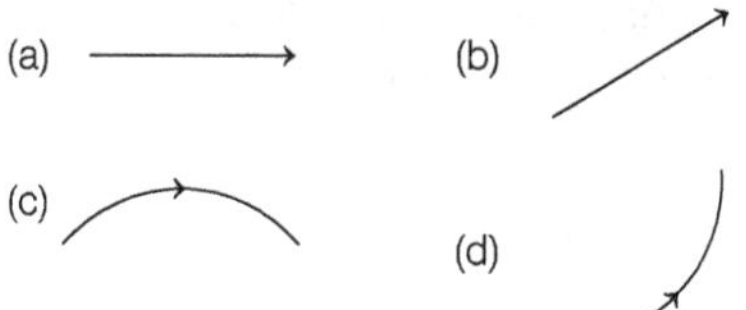

17. Potential energy of a system as a function of a parameter x is $U(x) = (x + 1)(x + 2)$.

Then, consider following statements:

  I. Point $x = \dfrac{-3}{2}$, corresponds to an equilibrium position.

  II. Points $x = -1$ and $x = -2$, corresponds to equilibrium position of system.

  III. At point $x = \dfrac{-3}{2}$, system is in stable equilibrium.

  IV. At point $x = \dfrac{-3}{2}$, system is in unstable equilibrium.

(a) All statements are correct
(b) Statements I and IV are correct
(c) Statements I and III are correct
(d) Only statement II is correct

18. On a temperature scale X, water boils at $-60°$ X and freezes at $-180°$ X. What would be a room temperature of $25°$ C on X-scale?

(a) $-18°$ X   (b) $-38°$ X   (c) $-150°$ X   (d) $-130°$ X

19. In given nuclear reaction,
$^{9}_{4}\text{Be} + \alpha \rightarrow {}^{12}_{6}\text{C} + X$, particle X is

(a) $^{4}_{2}\text{He}$ (b) $^{0}_{-1}e$ (c) $^{1}_{1}\text{H}$ (d) $^{1}_{0}n$

20. Two blocks of masses 0.2 kg and 0.5 kg are placed 22 m apart on a rough flat horizontal surface ($\mu = 0.5$). At time $t = 0$, blocks are pushed towards each other with equal forces of 3 N on each of the block. Blocks collide with each other in time duration

(a) 1 s   (b) $\sqrt{2}$ s
(c) $\sqrt{3}$ s   (d) 2 s

21. A table-tennis ball is floating in air by a jet of water emerging from a nozzle.

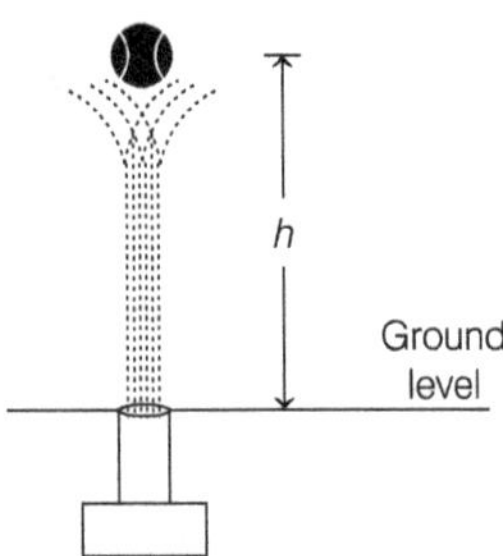

If mass of ball is m and water stream rises to height h above ground, then water flow rate is

(a) $\dfrac{m}{\sqrt{2}}\sqrt{\dfrac{g}{h}}$

(b) $\dfrac{m}{\sqrt{2}}\sqrt{\dfrac{h}{g}}$

(c) $m\sqrt{2gh}$

(d) $m\sqrt{\dfrac{2h}{g}}$

22. A system under goes three processes listed in table below. All quantities are (in kJ).

Process	ΔQ	ΔW	ΔU
Process $1 \to 2$	a	100	100
Process $2 \to 3$	b	-50	c
Process $3 \to 1$	100	d	-200

Then, value of c is

(a) 200 kJ   (b) 50 kJ
(c) 100 kJ   (d) 0 kJ

23. Force necessary to accelerate a mass of 1 kg at 10 ms^{-2} vertically upwards is (Take, $g = 10 \text{ ms}^{-2}$)

(a) 1 N   (b) 2 N   (c) 10 N   (d) 20 N

24. In Rutherford's scattering experiment, choose the correct statements are given below.

    I. Only α-particles are scattered backwards but not protons.

    II. α-particles cannot be effectively scattered by electrons because α-particles are positively charged.

    III. Radius nucleus of target is between 9.6×10^{-15} m to 4.8×10^{-15} m.

    IV. α-particles with energy greater than a certain critical value are not scattered back.

(a) Only statement II is correct
(b) Only statement III is correct
(c) Statements I, III and IV are correct
(d) All statements are correct

25. The ratio of the height above the surface of earth to the depth below the surface of earth for gravitational acceleration to be same (assuming small height) is

(a) 1   (b) 0.5
(c) 0.25   (d) 1.25

26. If a low pressure centre is developed in atmosphere (very common in India in summer), the wind will flow radially towards centre. The whirlpool of wind formed will rotate in India as

(a) clockwise only
(b) anti-clockwise only
(c) clockwise or anti-clockwise
(d) whirlpools are not formed in India

27. Which of these paths correctly describes motion of moon around observed from a space station?

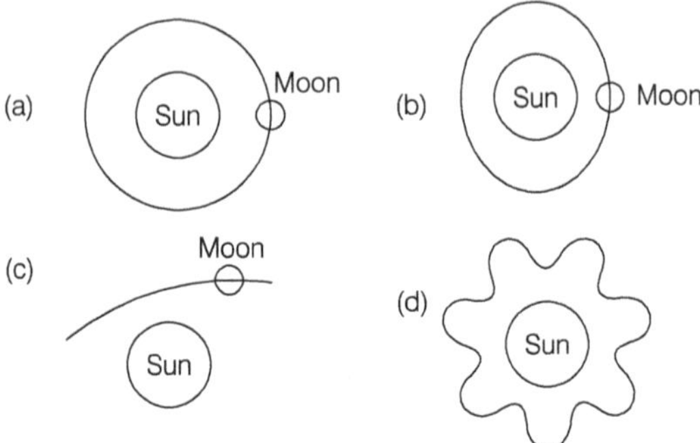

28. Correct variation of velocity of a table-tennis ball dropped from top of a 14-story building is

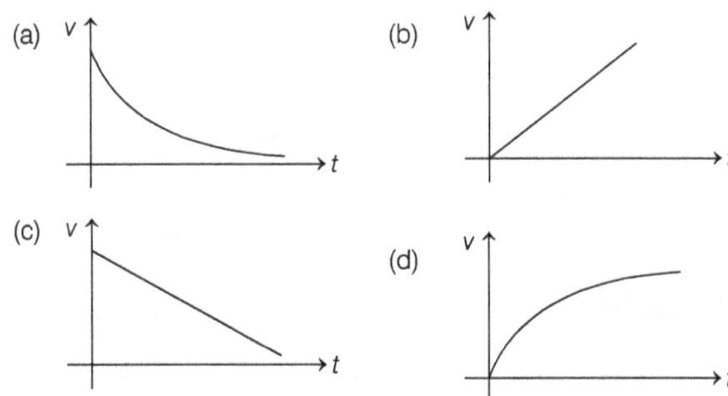

29. A vessel with water is placed on a weighing pan, it reads 600 g. Now a hollow ball of mass 40 g and volume 50 cm^3 is kept immersed in water by tying it to bottom with a thread of negligible mass.

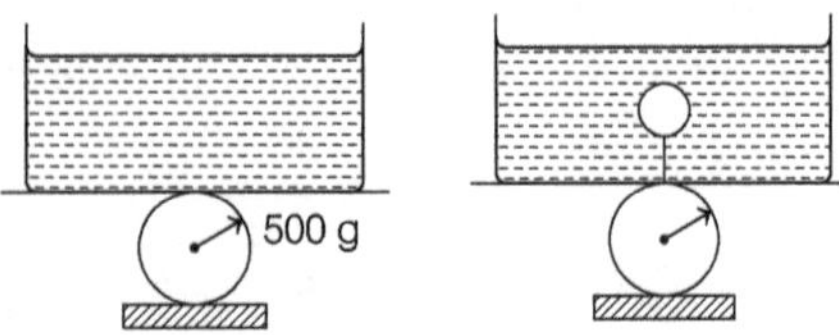

Reading of pan is now

(a) 690 g
(b) 550 g
(c) 650 g
(d) 610 g

30. Plane face of a plano-convex lens is silvered. Given, radius of convex face is 12 cm and refractive index of medium is 3 / 2.

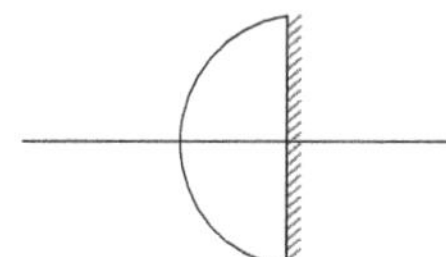

Power of resulting system is

(a) $\dfrac{25}{3}$ D

(b) $-\dfrac{25}{3}$ D

(c) $\dfrac{-25}{3}$ m

(d) $\dfrac{25}{3}$ m

CHEMISTRY

31. By heating 10 g $CaCO_3$, 5.6 g CaO is formed. The weight of CO_2 obtained in this reaction is closest to

(a) 5.6 g　　　　　　　(b) 2.4 g

(c) 4.4 g　　　　　　　(d) 3.6 g

32. Which of the following plot obeys the Raoult's law at all concentration?

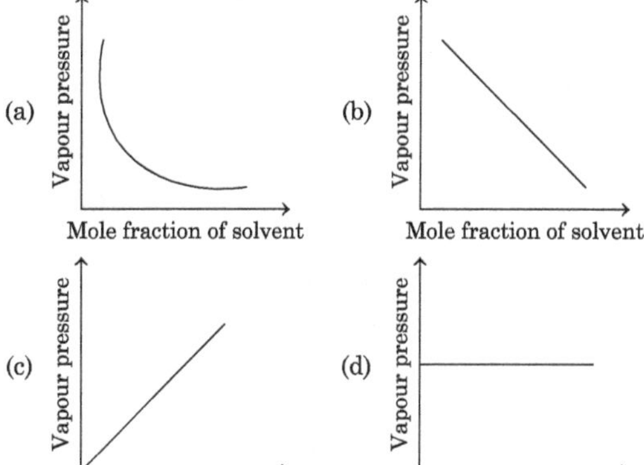

33. The correct order of increasing ionic character is

(a) $BeCl_2 < MgCl_2 < CaCl_2 < BaCl_2$

(b) $BeCl_2 < MgCl_2 < BaCl_2 < CaCl_2$

(c) $BeCl_2 < BaCl_2 < MgCl_2 < CaCl_2$

(d) $BaCl_2 < CaCl_2 < MgCl_2 < BeCl_2$

34. In the reaction,

$$3Br_2 + 6CO_3^{2-} + 3H_2O \longrightarrow 5Br^- + BrO_3^- + 6HCO_3^-$$

(a) Bromine is oxidised and the carbonate radical is reduced

(b) Bromine is reduced and the carbonate radical is oxidised

(c) Bromine is neither reduced nor oxidised

(d) Bromine is both reduced and oxidised

35. IUPAC name of the following compound

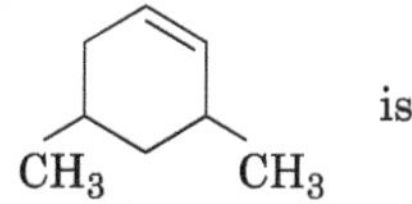

is

(a) 3, 5-dimethyl cyclohexene

(b) 3, 5-dimethyl-1-cyclohexene

(c) 1, 5-dimethyl-5-cyclohexene

(d) 1, 3-dimethyl-5-cyclohexene

36. Which of the following isomerisms is shown by pentan-2-one and 3-methylbutanone?

(a) Stereoisomerism　　　(b) Position isomerism

(c) Functional isomerism　(d) Chain isomerism

37. What is the maximum number of orbitals that can be identified with the following quantum numbers?

$$n = 3,\ l = 1 \text{ and } m_l = 0$$

(a) 1　　　　　　　　　(b) 2

(c) 3　　　　　　　　　(d) 4

38. The major product of the following reaction is

$$CH_3CH{=}CHCH_2CH_3 \xrightarrow[\text{(ii) hydrolysis, Zn}]{\text{(i) } O_3}$$

(a) $CH_3CHO + CH_3CH_2CHO$

(b) $CH_3COOH + CH_3COCH_3$

(c) $CH_3COOH + CH_3CH_2COOH$

(d) $CH_3COOH + CO_2$

39. Among the following, which is an incorrect statement.

(a) PH_5 and $BiCl_5$ do not exist

(b) $p\pi - d\pi$ bonds are present in SO_2

(c) SeF_4 and CH_4 have same shape

(d) I_3^+ has bent structure

40. Predict the effect of increased pressure on the following reaction equilibrium,

$$2SO_2(g) + O_2(g) \rightleftharpoons 2SO_3(g)$$

(a) equilibrium shift to the right

(b) equilibrium shift to the left

(c) no effect on equilibrium

(d) reaction stops

41. The solubility product of $BaCl_2$ is 4×10^{-9}. Its solubility in mol L^{-1} is

(a) 4×10^{-3}　　　　　(b) 4×10^{-9}

(c) 1×10^{-3}　　　　　(d) 1×10^{-9}

42. Chlorobenzene on treatment with sodium in dry ether gives diphenyl. The name of the reaction is

(a) Fittig reaction

(b) Wurtz-fittig reaction

(c) Sandmeyer reaction

(d) Gattermann reaction

43. A sample of unknown gas is placed in a 2.5 L bulb at a pressure of 360 torr and at a temperature of 22.5°C and is found to weight 1.6616 g. The molecular weight of the gas is closest to

(a) 80 g　　　　　　　(b) 55 g

(c) 34 g　　　　　　　(d) 55 g

44. Consider the isoelectronic ions

$$K^+, S^{2-}, Cl^- \text{ and } Ca^{2+}$$

The radii of these ionic species follow the order

(a) $Ca^{2+} > K^+ > Cl^- > S^{2-}$　　(b) $Cl^- > S^{2-} > K^+ > Ca^{2+}$

(c) $S^{2-} > Cl^- > K^+ > Ca^{2+}$　　(d) $K^+ > Ca^{2+} > S^{2-} > Cl^-$

45. The reaction of toluene with Cl_2 in the presence of $FeCl_3$ gives predominantly
(a) benzoyl chloride   (b) benzyl chloride
(c) *o* and *p*-chlorotoluene   (d) *m*-chlorotoluene

BIOLOGY

46. Most common type of phospholipids in the cell membrane of nerve cell is
(a) phosphatidylcholine   (b) phosphatidylinositol
(c) phosphatidylserine   (d) sphingomyelin

47. Graft rejection does not involve
(a) erythrocytes
(b) T-cells
(c) macrophages
(d) polymorphonuclear leukocytes

48. Horse-shoe crabs belong to the group
(a) Onychophora   (b) Chelicerata
(c) Uniramia   (d) Crustacea

49. The first living being on the earth were anaerobic because
(a) there was no oxygen in air
(b) oxygen damages proteins
(c) oxygen interferes with action of ribozymes
(d) they evolved in deep sea

50. The presence of *Salmonella* in tap water is indicative of contamination with
(a) industrial effluents   (b) human excreta
(c) agricultural waste   (d) None of these

51. The secondary order of protein structure is
(a) the sequence of amino acids in the polypeptide chain
(b) the formation of peptide bonds between amino acids
(c) the coiling of the polypeptide chain
(d) the folding of the coiled polypeptide chain

52. The amount of DNA in a mammalian cell in early prophase-I is x. What is the amount of DNA in the same cell in anaphase-I of mitosis?

(a) $\dfrac{x}{4}$ (b) $\dfrac{x}{2}$ (c) x (d) $2x$

53. Kreb's cycle was discovered by Krebs in pigeon muscles in 1940. Which step is called gateway step/link reaction/transition reaction in respiration?
(a) Glycolysis
(b) Formation of acetyl Co-A
(c) Citric acid formation
(d) ETS terminal oxidation

54. Which homeostatic function of the liver is controlled and monitored in the pancreas?
(a) Deamination of amino acids
(b) Release of glucose
(c) Release of iron
(d) Release of toxins

55. During generation of an action potential, depolarisation is due to
(a) K^+ efflux   (b) Na^+ efflux
(c) Na^+ influx   (d) K^+ influx

56. If liver from body is removed then which component of blood increases?
(a) Ammonia   (b) Protein
(c) Urea   (d) Uric acid

57. In his classical experiments on pea plants, Mendel did not use
(a) seed shape   (b) flower position
(c) seed colour   (d) pod length

58. In phylum, which group contains the greatest number of species?
(a) Class   (b) Family   (c) Genus   (d) Order

59. Cell division is initiated by
(a) centrosome   (b) centromere
(c) centriole   (d) None of these

60. The part of human hindbrain that is responsible for hand-eye coordination is
(a) cerebellum   (b) pons Varolii
(c) medulla oblongata   (d) thalamus

↺ PART-II (2 Marks Questions)

MATHEMATICS

61. A circle is inscribed in an equilateral triangle with side length of 6 units. Another circle is drawn inside the triangle (but outside the first circle), tangent to the first circle and two of the sides of the triangle. The radius of the smaller circle is

(a) $\dfrac{1}{\sqrt{3}}$ (b) $\dfrac{2}{3}$ (c) $\dfrac{1}{2}$ (d) 1

62. If $x^2 y^3 = 6$. Then, the minimum value of $3x + 4y$ for positive values of x and y is
(a) 6   (b) 8   (c) 10   (d) 12

63. If there are three different kinds of mangoes for sale in a market. Then, number of ways of purchase of 25 mangoes are
(a) 2925   (b) 325
(c) 351   (d) 2600

64. Four natural number m, n if
$(1 - y)^m (1 + y)^n = 1 + a_1 y + a_2 y^2 + \ldots$ and $a_1 = a_2 = 10$,
then (m, n) is
(a) (20, 45)   (b) (35, 20)
(c) (45, 35)   (d) (35, 45)

65. In a $\triangle ABC$, with $\angle A = 90°$, the bisector of the angle B and C meet at P. The distance from P to the hypotenuse is $4\sqrt{2}$. The distance AP is

(a) 8   (b) 4   (c) $8\sqrt{2}$ (d) $4\sqrt{2}$

PHYSICS

66. A planet contains a single type of gas in its atmosphere having molecular mass of 1.38×10^{-28} kg. Distribution of speeds in atmosphere is given below.

Speed (ms^{-1})	Percentage of molecules
100	10
200	30
500	20
800	20
1000	20

Escape speed for the planet is 900 ms^{-1}. Assuming stable atmospheric conditions, the possible estimated reduction in temperature of the planet in few years will be (Use, temperature,

$$T = \frac{mv_{\text{rms}}^2}{3K_B} \text{ and } K_B = 1.38 \times 10^{-23})$$

(a) 100 K   (b) 200 K   (c) 70 K   (d) 20 K

67. A right angle ruler used generally in tailoring or drafting hangs from rest from a peg P as shown below.

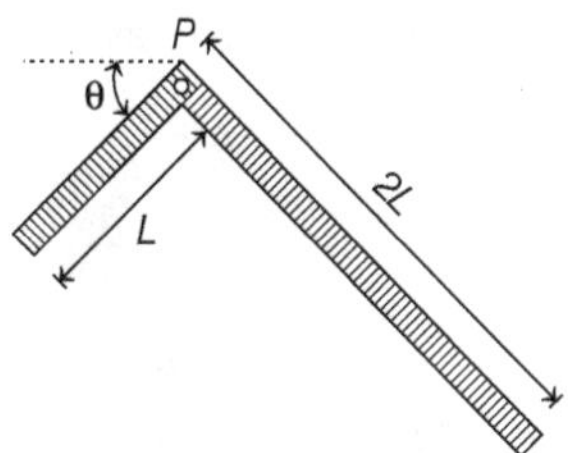

One arm is L cm long and other arm is $2L$ cm long. Value of angle θ is such that

(a) $\tan\theta = \dfrac{1}{4}$ (b) $\sin\theta = \dfrac{1}{4}$

(c) $\cos\theta = \dfrac{1}{4}$ (d) $\sec\theta = \dfrac{1}{4}$

68. 1 kg of steam at 100°C and 101 kPa occupies 1.68 m^3 space. What per cent of heat of vaporisation of water is used for expansion of water into steam?

(a) Nearly 7%   (b) Nearly 17%

(c) Nearly 70%   (d) Nearly 12%

69. A telephoto lens system consists of a converging lens ($f = +6.0$ cm) placed 4 cm in front of a diverging lens ($f = -2.5$ cm).

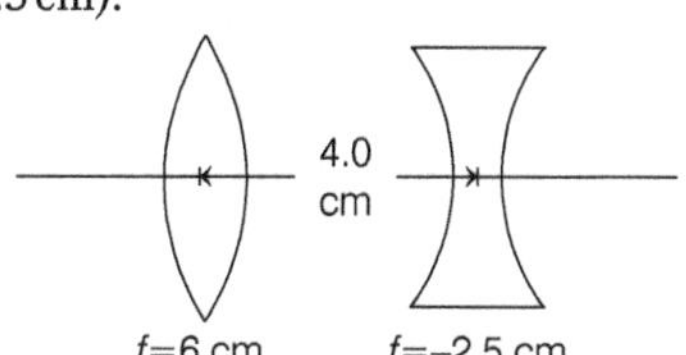

When a very distant object is viewed by this lens system, choose the correct option.

(a) Final image is formed at mid-point of lens separation

(b) Final image is virtual

(c) Diverging lens increases the magnification five times

(d) Final image is inverted and diminished

70. Current is flowing through a uniform thick rod of cross-sectional area A, under an applied potential difference V across its ends.

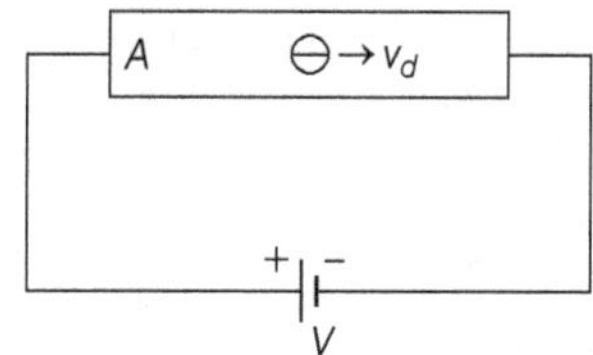

Let electrons flow through the thick rod with velocity v_{d_1}. A hole is drilled in the rod and its central portion of area $\dfrac{A}{2}$ is removed.

Let electrons flow through the hollow rod with velocity v_{d_2}. Then, ratio v_{d_2} / v_{d_1} will be

(a) 2   (b) $\dfrac{1}{2}$ (c) 1   (d) 4

CHEMISTRY

71. A bomb calorimeter has a heat capacity of 783 J°C^{-1} and contains 254 g of water, which has a specific heat of 4.184 g^{-1} °C^{-1}. Heat absorbed/evolved by a reaction when the temperature changes from 23.73°C to 26.01°C is closest to

(a) 1.78 kJ absorbed   (b) 2.42 kJ absorbed

(c) 1.78 kJ evolved   (d) 4.21 kJ absorbed

72. Isostructural species are those species which have the same shape and hybridisation. Among the given species, identify the isostructural pairs.

(a) NF_3 and BF_3 (b) BF_4^- and NH_4^+

(c) BCl_3 and $BrCl_3$ (d) NH_3 and NO_3^-

73. Which among the following will form geometrical isomers?

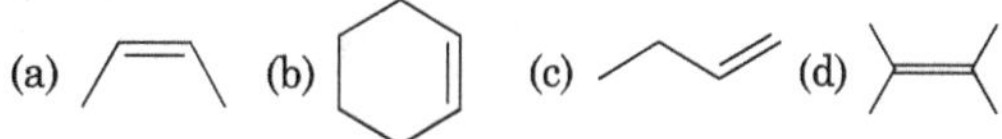

74. Consider the following reaction,

$$\underset{\text{(Major)}}{B} \xleftarrow[\text{(CH}_3\text{CH}_2\text{OH)}]{\text{(CH}_3\text{CH}_2\text{O}^-\text{Na}^+)} \underset{\text{CH}}{\overset{\text{CH}}{CH_3\,C-Br}} \xrightarrow{\text{CH}_3\text{CH}_2\text{OH}} \underset{\text{(Major)}}{A}$$

A and B respectively are

(a) $(CH_3)_3 COCH_2CH_3$ in both cases

(b) $(CH_3)_2 C = CH_2$ in both cases

(c) $(CH_3)_3 COCH_2CH_3$ and $(CH_3)_2 C = CH_2$

(d) $(CH_3)_2 C = CH_2$ and $(CH_3)_3 COCH_2CH_3$

75. Which of the following species contains equal number of σ and π-bonds?
(a) HCO_3^-
(b) XeO_4
(c) $(CN)_2$
(d) $CH_2(CN)_2$

BIOLOGY

76. A piece of mammalian tissue was homogenised and subjected to differential centrifugation. The diagrams below indicate the relative activity certain biochemical processes in these fractions. Which of the following fractions indicates the maximum hydrolytic enzyme activity?

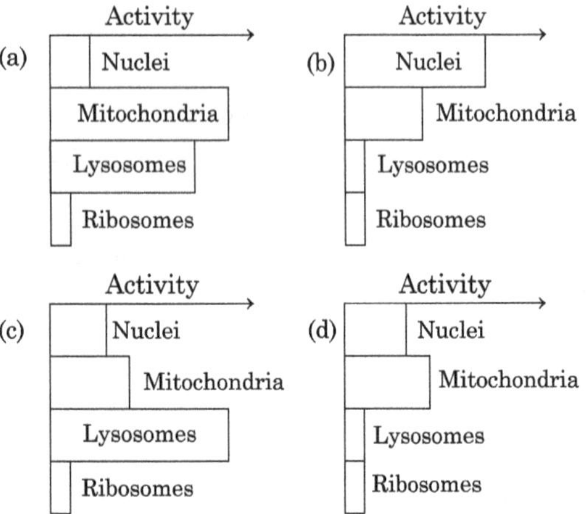

77. Which one of the following genotypes cannot occur amongst the offspring from a mating between a person of blood group A and a person of blood group B?
(a) AA
(b) AB
(c) AO
(d) BO

78. The weed killer DCMU blocks the flow of electrons from the electron transport chains in photophosphorylation. Why does this kill the plant?
(a) Active transport of mineral ions is prevented
(b) ATP and reduced NADP are not produced
(c) Photoactivation of the chlorophyll cannot occur
(d) Photolysis of water does not occur

79. Which one of the following is the correct description of a certain part of a normal human skeleton?
(a) Parietal bone and the temporal bone of the skull are joined by fibrous joint
(b) First vertebra is axis which articulates with the occipital condyles
(c) The 9th and 10th pairs of ribs are called the floating ribs
(d) Glenoid cavity is a depression to which the thigh bone articulates

80. Which of the following statements correctly describes a codon?
(a) A length of DNA which codes for a particular protein
(b) A part of the transfer RNA molecule to which a specific amino acid is attached
(c) A part of the transfer RNA molecule which recognises the triplet code on the messenger RNA
(d) A part of the messenger RNA molecule that has a sequence of bases coding for an amino acid

Answers

PART-I

1 (b)	2 (a)	3 (c)	4 (a)	5 (b)	6 (b)	7 (c)	8 (b)	9 (d)	10 (c)
11 (a)	12 (b)	13 (a)	14 (b)	15 (b)	16 (b)	17 (c)	18 (c)	19 (d)	20 (d)
21 (a)	22 (c)	23 (d)	24 (c)	25 (b)	26 (b)	27 (d)	28 (d)	29 (c)	30 (b)
31 (c)	32 (c)	33 (a)	34 (d)	35 (a)	36 (d)	37 (a)	38 (a)	39 (c)	40 (a)
41 (c)	42 (a)	43 (c)	44 (c)	45 (c)	46 (a)	47 (a)	48 (b)	49 (a)	50 (b)
51 (c)	52 (c)	53 (b)	54 (b)	55 (c)	56 (a)	57 (d)	58 (a)	59 (a)	60 (a)

PART-II

61 (a)	62 (c)	63 (c)	64 (d)	65 (a)	66 (c)	67 (a)	68 (a)	69 (c)	70 (c)
71 (d)	72 (b)	73 (a)	74 (c)	75 (b)	76 (c)	77 (a)	78 (b)	79 (a)	80 (c)

Solutions

1. *(b)* $5^{99} = 5^{98} \cdot 5 = (5^2)^{49} \cdot 5$

$\qquad = (25)^{49} \cdot 5 = 5(26 - 1)^{49}$

$\qquad = 5(26k - 1) \, [\because (a - b)^n = nk - (b)^n]$

$\qquad = 5 \times 26k - 5 = 5 \times 26k - 13 + 8$

$\qquad = 13(10k - 1) + 8$

$\therefore$ When 5^{99} is divided by 13 the remainder is 8.

2. *(a)* Let

$\quad p(x) = q(x)(x^2 - 3x + 2) + (2x - 3)$

$\quad p(x) = q(x)(x - 1)(x - 2) + (2x - 3)$

$\quad p(1) = 0 + (2 - 3) = -1$

$\quad p(2) = 0 + (4 - 3) = 1$

$\therefore \ p(1) < 0$ and $p(2) > 0$

$\therefore \ p(x)$ has one root lie between 1 and 2.

$\therefore p(x)$ must have a root lie between 0 and 3.

3. *(c)* Let the original price of commodity
$\qquad\qquad\qquad\qquad\qquad = P$

Price of commodity when price $x\%$ increase

$\quad = P + x\%$ of $P = \dfrac{P(100 + x)}{100}$

Price of commodity when price $Y\%$ decrease from the increase of $x\%$

$\quad = P\left(\dfrac{100 + x}{100}\right) - \dfrac{Y}{100} \times \dfrac{P(100 + x)}{100}$

$\quad = \dfrac{P(100 + x)}{100}\left(\dfrac{100 - y}{100}\right)$

Given, the reduces price is equal to original price.

$\therefore \quad P\left(\dfrac{100 + x}{100}\right)\left(\dfrac{100 - y}{100}\right) = P$

$\quad \left(\dfrac{100 + x}{100}\right)\left(\dfrac{100 - y}{100}\right) = 1$

$\Rightarrow \quad 1 + \dfrac{x}{100} - \dfrac{y}{100} - \dfrac{xy}{(100)^2} = 1$

$\Rightarrow \qquad \dfrac{x}{100} - \dfrac{y}{100} = \dfrac{xy}{(100)^2}$

$\Rightarrow \qquad x - y = \dfrac{xy}{100}$

Divide by xy, we get $\dfrac{1}{y} - \dfrac{1}{x} = \dfrac{1}{100}$

4. *(a)* Let α, β are roots of equation

$\qquad x^2 + ax + b = 0$

$\therefore \qquad\qquad \alpha + \beta = -a, \alpha\beta = b$

and γ, δ are roots of equation

$\qquad x^2 + bx + a = 0$

$\therefore \qquad\qquad \gamma + \delta = -b, \gamma\delta = a$

Given, $\quad |\alpha - \beta| = |\gamma - \delta|$

$\qquad\qquad (\alpha - \beta)^2 = (\gamma - \delta)^2$

$\Rightarrow \alpha^2 + \beta^2 - 2\alpha\beta = \gamma^2 + \delta^2 - 2\gamma\delta$

$\Rightarrow (\alpha + \beta)^2 - 4\alpha\beta = (\gamma + \delta)^2 - 4\gamma\delta$

$\Rightarrow \qquad a^2 - 4b = b^2 - 4a$

$\Rightarrow (a^2 - b^2) + 4(a - b) = 0$

$\Rightarrow \ (a - b)(a + b + 4) = 0$

$\Rightarrow \qquad a + b + 4 = 0 \qquad [\because a \neq b]$

5. *(b)* P be an interior point of rectangle $ABCD$.

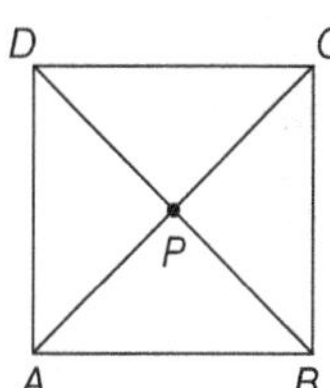

$\therefore$ Area of ΔAPB + area of ΔPCD

$\qquad =$ Area of ΔPBC + Area of ΔPAB

$\therefore$ In option (b), $21 + 6 = 15 + 12$

$\therefore$ Option (b) is correct.

6. *(b)* We have,

$$\sum_{i=1}^{n} x_i^2 = 400 \text{ and } \sum_{i=1}^{n} x_i = 80$$

We know,

$\Rightarrow \dfrac{x_1^2 + x_2^2 + x_3^2 + \dots + x_n^2}{n}$

$\qquad\qquad \geq \left(\dfrac{x_1 + x_2 + x_3 + \dots + x_n}{n}\right)^2$

$\Rightarrow \qquad \dfrac{\Sigma x_i^2}{n} \geq \dfrac{(\Sigma x_i)^2}{n^2}$

$\Rightarrow \qquad \dfrac{400}{n} \geq \dfrac{(80)^2}{n^2} \Rightarrow n \geq \dfrac{6400}{400} = 16$

$\therefore \qquad\qquad n \geq 16$

7. *(c)* The set S is divided into three equal size.

$\therefore$ Each set has 4 elements.

$\therefore$ Total number of ways in partition is

$^{12}C_4 \times {}^8C_4 \times {}^4C_4$.

$\dfrac{12!}{4! \, 8!} \times \dfrac{8!}{4! \, 4!} \times \dfrac{4!}{0! \, 4!} = \dfrac{12!}{(4!)^3}$

8. *(b)* Put x time of water of 110 ml to container and take y time of water of 25 ml from container.

Then, container contains $110x - 25y$

$\qquad\qquad = 5(22x - 5y)$

$\therefore$ Container contains multiple of 5.

$\therefore$ Smallest amount of water be measure accurately 5 ml.

9. *(d)* Given, $ABCD$ is collinear.

$\therefore AB + BC + CD = AD$

$\qquad\qquad \dfrac{AB}{CD} = \dfrac{3}{2}$

and $\qquad\qquad \dfrac{BC}{AD} = \dfrac{1}{5}$

$\Rightarrow \qquad\qquad \dfrac{AB}{CD} = \dfrac{3}{2}$

$\Rightarrow \qquad\qquad \dfrac{AC - BC}{BD - BC} = \dfrac{3}{2}$

$\Rightarrow \qquad 2AC - 2BC = 3BD - 3BC$

$\Rightarrow \qquad\qquad BC = 3BD - 2AC \qquad ...(i)$

and $\qquad\qquad \dfrac{BC}{AD} = \dfrac{1}{5}$

$\qquad\qquad\qquad 5BC = AD$

$\Rightarrow \qquad 5BC = AB + BC + CD$

$\Rightarrow \qquad 4BC = AB + CD$

$\Rightarrow \qquad 4BC = AC - BC + BD - BC$

$\Rightarrow \qquad 6BC = AC + BD \qquad ...(ii)$

From Eqs. (i) and (ii), we get

$\qquad 6(3BD - 2AC) = AC + BD$

$\Rightarrow \ 18BD - 12AC = AC + BD$

$\Rightarrow \qquad 13AC = 17BD$

$\Rightarrow \qquad \dfrac{AC}{BD} = \dfrac{17}{13}$

10. *(c)* We have,

In ΔABC,

$\qquad\qquad AB = AC = 6$

Circumradius $(R) = 5$

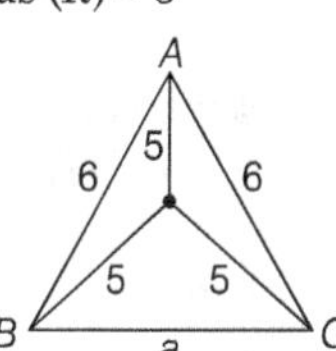

We know,

$\qquad R = \dfrac{abc}{4\Delta}$

$\quad 5 = \dfrac{(a)(6)(6)}{4\sqrt{\left(\dfrac{12 + a}{2}\right)\left(\dfrac{12 + a}{2} - 6\right)\left(\dfrac{12 + a}{2} - 6\right)\left(\dfrac{12 + a}{2} - a\right)}}$

$\Rightarrow \quad 5 = \dfrac{36a}{4\sqrt{\dfrac{(12 + a)(a)(a)(12 - a)}{16}}}$

$\Rightarrow \quad 5 = \dfrac{36}{\sqrt{144 - a^2}}$

$\Rightarrow 144 - a^2 = \left(\dfrac{36}{5}\right)^2$

$\Rightarrow \qquad a^2 = 144 - \left(\dfrac{36}{5}\right)^2$

$= 144\left(1 - \dfrac{9}{25}\right) = \dfrac{144 \times 16}{25}$

$\Rightarrow \qquad a^2 = \sqrt{\dfrac{144 \times 16}{25}} = \dfrac{48}{5}$

11. *(a)* Let the second car overtakes in t hours.

$\therefore$ Distance covered by first = Distance covered by second car

$10t = 8 + \left(8 + \dfrac{1}{2}\right) + \left(8 + 2\left(\dfrac{1}{2}\right)\right)$
$\qquad + \left(8 + \dfrac{3}{2}\right) + \ldots + \left(8 + \left(\dfrac{t-1}{2}\right)\right)$

$\Rightarrow \quad 10t = 8t + \dfrac{1}{2}(1 + 2 + 3 + \ldots + t - 1)$

$\Rightarrow \quad 10t = 8t + \dfrac{1}{2}\dfrac{(t)(t-1)}{2}$

$\Rightarrow t^2 - t = 8t \Rightarrow t - 1 = 8 \Rightarrow t = 9$

$\therefore$ The second car overtake the first car in 9 h.

12. *(b)* We have,

$\Rightarrow \qquad x^2 + 2013 = y^2$

$\Rightarrow \qquad y^2 - x^2 = 2013$

$\Rightarrow \quad (y + x)(y - x) = 3 \times 11 \times 61$

xy is minimum when

$\qquad y - x = 33 : y + x = 61$

$\therefore \qquad\qquad x = 14, y = 47$

$\therefore$ Minimum value of $xy = 14 \times 47 = 658$

13. *(a)* We have,

Edge of cube = 2 cm

$\therefore$ Total surface area of cube

$\qquad = 6\,(\text{side})^2 = 6(2)^2 = 24\,\text{cm}^2$

Length, breadth and height of cuboid are 1, 2 and 3 respectively

Total surface area of cuboid

$\qquad = 2(lb + bh + hl)$
$\qquad = 2(2 + 6 + 3)$
$\qquad = 22\,\text{cm}^2$

Total surface area of both cube and cuboid is $24 + 22 = 46$

which is less than $54\,\text{cm}^2$.

$\therefore$ Both cube and cuboid can be painted.

14. *(b)* Given, $(x)^{x\sqrt{x}} = (x\sqrt{x})^x$

$\qquad = (x)^{x^{\frac{3}{2}}} = x^{\frac{3x}{2}}$

Case I When base $x = 1$

Case II When base $x \neq 1$

Then, $x^{3/2} = \dfrac{3x}{2}$

$x\left(\sqrt{x} - \dfrac{3}{2}\right) = 0$

$\Rightarrow \quad \sqrt{x} = \dfrac{3}{2}, x \neq 0 \Rightarrow x = \dfrac{9}{4}$

$\therefore$ Hence, two solution $x = 1, \dfrac{9}{4}$

15. *(b)* Given, $0 < a < b < c$

Here, a, b, c are distinct.

$\therefore$ Three digits number formed by using a, b, c where digits are not repeated is $3! = 6$

Sum of all the three digits number are

$\quad 2!\,(a + b + c)\,(10^2 + 10 + 1)$
$\qquad = 2(a + b + c)\,(100 + 10 + 1)$
$\qquad = 222(a + b + c)$

Given, $222(a + b + c) = 1554$

$\qquad a + b + c = \dfrac{1554}{222} = 7$

The possible digits whose sum seven are 1, 2, 4

$\therefore \qquad\qquad b = 2$

16. *(b)* With respect to observer, there is no acceleration in the vertical velocity component. So, path of particle is a straight line as in option (b).

17. *(c)* $F = -\dfrac{dU}{dx} = -(2x + 3)$

For stable equilibrium,

$\qquad F = 0 \Rightarrow x = -\dfrac{3}{2}$

Also, $\qquad \dfrac{d^2U}{dx^2} = 2$

So, there is a minima of U.

i.e. system is in stable equilibrium.

18. *(c)* By principle of thermometry,

$\dfrac{X - (-180°\,\text{X})}{-60°\,\text{X} - (-180°\,\text{X})} = \dfrac{25 - 0}{100}$

$\Rightarrow \qquad \dfrac{X + 180°\,\text{X}}{120°\,\text{X}} = \dfrac{1}{4}$

$\Rightarrow \quad X + 180°\,\text{X} = \dfrac{120°\,\text{X}}{4} = 30°\,\text{X}$

$X = -180°\,\text{X} + 30°\,\text{X} \Rightarrow X = -150°\,\text{X}$

19. *(d)* Following conservation of mass number and atomic number, we have

$\qquad {}^{9}_{4}\text{Be} + {}^{4}_{2}\text{He} \longrightarrow {}^{12}_{6}\text{C} + {}^{1}_{0}n$

So, particle ${}^{1}_{0}n$ is a neutron.

20. *(d)*

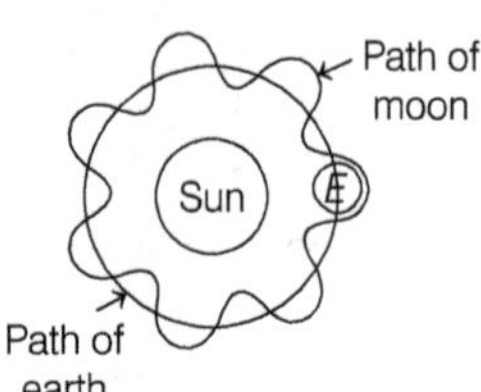

Acceleration of blocks are

$a_1 = \dfrac{F - f_1}{m_1} = \dfrac{F - \mu m_1 g}{m_1} = 10\,\text{ms}^{-2}$

$a_2 = \dfrac{-F + \mu m_2 g}{m_2} = -1\,\text{ms}^{-2}$

Now, from equation of motion, we have

$\qquad s = ut + \dfrac{1}{2}at^2$

$\quad 22 = 0 + \dfrac{1}{2}(10 - (-1))\,t^2$

$\Rightarrow \qquad t = 2\,\text{s}$

21. *(a)* Force on ball, $F = v\dfrac{\Delta m}{\Delta t}$

where, $\dfrac{\Delta m}{\Delta t}$ = flow rate of water.

$\Rightarrow \qquad v\dfrac{\Delta m}{\Delta t} = mg$

$\Rightarrow \qquad \dfrac{\Delta m}{\Delta t} = \dfrac{mg}{\sqrt{2gh}} = \dfrac{m}{\sqrt{2}}\sqrt{\dfrac{g}{h}}$

22. *(c)* For a cyclic process,

$\qquad 1 \rightarrow 2 \rightarrow 3 \rightarrow 1$

$\qquad \Sigma \Delta U = 0$

$\Rightarrow 100 + c + (-200) = 0$ or $c = 100\,\text{kJ}$

23. *(d)* From free body diagram,

$F - mg = ma$

$\Rightarrow \qquad F = m(g + a)$
$\qquad = 1\,(10 + 10)$
$\qquad = 20\,\text{N}$

24. *(c)* Electrons are not effective in scattering α-particles because they are about 7000 times lighter than α-particles.

25. *(b)* $\qquad g_h = g\left(1 - \dfrac{2h}{R}\right)$

and $\qquad g_d = g\left(1 - \dfrac{d}{R}\right)$

$\Rightarrow \qquad g_h = g_d \Rightarrow 2h = d$

$\Rightarrow \qquad \dfrac{h}{d} = \dfrac{1}{2} = 0.5$

26. *(b)* India is in northern hemisphere and due to rotation of earth, radially rushing wind will tend to rotate in anti-clockwise sense.

27. *(d)* Imagine earth rotating around sun and moon around earth.

28. *(d)* Velocity increases with time and then reaches terminal velocity. Velocity remains constant after reaching terminal speed.

29. *(c)* As density of ball $\left(=\dfrac{40}{50}=0.8\,g\,cm^{-3}\right)$ is less than water, it tends to float.

When ball is kept immersed, downthrust = weight of $50\,cm^3$ of water = $50\,g$

So, scale reading = $600 + 50 = 650\,g$

30. *(b)* $P_{combination} = 2(P_{lens}) + P_{mirror}$

$$= \dfrac{2 \times 100}{f_{lens}(\text{in cm})} + 0$$

$$= \dfrac{200}{-12/(1.5 - 1)}$$

$$= \dfrac{100}{-12} = -\dfrac{25}{3}\,D$$

31. *(c)* $CaCO_3 \longrightarrow CaO + CO_2$

Molar mass of $CaCO_3$

$$= 40 + 12 + 16 \times 3 = 100\,g$$

Molar mass of $CaO = 40 + 16 = 56\,g$

Molar mass of $CO_2 = 12 + 16 \times 2 = 44\,g$

$100\,g$ of $CaCO_3$ produces $44\,g$ of CO_2

$\therefore$ $10\,g$ of $CaCO_3$ produces $= \dfrac{44}{100} \times 10 = 4.4\,g$

32. *(c)* According to Raoult's law the vapour pressure of volatile component is directly proportional to its mole fraction. If the solution obeys Raoult's law at all concentration its vapour pressure would vary linearly from zero to the vapour pressure of pure solvent. Thus, the correct plot will be (c).

33. *(a)* The ionic character is decided by Fajan's rule. According to this rule, larger is size of cation, smaller the size of the anion and lesser is the charge on the cation or high, thus more will be the ionic character. As the anion and charge of n the cation in all the given compounds are same. So, the ionic character is only dependent on the size of cation. As the size of cation increases in the order

$$Be^{2+} < Mg^{2+} < Ca^{2+} < Ba^{2+}$$

$\therefore$ The ionic character will also increase in the same manner, i.e.

$$BeCl_2 < MgCl_2 < CaCl_2 < BaCl_2$$

34. *(d)* $3\overset{0}{Br_2} + 6CO_3^{2-} + 3H_2O \longrightarrow 5Br^-$
$$+ \overset{+5}{Br}O_3^- + 6HCO_3^-$$

In the reaction, Br_2 is reduced to Br^- (oxidation number decreases from zero to -1) and Br_2 is oxidised to BrO_3^- (oxidation number increases from zero to $+5$).

35. *(a)*

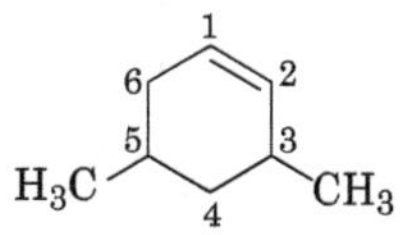

The IUPAC name of the above given compound is 3, 5-dimethyl cyclohexene.

36. *(d)* As pentan-2-one ($CH_3COCH_2CH_2CH_3$) and 3-methyl butanone ($CH_3COCH(CH_3)CH_3$) have similar molecular formula, but different carbon skeletons. Thus, they are chain isomers and will exhibit chain isomerism.

37. *(a)* The given value of $n = 3$ suggests that the shell is 3. For $n = 1$, l has 3 values, i.e. $+1$, 0 and -1 hence there occur 3 orbitals in p-subshell namely p_x, p_y and p_z. Thus, the given values for $n = 3$, $l = 1$ and $m_l = 0$ suggests that the orbital is $3p_y$. Hence, the maximum number of orbitals that can be identified with given quantum number is only 1.

38. *(a)*

$$CH_3CH{=}CHCH_2CH_3 \xrightarrow{O_3}$$

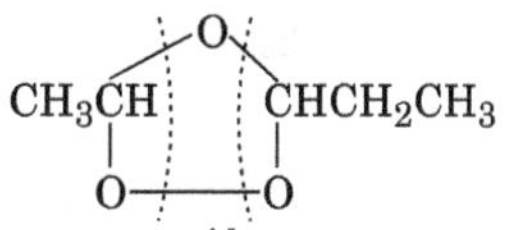

$$\underset{\text{ozonide}}{CH_3\overset{|}{\underset{|}{CH}}\overset{O}{\underset{O}{\diagdown\diagup}}\overset{|}{\underset{|}{CH}}CH_2CH_3}$$

$$\downarrow H_3O^+/ZnO$$

$$CH_3CHO + OHCCH_2CH_3$$

This reaction is known as ozonolysis reaction in which the addition of ozone molecule to alkene gives ozonide and then cleavage of ozonide by Zn—H_2O to smaller molecules occurs.

39. *(c)* PH_5 does not exist due to very less electronegativity difference between P and H. Hydrogen is slightly more electronegative than phosphorus, thus could not hold significantly the sharing electrons. On the other hand, $BiCl_5$ does not exist due to inert pair effect. This is because on moving down the group, +5 oxidation state becomes less stable while +3 oxidation state become more stable due to inert pair effect.

In SO_2, $p\pi$-$d\pi$ and $p\pi$-$p\pi$ both types of bonds are present.

SeF_4 has sp^3d-hybridisation whereas CH_4 has sp^3-hybridisation. Thus, they both have different geometry.

I_3^+ has a bent shape due to the presence of 2 lone pairs on central I atom.

40. *(a)* Any change in the concentration, pressure and temperature of the reaction results in change in the direction of equilibrium. This change in the direction of equlibrium is governed by Le-Chatelier's principle.

On increasing pressure, volume decreases. The reaction will move in the direction where there are less number of moles (according to Le-chatelier principle).

$$2SO_2(g) + O_2(g) \rightleftharpoons 2SO_3(g)$$

Hence, the reaction will more towards right.

41. *(c)* Given,

solubility product of $BaCl_2, K_{sp} = 4 \times 10^{-9}$

Let the solubility of $BaCl_2$ be S.

$$BaCl_2 \rightleftharpoons \underset{S}{Ba^{2+}} + \underset{2S}{2Cl^-}$$

$$K_{sp} = [Ba^{2+}]\,[Cl^-]^2 = (S)\,(2S)^2 = 4S^3$$

$$S = \left(\dfrac{K_{sp}}{4}\right)^{\frac{1}{3}} = \left(\dfrac{4 \times 10^{-9}}{4}\right)^{1/3}$$

$$= 1 \times 10^{-3}\ mol\ L^{-1}$$

42. *(a)* Chlorobenzene on treatment with sodium in dry ether gives diphenyl. The reaction is known as Fittig reaction.

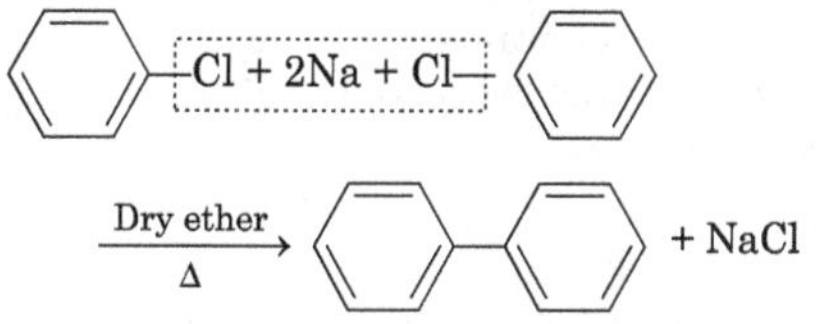

$$\text{Cl} + 2Na + \text{Cl}$$

$$\xrightarrow[\Delta]{\text{Dry ether}} \underset{\text{Diphenyl}}{\bigcirc\!\!-\!\!\bigcirc} + NaCl$$

43. *(c)* According to ideal gas equation,

$$pV = nRT$$

Given,

Pressure = $360\,torr = \dfrac{360}{760}\,atm$

Volume = 2.5

Temperature = $22.5 + 273 = 295.5\,K$

Weight of a gas = 1.6616

$\therefore$ $$n = \dfrac{pV}{RT}$$

Also $n = \dfrac{W}{M} \Rightarrow \dfrac{W}{M} = \dfrac{pV}{RT} = M = \dfrac{WRT}{pV}$

Substituting the values,

$$M = \dfrac{1.6616 \times 0.082 \times 295.5}{\dfrac{360}{760} \times 2.5} = 34.26\,g$$

$$\approx 34\,g$$

44. *(c)* Isoelectronic species are those species which have same number of electrons.

As all the given elements are isoelectronic with each other. Thus, the radii/size of isoelectronic species is inversely proportional to the atomic number, i.e. size $\propto \dfrac{1}{Z}$

Thus, the correct order is

$$S^{2-} > Cl^- > K^+ > Ca^{2+}$$

45. *(c)* The reaction of toluene with Cl_2 in the presence of $FeCl_3$ gives predominantly o and p chlorotoluene. This reaction follows electrophilic substitution mechanism and Cl^+ act as as electrophile.

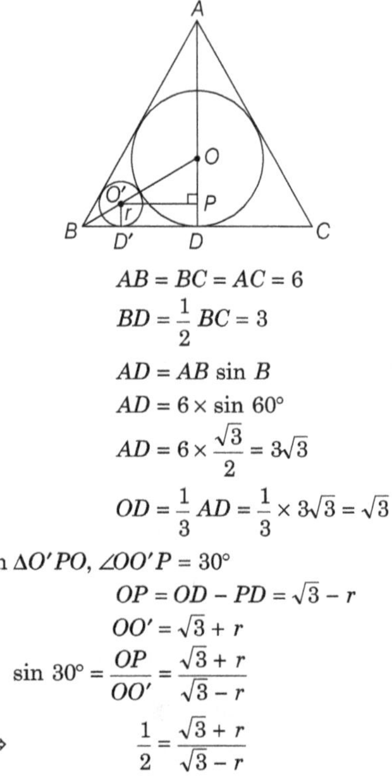

46. *(a)* Phosphatidylcholine is a class of phospholipids that are a major component of biological membranes (i.e. nerve cell membrane). It functions in the production of brain chemical called acetylcholine used for nerve impulse transmission at the synapse.

47. *(a)* Graft rejection does not involve erythrocytes. Transplant or graft rejection occurs when transplanted tissue is rejected by the recipient's immune system, which destroys the transplanted tissue. Rejection is an adaptive immune response *via* cellular immunity (mediated by killer T-cells), macrophages and polymorphonuclear leukocytes (i.e., neutrophils, eosinophils and basophils).

48. *(b)* Horse-shoe crabs are marine and brackish water arthropods. They resemble crustaceans but belong to separate subphylum of the arthropods, i.e. Chelicerata. The entire body of the horse-shoe crab is protected by a hard carapace.

49. *(a)* The first living being on the earth were anaerobic or heterotrophic bacteria because the primordial atmosphere was virtually oxygen-free. These organisms must have degraded simple compounds present in the primordial oceans. They may have had RNA genomes and used RNA as biological catalysts.

50. *(b) Salmonella* bacterium causes salmonellosis infection. The bacteria spread through human or animal faeces. Thus, the presence of *Salmonella* in tap water is due to contamination through human excreta. *Salmonella* outbreaks are commonly associated with eggs, meat and poultry, but these bacteria can also contaminate other foods such as fruits and vegetables.

51. *(c)* The structures adopted by polypeptides can be divided into four levels of organisation, i.e., the primary, secondary, tertiary and quaternary structures. The secondary structure pertains to the coiling of the polypeptide chains into regular structure such as α-helices and β-pleated sheets.

52. *(c)* At prophase-I, DNA replication has already occurred and the original amount of DNA has been doubled to x. At anaphase-I, the amount of DNA in the cell remains the same because no cytokinesis has occurred yet to separate the cytoplasm.

53. *(b)* If O_2 is not available, pyruvic acid undergoes anaerobic respiration / fermentation, but under aerobic condition, the pyruvic acid enters into mitochondria and converted to acetyl Co-A. Acetyl Co-A functions as substrate entrant for Krebs' cycle. So, it is a connecting link between glycolysis and Kreb's cycle.

54. *(b)* Glucose is stored in the liver as glycogen. Glycogen can be converted to free glucose by the process of glycogenolysis, which involves the activation of a phosphorylase enzyme by the hormone glucagon. Glucagon is made by the pancreas and is released when the blood sugar levels fall. There release of glucose is a homeostatic function of liver that is controlled and monitored in the pancreas.

55. *(c)* As the membrane potential is increased, sodium ions channels open, allowing the influx of Na^+ ions into the cell. The inward flow of sodium ions increases the concentration of positively charged cations in the cell and causes depolarisation, where the potential of the cell is higher than the cell's resting potential.

56. *(a)* Ammonia is toxic waste product which is converted into urea in the liver. This urea then enters the excretory system to get eliminated from the body. High levels of ammonia in blood is an indication of liver damage.

57. *(d)* Mendel did not choose pod length. The seven contrasting traits he took were
- Plant height
- Pod colour
- Flower colour
- Seed colour
- Flower position
- Pod shape
- Seed shape

58. *(a)* The levels of classification from the broadest to the narrowest, i.e. in term of having highest members to the lowest members are kingdom, phylum, class, order, family, genus and species.

59. *(a)* Centrosomes are made up of a pair of centrioles and other proteins. The centrosomes are important for cell division and produce microtubules that separate DNA into two new identical cells.

60. *(a)* The cerebellum is the part of hindbrain responsible for hand-eye coordination. It is responsible for maintaining equilibrium, transfer of information, fine adjustments to motor actions, coordinating eye movements, etc. Coordination and body balance, posture during walking, riding, standing, swimming, running are all maintained by the cerebellum.

61. *(a)* Given, ABC is an equilateral triangle.

$$AB = BC = AC = 6$$
$$BD = \frac{1}{2} BC = 3$$
$$AD = AB \sin B$$
$$AD = 6 \times \sin 60°$$
$$AD = 6 \times \frac{\sqrt{3}}{2} = 3\sqrt{3}$$
$$OD = \frac{1}{3} AD = \frac{1}{3} \times 3\sqrt{3} = \sqrt{3}$$

In $\Delta O'PO$, $\angle OO'P = 30°$
$$OP = OD - PD = \sqrt{3} - r$$
$$OO' = \sqrt{3} + r$$
$$\therefore \quad \sin 30° = \frac{OP}{OO'} = \frac{\sqrt{3} + r}{\sqrt{3} - r}$$
$$\Rightarrow \qquad \frac{1}{2} = \frac{\sqrt{3} + r}{\sqrt{3} - r}$$
$$\Rightarrow \qquad \sqrt{3} - r = 2\sqrt{3} + 2r$$
$$\Rightarrow \qquad r = \frac{1}{\sqrt{3}}$$

62. *(c)* We have, $x^2 y^3 = 6$

$$\frac{\frac{3x}{2} + \frac{3x}{2} + \frac{4y}{3} + \frac{4y}{3} + \frac{4y}{3}}{5} \geq \left(\frac{9x^2}{4} \times \frac{64y^3}{27} \right)^{1/5}$$
$$[\because AM \geq GM]$$
$$\Rightarrow \qquad 3x + 4y \geq 5 \left(\frac{16}{3} \times 6 \right)^{1/5} \quad [x^2 y^3 = 6]$$
$$\Rightarrow \qquad 3x + 4y \geq 10$$

$\therefore$ Minimum value of $3x + 4y$ is 10.

63. *(c)* We have three different kinds of mangoes and we can select 25 mangoes in all. Hence, we select 0 or 1 or 2 or 3 ... mangoes from each kind of mangoes.

Let x_1, x_2 and x_3 be different kinds of mangoes.

$\therefore x_1 + x_2 + x_3 = 25 \Rightarrow x_1, x_2, x_3 \geq 0$

$\therefore$ Total number of selection $= {}^{25 + 3 - 1}C_{3-1}$

$= {}^{27}C_2$

$= \dfrac{27 \times 26}{1 \times 2} = 351$

64. *(d)* We have, $(1 - y)^m (1 + y)^n$

$= \left(1 - my + \dfrac{m(m-1)}{2} y^2 + ...\right)$

$\quad \left(1 + ny + \dfrac{n(n-1)}{2} y^2 + ...\right)$

$\Rightarrow (1 - y)^m (1 + y)^n = 1 + (n - m) y$

$+ \left(\dfrac{n(n-1)}{2} + \dfrac{m(m-1)}{2} - nm\right) y^2 + ...$

Here, $\qquad a_1 = n - m = 10 \qquad$ ...(i)

$a_2 = \dfrac{n(n-1)}{2} + \dfrac{m(m-1)}{2} - nm = 10$

$\Rightarrow a_2 = \dfrac{n^2 - n + m^2 - m - 2mn}{2} = 10$

$\Rightarrow \qquad (n - m)^2 - (n + m) = 20 \qquad$ ...(ii)

From Eqs. (i) and (ii), we get

$\qquad\qquad n + m = 80 \qquad$ ...(iii)

From Eqs. (i) and (ii), we get

$\qquad\qquad n = 45, m = 35$

$\therefore \qquad (m, n) = (35, 45)$

65. *(a)* We have,

ABC is a right angle triangle.

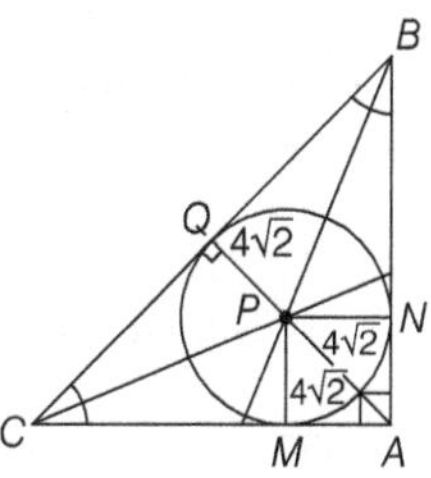

$\angle A = 90°$, the angle bisector of B and C meet at P

The distance from P to hypotenuse is $4\sqrt{2}$

$\therefore \qquad\qquad PQ = 4\sqrt{2}$

Here, PQ is the radius of incircle of ΔABC.

$\therefore PQ = PM = PN =$ radii of incircle of

$\qquad\qquad\qquad\qquad \Delta ABC$

$\therefore \qquad AP^2 = PM^2 + AM^2$

$\qquad AP^2 = (4\sqrt{2})^2 + (4\sqrt{2})^2$

$\qquad\qquad\qquad\qquad [\because AM = PN]$

$\qquad AP^2 = 32 + 32$

$\qquad AP = \sqrt{64} = 8$

66. *(c)* Present temperature,

$$T_1 = \dfrac{\begin{matrix}1.38 \times 10^{-28} \times (10 \times (100)^2 + 30 \times (200)^2 \\ + 20 \times (500)^2 + 20 \times (800)^2 + 20 \times (1000)^2)\end{matrix}}{3 \times 1.38 \times 10^{-23}}$$

$$= \dfrac{\begin{matrix}10^{-5} \times 10^4 (10 + 30 \times 4 + 20 \times 25 + 20 \\ \times 64 + 20 \times 100)\end{matrix}}{3}$$

$$= \dfrac{10^{-1} \times (10 + 120 + 500 + 1280 + 2000)}{3}$$

$$= \dfrac{3910}{30} = 130.33 \approx 130 \text{ K}$$

In few years, all the molecules with speed $> 900 \text{ ms}^{-1}$ will left the atmosphere.

So, then temperature will be

$$T_2 = \dfrac{\begin{matrix}1.38 \times 10^{-28} \times (10 \times (100)^2 + 30 \times (200)^2 \\ + 20 \times (500)^2 + 20 \times (800)^2)\end{matrix}}{3 \times 1.38 \times 10^{-23}}$$

$$= \dfrac{\begin{matrix}10^{-5} \times 10^4 \times (10 + 30 \times 4 \\ + 20 \times 25 + 20 \times 64)\end{matrix}}{3}$$

$$= \dfrac{10^{-1} \times (10 + 120 + 500 + 1280)}{3}$$

$$= \dfrac{1910}{30} = 63.66 \text{ K}$$

Reduction in temperature is nearly,

$\Delta T = T_1 - T_2 = 130 - 63.66$

$\qquad\qquad = 66.34 \text{ K} \approx 70 \text{ K}$

67. *(a)* Let $x =$ mass per unit length of ruler.

Forces on ruler are as shown below.

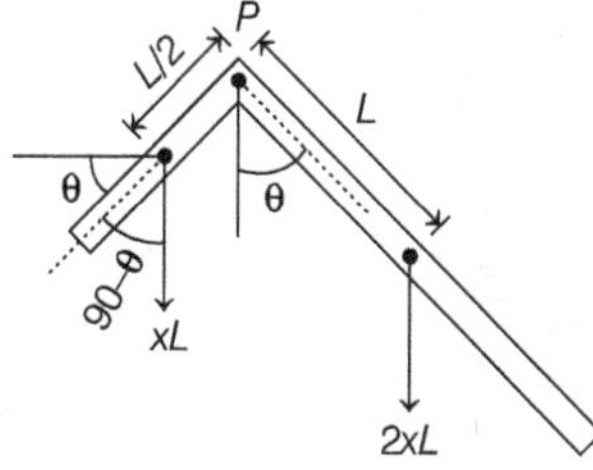

Equating moments about P,

$\dfrac{L}{2} (x \cdot L) \sin(90 - \theta) = L (2xL) \sin\theta$

$\Rightarrow \qquad \dfrac{\sin\theta}{\cos\theta} = \tan\theta = \dfrac{1}{4}$

68. *(a)* 1 kg of water expands from 1000 cm^3 to 1.68 m^3.

$\therefore \qquad \Delta V = 1.68 - 0.001 \approx 1.68 \text{ m}^3$

So, work done in expanding against pressure is

$\Delta W = p\Delta V = 1.01 \times 10^3 \times 1.68 = 169 \text{ kJ}$

Now, $\dfrac{\Delta W}{mL_V} = \dfrac{169}{1 \times 2260} = 0.0748$

69. *(c)*

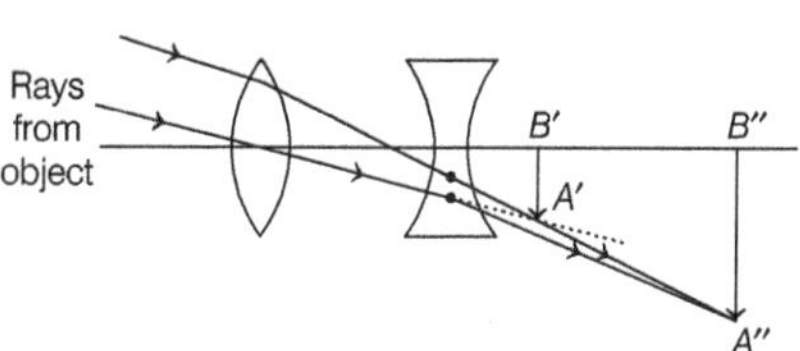

For convex lens, image is at focal distance 6 cm from the lens.

For concave lens,

$\qquad u = + 2 \text{ cm}, f = - 2.5 \text{ cm}$

$\Rightarrow \qquad \dfrac{1}{v} = \dfrac{1}{f} + \dfrac{1}{u} = \dfrac{1}{-2.5} + \dfrac{1}{2}$

$\Rightarrow \qquad v = + 10 \text{ cm}$

Linear magnification, produced by diverging lens is $m = \dfrac{v}{u} = \dfrac{10}{2} = 5$

So, diverging lens increases the magnification five times.

70. *(c)* $\qquad\qquad I = nev_d A$

$\Rightarrow \qquad v_d = \dfrac{I}{neA} = \dfrac{V/R}{neA}$

$\Rightarrow \qquad v_d = \dfrac{V}{\rho lne}$

So, drift speed is independent of area of conductor.

Hence, the ratio of v_{d_2} / v_{d_1} is 1.

71. *(d)* Given, specific heat of water

$\qquad\qquad = 4.184 \, g^{-1} \, ^\circ C^{-1}$

Heat capacity of calorimeter $= 783 \, \text{J} ^\circ C^{-1}$

Mass of water $= 254 \, g$

$\qquad \Delta T = 26.01 - 23.73 = 2.28 ^\circ C$

$q_{\text{bomb}} = C\Delta T = 783 \times 2.28 \, \text{J} = 1785.24 \, \text{J}$

$q_{\text{water}} = m \times \text{specific heat} \times \Delta T$

$\qquad = 254 \times 4.184 \times 2.28$

$\qquad = 2423.04 \, \text{J}$

Heat absorbed $= 1785.24 \, \text{J} + 2423.04 \, \text{J}$

$\qquad\qquad = 4208.28 \, \text{J} \approx 4.21 \, \text{kJ}$

72. *(b)* The hybridisation of any molecule can be calculated using formula

$X = \dfrac{1}{2}$ (valence electrons number of atoms

monoatomic $\pm$ anion/cation)

The shape and hybridisation of given molecules are as follows

Molecule	Shape	Hybridisation
NF_3	Pyramidal	sp^3
BF_3	Triangular planar	sp^2
BF_4^-	Tetrahedral	sp^3
NH_4^+	Tetrahedral	sp^3

Molecule	Shape	Hybridisation
BCl_3	Triangular planar	sp^2
$BrCl_3$	T-shaped	sp^3d
NH_3	Pyramidal	sp^3
NO_3^-	Triangular planar	sp^2

As BF_4^- and NH_4^+ have same shape and hybridisation. Thus, they are isostructural pair.

73. *(a)* Geometrical isomers are those isomers, which have same molecular formula, but different spatial arrangement of atoms about the double bond. In geometrical isomers, both the carbon atoms of a double bond should contain different substituents.

(a)

$$xH\,\diagdown\diagup Hx$$
$$y H_3C \diagup \diagdown CH_3\, y$$

As both the substituents are different hence, they will show geometrical isomerism.

(b)

$$y H_3C \diagdown \diagup CH_3\, x$$
$$y CH_3 \diagup \diagdown CH_3\, x$$

It does not show geometrical isomerism.

(c)

$$x \diagup \diagup Hx$$
$$y\, H \diagup\diagdown Hx$$

It does not show geometrical isomerism.

(d)

$$\diagup H\,x$$
$$\diagdown H\,x$$

It does not show geometrical isomerism.

74. *(c)* $CH_3\!-\!\overset{\displaystyle CH_3}{\underset{}{C}}\!=\!CH_2 \xleftarrow[E_1]{CH_3CH_2O^-Na^+}$

$$H_3C\!-\!\overset{\displaystyle CH}{\underset{\displaystyle CH_3}{C}}\!-\!Br \xrightarrow[S_N1]{CH_3CH_2OH}$$

$$CH_3\!-\!\overset{\displaystyle CH_3}{\underset{\displaystyle CH_3}{C}}OCH_2CH_3$$
(Major)
(A)

As in the given compound is 3°alkyl halide, so it can either go S_N1 or E_1 reaction, which is dependent on the nutrophile. As $CH_3CH_2O^-Na^+$ is a strong $Nu^\ominus$, so it will prefer to undergo E_1 reaction whereas CH_3CH_2OH is a weak $Nu^\ominus$ which undergoes S_N2.

75. *(b)* Number of π and σ bands in given species are as follows :

	Structure	No. of σ and π bonds
(a)	$-O\overset{\sigma}{\diagup}\underset{\sigma\|\pi}{C}\overset{\sigma}{\diagdown}O\overset{\sigma}{-}H$	σ bonds = 4 π bonds = 1
(b)	$O\overset{\sigma}{\underset{\sigma\|\pi}{\diagup}}\overset{\sigma\|\pi}{\underset{\sigma\|\pi}{Xe}}\overset{\sigma}{\diagdown}O$ (with O above and below)	σ bonds = 4 π bonds = 4
(c)	$N\overset{2\pi}{\underset{\sigma}{\equiv}}C\overset{\sigma}{-}C\overset{2\pi}{\underset{\sigma}{\equiv}}N$	σ bonds = 3 π bonds = 4
(d)	$N\overset{2\pi}{\underset{\sigma}{\equiv}}C\overset{\sigma}{-}\overset{\displaystyle H}{\underset{\displaystyle H}{\overset{\sigma}{\underset{\sigma}{C}}}}\overset{\sigma}{-}C\overset{2\pi}{\underset{\sigma}{\equiv}}N$	σ bonds = 6 π bonds = 4

76. *(c)* The graph (c) is correct as, it shows the highest biochemical activity in the lysosomes. These are membrane bound organelles which contain enzymes that degrade polymers into their monomeric subunits, i.e. hydrolytic enzymes.

77. *(a)* There are four possible mating crosses which can occur with persons of blood group *A* and blood group *B*.

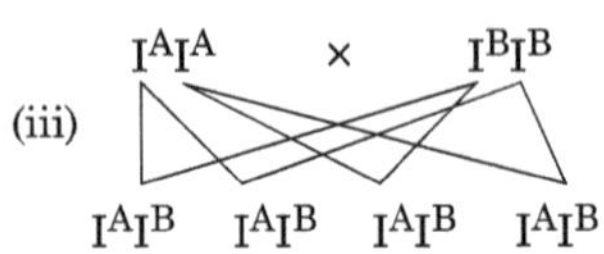

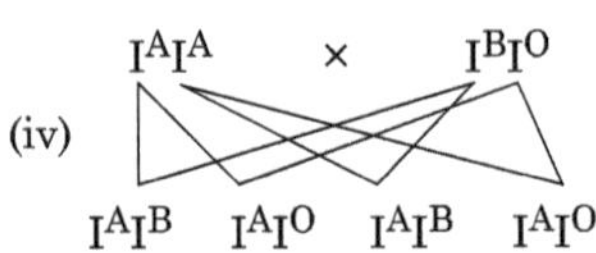

(i) $I^AI^O \times I^BI^O$: I^AI^O, I^AI^O, I^BI^O, I^OI^O

(ii) $I^AI^O \times I^BI^B$: I^AI^B, I^AI^B, I^BI^O, I^BI^O

(iii) $I^AI^A \times I^BI^B$: I^AI^B, I^AI^B, I^AI^B, I^AI^B

(iv) $I^AI^A \times I^BI^O$: I^AI^B, I^AI^O, I^AI^B, I^AI^O

Thus, in all four possibilities for F_1-generation can be I^AI^B, I^AI^O, I^BI^O, I^OI^O but never I^AI^A or AA.

78. *(b)* Only the electron transport system produces ATP and reduced NADP in the plant. Without these compounds, the Calvin cycle cannot proceed and carbon-fixation cannot occur and their is no respiratory substrate available for respiration.

79. *(a)* Immovable / fixed / fibrous joints are present between the skull bones. So, between parietal bone and the temporal bone of the skull are joined by fibrous joint. Other statements can be corrected as First cervical vertebra is atlas not axis. The 11th and 12th pairs of ribs are called floating ribs. Glenoid cavity is located at the end of scapula close to coracoid process.

80. *(c)* The triplet codon is made up of 3 nucleotide bases and is located at the centre of the middle loop of *t*RNA molecule and base pairs with the complementary bases on an *m*RNA molecule during protein synthesis.

PRACTICE SET 3
Stream : SA

MM : 100

Instructions

1. There are 80 questions in this paper.
2. This question paper contains two parts; Part I and Part II. There are four sections; Mathematics, Physics, Chemistry and Biology in each part.
3. Out of the four options given with each question, only one is correct.

➔ PART-I (1 Mark Questions)

MATHEMATICS

1. Let $E(n)$ denote the sum of the even digits of n. For example $E(1243) = 2 + 4 = 6$, then the value of $E(1) + E(2) + E(3) + \ldots + E(100)$ is equal to
(a) 200   (b) 300   (c) 400   (d) 500

2. The greatest possible perimeter of right angle triangle with integer side length if one of the sides has length 12 is
(a) 80   (b) 84   (c) 72   (d) 82

3. In a party, each man danced with exactly four women and each woman danced with exactly three men. Nine men attended the party, then number of woman attended the party is
(a) 12   (b) 9   (c) 6   (d) 8

4. If $3^x + 2^y = 985$ and $3^x - 2^y = 473$, then the value of xy is
(a) 36   (b) 72   (c) 48   (d) 54

5. A certain school has 300 students. Every student reads 5 newspapers and every newspaper is read by 60 students. Then, the number of newspaper
(a) is at least 30
(b) is at least 20
(c) is exactly 25
(d) cannot be determined by the data

6. Let a, b and c such that $a + b + c = 0$ and is defined as
$$P = \frac{a^2}{2a^2 + bc} + \frac{b^2}{2b^2 + ac} + \frac{c^2}{2c^2 + ab},$$ then the value of P is equal to
(a) 1   (b) $\frac{1}{2}$
(c) $\frac{1}{4}$ (d) 2

7. In a rectangle $ABCD$, $AB = 8$ and $BC = 20$, let P be a point on AD such that $\angle BPC = 90°$. If r_1, r_2 and r_3 are radii of the incircles of $\triangle APB$, BPC and CPD respectively, then the value of $r_1 + r_2 + r_3$ is equal to
(a) 6   (b) 8   (c) 10   (d) 12

8. If $\sin\theta + \cos\theta = \sqrt{3}$, then the value of $\tan\theta + \cot\theta$ is
(a) 1   (b) $\sqrt{2}$
(c) 2   (d) None of these

9. Numbers 1, 2, 3, ... 100 are written down each of the cards A, B and C. One number is selected at random from each of the cards. The probability that the numbers so selected can be the measures (in cm) of three sides of the right angled triangles no two of which are similar is

(a) $\dfrac{4}{100^3}$ (b) $\dfrac{3}{50^3}$ (c) $\dfrac{3!}{100^3}$ (d) None of these

10. In a triangle with integer side length, one side is three times as long as a second side and the length of the third side is 17. What is the greatest possible perimeter of the triangle?

(a) 46   (b) 47   (c) 48   (d) 49

11. One morning, each member of Kanchan's family drank 8 ounce mixture of coffee and milk. The amount of coffee and milk varied from cup to cup, but were never zero. Kanchan drank $\dfrac{1}{7}$th of the total amount of milk and $\dfrac{2}{17}$th of the total amount of coffee, then the number of people are there in Kanchan's family are

(a) 8   (b) 9   (c) 7   (d) 17

12. Let ABC be a triangle with $\angle ABC = 90°$. Let P and Q are mid-point of legs AB and BC, respectively. Suppose that $AQ = 19$ and $PC = 22$, then length of AC is equal to

(a) 24   (b) 25   (c) 26   (d) 30

13. Number of natural numbers n between 1 and 2019 (both inclusive) is $\dfrac{8n}{9999 - n}$ an integer is

(a) 0   (b) 1   (c) 2   (d) 3

14. A ray of light originating at the vertex A of a square $ABCD$ passes through the vertex B after getting reflected by BC, CD and DA in that order. If θ is the angle of the initial position of the ray with AB, then $\sin\theta$ equals

(a) $\dfrac{2}{\sqrt{13}}$ (b) $\dfrac{3}{\sqrt{13}}$ (c) $\dfrac{3}{5}$ (d) $\dfrac{4}{5}$

15. Let m be the number of ways in which two couples can be seated on 4 chairs in a row, so that no wife is next to her husband and n be the number of ways in which they can be seated in 4 chairs in a circle. In the other case rotation are considered different configurations. Then,

(a) $m = n$ (b) $m = 2n$ (c) $m = 4n$ (d) $m = 8n$

PHYSICS

16. A sample of pure ice is taken and following are recorded.

    I. Heat to melt the ice.

    II. Heat to warm ice cold water to 100°C.

    III. Heat to vaporize the water at 100°C.

The correct option is

(a) $H_I > H_{II} > H_{III}$

(b) $H_I < H_{II} < H_{III}$

(c) $H_I = H_{II} < H_{III}$

(d) data insufficient to conclude

17. Potential energy of a spring when stretched through a distance x is 10 J. Ratio of work done for every additional distance is

(a) $1 : 1 : 1 : ....$ (b) $1 : 2 : 4 : .....$

(c) $1 : 3 : 5 : ....$ (d) $1 : 4 : 9 : 16 : ...$

18. At what temperature, the celsius and farenheit scale give the same temperature value?

(a) 0°C   (b) −10°F

(c) −40°C   (d) −20°C

19. In given nuclear transformation,

$$_{92}U^{238} \xrightarrow{\ \alpha\ } {}_B Th^A \xrightarrow{\ \beta^-\ } {}_D Pa^C \xrightarrow{\ E\ } {}_{92}U^{234}$$

A, B, C, D and E are

(a) $A = 234, B = 90, C = 234, D = 91, E = \beta$

(b) $A = 234, B = 90, C = 238, D = 94, E = \alpha$

(c) $A = 238, B = 93, C = 234, D = 91, E = \beta$

(d) $A = 234, B = 90, C = 234, D = 93, E = \alpha$

20. A particle is subjected to two simple harmonic motions

$$(x = \sqrt{2}\,\sin\omega t)\ \text{cm and}\ \left[x = \sqrt{2}\,\sin\left(\omega t + \dfrac{\pi}{3}\right)\right]\text{cm}$$

time t is in seconds. Maximum speed of the particle, if $\omega = 1\,\dfrac{\text{rad}}{\text{s}}$ is

(a) $\sqrt{6}\,\dfrac{\text{cm}}{\text{s}^2}$ (b) $\sqrt{3}\,\dfrac{\text{cm}}{\text{s}^2}$

(c) $\sqrt{2}\,\dfrac{\text{cm}}{\text{s}^2}$ (d) $\dfrac{1}{\sqrt{2}}\,\dfrac{\text{cm}}{\text{s}^2}$

21. A man crosses a 320 m wide river perpendicular to the current in 4 min. If in still water, he can swim with a speed $\dfrac{5}{3}$ times that of the current, then the speed of the current (in m/min) is

(a) 30   (b) 40   (c) 50   (d) 60

22. Consider a 16 cm × 8 cm uniform rectangular sheet with its sides parallel to axes and its centre at origin.

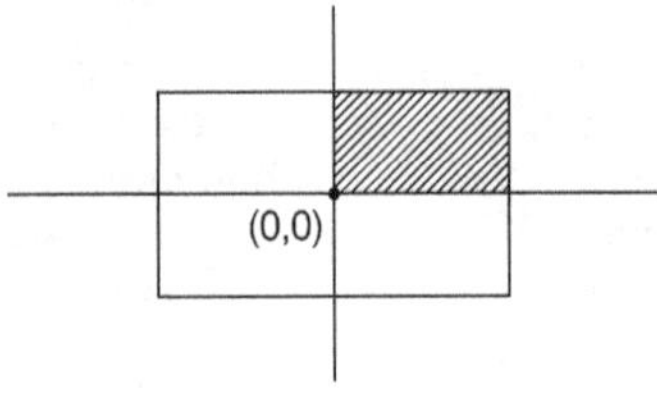

If exactly one quarter of this sheet is removed, coordinates of centre of mass of remaining sheet are

(a) (4/3, 2/3)   (b) (0, 2/3)

(c) (4/3, 0)   (d) $\left(\dfrac{-4}{3}, \dfrac{-2}{3}\right)$

23. For four processes A, B, C and D, $\log_e p$ *versus* $\log_e V$ graph are given below.

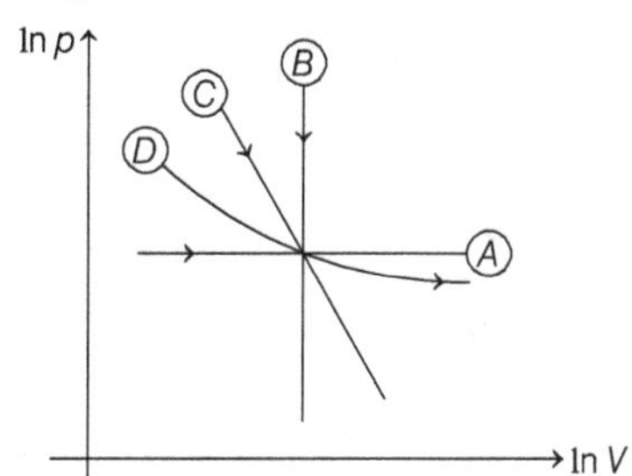

Isothermal process is
(a) A (b) B (c) C (d) D

24. In given set up,

focal length of mirror $= 20$ cm,

focal length of lens $= 15$ cm

and separation of mirror and lens $= 40$ cm.

A point source S of light 'S' is placed on principal axis at distance d from lens.

If the final beam comes out parallel to the principal axis, then value of d is

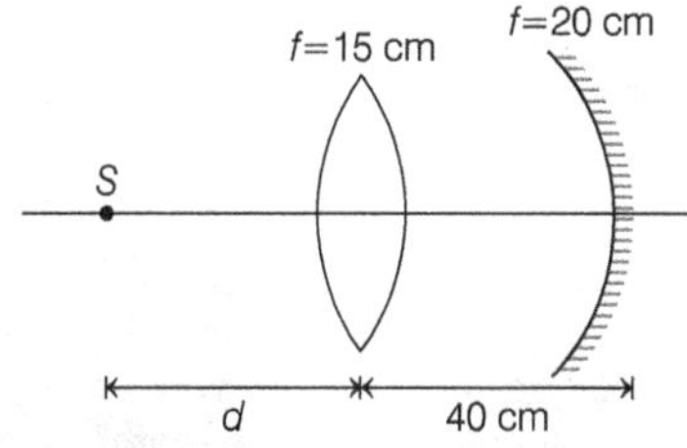

(a) 4 cm   (b) 8 cm   (c) 12 cm   (d) 16 cm

25. A gas satisfies the relation $pV^{5/3} = K$, where $p =$ pressure, $V =$ volume and $K =$ constant. The dimensions of constant K are
(a) $[ML^4T^{-2}]$ (b) $[ML^2T^{-2}]$ (c) $[M^0L^0T^0]$ (d) $[MLT^{-2}]$

26. When temperature of a semiconductor is raised, then choose the correct option.
(a) None of electron jump to higher energy level
(b) All electrons likely to jump at higher energy levels
(c) Electrons whose energies are close to fermi energy are likely to jump to higher energy levels
(d) Electrons having lesser energy than fermi energy are likely to jump to higher energy level

27. An incense stick is lighted in a closed room in which there is no flow of air. Then, choose the correct option given below.
(a) Flow of smoke is initially turbulent, then laminar
(b) Flow of smoke is initially laminar, then turbulent
(c) Flow of smoke is turbulent only
(d) Flow of smoke is laminar only

28. Which of these graphs correctly shows potential energy and force between two atoms in a diatomic molecule? ($U =$ potential energy, $F =$ force, $r =$ distance)

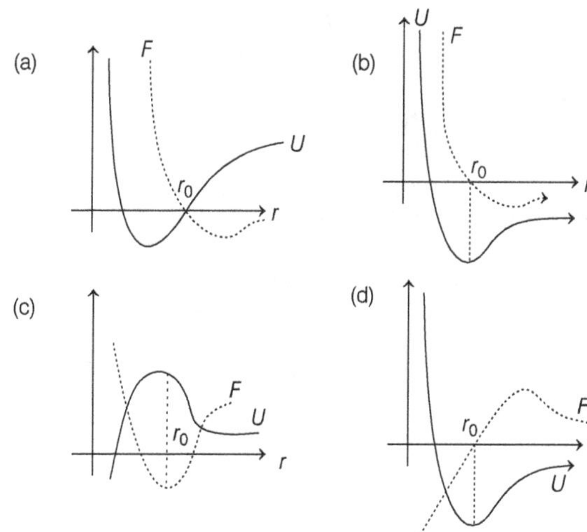

29. A metal sphere is held suspended along a wall as shown below.

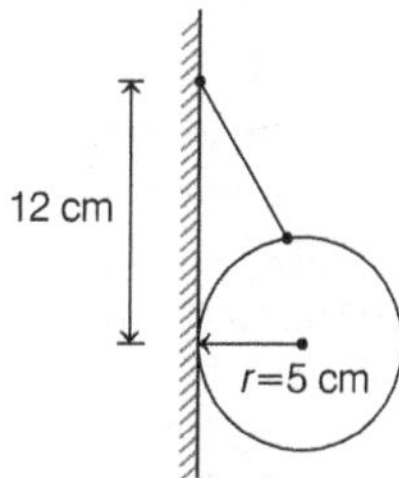

If string can break at a pull of 15 N, then maximum density of material of sphere can be
(a) 44 kg m^{-3} (b) 64 kg m^{-3} (c) 54 kg m^{-3} (d) 74 kg m^{-3}

30. An object at infinity forms an image of size 2 cm by a convex lens of focal length 30 cm.

Now, a concave lens of focal length 20 cm is placed between the convex lens and image at a distance of 26 cm from convex lens. Image size now will be
(a) 1.25 cm   (b) 2.5 cm   (c) 1.05 cm   (d) 2 cm

CHEMISTRY

31. If 500 mL of a 5M solution is diluted to 1500 mL. What will be the molarity of the solution obtained?
(a) 1.5 M   (b) 1.66 M   (c) 0.017 M   (d) 1.59 M

32. A plot of volume (V) *versus* temperature (T) for a gas at constant pressure is a straight line passing through the origin.

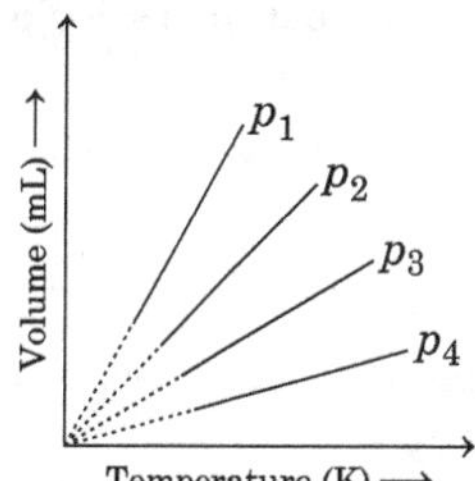

The plot of different values of pressure are shown in figure. Which of the following orders of pressure is correct?

(a) $p_1 > p_2 > p_3 > p_4$ (b) $p_1 = p_2 = p_3 = p_4$
(c) $p_1 < p_2 < p_3 < p_4$ (d) $p_1 < p_2 = p_3 < p_4$

33. A substance X gives brick red flame and breaks down on heating to give oxygen and a brown gas. The substance X is

(a) magnesium nitrate   (b) calcium nitrate
(c) barium nitrate   (d) strontium nitrate

34. The major product obtained when 1 butyne reacts with excess HBr is

(a) 2, 2-dibromobutane
(b) 2-bromobutane
(c) 1, 1, 2, 2-tetrabromobutane
(d) 1, 2-dibromobutene

35. Which of the following sulphides when heated strongly in air gives the corresponding metal?

(a) Cu_2S (b) CuS   (c) Fe_2S_3 (d) HgS

36. Sulphur in + 3 oxidation state is present in

(a) dithionous acid   (b) sulphurous acid
(c) dithionic acid   (d) pyrosulphuric acid

37. The correct order of boiling points of given compounds is n-butylamine (I), diethyl amine (II), N, N-dimethylethylamine (III).

(a) III < II < I   (b) I < II < III
(c) III < I < II   (d) II < I < III

38. The value of Planck's constant is 6.63×10^{-34} Js. The velocity of light is 3×10^8 ms^{-1}. Which value is closest to the wavelength in nanometer of a quantum of light with frequency of 8×10^{-15} s^{-1}?

(a) 2×10^{-25} (b) 3×10^7
(c) 4×10^1 (d) 5×10^{-18}

39. The correct order of electron affinities of N, O, S and Cl is

(a) N < O < S < Cl   (b) O < N < Cl < S
(c) O ≈ Cl < N ≈ S   (d) O < S < Cl < N

40. The number of lone pairs on central metal atom Xe in XeF_2, XeF_4 and XeF_6, respectively are

(a) 2, 3, 1   (b) 1, 2, 3   (c) 4, 1, 2   (d) 3, 2, 1

41. When aqueous solution of benzene diazonium chloride is boiled, the product obtained is

(a) $C_6H_5CH_2OH$ (b) $C_6H_6 + N_2$
(c) C_6H_5COOH (d) C_6H_5OH

42. The set of quantum number for 19th electron of chromium $(Z = 24)$ is

(a) $4, 0, 0, +\dfrac{1}{2}$ (b) $4, -1, 1, -1, +\dfrac{1}{2}$
(c) $3, 2, 2, +\dfrac{1}{2}$ (d) $3, 2, -2, +\dfrac{1}{2}$

43. Among the given carbocations, the most stable carbocation is

(a) methyl   (b) allyl   (c) benzyl   (d) vinyl

44. The correct IUPAC name of the following compound

is

(a) 3-(1-ethyl propyl) hex-1-ene
(b) 4-ethyl-3-propyl hex-1-ene
(c) 3-ethyl-4-ethenyl heptane
(d) 3-ethyl-4-propyl hex-5-ene

45. The period number in the long form of the periodic table is equal to

(a) magnetic quantum number of any element of the period
(b) atomic number of any element of the period
(c) maximum principal quantum number of any element of the period
(d) maximum azimuthal number of any element of the period

BIOLOGY

46. Which of the following biomolecules is common to respiration-mediated breakdown of fats, carbohydrates and proteins?

(a) Glucose-6-phosphate
(b) Fructose-1,6-bisphosphate
(c) Pyruvic acid
(d) Acetyl Co-A

47. You are given a tissue with its potential for differentiation in an artificial culture. Which of the following pairs of hormones would you add to the medium to secure shoots as well as roots?

(a) IAA and gibberellin
(b) Auxin and cytokinin
(c) Auxin and abscisic acid
(d) Gibberellin and abscisic acid

48. The partial pressure of oxygen in the alveoli of the lungs is

(a) equal to that in the blood
(b) more than that in the blood
(c) less than that in the blood
(d) less than that of carbon dioxide

49. When cell has stalled DNA replication fork, which checkpoint should be predominantly activated?

(a) G_1 / S
(b) G_2 / M
(c) M
(d) Both G_2/M and M

50. Which of the following is the least likely to be involved in stabilising the three-dimensional folding of most proteins?

(a) Hydrogen bonds
(b) Electrostatic interaction
(c) Hydrophobic interaction
(d) Ester bonds

51. Name a peptide hormone which acts mainly on hepatocytes, adipocytes and enhances cellular glucose uptake and utilisation.
(a) Insulin (b) Glucagon
(c) Secretin (d) Gastrin

52. If a colourblind man marries with a woman who is homozygous for normal colour vision, the probability of their son being colourblind is
(a) 0 (b) 0.5
(c) 0.75 (d) 1

53. One of the major components of cell wall of most fungi is
(a) peptidoglycan (b) cellulose
(c) hemicellulose (d) chitin

54. A tall true breeding garden pea plant is crossed with a dwarf true breeding garden pea plant. When the F_1-plants were selfed, the resulting genotypes were in the ratio of
(a) 1 : 2 : 1 :: Tall heterozygous : Tall homozygous : Dwarf
(b) 3 : 1 :: Tall : Dwarf
(c) 3 : 1 :: Dwarf : Tall
(d) 1 : 2 : 1 :: Tall homozygous : Tall heterozygous : Dwarf

55. Reduction in pH of blood will
(a) reduce the blood supply to the brain
(b) decrease the affinity of haemoglobin with oxygen
(c) release bicarbonate ions by the liver
(d) reduce the rate of heartbeat

56. Lack of relaxation between successive stimuli in sustained muscle contraction is known as
(a) fatigue (b) tetanus
(c) tonus (d) spasm

57. Which of the following guards the opening of hepatopancreatic duct into the duodenum?
(a) Ileocaecal valve (b) Pyloric sphincter
(c) Sphincter of Oddi (d) Semilunar valve

58. Which one of the following cell organelles is enclosed by a single membrane?
(a) Chloroplasts (b) Lysosomes
(c) Nuclei (d) Mitochondria

59. Which of the following features is not present in the phylum Arthropoda?
(a) Metameric segmentation
(b) Parapodia
(c) Jointed appendages
(d) Chitinous exoskeleton

60. Water soluble pigments found in plant cell vacuoles are
(a) chlorophylls (b) carotenoids
(c) anthocyanins (d) xanthophylls

➲ PART-II (2 Marks Questions)

MATHEMATICS

61. Let S be a set of real numbers with mean m. If the means of set $S \cup \{15\}$ and $S \cup \{15, 1\}$ are $m + 2$ and $m + 1$ respectively. Then, number of elements S has
(a) 4 (b) 5 (c) 6 (d) 7

62. For natural numbers x and y, let (x, y) denote the greatest common divisor of x and y. The pairs of natural number x and y with $x \le y$ satisfy the equation $xy = x + y + (x, y)$ is
(a) 2 (b) 3 (c) 4 (d) 5

63. In a $\triangle ABC$, X and Y are points on the segment AB and AC respectively, such that $AX : XB = 1 : 2$ and $AY : YC = 2 : 1$. If the area of $\triangle AXY$ is 10, then the area of $\triangle ABC$ is
(a) 30 (b) 45 (c) 60 (d) 27

64. Let $x_1, x_2, x_3, \ldots, x_{2019}$ be the real numbers different from 1, such that $x_1 + x_2 + x_3 + \ldots + x_{2019} = 1$ and
$$\frac{x_1}{1 - x_1} + \frac{x_2}{1 - x_2} + \ldots + \frac{x_{2019}}{1 - x_{2019}} = 1, \text{ then the value of}$$
$$\frac{x_1^2}{1 - x_1} + \frac{x_2^2}{1 - x_2} + \ldots + \frac{x_{2019}^2}{1 - x_{2019}} \text{ is equal to}$$
(a) 0 (b) 1 (c) 2019 (d) None of these

65. In a $\triangle ABC$, let I denotes the incenter. Let the line AI, BI and CI intersects the incircle at P, Q and R, respectively. If $\angle BAC = 40°$, then the value of $\angle QPR$ in degree is
(a) 50° (b) 65°
(c) 55° (d) 60°

PHYSICS

66. Power is given by $P = a + bt^2 + \left(\dfrac{c + t^3}{d} \right)$, where t is time. Then,

   I. $[a] = [\text{ML}^2\text{T}^{-3}]$

   II. $[b] = [\text{ML}^2\text{T}^{-5}]$

   III. $[c] = [\text{T}^3]$

   IV. $[d] = [\text{ML}^{-2}\text{T}^{-6}]$

Which of the above statements are correct?
(a) Statements I and IV are correct
(b) Statements I and III are correct
(c) Statements I, II and III are correct
(d) All statements are correct

67. A rolling sphere collides with a cube of equal mass. Surface is frictionless. Radius of sphere is 1 cm and its initial angular speed is 1 radian per second.

If side of cube is 2 cm and collision is elastic, then after collision,

(a) $\omega_{sphere} = 0$ and $v_{cube} = 0.01\,ms^{-1}$

(b) $\omega_{sphere} = 1\dfrac{rad}{s}$ and $v_{cube} = 0.01\,ms^{-1}$

(c) $\omega_{sphere} = 0$ and $v_{cube} = 0$

(d) $\omega_{sphere} = 1\dfrac{rad}{s}$ and $v_{cube} = 1\,ms^{-1}$

68. A current of 1 mA enters the network of resistors as shown below.

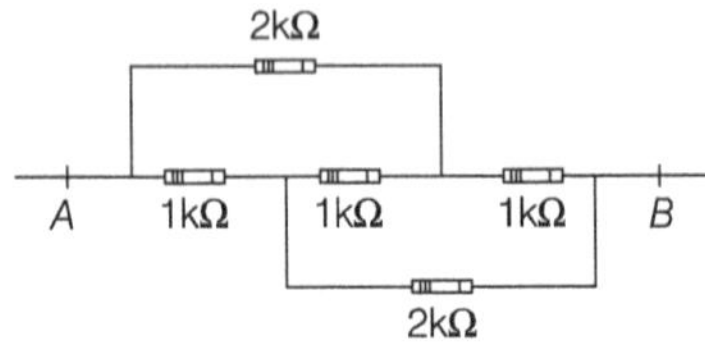

Now, consider the following statements:

I. Current through 2 kΩ resistor is $\dfrac{2}{5}$ mA.

II. Current through lower 2 kΩ resistor is $\dfrac{1}{5}$ mA.

III. Current through middle 1 kΩ resistor is $\dfrac{1}{5}$ mA.

IV. Current through middle 1 kΩ resistor is $\dfrac{3}{5}$ mA.

Which of the above statements are correct?

(a) Only statement I is correct
(b) Statements II and III are correct
(c) Statements I and III are correct
(d) Statements III and IV are correct

69. A steel ball travels through a hollow U-tube with separation in limbs 1 m, as shown below.

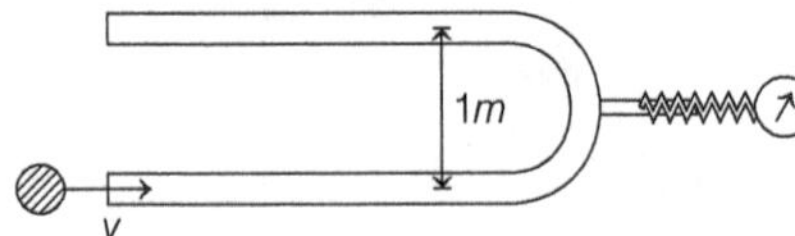

Radius of U-tube is slightly greater than ball such that ball travels through it and leaves from other end with same uniform speed of 3 ms⁻¹.

Mass of steel ball is 0.02 kg. What is the approximate reading on spring balance attached to the tube?

(a) 0.1 N (b) 0.2 N (c) 0.5 N (d) 0 N

70. A body of mass m ($= 5\,g$), is moving in one dimension under influence of a conservative force. Potential energy of the body is given by

$$U = \dfrac{-2x}{x^2 + 4}$$

Then, angular frequency of small oscillations of the body about the position of stable equilibrium is

(a) 5 rad s⁻¹ (b) 10 rad s⁻¹
(c) π rad s⁻¹ (d) 25 rad s⁻¹

CHEMISTRY

71. The heat of formation of $C_{12}H_{22}O_{11}(s)$, $CO_2(g)$ and $H_2O(l)$ are $-530, -94.3$ and -68.3 kcal/mol, respectively. The amount of $C_{12}H_{22}O_{11}$ required to supply 2700 kcal of energy is

(a) 382.70 g (b) 832.74 g
(c) 463.9 g (d) 682.6 g

72. The following alcohol after treatment with acid gives compound A. Ozonolysis of A gives nonan -2, 8 dione. The compound A is

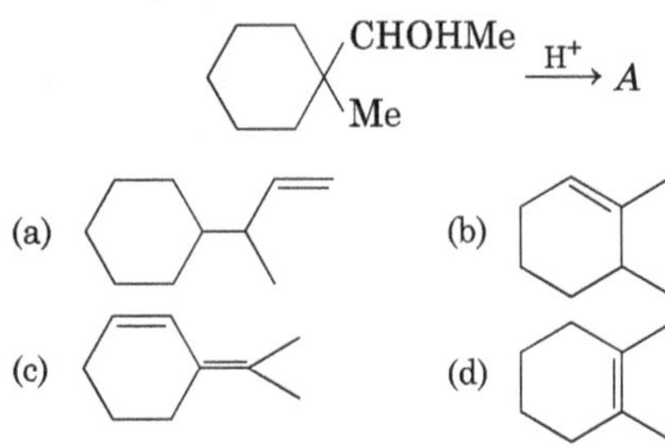

73. An electric current is passed through silver nitrate solution using silver electrodes. 10.79 g of silver was found to be deposited on the cathode. If the same amount of electricity is passed through copper sulphate solution using copper electrodes, the weight of copper deposited on the cathode is

(a) 1.6 g (b) 2.3 g
(c) 3.2 g (d) 6.4 g

74. Suppose 10^{-17} J of light energy is needed by the interior of human eye to see on object. Calculate the number of photons of green light ($\lambda = 550$ nm) needed to generate this minimum amount of energy.

(a) 26 (b) 27 (c) 28 (d) 29

75. The Gibbs' free energy change, $\Delta G°$, for the following reaction is 63.3kJ

$$Ag_2CO_3\,(s) \rightleftharpoons 2Ag^+\,(aq) + CO_3^{2-}\,(aq)$$

The K_{sp} of $Ag_2CO_3\,(s)$ in water at 25°C is closest to

(a) 3.2×10^{-26} (b) 8×10^{-12}
(c) 2.9×10^{-3} (d) 7.9×10^{-2}

BIOLOGY

76. Impulses travel very rapidly along nerves to the leg muscles of a mammal. Which fact accounts for the speed at which they travel?

(a) A nerve impulse is an all-or-nothing phenomenon
(b) The nerves contain myelinated fibres
(c) There is high concentration of Na^+ ions inside the axons
(d) There is a potential difference across the axon membranes

77. In a certain plant, yellow fruit colour (Y) is dominant to green (y) and round shape (R) is dominant to oval (r). The two genes involved are located on different chromosomes. Which of the above will result when plant YyRr is self-pollinated?
(a) 9 : 3 : 3 : 1 ratio of phenotypes only
(b) 9 : 3 : 3 : 1 ratio of genotypes only
(c) 1 : 1 : 1 : 1 ratio of phenotypes only
(d) 1 : 1 : 1 : 1 ratio of phenotypes and genotypes

78. Which graph shows the expected relationship between enzyme activity and substrate concentration?

(a) 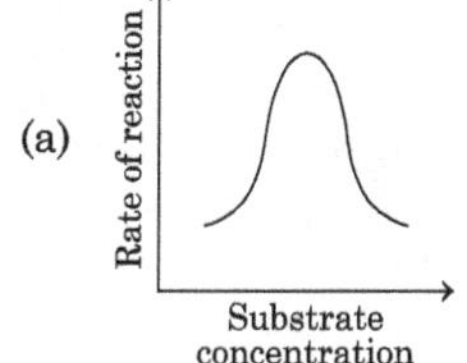

(b) 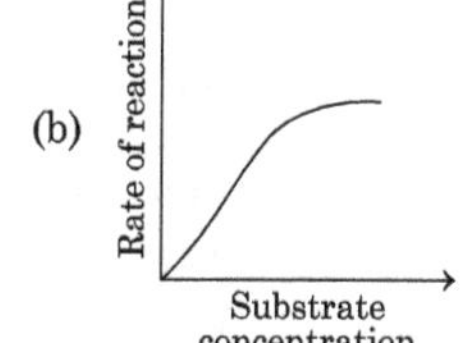

(c) 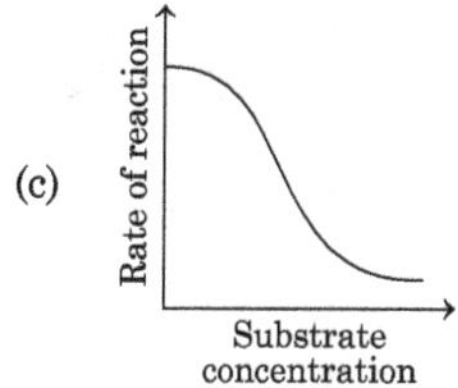

(d) 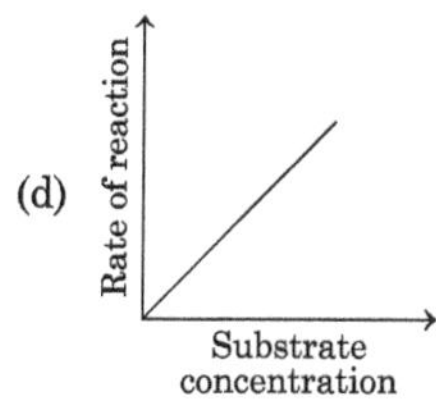

79. Assume that the average amino acid residue have a molecular weight of 110. The DNA strand coding for a polypeptide chain of molecular weight 20,000 has a length of
(a) 182 nucleotides
(b) 252 nucleotides
(c) 540 nucleotides
(d) 760 nucleotides

80. Which of the following is a correct statement?
(a) *Salvinia*, *Ginkgo* and *Pinus* all are gymnosperms
(b) *Sequoia* is one of the tallest trees
(c) The leaves of gymnosperms are not well-adapted to extremes of climate
(d) Gymnosperms are both homosporous and heterosporous

Answers

PART-I

1 *(c)*	2 *(b)*	3 *(a)*	4 *(c)*	5 *(c)*	6 *(a)*	7 *(b)*	8 *(d)*	9 *(d)*	10 *(d)*
11 *(a)*	12 *(c)*	13 *(b)*	14 *(a)*	15 *(c)*	16 *(b)*	17 *(c)*	18 *(c)*	19 *(a)*	20 *(a)*
21 *(d)*	22 *(d)*	23 *(c)*	24 *(c)*	25 *(a)*	26 *(c)*	27 *(b)*	28 *(d)*	29 *(a)*	30 *(b)*
31 *(b)*	32 *(c)*	33 *(b)*	34 *(a)*	35 *(d)*	36 *(a)*	37 *(a)*	38 *(c)*	39 *(a)*	40 *(d)*
41 *(d)*	42 *(a)*	43 *(c)*	44 *(b)*	45 *(c)*	46 *(d)*	47 *(b)*	48 *(b)*	49 *(a)*	50 *(d)*
51 *(a)*	52 *(a)*	53 *(d)*	54 *(d)*	55 *(b)*	56 *(b)*	57 *(c)*	58 *(b)*	59 *(b)*	60 *(c)*

PART-II

61 *(a)*	62 *(b)*	63 *(b)*	64 *(a)*	65 *(c)*	66 *(c)*	67 *(b)*	68 *(b)*	69 *(b)*	70 *(a)*
71 *(d)*	72 *(d)*	73 *(c)*	74 *(c)*	75 *(b)*	76 *(b)*	77 *(a)*	78 *(b)*	79 *(c)*	80 *(b)*

Solutions

1. *(c)* $E(1) + E(2) + E(3) + ... + E(100)$

= Sum of all even digits from 1 to 100

= Sum of all even digits in

$$[01 + 02 + 03 + ... + 98 + 99 + 100]$$

$$= 0 \times 20 + 2 \times 20 + 4 \times 20 + 6 \times 20 + 8 \times 20$$

$[\because$ there are $2 \times 100 = 200$ digits and

each digit appears $\dfrac{200}{10} = 20$ times]

$$= (2 + 4 + 6 + 8) \times 20 = 20 \times 20 = 400$$

2. *(b)* Let the other sides of right angle triangle be x and y.

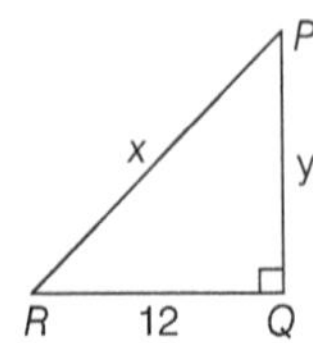

$$\therefore \qquad x^2 = 12^2 + y^2$$

$$\Rightarrow \qquad x^2 - y^2 = 144$$

$$\Rightarrow \quad (x + y)(x - y) = 72 \times 2$$

x and y are integer.

$\therefore$ Maximum value of $x + y = 72$

$\therefore$ Maximum perimeter of triangle

$$= 12 + x + y$$

$$= 12 + 72 = 84$$

3. *(a)* There are 9 men and each man danced with 4 women.

$\Rightarrow$ Number of dancing pairs $= 9 \times 4 = 36$

Now, let number of women $= x$

$\therefore$ Each woman danced with 3 men.

$\therefore$ Number of dancing pairs $= 3x$

$$\therefore \qquad 3x = 36, x = 12$$

Hence, 12 women attended the party.

4. *(c)* Given,

$$3^x + 2^y = 985 \qquad ...(i)$$

$$3^x - 2^y = 473 \qquad ...(ii)$$

On adding Eqs. (i) and (ii), we get

$$2 \cdot 3^x = 1458$$

$$3^x = 729$$

$$3^x = 3^6$$

$$\Rightarrow \qquad x = 6$$

On subtracting Eq. (ii) from Eq. (i), we get

$$2 \cdot 2^y = 512$$

$$2^y = 256$$

$$2^y = 2^8$$

$$\Rightarrow \qquad y = 8$$

$$\therefore \qquad xy = 6 \times 8$$

$$= 48$$

5. *(c)* We have,

Total number of students = 300

One student read = 5 newspapers

Number of newspaper read by 300 students $= 5 \times 300 = 1500$

Number of different newspaper

$$= \dfrac{1500}{60} = 25$$

6. *(a)* Given, $a + b + c = 0$

$$\therefore \qquad a^3 + b^3 + c^3 = 3abc$$

Now, $P = \dfrac{a^2}{2a^2 + bc} + \dfrac{b^2}{2b^2 + ac} + \dfrac{c^2}{2c^2 + ab}$

Let $a = 1, b = -1, c = 0$

$$\therefore \qquad P = \dfrac{1}{2 + 0} + \dfrac{1}{2 + 0} + 0$$

$$\Rightarrow \qquad P = \dfrac{1}{2} + \dfrac{1}{2} = 1$$

7. *(b)* Given, $ABCD$ is a rectangle.

$$AB = 8, BC = 20$$

Let $\qquad AP = x$

$$\therefore \qquad PD = 12 - x$$

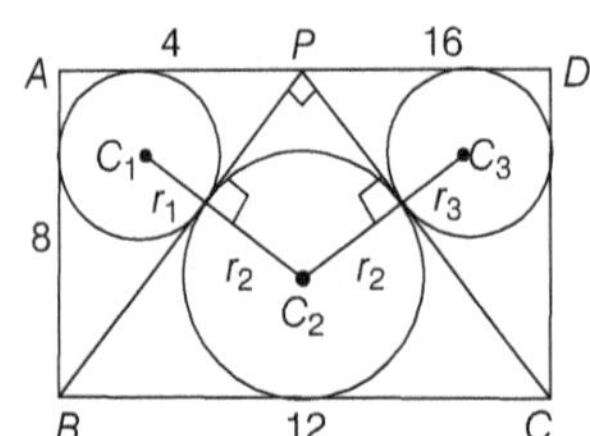

In $\triangle APB$ and $\triangle DPC$,

$$\triangle PBA \sim \triangle CPD$$

$$\therefore \qquad \dfrac{AB}{PD} = \dfrac{AP}{CD}$$

$$\Rightarrow \qquad \dfrac{8}{12 - x} = \dfrac{x}{8}$$

$$\Rightarrow \quad x^2 - 20x + 64 = 0$$

$$\Rightarrow \quad (x - 16)(x - 4) = 0$$

$$x = 4, 16$$

In $\triangle APB$,

$$r_1 = \dfrac{\Delta}{s} = \dfrac{\dfrac{1}{2} \times AB \times AP}{\dfrac{1}{2}(AB + PB + BP)}$$

$$r_1 = \dfrac{8 \times 4}{8 + 4 + 4\sqrt{5}}$$

$[\because BP^2 = AP^2 + BA^2$

$BP = \sqrt{16 + 64} = 4\sqrt{5}]$

$$r_1 = 12 - 4\sqrt{5}$$

Similarly,

$$r_2 = 6\sqrt{5} - 10$$

$$r_3 = 6 - 2\sqrt{5}$$

$$\therefore r_1 + r_2 + r_3 = 12 - 4\sqrt{5} + 6\sqrt{5} - 10 + 6 - 2\sqrt{5}$$

$$= 8$$

8. *(d)* Given, $\sin\theta + \cos\theta = \sqrt{3}$

Squaring both sides,

$$\sin^2\theta + \cos^2\theta + 2\sin\theta\cos\theta = 3$$

$$\Rightarrow \qquad 1 + 2\sin\theta\cos\theta = 3$$

$$\Rightarrow \qquad \sin 2\theta = 2$$

$\therefore$ Maximum value of $\sin\theta = 1$

Hence, $\sin\theta + \cos\theta = \sqrt{3}$ not possible.

9. *(d)* Given,

Number 1, 2, 3, ... 100 are written on card A, B and C.

$\therefore$ Total number of outcomes

$$= 100 \times 100 \times 100 = 100^3$$

Numbers are selected such that formal three sides of right angle triangle and triangle are not similar.

For a right angle triangle

$$(2n + 1)^2 + (2n^2 + 2n)^2 = (2n^2 + 2n + 1)^2,$$

$$n \in N$$

for $n = 1, 2, 3, 4, 5, 6$. If $n > 6$ then length of longest side is greater than 100.

$$\therefore \quad n(E) = 6 \times 3!$$

$$P(\in) = \dfrac{6 \times 3!}{(100)^3}$$

$$= \dfrac{6 \times 6}{2^3 \times (50)^3} = \dfrac{9}{2(50)^3}$$

10. *(d)* Given,

One side of triangle is three times the second side and third side is 17.

Let the sides of triangle are x, $3x$, 17.

We know, in triangle sum of two sides is greater than third side.

$$\Rightarrow \qquad x + 3x > 17$$

$$\Rightarrow \qquad x > \dfrac{17}{4}$$

and $\qquad x + 17 > 3x$

$$\therefore \qquad x < \dfrac{17}{2}$$

$$\therefore \qquad \dfrac{17}{4} < x < \dfrac{17}{2}$$

$$4.25 < x < 8.5$$

Since, sides of triangle are integer.

$$\therefore \qquad x = 5, 6, 7, 8$$

$\therefore$ Maximum value of $x = 8$

$\therefore$ Sides of triangle are 8, 24, 17

$\therefore$ Perimeter $= 8 + 24 + 17 = 49$

11. (*a*) Let the total milk is 7M ounce and total coffee is 17C ounce.

The ratio of total milk and coffee drank by Kanchan's must be integer.

$\therefore \dfrac{7M + 17C}{M + 2C}$ be an integer (which is the Total number of people in Kanchan's family)

$$\dfrac{7M + 17C}{M + 2C} = 7 + \dfrac{3C}{M + 2C}$$

$\therefore \qquad 0 < \dfrac{3C}{M + 2C} < \dfrac{3}{2}$

$$\dfrac{3C}{M + 2C} = 1$$

$\left[\because \dfrac{3C}{M + 2C} \text{ is integer less than } \dfrac{3}{2}\right]$

$$C = M$$

$\therefore$ Total number of people in Kanchan's family $\dfrac{7M + 17M}{M + 2M} = 8$

12. (*c*) Given,

ABC is a right angled triangle

$$\angle ABC = 90°$$

P and Q are mid-points of sides AB and BC respectively.

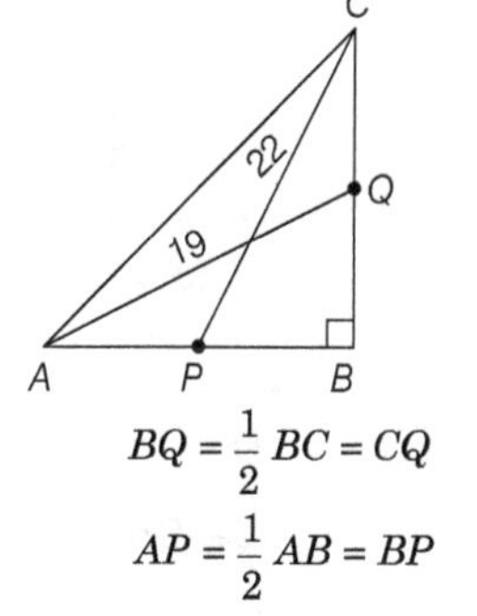

$\therefore \qquad BQ = \dfrac{1}{2} BC = CQ$

$$AP = \dfrac{1}{2} AB = BP$$

In $\triangle PBC$,

$$PC^2 = BC^2 + PB^2$$
$$PC^2 = BC^2 + \dfrac{1}{4} AB^2 \qquad ...(i)$$

In $\triangle AQB$,

$$AQ^2 = AB^2 + \dfrac{1}{4} BC^2 \qquad ...(ii)$$

On adding Eqs. (i) and (ii), we get

$$PC^2 + AQ^2 = \dfrac{5}{4}(AB^2 + BC^2)$$

$\Rightarrow PC^2 + AQ^2 = \dfrac{5AC^2}{4}$

$\Rightarrow \qquad AC^2 = \dfrac{4}{5}(PC^2 + AQ^2)$

$\Rightarrow \qquad AC^2 = \dfrac{4}{5}(19^2 + 22^2)$

$[\because PC = 19, AQ = 22]$

$\Rightarrow \qquad AC^2 = \dfrac{4}{5}(361 + 484) = \dfrac{4}{5} \times 845$

$\Rightarrow \qquad AC^2 = 4 \times 169$

$\Rightarrow \qquad AC = \sqrt{4 \times 169} = 26$

13. (*b*) Let $\dfrac{8n}{9999 - n} = \lambda$

$\therefore \qquad 8n = 9999\lambda - \lambda n$

$\Rightarrow \qquad n = \dfrac{9999\lambda}{8 + \lambda}$

$\Rightarrow \qquad n \in [1, 2019]$

$\therefore \qquad 1 \le \dfrac{9999\lambda}{8 + \lambda} \le 2019$

$\Rightarrow \qquad \dfrac{9999\lambda}{8 + \lambda} \ge 1$

$\Rightarrow \qquad 9999\lambda \ge 8 + \lambda$

$\Rightarrow \qquad \lambda \ge \dfrac{8}{9998}$ and $\dfrac{9999\lambda}{8 + \lambda} \le 2019$

$\Rightarrow \qquad 9999\lambda \le 16132 + 2019\lambda$

$\Rightarrow \qquad \lambda \le \dfrac{16132}{7990}$

$\therefore \qquad \dfrac{8}{9998} \le \lambda \le \dfrac{16132}{7990}$

$\therefore \qquad \lambda = 1, 2, \lambda$ is an integer.

For $\lambda = 2$, n is not an integer.

Hence, only one value is possible.

14. (*a*) Let side of square $ABCD$

$$AB = x$$

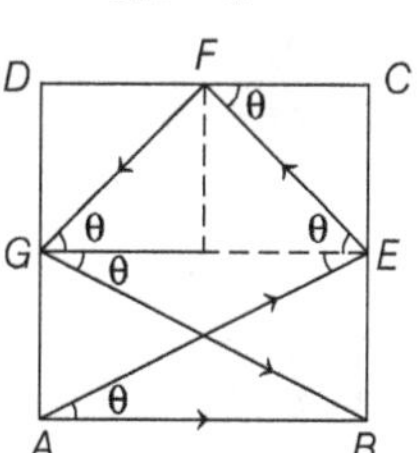

In $\triangle ABE$,

$$\tan\theta = \dfrac{BE}{AB}$$
$$BE = x\tan\theta$$
$$CE = BC - BE = x(1 - \tan\theta)$$

In $\triangle CEF$,

$$\tan\theta = \dfrac{CE}{CF} \Rightarrow CF = x(\cot\theta - 1)$$

Now in $\triangle GHF$,

$$\tan\theta = \dfrac{FH}{GH} = \dfrac{CE}{DF}$$
$$= \dfrac{CE}{DC - CF} = \dfrac{x(1 - \tan\theta)}{x(2 - \cot\theta)}$$
$$\tan\theta = \dfrac{1 - \tan\theta}{2 - \cot\theta}$$

$\Rightarrow \quad 2\tan\theta - 1 = 1 - \tan\theta \Rightarrow \tan\theta = \dfrac{2}{3}$

$\therefore \qquad \sin\theta = \dfrac{2}{\sqrt{13}}$

15. (*c*) m = Number of ways in which two couples can be seated in 4 chairs in a row such that no wife is next to husband.

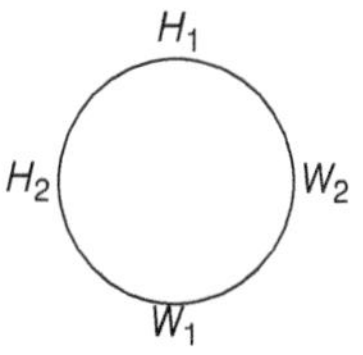

$\therefore \ m = 2! \times 2! \times 2! = 8 \,\text{ways} \ H_1 \times W_1 X$

n = Number of ways in circular permutation = $2! = 2$

$\therefore \qquad\qquad m = 4n$

16. (*b*) Let m kg of ice is taken.

Then, $H_I = mL_f = 334m\,J$

and $H_{II} = mc\Delta T = m\,(4.19)\,(100)$
$$= 419\,mJ$$
$$H_{III} = mL_V = m\,(2260) = 2260\,m\,J$$

$\therefore \ H_I < H_{II} < H_{III}$.

17. (*c*) For additional extension x, work done is

$$W = \dfrac{1}{2}k\,(2x)^2 - \dfrac{1}{2}kx^2$$
$$W = \dfrac{1}{2}k(4x^2) - \dfrac{1}{2}kx^2 = \dfrac{1}{2}k\,(3x^2)$$

$\therefore$ Ratio is $1 : 3 : 5 : ....$

18. (*c*) Let x = temperature value.

Then,

$$\dfrac{C - 0}{100 - 0} = \dfrac{F - 32}{212 - 32}$$

when $\qquad C = F = x$,

$\Rightarrow \qquad \dfrac{x}{100} = \dfrac{x - 32}{180} \Rightarrow x = -40$

$\therefore \qquad -40°C = -40°F$

19. (*a*) We have,

$$_{92}U^{238} \xrightarrow{\ \alpha\ } {}_{90}Th^{234} \xrightarrow{\ \beta^-\ } {}_{91}Pa^{234}$$
$$\xrightarrow{\ \beta\ } {}_{92}U^{234}$$

20. (*a*) Amplitude of resultant motion is

$$A = \sqrt{A_1^2 + A_2^2 + 2A_1A_2\cos\phi}$$
$$= \sqrt{2 + 2 + 2 \times \sqrt{2} \times \sqrt{2} \times \dfrac{1}{2}} = \sqrt{6}$$

So, maximum acceleration = $\omega^2 A$
$$= 1^2 \times \sqrt{6} = \sqrt{6}\ \dfrac{\text{cm}}{\text{s}^2}$$

21. (*d*) $v_r^2 = v_m^2 - v^2$

$$v = \dfrac{320}{4} = 80\,\text{m/min}$$

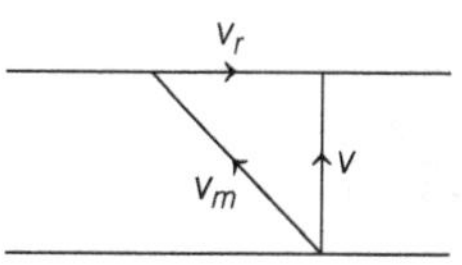

$$v_m = \frac{5}{3} v_r$$

$$v_r^2 = \left(\frac{5}{3} v_r\right)^2 - (80)^2$$

$$\frac{16}{9} v_r^2 = (80)^2$$

$$v_r = \frac{80 \times 3}{4} = 60 \text{ m/min}$$

22. *(d)* $X = \dfrac{Mx - mx'}{M - m} = \dfrac{4M(0) - M(4)}{4M - M}$

$$= -\frac{4}{3}$$

$$Y = \frac{My - my'}{M - m} = \frac{4M(0) - M(2)}{4M - M} = -\frac{2}{3}$$

23. *(c)* For isothermal process,

$$pV = \text{constant}$$

$$\Rightarrow \quad p = \frac{K}{V} \Rightarrow \log p = -\log V + \log K$$

This is a straight line with negative slope.

24. *(c)* As emergent beam is parallel, so mirror must forms image at focus of lens.

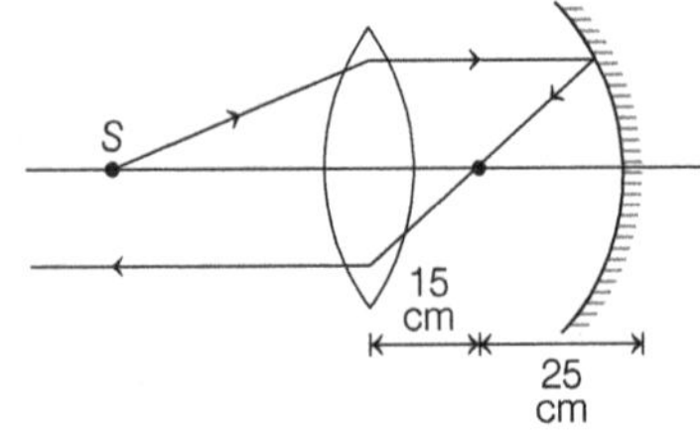

Clearly, $d = 12$ cm.

25. *(a)* $[K] = [p][V^{5/3}] = \dfrac{[MLT^{-2}]}{[L^2]} \cdot [L^3]^{5/3}$

$$= [ML^4T^{-2}]$$

26. *(c)* Electrons which have maximum energies are near to fermi energy level. These electrons can jump to higher energy levels.

27. *(b)* As smoke rises up in air, speed of smoke increases and flow becomes turbulent.

28. *(d)* As, $F = -\dfrac{dU}{dr}$, option (d) is correct.

29. *(a)* $T \cos\theta = mg$ and $T \sin\theta = N$

$$\Rightarrow \quad T = \frac{w}{\cos\theta} = \frac{13}{12} w$$

At $\quad T = 15$ N and $w = mg$,

$$15 = \frac{13}{12} mg \quad [\because g = 10 \text{ ms}^{-2}]$$

$$15 \times 12 = 13 \times 10 m$$

$$\Rightarrow \quad m = \frac{12 \times 15}{13 \times 10} \approx 1.4 \text{ kg}$$

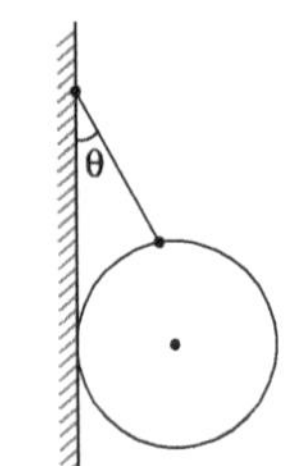

Density of sphere $= \dfrac{1.4}{4\pi \times (5)^2 \times (10^{-4})}$

$$= 44 \text{ kg m}^{-3}$$

30. *(b)*

For concave lens using, $\dfrac{1}{v} - \dfrac{1}{u} = \dfrac{1}{f}$

we have $\dfrac{1}{v} - \dfrac{1}{4} = \dfrac{1}{-20} \Rightarrow v = 5$ cm

Magnification of concave lens $= \dfrac{v}{u} = 1.25$

As size of I_1 is 2 cm.

$\therefore$ Size of $I_2 = 2 \times 1.25 = 2.5$ cm

31. *(b)* Given that,

$$M_1 = 5 \text{ M}, V_1 = 500 \text{ mL},$$

$$V_2 = 1500 \text{ mL}$$

For dilution, $M_1 V_1 = M_2 V_2$

$$5 \times 500 = M \times 1500$$

$$M = \frac{5}{3} = 1.66 \text{ M}$$

32. *(c)* According to Boyle's law, at constant temperature, the volume of a given mass of a gas is inversely proportional to its pressure, i.e. $p \propto \dfrac{1}{V}$

As, $V_1 > V_2 > V_3 > V_4$

$\therefore \qquad p_1 < p_2 < p_3 < p_4$

33. *(b)* Calcium nitrate gives brick red flame which breaks down on heating to give oxygen and NO_2 which is a brown gas $2Ca(NO_3) \xrightarrow{\Delta} 2CaO + O_2 + 4NO_2$

34. *(a)* When but-1-yne reacts with excess HBr, the major product obtained is 2,2 dibromobutane. This reaction follows Markownikoff's rule

$$\underset{\text{Butyne}}{CH_3 CH_2 C \equiv CH} + HBr \longrightarrow$$

$$\underset{\underset{Br}{|}}{CH_3 CH_2 C} = CH_2 \xrightarrow{HBr}$$

$$\underset{\underset{Br}{|}}{\overset{\overset{Br}{|}}{CH_3 CH_2 - C - CH_3}}$$

2, 2 dibromobutane

35. *(d)* HgS, when heated strongly in air gives mercury and sulphur dioxide.

$$HgS + O_2 \xrightarrow{\text{Roasting}} Hg + SO_2$$

The process is known as roasting where the sulphide ore is directly heated in presence of air (O_2) to get the respective metal.

36. *(a)* The oxidation state of S in the given options are as follows

(i) Dithionous acid

$$\underset{}{\overset{\overset{O}{\|} \quad \overset{O}{\|}}{HO - S - S - OH}}$$

$$2(x) + 2(-2) + 2(-1) = 0$$

$$2x - 4 - 2 = 0$$

$$2x = 6$$

$$x = +3$$

(ii) Sulphurous acid

$$\overset{\overset{O}{\|}}{HO \diagup S \diagdown OH}$$

$$1(x) + 1(-2) + 2(-1) = 0$$

$$x = +4$$

(iii) Dithionic acid

$$\underset{\underset{O \quad O}{}}{\overset{\overset{O \quad O}{\| \quad \|}}{HO - S - S - OH}}$$

$$2(x) + 2(-1) + 4(-2) = 0$$

$$2x - 2 - 8 = 8$$

$$2x = 10$$

$$x = +5$$

(iv) Pyrosulphuric acid

$$\underset{\underset{O \qquad O}{}}{\overset{\overset{O \qquad O}{\| \qquad \|}}{HO - S - O - S - OH}}$$

$$2(x) + 5(-2) + 2(-1) + = 0$$

$$2x - 10 - 2 = 0$$

$$2x = +12$$

$$x = +6$$

Thus, the correct option is (a).

37. *(a)* Boiling point of a compound is dependent of on H-bonding present in it. Intermolecular H-bonding is more in primary than in secondary amines as there are two H-atoms available for H-bonding. Tertiary amines do not have intermolecular H-bonding due to the absence of H-atom. Therefore, the order of boiling points of the given amines is as follows

$$n C_4 H_9 NH_2 > (C_2 H_5)_2 NH > C_2 H_5 N(CH_3)_2$$

n-butylamine   diethylamine   N,N dimethylethylamine
(1°)   (2°)   (3°)

38. (c) Given velocity of light
$$= 3 \times 10^8 \ ms^{-1}$$
Frequency of light $= 8 \times 10^{15} \ s^{-1}$

As we know, $\lambda = \dfrac{C}{\nu} = \dfrac{3 \times 10^8 \ ms^{-1}}{8 \times 10^{15} \ s^{-1}}$

$$= 3.75 \times 10^{-8} \ m$$
$$1 \ m = 10^9 \ nm$$
$$\therefore 3.75 \times 10^{-8} m = 3.75 \times 10^{-8} \times 10^9 \ nm$$
$$= 3.75 \times 10^1 nm \approx 4 \times 10^1 nm$$

39. (a) Electron affinities of II period element are less negative as compared to corresponding III period element. This is because of small size of II period elements. Also, nitrogen has the least electron affinity due to stable half-filled configuration. Thus, the correct order of electron affinity is $N < O < S < Cl$.

40. (d) Xe atom has 8 electrons in its outermost shell. In case of XeF_2, out of these 8 electrons, 2 are used for bond formation, while 3 pairs remains non-bonded, i.e. it has 3 lone pairs.

In case XeF_4, 4 electrons of Xe are used for bonding. Thus it has 2 lone pairs.

In case XeF_6, 6 electrons are involved for bond formation, thus, it has only 1 lone pair.

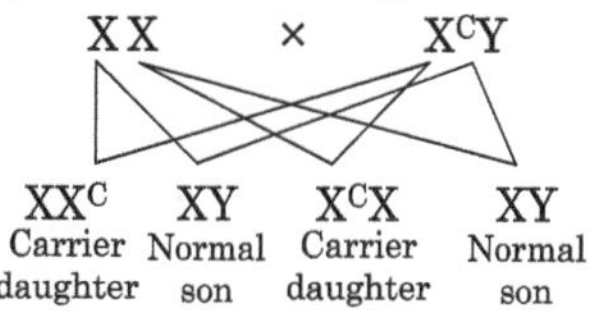

XeF_2 (3 lone pairs)   XeF_4 (2 lone pairs)   XeF_6 (1 lone pair)

41. (d) When aqueous solution of benzene diazonium chloride is boiled, it gives phenol.

Benzene diazonium chloride → Phenol

42. (a) The electronic configuration of chromium $(Z = 24)$ is
$$1s^2 \ 2s^2 \ 2p^6 \ 3s^2 \ 3p^6 \ 4s^1 \ 3d^5$$
for 19th electron the orbital is 4s

Thus,
$$n = 4$$
$$l = 0 \ to \ 3$$
$$m = -3 \ to \ 3$$
$$s = +\dfrac{1}{2}$$

Thus, among the given options, only (a) corresponds to the above given values. So, option (a) is correct.

43. (c) Among the given carbocations benzyl and allyl carbocations are more stable than methyl and vinyl carbocations because they have delocalised electrons. An allylic carbocation has two resonance structures whereas in benzylic carbocation has five resonance structures. Thus, benzyl carbocation is the most stable one.

$$RCH \overset{\frown}{=\!=\!=} CH\overset{+}{C}H_2 \longleftrightarrow RC\overset{+}{H}\!-\!CH\!=\!CH_2$$
(Allylic carbocation)

(Benzyl carbocation)

44. (b)

Thus, the correct IUPAC name of the given compound is 4-ethyl-3-propyl hex-1-ene.

45. (c) Since, each period starts with the filling of electrons in a new principal quantum number, therefore the period number in the long form of the periodic table refers to the maximum principal quantum number of any element in the period. Thus, period number = maximum n of any element.

(where, n = principal quantum number)

46. (d) Carbohydrates, fats and proteins all can be used as a substrate in cellular respiration. All of them first get converted to acetyl Co-A to enter Kreb's cycle of aerobic cellular respiration. Thus, it is the common factor of respiration entering Kreb's cycle after breakdown of carbohydrates, fats and proteins.

47. (b) When a tissue with a potential of differentiation is grown in an artificial medium containing auxin and cytokinin in a specific ratio, it starts differentiating. Thus, root and shoot differentiation occurs. Auxin initiates root formation while cytokinin starts shoot formation.

48. (b) The partial pressure of oxygen (pO_2) in alveoli of lungs is 104 mm Hg, which is more than that of blood in the blood capillaries of lung alveoli (40 mm Hg). This difference allows passive diffusion of O_2 from air filled in the lungs to the blood vessels of lung alveoli.

49. (a) Stalled fork activates checkpoint signaling and pauses replication. Since G_1 / S checkpoint checks DNA damage, cell size prior to S-phase (i.e. DNA replication phase) this checkpoint would be activated by stalled DNA replication fork.

50. (d) Ester bonds are the least likely to be involved in stabilising the 3-D folding of most proteins. A long protein chain gets folded upon itself like a hollow woolen ball, giving rise to a tertiary (3D) structure. This structure is stabilised by several types of bonds, i.e. hydrogen bonds, ionic bonds, van der Waal's interactions, covalent bonds and hydrophobic bonds.

Ester bond is formed between sugar and phosphate in a nucleotide and is not involved in stability of a polypeptide chain. Thus, option (d) is correct.

51. (a) Insulin is the peptide hormone which enhances the uptake of glucose molecules by liver cells (hepatocytes) and fat cells (adipocytes) for its cellular utilisation. Such an activity of insulin brings down the level of glucose in the blood.

52. (a) The cross for the question is

XX × X^{C}Y

XX^C XY   X^{C}X   XY
Carrier daughter   Normal son   Carrier daughter   Normal son

Since the male offsprings get X-chromosome from their mother who is normal homozygous, thus, none of the son would be colourblind.

53. (d) Cell wall of the most fungi is made up of chitin. Chemically it is N-acetyl glucosamine. It is found in the exoskeleton of insects.

54. (d)

Parents	TT (Tall)	×	tt (Dwarf)

F_1-generation — Tt (Heterozygous tall On selfing)

	T	t
T	TT (Tall)	Tt (Tall)
t	Tt (Tall)	tt (dwarf)

F_2-generation

Phenotypic ratio 3 : 1 [Tall : Dwarf]
Genotypic ratio 1 : 2 : 1

55. *(b)* Reduction of pH of blood, i.e. increase in acidity favours the dissociation of oxyhaemoglobin thereby giving up more O_2. When this phenomenon occurs due to increase in CO_2 concentration, then it is called Bohr effect.

56. *(b)* Sustained muscle contraction due to repeated stimulus is known as tetanus. This results due to muscle fatigue.

57. *(c)* Sphincter of Oddi guards the opening of hepatopancreatic duct into the duodenum. Hepatopancreatic duct brings secretion of liver as well as pancreas to the duodenum.

58. *(b)* Lysosomes are hydrolytic enzymes containing cell organelles which are bounded by a single membrane. Other organelles like chloroplast, mitochondria and nuclei have double membrane system.

59. *(b)* Parapodia are present in aquatic animals, i.e. annelids like *Nereis* which help them in swimming. Other three features, i.e. metameric segmentation, jointed appendages and chitinous exoskeleton are present in phylum Arthropoda. Out of these, metameric segmentation is visible as tagmetisation.

60. *(c)* Anthocyanins are water soluble vacuolar pigments that may appear red, purple or blue depending on pH. It is impermeable to cell membranes of plants and can leak out only when membrane is damaged or dead.

61. *(a)* Let the set S has n elements.

$\therefore$ Mean of S and $\{15\}$

$$m + 2 = \frac{S + 15}{n + 1}$$

$\Rightarrow \quad (n + 1)(m + 2) = S + 15$

$(n + 1)(m + 2) = nm + 15 \quad \left[\because m = \dfrac{S}{n}\right]$

$\Rightarrow \quad m + 2n = 13 \qquad \ldots(i)$

Also, mean of S and $\{15, 1\}$ is

$$m + 1 = \frac{S + 15 + 1}{n + 2}$$

$\Rightarrow \quad (n + 2)(m + 1) = S + 16$

$= nm + 2m + n + 2 = nm + 16$

$\Rightarrow \quad n + 2m = 14 \qquad \ldots(ii)$

From Eqs. (i) and (ii), we get

$$n = 4$$

$\therefore S$ has 4 elements.

62. *(b)* We have, $(x, y) = $ GCD of x and y.

Given, $xy = x + y + (x, y)$

$xy - x - y = (x, y)$

$xy - x - y + 1 = (x, y) + 1$

$(x - 1)(y - 1) = (x, y) + 1$

Put $x = 2, y = 3$

$(2 - 1)(3 - 1) = $ GCD of $(2, 3) + 1$

$2 = 1 + 1$

$\therefore (2, 3)$

$x = 3, y = 3$

$(3 - 1)(3 - 1) = 4 = $ GCD of $(3, 3) + 1$

$x = 2, y = 4$

also satisfies

When $x > 3$ not satisfies the equation.

$\therefore$ Only 3 pairs $(2, 3)$, $(3, 3)$ and $(2, 4)$ satisfy the equation.

63. *(b)* In $\triangle ABC$, X and Y are points on AB and AC respectively.

$$\frac{AX}{XB} = \frac{1}{2} \text{ and } \frac{AY}{YC} = \frac{2}{1}$$

$$\frac{\text{Area of } \triangle AXY}{\text{Area of } \triangle BXY} = \frac{1}{2}$$

$\Rightarrow \quad$ Area of $\triangle BXY = 20$

$$[\because \text{area of } \triangle AXY = 10]$$

$\Rightarrow \quad$ Area of $\triangle ABY = $ Area of $\triangle AXY$

$$+ \text{ Area of } \triangle BXY$$

$$= 10 + 20 = 30$$

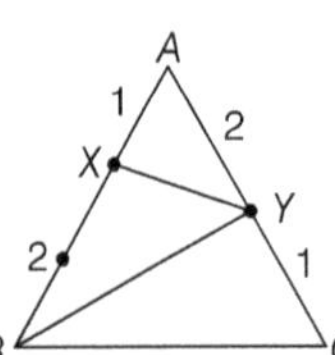

$\Rightarrow \quad \dfrac{\text{Area of } \triangle ABY}{\text{Area of } \triangle CBY} = \dfrac{2}{1}$

$\therefore \quad$ Area of $\triangle CBY = \dfrac{30}{2} = 15$

$\therefore$ Area of $\triangle ABC = $ Area of $\triangle ABY$

$$+ \text{ Area of } \triangle CBY$$

$$= 30 + 15 = 45$$

64. *(a)* We have,

$x_1 + x_2 + x_3 + \ldots + x_{2019} = 1$

and $\dfrac{x_1}{1 - x_1} + \dfrac{x_2}{1 - x_2} + \ldots + \dfrac{x_{2019}}{1 - x_{2019}} = 1$

$\Rightarrow \dfrac{x_1^2}{1 - x_1} + \dfrac{x_2^2}{1 - x_2} + \dfrac{x_3^2}{1 - x_3} + \ldots + \dfrac{x_{2019}^2}{1 - x_{2019}}$

$= \dfrac{x_1^2 - x_1 + x_1}{1 - x_1} + \dfrac{x_2^2 - x_2 + x_2}{1 - x_2} + \ldots$

$$+ \dfrac{x_{2019}^2 - x_{2019} + x_{2019}}{1 - x_{2019}}$$

$= \dfrac{x_1(x_1 - 1)}{1 - x_1} + \dfrac{x_1}{1 - x_1} + \dfrac{x_2(x_2 - 1)}{1 - x_2} + x_2$

$$+ \ldots + \dfrac{x_{2019}(x_{2019} - 1)}{1 - x_{2019}} + \dfrac{x_{2019}}{1 - x_{2019}}$$

$= -(x_1 + x_2 + \ldots + x_{2019})$

$$+ \left[\dfrac{x_1}{1 - x_1} + \dfrac{x_2}{1 - x_2} + \ldots + \dfrac{x_{2019}}{1 - x_{2019}}\right]$$

$= -1 + 1 = 0$

65. *(c)* Given,

In $\triangle ABC$, I is incentre of $\triangle ABC$.

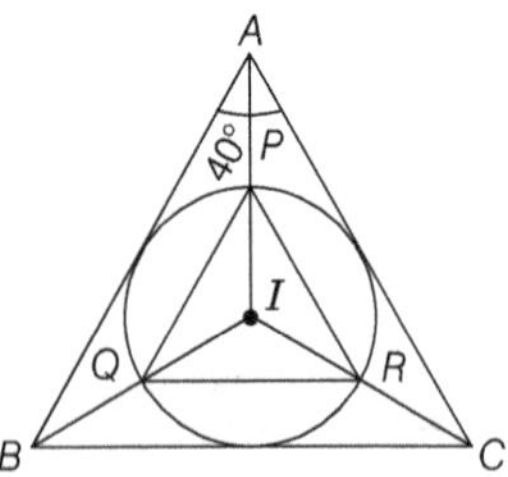

AI, BI and CI intersect the circle at P, Q, R respectively.

In $\triangle IBC$, $\angle BIC + \angle IBC + \angle ICB = 180°$

$$\angle BIC + \frac{\angle B}{2} + \frac{\angle C}{2} = 180°$$

$$\angle BIC = 180° - \left(\frac{\angle B + \angle C}{2}\right)$$

$$= 180° - \left(\frac{180 - \angle A}{2}\right)$$

$$= 90° + \frac{\angle A}{2} = 90 + 20 = 110$$

$$[\because \angle A = 40°]$$

$\angle BIC = \angle QIR = 40°$

$\angle QPR = \dfrac{1}{2} QIR$

[$\because$ angle in a segment is half of angle on a centre segment of circle]

$\angle QPR = \dfrac{1}{2} \times 110° = 55°$

66. *(c)* By homogenity principle,

$[a] = $ dimensions of power

$\dfrac{W}{T} = [ML^2T^{-3}]$

$[bt^2] = $ dimensions of power

$\Rightarrow \quad [b] = \dfrac{[ML^2T^{-3}]}{[T^2]} = [ML^2T^{-5}]$

$[c] = $ dimensions of $t^3 = [T^3]$

$[d^{-1}t^3] = $ dimensions of power

$\Rightarrow \quad [d] = \dfrac{[T^3]}{[ML^2T^{-3}]} = [M^{-1}L^{-2}T^{-6}]$

So, statement IV is incorrect.

67. *(b)* Before collision, velocity of translation of sphere

$$= v_{\text{cube}} = r\omega = 1\,\text{cms}^{-1} = 0.01\,\text{ms}^{-1}$$

As collision is elastic, translational kinetic energy of sphere is transferred to the cube but its rotational kinetic energy remains constant.

$\therefore$ After collision, $v_{\text{sphere}} = 0$,

$v_{\text{cube}} = 0.01\,\text{ms}^{-1}$ and $\omega_{\text{sphere}} = 1\,\text{rad s}^{-1}$.

68. *(b)* By KVL,

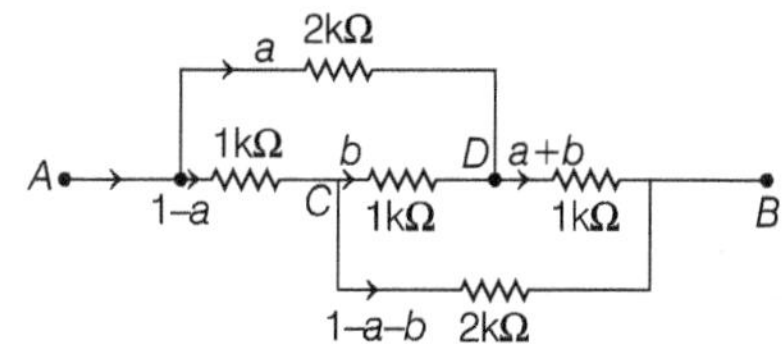

we have, $V_{AD} = 2a = 1 - a + b$

Also, $V_{CD} = 2(1 - a - b) = b + a + b$

$\therefore \qquad a = \dfrac{2}{5}$

and $\qquad b = \dfrac{1}{5}$

Hence, current through 2 kΩ resistor

$$= a = \dfrac{2}{5}\,\text{mA}.$$

and current through middle 1 kΩ resistor

$$= b = \dfrac{1}{5}\,\text{mA}.$$

69. *(b)* Change in momentum of steel ball $= -2mv$

Force on U-tube $= \dfrac{2mv}{\Delta t} = \dfrac{2mv}{\left(\dfrac{\pi d}{2v}\right)}$

$$= \dfrac{4mv^2}{\pi d} = \dfrac{4 \times 0.02 \times 9}{3.14 \times 1}$$

$$\approx 0.23\,\text{N}$$

$$= 0.2\,\text{N}$$

70. *(a)* As, $\quad U = \dfrac{-2x}{x^2 + 4}$

$\Rightarrow \qquad \dfrac{dU}{dx} = \dfrac{-2}{x^2 + 4} + \dfrac{(-2x)(-1)(2x)}{(x^2 + 4)^2}$

$$= \dfrac{-2}{x^2 + 4} + \dfrac{4x^2}{(x^2 + 4)^2}$$

$\dfrac{dU}{dx} = 0$ when $\dfrac{2}{x^2 + 4} = \dfrac{4x^2}{(x^2 + 4)^2}$

$\Rightarrow \qquad 2(x^2 + 4) = 4x^2$

$\Rightarrow \qquad 2x^2 = 8$

$\Rightarrow \qquad x = \pm\,2$

As U is minimum at $x = +2$.

$\therefore \qquad F = \dfrac{-dU}{dx} = 0$

Now, restoring force constant.

$$k = \dfrac{d^2 U}{dx^2}\bigg|_{\text{at } x = 2} = \dfrac{1}{8}\,\text{units}$$

$\therefore \quad \omega = \sqrt{\dfrac{k}{m}} = \sqrt{\dfrac{1}{8m}} = \sqrt{\left(\dfrac{1}{8 \times 5 \times 10^{-3}}\right)}$

$$= \sqrt{\dfrac{100}{4}}$$

$$= 5\,\text{rad s}^{-1}$$

71. *(d)*

$$C_{12}H_{22}O_{11}(s) + 12O_2(g) \longrightarrow 12CO_2(g)$$
$$+ 11H_2O(l)$$

$\Delta H_{\text{C}}^{\circ} = [12\Delta_f H^{\circ}(CO_2) + 11\Delta_f H^{\circ}(H_2O)]$
$$- [\Delta_f H^{\circ}(C_{12}H_{22}O_{11})]$$
$$= [12(-94.3) + 11(-68.3)] - [-530]$$
$$= -1352.9\,\text{J kcal mol}^{-1}$$

Thus, number of moles of $C_{12}H_{22}O_{11}$ required for 2700 kcal of energy

$$= \dfrac{2700}{1352.9} \approx 2\,\text{mol} = 682.6\,\text{g}$$

72. *(d)* The alcohol on treatment with acid gives an alkene *(A)* which on ozonolysis will give nonan-2, 8 dione. The reaction can be shown as

73. *(c)* Number of equivalents of silver formed = number of equivalents of copper formed.

In $AgNO_3$, Ag is in + 1 oxidation state.

In $CuSO_4$, Cu is in + 2 oxidation state.

$\therefore$ Equivalent weight of Ag $= \dfrac{108}{1} = 108$

Equivalent weight of Cu

$$= \dfrac{63.6}{2} = 31.8$$

$$\dfrac{\text{Weight of silver}}{\text{Weight of copper}} = \dfrac{\text{Eq. wt of silver}}{\text{Eq. wt of copper}}$$

$$\dfrac{10.79}{w_{Cu}} = \dfrac{108}{31.8}$$

$$w_{Cu} = \dfrac{10.79 \times 31.8}{108}$$

$$= 3.2\,\text{g}$$

74. *(c)* Energy of one photon $= \dfrac{hc}{\lambda}$

$$= \dfrac{6.626 \times 10^{-34}\,\text{Js} \times 3 \times 10^8\,\text{ms}^{-1}}{550 \times 10^{-9}\,\text{m}}$$

$$= 3.61 \times 10^{-19}\,\text{J}$$

$\therefore$ Number of photons

$$= \dfrac{\text{energy required}}{\text{energy of one photon}}$$

$$= \dfrac{10^{-17}}{3.61 \times 10^{-19}}$$

$$= 27.67 \approx 28$$

75. *(b)* ΔG° is related to K_{sp} by the equation

$\Delta G^{\circ} = -2.303\,RT \log K_{sp}$

$\Delta G^{\circ} = +63.3\,\text{kJ} = 63.3 \times 10^3\,\text{J}$

$63.3 \times 10^3 = -2.303 \times 8.314 \times 298 \times \log K_{sp}$

$\log K_{sp} = -11.09$

$K_{sp} = 8.0 \times 10^{-12}$

76. *(b)* The nerves are myelinated with unmyelinated segments called nodes of Ranvier. The high phospholipid content of the myelin sheath offers electrical insulation, thus saltatory conduction occurs as impulse jumps from one node to the next. This form of conduction facilitates a very rapid transmission of impulses.

77. *(a)* The cross for the question is

♀ \ ♂	YR	yR	Yr	yr
YR	YYRR	YyRR	YYRr	YyRr
yR	YyRR	yyRR	YyRr	yyRr
Yr	YYRr	YyRr	YYrr	Yyrr
yr	YyRr	yyRr	Yyrr	yyrr

The given Punnett square shows 9 : 3 : 3 : 1 ratio of the phenotypes only.

78. *(b)* As the substrate concentration increases, the rate of reaction increases until a maximum, when saturation of all the enzymes active sites occurs. When this happens, the limiting factor is enzyme concentration. Thus, graph (b) is correct.

79. *(c)* Average amino acid residues molecular weight = 110

Polypeptide chain of molecular weight

$$20{,}000 = \dfrac{20{,}000}{110} = 182\,\text{amino acids}$$

A triplet of bases in the DNA molecule codes for one amino acid in a polypeptide chain.

To translate 182 amino acids, there must be a minimum of $182 \times 3 = 546$ nucleotides.

80. *(b)* *Sequoia* is one of the tallest tree species, known as red wood tree. It is a gymnospermic plant.

Salvinia is an angiosperm, but *Ginkgo* and *Pinus* are gymnosperms. Gymnosperms are well-adapted to extremes of climate and are heterosporous.

PRACTICE SET 4
Stream : SA

MM : 100

Instructions

1. There are 80 questions in this paper.
2. This question paper contains two parts; Part I and Part II. There are four sections; Mathematics, Physics, Chemistry and Biology in each part.
3. Out of the four options given with each question, only one is correct.

➲ PART-I (1 Mark Questions)

MATHEMATICS

1. A natural number K is such that $K^2 < 2019 < (K+1)^2$. Then, the largest prime factor of K is
(a) 11 (b) 13 (c) 7 (d) 5

2. If real number a, b, c, d, e satisfy
$a + 1 = b + 2 = c + 3 = d + 4 = e + 5$
$= a + b + c + d + e + 3$, then the value of
$a^2 + b^2 + c^2 + d^2 + e^2$ is equal to
(a) 8 (b) 9 (c) 10 (d) 11

3. Let a semi-circle with centre O and diameter AB. Let P and Q be points on the semi-circle and R be a point on AB extended such that $OA = QR < PR$ if $\angle POA = 102°$, then $\angle PRA$ is equal to
(a) 51° (b) 34°
(c) 25.5° (d) None of these

4. If $x = \cos 1° \cos 2° \cos 3° \dots \cos 89°$ and
$y = \cos 2° \cos 6° \cos 10° \dots \cos 86°$, then the integer nearest to $\dfrac{2}{7} \log_2 \left(\dfrac{y}{x} \right)$ is
(a) 16 (b) 17 (c) 18 (d) 19

5. If $a, b, c \geq 4$ are integers, not all equal and $4abc = (a+3)(b+3)(c+3)$, then $(a+b+c)$ is equal to
(a) 14 (b) 15 (c) 16 (d) 18

6. In a $\triangle ABC$, right angled at A, the altitude through A and the internal bisector of $\angle A$ have lengths 3 and 4 respectively. Then, the length of median through A is
(a) 20 (b) 24 (c) 15 (d) 10

7. A rectangular floor that is 10 feet wide and 17 feet long is tiled with 170 one-foot square tiles. A bug walks from one corner to the opposite corner in a straight line including the first and the last tile, how many tiles does the bug visit?
(a) 17 (b) 25 (c) 26 (d) 27

8. Ashwani computes the mean μ, the median M and the modes of the 365 values that are the dates of 2019. Thus his data consists of 12 1s, 12 2s ..., 12 28s, 11 29s, 11 30s and 7 31s. Let d be the median of modes. Which of the following is correct?
(a) $\mu < d < M$ (b) $M < d < \mu$
(c) $M = d = \mu$ (d) $d < \mu < M$

9. A sequence of numbers is defined recursively by
$$a_1 = 1, a_2 = \frac{3}{7} \text{ and } a_n = \frac{a_{n-2} \cdot a_{n-1}}{2a_{n-2} - a_{n-1}} \text{ for all } n \geq 3.$$
Then, a_{2019} can be written as $\frac{p}{q}$, where p and q are relatively prime number, then the value of $p + q$ is equal to
(a) 6057   (b) 8087   (c) 8078   (d) 4039

10. A child builds towers using identically shaped cube of different color. Then, number of different tower with a height 8 cubes can the child build with 2 red cubes, 3 blue cubes and 4 green cubes (one cube is left out) is
(a) 24   (b) 288   (c) 312   (d) 1260

11. The least possible value of
$(x+1)(x+2)(x+3)(x+4) + 2019$ is (where, x is real)
(a) 2017   (b) 2018   (c) 2019   (d) 2020

12. Two circles of radius 5 are externally tangent to each other and are internally tangent to a circle of radius 13 at points A and B, as shown in the figure. The distance AB can be written in the form $\frac{m}{n}$, when m and n are relatively prime.

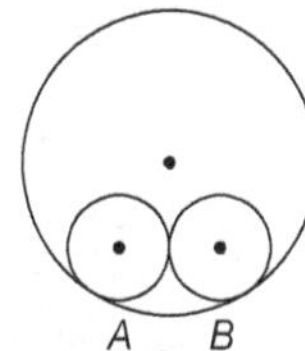

Then, $m + n$ is
(a) 21   (b) 29   (c) 69   (d) 58

13. A person X is running around a circular track completing one round in 40 s. Another person Y running in opposite direction meets X every 15 s. The time, expressed in seconds, taken to Y to complete one round is
(a) 12.5   (b) 24   (c) 25   (d) 55

14. Consider all 6-digit numbers of the form $abccba$, where b is odd. Then, number of all such 6-digit numbers that are divisible by 7 is
(a) 70   (b) 80   (c) 75   (d) 85

15. Let $ABCD$ be trapezium in which AB is parallel to CD and AD is perpendicular to AB. Suppose $ABCD$ has incircle which touches AB at Q and CD at P. Given that $PC = 36$ and $QB = 49$, then length PQ is
(a) 85   (b) 84   (c) 76   (d) 80

PHYSICS

16. Velocity-time graph of a particle of mass 10 kg pushed along a frictionless surface by an external force is as shown below.

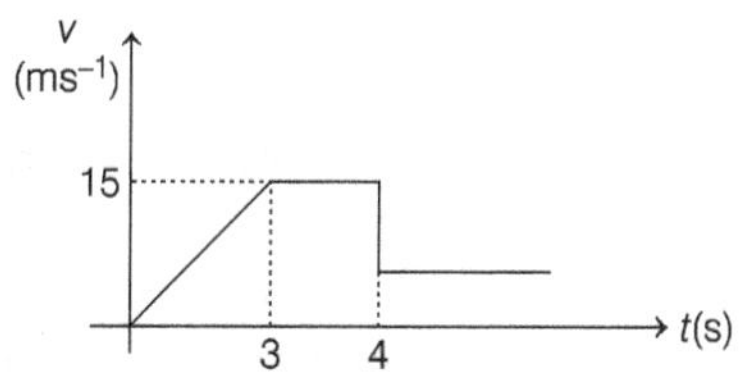

Now, consider the following statements:
   I. Force acting on particle is 50 N.
   II. Force stops at $t = 3$ s.
   III. Force stops at $t = 4$ s.
   IV. Particle receives an impulse at $t = 4$ s.
Which of the above statements are correct?
(a) Statements II and IV are correct
(b) Statements I, II and IV are correct
(c) Statements I, III and IV are correct
(d) Statements III and IV are correct

17. Correct graph of experimental values of specific heat of a constant volume of hydrogen gas is

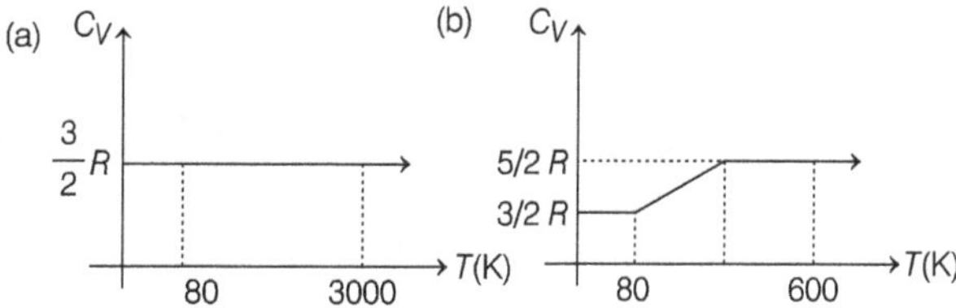

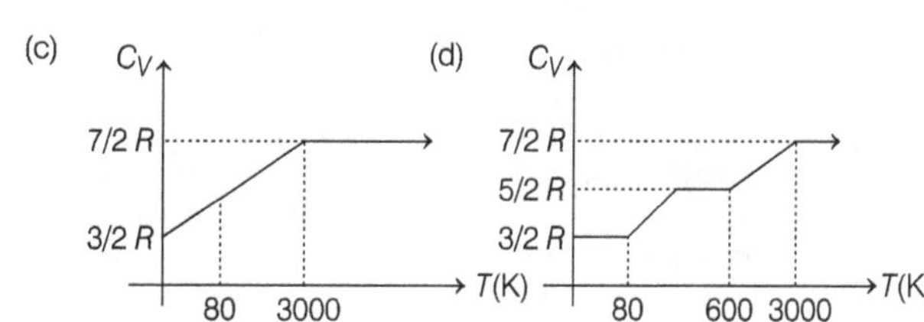

18. Ratio of nuclear density of nuclei $^{142}_{53}$I and $^{139}_{56}$Ba is
(a) 142 : 139   (b) 53 : 56
(c) 139 : 142   (d) None of these

19. A particle starts from origin, it accelerates first t_0 second and then deaccelerates at same rate till $2\,t_0$ second along the positive x-direction. Variation of displacement x with time t for the particle is given by

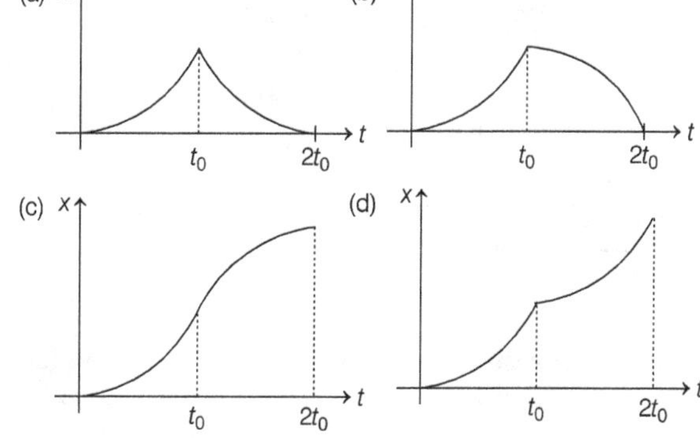

20. A mass m initially at rest is pulled with a force F. If force is proportional to instantaneous time t, then kinetic energy of the particle is proportional to
(a) t^2 (b) t^{-2} (c) t^4 (d) t^0

21. Density of ice is x (g/cc) and that of water is g (g/cc). Change in volume in cc when m grams of ice completely melts is
(a) $m(y - x)$
(b) $(y - x)/m$
(c) $mxy\,(y - x)$
(d) $m\left(\dfrac{1}{y} - \dfrac{1}{x}\right)$

22. How much work is required in units of electron-volt to carry an electron from the positive terminal of a 12 V battery to the negative terminal in external circuit?
(a) 12 eV
(b) -12 eV
(c) 6 eV
(d) -6 eV

23. Following graph shows atmospheric pressure, gauge pressure and absolute pressure.

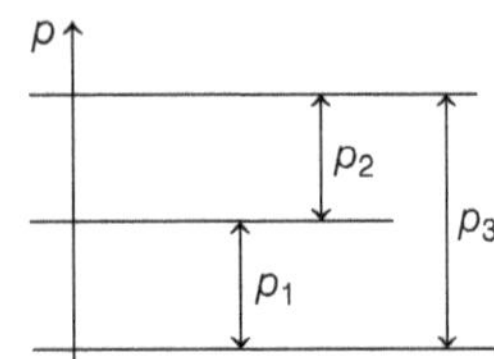

Then, choose the correct option.
(a) p_1 = gauge pressure, p_2 = atmospheric pressure, p_3 = absolute pressure
(b) p_1 = atmospheric pressure, p_2 = gauge pressure, p_3 = absolute pressure
(c) p_1 = absolute pressure, p_2 = atmospheric pressure, p_3 = gauge pressure
(d) p_1 = gauge pressure, p_2 = absolute pressure, p_3 = atmospheric pressure

24. A man can walks on hard ground with a speed of $5\ \text{ms}^{-1}$ and on sandy ground with $3\ \text{ms}^{-1}$.

Let he is standing on border of sandy and hard ground and wishes to reach the tree situated on the sandy ground as shown below.

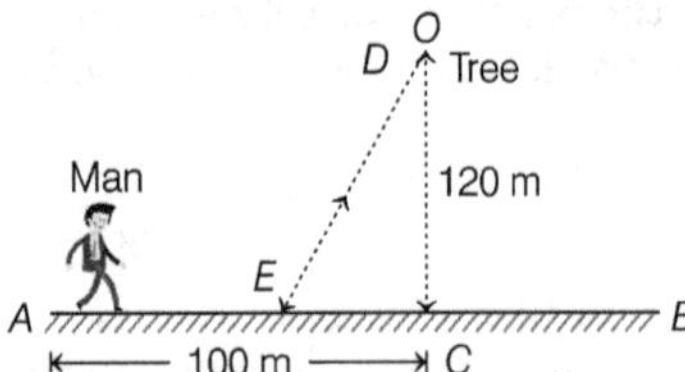

He can reach tree in least time when he walks on hard ground upto point E and then he walks straight towards tree along EO. Distance AE is
(a) 10 m
(b) 20 m
(c) 30 m
(d) 50 m

25. Equivalent resistance between A and B is $6\,\Omega$. Value of resistance R_1 is

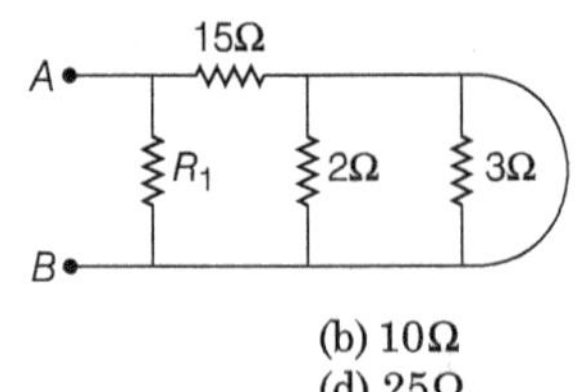

(a) $20\,\Omega$
(b) $10\,\Omega$
(c) $5\,\Omega$
(d) $25\,\Omega$

26. Fermi energy level for an electron is
(a) a possible energy value that an electron can have in free state
(b) an unfilled energy level that can be occupied by two electrons of opposite spins
(c) lowest energy value possible for a bound electron
(d) highest occupied energy level at absolute zero kelvin upto which every possible energy levels are filled

27. Solar cookers are not very popular because
(a) they are bulky
(b) they are not put into kitchen
(c) they cook food in large time
(d) sun changes its position rapidly

28. A cubical block of side 1 m and mass 10 kg is placed on a rough surface. Block can be toppled by applying a force horizontally at its upper edge. Minimum value of F is

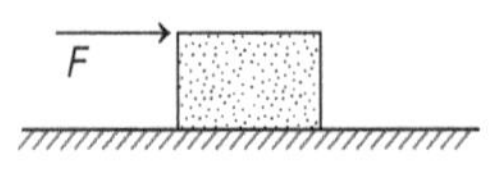

(a) 100 N
(b) 200 N
(c) 50 N
(d) 25 N

29. Potential energy between two molecules as a function of their separation is as shown below.

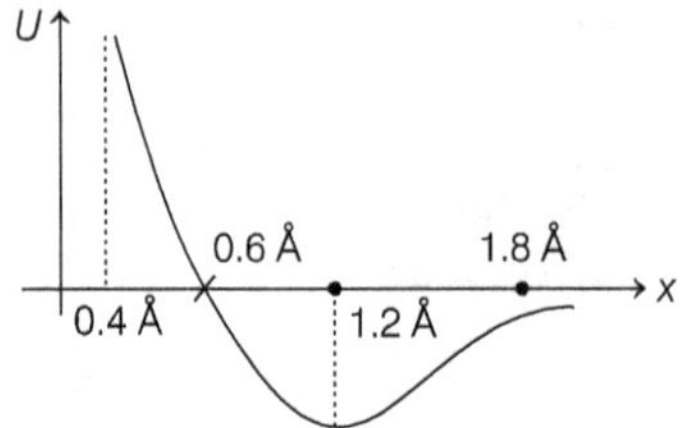

Force between particles is zero at
(a) $x = 0.4\,\text{Å}$
(b) $x = 0.6\,\text{Å}$
(c) $x = 1.2\,\text{Å}$
(d) $x = 1.8\,\text{Å}$

30. Using following figures,

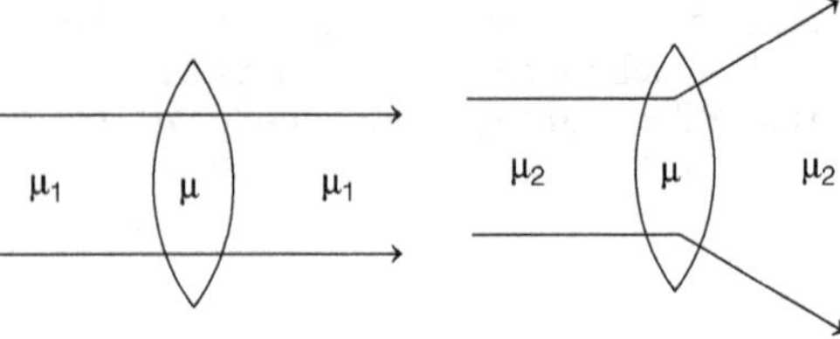

Relation between refractive indices μ_1 and μ_2 is
(a) $\mu_1 < \mu_2$
(b) $\mu_1\mu_2 = \mu^2$
(c) $\mu_1 > \mu_2$
(d) $\mu_1 = \mu_2$

CHEMISTRY

31. How many moles of magnesium phosphate $Mg_3(PO_4)_2$ will contain 0.25 mole of oxygen atom?
(a) 0.02
(b) 3.125×10^{-2}
(c) 1.25×10^{-2}
(d) 2.5×10^{-2}

32. At what temperature will the r.m.s velocity of SO_2 be the same as that of O_2 at 303 K ?
(a) 350 K
(b) 505 K
(c) 606 K
(d) 100 K

33. When acidified sodium extract of organic compound is treated with acetic acid and lead acetate, a black precipitate is obtained. This suggests that the organic compound contains
(a) chlorine
(b) phosphorus
(c) sulphur
(d) nitrogen

34. Acetone is treated with excess of ethanol in the presence of hydrochloric acid. The product obtained is

(a) 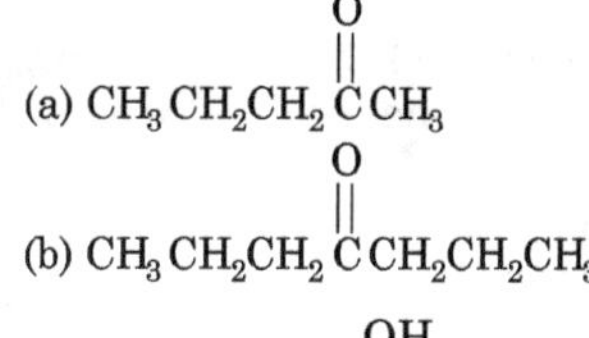

(b) 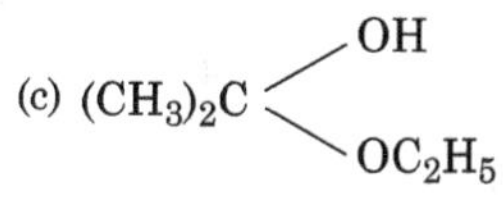

(c) 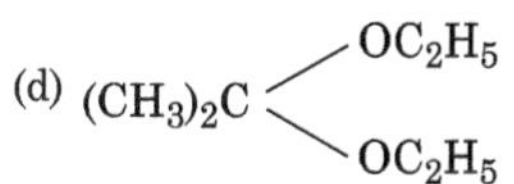

(d) $(CH_3)_2C\begin{smallmatrix}OC_2H_5\\OC_2H_5\end{smallmatrix}$

35. The electronegativity of the following elements increases in the order
(a) $C < N < Si < P$
(b) $N < Si < C < P$
(c) $Si < P < C < N$
(d) $P < Si < N < C$

36. The de-Broglie wavelength associated with particle of mass of 10^{-6} kg moving with a velocity of $10\ ms^{-1}$ is
(a) 6.63×10^{-7} m
(b) 6.63×10^{-16} m
(c) 6.63×10^{-21} m
(d) 6.63×10^{-29} m

37. The product formed when 1-bromo-3-chlorocyclobutane reacts with two equivalents of metallic sodium in ether, is

(a) 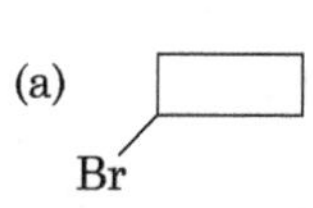

(b) 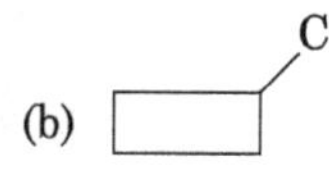

(c) 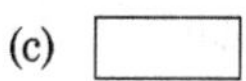

(d)

38. E° values of some redox couples are given below. On the basis of these values choose the correct option.
$$Br_2/Br^-, E^\circ = +1.90$$
$$Ag^+/Ag(s), E^\circ = +0.80$$
$$Cu^{2+}/Cu(s), E^\circ = +0.34$$
$$I_2(s)/I^-, E^\circ = +0.54$$
(a) Cu will reduce Br^-
(b) Cu will reduce Ag
(c) Cu will reduce I^-
(d) Cu will reduce Br_2

39. The carboxylic acid which reduces Tollen's reagent is
(a) acetic acid
(b) oxalic acid
(c) formic acid
(d) lactic acid

40. The correct order of C—O bond length among CO, CO_3^{2-}, CO_2 is
(a) $CO_2 < CO_3^{2-} < CO$
(b) $CO < CO_3^{2-} < CO_2$
(c) $CO_3^{2-} < CO_2 < CO$
(d) $CO < CO_2 < CO_3^{2-}$

41. When 22.4 L of $H_2(g)$ is mixed with 11.2 L of $Cl_2(g)$ each at STP, the moles of $HCl(g)$ formed is equal to
(a) 1 mole of HCl (g)
(b) 2 moles of HCl (g)
(c) 0.5 mole of HCl (g)
(d) 1.5 moles of HCl (g)

42. A 1 L flask contains 32g of O_2 gas at 27°C. What mass of O_2 must be released to reduce the pressure in the flask to 12.315 atm?
(a) 8 g
(b) 16 g
(c) 24 g
(d) 0 g

43. What is the orbital angular momentum of an electron in f-orbital ?
(a) $\dfrac{15h}{\pi}$
(b) $\dfrac{\sqrt{6h}}{\pi}$
(c) $\dfrac{\sqrt{3h}}{\pi}$
(d) $\dfrac{\sqrt{3h}}{\pi}$

44. Aluminium trifluoride is treated with anhydrous HF and then with NaF. When gaseous BF_3 is passed through the solution obtained, a precipitate X is formed. The formed pricipitate X is
(a) $Na_3[AlF_6]$
(b) $Na[BF_4]$
(c) AlF_3
(d) $H_3[AlF_6]$

45. Which one of the following will be aromatic?

(a) 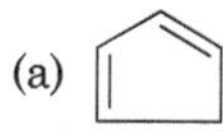

(b) 

(c) 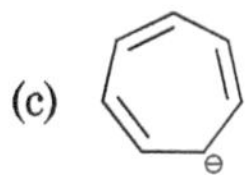

(d) 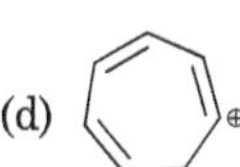

BIOLOGY

46. Which cells of 'crypts of Lieberkuhn' secrete antibacterial lysozyme?
(a) Argentaffin cells
(b) Paneth cells
(c) Zymogen cells
(d) Kupffer cells

47. Which among the following are the smallest living cells, known without a definite cell wall, pathogenic to plants as well as animals and can survive without oxygen?
(a) *Bacillus*
(b) *Pseudomonas*
(c) *Mycoplasma*
(d) *Nostoc*

48. The cell organelle responsible for extracting energy from carbohydrates to form ATP is
(a) lysosome
(b) ribosome
(c) chloroplast
(d) mitochondrion

49. DNA fragments are
(a) positively charged
(b) negatively charged
(c) neutral
(d) either positively or negatively charged depending on their size

50. An important characteristic that hemichordates share with chordates is
(a) absence of notochord
(b) ventral tubular nerve cord
(c) pharynx with gill slits
(d) pharynx without gill slits

51. Lungs are made up of air-filled sacs, the alveoli. They do not collapse even after forceful expiration, because of
(a) Residual Volume (RV)
(b) Inspiratory Reserve Volume (IRV)
(c) Tidal Volume (TV)
(d) Expiratory Reserve Volume (ERV)

52. Viroids differ from viruses in having
(a) DNA molecules with protein coat
(b) DNA molecules without protein coat
(c) RNA molecules with protein coat
(d) RNA molecules without protein coat

53. Plants, which produce characteristic pneumatophores and show vivipary belong to
(a) mesophytes   (b) halophytes
(c) psammophytes   (d) hydrophytes

54. Spliceosomes are not found in cells of
(a) plants   (b) fungi
(c) animals   (d) bacteria

55. Fruit and leaf drop at early stages can be prevented by the application of
(a) cytokinins
(b) ethylene
(c) auxins
(d) gibberellic acid

56. Which one of the following options best represents enzyme composition of pancreatic juice?
(a) Amylase, peptidase, trypsinogen, rennin
(b) Amylase, pepsin, trypsinogen, maltase
(c) Peptidase, amylase, pepsin, rennin
(d) Lipase, amylase, trypsinogen, procarboxypeptidase

57. In the fruit fly, *Drosophila melanogaster*, the diploid number of chromosomes is 8. In the absence of crossing over or mutation, how many genetically unique kinds of gamete might be formed by one individual?
(a) 4   (b) 8
(c) 16   (d) 32

58. Biochemical analysis of a sample of DNA shows that cytosine forms 40% of the nitrogenous bases. Which percentage of the bases is adenine?
(a) 10%   (b) 20%
(c) 40%   (d) 60%

59. The first stable product of fixation of atmospheric nitrogen in leguminous plant is
(a) NO_2^- (b) ammonia
(c) NO_3^- (d) glutamate

60. *Treponema pallidum* pathogen is a cause of
(a) leprosy   (b) plague
(c) syphilis   (d) pertussis

Ꙩ PART-II (2 Marks Questions)

MATHEMATICS

61. Integer a, b, c satisfy $a + b - c = 1$ and $a^2 + b^2 - c^2 + 1 = 0$, then the sum of all possible values of $a^2 + b^2 + c^2$ is equal to
(a) 17   (b) 18   (c) 20   (d) 24

62. There are several tea cups in the kitchen, some with handles and others without handles. The number of ways of selecting two cups without a handle and three with a handle is exactly 1200. Then, the maximum possible numbers of cups in the kitchen is equal to
(a) 25   (b) 27   (c) 28   (d) 29

63. Let D be an interior point of the side BC of a $\triangle ABC$. Let I_1 and I_2 be the incenters of $\triangle ABD$ and $\triangle ACD$ respectively. Let AI_1 and AI_2 meet BC in E and F respectively. If $\angle BI_1E = 60°$, then $\angle CI_2F$ is (in degree)
(a) 30°   (b) 45°   (c) 75°   (d) 60°

64. Let $P(x) = a_0 + a_1 x + a_2 x^2 + \ldots + a_n x^n$ be a polynomial in which a_i is a non-negative integer for each $i \in (0, 1, 2, 3, \ldots, n)$. If $P(1) = 4$ and $P(5) = 136$, then $P(3)$ is
(a) 25   (b) 30   (c) 32   (d) 34

65. In a quadrilateral $ABCD$, it is given that $AB = AD = 13$, $BC = CD = 20$, $BD = 24$. If r is the radius of the circle inscribed in the quadrilateral, then the integer closest to r is
(a) 6   (b) 8   (c) 9   (d) 10

PHYSICS

66. Two earthworms climb over a rough thin wall of an earthen pot 10 cm high placed in a lawn.

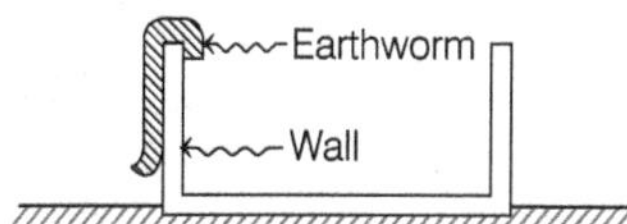

One of the worm is 20 cm long and other is only 10 cm long and mass of both earthworms is 20 g.

Ratio of work done by worms when they crosses half of their length across top of the wall is

(a) $1:1$ (b) $2:3$
(c) $2:1$ (d) $1:2$

67. A jar of height 20 cm is filled with water ($n_w = 4/3$). At centre of jar on the bottom surface, a red dot is made.

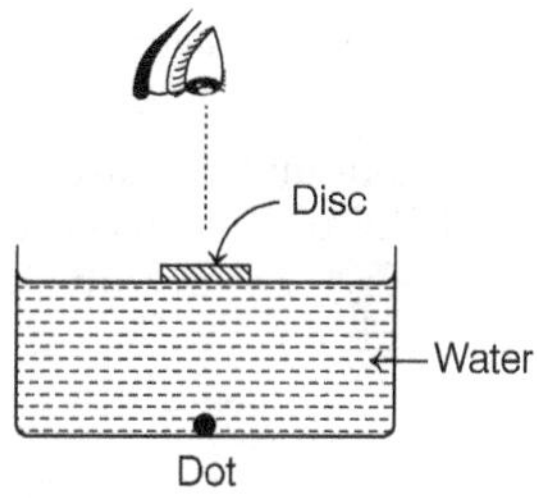

Minimum radius of an opaque plastic disc that makes the dot invisible from top is

(a) 20 cm   (b) 23 cm
(c) 12 cm   (d) 2 cm

68. Consider arrangements A and B for making a torch:

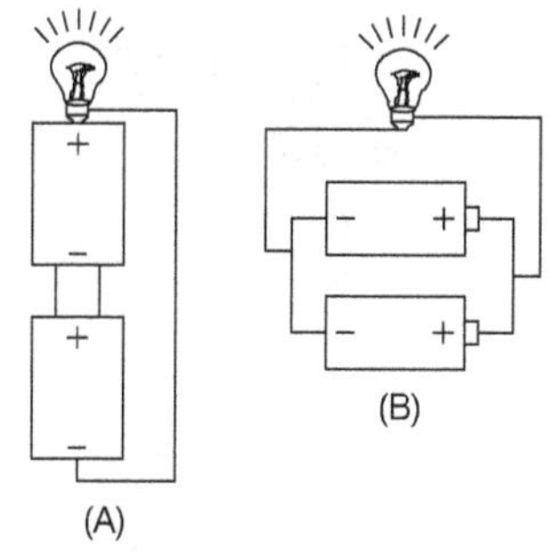

Now, consider the following statements.

  I. Torch A is brighter.

  II. Torch B is brighter.

  III. Torch A lasts longer.

  IV. Torch B lasts longer.

Which of the above statements are correct?

(a) Statements I and III are correct
(b) Statements II and IV are correct
(c) Statements I and IV are correct
(d) Statements II and III are correct

69. Velocity-time graph of an object moving along a straight line is as shown below.

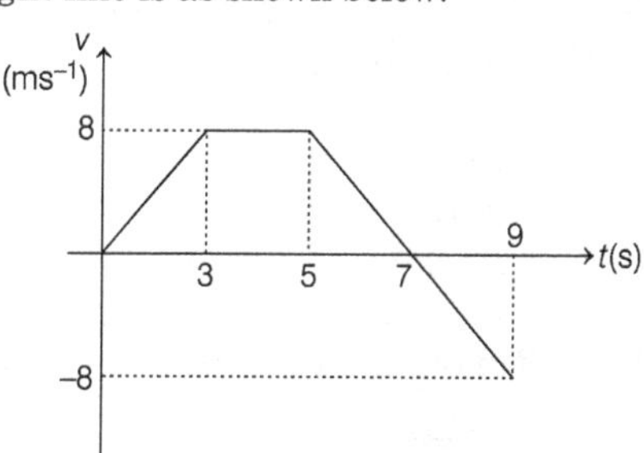

If x = displacement (in m) and a = acceleration (in ms^{-2}). Then, correct graph is

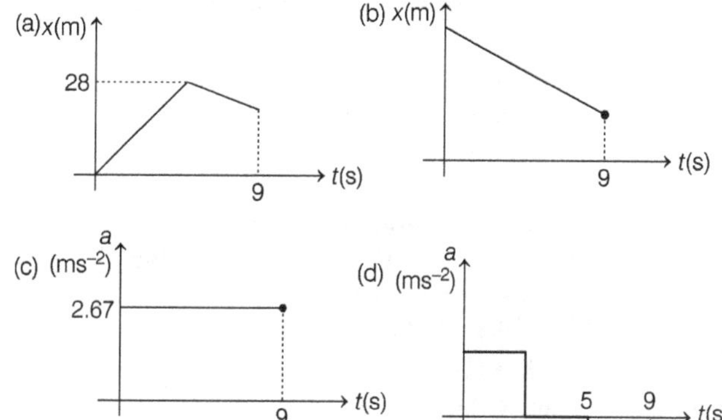

70. A vessel has a hole of radius $r = 1$ cm. Vessel is initially full of water and hole is sealed by a ball of mass $m = \pi$ g. Depth of water is now slowly reduced using a syphon and when it reaches a certain value h_0, the ball rises out of the hole.

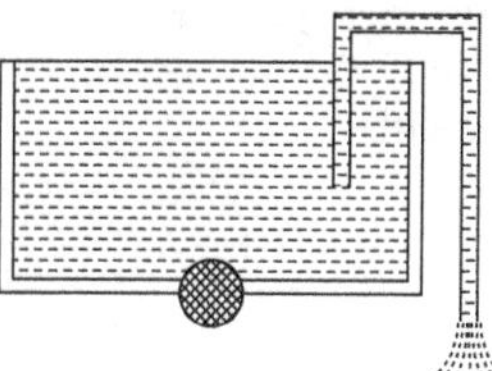

Value of h_0 is

(Radius of ball is slightly larger than hole but for calculation both can be taken same, $g = 10$ ms^{-2})

(a) 65 cm   (b) 72 cm   (c) 84 cm   (d) 110 cm

CHEMISTRY

71. A solid compound X on heating gives CO_2 gas and a residue. The residue mixed with water form Y. On passing an excess of CO_2 through Y in water, a clear solution Z is formed. On boiling Z, compound X is reformed. The compound X is

(a) $Ca(HCO_3)_2$ (b) $CaCO_3$ (c) Na_2CO_3 (d) K_2CO_3

72. Standard entropies of X_2, Y_2 and XY_3 are 60, 40 and 50 $JK^{-1}mol^{-1}$, respectively. For the reaction,

$$\frac{1}{2}X_2 + \frac{3}{2}Y_2 \rightleftharpoons XY_3 \; ; \Delta H = -30\,kJ$$

To be at equilibrium, the temperature should be
(a) 750 K   (b) 1000 K   (c) 1250 K   (d) 500 K

73. $A\,(C_4H_6) \xrightarrow[\text{1 mol}]{H_2/Ni} B\,(C_4H_8) \xrightarrow{O_3/H_2O/Zn} CH_3CHO$

Identify A and B in the above reaction.

(a) ⬚ and ⬚

(b) ⬚ and ⬚

(c) $CH_3CH_2C \equiv CH$ and $CH_3CH = CHCH_3$
(d) $CH_2 = CHCH = CH_2$ and $CH_3CH = CHCH_3$

74. In the Kjeldahl's method for the estimation of nitrogen present in a soil sample, ammonia evolved from 0.75 g of sample neutralised 10 mL of 1 M H_2SO_4. The percentage of nitrogen in the soil is
(a) 37.33   (b) 45.33   (c) 35.33   (d) 45.33

75. A carbon compound contains 12.8% of carbon, 2.1% of hydrogen and 85.1% of bromine. The molecular weight of the compound is 187.9. The molecular formula of the compound is

[Atomic weight of H = 1.008, C = 12.0 and Br = 79.9]
(a) CH_3Br (b) CH_2Br_2 (c) $C_2H_4Br_2$ (d) $C_2H_3Br_3$

BIOLOGY

76. The complete oxidation of one mole of glucose yields 2880 kJ of energy. The addition of one phosphate molecule to ADP requires 30.6 kJ of energy per mole. In aerobic respiration, 38 molecules of ATP are formed as a result of the breakdown of each glucose molecule. Which figure best represents the efficiency of aerobic respiration in trapping the energy released by the glucose molecule?
(a) 23%   (b) 36%   (c) 40%   (d) 45%

77. Haemophilia is caused by a sex-linked, recessive allele. A couple have a haemophilic son, a normal son and a haemophilic daughter. What are the most likely genotypes of the parents?

Mother Father
(a) $X^H X$ $X^H Y$
(b) $X^H Y$ $X^H Y$
(c) $X^H X^H$ $X^H Y$
(d) $X^H Y^H$ $X^H Y$

78. Which of the following statements is correct in relation to the endocrine system?
(a) Adenohypophysis is under direct neural regulation of the hypothalamus
(b) Organs in the body like gastro-intestinal tract, heart, kidney and liver do not produce any hormones
(c) Non-nutrient chemicals produced by the body in trace amount that act as intercellular messenger are known as hormones
(d) Releasing and inhibitory hormones are produced by the pituitary gland

79. If the nucleus of a human motor neuron contains 6.8 picograms (pg) of DNA, what mass of DNA is the nucleus of an actively dividing human skin cell likely to contain at the end of interphase?
(a) 3.4 pg   (b) 6.8 pg
(c) 13.6 pg   (d) 20.4 pg

80. The diagram represents a reaction with and without an enzyme. What is the activation energy of the enzyme catalysed reaction?

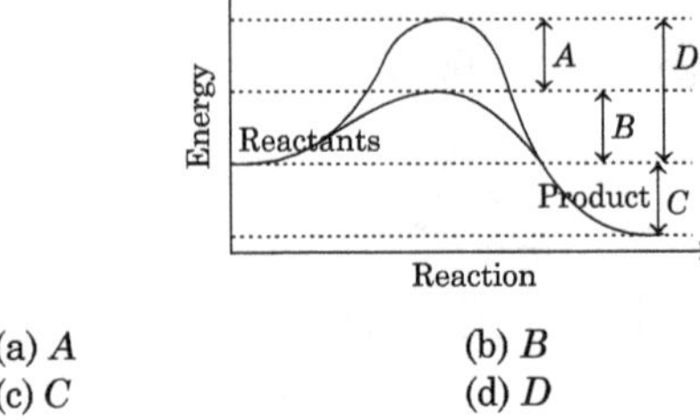

(a) A (b) B
(c) C (d) D

Answers

Solutions

1. *(a)* We have,
$$K^2 < 2019 < (K+1)^2$$
$$\therefore \quad K^2 < 2019$$
$$\Rightarrow \quad K < \sqrt{2019}$$
$$\Rightarrow \quad K < 44.93$$
$$\therefore \quad K = 44$$
$$\Rightarrow \quad K = 4 \times 11$$
The largest prime factor of K is 11.

2. *(c)* We have,
$$a + 1 = b + 2 = c + 3 = d + 4 = e + 5$$
$$= a + b + c + d + e + 3$$
$$\therefore \quad b = a - 1, c = a - 2, d = a - 3, e = a - 4$$
$$\Rightarrow \quad a + b + c + d + e = a - 2$$
$$a = 2, b = 1, c = 0, d = -1, e = -2$$
$$\therefore a^2 + b^2 + c^2 + d^2 + e^2$$
$$= (2)^2 + (1)^2 + (0)^2 + (-1)^2 + (-2)^2$$
$$= 4 + 1 + 0 + 1 + 4 = 10$$

3. *(d)* Given, AB is diameter of semi-circle.

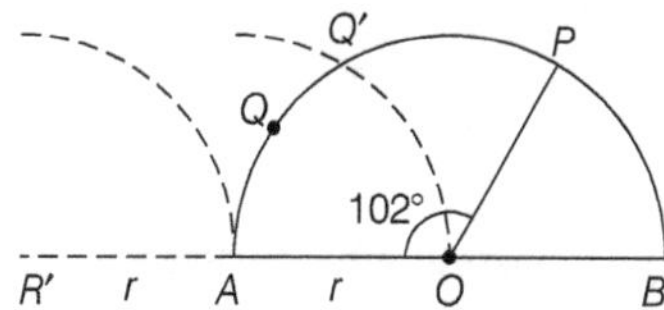

Since, R can be any point. Let A and R' and hence, its corresponding point Q lie on the arc AQ'.

Hence, $\angle PRA$ cannot be determined.

4. *(d)* We have,
$$x = \cos 1° \cos 2° \cos 3° \ldots \cos 89°$$
and $\quad y = \cos 2° \cos 6° \cos 10° \ldots \cos 86°$

Let $\quad x = \prod_{r=1}^{89} \cos r°$

$$\Rightarrow x = \sqrt{\prod_{r=1}^{89} \cos r° \cos (89 + 1 - r)°}$$

$$= \sqrt{\frac{1}{2^{89}} \prod_{r=1}^{89} \sin 2r°}$$

$$= \sqrt{\frac{1}{2^{89}} (\prod_{r=1}^{44} \sin 2r°)^2 \sin 90°}$$

$$= \frac{1}{2^{44}\sqrt{2}} \prod_{r=1}^{44} \sin 2r°$$

$$= \frac{1}{2^{44}\sqrt{2}} \sqrt{\prod_{r=1}^{44} \sin 2r° \sin 2(44+1-r)}$$

$$= \frac{1}{2^{66}\sqrt{2}} \sqrt{\prod_{r=1}^{44} \sin 4r}$$

$$= \frac{1}{2^{66}\sqrt{2}} \sqrt{(\prod_{r=1}^{22} \sin 4r)^2}$$

$$= \frac{1}{2^{66}\sqrt{2}} \prod_{r=1}^{22} \sin 4r$$

$$= \frac{1}{2^{66}\sqrt{2}} \prod_{r=1}^{22} \sin (92 - 4r)$$

$$= \frac{1}{2^{66}\sqrt{2}} \prod_{r=1}^{22} \cos (4r - 2)$$

$$\Rightarrow x = \frac{1}{2^{66}\sqrt{2}} y$$

$$\Rightarrow \frac{y}{x} = 2^{66 + \frac{1}{2}} = 2^{\frac{133}{2}}$$

$$\therefore \quad \frac{2}{7} \log_2 \frac{y}{x} = \frac{2}{7} \times \frac{133}{2} = 19$$

5. *(c)* We have,
$$4abc = (a + 3)(b + 3)(c + 3)$$
$a, b, c \geq 4$, a, b, c are integers.
$$\left(1 + \frac{3}{a}\right)\left(1 + \frac{3}{b}\right)\left(1 + \frac{3}{c}\right) = 4$$
$$\Rightarrow \quad 4 \leq a \leq b \leq c$$
$$\Rightarrow \quad \frac{1}{a} \geq \frac{1}{b} \geq \frac{1}{c}$$
$$\Rightarrow \quad 1 + \frac{3}{a} \geq 1 + \frac{3}{b} \geq 1 + \frac{3}{c}$$
$$\therefore \quad \left(1 + \frac{3}{a}\right)^3 \geq 4 \Rightarrow 1 + \frac{3}{a} \geq (4)^{1/3}$$
$$\Rightarrow \quad a \leq \frac{3}{4^{1/3} - 1} = \frac{4 - 1}{4^{1/3} - 1}$$
$$= 4^{2/3} + 4^{1/3} + 1$$
$$\Rightarrow \quad a \leq 3 + 2 + 1$$
$$\therefore \quad a < 6 \Rightarrow a = 4 \text{ or } 5$$
For $a = 5$, $\left(1 + \frac{3}{b}\right)\left(1 + \frac{3}{c}\right) = \frac{5}{2}$
$$\left(1 + \frac{3}{b}\right)^2 \geq \frac{5}{2}$$
$$\Rightarrow \quad b \leq \frac{3}{\left(\frac{5}{2}\right)^{1/2} - 1}$$
$$= 2\left(\sqrt{\frac{5}{2}} + 1\right) < 2(2 + 1) = 6$$
$$\Rightarrow \quad b < 6 \Rightarrow b \leq 5, b = 5 \ (b \geq a)$$
$$\Rightarrow \quad 1 + \frac{3}{c} = \frac{25}{16}$$
$$\Rightarrow \quad c = \frac{16}{3} \notin \text{integer}$$
$$\Rightarrow \quad a \neq 5$$
For $a = 4$, $\left(1 + \frac{3}{b}\right)\left(1 + \frac{3}{c}\right) = \frac{16}{7}$

$$\left(1 + \frac{3}{b}\right)^2 \geq \frac{16}{7}$$
$$\Rightarrow \quad b \leq \frac{3}{\frac{4}{\sqrt{7}} - 1} < 6$$
$$\Rightarrow b = 4 \text{ or } 5 \text{ for } b = 4, c = \frac{49}{5} \in I$$
For $b = 5, c = 7$
$$\Rightarrow \quad a + b + c = 4 + 5 + 7 = 16$$

6. *(b)* Given,
ABC is a right angled triangle
$$\angle A = 90°$$

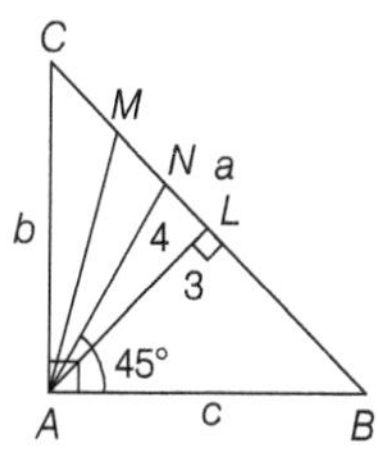

Altitude $AL = 3$
$AN = 4$ (AN is angle bisector of $\angle A$)
AM is median of $\triangle ABC$
$$\text{Area of } \triangle ABC = \frac{1}{2} bc = \frac{1}{2} AL \ a$$
$$\Rightarrow \quad bc = 3a$$
Area of $\triangle ABC$ = Area of $\triangle ABN$ + Area of $\triangle ANC$
$$\Rightarrow \quad \frac{1}{2} bc = \frac{1}{2} AB \cdot AN \sin 45°$$
$$+ \frac{1}{2} AC \cdot AN \sin 45°$$
$$\Rightarrow \quad \frac{1}{2} bc = \frac{1}{2} \times 4 \times \frac{1}{\sqrt{2}} (b + c)$$
$$\Rightarrow \quad bc = 2\sqrt{2} (b + c)$$
$$\Rightarrow \quad b^2 c^2 = 8(b^2 + c^2 + 2bc)$$
$$\Rightarrow \quad 9a^2 = 8(a^2 + 6a)$$
$$\Rightarrow \quad 9a^2 - 8a^2 = 48a$$
$$\Rightarrow \quad a = 48$$
$$\because \quad AM = MC = MB = \frac{BC}{2} = \frac{a}{2}$$
$$\because \quad AM = \frac{48}{2} = 24$$

7. *(c)* The number of tiles the bug visits is equal to 1 plus the number of times it crosses a horizontal or vertical line. As it must cross 16 horizontal lines and 9 vertical lines. It must be that bug visits a total of $16 + 9 + 1 = 26$ squares.

8. *(d)* Mean (μ) of 365 values of the takes 2019 are

$$12(1 + 2 + 3 + \ldots + 28)$$

$$\mu = \dfrac{+\ 11 \times 29 + 11 \times 30 + 7 \times 31}{365}$$

$$\mu = \dfrac{\dfrac{12 \times 28 \times 29}{2} + 319 + 330 + 217}{365} = 15.7$$

$$\text{Median} = \dfrac{366\text{th}}{2} \text{ observation}$$

$$= 183 \text{ th observation}$$

$$= 16$$

d (Median of modes)

Mode of data $= 1, 2, 3, \ldots, 28$

$$\text{Median of data} = \dfrac{\left(\dfrac{28}{2}\right)\text{th} + \left(\dfrac{28}{2} + 1\right)\text{th}}{2}$$

$$= \dfrac{14 + 15}{2} = 14.5$$

$\because \quad d < \mu < M$

9. *(c)* We have,

$$a_1 = 1, a_2 = \dfrac{3}{7}$$

$$a_n = \dfrac{a_{n-2} \cdot a_{n-1}}{2a_{n-2} - a_{n-1}}$$

$$a_3 = \dfrac{a_1 \cdot a_2}{2a_1 - a_2} = \dfrac{1 \cdot \dfrac{3}{7}}{2 - \dfrac{3}{7}} = \dfrac{3}{11}$$

$$a_4 = \dfrac{a_2 - a_3}{2a_2 - a_3}$$

$$= \dfrac{\dfrac{3}{7} - \dfrac{3}{11}}{2\left(\dfrac{3}{7}\right) - \dfrac{3}{11}} = \dfrac{3}{15}$$

$\because$ Sequence are $1, \dfrac{3}{7}, \dfrac{3}{11}, \dfrac{3}{15}, \dfrac{3}{19}, \ldots, \dfrac{3}{4n-1}$

$$\because \quad a_n = \dfrac{3}{4n - 1}$$

$$\Rightarrow a_{2019} = \dfrac{3}{4(2019) - 1} = \dfrac{3}{8075}$$

$\because \quad p = 3, q = 8075$

$\therefore \quad p + q = 8078$

10. *(d)* We have,

Total number of cubes $= 9$

2 Red cubes, 3 Blue cubes, 4 Green cubes

Number of ways making tower of height 8 cubes

$$^9C_2 \ ^7C_3 \ ^4C_4$$

$$\Rightarrow \dfrac{9!}{2! \ 7!} \times \dfrac{7!}{3! \ 4!} \times 1 = \dfrac{9!}{2! \times 3! \times 4!}$$

$$= \dfrac{9 \times 8 \times 7 \times 6 \times 5 \times 4!}{2 \times 3 \times 2 \times 4!} = 1260$$

11. *(b)* We have,

$$(x + 1)(x + 2)(x + 3)(x + 4) + 2019$$
$$= (x + 1)(x + 4)(x + 2)(x + 3) + 2019$$
$$= (x^2 + 5x + 4)(x^2 + 5x + 6) + 2019$$
$$= (x^2 + 5x)^2 + 10(x^2 + 5x) + 24 + 2019$$
$$= (x^2 + 5x)^2 + 10(x^2 + 5x) + 25$$
$$\qquad\qquad - 25 + 24 + 2019$$
$$= (x^2 + 5x + 5)^2 + 2018$$

$\therefore$ Minimum value of $x^2 + 5x + 5$ is 0

$\therefore$ Minimum value of $(x + 1)(x + 2)(x + 3)$ $(x + 4) + 2019$ is 2018.

12. *(c)* Given, $PA = 13 = PB$

$$QA = RB = 5$$

$\because$

$$PQ = PA - QA$$
$$= 13 - 5 = 8$$
$$PR = PB - RB = 8$$
$$QR = 2QA = 10$$
$$\Delta PQR \sim \Delta PAB$$

$\because$

$$\dfrac{PQ}{PA} = \dfrac{QR}{AB}$$

$$\Rightarrow \qquad AB = \dfrac{10 \times 13}{8} = \dfrac{65}{4}$$

$\because \qquad m = 65, n = 4$

Hence, $\quad m + n = 65 + 4 = 69$

13. *(b)* Distance travelled by X in 40 s.

$$\theta = \dfrac{2\pi}{40} \times 15 \qquad \ldots\text{(i)}$$

Distance travelled by Y in n second

$\because$

$$\theta = 2\pi - \left(\dfrac{2\pi}{n} \times 15\right) \qquad \ldots\text{(ii)}$$

From Eqs. (i) and (ii), we get

$$\dfrac{2\pi}{40} \times 15 = 2\pi - \left(\dfrac{2\pi}{n} \times 15\right)$$

$\therefore \qquad n = 24$

14. *(a)* We have, 6-digit numbers

$abccba$, b is odd.

If $abc - cba$ is divisible by 7

$\Rightarrow abc - cba = 99(a - c) = 7M$

So, $(a, = \{(9, 2) (8, 1) (7, 0) (2, 9) (1, 8)$
$(9, 9) (8, 8) (7, 7) (6, 6) (5, 5) (4, 4) (3, 3)$
$(2, 2) (1, 1)\}$

Number of pairs of $(a, b) = 14$

Also b can be 5

$\because$ Total number of 6-digit number
$$= 14 \times 5 = 70$$

15. *(b)* Given, $\quad PC = 36$

$$BQ = 49$$

$\therefore$

$$BT = BQ - TQ$$
$$= 49 - 36 \quad [\because TQ = PC]$$
$$BT = 13$$

In ΔBTC, $BC^2 = TC^2 + BT^2$

$$\Rightarrow \qquad (85)^2 = PQ^2 + (13)^2 \quad [\because TC = PQ]$$
$$\Rightarrow \qquad PQ^2 = (85)^2 - (13)^2$$
$$\Rightarrow \qquad PQ^2 = (85 + 13)(85 - 13)$$
$$\Rightarrow \qquad PQ^2 = 98 \times 72$$
$$\Rightarrow \qquad PQ = \sqrt{49 \times 2 \times 36 \times 2}$$
$$\Rightarrow \qquad PQ = 7 \times 6 \times 2 = 84$$

16. *(b)* $F = \dfrac{\Delta p}{\Delta t} = \dfrac{10 \times 15}{3} = 50 \, \text{N}$

As velocity is constant after $t = 3$ s, hence force stops.

17. *(d)* At low temperature, H_2 molecule has only translational degrees of freedom

$\therefore \qquad f = 3$

Above 600 K molecule be given to vibrate and at above 3000 K molecule dissociates.

18. *(d)* Nuclear density is a constant ($\rho = 2.38 \times 10^{17}$ kg m^{-3}). It is independent of nuclear size and number of nucleons. So, ratio is 1:1.

19. *(c)* $x_0 = \dfrac{1}{2} at_0^2$

and $\quad x = x_0 + at_0(t - t_0) - \dfrac{1}{2}a(t - t_0)^2$

So, correct graph is (c).

20. *(c)* $\therefore \qquad F = kt$

$$\Rightarrow \qquad m\int_0^v dv = k\int_0^t t \, dt$$
$$\Rightarrow \qquad mv = kt^2$$
$$\Rightarrow \qquad v = \dfrac{k}{m}t^2$$

Kinetic energy is

$$K = \dfrac{1}{2}mv^2 \Rightarrow K \propto t^4$$

21. (d) $\dfrac{\text{Mass}}{\text{Volume}} = \text{Density}$

As mass remains same,

$$V_{\text{ice}} \times \rho_{\text{ice}} = V_{\text{water}} \times \rho_{\text{water}}$$

$\Rightarrow \qquad V_{\text{water}} = \dfrac{m}{y}$

$\Rightarrow \qquad \Delta V = V_{\text{water}} - V_{\text{ice}}$

$$= \dfrac{m}{y} - \dfrac{m}{x} = m\left(\dfrac{1}{y} - \dfrac{1}{x}\right)$$

22. (a) $W = q\Delta V = e\,[(V_-) - (V_+)]$

$$= -e\,(0 - 12) = +12\,\text{eV}$$

An electron will move from negative to positive terminal by itself. So, positive work is required to carry electron in reverse direction.

23. (b) $p_{\text{absolute}} = p_{\text{atmospheric}} + p_{\text{gauge}}$

Also, $p_{\text{gauge}} > p_{\text{atmospheric}}$.

24. (a) Let $AE = x$, then $EC = 100 - x$.

So, $ED = \sqrt{(100 - x)^2 + (120)^2}$

$\therefore$ Time taken $= \dfrac{x}{5} + \dfrac{\sqrt{(100 - x)^2 + 120^2}}{3}$

This is minimum when $t = 10$ m.

25. (b) $\qquad R_{AB} = \dfrac{15 \times R_1}{15 + R_1}$

$\Rightarrow \qquad 6 = \dfrac{15R_1}{15 + R_1}$

$\Rightarrow \qquad \dfrac{6 \times 15}{9} = R_1 \Rightarrow R_1 = 10\,\Omega$

26. (d) Fermi energy level is last filled energy level at zero kelvin.

27. (d) As sun changes its position rapidly, so reflector of solar cooker is to be adjusted nearly in every $\dfrac{1}{2}$ hour duration.

28. (c)

Rotational equilibrium about O gives,

$$F \times l = mg\,\dfrac{l}{2}$$

$\Rightarrow \qquad F = \dfrac{mg}{2} = 50\,\text{N}$

29. (a) Force is zero when potential energy is minimum.

30. (a) From first ray diagram,

$$\mu = \mu_1$$

From second ray diagram,

$$\mu < \mu_2 \Rightarrow \mu_1 < \mu_2$$

31. (b) $Mg_3(PO_4)_2 \longrightarrow 3Mg + 2P + 8O$

As 8 moles of O-atoms are present in 1 mole of $Mg_3(PO_4)_2$.

$\therefore$ 0.25 moles are present in $Mg_3(PO_4)_2$

$$= \dfrac{1}{8} \times 0.25 = 3.125 \times 10^{-2}\,\text{mol}\,.$$

32. (c) From kinetic gas, $v_{\text{rms}} = \sqrt{\dfrac{3RT}{M}}$

v_{rms} of $SO_2 = \sqrt{\dfrac{3RT_{SO_2}}{M_{SO_2}}} = \sqrt{\dfrac{3RT_{SO_2}}{64}}$

v_{rms} of $O_2 = \sqrt{\dfrac{3RT_{O_2}}{M_{O_2}}} = \sqrt{\dfrac{3RT \times 303}{32}}$

According to question, $v_{\text{rms}\,(SO_2)} = v_{\text{rms}\,(O_2)}$

$$\sqrt{\dfrac{3RT_{SO_2}}{64}} = \sqrt{\dfrac{3RT \times 303}{32}}$$

$$T_{SO_2} = \dfrac{303 \times 64}{32}$$

$$T_{SO_2} = 606\,\text{K}$$

33. (c) The formation of black precipitate indicates the presence of sulphur in an organic compound. The sodium extract of organic compound contains Na_2S which forms a black precipitate of PbS when treated with lead acetate.

$$\underset{\substack{\text{Sodium} \\ \text{extract}}}{Na_2S} + \underset{\substack{\text{Lead} \\ \text{acetate}}}{(CH_3COO)_2Pb} \longrightarrow \underset{\substack{\text{Lead sulphide} \\ \text{(black ppt.)}}}{PbS\downarrow}$$

$$+ 2\,CH_3COONa$$

34. (d) When carbonyl compounds are treated with excess of alcohol, first hemiacetals are formed and then acetals are formed, i.e.

$$\underset{\text{Acetone}}{CH_3\!-\!\underset{\underset{O}{\|}}{C}\!-\!CH_3} + \underset{\text{Ethanol}}{C_2H_5OH}$$

$$\downarrow$$

$$\underset{\text{Hemiketal}}{(CH_3)_2C\!\!\begin{array}{l}\diagup OH \\ \diagdown OC_2H_5\end{array}}$$

$$\downarrow C_2H_5OH(\text{Excess})$$

$$\underset{\text{Acetal}}{(CH_3)_2C\!\!\begin{array}{l}\diagup OC_2H_5 \\ \diagdown OC_2H_5\end{array}}$$

35. (c) On moving across a period from left to right in periodic table electronegativity increases. This is because across the period the size of an atom decreases. While on moving down the group, electronegativity decreases. Thus, the correct order of electronegativity is

$$\underset{(1.8)\ \ (2.1)\ \ (2.5)\ \ (3.0)}{Si < P < C < N}$$

36. (d) According to de-Broglie relation,

$$\lambda = \dfrac{h}{mv}$$

$$= \dfrac{6.63 \times 10^{-34}}{10^{-6} \times 10} = 6.63 \times 10^{-29}\,\text{m}$$

37. (d) The product formed when 1-bromo-3-chlorocyclobutane reacts with two equivalents of metallic sodium in ether is bicyclo [1.1.0]. This reaction is known as Wurtz reaction.

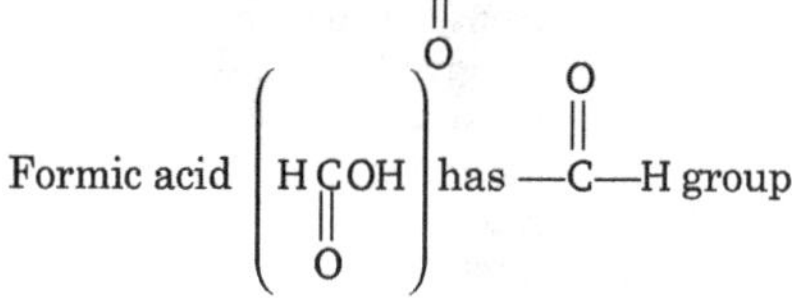

38. (d) Given $E°$ values are

$$Br_2\,/\,Br = +1.90\,\text{V}$$
$$Ag\,/\,Ag^+ = -0.80\,\text{V}$$
$$Cu^{2+}\,/Cu(s) = +0.34\,\text{V}$$
$$I^-\,/I_2(s) = -0.54$$

If the $E°_{\text{cell}}$ values of the redox reaction is positive, then only copper can reduce that element. (the reaction will be feasible)

For the reaction,

$$Cu \longrightarrow Cu^{2+} + 2e^- \quad E° = -0.34\text{V}$$
$$\underline{Br_2 + 2e^- \longrightarrow 2Br^-\,;\ E° = +1.09\,\text{V}}$$
$$Cu + Br_2 \longrightarrow CuBr_2\,;\ E° = +0.75\,\text{V}$$

Since, $E°_{\text{cell}}$ of this reaction is positive, therefore Cu can reduce Br_2. While in other reaction $E°_{\text{value}}$ will be negative and hence Cu cannot reduce other elements.

39. (c) Tollen's reagent is ammoniacal silver nitrate. It is reduced to silver by compounds having $-\!\underset{\underset{O}{\|}}{C}\!-\!H$ group.

Formic acid $\left(H\underset{\underset{O}{\|}}{C}OH\right)$ has $-\!\underset{\underset{O}{\|}}{C}\!-\!H$ group.

Thus, it reduces Tollen's reagent.

$$[2Ag(NH_3)_2]^+ + HCOOH \longrightarrow \underset{\text{Silver}}{2Ag\downarrow} + CO_2$$
$$+ 2NH_4^+$$

40. (d) Greater is the s-character, shorter is the bond length. The C-atom in CO_3^{2-} is sp^2-hybridised as shown.

$$O\!=\!C\!\!\begin{array}{l}\diagup O^- \\ \diagdown O^-\end{array} \longleftrightarrow O^-\!-\!C\!\!\begin{array}{l}\diagup O \\ \diagdown O^-\end{array}$$

$$O\!-\!C\!\!\begin{array}{l}\diagup O^- \\ \diagdown O\end{array}$$

The C-atom in CO_2 is sp-hybridised with bond distance of carbon oxygen is 122 pm.

$$O\!=\!C\!=\!O \longleftrightarrow O^+\!\equiv\!C\!-\!O^-$$
$$\longleftrightarrow O^-\!-\!C\!\equiv\!O^+$$

The C-atom in sp-hybridised with C—O bond distance 110 pm.

$$C\!\equiv\!O$$

Thus, the correct order of bond length is

$$CO < CO_2 < CO_3^{2-}$$

41. *(a)* $H_2(g) + Cl_2(g) \longrightarrow 2HCl(g)$

22.4 L at STP is occupied by 1 mole of Cl_2

$\therefore$ 11.2 L will be occupied by Cl_2

$$= \frac{1 \times 11.2}{22.4} = 0.5 \text{ mol}$$

As per equation,

1 mole of Cl_2 produces 2 mole of HCl

$\therefore$ 0.5 mole of Cl_2 produces $= 2 \times 0.5 = 1.0$ mole of HCl.

42. *(b)* From ideal gas equation,

$$pV = nRT$$

Also, $\qquad n = \dfrac{w}{M}$

$\therefore \qquad pV = \dfrac{w}{M} RT$

$$w = \frac{pVM}{RT}$$

Substituting the values, we get

$$\frac{12.315 \times 1 \times 32}{0.0821 \times 300} = 16 \text{ g}$$

$\therefore O_2$ to be released $= 32 - 16 = 16$ g

43. *(d)* Orbital angular momentum

$$= \frac{h}{2\pi} \sqrt{l(l+1)}$$

For f-orbital, $l = 3$

$\therefore$ Orbital angular momentum for f-orbital

$$= \frac{h}{2\pi} \sqrt{3(3+1)} = \frac{\sqrt{3}h}{\pi}$$

44. *(b)* Anhydrous HF is a covalent compound and is strongly H-bonded. Therefore, it does not give F^- ions and hence AlF_3 does not dissolve in HF. NaF is an ionic compound. It contains F^- ions which combine with electron deficient AlF_3 to form the soluble complex.

$$3NaF + AlF_3 \longrightarrow Na_3[AlF_6]$$

Boron due to its small size and higher electronegativity has greater tendency to form complexes than Al. Hence, precipitation of AlF_3 takes place when BF_3 is passed through $Na_3[AlF_6]$ solution.

$$Na_3[AlF_6] + 3BF_3 \longrightarrow \underset{(X)}{3Na[BF_4]}\downarrow + AlF_3 (s)$$

45. *(d)* The compound which follows Huckel's rule $[(4n + 2)\pi]$ will be aromatic in nature.

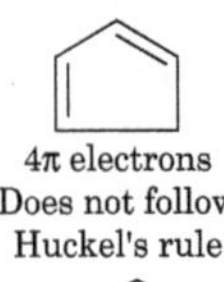
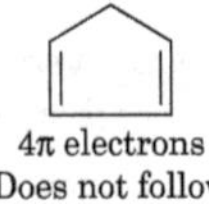

4π electrons   4π electrons
Does not follow   Does not follow
Huckel's rule   Huckel's rule

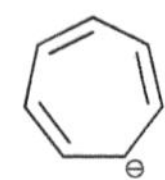

8π electrons   6π electrons
Does not follow   Follow
Huckel's rule   Huckel's rule

As compound given in option (d) follows Huckel's rule. Thus, it is aromatic in nature.

46. *(b)* The mucosa present in between the bases of villi of small intestine (crypts of Lieberkuhn) contain Paneth cells, which secrete antibacterial lysozyme. Kupffer cells are phagocyte cells of liver. Zymogen cells produce enzyme. Argentaffin cells produce hormones.

47. *(c)* Mycoplasma is triple layered smallest living cells. It does not have definite cell wall. It is an anaerobic organism. It causes disease in plants (little leaf of brinjal) as well as in animals (pleuromorphic pneumonia in man).

48. *(d)* Mitochondria is referred as powerhouse of the cell. It contains the enzymes for cellular respiration. It oxidises carbohydrate to produce ATP molecules in the process of aerobic respiration.

49. *(b)* DNA fragments are negatively charged molecules. The reason why DNA is negatively charged is the phosphate (PO_4^{2-}) group that constitutes every nucleotide.

During the formation of phosphodiester bond, nucleotides retain one of the two negative charge, while the other is lost to form ester bond to new pentose.

50. *(c)* The important characteristic that hemichordates share with chordates is pharynx with gill slits. These slits are narrow openings in the pharynx. The position of these pharyngeal gill slits is lateral in chordates, while dorsal in hemichordates.

51. *(a)* In lungs, even after the most forceful expiration, some of the volume of air remains. This volume is termed Residual Volume (RV). Due to this, lungs do not collapse even after the most forceful expiration. RV is about 1100-1200 mL.

52. *(d)* Viroids differ from viruses in having RNA molecules without protein coat. Viruses on the other hand possess DNA or RNA with a protein coat as their genetic material. Viruses can infect a wide range of organisms including plants, animals or bacteria, while viroids infect only plants.

53. *(b)* Plants that produce pneumatophores i.e. negatively geotropic roots and show vivipary i.e. germination of seeds inside the fruits are halophytes. These plants are adapted to grow in highly saline areas such as mangroves. Pneumatophores help these plants in respiration as they do not get sufficient oxygen from the soil. On the other hand vivipary aids in perennation.

54. *(d)* Spliceosome is a large molecular complex found in nucleus of eukaryotic cells of plants, animals and fungi, etc. It is assembled from *sn*RNAs and protein complexes that play an important role in splicing of introns. Spliceosome is absent in the cells of bacteria.

55. *(c)* Auxin delays abscission of leaves and fruits at early stages. Whenever leaf or fruit fall occurs, the organ concerned stops producing auxin. However, it promotes abscission of older, mature leaves and fruits.

56. *(d)* Pancreas consists of exocrine and endocrine parts. Exocrine part secretes alkaline pancreatic juice. This juice contains trypsinogen, chymotrypsinogen, procarboxypeptidase, lipase, amylase and elastase.

57. *(c)* As the diploid number is 8, there would be 4 pairs of homologous chromosome pairing. This gives rise to a combination of $4^2 = 16$ kinds of gametes.

58. *(a)* According to Chargaff's rule, $A + T = G + C$ and $A = T$ and $G = C$.

$\therefore \qquad$ Guanine + Cytosine

$\qquad\qquad$ 40% $\qquad\quad$ 40%

$\qquad\qquad$ Adenine + Thymine

$\qquad\qquad$ 10% $\qquad\quad$ 10%

59. *(b)* $\underset{\text{Nitrogen}}{N_2} \rightarrow \underset{\text{Dimide}}{N_2H_2} \rightarrow \underset{\text{Hydrazine}}{N_2H_4} \rightarrow \underset{\text{Ammonia}}{2NH_3}$

The fixation of atmospheric nitrogen to ammonia is given as

$$N_2 + 8e^- + 8H^+ + 16ATP \xrightarrow[\text{Nitrogenase}]{\text{Mo Fe}}$$

$$2NH_3 + H_2 + 16ADP + 16Pi$$

The process in which atmospheric nitrogen gets converted into inorganic nitrogenous (nitrate, ammonia) compounds through microorganisms is called biological nitrogen-fixation.

60. *(a)* *Treponema pallidum* pathogen is a cause of syphilis. It is a sexually transmitted infection that causes infected sores, blisters or ulcers on your genitals, anus (bottom) or mouth.

61. *(b)* Given, $a + b - c = 1$ $\qquad$ ...(i)

and $\quad a^2 + b^2 - c^2 + 1 = 0$ $\qquad$ ...(ii)

From Eqs. (i) and (ii), we get

$$a^2 + b^2 - (a + b - 1)^2 + 1 = 0$$

$\Rightarrow a^2 + b^2 - a^2 - b^2 - 1 - 2ab + 2a$
$$+ 2b + 1 = 0$$
$\Rightarrow \qquad (a + b) - ab = 0$
$\Rightarrow \qquad (a - 1)(b - 1) = 1$
$\Rightarrow \qquad a - 1 = 1 \text{ and } b - 1 = 1$
$\Rightarrow \qquad a = b = 2 \Rightarrow c = 3$
$\Rightarrow \qquad a - 1 = -1 \text{ and } b - 1 = -1$
$\Rightarrow \qquad a = b = 0 \text{ and } c = -1$
$\therefore a^2 + b^2 + c^2 = (2)^2 + (2)^2 + (3)^2$
$$= 4 + 4 + 9 = 17$$
$$a^2 + b^2 + c^2 = (0)^2 + (0)^2 + (-1) = 1$$
$\therefore$ Sum of all possible value is 18.

62. *(d)* Let the number of cups with handle be m and number of cups without handle be n.

$\therefore \qquad {}^mC_2 \, {}^nC_3 = 1200$

Let ${}^nC_3$ is divisible by 1200.

$\therefore n \le 20$ when $n = 21$, then ${}^{21}C_3 > 1200$

$\therefore {}^nC_3 = \dfrac{n(n-1)(n-2)}{3}$ is divisible by 1200

$\Rightarrow n \ne p, p+1, p+2$, where p prime ≥ 7

$\Rightarrow n \ne 7, 8, 9, 10, 11, 12, 13, 14, 15, 17, 18, 19, 20$

$\therefore$ Possible value of $n = 3, 4, 5, 6$

When $n = 4$, then $m = 25 \Rightarrow m + n = 29$

and $n = 10$, then $m = 5 \Rightarrow m + n = 15$

and $n = 5$, then $m = 16 \Rightarrow m + n = 21$

$\therefore \quad$ Maximum value of $(m + n) = 29$

63. *(a)* Let $\angle CI_2F = \theta$

$\qquad \angle BAE = x = \angle EAD$

and $\quad \angle DAF = y = \angle FAC$

$\qquad \angle A = 2x + 2y$

$\Rightarrow \qquad x + y = \dfrac{\angle A}{2}$

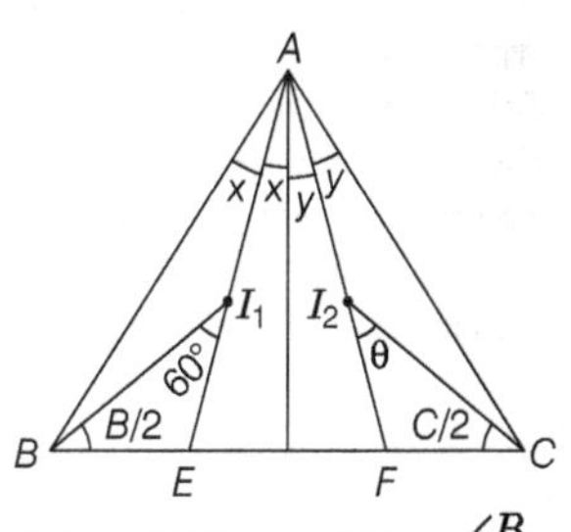

$\angle AEF = \angle EBI_1 + \angle BI_1E = \dfrac{\angle B}{2} + 60°$

and $\angle AFE = \dfrac{\angle C}{2} + \theta$

In $\triangle AEF$,

$\dfrac{\angle B}{2} + 60° + \theta + \dfrac{\angle C}{2} + \dfrac{\angle A}{2} = 180°$

$\Rightarrow \quad \theta = 180° - 60° - 90° \Rightarrow \theta = 30$

$\therefore \quad \angle CI_2F = 30°$

64. *(d)* We have,

$P(x) = a_0 + a_1x + a_2x^2 + \ldots + a_nx^n$

$P(5) = a_0 + 5a_1 + 25a_2 + 125a_3 +$
$$\ldots + (5)^n \, a_n$$

$\Rightarrow 136 = a_0 + 5a_1 + 25a_2 + 125a_3 +$
$$\ldots + (5)^n \, a_n$$

$a_i \ge 1$ for $i \ge 4$, then RHS > 136

$\therefore a_4 = a_5 = a_6 \ldots = a_n = 0$

$\therefore \quad a_0 + 5a_1 + 25a_2 + 125a_3 = 136 \qquad \ldots\text{(i)}$

$\therefore a_3$ can be 0 or 1 only

Now, $P(1) = a_0 + a_1 + a_2 + a_3 = 4 \qquad \ldots\text{(ii)}$

If $a_3 = 0$, then

$a_0 + 5a_1 + 25a_2 \le 4 + 20 + 100$
$$= 124 < 136$$

If $\qquad\qquad a_3 = 1$

$\Rightarrow \quad a_0 + 5a_1 + 25a_2 = 11 \qquad$ [from Eq. (i)]

$\Rightarrow \qquad\qquad a_2 = 0$

$\Rightarrow \qquad\qquad a_0 + 5a_1 = 11$

Also from Eq. (ii), $a_0 + a_1 = 3$

$\Rightarrow \qquad\qquad a_1 = 2, a_0 = 1$

Hence, $\qquad P(x) = 1 + 2x + x^3$

$\therefore \qquad\qquad P(3) = 1 + 6 + 27 = 34$

65. *(b)* Given, in quadrilateral $ABCD$

$\qquad AB = AD = 13$

$\qquad BC = CD = 20$

$\qquad BD = 24$

Area of $\triangle ABD$
$$= \sqrt{25(25 - 13)(25 - 13)(25 - 24)}$$
$$= \sqrt{25 \times 12 \times 12 \times 1}$$
$$= 60$$

Area of $\triangle BCD$
$$= \sqrt{32(32 - 20)(32 - 20)(32 - 24)}$$
$$= \sqrt{32 \times 12 \times 12 \times 8}$$
$$= 192$$

$\therefore$ Area of quadrilateral $ABCD$
$$= \text{Area of } \triangle ABD + \text{Area of } \triangle BCD$$
$$= 60 + 192$$
$$= 252$$

Radius of incircle
$$= \frac{\text{Area of quadrilateral}}{\text{Semiperimeter of quadrilateral}}$$
$$= \frac{252}{33} = 7.63$$

$\therefore$ Nearest integer of r is 8.

66. *(b)*

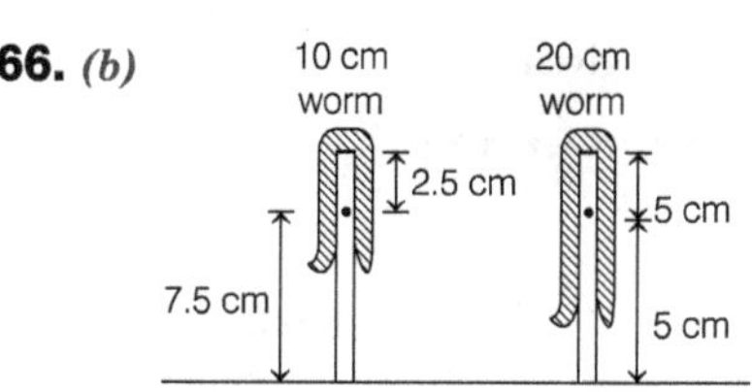

For 10 cm worm centre of mass is raised upto height of 7.5 cm, while for 20 cm worm height of centre of mass is 5 cm from ground.

So, ratio of work done by 20 cm worm to that of 10 cm worm is
$$\frac{W_1}{W_2} = \frac{mgh_1}{mgh_2} = \frac{5}{7.5} = \frac{50}{75} = 2 : 3$$

67. *(b)* Let d = diameter of disc. Spot is invisible, if incident rays from dot reaching top surface at $\dfrac{d}{2}$ are at the critical angle.

Then by $\sin i_c = \dfrac{1}{\mu}$

and $\dfrac{d/2}{h} = \tan i$

$\Rightarrow \qquad d = \dfrac{2h}{\sqrt{\mu^2 - 1}} = \dfrac{2 \times 20}{\sqrt{\dfrac{16}{9} - 1}} \approx 46 \, \text{cm}$

So, minimum radius of disc = 23 cm.

68. *(c)* In case A, voltage across bulb is higher, so lamb will burn brighter.

In case B, voltage is same as either of battery but each battery supplies only half of current, hence the batteries will lasts twice as long.

69. *(d)* From v-t graph,

For $0 < t < 3\,\text{s}$,
$$a = \frac{8 \, \text{ms}^{-1}}{3 \, \text{s}} = 2.67 \, \text{ms}^{-2}$$

For $3\text{s} < t < 5\text{s}$, $a = 0$

For $5\text{s} < t < 9\text{s}$,
$$a = \frac{-16 \, \text{ms}^{-1}}{4 \, \text{s}} = -4 \, \text{ms}^{-2}$$

70. *(a)* Forces on the ball are

(i) weight of ball = mg

(ii) weight of fluid column above ball
$$= \pi r^2 \rho g h$$

(iii) Buoyant force $= \left(\dfrac{2}{3} \pi r^3\right) \rho g$

when $mg = \dfrac{2}{3} \pi r^3 \rho g - \pi r^2 \rho g h$, ball will tend to rise corresponding height h_0 of water in vessel is given by
$$mg = \frac{2}{3} \pi r^2 \rho g - \pi r^2 \rho g h_0$$

Substituting given values, we get

$$\pi \times 10^{-3} \times 10 = \frac{2}{3} \times \pi \times \left(\frac{0.1}{100}\right)^2 \times 1000 \times 10$$

$$- \pi \left(\frac{1}{100}\right)^2 \times 1000 \times 10 \times h_0$$

$$\Rightarrow \quad \frac{1}{100} = \frac{2}{3} - h_0$$

$$\Rightarrow \quad h_0 = (0.66 - 0.01)\,\text{m} = 65\,\text{cm}$$

71. *(b)* Compound X is $CaCO_3$

$$CaCO_3 \underset{X}{\xrightarrow{\Delta}} \underset{\text{Residue}}{CaO} + CO_2 \uparrow$$

$$\underset{\text{Residue}}{CaO} + H_2O \longrightarrow \underset{Y}{Ca(OH)_2}$$

$$\underset{Y}{Ca(OH)_2} + \underset{\text{Excess}}{CO_2} + H_2O \longrightarrow Ca(HCO_3)_2$$

$$Ca(HCO_3)_2 \xrightarrow{\Delta} \underset{X}{CaCO_3} + H_2O + CO_2 \uparrow$$

72. *(a)* For the reaction,

$$\frac{1}{2}X_2 + \frac{3}{2}Y_2 \rightleftharpoons XY_3 \quad (\Delta H = -30\,\text{kJ})$$

$$\Delta S^\circ = \Delta S^\circ_{(XY_3)} - \left[\frac{1}{2}S^\circ_{X_2} + \frac{3}{2}S^\circ_{Y_2}\right]$$

$$= 50 - \left[\frac{1}{2} \times 60 + \frac{3}{2} \times 40\right]$$

$$= 50 - [30 + 60]$$

$$= 50 - 90 = -40\,\text{JK}^{-1}\,\text{mol}^{-1}$$

Also, $\Delta G^\circ = \Delta H^\circ - T\Delta S^\circ$

At equilibrium, $\Delta G^\circ = 0$

$$\Delta H = T\Delta S$$

$$T = \frac{\Delta H^\circ}{\Delta S^\circ}$$

$$= \frac{-30 \times 10^3\,\text{J mol}^{-1}}{-40 \times \text{JK}^{-1}\,\text{mol}^{-1}} = 750\,\text{K}$$

73. *(d)* (A) $(C_4H_6) \xrightarrow[\text{1 mole}]{H_2/Ni} (C_4H_8)$

$$\xrightarrow{O_3/H_2O/Zn} CH_3CHO$$

By considering the molecular formula C_4H_6. We can conclude that, it is an alkene, $CH_2 = CH—CH = CH_2$ which on reduction with H_2 gives $CH_3 CH = CH—CH_3$. Also ozonolysis of $CH_3 CH = CHCH_3$ will only give 2 moles of acetaldehyde.

Thus, the correct option is (d).

$$CH_2 = CH—CH = CH_2 \xrightarrow[\text{1, 4-addition}]{H_2/Ni}$$
$$\underset{(A)}{}$$
$$\underset{(B)}{CH_3 CH = CH— CH_3}$$

$$\downarrow O_3/H_2O/Zn$$

$$2CH_3CHO$$

74. *(a)* In Kjeldahl's method, percentage of N is given by

$$= \frac{1.4 \times \text{normality of acid} \times \text{volume of acid}}{\text{weight of compound}}$$

Also, $1\,M\,H_2SO_4 = 2\,N\,H_2SO_4$

$$[M = N \times \text{Basicity/Acidity}]$$

$$\therefore \%\text{ of N} = \frac{1.4 \times 2 \times 10}{0.75} = 37.33\,\%$$

75. *(c)*

Element	% of element	Atomic weight	No. of moles	Simple ratio
C	12.8	12	12.8/12 = 1.06	1.06/1.06 = 1
H	2.10	1	2.10/1 = 2.10	2.10/1.06 = 2
Br	85.1	80	85.1/80 = 1.06	1.06/1.06 = 1

Hence, the empirical formula becomes CH_2Br

Empirical weight of CH_2Br

$$= 12 + 2 + 80 = 94$$

As we know that,

$$n = \frac{\text{molecular wt.}}{\text{empirical wt.}}$$

$$= \frac{187.9}{94} = 2$$

Thus molecular formula

$$= n \times \text{empirical formula}$$

$$= 2 \times (CH_2Br)$$

$$= C_2H_4Br_2$$

76. *(c)* The total amount of energy used in forming 38 ATP is

$$38 \times 30.6\,\text{kJ} = 1162.8\,\text{kJ}$$

Thus efficiency of aerobic respiration is

$$\frac{1162.8}{2800} \times 100\% = 40\%$$

77. *(a)* Since there is both a haemophilic and normal son, the mother must have a heterozygous genotype.

Since there is a haemophilic daughter, the X-chromosome from the father must have the recessive allele.

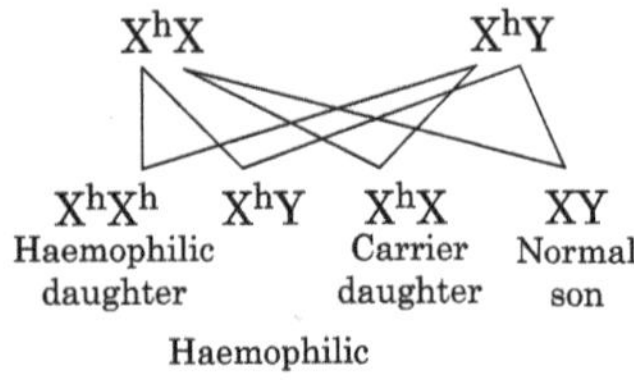

78. *(c)* Endocrine cells are present in different parts of the gastro-intestinal tract, e.g., gastrin, secretin, GIP. Atrial wall of our heart secretes a peptide hormone called ANF (Atrial Natriuretic Factor). Releasing and inhibitory hormones are released by hypothalamus. Adenohypophysis is not under direct control of hypothalamus.

79. *(c)* The amount of DNA in the 2 somatic cells, the motor neuron and the skin cell should be the same.

After interphase where DNA has already replicated, the amount of DNA is doubled, i.e. $6.8 \times 2\,\text{pg} = 13.6\,\text{pg}$.

80. *(b)* The reaction that is enzyme-catalysed has lower activation energy and is represented by the dotted line. The energy input required to raise the energy of the reactants to a certain level before the reaction is triggered is called the activation energy. This is represented by the increase in energy of the reactants to the top of the 'hill', B.

PRACTICE SET 5
Stream : SA

MM : 100

Instructions

1. There are 80 questions in this paper.
2. This question paper contains two parts; Part I and Part II. There are four sections; Mathematics, Physics, Chemistry and Biology in each part.
3. Out of the four options given with each question, only one is correct.

➔ PART–I (1 Mark Questions)

MATHEMATICS

1. How many positive integers less than 1000 are 6 times the sum of their digits?

(a) 0   (b) 1   (c) 2   (d) 3

2. Divya inscribed a circle inside a regular pentagon, circumscribed a circle around the pentagon, and calculated the area of region between the two circles. Mansi did the same with a regular heptagon. The areas of two regions A and B respectively. Each polygon had a side length of 2. Which of the following is true?

(a) $7A = 5B$ (b) $5A = 7B$
(c) $A = B$ (d) $25A = 49B$

3. A box contains a collection of triangular and square tiles. There are 25 tiles in the box containing 84 edge total. The number of square tiles in the box are

(a) 5   (b) 7   (c) 9   (d) 11

4. Define a function on the positive integers recursively by $f(1) = 2$, $f(n) = f(n-1) + 2$ if n is even, and $f(n) = f(n-2) + 2$ if n is odd and greater than one. Then, $f(2019)$ is equal to

(a) 2019   (b) 2020   (c) 2021   (d) 2018

5. The parabola $y = ax^2 - 2$ and $y = 4 - bx^2$ intersect the coordinate axes in exactly four points and these four points are the vertices of area 12, then $a + b$ is equal to

(a) 1/2   (b) 1   (c) 3/2   (d) 2

6. Let AB be a chord of circle with centre O. Let C be a point on the circle such that $\angle ABC = 30°$ and O lies inside the $\triangle ABC$. Let D be a point on AB such that $\angle DCO = \angle OCB = 20°$, then the measure of $\angle CDO$ in degree is

(a) 110°   (b) 70°   (c) 80°   (d) 20°

7. Let a and b be natural numbers such that $2a - b$, $a - 2b$ and $a + b$ are all distinct squares, the least possible value of b is

(a) 21   (b) 22   (c) 24   (d) 25

8. The wealth of a person A equals the sum of that of B and C. If he distributes half of his wealth between B and C in the ratio 2 : 1, then the wealth of B equals the sum of that A and C. Then, the fraction of wealth that A should distribute between B and C in the ratio 1 : 2, so that the wealth of C equals the sum of that of A and B is

(a) $\dfrac{1}{2}$ (b) $\dfrac{2}{3}$ (c) $\dfrac{3}{4}$ (d) 1

9. For some positive integer K, the repeating base-K representation of the (base-ten) fraction $\dfrac{7}{51}$ is $0.\overline{23}_K = 0.232323\ldots K$, then the value of K is

(a) 13　　(b) 14　　(c) 15　　(d) 16

10. The number 1, 2, 3, ..., 9 are randomly placed into the 9 square of a 3×3 grid. Each square gets one number and each of the numbers is used once. What is the probability that the sum of the numbers in each row and each column is odd?

(a) $\dfrac{1}{21}$　　(b) $\dfrac{1}{14}$　　(c) $\dfrac{5}{63}$　　(d) $\dfrac{2}{21}$

11. A quadrilateral is inscribed in a circle of radius $200\sqrt{2}$. Three sides of this quadrilateral have length 200, then length of the fourth side is

(a) 200　　(b) $200\sqrt{2}$　　(c) 400　　(d) 500

12. Let T be the smallest positive integer which, when divided by 11, 13, 15 leaves remainder in the sets $\{7, 8, 9\}, \{1, 2, 3\}, \{4, 5, 6\}$ respectively. The sum of squares of the digit of T is

(a) 50　　(b) 81　　(c) 89　　(d) 90

13. If roots of equation $x^2 - bx + c = 0$ be two consecutive integers, then $b^2 - 4c$ equals

(a) -2　　(b) 3　　(c) 2　　(d) 1

14. How many different words can be formed by jumbling the letters in the word MISSISSIPPI in which no two 'S' are together

(a) $8 \cdot {}^6C_4 \cdot {}^7C_4$　　(b) $6 \cdot {}^7{}^8C_4$
(c) $7 \cdot {}^6C_4 \cdot {}^8C_4$　　(d) $6 \cdot 8 \cdot {}^7C_4$

15. A man standing on a railway platform noticed that a train took 21 s to cross the platform which is 88 m long and that it took 9 s to pass him. Assuming that the train was moving with uniform speed. What is the length of the train in meters?

(a) 55　　(b) 60　　(c) 66　　(d) 72

PHYSICS

16. p-T curve representing phase equilibrium is given by;

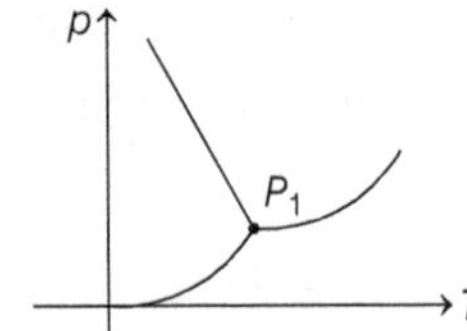

The point P_1 is
(a) boiling point of liquid
(b) condensation point of vapour
(c) melting point of solid
(d) triple point of phase equilibrium

17. In the cyclic process, process $A \to B$ is isothermal.

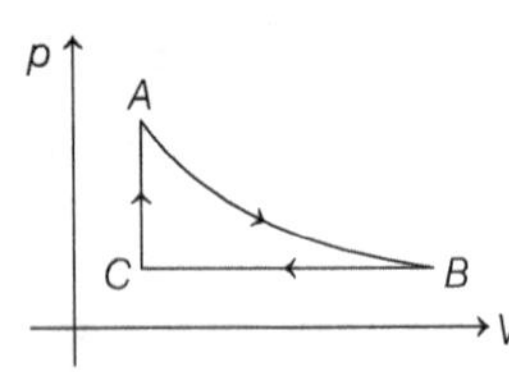

Correct V-T graph for the cycle is

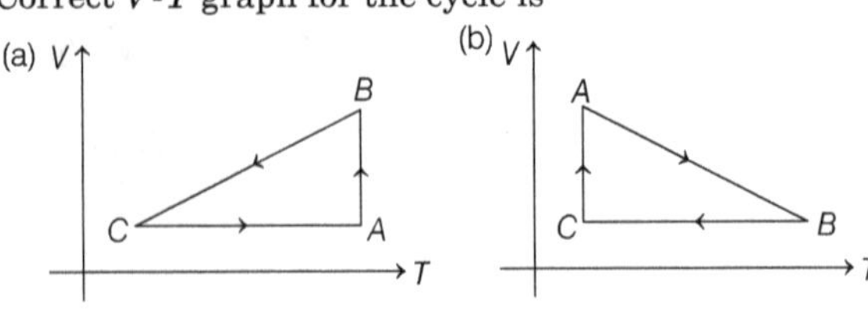

18. Consider the following nuclei:
$$_2\text{He}^3, {}_7\text{N}^{14}, {}_{92}\text{U}^{238}$$
$$_1\text{H}^3, {}_6\text{Cl}^{13}, {}_{92}\text{U}^{235}$$

Choose the correct statements given below.

I. $_2\text{He}^3$ and $_1\text{H}^3$ are isotopes.

II. $_{92}\text{U}^{235}$ and $_{92}\text{U}^{238}$ are isobars.

III. $_6\text{Cl}^{13}$ and $_7\text{N}^{14}$ are isotones.

(a) All statements are correct
(b) Both statements I and II are correct
(c) Both statements II and III are correct
(d) Only statement III is correct

19. Consider two identical copper spheres A and B. One is placed over a thermally insulating plate, while the other hangs from an insulating thread.

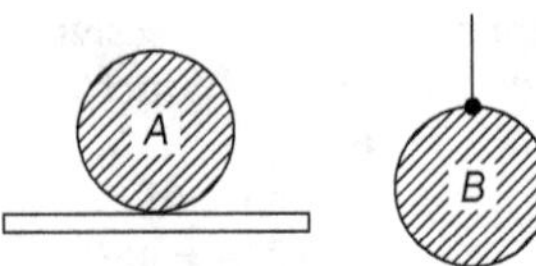

Equal amounts of heat are given to the two spheres and temperatures are recorded, then
(a) $T_A = T_B$　　(b) $T_B < T_A$
(c) $T_B > T_A$　　(d) cannot be concluded

20. A boy throws a stone to hit a pole at some distance. Kinetic energy K of stone varies with horizontal displacement x as shown in figures given below.

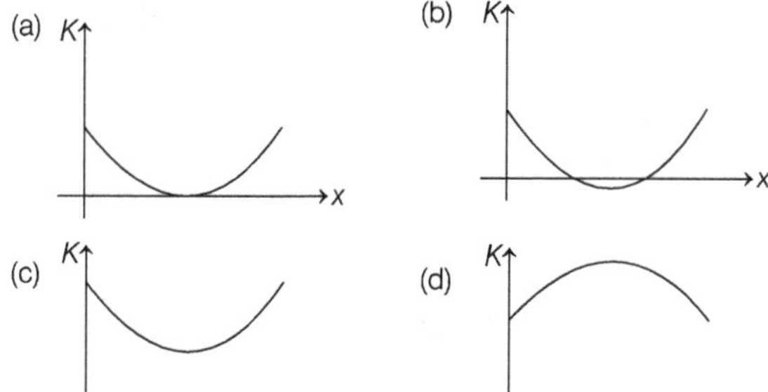

21. Ratio of time periods of small oscillations of the insulated spring and mass system (shown) before and after charging the mass is

(a) equal to one   (b) greater than one
(c) less than one   (d) greater than or equal to one

22. The lights on a car are inadvertently left on. They dissipate 95 W.

Fully charged 12 V car battery is rated 150 Ah. Time after which the car lights go OFF due to battery run down is

(a) 12 h   (b) 24 h   (c) 18 h   (d) 36 h

23. In the arrangement shown below.

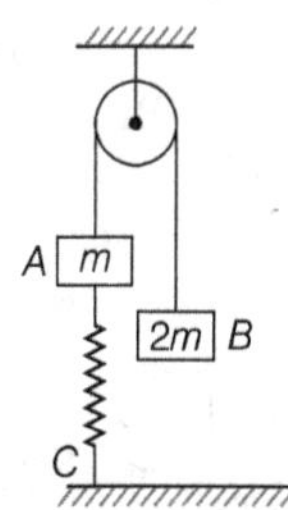

Accelerations of masses A and B just after cutting the string C are

(a) $0, g$ (b) g, g (c) $\dfrac{g}{2}, g$ (d) $2g, g$

24. For streamlined flow of water, consider the following statements.

I. Two streamlines does not cross each other.

II. Streamlines are straight.

III. Streamlined flow is more likely for fluids with low density and high viscosity.

IV. Streamlined flow is more likely for liquids with high density and low viscosity.

Which of the above statements are correct?

(a) Statements I and III are correct
(b) Statements II, III and IV are correct
(c) Statements III and IV are correct
(d) Statements I, III and IV are correct

25. Given, A = Boltzmann constant, B = Planck's constant and C = speed of light.

Then, quantity with dimensions of $A^4 B^{-3} C^{-2}$ is

(a) universal gas constant
(b) specific heat capacity
(c) Stefan's constant
(d) heat energy

26. Considering air resistance, if t_1 = time for a thrown ball in upward journey and t_2 = time taken for downward journey, then

(a) $t_1 = t_2$ (b) $t_1 > t_2$
(c) $t_2 > t_1$ (d) $3t_2 = 2t_1$

27. A car accelerates from rest at a constant rate α for sometime after which it deaccelerates at a constant rate β to come to rest.

If total time is t, then maximum speed of car is

(a) $\left(\dfrac{\alpha\beta}{\alpha+\beta}\right)t$ (b) $\left(\dfrac{\alpha+\beta}{\alpha\beta}\right)t$ (c) $\left(\dfrac{\alpha^2+\beta^2}{\alpha\beta}\right)t$ (d) $\left(\dfrac{\alpha^2-\beta^2}{\alpha\beta}\right)t$

28. A lawn roller of mass 10 kg, radius 1 m is pulled horizontally by a handle attached to axle of the roller.

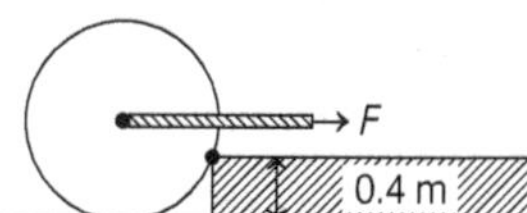

Necessary minimum pull to raise roller above a step of 0.4 m is

(a) 128 N   (b) 134 N
(c) 213 N   (d) 112 N

29. Geodesic is a
(a) straight line
(b) curve
(c) circle
(d) may be a straight line or curve

30. In given combination of lenses, a parallel beam is made incident from left as shown below.

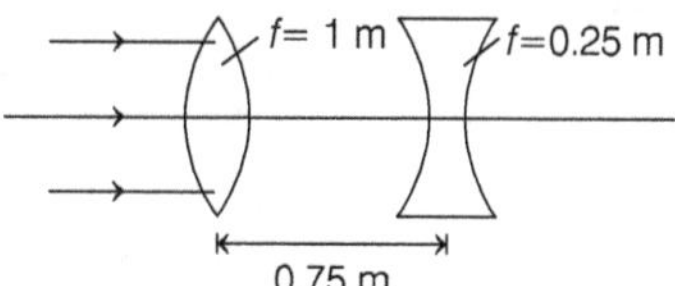

Emerging light rays are as shown by

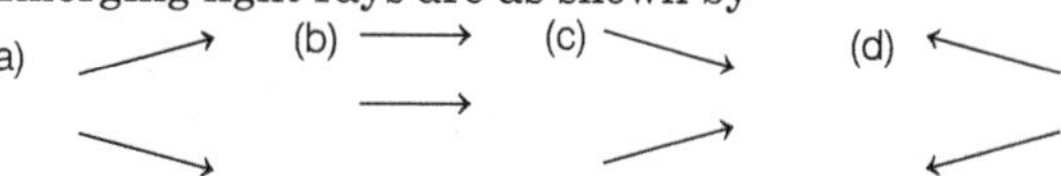

CHEMISTRY

31. Haemoglobin contains 0.33% of iron by weight. The molecular weight of haemoglobin is approximately 67200. The number of iron atoms (at. wt. of Fe is 56) present in one molecule of haemoglobin is closest to

(a) 1   (b) 6   (c) 4   (d) 2

32. Which of the following statements is incorrect?
   (a) Angular quantum number signifies the shape of the orbital
   (b) Energies of stationary states in hydrogen like atoms is inversely proportional to the square of the principle quantum number
   (c) Total number of nodes for $3s$-orbital is three
   (d) The radius of first orbit of He^+ is half that of the first orbit of hydrogen atom

33. The solubility of saturated solution of calcium fluoride is 2×10^{-4} mol L^{-1}. Its solubility product is closest to
   (a) $12 \times 10^{-2}\,M^3$ (b) $14 \times 10^{-4}\,M^3$
   (c) $22 \times 10^{-11}\,M^3$ (d) $32 \times 10^{-12}\,M^3$

34. The brown ring complex compound is formulated as $[Fe(H_2O)_5(NO)]\,SO_4$. The oxidation state of iron is
   (a) 1   (b) 2   (c) 3   (d) 0

35. Which one of the following has the maximum dipole moment?
   (a) CO_2 (b) CH_4 (c) NH_3 (d) NF_3

36. Which of the following is a chiral?
   (a) 1,1-dibromo-1-chloropropane
   (b) 1, 1 - dibromo -3-chloropropane
   (c) 1, 3-dibromo-1-chloropropane
   (d) 1, 3-dibromo-2-chloropropane

37. The correct order of acidic character of the following compounds is
   I. phenol,   II. o-cresol
   III. p-nitrophenol   IV. p-chlorophenol
   (a) I > II > III > IV   (b) III > IV > I > II
   (c) IV > III > II > I   (d) III > II > IV > I

38. Which of the following is the correct order of size of the given species?
   (a) $I > I^- > I^+$ (b) $I^+ > I^- > I$
   (c) $I > I^+ > I^-$ (d) $I^- > I > I^+$

39. Which of the following is the correct representation of Gay-Lussac's law?

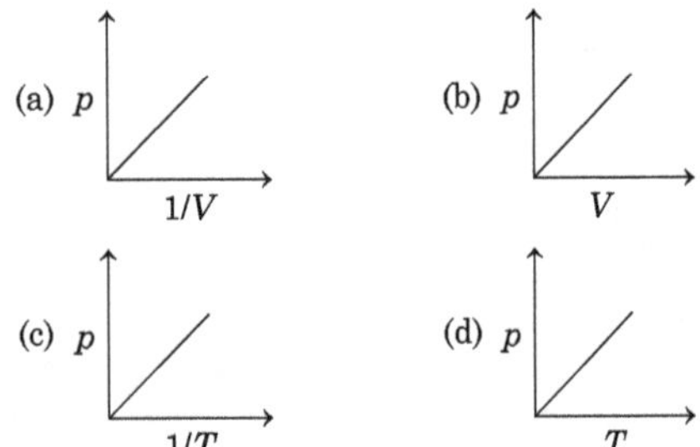

40. A compound that gives a positive iodoform test is
   (a) pentanol   (b) pentan-3-one
   (c) pentan-2-one   (d) pentanal

41. Which of the following compounds of xenon has pyramidal geometry?
   (a) $XeOF_4$ (b) XeF_2 (c) XeO_3 (d) XeF_4

42. Sodium peroxide which is a yellow solid, when exposed to air becomes white due to the formation of
   (a) H_2O_2 (b) Na_2O
   (c) Na_2O and O_3 (d) NaOH and Na_2CO_3

43. The products formed when the following compound is treated with Br_2 in the presence of $FeBr_3$ are

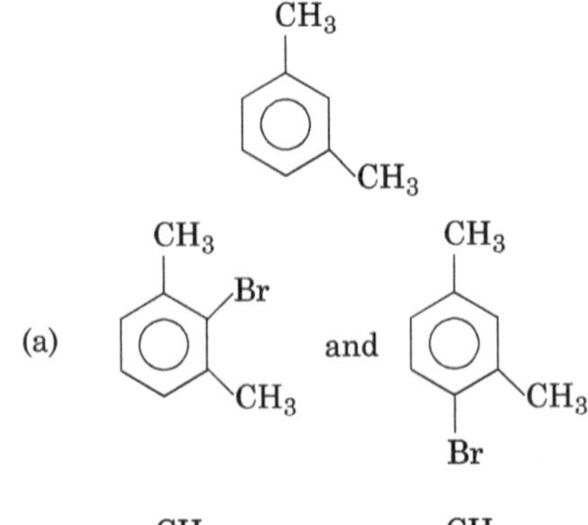

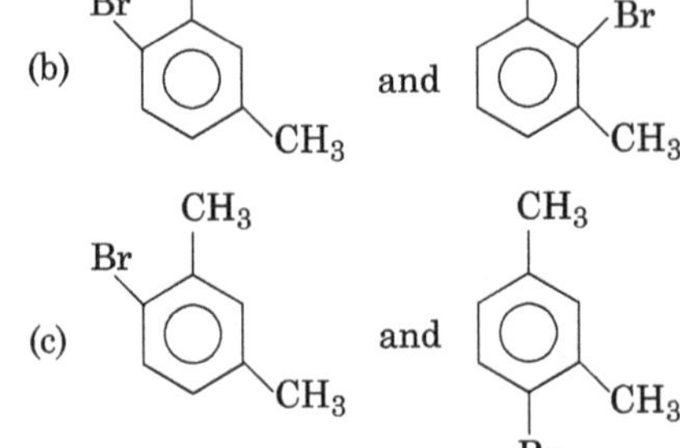

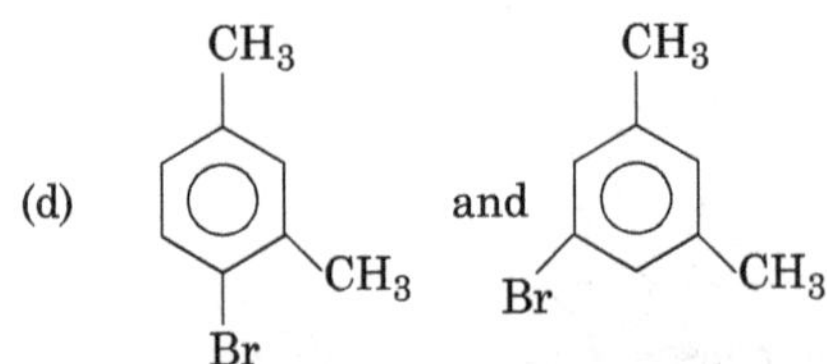

44. How many enantiomeric pairs are obtained by monochlorination of 2, 3-dimethyl butane ?
   (a) 4   (b) 2   (c) 3   (d) 1

45. If bond enthalpies of Cl—Cl bond, H—H bond and H—Cl bond are 243, 435 and 431 kJ mol^{-1} respectively, then calculate the $\Delta_f H°$ in kJ mol^{-1} of HCl.
   (a) -184 (b) -92 (c) 170   (d) -88

BIOLOGY

46. Which of the following components provides sticky character to the bacterial cell?
   (a) Cell wall   (b) Nuclear membrane
   (c) Plasma membrane   (d) Glycocalyx

47. Life cycle of *Ectocarpus* and *Fucus* respectively are
(a) haplontic, diplontic
(b) diplontic, haplodiplontic
(c) haplodiplontic, diplontic
(d) haplodiplontic, haplontic

48. Which of the following are not polymeric?
(a) Nucleic acid   (b) Proteins
(c) Polysaccharides   (d) Lipids

49. In case of poriferans, the spongocoel is lined with flagellated cells called
(a) ostia   (b) oscula
(c) choanocytes   (d) mesenchymal cells

50. A decrease in blood pressure/volume will not cause the release of
(a) renin   (b) atrial natriuretic factor
(c) aldosterone   (d) ADH

51. The vascular cambium normally gives rise to
(a) phelloderm   (b) primary phloem
(c) secondary xylem   (d) periderm

52. Which of the following options best represents enzyme composition of pancreatic juice?
(a) Amylase, peptidase, trypsinogen, renin
(b) Amylase, pepsin, trypsinogen, maltase
(c) Peptidase, amylase, pepsin, renin
(d) Lipase, amylase, trypsinogen, procarboxypeptidase

53. Which of the following are found in extreme saline conditions?
(a) Archaebacteria   (b) Eubacteria
(c) Cyanobacteria   (d) Mycobacteria

54. Anaphase Promoting Complex (APC) is a protein degradation machinery necessary for proper mitosis of animal cells. If APC is defective in a human cell, which of the following is expected to occur?
(a) Chromosomes will not condense
(b) Chromosomes will be fragmented
(c) Chromosomes will not segregate
(d) Recombination of chromosome arms will occur

55. Zygotic meiosis is a characteristic of
(a) *Marchantia*   (b) *Fucus*
(c) *Funaria*   (d) *Chlamydomonas*

56. Which one of the following generally acts as an antagonist to gibberellins?
(a) Zeatin   (b) Ethylene
(c) ABA   (d) IAA

57. The ornithine cycle removes two waste products from the blood in liver. These products are
(a) CO_2 and urea   (b) ammonia and urea
(c) CO_2 and ammonia   (d) ammonia and uric acid

58. Phellogen and phellem respectively denote
(a) cork and cork cambium
(b) cork cambium and cork
(c) secondary cortex and cork
(d) cork and secondary cortex

59. Which one of the following enzymes shows the greatest substrate specificity?
(a) Lipase   (b) Nuclease
(c) Pepsin   (d) Sucrose

60. Albinism in humans is controlled by a recessive allele. How many copies of this allele will be found at one of the poles of a cell at telophase-I of meiosis in an albino person?
(a) 23   (b) 4   (c) 2   (d) 1

☉ PART-II (2 Marks Questions)

MATHEMATICS

61. A positive integer K is said to be good if there exists a partition of $\{1, 2, 3, \dots, 20\}$ in to disjoint proper subsets such that the sum of the numbers in each subset of the partition is K. Then good number are there
(a) 5   (b) 6   (c) 7   (d) 4

62. Let C_1 and C_2 be circles defined by $(x - 10)^2 + y^2 = 36$ and $(x + 15)^2 + y^2 = 81$ respectively. The length of the shortest line segment PQ that is tangent C_1 at P and to C_2 at Q is
(a) 15   (b) 18   (c) 20   (d) 24

63. Suppose that a and b are digits, not both nine and not both zero, and the repeating decimal $0.\overline{ab}$ is expressed as a fraction in lowest terms. Then, the different denominators are possible, are
(a) 3   (b) 4   (c) 6   (d) 5

64. If $\triangle ABC$ is a right angle triangle with $\angle ACB$ as its right angle. The measure of $\angle ABC = 60°$ and $AB = 10$. Let P be randomly chosen inside ABC, and extend BP to meet AC at D. Then, the probability that $BD > 5\sqrt{2}$ is
(a) $\dfrac{1}{2}$ (b) $\dfrac{2 - \sqrt{2}}{2}$ (c) $\dfrac{3 - \sqrt{3}}{3}$ (d) $\dfrac{5 - \sqrt{5}}{5}$

65. Let $P(x) = (x - 1)(x - 2)(x - 3)$. For how many polynomials $Q(x)$ does there exist a polynomial $R(x)$ of degree 3 such that $P(Q(x)) = P(x) \cdot R(x)$?
(a) 22   (b) 24   (c) 27   (d) 32

PHYSICS

66. Two stones are thrown up simultaneously from the edge of a cliff 200 m high with initial speeds 15 ms^{-1} and 30 ms^{-1}.

Correct graph of time variation of the relative position of the second stone with respect to first is

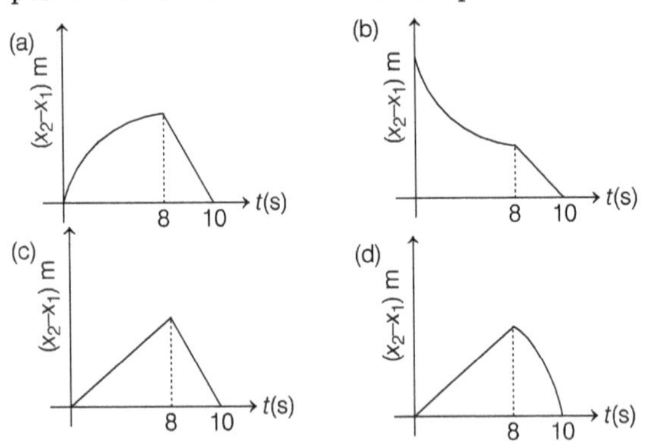

67. In an experiment of finding focal length of a concave mirror by u-v method, a student prepares following graph of u *versus* v graph.

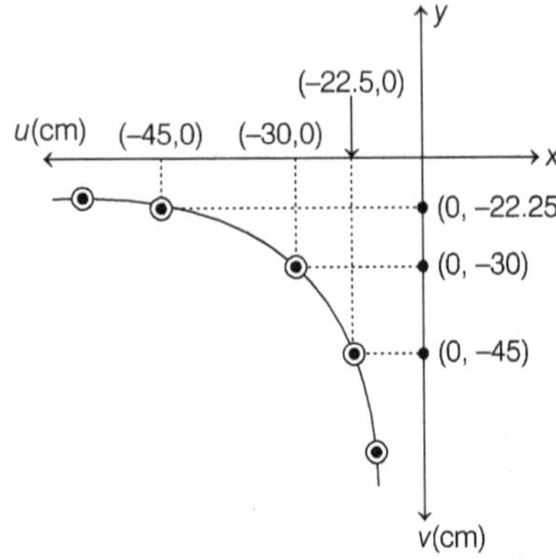

Focal length of mirror is nearly

(a) $-45\,cm$ (b) $-30\,cm$ (c) $-22.25\,cm$ (d) $-15\,cm$

68. In given circuit, bulb that glows with maximum intensity is

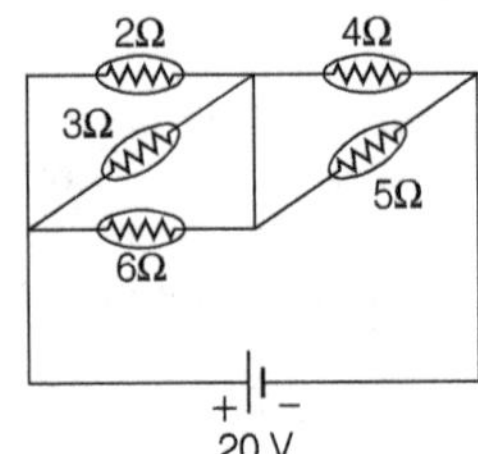

(a) 4Ω bulb (b) 2Ω bulb
(c) 3Ω bulb (d) 6Ω bulb

69. For a linear oscillator, potential energy as a function of its displacement x is

$$U(x) = \frac{kx^2}{2}$$

where, $k =$ spring constant $= 0.5\,Nm^{-1}$.

If total energy of the particle is 1 J, then maximum amplitude of oscillation of particle is

(a) 1 m (b) 2 m (c) 3 m (d) 1.5 m

70. A calorimeter contains some ice and 10 kg water. This calorimeter is heated over a slow burner which provides heat at a constant rate.

Temperature of calorimeter and its contents varies with time as shown below.

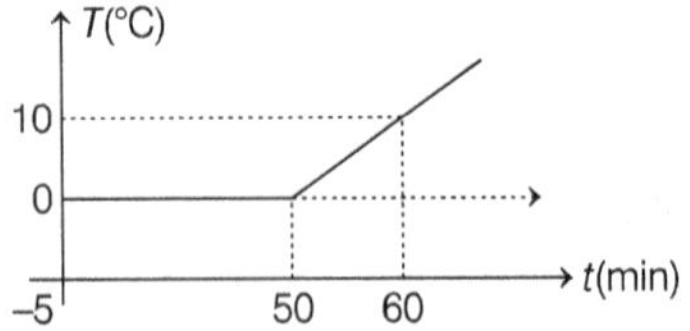

Amount of ice initially present is nearly

(a) 17 kg (b) 14 kg (c) 10 kg (d) 5 kg

CHEMISTRY

71. The heat liberated from the combustion of 0.5 g of carbon raised the temperature of 2000 g of water from 24°C to 26°C. The heat of combustion of carbon (per mole) is

(a) $-4\,kcal$ (b) $-8\,kcal$
(c) $-62\,kcal$ (d) $-96\,kcal$

72. An organic compound of molecular formula C_4H_6. A forms precipitates with ammoniacal silver nitrate and ammoniacal cuprous chloride. A is an isomer B, one mole of which reacts with one mole of Br_2 to form 1, 4-dibromobut-2-ene. A and B are

(a) $CH_3CH_2C \equiv CH$ and $CH_2 = CHCH = CH_2$

(b) $CH_3C \equiv CCH_3$ and $CH_3CH = C = CH_2$

(c) $\begin{array}{c} CH_2 \\ | \quad\ \ \diagdown \\ CH_2 \diagup \end{array} C = CH_2$ and $\begin{array}{c} CH_2 - CH \\ | \qquad\ \ \| \\ CH_2 - CH \end{array}$

(d) $CH_3C \equiv CCH_3$ and $\begin{array}{c} CH \\ \diagup\ \ | \ \ \diagdown \\ CH_2 \quad\ \ CH_2 \\ \diagdown\ \ | \ \ \diagup \\ CH \end{array}$

73. A gas bulb of 1 mL capacity contains 2.0×10^{21} molecules of nitrogen exerting a pressure of 7.57×10^3 Nm^{-2}. The root mean square speed of the gas molecules is

(a) $274\,ms^{-1}$ (b) $494\,ms^{-1}$
(c) $690\,ms^{-1}$ (d) $988\,ms^{-1}$

74. Which of the following statements is not correct from the view point of molecular orbital theory?

(a) Be_2 is not a stable molecule

(b) He_2 is not stable, but He_2^+ is expected to exist

(c) Bond strength of N_2 is maximum amongst the homonuclear diatomic molecule belonging to the second period

(d) The order of energies of molecular orbitals in N_2 molecule is

$\sigma 2s < \sigma^* 2s < \sigma 2p_z\ (\pi 2p_x \approx \pi 2p_y) < (\pi^* 2p_x \approx \pi^* 2p_y) < \sigma^* 2p_z$

75. The atomicity of a molecule, M, if 10 g of it combine with 0.8 g of oxygen to form an oxide is closest to [specific heat of molecule, M is 0.033 cal $deg^{-1}g^{-1}$ and molecular mass of molecule is 199.87 g]

(a) 1　　　(b) 2　　　(c) 3　　　(d) 8

BIOLOGY

76. The following statements describe the structure of certain protein molecule.

(I) The molecule consists of two polypeptide chains which are folded around each other.

(II) In each chain the amino acids are held in a helix by hydrogen bonds.

Which orders of structure are described by these statements?

	Statement (I)	Statement (II)
(a)	Primary	Tertiary
(b)	Secondary	Tertiary
(c)	Tertiary	Secondary
(d)	Quaternary	Secondary

77. The graph shows the relationship between oxygen production in photosynthesis and light intensity for a unicellular green organism in 0.02% sodium hydrogencarbonate solution

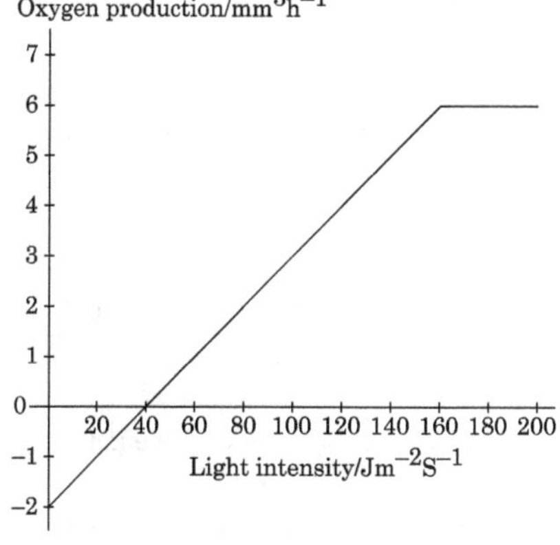

The most likely explanation of the fact that the graph levels off at 180 $Jm^{-2}s^{-1}$ is that the system is

(a) light limited and carbon dioxide saturated
(b) light limited and the temperature is below optimum
(c) light saturated and carbon dioxide is unlimited
(d) light saturated and the temperature is above optimum

78. Certain drug acts at synapses and affects the action of neurotransmitter substances. The table shows the effects of four different drugs.

Drug Effect

I. Inhibits the enzyme cholinesterase.

II. Prevents the release of acetylcholine.

III. Competes with acetylcholine at receptor sites.

IV. Inhibits the enzyme which destroys nor-adrenaline.

Which two drugs would prevent a skeletal muscle from responding to an electrical stimulus in the presynaptic neuron?

(a) I and II　　　　　(b) I and IV
(c) II and III　　　　(d) II and IV

79. The diagram shows some chromosomes at late prophase of mitosis.

How many chromosomes would be present in one nucleus at telophase-II of meiosis?

(a) 6　　　　　　　(b) 12
(c) 18　　　　　　(d) 24

80. Pyrimidine bases contain four carbon atoms and purine bases contain 5.

How many carbon atoms are there in a nucleotide containing cytosine?

(a) 8　　　(b) 9　　　(c) 10　　　(d) 11

Answers

PART-I

1 (b)	2 (c)	3 (c)	4 (b)	5 (c)	6 (c)	7 (a)	8 (d)	9 (d)	10 (b)
11 (d)	12 (b)	13 (d)	14 (c)	15 (c)	16 (d)	17 (a)	18 (d)	19 (c)	20 (c)
21 (a)	22 (c)	23 (d)	24 (a)	25 (c)	26 (c)	27 (a)	28 (b)	29 (d)	30 (b)
31 (c)	32 (c)	33 (d)	34 (a)	35 (c)	36 (c)	37 (b)	38 (d)	39 (d)	40 (c)
41 (c)	42 (d)	43 (c)	44 (d)	45 (b)	46 (d)	47 (c)	48 (d)	49 (c)	50 (d)
51 (c)	52 (d)	53 (a)	54 (c)	55 (d)	56 (c)	57 (b)	58 (b)	59 (d)	60 (c)

PART-II

61 (b)	62 (c)	63 (d)	64 (c)	65 (a)	66 (d)	67 (d)	68 (a)	69 (b)	70 (a)
71 (d)	72 (a)	73 (b)	74 (d)	75 (a)	76 (d)	77 (d)	78 (c)	79 (a)	80 (b)

Solutions

1. *(b)* Number less than 1000 can write

$$abc = 100a + 10b + c$$

where $a, b, c \in \{0, 1, 2, 3, ..., 9\}$ and $a + b + c > 0$

The sum of digits of this number is $(a + b + c)$.

Given, $100a + 10b + c = 6(a + b + c)$

$\therefore \quad 94a + 4b - 5c = 0$

Clearly, $a > 0$. No solution

$\therefore \quad a = 0$ then $4b = 5c$

This is possible only

$$b = 5 \text{ and } c = 4$$

$\therefore$ Number is 54.

Hence, only one number *i.e.*, 54.

2. *(c)* In ΔOPB,

$$\cos \frac{\pi}{5} = \frac{r}{R} \Rightarrow r = R \cos \frac{\pi}{5}$$

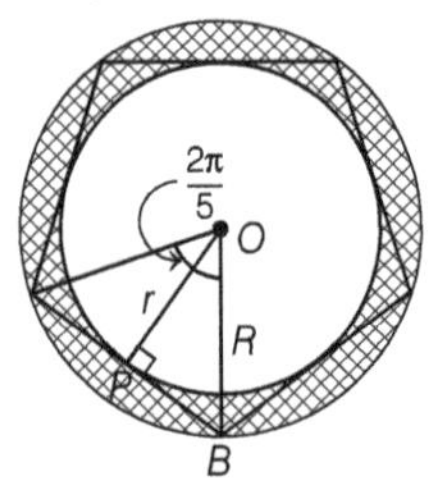

Area of region $= \pi (R^2 - r^2)$

$$= \pi R^2 \left(1 - \cos^2 \frac{\pi}{5} \right)$$

$$= \pi \csc^2 \frac{\pi}{5} \left(1 - \cos^2 \frac{\pi}{5} \right)$$

$$\left[\because \sin \frac{\pi}{5} = \frac{1}{R} \right]$$

$$= \pi \left(\csc^2 \frac{\pi}{5} - \cot^2 \frac{\pi}{5} \right) = \pi$$

Similarly in heptagon,

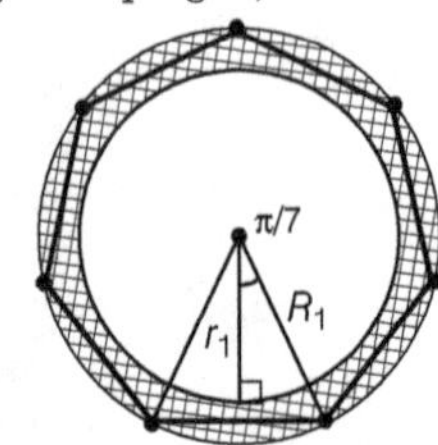

Area of region $= \pi \csc^2 \frac{\pi}{7} \left(1 - \cos^2 \frac{\pi}{7} \right)$

$$= \pi \left(\csc^2 \frac{\pi}{7} - \cos^2 \frac{\pi}{7} \right)$$

$$= \pi$$

$\therefore$ Both have same area.

$\therefore \qquad A = B$

3. *(c)* Let the number of triangular tiles

$$= x$$

and the number of square tiles $= y$

A triangle has three edges and square has four edges.

$\therefore \qquad x + y = 25 \qquad \text{...(i)}$

and $\qquad 3x + 4y = 84 \qquad \text{...(ii)}$

On solving Eqs. (i) and (ii), we get

$$x = 16, y = 9$$

Hence, number of square tiles in box is 9.

4. *(b)* We have, $f(1) = 2$

and $\quad f(n) = f(n - 2) + 2$, n is odd

$\therefore \quad f(3) = f(1) + 2 = 2 + 2 = 4$

$\quad f(5) = f(3) + 2 = 4 + 2 = 6$

$\therefore$ Similarly, $f(2019) = 2020$

5. *(c)* We have,

Equation of parabola

$$y = ax^2 - 2 \qquad \text{...(i)}$$

and $\qquad y = 4 - bx^2 \qquad \text{...(ii)}$

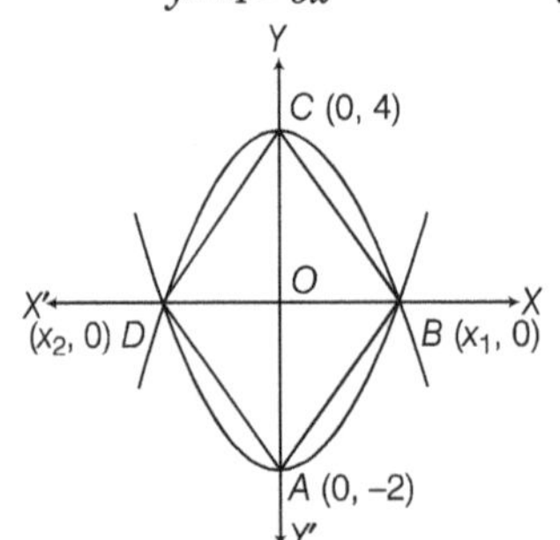

On solving Eqs. (i) and (ii), we get

x intercept are $\pm \sqrt{\dfrac{6}{\sqrt{a + b}}}$

i.e. coordinate of points

$$A (0, - 2), B \left(\sqrt{\frac{6}{a + b}}, 0 \right), C (0, 4)$$

and $D = - \sqrt{\dfrac{6}{a + b}}$

Area of kite $ABCD = \dfrac{1}{2} AC \times BD$

$$\Rightarrow \quad 12 = \frac{1}{2} 6 \times 2 \sqrt{\frac{6}{a + b}} \Rightarrow \sqrt{\frac{6}{a + b}} = 2$$

$$\Rightarrow \quad \frac{6}{a + b} = 4$$

$$\Rightarrow \quad a + b = \frac{6}{4} = \frac{3}{2}$$

6. *(c)* Given, $\angle ABC = 30°$

$$\therefore \qquad \angle AOC = 2 \angle ABC = 60°$$

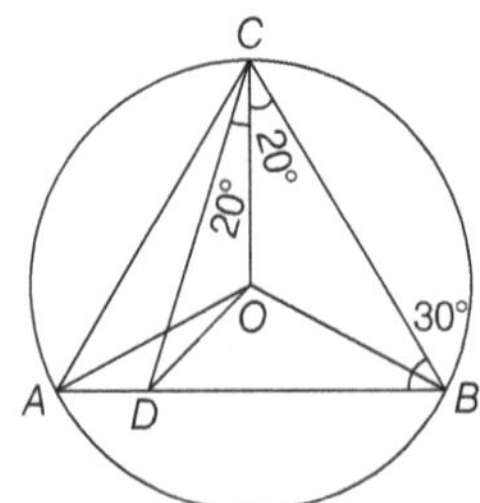

Now, $\qquad OA = OC$

ΔOAC is an equilateral

$\Rightarrow \qquad \angle CAO = \angle ACO = 60°$

$\Rightarrow \qquad \angle ACD = 60° - 20° = 40°$

$$OC = OB$$

$\therefore \qquad \angle OBC = \angle OCB = 20°$

$\Rightarrow \qquad \angle OBA = 10° = \angle OAB$

$\Rightarrow \qquad \angle DAC = 70°$

In ΔACD, $\quad \angle CDA = 70°$

$\Rightarrow \qquad \angle CDA = \angle CAD = 70°$

$\Rightarrow \qquad CD = CA = CO$

In ΔCDO, $CD = CO$ and $\angle DCO = 20°$

$\Rightarrow \qquad \angle CDO = \dfrac{180° - 20°}{2} = 80°$

7. *(a)* We have,

$2a - b$, $a - 2b$ and $a + b$ are squares.

$\therefore$ Let $\qquad 2a - b = x^2 \qquad \text{...(i)}$

$\qquad a - 2b = y^2 \qquad \text{...(ii)}$

and $\qquad a + b = z^2 \qquad \text{...(iii)}$

where $x, y, z \in N$

From Eqs. (ii) and (iii), we get

$$2a - b = y^2 + z^2$$

$\therefore \qquad x^2 = y^2 + z^2 \qquad \text{...(iv)}$

From Eqs. (i) and (iii), we get

$$3a = x^2 + z^2$$

$x^2 + z^2$ is multiple of $3 \Rightarrow x$ and z is also multiple of 3.

From Eqs. (ii) and (iii), we get

$$3b = z^2 - y^2 \qquad \text{...(v)}$$

$z^2 - y^2$ is a multiple of $3 \Rightarrow y$ and z is also multiple of 3.

Let $x = 3x_1$, $y = 3y_1$, $z = 3z_1 \Rightarrow x_1^2 = y_1^2 + z_1^2$

Let us assume every two of x, y, z are coprime.

$\Rightarrow x_1, y_1, z_1$ are pythagorean triplet.

$\Rightarrow$ Out of y_1 and z_1, one even ≥ 4 and other odd ≥ 3.

From Eq. (v), we get

$$b = 3(z_1^2 - y_1^2) = 3(z_1 + y_1) (z_1 - y_1)$$

$\Rightarrow \min b = 3(4 + 3) (4 - 3) = 21$

8. *(d)* Let the wealth of A, B and C are x, y and z respectively.

Given, $\qquad A = B + C$

$\therefore \qquad\qquad x = y + z$

A distributes half of his wealth to B and C in the ratio 2 : 1.

Wealth of $B = y + \dfrac{2}{3}\left(\dfrac{x}{2}\right)$ and $C = z + \dfrac{1}{3}\left(\dfrac{x}{2}\right)$

Now, $\qquad B = A + C$

$\therefore \quad y + \dfrac{x}{3} = \dfrac{x}{2} + z + \dfrac{x}{6} \ \Rightarrow \ y - z = \dfrac{x}{3}$

Let 'a' be the fraction that A should distribute and the ratio of distribution is 1 : 2.

$$\dfrac{1}{3} < \dfrac{2}{3}$$

Now, $\qquad A = (1 - a)\, x$

$$B = y + \dfrac{ax}{3}$$

$$C = z + \dfrac{2ax}{3}$$

$\therefore \quad z + \dfrac{2ax}{3} = y + \dfrac{ax}{3} + (1 - a)\, x$

$\Rightarrow \quad 3z + ax = 3y + 3x - 3ax$

$\Rightarrow \quad 4ax = 3(y - z) + 3x$

$\Rightarrow \quad 4ax = 3\left(\dfrac{x}{3}\right) + 3x \quad \left[\because y - z = \dfrac{x}{3}\right]$

$\Rightarrow \quad 4ax = 4x \Rightarrow a = 1$

9. *(d)* We can expand the fraction $0.\overline{23}K$ as follows

$0.\overline{23}K = 2 \cdot K^{-1} + 3 \cdot K^{-2} + 2 \cdot K^{-3}$
$\qquad\qquad\qquad\qquad + 3 \cdot K^{-4} + \dots$

$= 2(K^{-1} + K^{-3} + K^{-5} + \dots) + 3(K^{-2} + K^{-4}$
$\qquad\qquad\qquad\qquad\qquad\qquad + K^{-6} + \dots)$

$= \dfrac{2}{K}\left(1 + \dfrac{1}{K^2} + \dfrac{1}{K^4} + \dots\right)$

$\qquad\qquad + \dfrac{3}{K^2}\left(1 + \dfrac{1}{K^2} + \dfrac{1}{K^4} + \dots\right)$

$= \left(\dfrac{2}{K} + \dfrac{3}{K^2}\right)\left(\dfrac{1}{1 - \dfrac{1}{K^2}}\right) = \dfrac{2K + 3}{K^2 - 1}$

Given, $\qquad 0.\overline{23}K = \dfrac{7}{51}$

$\therefore \qquad \dfrac{2K + 3}{K^2 - 1} = \dfrac{7}{51}$

$\Rightarrow 7K^2 - 102K - 160 = 0$

$\Rightarrow 7K^2 - 112K + 10K - 160 = 0$

$\Rightarrow \qquad (7K + 10)\,(K - 16) = 0$

$\Rightarrow \qquad\qquad K = 16,\ K \neq \dfrac{-10}{7}$

10. *(b)* Sum odd only be formed (even, even, odd) or (odd, odd, odd). So can focus on placing evens, we need to have

each even be with another even in each row or column. There are 9 ways to this. They are 5! ways to permute odd and 4! ways to permute even number.

$\therefore$ Required probability $= \dfrac{5! \times 4! \times 9}{9!} = \dfrac{1}{14}$

11. *(d)* Given,

$$AB = BC = CD = 200$$
$$OA = OB = OC = OD = 200\sqrt{2}$$
$$\angle AOB = \angle BOC = \angle COD$$

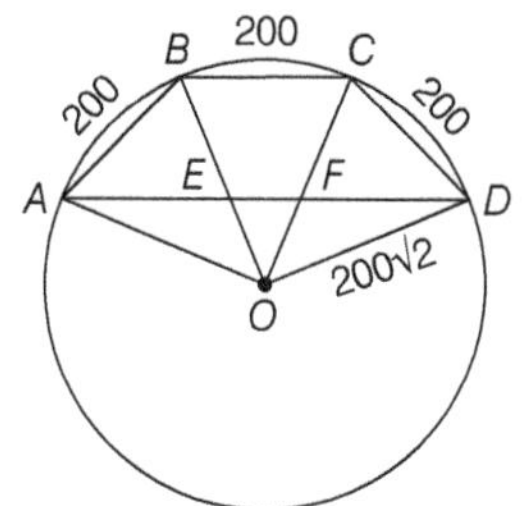

In ΔOAB and ΔABE,

$$\angle BAE = \angle AOB$$
$$\angle ABO = \angle ABE$$

$\therefore \qquad \Delta OAB \sim \Delta ABE$

$$\dfrac{OA}{AB} = \dfrac{AB}{BE} = \dfrac{OB}{AE}$$

$$AB = AE \qquad\qquad [\because OA = OB]$$

Similarly in ΔOCD and ΔDFE,

$$CD = DF$$

$\therefore \qquad OE = 100\sqrt{2} = \dfrac{OB}{2}$

and $\qquad EF = \dfrac{BC}{2} = 100$

$\therefore \qquad AD = AE + EF + FD$
$$= 200 + 100 + 200 = 500$$

12. *(b)* $T = \{4, 5, 6\}$ (mod 15)

or $T = \{19, 20, 21\}, \{34, 35, 36\}, \{49, 50, 51\},$
$$\{64, 65, 66\}$$
$$\{79, 80, 81\}, \{94, 95, 96\}, \{109, 110, 111\},$$
$$\{124, 125, 126\}$$
$$\{139, 140, 141\}, \{154, 155, 156\},$$
$$\{169, 170, 171\}, \{184, 185, 186\} \,(\text{mod}\,15)$$

Now, by direct checking we get smallest

$$T = 184$$

$\therefore$ Required sum $= 1^2 + 8^2 + 4^2 = 81$

13. *(d)* We have,

$$x^2 - bx + c = 0$$

Let α, β are the roots of the equations.

$\therefore \qquad\qquad \alpha + \beta = b,\, \alpha\beta = c$

Given, $\qquad\qquad \alpha - \beta = 1$

$\therefore \quad (\alpha + \beta)^2 - (\alpha - \beta)^2 = 4\alpha\beta$
$$b^2 - 1 = 4c$$

$\Rightarrow \qquad\qquad b^2 - 4c = 1$

14. *(c)* We have, MISSISSIPPI

Other than S, seven letters, M, I, I, I,P, P, I can be arranged in

$$\dfrac{7!}{4!\,2!} = 7 \times 5 \times 3$$

Now, 4 S can be placed in 8 spaces, i.e. $^8C_4$.

$\therefore$ Total number of arrangement

$$= 7 \cdot 5 \cdot 3 \cdot {}^8C_4$$
$$= 7 \times 15 \times {}^8C_4$$
$$= 7 \times {}^6C_4 \times {}^8C_4$$

15. *(c)* Let the length of train is x m.

Length of train and platform $= (x + 88)$ m

Time taken by train to cross the platform
$$= 21\,\text{s}$$

$\therefore \qquad\qquad \text{Speed} = \dfrac{x + 88}{21} \qquad \dots(i)$

Time taken by train to cross the man $= 9\,\text{s}$

$\therefore \qquad\qquad \text{Speed} = \dfrac{x}{9} \qquad \dots(ii)$

From Eqs. (i) and (ii), we get

$$\dfrac{x + 88}{21} = \dfrac{x}{9} \Rightarrow 12x = 88 \times 9$$

$\Rightarrow \qquad\qquad x = \dfrac{88 \times 9}{12} = 66\,\text{m}$

16. *(d)* Point P_1 is called triple point, where fusion curve vaporisation curve and sublimation curve meets.

17. *(a)* Process AB is isothermal expansion, so

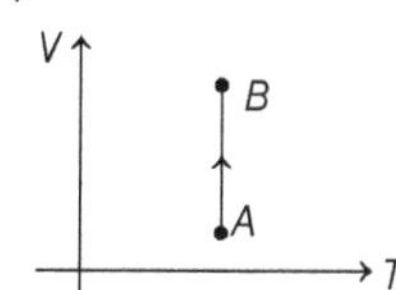

Process BC is isobaric, so

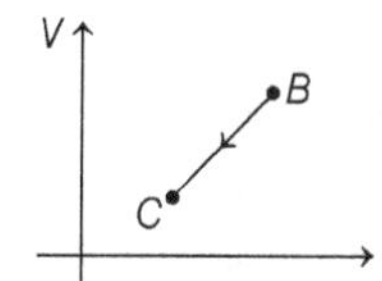

18. *(d)* Number of neutrons,
$$N = A - Z$$

For $_6\text{Cl}^{13}$, $N = 13 - 6 = 7$

and $_7\text{N}^{14}$, $N = 14 - 7 = 7$

So, they contains same number of neutrons.

19. *(c)* Part of heat given to A is used up in doing work (against) gravitational force.

So, temperature of B will be slightly higher.

20. *(c)* Kinetic energy of stone decreases then increases. It is never zero in entire flight of stone.

21. *(a)* In absence of charge, time period

$$T_1 = 2\pi\sqrt{\frac{m}{2k}}$$

In presence of charge, time period

$$T_2 = 2\pi\sqrt{\frac{m}{2k}}$$

So, ratio of time period is equal to one.

22. *(c)* Total output energy of battery

$$= V(It) = 12\,V \times 150\,Ah$$
$$= 12 \times 150 \times 3600\,J$$
$$= 6.48 \times 10^6\,J$$

Energy consumed by car lights in time t
$$= 95t$$

Equating both values, we get

$$t = \frac{6.48 \times 10^6}{95} \approx 18.9\,h$$

23. *(d)* When string C is cut, spring snaps back to regain its unstretched length. So, spring force on m remains same. Hence, accelerations of m and $2m$ are $2g$ and g, respectively.

24. *(a)* Streamlines may be straight or curved.

In fluids, with low viscosity streamlined flow occurs only at low flow speed.

25. *(c)* $[A^4 B^{-3} C^2]$

$$= [ML^2T^{-2}K^{-1}]^4 \cdot [ML^2T^{-1}]^{-3} \cdot [LT^{-1}]^{-2}$$
$$= [M^{4-3}L^{8-6-2}T^{-8+3+2}K^{-4}]$$
$$= [ML^0T^{-3}K^{-4}]$$
$$= \text{Stefan's constant.}$$

26. *(c)* Time for downward journey is higher as ball can be thrown with any velocity but its downward velocity is always less than or equal to terminal velocity.

27. *(a)* Let car accelerates for time t_1 and then it deaccelerates for time t_2.

Then, $\alpha t_1 - \beta t_2 = 0$ and $t = t_1 + t_2$

Maximum speed, $v = \alpha t_1 = \left(\dfrac{\alpha\beta}{\alpha+\beta}\right)t$

28. *(b)* Taking moments about point of contact O.

$$F \times 0.6 = 100 \times 0.8$$
$$\Rightarrow \quad F = \frac{100 \times 0.8}{0.6} = 133.3\,N \simeq 134\,N$$

29. *(d)* Shortest distance between two points is called Geodesic.

If surface over which points are located is a plane, then Geodesic is a straight line. On the surface of a planet, Geodesic is a great circle joining two points.

30. *(b)* Image of first lens is formed at focal point of second lens.

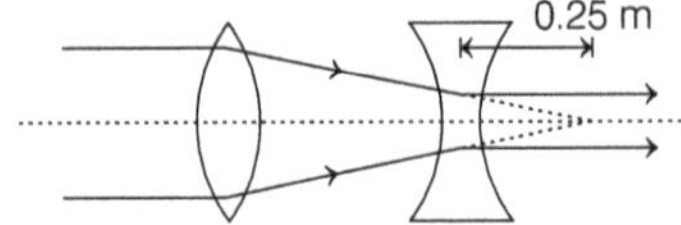

So, emerging rays are parallel.

31. *(c)* 100 g of haemoglobin contains
$$= 0.33\,g\,Fe$$

$\therefore$ 67200 g of haemoglobin contains
$$= \frac{0.33 \times 67200}{100}\,g\,Fe$$
$$= 221.76\,g\,Fe$$

$\therefore$ Number of Fe atom present in one molecule of haemoglobin $= \dfrac{221.76}{56} \approx 4$

32. *(c)* (a) Angular quantum number, l signifies the shape of the orbital. e.g.

When $l = 0$, the shape of orbital is spherical.

When $l = 1$, the shape of orbital is dumb-bell.

Thus, statement (a) is correct.

(b) According to Bohr's theory

For hydrogen like atom

$$E_n = -13.6\left[\frac{Z^2}{n^2}\right]\,eV$$

Thus, statement (b) is correct.

(c) Total number of nodes in orbital
$$= n - l - 1$$

For $3s$-orbital, $n = 3, l = 0$

Number of nodes $= 3 - 0 - 1 = 2$

Thus, statement (c) is incorrect.

(d) According to Bohr's radius

$$r = \frac{a_0 n^2}{Z}$$

$$r_{He^+} = \frac{a_0(1)^2}{2}, \; r_H\,\frac{a_0(1)^2}{1}$$

Thus, statement (d) is correct.

33. *(d)* Let the solubility of CaF_2 be S.

For the reaction,

$$CaF_2 \rightleftharpoons \underset{S}{Ca^{2+}}(aq) + \underset{2S}{2F^-}(aq)$$

$$K_{sp} = [Ca^{2+}][F^-]^2 = (S)(2S)^2 = 4S^3$$

$\therefore \quad K_{sp} = 4(2 \times 10^{-4})^3 = 32 \times 10^{-12}\,M^3$

34. *(a)* Let, the oxidation state of Fe in $[Fe(H_2O)_5\,(NO)]\,SO_4$ be x.

$\therefore \quad x + 5(0) + 1 = +2$

$\Rightarrow \qquad x = +1$

35. *(c)* CO_2 and CH_4 have zero dipole moment as these are symmetrical in nature. Between NH_3 and NF_3, NH_3 has greater dipole moment though in both NH_3 and NF_3, N possesses one lone pair of electrons.

This is because in case of NH_3, the net N—H bond dipole is in the same direction as the direction of dipole of lone pair but in case of NF_3, the direction of net bond dipole moment of three N—F is opposite to that of the dipole moment of the lone pair which cancel out the resultant dipole.

36. *(c)* A molecule is set to be chiral, if all the four groups attached to central carbon atom are different.

(a) $\overset{3}{H_3C}\!-\!\overset{2}{CH_2}\!-\!\overset{1}{\underset{\underset{Br}{|}}{\overset{\overset{Br}{|}}{C}}}\!-\!Cl$

1, 1-dibromo-1-chloropropane
It is an achiral molecule.

(b) $Cl\!-\!\overset{3}{CH_2}\!-\!\overset{2}{CH_2}\!-\!\overset{1}{\underset{\underset{Br}{|}}{\overset{\overset{Br}{|}}{CH}}}$

1, 1-dibromo-3 chloropropane
It is an achiral carbon.

(c) $\overset{3}{BrCH_2}\!-\!\overset{2}{CH_2}\!-\!\overset{1}{\underset{\underset{Cl}{|}}{\overset{\overset{Br}{|}}{*CH}}}$

1, 3-dibromo-1-chloropropane
It is a chiral molecule with chiral carbon position at 1(*).

(d) $\overset{3}{H_2C}\!-\!\overset{2}{\underset{\underset{Cl}{|}}{\overset{\overset{Cl}{|}}{C}}}\!-\!\overset{1}{\underset{\underset{Br}{|}}{\overset{\overset{Br}{|}}{CH_2}}}$

1, 3-dibromo-2-chloropropane
It is an achiral molecule.

37. *(b)* When an electron withdrawing group, like NO_2, Cl is attached to the phenol ring, it stabilises the negative charge on the oxygen of the phenoxide ion. Due to this reason, acidic character of phenol increases. Between compound III and IV, III is more acidic as NO_2 is more stronger EWG than Cl.

But when an electron donating group, like CH_3 is attached to the phenol ring, it destabilises the ring and hence acidic character of phenol decreases. Thus, the correct order of acidic character is

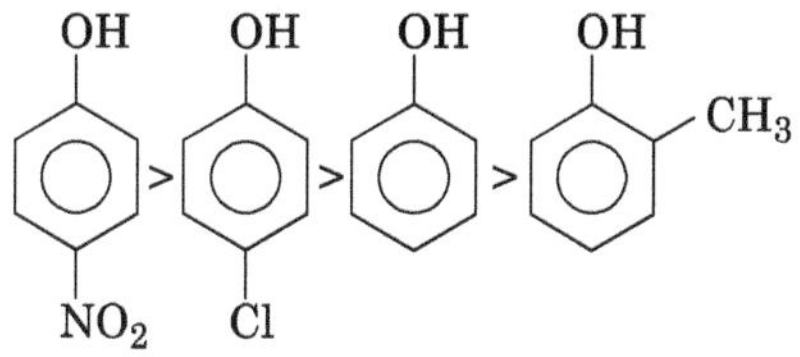

OH　　OH　　OH　　OH

(III) > (IV) > (I) > (II)

NO_2　　Cl

III　　IV　　I　　II

38. *(d)* Anion is formed by the gain of electron to the neutral atom and cation is formed after the loss of electron from the neutral atom. Hence, cation has smaller size due to increased nuclear charge whereas anion has bigger size than its neutral atom.

Thus, the correct order of size is $I^- > I > I^+$.

39. *(d)* According to Gay Lussac's law, at constant volume, the pressure of given mass of the gas is directly proportional to its absolute temperature, i.e.

$$p \propto T \text{ or } p = kT$$

Thus, the correct representation is given in option (d).

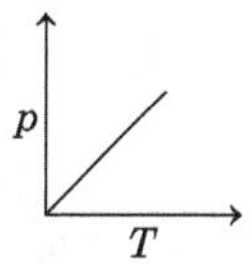

40. *(c)* Positive iodoform test are given by those carbonyl compounds which contain CH_3—$\overset{\text{O}}{\underset{||}{C}}$ group.

(a) $CH_3CH_2CH_2CH_2CH_2OH$

(Pentanol)

It gives negative iodoform test.

(b) H_3C—CH_2—$\overset{\text{O}}{\underset{||}{C}}$—$CH_2$—$CH_3$

(Pentan-3-one)

It does not show iodoform test.

(c) H_3C—CH_2—CH_2—$\overset{\text{O}}{\underset{||}{C}}$—$CH_3$

(Pentan-2-one)

As it contains —$\overset{\text{O}}{\underset{||}{C}}$ CH_3 group.

Thus, it will show positive iodoform test.

(d) $CH_3CH_2CH_2CH_2CHO$

(Pentanal)

It gives negative iodoform test.

41. *(c)* The structures of given species are shown below:

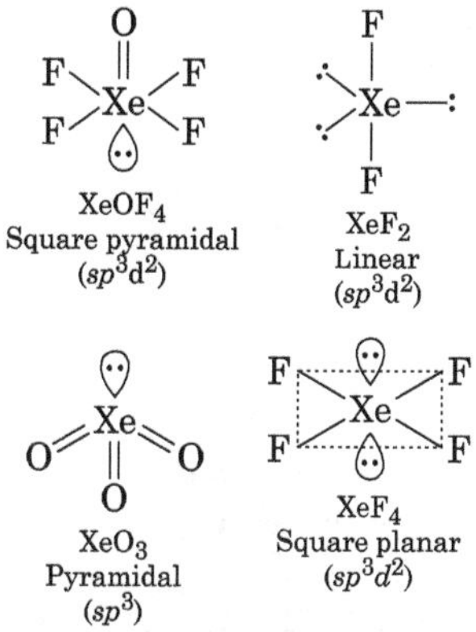

$XeOF_4$
Square pyramidal
(sp^3d^2)

XeF_2
Linear
(sp^3d^2)

XeO_3
Pyramidal
(sp^3)

XeF_4
Square planar
(sp^3d^2)

42. *(d)* Sodium peroxide which is a yellow solid, reacts with moisture and CO_2 of air (when exposed to air) and becomes white due to the formation of NaOH and Na_2CO_3.

$$2Na_2O_2 + H_2O \longrightarrow 4NaOH + O_2$$
$$2NaOH + CO_2 \longrightarrow Na_2CO_3 + H_2O$$

43. *(c)* As CH_3 group is *ortho-para* directing, so the major products will be formed at *o* and *p*-position only.

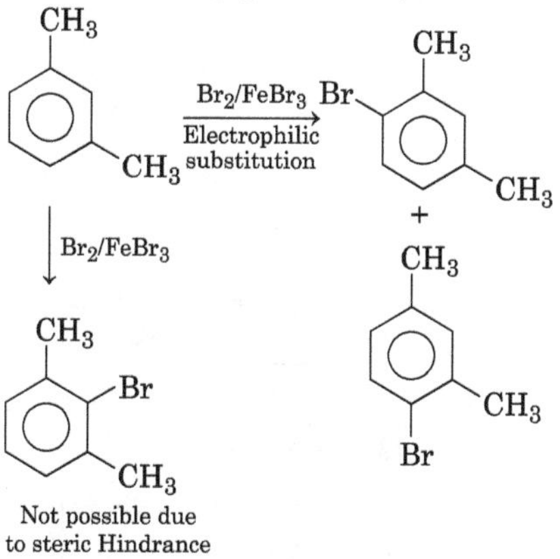

(with $Br_2/FeBr_3$, Electrophilic substitution)

Not possible due to steric Hindrance

Thus, the correct option is (c).

44. *(d)* CH_3—CH—CH—CH_3 + Cl_2
　　　　　　　|　　|
　　　　　CH_3　CH_3

2, 3-dimethyl butane

$\longrightarrow$ CH_3—CH—$\overset{*}{CH}$—CH_2Cl
　　　　　　　　|　　|
　　　　　　　CH_3　CH_3

1–chloro-2, 3 dimethyl butane

Due to the presence of chiral centre (*), it shows the optical activity and its mirror image are non-superimposable.

Hence, it shows one enantiomeric pair.

45. *(b)* $H_2(g) + Cl_2(g) \longrightarrow 2HCl(g)$

$\Delta H = [(BE)_{H-H} + (BE)_{Cl-Cl}] - 2[(BE)_{HCl}]$
$= [435 + 243] - 2[431] = -184 \text{ kJ mol}^{-1}$

The moles of $HCl(g)$ are formed from its element, hence

$$\Delta_f H°_{(HCl)} = \frac{-184}{2} = -92 \text{ kJ mol}^{-1}.$$

46. *(d)* **Glycocalyx** is the outermost mucilage layer of the cell envelope. It gives sticky character to the bacterial cell.

47. *(c)* *Ectocarpus* and *Fucus* respectively show **haplodiplontic** and **diplontic** life cycle. In *Ectocarpus*, sporic meiosis occurs and haploid biflagellate meiozoospores are formed. They germinate to produce gametophytic thalli. The gametophytes liberate gametes which fuse to form diploid zygote which gives rise to a diploid plant.

In *Fucus*, there is a single somatic phase. It is diploid and produces haploid gametes. They fuse during fertilisation to give rise to diploid individual.

48. *(d)* Among the given options, except **lipids** all are polymers. These are formed by the polymerisation of monomers. The basic unit of lipid are fatty acids and glycerol molecules that do not form repetitive chains. Instead they form triglycerides from 3 fatty acids and one glycerol molecules. Protein monomers are amino acids and they bond together in repetitive chains just as carbohydrate monomers are monosaccharides.

49. *(c)* The body wall of a common sponge consists of three layers i.e. pinacoderm, choanoderm and mesophyll layers. Choanoderm is inner cellular layer which consists of highly specialised flagellated cells called choanocytes. The beating of their flagella creates water current.

50. *(d)* A decrease in blood pressure/volume stimulates the hypothalamus to release ADH (Antidiuretic Hormone) as well as JGA cells to release renin. Renin by renin angiotensin mechanism activates the adrenal cortex to release aldosterone. ANF (Atrial Natriuretic factor) is produced by atria of heart during increased blood pressure. It can cause vasodilation and thereby decrease the blood pressure. Therefore, option (d) is correct.

51. *(c)* Vascular cambium located between xylem and phloem in the stems and roots of vascular plants. It produces secondary xylem towards the pith and secondary phloem towards the bark.

52. *(d)* Pancreas consists of exocrine and endocrine parts. Exocrine part secretes alkaline pancreatic juice. This juice contains trypsinogen, chymotrypsinogen, procarboxypeptidase, lipase, amylase, elastase.

53. *(a)* **Archaebacteria** are the most primitive form of bacteria. These live in diverse habitat, e.g. extreme hot temperature, saline condition, variable pH, etc. Saline bacteria are called halophiles (e.g. *Halobacterium*, *Halococcus*).

54. *(c)* If anaphase promoting complex is defective in a human cell, the **chromosome will not segregate** during anaphase of mitosis. APC triggers the transition from metaphase to anaphase by tagging specific proteins for degradation.

55. *(d)* Zygotic meiosis is represented in the haplontic life cycle of many algae including **Chlamydomonas**. In such a life cycle, all cells are haploid except zygote. This is because meiosis occurs in the zygote itself resulting into four haploid cells that give rise to haploid plants.

56. *(c)* Gibberellins and ABA are antagonistic to each other. Gibberellins promote seed germination whereas ABA promotes seed dormancy.

57. *(b)* Ornithine cycle removes both ammonia and urea from the blood. It converts ammonia into urea (in liver) and transports it to kidneys by the blood. Hence, it plays a key role in detoxification of our blood. This cycle occurs in the liver.

58. *(b)* In the dicot stem, the cortical cells get differentiated to give rise to another meristematic tissue, which is called cork cambium or phellogen. On the other side, it forms phellem (cork) and in the inner region it forms secondary cortical cells (phelloderm).

59. *(d)* Sucrose shows the most substrate specificity since it hydrolyses only the disaccharide, sucrose.

60. *(c)* Since the allele is recessive, both homologous chromosomes in a somatic cell of an albino person would have the allele. After meiosis-I, each end would have a homologous chromosome with the allele. As the chromosome is existing as a

pair of sister chromatids at this stage each chromosome and hence each end would have two copies of the allele.

61. *(b)* Let us partition in to n parts and each part has sum $= K$, then
$$nK = 1 + 2 + 3 + \ldots + 20$$
$$\Rightarrow \qquad nK = 210$$
$\therefore K$ divides 210.

Also, K must be ≥ 20.

Now, $210 = 2 \times 3 \times 5 \times 7$

So, proper divisor of 210 are $\{1, 2, 3, 5, 6, 7, 10, 14, 15, 21, 30, 35, 42, 70, 105, 210\}$

$\Rightarrow K$ can be 21, 30, 35, 42, 70, 105

For $K = 21$, we have $(1, 20)\ (2, 19) \ldots$
$$(10, 11)$$
$\Rightarrow 21$ is a good number.

For $K = 42$, join two-two pairs

For $K = 105$, join five-five pairs

$\Rightarrow 42$ and 105 are also good numbers

For $K = 30$, we have
$\{20, 10\}, \{19, 11\}, \{18, 12\}, \{17, 13\}, \{16, 14\},$
$\{15, 9, 6\}, \{1, 2, 3, 4, 5, 7, 8\}$

$\Rightarrow K = 30$ is also good number

Similarly, 35 and 70 also good numbers.

$\therefore$ There are total 6 good numbers.

62. *(c)* We have,
$$C_1 : (x - 10)^2 + y^2 = 36$$
$$C_2 : (x + 15)^2 + y^2 = 81$$
Centre of $C_1 = (10, 0)$ and radius $= 6$

Centre of $C_2 = (-15, 0)$ and radius $= 9$

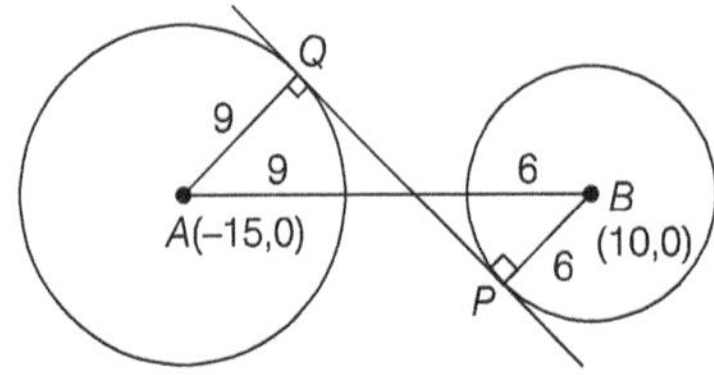

The length of smallest line segment PQ is the indirect common tangent of circle
$$\therefore \qquad PQ = \sqrt{AB^2 - (r_1 + r_2)^2}$$
$$\Rightarrow \qquad PQ = \sqrt{(25)^2 - (9 + 6)^2}$$
$$[\because AB = \sqrt{(10 + 15)^2 - 0^2}, AB = 25]$$
$$\Rightarrow \qquad PQ = \sqrt{625 - 225}$$
$$\Rightarrow \qquad PQ = \sqrt{400} = 20$$

63. *(d)* The repeating decimal $0.\overline{ab}$ is equal to
$$x = 0.abababab \qquad \ldots(i)$$
$$100x = ab \cdot abababab \qquad \ldots(ii)$$
On subtracting Eq. (i) from Eq. (ii), we get
$$99x = ab$$
$$\Rightarrow \qquad x = \frac{ab}{99} = \frac{10a + b}{99}$$

When expressed in lowest term, the denominator of this fraction will always be a divisor of $99 = 3 \cdot 3 \cdot 11$

This gives us the possibilities $\{1, 3, 9, 11, 33, 99\}$. As a and b both are not both 9 and not both zero the denominator 1 cannot be possible.

$\therefore$ Possible denominators are $\{3, 9, 11, 33, 99\}$.

64. *(c)* In $\triangle ABC$,
$$\angle C = 90°, AB = 10, \angle B = 60°$$

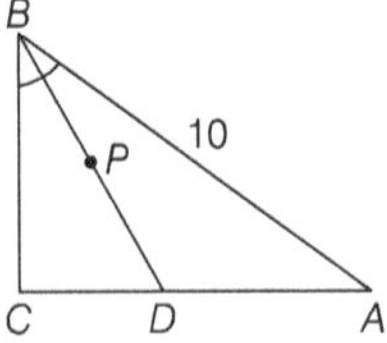

In $\triangle ABC$,
$$BC = AB \cos B = 10 \times \cos 60° = 5$$
$$AC = AB \sin B = 10 \times \sin 60° = 5\sqrt{3}$$

Choose a P' and get a corresponding D' such that $BD' = 5\sqrt{2}$
$$BD > 5\sqrt{2} > \sqrt{BC^2 + CD^2} > \sqrt{25 + CD^2}$$
$$\Rightarrow \quad CD > 5$$

Thus, the point P may only lie in the $\triangle ABD'$

Required probability $= \dfrac{\text{Area of } \triangle ABD'}{\text{Area of } \triangle ABC}$

The ratio of AD' to AC because the triangle have identical altitudes.

So, ratio $= \dfrac{AD'}{AC} = \dfrac{AC - CD'}{AC}$
$$= 1 - \frac{CD'}{AC} = 1 - \frac{5}{5\sqrt{3}} = \frac{\sqrt{3} - 1}{\sqrt{3}}$$

$\therefore$ Required probability
$$= \frac{(\sqrt{3} - 1) \times \sqrt{3}}{\sqrt{3} \times \sqrt{3}} = \frac{3 - \sqrt{3}}{3}$$

65. *(a)* We have,
$$P(x) = (x - 1)\ (x - 2)\ (x - 3)$$
and $\qquad P[Q(x)] = P(x) \cdot R(x)$
$\therefore \quad P[Q(x)] = [Q(x) - 1]\ [Q(x) - 2]\ [Q(x) - 3]$
$$= (x - 1)\ (x - 2)\ (x - 3)\ R(x)$$
Since, degree of $P(x) = 3$

and $\quad$ degree of $R(x) = 3$

$\therefore$ Degree of $[P(x) \cdot R(x)] = 6$

Thus, degree of $P(Q(x)) = 6$, so degree $Q(x) = 2$
$$P(Q(1)) = (Q(1) - 1)\ (Q(1) - 2)\ (Q(1) - 3) = 0$$
$$P(Q(2)) = (Q(2) - 1)\ (Q(2) - 2)\ (Q(2) - 3) = 0$$
$$P(Q(3)) = (Q(3) - 1)\ (Q(3) - 2)\ (Q(3) - 3) = 0$$
Hence, we conclude $Q(1), Q(2)$ and $Q(3)$ must each be 1, 2, 3. Since, a quadratic is uniquely determined by the three points.

There can be $3 \times 3 \times 3 = 27$ different quadratic.

However, we have included $Q(x)$ which are not quadratic. They are line.

Then, $Q(1) = Q(2) = Q(3) = 1$

$\Rightarrow \quad Q(x) = 1$

$\qquad Q(1) = Q(2) = Q(3) = 2$

$\Rightarrow \quad Q(x) = 2$

$\qquad Q(1) = Q(2) = Q(3) = 3$

$\Rightarrow \quad Q(x) = 3$

$\qquad Q(1) = 1, Q(2) = 2, Q(3) = 3$

$\Rightarrow \quad Q(x) = x$

$\qquad Q(1) = 3, Q(2) = 2, Q(3) = 1$

$\Rightarrow \quad Q(x) = 4 - x$

So, these linear function are not included

$\therefore$ Total number of polynomials

$\qquad = 27 - 5 = 22$

66. *(d)* For first stone,

$$x_1 = ut + \frac{1}{2}at^2$$

$$= 15t - 5t^2 \quad [\because a = g = -10 \text{ ms}^{-2}]$$

Now, $x_1 = -200 \text{ m}$

$\Rightarrow \qquad 15t - 5t^2 = -200$

$\Rightarrow \qquad 5t^2 - 15t - 200 = 0$

$\Rightarrow \quad 5t^2 - 40t + 25t - 200 = 0$

$\Rightarrow \quad 5t\,(t - 8) + 25\,(t - 8) = 0$

$\Rightarrow \qquad t = 8 \text{ s or } t = -5 \text{ s}$

$(\because t = -5 \text{ s not acceptable})$

$\therefore$ Time for which first stone remains in air $= 8$ s.

So, graph is $x_2 - x_1 = 15t$

$\qquad\qquad$ (For $t = 0$ to $t = 8$ s)

and $x_2 - x_1 = 200 + 30t - 5t^2$

$\qquad\qquad$ (For $t > 8$ s to $t = 10$ s)

67. *(d)* When object is placed at $2f$ distance, image formed is also at $2f$.

So, from graph,

$$2f = -30 \text{ cm}$$

$\Rightarrow \qquad f = -15 \text{ cm}$

68. *(a)* Circuit can be redrawn as

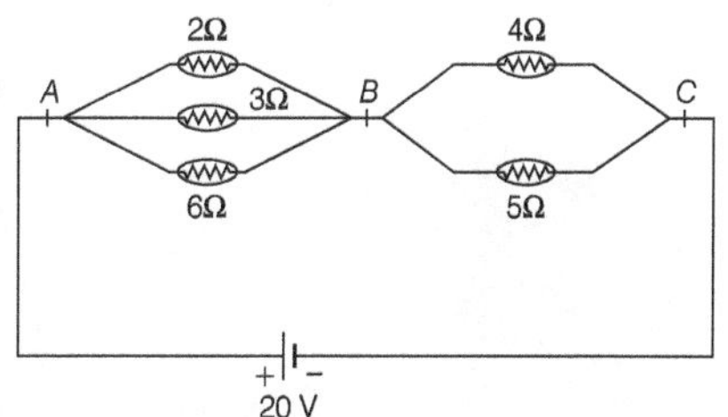

As R_{AB} and R_{AC} are nearly $1\ \Omega$ and 2Ω respectively, a larger potential drop occurs across BC. As AB and BC are in

series and current remains same in both, so $IR_{AB} < IR_{BC}$.

Now, for a parallel combination,

$$P = \frac{V^2}{R} \text{ or } P \propto \frac{1}{R}.$$

Hence, a larger potential drop occurs across 4Ω bulb.

Hence, 4Ω bulb glows brightest in given circuit.

69. *(b)* At extreme positions, total energy is potential energy.

So, $\qquad U(x) = \frac{kx^2}{2} \Rightarrow 1 = \frac{0.5x^2}{2}$

$\Rightarrow \qquad x^2 = 4 \Rightarrow x = \pm 2\text{m}$

So, particle turns back after reading 2 m mark.

$\therefore$ Amplitude of oscillation of particle is 2 m.

70. *(a)* Let m = mass of ice initially present.

Heat absorbed from $t = 0$ to $t = 50$ min is

$$Q_1 = m_{\text{ice}} L$$

$$= m\,(\text{kg})\,333\,(\text{J/g})$$

$$= m\,(3.33 \times 10^5)\,\text{J}$$

and heat absorbed from $t = 50$ min to $t = 60$ min,

$$Q_2 = ms\Delta T$$

$$= (10 + m)\,(4.186 \times 10^3)\,(10 - 0)$$

$$= (10 + m)\,(4.186 \times 10^3)\,(10)$$

Given that, rate of heat supply is constant.

So, $\qquad \dfrac{Q_1}{\Delta t_1} = \dfrac{Q_2}{\Delta t_2}$

$$\frac{m\,(3.33 \times 10^5)}{50} = \frac{(10 + m)\,(4.186 \times 10^3)\,(10)}{10}$$

$\Rightarrow \qquad \dfrac{m(33.33)}{5} = (10 + m)(4.186)$

$\Rightarrow \qquad 33.33\,m = 209.3 + 20.93\,m$

$\Rightarrow \qquad 12.4\,m = 209.3$

$\Rightarrow \qquad m = 16.87 \text{ kg}$

71. *(d)* Amount of heat liberated by 0.05 g of C

$$= mC\Delta T$$

$$= 2000 \times 1\,(26 - 24)$$

$$= 4000 \text{ cal} = 4 \text{ kcal}$$

Calorific value $= \dfrac{4 \text{ kcal} \times 1}{0.5} = 8$ kcal per g

$\therefore$ Heat of combustion $= -8 \times 12$

$$= -96 \text{ kcal per mol}$$

72. *(a)* As the organic compound forms white precipitate with $AgNO_3/NH_4OH$ and red precipitate with Cu_2Cl_2/NH_4OH, it must be a terminal alkyne.

Thus, terminal alkyne (A) with molecular formula C_4H_6 is $CH_3CH_2C \equiv CH$. Thus, option (a) is correct.

$$CH_2\!=\!\!CH\!-\!\!CH\!=\!\!\overset{.}{C}H_2$$
$$B$$
$$\text{(Isomer of } A\text{)}$$

$$\overset{+}{C}H_2\!-\!CH\!=\!\!CH\!-\!\overset{-}{C}H_2$$

$\qquad\qquad \downarrow Br_2$

$$CH_2\!-\!CH\!=\!\!CH\!-\!CH_2$$
$$|\qquad\qquad\qquad\quad |$$
$$Br \qquad\qquad\qquad Br$$

1, 4 dibromobut-2-ene

73. *(b)* Number of moles of the gas

$$= \frac{2.0 \times 10^{21}}{6.023 \times 10^{23}} \text{ mol}$$

$$= 3.32 \times 10^{-3} \text{ mol}$$

From ideal gas equation

$$pV = nRT$$

$$T = \frac{pV}{nR} = \frac{7.57 \times 10^3 \times 10^{-3}}{3.32 \times 10^{-3} \times 8.314}$$

$$= 274.25 \text{ K}$$

Root mean square speed,

$$v_{\text{rms}} = \sqrt{\frac{3RT}{M}}$$

$$= \sqrt{\frac{3 \times 8.314 \times 274.25}{28 \times 10^{-3}}}$$

$$= 494.26 \text{ ms}^{-1}$$

74. *(d)* (a) Electronic configuration of

$$Br_2 = \sigma 1s^2\,\sigma^*\,1s^2\,\sigma 2s^2\,\sigma^*\,2s^2$$

$$\text{B.O} = \frac{4 - 4}{2} = 0$$

Thus, it does not exist. Hence, statement (a) is correct.

(b) $He_2 = \sigma 1s^2\,\sigma^*\,1s^2$ $\text{B.O} = \dfrac{2 - 2}{2} = 0$

Hence, it will not exist.

$\qquad He_2^+ = \sigma 1s^2 \sigma^* 1s^2$, $\text{B.O} = \dfrac{2 - 1}{2} = 0.5$

Since, the bond order is not zero, this molecule is expected to exist.

(c) $N_2 = \sigma 1s^2 \sigma^* 1s^2\,\sigma 2s^2\,\sigma^*\,2s^2$

$$\pi 2p_x^2 \approx \pi 2py^2\,\sigma 2p_z^2$$

$$\text{B.O} = \frac{10 - 4}{2} = 3$$

Thus, it has the maximum bond strength among the other diatomic molecule belonging to the second period.

(d) The correct electronic configuration of N_2 is $\sigma 1s^2\,\sigma^*\,1s^2 \sigma 2s^2 \sigma^*\,2s^2$

$\pi 2p_x^2 \approx \pi 2p_y^2\,\sigma 2p_z^2$

Thus, statement (d) is incorrect.

75. *(a)* Equivalent mass of M

$$= \frac{\text{mass of metal}}{\text{mass of oxygen}} \times 8$$

$$= \frac{10}{0.8} \times 8 = 100$$

Approximate atomic mass

$$= \frac{6.4}{\text{specific heat}} = \frac{6.4}{0.033} = 193.3\,g$$

Valency of $M = \frac{193.93}{100} = 1.98 \approx 2$

So, accurate atomic mass

$$= \text{equivalent mass} \times \text{valency}$$

$$= 100 \times 2 = 200\,g$$

$$\text{Atomicity} = \frac{\text{molar mass}}{\text{atomic mass}} = \frac{199.87}{200} = 1$$

76. *(d)* The folding of two or more polypeptide chains constitutes the quaternary structure. Tertiary structure of protein is a single polypeptide chain folded and twisted. Primary structure of protein is amino acids joined end to end with each other. Secondary structures are folded into α-helix and β-pleated sheets.

77. *(d)* The amount of light given is saturated, not limited. Therefore the answer is (d). The concentration of carbon dioxide is in short supply, hence limiting the rate of photosynthesis.

78. *(c)* The drugs will only prevent the response of the muscle to an electrical stimulus if it prevents the release of acetylcholine and so inhibits the increase in membrane permeability to sodium ions, and if the drug competes with acetylcholine at the receptor sites.

79. *(a)* There are 12 chromosomes present. In a mitotic division, the number of chromosomes remains the same, i.e. $2n \to 2n$. In a meiotic division, the number is halved, i.e., $2n \to n$ so, there should only be 6 chromosomes in the nucleus.

80. *(b)* Phosphate group, ribose or deoxyribose group and cytosine group form the nucleotide.

Phosphate (H_3PO_4)

Ribose $(C_5H_{10}O_5)$

Deoxyribose $(C_5H_{10}O_4)$

Cytosine has 4 carbon atoms, as it is a pyrimidine.

Therefore, the nucleotide should have

$5C + 4C = 9C$

CPSIA information can be obtained
at www.ICGtesting.com
Printed in the USA
BVHW060001100623
665688BV00015B/957